THE OXFORD HISTORY OF
THE CHRISTIAN CHURCH

Edited by
Henry and Owen Chadwick

Church and Society in Eighteenth-Century France

VOLUME 1

THE CLERICAL ESTABLISHMENT AND ITS SOCIAL RAMIFICATIONS

JOHN McMANNERS

OXFORD
UNIVERSITY PRESS

OXFORD
UNIVERSITY PRESS

Great Clarendon Street, Oxford OX2 6DP

Oxford University Press is a department of the University of Oxford.
It furthers the University's objective of excellence in research, scholarship,
and education by publishing worldwide in

Oxford New York

Athens Auckland Bangkok Bogotá Buenos Aires Calcutta
Cape Town Chennai Dar es Salaam Delhi Florence Hong Kong Istanbul
Karachi Kuala Lumpur Madrid Melbourne Mexico City Mumbai
Nairobi Paris São Paulo Singapore Taipei Tokyo Toronto Warsaw

and associated companies in Berlin Ibadan

Oxford is a registered trade mark of Oxford University Press
in the UK and in certain other countries

Published in the United States
by Oxford University Press Inc., New York

British Library Cataloguing in Publication Data

Data available

Library of Congress Cataloging in Publication Data
The church in eighteenth-century France / John McManners.
(The Oxford history of the Christian Church)
Includes bibliographical references.
Contents: 1. Clergy and people—2. Church, power, and politics.
1. Catholic Church—France—History—18th century. 2. France—
Church history—18th century. I. Title. II. Series.
BX1529.M36 1998 282'.44'09033—dc21 97-47458

ISBN 0-19-827003-8

1 3 5 7 9 10 8 6 4 2

Typeset by Regent Typesetting, London
Printed in Great Britain on acid-free paper by
Bookcraft (Bath) Ltd., Midsomer Norton

To Sarah

ACKNOWLEDGEMENTS

The editors of this Series generously allowed me to make an idio-syncratic, maverick contribution, and encouraged me to write at my own length and pace. The Delegates of Oxford University Press courageously accepted the enormous book which I finally presented. Thereafter, all concerned at the Press have exceeded the bounds of duty in assisting me: Hilary O'Shea, Editor for Theology and Classics, Elizabeth Alsop who set in train the processes of pro-duction, and Enid Barker who sportingly came out of retirement to bring the work to conclusion when Elizabeth moved to new fields of endeavour in London, Jean van Altena the copy-editor, Judith Colleran the proof-reader, and Meg Davies who compiled the index. To all I am deeply grateful. I am also especially indebted to friends who read over, with critical and discerning eyes the chapters falling within the areas of their research: Robin Briggs (Chs. 30, 31), Scott Mandelbrote (Chs. 33, 44), Margaret Bent (Ch. 15), John Rogister (Chs. 39, 40, 41), Nigel Aston (Chs. 48, 49, 50). Chapter 21, difficult to write, was read by Richard Fargher, Robert Darnton, and Nicolas Cronk—they saved me from many an error, though I suspect they will not be entirely happy with the final version. Finally, I must express my thanks to All Souls College, where I have been granted an academic home since retiring from the chair of Ecclesiastical History. Successive secretaries have typed my ill-written manuscripts in their various recensions, and Margaret Lord has completed the task with a blend of intuition and accuracy. For the final proof-reading the college enabled me to employ Genevieve Hawkins, famous in the Faculty of Modern Languages for her expertise. Here in All Souls I have found friendship and intellectual companionship, with many an opportunity to discuss the problems of interpreting the French eighteenth century. It has been a rare privilege, making the fourteen years since I retired the happiest of my life.

J.M.

CONTENTS

ABBREVIATIONS

PRIMARY SOURCES

D'Argenson	R.-L. de Voyer, marquis D'Argenson, *Journal et mémoires*, ed. E. J. B. Rathery (9 vols., 1859–67).
Bachaumont	L. P. de Bachaumont, Pidanset de Mairobert, and Mouffle d'Angerville, *Mémoires secrets pour servir à histoire de la République des lettres en France* (36 vols., 1779–89).
Barbier	E.-J.-F. Barbier, *Chronique de la Régence et du règne de Louis XV, 1718–1763* (8 vols., 1857–8).
Grimm	F.-M. Grimm, *Correspondance littéraire, philosophique et politique*, ed. M. Tourneux (16 vols., 1871–80).
Guyot	P.-J. Guyot, *Répertoire universel et raisonné de jurisprudence civile, criminelle, canonique et bénéficiale* (64 vols., 1775–83, + 14 vols. supp. 1786).
Luynes	C.-P. d'Albert, duc de Luynes, *Mémoires du duc de Luynes sur la cour de Louis XV*, ed. L. Dussieux and E. Soulié (11 vols., 1860–5).
Marais	M. Marais, *Journal et mémoires*, ed. M. de Lescure (4 vols., 1863).
Métra	L.-F. Métra *et al.*, *Correspondance secrète, politique et littéraire* (18 vols., 1781–90).
P.V. Ass.	*Collection des procès verbaux des Assemblées générales du clergé de France* (10 vols., 1767–78).
Saint-Simon	Louis de Rouvroy, duc de Saint-Simon, *Mémoires* (21 vols., 1829).
Saint-Simon (Pléiade)	Louis de Rouvroy, duc de Saint-Simon, *Mémoires*, ed. G. Truc, Pléiade (9 vols., 1950).
Voltaire, *Corresp.*	Voltaire, *Correspondance*, ed. Th. Besterman (101 vols., Geneva, 1953–65). References to this edition unless stated otherwise. *Correspondance*, new augmented edition by Th. Besterman (135 vols., Paris, 1963–77).
Voltaire, *Œuvres*	François-Marie Arouet, Voltaire, *Œuvres complètes*, ed. L. Moland (52 vols., 1877–85).

Abbreviations

Am. Hist. Rev.	American Historical Review (Washington)
Amis Chinon	Les Amis du vieux Chinon: Bulletin (Chinon)
Anal. cist.	Analecta cisterciensia (Rome)
L'Anjou hist.	L'Anjou historique (Angers)
Ann.	Annales. Économies. Sociétés. Civilisations. (Paris)
Ann. Acad. Mâcon	Annales de l'Académie de Mâcon (Mâcon)
Ann. Bourgogne	Annales de Bourgogne (Dijon)
Ann. Bretagne	Annales de Bretagne et des pays de l'Ouest (Rennes)
Ann. Clermont-Ferrand	Annales de Clermont-Ferrrand (Clermont-Ferrand)
Ann. dém. hist.	Annales de démographie historique (Paris)
Ann. Est	Annales de l'Est (Nancy)
Ann. Haute-Provence	Annales de Haute-Provence (Dijon)
Ann. hist. Rév. fr.	Annales historiques de la Révolution française (formerly Revue historique de la Révolution française) (Paris)
Ann. internat. crim.	Annales internationales de criminologie (Paris)
Ann. Malte	Annales de l'Ordre souverain militaire de Malte (Rome)
Ann. Midi	Annales du Midi (Toulouse)
Ann. Normandie	Annales de Normandie (Caen)
Ann. rév.	Annales révolutionnaires (Société des études robespierristes) (Paris)
Ann. Soc. Cannes	Annales de la Société scientifique et littéraire de Cannes et de l'arrondissement de Grasse (Cannes)
Ann. Soc. Rousseau	Annales de la Société Jean-Jacques Rousseau (Geneva)
Ann. Soc. Saint-Malo	Annales de la Société d'histoire et d'archéologie de l'arrondissement de Saint-Malo (Saint-Malo)
L'Année canonique	L'Année canonique (Inst. cath. fac. de droit canonique, Paris)
Arch. Église Alsace	Archives de l'Église d'Alsace (Strasbourg)
Arch. Hist. Soc. Jesu	Archivum Historicum Societatis Jesu (Rome)
Arch. juives	Archives juives
Bibl. École Chartes	Bibliothèque de l'École des Chartes (Paris)
Le Bugey	Le Bugey (Belley)
Bull. Acad. delph.	Bulletin (mensuel) de l'Académie delphinale (Grenoble)
Bull. ann. Cluny	Bulletin annuel des amis de Cluny (Dijon)
Bull. Auvergne	Bulletin historique et scientifique de l'Auvergne (Clermont-Ferrand)

Bull. Belley	*Bulletin d'histoire et d'archéologie du diocèse de Belley* (Bourg-en-Bresse)
Bull. Com. Nîmes	*Bulletin du Comité de l'art chrétien de Nîmes* (Nîmes)
Bull. Com. Paris	*Bulletin du Comité d'histoire et d'archéologie du diocèse de Paris* (Paris)
Bull. Comm. Seine-et-Oise	*Bulletin de la Commission des antiquités et des arts de Seine-et-Oise* (Versailles)
Bull. Diana	*Bulletin de la Diana* (Montbrison)
Bull. Fac. cath. Lille	*Bulletin des Facultés catholiques de Lille* (Lille)
Bull. Féd. Franche Comté	*Bulletin de la Fédération des sociétés savantes de Franche Comté* (Besançon)
Bull. Hist. Med.	*Bulletin of the History of Medicine* (Baltimore)
Bull. litt. ecclés.	*Bulletin de littérature ecclésiastique* (Institut catholique: Toulouse)
Bull. Lyon	*Bulletin historique du diocèse de Lyon* (Lyon)
Bull. méms. Soc. Côtes-du-Nord	*Bulletin et mémoires de la Société d'émulation des Côtes-du-Nord* (Saint-Brieuc)
Bull. méms. Soc. Ille-et-Vilaine	*Bulletin et mémoires de la Société archéologique du département d'Ille-et-Vilaine* (Rennes)
Bull. Soc. Aube	*Bulletin (mensuel) de la Société académique d'agriculture, sciences, arts et belles-lettres du département de l'Aube* (earlier *Mémoires*) (Troyes)
Bull. Soc. Basses-Alpes	*Bulletin de la Société scientifique et littéraire des Basses-Alpes* (Digne)
Bull. Soc. Bayonne	*Bulletin (trimestriel) de la Société des sciences, lettres et arts de Bayonne* (Bayonne)
Bull. Soc. Borda	*Bulletin (trimestriel) de la Société de Borda* (Dax)
Bull. Soc. Bretagne	*Bulletin de la Société d'histoire et archéologie de Bretagne* (Rennes)
Bull. Soc. Draguignan	*Bulletin de la Société d'études scientifiques et archéologiques de Draguignan* (Draguignan)
Bull. Soc. Drôme	*Bulletin de la Société d'archéologie et de statistique de la Drôme* (Valence)
Bull. Soc. Eure-et-Loire	*Bulletin de la Société archéologique et historique d'Eure-et-Loire* (Chartres)
Bull. Soc. Gers	*Bulletin de la Société archéologique, historique, littéraire et scientifique du Gers* (Auch)
Bull. Soc. Guyenne	*Bulletin de la Société des Bibliophiles de Guyenne* (Bordeaux)
Bull. Soc. Hautes-Alpes	*Bulletin de la Société d'études historiques, scientifiques et littéraires des Hautes-Alpes* (Gap)
Bull. Soc. hist. mod.	*Bulletin de la Société de l'histoire moderne* (Paris)
Bull. Soc. hist. prot. fr.	*Bulletin de la Société de l'histoire du protestantisme français* (Paris)

Bull. Soc. Meuse	Bulletin des Sociétés d'histoire et archéologie de la Meuse (Bar-le-Duc)
Bull. Soc. Montargis	Bulletin de la Société d'émulation de l'arrondissement de Montargis (Montargis)
Bull. Soc. Morbihan	Bulletin (mensuel) de la Société polymathique du Morbihan (Vannes)
Bull. Soc. Morinie	Bulletin historique de la Société des antiquaires de la Morinie (earlier Mémoires) (Saint-Omer)
Bull. Soc. Nantes	Bulletin de la Société archéologique et historique de Nantes et de la Loire-Inférieure (Nantes)
Bull. Soc. Normandie	Bulletin de la Société des antiquaires de Normandie (Caen-Rouen)
Bull. Soc. Oise	Bulletin de la Société académique d'archéologie, sciences et arts du département de l'Oise (Beauvais)
Bull. Soc. Orléanais	Bulletin (trimestriel) de la Société archéologique et historique de l'Orléanais (Orléans)
Bull. Soc. Orne	Bulletin de la Société historique et archéologique de l'Orne (Alençon)
Bull. Soc. Ouest	Bulletin de la Société des antiquaires de l'Ouest et des Musées de Poitiers (earlier Mémoires) (Poitiers)
Bull. Soc. Paris	Bulletin de la Société de l'histoire de Paris et de l'Île-de-France (Paris)
Bull. Soc. Pau	Bulletin de la Société des sciences, lettres et arts de Pau (Pau)
Bull. Soc. phil. vosgienne	Bulletin de la Société philomatique vosgienne (Saint-Dié)
Bull. Soc. Sarthe	Bulletin de la Société d'agriculture, sciences et arts de la Sarthe (Le Mans)
Bull. Soc. Seine-et-Marne	Bulletin de la Société d'archéologie, sciences, lettres et arts du département de Seine-et-Marne (Meaux)
Bull. Soc. Sens	Bulletin de la Société archéologique de Sens (Sens)
Cahiers hist.	Cahiers d'histoire (Lyon: universities of Clermont, Lyon, and Grenoble)
Cahiers hist. enseign.	Cahiers de l'histoire de l'enseignement (Rouen)
Cahiers Bazadais	Les Cahiers du Bazadais (Bazas)
Cahiers Vitrezais	Les Cahiers du Vitrezais: revue historique, archéologique et littéraire des Hauts de Gironde (Paris)
Cath. Hist. Rev.	The Catholic Historical Review (Washington)
Chron. Port-Royal	Chroniques de Port-Royal (Paris)
Church Hist.	Church History (Chicago)
Cîteaux	Cîteaux, commentarii cistercienses (Achel)
Coll. cist.	Collectanea cisterciensia (Rome)

Comptes Soc. Clermont-en-Beauvaisis	*Comptes rendus et mémoires de la Société archéologique et historique de Clermont-en-Beauvaisis* (Clermont-en-Beauvaisis)
Divus Thomas	*Divus Thomas, commentarium de philosophia et theologia* (Plaisance)
Eng. Hist. Rev.	*English Historical Review* (London)
Ensembles d'Écoles	*Ensemble d'Écoles supérieures et Facultés catholiques (Fédération universitaire et polytechnique de Lille)* (Lille)
Études rurales	*Études rurales* (École des Hautes Études) (Paris)
Études XVIIIᵉ siècle	*Études sur le dix-huitième siècle* (Univ. libre, Brussels)
Eur. J. Population	*European Journal of Population* (Amsterdam)
Eur. St. Rev.	*European Studies Review (European History Quarterly)* (London)
Fr. Hist.	*French History* (Oxford)
Fr. Hist. St.	*French Historical Studies* (Raleigh, NC)
Fr. St.	*French Studies* (Oxford)
Genava	*Genava* (Geneva)
Hist. J.	*The Historical Journal* (Cambridge)
L'Information hist.	*L'Information historique* (Paris)
JAMS	*Journal of the American Musicological Society* (Richmond, Va.)
J. Eccles. Hist.	*Journal of Ecclesiastical History* (London)
J. hist.	*Journal historique*
J. Interdisc. Hist.	*Journal of Interdisciplinary History*
J. Mod. Hist.	*Journal of Modern History* (Chicago)
J. Ren. Mod. St.	*Journal of Renaissance and Modern Studies* (Nottingham)
Lettres romanes	*Lettres romanes* (Louvain)
Maison-Dieu	*La Maison-Dieu* (Centre de Pastorale liturgique: Paris)
Mélanges sc. relig.	*Mélanges de science religieuse* (Lille)
Méms. Acad. Besançon	*Mémoires de l'Académie des sciences, belles-lettres et arts de Besançon* (Besançon)
Méms. Acad. Lyon	*Mémoires de l'Académie des sciences, belles-lettres et arts de Lyon* (Lyon)
Méms. Acad. nat. Angers	*Mémoires de l'Académie nationale des sciences, arts et belles-lettres d'Angers* (Angers)
Méms. Acad. nat. Caen	*Mémoires de l'Académie nationale des sciences, arts et belles-lettres de Caen* (Caen)
Méms. Acad. nat. Dijon	*Mémoires de l'Académie nationale (impériale) des sciences, arts et belles-lettres de Dijon* (Dijon)
Méms. Acad. nat. Metz	*Mémoires de l'Académie nationale des sciences, arts et belles-lettres de Metz* (Metz)

Méms. Acad. nat. Toulouse	*Mémoires de l'Académie nationale des sciences, inscriptions et belles-lettres de Toulouse* (Toulouse)
Méms. Comm. Côte-d'Or	*Mémoires de la Commission des antiquités de la Côte-d'Or* (Dijon)
Méms. Soc. Alais	*Mémoires et comptes rendus de la Société scientifique et littéraire d'Alais* (Alais)
Méms. Soc. Aube	*Mémoires de la Société académique d'agriculture, des sciences, arts et belles-lettres du département de l'Aube* (later *Bulletin*) (Troyes)
Méms. Soc. Bretagne	*Mémoires de la Société d'histoire et d'archéologie de Bretagne* (later *Bulletin*) (Rennes)
Méms. Soc. Cambrai	*Mémoires de la Société d'émulation de Cambrai* (Cambrai)
Méms. Soc. Carcassonne	*Mémoires de la Société des arts et des sciences de Carcassonne* (Carcassonne)
Méms. Soc. Côtes-du-Nord	*Mémoires de la Société d'émulation des Côtes-du-Nord* (Saint-Brieuc)
Méms. Soc. Doubs	*Mémoires de la Société d'émulation du département du Doubs* (Besançon)
Méms. Soc. Marne	*Mémoires de la Société d'agriculture, commerce, sciences et arts du département de la Marne* (Châlons-sur-Marne)
Méms. Soc. Morinie	*Mémoires de la Société des antiquaires de la Morinie* (later *Bulletin*) (Saint-Omer)
Méms. Soc. Nord	*Mémoires de la Société centrale d'agriculture, sciences et arts du département du Nord* (Douai)
Méms. Soc. Orléans	*Mémoires de la Société d'agriculture, sciences, belles-lettres et arts d'Orléans* (Orléans)
Méms. Soc. Ouest	*Mémoires de la Société des antiquaires de l'Ouest* (later *Bulletin*) (Poitiers)
Méms. Soc. Paris	*Mémoires de la Société de l'histoire de Paris et de l'Île-de-France* (later *Bulletin*) (Paris)
Méms. Soc. Rambouillet	*Mémoires de la Société archéologique de Rambouillet* (Rambouillet)
Méms. Trav. Fac. cath. Lille	*Mémoires et Travaux des Facultés catholiques de Lille* (later *Bulletin*) (Lille)
Mentalités	*Mentalités: histoire des cultures et des sociétés* (Paris)
Le Monde alpin	*Le Monde alpin et rhodanien* (Nyons)
La Montagne Sainte-Geneviève	*La Montagne Sainte-Geneviève et ses abords: Société historique et archéologique du Ve arrondissement* (Paris)
Music & Letters	*Music & Letters* (Taunton)
Neophilologus	*Neophilologus* (New York)
Nice hist.	*Nice historique* (Nice)

Nouv. Rev. Champagne et Brie	*La Nouvelle Revue de Champagne et de Brie* (earlier, just *Revue*) (Châlons-sur-Marne)
Pays d'Auge	*Le Pays d'Auge* (Lisieux)
Population	*Population* (Paris)
Provence hist.	*Provence historique* (Marseille)
Province du Maine	*La Province du Maine* (Le Mans)
Rev. Alsace	*Revue d'Alsace* (Strasbourg)
Rev. Anjou	*Revue de l'Anjou* (from 1880; earlier titles included *Maine-et-Loire* and *Maine*) (Angers)
Rev. Auvergne	*La Revue d'Auvergne* (Clermont-Ferrand)
Rev. Bas-Poitou	*Revue de Bas-Poitou* (Fontenay-le-Comte)
Rev. belge phil. hist.	*Revue belge de philologie et d'histoire* (Brussels)
Rev. bénédictine	*Revue bénédictine* (Abbey of Maredsous, Belgium)
Rev. Bordeaux	*Revue historique de Bordeaux et du département de la Gironde* (Bordeaux)
Rev. Champagne et Brie	*Revue de Champagne et de Brie* (revived as *Nouvelle*) (Châlons-sur-Marne)
Rev. Clergé fr.	*Revue du Clergé français* (Paris)
Rev. Comminges	*Revue de Comminges* (Toulouse)
Rev. études juives	*Revue des études juives* (Société des études juives) (Paris)
Rév. fr.	*La Révolution française* (Paris)
Rev. Gascogne	*Revue de Gascogne: Bulletin de la Société historique de Gascogne* (Auch)
Rev. Gévaudan	*Revue du Gévaudan, des Causses et des Cévennes* (Mende)
Rev. Haute-Auvergne	*Revue de la Haute-Auvergne* (Société des lettres, sciences et arts de la Haute-Auvergne) (Aurillac)
Rev. hist.	*Revue historique* (Paris)
Rev. hist. armée	*Revue historique de l'armée* (Paris)
Rev. hist. droit fr.	*Revue historique de droit français et étranger* (Paris)
Rev. hist. ecclés.	*Revue d'histoire ecclésiastique* (Louvain)
Rev. hist. écon. sociale	*Revue d'histoire économique et sociale* (earlier *Annales*) (Paris)
Rev. hist. Église Fr.	*Revue d'histoire de l'Église de France* (Paris)
Rev. hist. litt. Fr.	*Revue d'histoire littéraire de la France* (Paris)
Rev. hist. missions	*Revue de l'histoire des missions* (Paris)
Rev. hist. mod. contemp.	*Revue d'histoire moderne et contemporaine* (Paris)
Rev. hist. religions	*Revue de l'histoire des religions* (Paris)
Rev. hist. théâtre	*Revue d'histoire du théâtre* (Paris)
Rev. internat. enseign.	*Revue internationale de l'enseignement* (Paris)
Rev. Libournais	*Revue historique et archéologique du Libournais* (Libourne)

Rev. Lyon	Revue d'histoire de Lyon (Lyon)
Rev. Mabillon	Revue Mabillon (Ligugé)
Rev. Maine	Revue historique et archéologique du Maine (Le Mans)
Rev. monde cath.	Revue du monde catholique (Paris)
Rev. mus.	Revue musicale (Paris)
Rev. Nord	Revue du Nord (Paris)
Rev. quest. hist.	Revue des questions historiques (Paris)
Rev. Rouergue	Revue du Rouergue (Rodez)
Rev. sc. hum.	Revue des sciences humaines (Lille)
Rev. sc. philos. théol.	Revue des sciences philosophiques et théologiques (Paris)
Rev. Soc. Villiers-sur-Marne	Revue de la Société historique de Villiers-sur-Marne et de la Brie française (Villiers-sur-Marne)
Rev. Socs. Haute-Normandie	Revue des Sociétés savantes de Haute-Normandie (Rouen)
Rev. Versailles	Revue de l'histoire de Versailles et de Seine-et-Oise (Versailles)
Rev. Vivarais	Revue historique, archéologique et scientifique du Vivarais (Annonay)
Soc. sav. hist. arch.	La Société savoisienne d'histoire et d'archéologie: Mémoires et documents (Chambéry)
St. 18th C. Culture	Studies in Eighteenth-Century Culture (Cleveland)
S.V.E.C.	Studies on Voltaire and the 18th Century (Voltaire Foundation, Oxford)
Theol. Zeitschrift	Theologische Zeitschrift (Basel)
Trav. Acad. nat. Reims	Travaux de l'Académie nationale de Reims (Reims)
XVIIIe Siècle	Dix-huitième Siècle (Paris)
XVIIe Siècle	Dix-septième Siècle: Bulletin de la Société d'études du XVIIe siècle (Paris)
Yale Fr. St.	Yale French Studies (New Haven)

THE THEME

This book attempts to give a picture of the religious life of the people of eighteenth-century France, to recapture the atmosphere of the times, and to appreciate the beliefs, aspirations, hopes, and fears of four generations. It is written out of interest and sympathy, adopting the approach of the portrait painter rather than that of the clinical diagnostician, aiming for friendly realism rather than morbid analysis. To be fair, and if erring, erring on the side of generosity, presentation in detail is required; individuals and groups come out less well in history written in broad generalizations. Their justification lies in the small print of the historical record rather than in the formal pages. This approach fits with the methodology which the nature of the subject imposes, for the enormous wealth of the Gallican Church, its alliance with the State, and its close, almost symbiotic, integration with the social order mean that it cannot be treated as a self-contained unit. There is no escape from exploring the detailed context of how everything worked (taxation, property holding, the legal system, the hierarchy of classes) and how everyone lived (customs, communities, families, sociability). The history of the Church cannot be separated from the history of society generally.

The constant pressure of worldly interests influenced almost everything that happened in the life of the Church; one of the driving themes in these studies, religious vocation and allegiance among both clergy and laity, is no exception. The century provides many examples of dramatic renunciations, saintly conduct, and sacrificial dedication—glimpses of souls destined to break through all the webs of self-interest in the human situation in any age. But giving realistic consideration to allegiance to the Church and the call to serve it in the material circumstances of the day, with rewards to be won and social status to be achieved, vocation appears in a more complex, variant form, a mutation to be judged by adjusted criteria. The choice of the monastic life took place against the background of families making arrangements for the careers and maintenance of their children. Candidates called to the parochial ministry were considering it as a career, useful to their family and giving opportunities for local leadership. The aristocratic monopoly of bishoprics is explained by the dynastic policies of noble families, the policies of the Crown, and the protocol of Versailles, and something of a justification becomes apparent when the secular and social obligations of bishops are reviewed. These are obvious examples among many. With the interdependence of Church and society a dimension of ambiguity creeps into reflections on religious motivation. It could be that in what follows the emphasis has leaned too far towards material factors, for just as the Devil has the best tunes, so the affairs of the world provide the historian with better evidence than fervour and devotion.

Yet inspiration is only seemingly devalued by being seen in its worldly milieu. In subtle ways self-interest operates in Church affairs everywhere, in whatever social environment; in an age of ecclesiastical wealth and power it is simply more evident. Saints and fanatics excepted, motivation is rarely single-minded, and it is the mark of a civilized mind to follow an ideal yet be conscious of worldly advantages, and to know when they ought to be repudiated and when they may be accepted. Sacrificial certainty driving to its goal evokes admiration, but sympathy is more readily accorded to routine, ambiguous, or provisional commitments, sometimes managing to transcend personal gain, sometimes transmuting it into opportunity, or, taking the easiest path, accommodating it into a workable compromise.

Under the *ancien régime*, we find clerics who are totally cynical, some scandalous to boot; but there are many more who are paradoxically edifying—unbelievers meticulously fulfilling their duties, dubious characters who change course, routine careerists, believers without enthusiasm who refuse to let the side down, and a multitude of good men and women drawn to the Church for both self-interested reasons and the desire to serve it, who would be astonished if asked to distinguish between the two.

As the picture of Church life builds up, a pattern of development becomes apparent. The old social order was evolving, and stirrings of division and discontent demonstrated that it had to change more rapidly to avert disaster. As the royal government creaked on towards eventual bankruptcy, the archaic machinery of the Gallican Church was slowing down every initiative for pastoral efficiency: benefice law put a premium upon guile and influence; the confusions of diocesan and parochial structure handicapped the clergy in coping with shifts of population; and the chaotic conventions of rule in so many of the monastic orders made reforming schemes illusory.

It was becoming evident that the nobility would have to surrender its privileges, voluntarily or under pressure from the Crown or, if the crust of tradition and order cracked, in revolutionary turmoil. Nowhere was this more certain than in the Church, where the build-up of the challenge to aristocratic monopoly gained apostolic force when a corpus of theological arguments came in to reinforce those from natural law, with the curés as propagandists and leaders. Opposition to the riches and exemptions of ecclesiastics was growing. While the scepticism of the Enlightenment did not endanger the Church in the short term—it was a spectacular firework display on the horizon—the earthy realities of anticlerical feeling accumulated over questions of taxation, tithe, church fees and rates, leasehold and feudal dues—envy was intensified by oppressiveness. Stories of luxurious living and idleness, the hypocrisy and uncharitable bitterness of the Jansenist–Jesuit struggle, and revulsion against the persecution of the Protestants influenced public opinion (with Rousseau as its prophet) to separate the Christianity of the gospels from the claims of the institutional Church. The standard arguments from divine ordinance, the Scriptures, and immemorial tradition in defence of clerical wealth and privilege sounded hollow.

Yet in many ways, this was the golden age of the French Church. An increasing number of bishops, some showing little zeal in their own lives, strove to improve standards among their clergy. Never before had the parish priests been so moral and well educated, and never before or since had they been drawn from such reputable families and enjoyed so much respect. Never had there been so many Easter confessions and communions, and so many laymen living lives of well-informed belief and pious practice. The work of religious institutions in education and care for the sick reached a new level of dedication and expertise. Liturgical observances were conducted with unsurpassed splendour, and church music achieved a unique professional sophistication. But this was the mellow autumn season adorning the landscape with rich colours before the leaves began to fall and winter came. And this golden age had a contradiction at its heart. The clergy, so many of them touched with Counter-Reformation zeal, were trying to enforce the austerities of piety on the confraternities, pilgrimages, and manifold traditional observances of the people; by so doing they were hastening the breakdown of mass conformity. They were unwilling to accept the compromises with the world on which the Gallican Church's monolithic splendour rested.

The four generations of this century were the last to profit by—

and be oppressed by—the majestic worldly greatness of the Gallican Church and the (at least nominal) deference of authority to other-worldly principles resulting from the accumulated understandings between religion and power which had tamed barbarism and given Europe its distinctive Christian civilization. A new order was coming in by stealth and osmosis, then, finally, in a brutal cataclysm. In it, the injustices of the past were swept away, and injustices more logically based replaced them. As the reverberations of the clash of ideals, the interventions of circumstance, and the play of individual ambitions fade into retrospect, at the core of the Revolution is seen a vast seizure and transfer of property, the patrimony of the Church that had underpinned so many vocations, kept so many decent families in the fashion to which they were accustomed, and enabled the kings to tie in the feuding aristocracy to the service of the nation. Shorn of its wealth and the influence and temptation which wealth brings, and with the old routines of conformity shattered by war and social overturn, the Church was to become a minority group following more closely its divine inspiration, but with its authority confined to its own voluntary adherents, while the State and the majority went their way with only fading nuances of religion to direct consciences and restrain conduct. Though the sphere of individual opportunity and general liberty has been widened, to the benefit of so many, the old decencies and certainties have decayed, and there is no way back to them. There is always a price to pay for freedom.

I

CHURCH AND STATE

I

THE CORONATION:
REFLECTIONS ON THE
ALLEGIANCE OF THE CLERGY

I

On Friday, 9 June 1775, Louis XVI came to Reims for the *Sacre*, the ceremony of his coronation. The civilian militia paraded outside the city gates, where the provincial governor, the duc de Bourbon, and the municipal officers in scarlet gowns met him. The king changed over from his huge travelling coach to a gala carriage, all glass, paintings, and embroidery, surmounted by plumes. Salvoes of artillery were fired, and the bells pealed, as he was escorted to the cathedral square between the ranks of the Gardes Françaises in their blue, white, and red uniforms.[1] The bishops of the ecclesiastical province, led by the archbishop of Reims, Cardinal La Roche-Aymon, met Louis in the shadow of the vast ornate façade of the cathedral. The cardinal was old and feeble, but he had girded himself to preside over the ceremonies of the coming days, when an archbishop of Reims was the most prestigious figure in France after the king. A mediocre and compliant man ('on ne se brouille pas avec moi'[2]), he had risen to monopolize the greatest ecclesiastical offices and sinecures Versailles could confer: *grand aumônier du Roi*, holder of the *feuille des bénéfices* and the titular abbacy of Saint-Germain, as well as the prelacy of Reims. The king knelt before the bishops to receive aspersion with holy water and to kiss the gospel book. A Te Deum was sung, then the royal cortège adjourned to the episcopal palace for loyal harangues. On the Saturday evening, the king attended a sermon. With apostolic rigour and fashionable reformist zeal, Boisgelin, archbishop of Aix, preached on the duties of rulers; Louis commended him, though the Court did not allow his liberal sentiments to be published.[3]

The coronation took place on 11 June, Trinity Sunday. The Gothic aspect of the cathedral interior was masked by tapestry draping the pillars, by statues and ornaments, and by a lofty woodwork of Corinthian orders with richly gilded fluting and grooving, encasing the walls of the choir. Above the royal throne was a cupola of violet velvet drapery. An orchestra of a hundred players was concealed behind the altar. The canons of Reims were in their stalls, for they had a prescriptive right to their own places. On the epistle side of the choir were packed ministers of state, high ecclesiastics, and nobles of the robe; on the gospel side, peers, marshals of France, and wearers of the cordon bleu. The duc de Croÿ made a quick check to ensure that no one had manœuvred into a higher place than his rank justified: 'qu'il n'y avait point d'embarras pour le rang'.[4] Ensconced among the reverend canons was the 21-year-old Charles-Maurice, abbé de Périgord, on the first stage of an ecclesiastical career forced on him by his family because of his lameness. His uncle, the coadjutor of Reims, had arranged a canonry for him five weeks before, barely a month after he had been made a subdeacon.[5] In his memoirs, the young abbé says nothing about the *Sacre* except that the festivities gave him the opportunity to cultivate the friendship of three influential ladies of the Court.[6] Within fifteen years of hearing the king at Reims swearing to defend the privileges of the Church, Charles-Maurice, now bearing the name of Talleyrand and bishop of Autun, was to propose the sale of ecclesiastical property in the revolutionary assembly, and within thirty years he was to wear the splendid habit of *Grand Chambellan* at the coronation of Napoleon, and to parade in the same office at the coronation of the last Bourbon king twenty-one years later still.

Everyone was in place by 7 o'clock in the morning. Then, a procession set off down the newly constructed covered way to the archbishop's palace to bring back the king—the *grand maître des cérémonies*, the canons of Reims, players of music, and the bishops of Laon and Beauvais. The precentor of the cathedral hammered on the door. 'Que demandez-vous?' 'Nous demandons le roi.' 'Le roi dort.' But at the third time of asking—'Nous demandons Louis XVI que Dieu nous a donné pour roi'—the door was opened.[7]

The king in a silver cloak over a crimson shirt and wearing a black velvet hat adorned with diamonds was brought to the cathedral and set before the altar. Holy water was sprinkled over him, and the prayer was said: 'God almighty and eternal, who hast elevated to the kingdom thy servant Louis, grant that he may ensure the good of his subjects in all the course of his reign, and never depart from the paths of justice and of truth.'[8]

The *Veni Creator* was sung while the archbishop of Reims proceeded to the cathedral porch to meet the procession of the *Sainte*

Ampoule.[9] The holy oil for the king's anointing, brought down from heaven by a dove at the prayer of Saint-Rémy for the baptism of Clovis, was kept in the *Sainte Ampoule*, a tiny crystal flask silvered inside and carried, for safety's sake, in a golden holder shaped like a dove, enamelled white with red beak and claws. The revered object was brought to the cathedral by the *grand prieur* of the abbey of Saint-Rémy, riding a white horse and dressed in a golden cope. He was sheltered by a canopy borne aloft by the four *chevaliers de la Sainte Ampoule* (vassals of fiefs of the abbey), and at each corner rode the *barons otagers*, hostages for the safe return of the flask, dressed in cloth of gold, each escorted by a groom. Ahead of the *grand prieur* went his monks in white albs and the Minims with their cross, and ahead of them marched a military escort of musketeers with their band, and first of all, a rustic guard of the men of the parish of Le Chesne, dressed in blue, wearing gaiters, with cockades and oak leaves in their hats, muskets on shoulder. This was their peculiar privilege, for their ancestors in the village had preserved the *Sainte Ampoule* from destruction in the Hundred Years War.

The coronation service began with the king taking the oaths. He promised to 'preserve the canonical privilege, law and justice due' to the 'bishops and the churches committed to their charge', to preserve all Christian people in peace, to prevent rapine and iniquity, to be merciful and equitable in judgement, and to do all in his power 'to exterminate, in all lands subjected to my rule, the heretics declared to be so by the Church (*nommément condamnés par l'Église*)'.[10]

The bishops of Laon and Beauvais then asked the congregation if it received its king, and respectful silence ensued; Louis then took the oath to preserve the two great orders of chivalry—that of the Saint-Esprit and that of Saint-Louis—and to enforce the edicts against duelling (a solemn gesture against aristocratic lawlessness introduced by Louis XIV).

The king had made his promises, and he was now invested with the first instalment of the panoply of office.[11] The spurs (which came from the early days of the Capetian monarchy), the sword (supposedly that of Charlemagne, though the oldest part, the hilt, with two winged heads guarding the tree of life, dated only from the eleventh century), the long sceptre (surmounted by an effigy of Charlemagne, though dating only from the High Middle Ages), lay on the altar. Between coronations, these regalia were kept in the Parisian abbey of Saint-Denis, whose abbot was in proud attendance, standing by his treasures. The senior lay peer affixed the spurs, and the archbishop girded on the sword, after solemnly consecrating it to noble deeds. The king held it, drawn, while an anthem was sung; thereafter it was borne before him by a nobleman for the rest of the ceremony.

Kneeling on a vast carpet of violet velvet scattered with golden fleurs-de-lis, the king received the seven unctions. A drop of resin from the *Sainte Ampoule* was taken out on a golden needle and mixed with the *sainte chrême*, the oil used in the cathedral for baptisms, confirmations, and ordinations. What was left on the paten after the ceremony was returned to the flask, so the supply of the sacred balm would continue to be available at the coronations of kings of France for all time.[12] The six ecclesiastical peers stood around; the archbishop of Reims, assisted by the bishop of Laon, administered the unctions; the prelates of Beauvais, Langres, Châlons, and Noyon arrayed their monarch in a tunic and dalmatic, vestments of a priestly type. Then came the unctions on the palms, unctions appropriate for a bishop. The great ermine-braided mantle was thrown over the king's shoulders, and he was then given the remaining symbols of office: the sceptre, the ring, and the *main de justice.*

It was time to call in the laity. The Garde des Sceaux invited the lay peers to assemble, summoning them for the occasion under the archaic titles of dukes of Normandy, Burgundy, and Aquitaine, and counts of Toulouse, Flanders, and Champagne—evoking the memories of the war lords who had built the West in distant centuries, oddly contrasting with the present luxurious generation: the king's two brothers, and the duc d'Orléans and his son the duc de Chartres, and the prince de Condé and his son the duc de Bourbon.[13]

Then came the actual coronation. The archbishop of Reims took the crown from the altar and placed it on the royal brow. All the peers, ecclesiastical and lay, gathered round and put out a hand to steady it. Crowned and vested with the garments and insignia of office, Louis moved off to his throne. As he sat there, the archbishop, now mitre-less, paid him the homage of a kiss and cried 'Vivat rex in aeternum!'—a cry which was echoed by all the peers. This was the signal for unrestrained public rejoicing. The air thundered with fanfares of trumpets, the crash of artillery, and the pealing of all the bells of the city, and the great doors of the cathedral were flung open to let the people surge in to catch a glimpse of their ruler on his throne, adorned with the diadem of Charlemagne.[14] Among them (or was he stranded in the throng in the streets outside?) was an ugly 16-year-old playing truant from school at Troyes; on his return, he was to write a well-informed essay on the *Sacre* for his teacher, an early venture into eloquence by Georges-Jacques Danton.[15]

There were lengthy prayers, and the Te Deum was sung, a prelude to the celebration of the coronation mass—dramatically, a quiet anticlimax to the ceremony; spiritually, the true heart of it. The king recognized his insignificance and mortality by taking off his crown when the gospel was read; then the Church received him into the circle of its chosen ministry by giving him communion in both kinds, a prerogative of the clergy.

As the royal procession left the cathedral, hundreds of little birds were released from their cages to flutter under the vaults, and the heralds scattered commemorative medals among the people.

Though the comte d'Artois and some libertine nobles had laughed and gossiped,[16] the overwhelming impression was one of splendour, dignity, and rejoicing, a vast pageant of national loyalty. As she saw her husband crowned, Marie Antoinette had broken down and wept. It was astonishing, she reflected, that the king should be so received by his people only two months after starvation had driven so many to riot; we must work for their happiness, she wrote to the empress, her mother. It had been a day she would never forget. 'Je sais bien que je n'oublierai de ma vie (dût-elle durer cent ans) la journée du Sacre.'[17] The royal couple were drawn together: Louis by the sight of her tears, Marie Antoinette by the vision of his great calling; but the attraction lasted but a day, and desire failed.

Cardinal La Roche-Aymon, sustained through the rigours of the long ceremonial by coffee and stimulants, ended the day feeling fine. Solicitously, the king asked him if he was tired. 'O non, Sire! prêt à recommencer'; a fatuous answer which delighted the courtiers for long afterwards.[18]

From henceforth, Louis, the Lord's anointed, was endowed with the power of healing the victims of scrofula. Renan was to exaggerate when he described the 'touching' for 'the king's evil' as the 'eighth sacrament', but it was true enough that the monarch, once crowned, was regarded as the channel of divine mercy (he could act only if he was in a state of grace and had received communion). Three days after the *Sacre*, on 14 June, a procession[19] set off for the abbey of Saint-Rémy, a procession with a military flavour—the Musketeers, the Swiss Guards, the *Chevaux-légers*, and the Royal Pages, with Louis on his famous horse 'Vainqueur' (a corpulent young man, but a fearless horseman, he looked his best in the saddle). The Benedictines of Saint-Rémy had gathered a multitude of sufferers from miles around into various hospitals awaiting the great day—there were many, alas, for the tumours massed behind ears and under jaws were the effect of malnutrition. The scrofulous were gathered together in the open air, 1,000, perhaps 2,000 of them. The task of touching was repulsive. The royal person was protected, in so far as the head of each scrofulous person was held by a doctor, and the supplicants' hands were clasped within the gloved hands of the captain of the Guard, but the day was hot and the vast assembly stank. Louis was relieved to complete the exhausting round and wash in vinegar and water scented with orange blossom.[20]

The message of the *Sacre* was: the king's power comes from God. His servants only open the door to the summons to attend the cathedral when the formula is used 'whom God has given us for king'. The symbols of office (the spurs excepted) are handed over by the ecclesiastical peers; even the sword is a gift from God. More than this, the king is a sacerdotal figure. The anointings, the priestly vestments, the reception of the Sacrament in both kinds, the gift of healing, and perhaps some minor details—the hands of the bishops outstretched to steady the crown, the sceptre as long as a bishop's pastoral staff—all imply that he belongs to the ranks of the clerical estate, those whose peculiar vocation comes intensely, uniquely, and directly from Heaven. Being called by God and instituted by God's servants, however, brings special obligations; the sovereign solemnly swears to preserve the privileges of the ecclesiastical order and to suppress heresy. Throne and altar are allied and interdependent. The prayers,[21] a richly layered historical accumulation, place the monarch in the lineage of Abraham, Moses, David, and Solomon: called by God, favoured by God, and exercising power in the shadow of the divine authority. The manifold intercessions have a threefold emphasis. First, the king is exhorted to fulfil his obligations, and God is implored to help him to do so. Louis is told that he must govern his passions, set a good example, and be magnanimous. May he be a defender of the Church, a 'munificent patron' of ecclesiastical foundations; may he drive out 'false Christians, enemies of the name of Jesus Christ and heretics'. To all, he must give impartial justice, and he must wreak vengeance on the unjust. To the 'princes and seigneurs' of his realm, he must be 'liberal and kind', but his most especial solicitude must be shown to the poor, pilgrims, widows, and orphans. Secondly, the Church reciprocates by calling down on the king the blessings of Heaven, in this life and the next. No fewer than twelve prayers ask for the boon of eternal felicity in the afterlife. But an equal number ask for the overthrow of his enemies in this (including the famous archaic supplication for the strength of the rhinoceros). Six petitions ask for the king to be granted a long life; others ask that he be granted forgiveness for his sins, be delivered from infirmity, and that his descendants may reign for long after him. Thirdly, the prayers ask for material blessing to be shed upon the people of the kingdom. There are several references to the blessing of peace, one specific appeal for the multiplication of population, and two appeals (in the words of the blessings in the Old Testament) for the dew of heaven, the fatness of the earth, and an abundance of corn and oil for the consolation of the people.

The *Sacre* was too solemn a national institution to be ridiculed, but anticlericals and lawyers were not prepared to allow the clergy to make capital out of the manifestly religious implications of the ceremonies. A journalist heaved a sigh of relief when he described how the lay peers were finally summoned to come forward: 'here is the moment when the clergy ceases to attribute to itself the right of conferring unlimited power on the king.' To his disillusioned eye, the unctions and the arrayal in sacerdotal vestments constituted the supreme moment for clerical pretensions—'symbols by which the order of clergy seeks, no doubt, to prove it is united to the royal power'.[22] He was right; the unctions could imply a certain subordination of the monarch—as the Epistle to the Hebrews had said, 'the less is blessed of the better'. And in France, as distinct from England, it was accepted that the king could not exercise his healing touch until he became the Lord's anointed.[23] Laymen, therefore, preferred not to enthuse over this aspect of the liturgical observances. Scholars, in the safe obscurity of Latin, had doubts about the provenance of the *Sainte Ampoule* and the story of the dove.[24] Voltaire could not see how 'a few drops of oil' made any difference to an essentially secular ceremony[25]—in fact, the clergy did not claim that they did in so far as the rights of sovereignty were concerned.[26]

Those who had reservations about the unctions went even further in their scepticism about the magical touch of kings.[27] Saint-Simon has a story, untrue and evilly sardonic, about Mme de Soubise being the mistress of Louis XIV, yet dying from scrofula. Montesquieu was ironical in the *Lettres Persanes*; the *Encyclopédie* expressed disbelief; Voltaire urged the French monarchs to follow the example of William of Orange and renounce the claim to work miracles.[28] At the beginning of the reign of Louis XV the formula was indeed changed, from the absolute 'Dieu te guérit' to the hopeful 'Dieu te guérisse', and from 1739 onwards, Louis XV's private life ensured that he was disqualified from exercising healing powers. On Christmas Day 1736 he communicated and touched for the king's

evil according to usage; the next Christmas, 'illness' provided an
excuse to do neither. His last Easter duty was performed in 1738, and
there was scandal at Eastertide in 1739 when he did not call the
scrofulous to appear before him.[29] Thus there was a gap of thirty-six
years before Louis XVI touched the sick after his coronation. Three
or four certificates about people he had cured were welcomed at
Versailles, but it is doubtful if he convoked any further ceremonies
of healing.

To the lawyers, the essential, decisively anticlerical point about
the coronation was: whatever else the clergy bestowed upon the
monarch in the name of God, they certainly did not make him king.
From the end of the thirteenth century, the legal beginning of
a royal reign was dated from the accession, not from the *Sacre*.[30]
Skilfully taking the ceremonies as a whole and avoiding precise
language so as to give little opportunity for magnifying the role of
the Church, chancelier d'Aguesseau defined what he supposed were
the religious implications: 'Kings protest publicly before the altar
that it is by God that they reign . . . the people, receiving the king
in a fashion (*en quelque manière*) from the hands of God, are more
disposed . . . to revere and obey him, not only by motives of fear or
hope, but by a sentiment and principle of religion.'[31] Similarly, the
Encyclopédie, welcoming the legal point that the king ruled already by
his birth and right of succession, treated the *Sacre* as a picturesque
parable to instruct the multitude. 'Doubtless, the object of this pious
ceremony is to teach the people, by a striking spectacle, that the
king's person is sacred, and threats against his life are forbidden
because, as the Scripture says of Saul, he is the *Lord's anointed*.'[32]

Apart from minimizing the importance of the religious aspects of
the *Sacre* in general, on two specific points men of the Enlightenment accused the clergy of impropriety. One concerned an
omission—deliberate or accidental we cannot know—from the
traditional usages.[33] After the two bishops had asked the congregation if it received its king, the silence that ensued ought to have been
followed by the announcement of the Archbishop of Reims: 'quia
populus acclamavit te, te sacro regem'—a formula transmitted from
prelate to prelate since Saint-Rémy. A substantial volume published
later in the year, *Le Sacre royal, ou les droits de la nation française
reconnus et confirmés par cette cérémonie*, declared that the omission was
engineered by a 'party of reaction', a conspiracy which included the
higher clergy. Other pamphleteers took up the theme: the monarchy, they argued, was founded on a social contract, to which the
people in general gave formal assent. There were similar sentiments

in the account of the *Sacre* given by a radical journalist at the point where he described how the peers, lay and ecclesiastical, put out their hands to touch the crown—'a truly noble and expressive allegory, but one which would be much more appropriate if delegates of the people also joined in supporting the crown with the same allegorical implication'.[34]

The second point of criticism concerned the maintenance of a traditional observance which enlightened opinion regarded as no longer civilized—the oath to extirpate heresy. In the space of the three generations since Louis XIV, the persecutions had died away, and the law courts had found ways and means of—virtually—giving civil rights to Protestants.[35] Turgot urged the young king to take a revised form of coronation oath: 'I promise God and my people to govern my kingdom with justice according to the laws; never to wage war except in a just and indisputable cause; to employ all my authority to maintain the rights of each of my subjects; and to work all my life to render them as happy as is in my power.'[36] Louis was sympathetic, but in the end he dared not do it—he mumbled the offensive formula almost inaudibly. The Assemblies of Clergy continued their hollow exhortations for action against heretics; 'under the government of a monarch', they argued, 'troubles are practically always inseparable from the diversity of religious opinions', and the coronation oath was 'the foundation of public peace', with its obligations to 'enforce morality and protect religion'.[37] When, in 1787, the long overdue grant of civil rights to Protestants was made, the clergy mostly acquiesced, though there were protests that Louis had betrayed his mission and broken his promises. In January 1788 the bishop of Dol scandalously used the opportunity of a Breton delegation to Versailles to denounce his sovereign to his face. Constantine, Theodosius, and Charlemagne, he declared, would have convoked a national council of the Church before embarking on a measure 'that threatened the collapse of the arches of the sanctuary'.[38]

II

The interdependence of Church and State, rehearsed in the *Sacre* once in a lifetime, was continually demonstrated anew in the multitudinous official ceremonies of the *ancien régime*. The great occasions of secular rejoicing were marked by the solemn chanting of the Te Deum. This fourth-century hymn of praise and credal affirmation had been drawn out of its devotional and liturgical context to be made the propaganda manifestation of the monarchy. From the late fourteenth century it had been central in the coronation ceremony, and thereafter it became the general official observance of the cities of France when rejoicing for fortunate occasions in the life of the royal family and, above all, for military victories. In Toulouse, the Te Deum was prescribed (with all the magistrates and great ones of the city processing into the cathedral to hear it) on seventy-two recorded occasions between 1738 and 1780. Only nine of these were religious events (a new archbishop welcomed, a new saint canonized, a new relic acquired, or a new altar consecrated); nineteen concerned the royal family (ten being to give thanks for the king's recovery of health, seven for royal births); thirty-seven were celebrations of military victories (including three peace treaties).[39] In the heady days of the early Revolution, when the Nation and the Law were being co-opted with the monarchy into the triple symbol of patriotic ardour, the Te Deum remained indispensable. At the festival of the Federation on 14 July 1790, everywhere in France it was sung as the local community gathered to take the new civic oath at the 'autel de la patrie'. It took another year before the pageant masters of the Revolution conceived of national rejoicing in purely secular terms with a pagan, neo-classical décor.

By contrast, in times of national disaster, dearth, defeat, royal illness, the Church was called on to recite services of liturgical penitence, and to invite the faithful to fervent intercessions. Thus, the joys and sorrows of the royal family can be chronicled from the liturgical record of the Parisian churches. On 11 September 1729, Louis XV went to Notre-Dame to give thanks for the birth of the dauphin, and all chapters, parishes, and religious communities processed to the cathedral, and from thence to the Sainte-Chapelle, to worship before its prestigious relic, the fragment of the True Cross. Churchmen reminded the laity that only eleven months before, the Queen had paid her first visit to Notre-Dame to pray for a male heir. The collapse of the popularity of Louis XV can be documented in the attendances at the intercessions for his recovery from illness. In 1744, the whole capital came, and when he was pronounced out of danger, every guild commissioned a Te Deum, the coal heavers outdoing all rivals by hiring the municipal oboes and trumpets. In his last illness, thirty years later, hardly anyone attended the intercessions or prayed before the relics of Ste Geneviève, displayed for the purpose. As with the monarch, so with the institutions which, under him, regulated society. When the law courts reassembled after the vacation, proceedings began with a mass, the *messe rouge* of the parlement of Paris, so called because the lawyers wore their scarlet and ermine. If there had been an involuntary vacation because the magistrates had been exiled by the king, the *messe rouge* would be celebrated before they administered justice again; great was their delight on such an occasion, on 1 December 1732, when the verse for the day was Isaiah 1: 26: *Restituam tuos judices*: 'I will restore thy judges as at first, and thy counsellors as at the beginning; afterwards, thou shalt be called the city of righteousness, the faithful city.'[40] The terms and examinations of the universities, the commemorative days of individual faculties, municipal elections, the opening of a new building or bridge, the laying of the keel of a warship, the blessing of the colours of a regiment—the whole official life of the country was marked by religious observances. The directors of the most unpopular of the instruments of government were the most scrupulous about paying deference to God. The lease of the Ferme Générale of the taxes always ended with an article according alms to the poor, 'and that it might please God to bless this Association, a mass shall be said every day in the chapel of the *Hôtel des Fermes* at Paris, paid for at the ordinary tariff'.[41]

The celebration of this alliance of Church and State, so evident in ceremonies, was a commonplace of ecclesiastical eloquence. The people were brought to obedience by the teachings of religion, and the Church was preserved in safety under the shadow of the secular power: 'God subjects peoples to the authority of kings and the authority of kings ought to keep the peoples submissive to God,' said the Jesuit Charles de Neuville preaching before Louis XV: 'Religion is the support of the throne, and the throne gives protection to religion.'[42] As the century progressed, it became injudicious for the clergy to define this 'protection'; liberal journalists were outraged when ecclesiastical obituarists, short of other material to praise Louis XV, instanced in his favour the censorship of irreligious books and the penalizing of Protestants.[43] Preachers used extravagant language in expressing loyalty to the hereditary monarchy of France. 'Vous êtes des Dieux,' said Bossuet of kings,[44] though the context in which he said it hardly gave monarchs cause for complacency. The pastoral letters of bishops might stray over the borderline which separated sycophancy from blasphemy—like using New Testament phrases about the incarnation of the Saviour to greet the birth of a new royal prince.[45] Unconditional loyalty to the person of the monarch was expressed in the oath of allegiance taken by a bishop: he would not take part in any treasonable design 'and if any such

comes to my notice, I will make it known to your Majesty'.[46] The
law-books define what was involved; the only case in which the
secret of the confessional could be violated was when a crime of 'lèze
majesté au premier chef' was involved.[47]

Looked at from a doctrinal point of view, loyal rhetoric wandered
furthest from orthodoxy in the routine assertions so commonly
found, that religion would fail if it did not have the support of the
monarchical State. Massillon had declared: 'Religion grows feeble
and collapses . . . wherever civil harmony is destroyed.'[48] 'I will not
separate religion from the State,' said Archbishop Boisgelin to Louis
XVI in December 1790, 'nor the State from your person, because
religion and the State fall with the king.'[49] These statements were
leaving a great truth unsaid: the Church had an eternal mission, and
if the secular order fell or the State lost its monarchical organization,
the Church would go on. Even as Boisgelin spoke, the time was
rapidly approaching when churchmen would be obliged to dig into
the unspoken assumptions behind their political theory and adjust to
a world in revolution; essentially, it was public order that was sacred,
and a *de facto* government had to be obeyed. The mystique of royal
sovereignty was real enough, but fragile. Churchmen did not say
that the quasi-sacerdotal status received by kings at their coronation
was the origin of their sovereignty, though it 'rendered their power
more acceptable to the subjects and less dangerous to themselves'.[50]
Power had a divine origin, but this did not mean that God gave it as
a peculiar personal gift to the ruler; power came from God in his
general activity as creator: he made man of a nature demanding life
in society, and life in society demanded a final secular authority. 'In
all this', Suarez had said, 'there is no divine action distinct from
creation.' The greatest French theologian of the century, Bergier, in
his *Quelle est la source de toute autorité?* (1789), ridiculed theories of
political contracts made among men who had sprung up from the
earth as isolated individuals; in reality, God created men with
reciprocal rights and duties from the beginning. There was an
original social nexus, and from it systems of government had arisen;
we must accept them, since 'the harshest of governments is a lesser
evil than anarchy'. The ideal is the 'conservation of the people', not
their 'absolute liberty', a dream of 'an imaginary happiness which no
nation has ever enjoyed since the creation'.[51] The argument from
anarchy is strong, but ambiguous so far as monarchy is concerned.
Any port will do if the storm is wild enough.

The raw, utilitarian antithesis between anarchy and government
which underlay the Christian doctrine of obedience was an argu-

ment of last resort, to be drawn on in desperate, revolutionary days. The divinity that hedged a king implied some sense of more direct divine election. This election was more often assumed than defined. An attempt to do so was made, at the end of the seventeenth century, by Quesnel the Jansenist, arguing on Thomist lines and anxious to show that the authority of Louis XIV had nothing to fear from his party; what he said was the quintessence of current ortho-doxy, though more logically put.[52] Essentially, he appealed to the operation of the providential hand of God in history. A king may be elected; 'this instinct by which a multitude of persons of different temperaments agree to choose a man to command them and by which they focus their choice on a single man . . . can only be regarded as a singular effect of the guidance of God, who holds in his hand the hearts of all men'. Another way a monarch may achieve power is by conquest in a just war, for all peoples, even pagans, accept God as 'the sovereign arbiter of battles'. But there is a third way, superior to the others: 'legitimate succession', as in France. The caprice of peoples, cabals, and violence can vitiate an election, and a tyrant with an army of barbarians can win a war. God may not be actually operating in a particular election or on a particular battlefield. But children are always a gift of God, and he sends to kings the heirs destined to succeed them in their sovereignty. 'This way of entering into authority is more excellent, and it imitates . . . the manner in which the Son of God received from his Father all his power and authority, by way of birth; for God the Father, engender-ing the Son, communicates to him all that is in his own essence.' Hereditary government also resembles the rule of God, as it is eternal. And in whatever way a king comes to rule, whether by election, battle, or—more surely—by legitimate succession, he is 'God's minister', as St Paul said, and as Aquinas taught. There was, of course, a difficulty. As in any view of the workings of Providence, there was a twilight area where the divine purpose seemed to falter. An election might be fraudulent or a victory mere brute force; as for hereditary monarchy, what of a barren queen or an imbecile or vicious heir? These were further examples of crisis, where the theologians had to fall back on the argument from anarchy to main-tain the obligation of obedience. France, however, was fortunate: a thousand years of monarchy were evidence to demonstrate the long-continuing providence of God underlying the accidents of history.

There had once been a time when the Church had obeyed—or suffered beneath—an alien and unsympathetic government only because the alternative was anarchy; churchmen, said the archbishop of Tours, in a speech to the General Assembly of the Clergy in 1745, had then appeared in the courts of emperors only to defend their conduct and, maybe, face martyrdom. 'Since Constantine and Clovis', however, these unhappy days had ended, and the two powers were 'in firm alliance'.[53] When they reflected on the role of the temporal power in this alliance, the clergy, like the magistrates, held that the king, though absolute, was not arbitrary. Bossuet had listed the obligations of kings: to obey Christian precepts, observe the fundamental laws of France, protect the Church, and defend the poor.[54] As a mere man, no better than all the others, the ruler ought to be 'submissive to [the prelates] in the order of religion' and open-hearted towards the miseries of his fellows. Both the human being and the wearer of the crown were under the shadow of the judgement of God. The language of adulation addressed by churchmen to kings was generally ambiguous. The phrase 'Ye are gods' in Bossuet's great Palm Sunday sermon (1662) comes from Psalm 82, in which God speaks to unjust judges: 'Ye are gods . . . nevertheless ye shall die like men and fall like one of the princes.' Ironically, the orator thunders on: 'Oh gods of flesh and blood, gods of dust and mud', you will die, and what is godlike and continuous is your authority. 'The man dies, it is true, but the king, as we say, never dies, the image of God is immortal.'[55] It was hardly a declaration of the divine right of kings.

But there were no earthly sanctions against the misdemeanours of a sovereign. Bossuet's 'Ye are gods' was less a declaration of adoration, than a threat of mortality and the judgement of the next world, allied to an admission of impotence on the part of the subject in this. A Christian could remonstrate and, even, disobey if he was prepared to be struck down, but he was not entitled to revolt. Even as late as 1663, the Sorbonne had defended the possibility of launching an ecclesiastical excommunication against a tyrant. But the need for an assured principle of order in society was pressing all the while towards a doctrine of non-resistance: memories of the murders of Henri III and Henri IV and the civil wars of the sixteenth and seventeenth centuries were never far from the minds of Frenchmen. The Third Estate of the Estates General of 1614 had advanced the proposition: kings could not be deposed by the Church, and subjects could not be released from their oath of allegiance. This declaration was accepted by the Assembly of Clergy of 1682 as the first of its Four Gallican Articles, which were to be taught in all universities, colleges, and seminaries.[56] The Assemblies of Clergy in 1750 and 1756 renewed the formal statement that Christians are not entitled

to revolt against duly constituted authority; this was said categor-
ically, without reservations admitting the marginal possibility of
tyrannicide which could be found in Aquinas and which for long
had been included in Christian political theory.

The doctrine of non-resistance had nothing to do with absolutism:
France was not a 'despotisme à la Turque'. The actors in the pageant
of the *Sacre*—from the peers ecclesiastical and lay to the abbots of
Saint-Rémy and Saint-Denis, from the canons of Reims down to the
humble peasants of Le Chesne—played their parts by traditional right
and privilege. It was a demonstration of how France was a monarchy
hedged around by convention and vested interest. As Jean Bodin had
said long ago, his country was not ruled by a 'seigniorial monarchy'
or a tyranny, but by a royal or legitimate one, in which 'natural liberty and the natural right to property are secured to all'.[57] The lesson
was enhanced by the spectacle of the monarch taking solemn oaths
before he was crowned—though Louis XV held he had taken them
'to God alone', implying that only Heaven could call him to a
reckoning. Though they did not claim that any sublunary authority
could enforce accountability upon the king, the parlements certainly
disagreed with this view of the coronation oaths—they were taken
'to the nation'.[58] Furthermore, the jurists were prepared to elaborate
the royal obligations. They held that, in addition to the coronation
oaths, there were other 'fundamental laws'—concerning the succession to the Crown, the age at which the king ceased to be a
minor, the exact time when his reign began, the Catholicity of the
monarchy, and the inviolability of the Crown demesne. More
vaguely, they talked of the traditions and 'maximes du royaume'—
for example, laws should be published in due form, and officials
should not be dismissed without due process. From time to time they
tried to add the parlement's right to register royal edicts and remonstrate against them. (Louis XV flatly denied this in 1766.) This claim
to a role of verification and criticism was given a wider justification
by the theories of Montesquieu; in 1766 Joly de Fleury declared that
traditional corporations within the State were indispensable to
liberty—'it is of the essence of a monarchy that there be intermediary
bodies'.[59] The struggle of the parlement of Paris with the Crown
throughout the eighteenth century was, in a sense, the attempt of the
magistrates to establish themselves as the intermediary body which
was the interpreter of a set of fundamental understandings between
monarch and people, more especially since the Estates General no
longer met. Their claims, it has been said, were 'a middle term in the
development of the idea of national sovereignty'.[60]

The parlements formulated a version of liberty, but this idea was not their monopoly. After the coronation of Louis XVI, a journalist described the popular anger at the omission of the question to the people asking if they accepted Louis as their king. 'However vain and derisory this formula today, there is great disapproval of the fact that the Clergy, for whom this pious spectacle seems especially designed, should have ventured on its own initiative to cut out this particular part and preserve only that which especially concerns its own interests.'[61] *Le Sacre royal, ou les droits de la nation française reconnus et confirmés par cette cérémonie* (1775) pointed to the announcement which the bishops had omitted from the ritual as confirmation of the idea that the monarchy was founded on a social contract; other pamphleteers followed, taking the same line. These writers were not intending to preach revolution. They deplored Louis XV's attempt to abolish the parlements, and they were anticlerical, wanting to give power a rational and mundane origin, not a divine one. True, there was a 'republicanism' abroad at the end of the *ancien régime*; but it was, in reality, a cult of devotion to the ideal of liberty and patriotism under the monarchy. Its manifestation at the beginning of the Revolution was the idolizing of one of those far distant and dubiously relevant heroes of the Roman history taught in the *collèges*: Lucius Junius Brutus, who fought against Tarquin. He it was who figured in David's picture exhibited in September 1789 and in Voltaire's play revived in Paris in November 1790.[62]

Like the magistrates of the parlements, the clergy claimed to have the right to collaborate with and guide the monarchy; nor did the fresh breeze of liberty that was blowing towards the end of the *ancien régime* leave them indifferent. But the jurists who were so fond of fundamental laws, traditions, maxims, and intermediary bodies to hedge in the royal absolutism had no enthusiasm for lending the benefit of these concepts to churchmen. 'C'est l'Église qui est dans l'État, et non pas l'État dans l'Église.'[63] An *arrête* of the parlement of Paris in September 1731 defined the relationship of the two powers.

The temporal power, established directly by God, is absolutely independent of all other powers . . . it is not the business of the ministers of the Church, under whatever pretext, teaching or otherwise, to fix the boundaries God has placed between the two powers, and . . . the canons and regulations that the Church is entitled to make do not become laws of the State except in so far as they are endowed with the sovereign's respectable authority . . . To the temporal power alone belongs the jurisdiction which has the right to employ visible and exterior force to compel obedience by the subjects of the King. The ministers of the Church are accountable to the King, and in case of abuse, to the law courts, for the exercise of the jurisdiction which they hold from the King and, even, for the exercise of the power they hold directly from God, in anything which might endanger public safety, the laws or the maxims of the Kingdom.[64]

The temporal power, then, was autonomous, supreme in its own sphere, and the sole judge of the extent of its own dominion. Customary boundaries between the two powers could always be revised by the secular ruler; the Church was a ship with an ecclesiastical pilot who did the everyday navigation, but there was a captain in charge of security who would intervene if there was trouble aboard which might lead to shipwreck.[65] 'All exterior and public authority is but an emanation of the power (of kings). The Crown is the source of all magistracy, political, civil and ecclesiastical.'[66] Thus, according to the standard law dictionary, 'the rank, precedences, property, possessions, rights, prerogatives and privileges of the clergy are held solely from the generosity, the piety and will of the sovereigns'.[67]

These sweeping views of secular pre-eminence were invoked against the pretensions of churchmen in general and of the Roman Curia in particular, in an uncompromising fashion. The Church was regulated by canon law (the collection which Pope Hadrian II had given to Charlemagne, the canons assembled by Gratian, the decretals of Gregory IX, and so on), but only in so far as these prescriptions were not contrary to the liberties and usages of France and the ordinances of her kings. Constitutions of popes of the last 300 years were not binding, and new papal bulls needed letters of confirmation from the king (issued after due examination by the parlements)—a rule reaffirmed by the parlement of Paris in 1703, 1716, 1764, and 1765.[68] Every Maundy Thursday the Pope reissued the thunderous bull *In coena Domini*, proclaiming the immunities of ecclesiastics, their jurisdictions, and their properties. Not a word of this was valid in France; nor was the kingdom subject to the decrees of the Holy Office or of the Congregation of the Index. The Crown had the oversight of the use of all ecclesiastical property and, maybe, had a right in reserve to pronounce on its very existence. The king named to 'all the prelacies of the kingdom', not, as the Pope might imagine, by virtue of the Concordat, but as 'founder, donor, suzerain and protector'.[69]

To enforce these Erastian maxims against the clergy, one of the ploys of the lawyers was to undermine them with pious deference; they served a master whose kingdom was not of this world: God would look after them, so no one else need bother. This was the principle behind the verdicts in lawsuits in the first half of the century about 'la cause de Dieu'; evidence of a vow before God to give money to a hospital, or of an entry in a parish register promising to pay for a new pulpit, was not an argument at law—only a last will and testament was enforceable against the heirs.[70] The same device helped to whittle down the precedence enjoyed by ecclesiastics as members of the First Estate.[71] Servants of another world, they were accorded first place because for long people had admired their virtues; there was always an impropriety, then, in any attempt to enforce a priority which was not freely offered. The Crown was the fountain of honour, of course, and Louis XIV's edict of 1695 gave the dignitaries of chapters precedence over presiding officers of law courts, and canons over ordinary magistrates. The lawyers, however, interpreted the sovereign's will restrictively: only cathedral chapters were meant; the 'second order' clergy, curés, and the like were excluded, and the *cour des comptes* of Montpellier by tradition took pride of place over the cathedral of that city, and so on.[72]

Readers of Montesquieu, converted to the necessity of intermediary powers to prevent monarchy becoming despotism, might have encouraged the clergy to think of themselves in this mediating role. The dauphin, son of Louis XV, was said (by Père Griffet) to have derived this lesson from *L'Esprit des lois*: 'le pouvoir du Clergé y est très convenable; il sert de borne au despotisme sans y opposer de violence'.[73] But the lawyers reserved this task for the parlements, and tended to subject ecclesiastics to the will of the sovereign.

The evolution of the lawyers towards a view of monarchy as absolute yet hedged with restrictions, open to remonstrance and criticism yet never endangered by armed resistance, had run parallel with the thinking of the clergy. So far, churchmen and magistrates were in agreement, though each side would have claimed the leadership in remonstrance and presenting the case for the people. The lawyers were also in agreement with the Assembly of Clergy's statement of 1765: 'within the alliance of temporal and spiritual, each power is sovereign and absolute in what concerns it'.[74] But the point of disagreement came with the question: 'who defines the boundaries within which this sovereign and absolute sway is exercised?' In the last resort, the clergy were not prepared to leave the definition in the hands of the secular power. Their case was squarely put by the Assembly of 1765 in its 'Exposition of the rights of the Spiritual Power'. They agreed that the sovereign could examine religious institutions from their temporal side and admit or not admit

them,[75] and they conceded that the secular authority had a special
interest in ecclesiastical property, though with two provisos: first,
such property was 'legitimately acquired',[76] so was protected by the
same safeguards which private individuals and corporations enjoyed,
and second, there were sanctifying circumstances of biblical warrant
and charitable obligations which the State was obliged to respect.
(Even so, in practice, pleading sanctity could not get churchmen out
of contractual obligations—a test case was settled by ordinance of the
parlement of Paris in 1603 establishing the right of a bell-founder
whose bill had not been paid to confiscate the bells from the steeple,
even though they had been solemnly consecrated.[77]) But doctrine,
morals, and the administration of the sacraments the clergy declared
to be exclusively within the spiritual sphere. On such matters, a
bishop could not be restrained from speaking freely: 'silence can
never be imposed on those whom God has instituted as his spokesmen'—so much for the royal resort to a 'law of silence' in
September 1754. The secular power was never entitled to suspend
the execution of the judgements of the Church. Though external
circumstances concerning the administration of the sacraments
might have major secular repercussions, the lay courts could not
intervene:[78] they could not determine, for example, if consent had
been given to a marriage. Nor could they rule a refusal of communion to be a deprivation of individual rights or an actionable defamation of a citizen—'the refusal of the most august of our sacraments
can never be within the competence of the civil authority'. This ill-
considered and unrealistic proclamation of clerical authority was
promptly suppressed by the parlement of Paris, while the king,
anxious to extract a substantial subsidy from the ecclesiastical
Assembly, made haste to annul the parlement's pronouncement—
without, of course, endorsing that of the clergy. There was a storm
of controversy.[79] The canonists, Le Paige and Maultrot, reaffirmed
the right of the magistrates to 'guarantee citizens in the possession of
the exterior advantages enjoyed by all Christians'. Jansenist pamphleteers, long accustomed to extracting questions of 'fact' from the
domain of spiritual infallibility, enlarged the sphere of the secular
power, by listing the matters of 'fact' which the prince was entitled
to decide, like interpreting ambiguities of language, verifying the
correct performance of canonical procedures, and, indeed, ruling
what was fact and what was doctrine in the first place. Other
polemicists were ruthlessly anticlerical. There was Richer (*De
l'autorité du Clergé et du pouvoir du magistrat politique sur l'exercice des
fonctions du ministère* (2 vols., 1766)), the marquis de Puységur

(*Discussion intéressante sur la prétention du clergé d'être le premier ordre d'un état*, 1767), and Cerfvol (*Du droit du souverain sur les biens fonds du Clergé et des moines*, 1770). Christians are pilgrims on the earth on their way to another country, was Richer's theme. The prince examines their beliefs and, if satisfied, makes a contract with them guaranteeing them safe conduct through his dominions. Bound by this contract, churchmen cannot innovate in doctrine—cannot, say, add a bull like *Unigenitus* to the original declaration of belief which has been verified. Further, being responsible for good order, the temporal sovereign imposes rules on the travellers for their journey; their conduct was likely to be better in future, for example, if he decided to legalize divorce among them, to order their priests to marry, and confiscate ecclesiastical property. The idea of selling off the landed domain of the Church appealed to Puységur and Cerfvol, the marquis because the clergy are 'strangers in the world', Cerfvol because of the precepts of the gospel—we are ordered to sell all we possess and give to the poor, and if the rest of us cannot realistically do this, the ordained ministers at least should obey. In his *Défense des Actes du Clergé de France* (1769), Le Franc de Pompignan, bishop of Le Puy, made something of a reply to the Gallican canonists, but he could only express panic and foreboding at the theorizing of Richer; there was a design, he said, to subject religion to the State along the lines of English Erastianism or, worse still, Rousseau's 'Civil Religion'.

The arguments of the clergy in defence of their rights were feeble by the standards of the Enlightenment, but respectable by those of the law-books. They cited 'authorities', specific texts from the New Testament and from the Fathers. There was the charge to 'teach all nations', 'to bind and to loose', and to speak in Christ's name—'he that heareth you heareth me'. St Paul was cited as evidence that the Holy Spirit had established bishops 'to govern the Church of God'. There were citations from Ambrose, Gregory Nazianzus, Pope Gelasius, and a few other writers, and Charlemagne's dictum that those who did not show submission to their pastors were hardly likely to be faithful to him.[80] Churchmen were conscious, however, that the sort of precedents capable of transforming sweeping Dominical charges into mundane practical authority were thinly spread. The Assembly of 1775 complained of the failure of historians and canonists to make full use of the laws of the first Christian emperors, 'so favourable to episcopal jurisdiction and to religion. It is astonishing that they have been regarded as foreign to the Gallican Church.'[81] The Assembly did not say how this relevance could be established. The instinct of the lawyers had been right: if they loaded the Church with praise as a virtuous institution proclaiming a 'kingdom not of this world', it would not be easy for bishops to claim final authority in matters which had a tincture of secular involvement.

What the Church needed was a Montesquieu, a genius who could ally erudition with theoretical speculation to justify the Church's position in society and its claims against the temporal power. Fénelon, relativist, utilitarian, pessimistic, ready to argue from first principles rather than Scripture,[82] could have done it; but his dreams of a Church freed from State control and a State liberalized by aristocratic councils and estates were removed from reality and, mostly, confined to private circulation. At the end of the *ancien régime*, Loménie de Brienne, in his *Mémoire sur les Assemblées Provinciales*, faced the Church's problem and adapted the ideas of Montesquieu and Fénelon towards a solution. The argument from being the First Order in the State was dead, and he avoided using it. Before Sièyes said it, the idea was current that the Third Estate was, in fact, the foundation of the nation. Of the Tiers État the marquis de Mirabeau had said, 'celui-ci comprend tout le reste, et quel reste! . . . Ce reste est tout de fait, et rien de droit.'[83] And in a pamphlet of 1787, the genealogist Maugard declared: 'There are two principal Orders in the State, the Nobles, which include the Clergy because their privileges are almost identical, and the People.'[84] Loménie de Brienne recognized the validity of these two observations, and combined them into a theory giving the clergy a lofty political role. In a popular State, he said, everyone claims to be equal, and in a despotism the ruler forces them to be so. These are unsatisfactory forms of government. France is fortunate in being a monarchy founded on 'honour'; 'les grands', the great ones of the land, inspired by this principle, defend the people from the abuses of authority, and uphold the throne against the fickleness of the people. So, in setting up the new provincial assemblies, there must be a clear recognition of distinctions of rank. True, in accordance with the spirit of the times, the Tiers État must have more than a third of the representation, and voting must be in common. 'Je repousse absolument les délibérations par ordres.' But the presidency must be given to 'les grands', and they must give leadership. These great ones are defined as the nobles and the clergy—all the clergy, irrespective of birth or rank. 'Properly speaking, there are only two Estates in France, nobles and non-nobles.' The merits of the clergy, their good education, their hard work, their 'attachment to authority by interest and duty', their friendship with the people, their willingness to tell the truth to the king, and the 'excellency of their functions' generally give them the right to noble privileges and to belong to 'the great', the leadership cadre of the nation.[85]

This was a defence of the claims of churchmen purely on Enlightenment principles, but it was unrealistic in treating the clergy as a unified body standing solemnly by to play its role in the new constitutional arrangements. In any deliberative assembly, if the lower clergy had representatives, they would sooner or later discover that their place was not with 'les grands', but with the people.

2

THE RELIGION OF VERSAILLES

I

Isolated from the real life of their people within the crowded, unhygienic splendours of Versailles, the kings of France had two preoccupations besides ruling: to maintain decorum and to keep boredom at bay. Nine thousand soldiers provided pomp and security. Among the 6,000 civilian officials and servants were 200 ecclesiastics. There were as many grooms in the stables, and almost as many musicians in the *musique du Roi*; for hunting and theatrical performances vied with religious ceremonies as the chief pastimes. The greatest ecclesiastic of all was the *grand aumônier*, his office 'almost as ancient as the monarchy itself'.[1] He walked on the king's right in processions, attended (though he did not always say) the prayers at the royal *lever* and *coucher* and the grace at meals, baptized the royal children, and conducted the nuptials of princes and princesses of the blood (always in the presence of the curé of Versailles, for no one, however great, could infringe the rights of parish priests). By virtue of his appointment, he was a commander in the most honourable of all the orders of chivalry, the Ordre du Saint-Esprit. Without having to make the profession of faith or to produce his proofs of nobility, he joined the 100 greatest nobles in the land and the eight other ecclesiastics whom the king delighted to honour, and wore the prestigious cordon bleu (for knights, the riband ran from the right shoulder across to the sword guard; for prelates, the cross, with its dove and fleurs-de-lis, hung on a blue ribbon around the neck).[2] The memoirs and correspondence of courtiers are full of envious yearnings and conspiracies to gain promotion to this inner circle of the great.[3] There were revenues and patronage attached to the *grande aumônerie*,[4] but these could hardly matter to one who would already be a bishop, a cardinal, and the holder of at least one rich abbey *in commendam* (in 1789 aristocratic court chaplains held no fewer than eighty-three abbeys between them).[5] Early in the eighteenth century the Rohan family, which had made the see of Strasbourg its fief, seemed to have appropriated the *grande aumônerie* as family property also; but in 1756 their monopoly was broken. In the beginning of the reign of Louis XVI they rescued it, though with difficulty—the story of how this was done being a good illustration of the way in which great families treated ecclesiastical office as a perquisite of birth.[6] The comtesse de Marsan, sister of the prince de Soubise, persuaded Louis XV to promise the reversion of the office to her cousin, Prince Louis de Rohan, coadjutor of Strasbourg, and when Louis XVI ascended the throne, persuaded him to renew his grandfather's promise. Marie Antoinette hated Louis de Rohan (believing him to have written to Mme du Barry ridiculing her mother, the empress); she insisted that the king change his mind. When Cardinal de la Roche-Aymon, the *grand aumônier*, finally died, there was a tremendous confrontation between the king and the comtesse de Marsan; she won, Rohan receiving the office, though on condition that he would resign after two years if he still was not wanted. The question did not arise, since in his naïve and unprincipled attempt to win the queen's favour, Cardinal Louis de Rohan was implicated in the diamond necklace scandal and was banished from court, Montmorency, bishop of Metz, succeeding as the chief of the chaplains to the Crown.

Next in the ecclesiastical hierarchy at Court was the *premier aumônier du Roi*, whose chief duty was to greet the king when he arrived at his place in chapel, take his hat, and hand it to the *aumônier de quartier*.[7] The importance of the office was that it gave access to the monarch, the fountain of promotion. For this reason, and from pride and royalist principles, the bishops competed for it. Like so many offices, this was bought and sold (the price was 300,000 livres, and the salary was 12,000, so there was an average return on the investment).[8] Under the jurisdiction of this 'first' chaplain were eight other *aumôniers du Roi*, serving in pairs for a quarter of the year. They gave the king communion, marked the brows of royalty with ashes on Ash Wednesday, said the prayers at the *lever* and *coucher* and the grace at formal meals, and were present at the king's daily mass, holding his hat, not entitled to take it from him, but with the privilege (absolute except as against the *grand aumônier*) of giving it back directly. Their perquisites were 300 livres and meals at a special table, and their offices changed hands at about 30,000 livres.[9] Parallel to them, though less distinguished, were the chaplains of the queen and of other members of the royal family. These were offices suited to bishops. Of the daughters of Louis XV, Mme Victoire had the bishop of Evreux as her *premier aumônier*, Mme Sophie the bishop of Chartres, while Mme Adélaïde, appointing a chaplain in 1772, could

not find an existing diocesan bishop, so had to settle for the grant of
a title of bishop *in partibus* for her candidate (that is, an episcopal title
attached to some ancient city in lands now ruled by infidels). She
insisted he must not be given 'one of those names which give rise to
jesting'. The Roman chancellery wanted 'Paphos', but in the end he
got 'Pergame'. Eight years later, the comte d'Artois wanted his
chaplain elevated, and the foreign minister wrote to the ambassador
in Rome: 'organize it, Monseigneur, so they do not resurrect the
title of "Paphos"'. This great diplomatic matter was resolved, and
the abbé Gaston became bishop of Terme in Cappadocia.[10] In
addition to this crowd of chaplains to the royal family with episcopal titles resonant with the splendours of Nestorian Christianity,
there was also the *maître de l'oratoire du Roi*, a priest with no functions, but with the right to a place near the monarch's prayer-desk
in the chapel and to a salary of 4,800 livres; in 1746, gossips of the
Court were delighted to recount how the abbé d'Oppede had sold
the office to the abbé Honolstein for 80,000 livres, having bought it
five years previously for half the price.[11] Below these were minor
clergy acting as assistant chaplains, sacristans, acolytes, chaplains to
the military establishment and to the stable grooms—there were
even two concerned with the spiritual welfare of the employees of
the *venerie*, the department organizing the royal hunts.

Louis XV inherited and—with occasional variations—followed
the daily routine of religious observances which Louis XIV had
imposed on the Court: formal prayers before rising, informal ones
after breakfast, mass at noon (Louis XIV had changed to 10 a.m. in
his later years, but his successors changed back to midday), evening
prayers following the afternoon's hunting or promenades, and prayer
in bed after supper late at night.[12] There were also special observances. On Maundy Thursday, both the king and the queen, in
separate ceremonies, washed the feet of a selected band of deserving
poor: the *Miserere* in fauxbourdon was followed by a sermon and the
grand aumônier pronouncing an absolution and a blessing, while after
the washing, dukes and duchesses presented the poor with dishes
chosen from the Lenten menu, fried carp and the like.[13] On Good
Friday, the courtiers would come forward individually for the
adoration of the Cross—the officiant, deacon and subdeacon, the
royal confessor and chaplains, then the king himself, followed by
the laity in descending order of rank.[14] Versailles had its own
deferential additions to liturgical practice. When the queen was to
receive communion, she chose a Host to be consecrated from a box
containing many which was proffered to her; immediately after the

reception, the celebrant would take a gilded cup of wine from a servant, the *premier maître d'hôtel* would taste it, then it would be presented to Her Majesty to drink; at the end of the service, the celebrant would place the end of his stole on the queen's head while he read the Gospel according to St John. (There were variants when the king or the dauphin communicated.[15]) On ordinary days, the royal couple would hear mass from their elevated tribune facing the high altar; on great festivals their chairs were on the level, but on a velvet carpet fringed with gold.[16] The greatest in the land were called on to play their role in liturgical observances; dukes would be required to hold the communion cloth before the dauphin when he received the sacrament,[17] and the queen nominated ladies to take the collection on festival days. In April 1746, Mme de Pompadour proudly confided to the duchesse de Luynes that she expected to be named for this duty at Easter: 'tout le monde dit que je quêterai le jour de Pâques'. But the long-suffering queen passed her over.[18]

The religion of the palace was closely connected with the 'royal parish' of Notre-Dame of Versailles, in which, strictly speaking, the king was a parishioner. Louis XIV had established the Lazarists in the cure of the growing town in 1674, giving them the abbot's share of the revenue of the abbey of Saint-Rémy of Sens, and the building of the new church began in 1684. Two years later, the abbé Hébert was brought from ruling the seminary at Arras to be curé, an austere man who, before he became a bishop in 1704,[19] had organized the parish pastorally and integrated it with the life of the Court. Royal generosity, generally at the expense of some ecclesiastical foundation, and the great growth of population made Notre-Dame of Versailles one of the most splendid parishes in the kingdom by the 1780s. There were 55,000 souls within its boundaries; the *fabrique* had a revenue of 36,000 livres; and in the presbytery, with its extensive gardens and library, no fewer than twenty-three priests resided.[20] On occasion, the king would attend the parish church. It was here, certainly, that he ought to perform his Easter duty; in his pious later years, Louis XIV communicated there every Easter (one of his five annual communions).[21] In 1722, Louis XV made his first Easter communion there, and in 1738, his last.[22] More usually, it was when a Te Deum was being sung for a national occasion, or when the annual Corpus Christi procession took place, that a royal party came to the parish. On 11 September 1729, the king was there to give thanks for the baptism of the dauphin; the royal music came to provide the accompaniment, and the churchwardens invested in 200 candles (the vergers had to start lighting at five in the evening to be ready for the Te Deum at six).[23] The Corpus Christi procession was a regular engagement. That of 4 June 1744 was noted for the anarchical display of the variegated colours of the ladies' parasols—someone had forgotten to prescribe uniformity.[24] In 1759, the parish used for the first time the new canopy of crimson velvet fringed with gold and worked with scriptural subjects in silken embroidery—it cost 90,000 livres; the king did what was expected of him, and gave 14,000 as his personal contribution.[25]

From time to time, the curé would attend at the château. When there was a dearth, the king was the first person to apply to for alms. The ladies of the court supported a charitable association in the parish of Notre-Dame (as also in that of Saint-Louis, the other, newer parish in town); the king paid for a physician (*chirurgien des pauvres*) in each, and sent to both curés regular gifts of firewood from the royal demesne.[26] When, in 1777, the parish set up a manufactory of lace to provide employment for poor children, the maréchal de Mouchy persuaded Louis XVI to endow it with 3,000 livres of annual income.[27] At the same time, the queen extended a standing invitation to the curé of Notre-Dame to attend, alms bag in hand, at 7 p.m. on Sundays at the Salon de Paix, where her weekly gambling sessions were held.[28] Before play began, Marie Antoinette would go round with the bag—'Pour les pauvres, s'il vous plaît'. The ladies gave 6 livres, and the men 24, enough usually being taken to pay for the maintenance of a hundred families in the coming week.

There were times when the curé entered the palace as of right, armed with his parish registers to record royal baptisms, funerals, and weddings. When the future Louis XVI married Marie Antoinette, after the nuptial mass the *grand aumônier* took the register from the hands of the curé and presented it to Louis XV, who signed as first of the witnesses—last of all came the signature of the humble parish priest.[29] Ceremonies which took place in other royal châteaux would, of course, come under the jurisdiction of the appropriate local curé. When Louis XV married Marie Lecsynska in the chapel of Fontainebleau, the curé of Fontainebleau was there with his register.[30] Similarly, when the dauphin, son of Louis XIV, died of smallpox in 1711, the fear of infection was so great that an *ad hoc* funeral procession went off to Saint-Denis by night with the coffin in an ordinary carriage, and the curé of Meudon had the dangerous honour of riding up front along with the official court chaplain.[31]

When a courtier was dying, the Holy Sacrament and the conse-crated oils had to be sent for from the parish church. On Sunday, 29

June 1740, Mme de Sourches collapsed; the king left his evening meal to go to the parish, and led the procession which brought the Holy Sacrament; after the administration, he returned with the curé and attended Benediction before recommencing his supper.[32] In February 1752, when Madame, Louis XV's daughter, was dying, the viaticum was administered by her *premier aumônier*, the bishop of Meaux. But the prelate took over the ciborium from the curé, who had brought it in procession, dukes bearing the canopy over it, and the royal family, escorted by lackeys with torches, walking before. When extreme unction was administered, again the bishop sent for the parish priest, who brought the holy oils from their niche in his church.[33] Mme de Pompadour died at the palace, and was buried in Paris at the Capuchins of the Place Vendôme, but her funeral service took place in the parish of Notre-Dame. Her coffin was taken from her apartments near the king to her private mansion in Versailles, and thence, in a procession with her forty-two servants, to the parish church (this chronology is important, as it absolves Louis XV from the charge of heartlessness; he wept on the freezing balcony when she was first taken away—'voilà les seuls devoirs que j'ai pu lui rendre'. If he asked how long the procession would take to reach Paris, it was at the time of the departure from the parish church two days later).[34]

Being a parishioner of Notre-Dame of Versailles, the monarch was a member of the flock of the archbishop of Paris. The confessors chosen by the king and queen were approved by the archbishop, and permission to infringe the strict rules of fasting in Lent came by way of the curé, who transmitted the diocesan ordinances. When, on national occasions, the royal family went to Paris for services of intercession or rejoicing, arrangements had to be made with the chapter of Notre-Dame, the canons of Sainte-Geneviève, or who-ever else was concerned.[35] But routine ecclesiastical matters within the palace were regulated by the *grand aumônier*, free from diocesan interference: there was always a possibility of dispute, for it was impossible to exclude the ordinary altogether. In 1710, when the new chapel was finished, Noailles, the archbishop, won the right to consecrate it, to the chagrin of Cardinal de Janson, the *grand aumônier*.[36] There was always a problem whenever the prelate of the see of Paris was deemed worthy to become a member of the Ordre du Saint-Esprit: he would have to come to the royal chapel for investiture, and he would wish to have his cross carried before him, and as this signified pre-eminent jurisdiction, the *grand aumônier* would never accept it. The solution adopted in 1747 was to allow the cross, but to put a note in the registers of the Order that this was 'without prejudice' to the conflicting claims.[37]

The affair of the archbishop's cross was typical. Prickliness about precedence was an occupational disease of courtiers, and religious ceremonies were the same as any others where pride was concerned. Under the Regency, the dukes warred against slights on their superiority—that was why those who did not have indispensable duties to perform at the coronation of Louis XV stayed away.[38] Thereafter, they boycotted the Maundy Thursday foot-washing (*la Cène*) of the king: some of them went instead to the queen's. In 1746, they boiled over with rage because the boy duc d'Antin, merely for the fun of it, carried the king's dishes to the poor; they blamed his mother for letting him out that morning. In the following year, however, the ducal claim was recognized, and they turned up at the *Cène*, not without disputes about seniority among themselves, however.[39] At royal funerals, the ducal interest mustered again to outmanœuvre the princes of Lorraine, the Rohans, and the Bouillons, to be first in splashing holy water on the coffin.[40] At the funeral of the maréchal d'Estrées in 1737, to defeat the claim of the marshals to walk 'as a corporate body' close behind the coffin and to have the holy water precedence, the dukes got to the church of Saint-Sulpice early to monopolize the front seats; the marshals persuaded the vergers to move their chairs in front of the intruders; two dukes therefore pushed into the narrow gap between the distinguished soldiery and the sanctuary balustrade, upon which the maréchal de Noailles rushed off to find the curé and forbid any aspersions with holy water whatever.[41] Since their claims were so grievously flouted, in November 1744 the marshals stayed away from the funeral of the maréchal de Chaulnes, all except one, who was a close relative.[42]

The clergy were as competitive as the lords temporal in these ceremonial feuds and forays. In 1723, in view of the continual contests between prelates for the seats of honour, the king directed that the *grand maître des cérémonies* or his deputy must always be present in the chancel of whatever church the royal family were attending to check that due order was being observed; only when all was calm was he to go to the sacristy to escort the officiant to the altar. Rules create new possibilities of infringement, of course; in 1746, at the anniversary service for Louis XIV at Saint-Denis, the clergy accused the *grand maître* of disrespect by failing to advise the celebrant that the service could begin.[43] When he attended mass, the king would kiss the gospel book, which was held out to him—not by the celebrant, but by the senior bishop present.[44] In 1745, the Court, assembled in the cathedral of Notre-Dame in Paris, was delighted to hear Louis XV rejecting the gospels proffered by the _aumônier de quartier_: 'Ce n'est point à vous, c'est à M. le cardinal d'Auvergne.'[45] There were complexities, however. If the celebrant was himself a bishop, he yielded place to no one, and in 1748 Cardinal de Rohan added tricky provisos giving precedence within the episcopate to cardinals and to the _grand_ and _premier aumôniers_.[46] Cardinals, entitled to more exalted feuds than other prelates, had their own running battle with the king, for they claimed the royal prerogative of wearing purple mourning instead of black. Louis XIV, nettled because he had mistaken the purple-draped sedan-chair of Cardinal de Bouillon for his own, deprived them of their singular privilege;[47] but in 1746 they were still clinging to it. In July of that year, when the Court was in mourning for the wife of the dauphin, they refused to put drapes on their carriages or chairs since the prohibition of purple was still being maintained.[48]

Cardinals were secure in their superiority over the episcopate generally, though bishops who sat on folding chairs at royal funeral services would not concede to them the right to repose on more solid seats with high backs.[49] And there were six bishops who enjoyed the status of peers of France with special duties to perform in the coronation, and they would not yield place to red hats and Roman titles. When Dubois, the regent's low-born minister, was made a cardinal, their rage was boundless. If he comes to the parlement for a royal _lit de justice_, said Clermont-Tonnere, bishop and comte of Noyon and peer, 'I will throw him from the upper seats to the lower ones, whatever may be the consequences, and I'll be aided and abetted by the lay peers, with whom measures have been concerted'.[50] No doubt wisely, Dubois never came. Lower down the scale, the chaplains haunted the _premier aumônier_ over the right to say the royal grace; they conceded his pre-eminence, but what if he was late and the _aumônier de quartier_ had already launched on the _Benedicite_ which was the prelude to the grace proper? And the queen's chaplain in his turn would insist on taking over the grace on the days when the queen's kitchen staff were serving the king's dinner because the Court had just returned from Fontainebleau.[51] In their turn, the _aumôniers_ were being pressed by the minor chaplains on their staff, anxious not to have to give way if they had once begun to say a grace in the presence of the royal family.[52] When the future cardinal Fleury became chaplain to the wife of the dauphin, an Oratorian father told him: 'assotissez votre esprit et endurcissez votre coeur'.[53] Everyone knew that these contests were unfitting for good men or men of intelligence, yet the ethos of a hierarchical society and the obsession with proximity to the monarch ensured that they continued, with minds stupefied and hearts hardened.

Sermons were preached before the king at Christmas, Easter, Pentecost, the feasts of Our Lady, All Saints' Day, the *Cène* on Maundy Thursday, and in two complete courses, one for Advent (on the four Sundays) and one, much longer, for Lent (on the Sundays and two other days each week).[54] The regent, to lighten the burden on the boy king—not to mention himself—had reduced the Lenten course to Sundays only (hence, the *Petit Carême*), but the Court soon returned to three sermons a week.[55] In 1751 Louis XV fixed the Lent weekdays as Tuesdays and Thursdays, when he did not hunt, and in his reign the practice became firm of always holding the sermons in the chapel at Versailles—Louis XIV having wandered around to Fontainebleau, Saint-Germain, the Palais Royal, and the two chapels of the Louvre.[56] The payment to the Court preacher, 1,500 livres for Advent and double for Lent,[57] was considerable, and the king sometimes added a pension. But there were more glittering possibilities: a successful preachment might be a stepping-stone to an abbey, or even a bishopric. Certainly, the performance was much discussed at Court afterwards: Père Neuville excelled at portraiture but was voluble and monotonous; Père Chapelin was sound in doctrine but wooden in gesture; Père Teinturier had authority but slipped into familiarity; Père Laugier had a fine presence and a sonorous voice, but lacked discretion.[58] The preacher was supposed to begin with a 'compliment' to the highest-ranking member of the royal family present. Finding apposite phraseology was difficult. Inadequate praise was not to be thought of, but too much would be in poor taste. The humble Capuchin who walked from Montfort to preach at the queen's Maundy Thursday in 1742 and walked back afterwards had no fewer than four compliments to the queen and another to the king; no one approved of this prophet from the wilderness so gauchely sycophantic.[59] The curé who spoke of French conquests in November of the same year found he had struck a false note;[60] so too did the Jesuit who compared the dauphin to Solomon ten years later.[61] And what if, contrary to expectation, the king failed to turn up? A provident preacher would have a reserve compliment to the queen up his sleeve, but if she caught the royal cold and stayed away as well, he was not likely to be ready for the dauphin.[62] Canon Boismont was particularly unlucky. He arrived to preach before the queen on

Maundy Thursday 1748, only to be whisked away to give his discourse before the king (the Cordelier nominated for the *Cène du Roi* having failed to appear).[63] Louis XV received no encomium that day: if the good canon had prepared an alternative compliment, it was downwards, without a thought that his sermon might be promoted.

After a compliment to the monarch, it was allowable to censure him. 'Let him vanquish his passions to merit the true glory, which is the happiness of the saints'[64] was an easy, oblique way of doing it. In his Lenten course of 1734, Père Teinturier urged the king to supervise his ministers and to go out and command his armies (it was said that Fleury was behind this exhortation, wishing to push his young master into accepting responsibility).[65] Père Griffet in 1751 thundered against adultery, and Mme de Pompadour trembled.[66] Three years later, another Jesuit, Laugier, denounced Louis XV's idleness and extravagance, and at Easter, instead of talking of the Resurrection, spoke of the duties of the great towards religion.[67] Two years after that, the abbé de Boismont drew a sharp contrast between the life of the Court and the way of true Christianity.[68] At the very end of Louis XV's reign, in 1773, came the most sensational censure of all, the abbé de Beauvais describing Solomon, weary of pleasures, turning to 'les vils restes de la licence publique', generally taken to be a reference to Mme du Barry.[69] 'Tell me, Richelieu,' said the king to that other notorious womanizer of the century, 'it seems that the preacher threw quite a number of stones into your garden.' 'Yes, Sire, and some thrown with such vigour that they bounced almost into the park of Versailles.'[70] Sophisticated presentation and emphasis were needed to bring these sorts of censures within the conventions of the Court. Laugier was exiled for his pains, while the abbé de Beauvais was rewarded with a bishopric, even though he was not of noble birth (true, it was a miserable little diocese amidst wild mountains). Eleven days after his promotion was announced, he preached again, and was in honour bound to demonstrate that he had not been bought off. 'Sire, my duty as a minister of the Gospel of truth is to tell you that your people are unhappy, that you are the cause, and that no one dare tell you.' And, he said, using the threat of Jonah, 'in 40 days Nineveh will be destroyed.' (In fact, 40 days later, Louis XV died.)[71] A journalist, reflecting on the 'vigorous and astringent style' which had earned the abbé de Beauvais the see of Senez, described how the abbé Rousseau, preaching before the king in February 1774, had imitated him, 'with a holy courage, as the devout will have it, but with cynicism, in the view of the courtiers'.[72] He was prepared to take the risks, in the hope of the reward.

Court sermons were, indeed, feats of apostolic brinkmanship: the preacher was expected to censure, but could he do it without vulgar disrespect? From the early seventeenth century, there had been a tradition of 'political eloquence' associated with the pulpit. 'There are occasions,' said Guéret's handbook of 'eloquence' in 1666, 'rare it is true, but necessary none the less, when nothing ought to confine the preacher's zeal, when he is permitted to say all, and when, rather than risk betraying the cause of God, he must pay no regard to the majesty of the king or to his sovereign authority.'[73] Louis XIV had set the seal of his majestic approval on this convention of sophisticated candour: 'the preacher has done his duty, it is now for us to do ours'.[74] The abbé Soldini, confessor to the dauphin, the future Louis XVI, looked with suspicion on the tradition of the Court sermon, and he warned his royal penitent not to encourage preachers either in their compliments or in their criticisms of the king. The sermon, his view seemed to be, should be emancipated from this unhealthy, ritualistic fixation on the doings of a single man. 'Let each take to himself what is personal to him in a sermon and not concern himself with what is relevant only to others.'[75] When, eventually, the dauphin was crowned as Louis XVI, the preachers no longer had an obvious royal target, but they could always—maybe with implied censure—exhort the king to repress irreligious propaganda and to alleviate the miseries of the people. The abbé Maury's sermon at the *Cène du Roi* in 1778 was one of the masterpieces of the new fashion of *bienfaisance* and *sensibilité*—even the useless comte d'Artois was reputed to know it by heart. Significantly, one of the *aumôniers du Roi* told Maury that he ought to have hammered the philosophes as well. 'Vous oubliez, M. l'abbé', was the reply, 'que je prêchois sur la charité.'[76]

Princes and princesses of France had their confessors whose names were published in the *Almanach royal*.[77] These confessors had established posts with a substantial salary and individual perquisites—two horses, as available, for the queen's, and four for the king's entirely under his own control.[78] Even for royalty, the established rules giving diocesan bishops the power of pastoral oversight could not be waived: the keeper of the king's conscience had to have the licence of the archbishop of Paris to hear confessions in the diocese. In 1722,[79] when Claude Fleury, a learned and conciliatory Gallican, became too old to carry on, Cardinal Noailles for more than a year refused to grant powers to his successor, Taschereau de Linières, no doubt because he was a Jesuit. This put the Court to great inconvenience. Linières was transferred to the Jesuit house at Pontoise,

under the jurisdiction of the archbishop of Rouen, and when the
king made his confession before his First Communion, he had to go
outside the diocèse of Paris to Saint-Cyr, under the authority of the
compliant bishop of Chartres. So long as he held the office, the confessor had the monopoly of the royal conscience, unless illness prevented him from acting—Louis XIV had been able to fulfil his
Easter duties, mistresses and all, because this was the season of the
year when a tactical indisposition incapacitated Père La Chaize.
When, in 1757, Louis XV was stabbed by Damiens, he received
immediate absolution from the first priest available, then again from
Desmaretz, his official director of conscience.[80] Louis XIV had
established the custom of having Jesuits in the office, and with Père
Linières in the reign of his successor, the Jesuit monopoly began
again, with Peyrusseau succeeding from 1743 to 1753, and Desmaretz
thereafter. When the Jesuits were banned in France, Louis XV
turned for a confessor to a curé reported to be their protégé.[81] So did
his pious daughters, Mesdames Adélaïde, Victoire, and Sophie, who
put themselves under the direction of the abbé Madier, curé of
Saint-Séverin, a pupil of the Society of Jesus whose bitter warfare
against his Jansenist parishioners had earned him three years' exile
from the parlement of Paris. In 1774, his duties at Court were interrupted because he had refused the Sacraments to a dying Jansenist
and had no alternative but to flee again from the wrath of the vengeful magistrates—leading a procession of four carts laden with his
furniture, to save it from confiscation by the agents of the law.[82]

Under the Bourbons, the 'two powers' at Court, according to
Montesquieu, were 'the mistress and the confessor'.[83] In Louis XIV's
earlier years, the first power had prevailed, and his Jesuit directors
incurred reproach for their feebleness, Père La Chaize being
unkindly named 'la chaise de commodité'. To avoid further accusations of laxity, the confessors of Louis XV were stern about his
sexual liaisons. When the king fell ill while with the armies at Metz
in August 1744, Père Peyrusseau allied with the Jansenistically
inclined bishop of Soissons, Fitz-James, to ensure that the duchesse
de Châteauroux and her sister were sent away before the last sacraments were administered.[84] Long after Louis XV had ceased to have
sexual relations with Mme de Pompadour, Père Desmaretz refused
to allow him to take communion so long as she remained at Court.
'If the Jesuits were Molinists on this point under Louis XIV,' said
Bernis, 'they are Jansenists in our time.'[85]

What passed between monarch and confessor we cannot know
directly, but we may guess that political matters rarely entered into

their discussions. Aquaviva, general of the Jesuits, in 1602 had laid down a realistic rule for those of his Order called to direct the consciences of kings: they could draw attention to abuses coming to their notice, but 'take care not to meddle in political affairs'. In the eighteenth century, when the ideal of religious toleration was winning over educated opinion, this rule was reinforced by the memory of the confessors who had broken it: the fanatical haters of Protestants pushed into office at Court by the Guise faction during the Wars of Religion, the two Jesuits who had encouraged the young Louis XIV to detest Calvinists and Jansenists, and even Père La Chaize, colourlessly detached rather than culpable. Le Tellier, keeping the royal conscience at the end of the reign, the implacable foe of Cardinal Noailles and Jansenism, could not possibly have been the malevolent desperado he appears to be in Saint-Simon's demonological gallery; but the odium he had incurred was a warning to his successors to stick to the rules of Aquaviva. Certainly, once the Sun King was gone, the *feuille des bénéfices* was taken out of the confessor's domain, and from henceforth he was excluded from decisions on the award of ecclesiastical promotions.

By the time of Louis XVI, the confessor was outside the political sphere altogether. There was nothing for court gossips to seize on; in the previous reign, the exclusion of the monarch from communion had been standing evidence of the working of the discipline of the confessional, but Louis XVI's sexual life was blameless, and open scandal ceased. As the duc de Berry before his accession, the future king[86] had been schooled in the wisdom of Fénelon by his director of conscience, the abbé Soldini, drawing from the *Télémaque* lessons of political guidance based on the fundamental principle of justice. But it was understood that these indicated no more than broad lines of thinking, and that the confessor would not intervene if specific political issues came up. Soldini's notes show the points of personal conduct he insisted on: conjugal fidelity, avoiding reading literature hostile to the Church, directing the royal hunt away from sown fields, abstention from the theatre, but compensation by enjoying hunting, cards, and dice to the full. A few months after his penitent came to the throne, the good abbé died, and his successor was Poupart, curé of Saint-Eustache, simple and virtuous, living all the while in his parish and never appearing at Court except for his private sessions with the king. By contrast, there was a throw-back to the discredited tradition of meddling in politics in the person of Marie Antoinette's confessor, the abbé Vermond, doctor of the Sorbonne and former *grand vicaire* of Loménie de Brienne at

Toulouse, an intriguer in the corridors of Versailles. The king had no director to steel his weak will in affairs of State, and the queen had no mentor to curb her frivolity.

II

The royal chapel at Versailles provided a fitting setting for the curiously formalized religion of the Court.[87] The fourth chapel on the site, it was a creation of Louis XIV, begun in 1698 by Mansart and finished in 1710 by Robert de Cotte, the two greatest architects of the day. All the eminent sculptors of the end of the reign contributed, except Girardon, who was too old, and Coysevox, who was entirely occupied in providing nymphs and river-gods for the gardens of Marly. The exterior was adorned with sculptures and bas-reliefs, and the interior, in bright, white stone, with paintings, marbles, gilt, and bronzes. The more sombre aspects of the Christian message were muted. The three ceiling paintings—the descent of the Holy Spirit by Jouvenet over the royal tribune, the Father in his glory by Noël Coypel in the centre, and Delafosse's Resurrection on the far side—were triumphalist, and the bas-relief by Coustou on the high altar, of the dead Christ on the knees of his mother, was overwhelmed by the Gloire designed by Van Clève. Around the chapel were bas-reliefs which constituted a 'Way of the Cross', from the foot-washing and the Last Supper to Gethsemane, the trials before Annas and Pilate, Peter's repentance and the descent from the Cross; but the sheer agony of the Crucifixion was absent, and there were attendant angels with floating drapery and cloud-borne cherubim. 'It is a Way of the Cross of a particular kind,' it has been said, 'in which the artist proceeds by discreet allusions, avoiding giving offence to the eyes of a fastidious Court.'[88] Royal symbols abounded. The monogram of Louis XIV and the armorial bearings of France filtered the light through the windows. There were fleurs-de-lis and cartouches bearing the royal arms. The royal tribune was more prominent than the altar; at each end there was a sort of pagoda of gilded wood set in a semi-circular projection—the king knelt in the left-hand one, the queen in the right. According to La Bruyère, on occasion,

the great nobles formed a vast circle at the foot of the altar and stood, backs towards the priest and the holy mysteries, their faces turned towards their King, who is seen kneeling in a tribune, and to whom they seem to be directing all their mind and all their heart. This usage, you can hardly avoid realizing, implies a sort of subordination, for the people seem to be worshipping the prince, and the prince worshipping God.[89]

This was under Louis XIV, of course; the forms remained, but lost their intensity of meaning under his successor.

The ceremonies which rolled on daily in the chapel combined exactitude with boredom and irreverence. Louis XIV had put the imprint of discipline on the religious observances of his Court as upon all others. Though idle and inclined to informality, Louis XV continued to be exacting so far as the routine of his chapel was concerned. 'The rites and ceremonies of the Church, the details of the Calendar are rather too often the subject of his conversations,' said the duc de Luynes; 'you can't imagine the degree to which he is well informed on these matters.'[90] The tradition continued under Louis XVI. There was no question of the royal family postponing mass when the launching of the Montgolfier balloon on 19 September 1783 had reached its crucial stage: everything had to be delayed until Marie Antoinette came back from the chapel to the terrace and Louis to the balcony with his telescope.[91] One of the sticklers for religious punctilio was the king's brother, the comte de Provence, in this resembling his royal grandfather. 'That's not how you ought to begin,' he said, when the *grand aumônier* was baptizing one of the royal children; 'the first thing to ask is who are the father and mother—that's what the *Rituel* prescribes.'[92] No doubt he was also gaining satisfaction from dragging in an allusion to the rumours about the conduct of Marie Antoinette. The king's other brother, the comte d'Artois, played the fool at the coronation;[93] it was he, too, who 'sniggered indecently and made the king laugh' in chapel on the day of Necker's dismissal.[94] Versailles was a machine in perpetual motion, producing recurrent patterns of boring magnificence. 'Always the same pleasures,' said a lady at the Court of Louis XIV, 'always at the same times, always with the same people.'[95] Behind the façade was a world of confusion and dirt: courtiers crammed into attics, servants sleeping in sheds and stables, rogues who cut the gold fringes from the curtains, and pilferers who took provisions from the kitchens and ice from the storage pits.[96] Louis XV, whose design for living was to separate Louis de Bourbon from the king of France,[97] built himself an independent life doubly insulated from harsh realities by being hidden away within the hollow shell of splendid ceremony.[98] After a public *coucher* with the standard prayers in the official bed in the *chambre de parade* where Louis XIV had died, he went off to the Petits Appartements; in the morning, his valet woke him, and he went through the empty rooms, over the balustrade and back into the official bed; the door to the Œil de Bœuf was then opened, and the courtiers flooded in, led by the *grand aumônier* to preside over morning prayers. The chapel was part of the official external ceremonial in which everyone had his hierarchical place, a sham which everyone endured while real life went on elsewhere. 'When I return from Versailles,' said a courtier, 'I sometimes stop in the street just to watch a dog gnawing a bone'[99]—this at least was a real happening.

How should a Christian conduct himself in this artificial, heartless environment, where religious observances rolled on in a routine that for so many had no personal relevance? A casuistry of the Christian at Court had been subtly developed in the circle of Fénelon in the reign of Louis XIV, but, for laymen at least, the formula was simple: to follow Soldini's advice, to apply the gospel precepts to one's own life and leave others to do what they conceived to be their duty. In practice, there were two ways of psychological adjustment. One was to follow the daily observances of religion in the royal circle with exactitude, seeking the inner meaning behind the routine; this was the way of the pious duc de Luynes. The other was to serve the king in all the details of Versailles, but to be, as it were, a spiritual *émigré* and find religious reality outside the system. This was Saint-Simon's way. His spiritual mentor had been Rancé, and he found his peace in retreats at La Trappe in Holy Week, and in Easter sojourns on his estates at La Ferté. His sole true happiness was with his wife: they were joined in bonds of affection as strong as the iron bands which he prescribed to rivet their coffins together for ever. He was one of those who hated Versailles, but could think of nothing else, even when away from it in his later years—a classic case of one of the La Bruyère characters 'que la Cour ne rend pas contents, mais qu'elle empêche de l'être ailleurs'.[100] His mind was full of the affairs of Versailles, but he was apart from its life. He detested the official religious policies which persecuted Jansenists and Protestants; he repudiated the amusements—he did not gamble, hunt, or woman-ize, and early on he gave up dancing; though he sought formal honours, he refused to do what everyone else did and ask for pensions and sinecures—what was called 'faire des affaires'. He saw everything, but it was not a world which involved his own Christian destiny among striving fellow sinners. Hypocrisy ruled, everyone was masked, and he watched for the single false move that betrays meanness of the soul. His hatreds were more than un-Christian; they

were perversely Augustinian. His enemies, described with 'demonological verve', were predestined to evil; there was no forgiveness
for them—not from him after thirty years, not from God in all
eternity.[101]

There was one person who took the religious ceremonies of the
Court with unspiritual, downright literalness—and who believed
above all in forgiveness: Louis XV. He was obsessed with death. If
he passed a cemetery, he wished to know if there were any newly
dug graves. 'This is the King's way,' said Mme de Pompadour; 'he
loves to talk about death.'[102] 'It often happened', said the duc de
Croÿ, 'that the King would speak only of sudden death, of the
prayers said over the dying and so on.'[103] He tormented others with
the fears that tormented him. 'Look at his colour'—this said within
the hearing of the subject—'his liver is obstructed, he has only a
month to live.'[104] 'Beware of that nosebleed,' he observed to someone else; 'at your age it is the forerunner of apoplexy.'[105] His macabre
insensitivity met its match with the aged marquis de Souvré. 'Where
do you wish to be buried?' 'At your feet, Sire.'[106] This obsession with
death reflected the strict logic of Louis' religion. He took literally the
Christian doctrine of instant forgiveness available to the penitent,
even at the very last moment,[107] and gave himself up to womanizing.
'He had made a calculation on the matter,' said the duc de Croÿ,
'and thought that, provided at death he repented and received the
sacraments, these [sexual immoralities] were unimportant things . . .
He counted always on the last minute, on a good *peccavi* to cover
everything amiss.'[108] The formal religion of the chapel at Versailles
was, then, all the religion that Louis XV had, but within its narrow
unspiritual limits, he was sincere. He was an official believer, conforming to all the routines,[109] a deliberate sinner keeping in touch
until the dread moment when he would have to break through to
the interior meaning. From 1738, he made no Easter communion.[110]
On his system, the great danger he ran was the sudden onset of death
without time for amendment (he was panic-stricken in 1773 when
the marquis de Chauvelin dropped dead at the card-table; they
pacified him with the story that there had been a flicker of pulse
when conditional absolution was given).[111] A nice calculation would
be required to judge when an illness was sufficiently serious to
warrant sending for the ministrations of the Church, for to promise
amendment of life, then to recover health and relapse into
immorality, would be a serious affair, casting new doubts on the
scheme of a planned conversion which was dubious enough already.
When, in 1744, the king fell ill when he was campaigning with the

armies, the reigning mistress, the duchesse de Châteauroux, had to be sent away;[112] when, in 1757, Damiens stabbed the king, it was touch and go whether Mme de Pompadour would be dismissed.[113] Her case was peculiar, in that sexual relations with Louis had ceased, and for a year she had been deep in conversations with the Jesuit Père Sacy, going with the queen (as a lady-in-waiting) to mass every day,[114] fasting, encouraging Voltaire to compose a verse translation of the Psalms,[115] writing to her husband offering to return to him (no doubt aware that he would not dare to accept).[116] She remained the king's companion and was not admitted to the sacraments until 1764, when she was dying; once she had received the viaticum, Louis could visit her no more.[117]

As between supporters of the official mistress and the familiars of the queen, there was, inevitably, a polarization of court groupings. Marie Lecsynska, Louis XV's consort, was deeply pious; the Pope rewarded her with the golden rose, and the courtiers complained of the inconvenience caused by her interminable devotional obser-vances.[118] Her meditations before a skull, said to be that of Ninon de l'Enclos, set a fashion for the ladies; a be-ribboned death's head, illuminated from within, became an ornament for dressing-tables.[119] Of the royal children, the dauphin, fat and idle, was given to ostentatious genuflections and open censure of his father's pleasures, though he fell into infidelities himself in due course.[120] Of the daughters, Mme Louise became a Carmelite nun, and the other three—Mesdames Adélaïde, Sophie, and Victoire—lived in a severe court of their own (puritanical except where food was concerned),[121] and won public appreciation for their devotion to religion. In February 1752, they not only stopped their carriage outside the church of Saint-Roch in Paris as the Holy Sacrament went by, they got out and knelt in the mud—'Ah! les adorables princesses!'[122] It was about this time, in the early 1750s, that a *parti dévot* began to form, ostensibly giving allegiance to the pious members of the royal family.[123] Marie-Louise-Geneviève de Rohan-Soubise, widow of the comte de Marsan, and the duc de Vauguyon (both bearing respon-sibilities for the education of the dauphin's children) were of the cabal, and among 'ces vilains dévots' D'Argenson also mentions the maréchal de Duras, the prince de Conti, the bishops around the Court, and Père de la Tour, the principal of the *collège* Louis-le-Grand; they put up the Jesuit Dumas as Lent preacher in 1752 to be eloquent on the theme of David and Bathsheba, hoping to oust Pompadour. Meanwhile, the marquise was trying to persuade Père de Sacy to admit her to communion; had she succeeded, the *dévots* would have been outmanœuvred. As it was, said the gossips, she took her revenge by allying with Choiseul to ruin the Jesuits.[124]

The new alignment of court factions at the end of the reign showed how little piety had to do with the politics of the *dévots*, for the comtesse de Marsan and the duc de Vauguyon became supporters of Mme du Barry, the new mistress. To them, it was more important to go along with Richelieu and d'Aiguillon to oust Choiseul and reduce the importance of the Austrian princess he had brought to France, than to demonstrate for rectitude.[125] Mme du Barry had been a high-class prostitute before she met the king;[126] Mme Adélaïde would have nothing to do with her, and joined the circle of Marie Antoinette.[127]

In 1774, when Louis XV was struck down by smallpox, the Court was divided into bitter factions over the question of confession, communion, and sending away Mme du Barry. Once the mistress had gone, she could never come back, and the alignment of forces at Versailles would be radically changed under a 'converted' king if he happened to survive.[128] The dissolute maréchal de Richelieu threatened curé Maudoux, the confessor, to try to keep him away from the royal bedside, and offered to obtain a cardinal's hat for the archbishop of Paris if he would only mind his own business. 'If you want to preside over a confession,' he said, 'listen to mine and you will learn of such sins as you never heard of before.' The devout party wanted to get Mme Louise, the king's Carmelite daughter, to come to the rescue, but hers was a closed Order and she could not leave her convent. The *grand aumônier* failed to stand up to the maréchal, and the bishop of Carcassonne rebuked him. On the eighth day of his illness, Louis made his own decision, sent for the abbé Maudoux, and confessed. The Holy Sacrament was brought from the parish; the ciborium was carried by the *grand aumônier*, the clergy of parish and chapel going before, the royal family and the courtiers following, all with lighted candles. The French guards lined the courtyard and the Swiss the staircase, their drums beating the retreat. Louis received communion holding the crucifix which Mme Louise had sent him.[129] The *grand aumônier* came to the door of the room to announce: 'Gentlemen, the King charges me to tell you that he asks pardon of God for having offended him and for the scandal he has caused among his people; if God gives him his health again, he will occupy himself in penitential exercises, in the maintenance of religion, and the relief of his people.'[130] Richelieu cursed. Two days later, the holy oils were brought, and extreme unction given.[131] By then, the king's face was

swollen and encrusted beyond recognition—a 'bronze mask'. He
lasted two more hours and then died: 'the most courageous death
you would ever see', said the duc de Croÿ, 'and a very Christian
one'.[132] The bishops had a difficult task composing their pastoral
letters for the occasion.[133] Some spoke of the 'good king', more of
his 'penitence'. The bishop of Lodève said he would not 'betray his
ministry' by 'portraying vice without its deformity'. The final
destiny of this prince, said the bishop of Alais, 'is concealed from our
eyes by an impenetrable veil'. According to Voltaire, the curé of
Neuilly preached a funeral sermon that was better than all the rest.
Louis, he said, 'would have paid his debts if he had had the money';
he built the bridge at Neuilly, and he had a valet 'to whom I owe
the appointment to my benefice'.[134] It was a fair summary of the
duties of monarchs of the *ancien régime*: to do some public works and
confer many private favours, to maintain the hierarchy of society,
and to manœuvre along the fringes of bankruptcy.

III

The principal resource available to the king to do favours to individuals was the immense wealth of the Gallican Church. By the
Concordat of 1516, the Crown appointed to the bishoprics (except
Strasbourg, which remained in theory elective)[135] and to the headship of the great abbeys, more than 800 in number. Various other
benefices—canonries, cures, and chapels—were disposed of by the
Crown by rights of patronage and customs of a pre-emptive kind.[136]
Such benefices as did not carry with them the cure of souls could be
conferred on those nominal ecclesiastics whose sole qualification was
the tonsure; the office of abbot of a great monastery, for example,
was a dignity held *in commendam* with no obligations beyond supervising the arrangements that drew off something like a third of the
revenue of the house. It was also customary for the king to allocate
pensions to named individuals, to be deducted from the revenues of
a bishopric or monastery. The list of current vacancies in this manifold patronage available to the Crown was called the *feuille des
bénéfices*; a great deal of the intrigue, the ecclesiastical politics, and,
indeed, the genuine piety of the Court swirled in a whirlpool around
this notorious list. It was one of the principal reasons why the
great nobles demonstrated their loyalty by dancing attendance at
Versailles.

A foreign envoy at the court of Louis XIV in 1690 referred to the right to present to the benefices in the *feuille* as 'one of the most splendid possessions of the Crown'. Families which gave distinguished service in war, in the administration of justice, in finance, or at Court, he said, were rewarded by ecclesiastical promotion for their sons, 'without a penny coming out of the Treasury'.[137] This was only part of the story, of course. The Church had to be kept going as an administrative organization, if not as a spiritual one, so attention had to be given to ability; there were parties within the Church which lobbied for positions of authority, just as there were political cabals and aristocratic alliances pushing for influence or perquisites. There was, too, the matter of the king's conscience. If there was one sin for which damnation was sure, said the handbooks of the confessional, it was the conferring of ecclesiastical benefices for worldly motives. A monarch who was truly pious, as was Louis XVI, would be restrained by painful scruples; a monarch who was a notorious womanizer, as were Louis XIV and Louis XV, did well not to tie a second, major weight to his soul to drag it down to Hell.

Louis XIV began in 1661 by using a *conseil de conscience*, consisting of his confessor, the *grand aumônier* and three other bishops, to advise him on Church appointments.[138] As its members died off, they were not replaced, and the king and his confessor ran the business alone, except for a period in the 1690s, when Desmarais, bishop of Chartres, was taken on as an extra adviser. During his final illness Louis refused to make any further nominations. 'Mon père', he told Le Tellier, his confessor, 'I find myself burdened enough already by the large number of nominations to benefices that I have made during my reign; I fear greatly that I have been misled in the choice of candidates recommended to me, concerning which I may, very soon, have to render my account before the judgement of God.'[139]

After the Sun King's death, under the regent Orléans and subsequently, up to 1732, ecclesiastical appointments were discussed in a *conseil de conscience* of prelates. Two different sorts of anecdote are told about the attitude of the regent himself. A churchman with heavy debts appealed for a bishopric, without whose revenues, he said, 'I'll be dishonoured'. 'Better you than me,' said Orléans. To a canon who boasted that he was 'of episcopal timber', the reply came: 'Eh bien, when they start making wooden bishops, I won't fail, *monsieur*, to mention your name to the king.'[140] As against these tales of honesty, there is one of the regent announcing, over his morning cup of chocolate: 'the King has just signed the *feuille*; the Jansenists ought to be pleased with me this time, for I've given all to Grace and nothing to merit.'[141] There is no necessary contradiction between these two aspects of anecdotal evidence; the duc d'Orléans hoped, maybe, that the best man would be found on most occasions by the deliberations of the *conseil de conscience*, provided a corrupt promotion could be made when it suited his personal interests. The most notorious of his appointments without merit were those of Dubois, and after him, of the abbé de Saint-Albin, his illegitimate son by the actress Florence, to the wealthy see of Cambrai—in the wake of the saintly and sophisticated Fénelon. Parisian gossips rejoiced in scandals like this. The regent, they also noted, kept the abbey of Hautevillers in his family, because its lands produced the best champagne, and the bishop of Rennes moved to Nantes, thus tripling his income, after frequenting the company of the Regent's valet. And why did a Prussian diplomat enjoy a pension from the bishopric of Verdun, and a notorious gambler be given 2,000 livres a year from an abbey, having belatedly remembered that he had been tonsured in his youth?[142]

The regent died in December 1723, and after a brief interval of rule by the duc de Bourbon, Fleury, the king's tutor and a bishop, took over the administration in the summer of 1726. A few months later he was made a cardinal, as an enhancement of his authority and to give him precedence in the council. A long new era of stability began. Its outward symbol was the complex old ceremonial routine of the days of Louis XIV, interrupted from 1715 to 1722 when the Court had moved to Paris and the fountains ran dry and the trees withered at Versailles, but now restored amidst all its ancient splendours. Fleury took over the *feuille des bénéfices* himself, and made ecclesiastical appointments with the collaboration of the *conseil de conscience*—at least in theory—for six years or so. After that, he relied solely on the advice of M. Couturier, the superior of the seminary of Saint-Sulpice. As a churchman, Fleury paid due regard to merit in his promotions, and as an orthodox churchman, due regard to the exclusion of Jansenists. In a century famous for its insolent wit, the reply of the frivolous abbé de Bernis to the octogenarian cardinal was remembered. 'You will never receive an ecclesiastical benefice so long as I live!' 'Eh bien, Monseigneur, j'attendrai.'[143] By the standards of the *ancien régime* it might have been assumed that Fleury's nephew, the abbé Henri de Rosset de Ceilhas would be a certainty for the vacant bishopric of Lodève; the town and the chapter were supposed to be asking for him, and the archbishop of Narbonne pressed for his appointment: 'act with an urgency that recalls the elections of the Early Church', he wrote quaintly, recommending this piece of nepotism. Pons de Rosset, chevalier de

Rocozals, maréchal de camp, the candidate's brother, wrote to Fleury on 27 April 1732:

I can certify to you truthfully that he has piety and a great love for the poor, virtues he has inherited from your family. I noticed also that, since his return from Paris, he applies himself greatly to the reading of the Holy Scriptures. Your Eminence once honoured me with the confidence that you had heard that he allowed his subordinates to lead him. Since he has an excellent nature and is full of kindness, some enemy of his has ascribed this ridiculous trait to him. I know for a fact that if Your Eminence deemed it right to honour him with the dignity of a bishop, he would choose a grand vicaire and a chaplain who would edify the public by their morals and would be very knowledgeable.[144]

(In short, he is the twit of the family, but we'll get him good advisers.) Fleury turned him down. 'I pay more attention to looking for candidates suitable to serve the Church efficiently than to helping my own family.' Nevertheless, it was no disadvantage to be related to the cardinal-minister. Two great-nephews of Fleury eventually became archbishops.[145]

Fleury died in 1743. Tencin, a worldly prelate living down a seamy past, but strictly orthodox and with a head for business, was spoken of as a candidate to hold the *feuille*, and thought he had got it when the cardinal, approaching death, offered 'to do something' for him—but it was only to get him into the Academy.[146] The *feuille* went instead to Boyer, bishop of Mirepoix, a Théatin monk who had risen from obscurity by the lucky accident which had made him confessor to the duchesse de Lévis. He was an honest man, who imposed tests on candidates for bishoprics: interviews with a curé of Paris, reforming a nunnery, presiding over a difficult general-chapter of a monastic Order.[147] He excluded Jansenists, of course, leading D'Argenson to call him 'a persecutor for bagatelles' who put 'the Constitution *Unigenitus* above the Gospel'.[148] His ruthless ortho-doxy apart, he was probably as fair as the pressures and prejudices of Versailles allowed. On the one hand, D'Argenson accused him of favouring the great nobles;[149] on the other, Bernis said that he did not even know the names of the pre-eminent aristocratic families—'he did not like the *noblesse*, and preferred to be deceived by men of obscure family'.[150] Louis XV, now his own master, 'worked' with Boyer on the *feuille*, and was said by the pious duc de Luynes to be conscientious in awarding benefices. 'I do not give bishoprics to either name or favour,' wrote Louis in 1764, 'but to those who, I believe, can do the most for religion and towards the peace of the kingdom—though I'm far from being infallible.'[151]

After Boyer, for two years, 1755–7, the *feuille* was held by old La Rochefoucauld, the worthy archbishop of Bourges, and on his death, it was transferred to Jarente, bishop of Digne. Unlike his two predecessors, Jarente was essentially a politician. He established himself at Versailles, and his new diocese, Orléans, saw him but rarely. Mlle Guimard, the dancer, was rumoured to be his mistress. (She was thin: 'Je ne conçois pas comme ce petit ver à soie n'est pas plus gras; il vit sur une si bonne feuille'.[152]) The papal nuncio hesitated to believe this and other stories: 'in this country, people easily pass adverse verdicts on those against whom a prejudice has formed'.[153] The prejudice, no doubt, arose from the gossip of Versailles. The king and Choiseul played practical jokes on their minister of the *feuille*; Louis had him knocked up in the middle of the night to order him to send to Orléans for some jars of the local marmalade for his daughters (the story comes with comic trimmings—'the Archbishop of Paris must have died', the search for the episcopal spectacles, the king's daughters have drawn a sedan chair on the letter). Choiseul sent two actresses dressed as abbés to call on him to ask for benefices and to claim the kiss of peace.[154] The *dévots* at Court decried Jarente's nominations for ecclesiastical office. 'He took the opposite line to his predecessor who wanted an exemplary clergy attached to religion,' said the dauphin; 'M. de Jarente chose too many people like himself.'[155] This reputation lingered on after his fall. A pamphleteer described him as 'an amiable and voluptuous brigand who spent more time in arranging a supper party than in appointing to a bishopric'.[156] In fact, his appointments were no worse than Boyer's; his worldliness was manifested chiefly in his favouring conciliatory candidates for the episcopate rather than harshly orthodox anti-Jansenists.

Jarente had been the nominee and agent of Choiseul; on Choiseul's fall and exile at the end of 1770, his position at Court became precarious, and he lost the *feuille* on 20 March 1771. He was succeeded by the highest-ranking prelate of the kingdom, La Roche-Aymon, archbishop of Reims, abbot of Saint-Germain, *grand aumônier* of France, soon to be made cardinal. His greatness had arisen, it was said, from a lifetime of servility—to Choiseul, then to Mme du Barry, then, after the accession of Louis XVI, to Maurepas. 'The triumph of mediocrity', said Mme du Deffand, wondering how he had contrived to do it 'without merit, without backers and, so to speak, without intrigue'.[157] The courtiers conspired to see the fatuous side of his universal pliability. 'On ne se brouille pas avec moi'—'Nobody falls out with me,' he said. According to the abbé de Véri, when Maurepas dominated in politics, La Roche-Aymon took up residence in the minister's study and in his wife's salon, and 'obeyed them in everything in the awarding of benefices'. Yet, said Véri, 'the choices he made for benefices were always good ones. The silence he has maintained among the clergy is evidence of his wisdom.'[158] The best way to end the feuds and divisions in the Gallican Church was to let politicians direct ecclesiastical appointments.

In 1777, Yves-Alexandre de Marbeuf, bishop of Autun, succeeded to the *feuille*.[159] He was known to have been strict about promotions in his diocese, getting his advisers to prepare lists of well-qualified vicaires to be recommended to the attention of lay patrons. As minister, he retained the bishop of Senez, himself a famous preacher, to report on sermons in the capital, and he tried to prohibit the accumulation of abbeys (he set an example by twice giving up an abbey on promotion to a better one, though it is true that he finished up with Ourscamp, enormously lucrative). Louis XVI, solidly insisting on sound morals as a basic qualification, backed him in providing Cambrai with its first good bishop since Fénelon, and in excluding Loménie de Brienne from the see of Paris ('the archbishop of Paris must at least believe in God'). The abbé de Bourbon, illegitimate son of the previous monarch, had fourteen bishops present when he said his first mass at Saint-Magloire, but no promotion from the *feuille* followed.[160] Yet Marbeuf's administration was savagely attacked in a series of pamphlets, the *Lettres secrètes*, between 1781 and 1784, and the truth was that his appointments were no better than anyone else's had been. The affairs of the *feuille* went best when the political direction at Versailles was firm: a king making appointments knowing that the price of dishonesty was eternal damnation, or a minister anxious to keep Church affairs decent and uncontroversial. Louis XVI was weak; Marie Antoinette and her *lecteur*, the abbé de Vermond, intervened too often to obtain rewards for the ecclesiastics of her circle,[161] while the aristocrats around the Court were more insistent than ever upon their perquisites from the wealth of the Church.[162]

On 4 August 1789, Marbeuf stepped down to give way to Le Franc de Pompignon, archbishop of Vienne. The *feuille* was now in the hands of a pious character who gave up his archbishopric because he had to live at Versailles. Under him, for the second time in the century, an episcopal see went to a commoner, with the elevation of the learned Asseline to Boulogne. By now the old system of appointments was nearing its end: by the Civil Constitution of the

Clergy, dioceses were to coincide with the new political units, the *départements*, and the departmental electors were to choose their bishops.

The history of the *feuille des bénéfices* is unedifying. In mid-century, D'Argenson thought it would be better to withdraw the custody of this famous list from ecclesiastics, and leave it to a lawyer from the Royal Council—just as the Ministry of War always worked better when a civilian was in charge, rather than a professional soldier.[163] Multitudes strove to attract the attention of the holder of the *feuille*, with servility, sanctimonious zeal, *bonhomie*, or insouciance according to their rank in society. 'There is no seigneur at court, however great he may be', reported the papal nuncio in 1766, 'who has not need of this prelate (Jarente) for the benefit of his relatives and friends.'[164] An indispensable qualification to be the dispenser of Crown patronage was the ability to devise a suave letter of refusal to the mighty. Thus Jarente wrote to the duchesse d'Ayen in 1750 concerning his failure to find a benefice for the abbé Saint-Just:

I am sure that I can justify myself to you whenever you are free to listen and to allow me to explain my position to you. I lament my situation: I am like a miserable debtor who owes more than he has money available to pay. Time is the only remedy, and I flatter myself that in due course it will demonstrate to you the respectful attachment with which I have the honour to be, Madame.[165]

On 15 August 1780, Turgot wrote to the duchesse d'Enville to tell her that he was going to see Marbeuf on the following day 'to find out if he has done something for those he promised to help. I have little hope that he has'—he had deceived people before.[166] Ordinary ecclesiastics presented themselves humbly in the antechambers of the minister of the *feuille*. A down-at-heel abbé, an ex-Cordelier forced into a friary by his parents and secularized after they died, wrote to Voltaire begging him to provide some verses congratulating La Roche-Aymon of the *feuille* on being made a cardinal: it might be a way to win a benefice and move to more salubrious quarters than his present lodgings above the pastry cook's opposite the rue des deux portes Saint-Sauveur.[167] In 1757, Canon Le Gouz of Dijon abandoned his quest for a supplementary benefice to finance his long stays in Paris. Jarente had taken over the *feuille*; and having buttered up the two previous holders, Le Gouz was unwilling to start again with a third. 'I am tired of supplicating and sweeping the floors of these disposers of Church property with the hem of my cassock. So I don't think that I'll go to clean up the spittle from the antechamber of the bishop of Digne with my clerical mantle.'[168] A pamphleteer described the scene in Marbeuf's waiting-room:

Picture it: a bizarre collection of monks, abbés, curés, soldiers, women. All these people are asking for bread. 'Pension!' 'Abbey!'. The words circulate and echo resoundingly from every mouth. Monseigneur has promises and consolations for everyone. 'M. le chevalier', he says to a respectable-looking soldier, 'these are hard times, don't get impatient, everything will work out'. 'M. le curé, you know my intentions: use them as a pillow for your repose, and believe me, the moment of happy awakening is not far away. I foresee . . . yes, go along, don't worry'. 'Mon cher abbé, you are displeased, and so am I. The Queen is getting hold of everything, I control nothing. But leave it to me, I have my plan . . . good day to you, be discreet and count on my help.'

Sometimes, the suppliants were so numerous that he could not give them this individual attention, and had to embark on an edifying collective oration before sending them away for another day.[169]

The system worked better than might have been expected. Whether it was the royal confessor, a *conseil de conscience*, the cardinal-first minister, a severe ex-monk, a cynical political church-man, some prestigious old archbishop, or a conscientious diocesan that held the *feuille* did not seem to make much difference. Probably things went best when there was a firm hand on the helm at Versailles, with the king or his chief political adviser well aware of direct personal responsibility. No doubt political designs would then be important, but what could be more wisely political than the desire to make appointments to pacify feuds between churchmen and to improve the climate of relations between clergy and laity? It was better than seeking out austere zealots who would reform with lofty insensitivity. The Church was rich, and there were sinecures and pensions enough to placate the lukewarm, vocationless, or use-less sons of the aristocracy, to support government business, promote learning, and gratify local worthies. Bishoprics and other important offices with cure of souls were mostly awarded—within the system of aristocratic monopoly that prevailed at Versailles—with regard to merit and the interests of the Church. Any system of running ecclesiastical preferment, however honest the electoral procedures, whatever prayerful or charismatic formulas are prescribed or sponta-neously invented, ends up looking frayed and finger-marked when the human aspects of rivalry and manipulation are detected. At Versailles, this human side was unashamedly evident, and anti-clericals had easy fun mocking the strange detours of the workings

of the Holy Spirit. But we have to remember that the men of the
eighteenth century took the Church seriously, at once as an instrument of temporal rule, a socially necessary institution, and the intermediary of personal salvation. It is obvious to us how they pushed
for families and friends; but we do not so easily understand the
psychological restraints within which their pursuit of self-interest
operated.

3

THE WORKING OF THE
CHURCH–STATE ALLIANCE

When a Church becomes rich and powerful, it is infiltrated by the world. For the most part without hypocrisy, individuals realize their ambitions within it, and without undue cynicism, the State makes use of ecclesiastical wealth, personnel, and prestige. The Church gains from the recruitment of ability and the support of secular force in its labours, while it loses in so far as its mission of conversion becomes a routine, its mysteries social observances, and its moral teaching a utilitarianism with supernatural sanctions. Religious perfectionists regret this, but a religion white hot and purified can never be a creed of the majority. Reformations and renewals will revive the traditions of sanctity in the Church, but a powerful established religion infiltrated by the world may yield more quiet decency in human behaviour and, perhaps, a greater sum of human happiness. In the nature of things, in the alliance of Church and State the secular power will be the gainer, for it is bent on achieving immediate and realizable ends, while the spiritual power is aiming for a perfection never attainable in this life, and looks to a mysterious eternal destiny. But there is always a reciprocity, and the balance of advantage is ever changing. In the eighteenth century, behind all the archaic complexities and convolutions of the relationship, the balance was tilting inexorably in favour of the secular power, and as events unfolded, it began to look as if the swing was irreversible.

I Ecclesiastics in State Service

During the eighteenth century, three First Ministers of the Crown were ecclesiastics. It was a question of making use of available talent. Dubois was a libertine, Fleury a man of piety, and Loménie de Brienne a sceptic; but all were outstanding for ability and tireless efficiency, and all three, in the tradition of Richelieu and Mazarin, were rewarded with the red hat of a cardinal. There never was a clash of loyalties. With Dubois, there hardly could have been, for the only moral anchor in his life was his friendship with the regent; Fleury, however, was passionately devoted to papal orthodoxy, and Brienne was a partisan of the Church whose doctrine he hardly believed. Yet they put the interest of the king above all others. It was a French and Gallican attitude. When Vergennes, devout to the point of scrupulosity, was Foreign Minister, his chief clerk wrote of him: 'the clergy counted him in the number of the pious, but they dared not propose anything to him which tended to put the altar on the level of the throne'.[1]

This Gallican devotion to the monarch encouraged the king to turn to ecclesiastics when recruiting diplomats: again, a question of enlisting talent where it could most obviously be found. Talleyrand, who enjoyed a shady success in both careers, analysed the reasons why churchmen make good ambassadors: they are used to dialectic and detecting the nuances of argument; they have the confessor's art of finding out secrets and keeping them; they enjoy ceremony and protocol; they know all about women, yet have no wives.[2] Louis XIV had used cardinal-prelates as envoys—d'Estrées to Bavaria, Forbin-Jansen to Poland, Bonzi to Rome—but in the eighteenth century there were few appointments of this kind, the notable exceptions being Rohan, sent on a brief, glittering, and incompetent foray to Vienna, and Bernis, making a long sojourn at Rome, where, he said, he 'kept the French inn at the crossroads of Europe' and gave lavish receptions—significant in the development of the Italian ice-cream trade. Perhaps Louis XV refrained from choosing great prelates because he suspected they would be too concerned in lobbying for a cardinal's hat, whether by the favour of Rome or on the nomination of a Catholic sovereign—certainly, this was why he refused to make Bernis his ambassador to Poland.[3] But churchmen of lower pretensions were still frequently employed in the diplomatic service. Through some contact, probably with a French cardinal, they might be invited into the mission to Rome, like the abbé Dufour, a *grand vicaire* of Angers, who was employed by the Foreign Ministry from 1760 to 1767 to report on various cardinals of the papal Curia.[4] Others made a deliberate choice of a diplomatic career, putting the Church behind them except for its rewards. Bernis did this, refusing Massillon's offer to make him a *grand vicaire* because he felt no pastoral vocation; the bishop, he said, approved of his honesty, and 'counselled me to devote myself to foreign affairs, saying I would have great success in a career as a negotiator'.[5] This was also the choice of the abbé Véri, doctor of the Sorbonne, canon of Narbonne, *grand vicaire* of Bourges, a certain candidate for a bishopric. In 1756, he changed course: 'je quitta tout à fait la carrière ecclésiastique'.[6] He was appointed an *auditeur de Rote*, the representative of the French king on a Roman tribunal concerned with boring diplomatic and judicial affairs, an office with the virtue of attracting rich benefices to its holder. In 1772 he came back to Paris 'to enjoy the considerable fortune in benefices that this employment had procured for me'. Thereafter he could saunter round Versailles, a confidant of royalty, giving judicious advice on matters unimportant. His career is an example of another reason why churchmen were welcome in royal service: they were paid from ecclesiastical revenues. The abbé de Pomponne (1669–1756), ambassador to Venice and envoy extraordinary to other Italian states, enjoyed the revenue of two abbeys, one, Saint-Médard at Soissons, prodigiously rich.[7] The abbé de Ville (1701–74), an ex-Jesuit, graduated from tutor to the sons of the French representative in the United Provinces, to cipher clerk, chargé d'affaires, and ambassador; then from 1748 for long he was the *premier commis* at the Foreign Ministry, running the administration and co-ordinating information. His rewards were extensive monastic revenues and the episcopal title of 'bishop of Tricomium'; in his leisure he published translations of English political treatises and, remembering he was a churchman, edited Fénelon's spiritual writings.

The revenues of the Church also supported another sort of public servant, though not directly in the service of the Crown, the *conseillers clercs* of the highest law courts, the so-called sovereign courts. In each parlement, a number of magisterial posts (six in the parlement of Bordeaux, twelve in that of Paris) were reserved for clerics, who might be in priestly orders or, with dispensation, in minor orders or just tonsured. By background they had lower social standing than the nobles of the robe who were the lay *conseillers*, but they came from families of note, none the less.[8] The famous abbé Pucelle was a commoner, but his father was a wealthy *avocat*, and his mother a daughter of the maréchal de Catinat. They were more learned than their lay colleagues, and it was the longer time they spent in acquiring educational qualifications as much as their lower social origins which accounted for their average age on appointment being higher—28 years, 6 months, as against 22 years, 7 months, in the parlement of Paris. Their families had bought the office for them, and they drew a revenue from its perquisites. But all had other resources: for example, the abbé Salabery was chairman of the committee running the financial and legal affairs of the duc de

Penthièvre, though his efforts over seven years did not save this great nobleman from bankruptcy. Most important of all, in every case, however, was money from the Church. There were the abbatial monies held *in commendam*: Salabery had the abbey of Coulombes in the diocese of Chartres, while Voltaire's portly and philanthropic nephew the abbé Mignot, who walked unpretentiously every day to the *grand chambre* of the parlement and spent his nights in writing inaccurate history, drew 4,000 livres a year from the abbey of Scellières—the refuge where he took the body of his illustrious uncle for burial, to the rage of those clergy who had been looking forward to seeing the great philosophe denied a Christian resting-place. Probably more of the *conseillers clercs* found their ecclesiastical income from canonries, certainly in Paris, with the special privilege of being able to draw the fruits of their prebends *in absentia*. The chapter of Notre-Dame challenged this right in 1771, but the Royal Council reaffirmed it. Sometimes, though rarely, a *conseiller clerc* moved on into the direct service of the Crown: during the eighteenth century the parlement of Paris lost two of them to the diplomatic service, three to the corps of the *maîtres des requêtes*, one to membership of the Conseil d'État, and another to the great office of controller-general (the sinister, unbelieving abbé Terray). For the most part, however, they stayed with the parlement for life. With their learning, clerical status, and expertise, they provided leaders for the tiny 'Jansenist' clique on the magisterial benches—the abbé Chauvelin, 'coryphée tour à tour du théâtre et du jansénisme', and, above all, the choleric and eloquent abbé Pucelle. Both as magistrates and as churchmen, these clerical lawyers were self-consciously dignified. Pierre de Laffayart, who took up the theatre and had a comedy performed, was an aberration from type to be gossiped about. Laffayart's play was a flop: the title, *Le Fat*, was unfortunate— 'a man never knows himself well enough to produce a convincing self-portrait', said Piron.

From the court at Versailles to a provincial workhouse, all government and municipal institutes had their chaplains, ranging from splendid gilded clerics in lofty office to threadbare abbés called in when needed. The observances of religion, available and indeed compulsory for the sick and poor in institutions, extended also to the prisons. When, in 1789, the Bastille was stormed and pulled down by enthusiastic volunteers, three priests lost their lodgings and employment, and were awarded pensions by the Crown as compensation.[9] As they were as numerous as the prisoners, presumably most of their work was with the garrison. And when the State executed a criminal, the clergy were present on the scaffold.[10] The confessor came to the prison cell to hear the last confession—under regulations which, strictly speaking, were incompatible with the Church's doctrine of forgiveness. Absolution was not given unless the criminal revealed the names of his accomplices (the Capuchins were said to err on the side of mercy here), and communion and extreme unction were withheld. This was because the death penalty was normally carried out on the day of the sentence, and 'it was not fitting to unite the adorable Body of Jesus Christ to a body soon to be subjected to loathsome indignities'. In 1788, the delay of a month between sentence and execution was decreed; yet the rule concerning the viaticum was not changed, and three of the *cahiers* of the clergy in 1789 complain of this. The confessor would accompany the condemned man on the cart on the way to execution, presiding when, at the portals of the cathedral he knelt to ask pardon of God, the king, and justice, and on the scaffold would stay with him to the end; if it was breaking on the wheel, he offered the crucifix to kiss as the agony intensified. On rare occasions, a hardened sinner refused the ministrations of religion; in 1755, the heroic smuggler Mandarin sent away the solicitous friar as 'too fat for a man who preaches penitence', and in 1784 two murderers turned their backs on the priest to address the executioner: 'c'est à vous que nous avons affaire'. There was a sanction to encourage an edifying conformity on the scaffold, for the executioner might shorten the agony of breaking or burning by merciful strangulation; when, in 1721, the bandit Cartouche was on the wheel, the executioner failed to act, and it was the confessor who ordered one of the guards to pull the rope tight. In 1781, a lawyer proposed that priests should be withdrawn from these scenes of cruelty, as the criminals blasphemed and the spectators cursed the confessor as if he was in league with the judges. But it was more usual to admire the clergy who performed such grim duties. 'I saw him embrace the wretch,' says Restif of such a one, 'devoured with fever, as infected as the dungeons from which he was taken, covered in vermin. And I said to myself, "O religion, here is your triumph."'

In the army and navy, chaplains were indispensable, for it was a maxim that discipline and morals require religion, and men who by profession were required to die for their king had a right to spiritual consolation before the final moment. The idea of sudden death as the easiest way was counterbalanced by the fear of dying unshriven. When the duchesse de Longueville heard her soldier-son had been killed, she did not ask if his end had been painless. 'Ah, mon cher fils! Est-il mort sur-le-champ? N'a-t-il pas eu un seul moment? Ah mon Dieu, quel sacrifice!'[11] A bishop dedicating regimental standards declared that 'the penance of blood' could wash away the stain of sin, but this dispensation to soldiers was not to be presumed on, and a man must make his peace so far as he could beforehand; this was provided for in the chaplain's prayers before battle, ending with the pronouncing of the general absolution.

From the early seventeenth century, most warships had chaplains, the Capuchins serving on the ships of the line and the Lazarists, directed to the duty by Vincent de Paul, on the galleys. Richelieu called on the Jesuits to take over service in the fleet, and one of them, Père Georges Fournier, a professor of mathematics at the *collège* of La Flèche, became an *aumônier de la marine*, and in 1643 published a famous treatise, *Hydrographie, contenant la théorie et la pratique de toutes les parties de la Navigation.*[12] At the end of the century, royal regulations made it mandatory for all warships to have chaplains, as well as merchant ships on long voyages. To provide priests for these duties, Louis XIV set up three seminaries: one, inadequately endowed, at Rochefort (1683) under the Lazarists, the others at Brest and Toulon under the Jesuits (1686). The training programmes were—officially—relentless. At Rochefort there was a year's probation followed by three years' instruction, with a daily schedule running from 5 a.m. to 9 p.m., the entire waking hours being filled with liturgical observances, meditation, self-examination, and lectures, except for two breaks of one and a half hours each for meals and recreation. In 1701 the shipping regulations were codified with a realistic proviso: the rules about chaplains were to apply only to vessels with a crew of thirty or more.[13] Even so, the bishops of the seaboard dioceses of Vannes, Saint-Malo, La Rochelle, Coutances, Bayonne, and Bordeaux protested to the king that it was impossible to find priests in the numbers required. The salary laid down in 1701 for the chaplain of a merchant ship was 30 livres a month, with meals at the captain's table;[14] this was not enough to attract candidates, and those who volunteered, said the bishop of Coutances, were motivated 'rather by libertinage than by piety'.[15] No single Order came forward to devote itself to the pastoral care of sailors, most of the *aumôniers* on the galleys being Lazarists, on the other ships Lazarists, Capuchins, Récollets, Jesuits, and seculars, some of them in flight from normal ecclesiastical discipline, though not always the worse for that. The hardships and dangers of life afloat deterred recruitment. Many of those going on a long voyage would not return. A warship patrolling the Atlantic and Indian oceans for four years between 1780 and 1784 lost 228 out of its crew of 430, only thirty of them killed in battle.[16] The conditions were appalling, especially in the galleys, with their oarsmen in chains—criminals, Turkish prisoners of war, and victimized Protestants. A chaplain hearing the confessions of the sick did so in a cavity three feet high in the poop, with his penitents lying in their excrement and covered in vermin, and all around were scenes of savagery—it was the selective flogging of Protestants which led the abbé Bion to renounce his chaplain's role and flee to Geneva to become a Calvinist.[17] Though the French Company of the Indies had the resources to pay well to fulfil its obligation to send a priest out with every argosy, sometimes a ship had to sail without one, and in 1766 the directors applied to the Irish seminary at Nantes for volunteers. At Saint-Malo in the 1730s, 2,600 fishermen left every year for the Newfoundland banks, and only sixteen priests accompanied them, and at the end of the *ancien régime* there were 3,700 fishermen and only six chaplains available.[18]

There were picturesque ceremonies when a ship was commissioned, solemn blessings according to the *Rituel* of the particular maritime diocese (all based on Pope Paul V's liturgy of 1614) with the inevitable references to Noah and the ark and Christ walking on the waters. When a vessel returned from a long voyage, there would be a high mass with Te Deum in the parish church, and while the crew roistered in port, they would be the target of mission sermons by the local Jesuits or Capuchins or, in Brittany, by the Montfortians. These interesting liturgical and evangelistic occasions were monopolized by the coastal clergy, and the *aumônier* would take over when the ship left port—if he had obeyed the rules, he would have observed a retreat of ten days beforehand to prepare himself. At sea, he had to say daily prayers before the mainmast, offering thanks for preservation, making an act of dedication for the day's work, and praying for the ship's company to be given strength to overcome temptation, especially the sin of cursing and swearing, and ending with the psalm for the king, *Domine salvum fac regem*. An effort would be made to observe the great feasts of the Church—for the Fête-Dieu, a procession round the decks and the firing of a cannon salvo. If a sailor fell gravely ill, the chaplain would take the Sacrament to him, observing regulations to ensure decorum: the Host must be in a ciborium or decent box, not openly on the paten, and a sailor with lantern and handbell would go before, while the officer of the watch would ensure that all members of the crew, Protestants included, removed their hats and knelt as the procession passed. A funeral would require a requiem mass with a *De profundis* and *Libera*, and if it was the captain who had died, there would be volleys of musket-shots and the firing of a single cannon. Before battle, or when the sky was lowering with imminent storm, the chaplain would offer prayers, recite the *Confiteor*, and give the assembled crew a general absolution. According to Fournier, they could be sure of God's forgiveness at these desperate moments, for penitence is sincere in proportion to the grimness of the danger— not a view the theologians generally accepted. The captain of a warship would also expect his chaplain to add a word to encourage his men to fight bravely. Before an engagement in the American War of Independence, the chaplain of the *Astrée* gave a famous oration in a single sentence: 'Mes amis, tous les braves gens vont au paradis, et tous les jean-foutres en enfer'.[19] On shipboard, all faced the same perils and had to contrive to live together. If the *aumôniers* were suspect to the bishops safe on dry land as reckless characters wearing lay dress on board and going along with a modicum of drink and swearing, it may be that, according to their lights, they did their duty.

As with the navy, so with the army, the royal government pro- vided military chaplains, in time of war paying them realistically, more than the clergy ministering to the crews of ships. In the artillery and infantry, about 700 livres a year was given, calculated on a daily basis; this was the wage of a sergeant and rather better, for there was a superior ration allowance—a total income about equal to one of the poorer curés on the *congrue* (the official stipend for a parish priest who did not draw the tithe).[20] In the cavalry and dragoons, the salaries were slightly less. But in peacetime, the chaplains serving in the infantry and artillery were on half pay, while those in the mounted regiments got nothing at all. There was no retirement pension, a notable disadvantage, for bishops distrusted clergy who had been associated with the military[21] and were reluc- tant to collate them to parochial benefices. The government mooted the idea of a levy on ecclesiastical property to provide larger and more regular salaries, but nothing was done.[22] Some colonels, however, especially those recruiting in Lorraine and the Auvergne, raised money to pay much more, offering as much as 2,000 livres a year, with a retirement pension after thirty years' service. Under Richelieu, it was the Jesuits and a few Capuchins who had served with the armies; by the eighteenth century, chap- lains came from a variety of backgrounds, though most of them were Récollet friars. In a *Mémoire abrégé sur les aumôniers de l'infanterie française* (1782), the duc de Mortemart, colonel of the regiment of

Lorraine, said that the priests who took service with the infantry 'seem to be drawn from the lowest class of clergy, at best useless, and sometimes a nuisance because of their ignorance and lack of morals'. The remedies he proposed were higher salaries to attract better men and the setting up of a seminary in a garrison town like Metz or Strasbourg to give a three-year course to ordinands destined for the army, with lessons in theology reinforced by history, geography, draughtsmanship, and fortification. As he said, it was not just the poor quality of the *aumôniers* giving cause for concern; they were also too few, only a hundred or so in all the infantry regiments in peacetime.[23]

When the puritanical comte de Saint-Germain had been Minister for War (1775–7), a seminary had indeed been set up, in concert with the archbishop of Paris, but it had lasted for only a few years.[24] Apart from the zealous minister himself, both government officials and churchmen thought enough had been done when the army had a minimum of formal liturgical offices and opportunities for every soldier to go shriven to his grave. Had there been genuine enthusiasm for the seminary, there would have been unions of benefices and diversion of monastic revenues sufficient to guarantee its success. The government similarly parsimoniously refused to make provision for retired soldiers—officers who were awarded the cross of St Louis received a small pension, and a few rankers obtained an abusive 'corrody' at the expense of a monastery; but most left the army without any means of support. There was, however, a splendid exception to the government's meanness, an institution where a selected group of officers and men lived in comfort for the rest of their lives—Louis XIV's prestigious foundation of the Invalides, a showpiece for the rest of Europe to admire.[25] The inmates lived well, with prodigious provision of bread, meat, and wine, comfortable quarters, and smart uniforms (blue coat and grey breeches, the officers having red facings and linings to the coats and silver braid stripes of rank). Thirty sisters of St Vincent de Paul administered the institution and supervised the care of the sick. As a result of good food and comfort, the inmates lived long: the average age of death in the last three years of the *ancien régime* was between 65 and 69 years of age.[26] The price paid by the retired warriors for their ease and distinction was conformity to a strict religious regimen—they were all Catholics, for after the revocation of the edict of Nantes, Protestants were excluded. They had to be present at mass and vespers on Sundays and saints' days, and at morning and evening prayers daily. If their knowledge was deemed insufficient, they could be summoned to a catechism session. To be allowed a day pass or longer leave, they had to show a *billet de confession* and a certificate of Easter communion. Two months in a punishment cell was the penalty for swearing, and expulsion for a second offence. Realistically, eight bouts of drunkenness were allowed, but once the quota was exceeded, the offender was transferred for a year to the grim institution for disciplining libertines, the criminally insane, and prostitutes, the Bicêtre. To what extent was this puritanical and pious life-style enforced? The twenty-six Lazarist priests of the original establishment were reduced in numbers by subsequent economies, and by the reign of Louis XVI they were down to five—though of the chapel musicians, the precentor, organist, and four choirboys were retained. The *pension* in which the clergy lived was in confusion, running deeper and deeper into debt and haunted by minor clerics of Paris who insinuated themselves to get cheap quarters. Probably, the clergy did little more eventually than keep the routine liturgical services going and hear Easter confessions. But a tourist in 1713 reported that at every hour of the day in the chapel of the Invalides there were numerous old soldiers sunk in reflective prayer.[27] If the compulsory piety was observed in a perfunctory fashion, there were some who sought the consolations of religion as they remembered the cruelties of war.

Soldiers were notoriously immoral, proverbially corrupting the inhabitants of any town where they were stationed. The chaplains despaired of making much impression on them in peacetime, and had the reputation of performing the necessary formalities of religion in a minimal fashion—rushing the men of a whole battalion through their individual confessions in a single morning, pronouncing rapid-fire absolutions like a series of 'bonjours'.[28] If the troops were to be converted, it would be by the descent of teams of Jesuits, Lazarists, or Capuchins on evangelistic missions. Commanding officers did not mind their *aumôniers* compressing spirituality into brusque formalities—what they especially required in quiet periods was for them to liaise with the local authorities to agree measures to keep the prostitutes away, lest the unit be decimated by venereal disease. On the march, when crossing the boundary of a diocese, the chaplain would be sent to call on the bishop, whether French or foreign, to request formal permission—always given—to enter his territory.[29] When battle was imminent, the army chaplains, like their colleagues at sea, had to conduct prayers and pronounce a general absolution, ending with a harangue to inspire courage.[30] These would-be encouraging talks were unpopular, so it was safest to keep them brief. One ran: '*Enfants de guerre*, though your hearts are filled with proud courage, humble yourselves before the Lord, for it is he alone who gives victory.' There is more than one version of the story about the lieutenant-colonel cutting the sermon short: 'Soldiers! M. l'abbé means to say, there is no salvation for cowards, *en avant!*'—or, as a variant, 'Vive le Roi!' Once the battle was joined, the *aumônier* was 'to hold himself available during the fighting to help the wounded and dying'. Perhaps he would find his post with the *hôpital ambulant* keeping up close to the firing line, or he would be sent back to one of the field ambulances in third echelon.[31] At the Battle of Fontenoy, the main hospital had a chief surgeon with thirty assistants, ten apothecaries, sixty-six male nurses, and eleven chaplains, eight being Récollet friars. The hospital routine included a mass in the morning and prayers at night followed by a round of the wards; all Catholic soldiers were required to make their confession every three days. The chaplains buried those who died, recording their names in a register, and were responsible for sending death certificates to the family and to regimental headquarters. François de Chennevières, the inspector-general of military hospitals, published a four-volume study of their working in 1742, in which he declared that the chaplains 'acquitted their duties to the general edification'. Perhaps the duc de Mortemart's unfavourable verdict concerned the peacetime conduct of the chaplains, while François de Chennevières was referring to them amid the grim butchery of the hospitals as the casualties were brought in. With all their faults, they measured up to the decisive test of war.

When we catch a glimpse of individuals, they appear worthy, maybe eccentric, though it is true that evidence tends to survive about those who in some way distinguished themselves. It is true also that those of ability had often been driven unwillingly into a military career, having through no fault of their own lost their niche in the ecclesiastical establishment—Jansenists ousted by the government, orthodox pursued by the parlements, Jesuits seeking employment after the destruction of their Order. Dom Pierre Toussaint, a Benedictine of the Congregation of Saint-Vanne and teacher at one of their *collèges*, was imprisoned for eleven months in the citadel of Verdun (no doubt for Jansenism); on coming out, he rehabilitated himself by serving as a chaplain in an artillery regiment for six years, then became principal of the *collège* at Metz.[32] J.-B.-J. Adent was a mendicant who got himself secularized and served two years in a parish, then ten years as a chaplain to the Languedoc dragoons, moving on to become a curé by the resignation of the previous incumbent in his favour; during the Revolution, he was elected a councillor of the district at Versailles.[33] Nicolas Segretier, curé of Meung-sur-Loire, on the orders of his bishop, refused the last sacraments to a dying Jansenist and had to flee from the wrath of the parlement of Paris. In 1756, he became *aumônier* to the duc de Beauvillier in the campaign in Germany, having two narrow escapes from cannon-balls, one passing so close that the wind of it paralysed his left leg for a month, the other spattering him with soil when it hit the ground. When the duke was wounded and a prisoner, he stayed with him, and when his master died, he took the sad news back to the family and stayed some months with the duchess—finally venturing back to his parish again.[34] The abbé Robin, chaplain to a regiment in Canada, came back to France, and in 1781 published an account of his American explorations and a brochure on freemasonry, then became *aumônier* to the vicomte de Noailles, the colonel of a cavalry regiment—Noailles set up a 'club' for his officers with books and newspapers available, and made Robin its presiding welfare officer.[35] The colonels of regiments were young aristocrats of the Court arrived directly into higher commands by a combination of privilege and purchase. Their personal chaplains, like Segretier and Robin, moved in loftier circles than the Récollets lower down under the orders of the hard-bitten professional officers, mostly poor provincial nobles, who ran the real work of the army, and the surgeons, who hacked away in the field hospitals. Even so, when battle was joined, cannon-balls and musket-shots were no respecters of persons.

II *Marriage and Parish Registers*

In high religious theory, the Church alone had the right to prescribe rules for marriage—affirmed in a papal brief of 1788 condemning Jansenist views recently put forward at a synod in Italy. To most appearances, this was the case in France. The clergy called the banns, perhaps checking on the degree of Christian instruction of the affianced pair, and conducted the ceremony. The laws of the Church determined the relationships within which marriage was allowed, and defined the impediments, citing the code of the Old Testament, equated, from its origin in remote antiquity, with natural law. It was not just immemorial custom which suggested the rules must be 'natural', for the theologians argued that the obligation to marry outside the family clan extended the boundaries of friendship and charity: exogamy was part of the social machinery prescribed by God for achieving the Christian aim of 'goodwill towards men'. The prohibited degrees were wider then than now, and the clergy added to them the impediment of 'spiritual affinity': that is, the relationship between godparent and godchild. This could not be justified from the code of the Old Testament, and came only marginally under the rubric of the expansion of the sphere of charity. Voltaire made fun of its illogicality: his noble savage is unable to marry the charming girl who converted him to Christianity, as she had unthinkingly stood sponsor for him at his baptism. The best that could be done to justify the prohibition was to cite the danger of undue influence, the possibility of misusing a duty of pastoral oversight to forward the desires of the flesh and social ambitions. These multitudinous restrictions on choice of partner caused hardship to many, especially in isolated rural communities, so there was a stream of applications for dispensations, giving a great deal of business to diocesan officials and the ecclesiastical courts.

But while marriage was the work of God joining a man and woman in unbreakable union, the institution was also the bedrock of the social order, ensuring the continuation of the race in a disciplined fashion and the transmission of property through the generations. As such, the State claimed a right of regulation, in the process necessarily treating marriage not as a sacrament, but a contract. Government legislation guaranteed the rights of the heads of households in setting a late age before parental prohibition could be overridden by the two contracting parties; there was a legal procedure (the *rapt de séduction* charge) to give respectable families protection against matrimonial adventurers; the law courts investigated the validity of marriages in suits concerning inheritance; the legal systems of the various provinces apportioned the control of the joint property and dowry between husband and wife; the secular courts as well as the ecclesiastical could pronounce a decree of separation when a marriage had foundered; the king could intervene by *lettre de cachet* in matrimonial relations where the honour of a family was concerned. The philosophes, concerned to diminish the importance of the clergy in the lives of individuals and in the community, put marriage firmly in the control of the State, making the contribution of the Church an optional extra.[36] Voltaire stated the case clearly in the *Dictionnaire philosophique*: 'Marriage is a contract by natural law (*droit des gens*); the Roman Church has made a sacrament of it. But the contract and the sacrament are two very different things: the one has civil consequences, the other qualifies for the blessings of the

Church.' Two legal treatises of mid-century (1753 and 1760) provided an array of learned arguments to support the Voltairean
inference from the nature of things.

The basic principles of the theologians could be used to justify
both the high ecclesiastical view of marriage as a sacrament and the
secular view of marriage as a contract. The three ends of marriage,
as St Augustine had defined them, were mutual self-giving, the pro-
creation of children, and the sacramental union signifying the union
of Christ with his Church. Everything else followed from the
mutual self-giving. The celebrants of the sacrament were the man
and woman themselves, their mutual consent and sexual congress
constituting the marriage in the eyes of God. The Jansenists[37] used
these principles to argue that the final word in marriage regulations,
even where the prohibited degrees of affinity were concerned,
should rest with the secular sovereign. In 1676, Jean de Launoy took
this as a typical instance in which, in a Christian nation, the prince
is the Church's agent for executive action. In Jansenist circles in the
eighteenth century, the argument was given a full theological
development. It is not the actions of the Church which make a
union indissoluble, for St Paul had declared marriages with infidels
to be valid, and in the first eight centuries in the West and the first
ten centuries in the East, validity had not depended on the ministrations of the clergy. Thus the State was entitled to take the essence of
marriage to be contractual and to regulate it accordingly.

Given that the free consent and self-giving of the two parties
created the union in the eyes of God, provided the consent and self-
giving could be established by evidence, the marriages of heretics
and pagans were valid. The case of Protestants in France was odd,
for Louis XIV had imposed the intolerant fiction that they did not
exist, so it was Catholic marriage for them or nothing. Protestants
who married before their own pastors risked the future of their
children if rapacious Catholic relatives went to law to claim the
inheritance. As the century went on, the law courts revolted against
this manifest injustice by twisting every possible circumstance to disqualify the suit of the would-be plunderers. Protestant marriages
were made legitimate in 1787; meanwhile, at mid-century, the great
test for the liberal principle of the theologians arose. A Jew of Alsace,
proclaiming his conversion to Christianity, maintained that his
Jewish marriage was now null, so he was free to marry again in a true
Christian union.[38] Two Parisian curés were approached and refused
to call the banns, declaring his previous union with its two children
to be permanent in the eyes of God. The archbishop backed them.

The parlement of Paris took the side of the convert, and when he was baptized on 10 August 1752, magistrates of the Court were among his godparents. The archbishop, regarding the conversion (given the design to marry again) as fraudulent, banned the curé who administered the baptism, to the rage of the parishioners, whom he had served faithfully for thirty-three years. The parlement denounced the episcopal sentence, on the ground that a parish priest is the sole judge of applications for baptism. On 7 November 1754 the front of theological principle was breached when the *officialité*, the court of the bishop of Strasbourg, was persuaded to declare the Jewish marriage null. With this verdict in hand, the new convert proposed to remarry in the diocese of Soissons; the bishop, Mgr Fitz-James, austere and Jansenistically inclined, turned him down, and reversed the Strasbourg decision. The *appel comme d'abus* went to the parlement of Paris, but the magistrates at last listened to the opinions of theologians and the cry of natural justice: a non-Christian marriage celebrated in good faith was declared indissoluble.

During the Revolution a multitude of cases arose to establish this finding.[39] The exiled bishops at first tried to argue that a marriage before one of the Constitutional Clergy was invalid, but they knew theological principle was against them, and they had to retreat; indeed, they conceded that even a union contracted in the presence of a municipal officer was valid—though, with a certain failure of logic, they added the proviso: so long as resort to a priest was not possible. The bishop of Langres, followed by other bishops and approved by Rome, urged Christians who wished to be faithful to orthodoxy as against the State-sponsored Constitutional Church, to marry before their own priests and register the event with the municipal officials, as Protestants had done under the 1787 edict. On the side of the new revolutionary government, the recognition that marriage was simply a contract came from a report by the canonist Durand de Maillane to the Assembly concerning a petition of the actor Talma against the refusal of the curé of Saint-Sulpice to call his banns because of his profession. The State, the report argued, is concerned only with the contract; the sacrament needs other dispositions, and is no affair of the legislator. Even so, no action was taken until 20 September 1792, when the Legislative Assembly, on the last day of its existence, legalized divorce and laicized the *état civil*—the keeping of the registers of births, marriages, and deaths. A Jansenist lawyer of the *ancien régime*, still writing on legal subjects in 1800, summed up the situation: marriage is established as a contract ruled by civil law, and not a sacrament; yet there still remains a distinction between unions Christians accept as made by the mutual consent of the two parties, and those they themselves celebrate within the Church with a specific dedication to the God of Christianity.

Church and State had a mutual interest in keeping permanent records of marriages. The clergy needed them for pastoral purposes and to prevent unions within the prohibited degrees, while the lawyers of the royal tribunals had to have formal documentation available to supervise the structure of family relationships and the transmission of rights to property. As ever, the government put the expense and effort on somebody else. In 1569, the curés were ordered to keep registers of births and baptisms and to deposit them from time to time at the *greffe*, the record office of the nearest royal law court.[40] In 1579, the regulation was extended to include marriages and deaths. The question of expense was clarified in 1667: the churchwardens (*fabriques*) of parishes had to provide two registers, one to stay in the parish archives, the other to be sent to the clerk of the magistrates. To extract State profits from these trans-actions over and above having other people pay for them, absurd offices were created for sale with the nominal duty of filing the information. The curés fulfilled their responsibilities with a mini-mum of zeal. They would fail to hand the copy to the royal court, or mislay their parish version. Often, their entries were full of erasures and unsigned corrections, or, indeed, were illegible altogether. The law-books cited the 'affaire Bouteville', a lawsuit turning on an undecipherable marginal note concerning a marriage. Why was it, asked the author of a legal handbook, that notaries deposited such well-written documents at the *greffe*, while the clergy are guilty of culpable carelessness: 'why are the children of this world wiser than the children of light?'[41] An answer was not far to seek: the notaries pocketed fees, and the curés got nothing. A register with its parchment leaves and official stamps was expensive (15 livres for a big town parish and 3 to 6 livres for a small country one); the lawyers were presented with their copy at the expense of the parishioners, who also had to pay a fee to the clerk who numbered the pages.[42] A curé might amuse himself by chronicling local events in his parish copy of the register,[43] but he was unenthu-siastic about acting as the unpaid servant of the government.

A royal declaration of 9 April 1736 tried to compel efficiency by laying down stern regulations.[44] A register was to cover a single year only. A month before the year began, the curé had to obtain two of them, one with stamped leaves, one with plain; both were to be taken to the nearest royal jurisdiction for checking and pagination. Blanks must not be left, and loose leaves must not be inserted. Entries must be precisely dated. Baptisms are to be verified with the signature of the priest, the father, and a godfather, weddings with those of the curé and two witnesses. At the end of each year, the stamped version was to be taken to the *greffe*. (Religious houses were also to keep separate registers of accessions to the noviciate and of professions; in each case a duplicate had to be kept to be handed in at the registry of the law court every five years.) The curés of Paris leagued together to sign no fewer than three successive protests against these regulations. Granted, a simple record was indispensable, but they saw no need for these bureaucratic elaborations. For one thing, they had not the time to do this amount of paperwork. Often, they had ten marriages a day, and, approaching Advent and Lent, when marriages were forbidden, twenty-five to thirty. Baptism parties arrived at the church unannounced, and a curé who thought he was turning out to baptize one child might find as many as eight with parents and godparents lined up waiting. To get the details of these ceremonies and the names of the witnesses was difficult enough, but to have to make a copy for the lawyers was a vexatious addition. Besides, depositing these records at the *greffe* left the secrets of families open to ill-intentioned curiosity, and the new precision of entry increased the danger. No longer could curés fudge the date of a marriage 'for the honour of families'—pre-nuptial conceptions would be obvious, illegitimate children would stand out from the others, and hasty, renewed ceremonies to cover up a wedding which some technicality had nullified would leave a jarring memorial. These complaints against the lust for accuracy and the frank justifications of pastoral subterfuges were unacceptable to the government, which insisted on compliance, though it was not until the end of July 1738 that all the parishes of the capital had conformed to the declaration and bought their double registers.

There was improvement, but scandal still occurred. In a comic lawsuit in 1768, a girl wanting to marry had to go to court to prove her sex, since her baptismal certificate, by some 'étourderie de sacristan', had her down as a boy.[45] Isolated errors became unusual; if something went wrong it was when some curé, worn out or drifting into irresponsibility in some rural backwater, gave up the struggle altogether. In such a case there had to be laborious interrogations of all the inhabitants to reconstitute the missing registers. The little town of Guémené in Brittany was pastorally served by the collegiate church of Notre-Dame-de-la Fosse. In 1774, the chapter decided that the canon in residence must sign the registers as correct every day before he left the sacristy: 'Otherwise, we will inevitably find ourselves back in the position of having to run round the town as we used to, to remedy omissions.'[46] Some of the *cahiers* of the clergy in 1789 admitted all was not well, and asked for remedial measures, perhaps sending round specimen entries for imitation.[47] At least one lay *cahier* asked for the recording of births, marriages, and deaths to be taken from the clergy and put in the hands of public officials, which in fact was what happened, marriage becoming a civil contract. The old monarchy had treated it as such without being willing to find the money to secularize the registration process.

III *Police Procedures and Religious Conformity*

'Que la Religion est le premier et le principal objet de la Police; que dans tous les temps les soins en ont été confiez aux deux Puissances, la spirituelle, et la temporelle.' So said Delamare's *Traité de la Police*.[48] The State had to support religion by its laws, its law courts, and their penalties, since 'the punishments at the disposal of the ministers of religion are not severe enough to vanquish the indocility of human nature'. There was an age-long justification for the use of coercion, since the Church was assumed to have inherited the privileged position of the synagogue in the Old Testament. True, Delamare concedes, for three centuries the Christian gospel was preached without the aid of the secular power, but as Chrysostom had said, this was a dispensation of Providence to demonstrate the ability of true religion to make its way in a hostile world independently of all human aid. Thereafter, the partnership of Church and State was renewed, to the benefit of mankind and the saving of souls. St Augustine, in controversy with the Donatists, had established the legitimacy and necessity of this alliance. Such was the theory of Church–State relationships in the standard handbook of police procedures of eighteenth-century France.

   In practice, what ought the police to do to assist religion in its mission? We can obtain an answer to this question by abstracting the relevant points from Delamare's review of the duties of the *commissaires examinateurs* who are the 'eyes' of the Parisian magistrates.[49] For the moment we are not concerned with their collaboration with churchmen in enforcing the laws against Protestants or in suppressing immorality—they also had specific duties concerning the supervision of outward religious practice. They were to arrest perpetrators of acts of blasphemy and sacrilege. On Sundays and great feasts of the Church they were to roam at large to prevent commercial activities, and to close down wine bars, tennis courts, and theatres during the hours of divine service. In Lent, they had to watch the butchers' shops to spy out illicit sales of meat, and pop into cafés and hostelries ready to prosecute if meat dishes were being served. When a major religious procession was to take place, they were to go round ordering householders to decorate their street. In short, they were to protect religion against insult and outrage, and to ensure a decent outward conformity to Catholic customs and discipline.

During the sixteenth century, with religious warfare raging, the offence of blasphemy became more heinous than it had been.[50] So much so that it passed out of the jurisdiction of the ecclesiastical courts and was taken over by the secular magistrates, whose punishments reflected the hatred aroused by those who not only insulted God, but also destroyed the national unity. Yet, grave as it was taken to be, blasphemy was not a sin of interest to the casuists—it was too obvious, and not a matter for finely tuned distinctions. The standard manual of Pontas has no entry 'blasphème', and its readers would have to seek under 'jurer' or ponder on the single example given under the general heading of 'péché'.[51] In 1666, Louis XIV issued an edict defining the crime and setting a scale of punishments for it— possibly provoked to do so by the scandal aroused by a scene in Molière's *Don Juan* (soon suppressed) where the hero gives money to a poor man to induce him to curse God. The edict said that blasphemy consisted in insults proffered to God, the Eucharist, the Blessed Virgin, and the saints, and was punishable with fine and imprisonment for the first four offences; for the fifth, with exposure in the pillory from eight in the morning to one o'clock in the afternoon on a Sunday or holiday; for the sixth, by branding with a hot iron on the upper lip, for the seventh on the lower; for the eighth, by amputation of the tongue. In the nature of the case, detection of the full accumulation of successive offences was unlikely, and the magistrates were not enthusiastic about enforcing the law on every occasion. From 1700 to 1790, only ninety-one cases came on appeal to the parlement of Paris.[52] Though the law-books have an example of the exaction of the full, final penalty by the parlement in 1724, this was as a prelude to an execution by burning, indicating that the offence had been committed in association with the more serious crime of sacrilege; probably, it was only with the occurrence of such a combination of insults to religion that the extreme penalty for

blasphemy was invoked.[53] The army had its own peculiar savage prescription, laid down by a declaration of 1681, renewed in 1727: the
piercing of the tongue with a hot iron, a variant punishment
designed to leave the offender still capable of shouting a warning or
giving a command.[54] The threat of the burning iron does not seem
to have had much influence on the proverbially outrageous language
of military men. 'To give themselves a lively and cavalier style and
air,' said the bishop of Lodève in 1749, 'many Christians among the
soldiery adopt the affectation of swearing in God's name; and many
others, in all walks of life, try to supplement their lack of facility and
inventiveness in conversation by the profane use of this adorable
name.'[55]

The punishments for sacrilegious crimes were horrendous. This
was an age when authority, lacking effective machinery for law
enforcement, used exemplary penalties in a sort of 'calculus of deter-
rence', culminating in breaking on the wheel for crimes which
seemed to threaten the social order, with a longer or shorter time of
agony prescribed before merciful strangulation was allowed.[56] In this
graduated tabulation of terror, the maintenance of the hierarchy of
society was taken into account: unbelievable torments were inflicted
on Damiens in 1757 because he had lifted his hand against the king,
and the penalty for stealing a mere handkerchief within the sacred
precincts of the parlement of Paris was branding and three years in
the galleys.[57] This sort of special and odious protection was afforded
to religion. A declaration of 4 May 1724 allowed sentences of up to
lifetime slavery in the galleys for thefts in churches.[58] These were
ordinary thefts—say, by pickpockets, or by the ingenious rogues
who extracted money from offertory boxes with flat pieces of wood
and glue.[59] Sentences to the galleys tended to range from two to
twelve years.[60] Outside churches, there were various sorts of conduct
which the courts might treat as sacrilegious on the way to inflicting
savage punishment. The man who fired a pistol at a crucifix in
Reims in 1725 had his hand cut off and was burned at the stake—
'he made a religious end under the ministrations of a friar of the
Cordeliers', the local annalist recorded.[61] The year before, at
Charolles, Angélique Lombard, a vagabond convicted of having had
herself baptized several times (no doubt as a fund-raising technique),
was condemned to the *amende honorable*, branding with a fleur-de-lis
mark on the left shoulder, floggings at four street corners, and perpetual banishment.[62] By contrast, one 'Popo' in the village of
Sennely in 1758, who insulted the curé, turned his back on the
Sacrament, beat his wife, and 'had carnal knowledge of her on the

public square', was condemned only to burning a candle as a gesture of repentance[63]—clearly, the court had taken his inebriation to be a mitigating circumstance.

Drunken frolics apart, sacrilegious crimes were most often committed in the course of thefts of church plate and silver. Sometimes, the thieves were guilty of a double sacrilege when they stole or profaned the reserved Sacrament in the course of their depredations—as did the soldier who made away with a golden ciborium during the great fire of Rennes in 1720.[64] The revulsion aroused by such crimes inspired the various foundations of devotions 'for the reparation of the insults proffered to Our Saviour Jesus Christ in the Holy Sacrament of the Altar'; a curé of Paris in 1724 gave no less than 4,000 livres for this purpose.[65] And this was why the police of Paris from time to time held special sessions with the *premier président* of the parlement concerning the growing number of thefts from churches.[66] The penalty for stealing 'sacred vases with profanation' was the cutting off of the right hand and burning at the stake. In 1714 (a priest),[67] in 1768 (three thieves),[68] and in 1781 (a burglar of Amiens)[69] were executed in this way on the orders of the parlement of Paris. When such thefts 'with profanation' took place, there was sometimes a suspicion—spoken of in a whisper—that the ultimate sacrilege had been committed, the deliberate appropriation of a consecrated Host for use in the ceremonies of black magic. (There was such a case among the garrison at Lille in 1713, ending with three soldiers burned and one shot; fifty years later a solemn procession of expiation was held to mark the 'jubilee', as it were, of this disgrace to the city.)[70]

What was the good of these cruel punishments? In *L'Esprit des Lois*, Montesquieu coolly contrasted the practice of Catholic Europe with that of ancient Rome, where stealing sacred vases from a temple was treated as simple theft.[71] If there is an incident which constitutes an offence to religion, the proper penalties are not those imposed by the secular magistrates on ordinary criminals, but exclusion from public places of worship and from the society of faithful believers. And the magistrate should assess the outward action only; whatever sacrilege is committed in secret is a matter between the offender and God alone. Mere men cannot avenge the majesty of God: 'il faut honorer la Divinité, et ne la venger pas'.[72] No doubt Voltaire believed the same, but he found more fun in emphasizing the ridiculous side of official conformity, yet sardonically recommending it. What is blasphemy in Rome and Notre-Dame of Loretto, he says, is piety in London, Amsterdam, Berlin, and Berne,[73]

and what is holy in Tibet is contemptible in China. No matter—
when the Grand Lama orders his subjects to kiss a gold-wrapped
dollop of his excrement, they ought to obey, though the emperor of
China, independent and outside his boundaries, will rightly throw
the ludicrous contraption into his privy.[74] In fact, the magistrates of
France, while accepting the principle that it was futile to attempt to
'avenge the Divinity',[75] were still prepared on occasion to enforce
hand-chopping and burning. There can be little doubt of their
motivation. Whether they cared for Catholic belief or merely
respected the established customs of their country, like Voltaire, they
all regarded religion as an essential part of the hierarchical structure
of society; they feared all sacrilegious acts as subverting the decencies
and deference that helped to preserve the stability of the social
order.[76]

   So long as sacrilege was regarded as a threat to public order, anticlericals had only limited opportunities to denounce the secular
cruelties exercised on religion's behalf—until the execution of the
chevalier La Barre in 1766 horrified the enlightened opinion of
Western Europe. This young man was brought before the court of
the *sénéchaussée* of Ponthieu in October 1765 on suspicion of being
implicated in the mutilation of a crucifix on the bridge at Abbeville.
The investigation failed to prove his complicity in this particular act
of sacrilege, but established the truth of other charges: he had kept
his hat on in the presence of the Sacrament, had sung outrageous
songs, possessed dangerous books, had made the sign of the cross
with obscene remarks, and parodied the priestly actions of consecration at mass.[77] He was sentenced to the standard preliminary tortures
that preceded an execution (to extract an avowal and the names of
accomplices), to have his tongue torn out, and to be decapitated;
when all this was over, the corpse was to be burned. The parlement
of Paris confirmed the sentence on 4 June 1766, and it was carried
out on 1 July, in front of an immense crowd that had poured in from
twenty leagues around and had waited a night and most of a day in
the rain. The *question* (crushing the legs between planks by driving
in wedges) was applied at five in the morning, and the decapitation
took place at five in the evening (the executioner merely simulating
the tearing out of the tongue). Clerical fanaticism had little to do
with the tragic outcome; it was essentially an affair of legal red tape,
corruption, and confusion.[78] M. de Belleval, a legal official of
Ponthieu, had pressed the case against La Barre as a personal
vendetta (the chevalier had been provided with a home by his
cousin, the abbess of Willancourt, and his presence in her house had

broken off her old friendship with Belleval—a miserable provincial feud worthy of inclusion in *Madame Bovary*). La Barre, unlike his partner in riot, d'Etallonde, who fled and became an officer in the Prussian army, had failed to do the usual thing and run away—had he done this, he would have been executed in effigy, and the affair would have been forgotten. The parlement of Paris had put on a special show of ferocious zeal to counterbalance the anticlerical reputation it was enhancing by attacking the Jesuits. The clergy had tried to stop the execution; the diocesan bishop[79] had asked for commutation to life imprisonment (the papal nuncio said that in Rome a year in gaol would have sufficed), and the Assembly of the Clergy of France asked for clemency.[80] The *procureur général* of the parlement had prepared an order to suspend the execution, but it was never sent—the bureaucrats of the scaffold delayed on 1 July from early morning to evening expecting it would arrive.

The cruel death of La Barre gave Voltaire yet another of his great anticlerical opportunities. He was eloquent on the laws which punished mere deviations from 'the dominant opinion' of the nation as if they were crimes of poisoning or parricide. It was absurd for the clergy to erect a crucifix on a bridge where it formed a temptation to every drunken reveller.[81] The bishop, who had presided at a ceremony of expiation when he had described the insult to the sacred figure as 'worthy of the most extreme punishments which this world affords', was blamed for inflaming public opinion, so that a single malicious judge (Belleval) and two stupid ones (a pig dealer and a nonentity) had been influenced to pass a viciously cruel sentence.[82] Voltaire had done some legal research, and he doubted whether this and most other executions for sacrilege were legitimate: the royal ordinance of 1682 spoke of 'sacrilège joint à la superstition', and this surely meant the profanation of Christian objects for the purpose of sorcery, and nothing more. His conclusion was that of Montesquieu, though he chose to quote Vauvenargues: 'ce qui n'offense pas la société n'est pas du ressort de la justice'.[83] The sole task of the police was to protect society—he implied that religion must stand or fall by the allegiance it can win in free intellectual debate.

In a work published in 1686, a parish priest of a rigorist turn of mind listed the activities appropriate for Sunday and other religious festivals. The faithful must attend mass and vespers and hear a sermon. In what time remained, they were recommended to attend the observances of churches other than their own and to visit the sick and the poor.

They may also see their friends or pay necessary social calls, go for walks, converse in an edifying way on the Christian instruction they have received, read some useful books (if they know how to read, otherwise get others to read to them), . . . enjoy sober and moderate repasts, . . . and even play games or indulge in other relaxations, provided these . . . are respectable and fitting to their station in life, and that they do not involve any dubious circumstances.[84]

The law of the land would hardly enforce such worthy activities, but the legislator did his best to circumscribe profane pastimes and to limit the 'dubious circumstances' which curé Thiers feared. Restrictions concerning Sundays and feast-days had been laid down by royal ordinances of 1560 and 1579 and various edicts of Louis XIV (renewed by the parlement of Paris in December 1734); these prohibitions were codified in the major police ordinance of 30 April 1778.[85] Work was forbidden, except when ecclesiastical authority certified a particular task as necessary: there were, however, various customary exemptions in which the necessity was regarded as permanently established. Though the actual baking of bread had to take place on a weekday, loaves could be sold on Sundays, provided the shop was shut to outward appearances. The *pâtisseurs* were allowed to stay open, for holidays were their principal trading times, but they had to close at Easter, Pentecost, All Saints, and the feast of St Laurent, their patron.[86] Barbers could wield their razors after divine service finished (presumably because they had once been surgeons); butchers could sell meat in the hot weather from the first Sunday after Trinity to the first Sunday in September, inclusive. Most judicial proceedings were null if conducted on a Sunday (the agents-general of the clergy in 1722 demonstrated the rule by getting the Royal Council to cancel a writ served on a curé of Rouen by a local monastery). By contrast, assignations to justice of a whole community were always served on Sundays at the end of Sunday mass or vespers, for that was when most people were there to hear the bad news. Barges[87] carrying grain to Paris passed down the waterways continuously, except during the four most solemn feasts of the year, for the provisioning of the capital was too vital a matter to risk any delay. For similar reasons, the parlement of Paris tended to allow millers to work on holy days, and in a case of 1765 accepted the plea that a shop could stay open to sell articles of necessity.[88] At Versailles, Sceaux, and a few other places near Paris, weekday markets were allowed to stay open when they fell on saints' days, though the archbishop in 1787 prevented the fair of Brie-Comte-Robert from gaining this privilege.[89] As for harvest time in the countryside, a sensible parish priest would try to accommodate the needs of his peasants, though maybe not so sweepingly as Restif's curé Pinard, who advanced the hour of mass, cancelled the sermon, and said that the schoolmaster and a few old people would be a sufficient congregation for vespers. 'Bind up your sheaves in this sunny weather,' he said; 'the people subject to the law of Moses were not allowed to violate the Sabbath in this way, but you, children of the regeneration, are free from the letter that killeth . . . God imposes one duty: that is, to love Him.'[90]

It was unrealistic to attempt to close wine bars, cafés, theatres, billiard saloons, and tennis courts all day on Sundays; besides, the authorities were well aware that men congregating on a holiday might resort to activities more dangerous to public order than getting drunk, watching entertainments, or playing games. The law therefore closed places of refreshment and amusement only during the hours of divine service.[91] At these times, dances were also forbidden, on pain of a fine of 500 livres and confiscation of the musical instruments.[92] If a new recreation was devised, the local authorities would regulate it as, in the summer of 1781, the *capitouls* of Toulouse banned the launching of a Montgolfier balloon on St Stephen's Day, on penalty of a fine of 1,000 livres for non-compliance. 'The curiosity to see the ascent of the balloon whose manœuvres will take a long time, might divert the people from fulfilling the acts of worship required by religion.'[93] It was customary to hold the threat of large fines over the heads of potential offenders. In 1719, the assizes of the seigneurial court of the village of Franxault in Burgundy ordained a penalty of 100 livres for serving drinks to customers during church time: the actual fines levied varied from 10 to 50 livres.[94] Police intervention against untimely Sunday drinking was quite frequent. The parish priest might insist on it, as he did at Bouzigues in 1744; twenty or so local inhabitants were found regaling themselves in the bar of one Goudard as the strains of the Magnificat resounded from the church—the customary fine of 3 livres went to the fund for the upkeep of the light before the Holy Sacrament.[95] In the Paris area, the parlement itself sometimes judged an indictment, with exemplary punishment resulting, but mostly, Sunday drinking cases were dealt with by the *chambre de police*, whose chief other task was to fine citizens who failed to sweep the street outside their doorstep.[96] The number of cases dealt with diminished in the early years of the century, but began to rise from 1725, with a still greater increase after 1740. By contrast, in 1755, the standard

fine was reduced from 2 livres per customer detected to 1 livre, 10
sous, while the fine for failure to sweep the street doubled, from 2
livres to 4 livres. Nor did renewed drinking infringements attract
heavier penalties, and there was no closing down of the premises of
habitual offenders.[97] One might infer that the police were becoming
more efficient—or officious—but that the actual offence was
becoming less seriously regarded. The fine for illegal Sunday drinking was settling down into a sort of licence fee.

No doubt there were pious folk who observed Sunday with the
piety that curé Thiers recommended, and others who at least liked
to appear respectable. A cobbler of Chartres called on by an ecclesiastic (a future archbishop) for an urgent shoe repair on a Sunday
professed to be scandalized.[98] Perhaps his trade had special pretensions. 'We aren't like the *canaille* and the dregs of the populace who
employ Sundays and feast-days in going for walks and amusing
themselves at fairs and assemblies, in wine bars and country inns,'
said a pamphlet in defence of the shoemaker's profession; 'for our
part, we are occupied solely on those days in doing useful work in
churches, as bell-ringers, making the offering of *pain bénit*, and
supervising the letting of chairs.'[99] The peasants sometimes worked
on Sundays, sometimes enjoyed the holiday, according to the
weather, the season, local tradition, and the character and exigencies
of their curé;[100] town artisans would have less latitude, but be more
influenced by the degree of their necessity. But clearly absenteeism
from work was the rule—and it did nothing to increase the incidence of practices of piety.

Early in the century, a mission preacher complained of 'the
false idea of most contemporary Christians that it suffices to have
attended Holy Mass to be able to be free to employ all the rest of the
day in business, amusement and idleness'.[101] In 1722, the parlement
of Rennes described the typical Sunday of the lower orders as consisting of 'impious conversations in cemeteries' (being places of
general resort near the church), wandering from wine bar to wine
bar, playing boule and billiards during the hours of divine service,
and indulging in 'execrable oaths and swearing'.[102] Things were presumably getting worse, for after a whole century of silence on the
matter, the Assembly of the Clergy of France began to complain, in
1755, of the failure 'to sanctify Sundays'. 'In the past, disobedience
was carefully concealed . . . now it shows itself openly.'[103] English
travellers to France were struck by the light-hearted fashion in which
the day of rest was enjoyed across the Channel. In 1776, Thomas
Bentley took a drive through the Bois de Boulogne to Saint-Cloud

and back. 'The most striking thing we saw here and all the way', he said,

> was the immense crowds of people and the manner of their Sunday amuse-
> ments. Many kinds of shops were open as on other days; everybody was
> taking the air in their holiday clothes; close to the terrace leading to the
> gardens of St Cloud under the shade of a grove a large party of young men
> and women clean and decently dressed were dancing country dances and
> minuets of three couples alternately with all the ease and decorum of a
> genteel assembly. Multitudes were sitting upon the terrace conversing and
> enjoying the open air; in the woods of Boulogne as we returned back we
> observed many small parties enjoying themselves under the shade of the
> trees and dancing away.[104]

Bentley's naïve enthusiasm for the innocent recreations of the people was not shared by the philosophes; with them, the dominant view was: if only the lower orders could be dissuaded from amusing themselves on Sundays and, indeed, not be pressed overmuch to go to church, they would be able to add an extra day of toil per week to increase the national wealth. Reforming bishops had reduced the number of saints of dubious authenticity: Turgot and the *Encyclopédie* wanted further retrenchments in the calendar in the name of utility.[105] A petition of the labouring classes to the king in 1770 asked for 'permission to work'—this was a concoction of Voltaire,[106] who could not abide idleness and was repelled by vulgar swilling in taverns. This had been one of the abbé de Saint-Pierre's remedies for the ills of France: fill Sundays with work and educational lectures as well as church-going, to leave no time for drinking.[107] A pamphlet-eer of 1789 renewed the proposal, asking for secular Sunday schools teaching law, anatomy, and botany to the ignorant multitude, along-side the usual catechism classes.[108] It is refreshing to turn from these improving schemes to Necker, who saw no reason for the poor to work an extra day since, sadly, their employers would pay them the same subsistence wages whatever extra efforts they made. As it was, on one day in the week they dressed like other citizens and did as they pleased, enjoying the brief illusion of freedom. 'Et moi aussi,' they could say, 'je suis libre.'[109]

One of the tasks of the police was to enforce outward conformity to the Lenten fast, keeping a watch more particularly on butchers' shops and eating-houses. A Parisian police ordinance of January 1768 clarified some details. An innkeeper serving meat dishes (for foreigners and people with special authorizations) had to have a document specifying the permission of his curé and countersigned by the lieutenant-general of police, and he had to serve the privileged few at a separate table. A dignified police official, *L'exempte de la compagnie du prévôt de l'île de France*, was authorized to visit the houses of princes and *grands seigneurs* and to confiscate illegal joints from their kitchens.[110] Strictly speaking, eggs were banned in Lent, though most bishops issued an annual pastoral letter authorizing them. This relaxation only gradually became established in the stern diocese of Paris. There had been no more than two instances in sixty years, when, early in 1729, a tremendous frost extracted the jealously guarded privilege; Parisians rejoiced to find it was not cancelled when the thaw came unexpectedly quickly.[111] Thereafter, permissions became frequent—in 1731, 1732, 1735, then three years running from 1739 to 1741, then nine consecutive years from 1745 to 1753.[112] A solemn ritual was followed by the civil and ecclesiastical powers when such relaxations were being sought: the municipal authorities would draw up a petition, using the conventional formula, 'vu la misère des temps' (which meant that bad weather or famine was rendering the provisioning of the capital difficult); the lieutenant-general of police would support this, referring the application to the parlement, which would send a deputation to the archbishop.[113] When the prelate had issued his pastoral letter giving permission, the magistrates would pass on an *arrêt* authorizing the execution of the episcopal decree, just to show the supremacy of the temporal power.[114] In 1754, all was confusion, since parlement and archbishop were at war with each other. Seeing that the magistrates were so busily engaged in encroaching on spiritual matters, said the old duchesse de Villars, she was asking the *premier président* of the parlement for his permission to eat eggs that year.[115]

Individuals could be exempted from fasting, provided they had an ecclesiastical authorization, generally given on the production of medical evidence. The profits on the sale of meat to such privileged folk were supposed to go to charity. The bishop would fix the prices,[116] and in provincial towns a single butcher would be named, *le boucher de carême*, who paid a fine to the local hospitals. In Paris, the *hôtel-Dieu* had the privilege of overseeing the meat trade in Lent and made 50,000 livres a year from it: this was the compensation decreed by the Crown in 1774 when the monopoly was ended.[117] In desperate times—famine or terrible weather—an episcopal ordinance might even allow meat to everyone. In Lorraine in 1720, with no vegetables available, the price of eggs soaring, and butter said to have lost its nourishing qualities, 'la crainte de voir les maladies succéder à la disette' led to the authorization of meat four days in the week.[118] The first such general permission in Angers was given in January 1766, for every day 'up to and including Maundy Thursday'; for a whole month the Loire had been frozen so hard that horsemen could gallop across the ice.[119] In the same harsh year, the archbishop of Toulouse[120] allowed meat on three days in the week—for the first time within living memory, said a local annalist. The two prelates concerned, Jacques de Grasse and Loménie de Brienne, were suspected of having no serious Christian beliefs; no doubt they had more reasons than one for welcoming the opportunity to be generous to the shivering population of their dioceses.

The Lenten fast was an easy target for the anticlericals of the Enlightenment. It was a burden devised by churchmen, they pointed out, having nothing to do with the essence of religion in general or with the teachings of the founder of Christianity in particular. Christ did not forbid omelettes to his apostles, said Voltaire; on the contrary, he advised them, whatever city they entered, to 'eat such things as they set before you'.[121] Jesus fasted for forty days in the wilderness, a lawyer speculated; the Israelites wandered in the desert for forty years; the Flood lasted forty days; and Nineveh was allowed forty days in which to repent: perhaps Lent is a commemoration of one of these times, without—it is implied—a great deal of relevance to modern conditions.[122] Voltaire did not mind if the State imposed a sort of political Lent—it was, indeed, a civilized idea to stop the fearful carnage of animals for once in a year—but where was the authority of the Church in such a matter? In 1769, Jean-Baptiste Cloots (later to call himself 'Anarcharsis'), a boy of 14 who was being educated in Paris, led his schoolboy companions astray with prohibited Lenten fare by using the standard anticlerical argument: 'to do an action which is in itself innocent, and which becomes criminal only because it is prohibited, is not to sin, so long as one cannot discover whether or not the pro-hibition emanates from a legitimate tribunal'.[123] In any case, said Voltaire, the Lenten discipline of the clergy was suspect because of the manifest inequality of the sacrifices they were trying to impose on the different classes of society. While the rich were eating their way to salvation with sole and salmon, turbot and sturgeon, the poor were deprived of such miserable scraps of meat as might come their way, and were dependent on special permission to eat eggs and butter—what else had they got to nourish them and make their black bread and chestnuts palatable?[124] It was one of the high points of the year for Parisian anticlericals when the post brought in the

Lenten pastoral letters of various bishops from the provinces—full of
thunders of the Last Judgement and the Great Abyss, or of massive
learning from the New Testament and the Fathers, leading usually
to a splendid anticlimax as conclusion: authorizing the eating of
cheese and butter—nay, even, of eggs—in the forthcoming forty
days. If one of these publications survives, what will our descendants
make of it in 2,000 or 3,000 years time, asked the *Correspondance
littéraire* of the pastoral of the archbishop of Lyon in 1768. 'Ils se
casseront la tête pour découvrir la liaison et la logique de ces idées.'[125]
To what extent was the fast of Lent observed? It was commonly said
that the austerities of the penitential season were endured only by
the poor. According to the Lenten pastoral letter of the archbishop
of Sens in 1779, the rich often obtained medical certificates allowing
them to eat what they liked.[126] This was the fashionable thing to do.
'Look at our bourgeois citizen and his wife in their (draper's) shop,
observing Lent strictly,' said the Jesuit Père Croisset in his *Parallèle
des mœurs de ce siècle et la morale de Jésus-Christ* (1727); 'their fortune
changes . . . and scarcely has the tape measure dropped from their
hands than you see them putting on airs like people of quality and
asking for dispensations from fasting.'[127] This class distinction was
observed even in the kitchens of the Bastille: on the first Friday of
his imprisonment, Marmontel gloomily ate the meatless meal provided, not knowing that it had been meant for his servant.[128] In any
case, there were plenty of succulent dishes within the rules, for those
who could afford them. Lent was the season to have tubs of fresh
butter sent in from the countryside,[129] and to ensure plentiful supplies
of fish and water birds (the test of an allowable fowl was: did the
gravy remain uncongealed after fifteen minutes?—so a bishop
gravely advised Mme Victoire, Louis XV's pious but comfortable
daughter[130]). The peasant, whose existence is a perpetual Lent
anyway, said Voltaire, awaits episcopal permission to eat his farmyard
eggs, while the bishop himself looks forward to expensive dishes of
soles.[131] Certainly, things were well organized at Versailles. 'A ray of
grace has descended on us,' wrote the duc de la Vallière in April
1756; 'we fasted for three days a week during the whole of Lent, but
on condition that we suffered no deprivations.'[132] Preachers were
well aware that those with money and leisure could organize an
attractive Lent for themselves: an occasional walk in a procession
(a penitent's garb was no disadvantage to a good-looking woman),[133]
extra time in bed to recuperate from privations, and food more
delicately cooked and served than usual. 'For some—God grant
there are none in my congregation today,' thundered the Oratorian

Surian, 'Lent is a more agreeable time, in a sophisticated way, than the other seasons of the year.'[134]

In the second half of the eighteenth century, contemporaries recorded a widespread decline of scruples about fasting in Paris, and the beginnings of a decline in Angers.[135] Mercier in the 1780s describes how the police of the capital had relaxed their vigilance: when he was a boy, they had confiscated the dinner sent to the prince de Condé from his private kitchens to the tennis court in the rue Mazarine, and a citizen taking broth to an ailing friend on a Friday did well to conceal it in a hat box; now, the butchers' shops openly sold meat without hindrance.[136] The king, however, still intervened to stop outrageous violations of decency by the great: the lavish subscription dinner organized by certain courtiers in 1776 for the first Thursday in Lent was whipped away and given to the poor of the parish of Saint-Roch (as it had cost five louis a head, the wits called it 'le repas des Chevaliers de Saint-Louis'[137]). In spite of the gulf between rich and poor, there was a sense in which the social life of Paris constituted a unity; there were occasions when the irreligious ostentation of the great provided a celebration of revolt for everyone. Such was the promenade of Longchamps which became a fashion in the last two decades of the *ancien régime*. It began with excursions through the Bois-de-Boulogne, on the Wednesday of Holy Week, Maundy Thursday, and Good Friday to hear *Tenebrae* sung by the nuns at the abbey of Longchamps—young bloods rode there on horseback, and the ladies in their carriages. The abbey, which had rejoiced in its fame and fortified its choir with opera singers, soon changed its policy in accordance with the solemnity of Lent, but the promenade had become an institution.[138] The rich vied in their splendour, the others crowded to watch them, and the police turned out in force to keep order, the city watch lining the streets from the Place Louis XV to the Porte Maillot, and the *maréchaussée* patrolling the woods beyond. The chief competition in ostentation was among the *filles entretenues* of court nobles and financiers. Mlle Guimard the dancer, 'la belle Damnée', won in 1768 with her invented coat of arms, supported by Graces and surmounted by cherubs, painted on the doors of her carriage.[139] In 1774, two dancers (one the mistress of the Spanish ambassador) scored off all other rivals by having no fewer than six horses pulling their carriages; the next year, Mlle Duthé tried the same gambit, adding blue morocco harness adorned with polished steel, and got hooted for ostentation;[140] in 1780, the daughter of the duchesse de Mazarin, pulled by four greys caparisoned in crimson silk, had to brook comparisons with a *fille* in a porcelain carriage and another who had the distinction of the duc de Chartres riding alongside her all the way.[141] In 1787, Mlle Rozalie of the Comédie-Italienne misbehaved so badly in the parade that the lieutenant of police sent her to the prison of For l'Évêque, where the young seigneurs of the Court visited her and she took charitable collections for the release of debtors, which made her universally popular.[142] Such were the subjects of Holy Week gossip in Paris.

Concerning fasting and ordinary people, while there is a broad assumption that they unenthusiastically gave some compliance, we cannot hope to know what happened in their houses. Yet, oddly enough, we do know about their reactions to the Church's precepts to abstain from sexual intercourse in penitential seasons. Counting backwards from dates of birth, we can infer[143] that sexual activity was at its minimum in the early autumn (through preoccupation with harvesting and sheer exhaustion) and in Lent (presumably principally for religious reasons), while it was at its maximum in spring, once Lent was over. Advent was not respected (though in French Canada it was), but the rule of abstention in Lent was still taken seriously—and in a branch of enjoyment which escaped the surveillance of the police. It was, no doubt, natural to resort to—or to applaud—brinkmanship in words and gestures banned by the police in association with the clergy, to find ways of enlivening Sunday with profane merriment, to evade the austere regulations of penitential seasons, and to laugh at the irreligious and anticlerical gestures of *grands seigneurs* and philosophes. But to the mass of people who enjoyed no privacy for reflection or devotion and owned so very little they could offer as a gift, the Church's call to self-denial as a spiritual exercise and a self-offering struck a chord of human need and led to a degree of conformity to ecclesiastical discipline which was the result neither of the coercion of the mind by habit nor the outward act by the police. The flavour of this sort of conformity is rarely evoked by the handbooks of spirituality read by the leisured classes or in statistics of conduct; the historian is grateful for a glimpse of it, even if he can only guess at its significance.

IV *The Church and Law Enforcement*

Just as the police powers of the State protected the observances of religion, so the Church was expected to second the officers of the State in the enforcement of the laws. Though the ecclesiastical courts exercised jurisdiction over clerics, in the last resort royal jurisdiction could take over—the *appel comme d'abus* was the decisive weapon of the lay magistrates to defeat the pretensions of churchmen. The king's writ ran against all persons and in all places of his dominions. The ancient right of sanctuary was lost to the churches and convents of France—a criminal could be arrested in a church just as anywhere else.[144] It is true that there remained some oases of feudal jurisdictions in the cities, often enough owned by collegiate churches, in which the municipal police did not operate in non-criminal matters, though they were being taken over by the civic authorities whenever opportunity offered. This is what happened to the *sauvetés* of Saint-André and Saint-Seurin at Bordeaux at the end of the *ancien régime*.[145] Until then, under the lax policing of the canons, gambling dens and unpleasant and dangerous industrial establishments like iron foundries and tanneries had flourished, and dubious women had plied their trade in the very cloisters of the chapters and in the capitular prisons. There was a 'sanctuary' of a sort in Paris, the *enclos du Temple*, belonging to the knights of Malta, who had inherited it from the Templars. In this 'lieu d'asile', ordinary criminals could be arrested, but debtors, duellists, and writers who had fallen foul of the censorship were safe, provided they entered their names and the reason for their application for sanctuary in the register kept by the *bailli* of the Order. Gudin, friend of Beaumarchais, fled there in 1778, pursued by the police for verses satirizing the parlement Maupeou; he lived there together with Mme de Goodville, who had taken refuge in the Temple to escape her creditors, and they amused themselves by writing lampoons on the great, sending them to the lieutenant of police with their compliments.[146]

The clergy had no immunity from criminal prosecution and could not offer asylum to others; they could, however, give advice and comfort in the confessional under the seal of absolute secrecy. But the secular authorities, in every circumstance outside the confessional, expected the clergy to co-operate in law enforcement. They regarded the parish priests as having the duty of making government legislation known to their people, and ancient ordinances of the kings had laid on the curés the duty of reading out official announcements during the Sunday mass, when all the parishioners would be assembled.[147] The law courts also demanded the publication of their verdicts in significant cases, and the great came to insist on having notices read warning the public to respect their rights—as when a boundary dispute had been settled in their favour. The clergy, concerned to elevate the Sacrament of the altar to a pinnacle of reverence, challenged the old ordinances and established customs. Bishops directed curés[148] to limit notices during the mass to listing ecclesiastical feasts and fasts and the foundation masses for the coming week, relegating anything else to after the post-communion prayers or, better still, to the porch or churchyard after the congregation had left the church. In the case of a private announcement, let the individual concerned hire a notary or *huissier* to read out his notice, instead of imposing on the clergy. (Truth to tell, in the depths of the country curés did not regard such notices as a nuisance, especially where they charged a small fee for them, a practice continuing all through the century.) These episcopal rules were given official standing by the royal edict of 1695, freeing the curés from any obligation to mention private affairs, and the declaration of 1698 extended this to all secular affairs, even if the business of the king was concerned.[149] Curés were still subjected to pressure by local magistrates and nobles, and no doubt often yielded for the sake of a quiet life, but if they complained to the agents general of the clergy at Paris, they could be sure the Royal Council would intervene on the side of the Church. In 1742 the parlement of Pau ordered a curé to read out a newly surveyed documentation of the boundaries and feudal rights of the 'sieur de Capdeville'; a year later, the council cancelled the parlement's ruling.[150] Five years later, another case was won against the Maîtrise des Eaux et Forêts of Dôle. In 1775, a curé of the diocese of Chartres successfully defied the *chambre des comptes* which was demanding publication of its arbitration settling the boundaries of the royal forest of Senonches.[151] About this time, the parlement of Toulouse tested the established jurisprudence deriving from the edicts of 1695 and 1698 by demanding the reading of a verdict, alleging the subject to be morals and religion. The magistrates, who had sentenced three girls to death for concealing their pregnancies, so that their babies died, wanted the judgement widely disseminated as a warning to others. The agents-general of the clergy defeated the claim using an interesting new argument: granted the Church had the duty of assisting to maintain public morality, it was improper to do so by dishonouring private families by naming them in the house of God. Yet the idea that the clergy had to read out government regulations in church was deeply ingrained, and in 1789, the National Assembly, determined to claim for itself the full sovereign rights of the old monarchy, prescribed the reading of its decrees at *prône*. Local authorities, full of revolutionary self-importance, began to do the same. 'They are assimilating our ministry to that of town criers,' complained the bishop of Senez.[152]

When Church property was to be sold, however, the assembly recognized that it would be indecent for curés to have to read from the pulpit the list of ecclesiastical lands and buildings for auction, though there were anticlerical local authorities reluctant to recognize the incongruity.

There was a peculiar kind of public announcement detested by the clergy even more than the reading of government edicts; though it concerned secular business, it could not be excluded from the parish mass, for its essence was the proclamation of a threat of ecclesiastical penalties. The *monitoire*[153] was an injunction of the Church, issued on the request of a secular magistrate, ordering all Christian people to reveal whatever they might know about the circumstances and perpetrators of a particular criminal act, under pain of excommunication. The lawyers held certain crimes to be especially suitable for investigation in this fashion: the suppression of a last will and testament or the concealment of possessions in the inheritance; fraud, more especially fraudulent bankruptcy; usury; monopolistic conspiracy to force up prices—all involving clandestine manœuvres. Other suitable offences were those in which the perpetrators were known but no one would give evidence, as when cattle had broken through hedges and trampled a sown field or had been surreptitiously grazed on a meadow. A rumour of a duel, condoned by certain sections of public opinion, but held to be a threat to society by the government, was considered to be eminently worthy of investigation, and the procedures for obtaining a *monitoire* were made correspondingly easier. But in every case, the will of the secular court had to prevail: the *officiel*, the legal registrar of a diocese, had to comply with the request of the lay judge on pain of seizure of his property. The ecclesiastical courts could also resort to the *monitoire*, the standard examples being simony or the illegitimate appropriation of the title to a tithe by a layman. There were safeguards, however. A court, lay or ecclesiastical, could not embark on a 'fishing expedition': the judges must have made arrangements to prosecute or at least have a 'plainte répondue' before them, indicating that a civil case would be pursued. Offences concerning movable property were excluded, as were evasion of taxes or customs duties (there was also a papal ruling, not accepted in France, excluding small sums of money).[154] Except in cases of adultery, the names of individuals could not be mentioned in a derogatory fashion. Doctors and midwives had no obligation to proffer information (it went without saying that confessors could not do so); servants could not incriminate their masters; and the relatives of a criminal up to the fourth degree were free to remain silent.

When a *monitoire* was called for, the curé had to publish it on three successive Sundays, giving a certificate of performance to the *officiel* or to the lay tribunal; if any revelations were made to him as a result of the proclamation, he forwarded them to the court in a sealed envelope. Some diocesan *Rituels* provided a formula for a *monitoire* in which the excommunication was automatically incurred after a stated lapse of time (in the diocese of Bâle, it was thirty days, except for a murder, when it was three days only).[155] Or the *Rituel* might provide for the separate pronouncement of the excommunication, possibly in two stages of increasing gravity. The final step would be the proclamation of the *aggrave* (sometimes called the *réaggrave*), the major excommunication, consignment to total damnation. This could be done with sinister ceremonies—a white baptismal robe trampled under foot, a crucifix or a lighted candle thrown down; perhaps a coffin would be brought into the nave as stage scenery for the fulmination, then taken out and put on a bonfire, with two priests each throwing six stones (two and six being numbers short of the ecclesiastical golden norm, three and seven). While the flames roared, Psalm 109 would be recited: 'let Satan stand at his right hand. When he shall be judged, let him be condemned, and let his prayer be turned into sin. Let his days be few and another take his office. Let there be no man to pity him, nor have compassion on his fatherless children.'

These macabre, archaic thunders often enough failed to produce revelations. The excommunication of named persons for known transgression[156] (rarely possible in France except for open and continuous adultery) could be effective, as incurring social ostracism, but it was unlikely that undetected people whose only crime was to keep their own counsel would tremble. Officials and men of property using the *monitoire* in an attempt to break through the popular conspiracy of silence rarely succeeded. Year after year the municipality of Angers[157] uselessly had the clergy calling for the names of the scoundrels who broke up seats on the public promenades and damaged trees to get fuel in winter—the freezing poor were leagued together to survive. In 1736 the parlement of Brittany used the *monitoire* in an attempt to prevent the filling in of the ditches and the pulling down of the fences of a nobleman who had enclosed the common land at Plourivo; the peasants erected a gallows and dug a grave at its foot, with the notice 'It is here we will bury those who talk'—no one did.[158] A *monitoire* in the diocese of Gap led to the women of the parish pulling the priest out of his pulpit, tearing his cassock, throwing away his wig, and beating him with the processional cross, for they feared his anathemas might do damage to the crops.[159] Some *monitoires* were not only futile, but frivolous. Everyone except the victims enjoyed the lampoons circulating in provincial towns against the great; why should the terrors of Hell be invoked against the jester who put out a broadsheet ridiculing the canons of Reims, the satirist who described in verse the follies of the élite of Angers at a pretentious ball, the artist at Séez who painted a poster denouncing a local physician adorned with a border of knives dripping blood?[160] When anathemas were effective, it was because the criminals were well-known rogues without local sympathy, as at Auxerre in 1739, when Pierre Fleury, his wife, and three accomplices were identified as the nocturnal thieves who had stolen the iron grilles over cellar entrances, and were duly flogged, branded, and banished.[161] If a *monitoire* had the justification of being directed at a grave crime executed by stealth—a man killed by a pistol shot in an empty street in Paris,[162] musket balls fired through the windows of an unpopular seigneur,[163] the many revenges taken by arson in the countryside—almost by definition the chances of finding the criminal were small. Yet the law courts were happy to requisition the thunders of the Church, however useless, for it was a demonstration that the magistrates were at least doing something, expressing some concern. For their part, the clergy felt they were degrading their office and the majesty of religion by evoking superficial and superstitious *frissons* of terror demonstrably ineffective.

There were simple parish priests in remote places who entered into the spirit of these thunderous performances and improved them with threatening discourses, adding transformation into werewolves to the prescribed liturgical penalties.[164] But the better-educated and those in touch with urban opinion could do no other than regard the proceedings as theologically dubious and verging on the ridiculous, so they dissociated themselves as far as possible, and did no more than the bare minimum to conform to the law. This was more particularly so after the storm broke over the unjust condemnation of the Protestant Calas, in which the *monitoire* was revealed as the instrument of prejudiced judges; the magistrates of Toulouse had used it to ask for information about the 'assassins' of Marc-Antoine Calas, excluding the possibility of what really happened—suicide.[165] 'A monitoire can be a proscription,' Voltaire was to say.[166] This was the beginning of the road to the vicious verdict condemning Marc-Antoine's father to breaking on the wheel on the ground that he had murdered his son to prevent him converting to the Roman faith. In addition to high principle and the odium of the Calas affair, there

was also a material consideration to encourage clerical resentment.
Here was yet another instance of the clergy being obliged to work
for derisory remuneration in State service, to the profit of the
lawyers.[167] The registrar of a lay tribunal ordering a *monitoire* got a fee
of 30 sous, and his clerk 10 sous. The curé, who went through the
repeated ceremonies, wrote the certificate, copied down the evidence, and forwarded it, in the process making himself ridiculous
and, possibly, unpopular, got the same as the clerk, 10 sous. When
in Brittany the parish priests leagued together to ask a fee of three
livres, the magistrates of the parlement (who exacted considerable
épices from litigants) described their request as 'sordid avarice'. There
was also the matter of pride, of the dignity of the office of pastor, of
the majesty of the ceremonies of religion. Judging by their *cahiers* in
1789, this is what piqued the curés most. They were ashamed to see
'the sword of excommunication being unsheathed in executing the
sentence of a village judge', and angered at 'the frivolity and indis-
cretion with which *monitoires* are ordered, sometimes for absurd
reasons'.[168] 'Is it decent for the Church', asked the clergy of
Clermont-Ferrand, 'to be obliged, at the discretion of a simple
seigneurial judge, to deploy all the most formidable weapons in its
armoury, sometimes for matters bordering on the ridiculous?'[169]

4

THE WEALTH OF THE CHURCH

The Gallican Church was enormously wealthy. In the seventeenth century, envious estimates had accused churchmen of monopolizing a quarter of the wealth of the kingdom, more than the king, who enjoyed only a ninth.[1] According to more sober guesses at the beginning of the Revolution, ecclesiastics disposed of a total income twice as large as the yield of the basic land tax, the *taille*; if this was so, though not quite as rich as the Crown, the Church was not far from it. These splendid revenues were derived from two sources: property on the one hand and tithe on the other. Probably, tithe brought in rather more, but the balance between tithe and landed estates varied throughout France. There was an infinity of local differences and one broad, overwhelming contrast: in the North, where there were vast tracts of ecclesiastical property, tithe played a lesser part than in the South, where in some dioceses, it was the primary and indispensable support of the clergy. It formed three-quarters of their revenues in the dioceses of Albi, Castres, and Lavaur. The canons of the cathedral of Toulouse and the bishop of Pamiers would have been in penury without it.[2] Where the impact of ecclesiastical riches on public opinion is concerned, it is difficult to generalize about the estates of the Church, since they were so unevenly distributed throughout the country. More comprehensive statements can usually be made about tithe. Therefore, in this chapter, these two sources of income will be considered separately.

Though in some respects such separate consideration will bring clarity, it will also distort the picture. Those who paid were more concerned about the total amount dragged from their pockets than about the headings under which the various levies were made. The peasant who looked enviously on the broad acres of some great abbey and, maybe, paid rents and feudal dues to it was also paying tithe to churchmen. The total burden could be heavy. In one village in the mid-eighteenth century, where there were 62 houses and 240 inhabitants, with a gross income of 11,000 livres, the clergy took 2,400, the seigneur 1,900, and direct royal taxation 1,975. In another, of 212 houses and 630 inhabitants, with a gross income of

24,000 livres, the corresponding figures were 4,700, 4,150, and 4,230.[3] The clergy were making away with a fifth of the produce of the parish; the 'establishment' generally, including the clergy, with half. These are the sophisticated calculations of a modern historian, but the peasant, isolated and ignorant as he was, knew how much he harvested and who got what. This was his fate, accepted with bitterness.

A consideration of his lot may serve as a warning. In our fashionable enthusiasm for the study of nuances of social structure, we should never lose sight of the sheer oppressiveness of the *ancien régime*. It requires an effort of the imagination to understand how these unjust arrangements were stolidly and fatalistically accepted from below, and imposed, with only rare tremors of conscience, from above: the gilded world of Versailles, the crystalline salons of the Enlightenment, the rich and varied liturgical, spiritual, social, and cultural activities of the Gallican Church can be regarded, if we so wish, as self-contained subjects for historical study, taking for granted the complex underpinning of law, tradition, and coercion holding together the system of tribute that paid the bills. In this chapter on the wealth of the Church, we clamber, as it were, amid the joists and beams of this multifarious underpinning. The temptation is to hasten out of the obscurity up to the Church itself, that great autonomous institution, with its organization, its clergy, its role in society, its aspirations towards eternity. For the most part, indeed, the nature of the evidence available obliges us to do so. Yet, groping on the under-side of ecclesiastical history, we come into touch with rural France, and with the peasants, the vast majority of the population. Their role was to pay. Along rutted lanes, paths through cornfields, and sheep tracks in the mountains, we meet continually a multitude of weather-beaten figures, a spectacle of broken teeth, gnarled hands, rags, clogs, coarse woollen stockings, and homespun cloaks. These folk not only support the Church; they constitute it and justify its existence. If we can discover how they believed and felt, and what charity and hope religion brought into their living and their dying, this would be the quintessential ecclesiastical history—a history which, alas, will largely remain unwritten, though on a plane not accessible to terrestrial historians it is recorded and will not be forgotten.

I *Property*

According to Barbier, the early eighteenth-century diarist, a third of the whole territory of France was in ecclesiastical hands.[4] A cynical and irreverent *avocat*, he delighted in anticlerical exaggeration. When, at the beginning of the Revolution, it was a question of proposing the sale of the sacred acres to pay off the State debt, estimates of the assets to go to auction varied from 60 to 170 million. Talleyrand who, as a bishop, a former *agent général* of the clergy, a financial expert, and the deviser of the great spoliation, was likely to be well informed, spoke of 80 million. Lavoisier, both a scientist and one of the financiers collecting the taxes, thought 70.[5] In 1750, the reforming minister Machault, designing to subject the Church to ordinary taxation, had done sums coming to a higher total than even the most reckless estimates of 1790. He had probably been relying on documents in the royal archives which are now lost, the records of the *Économat*, the department in charge of the collection of the revenues of abbeys of royal foundation and bishoprics during vacancies, for the benefit of the Crown. Starting with the value of these opulent benefices and multiplying to take cognizance of the others would account for his figure being unreasonably high.[6] In fact, the quest for a reliable global assessment was hopeless. Agriculturally based revenues were subject to steep fluctuation; good or bad weather, good or bad management, could make all the difference. Few incomings were clear profit—there were always repairs to be done, pensions to be paid, obligations to be fulfilled. The estates of the Church were leased and sublet in various fashions according to the changing policies of institutions and the coming and going of personalities, while the true value of leases was obscured by the custom of giving unrecorded gratifications to proprietors at each renewal. And whatever government has ruled, Frenchmen have never willingly entrusted details of income and possessions to its agents. One can take it as a rule that the almanacs of the eighteenth century understate the revenues of bishoprics by at least 50 per cent. Efforts within the Church to get correct figures—for the diocesan list of benefices, the *pouillé*, for example—had only limited success, for clerical taxation in detail was as repugnant to the individual benefice holder as government exactions were to the Church in general.

Historians of our own century, with the documentation of the Revolutionary inventories, estimates, and sales available, have, with a great deal of burrowing in series Q of departmental archives, worked out the proportion of land held by the Church in particular areas. By the conflation of such studies, reasonably reliable calculations have been made applying to the whole cultivated area of France—somewhere between Henri Sée's 6 per cent and Georges Lefebvre's 10 per cent.[7] This average, like all averages, conceals variations—in this case, very great ones. Churchmen owned much more property in the towns than in the countryside. A third of the area of the cities of Toulouse and Rennes belonged to them, while all around Revel, near Toulouse, they had only 3.02 per cent, and in 130 rural parishes in the Rennes–Fougères–Vitré area, only 3.41 per cent.[8] Ecclesiastical property was also much more extensive in the North than in the South. In the plain of Picardy and around Laon and Cambrai, it totalled 30–40 per cent,[9] in the diocese of Arras, 19 per cent.[10] Here was tremendous wealth, obvious at first glance to the most hasty tourist; Thomas Bentley, posting from Calais to Paris in 1776, was astonished to see no châteaux or mansions of the gentry, 'but magnificent abbeys and churches everywhere, especially in Artois, which seems to be the paradise of the monks'.[11] Going south and west, the picture changed. Around Sens, the figure was 12 per cent,[12] in Touraine 10 per cent,[13] in the intendancy of Limoges 3 per cent,[14] in the *bocage* country of the West, in Quercy[15] and in the diocese of Auch, around 2 per cent.[16] Not surprisingly, the clergy of Auch fought hard to conserve every jot of tithe income. In Béarn, the clergy's share of the land was minute (0.003 per cent), chiefly consisting of gardens belonging to curés.[17]

Peasant anticlericalism might be supposed to be a collective passion which grows more bitter in proportion to the amount of ecclesiastical property in and around the parish. There would obviously be less provocation to envy in the Breton canton of Fougerai, with only one acre in each thousand belonging to priests,[18] than in Saint-André-de-la-Marche in the Angevin Vendée, where the figure was one in three, or in the little town of Montfaucon nearby, where a third of the inhabitants were paupers and two-thirds of the land belonged to the curés or to religious houses.[19] Yet, while there is truth in this broad generalization, there are distinctions to be made. The peasant assessed the quality of land with a professional eye, well aware of differences in value, and of the amount of labour that each patch would require to earn a living. Around Sens, the best arable land seemed to have fallen to the clergy and the nobles, and the clergy predominated in the ownership of forests and meadows— forests supplying the timber and firewood which were in short supply and requiring little labour, and meadows usually taken to be worth double or triple the same area under the cultivation of cereals.[20] Around Paris, where churchmen owned 14 per cent of the soil, their wealth was more manifest and more censured because some great religious institutions owned conspicuous blocs: the abbey of Saint-Denis was seigneur in seven parishes, the chapter of Sainte-Croix d'Orléans in five, Notre-Dame of Paris in three, and the Dames de Saint Cyr in fourteen. Here, there was also a sort of guilt by association, since Court nobles and magistrates of the parlement had bought up seigneuries, often with hunting rights in mind, over the years. (The prince de Condé had twelve, the prince de Conti, fourteen). Extensive clerical domains looked like part of the conspiracy of the great against the poor.[21] So it was in the Mauges area of Anjou. The wretched peasants had only 18 per cent of the land, but it was not the clergy (with 5.13 per cent) who stood in the way; the nobles had 60 per cent, and the bourgeoisie 17 per cent. Yet in 1789, the *cahiers* were virulently anticlerical, unanimously denouncing tithe and clamouring for the suppression of religious houses.[22]

As a rule, throughout the eighteenth century, the profits of landowners were rising, slowly in the first half of the century, rapidly after 1760. In Metz, there were four great abbeys of the Benedictine congregation of Saint-Vanne; we have figures for the rise in the revenues of three of them between 1766 and the beginning of 1789. Rounded off to the nearest thousand they are: a rise from 25,000 livres to 63,000 livres, from 24,000 to 65,000, and from 16,000 to 50,000.[23] Similarly, we have figures for the rise in the abbot's income in three of the four Benedictine abbeys of the congregation of Saint-Maur in the diocese of Sens between 1753 and 1789: in one it tripled, in another quadrupled, and in the third it remained stationary.[24] Studies of three great abbeys in the West (Saint-Aubin of Angers, Saint-Georges of Rennes, and Saint-Sauveur of Redon) show a slow rise from 1720 to 1760, then an explosive expansion in the reign of Louix XVI; Saint-Aubin doubled its income.[25] The lands of such well-endowed institutions often consisted of sizeable farms (some being *métairies* run by tenants on a share-crop basis), and these would be grouped into 'domains'; the abbey of Saint-Vincent at Le Mans owned fifty-five farms divided into six domains.[26] Around Tours, where such a major agricultural unit was called a 'terre' or a 'lieu', the basilica of Saint-Martin owned 'le lieu des Ligneries' in the parish of Charentilly, comprising a seigneurie with a clutter of feudal dues, seven farms, ponds, and a fulling mill; at the Revolution, the entrepreneur who leased the whole concern, one Bourreau, tried to buy it, but was outbid by a bourgeois of Tours.[27]

Property of this kind was conveniently disposed for exploitation on the large scale, and the holders—normally, abbeys, bishops, or chapters—were accustomed to negotiate leases with businessmen like Bourreau, who would sublet the land and organize the collection of the disparate revenues. Given the increasing opportunities for profit, there was no lack of takers, and this 'farming' of Church property (as of the tithe) was one of the surest ways for an enterprising monied family to move up into the higher reaches of finance and towards the purchase of noble status.

No doubt this was the most effective method for ecclesiastical institutions to improve their income, but ordinary folk regarded the monopoly of the capitalist *fermier* as a social evil:[28] arable land was turned into pasture, buildings were demolished, subtenants squeezed, local traditions broken, and local charitable obligations ignored. About a third of the peasants had not enough land of their own to live on; they had less than the standard five hectares regarded as the minimum plot to grow enough grain to feed a family. Many others had not a great deal more. These folk survived by day-labouring, practising part-time trades, grazing an animal on the common, following the harvesting round to get temporary reaping jobs, by vagabondage and outright begging; it was 'an economy of make-shifts'.[29] Ideally, their best resource was to find a complaisant land-owner who was willing to lease out a small plot for a not too severe rent. And often enough, there was fragmented property of this kind available, belonging to chapters, parish priests, and parish vestries rather than to monasteries—odd fields, houses, gardens, and orchards which had been given by pious donors to pay for masses, to support a chapel, a confraternity, or some religious observance. In the district around Caudebec, where ecclesiastical property constituted only slightly over 5 per cent of the total cultivated land, its patchwork nature can be inferred from the fact that there was at least one item to reckon in no fewer than 132 out of 136 parishes.[30] In the Sarthe, we find a curé who has twenty-four separate plots, and another with no fewer than fifty.[31] Not all were suitable for leasehold, of course. Putting a tenant into a vineyard could be bad business, since he might let the vines run on to become woody, realizing quick profits but ruining long-term prospects.[32] Curés tended to use their local knowledge to cultivate their land with hired labour; on the other hand, vestries (*fabriques*) preferred to auction the leases to the highest bidder, which saved the churchwardens trouble and pleased the villagers. All in all, when there were small plots, there was a likelihood that some would be available for letting, and this is what the rural folk wanted. It was not so much the amount of property held by ecclesiastics, as the use they made of it, which determined peasant attitudes. Prelates and abbeys leasing out their estates in large units to capitalist contractors were hated, and even curés were frowned on if they insisted on tilling the odd field belonging to their benefices.[33] A parish containing lots of corners of land leased out at old traditional rents was one which agricultural reformers and the big entrepreneurs would condemn as backward and unproductive but for the mass of peasants it was ideal. Where approximations to this ideal existed, the sale of church lands at the Revolution swept them away.

It was a maxim in rural society that churchmen ought to lease their property to the laity. 'It is scandalous, and against both civil and canon law', says a *cahier* in 1789, 'that a priest, a curé should become a merchant. Let them be compelled to lease out their possessions, except those necessary to and dependent upon their dwellings.'[34] 'Let the clergy be no longer permitted to administer their property,' says another; 'this is incompatible with their ministry. In future, let their leases be put up to auction under the supervision of the nearest royal magistrate, and let these auctions be public. The people of the commonality, in taking over these leases, will find in them resources to enable them to bring up their families.'[35] The lust for leasehold was universal. The poor could not feed themselves without more land, and the richer sort saw handsome profits to be made from the bigger units. When Church property was sold under the Revolution, the successful bids at the auctions were normally well in excess of the official estimated prices, which had been calculated on the value of the leases.[36] One might conclude that most churchmen could probably have extracted more from their tenants if they had insisted on the strict market price and kept it up to date. In Artois, Picardy, and around Laon, and no doubt in some other places, the leases of ecclesiastical property had become virtually hereditary possessions within certain families; whether by customary deference or because of intimidation, rivals did not come forward to compete at renewal time.[37] When a tenant got into difficulties as a result of a natural disaster, or even from miscalculation, ecclesiastical institutions were more likely to be generous than secular landlords. Such had been the old days in Lorraine, said a report of 1790 looking back nostalgically:

The canons of Nancy had kept the ancient usage of according reductions and compensations to their leaseholders. Often enough, under these

canons of former times, tenants who, by the terms of their leases were
formally excluded from such remissions, nevertheless asked for them and
got them as before. These reductions often saved them from ruin. That is
one of the reasons why cultivators prefer to manage the lands of the
clergy rather than those of the proprietors; among those who go bankrupt
you rarely find one of the tenants of the clergy.[38]

When deploring the failure of eighteenth-century churchmen to
devote more of their wealth to charity, we too easily overlook the
hidden, almost involuntary contributions which an easygoing and
decent tradition imposed on them.

The property of a benefice was vulnerable to depredation: an
unscrupulous cleric might neglect repairs or anticipate revenues.
There were, therefore, legal safeguards to protect future holders
against present ones. Thus priority was given to repairs as against the
claims of ordinary creditors—a precaution much to the disadvantage
of tradesmen, money-lenders, and other laymen who had been too
trusting. When that dubious prelate, Jacques de Grasse, bishop of
Angers, died, the new bishop, Mgr Couet du Vivier de Lorry, was
left with 100,000 livres worth of repairs to do and only half that
amount available from the sale of the furniture of his predecessor.
This was bad news for the baker, who had not been paid for years,
and the good lady who owned the butcher's shop near the palace.
That 'petit livre particulier que la demlle Coudray tenait exprès pour
M. De Grasse' showed 1,891 livres, 10 sous, and 9 deniers owing;
one fears she got none of it.[39] Another safeguard against depredation
was that leases granted by benefice holders were automatically
annulled on the death or resignation of the titular. Economic
thinkers condemned this rule as a hindrance to efficient agriculture,
since farmers on a precarious tenure are unlikely to embark on major
improvements. Talleyrand, making a show as a man of progress, did
not fail to elaborate the point in his speech of 10 October 1789,
proposing the sale of the property of his Order.[40] In their *cahiers* the
peasants took a more personal view of the disadvantage, and alleged
sharp practice. In the *bailliage* of Amiens, eighty families had been
evicted because the holders of two abbeys happened to resign
simultaneously.[41] The inhabitants of Givry-sur-Aisne (near Reims)
claimed to have seen many examples of a tenant losing his lease just
as he was about to reap his first crop.[42] In fact, it was not easy to turn
out a tenant: such ruthlessness would meet with *mauvais gré*—wilful
damage, concerted local hostility.[43] Provided there were funds
available to meet the extra costs of renewing the lease, eviction was
hardly likely. But these costs were considerable because of the way

the leasehold system operated. It was customary to draw up an agreement for a term of nine years or so, adding little or nothing to the annual rent which was specified, as this would attract a heavier State registration tax, but exacting a substantial lump sum as a sort of signing fee, the so-called *pot de vin*. This was a single, non-returnable payment. Thus, if a benefice fell vacant before the term prescribed in its lease, the tenant had paid excessively for a short tenure, while the departing benefice holder (or if he had died, his heirs) would be rejoicing in bearing off a comfortable, disproportionately large lump sum. So the strategic time to migrate from one benefice to another was shortly after the renewal of the leases. When this happened, there would be dark suspicions locally that the move at this particular moment was not an accident. The titular abbot of Saint-Jean at Amiens offered the tenants of his six large farms advantageous leases for the term of their individual lives—on condition of a substantial signing fee, of course. It was 'perfidious generosity' said the *cahier* of La Chaussée de Picquigny. 'Never was a proposal more enthusiastically accepted. Immediately, leases changed hands for the consideration of a *pot de vin*. What then did M. de Crillon (the abbot) do? In that very same year he resigned his abbey into the hands of the king to obtain a richer one'—and the tenants had to fork out all over again to conclude leases with his successor. This was a notable case of injustice, and M. de Crillon's victims went to law, with what result we know not.[44] It was not entirely impossible for an enlightened benefice holder to contrive a longer lease which was not cancelled, but the procedures were difficult, and examples are rare.[45] The broad picture over rural France is one of peasants, rich and poor, yearning to get hold of Church lands on leasehold, yet anxious not to pay the full economic rent, and complaining bitterly when the gamble over the initial outlay on signing a lease turned out unluckily for them.

Tocqueville approved of a land-owning clergy.[46] The possession of agricultural property would prevent them from becoming other-worldly, and would keep them in practical daily contact with their people; the Church, a popular institution, would be able to stand for liberty against tyrants and bureaucrats. One may argue about whether the political results he anticipated followed; but it is true that the clergy of eighteenth-century France came quite near to his specifications. Some curés had a good deal of land attached to their benefices. Of 352 parishes in the Sarthe, in only 15 was the parish priest limited to a simple garden, and in only 60 more did he have less than the five hectares which could feed a family. In 165 he had

between 10 and 29 hectares, and in 37 between 30 and 50, while one
had quite an estate, 200 hectares. About half the total also had a vineyard, and there were some who held additional benefices whose
revenue came from agricultural property nearby.[47] But even those
curés who had no land to till or to lease were still tied up with the
success or failure of the harvest if they drew all or a portion of the
tithe. Thus France was full of priests who were knowledgeable about
agriculture, in touch with their parishioners and the life of the
countryside, looking at the weather, the progress of the crops, the
health of the cattle, and the state of the market with the expert and
apprehensive eye of the peasants. In his *Essai d'éducation nationale* in
1763 La Cholotais listed the secular expertise he required of a curé;
he must know something of medicine and law, and above all must
be well informed on methods of improving cultivation and on the
art of surveying. When, in the second half of the century, the vogue
for theorizing about agricultural improvements swept the country,
and agricultural societies were founded, the clergy were prominent
in their membership. Chief of them was the abbé François Rozier,
who published a solid textbook on botany for the Royal Veterinary
School in 1766, and won the first prize of the Royal Agricultural
Society of Limoges in 1770 and that of the Society of Lyon in 1787.
After publishing on 'the fermentation of wine and the best way to
make eau-de-vie', on the cultivation of hemp and of rape (and how
to 'extract an oil with the bad taste and disagreeable odour refined
out of it'), from 1781 he began publishing a vast *Cours complet
d'agriculture théorique, pratique, économique et de médecine rurale et
vétérinaire* which had reached volume 8 by 1789.[48] At the invitation
of the Royal Bureau of Agriculture of Le Mans, in 1769, Froger, a
local curé, published his *Instructions d'agriculture et d'économie, pour les
habitans de la campagne*. It was a moralizing book to encourage
country people to read, and to convert them to the ethic of work,
including useful tips like: in bad weather, don't be idle, clean out the
stables and repair the hedges.[49] Humble curés tried their hand at
essays for prize competitions, like the incumbent of a parish near
Vienne who, early in 1789, submitted to the Agricultural Society of
Paris his reflections on the introduction of potatoes. Baked in the
oven with milk, salt and pepper, he said, they were 'mana' last
winter, and they fattened the pigs 'd'une manière prodigieuse'.[50] No
prize for these anecdotes; the Society preferred scientific analyses like
those of the abbé de Commerell who, from just across the Alsace
border, sent in his *mémoire* on the wastefulness of leaving land fallow,
and was already well known for his brochure 'on the cultivation, use

and advantages' of mangel wurzels as a last resort in times of crop failure—printed and reprinted by the government.[51] Many a monastery, and, even, parish priest, gained fame as improvers of vintages. The best vineyards around Beaune belonged to the monks of Citeaux,[52] and the best ones near Barr to the Antonists (producing the famous wine, the story ran, which Cardinal de Lorraine had dispensed to the Fathers of the Council of Trent to persuade them to vote on his side).[53] The authoritative guide to the wine-growing areas around Bordeaux was published by a cleric, the abbé Baurein, in 1784–6.[54] The curé of Cantenac (Médoc) sold 25,000 livres worth of wine annually in mid-century,[55] and the Benedictine monks of the abbey of Sainte-Croix exported their product to the abstemious Sons of the Prophet in the Levant in bottles labelled 'Eau minérale de Sainte-Croix'.[56]

Some of the great abbeys and bishoprics progressed from the ownership of extensive woods to becoming proprietors of iron-smelting furnaces: the bishops of Châlons, Évreux, Langres, Saint-Pol-de-Léon (the latter in a company with six nobles as associates), the chapter of the cathedral of Besançon, the abbeys of Clairvaux, Chalôns, and so on.[57] This natural progression from timber merchant to iron master is illustrated in the adventures of the Benedictines of Liessies in Hainault. The owners of smelting furnaces there were in a ring to keep down the price of fuel, so the monks refused to sell wood to them and set up their own ironworks. A great lawsuit ensued. Dom Gérard, who detested being away from home, lived miserably in Paris to prosecute it, doling out cheeses and snuff-boxes (and once the carcase of a whole wild boar) as bribes, and flourishing a statement signed by his abbot offering 2,000 écus to the lawyer who could win the case. The case was indeed won, and the monks kept their furnace, but Dom Gérard died in the capital away from his comfortable cell.[58] The clergy were as interested as the laity in schemes to enhance their profits. From 1719 the Discalced Carmelites of the rue de Vaugirard in Paris were exploiting their urban site by building five mansions for letting; in 1728 the Comte de Rottembourg took one, followed in his tenure by the Sicilian ambassador and by the princess de Croÿ, who entered on a nine-year lease at 7,000 livres a year.[59] A more picturesque venture into commercial enterprise is recorded by a traveller in the South. The abbey of Sylvanes had a thermal spring on its territory; when a medical report in 1772 praised the water as beneficial for those in ailing health or of a melancholy temperament the monks borrowed money to construct two pools and twenty guest-rooms, with further additions in 1786. A constant procession of well-off invalids came to stay, sent by the prestigious Medical Faculty of Montpellier.[60] To understand the clergy of eighteenth-century France and their place in society, we must remember, for better and for worse, their zestful entanglement in agricultural, commercial, and financial activities. Sometimes, these involvements could discredit their spiritual mission and their local standing. Not everyone approved of the curé of Franche Comté who 'appears at fairs among the pigs like a dealer'; much worse was the one who loaned money to the peasants at an interest of 30 per cent a month and had labourers working in his fields on Sundays and saints' days.[61] Property owning at once identified the clergy with lay society and alienated them from it. The occasional curé who was censured in the *cahier* of his parishioners, or the abbey more frequently denounced, had not usually been guilty of notable meanness or oppression. They had, however, transgressed some psychological boundary, and had done what was legal for everyone rather than what was considered fitting for ecclesiastics. Churchmen who were proprietors had special obligations, mostly of an informal and unenforceable kind, concerning fair rents, traditional procedures, debts, arrears, litigation, almsgiving. And, as we have seen, the greatest of all these half-understood obligations, so far as the mass of ordinary folk in the countryside was concerned, was that of making land available to the laity for leasehold on reasonable terms and in small lots.

So far we have considered the ownership of land in eighteenth-century France as if it was absolute property in our modern sense, even though the patterns of landholding were fantastically complicated. In fact, however, most property was in some way subject to feudal obligations, and part of the vast inheritance of the Gallican Church was its feudal dues from lands it did not own, but were within its fiefs and seigneuries. This sort of proprietary right did not come within Tocqueville's definition of an ownership which improves social relationships; on the contrary, he considered the survival of feudal obligations as destructive of respect between those who levied them and those who paid them. They had arisen as tributes to powerful lords in return for protection; now the king's writ ran in all the land, their justification was ended. As a simplified model of how feudalism still operated in the age of the Enlightenment we may imagine a village which has a nobleman (or a prelate or an abbey) as its seigneur. The lord of the manor's lawyers will attend to hold 'assizes', and though the Crown had taken away most of the powers of feudal justice, the villagers could be fined small sums and ordered to do various chores (like sweeping their chimneys, ringing the church bells in thunderstorms, or appointing a communal herdsman). The seigneur would announce in his court the date fixed for harvesting or grape gathering (starting earlier himself to get in first for hiring labour), and his legal assessors could impose their will in disputes concerning his rights (the inhabitants having a routine, but expensive, resort of appeal to royal courts). The lord's agents would collect various dues, like the *cens*, or quit rent, generally small but important as proof of feudal dependence, or tributes in kind such as chickens or eggs, and sometimes, though rarely, an onerous levy on crops at harvest time (*champart*). The lord might enjoy exclusive hunting or fishing rights, or the right to keep pigeons protected by law from the guns of the folk whose crops they raided; he might have the monopoly of the stud bull, the mill, or the communal oven (*banalités*); he might levy a toll on a bridge or side-road. Of course, nothing was ever quite as simple as this under the *ancien régime*. There might be a seigneur haut justicier over the seigneur with peculiar rights (for example, to saw down and sell roadside trees in the area of his jurisdiction). Several seigneurs might rule in a single village, or several villages be compounded in a single seigneurie: there would be enclaves and detached fragments; there would be odd local dues peculiar to one area (consider some curious items in the mass of feudal incidents owed to the bishop of Lodève: a *droit de pulvérage* on flocks in transit, a fine paid by those who pierced doors or windows in the old city walls, a *droit de coupe* on strangers who brought grain into the city to sell—this latter exaction bought off by the city for 600 livres a year).[62] Furthermore, urban fiefs and overlordship differed in various respects from rural ones, more especially because their chief revenue was usually derived from *lods et ventes*, a stiff tax on every house sale.

In all this archaic structure of vexatious jurisdictions and dues, the Church was inextricably involved. An ecclesiastic whose revenues came from straightforward landowning was lucky; some were dependent on the feudal incidents which everyone hated. The bishop of Quimper (until an abbey was united to his see in 1782 to boost the revenues) had only about 4,000 livres a year from his estates; he had twice as much from tithe (unpopular always) and about 21,000 from secular jurisdictions and feudal dues (even more unpopular).[63] In the seventeenth century, two-thirds of the immense revenues of the see of Paris were derived from *lods et ventes* on the houses of 500 streets of the capital; in 1674 the archbishop gave up most of his manifold feudal jurisdictions for a limited compensa-

tion—a financial loss, but a great improvement in public relations.[64]
A study of ten abbeys in Normandy shows that only a third of their
total revenues came from agricultural property; two-thirds came
from feudal dues and tithe[65]—how could these monks ever hope to
be popular in the countryside? Certain cities seemed to be locked
within a strait-jacket by the feudal jurisdictions of ecclesiastics.
Reims was one of them.[66] The archbishop's *ban* covered the *cité*, the
old Gallo-Roman centre, and the cathedral chapter ruled in the
cloisters and in two 'cantons' within the episcopal segment and in
two outside it; the abbeys of Saint-Rémy and Saint-Nicaise and the
hôtel-Dieu all had their seigneurial courts, while an official of the
cathedral, the *vidame*, had a peculiar jurisdiction over the saddlers,
glass-blowers, coopers, and tinkers wherever they dwelt. The
archiepiscopal tribunal, meeting twice weekly, had no fewer than
twenty-three officials, though truth to tell, they were all part-time
and doubled up in other seigneurial courts wearing different hats. By
contrast, in the town of Angers,[67] it was the cathedral chapter, rather
than the bishop, which enjoyed the splendour of feudal superiority.
The cité was its fief. Here, the canons of Saint-Maurice levied the
cens on all householders, and from time to time imposed disciplinary
regulations on them, such as ordering them to have the street swept
in front of their own doorstep. Tradesmen had to apply to the
chapter for permission to put up their signs, and the property of
persons who died without direct heirs fell to the cathedral by
escheat. As a reciprocal obligation, the chapter had to pay for
improvements like street lighting, and had to rear children who were
abandoned within the fief. This feudal jurisdiction was reinforced
(which was unusual) by a spiritual one, since the cathedral enjoyed
episcopal powers in the enclave around its walls; it held synods to
which it summoned its dependent curés, and its ecclesiastical court
issued dispensations, as for marrying within the lower reaches of the
prohibited degrees or for eating meat in Lent. There were fifteen
other seigneurial courts in Angers, all dependent upon ecclesiastical
jurisdictions.[68] The chief were the penurious chapters of Saint-
Maurille and Saint-Martin, which levied *lods et ventes* at a fifteenth
of the selling price of houses, a fluctuating revenue averaging out at
about 3,000 livres a year for Saint-Martin and a third of this for
Saint-Maurille. The canons, aware how bitterly this tax was hated,
tried to ingratiate themselves with their victims by granting remissions of 25 per cent. This was all very well for Saint-Maurille, enjoying rents on twenty houses built on the site of its old cemetery; being
poorer, the canons of Saint-Martin in 1783 called a halt to this

customary rebate. 'The charges they are at in respect of their fiefs are many in number, and are constantly augmenting.' This was true. As many as twenty children might be abandoned to their care annually (most would die, of course, but the cost of signing on an adoptive parent was about 100 livres), while the expenses of administering justice were not negligible. It was unfortunate to be levying unpopular and unjustifiable dues and yet be able to enjoy barely half the yield.

As, towards the end of the *ancien régime*, feudal dues appeared more obviously unreasonable and were more widely decried, the value of those that had not been fixed as a precise sum of money became much greater. It has been estimated that the yield of *lods et ventes* doubled between 1760 and 1790.[69] Dues in kind, reckoned as a proportion of the crop, albeit at a small fraction, became well worth having. Since the late seventeenth century, antiquarian studies had been flourishing; now, delving in the archives became an occasion of profit. Technical handbooks were published on the art of checking on the past history and present legality of feudal incidents, and *feudistes* arose, professional researchers who were paid by results. One such was appointed by the chapter of Sainte-Radegonde of Poitiers in 1785: a *feudiste-géographe*, to be paid 2,000 livres a year for six years, and half of all sums he recovered.[70] In other places, ecclesiastics themselves reorganized their charters, and, as Richeprey observed, he had yet to come across a feudal investigator who published any discoveries which would benefit the peasants who had to pay.[71] Fortified by technical expertise, seigneurs began to make more use of their right to 'renew' the *terriers*, the documents showing the boundaries of properties and the nature of the obligations attached to them. The peasants hated having to find their share of the expense of these renewals, and they feared the 'declarations' which they had to make: if they overstated their extent, they would be fined; if they understated it, they might be taken at their word. In 1781 both the archbishop of Cambrai and his metropolitan chapter took out letters patent for the renewal of *terriers* on their lands, causing anger and unrest among the rural population of the diocese.[72] Three years later, the archbishop of Embrun initiated a series of lawsuits before the parlement of Grenoble in an attempt to establish his right to *lods et ventes* on certain allodial lands which had remained outside the feudal nexus.[73] Travelling in the South in 1780, Richeprey described the *corvées* (labour dues) of four days a year 'enforced with extreme rigour' by the abbey of Aubrac, and how, when the vassals were unable to pay a peculiar rent reckoned in salt and apples, the monks would demand an unreasonable sum in its place. At Trémouille, his inn was besieged by angry peasants led by a man with an axe—they thought he had come to demand arrears of the *commun de paix*, a twelfth-century tax originally paid to repair the damage done by wandering mercenaries and now providing some financial solace to the bishop of Rodez and other great personages.[74] There would have been riots at Reims in 1770 in any case, but a contributory factor was the archbishop's *droit de stellage*, an impost on all grain brought into the city for sale. The contractor who levied this tax on the bread of the people was entitled to ban all marketing of grain within four leagues of the city walls and to imprison those suspected of breaking the regulations. The prelate got 14,000 livres a year from his *droit de stellage*, and at least 14,000 livres worth of unpopularity with it.[75] There was deep-seated economic malaise behind the riots at Lyon in 1786, but one of the superficial causes which provoked the mob was the archbishop's attempt to collect the arrears on his *droit de banvin*, an impost on wine sales, which drove the owners of bars and taverns to put up their shutters.[76] When a riot is inevitable, both drink and lack of it are dangerous.

Ecclesiastical institutions, organized to survive in perpetuity, furnished with rich archives with literate custodians, and never forgetting a precedent, were regarded as permanent menaces to the ordinary carefree citizen. When in Angers in the 1770s the canons of Saint-Martin and of Saint-Maurille and the monks of Saint-Nicolas were all engaged in lawsuits over escheats, the opposition lawyers made the point: 'Your courts will resound with disputes of this kind, always burdensome to citizens of limited means, though the chapters of Angers, opulent feudal lords, count outlay on a lawsuit a mere nothing if it can bring them some pickings from their fiefs.'[77] Citizens of limited means, indeed, did well to count the cost before they challenged some ecclesiastical institution. The village community of Donchery challenged the prior of the local monastery (who was also the bishop of Nancy) over his feudal control of the village oven and lost, at a cost of 1,440 livres, 14 sous, 8 deniers. This episcopal prior was a difficult man—witness the affair of the bridge which the floods had swept away. As seigneur, he was supposed to 'repair' it, but he refused to do anything, as 'repair' did not mean 'replace'. The *cahier* of Donchery is full of complaints against this 'usurper', who 'relies on the right of the strongest'.[78] And even if a case was won, a village might impoverish itself in the process. When the villagers of Saint-Maurice-aux-Riches-Hommes won a lawsuit against their seigneur, the bishop of Châlons, with damages of 2,000

livres, they found that they owed their parish priest 3,500 livres for
expenses for the thousand days he had spent away from home prosecuting the case. It was a sum almost as large as the community's
annual payment in direct taxation.[79]

Anticlerical propagandists were glad to remind their readers how
churchmen profited from feudal payments given to them in return
for non-existent services which would have been incompatible with
their pious vocation anyway. Historical excursuses, Velly's *Histoire
de France* and Renauldon's *Traité historique et pratique des droits
seigneuriaux*, traced the incongruous alliance of Christianity and
feudalism to the superstition of the laity and the worldliness of
priests. There was scope for irony in listing the more ridiculous
feudal obligations, like the mythical *droit du seigneur*, supposedly
arrogated at the time of the crusades, that epoch of misguided
religious zeal and cynical designs of plunder.[80] But there was one
actual and scandalous feudal survival which anticlerics relished above
all: that was 'serfdom'. In fact, it was not personal servitude, but a
mode of servile tenure chiefly concerned with inheritance, though
none the less hated for that. In Brittany, on the lands of the abbeys
of Rellec and Bégard, and in one or two other ecclesiastical jurisdictions in the diocese of Tréguier, it took the form of *quevaise*.[81]
The tenant, the *quevaisier*, paid a heavy *champart* of one sheaf in
seven. When he died, the youngest son inherited, followed by the
other sons, then by the youngest daughter, provided they were
resident on the property. If there was no direct heir actually present,
everything fell to the seigneur. If the *quevaisier* sold out to escape
from his onerous tenure, the lord collected a quarter of the selling
price; if he ceased to cultivate the land, the lord could confiscate it
after a year and a day. Though the abbey of Rellec had given up
most of its *champart* (after a revolt in 1727, when the house was
burned down) and had begun to relax the terms of escheat, allowing
inheritances to go to collateral heirs, there was continued friction
and ill will. In 1774, the monks had sixteen lawsuits against their
quevaisiers pending before the parlement of Rennes, with others on
the way up through their own feudal court.

As it happened, this survival of a servile tenure in Brittany
remained a curiosity of the law-books; the great exposures of
'serfdom' came in revelations about the injustices suffered by the
peasants on the lands of two abbeys in the Jura Mountains—the
Benedictine houses of Luxeuil[82] and Saint-Claude. (The latter was
secularized in 1742 to form a chapter of exclusively noble canons;
but the monks stayed on for the term of their lives, forming a joint

institution.) The vassals of these two great foundations held their
land subject to 'mainmorte'. They needed the consent of their
seigneur to marry outside the fief, and could bequeath their property
only to direct heirs actually living at home with them. To shake off
these obligations, a man had to make a *désaveu*, a formal surrender of
all his possessions. There were approximations to this sort of servile
tenure in Franche Comté, Bourgogne, the Auvergne, and the
Nivernais.[83] From this latter province, in 1756, there arose an outrageous lawsuit to set all Paris talking: a citizen of the capital died,
and an obscure nobleman from the country round Nevers came
forward to claim his not-inconsiderable inheritance on the ground
that the dead man's father had been one of his tenants long ago. The
magistrates of the Châtelet threw out the claim amidst the applause
of bourgeois opinion.[84] In 1770, Voltaire was called in to champion
the 'serfs' of Saint-Claude, and he joined forces with their lawyer,
M. Christin, who was pleading a suit on their behalf before the
parlement of Besançon. Two years later, Christin published an
account of his investigations into the documentation put forward by
the abbey: the title, *Dissertation sur l'abbaye de Saint-Claude, ses
chroniques, ses légendes, ses chartes, ses usurpations, et sur les droits des
habitants de cette terre*, is self-explanatory. It was one of those revelations of the pious forgeries of distant 'gothic' times which so
delighted the erudite wits of the Enlightenment. For his contribution, Voltaire published *La Voix du curé*.[85] A priest is installed in his
new parish on the feast of St Louis, 1772, and is astonished when his
wretched parishioners complain to him that they are serfs to the
abbey of Saint-Claude. 'Est-ce qu'il y a des esclaves en France?' asks
the man of God. How can this be? St Louis crusaded to deliver
Christians from slavery, and the Pères de La Merci risk their lives
daily on the Barbary coast to ransom them. Well, they had better
send these good Fathers to ransom us, says the village patriarch. The
curé then recounts the findings of his enquiry into this ancient abuse.
The name *mainmorte* given to this tenure arose, he assures us, because
in the Middle Ages, seigneurs expected to confiscate the chattels of
their dead vassals, and if there was nothing to take, they showed their
displeasure by cutting off a hand from the corpse as a trophy. If an
unsuspecting outsider settled within the jurisdiction of Saint-Claude
for a year and a day, for ever after his inheritance would be in
danger from the monks, even if he migrated far away, for the abbey
enjoyed the 'right of pursuit' against its vassals. A woman told him
how the abbey had tried to deprive her of a legacy because she had
broken the feudal rule and slept the first night after her marriage in

the house of her husband, not of her father; evidence of the fact had been obtained by threats of excommunication against recalcitrant witnesses. The good curé has a vision of Christ upbraiding the cellarer of the monastery for his oppression. 'You were the suffering Church,' says the cellarer; 'we are the Church triumphant . . . We gave them the hope of heaven, so we took their land from them.' To protest, the curé calls on one of the canons of Saint-Claude and gets a friendly reception, for the newly created canons 'had not contracted that hardness of heart, that greed, that secret hatred of the human race' which the monastic way of life engenders. Two local lawyers and a nobleman who own seigneuries containing serfs have just volunteered to renounce their rights, and the canons would have wished to do the same. But they were outvoted by the surviving monks, who refused to abandon their archaic privileges.

Four years later, Voltaire returned to the attack, this time drawing up a petition on behalf of the serfs of the Bernardine monks of Chézery. As a result of the frontier changes of 1760, they had been transferred from Savoy and incorporated into France, thus just missing being enfranchised by the king of Sardinia's edict abolishing serfdom two years later.[86] This foreign example and the march of enlightened ideas prevailed at Versailles, and in 1779 Necker abolished the *droit de poursuite*. On Crown lands, where he was completely free to take action, he ended the tenure by *mainmorte* altogether. A few seigneurs followed suit, including the penurious missionary priests of Beaupré, but not the two great abbeys. Clermont-Tonnerre, abbot of Luxeuil, proclaimed liberal sentiments. For the thirty years he had held his office, he said in 1775, he had seen how his tenants were 'dull, indolent, discouraged, downtrodden, their fields neglected . . . while the inhabitants of free villages, their neighbours, are busy and hard-working'.[87] Even so, fourteen years later he had still got no further than approaching three of his twenty-two villages with proposals for change. In fact, the enthusiasm at Luxeuil and Saint-Claude for reform was conditional upon substantial compensation being offered, and this had not been forthcoming. By 1789, the outcry against *mainmorte* was general. In their *cahier*, the peasants of Saint-Claude still remembered the woman who had slept at her husband's the first night.[88] 'The possessors of fiefs, most of them ecclesiastics,' the *cahier* of the Jura area began, 'obstinately insist, despite your (Majesty's) paternal invitation, to keep in the chains of servitude more than a million Frenchmen'.[89] A curé of Franche Comté, Clerget, published a powerful 'Cry of reason' against serfdom: *Cri de la Raison ou examen approfondi des lois et des coutumes qui tiennent dans la servitude mainmortable 1,500,000 sujets du Roi.* If these figures of a million to a million-and-a-half serfs are near the truth, there must have been quite a number of seigneuries held by laymen or minor ecclesiastics in which the 'cry of reason' and the 'paternal invitation' of the monarch had been ignored. But the abbeys of Luxeuil and Saint-Claude were so rich that it was not unreasonable that they should bear the brunt of public reprobation. In the rural rioting of July 1789, the peasants of Luxeuil paid off old scores: the books from the library (did they include the 'chronicles, legends and charters' Christin had denounced?) were burned, and the contents of the cellars drunk by the angry *mainmortables.*[90]

In eighteenth-century France, the question of the theoretical justification of property was much discussed from *L'Esprit des Lois* onwards.[91] There were two views. Its origin may be seen as 'natural'—the physiocrats embraced this opinion, and the revolutionary Declaration of Rights was to consecrate it; or its origin may be seen as 'social'—this supposition is found in Montesquieu, Voltaire, and Rousseau. In the debates of the Revolution, Camus and Mirabeau drew the inference from the 'social' theory that property could be taken over by the nation in urgent cases. Other orators, not denying this proposition so far as corporate bodies are concerned, rejected its severities as regards individuals. On the whole, the legislation of the Revolution (as distinct from the practice of a war for survival) did not interfere with the proprietary rights of individuals, except to forbid long leases (protecting the owner against himself) and by putting mining rights at the disposition of the nation, instead of in the power of the owner of the surface. The theory of 'social' creation was reserved for application to the estates of the Gallican Church, auctioned to pay the nation's debts. But the way towards this great expropriation had been prepared by the long-standing policy of the French monarchy, pragmatic and authoritarian, and little concerned with social theory. According to the lawyers,[92] the clergy were *usufruitiers* of their property, not absolute owners, and Church lands were a special case, peculiarly subject to royal oversight and control. One aspect of this control concerned the protection of the Church, and of all the pious families who had contributed to its endowments, against the carelessness or rapacity of the present holders of benefices. This was done partly by the granting of privileges—the cancellation of leases on a change of titular, and repairs being a privileged debt—and partly by restriction, since ecclesiastical property could not be alienated without the king's agreement. There had to be an enquiry *de commodo et incommodo*, and if sale was recommended, the decision had to be authorized by the local judges of the Crown or, for great benefices, by letters patent registered in the relevant parlement.[93] In this fashion, the archbishop of Aix got permission to sell half of a huge fief in 1782, and about the same time, the bishop of Nevers, as abbot of Saint-Cyran, was allowed to grant permanent leases of four *métairies* belonging to his abbey; these concessions were made because the properties concerned were difficult to manage.[94] An ecclesiastic could not cut the woods of his benefice without letters patent duly registered, and inspectors of the Eaux et Forêts made visitations every fifteen years to check that no illegal timber felling had taken place.[95]

These official procedures of enquiry, letters patent, and magisterial verification were also obligatory for churchmen who wished to acquire new property. In addition, there was a *droit d'amortissement* levied on any extension or improvement made to existing possessions; repairs, the signing of a new lease, the changing of a building to a different use—almost any sort of amelioration was regarded as taxable.[96] It was a question here, not of protecting the Church, but of protecting the State and the laity against its aggrandizement. This restrictive code was fortified by the royal edict of August 1749,[97] which was the culmination of the process of tightening up the laws of mortmain. (The word had two meanings in France: the notorious servile tenure in the Jura and the more general meaning, found also in England, of legislation to relax the grip of the 'dead hand' of the Church.) The bishops were indignant at the edict of 1749. 'It seems', said the bishop of Angers, 'that churchmen are foreigners, and not the children and relatives of the King's subjects, and as if their income is not spent in the Kingdom, or used to help the other subjects of the King and the poor, and all of us who are subject to mortmain are depicted as men who have no other aim than getting hold of the property of the laity.'[98] D'Argenson was one of the few laymen who sympathized with episcopal complaints. 'It's always said the Church is too rich, but I don't see who this harms.'[99] The general view was that an enduring corporation which already had vast possessions, would expand continually unless limitations were maintained. This being so, permission to acquire new property was hardly ever granted; indeed, if churchmen applied for ordinary compensation for encroachments by the Crown, the Royal Council was reluctant to grant it.[100]

From regulation and restriction for reasons of social utility, it was a short step to ideas of a limited confiscation in cases of necessity.

Had ecclesiastical property been evenly distributed over the country, the claustrophobic sense of monopoly in certain areas would not have been so pervasive; had the patterns of landowning been less complex, occasions for conflict would have been fewer. The number of skirmishes was in proportion to the length and illogicality of the frontiers between the possessions of the clergy and those of the laity. Anyone with an improving scheme for a road, a canal, or a public building, or wanting to round off his heritage or expand his business, would be likely to run athwart some ecclesiastical property owner. Thus, when in 1772 the marquis de Pérusse proposed a scheme for settling Acadian refugees on his moorland acres in Poitou, the government inspection party asked for 630 *arpents* of the lands of the marquis, 2,400 belonging to the bishop of Poitiers, and 980 belonging to the abbey of Fontevrault.[101] Similarly, when space was cleared to show off the colonnade of the Louvre in 1756, and a site for new stables for the Poste aux chevaux (the mounted courier's department of the postal service) had to be found, almost inevitably, it was acquired from a monastery.[102]

This is what one would expect in Paris, a crowded city of half a million inhabitants in which there were thirteen great abbeys and two hundred other religious houses. Such was the multitude of ecclesiastical buildings, monastic and others, that in August 1792, the commissioners charged with the task of removing the ornaments and symbols of the *ancien régime* despaired of finding them all, and called for local assistance: 'comme il y a trop grand nombre d'églises à Paris, il faut que les Sections viennent à notre secours'.[103] What was true of the capital was true, *mutatis mutandis*, of nearly all the towns of France, great and small. Marseille with its 88,000 population had thirty-four monastic establishments; Toulouse, rather less than half its size, had forty-six; Grenoble, Troyes, Reims, and Douai, half the size again, had twenty-six, nineteen, seventeen, and twenty-eight respectively; Aix, with 10,000 inhabitants, had six monasteries and twelve nunneries.[104] This was the sort of disproportion to catch the eye of an English traveller; passing through Coutances, Wraxall observed that the place was 'large, but the convents form a considerable part of its size, and the religious of different Orders a great part of its inhabitants'.[105] And in all these places, in addition to the enclosures of monks and nuns, there were also collegiate and parish churches, hospitals, *collèges*, and chapels. The picture is the same when we go down byways to seek out the tiny towns, hardly worthy of the name, except for a core of a few prestigious buildings. Montreuil-sur-Mer with 4,000 residents had eight religious houses.

'As is well known,' said the municipal officers in 1780, 'the town is composed largely of ecclesiastics, nobles, army officers and legal officials, and the people are few in number and poor because it is impossible to carry on any sort of commercial activity.'[106] Avallon, of the same size, agreeably and loftily situated, its ramparts looking down on vineyards and woods below, had two parishes, four religious houses, and a *collège*.[107] Pontivy in Brittany, rather smaller, could be summed up as a social entity briefly: the duc de Rohan's castle overlooking everything, thirty-two rich families, the recteur and a confraternity of six priests, the houses of the Ursulines and the Récollets, and a *collège* where the sons of decent families were educated.[108] Clermont, a miserable squalid place built on inhospitable volcanic rock, had a chapter of canons, a *collège*, a monastery, and a nunnery for its 2,000 inhabitants.[109] This was the same size as Belley, and here there were no fewer than five religious houses and, being the seat of a bishop, a cathedral too.[110]

Given the ground plan of so many towns, it was not surprising that diplomatic incidents and boundary skirmishes over the issue of Church property were frequent; indeed, these conflicts often hardened into an institutionalized feud. The eighteenth century was the great age of municipal improvements: town councils engaged in demolishing ancient ramparts and opening up promenades and straight, sweeping avenues, constructing fountains and statues, naming and numbering streets, installing street lighting, and planting trees in regimented ranks in newly created squares.[111] Zealous aldermen in search of *lebensraum*, and of the commercial profits that would accrue from institutional expansion, were thwarted at every turn by the extensive property of churchmen. We can see how the tensions developed in Angers.[112] There, religious foundations were popularly supposed to own 'three-quarters of the town'. Half-empty monasteries hired out their staterooms for meeting-places for guilds, university faculties, and professional associations; rich laymen like the Englishmen Mr Swinfort and Milord Southwell rented abbatical mansions, as local citizens rented less prestigious houses; old ladies took rooms in convents, and artisans hired sheds to store their gear. 'The Church was shrinking back inside its territory, leaving a fringe of secular leaseholders on its boundaries.' The city fathers cast envious eyes on so many splendid façades, spacious gardens, and strategic building sites. At one time it was a question of opening up a pedestrian way, at another enlarging a square, at another finding storage space for municipal property. Greater issues were: finding a meeting-hall for an agricultural society (hopeless negotiations with the abbey of Saint-Aubin), a site for a botanical garden (unsuccessful pleas to the abbey of Saint-Serge), a building for a new boarding-school (Saint-Aubin again for both buildings and teachers, and no success), a foundling hospital (could the decayed friary of Lesvière be taken for such a charitable object?), a barracks (no fewer than seven monastic houses were considered for confiscation). Let the Augustinian friars retire into a corner of their large enclosure, leaving the rest for the soldiers: 'the greater good is that which turns to the profit of society in general. No corporation or community can be allowed to go on living in a property which is useless to it, and which is rendered profitless to the State by the mere fact of their retaining it.' Or let the Benedictines of Saint-Serge move out; their Order would still retain three houses in Angers: 'when it is a question of the general interest, an opulent congregation ought to be disposed to make sacrifices'.

Eloquence of this sort about the greatest happiness of the greatest number was the house style of aldermen the world over when they complained about the possessions of the clergy. Vannes was a decayed and ancient city, whose population of 14,000 consisted of 1,000 paupers at one end of the scale and 300 nobles, 62 secular priests, and 300 monks and nuns at the other.[113] 'Ours is a little town', the municipal officers lamented in 1769, 'whose every building is on the verge of tumbling down, surrounded on every side by superb monasteries which hardly leave room for traffic to get in and out of the place. The monasteries form . . . a chain which binds tightly a constricted city of gothic construction, with few viable streets and a polluted atmosphere. We breathe contaminated air . . . the monks enjoy spacious enclosures.'[114] Dijon was another archaic town, its skyline dominated by the thirty-two bell towers of its churches and monasteries, its affairs dominated by nobles of the robe and churchmen. It produced little: no less than 13 per cent of its population were domestic servants.[115] Once again, it was the clergy who were blamed for this backwardness. In 1786, the intendant (supporting the municipality's plan to drive a road through the convent of the Jacobins) wrote: 'In this town, where rents are so high, there could hardly be a more important improvement than to put land up for sale whenever this is possible, for the dead hand of churchmen controls over two-fifths of the area.'[116]

The concentration of ecclesiastical property in so many towns promoted anticlerical feeling. Public opinion was formulated in the urban milieu: here, instinctive and envious emotions were fostered and transmuted into the sort of logical coherence that could lead to legislative action in revolutionary times. When, however, early in the Revolution, the sale of ecclesiastical property was proposed, townsfolk suddenly realized that there was something to be said for the 'dead hand' of the Church after all. The chapters and abbeys whose walls and gardens blocked the avenues of municipal improvement were also owners of vast estates in the countryside, from whence they drew in wealth to be spent in the city. Artists, goldsmiths, organ builders, bell-founders, lawyers, and estate agents profited from their commissions; respectable families competed to have their sons accepted as choirboys or to find a place in the *collège* or, when they were older, to receive ecclesiastical sinecures; daughters with only limited dowries would go into nunneries; artisans, tradesmen, provision sellers, and candlemakers rejoiced in the steady custom of ecclesiastical institutions, and ordinary folk found employment as cooks and domestic servants, as well as bell-ringers, sacristans, and beadles. Churchmen were better employers than most, sometimes finding a niche for the infirm or simple-minded, and keeping on the aged after their real usefulness was over. What would happen when the sources of all this expenditure were auctioned off to private individuals—where would the buyers live, and whom would they employ? At Angers, there was a cry for some major law court, a barracks, or some other institution of central government to be established to replace 'the losses which the town must bear by the suppression of its religious houses, which are very numerous and which spend all their revenue here'.[117] Bayeux, with 10,000 inhabitants a third of the size of Angers, was even more dependent, economically, upon the Church.[118] On 11 November 1790 the municipality declared: 'The town of Bayeux is absolutely without commerce, without manufactures and without industry; it is a cathedral city, and as the ecclesiastics of this town were in a position to spend 400,000 to 500,000 livres here annually, this sum, distributed and spread around in the hands of tradesmen, constituted the greater part of the public fortune of the town.' As for the more notable citizens, 'the Church and the Bar were the only professional outlets for their children'.[119]

Two major reforms of the second half of the century drew attention to the unreasonable extent of ecclesiastical possessions. One was the setting up of the Commission des réguliers in 1768 to reform the monasteries. Its investigations concerned not only the usefulness and discipline of each house, but also the number of its inmates as compared with the size of its buildings and income. Numerous possibilities of suppressions and transfers of monastic population were considered; some were proposed, and a limited number carried out. The laity watched these proceedings with interest, and were sometimes consulted. For long, unions of benefices had been taking place at the behest of reforming bishops, always after an enquiry *de commodo et incommodo* in which parishes, municipalities, and other interested parties had a chance to state their views. To provide extra funds for an educational establishment, for a hospital, to increase the revenues of a poor bishopric, or to found an endowment for a new parish—for purposes like these, chapels and priories without cure of souls, or even the abbatial manse of an abbey would be annexed. Often, laymen approved of these transfers and sometimes clamoured for them, though not if the money was to go out of the area, or if local families were going to be deprived of ecclesiastical sinecures for their sons. With the advent of the Commission des réguliers, the laity were encouraged to reflect more generally on the endowments of nearby monasteries and on what better use might be made of them.

The other reform was the edict of 1776 ordering the removal of cemeteries from populated areas, a result of horror stories about crowded graveyards, with their open burial pits, and the campaign of medical experts for hygienic improvements, and of an increasing refinement of sensibility with deep psychological roots in the changing patterns of human relationships.[120] Parsimonious churchwardens and parish assemblies, reluctant to pay the heavy expenses of acquiring new land and walling and gating it, did their best to avoid compliance, and landowners were usually incensed at any proposal that they should sell any of their heritage to provide a site for a new cemetery. There was a customary rule of jurisprudence which allowed the confiscation, against compensation, of land needed for public use: the 'vente forcée pour utilité publique'. There was universal resentment among proprietors whenever any resort to this device was mentioned, so municipal authorities preferred to apply for permission to exercise it against the extensive acres of the Church, rather than against their fellow citizens. What could be more appropriate, they argued, when they were searching for a cemetery? The aldermen of Angers and of Tours were in correspondence, conspiratorially, on this subject.[121] There was a difficulty about this policy, however. Since, by the mortmain legislation, churchmen were prevented from acquiring new property with the compensation money they would obtain, a forced sale of land was a notable disadvantage to them. The parlements, on grounds of equity, generally ruled, if other things were equal, that the property of laymen must be taken. With this security at law, the Benedictines of Bar-sur-Seine and the Dominicans of Grenoble turned down requests for some of their land, and the nuns of the Visitation at Angers even refused to allow a path to a new cemetery site to run through their grounds.[122] The best chance of getting hold of an ecclesiastical site was to persuade the curé to give a field (if he had one) in return for the old cemetery as an eventual extension to his garden. The intendant of Limoges said, sardonically, that in his rural parishes, the translation of cemeteries never took place except when such a deal was possible between the curé and the churchwardens.

The arguments of anticlericals against a wealthy, property-owning Church were predictable. The philosophes cited the gospel prohibitions against the amassing of riches;[123] they searched the Middle Ages for the donations of superstitious kings under the influence of wily priests. The Church is 'always gathering, never giving': it prevents the circulation of wealth and the development of manufactures.[124] Wealthy corporations must always be subject to the law of public utility as interpreted by the State. Turgot's article 'Fondation' in the *Encyclopédie* insists on the interests of the present over the past; a donor cannot tie up his gift for ever, to the prejudice of the human race—'society does not always have the same needs'.[125] Lawyers proclaimed the rights of the State over the property of the Church; whether from reforming or Gallican motives, some churchmen did the same. Between 1755 and 1757, the Jansenist abbé Mignot published a six-volume treatise on 'the rights of the State and of the Prince on the property of the clergy', with a separate supplementary volume giving the history of the feud between Henry II of England and Thomas à Becket, archbishop of Canterbury, as a special case history concerning the overweening pretensions of churchmen. He denied that the clergy had any justification, natural or divine, for escaping ordinary taxation. Councils, he said, denounced those who usurped the sacred acres, but they never denied the right of the prince to use them for the good of his people.[126] Pamphleteers began to make practical proposals for action on these principles. In 1770 was published the *Droit du souverain sur les bien fonds du clergé*: let all Church lands be sold by the sovereign, and the clergy become 'pensioners of the State'.[127] Other pamphlets followed. A common theme is that parish priests, the most useful and deserving of the clergy, should be given their fair share of the endowments. The rest, more particularly the monks, should be reduced in numbers and should own less.[128] Here we come to the final, irrefutable challenge to the vast endowments of the Gallican Church. They were being misapplied. They were divided among the clergy by the accidents of history and the self-seeking of the influential, in an unequal fashion which was against all possible interpretions of the gospels, and to the serious detriment of the Church as an institution.

II *Tithe*[129]

According to informed observers, tithe brought in rather more revenue to the Gallican Church than its landed property.[130] In 1784, Necker estimated this traditional tribute of the laity to be worth 130 million livres a year; at the beginning of the Revolution, when such calculations suddenly became relevant to schemes for staving off national bankruptcy, estimates stood at 120–3 million.

In theory, the levy was a tenth of the crop; in practice, said Arthur Young, it was less.[131] This was indeed the case in many areas; in Maine, Berry, and Champagne, it averaged one-thirteenth, around Orléans only one-thirtieth, even less in parts of Dauphiné and Provence.[132] On the other hand, there were places where tithe outran the fraction implied by its formal definition, reaching one-seventh in Lorraine and one-eighth sometimes in Gascony. Such cases of an unusually high proportion need analysis, however: they may represent a composite levy, including other dues of a seigneurial kind.[133] Local custom sometimes reduced the formal burden; there were villages where it was understood that the curé must accept less than his legal entitlement,[134] and others where the community was accustomed to buy off the tithe by paying a lump sum annually. This is what happened in the little town of Gap,[135] in two villages in the diocese of Lodève, and commonly in mountain hamlets in Auvergne, where the rugged terrain made direct collection difficult.[136] Where such commutations were made, the payers got off lightly (and, according to a government tax official in 1778, their land was always more efficiently cultivated).[137] Even so, when all corrections have been made, there were wide disparities between the highest fractions levied and the lowest, all the more illogical and vexatious when they coexisted—as they often did—within a narrow area, even in adjoining parishes.

Tithes were of various kinds, according to the produce on which they were levied: the *grosses dîmes*, the 'great tithes', on the main cereal crops; the *menues dîmes*, the 'small tithes', divided into the *dîmes vertes* on vegetables and fruits and the *dîme de sang* on animals and wool. Different provinces had different rules about what was included under each heading, and within each category the tariff could vary.[138] There were places where there was a due paid to the clergy as an alternative to the tithe. In Brittany, it was a tax collected by recteurs on the inheritance of moveable property, the so-called *neûmes*.[139] In some parishes in the *bocage* country and coastal marches of Bas-Poitou, chiefly in the diocese of Luçon, the place of tithe was taken by the *boisselage*, an unjust levy paid at a fixed amount of grain by all households, irrespective of the extent of their property or of the state of the year's harvest (in fifteen parishes, it was a supplement to the tithe, not a substitute for it). When a royal edict of 1769 replaced the *boisselage* with a tithe at one-sixteenth, the inhabitants protested so vehemently that the reform was withdrawn (the rich liked the old system because they got off cheaply, the poor because it was so unjust that the curé dared not make them pay).[140] In some places, there was an extra little tithe over and above the usual ones, like the *prémice* occasionally found in Brittany and the diocese of Lodève (one sheep in every sixty or so, or a piglet from the first litter of the season).[141] Voltaire also cites the *droit de moisson* in Franche Comté, paid by villagers to their curé in parishes where the orthodox *grosses dîmes* had fallen into the hands of monastic houses.[142]

The tithes within a parish were often levied by several different tithe owners. They might include—though not always—the parish priest himself, a bishop, chapter, monastery, priory, or other ecclesiastical foundation, or, maybe, a layman. The *dîmes inféodées*, tithes held by lay proprietors, were an old-established anomaly, and the law was strict about them: to prove his title, a layman had to demonstrate no less than 100 years' prescription—hence, one of the few victories of the clergy over Voltaire. When he bought his seigneurie at Ferney, he inherited a *dîme inféodée*, coming to the lord of the manor from the Bernese confiscation of ecclesiastical property at the Reformation, but not recognized by the parlement of Dijon when the Pays de Gex came under French overlordship. In spite of influence at court and well-organized litigation, the patriarch of Ferney had to agree to an inglorious compromise with his curé. As ever, he made the best of his discomfiture, adjuring the warring factions of Geneva to make peace by instancing his own sweet reasonableness, meeting with his parish priest to settle their differences over a friendly glass of wine.[143] Strict though the law was, a goodly proportion of the tithe of France—perhaps a twelfth—was held by laymen; had this been exclusively in the hands of the seigneurs descended from the founders of churches, the position would have been easier to justify, but by dint of having been sold and subdivided, the *dîmes inféodées* had passed to all sorts of people[144]—they had become property, just as feudal dues were property. Tithes held by churchmen other than the parish priest were open to similar censures whenever, as was often the case, the bishops, canons, or monks concerned enjoyed excessive riches. More than a third of the curés of France were paid the officially pre-scribed dole, the *portion congrue*, by the holders of the great tithes; and throughout the century, their complaints about the misappropriation of ecclesiastical wealth became more insistent, and received increas-ing popular support.[145]

In many parishes, the division of the tithes had reached an astonishing complexity. In one place near Sedan, the curé was entitled to two-fifths, the prior of Donchery, the chapter of Reims, and the local seigneur to one-fifth each. In the nearby parish of Torcy, the curé had half, the prior of Donchery thirteen-thirty-seconds, another prior one-sixteenth, and a seigneur one-thirty-second.[146] In the little village of Courbesseaux in Lorraine, the curé collected a quarter, a seminary seven-twenty-fourths, an abbot five-twenty-fourths, a prior one-eighth, and two lay lords three-forty-eighths each.[147] In the diocese of Toulouse, of 109 parish priests who owned tithes, only three were the exclusive collectors; 60 had half shares, 29 had thirds, and so on.[148] Confronted with problems of division, some tithe owners made peace among themselves by adopting a system of rotation, whether chronological (the curé to levy every third year, his lay rival in the other two)[149] or geographi-cal (the parish divided into halves with the two tithe owners col-lecting in alternate years in each).[150] In the diocese of Châlons-sur-Marne and in odd places elsewhere, a custom of division prevailed which must surely have been invented by lawyers anxious for fees: the right of the *suite de fer*. The curé of a parish in which a farmer stabled his horses or oxen during the winter had a right to collect half the tithes (and the whole of the tithes on animals and wool) in fields of another parish where these animals were used to do the ploughing. There were conditions, however: the boundaries of the parishes must run alongside at some point; the plough must be able to cross the border without encountering a stream or other natural obstacle; and the farmer must be self-employed.[151] In a tiny parish near Reims, this right to 'follow the plough' was divided equally between the curé, another parish priest, and the cathedral chapter, with the two curés owing small fractions of their portion to three different monastic institutions.[152] A whole history of distrust and litigation lay behind these confusions. Yet the story of such labyrinthine arrangements was not always a sordid one. In one Angevin parish a simple tripartite division had prevailed until a great nobleman listened to the stirrings of conscience and complicated everything by giving a ninth of his third share to the curé, and an eighth of it to maintain a local chapel.[153]

Whether there were various tithe owners or just one, the whole business of collection might be leased to a *fermier*. Since prices tended to rise and leases to be traditional, an entrepreneurial family which established itself in the tithe-farming business was likely to do well.[154] Collecting for a modest nunnery, then on to service with more opulent institutions, and eventually farming the *taille* for the government—this was how Cardinal Fleury's family had climbed up into the world of finance in the seventeenth century.[155] The list of *fermiers* who undertook to collect the archbishop of Albi's tithes shows that it was not artisans or peasants who competed for the contracts, but merchants and entrepreneurs, one-third of them from Albi itself and the others from smaller towns. Frequently, in this area of France, within reach of the great canal crossing the whole country, it was the professional grain merchants who took up the collection; a typical case is at Calmont in 1770, where the auction stood at just over 6,000 livres—a grain merchant took it up in alliance with an innkeeper and two other local worthies who would oversee the collection for him.[156] In the diocese of Auch, a fifth of the contractors were peasants, but always the richer, 'les plus aisés', of their villages. Most of the rest were bourgeois, and, significantly, when collection became difficult because of 'strikes' of tithe payers towards the end of the *ancien régime*, it was the richer merchants and lawyers who were able to stay in competition for the contracts. In 1786, the archbishop of Auch farmed the whole of his tithes (in more than 300 parishes) to an *avocat* of Paris for the huge sum of 306,000 livres and 706 sacks of barley. It is easy to see why the auction of the tithes of the bigger tithe owners should so often be won by the better-off bidders. To sign a contract, often for half a dozen years ahead, was too risky a business for a family without substantial resources, and a single rich entrepreneur could afford to finance a lawsuit against selected individuals, and could settle the matter of a rebate from the tithe owner for unpaid sums in one comprehensive negotiation.[157] To make the peasants fork out, it was as well to have a man of influence accustomed to hobnobbing with lawyers, and if he lived out of the parish, so much the better for his peace of mind.

Instead of contracting out the collection, a tithe owner might

decide to exercise a general oversight himself, but employ one or
two professionals to share the odium of getting the produce safely
into his barn. In Anjou, these characters, called *métiviers*, were substantially remunerated, retaining between a tenth and a sixth of all
they garnered.[158] Even doing it oneself, collecting a tithe could be an
expensive business. One curé, in a year when he took up 2,178
livres' worth of produce, reckoned that the operation had cost him
435 livres: engaging two labourers and plying them with wine,
hiring carts and extra help to unload them, and getting in a thresh-
ing expert had run away with a fifth of his income.[159] This was a high
proportion: according to an official record in the diocese of
Clermont in 1763, the cost of collection was normally one-tenth.[160]
In 1786, a curé of the diocese of Comminges complained to his
bishop about the alacrity of his parishioners in joining his rejoicing
on the day his sheaves came home; by tradition, he had to furnish
twelve jars of wine, twelve pounds of matured cheese, and a dinner
to the municipal officers—after deducting these expenses and other
largesse which he had to furnish at Christmas and on All Saints' Day,
and the wages of a vicaire, he was left with only 512 livres to live
on.[161] Another peculiar obligation afflicted the tithe owners of
Lorraine, who had to provide their villagers with stud animals, and
these, like aldermen invited to a tithe banquet, had voracious
appetites. At Montiers-sur-Saulx,[162] in the diocese of Toul, where
the tithe was shared between the curé and two abbeys, by tradition
the parish priest provided the ram, the abbey of Ecurey the bull, and
the abbey of Montier-en-Der the boar. But in 1714 the Benedictines
of Ecurey refused to pay for a bull and persuaded the local court to
order the curé to contribute towards it as he alone drew the *menues
dîmes*. A new curé appealed against the verdict, and obtained a legal
ruling obliging all three tithe owners to pay equally towards all three
animals. The monks, on appeal to the *bailliage* court, got the curé
condemned to pay one-third towards the bull and to pay entirely for
the ram and the boar. But in 1730 the parish priest finally turned the
tables; the system of pre-1714 was restored, and the conspiratorial
Benedictines, in addition to having to pay all the expenses of
furnishing the bull, incurred costs and damages to the curé and the
inhabitants.

But the owner of the *grosses dîmes* had obligations going far
beyond the provision of cheese and wine, bulls and boars. Any tithe
owner who drew the revenues to the exclusion of the curé had, as
his first obligation, to pay the officially prescribed salary to the parish
priest—the so-called *congrue*. The *gros décimateur*, whether he was the

parochial minister or not, was also responsible for the repairs to the church, at one time solely responsible. The edict of 1695 limited this obligation to the chancel and the choir, an injustice to parishioners which was not entirely forgotten in the *cahiers* of 1789.[163] In addition, if the parishioners were poor, chalices, ornaments, and liturgical books had to be provided, possibly candles also, and laundry expenses. Royal edicts of 1771 and 1772 made these obligations more precise. By contrast, an edict of May 1768, purporting to excuse tithe holders from having to pay out more than a third of their annual profit on repairs, was sufficiently ambiguous in its wording to cause confusion.[164] There was, however, some safeguard for a parish priest, as distinct from other tithe owners: by tradition, he ought always to be left with a reasonable living wage.[165] Doubtful questions abounded, with corresponding scope for litigation. What redress was available if the tithe owner was the Crown, and the administrators of the royal demesne refused to provide 'what is necessary for the celebration of the holy mysteries'?[166] Could a parish sue for past negligence? In 1740, a village in Dauphiné went to law for arrears of candles back to 1672.[167] Did 'what is necessary' include the salary of a parish clerk, as the parlement of Toulouse was trying to prove in the mid-eighteenth century?[168] Did repairing responsibilities accompany the enjoyment of the *menues dîmes*? Generally not, and the matter was finally settled by a ruling of the Grand Conseil in 1748—a verdict which rescued a country curé who was being haunted by the archbishop of Cambrai and the chapter of Notre-Dame of Paris (no less) to contribute to chancel repairs on the strength of a miserable tithe on beans and lentils and a mere bushel of grain allotted to him from the great tithes.[169] Towers and spires were ruinously expensive: if the tower was over the nave, the parishioners had to pay, if over the choir or chancel, the tithe owners. But what of the tower at Guyancourt, with two supporting pillars on one side and two on the other? It took lawsuits from 1769 to 1775 to get to the common-sense solution of dividing the cost.[170] What if the tower fell, damaging the nave? In 1751, the spire of Mortagne in Poitou was blown down, and the Benedictine monks who tithed there refused to rebuild it, as 'unnecessary'. The parish went to law, alleging that it had been a landmark for travellers and a look-out post when the English had attacked La Rochelle; in the end, the Benedictines escaped their obligation on the aesthetic ground that the architecture had been Gothic, and therefore of dubious value.[171] The edict of 1695 had favoured tithe owners, but it had not repealed certain provincial customs benefiting parishes;

more especially, it had not changed the old jurisprudence of Flanders.[172] Here, the exploiter of the great tithes was responsible for the whole of the church building, and was obliged to allocate two years' revenue out of every six for the purpose. The parlement of Flanders repelled all manœuvres of the tithe owners to bring the province under the law of 1695; indeed, the magistrates went further, and in a series of lawsuits ruled that the salaries of curés and repairs to vicarages and churches were expenses which holders of the *grosses dîmes* had to pay, however much they exceeded the compulsory two years' contribution.

Where the tithe of a parish went to the curé, his people looked to him to give proportionately to the poor. Whether by Christian charity or by the pressure of public opinion, most parish priests did something—and in times of famine, a great deal. But what of the absentee chapters, monasteries, and laymen whose contractors' carts trundled off the sheaves or the wine jars at the appropriate harvest season? In some places, more especially in Dauphiné, the holder of the great tithe on cereals was, by custom, expected to hand over a fixed proportion to the curé for the poor.[173] In others, the courts had intervened to make custom into obligation. In this way, great abbeys had been saddled with compulsory alms; Lessay in Normandy, for example, was under the orders of the parlement of Rouen to pay 6,000–7,000 livres a year 'without prejudice to ordinary almsgiving as circumstances require, or to the exercise of hospitality'.[174] When farming out its estates, an ecclesiastical institution might impose a tariff of charity on its contractor—in this way, perhaps, losing credit for its generosity among local people at the time and among historians subsequently.[175] In various other ways, friendly gestures were made by tithe owners to their villages; the *collège* of Pélegri near Cahors had set up exhibitions limited to the children of the three parishes where it collected half the tithe.[176] But except in crises of dearth, and not always then, the absentee tithe owners were rarely generous. 'I haven't received a *sou* from anybody at all to help me to aid the destitute in my parish,' said a curé of Guyenne in 1789; 'not even from le sieur Thyerri, who draws the great tithe . . . which Thyerri I must leave to the judgement of his own conscience.'[177] An enquiry, towards the end of the *ancien régime*, by the archbishop of Rouen throughout his diocese, was full of such complaints: the great abbey of Bec gives 72 livres a year only, that of Jumièges nothing at all; 'the poor get more aid from the most insignificant of Protestant families than they do from a celebrated abbey which plunders 800 acres of my parish'. 'It appears to me to be simple justice', said another curé, 'that the holders of the *grosses dîmes* should contribute to helping their brethren, seeing they enjoy crops that have been fertilized by the sweat of the poor.'[178] Similar complaints abound in the *cahiers* of 1789. The villagers of Cumières, near Reims, had an ancient tradition that the tithe which they paid at one-eleventh had, long ago, been as little as one-sixtieth, until their ancestors, 'as honest and trusting as monks and ecclesiastics are sly and crafty', had agreed to an increased payment for the rebuilding of the abbey of Hautvilliers, an increase which had been illegally perpetuated. Even so, the abbey gave no alms. 'The abbot of Hautvilliers does nothing to help to pay for the expenses of religious services in Cumières. We tried to stir up his charity on behalf of the poor, but there has been no reply; his heart of bronze remains deaf—it hears only the chink of gold pieces.'[179]

The motivation to contest the levy of tithe was universal, and confusions and ambiguities providing grounds for litigation were legion.[180] Mines and quarries were exempt, so were woods, though under certain circumstances a major cut of trees became taxable. Fruit-trees were exempt in most of France, but were all chargeable in Gascony, and certain fruits in some other places. Why, in Auvergne, should hemp pay so generally and hay so rarely, and why, when new crops in that province were mostly exempt, did turnips and sainfoin occasionally slip into the tithe gatherer's net?[181] The produce of hunting escaped, so too of fishing, except in certain Norman ports. Crops cut before due time were free if used to feed the working animals, but not if used to fatten beasts for sale to butchers. An enclosed private garden adjoining a house was free, but not if it was newly created from land that had once been ploughed and sown. Needless to say, there were regulations to stop the laity enclosing whole fields and calling them gardens; logical in injustice, the parlement of Bordeaux allowed one size of garden to a man who ploughed with two oxen, and double this amount to one who ploughed with four. Private parks did not pay tithe, but if they were created from arable land, compensation had to be paid; Louis XIV gave annuities to curés and the abbey of Sainte-Geneviève when he created the Trianon park in 1668—these fell steadily in value, and were a cause of complaint in the eighteenth century.[182]

Odd local circumstances could intensify ill will and provide occasions for tragi-comic feuds and litigation. Not every village had an established, clear procedure for allocating the tithe owners' share—like Blairy in Burgundy, where each proprietor had to stack his sheaves in a straight row, so that the *dixmeur* could start counting at any one he chose and collect every thirteenth sheaf thereafter,[183] or Heuilley, where the payment was a fixed measure of grain according to the amount of land under cultivation, the area to be declared by the proprietor, with the curé having the right to challenge (surveyor's fees paid by the party which was mistaken).[184] In some places, the size of sheaves was argued about; in others, whether they were properly tied, whether the necessary warning of the harvesting date had been given, whether the sheaves had remained available long enough in the field for inspection.[185] What of new crops— clover, potatoes, maize? What of crops planted between rows of vines?[186] Who was to dictate which of two alternative local measures of grain should be used—like the bushel of Falaise, marginally bigger than that of Briouze?[187] What if a crop of rye had been harvested green to be used as ties for the bundles of ripe grain later on? What of windfall fruit, fallen to the ground before it was ripe?[188] One thing was sure; if the tithe owner let things slip, a precedent would be created against him, and what was allowed to one individual in one year would be demanded by everyone the next. In 1770, a canon of Saint-Omer sued a proprietor of Helfaut for tithe on a few tobacco plants; a derisory sum was involved, but the crop might have become significant in a few years' time.[189] And in any case, there was the whole principle of tithe to be upheld, so that even the most improbable windfall was worth pursuing. In 1747 the curé of Issy won a lawsuit before the parlement of Paris for 'la dîme des sangliers élevés dans les maisons'—the severe winter had driven wild boars into the village for refuge. 'It is true', said the lawyers, 'that there is no custom of tithing wild boars, but that is not an argument for saying the claim is unfounded because up to now there has been no custom of rearing wild boars in houses.'[190] It was important to seize the right moment for litigation, and also to choose the appropriate adversary. In 1788, a curé wrote to the abbot of the Cistercian abbey of La Ferté-sur-Grosne proposing a joint onslaught on 'le sieur Grassart', evidently a man of substance, who had been stirring up the parishioners to refuse a tithe which the abbey and the parish priest shared between them.[191] This was the strategy of staking everything on breaking through the enemy's centre. But it might be safer to begin with an attack on the flank, to pick off some miserable peasant, thus establishing a legal ruling to be used against the richer ones. The poor, we must remember, ran the danger of ruin if they contested a lawsuit, since they might have to pay the costs of the other side. In Voltaire's correspondence we read of the fate of five peasant families who foolishly disputed a tithe of 30 livres a year which came to them as a charity, in opposition to the grasping curé of Monëns, only to find themselves condemned to pay 1,300 livres in costs, including the curé's lodging and wine bills during the hearing of the case in Dijon.[192] In 1767, the recteur of Saint-Denoual noted in his journal that his tithe of one fleece from each flock invariably brought him in the most mangy specimens: 'on vole le Recteur en tout'. Though nobles were the meanest of all in this respect, he dissimulated his ire; the only way to proceed was to look out for a chance to cite before the *présidial* someone too poor to fight back, then to publish the sentence of the court (at a cost of ten écus, he notes gloomily), in the hope of frightening the others.[193]

One standard device for evading tithe which the richer cultivator could resort to was to change to a different crop—one which the lawyers recommended as having a chance to qualify for exemption. Thus Restif de la Bretonne's father, smarting at the rapacious forays of the bishop and canons of Auxerre among his corn sheaves, planted part of his non-ploughable hill terrain with vines, and in seven years was producing wine, a commodity not titheable by local custom.[194] M. de Goupillières, *directeur* of the Mint at Caen, was not so lucky. In 1734 he went down in person to his seigneurie of Saint-Hilaire to supervise the change of some arable land to pasture (catching a cold in the process), and wrote a smooth letter to the curé— 'Mon Révérend Père'—pointing out that he was within his legal rights since he had left two-thirds of his land under the plough. After four years of litigation, however, he was condemned to pay an annual compensation.[195] His lawyers had not done their homework. True, a declaration of 1657 protecting tithe owners against loss of revenue when meadows were created had never been registered, and the parlement and the Grand Conseil had ruled that a tithe owner could claim compensation only if he was losing more than a third of his revenue. But the essential point was—it was a third of the *whole* tithe from the parish which mattered; thus, landowners who were quick to create meadows might get away with it, but not the later ones.[196] In this same year, 1734, M. Grandjean de Lespine planted trees on a stretch of his arable land in Crevecœur-en-Brie. In this case the curé failed in his lawsuit as his losses, on all heritages taken together, still did not total a third.

Disputes of a like kind arose from government edicts[197] to encourage the extension of the area of cultivation by granting a limited suspension of tithe. In 1761, an exemption for ten years was offered for wasteland brought under the plough; three years later this was raised to fifteen. As for land reclaimed from marsh, this would enjoy

an exemption of twenty years, with tithe thereafter pegged at the
low figure of one-fiftieth. Foolishly, the clergy of the province of
Guyenne protested. 'The saying, you must sow before you can reap,
is unknown to them,' complained Quesnay, the physiocrat.[198] Most
ecclesiastics were more enlightened, and saw these concessions as a
source of future profit: a minor waiving of principle in the present,
and an increase of revenue in the long run. The chapter of Notre-
Dame of Paris and the clerical representatives at the estates of
Brittany were willing to improve on the government's regulations
and offer a twenty-one years' immunity in the areas where they
tithed. But what was 'wasteland'? Inevitably, any weedy patch that
had escaped the plough for a while was claimed to be such by its
owners, so an *arrêt* of 1766 laid down a definition of forty years without cultivation. The Assembly General of the Clergy still had to go
on protesting, however; the parlement of Bordeaux was allowing
proprietors to plough waste without giving the tithe owner notice
of intent, thus obliterating evidence of previous cultivation, while in
the *landes* the sand performed the function anyway. And what of the
crafty estate managers who ploughed up old-established meadows
and switched some of their old titheable arable land to pasture in
exchange? In Gascony and Quercy, it was the nobles who led the
way in manipulating the code concerning wasteland and marshes to
evade the tithe owner's levies; bourgeois entrepreneurs tended to be
mixed up in the business of collection, and therefore sided with the
clergy.[199] A Breton nobleman wrote to the controller-general in 1783
pointing out that the fifteen-year exemption granted in 1766 was
now running out for many proprietors.

The peasant proprietor, the laboureur [no doubt it was convenient not to
mention the drainers and enclosers among the nobility], panic-stricken,
can already see the Church annexing the fruit of his toil, and is deciding
to abandon the cultivation of land he had enclosed from the waste, and on
which he has become agreeably accustomed to pay nothing more than
taxes to the State.

Thus, he concluded, the king is going to lose revenue, simply
because the clergy are being allowed an unearned windfall—was
there not a royal edict in 1749 forbidding them to acquire new
property, and what is tithe but property of a sort?[200]

   Given this atmosphere of suspicion, fraud, and litigation, tithe
was inevitably hated. It was all the more grudgingly paid when the
peasant made comparisons. If he paid tithe at a high rate, he would
compare his burden with the lighter burden borne by others. Of a

group of thirty-six parishes in Champagne,[201] twenty-one paid a global sum equal to one-third of all State taxation levied, but four paid fully two-thirds of the total exactions of the Crown—an enormous disparity. The peasants were narrowly confined, physically and intellectually, within the boundaries of their village community, but where paying out was concerned, they knew when they were being unequally treated. In Brittany, where tithe in adjoining parishes could vary from one-tenth to one-thirty-sixth, this was a general complaint in the *cahiers*. That of the village of Comblessac asked for some reduction in its one-twelfth, 'seeing that the parishes around owe it only on the fiftieth or thirtieth sheaf, and their land is better quality than ours'.[202] Another comparison to be made was with the privileged few who escaped paying tithe altogether. A man whose income consisted solely in an official salary or house rents would pay nothing. Mills were exempt, and forests often escaped, and these were mostly owned by the privileged classes. In Provence nobles paid at a lower rate than commoners, even on non-noble lands which they might have purchased. The Orders of Malta, Cîteaux, Cluny, the Prémontrés, and the Chartreux held exemptions granted to them by popes, though there was a developing jurisprudence in the eighteenth century to limit their privilege. Oddly enough, some Protestants in Alsace were not liable, since the lawyers of Louis XIV had failed to list all provincial peculiarities that needed to be changed on annexation.[203] And finally, there was the most devastating comparison of all, between the poverty of the payer of tithe and the wealth of some great ecclesiastical institution which levied it—and if this institution collected seigneurial or other dues locally as well, the cumulative effect was overwhelming. Richeprey, touring the South, investigating inequalities of the taxation system, noted the nuns of Saint-Sernin (Rodez) tied up in lawsuits with a parish in which they levied a *champart* of one-quarter or one-fifth along with the tithe.[204] The cathedral chapter of Beauvais, in twelve parishes of its estates, enjoyed a tithe and a *champart* which together took 18 per cent of the peasants' crops; the *cahiers* of this area in 1789 overflow with bitterness.[205]

The peasant, enviously reflecting on his misery, was well aware that the true rate at which he paid his tribute to the Church was always higher than the ostensible official figure. As the villagers of Saint-André-du-Double in Périgord said in their *cahier*, they paid twice over when they paid a tithe on potatoes, then another one on the pigs that were fed on them; similarly when they paid on grain used to feed chickens. Furthermore, they were not allowed to deduct anything to cover the seed-corn which they planted.[206] This was an important point, for the yield of grain was often only one in four; that is, a tithe which appeared to be one-eighth would in fact be one-fifth.[207] Dupont de Nemours, drawing up the *cahier* of the Tiers État of his *bailliage*, declared that proprietors were paying as much as a third of their crop if all expenses were taken into account. 'You imagine, O complaining farmer, that it's one sheaf in ten they are taking out of your field,' said a pamphleteer of 1789, *L'Iniquité de la dîme*, 'Great is your error; they are taking one in five. Half of your crop goes in covering your advances, your cost of cultivation, your seed-corn.'[208] And an important item in this cost of cultivation was the manuring of the fields. Carting seaweed or the fragrant contents of municipal cesspits to the land was a toilsome expedient available only to those who lived near the sea-shore or suburbs. For the most part, the fields were fertilized by the dung-impregnated litter which had bedded the animals, more especially during the winter months. But straw was so often in short supply: 'la paille est toujours ce qui manque', said an agricultural reformer in a treatise of 1763.[209] To collect tithe 'au champ' instead of 'dans le sac' (that is, taking the stalk along with the grain) was a notable device of seigneurial oppression—used, for example, by a Catholic seigneur against a Protestant village in Alsace to force it to conversion.[210] Some of the parlements made regulations compelling tithe owners to sell back their straw to the inhabitants at low prices fixed by the local judicial officials.[211] This arbitrary intervention of the magistrates was not unreasonable. The least that wealthy chapters and monasteries could do was to refrain from hampering the cultivators who grew the crops which paid their tribute.

If tithe was collected by a contractor, it was likely that enforcement would be harsher, and if the contractor was from outside the village, no one was satisfied. The richer peasants saw a lucrative job escaping them, and the poorer saw wealth leaving the parish that might have provided them with employment or charity. In Flanders, by a cherished local custom, the job of collecting tithes was auctioned annually in separate details, enabling even humble peasants to have a chance to try their hand at this minor capitalist enterprise. By contrast, in the areas where the archbishop of Cambrai left his tithe collection in the hands of the manager who ran all his estates, there was a general clamour in the *cahiers* of 1789 for tithe to be farmed to parishioners only.[212] There was an exception—an illogical one—to this preference for a local contractor. Some parish priests held the tithe in their own hands and collected it: this was accepted as an inevitable evil, and it was satisfying, at any rate, to reflect that the profits stayed in the parish. But there were curés who did not enjoy the tithe, but who nevertheless volunteered to collect it, to obtain the contractor's percentage.[213] Thus, the abbey or chapter which had usurped the curé's true patrimony (for this was how everyone regarded it), and which now paid him a mere pittance, was able to make use of his local knowledge in levying its dues. What was worse, here was a man of God stepping out of his spiritual role to usurp a job which a layman of the parish might have hoped for. 'By taking holy orders, he had become the protector and father of the flock confided to his care; but he takes the bread from the hands of the hard-up individuals who used to collect the tithes, work which used to help them to earn a living and to pay their taxes'—this concerning the curé of Marche-Maisons near Alençon, in the village *cahier*.[214] Another variant of the pastor as professional collector is when he shared a tithe with others, drawing a fraction which, perhaps, was too small to be economically levied on its own. In this case, it was only common sense to offer to collect the lot and to arrange the share-out. In his memoirs, Marquis-Ducastel, curé of Sainte-Suzanne, describes how he inherited a comfortable arrangement of this kind, handing over two-thirds to the abbot of Evron, less 360 livres collector's charges. A new abbot, however, put the business into the hands of the city slickers—'intriguers from Laval'— who farmed his estates; Marquis-Ducastel lost something like 800 livres a year by having to hire a separate barn for storing his third.[215] He does not tell us what was the attitude of the parishioners of Sainte-Suzanne; there was no doubt about that of the inhabitants of Rumegies, in the diocese of Tournai, earlier in the century. Dubois, the curé, tells us how the abbey of Saint-Amand enjoyed a tithe of seven-hundredths in his parish, and he himself one of one-hundredth, a fraction too small to levy effectively; how in 1702 he bought the right to levy the abbey tithe as well as his own—'using the same collector, the same cart and the same efforts as before!' He soon wished he had not been so efficient.

On every side nothing was heard but threats—to burn him out, to kill him, to insult him, to drive him out of his cure. And even his best friends in the parish all made war on him. And unless God in his goodness touches their hearts, they will never pardon him! Indeed, if the curé had had the least inkling that he'd become so unpopular, he'd never have thought of taking over this tithe collecting.[216]

The lawyers who grew sleek by conducting the tithe suits of the

laity had accumulated theoretical and historical arguments; anticlericals in search of ammunition did not need to go further than the
law dictionaries. Was tithe of divine institution? In his edict of 1657,
Louis XIV had repeated this claim, but the parlement of Paris had
refused to register it. The lawyers insisted that here was a simple
tax 'for the maintenance of the ministers of the Church'.[217] True,
the Levites had enjoyed their tithes, as recorded in the books of
Leviticus and Numbers. But the Gallican Church was in a different
situation, having its own landed endowment. St Paul was much concerned about the maintenance of preachers of the gospel, yet he was
silent about this Levitical precedent; so too were the laws of the first
six centuries.[218] Christians, unlike Jews, are not obliged to pay a fixed
tribute, St Augustine had boasted. St Thomas Aquinas does not
accept the principle of divine institution. Indeed, the argument ran,
the variations in the rate at which tithe was levied suggest an accumulation of practical concessions rather than the imposition of a
theoretical obligation. The parlement of Franche Comté used these
arguments in 1725 to prevent a curé from levying tithe on a tiny
hamlet. Even though the rest of the parish paid, the inhabitants of
Boismurie were held to be exempt on grounds of prescription—they
had evaded payment for a long time. No tithe was levied in the early
centuries; the Eastern Church has never had it; it has not been paid
in India or America, said the parlement. Therefore it has arisen
purely by custom, and as it arose, so let it die, beginning maybe in
the hamlet of Boismurie.[219] Montesquieu added learning and Voltaire
irony to the concept of tithe as a purely human institution which the
law of the land could modify. Payment of a tenth among the Jews,
said Montesquieu, had been 'part of the plan of the foundation of
their republic', while in France it was a 'charge independent of
those involved in the establishment of the monarchy'. Before
Charlemagne, tithe was 'preached . . . but not established', and for
long after him payment was episodic. And tithe, as Charlemagne had
devised it, was divided between the bishop, the clergy, the church
building, and the poor. Since he had considered his gifts to the
Church less as a religious than as a 'political dispensation', there is
every reason to believe that the tithe is not exclusively for the
clergy; in its primitive allocation, half went to the church fabric and
the indigent.[220] Voltaire, as ever, had fun with the arrangements of
the Old Testament. The Levites tithed in the wilderness of Cades,
and Abraham gave to Melchizedek the tithes of Sodom; let us pack
off our modern tithe owners to collect their revenues in those distant, insalubrious places. This applies, however, only to the rich

monks and canons, who drink choice vintages, eat pheasant and par-
tridge, and sleep, not unaccompanied, on feather-beds; by contrast,
Voltaire laments (probably sincerely) the lot of the country curé
'obliged to dispute a sheaf of corn with his poor parishioners . . . to
be hated and to hate'. Surely, these unjust exactions do not spring
from the Christian gospel: 'did God come down to earth to award a
quarter of my income to the . . . abbot of Saint-Denis?' In northern
Europe, ministers of religion are paid from public funds, and everyone is happier.[221] These were hard words; even so, the clergy were
to be officially maintained. But why should this maintenance be
official? According to a more radical view—rarely found—the laity
should be left to contribute of their own free will. In his journal,
the abbé Véri explored the unavowed, subconscious cause of the
intolerance of the Gallican Church towards Protestants: the fear that
tithe would be lost. 'As soon as the exercise of religion is freely
allowed, each believer then ought to allot the tithe of his field to the
actual minister who exercises pastoral care over him.'[222] There is a
logical further step which Véri does not mention: unbelievers might
keep their crops for themselves; once this was allowed, their
numbers would be legion.

Criticism of tithe on grounds of history or principle was
reinforced by solid economic arguments from the physiocrats. The
theories of this dominant school of French economic thinkers were
dubious enough; they were mistaken about the declining population; they oversimplified when they made agriculture the sole source
of real wealth; their theoretical insistence that grain must be allowed
to rise to its natural price level disregarded the misery of the
common people. But they saw clearly what was wrong with the
French countryside; as a result of conspicuous waste, heavy taxation,
tithe, and the purchase of offices, investment in agriculture was
inadequate. So they proclaimed a new slogan, 'the inviolability of
agricultural capital'[223]—much discussed by provincial agricultural
societies. The owner of land ought not to push up the farmer's lease
to the limit, ought not to pass on to him the unpredictable burden
of State taxation. The actual tiller of the soil should enjoy a surplus,
growing in proportion to the intensity of his own efforts, and which,
in every sense of the word, he would plough back into the business.
Tithe clearly was a major drain of capital away from the land, and a
discouragement to enterprise and to the extension of the area of
cultivation. To the peasants' complaint that the true fraction of the
crops taken was greater than the apparent one, the physiocrats added
a further argument. The costs of agricultural production were

greatest in the least fertile areas, so that their tithe absorbed a greater fraction of the net crop than elsewhere: it was a levy falling most heavily on the poor.

The arguments of lawyers, philosophes, and physiocrats were but dimly grasped in rural France. Yet the peasants understood perfectly the basic principle at issue. Tithes were meant to pay the parochial ministers, to maintain the church building, and keep divine service going; but they had been diverted to other purposes. Properly used, they ought to provide a liberal maintenance for the curé, leaving him well enough off to feed the poor in time of dearth, and freeing him from the need to collect surplice-fees at weddings and funerals. *Dîme* and *casuel* (tithe and surplice-fees) were linked in the minds of the peasants: given the burden of the one, the other was unjustified. Representatives of the community of Gignac in the diocese of Aix-en-Provence in 1775 described how they paid tithe to the tune of 2,000 livres a year, and all they got back was 200 livres to pay a priest so ignorant that he did not know how to baptize; they applied, therefore, to be allowed to keep their money and use it to build up a real parochial life.[224] The *cahier* of Rougeon (diocese of Blois) gave a ruthless summary of peasant grievances:

We lament to see our parish priests in abjection, misery and necessity, while . . . a horde of monks of various sorts, abbots and canons take away our tithe and swindle our curés out of what is their due. The [tithe owners] on whom the benefice depends do not blush to see our churches without books, linen, ornaments, and on the verge of falling down, and dirtier than stables. Let their riches be cut back, and let our churches and our curé—the inspiration and support of our families—be properly endowed. And let us hear no more of surplice-fees—the tithe is sufficient to pay for the administration of the sacraments.[225]

In the last twenty years of the *ancien régime*, a revolt against tithe was smouldering in the south of France. In 1775, the Assembly General of the Clergy of France accused the parlement of Toulouse of an underhand design to encourage refusal to pay the *menues dîmes*. According to the magistrates, these could only be demanded if there was a clear title or long prescription, with proof that at least two-thirds of the inhabitants had been paying over at least two-thirds of the area of the parish, and that all had been paying at precisely the same rate (variations would show that the tribute was voluntary). Furthermore, these details had to be established by the testimony of witnesses other than the actual collectors. Since these were imposs-ible conditions, the government issued declarations to rescue the clergy, declarations which the magistrates refused to register.[226] To the assembly of the clergy of the ecclesiastical province of Auch in 1780[227] (one of the areas of France where tithe was levied at a high rate), the archbishop reported widespread refusals to pay any more than the literal tenth and to pay anything at all on maize, which was regarded as a new and exempt crop. 'This revolt is winning support from parish to parish, to the point that, if the approaching Assembly General of the Clergy fails to act in this respect, or acts unsuccessfully, payments will become purely a matter of individual choice, and refusals universal.' The parlement of Toulouse backed M. de Saint-Géry's defiance of the bishop of Lectoure over the payment of a tithe of two-seventeenths on millet, and other cases were on the way. At another assembly of the clergy of his province in September 1782, the archbishop of Auch spoke of 'an evident conspiracy', with 500 lawsuits pending before the parlement, and little doubt as to what the verdicts would be. The crisis came when the magistrates of Toulouse considered the plea of the villagers of Mouchez, who had refused to pay a tithe of four-thirty-firsts on wheat, offering to pay at one-tenth. The curé had won his case when he cited the three chief recalcitrants before the court of the *sénéchaussée* of Auch; but on appeal, the parlement reversed this verdict in March 1781. From then onwards there was a torrent of refusals. By December 1784, more than half the parishes of Auch and Comminges were offering to pay at a strict tenth and no more. The tensions are evident in the complaints of the curés to the bishop of Comminges in 1786. They spoke of 'fire' and 'fermentation' and 'visible' threats; the old days when the tithe owners could be brusque with their peasants were over—'il faut les traiter comme à des noces: de cette façon, ma portion est toujours petite'.[228] Not surprisingly, the clergy backed away from the desperate confrontation that seemed to be developing. Instead of 500 lawsuits being prosecuted, possibly only a dozen were fought through to a conclusion. Tithe owners avoided coming to a legal crunch unless they were confident about their documentary evidence; the curés urged the archbishop and chapters to be moderate, and were themselves willing to negotiate. In most places there was a 'transaction'; on the main cereal crops the payment was reduced to the strict one-tenth, and by way of compensation the clergy might be allowed peaceful possession of the *menues dîmes* in areas where these had been contested.[229] Other sovereign courts began to follow the example of Toulouse. In 1774, the parlement of Normandy declared that only the tithe on the four basic grain crops, wheat, rye, barley, and oats, could be levied as of right:

tithes on all other crops were 'insolites': that is, proof of forty years' possession was required.[230] The parlement of Burgundy had been accustomed to decide cases in favour of tithe owners; from 1770, it tended to find against them, and in 1775 issued an *arrêt* modelled on that of Normandy.[231] These were years of rising prices and of agricultural diversification. From both these developments (somewhat paradoxically coinciding) the tithe owners were gaining an enhanced income. Hence, given the pervasive anticlericalism of the countryside, an envious alliance of magistrates and cultivators formed against them.

At first sight it seems astonishing that the reformers of the early years of the Revolution abandoned their original idea of confiscating tithe for the coffers of the State, and simply suppressed it, thus making a handsome present to all landowners at a time of national bankruptcy. Yet it is not difficult to see why the intention of 4 August 1789[232] was never carried into effect. For long, there had been a vast, undeclared conspiracy over the whole of France to evade and outwit the tithe holders. On this issue landowners had become pathologically conditioned to be deaf to reason and religion, and, if need be, to patriotism. The history of the guerrilla war against tithe waged for so long in the law courts is essential evidence in any study of rural anticlericalism in France. A formula for calculating its intensity in any particular area may be suggested. Start with a standard, inevitable figure, then adjust it slightly for the worse in years of very bad or very good harvests, when tithe becomes especially hated as either a confiscation of the bread of the poor or a theft from the profits of diligence and enterprise. To this, add extra points of discontent if an ecclesiastical institution holds the tithe to the exclusion of the curé, more points still if that institution is scandalously rich, and still more if it levies seigneurial dues on the same people from whom it takes tithe, and a substantial bonus if it gives only derisory alms locally. All this to be multiplied by a coefficient based on the rate at which tithe is levied as compared with other places. The suppression of tithe by the representatives of the nation went far beyond what was suggested in the *cahiers*, yet was entirely compatible with them. Tithe had lost all religious overtones and associations, and had become just a set of dues authorized by the State and levied by a minority of citizens on all the others. As Condorcet said, it was 'un véritable revenu indépendant de tout service religieux'.[233]

5

THE GENERAL ASSEMBLIES OF THE CLERGY AND CLERICAL TAXATION

I

The clergy of France voted taxation to the Crown in their own elected assemblies. This independence, unique in the kingdom, was jealously defended. In the preface to the first volume of the collection of the minutes of past meetings, published in 1767, the status and rights of the 'first Order in the nation' are proudly asserted: 'accustomed to make its remonstrances to its august Sovereign, to bring before him its *cahiers* of grievances, to offer him the gifts which it levies independently—a right which is a precious survival of the Estates General (*reste précieux des États Généraux*)'. In these volumes of minutes, says the editor, 'you see the Assemblies of this illustrious corporation constantly conserving their forms and usages, as zealous to give their Sovereign glittering proofs of their fidelity and their affection, as courageous to defend the sacred rights of religion; in a word, participating in the majesty of the State and in the holiness of [ecclesiastical] Councils.'[1]

The assemblies, which eventually gave the clergy a degree of independence of the Crown, had arisen because the Church was taken into partnership with the monarchy as a collaborator in the extension of royal power over a divided country. The foundation of the alliance was the Concordat of 1516, by which the king named the bishops.[2] The Wars of Religion drew the interests of churchmen and administrators closer. After 1563, the Papacy, anxious to have the reforms of the Council of Trent implemented in France, connived at the strengthening of the Gallican hierarchy, since the Tridentine decrees, not officially accepted by the Crown, were adopted by reforming bishops in their dioceses. More prosaically, the king needed money. The clergy had paid *décimes* to him, with papal permission, from the twelfth century, but the royal ministers wanted the inflow of money made more systematic. On their side, churchmen, afraid that in desperate times the State might confiscate their property, were co-operative. Thus, labyrinthine financial trans-actions created a new and more predictable system of clerical taxa-tion, and the assemblies of the Gallican Church with it.

The clergy liked to think of their right to vote their own taxation as the remains of the old national franchises which the other orders in the State had failed to defend, or as the recognition by the secu-lar power of the just authority of the spiritual. In fact, their right was ensured by an immense structure of debt. The king found it easiest to borrow money by using the Church as an intermediary; the clergy were well organized, they did not default on payments, and rarely delayed them. The system began with the 'contrat de Poissy' of 1561,[3] by which they engaged themselves for the next sixteen years to redeem the royal domain lands pledged to the Hôtel de Ville of Paris. The government, finding life easier under this arrangement, contracted new loans to be serviced by annuities on the clergy, and the contrat de Poissy was renewed at ten-yearly intervals. At these times the assemblies maintained the fiction that they were not obliged to go on making payments on behalf of the State, but many bourgeois families came to depend on these *rentes*, and as is the way with debts, the creditors were concerned to keep going the arrange-ments which ensured their regular income. These *rentes de l'Hôtel de Ville de Paris* continued to be paid all through the seventeenth and eighteenth centuries.

The *rentes* were a matter of about 400,000 livres annually, which, comparatively speaking, was not a large sum. But the Assemblies of Clergy went on to contract new debts, partly because it would have been impossible to meet the exactions of Louis XIV without recourse to anticipations of revenue, but not without a quiet realiza-tion that the increase of indebtedness was a further guarantee of indispensability and of the sanctity of their independent arrange-ments. In 1689, the Great Monarch wanted 18 million for 43 years' arrears of the *droit d'amortissement*, the fines paid for extensions and improvements to ecclesiastical property; in 1693 it was 7 million in *amercements* for the illegal cutting of woods over the past twenty-four years. In 1710, Louis collected the immense sum of 24 million livres as a lump payment to buy off clerical liability to his new capitation tax. (In the end, the clergy did well out of this transaction; the capitation did not end when the war was over, but continued throughout the eighteenth century, so that for six years' purchase they had bought off a liability which would have totalled 310 million by 1789.[4]) The assemblies which borrowed in 1686 to set up a fund to aid in the conversion of Protestants went on to borrow more to meet the royal demands: five and a half million out of the twelve they had to raise in 1690, twenty-four for the capitation in 1710, eight million in 1711, and twelve in 1715. By the end of the reign, they were finding over 6,250,000 a year, of which nearly 4,000,000 was payment of interest on the debt.[5] This debt, augmented from time to time (and occasionally held in check by attempts to consolidate it), remained throughout the eighteenth century. It was more than the king would ever be able to pay off, and the interest went to creditors who knew that they were holders of the safest investment in France. 'Rien n'est mieux payé que ce qui est assis sur le clergé,' said the duc de Luynes in 1755.[6] In 1784, according to Necker, the annual payments of the clergy were 400,000 livres for the old *rentes* on the Hôtel de Ville of Paris, interest on the main debt of 134 million to the tune of 5,800,000, a sum of 4,100,000 designed to pay off some of the main debt, and 700,000 interest on borrowings by individual dioceses. When the Revolution came and the lands of the Church were to be sold, the debt which had to be taken over was more than 149 million. It was then seen how good the credit of the clergy had been, since 104 million of the loans were at the rate of 4 per cent, 37 million at 2 to 2½ per cent, and eight million at 5 per cent.[7]

Some organization for assessing individual dioceses, collecting taxes from the clergy, and paying them into the treasury of the central government would always have been necessary; indeed, lacking a single, recognized episcopal head, the Gallican Church needed a bureaucratic headquarters to act as a post office between bishops and a link between dioceses for the transaction of everyday financial and legal affairs. But it was the existence of the debt which encouraged the Crown to favour the rapid and complex development of such machinery. A meeting held in 1580[8] marks the beginning of regularly held and legally recognized assemblies of the clergy. For the first time, representatives of the rank and file were present, as well as bishops; details of ceremonies and voting procedures were fixed; and a system of correspondence from Paris to *syndics* in each diocese was established. The king promised to call such another assembly in ten years' time, and in the meantime he would not set up any other machinery to tax the clergy, and not ask for any other impositions beyond those already granted. These promises became common form, though when Louis XIV was on the throne, they meant less than might be supposed. He reserved the right to ask at any time for a benevolence, a *don gratuit*, which he did not count as ordinary taxation, and he did not brook argument in the assemblies about the amount of money he demanded. But under weaker successors, this would not always be so. And administrative machinery, as it increases in efficiency and complexity, engenders its own power to resist, whether by bureaucratic inertia or by the ability to mount concerted opposition and propaganda.

In its final form, the system of taxation had, as the base of the pyramid, the *bureaux des décimes* (also known, in various places, as *chambres des décimes* or *bureaux diocésains*). An edict of 1615 had ordered each diocese to establish such a committee, and gradually this was done, the dioceses of Brittany being late in complying (Saint-Malo in 1681, Nantes in 1682, Rennes in 1696).[9] These bureaux assessed all holders of benefices, and saw that the proceeds were used to pay the contribution laid upon the diocese by the Assembly of the Clergy, and to meet various diocesan expenses, including payment of interest on any local debts which had been incurred. In cases of disputed assessment, the bureau had power to settle definitively those involving no more than 20 or 30 livres. Complainants would be heard only if they had paid all past arrears and had put down the cash for half their current assessment, and if they produced statements of their revenues backed with documentary evidence (if not honestly done, double tax was chargeable).[10] The bureau had a *syndic*, some prominent ecclesiastic with a head for business, who had oversight of the taxation and conducted the correspondence with the central organization in Paris—indeed, the letters patent of 1616 and 1626 made him a sort of official defender of the interests of the diocese. The actual work of collecting and accounting was in the hands of a lay expert, the *receveur diocésain*, who sent up the money to the *receveur général* in Paris.[11] Like so many offices in seventeenth-century France, these diocesan receiverships had been put up for sale by the Crown. An edict of 1719 made a clean sweep of these venal posts, and allowed bishops and their bureaux to make their own nominations. Alas, in 1723 the Assembly of Clergy itself, faced with the payment of a heavy *don gratuit*, asked the king to sell the receiverships again to raise 1,500,000 livres; most dioceses bought them, and incurred heavy debts in the process.[12]

The diocesan bureaux were supposed to be 'representative' of the clergy. But the election of members by benefice holders was rare. Sometimes the bishop named the people he wanted, sometimes the existing group co-opted others or had a right to approve the bishop's choices. Often, the selection was made within a cadre of understandings about which institutions or classes of clergy were entitled to a voice—the cathedral, other chapters, a great abbey, curés of the town, curés of the countryside, and so on. In a few places, parish priests had obtained strong representation: eight out of ten in Lectoure, four out of seven in Lescar, three out of six in Montauban. But such democratic arrangements were rare; in most dioceses the bureau was the closed preserve of the clerical oligarchy around the bishop and the cathedral. In 1789, the *chambre ecclésiastique* of Paris consisted of the archbishop, the dean and two canons of Notre-Dame (one being the *syndic*), a canon of Saint-Honoré, the abbot of the canons regular of Sainte-Geneviève, and a single curé.[13] At Angers, there were two canons of the cathedral, one deputy for the four Benedictine abbeys, one for the canons regular of the abbey of Toussaint, one for the two royal chapters of the town, one for the other collegiate churches, and two curés—and these latter, being chosen by the bureau itself, were staid and peaceable characters, not the firebrands of the parishes. It was 'le comité particulier des chanoines' said a pamphleteer in 1789, denouncing the injustices under which the parish priests laboured.[14] This was an extreme case, but a law-book of 1769 regarded canonical domination as general— its recommended standard formula was: the bishop, two deputies of the cathedral, two of other chapters, and two others.[15] Bishops might chafe under the constraints of the diocesan oligarchy. In 1745, the bishop of Saint-Flour appealed to the Assembly to rescue him: he presided over a bureau with a fluctuating composition of about twenty, his cathedral having two representatives, the collegiate churches one each, and various abbots and priors also attending. At his request, the membership was reduced to seven, elected by the diocesan synod.[16] More commonly, however, there was an alliance of bishops and canons against the parish clergy, with the curés showing a growing discontent at their subordination. In 1770, a dispute in the diocese of Troyes led to the Assembly of the Clergy laying down new guide-lines for the composition of bureaux; in addition to the bishop, there would be one representative each for the cathedral, the other chapters, the religious houses, holders of benefices without cure of souls, and the curés—all to be elected.[17] Some dioceses reformed themselves along these lines, and some were compulsorily reformed by orders of the Royal Council; most remained unchanged or only superficially altered—hence, a continuing cause for discontent among the lower clergy.

If benefice holders who disputed their assessment had been able to resort to the secular courts, the autonomous system of clerical taxation would have become unworkable. There was nothing the magistrates relished more than running down hierarchical authority in the

Church and posing as the defenders of persecuted individuals. But the Church enjoyed the advantage of having special tribunals, largely under its own control, to handle tax appeals, the *chambres supérieures des décimes* at Paris, Lyon, Toulouse, Bordeaux, Rouen, Tours, Aix, and Bourges.[18] To these, each diocese of the ecclesiastical province sent a deputy, named by its bishop (and the bishops themselves could attend, except when a case concerning one of their own clergy was being heard). A representative of the archbishop presided at meetings, normally weekly. There were also three legal members, chosen by the *chambre* itself from the *conseillers* of the chief court of the town where the sessions were held, generally a parlement. It was sometimes possible to choose lawyers who were also clerics by status, the so-called *conseillers clercs*; but as these were few in number, the legal assessors were generally laymen. This ingenious combination of hand-picked lawyers and churchmen was an excuse to exclude the parlements from meddling, and the authority of these *chambres supérieures* was so solidly established, the standard law dictionary affirmed, that it was exercised even over institutions which enjoyed the specific right of taking all their litigation directly to the Crown. True, the Royal Council, in the last resort, could reverse any judgment, but generally it was content to send complaints to the Assembly for a final ruling.

At the summit of the taxation pyramid was the General Assembly of the Clergy of France. Decennially, in the years ending with the numeral '5', there would be a *Grande Assemblée*, while half-way through the interval, in the year ending with '0', there would be a *Petite Assemblée*. Theoretically, the former was for making great decisions, the latter for 'verifying the accounts'; in practice, important matters could be transacted at either. Their composition was different: to the 'great' Assembly each ecclesiastical province sent four deputies, two being bishops and two of the 'second order'; to the 'small' Assembly, each province sent one bishop and one other. There could also be an *assemblée extraordinaire*, called for some urgent reason, with deputies elected in the same numbers as for the small assemblies. This did not exhaust the emergency machinery, since the king could always ask for the summoning of an *ad hoc* gathering of such bishops as happened to be available. These were originally called assemblies of 'prélats à la suite de la Cour', and later came to be called assemblies of 'prélats présents à Paris'—perhaps one can infer that under Louis XIV the bishops came to play the courtier at Versailles, while under Louis XV they came to the capital to transact business and enjoy society. In 1749, when Machault d'Arnouville tried to compel the clergy of the frontier provinces to register their property for eligibility to a *vingtième*; in 1752, when the parlement of Paris published an *arrêt* against the archbishop; and in 1767, when the magistrates banished three ecclesiastics and confiscated their goods (over the refusal of sacraments to Jansenists), such emergency meetings of prelates were held. In 1767, there were three cardinals, nine archbishops, and twenty-four bishops present. Anticlerical wits, as usual, expressed their astonishment that so many zealous chief pastors were on hand, instead of being far away saving souls in their dioceses.

The election of deputies to assemblies was done in two stages. Each diocese sent its bishop (or his representative) and one other benefice holder to an assembly of the archiepiscopal province. In theory the non-episcopal delegate was 'elected', but hardly so in practice. In Angers, it was the so-called general assembly of the diocese, consisting of twenty-three monks and canons of the town and only two curés;[19] in some places, the prelate took whom he pleased. So the provincial meetings were packed with aristocratic dignitaries and members of the ruling oligarchy of the dioceses. The Gascon clergy, for example, meeting in 1755 (not at Auch as usual, but in Dax to mark the consecration of the new cathedral there), consisted of the bishops of Dax, Aire, Oloron, Bayonne, Tarbes, and Couseran, and the archbishop of Auch; of representatives of the bishops of Lescar, Comminges, Lectoure, and Bazas; of vicars-general from Auch, Bayonne, Bazas, and Tarbes; of canons from Aire, Comminges, Dax, and Couseran; and a single parish priest from the diocese of Oloron. (In 1756 there was one curé, in 1758 three, in 1775 two.[20])

The elections finally made in the ecclesiastical provinces were solemn manœuvres to find prestigious openings for ambitious young aristocrats. In the Gascon electoral meetings, there was an agreed rotation (not always observed) among the bishops; as for the other benefice holders, it was a question of string-pulling by prelates and whispered interventions from high society. In 1758, 1760, and 1787 it was nephews of local bishops who were elected; almost invariably in the second half of the century, all the elected were vicars-general. In the whole of France, during the reign of Louis XV, there was only one deputy to the Assemblies of the Clergy of France who was a straightforward parish priest (and the case is doubtful). The system of vicars-general (*grands vicaires*) around each diocesan bishop, apprentices to administration who were regarded as entitled to a monopoly of episcopal promotion, became universal in

France about 1720; a corporation of servants of the Crown was evolving into a self-perpetuating oligarchy. This development was rapidly reflected in the composition of the assemblies.[21] In 1725, of the thirty-two deputies of the second order, twenty-two had studied in Paris, eighteen were vicars-general, twenty-three were relatives of bishops in office, and fifteen later became bishops themselves. After 1750, it was rare for a deputy to be elected who was not a *grand vicaire*; in the assemblies of 1755–88, of the total of 128, no fewer than 115 held this rank in the dioceses, and the rest were on their way to it. They were going up to Paris to meetings of a club of the bishops and their circle. This was why the parliamentary system of the Gallican Church was so formidable, bringing together homogeneous gatherings of proud aristocrats linked by family ties and social relationships, proud of their traditions and well capable of defending the privileges and mission of the Church. Though there were some idle passengers, most were zealous for the interests of the Church and State alike, competing to show statesmanlike qualities deserving of promotion and the approbation of their peers. 'Ambition there took all its forms', said Talleyrand cynically of their meetings, 'and all its distinguishing colours—religion, humanity, patriotism and philosophy.' But the oligarchical composition of the assemblies appealed less and less to the rank and file of the working clergy who were outside the magic circle of privilege. In the form of a letter to a country parson, a pamphleteer of 1789 complained bitterly after meeting 'a young abbé just off his school bench, with no experience of life, no moral fibre, who aspires to Court favour and who has influence operating helping him to rise—likely as not a stranger to the diocese whose deputy he claims to be'. His conclusion was: 'the curés consider these so-called Assemblies of the Clergy of France as coalitions of prelates and of aspirants to the episcopate'.[22]

Under Louis XIV, the assemblies were kept in tutelage. The king would exclude a deputy he disliked by a *lettre de cachet*, or would demand that someone he favoured be elected, and he insisted that the archbishop of Paris should preside. Things were different after the Sun King died: the assemblies gained independence and control of their own procedures. They settled whatever disputes arose concerning the election of deputies; during the reign of Louis XV there were only two or three cases of exclusion by royal pressure, and these brought about by indirect means. Indeed, overt intervention would be resisted. The Assembly of 1740 nullified the election of the archbishop of Sens because he had given his archiepiscopal assemblies the impression that the king had forbidden voting for two of his fellow prelates.[23] From 1715, there was a system of alternating presidents from a panel of four to eight bishops, with one of them taking the lead in the most important business. From the deputies of the Second Order, the Assembly elected the officials who ran the day-to-day programme: the *promoteur* and the secretary. Proceedings were confidential. It was a relaxation of the rule when, in 1758, it was decided to allow bishops who were not members to be told the results of deliberations, though there was to be no revelation of the opinions expressed by individuals. Work went forward in committees, whose members were nominated (with equal numbers of bishops and others) by the senior president, who sat on all of them, along with the two *agents généraux* of the clergy. One of these bodies handled the apportionment of the tax burden among the dioceses, another scrutinized the contracts for loans, another dealt with the current application from the Crown for a *don gratuit*, and another with the verification of the debts of individual dioceses. If matters came to a vote in the full Assembly, it was usually taken by ecclesiastical provinces, a system which helped to prevent the gathering fissiparating into petty factions and competing family clans. The sense of purpose which might be expected to inspire a group of churchmen was intensified by the social homogeneity—abusive though it was—of the membership of the assemblies. Continuity was maintained because of the re-election of various bishops—not always by reason of their ability, it is true, since longevity and tenure of a see in a province with few dioceses helped. In particular, the role of leadership fell to the archbishops: of a total of 736 episcopal deputations from 1690 to 1787, 105 fell to them—or, rather, to thirteen of them, for the prelates of Embrun and of Albi were generally passed over, since their sees were undistinguished, and Lyon was hardly ever represented because its incumbents' claim to 'primacy' was rejected by the rest of the episcopate. One archbishop, Vintimille of Aix and Paris, was the senior president at all meetings from 1726 to 1745, and La Roche-Aymon of Narbonne and Reims from 1760 to 1775.[24] Both were vilified by memoir writers, but not because of any deficiency of worldly perspicuity. A comfortable permanent meeting-place helped to create a feeling of continuity and assurance in the meetings of assemblies. All through the eighteenth century, the deputies congregated at the monastery of the Grands Augustins, which provided a discussion chamber, committee rooms, and a corner for a running buffet, where less formal exchanges took place over tea, coffee, chocolate, bread, and cold meats.[25]

Proceedings were conducted with a solemn, established ceremony which affirmed the dignity and enduring tradition of the clerical hierarchy. The sessions opened with the mass of the Holy Spirit, attended by prelates in rochets and purple capes and the other clergy in long mantles and clerical hats (*bonnets carrés*), with the prior and monks of the Grands Augustins in copes bearing incense and holy water. After the gospel, all present came forward in order of seniority to kiss the book, before returning to their places to listen to a sermon which was not without its references to the conjoined poverty and loyalty of the clergy of the Gallican Church. When, after four to five months of deliberation in the case of great assemblies and two to three months for the lesser ones, the proceedings came to an end, all the battles fought were precisely recorded, and the record made available to the clergy in general. A year or two after the closure, minutes of the assembly were published in full, as well as the report of the agents of the clergy. In addition, reference works were published which made the information by which the Church could be defended easily available to the ecclesiastical lawyers. There was a collection of all legislation and legal texts, the *Mémoires du Clergé* (first edition in two volumes, 1595, the last in twelve volumes, 1700–30), and a collection of the minutes of assemblies drawn up by subjects to facilitate reference to precedents (10 volumes, 1767–81).[26]

II

The effectiveness of the assemblies in maintaining the privileges of the clergy depended, to a great extent, on the work of a small but, by eighteenth-century standards, efficient bureaucracy. The *receveur général* who was in charge of the collection of the taxes was a substantial financier (Boswell visited the one in office in 1775—'the house has no very large room', he observed, 'but is set with mirrors and covered in gold'[27]). But he was not an entrepreneur like the farmers-general of the indirect taxes of the State, making advances, then doing well out of the collecting; he was, rather, an employee, closely supervised. Ever since the Assembly of 1725, when the enraged deputies had discovered that their receiver had left 2,000,000 livres invested in the *billets* of Law's Scheme (rapidly declining in value) while borrowing real money for expenditure,[28] constant checks were made. The agents of the clergy were given a statement of income and disbursements every six months. Full accounts were rendered every five years to the regular assemblies, and by a two-thirds majority the deputies could dismiss their receiver and appoint someone else.

Between meetings of assemblies, affairs were in the hands of the *agents généraux* of the clergy,[29] able young clerics of aristocratic distinction, who were exercising their talents to qualify for a bishopric. They held office for a term of five years, being richly rewarded with a salary, expenses, gratifications, and benefices, with the final award of episcopal promotion to look forward to at the end of their tour of duty. From the king, the agents received letters of appointment as *conseillers d'état*, which gave them the right to attend the judicial branch of the Royal Council and to speak there, though not to vote. (Typically of the age, there were regulations about the type of hat they had to wear, and on 18 October 1770 the chancellor had to take the abbé Dulau aside and instruct him not to wear the aggressively ecclesiastical *bonnet carré*.[30])

Behind the agents was a well-organized bureaucracy. Its members were adept at feathering their own nests—an investigation of 1742 complained of 'the adroit avidity' of certain 'calculators of taxes' and 'couriers' who had pushed their wages up by a factor of thirty in as many years.[31] They were equally efficient, however, in looking after the affairs of the clergy. In 1748, the whole system was formalized under the *Bureau de l'agence*, which was to supervise the archives, consult the clergy's lawyers, send circulars to dioceses, and receive news from diocesan *syndics* in return.[32] Half the secret of the Gallican Church's success in maintaining its privileges lay in these archives. In 1715, the vaulted room with the barred windows and locking cupboards was organized, with an official archivist in charge, an inventory of contents, and a register which had to be signed for any document taken beyond the doors.[33] The other half of the secret was the council of six lawyers which gave consultations on judgments published by the various parlements or the Royal Council concerning Church affairs. The agents expected the diocesan *syndics* to send in all information concerning lawsuits about tithe or clerical privileges. If there was a defeat for the clergy, the causes were analysed and, maybe, an appeal against it lodged with the ministers of the Crown; if a victory, the news was circulated so all dioceses could profit by using the same arguments. In 1783, the *syndics* were invited to send in reports concerning lawsuits every three months, and there were plans, two years later, for setting up officers in each parlement town to collect information more directly. Agents came and went, but the whole process of fact-finding and indexing went on in the care of the *garde des archives*, M. de Beauvais, assisted in his latter years by M. Duchesne, his son-in-law, who succeeded him in office in 1775.[34] This legal family deserves its place in the history of the eighteenth-century Church alongside the great episcopal families, like the Rohans and the Luynes.

From 1780 to 1785, the two agents were Talleyrand and the abbé de Boisgelin de Kerdu. Effectively, the work was done by Talleyrand, since Boisgelin, discredited by his liaison with Mme de Cavanac, a former mistress of Louis XV, decided that he had already lost his hope of a bishopric and took things easily. Thus, the great diplomat served his apprenticeship manœuvring among bishops, royal ministers, and courtiers on affairs of tithe, parish registers, and unions of benefices. Now he was confronting Vergennes in defence of ecclesiastical temporalities, now standing up to the archbishop of Paris denying his right to call meetings of bishops over the heads of the agents. The king was pressed for legislation to improve the lot of the lower clergy by increasing the *congrue*,[35] to regulate the sale of books, to define the number of 'walled' towns whose benefices were reserved to graduates, to issue a declaration forbidding curés to league together against their superiors. The government was persuaded to withdraw a declaration concerning entries in baptismal registers which the parish priests had found unworkable. The parlements were persuaded to hasten the issue of letters patent confirming loans and unions of benefices. Tricky legal points were investigated: could a parlement lift a ban on a curé imposed by a bishop's diocesan court? Could a Jew of Colmar who had bought a seigneurie exercise the rights of patronage that went with it? Could a neglected meadow count as uncultivated land so that it escaped tithe when ploughed for a grain crop? All along the line, the privileges of the clergy had to be defended. Ecclesiastical property being inalienable, the lands of the abbey of Chaalis could not be sequestrated for debt: 'we defended [the monks] with regret', said the agents, 'because it seemed to us that they only invoked the privilege to protect themselves from being obliged to fulfil their obligations'.[36]

The agents were nominated by the ecclesiastical provinces in their assemblies (as will be remembered, two deputies, one being the bishop, came up from each diocese). There was an established rotation. In 1765, the provinces of Vienne and Bourges nominated one agent apiece; in 1770 the provinces of Lyon and Bordeaux, and so on at quinquennial intervals—Rouen paired with Toulouse, Tours with Aix, Sens and Auch, Paris and Albi, Embrun and Arles, Reims and Narbonne. These arrangements were the cadre within which the forces of aristocratic and episcopal influence operated. In 1775, the province of Rouen elected Pierre-Louis de la Rochefoucauld Bayers; his uncle was archbishop of Rouen, and his brother was bishop of Beauvais, where he served as *grand vicaire*. Meanwhile the province of Toulouse elected Louis-François-Alexandre de Jarente de Sénas d'Orgeval, a vicar-general of the diocese of Toulouse and nephew of the bishop of Orléans. When they retired from office five years later, the first became bishop of Saintes, and the second became coadjutor of his uncle at Orléans.[37] In 1780, the choice of the province of Aix lighted upon the abbé de Boisgelin de Kerdu, nephew of the archbishop and a *grand vicaire* in his diocese. About the same time, the province of Tours was electing Talleyrand, nephew of the archbishop of Reims. As usual, these elections had been settled quietly off the record long ago. In June 1772, the bishop of Dol had been writing to Bareau de Girac, bishop of Rennes, as he had to various other episcopal colleagues, soliciting his vote for his younger brother, a vicar-general of Nantes—'assuming always that you have not as yet contracted an engagement to someone else'.[38] The effort was vain. Among the prelates of Tours, Angers, Rennes, Quimper, Nantes, Le Mans, Saint-Brieuc, Tréguier, Saint-Malo, Léon, and Vannes, a majority had formed for Talleyrand by the meeting of 1775, where the real decision had been taken. There was a more dramatic confrontation in 1788 in the assembly of the province of Sens. The archbishop there was pushing for the abbé d'Osmond, brother of one bishop and nephew of another, to the chagrin of the bishop of Auxerre, who was recommending his own nephew, the abbé de la Bintinaye, a *grand vicaire* of his other uncle, the archbishop of Bordeaux. At the actual meeting, the archbishop of Sens was absent, supposedly overcome by the 'heat', so Cicé, bishop of Auxerre, had to preside. But he gained no advantage from his position as chairman, for a letter arrived from Versailles declaring that the king wished d'Osmond to be chosen. So he was, but the days when the clergy knuckled under to Louis XIV were gone—the Assembly annulled the proceedings, and ordered the province of Sens to make new elections.[39] There were regulations to ensure that candidates for the post of agent were in priest's orders, actually beneficed within the province sponsoring them, holding a true benefice and not just a chapel without cure of souls, and having resided there for a year before the election.[40] These rules, except for the residence, were observed, since elections were foreseen for a long time ahead, and minor details of a benefice here or there were easily adjusted. These were key posts, and they were awarded by the play of family influence within the episcopate, tempered by obscure political pressures and a determination to see the affairs of the Church efficiently run and its privileges preserved.

III

With the aid of this efficient bureaucracy, the Assembly strove to reform the archaic system of assessing and levying clerical taxes. Since the diocese was the unit of assessment, the numerous confusions over boundaries and jurisdictions compelled the Assembly to decide from time to time which diocesan bureau had the taxing authority over particular benefices. Could the dioceses of Boulogne and Amiens impose levies on their enclaves lying in more recently conquered territories which had not been incorporated within the financial jurisdiction of the clergy of France?[41] The diocese of Clermont taxed the abbey of Chaise-Dieu, but could it include the dependent priory of Poussan in the Montpellier area?[42] Could Arras, with its abbey of Saint-Vaast, include the *prévoté* of Mesnil in the see of Dijon?[43] A more serious problem was the varying loads of debt which had been incurred by individual dioceses. To raise the money for the benevolences given to Louis XIV in 1710, 1711, and 1715, the dioceses had been allowed to borrow on their own account, with the hope that they would obtain a lower rate of interest locally. Thereafter, the Assembly centralized borrowing and forbade independent initiative, and in 1735 took in hand the task of trying to force the dioceses back to solvency. Four failed to send in returns of their indebtedness, nine were found to be making no effort to repay the borrowed capital, and seven were trying, but behindhand. In 1742, the Assembly ordered the submission of a return of indebtedness every six months, and from then onwards had a standing item in its proceedings: a statement classifying the dioceses into six categories, the bottom one consisting of the hopeless defaulters. According to changes in local circumstances, these categories showed variations, but the hard core of failures always included Rieux, Beziers, Agen, Grasse, Vence, and Senez. They were all poor areas, and the benefice holders of Beziers took a long time to recover from disastrous floods, as those of Agen from famine, and those of Vence from warfare, while those of Grasse and more particularly of Senez suffered from scandalous overcharging to clerical taxation for more than a century.[44]

Here, indeed, was the most intractable problem of all, the long-standing injustice of the assessment breakdown between dioceses. Up to 1755, the assemblies shared out the burden on the basis of proportionality established long ago in 1516, revised in 1641 and 1646. Everyone knew that the figures were unreasonable. The area south of the Loire was known to pay more in proportion to its resources compared with the provinces north of that river. In 1701, the archbishop of Arles suggested drastic action to rectify the balance. Let all benefice holders be constrained to make a declaration of income, with the diocesan bureau entitled, in case of fraud, either to levy a punitive quadrupled tax, or simply to confiscate the revenues of the suspect and award him a pension of the amount shown on his return. A commission of prelates from north of the Loire would visit the south to check on procedures, and another from the south would go northwards.[45] Such an inquisitorial proposal was too unsporting to be accepted under the *ancien régime*, and anomalies grew worse. The clergy, better educated and with more contacts, compared notes with each other across diocesan boundaries; the legend in Autun was that the misdemeanours of a sixteenth-century bishop had brought down double impositions on his collaborators as a punishment.[46] Yet it was not Autun that made the running in complaining to the Assembly in the first half of the eighteenth century; it was Comminges, Narbonne, Glandève, Embrun (in alliance with Grenoble, Gap, and Saint-Paul-Trois-Châteaux), Grasse, and Poitiers. A mistake made in 1670 had been perpetuated, said Comminges; non-existent benefices were being counted, said Narbonne; Embrun and its three allied dioceses had a story of being taxed in local florins until 1515, and a mistake then being made when translating florins into livres.[47] The Assembly granted no remissions, except to Glandève, declaring that everyone should wait until a completely new taxation table was drawn up. Sure enough, the Assembly's own enquiries revealed anomalies even more scandalous than those complained of: the poor and tiny diocese of Senez had been paying four times as much as it ought,[48] and the diocese of Albi, which had barely a tenth of the revenues of Paris, had been paying as much and more.[49]

The will-o'-the-wisp of a comprehensive revaluation of all benefices of the kingdom based on the declarations of the holders as supervised by the diocesan *syndics* flitted through the discussions of various assemblies.[50] In the end, by one means or another—incomplete information of this kind, a pilot scheme in eight dioceses, information from the Crown about the value of the 'consistorial benefices' which were administered by the royal demesne in vacancies—a new tax assessment schedule was devised.[51] The concept of taxable income as against actual income was introduced, benefices being divided into categories, paying more in proportion to greater resources, but less according to greater weight of pastoral responsibilities. Taking the taxable wealth of the whole Church as rather more than 31 million, the diocese of Paris was reckoned to be worth just under 2 million, and so on down to Senez at 15,000, Vence and Glandève at 8,000, and Belley at 6,312.[52] The new tables fell far short of absolute justice; in particular, the admirable theory of exacting less from clergy engaged in the pastoral ministry was not carried into practice as comprehensively as parish priests desired and deserved. But given the complexities of the *ancien régime* and the almost universal indifference to the concept of simple honesty, it was an astonishing achievement.

IV

Apart from running the taxation system, the Assembly took upon itself, as a major duty, the presentation of the grievances of the Gallican Church on the occasion of granting supply. The complaints were always marshalled and processed ready for discussion, because the agents and the bureaucracy had been continually in session as a clearing-house and a centre for legal advice for all the dioceses. Many cases of ecclesiastics unfairly treated by the law courts or royal officials were settled by the agents themselves: it was only the more intractable instances that came to a full Assembly to be made a subject of official protest.

In the second half of the century, the assemblies were much concerned with the attempts of the secular magistrates to relieve the laity of some of their traditional obligations. The parlements of Toulouse and Grenoble were transferring from communities to tithe owner the duty of furnishing candles and other necessities for divine service, and that of Grenoble was trying to extend to all tithe the principle of compulsory alms; the parlement of Provence wanted the clergy to pay more towards the repair of their vicarages.[53] The magistrates of Brittany were the leaders of this lay attack. In 1721 they had declared the curés to be responsible for all vicarage repairs, great or small, and their ordinance stood unchanged in 1762,[54] while in 1735 they had annulled the new table of fees for marriages and funerals published by the bishops of the province.[55] Wherever the boundaries between ecclesiastical and secular jurisdiction were uncertain, the magistrates were encroaching. The archiepiscopal *chambres supérieures des décimes* dealt with disputes about clerical taxation, but if a diocesan *receveur* ran off with the cash, were the lay courts entitled to adjudicate on the financial obligations of his sureties?[56] After due investigation of faith and morals, a bishop could refuse a priest a visa for a benefice; the secular courts claimed the right to check if the refusal was justified, and if not to award the temporalities.[57] In an unprecedented intervention in 1771, the parlement of Dijon even claimed to give canonical institution as well.[58] Only the Church could lift the obligations of monastic or marriage vows; true, but the parlements argued that the civil consequences of these vows followed only upon genuine consent, and the fact of that 'consent' was a matter for purely lay enquiry.[59] Curés disciplined by their bishops could use the procedure of *appel comme d'abus* to go before the parlements; the judges might make the diocesan legal officials liable to damages for 'calumny',[60] or even lift the ecclesiastical censure altogether. Thus, in 1730, the Jansenist curé of Saint-Barthélemy in Paris, interdicted by his archbishop, was carrying on in his parish under warrant of the magistrates, 'giving invalid absolutions . . . and saying sacrilegious masses', said the Assembly.[61] This was just one of the incidents in the Jansenist furore, coming to its crisis with the Assembly's letter to the king of 20 June 1752; in denouncing the *arrêt* of the parlement forbidding the refusal of the sacraments to opponents of the bull *Unigenitus*, this letter claimed, with the full rigour of the Dominical texts, that the words of bishops are the words of Christ, and what they bind on earth is bound in heaven.[62]

The encroachments of the parlements fitted into a general pattern of developing anticlericalism which haunted the assemblies from the middle of the century. In 1745, the alarm was sounded against the illegal assemblies of Protestants and the marriages conducted by their pastors. The king was reminded of the Calvinists' 'love of a liberty that is the enemy of all authority', and was asked to enforce the laws against them, a request which was repeated in 1750 and 1775.[63] At the Assembly of 1750, the alarm was sounded against irreligious publications, especially the letters *Ne repugnate vestro bono*, on the theme of the social uselessness of the clergy.[64] Fifteen years later, it was the leading works of Voltaire and Rousseau that were condemned.[65]

In 1775, the theme of discussion was 'the decline of religion'. The Assembly refrained from lamentations about the propaganda of the philosophes, and took a practical view of the causes: there was a shortage of suitable vocations to the ministry, because of the high cost of an education lasting to the age of 24, the poverty of life on the *congrue*, the long wait for promotion, and the lack of adequate provision for retirement. The plan therefore was to confiscate benefices without cure of souls and to suppress the minor clergy of cathedrals, using the funds made available to provide free educational places, improved salaries, and official retirement pensions. Once these pensions were organized, the system of a resigning curé appointing his successor could be ended; bishops would gain more control over patronage, and would be able to encourage ability with promotion.[66]

This last proviso was typical: the assemblies were devoted to maintaining and increasing the power of the bishops. Abbeys like Cluny and cathedral chapters like Saintes, which enjoyed episcopal jurisdiction over certain parishes, were narrowly watched;[67] so too were curés who claimed the right to act collectively or to challenge the jurisdiction of their bishop.[68] In 1762, the proposal to delate the curés of Sées to the Royal Council was passed 'by acclamation'.[69]

Even so, it is remarkable how these gatherings of aristocrats fought for the Church as an institution against their own social class. Their brothers and cousins found sinecures in the Order of Malta and the Order of Saint-Lazare, but the prelates of successive assemblies waged war on these two abusive institutions. They opposed the knights of Malta's claims for freedom from tithe, for burials in their own chapels, for honorific distinctions in parish churches, for exemption for curés under their patronage from episcopal visitations.[70] The manœuvres of the Crown, from 1762 onwards, to reinforce the endowments of Saint-Lazare with the property of the decadent Order of Saint-Ruf and of the canons regular of Saint-Antoine met with unsparing condemnation. Must the clergy pay for 'the opulence and grandeur' of an institution that was 'of no sort of utility to the Church?', they asked. When the comte de Provence became grand master, increasing royal pressure compelled the clergy to offer something—but they did so with an ill grace, 'more by condescension than by justice', they bitterly minuted.[71]

V

In 1765, to forestall the condemnation by the Assembly of an injudicious pastoral letter he had written, the bishop of Alais argued that these gatherings were 'purely economic'. They were convoked solely to vote taxation to the Crown and to administer the financial affairs of the Church. If this had been true, the Gallican Church would have lived in administrative chaos, and, what is more, would not have been able to speak with a single voice in matters of doctrine and morals. Ideally, the forum for such pronouncements ought to have been a national council of bishops, but the Crown would not allow such a body to meet. The promise that some great doctrinal pronouncement by the Gallican episcopate would shed a vicarious splendour on the throne, as Nicaea had given lustre to the diadem of Constantine,[72] sounded unconvincing at Versailles. Requests for the convocation of provincial councils to deal with Jansenist bishops[73] were turned down—except for a meeting of the province of Embrun, which turned out to be a disreputable affair, not to be repeated. If the traditional councils of the Church were banned, however, there was an alternative—as the Assembly pointed out at length to the bishop of Alais. 'The right to teach and instruct is inseparable from the person of bishops and, far from diminishing their rights, their meeting together serves to give new force to their pronouncements.'[74] True, a bishop can be *judged* only by a provincial council, but when a pastoral letter has been published outside the individual diocese, it becomes a matter to be dealt with by the whole episcopate. The strict logic of this argument would demand that a doctrinal pronouncement of an Assembly should come from its episcopal members alone, and, indeed, this was what the procedures ensured. Deputies of the 'Second Order' were excluded from the settlement of matters of doctrine and morals unless their right to speak for the bishops of their province was explicitly stated in their letters of appointment. Conversely,[75] when such matters were discussed, bishops who were not members of the Assembly could attend. Thus at an extraordinary Assembly of forty-nine prelates in 1713–14, 'as only matters concerning doctrine were to be discussed, and not temporal affairs', the retired bishops of Avranches and of Tulle were present and signed the proceedings.[76] Normally, prelates took precedence according to the rank of their see, but in the Assembly they sat in order of the date of their consecration.[77] It was, as it were, a reminder that the worldly honours that went with ecclesiastical office were irrelevant: it was the interests of religion that were the essential concern of the delegates.

With this sort of justification, assemblies made the sort of pronouncements on doctrine and morals that might more appropriately have come from a national council of the episcopate. In the seventeenth century, the decrees of Trent, which had been refused endorsement by the Crown, were described, independently, as 'rules and oracles of the Church'. In 1700, various propositions of relaxed morality had been censured. A pastoral letter on the Jansenist issue for adoption in all dioceses was circulated five years later; nine years after that a statement on the doctrine of grace was issued. In 1765, all bishops were recommended to foster the cult of the Sacred Heart (the queen's favourite devotion); and, in the course of the century, applications were made to the Pope for the canonization of Mme Chantal, François Régis, Mère Agnès of Saint-Catherine de Lauzet, and Alain de Solmniac.[78] The Assembly of 1770 decided to sponsor its own venture into apologetics, issuing an *Avertissement* on 'the dangers of unbelief', followed five years later by another on 'the advantages of the Christian religion'.

The word 'catechism' is absent from the index of the collections of minutes. Maybe, as has been suggested, this is evidence of lack of interest in popular religion, but with so many diocesan catechisms available, and with orthodox and Jansenist controversialists lying in wait on either hand to pounce on any offending word, the deputies may be forgiven for letting sleeping dogs lie.

VI

Seen from Versailles, the whole point of the convocation of an Assembly was to obtain a vote of money.[79] Louis XIV established— almost—his right to have what he demanded without question. His *don gratuit* of 1665 was the last which was held up by discussion. Then, the royal commissioners had to present themselves three times, on the last occasion laying on the table the drafts of the edicts the clergy were demanding, before the grant was approved. Thereafter, the Great Monarch's absolute will prevailed: he received his vote 'without difficulty', or 'at once', as the minutes record. Even so, he renewed promises of exemption from ordinary taxation; when a *don gratuit* of 8 million was voted in 1711, it was recorded that the clergy would never have to pay to a *dixième*—'exempt in perpetuity . . . whatever may happen'. After the death of Louis XIV, supply was no longer automatic. The Crown proceeded as if it would be, but the Assembly always deliberated before agreeing, and might—just possibly—refuse if the privileges of ecclesiastics were threatened. In 1725, an edict proclaiming the levy of a new tax, the *cinquantième*, blandly included everyone, 'privileged or unprivileged . . . ecclesiastics or seculars'. The clergy had been in this situation before, in

1710–11 at the time of Louis XIV's *dixième*, and once again they managed to obtain a royal declaration exempting them. But it was a real fight and a real triumph this time. No supply was voted, and no arrangements to pay the *rentes* to State creditors were made at the 1725 Assembly, and a new one had to be called in the following year.[80] The declarations then extracted (for a *don* of 5 million) promised freedom from all ordinary taxes for the clergy in perpetuity, even if royal legislation specifically included them. Thereafter, amid the harsh demands of war, the clergy demonstrated patriotism—12 million in 1734, 10 million the next year, 3½ million in 1740, 12 million in 1742, 15 million in 1743, 11 million in 1747, and 16 million in 1748. But in May 1749, the controller-general, Machault, inserted yet another sinister preface in an edict establishing a *vingtième*—there would be 'no exceptions . . . all proprietors or *usufruitiers*, nobles or commoners, privileged or non-privileged' would pay. *Usufruitiers* presumably meant the clergy, and to establish the point circuitously, Machault ordered the *clergé étranger* (that is, of provinces annexed since 1561) to register their possessions with the *directeurs* of the *vingtième*. When, in the following year, Louis XV asked the Assembly for 7,500,000 livres, there was an outcry. D'Ormesson's speech[81] of application spoke of 'obligation', and he made formal the demand for declarations of clerical revenues, as well as revealing that the government was proposing to liquidate the debt of the clergy—no doubt as a first step in curtailing their financial autonomy. 'Our conscience and our honour', the Assembly told the king, 'will not permit us to consent to changing into an obligatory tribute a contribution which can only be the offering of our devotion.' The bishops of Languedoc forbade the intendant of their province to approach officials of their dioceses for tax information;[82] the aged bishop of Verdun published an open letter to the controller-general which was a masterpiece of sentimental obduracy;[83] the bishop of Grenoble rushed into print a three-volume defence of clerical immunities;[84] while the bishop of Metz excommunicated the intendant who was trying to extract clerical declarations.[85] The government unleashed a swarm of pamphleteers,[86] Voltaire included. 'Antichrist has come: he has sent numerous circular letters to the bishops of France, in which he has had the audacity to treat them as Frenchmen and subjects of the king.'[87] The clergy stood firm. 'On this occasion', said D'Argenson, 'the lower clergy . . . were absolutely solid with the higher, something never seen before,' and he refers to threats of putting the land under an interdict or, more practically, demanding the summoning of the

Estates General.[88] In the end, the king gave way: there was no hope
of supply from the Church unless he did. Because he had capitulated, the Assembly demonstrated its generosity in 1755, and because
of the war, further grants were made at an extraordinary Assembly
three years later, and also in 1760 and 1762. A proposal to include
ecclesiastics in a land census and their apparent inclusion in the edict
of December 1764 on the taxation of *rentes* led to a new battle of
wills; the long Assembly of 1765 withheld a third of the subsidy
requested until these threatening proposals were withdrawn.[89] Large
grants were made in 1770, 1772, and 1774; then Calonne's new
designs against clerical immunities led to a further part-refusal of
supply in 1785. Finally, in 1788, the clergy led the way in forcing the
bankrupt king to call the Estates General. Only 1,800,000 livres of
the 8,000,000 demanded was voted, and the remonstrance of the
clergy of 15 June 'lifted the aristocratic revolt on to a new plane of
dignity and universality'.[90] They had clung all the while to their
unique privilege of voting their own taxation, they said, not for
selfish reasons, but as custodians of 'the remains of the old national
franchises'. The whole nation ought to follow their example and
reclaim its rights, so long in abeyance. 'The glory of your Majesty is,
not to be king of France, but king of Frenchmen, and the heart of
your subjects is the finest of your domains.'

The downright refusal of supply was, however, abnormal.
Usually, the demands of the Crown were granted by dignified,
formal stages.[91] The clergy would go to Versailles to 'harangue' the
monarch, then six members of the Council would come to the
Grands Augustins on a courtesy visit. A few days later, the same six
would return bearing the actual royal demand. The president of the
Assembly would reply, saying how hard-up his constituents were,
and how difficult it would be to find the sum required; the councillors would then retire into an adjoining room and wait for the reply,
which was usually given on the same day. All the while, of course,
less formal discussions had gone on in the committees with the
government officials concerned. Seen from the *salle des séances* of the
Grands Augustins, the point of all that was happening was to proclaim clerical grievances alongside the grudging vote of the funds
demanded. Thus, at the extraordinary Assembly of 1782,[92] after the
bishop of Senez had preached on Exodus 35: 29, 'omnes obtulerunt
donaris', saying that paying up was a patriotic duty, the deputies proceeded to complain of the oppressions of the parlement of Toulouse
on tithe owners, of the parlement of Rennes on the bishop and
cathedral chapter of Saint-Malo, of the intendant of the *généralité* of

Caen who was trying to make the clergy pay towards the upkeep of roads, of the duc d'Orléans who was demanding payment of a feudal obligation, *foi et hommage*, from the lands of the Church within his *apanage*, of laymen who were evading tithe by switching areas of cultivation, of a peculiar new fraud concerning ecclesiastical benefices arising from a gap in the legislation on the subject, of the scoundrels who were circulating the works of Voltaire and Rousseau free of charge, and under the cover of night were throwing copies over the garden walls of nunneries. An Assembly also had a good deal of formal business to transact. The agents of the clergy would make their report, describing how the central bureaucracy had handled the matters which had arisen since the last meeting; the *receveur-général* would present his accounts, and there would be cases concerning disputed tax assessments coming up from the *chambres supérieures des décimes*. As befitted churchmen, there were charitable allocations to be made, 10,000 livres or so, partly from common funds and partly by the deputies forgoing four days' salary. In 1770, an extra 10,000 was found to give to the lieutenant of police of Paris for the families of those killed in the panic stampede at the fireworks for the marriage of the dauphin. There were pensions to be awarded to converted Protestant ministers, funds to a few favoured enterprises like missions to the Levant or seminaries at home, and gratifications to the authors of books defending religion. Less disinterested gifts were made to lawyers who had given consultations, and dignified rewards were proffered to great personages who had been helpful, in the form of 'bourses de jetons', purses of specially minted medallions.

VII

The subsidies voted by the Assemblies of the Clergy were not the only contributions made by churchmen to the State. Payments also came in from the so-called *clergé étranger*,[93] who were within the kingdom, but were not represented in the Assemblies and not subject to its assessments. The contrat de Poissy of 1561 applied only to the dioceses existing at that time; provinces united to France afterwards did not qualify for inclusion, though exceptions were made for Béarn and Navarre. Thus there was a separate taxation system for the provinces of Artois, Flanders, Hainault, Alsace, Franche Comté, Roussillon, and eventually for Lorraine. The clergy of Roussillon bought off royal taxes by the payment of agreed subscriptions. In Flanders, Artois, and Hainault, where the provincial estates voted taxation to the Crown, the clergy joined with the laity in paying their share. In Alsace,[94] ecclesiastical lands acquired after the Treaty of Munster of 24 October 1648 were liable to ordinary taxation, and lands held from before that date which were not directly cultivated by the benefice holder paid half tax. Capitation was due, though it was a special tax in Alsace, devoted to maintaining the *curés royaux*, the priests of the new parishes set up in Protestant areas. This levy could be heavy: in 1735 the bishop of Strasbourg paid 9,480 livres, nearly double his clerical taxation for that year. In addition, the Alsatian clergy, from time to time, paid a *don gratuit*. 'If the Government has been good enough to call their contributions a "free gift",' said a committee of clergy in 1788, 'it is a favour that makes no difference, for nothing could be further from being voluntary.' Even so, the dioceses of Alsace assessed themselves and, like the assemblies in the Grands Augustins, made difficulties about the level of contribution expected of them. The diocese of Bâle in 1735 audaciously offered only 3,500 livres; after a struggle it had to pay 20,000. Negotiations were complex. There were five dioceses in Alsace: Strasbourg and Bâle extensive, Spire, Besançon, and Metz smaller, and all having other parishes outside the province, and indeed, outside France altogether, under their jurisdiction. Five sets of arguments in dioceses which were not exclusively French and which were in fortress zones frequently suffering the ravages of war meant that the government could not be too exigent. In any case, in all the more recently acquired provinces the Crown was inclined to be lenient to woo the inhabitants. So the *clergé étranger* in Alsace and elsewhere escaped lightly. According to Necker, their income was about a fifth of the income of the clergy of France, but they paid only an eleventh part of the taxation voted by the general assemblies at the Grands Augustins. In 1749, Machault d'Arnouville attempted to compel the *clergé étranger* to furnish details of their possessions to the collectors of the *vingtièmes*, intending to subject them to ordinary taxation. The clergy of France held up supply until the government withdrew its claim, and the *clergé étranger* continued to pay at its modest rate until the Revolution came to absorb all individuals and corporations into a national taxation system.

When well-informed contemporaries estimated the amount that churchmen paid to national taxation, they included the votes of the *clergé étranger*; Necker, for example, put their contribution at 940,000 annually (though he was not including the capitation and the land which fell under the half-tax regulations). But there were other exactions of the Crown which were not normally included in the calculations. In times of war when the country faced defeat, the silver of churches could be requisitioned to be melted down to pay the armies. Louis XIV so ordered in 1689,[95] and Louis XV in 1759. Churches could retain such objects as were necessary for the decent performance of divine service, or to pay off debts. During the Seven Years War, some bishops obeyed Louis XV's orders with excessive zeal, instructing their curés to retain only the communion plate and a crucifix; the king had to issue new instructions authorizing the retention of everything necessary for divine service.[96] On Christmas Eve 1759, a curé of the diocese of Le Mans noted wryly that such sacrifices were not for his parishioners: 'as we have only what is necessary, indeed, not even that, we sent nothing'.[97] An extension of this emergency principle was the obligation for monasteries to receive within their walls aged or wounded soldiers, the 'oblats'. This was commuted by the Crown into a money tax. No doubt the change was to the relief of monks who cared for piety and decorum; what pleased the king was that something like a quarter of a million came in annually to the Treasury.[98] Then, there were the more indirect and stealthy impositions of the Crown. The absolute monarchy of France roared like a lion when demanding its heavy taxes, and as they were never enough, roamed like a jackal to find pickings to make up the deficit. From time to time, the dioceses, like municipalities, found that they had to buy up offices created by the Crown, or run the risk of ignorant practitioners confusing their affairs. That was why the diocese of Angers in 1778–9 paid good money to rescue the posts of apostolic notaries from the ordinary notaries, not being willing to leave applications and promotions in the hands of those unskilled in benefice law.[99] The State levied its fees on every legal transaction, and these were innumerable in a landowning Church in a litigious century. More especially, the government drew money from the clergy through its mortmain and leasehold legislation. When land came into the possession of an ecclesiastical foundation, there was a loss of secular taxation revenue to the Crown and of succession dues to the seigneurs; so compensation had to be paid. As far as the lord was concerned, churchmen might pay him *lods et ventes* one year in twenty, or they might designate 'un homme vivant, mourant et confisquant' whose death (or felony) would be taxable. For the State a compensation known as *amortissement* was paid. In November 1724 a royal edict regulated this as one-fifth of the capital value of 'noble' lands and one-sixth of that of commoners. The ruthless edict of 1749[100] made it difficult for the Church to acquire any new property at all, and what it did acquire (for example, by feudal escheat) had to be sold within a year and a day. But the *fermiers* of the royal demesne counted almost any change made in the use of ecclesiastical property as subject to the payment of *amortissement*: the rebuilding of a burnt-out house, unless it was precisely identical with the old one, unions of benefices, buildings acquired for charitable purposes, legacies in the form of annuities—all these were held to be chargeable. In 1774, one particular injustice in this programme of exactions was removed: canons and other churchmen who chose to live in smaller rented lodgings would not be charged on the leasing of their official houses. There was a catch, however—they would have to pay the *droit de nouvel acquêt*, one year's revenue out of every twenty.[101] The tax farmers of the State also collected a fee on the signing of a lease; ecclesiastics were obliged to make formal contracts before notaries, instead of evading taxation by agreements under private seal and signature. The law, perhaps, had not been clear; at least, in 1740 the Assembly paid the Crown 120,000 livres to buy off the arrears of the *droit de contrôle* which so many benefice holders had failed to render.[102] This did not prevent the intendant of Limoges, however, from charging the monks of Grandmont the usual tax on all the leases they had contracted privately since 1731.[103] Some of the demands of the *fermiers* of the tax were far-fetched indeed, and the wrath of the Assembly was correspondingly intensified: the documents establishing the dowries of nuns were held as chargeable,[104] and even curés who cultivated their own lands or gathered their own tithes were challenged to fork out on the leases that they *ought* to have been making.[105]

Did the Church of France pay its fair share of national taxation? We have seen how, quite apart from clerical subsidies freely voted, the government also extracted money indirectly under various pretexts—though it might be said that these harassments were the lot of most Frenchmen. The abbé Véri[106] argued that the *taille* and capitation paid by the contractors who farmed ecclesiastical property should also be taken into consideration; after all, these entrepreneurs took their expenses into account when bidding for their leases. What adjustments to total figures ought to be made for indirect payments of various kinds it is impossible to say. Thanks to the confusion of French finances, it is just as difficult to give exact figures for the total national burden. So only an impressionistic answer can be given on the question of 'fairness'. The monies levied by the general assemblies and by the *clergé étranger* during the reign of Louis XV averaged nearly 5 million a year, but this broad figure conceals a remarkable escalation of payments. In 1725–34, the clergy were making an annual contribution of 2,686,620; in 1765–74, of 7,352,108; in a period during which the State budget rather more than doubled, the clergy budget tripled.[107] According to Necker, in 1784 the Church was paying rather more than 10,000,000 a year; it is estimated that in the next few years the figure rose to between 16,000,000 and 18,000,000.[108] Sénac de Meilhan, an intendant in the latter years of the *ancien régime*, thought that 17,000,000 a year would have been a fair amount.[109] Thus, the Church was hardly paying its appropriate share earlier in the century, but came to be doing so in the reign of Louis XVI. As a different method of reckoning 'fairness', we might turn from comparing grand totals and look at the proportion of income paid by individual clerics as against, say, what provincial nobles paid. 'It is certain that no secular person pays as much as ecclesiastical property does,' said the abbé Véri in 1780. 'The tax demanded from benefice holders runs at a sixth or a fifth or even a quarter of the revenues of abbeys and at a twelfth, a tenth or an eighth for bishops and curés.'[110] True, assessments as between individual clerics were often unjustly calculated, giving undue favour to the great; even so, a modern calculation of the payments (after the tax reform of 1760) by eighty abbeys shows they did indeed pay a quarter to a sixth, while of thirty-nine bishops, sixteen paid over a tenth and thirteen between a tenth and a fifteenth.[111] This is more than nobles or many of the bourgeois paid. Significantly (once again, Véri points this out), the clergy, however grudgingly, almost always gave the ministers of the Crown the sum they demanded. No doubt, like the provincial estates which paid by *abonnement*, they got favourable terms because their credit was good and they could borrow to produce money quickly. Even so, had they been underpaying outrageously, one imagines that government pressure would have been more ruthless and disputes more frequent. The refusals of the clergy were in defence of their privileged independence, rather than to challenge the particular sum of money demanded. The general willingness of churchmen in their *cahiers* in 1789 to pay ordinary taxation (provided they remained an Order in the State) has been taken, rightly, as evidence of their affinities with the Third Estate and of their patriotism. But it was also evidence of their common sense: they knew they had little to lose, financially, by the change.

VIII

Lay society envied the privileges of churchmen, and was inclined to suppose—however unjustly—that they did well out of them. A hard-pressed taxpayer would see how ecclesiastics were exempt from the payment of *franc fief* (a due levied on commoners who bought noble land), from the *corvée* (forced labour, generally on the roads), the billeting of soldiers, local payments towards roads and bridges, taxes to pay off the debts of towns and provinces, and from municipal charitable levies. The lands of ecclesiastical benefices escaped tax when cultivated directly—an exasperating example would be to see a cleric selling off in bulk the wine from his vineyard exempt from the *aides*, the internal customs duties. An ecclesiastic rejoiced also in exemption on the patrimonial lands which came to him in direct succession, provided, once more, that he cultivated them directly; also on whatever property brought in the small income representing his clerical 'title', the sum needed to qualify for ordination. An envious onlooker on these accumulations of privilege might overlook the severe restrictions which, in fact, were applied to clerical immunities. Tenants who leased ecclesiastical lands paid ordinary taxation. So too did clerics on all property coming to them by collateral succession, or which they had purchased. And even that coming by direct succession could only be cultivated directly (and thus be privileged) if it lay in the actual parish of domicile; otherwise it had to be leased out to laymen subject to the *taille*. The tax farmers and officials were always hovering, ready to swoop. They argued that the possession of a benefice, as well as ordination, was a necessary condition to enjoy the immunity on patrimonial lands,[112] and if a cleric took up a lay occupation, he was conscripted forthwith for lay burdens like the *corvée*.[113]

The arguments of the laity for subjecting the clergy to ordinary taxation are found classified and enumerated in the treatises of the Gallican lawyers, who kept every precedent and every philosophical—and even theological—consideration handy for use to defend the purses of the laity. They were much the same arguments as were used to justify taking Church property in time of national emergency. A typical discussion would begin with a learned—and slanted—historical excursus.[114] In the earliest centuries, churchmen had held their possessions in common; in the fourth and fifth centuries they had divided them into four parts, with the poor and church buildings having a quarter each. Since then, laymen had been compelled to over-endow the Church by threats of excommunication and by superstitious preachments,[115] and accumulations of wealth had fallen into the hands of prelates and great abbeys. In short, we have now travelled a long way from the golden days when the austere missionary Church deserved a privilege like exemption from taxation. But in fact, the exemption had arisen along with the misapplication of the income. When the Franks conquered the Gauls, they freed the clergy from personal servitude, but not from ordinary taxation.[116] The immunity of clerics arose in the tenth century, and was maintained by the claim that the Church depended on the Pope alone.[117] The French State had never accepted this proposition, and the bull *In Coena Domini* of 1536, excommunicating those who taxed ecclesiastics without papal permission, had never been published in the kingdom. What dependence on Rome meant can be seen by looking at the unedifying causes for which popes had levied subsidies from their clergy—for crusades, onslaughts on heretics, campaigns against Christian princes, and even against rival popes.[118] Far better, like the Assembly of the Clergy in 1715, volunteer to support the king in defence of his frontiers.[119] The historical excursus would, throughout, be tailored to demonstrate how ecclesiastical immunities had arisen because of custom—by accident, not by divine right and scriptural tradition. Comparison would help here; look across the Channel to England, where the parsons pay taxes in the same way as everyone else. 'Rien n'est plus juste.'[120] Churchmen, it was always said, had the usufruct of their possessions rather than absolute ownership. The point could be taken a stage further. Their usufruct entitled them to draw an 'honest subsistence', no more; the surplus they were obliged to administer for the benefit of the poor. Church property, therefore, was 'the patrimony of the poor', who were the true, though passive owners.[121] In essence, a benefice is the right to preach, confess, and say mass, and its endowment is 'a fund that the Church has confided [to the holder] to employ for pious uses, and more especially to help the local poor'.[122] As patterns of social existence change, these various funds for pious uses need to be reallocated, and the Church authorities can do this. But who verifies that it is properly done, who checks that the subsistence taken is limited to what is 'honest', and who protects the rights of the poor? As these are questions of 'distributive justice' in society, the answer is clear: the secular sovereign must do so because he alone has the oversight of the whole social structure. 'The State is not in the Church, but the Church is in the State, which existed before it and which received it into its protection.'[123] The claim of the sovereign is double, for 'we must not confound the clergy with the Church . . . the Church is the assembly of the faithful under their legitimate pastors'.[124] The sovereign speaks for the mass of the faithful, as it were within the Church, just as he offers the Church his protection, as it were from outside it. 'Let every soul be subject to the higher powers,' says St Paul (Romans 13: 1; Titus 3: 1; cf. Peter 2: 13). St Augustine and St Ambrose say the same. Churchmen enjoying vast collective revenues need the protection of the secular arm more than other people,[125] and the gospels enjoin them to live austerely and humbly. They are, as Louis XIV observed, 'free from the dangers of war, from the wastefulness of luxury and the burden of rearing families'.[126] Therefore, they must contribute on an exceptional scale to the needs of the State and of society. And, as simple arithmetic shows, the less they pay, the more will have to come from the pockets of the laity.[127]

One of the arguments of the clergy in defence of their immunities was the need to preserve the dignity and independence of their ministry. Custodians of public morality who have the duty of rebuking sinners should not have to keep looking over their shoulders fearing the malice of the local notables and officials who assess and collect taxation.[128] Anticlericals had a ready reply: the whole independent assessment system of the clergy was run in the interests of a narrow oligarchy. Curés on the *congrue* were legally liable to pay up to 50 livres from 1690, and 60 from 1715, at a time when their pittance was only 300 a year.[129] The other curés were paying a seventh or an eighth of their income, in spite of all the pious platitudes about the indispensability of their ministry and their charitable obligations. By contrast, bishops tended to slip out of the net of strict accountability.[130] The automatic rebate of 6,000 livres to cardinals was at least according to a rule, but in the mid-eighteenth century some astonishing figures were current, which could be possible only by downright tax evasion: the bishop of Le Mans paying 1,050 livres on an income of 30,000, and his confrère at Verdun 180 on 60,000. Jacques de Grasse of Angers died in 1782 owing 16,000 from long ago, money that was never recovered.[131] Next after bishops in the hierarchy of underpayment came the canons of cathedrals, mostly aristocrats—in mid-century, those of Dijon and Besançon were paying about 1 per cent, those of Le Mans 5 per cent.[132] Reform of these abuses was slow. Benefice holders were ordered to make declarations of revenue to their diverse bureaux in 1727 and again in 1751. From this information the Assembly worked out a plan (accepted in 1760) for dividing benefice holders into eight categories of progressive taxation, taking into account both income and the usefulness of particular offices to the Church. This ought to have done much to reform abuses, but not everyone honoured the new prescriptions. A curé of Angers in 1785 accused the new bishop of paying less than a seventh of what he owed,[133] and the bishop of Quimper almost halved his contribution by having his episcopal estates and commendatory abbey assessed separately, thereby avoiding the higher rates of tax.[134]

All over France, tax officials, intendants, and municipal officers lay in wait, in a half-formulated anticlerical conspiracy, to trap the clergy into paying secular taxation. In the proceedings of the extra-ordinary Assembly of 1782[135] we hear of the benefice holders in the *généralité* of Caen, who had weakly agreed to pay a tax for the repair of the port of Grandville, because it was only for five years, and who were now being inscribed on the contribution rolls for works on the river banks. There was a bridge at Mareuil-sur-Ay (Champagne) for whose repair the curé was being charged 183 and a convent of nuns 1,650 livres. A curé of the diocese of Bourges was being compelled by the *fermiers* of the *gabelle* to buy the standard quantity of salt obligatory for commoners. 'Most often', the Assembly records, 'they attack our immunities in the persons of a few poor ecclesiastics who have no influence and are isolated from the advice they need to be able to defend themselves . . . one or two examples suffice to create a precedent.' The estates of Bresse (which came under French rule in 1601) were ordering the local clergy to pay to a *vingtième*, despite the fact that the Royal Council had ruled in 1626 that they must pay 3,000 livres annually to the clergy of France. The Assembly agreed to defend them, provided their contribution to clerical taxation was brought up to date and doubled. The estates of Provence were asking clergy and nobles to pay sixty-seven years' arrears of a local tax, having decided, belatedly, that they were liable.

Above all, there was the two-centuries-old feudal conspiracy by the Crown and the holders of royal *apanages* (in this case the duc d'Orléans and the comte d'Artois) to extract *foi et hommage, aveu et dénombrements*.[136] If they did such homage for their temporalities, the clergy would have fees to pay, and would render themselves liable to other feudal exactions. The dispute is worth lingering over, for it reveals with the sharpness of caricature the sort of rules of the game which governed the relations of Crown and Church in matters of taxation. For long—at least since 1674—churchmen had got away with evasive action, and from 1725 each Assembly had obtained a declaration of *surséance*—a stay of execution. The Assembly of 1750 had presented to it a masterly legal memorandum proving its case,

but craftily decided to postpone publishing it, given that passions
were then running so high against clerical privileges; instead, another
request for a five years' *surséance* was made.[137] In 1775, aware that the
sands were running out, the Assembly put on a brave face and asked
the king to name commissioners from his Council to adjudicate; a
committee of bishops was set up to prepare the clergy's brief, and to
this the abbé Bouquet and the ecclesiastical lawyers brought a mountain of documents.[138] In 1782, the king announced that the stay of
execution already granted to 1785 would be the last: the Council
would then judge the issue definitively on the basis of evidence
submitted by the clergy, on the one hand, and by the inspector-
general of the royal domain, on the other.

The memoranda of the two parties, published in 1785,[139] provide
contrasting views of State and society. On the royal side, the king is
said to enjoy a universal right of seigneurie, filling all empty spaces
in his kingdom wherever feudal authority is not evident; this is the
meaning of 'nulle terre sans seigneur'. Also, as 'Chef de la Police',
the monarch can enter anyone's territory to inspect, and as the
enforcer of public order he guarantees the property of each of his
subjects as against all the others. The 'liberty' the clergy ask for is that
of 'a naked savage'. The lawyers of the Assembly reply that most
Church property goes back to the days before feudalism was
invented, days of piety when a ruler would have considered it sacrilegious to impose any obligations on the free gifts of land he made
to the Church. Feudal tenures arose because of the weakness of the
monarchy; there is no reason to believe that kings now made their
gifts to religion in a feudal way, unless they specifically stated that
they were doing so. And to demonstrate that this was not done, the
clergy produced thousands of documents. They contrast their evidence with the inspector of the domain's generalities—he is proclaiming a theory of absolutism, within which he is confusing
sovereignty with suzerainty; he has no historical proofs. Laymen,
like churchmen, rely on the complex documentation of the past to
establish their ownership and their rights, so 'the interest of the
Clergy is the interest of all citizens'. It was a curious, archaic controversy which was still unresolved when Church lands were finally
put up for auction in the Revolution. In the form of a historical
debate, it summed up the contrast between the starkness of theories
of royal absolutism and State power dating from Louis XIV, and the
ancien régime's peculiar concept of liberty as a matter of tradition and
privilege, however abusive. And in another form it restated the
hypothesis which was to lead to the great Revolutionary confisca-

tion: that the clergy were *usufruitiers* of their riches, and not absolute proprietors. All roads of anticlerical debate seemed to lead in the end to this single proposition—a dry legal formula which summed up the instinctive suspicion and envy of lay society confronted by an institutional alliance of immense material wealth and lofty spiritual ideals.

PART II

THE RELIGIOUS ESTABLISHMENT

6

DIOCESES

I

In 1789, there were 130 dioceses in France.[1] Of these, 123 were grouped into twenty-eight provinces under the metropolitan jurisdiction of archbishops; the archbishop of Tours had eleven suffragans, his colleague at Sens only three—there was no uniformity. The seven other dioceses had their metropolitans outside France, for the kings had extended their borders while the ecclesiastical structure remained the same when all foreign secular authority had been annihilated. Metz, Toul, Verdun, Nancy, and Saint-Dié responded to the German see of Trier, and Strasbourg to that of Mayence, and Perpignan to Tarragona in Spain. This total of the 130 dioceses of the Gallican Church does not include Corsica, even though the island was ceded to France in 1768. Three of its dioceses were under the jurisdiction of the archiepiscopal see of Genoa, and the other was under Pisa, the last remnants of the Italian connection.[2] Though the bishops of Avignon, Carpentras, Cavaillon, and Vaison are occasionally heard of in French history, they bore no allegiance to Versailles, since they belonged to a papal enclave surrounded by French territory—an enclave occasionally occupied by the French kings, but always returned. Another bishopric mentioned as identified with French soil was that of Bethléem—the title, awarded independently by the Pope, was attached to a hospital building near Clamecy in the Niverais.[3] Just as metropolitan sway over French bishops was exercised by German and Spanish archbishops, so too French archbishops were the official ecclesiastical superiors of foreign prelates outside the national territory: Embrun was the metropolitan see of Nice; Cambrai of Namur and Tourai; Besançon of Bâle and Lausanne; and Vienne of Annecy and Saint-Jean de Maurienne.

There were extreme disparities in the size of dioceses. Rouen, with 1,385 parishes, outstripped all the others. Six had between 700 and 800 (Bourges, Sens, Dax, Clermont, Le Mans, Autun); another five had between 500 and 700 parishes (Limoges, Metz, Cambrai,

Reims, Langres). By contrast, there were tiny dioceses, mostly clustered in the South, the creation of popes who were either strengthening local church organization against the Albigensian heresy or accumulating votes on their side in some future Council to deal with the great Avignon schism. The tiniest of all were the six dioceses of Toulon, Orange, Mirepoix, Agde, Vence, and Senez, with between twenty and thirty parishes each. A bishop of a small diocese often, but not always, found himself in a provincial backwater. It was so at Senez; the episcopal town consisted of 177 houses and the cathedral—it was better to abandon the episcopal palace and lodge at Castellane, where there was a population of nearly 2,000 and pilgrims came through town to visit the sanctuary of Notre-Dame-du-Roc.[4] The town and cathedral of Glandève (a diocese with fifty-five parishes) existed no more, having been swept away in a flood; the bishops' palace still stood, but was deserted for Entrevaux two miles away, where there were 1,500 inhabitants and a cathedral whose canons were poorer than the poorest artisans, and could afford only two choirboys.[5] By contrast, there was the diocese of Toulon, consisting of only twenty parishes, but serving the naval port and dockyard, and Marseille, with thirty-eight parishes but centred on one of the biggest commercial ports of Europe.

The oddness and irregularity of the diocesan framework of ecclesiastical France were matched by the internal complexities of the individual dioceses. What appeared to be a boundary on a map[6] was not necessarily the limit of a bishop's visitation tours—he might have to go further afield to inspect parishes forming enclaves in other dioceses. In 1622, the archdiocese of Paris had been carved out of that of Sens, but the parishes of the rural deanery of Champeaux, allotted to Paris, were surrounded by the territory remaining under Sens. The bishop of Lisieux had two 'exemptions' to look after, parishes in the dioceses of Bayeux and Rouen.[7] Dol, in Brittany, was a bizarre example of geographical confusion. Of the ninety-six parishes, forty-nine were clustered round the episcopal city; the rest were enclaved elsewhere (three in the diocese of Rennes, twenty-three in Saint-Malo, eleven in Tréguier, four in Rouen).[8] Minor absurdities of boundary drawing were legion, slicing farms, seigneuries, and villages in two—like the town of Morlaix, which was half under the bishop of Léon and half under his colleague of Tréguier.

Along the frontiers of France, the complexities of ecclesiastical structure were of international importance, a concern of national foreign policy. Metropolitan authority was nominal, so the supremacy of German and Spanish archbishops over French bishops rarely presented problems. More significant difficulties arose where royal conquests had bitten deep into the territories of external dioceses, so that foreign prelates ruled over parishes under French secular sovereignty. The bishops of Ypres and of Tournai were in this position; indeed, the latter had the greater part of his clergy inside the boundaries of France. In 1789, these two splendid prelates, Charles-Alexandre d'Arberg, count, and Guillaume Florentin de Salm-Salm, prince, of the Holy Roman Empire, imposed their greatness on the clerical electors of their French areas, and so were able to present themselves as deputies to the Estates General of 1789. On 20 July the National Assembly annulled their elections and sent them packing.[9] The prince-bishop of Spire had forty-five parishes in Alsace, French by right of conquest. It was a rule of the Gallican monarchy to exclude foreign jurisdictions from operating in France without royal consent—even if the Pope himself was concerned; foreign bishops with parishes within the kingdom were required to set up separate *officialités* (ecclesiastical courts) for them, locally based. In 1749, the sovereign court of Colmar, at the instance of Versailles, took notice that the prince-bishop had failed to do so, and declared his jurisdiction in Alsace suspended.[10] Another foreign prelate with a multitude of parishes in Alsace was the prince-bishop of Bâle.[11] History had made his position interestingly anomalous. Because of the Reformation he had lost Bâle, his nominal episcopal city, and ruled from Porrentry; his metropolitan was the French archbishop of Besançon. His diocese consisted of twelve deaneries, six in Switzerland and six in Alsace. The Alsatian deaneries (totalling 237 parishes), rejoicing in resonant names (*ultra colles Ottonis, citra colles Ottonis, inter colles,* Sundgau, Masevaux, and Rhenum), were ruled by 'chapitres ruraux', which had their own coats of arms and were under the presidency of parish priests elected by their fellows. Since the patronage of benefices was unchanged by the conquest, some of the curés were presented to their livings by German noblemen, even Protestant ones; alongside them, however, the Crown had filled gaps in the parochial system with 'curés royaux', paid by the State and appointed, like secular officials, by the intendant. The system ran very largely independently of the prince-bishop at Porrentry, and in any case, he was expected to appoint a suffragan for the French part of his diocese. In the 1780s, this was Gobel, son of a Gallican lawyer of Alsace, an intriguer who was to finish up as the constitutional bishop of Paris during the Revolution. In 1786, he began his apprenticeship to ambition by laying information against the morals of the bishop of Bâle in the hope of getting a diocese separated off for himself. But changing ecclesiastical boundaries was no easy matter; what minister at Versailles could have done it for the sole reason that a bishop, making a visitation of a nunnery, had ordered singing and dancing to the music of a flageolet played by his registrar?[12]

The south-east frontier was more complex still. Here, the jurisdictional problem was the other way round, French bishops having parishes within the sovereignty of the dukes of Savoy. In Savoy itself, the diocese of Grenoble ruled a sizeable *décanat* centring on Chambéry, and the diocese of Belley had the thirty parishes of the so-called Petit-Bugey; in the comté of Nice, the dioceses of Senez, Embrun, Vence, and Glandève all had parishes—Glandève had thirty, more than it possessed in France itself.[13] At Nice and at Chambéry, the dukes of Savoy had *sénats*, courts equivalent to the French parlements and resembling them in being determined to defend the secular power against ecclesiastical encroachments and foreign interference. They claimed the right to confirm all nominations to benefices or offices made by the French bishops, gave permission or refused it for visitations of monasteries or for laymen to appear as witnesses before ecclesiastical courts.[14] The fiscal officers of the dukes, equally vigilant, confiscated the revenues of episcopal sees during vacancies, in so far as they arose from the territories of Nice and Savoy, and did not hasten to restore them when a new bishop was appointed.[15] At various times in the century France and Savoy made treaties involving the simplification of their borders. In 1713, Senez and Embrun had to surrender their parishes; in 1760, by the Treaty of Turin, Vence did so—but there was no change for Glandève. This was the treaty dividing in two the town of Pont-de-Beauvoisin, with the curious proviso that the Lenten sermons paid for by the municipality must be given on either side of the border in alternate years. In 1779, a deal was done allowing Savoy to have its own separate diocese at Chambéry independent of Grenoble; but the thirty parishes of the Petit-Bugey remained in the diocese of Belley, even though Charles Emmanuel III offered Versailles the French parishes of his diocese of Geneva in exchange. Pastoral concerns were all very well, but a fragment of ecclesiastical jurisdiction was a diplomatic lever worth retaining to gain advantages in future negotiations.

II

A map of the ecclesiastical dioceses with all their complexities is difficult to draw. One of the total structure of France, civil, ecclesiastical, and traditional, defies representation, and needs to be stored in a computer. The ecclesiastical system was not geared into the various secular systems, and, for that matter, these secular arrangements rarely fitted into each other. There were the traditional provinces, some with and some without provincial estates, and those with estates having peculiar administrative and taxation arrangements. There were the royal administrative areas, the *généralités* under *intendants* and their sub-units under the *subdélégués*; the judicial areas of appeal with hierarchies of courts going up to the various parlements; specialist courts quite apart from all these intervened to take off litigation concerning various subjects—some concerned with taxation, some with the seaports, some with customs duties, some with 'rivers and forests', others with commercial transactions. There were the various odd boundary lines within which *gabelles*, *octrois*, and local taxes were levied; there were policing areas separating the town *archers* from the countryside *maréchaussée*; seigneuries and other feudal units had their fiscal and judicial activities, and there were meaningless areas where obsolete officials by purchase did nothing importantly. All these systems operated independently. Sometimes there was a fitting together, but even then the coincidence was never exact. It was commonly said that the 'dioceses' of Languedoc were units of both spiritual jurisdiction and civil administration, with the bishop playing a dominant role in the secular business. True, but the civil and religious boundaries were only approximately the same.[16] The secular diocese of Uzès was the ecclesiastical one, with the addition of seventeen parishes owing spiritual allegiance to the papal bishop of Avignon. Similarly, Nîmes had Beaucaire and six rural parishes belonging to the archbishop of Arles. The estates of Toulouse, with the archbishop presiding, ran the secular affairs of the diocese minus part of the episcopal city itself.

In some areas, all is multilayered confusion, so that the working of accident in history seems to have been perverse. The province of Périgord had two dioceses, Périgueux and Sarlat; administratively, it was also divided into two *élections*; but there was no correspondence between these ecclesiastical and secular units.[17] The 210 parishes of the province of Roussillon centred around Perpignan, where the bishop had his seat; yet, while he had most of the parishes, he did not have all, four other bishops outside the province being involved, including a Spanish bishop who had twenty-five of them. If a bishop had an administrative dispute or a lawsuit, he might have to fight his battle in duplicate or triplicate.[18] The bishop of Quimper had fourteen *subdélégués* of the intendant in his diocese, three of them being responsible for other areas outside it; there were ten *sénéchaussées* (royal courts of first instance), appeals from three of them going outside the diocese to the episcopal towns of other bishops, Vannes and Rennes. The bishop of Tarbes presided over the estates of the province of Bigorre, with 201 of his 294 parishes within the provincial boundaries. But ninety-three of his parishes belonged to other territorial units: twenty-five to the vicomté de Nébouzan, seven to the Pays des Affites, six to the comté de Pardiac, and seventeen to the province of Béarn. The others were in the valleys of the Pyrenees where the mountain folk ruled themselves in village assemblies, paying more attention to their big local proprietors than to government officials, and having more affinities with the Spaniards grazing their flocks on the high pastures than with the French of the plains.[19] The bishop of Autun had two parlements to reckon with, Paris and Dijon, and two intendants, one based at Dijon, the other at Moulins; in addition, there was the complication of his eighty-four parishes within the quasi-independent comté of Charolais, and twenty others within the boundaries of the dioceses of Châlons and Mâcon.[20]

III

To bring some degree of logic into the diocesan structure, it might have seemed that the first step was to unite some of the tiny bishoprics clustered in the South. The difficulties in putting through a union were almost insuperable.[21] Local interests would muster to defend the *status quo*. The prestige of the episcopal city, employment, and expenditure with local tradesmen were involved; aristocratic families would have had the bishopric earmarked as an appointment for one of their sons. The legal procedures for a union ground along slowly. By the canonical rules the metropolitan and the neighbouring bishops had to be consulted, as well as their collegiate chapters; to this the secular lawyers added the proviso that the 'consent of the people' ought to be sought, whatever that might mean. Then the Pope had to approve and issue his bulls. And in any case, a double vacancy had to be contrived, holding one see under an administrator until the other fell available. It was easier to carve new units out of the excessively large dioceses: this would enlist local pride and aristocratic ambition, rather than alienating them. The advantages were obvious: from sprawling cumbersome areas more manageable pastoral units would be fashioned. On these grounds of pastoral efficiency the new dioceses of Paris (1622), Albi (1675), and Blois (1697) were created.[22] A different motive operated when Alais was detached from Nîmes in 1694, since Nîmes had been a diocese of modest size; the two new units were small indeed—eighty-four and eighty-eight parishes. Here was the devastated fortress country of the Protestants of the Cévennes, isolated in their mountains and embittered by their forced conversion—closer episcopal supervision was deemed to be needed to attempt to make their Catholicism real.[23] For over a century Langres, with 619 parishes, had seemed ripe for division, with Dijon the obvious new episcopal city and the existing archdeaconry of that name furnishing convenient boundaries. After six years of negotiations with Rome, bulls were received in April 1731 detaching 135 parishes (together with nineteen from Besançon in a rounding-off exercise) to form the new unit. The abbey of Saint-Etienne became the new cathedral, and its abbatial revenue supplied the basis of an episcopal income, with supplements from other monasteries. The difficulties inherent in establishing an entirely new administration were alleviated by the choice of Jean Bouhier, son of a magistrate of the parlement of Dijon and already dean of the Sainte-Chapelle there.[24] His legal expertise was called on again in 1741 when the new diocese of Saint-Claude was created, joining eighty-one parishes from Lyon and seven from Besançon. Heroically, at the age of 76, Bouhier accepted a translation to become the first bishop. He completed the organization and published statutes in a synod in 1743, then resigned to take a well-earned rest, which turned out to be brief. The town of Saint-Claude, with a rich abbey whose church provided a cathedral and whose abbatial revenues endowed the bishopric, was an excellent centre for episcopal administration for an area not easily accessible from Lyon. There was, however, a hidden agenda behind this new creation. The monks of the abbey, aristocrats living in comfort in independent little houses around their great church, were haunted by fears of reform: as they submitted to the king in 1691, 'if they lived in the rigour of a more severe rule, it would be difficult to find persons of quality—such as they are and always have been—who would wish to join'. Hence, they applied to be transformed into secular canons, and the change was part of the deal when the new diocese was formed. Far from being grateful for their conversion to canons of a cathedral, the ex-monks made life difficult for the inexperienced young bishop who succeeded tough old Bouhier.[25]

The huge diocese of Toul would long ago have been divided if pastoral considerations had ruled; but it straddled France and Lorraine, so politics prevailed. The dukes of Lorraine wanted their territories liberated from the jurisdiction of the French bishop by the creation of new dioceses at Nancy and Saint-Dié; the French king, unwilling to relinquish any levers of influence outside his boundaries, refused. In 1737, however, Lorraine fell to Stanislas, father of the French queen, and in 1766 reverted to France altogether. Now, Louis XV saw no objection to change—indeed, he saw advantages in pleasing the Lorrainers by letting them have their own bishops. In 1773, when the see of Toul fell vacant, he appointed a new prelate, brought from the poor see of Senez with the express provision that he agreed to sacrifice some of his territory. The cathedral chapter of Toul made difficulties; it was bought off by being granted 'noble' status, together with some extra endowments from monastic revenues, precedence over the chapters of Nancy and Saint-Dié (now to be elevated to cathedrals), and, not least, a mark of sartorial distinction for its canons. The canons of Saint-Dié had been given the right to wear a pectoral cross by Stanislas, but now Toul would out-vie them utterly, with an eight-pointed cross in gold and enamel, adorned with a fleur-de-lis and the figure of St Stephen, to be suspended round the neck on a red ribbon edged with purple. In 1777, papal briefs established the two new dioceses (Toul still had 645 parishes left). There was rejoicing in Lorraine and complaints in France. Some ecclesiastical business left the city of Toul. There were wrangles about which catechisms and liturgical books should be used, and news came of Saint-Dié and Nancy ousting the saints of Toul from their observances in favour of their own. Struggles for precedence among the clergy of the diocese of Nancy prevented the new bishop from organizing it into archdeaconries and rural deaneries. Two rural deans of Toul who had lost parishes from their jurisdiction embarked on lawsuits. The feather-bedding canons of Toul were regarded as traitors and pilloried as 'crucimanes'.[26]

By this readjustment of ecclesiastical boundaries and jurisdictions, the Crown was strengthening its power on the borderlands of the kingdom. It had been a subsidiary motive for creating Dijon and Saint-Claude earlier. In the 1780s another borderland project was mooted, a new diocese with Lille as the episcopal city. This was never done.[27] The last new creation before the Revolution was

Moulins, carved out of Autun (forty-seven parishes), Clermont (ninety), and Bourges (eighty). Here was a case where Louis XVI broke the rules of procedure to enforce speedy change, perhaps because of his concern for pastoral efficiency, perhaps because the case for the reform seemed so obvious, Moulins already being a major administrative centre, the seat of an intendant ruling a vast *généralité*, and of one of the new provincial assemblies. The arch-bishop of Bourges and his cathedral chapter and the chapters of Autun and Clermont registered opposition, and the bishop of Mâcon delayed his verdict. Even so, with only the bishops of Autun and Clermont agreeing, on 17 April 1788 the king signed the decree for the new diocese, and named the abbé Gallois de La Tour, dean of the chapter of Moulins, as the first bishop. Only on 27 April did the government ask for the Pope's consent.[28] There was ample material here for those endless lawsuits characterizing the *ancien régime*, but the Revolution intervened, and the National Assembly redrew the entire map of France, making new administrative units, the *départements*, and making all the dioceses conform to them. Among the motives of the vast majority of bishops for rejecting the Civil Constitution of the Clergy, here is one whose importance has been understated. By canon and civil law and by tradition, the universal change of all the diocesan boundaries by mere legislative fiat was an astonishing innovation.

IV

Amid all these complexities of structure, what held the Gallican Church together? It was a church with a highly developed sense of identity, and its aristocratic bishops were bound together in an oligarchical esprit de corps. Even so, there was no central direction, and the Crown was determined this would remain so. Though the Pope had authority in morals and doctrine, his rescripts could not be published in France without royal permission. National councils were not called, and provincial councils were rare. The eighteen archbishops had their ecclesiastical courts of appeal from the courts of the dioceses of their province, and certain rights of precedence when meetings were held to choose deputies to the Assembly General of the Clergy, but the rank-and-file bishops would not allow them any meaningful inherent superiority. On 10 January 1734, the archbishop of Narbonne, as president of the estates of Languedoc, had his cross carried before him at a Te Deum in

Montpellier. Colbert, the local bishop, began a lawsuit against him. The other bishops backed Colbert, even though he was a Jansenist under the ban of Versailles. On 30 October Massillon wrote to him:

The enterprise of Mgr de Narbonne concerns the whole episcopate. If it is allowed to stand it constitutes an overthrow of our rules, leaving us little more than the title of delegates of our metropolitans in our diocese. Established as bishops by the authority of Jesus Christ and not that of the Roman pontiff, they (the metropolitans) form with us a single united episcopate which we, as individuals, share with them.[29]

The most prestigious archbishopric of all was Paris. With 472 parishes it was far from being the biggest, but its revenues were immense, its population enormous, and the archbishop had all the great, from the king downwards, within his pastoral responsibilities. 'By your office you are not only charged with the care of the diocese of Paris, but also of the whole clergy of the Church of France,' wrote the bishop of Châlons to his brother, promoted to the capital.[30] 'Every archbishop of Paris', wrote a canon of Notre-Dame at about the same time, 'who has guile and style (*manège et élévation*) and who applies himself to win people's hearts, will always be considered as head of the Gallican Church, and the court will show him deference, even if not well disposed to him'.[31] But during two long reigns, those of Louis-Antoine de Noailles and Christophe de Beaumont, the see was held by a prelate who was head of a minority faction, the one of Jansenists, the other of ultramontanes. The patience of the Court wore thin with both of them, and in the end Versailles was using the ancient claims to 'primacy' of Lyon to end disputes in the diocese of Paris over the head of its intransigent archbishop.

In fact, seven archbishops claimed the title of 'primat'.[32] Bordeaux and Narbonne were simply 'primat', Bourges 'primat des Aquitaines', Lyon 'primat des Gaulles', Reims 'primat de Gaule-Belgique', Vienne 'primat des primats', which appeared to outrange all the others, but in fact meant nothing. Except in the case of Lyon, this claim to superior authority was largely unrecognized and rarely invoked. It might mean that there was a court to deal with appeals from the courts of the archbishops, or the possibility to intervene to grant a visa for a benefice if all other means of filling it had been blocked by legal obstacles; thus, in 1745, the archbishop of Bourges, using his claim to have the last word in jurisdiction in all the dioceses of Aquitaine, allowed the abbé Lahitère to proceed to a canonry in the cathedral of Aire—his provisions from Rome having been turned down by the local bishop and the archbishop of Auch.[33]

The archbishop of Lyon enjoyed the title of 'primat des Gaulles' from the bull of Pope Gregory VII of 1079; the lawyers defined his primatial jurisdiction as extending over the archbishops of Sens, Tours, and Paris and all bishops in the area of the jurisdiction of the parlement of Paris. A royal decree confirmed his precedence in 1661, on the occasion of the marriage of Louis XIV. Bull and decree notwithstanding, the archbishops of Sens, Tours, and Rouen always resisted these claims. At the end of the seventeenth century, after bitter words about precedence had been exchanged in the royal chapel, the archbishop of Lyon went to law against his colleague of Rouen, and lost with costs. In 1707, the Pope and the Royal Council confirmed the metropolitan of Normandy in his claim to independence.[34] For all its importance, however, Paris was firmly under the metropolitan jurisdiction of Lyon—it was just a question of whether the king would allow it to be exercised. When Cardinal Noailles refused to publish *Unigenitus* in 1714, Louis XIV was assured by his lawyers that the primate of Lyon could intervene by issuing three summations and, failing compliance, publish the bull in the diocese of Paris himself.[35] The weary king refused to stir up more trouble. From mid-century, it was a question of dealing with the fanatical intransigence of Archbishop Christophe de Beaumont. In 1758, the Royal Council got the new archbishop of Lyon, Montazet, to annul a decree of Beaumont prohibiting the nuns of La Miséricorde, faubourg Saint-Marceau, from electing a mother superior. Fresh from this triumph, Montazet published his *Lettre de M. l'archevêque de Lyon, Primat de France, à M. l'archevêque de Paris* (1760) setting forth his rights, changing 'Gaules' to 'France' to head off those who might doubt the scope of ancient phraseology. In 1765, Montazet was called in to validate the uniting of certain benefices to the *collège* of Louis-le-Grand, since Beaumont was refusing to co-operate because he objected to the expulsion of the Jesuits. In the same year the curé of Saint-Sulpice resigned, and the patron named one of the vicaires to succeed him. Beaumont rejected the nomination, Lyon gave the necessary provisions, and Beaumont therefore interdicted the new man from ministerial functions. Pastoral chaos at Saint-Sulpice was avoided by M. de Lau, the old curé, withdrawing his resignation and winning a lawsuit before the Grand Chambre for restitution to his altar and vicarage. About the same time the abbé Couvret moved into a canonry at Notre-Dame by resignation of the previous incumbent; at the instance of the parlement of Paris the archbishop of Lyon provided the visa, Beaumont refusing it, and the canons leaguing together to send the new man to Coventry.[36]

These contentious affairs of appointments, jurisdiction, and precedence were of great concern to the prelates, but in the last resort they did not involve the leadership of the Gallican Church. If this was found anywhere it was in the assemblies of the clergy convoked by the Crown for taxation purposes. In these meetings, the role of leadership which the archaic claims to 'primacy' did nothing to confer, fell to the archbishops—or rather, to those of certain sees who were able and willing to conduct high political business. Half the deputies from the ecclesiastical provinces were bishops, with the metropolitans predominating (of 736 deputies from 1690 to 1788, 205 were of archiepiscopal rank). Those of Albi, Embrun, and Lyon were hardly ever present (Lyon because the claim to primacy roused general suspicion), and Reims was represented only from 1766 to 1776, when La Roche-Aymon, dominant at Court, held the see. The metropolitans of the great and populous sees of Paris, Rouen, and Bourges were always there, so too those of Narbonne and Toulouse, who *ex officio* played a major secular role, as well as an ecclesiastical one, in the South.[37] Except from 1701 to 1716, when the archbishop of Paris was president, this high dignity fell to the senior archbishop present, who thus became the leading negotiator for the clergy with the ministers of the Crown and the magistrates of the parlement. Since the assemblies were indispensable to the monarchy for the voting of money, the prelates made them a forum for formulating the policies and grievances of the Gallican Church and pressing its demands upon the government. Continuity came from the two agents-general and their bureaucracy running business in the intervals between the quinquennial meetings. As so often under the *ancien régime*, ways of getting things done were found outside the archaic structures and hierarchies.

V

By ancient custom, dioceses (the episcopal town apart) were divided into the major administrative units of archdeaconries, *archidiaconés*. A small diocese might have two or, even, just one, but the correlation with geographical extent, population or number of parishes was distant. Reims and Quimper (517 and 263 parishes) each had two. Of dioceses with between 700 and 800 parishes, Autun had four,

Sens five, Le Mans seven, Bourges eight; the 1,385 parishes of Rouen were shared between only six *archidiaconés*. In their turn these major units were divided into deaneries, sometimes called 'rural deaneries' (*doyennés*, sometimes called *ruraux*, sometimes *champêtres*). There were other names for the deaneries—*archiprêtrés* was common; around Albi they were *claveries*, around Cahors and Comminges *congrégations*, around Rodez *voyages*. 'All this variety of names refers to exactly the same thing', said a writer in the *Mercure géographique* of 1678.[38] There was little logic beyond that of history in the size and number of these variously named groupings of parishes. In the diocese of Paris, each of the three *archidiaconés* was divided into two *doyennés*; the four *archidiaconés* of Autun had ten, six, five, and four *archiprêtrés* respectively; Reims had thirteen *doyennés* in one group and ten in the other; Quimper had three in one and two in the other. As ever, there were oddities and exceptions. In Paris, the parishes of the Cité, the island, and the right bank of the Seine were in the *archiprêtré* of La Madeleine, and the left bank and the south in that of Saint-Séverin, neither of those two units being within the scope of any of the *archidiaconés*. There was also in the Paris diocese a *doyenné* of Champeaux which was in Brie but not in the jurisdiction of the archdeacon of that name; nor was it in that of either of the other two, the *grand archidiacre* and the *archidiacre-de-Josas*.[39]

An archdeacon was generally a canon of the diocesan cathedral; he might receive the emoluments of a simple canon or have additional allowances as well; he might enjoy precedence among the dignitaries of the chapter or not.[40] In some cases, he was entitled to make ancient and unpopular exactions—the *droit de déport* (taking up to a year's revenue from a benefice in a vacancy) or the *droit de dépouille* (the right to certain perquisites on the death of a curé—his best bed, cassock, surplice, and horse, or a fee in lieu thereof).[41] The bishop appointed an archdeacon with the agreement of the cathedral chapter. The archdeacon's duties differed from diocese to diocese: according to the standard law dictionary of the day, 'usage and possession are the only rules to consult to know the rights of the different *archidiacres*'.[42] But whether his powers were extensive or limited, they could be broadly defined as exercising jurisdiction in the name of the bishop and conducting the visitation of parishes by his authority. If he descended on a parish in formal visitation, he was entitled to levy a fee, one which the local people were inclined to regard as excessive, considering that they did not wish to be visited anyway, but which appeared trivial to the recipient. One hamlet in Brittany had fifteen houses, and the parish priest had an income of

900 livres; another had ninety-six houses and the curé drew 1,000 livres; when the archdeacons (of Evreux and of Ouche) came on visitation, their fees were 7 livres, 7 sols, 6 deniers, in one case and 3 livres, 15 sols in the other. It was custom which fixed these sums, disproportionate between the two places and with the church-wardens paying most of the fee in the first case and the curé paying most in the second.[43] The *droit de visite* had originally consisted of the right to a good dinner, this having been generally commuted to a money payment. With the proverbial rapacity which medieval satirists attached to his office, the archdeacon of Rennes in 1718 tried to exact both the fee and the dinner; the *présidial* found for him, but the parlement overturned the verdict on appeal.[44] One of the demands of the curés of Le Mans in their *cahier* of 1789 was to be visited only by their bishops, never by the archdeacon—evidence that archidiaconal visitations still took place, but also for their unpopularity.[45]

Bishops were disinclined to work through archdeacons. Once appointed, they remained ensconced in their niches, maybe growing old in exactions or idleness. In spite of the potential importance of their office, they could dispose of it by resignation, as with any other benefice. Between 1760 and 1763 the three archdeacons of Lisieux named their successors in this way. A bishop might thus be confronted by a chief administrator he could not trust, or even face a dynasty growing accustomed to rule. Therefore, whether as zealous reformers, dictatorial aristocrats, or even as slothful prelates wanting a quiet life, the bishops turned against the archdeacons. From the end of the seventeenth century the bishops undercut their archdeacons' privileges and their role as visitors of the parishes in their archdeaconry. This was possible, for by law an archdeacon could not follow up his visitation by publishing ordinances or disciplining erring curés—all he could do was to report to diocesan head-quarters.[46] In 1741, the bishop of Langres issued orders to his archdeacons, putting them in their place; he wanted more detailed reports from them, but they were 'to observe and not to issue orders', except in emergency.[47] Three years later, in his synodal statutes, the bishop of Boulogne instructed his archdeacons to make annual visits 'in the places where we cannot go in person'— their role was supplementary. Also, he laid visitation duties more emphatically and directly upon his rural deans, giving them wide powers to absolve reserved cases, bless church ornaments, distribute the consecrated oils for use in baptism and extreme unction, and fill vacant cures with temporary incumbents.[48]

True, there were dioceses where the archdeacons remained active throughout the eighteenth century—Sées, for example. Under the reign of scandalous and negligent prelates, like Jarente at Orléans or Grimaldi at Noyon, archidiaconal visitations within the areas of their jurisdictions are the only ones we hear of. After the death of Noailles in 1729, visitations in the diocese of Paris were irregular, which left the way open for the archdeacon in the cathedral of Notre-Dame to emerge in a flurry of activity in the 1760s. Zealous bishops—Colbert at Montpellier, all those who ruled the tiny see of Orange, the occupants of the see of Nantes after 1746—did all their own visitations. When circumstances or inclination persuaded bishops to delegate, they were free to choose any of their clergy: to investigate the state of a chapel, for example, they might call in a neighbouring parish priest. In some dioceses, they bypassed the archdeacons and called on the rural deans to act. In Montpellier after Colbert, Berger de Charancy, a great visitor himself, used them (*archiprêtres*, as they were termed) to do 'verifications' as a follow-up to ordinances he had issued concerning a particular parish. His successor, in addition to travelling round himself, used the *archiprêtres* more widely, not only for verifications but also to make the visitations in the first place. Then came Raymond de Durfort (1766–74), not very active himself, but using the *archiprêtres* everywhere (with a resort to *grands vicaires* from 1770 to 1772). Malide (1774–91) continued the policy, though doing a great deal of the travelling himself. In the dioceses of Metz, Rodez, and Reims this same turning to rural deans is evident. But it was more usual to turn to a *grand vicaire*. When archdeacons are found on visitation tours, it is usually by virtue of a commission of *grand vicaire* rather than by their own authority—like Nicolas-Joseph de Paris, archdeacon of Pithiviers and vicar-general of bishop Fleuriau d'Armenonville at Orléans, right-hand man of his bishop and his assistant in constant visitations, and later his successor in the bishopric.[49] In the diocese of Langres in the first half of the eighteenth century, the bishops ordered visitations by both archdeacons and rural deans; by 1733, they were relying more on the rural deans; in the second half of the century they turned to their *grands vicaires*.[50] That cynical master of efficient administration, Loménie de Brienne, used *grands vicaires* exclusively in his archdiocese of Toulouse. It was the way to break through local torpor and assert episcopal authority.[51]

The *grands vicaires* were agents of the bishop pure and simple, commissioned to exercise jurisdiction in his name over the whole diocese, and revokable at will. If the see fell vacant, their powers lapsed at once.[52] Their office was unpaid, and they lived on some abbey held *in commendam* or canonry or ecclesiastical sinecure—whatever their patron was able to find for them. Throughout the eighteenth century, their numbers increased. There were six at Lisieux in 1717, nine in 1788; three at Rennes in 1710 and six in 1779; four at Bordeaux in 1730 and twelve in 1789. The importance of the office increased as the Crown came to choose its bishops from their number, after mid-century, almost exclusively. By 1725, half the non-episcopal deputies to the assemblies of clergy were *grands vicaires*; by 1750 practically all were.[53] The standard explanation for their multiplication is the Crown's insistence on administrative experience in a diocese as a qualification for the episcopate, leading to a rush of aristocratic candidates for the office and to the willingness of the aristocratic bishops to gratify their friends by appointing more of them. Even so, if there were extra passengers being added to the ship, the importance of key members of the crew was increasing, and the bishops needed more *grands vicaires* to help them run their dioceses.

The *doyens ruraux*, *archiprêtres*,[54] and so on were the bishop's confidential men in the oversight of a group of parishes. Even if, as was sometimes the case, they were put up by the archdeacon or proposed by election by their fellow curés, they were appointed by the bishop and revokable by him. The extreme limits of what their episcopally defined powers could be were listed by Bishop Roquette of Autun in 1690; they could absolve reserved cases in the confessional; if sent by the bishop, they could conduct a visitation; or they could go informally into parishes to help, for example, in training a schoolteacher or a catechist. If the bishop wanted to hold a synod, they would do the organization. Also—and this was probably their most important duty—they were to write to the bishop every three months to inform him of the state of the parishes and to report on any scandals. The commission of a rural dean would state specifically that it lasted only 'tant qu'il plaira à l'évêque', only so long as the bishop pleased.[55] There was thus no reason to distrust them (unlike the archdeacons), and in a well-organized diocese the bishop and his *grands vicaires* would make great use of them.

VI

Every diocese had its ecclesiastical court, the *officialité diocésaine*. Appeals could be made from its jurisdiction to the court of the archbishop of the province, the *officialité métropolitaine* (or *archiépiscopale*).

Where a *primat* had effective rights, as had the archbishop of Lyon, there was the theoretical possibility of taking a case further to the *officialité primatiale*. The system seemed straightforward, but nothing ever was under the *ancien régime*. There were *officialités* attached to ecclesiastical institutions other than dioceses: the chapter of Notre-Dame and the two Sainte-Chapelles at Paris, the cathedral of Saintes, the cathedral at Orléans all had their courts for the use of a dozen to a score of dependent parishes.[56] There was also a fossilized relic of one in the little town of Villedieu-les-Poêles serving the citizens and those of the nearby Villedieu-lès-Bailleul. For long, its legal personnel consisted only of the curé, and by 1782, he had ceased to act. The local people were angry at having to go further afield for dispensations to marry within the prohibited degrees, and in 1785 confusion ensued when a husband and wife petitioned for separation, one going to the *officialité* of Coutances, the other to that of Rouen.[57] The parlements would have no dealings with ecclesiastical courts located outside the boundaries of their jurisdictions; so where a diocese was divided between the spheres of different parlements, the bishop was obliged to have a second *officialité*, known as an *officialité foraine*, away from his episcopal city and on the other side of the dividing line.[58] Thus, while the dioceses of Autun, Limoges, Toul, and Sées had ecclesiastical courts near their cathedrals corresponding with their local parlements (Dijon, Bordeaux, Nancy, and Rouen), they had others corresponding with the parlement of Paris at Moulins, Gueret, Bar-le-Duc, and Mortagne. The dioceses of Lyon, Puy, and Tarbes were within the areas of different parlements, but the king had granted them exemption from the rule, since there was no subsidiary town of sufficient importance to house a law court. An archbishop was under the same constraints as an ordinary bishop: he had to duplicate his *officialité métropolitaine* if any of the dioceses of his province ran into the jurisdiction of other parlements. Thus, the archbishop of Bordeaux had an *officialité métropolitaine foraine* at Poitiers covering appeals from his suffragan dioceses of La Rochelle, Poitiers, and Luçon to correspond with the parlement of Paris. In two dioceses, without any explanation from conflicting areas of secular jurisdiction, an additional *officialité* just happened to exist: the bishop of Bayeux had an extra one at Caen, and the bishop of Coutances had two, at Saint-Lô and Vallogne.[59] Scattered around the frontiers were also the ecclesiastical courts of the foreign bishops who had parishes within France, as the archbishop of the papal enclave of Avignon had for the seventeen parishes under his ecclesiastical jurisdiction in Languedoc.[60] Similarly, outside France were the *officialités* of the French bishops who exercised pastoral sway over parishes in Nice, Savoy, and Germany; staffed by local lawyers, they figure only marginally in the history of the Gallican Church.

In addition to his main ecclesiastical court, a bishop had to have a diocesan registry.[61] Though this would probably be housed in the same building or, certainly, nearby, it was, strictly speaking, a royal institution, the clerk being a layman and a crown employee. Here, copies of all letters of ordination, signification of degrees to patrons, minutes of the taking possession of benefices, and so on had to be filed. All this documentation had to be on expensive government-stamped paper: in the first instance, this was a taxation office, though it also served as a place of ecclesiastical record, whose archives might well have to be consulted by the lawyers of the *officialité*.

The minimum staff for an *officialité* consisted of the *official* (that is, the judge) himself, the *promoteur* (the investigator and prosecutor), and their *greffier* (clerk). The *official* had to be a priest with a degree in law or theology and not belonging to a religious order (with the curious exception of any monk who came from the abbey of Fécamp).[62] Like as not, he would be a canon, probably of the cathedral. The *promoteur* had an unpleasant role to play, for he faced the inevitable difficulties of all those who have the duty of exercising discipline in society. As the learned abbé Bexon, refusing the office in the diocese of Toul, observed: if he reported the faults of the clergy to the bishop, he would be 'regarded as a hard man, perhaps even a persecutor', while if he failed to do so, the bishop would regard him as 'culpably tolerant'. There were other dangers too, for the secular judges would not countenance an 'odious inquisition' into the morals of the laity, and he was liable for damages if he challenged those of an ecclesiastic without convincing evidence.[63] In a populous diocese, additional staff were needed. Paris had a deputy for the *official*, two for the *promoteur*, and an administrative back-up of four attorneys, an usher, and a beadle. The *officialité métropolitaine*, with a different *official* and *promoteur*, used the same administrative services, so the meetings were set on Tuesdays and Fridays, with the diocesan court on Wednesdays and Saturdays. Taking into account the *officialités* of the cathedral, the Sainte-Chapelle, and the other Sainte-Chapelle out at Vincennes, the court of the cathedral chapter for its jurisdiction over elementary schools, the feudal court of the archbishop's *duché-pairie*, and the *bailliage du Banc du Chapître de l'Église de Paris* dealing with civil and criminal cases in and around the cathedral, the lawyers of the capital did well out of the affairs of the Church.[64]

The scope of ecclesiastical courts was wide in appearance, but in practice was constrained within strict boundaries set by the Crown and the secular magistrates. Crimes and offences against public order were matters for the lay judges: not just murder, rape, sodomy, and the like, but also offences which had ecclesiastical contexts—aggravated blasphemy, sacrilege, fighting in a sacred building, a priest marrying people outside his own parish, and so on.[65] Otherwise, priests, deacons, subdeacons, and monks were, as 'clercs', exempt from the lay courts—the summary justice of the *prévots des maréchaux* and the routine justice of the *présidiaux*. Quite often, however, a crime like murder would be dealt with conjointly by both lay and ecclesiastical justice, whether because an accused clerk exercised his right to insist on a dual review, or because the bishop issued letters of vicariate to enable the lawyers to proceed this way.[66] The broad immunity of clerks in civil cases was also subject to limitations: the clerk had to be the defendant, not the accuser, and the matter must not concern property, commerce, the payment of servants' wages, precedence in public places, and the interests of the Crown.[67] In some provinces, local custom also left the clergy open to a civil suit, as in Normandy, where the 'clameur de haro' could be raised. If two ecclesiastics were in litigation against each other, it might seem as if the ecclesiastical courts would have a monopoly—true, except where wills, church benefactions, the light before the reserved Sacrament, pew rents, the election of churchwardens, fights in church, the keeping of registers, the delineation of boundaries, and the sacking of vergers were concerned. The administration of the sacraments and the burial of the dead were the affairs of the clergy, but the secular magistrates were watchful all the same, for what if a lay parishioner was being insulted by a public refusal? Vows of religion were, more than any other matter, an exclusive affair of the *officialité*, but in these cases, as indeed in any others, there could always be the invocation of the *appel comme d'abus*, the final weapon by which the clergy could be defeated.

Much of the business of an ecclesiastical court concerned applications for dispensations to marry within the prohibited degrees, and these were numerous, for in small places everyone was related to all the others, and the prohibitions were extensive, including 'spiritual affinity', which precluded godparents from marrying their godchildren. The secular courts, however, monopolized marriage cases where the actual fact of the marriage was disputed, where promises had been broken, abduction was alleged, where dowries and inheritances were concerned. There was no divorce, the only remedy for marital breakdown being a decree of judicial separation, 'séparation de corps et d'habitation'. Generally, the petition would come from the wife, the husband having more severe means of getting rid of his wife if she had offended. She would usually go to the secular judges, who had the means to enforce their verdict and any settlement arising from it. But it was possible to go to the ecclesiastical court instead; this took advantage of the fact that canon law treated men and women as equal, adultery by either party being grounds for separation (though it is true that a woman would be sent to a convent for two years if she was the guilty party). In the diocese of Cambrai (probably because of the idiosyncratic character of the legal system there), the *officialité* was the court handling all these affairs, three-quarters coming from the wives, a tenth from the husbands, and a tenth being joint applications. The average number of separations decreed annually from 1737 to 1774 was nine—clearly, for most people marriage was simple and final, not a matter to take before lawyers.[68]

The power of the ecclesiastical courts was limited. They could not impose temporal penalties, though canonical penalties could be severe enough for a clerk, ranging from excommunication, interdiction from ministerial functions, deprivation of benefice, or imprisonment in a monastery. Laymen, without preferments or functions to be abrogated, could adopt a cavalier attitude to the fulminations of ecclesiastical judges. In most dioceses, the *officialité* no longer had a functioning prison, though at Lyon recourse could be made to the state fortress of Pierre en Cize, and at Paris there were cells in a tower in the first courtyard of the episcopal palace. In all the eighteenth century, no one was imprisoned in the gaol of the *officialité* at Montpellier—a dank underground cellar in the cloisters without a lock on the door. The laity were rarely prepared to co-operate with the diocesan lawyers when they went about their enquiries. In 1747, the bishop of Agde sent his *official* and *promoteur* to Celle to investigate allegations against a curé; there was a riot, the police would not help, and a magistrate who came down from Béziers interrogated witnesses and condemned the two ecclesiastical officers for defaming a worthy parish priest.[69] The sort of case an *officialité* could handle was the 'tumultuous incident' in the collegiate church of Saint-Géry in Cambrai in 1758. It concerned the chairs, the property of the chapter. When the curé was taking a catechism class, Michelle Noral, a lady of 50, the *chaisière*, burst in and tipped the children from their seats. The *promoteur* summoned witnesses, promising to make up the loss of their wages when attending the court. Noral said that Canon Mallet had ordered her to stack the chairs in a side chapel, and she had not understood the curé's protests because 'he spoke to her in Latin'. We do not know the verdict, but the *promoteur* asked for her to have to pay the costs and apologize to the curé in the presence of two witnesses.[70] To deal with a more serious case, a conjoint procedure of ecclesiastical and secular courts was needed if the penalty was to be severe. The priest who interrupted the sermon of the curé of Saint-André in Paris, declaring him to be preaching Luther and Calvin, was sentenced by the *official* to a period of prayer and fasting in a seminary, but the Châtelet insisted on a ceremony of reparation, a fine of 500 livres, and a five-year banishment from the city.[71] The affair in 1765 of the sermon of curé Papin of the village of Ormesson was more complex. The marquis d'Ormesson had pulled down the old church, which obstructed the entrance to his château, and built a new one, exhuming the bodies from the churchyard by warrant of the archbishop of Paris—Papin was accused of denouncing this as sacrilege. The *bailliage* court, alerted by the parlement of Paris, took up the case; the *officialité* intervened on grounds of clerical privilege, had Papin borne off to the ecclesiastical prison, and interrogated the witnesses, who turned out to have been prompted about the sermon by the marquis's estate manager. The *official* in a court reinforced by two canons of Notre-Dame and two barristers ordered the curé to a seminary for a month; the *bailliage* court fined him 10 livres for the poor of the parish. In short, he had been condemned by two jurisdictions, probably unjustly, and because a great nobleman was concerned; but his punishment was so light, it verged on acquittal.[72]

Given the cumbersome nature of conjoint procedures and the halting inefficiency of denunciations before the *officialité*, a bishop proposing to discipline an erring cleric would incline to short-circuit the old ways and act by the authority of the royal edict of 1698 giving him power to send a priest to a seminary for a period of penitence. The most common offenders were alcoholics, who would be sent to do a 'spiritual retreat' for forty days or so. Causing a public scandal in other ways (as losing money at tric trac to an officer of the garrison at Le Mans) might incur a longer period. For fornication, the customary rigours of the seminary might be supplemented by the humiliation of a public penance—like reciting the synodal ordinances and decretals on clerical conduct in front of the assembled ordinands before dinner on Fridays and dining on bread and water afterwards.[73] For graver breaches of discipline a *lettre de cachet* would be solicited from Versailles to send the offender to some

house of correction, like those run by the Frères des Écoles
Chrétiennes or the rigorous seminary of La Délivrande at Bayeux, or
the Bon Sauveur at Caen, whose nuns had disciplined prostitutes
before being changed to the task of taking in delinquent clergy. The
ancient structures of rule in France were falling into desuetude, and
new central officials had taken over, like the royal intendants running the *généralités*. In the same way, in the Church the episcopal
grands vicaires were doing the administering and inspecting which had
once been the prerogatives of the archdeacons, and bishops were
using arbitrary removals to seminaries and imprisonment by *lettres de
cachet* to root out scandal from the clerical estate without resort to the
cumbersome old *officialités*.

VII

The diocesan seminary[74] was the creation of the Counter-
Reformation, prescribed by the Council of Trent. In the course of
the seventeenth century, most bishops made an effort to comply
with the conciliar order. Finance was the problem. The initial
impetus might come from a pious donation of a site; thereafter, there
would be a continual search for benefices for union with the foundation. In theory, a bishop could tax his clergy to maintain the seminary, but this course was unpopular—'Why could not Monseigneur
find an abbey to annex?' was the cry. This search for 'unions' went
on all through the eighteenth century—an abbey was taken over by
Evreux in 1740, a priory in 1773 and an abbey in 1779 at Lisieux, an
abbey at Bayeux in 1781. These confiscations involved ruthless
utilitarian vandalism, demolishing the monastic church and buildings
and selling the fittings and debris.[75] There was also the problem of
finding endowments to provide maintenance grants for the poorer
students—150 livres a year for each of them was needed. Some
seminaries ran a *camérie*, a sort of cheap lodging-house (at Valonges,
a bed and soup twice a day for 3 livres a month).[76] Most, however,
shrank from this threadbare expedient, destructive of a common
spirit, and accepted only those who could pay or could win a
scholarship, whether by competition or favour. A seminarist accepting a *bourse* often had to undertake not to work outside the diocese
without the bishop's permission.[77] Thus, the number of grants
available from the seminary endowments was a significant factor in
the pastoral efficiency of the whole surrounding area.

According to the interpretation of the intentions of the Council of Trent and within the constraints of financial possibility, the concept of a seminary varied, both in the aims of the original foundation and the use to which it was eventually put. A royal declaration of 1698 summarized the wisdom built up by experience: bishops were ordered to set up a *grand séminaire* training and testing ordinands, and a *petit séminaire*[78] educating boys from the age of 12 as a preparatory school. These little seminaries, an invention of Vincent de Paul, had come late upon the scene, the first outside Paris being established by the bishop of Beauvais in 1648. New foundations were still being made in the late eighteenth century—at Boulogne in 1780, Toulouse and Oloron in 1784. Yet even by 1789, nearly half the dioceses were without one. From early on, these schools had two objects, often pursued in parallel. One was to provide boys with a basic education in the humanities, either by in-house teaching or by sending them to the local *collège* for most of their classes. The other was to enable boys of poor families to aspire to the priesthood. The content of the curriculum would correspond to the nature of the basic aim. In the one case, it would stop short at the end of philosophy, which completed the cycle of the humanities; in the case of the poor students, it would carry on with theology afterwards. Living cheaply at the little seminary, they could complete their formal theology, then move to the big seminary for their final instruction in pastoralia and the techniques of the ministry. Or, as a variant, some theology could be studied in both institutions; at Périgueux it was scholastic theology in the first, and moral theology, for three years, in the second. Not everyone who attended a little seminary or lodged there while attending a *collège* would go on to ordination, and some pupils were accepted who never had that intention. Most fathers, however, would not ask this privilege for their sons if they could afford to pay for education in a *collège*. Little seminary teaching concentrated on logic, metaphysics, and moral philosophy with only a reduced role for mathematics and physics. The range of prescribed authors was narrow; according to the abbé Carrel's *Science ecclésiastique* (1700), pagan authors ought to be avoided altogether. Courses were in Latin and were taught by way of dictation. Learning went at a snail's pace; one pupil remembered how a month went by reviewing the different definitions of 'philosophy'. But at least there was progress throughout the century; in spite of the fulminations of the parlement and the University of Paris, Cartesianism was winning, evident in the Latin courses of philosophy printed for Toul in 1769 and for Lyon in 1785.

There were 153 *grands séminaires* in France in 1760, and 130 in

1789, the main reason for the reduction in numbers being the expulsion of the Jesuits.[79] Half a dozen of the tiny dioceses had never managed to establish one, and another five dioceses had done so but had lost them by financial collapse—in the case of Mâcon, by fire destroying the buildings. On the other hand, a few dioceses had several, the precise count depending on the definition—three at Toulouse, four at Rouen, Rodez, and Lyon, and from eight to eleven in Paris. Outside this total of diocesan seminaries there were also some specialist institutions of the same kind. The Missions Étrangères had a small house in the rue du Bac in Paris training clergy for work in Canada and the Antilles. Up to 1786, when it went bankrupt, there was an English college in Paris, rue des Postes, drawing its students chiefly from the English school at Douai.[80] There was a similar Scottish institution in the rue des Fossés Saint-Victor. For the Irish, there were seminaries at Bordeaux, Nantes, Toulouse, Douai, Lille, and, especially, in Paris, the collège des Lombards, rue des Carmes, with an annexe of new buildings in the rue du Cheval-Vert put up by Laurence Kelly in 1770.[81] The mendicant orders also had houses devoted to the education of Irish friars in various countries; in France, there were Capuchin establishments at Bar-sur-Aube and Vassey and a Franciscan one at Boulay in Lorraine.[82] For the four Irish professors who taught at the Lombards and their French superior, the system was scandalous. The abbé Vaubrun and professor John Bourke protested to Rome in 1733, and the abbé de Nicholay renewed their complaints anonymously in mid-century. The Irish bishops insisted on ordaining their men before they left Ireland to study in France (presumably so that they could eke out a living by saying masses), and they showed no restraint over numbers. Consequently, said Bourke, there was a multitude of priests in Ireland 'without any function but to say mass, marry young couples and empty barrels'.[83] Scattered around France there were many others, some footloose adventurers, others useful to the bishops because willing to work in grim and lonely places where French priests were reluctant to stay. In Paris, there were 250 of them, most not living in the *collège* and some misbehaving. But pleas to Rome to suspend Irish ordinations for a while and to transform the Lombards into a genuine seminary for ordinands, not a lodging-house for unemployed priests, fell on deaf ears, though the Pope closed the Irish noviciates for friars from 1751 to 1773 and divided the Lombards into two sections, one for priests and one for ordinands. The Irish bishops remained incorrigible in their policy of ordaining; in the eyes of the hard-pressed Irish theologians in Paris trying to set up a dignified seminary, they were 'no better than a pack of cowboys'.[84]

There were also some special seminars to train penniless young men up to the priesthood, generally with the aim of directing them (like some of the Irish) to difficult areas. The seminary of Saint-Charles at Lyon was the prototype. In imitation of this successful venture, in 1740 the bishops of Grenoble, Viviers, Valence, and Gap collaborated to found a similar house at Grenoble to produce clergy for the remote mountain areas of the frontier.[85] In the diocese of Avranches there were experiments on a lesser scale with 'rural seminaries'. Paris, where young men from the provinces gravitated hoping to find a way into the priesthood, became a centre for such initiatives. In 1633, the Séminaire des Trente-Trois was founded, the title referring to the thirty-three years of the life of Christ, spent on earth in penury. Later in the seventeenth century, a student of Saint-Sulpice, François Chansiergues, founded a club for poor clerks lodging in the capital; they earned a living by copying sermons, giving tuition, walking in funeral processions, and doing other odd jobs on the fringes of the clerical world, supported each other, and worked together as best they might to qualify for ordination. Another student, the Breton abbé Poullart, bought a house in which he gave shelter to some of these poor clerks; by 1703 there were twelve of them, and soon their numbers had risen to seventy, and the Congrégation du Saint-Esprit was founded, inhabiting a seminary proper in the rue des Postes. Other communities of this kind sprang up, the so-called *Séminaires de la Providence*.[86] Archbishop Noailles and the wealthy curé of Saint-Jacques de la Boucherie, Louis de Marillac (son of a *maître des requêtes*), intervened, and united these ventures with the Chansiergues group to form the Seminary of Saint-Louis, the curé giving a house, and the prelate endowing forty free places.[87]

The *grands séminaires* in the dioceses were controlled by the local bishops, who prescribed the courses of study, appointed the *directeurs*, and made the final decisions about accepting individual candidates for ordination. Most bishops had confided the running of their seminaries to religious Orders; in 1760, a third of the total, sixty, were under the Lazarists, thirteen under the Eudistes (mostly in Normandy), fourteen under the Doctrinaires, fourteen under the Oratorians, twenty under the Sulpicians, and thirty-two under the Jesuits. Though each group of *directeurs* had its individual style, the establishments they ran were very much alike in discipline and atmosphere. But, according to what the diocese expected of them, there were *grands séminaires* of various kinds, though different functions might be fulfilled together in the same institution. The simplest case was a house of strict quiet discipline where the final preparation for ordination was made. It was assumed that those entering had already completed their quinquennium elsewhere—that is, two years of philosophy and three years of theology. The synodal ordinances of a bishop describe how this time of preparation must be spent: prayer, meditation, and spiritual reading for the cultivation of the inner life, acquiring the art of preaching and facility at plainchant, learning the rules of the Church about the administration of the sacraments and the customs and statutes of the diocese, analysing problems of casuistry for application in the confessional. Some episcopal regulations prescribe how the time before entrance to the seminary must be spent. At Tarbes,[88] during the five years of study of philosophy and theology at the local *collège*, the prospective ordinand, living at home or in lodgings, was to wear clerical bands on weekdays to mark out his vocation; on Sundays he had to attend services in the cathedral or the church of Saint-Jean; and twice a year he had to submit to an examination conducted by a *grand vicaire*, a professor of the *collège*, and a *directeur* of the seminary—this to last three days, with the closing session held in public. Thereafter, twelve months' attendance at the seminary was required, spread over two years. In other dioceses, the obligatory time of preparation for ordination was variously prescribed, but in roughly the same pattern—a certain time for the subdiaconate, another for the diaconate, another for the priesthood. In 1729, the bishop of Sées laid down eight months for the first, one for the second, one for the third. If he did not ask more, he said, it was because 'the faculties of the greater part of the ordinands are too mediocre'. And he ordered them all to buy the abridged version (it was four volumes all the same) of the theology of Poitiers; they were forbidden to sell it or to lend it to others.[89] At Paris, the preparation times were nine months, three months and three months; at Bayeux three, six, and three, all to be spread over three years; at Autun three, two, and three.[90] At Dol, the patriarchal Urbain d'Hercé, becoming bishop in 1767, was horrified to find that only three months altogether was needed; he immediately increased it to seven, with a vacation break in the middle followed by an examination. His seminarists all had to dine in his dining-hall and when they reached the subdiaconate, at his own table—here, they were expected to marvel at their bishop's ability to recite from memory the odes of Horace and the psalms between courses.[91]

Most of the diocesan seminaries were organized to provide more than this minimum preparation for ordination.[92] They would accept ordinands who had completed their humanities to do from two to four years of theology; sometimes they would take over philosophy from the humanities curriculum as well. The teaching might be given exclusively by the *directeurs*—this is how the Lazarists and Sulpicians liked to have it; or some of it might be given externally, especially in the earlier years, the students attending at the local *collège* or, if there was one, the university. Each diocese had its pattern of study, though the bishop would not necessarily insist on a particular individual following the whole of it. At Nevers,[93] there were four years of theology with the first two studied externally; at Poitiers two years of philosophy then two years of theology. At Angers, the seminarists went once a day to a lecture in the Faculty of Theology of the university, but were otherwise taught by their own masters. The seminary of Larressonne in the diocese of Bayonne from 1747 allowed its students leave of absence to affiliate to a Spanish university.[94] Bordeaux had its seminary of Saint-Raphael, a place of severe spiritual discipline; here for five or six years a student would attend classes at the Jesuit *collège*, and after passing his examinations transferred to the séminaire des Ordinands for the prescribed months of pastoralia and retreat before the priesthood.[95] The working of the system in the diocese of Rouen is illustrated in the story of Jean-Marie Absolom Lebay's progress to holy orders. He was from a peasant family, and paid his way through the Oratorian *collège* at Dieppe by spare-time tutoring (his efforts brought on a nervous breakdown, from which he was rescued by an English doctor, who cured him and then committed suicide). He ended up with four prizes, including the one for 'diligence'. He got a place in the seminary of Saint-Nicaise at Rouen—number seventeen out of eighteen candidates; had it not been for the local curé who knew the *directeurs*, he might not have made it. He was there for five years, doing one of philosophy and one of physics externally at the *collège*, and three years of theology internally. At the end of the first year he received the tonsure, at the end of the second minor orders, at the end of the third the subdiaconate and the diaconate— this committed him to celibacy. He was 22 years of age when he left, having two years to wait before he would be old enough for ordination to the priesthood. Three months teaching in a *pensionnat* proved intolerable, due to the long hours and the embarrassment of being shorter in stature than all the pupils. He then became manager of a small saltpetre and gunpowder factory. After 'a not very rigorous examination' he was ordained priest in 1785, and earned a meagre living as a *prêtre habitué* at home. He was a vicaire when the Revolution came; not until 1819 did he become a curé—in his native village.[96] For someone without influence, it had been a slow and penny-pinching progress.

By definition, seminaries were austere places. Lay critics called them 'prisons', 'noviciates for monks', 'barracks for galley-slaves'. Drunk or immoral clergy sent there for a period of discipline did not need a special regimen—it existed already. Priests who found themselves penniless at the end of their working days and who were not in dioceses like Paris, Langres, or Rouen where prescient bishops had set up rest-homes for them, dreaded having to join the ordinands—being 'buried in the darkness of your seminary', as some of them complained to the bishop of Lisieux.[97] The fare was solid and simple; though, as one who endured it observes, it was the seminarists from poorer families who had never fed well who led in complaining.[98] The received wisdom was to prevent familiarity among the students and reduce conversations to a minimum, the ideal represented in the new buildings at Viviers in 1777, a series of cells opening into galleries around a central hall, so that all the doors could be under surveillance.[99] Confession once a week to one of the *directeurs* was the rule; there was no escape to confessors in town. Apart from the Parisian houses attended by great aristocrats and, towards the end of the century, Saint-Nicolas du Chardonnet, scandal or slackness is rarely reported. An isolated instance of cards and drinking at midnight could happen anywhere. Wigs and hair powder, more and more creeping into acceptance, were harmless fashions. The seminarist sent down for reading *L'Esprit* in chapel and another rusticated for possessing works of J.-J. Rousseau, the billiard-players at Caen, the chapel orchestra at Toulouse which struck up the 'March of the Bandits' when the procession moved into the stalls, might win our approval rather than our censure.[100]

According to philosophes and Jansenists, seminaries were haunts of ignorance and superstition. Some clergy who had passed through the system complained of the lack of intellectual content. There was all about the shape of tonsures, genuflexions and ceremonies, and the old canons of the Church, said one, and nothing of St Paul and the gospels.[101] Another, wanting to set up an academy of preaching, complained of the absence of the study of patristic texts: 'on donne trop de temps à former les cœurs et pas assez à former l'esprit'.[102] Yet the opposite objection is found—too much time spent on theological controversy: 'a young candidate who in his examinations is able to give effective replies to all the sophisms of heresy and impiety passes, and is judged capable of directing the consciences of 300 country folk who have never heard of Luther or Calvin, Jansenius or Quesnel'.[103] In fact, intellectual qualifications were secondary in a seminary education. 'The bishops send their ecclesiastics to us', said Jean Bonnet (dd. 1735), superior-general of the Lazarists, 'not to make teachers of theology out of them, but just curés and vicaires capable of instructing and directing the faithful.'[104] The framework of each day was prayer in the morning and evening, mass at 11 a.m. when those who had been out to lectures came back, and an hour's meditation according to the Salesian, Ignatian, or Oratorian methods as systematized in handbooks by Beuvelet in 1657 and Bussée in 1700. There was training for preaching, with the emphasis on clarity and simplicity; sermons corrected by the *directeurs* were tried out in the chapel with the object of enabling each seminarian to build up a corpus of twenty to thirty to take out when he left for parish work. The catechist's art was learned either in front of a seminary audience pretending to be children or a real class. Ceremonies were studied in Beuvelet's manual (1654), which took account of the rituals of the various dioceses as well as the Roman. The choreography of the liturgy and its manual actions were rehearsed, a wooden doll being used in simulated baptisms. Plainchant was studied with careful tuition, very often from outside experts. There was also a good deal of study of casuistry and the duties of the priest in the confessional. As the century progressed, the time spent in some of these exercises was curtailed (meditation was reduced to half an hour, and chanting became less important); even so, the subjects of pastoral value remained the core of the curriculum.

If the length and solidity of the textbooks specially produced for seminary use are an indication, there was every intention of giving students an exhaustive survey of moral and dogmatic theology.[105] Given the menace of Jansenism, bishops prescribed the reading lists, sometimes even commissioned the writing of the manuals themselves. The Jansenist volumes of Louis Habert were progressively outlawed, and most seminaries came to rely on the theology of Poitiers (1708), then that written by Tournely in sixteen volumes (1725–39) as later revised by Collet and abridged by him and others. Though these works were anti-Jansenist, they were Gallican, holding that infallibility required the assent of a majority of the bishops. They were also rigorist as regards the confessional. The theology of Lyon (1780) moved on from episcopal Gallicanism towards clerical democracy, the view that the unanimous collaboration of all the pastors, parish priests included, was required for infallibility. What was lacking in the vast systematization of these volumes was Church history, the direct study of the text of the Bible, and the drawing out of apologetical arguments to confront the thought of the Enlightenment. Improvements came in the course of the century.[106] In place of edifying stories, real Church history was read in the refectories and came into class work; the New Testament was read morning and evening and commented on in discussion groups; while from the *De vera religione* which Collet added to his abridgement of Tournely in 1751, every theological textbook came to have an apologetical section. Bailly's two-volume *Tractatus* (1758) of such arguments arranged for the use of seminaries had the unusual virtue of analysing, in a well-informed way, what the sceptical writers actually were saying.

If it was a question of the minimum course of seven to twelve months to pass through the stages to ordination, very little intellectual ground could be covered. The abbé de Mondran found his year at Toulouse (in the 1730s) unsatisfying: 'in the short space of a year they hurried along, accumulated subjects were passed in review as rapidly as through a magic lantern'.[107] He had not suffered too much himself, since he already had his *baccalauréat* in theology. Here is the difficulty when generalizing about the intellectual content of seminary courses. A priest who had received no more than the minimum training of a year obviously knew little about intellectual problems. But most had spent more than that, sometimes a great deal more, on theology. If this had taken place exclusively in the seminary, the teaching may have had a deadening effect, for the old custom of dictating endlessly to pupils carried on long after it was officially frowned upon: the idea being to send out the clergy of the future with a set of theology *cahiers* as well as a clutch of sermons.[108] But more and more, enlightened ideas were prevailing; *conférences*, discussion groups, were becoming the approved method of teaching, and the need to sharpen the weapons of Christian apologetics was bringing in a liberal and critical spirit in place of the old lapidary affirmations. There were so many combinations of theological study: in the seminary alone and for varying periods of time up to four years, in conjunction with a *collège* or with a university, and in the minority of seminaries duly affiliated to a university, in courses which would lead to a university degree. In this case, the value of the study depended a great deal on which university it was and at what stage the student left—at the *maîtrise* of arts, the *baccalauréat* of theology, the *licence* of theology, or the doctorate. Like most organizations in eighteenth-century France, the seminary system was full of illogicalities and confusions, but candidates for ecclesiastical office manœuvred their way through it with the help of such influence as they could muster, and got as much qualifying learning as they needed for the fulfilment of their ambitions.

We need to know more about the *directeurs* of the seminaries. If they were secular priests, the rewards of the Church rarely came their way. Christophe de Lalane, who ran the seminary at Langres from 1738 to 1745, then that of Quebec, and finished up as superior at Dax and a *vicaire général* of the diocese, was rewarded by the gift of an abbey only at the age of 60.[109] If they were members of an Order, they had been chosen from the learned and austere minority among their colleagues. Though they were nominated to their way of service by authority, they remained, in the best sense of the word, volunteers, for Lazarists, Doctrinaires, and Oratorians, all in their different ways, had taken vows which might be binding on the interior conscience, but were not enforceable against them by secular or canon law if they chose to leave.[110] Theirs was a vocation requiring the abandonment of the companionship and comforts so many pastoral or monastic duties afforded, though it brought wide contacts with the parish priests of a diocese, including austere friendships of a sort. When the clergy of France were confronted with the oath to the revolutionary Civil Constitution of the Clergy, it was often the *directeurs* of their local seminary to whom they turned for advice. In the dark days of the Terror the dominant figure in the Gallican Church and the keeper of its conscience was M. Emery, who had ruled the seminaries of Orléans, Lyon, and Angers before taking over at Saint-Sulpice—a man who rose at four in the morning to meditate and wore hair shirts and iron bracelets, and gave them as presents to his friends.[111] Free from bias towards the spirit of the *ancien régime* or rancour against the Revolution, and with the insight of clear logic and unshakable rectitude, he advised the persecuted clergy on their attitude towards the various revolutionary oaths. Those who had ridiculed the seminaries as dens of logic—chopping casuistry and wrangles over unreal contingencies—could not have guessed that national events would catch up with the exercises of the classroom.

THE BISHOPS: ARISTOCRATIC VOCATIONS

I

The king nominated to all the bishoprics of France.[1] The Pope had granted the right by the Concordat of 1516. According to one school of Gallican lawyers, the treaty covered the dioceses in provinces subsequently annexed; this was not agreed at Rome, but as the Pope conceded the right in separate instruments, the dispute made no difference to the exercise of the royal power. In theory, if the titular of a French see died while visiting Rome, the right of appointing a successor would lapse to the Pope—a contingency which fortunately did not arise to trouble the diplomats and lawyers of the eighteenth century. The one other apparent exception to the patronage of the Crown was the continuing right of the cathedral chapter of Strasbourg to elect its bishop, but in practice, the canons always accepted the name sent to them from Versailles.

By the Concordat, the king's power of choice was limited to sons of Catholic parents, of at least 27 years of age (by canon law it was 30), who had studied at a famous university and had obtained the *licence* in theology or in law, including canon law. The formal procedures of appointment were solemn and measured.[2] The king signed three letters—to the Pope, the 'Cardinal Protector' of French affairs in Rome, and the ambassador there. The bishop-to-be had to go to the nuncio in Paris to fill in an 'information de vie et de mœurs' of twenty searching questions, and to his own diocesan bishop to make a profession of faith before him and to sign an 'information' concerning the see to which he was nominated. He then sent these three documents and the king's three letters to a *banquier expéditionnaire en Cour de Rome*. The *banquier* went to the French ambassador to get his *expediatur* on the royal letter to the Pope, then took it to the Datary for the Roman bureaucracy to process it and send it onwards. Armed with his own royal letter, the Cardinal Protector would give notice to the first Consistory meeting that occurred of his intention to propose the candidate at the next session (the *Préconisation*). At the following Consistory the proposition was put, the cardinals gave their advice, and the Pope thereafter ordered the nine bulls to be sent to France, the most important being the provisions to the bishop-to-be and the authorization to one or more bishops to consecrate him.

There were ample opportunities in the process for objections to be made to the candidate's morals, beliefs, or fitness. Before this process had begun, there had been the original enquiry made before he had been ordained priest (this had been a problem with Dubois, for Archbishop Noailles refused to give his *licet*, and in the end the archbishop of Rouen had been persuaded to degrade himself and do so). The nuncio had the duty of checking the *information de vie et de mœurs* by taking opinions from two leading churchmen—in the case of Talleyrand, Dugnani obtained certificates of moral conduct from Thémines, bishop of Blois, and Barral, the coadjutor of Troyes.[3] The diocesan bishop could challenge the profession of faith, the cardinals could make enquiries between Consistories and advance objections, and, finally, the bishops authorized to consecrate could refuse. Yet the system rolled on without these opportunities being taken or, if they were, without making any difference. Good men combined with worldly men to operate it. The devout Massillon tried to persuade Noailles to give Dubois his *licet*, then was one of the three prelates who consecrated the crafty and dissolute minister to the episcopate.[4] How did his mind work, and the minds of others like him, when facing candidatures which, by any standard, were unacceptable? Tronson, the severe head of Saint-Sulpice, wrote to Colbert, the great minister of Louis XIV, on 29 August 1679, in reply to his formal enquiry whether his second son, aged 25 and just out of seminary, might be consecrated as coadjutor archbishop of Rouen. 'With all the sincerity I can muster', said Tronson, 'there is nothing in him to make him unsuitable . . . and he can render the Church service.'[5] So the boyish Jacques-Nicolas in the following year was consecrated 'archbishop of Carthage' and coadjutor of the most splendid see in France; there were thirty-six bishops at the ceremony and six who were nominated but not yet in office—'there were no more at the Council of Nicea,' said Mme de Sévigné. Tronson's carefully worded recommendation had meant, quite simply: it was in the interest of the Gallican Church to serve the political designs of the State: the king's will must prevail.

II

If the Church is to be in servitude, said a seventeenth-century Jansenist, it had better be to secular princes than to ecclesiastics: 'I prefer to see bishoprics given by the Court of France than by that of Rome.'[6] In an established Church, there is no reason why the secular power should not appoint bishops as good as those ecclesiastics might elect for themselves, or ecclesiastical authority impose. The ruler and his ministers have nothing to gain and much to lose by making appointments which churchmen would regard as falling short of the best available. But there is always the problem of the constituency which the government wishes to please. The theoretically absolute monarchy of France, though becoming more responsive to public opinion throughout the eighteenth century, was primarily looking for approval to the aristocracy: Versailles, where the nobles glittered around the king in self-interested subordination, was the heart and symbol of the monarchy's power. Oversimplifying, it can be said that the nobles had yielded up their anarchical local domination in return for bribes offered by the Crown, and the source for the bribes was the wealth and splendour of the Gallican Church.

In 1516, at the time of the Concordat, of the 102 bishops in place, ninety were nobles (sixty being of a lineage going back to 1400), four were commoners, and the remaining eight are of uncertain status.[7] The aristocratic predominance carried on to the Revolution: of the 1,416 nominations from 1516 to 1789, 1,227 were nobles, 62 were commoners, and the exact status of the remaining 127 has not been determined. Half of the commoners and those who may possibly have been so obtained their sees during the Wars of Religion, from 1560 to 1588, when the grip of the Crown was faltering. Within these broad figures of aristocratic monopoly, however, two major changes had taken place, imposed by the Crown to promote royal power and administrative efficiency, and to aid the Gallican Church in its religious mission. In the early sixteenth century, the noble prelates were occupying sees in areas where their families were dominant, no fewer than seventy-two of them established in place by virtual inheritance, members of dynasties. Royal policy, ruthlessly pushed ahead by Richelieu, was to break these family chains of succession, and appoint bishops to dioceses away from their family sphere of influence. Louis XIV firmly established this principle, the last dynastic see to be liberated being Senlis in 1702; he did, however, allow exceptions for newly annexed territories and areas where knowledge of the local language was desirable. Le Camus, bishop of Grenoble from 1671 to 1702, noted the effect of this change on the standing of the bishop in the local community: 'a bishop is usually a man fallen from the skies into the midst of a province where he finds no support, no help; monks, chapters and parlement continually cause him difficulties, officials never put themselves out to assist him'.[8] It meant the bishop was now entirely a king's man, an agent of the royal power on which he was dependent.

The second major change in the character of the episcopate imposed by royal policy was to insist that nobles who sought to rule dioceses must make themselves professionally qualified to do so. The stipulation of the Concordat concerning the *licence* was enforced, and in the reign of Louis XIV it became understood that the degree had to be taken at the Sorbonne; from 1700 the custom arose of residing at Saint-Sulpice for part of the time. From 1680, Louis XIV was also making it a rule that an apprenticeship in the office of *grand vicaire* was necessary: from 1660 to 1690, seventeen of the forty-seven nominations had held these administrative posts in the dioceses, then from 1690 to 1715, seventy-six out of 107; after 1730, this qualification became routinely indispensable. The scandal of very young bishops, 'évêques à la bavette', was ended. From 1589 to 1623, the average age on appointment was 35; thereafter it became about 40. In the eighteenth century, few appointments were made under the age of 30—the abbé de Saint-Albin, the illegitimate son of the regent, taking the see of Cambrai at 25 was an outrageous exception to all the rules. Vacancies in the episcopate were few, and they became fewer as the prelates, a long-lived class to start with, began to live longer still. In the eighteenth century, the average age of death was between 65 and 70, and the number of vacancies was just over five a year, declining at the end of the *ancien régime* to three and a half. There were always going to be many more aspirants than successful candidates. The noble families enjoying the virtual monopoly of the royal patronage—say, 300 of them, for 793 of the 1,416 nominations from 1516 to 1589 were from 269 families—knew exactly what qualifications had to be gained by their sons, what the chances of an appointment were, and how long the time of waiting was likely to be.

Among the 300 families, the pattern of recruitment changed somewhat as the years went by. There are various ways of categorizing the nobility of France, none comprehensive, all overlapping and subject to exceptions. Going by genealogy, there were the newly ennobled, the established nobles with four generations to prove it, and the *nobles de race*, the feudal families tracing their descent back to 1400 and earlier and entitled to be presented at Court. Looking at the caste by function, there were nobles of the Court and high administration, the magistrates of the parlements and other sovereign courts (the 'robe'), and the provincial nobles. Looking at the nobility on the scale of wealth, the provincial nobles fragment into contrasting groups, from rural squires forced into penury by the operation of the inheritance laws, to well-off landed families and, even, splendidly affluent ones, living on their fiefs. There was also, on the fringe of the nobility, a penumbra of rich families, holders of important municipal offices, successful bourgeois who had purchased estates, spoken of technically as 'living nobly', and rated as noble by local opinion. In the eighteenth century the *nobles de race* were the favourites for the bishoprics, and for the most important ones. Of the bishops of 1789, ninety-nine were from old feudal families, eighty of them having proceeded to 'the honours of the Court'. Authentic documentation going back to the High Middle Ages had enormous force in society; there are stories of it, unsupported by wealth or connections, opening the way to high office—a bishop of Mende taking refuge from a thunderstorm in the hovel of a penurious squire and happening to ask to see the family title-deeds, with the result that one son came to command a regiment and another became a vicar-general.[9] Among the prelates of 1789 there was such a case. Jean-Baptiste Chabot, bishop of Saint-Claude, had been a curé until he found his family *preuves* and had them verified by Chérin, the court genealogist, thus making himself eligible to rise to the top of the ecclesiastical hierarchy. The thirty-one prelates of 1789 who lacked the cachet of great antiquity mostly had lineages going back for at least two centuries, and those whose ancestral tree had shallower roots were of undeniable distinction. The family of Couet du Vivier de Lorry (Angers) had risen in high administration before being recognized as noble in 1675. Courtois (Belley) was from a family acquiring instant transmissible nobility early in the eighteenth century by paying the immense sum required for the office of *secrétaire du roi*; since then it had provided three generals for the armies of the king. Chaumont de la Galaisière (Saint-Dié) had as a grandfather a rich grain merchant from the Low Countries who had loaned money to Louis XIV; he became naturalized in France in 1720, and bought nobility as a *secrétaire du roi*; his son, the bishop's father, had become intendant of Lorraine and married the daughter of Controller General Orry. Two of the prelates of 1789 (both appointed in 1771) came from the penumbra of families regarded as noble though they lacked the documentation.[10] Le Quien de Neufville (Dax) had relatives in high positions in the army and the administration, but the family *preuves* were 'lost'; the best that could be done was to point to the grandfather recognized as noble in Portugal. Hachette des Portes was of the rich patrician merchant class of Reims, holders of high municipal office—wealth and distinction enough to enable him to proceed to the minor see of Glandève.

In the eighteenth century, appointments to the episcopate from families of the Court and high administration declined, from 25 per cent or more under Louis XIV to 18 per cent after 1726. One possible reason was the rising incidence of birth control in the highest echelons of society: there were fewer sons in search of an establishment. There was a decline too in the representatives of the nobles of the robe.[11] This class had provided the intelligent and moral heart of the Jansenist movement, and the powers that be in Church and State were excluding Jansenists from all influential ecclesiastical posts. When vacancies occurred in the dioceses where the opposition to *Unigenitus* was centred—Paris, Boulogne, Tours, Orléans, Meaux, Nantes, Montpellier, Aix, and Senez—strictly orthodox prelates were appointed. By 1740, there were no Jansenist bishops left. Not surprisingly, then, there were fewer religious vocations among the sons of the magistrates. Throughout the century, the parlement of Paris battled against the Crown on political, as well as religious, issues. One of the penalties the king could impose was to look elsewhere for his bishops: in the reign of Louis XVI, all appointments from the robe were from the provincial parlements. It is easier to define the classes within the nobility which were providing fewer recruits to the episcopate than to generalize about those producing the majority, for outside Court, higher administration, and robe, the caste was complex and heterogeneous. But broadly speaking, they were very often 'provincial' nobles, mostly of old feudal families and enjoying substantial incomes from landed estates and with a long tradition of military service.[12]

In the reign of Louis XIV, commoners—given brilliant abilities or membership of a family coming to the king's notice in his domestic service—could still hope to become bishops. Even so, in some circles their birth was held against them. Saint-Simon, with his fanatical cult of ancestry, refers to them in savage terms—'an ill-bred pedant from the dregs of the populace', and the like. One, who became bishop of Dax, then of Périgueux, was said 'to have been born a beggar (*gueux*), lived as a beggar and wanted to die as a beggar (*périr gueux*)'. In 1712, Paris heard how Hébert, bishop of Agen, had received an official rebuke: 'they wrote to him as if he was a scoundrel (*faquin*) just because he is not a *grand seigneur* and has been curé of Versailles. He replied as a bishop should, briefly, precisely.'[13] According to one calculation (there is room for small divergencies), from 1682 to 1700 sixteen commoners entered the episcopate, from 1700 to 1743 only nine. Thereafter, up to 1789, there was only one, appointed in 1774, a very special case. The abbé de Beauvais,[14] son of an *avocat* pleading before the parlement of Paris, was 43 years of age, the greatest preacher of his generation, adored by the king's pious daughters, who pressed for his elevation. He was also well thought of by the higher clergy, for his uncle was the lawyer presiding over the office of the agents-general, the key man in advising the Assembly of Clergy how to resist encroachments on clerical privileges. The bishopric they gave him was Senez, consisting of thirty parishes among barren mountains, with a tiny income. The promotion, in fact, put him to great inconvenience, as he struggled to run his diocese and to travel back and forth to Paris to fulfil preaching engagements; after nine years he resigned and joined the staff of Archbishop Juigné in the capital. The abbé Maury, preaching in 1775, thundered against the 'blind prejudice' of those who talked of the new bishop of Senez with condescension as one of the 'hommes de fortune', 'while, on the contrary, they are the only bishops for whom fortune has done nothing'. It was an isolated breakthrough for talent.

In 1790 France was ruled by the National Assembly, and the future of the episcopate was in doubt. Le Franc de Pompignan, the honest old archbishop of Vienne, had become minister of the *feuille* (and had shown remarkable scrupulosity in resigning his see to do so). The bishopric of Boulogne fell vacant, and, in the dying months of the old order, another commoner was appointed, Jean-René Asseline, aged 48, a brilliant scholar who held the chair of Hebrew at the Sorbonne and for long had been a *grand vicaire* of the diocese of Paris.[15] The story goes that his low birth was argued against his elevation (he was a son of a domestic servant of the Orléans family), but Louis XVI merely asked, 'a-t-il autant de vertus qu'on l'assure?' He was consecrated in time to publish a pastoral letter against the Civil Constitution of the Clergy, and to be evicted from the see he so well deserved and which had come to him so late.

III

Anticlerical orators of the Revolution were to declaim against the selection of bishops under the *ancien régime* as a matter of Court intrigue, with valets and mistresses as intermediaries. In the nature of the old society, Court influence counted. There were families under the king's eye as notable servants of the Crown. Dillon, archbishop of Narbonne, was the son of a lieutenant-general and had two brothers killed in the wars: a passport to promotion in the Church was brothers who risked their lives. Others came to notice as they acquired a contact at Versailles: Boisgelin, archbishop of Aix, had a brother who married a matron of honour to the royal princesses and joined his wife doing official duties in their household. In the next reign, Marie Antoinette and her circle radiated favouritism.[16] The abbé d'Agoult, disqualified from promotion because of his weakness for the ladies, was absolved by his links with her friends Breteuil and the Polignacs, and became bishop of Pamiers in 1787. Since La Tour du Pin Montauban, bishop of Nancy, chaplain to the queen, was refused the prestigious office of tutor to the dauphin, Marie Antoinette got him compensated with the rich see of Auch. Nobles who stayed away from Versailles needed a lucky accident to bring them to this sort of preferential notice. Hercé is said to have got Dol in 1767 because of a meeting with the duc d'Aiguillon when the estates of Brittany convened at Nantes, where for long he had run the diocese for his bishop; Gabriel Cortois de Quincey, archdeacon of Dijon, became bishop of Belley in 1751 because he out-argued an *esprit fort* in the stage-coach going to Paris, with a Théatin monk in the corner seat who turned out to be Boyer, minister of the *feuille*.[17]

But when the king 'worked', as the phrase went, with his minister, there were other pressures to take into account, more ecclesiastical in their nature, at least in their veneer. The bishops, and especially the archbishops, constituted a web of influence, and the system of qualifying as *grands vicaires* on their staffs gave them additional opportunities for liaising together in a sort of selection process. Of the episcopal generation of 1789,[18] twenty-three had an episcopal uncle as patron, four an episcopal brother, others had brothers marrying the nieces of bishops or more distant connections of relationship or friendship. The bishops in place were pushing members of their family (and pushing each other's), but they were also concerned about the dignity of their order, anxious to see it fortified with outstanding talent. They knew all the possible candidates and selectively groomed them for royal consideration.

There were, of course, dioceses and dioceses. The great nobles wanted the most splendid sees for their sons, if not immediately, then certainly by promotion. And the assessment of splendour began, though it did not end there, with sheer material considerations: some bishoprics conferred enough to live on by the standards of a modest country estate owner, others conferred riches on a scale only enjoyed by grandees of the Court—and there were many gradations of income between. About 1760, according to the *Almanach Royal*, Paris was worth over half a million livres, and Strasbourg and Metz were prodigiously rich. Around 80,000 livres were Arras and Verdun, around 50,000 livres Vabres, Lodève, Dol, Fréjus, Mirepoix, and Marseille. The poorest of all was Vence, at a mere 12,000 livres. Two vague generalizations are possible: the very tiny sees tended to have small incomes, and most of the sees in the North were rich, while most in the South were poor—a contrast reflecting the very different productivity of the two areas. Those rewards did not correspond to either status or responsibilities. Vienne was an archbishopric, but worth only 29,000 livres, Langres of peerage rank was worth less still. Condom, Agen, and Lectoure were dioceses of about equal size, but Condom had double the income of either of the others. Everyone, including candidates for episcopal promotion, used the *Almanach* when discussing incomes, since it was at least broadly reliable in putting sees in order of profitability, but it was assumed that the figures were much too low. From the gossip of the time, Taine inferred that multiplication by two would not be excessive. It is safer, however, to assume that it was mostly the poorer bishoprics which were greatly understated. An astonishing case is Troyes, down in the *Almanach* of 1789 as worth 14,000 livres, but according to figures submitted by the bishop himself in October 1790, really worth 68,068 livres, 6 sols (a degree of precision arousing doubts). Early in the century, the Assembly of Clergy, anxious to establish true figures for taxation purposes, collected returns from the individual bishops, a method which had never worked in France. Given that the incomes were complex in derivation and fluctuating in yield, there was inevitably cautious understatement in offering a figure likely to become permanent. Finally, the agents-general hit upon a surer way, examining the accounts held in the *Régie des Économats*, the organization collecting the revenues of bishoprics during vacancies. A good deal depended, however, on when the vacancy had occurred, how long it lasted, and how long the principal leases had been in unrevised operation. Short of a detailed investigation of the financial archives of a bishopric (where available), exact statements are impossible. One thing, however, is sure: episcopal incomes rose greatly in the course of the eighteenth century, a rise beginning about 1730 and becoming rapid after 1760.[19] It was dioceses like Strasbourg, Chartres, La Rochelle, and Rodez, where rents from land were the core of the income, which did best. The leases of the bishop of Chartres doubled from 1742 to 1770, and doubled again from 1770 to 1780. In so far as the facts were known, none of this would endear the bishops to their flocks and to those of their curés who lived on modest tithes or, worse still, on the *congrue*, with its belated and meagre augmentations.

The king and his minister of the *feuille* organized the patronage of abbeys in conjunction with that of bishoprics. A bishop would expect abbeys *in commendam* to supplement his income, the great aristocrats in the wealthy sees because they were great, the lesser nobles in the poorer sees because they needed the money. It was the great who received the most and the most promptly. Etienne Saint-Jean de Prunières became bishop of Grasse in 1753, and drew its income of 14,000 livres, as the years went by accumulating pensions of 9,000 livres extra; not until 1788 did he get an abbey, and it was worth only 5,000 livres a year.[20] Among his contemporaries, Montmorency-Laval at Metz with fifteen times his episcopal income had a further 60,000 livres from abbeys.[21] Cardinal Dominique de la Rochefoucauld, archbishop of Rouen from 1755, had an income from his see of 172,000 livres and the abbey of Cluny worth almost as much; nevertheless, in 1778, the abbey of Fécamp came his way.[22] These lofty noblemen had no doubts about their right to collect such vast revenues from the Church, though there were unwritten rules to add a veneer of decency. The income of the archbishop of Paris was so great that it was understood he needed no supplements; also, when one of the very lucrative monastic prizes fell to a bishop, he would feel obliged to throw back into the Versailles pool of benefices the smaller ones he had accumulated. This was a rule that Dubois, a vulgar adventurer, did not accept: he wrote to the Pope explaining why he deserved the extra abbey which had just been awarded to him—Richelieu had had twenty and Mazarin twenty-two, while he still had no more than eight.[23] A proper bishop would be more decorous in flouting the canonical ordinances against pluralities—provided the limited number of abbeys he retained yielded substantial revenues.

Behind this system of granting favours graded according to aristo-cratic standing and Court influence, a royal policy of a broader kind was operating, working towards political and ecclesiastical ends.[24] The king could modify a bishop's revenues in three ways: increasing them by adding an abbey or a grant of a pension from some ecclesiastical source, or diminishing them by deducting a pension. These devices were used in concert to maintain an equilibrium. A bishop already provided richly with abbeys who was moved up to a wealthier see might keep his abbeys but find the Crown had deducted pensions from his new income. A prelate who accepted translation to a poorer see to suit royal policy could expect to have the difference promptly made up. Long and valuable service would be recognized: for one, there would be an automatic increase as pensioners died off; for another, the Crown might offer an additional abbey. Apart from Vence and Saint-Paul-Trois-Châteaux, always left in poverty, the very lowest episcopal incomes were pushed up to a more dignified level. Also, certain sees, some rich, some not, were marked down for special consideration: the half-dozen most influential archbishoprics, the six conferring the title of peer, and the frontier sees of Strasbourg, Metz, and Verdun, where the completion of the annexation policy involved granting favours.

The *noblesse de race* had the greatest chance of obtaining the wealthy sees, and, for other reasons, they had a virtual monopoly of certain dioceses. The five 'foreign' dioceses—Besançon, Cambrai, Saint-Omer, Strasbourg, and Metz—carried with them princely titles in the Holy Roman Empire, so it was unthinkable to give any of them to an ordinary candidate—unless it was Dubois, of course. There were also the six carrying with them the rank of 'peer', three as 'counts' and three as 'dukes'. There were others, perhaps as many as twenty in number, for which lofty status was desirable, as there were numerous noble families in the diocese, who would look down on a prelate of inferior lineage.

In a minority of dioceses, there were reasons why the king, at least sometimes, would consider appointing a local candidate. Backers of a particular candidate would argue that the neighbours had a great affection for the family and wanted someone they knew.[25] And it was axiomatic that a bishop would enjoy exercising his splendid office among familiar faces; the minister of the *feuille*, if making such an appointment, would be sure to put a courteous cliché about it in his letter: 'I thought this place would be doubly agreeable to you, in that it puts you in the neighbourhood of your family.'[26] Knowledge of the local dialect was important for some areas: it was impossible, for example, to preside over the estates of Béarn without speaking Basque, so a man of the province had to be found for Lescar. This was certainly a consideration, though not an overriding one, when appointing to the bishoprics of Provence. Brittany was an ambiguous case. For pastoral efficiency, Breton was desirable, but experience had shown that anyone appointed from within the province would soon become involved in the tumultuous political agitations of the nobles. As a result, 'foreigners' were appointed to the important sees of Nantes, Saint-Malo, and Vannes throughout the eighteenth century, while Bretons got the less important ones of Tréguier, Saint-Pol-de-Léon, and Quimper.[27]

A different set of considerations operated when the minister of the *feuille* looked away from the demands of royal policy and the preference of the dioceses and considered the effect a particular nomination would have on the structure of the episcopate as a whole. An archbishop of Paris must be capable of giving leadership to the Gallican Church and must therefore be experienced (there was surprise when Beaumont went there after only a few years at Bayonne).[28] Somewhere on the episcopal bench, there ought to be an expert theologian—a factor which helped the rise of Languet de Gergy, the great polemicist against Jansenism. Looking at the scene more broadly, it was important to keep the age structure of the episcopate constant, with readily predictable possibilities of operating promotions and bringing in new blood at reasonably spaced intervals. When a bishop died young, there seems to have been a preference for appointing a young successor; when old, an older one.[29] This helped to keep the age and career pattern uniform, and to compensate dioceses for an unexpectedly short term of office by awarding the possibility of a longer one.

From time to time the king would consider the possibility of transferring a prelate to another see. In strict old-fashioned parlance, a bishop was 'married' to his see and ought to stay with his people for life, though in the eighteenth century it was a 'Jansenist' sentiment to proclaim it. By contrast, in Court circles, such moves were cynically regarded as simple matters of calculation of personal interest. On 21 April 1758 Bernis was advising the comte de Choiseul that his brother should accept the first vacancy: 'this will be the bridge towards the first great see which falls vacant afterwards'.[30] A few days later, news of the death of the archbishop of Tours arrived, and Bernis was trying to get it for the abbé de Choiseul—or, if the archbishop of Albi was moving over to take it, Albi would do. On 13 May it was a question of Evreux, and the idea was to persuade the bishop of Toul to take it, leaving Toul available. 'But the great point is to make the abbé de Choiseul a bishop. The

king has promised not to leave him languishing in a minor see.' On
16 May, it was definitely Evreux: 'I won't congratulate you,' wrote
Bernis, 'it's a simple stepping-stone.'

This correspondence comes from a Court intrigue in the circle of
Mme de Pompadour; most translations were more decorously
arranged and for better reasons. The vast disparities in wealth and
importance meant that there was a ready-made ladder for promotion. As the bishop of poor and mountainous Glandève said in 1790,
'surely these translations can be regarded as the recompense for a
laborious life spent in harsh surroundings offering no consolations
but those we can hope to find in the fulfilment of our ministry'.[31] A
vast and prestigious archbishopric like Rouen had to be ruled by a
senior and experienced administrator—its five incumbents from
1709 to 1789 had served their apprenticeship in smaller bishoprics.[32]
Conversely, individuals marked out by their great abilities needed to
be moved to spheres of wider opportunity—thus Champion de Cicé
and Loménie de Brienne staged at Condom and Rodez before
taking over the great responsibilities of Bordeaux and Toulouse. And
then, of course, there were always men of families of great distinction who could not be left to 'languish' low down in the hierarchy—bishop of Saint-Omer in 1775 at the age of 35, of
Carcassonne three years later, and archbishop of Bourges ten years
later still, this was an appropriate run of promotion for a son of
the military aristocracy of the Court, Jean-Antoine Auguste de
Chastenet de Puységur. On rare occasions (there was a case in 1719,
and another in 1788) an episcopal appointment was resigned before
it was taken up, as a more splendid see suddenly became available.

By contrast, there were prelates who refused the king's offer of
promotion.[33] Belsunce, hero of the plague of Marseille, turned down
Laon in 1723 and Bordeaux in 1729; the bishops of Limoges and
Uzès refused offers in 1750 and 1754, preferring their peace of mind
among people who were devoted to them. The saintly bishop of
Orange agreed to move to Grenoble in 1788, then changed his
mind. It might have appeared that Henri de Fleury, who left Tours
for Cambrai in 1775, was drawn by the lure of the high income, yet
originally he had refused, wishing to stay at Tours where for
twenty-three years he had been happy. The king made him go, to
give Cambrai a break from its series of worldly bishops—'you must
accept, Fénelon has not yet been replaced'.[34] Some of the poorer
bishoprics got the name of 'sièges de passage', but this was simply
because of the accident of dates of vacancy; if there was no candidate of great family or conspicuous ability ready to begin his progress

over the 'stepping-stones', an appointment would be made of someone who might well stay there for life. During the century, Valence
had one episcopal reign of forty-five years, Pamiers of forty-six,
Carcassonne of fifty; in 1789, the bishop of Grasse had ruled for
thirty-seven years, of Bazas for forty-three, Saint-Paul-Trois-
Châteaux for forty-six, Saint-Dié for forty-seven; of the 130 bishops
of 1789, thirty-six had received translations, generally after a decent
interval of about ten years.[35] With the disparities between dioceses,
most bishops had an eye to promotion; there were important sees to
which the Crown had to move up experienced administrators; there
were some great families whose sons could not be left to 'languish'.
Given these factors, it is surprising that translations were the exception rather than the rule.

IV

Problem III Aristacus, an abbé of high birth and distinguished merit,
solicits a bishopric, desiring to serve the church usefully.
Reply He can not desire the office of bishop with the elevation to such a
high dignity in mind, without rendering himself guilty of ambition or presumption; he cannot desire it aiming to be honoured and respected, or to
become rich, without rendering himself guilty of ambition or avarice. In
addition, it is not enough to have a pure intention to be able to desire a
bishopric without sin; he must have all the virtues that the Apostle prescribes for a bishop.[36]

These episcopal virtues prescribed by St Paul were: to be vigilant,
sober, blameless, hospitable, apt to teach, and not to be a brawler or
a striker—the Pauline proviso about being the husband of one wife
having been tightened up subsequently by a presumably superior
authority. As for the right to solicit a bishopric, most casuists would
have said this was not allowed in any case, even by attempting to
give an impression of worthiness so as to be noticed for promotion.
Tronson of Saint-Sulpice called Fénelon to penitence when he was
made tutor to the duc de Bourgogne. You did not seek it, but
maybe you took care to show yourself in a favourable light; 'on a
souvent plus de part à son élévation qu'on ne pense . . . personne ne
saurait s'assurer entièrement qu'il ne se soit pas appelé soi-même'.[37]
Given the severity of the casuists, how could a young aristocrat seek
a bishopric with a sincere purpose? There was a single narrow gap in
the wall of prohibitions through which he could drag his conscience.
One of the factors in the clerical vocation was to be 'called'. The

Church needed well-qualified men for its service, and those with an 'inclination' had a duty to consider seriously, when they were invited; indeed, there was an obligation to accept 'if the Pope or another legitimate superior orders'.[38] Humility, fear, distrust of the worldly manœuvres of relatives, were not legitimate grounds for refusing an authentic call.[39] The way bishops were appointed in eighteenth-century France involved recommendation by existing prelates, nomination by the king, and confirmation by the Pope. The system was corrupt, yet formally correct. A *grand vicaire* offered a diocese of his own could, in a fashion, justifiably say he was 'called'.

Yet the system contrived to call only aristocrats. 'If I thought that noble birth was the principal condition required for episcopal office,' said Cardinal La Roche-Aymon, when appointing the abbé de Beauvais to Senez, 'I would trample my pectoral cross under foot.'[40] His cross remained undamaged, so there must have been good arguments to placate his conscience. They would start from the general theories by which the nobility justified its privileges. According to the lawyers, noble rank was a creation of the king as the reward for great past services, especially upon the battlefield—petitioners for royal favour in the Church and elsewhere would cite the members of their family who had died in their country's wars. There was also the argument, most strongly advanced in La Roque's *Traité de la noblesse* (new edn. 1735), that there was an inherent superiority of soul in certain families, transmitted in their 'semance'; there might be unfortunate accidents, but they did not vitiate the principle of a class inherently worthy to rule in Church and State. However, beyond the theorizing about worthiness derived from past generations, there was a basic proposition referring to the present: the episcopate was a secular institution with a crucial political role and social responsibility as well as a system for governing the Church. The simple apostolic days were gone for ever. The eighteenth-century view of the change was summed up by an English preacher in 1760: 'though the apostles for wise reasons were chosen from among men of low birth and parentage, yet times and circumstances are so changed that persons of noble extraction by coming into the Church, may add strength and ornament to it'.[41] This was the establishment view in France as well; it was the philosophes and revolutionary reformers who, somewhat disingenuously, recalled how Matthew and Luke were not called 'Monseigneur', and how a true Christian bishop, white of hair, furrowed of face, rustic staff in hand, would tramp round the lanes visiting his parishes.[42] In fact,

Matthew, Luke, and perambulating patriarchs could not have run an eighteenth-century diocese: collected the complex revenues, organized clerical taxation, directed the ecclesiastical courts, presided over provincial estates and the boards of hospitals and charities, out-faced intendants, parlements, military governors, municipal authorities and the powerful local nobility in defence of their clergy and the interests of the Church. It was to do tasks like this that the aristo-cratic aspirants to bishoprics were appointed.

Among the families accustomed to receiving bishoprics for their sons, vocation was a concept accepted with a nod, then left to the particular individual, who, no doubt, tended to think of it occasion-ally but not obsessively. In practice, young men of these families had a choice between two main careers, the Church and the armed forces. A stock figure in eighteenth-century literature is the younger son of a penurious noble house having to choose between them. An unpleasant mother in one of Marmontel's *Contes moraux* tells her second son: 'your father's fortune was not so considerable as was imagined; it will scarce suffice to settle your elder brother. For your part, you have simply to decide whether you will follow the career of benefices or of arms, whether you will have your head shaved or broken, whether you will take orders or a lieutenancy of infantry.'[43] In real life, the victims of such decisions are sometimes found look-ing back sadly on the mistake they had made: 'if I had taken the path of the Church, what tribulations, what toils I'd have spared myself,' says a soldier; a monk writes to his soldier brother of 'the fearful misery and harsh slavery to which I am reduced in this abominable monastery where schemes of ill-considered ambition have dragged me' (he finished up an abbot with comfortable apartments and his private town house).[44] But the young aspirants to the episcopate were not driven by necessity: their families were, for the most part, rich. It was not a question of pushing the youngest sons for bishoprics; the eldest inherited, of course, but it was the *second* son who was encouraged to follow an episcopal destiny, the preferred option for the prestige of the family. Of the bishops of 1789, sixty-one were second sons (twenty-one the second and last); twenty-four were third sons, ten fourth sons. These were families with long traditions of service—ninety-seven of these bishops had five genera-tions of unbroken ecclesiastical service preceding them, forty-three of them having had bishops among their number. They were proud to serve the king, whether providing colonels of regiments or rulers of dioceses.

Occasionally, a young man who had originally chosen the army would change his mind and seek ordination. After the Peace of Utrecht, Antoine-Pierre de Grammont left his colonelcy at the age of 28, and from 1735 he was a worthy archbishop of Besançon, succeeding his uncle. A very different case was Paul-Albert de Luynes, a colonel of infantry in 1719 at the age of 16; a brother-officer struck him, he refused to fight a duel, and his termagant mother ordered him either to avenge the insult or be ordained. He was bishop of Bayeux in 1729 and archbishop of Sens in 1753, a wealthy, decent, and simple prelate who got up early to attend the parish church when the Court was at Fontainebleau, and read to peasant congregations the homilies he had written in his seminary, warning them against velvet cushions and other trappings of luxury.[45] Of the bishops of 1789 Saint-Pol-de-Léon had been a captain in the Queen's regiment, leaving after the Peace of Aix-la-Chapelle; Soissons had been a musketeer, Périgueux a captain of artillery. Waiting in the wings, but deprived of great ecclesiastical promotion by the Revolution, were Guillaume-Jean-François Souquet de Latour, who left the *école militaire* of Beaumont-en-Ange and was ordained in 1789, and Guillaume-Honoré Rocques de Montgaillard, who had been crippled by an accident at the *école militaire* of Sorèze and was about to become a *grand vicaire* of Champion de Cicé.[46] About this time, Chateaubriand was thinking of an ecclesiastical career, but decided against, perhaps because his mother was afraid of having a scandalous priest in the family. He became a second lieutenant in the regiment of Navarre, and in December 1788 took the tonsure, not intending to proceed further as an ecclesiastic, but to qualify for an income as a knight of Malta: 'An abuse, no doubt, in the ecclesiastical order,' he wrote, 'but a useful arrangement in the political order of the old constitution.'[47]

The recipients of privilege can easily convince themselves that it is merited. The great aristocratic families talked of the bishoprics with easy, possessive familiarity—discussed the income, the agreeableness of the house, the distance from Paris, the chances of getting a better see later on. A mother paints an attractive picture of clerical life to a third son: time in a seminary in Paris, then pensions and abbeys, chaplain to the king, agent-general of the clergy, a bishop at 30, 'et enfin le plus riche de la famille'.[48] Another mother gives her son an intensive education so that he can rise in the Church and rescue the straitened family fortunes, rebuild the family château, and, perhaps, emulate the greatness of her grandfather, Secretary of State to Louis XIV—Loménie de Brienne realized her ambitions.[49] A grandmother presents her 15-year-old grandson to Morellet, who is to be his tutor: 'he is destined to become a bishop; you have to ensure he passes his *licence* in theology'. Bishoprics and abbeys were underpinnings of the family structure—the policy of the La Rochefoucaulds as Saint-Simon defined it: one son for inheriting all the property and marrying, the girls and younger sons remaining celibate and living off ecclesiastical revenues. 'I am old,' said a crudely frank seventeenth-century nobleman; 'I am not rich, I have many children, my duty as a father is to preserve them from want by placing them advantageously.' As for fitness for episcopal office, he did not see how this came into it. 'If my son has not got the qualities required to govern a diocese, he will always be able to have capable ecclesiastics around him whose counsels he will faithfully follow.'[50]

Once a son had gained the necessary academic qualifications and become a *grand vicaire*, the family would mobilize to hasten on the final promotion. At the age of 30, in 1760, Pierre-Augustin Godert de Belbeuf became *grand vicaire* of Verdun.[51] His brother, *procureur général* of the parlement of Rouen, took charge of his candidature. The bishop of Verdun wrote plausibly, saying he was pressing the case, but information came suggesting these recommendations were lukewarm. So the archbishop of Rouen was persuaded to give Pierre-Augustin the grand vicariate of Pontoise. In 1767, the bishop of Lescar wrote to say that his colleague at Tarbes had just died— 200 leagues away, but an agreeable niche. Jarente, minister of the *feuille*, wrote encouraging letters to Rouen, until in 1771 he sent a final note of regret saying he had just been dismissed. Finally, in 1774, Avranches was offered. It had been a long haul of fourteen years. The campaign for Jean-de-Dieu-Raymond de Boisgelin was run by his father, a *président à mortier* of the parlement of Brittany, an operation conducted with a blend of cynicism and sincerity.[52] Strings were pulled through the prince de Soubise and Mme de Pompadour to get an abbey, and great was the disappointment when four years went by without success. Then the abbey came, and another four years of lobbying ensued until the see of Lavaur was offered. The intriguing *président à mortier* genuinely wanted his son to be a good Christian, and he was not unaware of the fact that being seen to be one might help on the promotion. 'I expect a great deal of a son who has voluntarily embraced such a respectable state; I hope that he will have religion, morals and application to the studies relating to his profession, rather than to *belles lettres*, which adorn only the mind and which often corrupt the heart.' This to the 20-year-old student. Then, two years later, at the time of the subdiaconate: 'the public expects edification of you. You have ambition, but it must always be subordinate to religion; you will reap the fruits in this world and the next.' So he did—at least in this world. In 1780, as archbishop of Aix, Boisgelin had an income of 219,000 livres from the Church, as against a family pittance of 27,000 livres.

In these operations to obtain an episcopal promotion, a relative in episcopal orders (generally an uncle) could be invaluable—to offer an appointment as *grand vicaire*, to use influence with other bishops towards an election as agent-general of the clergy, to put in a good word with the minister of the *feuille*. The way this family patronage worked may be considered in the careers of some of the related prelates who occupied sees in 1789. The two Rohans, glittering names from the highest reaches of the Court, did not need such recommendations, and they proceeded as of right to hold the wealthy sees of Strasbourg and Cambrai in unworthy splendour. The two Duplessis d'Argentré had come up their separate ways, Jean-Baptiste getting Sées by his Breton connections, while Louis-Charles, brought up by a relative, the bishop of Limoges, inherited the see when Mgr de Coeslosquet resigned it to become tutor to the dauphin and, as such, having Court influence to fix his own successor.[53] Of the three La Rochefoucaulds, all conscientious rulers of dioceses, Dominique (archbishop of Albi in 1747, then of Rouen in 1759) had been helped in his career by an uncle who was archbishop of Bourges; in his turn he helped two brothers of another branch of the family, François-Joseph becoming bishop of Beauvais in 1772, Pierre-Louis of Saintes in 1781 (after serving as vicar-general at Beauvais under his brother).[54] The eldest of the Champion de Cicé became bishop of Troyes in 1758, and took his brother as vicar-general; the one was promoted to Auxerre in 1777, the other got Rodez as his first bishopric in 1770. When La Roche-Aymon died in 1777, his great see of Reims went automatically to the nephew he had established as his coadjutor, Alexandre-Angélique de Talleyrand-Périgord; in his turn, the new archbishop looked after his nephew, the Talleyrand who was to become notorious, making him a canon of Reims and arranging his election as agent-general of the clergy. This patronage, proven administrative ability, and a letter from Talleyrand's dying father to the king finally brought the bishopric of Autun.

As the example of Reims in 1777 showed, a bishop might exercise enough influence to ensure his nephew the succession to the diocese. The bishop of Oloron, who died in 1735, was followed by his nephew; the nephew, promoted to Auch in 1741, was followed by his great-nephew; the chain was broken in 1783 by an outsider—who was nephew and *grand vicaire* to Loménie de Brienne.[55] The case of Gilbert de Montmorin de Saint-Herem coming to the see of Aire in 1723 was an unusual variant, as he was inheriting from his father, who had left the army and taken holy orders after the death of his wife.[56] The certain way to ensure succession was to persuade the king to allow the nephew or other favoured relative to become coadjutor bishop. In 1788, Barral took over Troyes and Jarente d'Orgeval took over Orléans in this way, and in the same year Loménie de Brienne had his 25-year-old nephew consecrated as 'archbishop of Trajanopolis' and coadjutor of his archidiocese of Sens, a family contrivance broken by the Revolution.

A bishop was not likely to be able to foster the career of a nephew who had no talent, but he could give him experience and a chance to display such talent as he might possess, more especially by engineering his election as a representative of the ecclesiastical province to the Assembly General of the Clergy, or better still, as one of the two agents-general. To get this ultimate opportunity, the patronage of a bishop hardly sufficed—it needed an archbishop in the family. The ecclesiastical provinces were paired and took their turns in electing on a rota of forty years, the electing body being the metropolitan assembly of two deputies from each diocese meeting under the presidency of the archbishop. Thus in 1775, Rouen chose Pierre-Louis de la Rochefoucauld, nephew of the archbishop, and Toulouse chose François-Alexandre de Jarente, nephew of the bishop of Orléans and protégé and *grand vicaire* of the presiding archbishop. In 1780, Tours elected Talleyrand by influence exercised from Reims, and Aix the abbé de Boisgelin de Kerdu, nephew of the archbishop. Talleyrand, more slowly than he would have wished, reached the episcopate, but the abbé de Boisgelin had to be content with rich abbeys because he was caught in the bedroom of Mme de Cavanac and fought her angry husband, parrying the fire shovel with the tongs.

V

When, for whatever reasons, a young nobleman had decided he had a vocation to the episcopal state, he had to work to qualify himself for selection: that is, to carry through university studies to the point of obtaining the *licence*, and to serve an apprenticeship to diocesan administration as a *grand vicaire*.

By the standards of the day and in formal qualifications, the bishops were well educated. Of the 130 ruling the dioceses in 1789, all were *licenciés* of a major university, except two Bretons whose academic careers had stopped at the *baccalauréat* and Cardinal Bernis, who had risen through Court favour and the diplomatic service. Of the *licenciés*, all except seven had qualified at Paris (between 1755 and 1760, the examination of theses at the Sorbonne had been suspended, so some candidates had moved out to Reims or Orléans). The degrees were mostly in theology, though a third of them were in law (with canon law included).

The first academic hurdle to be negotiated was the *maîtrise-ès-arts*, the examination being taken at the completion of the final two years of philosophy at a *collège* affiliated to the university. In these Parisian institutions, the future bishop sat on the classroom benches with contemporaries destined for the highest offices in Church, Government, and Law. In mid-century, at the Collège du Plessis, six future bishops were together—in later life they were to rule the sees of Saint-Dié, Noyon, Strasbourg, Bordeaux, Cambrai, and Lyon.[57] The three years after the *maîtrise* were devoted to theology, the candidates either going back to their *collèges* to lodge or moving on to a seminary, generally that of Saint-Sulpice. This was the point at which a family was well advised to hire a tutor: Le Tonnelier de Breteuil, the future bishop of Rennes, studying theology at the Collège de Lisieux from 1705 to 1709, was coached by M. Langlois, who was paid a fee of 1,000 livres a year.[58] There was an oral examination on five subjects: the attributes of God, the Trinity, the angels, and two others chosen by the candidate, and a thesis, the *tentative*, examined in public in a five-hour session by ten doctors. The subjects prescribed may give an impression of restricted horizons of study, though in practice, speculation could range widely; a candidate defending a thesis on, say, the angels, would make it a starting-point for a polemic against atheists and materialists who had aired their sceptical doubts about such aspects of the faith.[59] A satisfactory performance gained the *baccalauréat en théologie*, opening the way to the *licence*, requiring at least two more years' study of theology. The candidate now had to enrol in the society of the Sorbonne or of Navarre or take the status of *ubiquiste*; he had to proceed to the subdiaconate, which brought the obligation of celibacy; he had to be present at all public examinations of theses and be prepared to join in the questioning, and had to attend the lectures of the professors, taking down the information they dictated and writing it up in *cahiers* handed in for inspection at the end of the course. There were two oral examinations, one on Aquinas, the other on Church history, and three theses had to be sustained: the 'minor' on the sacraments (with a six-hour viva), the 'major' on the Bible and ecclesiastical history (ten hours), and the 'sorbonique' on the Incarnation and grace (twelve hours). Success in the *licence* was virtually equivalent to a doctorate; true, a further thesis had to be sustained before the *bonnet* was awarded, but this was a formality— as the abbé Baston said, it was a question of 'paying 600 livres and a ceremony'. Some bishops proceeded to the doctorate (twenty-five of the 130 of 1789 had done so), but most stayed at the *licence*, the officially prescribed qualification for the highest offices in the Church.

Stories of painless degrees given for fees or favour come mainly in the first half of the century from provincial universities and in the Faculties of Law and Medicine (though Jean-Antoine de Tinseau, who became bishop of Belley in 1745, had obtained a doctorate at his local university of Besançon at the age of 15).[60] By 1750, the theological training of the episcopate had come to be centred in Paris, and was decorous according to the regulations. True, as everywhere in France, the university gave deference to those of aristocratic birth, but it was a formalized deference, obvious to every eye and deceiving no one, and falling short of obsequiousness except in the case of sons of the very greatest families of the Court.[61] In the awarding of places in the *licence*, the first went to the candidate with the longest genealogy, and the next three to those named in the Sorbonne and Navarre as the most distinguished, the real list of academic merit beginning at number five. Granting the initial abuse, it was honestly done. The longest genealogy meant what it said: the son of a penurious Gascon squire whose line went back to the Crusades came first on one occasion, with the son of a *grand seigneur* postponing his graduation so as not to have to come after him.[62] Aristocrats with good results chose to figure in places five, six, and seven, preferring to be recognized as intelligent rather than parading ancestry. François-Joseph Partz de Pressy (later bishop of Boulogne) took the *licence* in 1738 at number five, so did Pierre-Louis Leyssin (later archbishop of Embrun) in 1748, as also Loménie de Brienne in 1752. Loménie de Brienne's thesis, sustained on 30 October 1751, was a masterpiece of brinkmanship, winning the highest award from the examiners, yet pleasing the audience by incorporating the epistemology of Locke and a view of divine action in history appropriate to the ideas of the Enlightenment. A conservative theologian, alarmed by the abbé de Prade's notorious thesis of November of the same year, accused Brienne of being in the same plot to insinuate unbelief into the Faculty of Theology.[63] Clearly, there were nobles who were academic high-flyers, and there were others who had their theses compiled by their tutors and who hired substitutes to copy the lecture notes (presenting them with the handsome binding and laudatory title-page which always won the approval of the professors).[64] Yet, so dull was the teaching and so hidebound the procedures of the Sorbonne, that coaching by tutors was a superior way to learning, and the sleek young men on their way to bishoprics had all the pride of their ancestry to inspire them to try to shine before the fashionable audiences which came to their *soutenances*. At the end of the *ancien régime* the curés challenged the bishops as members of an aristocratic caste, but it was no longer justifiable to add to the charge the accusation of ignorance of theology; about one in ten parish priests had the *licence* or the doctorate, the standard episcopal qualification.

Provincial seminaries tried, however inefficiently, to give their ordinands a grounding in pastoralia, the casuistry of the confessional, and the practices of the spiritual life. To what extent did the future bishops receive this formation? In the second half of the century, 60 per cent of them lived from three to seven years of their period of academic study in the seminary of Saint-Sulpice, and these were probably subjected to more discipline than those who went elsewhere. With Louis Tronson as superior at the end of the seventeenth century, Saint-Sulpice had been—so far as he could make it—an austere place. His correspondence shows him banning wigs, the wearing of slippers in chapel, the drinking of wine undiluted with water, and imposing one and a half hours of meditation daily, fasting three days a week, and the wearing of hair shirts on one of them. The sending down of offenders, he said, gave him more joy than welcoming new recruits, as it proved he was carrying out reforms. In truth, he was always trying to enforce reforms and never succeeding, and after his death, Saint-Sulpice went downhill. The reasons were partly inherent in the peculiar nature of the institution itself. Unlike other seminaries, it was not under the jurisdiction of the diocesan bishop, being under the abbey of Saint-Germain-des-Prés; nor were its recruits mainly from the diocese, most of them coming from elsewhere in France. It was a metropolitan centre with a reputation as the place to attend with a successful career in mind.[65] Central control met with obstacles, for Saint-Sulpice was a federation of houses rather than one. Around the Grand Séminaire were La Maison des Philosophes in the rue Pot de Fer, the Robertins in the Impasse Féron, and, from 1738, the community which came to be called the Collège de Laon, while there was a country house at Issy, and further country retreats there and at Vaugiraud for the affiliated branches.[66] As Saint-Sulpice became the recognized gateway to the episcopate, more aristocratic recruits came in; they required extensive accommodation, brought their own furniture, and were attended by their own servants. Cardinal Fleury's patronage of the Sulpicians was dangerous: he made Issy his favourite residence, so the place became a resort for high society, and the seminarists, who went there once a week and for a period of several weeks in summer lost the sense of separation from the world. Under the weak rule of M. Couturier and M. Le Gallic, the aristocratic ordinands broke down the disciplinary code. Le Gallic was kept awake at night by explosive charges fired at random round the house, and the crowning indignity came at the Corpus Christi procession of the district, when the students cut the rope of a canopy, trapping him under the collapsing canvas. Talleyrand recounts how his liaison with a pretty young actress passed without rebuke from the directors—'the abbé Couturier had taught them the art of closing their eyes . . . and not reproaching a Seminarist destined for archbishoprics'.[67] Belatedly, reform came in 1782 when M. Emery arrived as superior.[68] The first explosion that was perpetrated led to twenty-five expulsions. Theatrical productions ended in the Grand Séminaire and were discouraged in the Robertins and Laon. But in matters of life-style rather than discipline, he often had to put up with expressing disapproval and finding it had little effect. The elaborate hair-styling that went on, especially on the night before an ordination, could not be suppressed, though Emery defined 'sin' as beginning when 'deux ou trois étages' were built up, and he urged the frequenters of the *perruquiers* to consider if their action was one they could offer to God for his glory, as one deserving of reward on the Day of Judgement.

The life of a seminary is not truly reflected in the scandalous incidents recorded by gossip writers; even in the decadent days, there were intelligent discussion groups, more useful than the course at the Sorbonne, said the abbé Baston;[69] there was the daily round of liturgical observances and of meditation (at mid-century reduced to half an hour). The directors were known to report on the suitability of their charges for ordination, which was a restraint on excesses, if not on comfortable living. Most candidates for high office in the Church would have learned about ecclesiastical routines and gained a familiarity with the practices of piety. According to Bernis, the

Sulpicians concentrated on 'little things' concerning 'conduct'. Saint-Simon spoke of them as excelling in 'minutiae and useless puerilities'—severe criticisms, but on the other side of the divide to those of laxity. What was wrong with the training of the future bishops was its atmosphere rather than its deficiencies. They had their valets and the comfortable life-style to which they were accustomed. They were not at one with their fellow seminarists, just as, when they came to rule dioceses, they were not at one with their curés. They had served no apprenticeship to humility.

After the *licence* and ordination to the priesthood, the next step for the episcopal aspirant was to negotiate an appointment as a *grand vicaire*. An uncle or some family friend would issue the invitation, though it might be better to move out of the family circle if some prelate could be found who was high in favour at Court or ruled over a more prestigious diocese. At Rouen in 1756–60, no fewer than six future bishops were serving together as *grands vicaires* (this includes one who had the quasi-independent archidiaconal administration of Pontoise). According to ill-disposed critics, these apprentices to the episcopate were gilded drones, just filling in time until a vacancy came their way. 'C'est une dérision qui fait gémir,' said the abbé Barruel in 1789; 'our bishops have eight, ten, twelve or twenty *grands vicaires*; two or three, at most, work; the others hardly ever appear—yet these are the only ones who aspire to bishoprics and get them.'[70] In an obvious sense, Barruel's picture is true to life, for a bishop who valued his peace of mind would hardly confide his administration to young men newly arrived from the Sorbonne—he would have a few professionals doing it, like Jullien Lailler, who was vicar-general, *official*, archdeacon, and superior of the seminary all in one at Coutances from 1676 to 1725, or Louis Daignan de Sendat (dd. 1764), who ran the diocese of Auch for fifty years under three archbishops, one a complete absentee and the others there only intermittently.[71] Some of these professionals were indigenous to the diocese, often from families of local distinction, chosen because of their ability from parochial curés or canonries; others came in from outside with the bishop when he first arrived, having been his tutor or one of the directors of his seminary in Paris. They would form the effective administrative stiffening in the corps of *grands vicaires*. Champion de Cicé at Bordeaux had two of them, along with his nephew and two sons of *grands seigneurs*; Boisgelin at Aix had four, along with eleven young aristocrats; Bernis at Albi had two out of a dozen. Under the haughty and distant Montmorency-Laval at Metz the diocese was run by the abbés Bertin and Ravaut and by Henri de Chambre d'Urgons (who was made suffragan bishop in 1780), while the other ten *grands vicaires* looked on or were absent.[72]

Yet Barruel's condemnation of the system is only half justified. It was a manifest abuse to allow aristocratic candidates to walk into the office of *grand vicaire* with little or no pastoral experience; no doubt some of these young men took more time away from the diocese than was reasonable, and sought out what amusements provincial society afforded—perhaps introducing Parisian taste by organizing concerts or demonstrating the new sport of hot-air ballooning.[73] Yet it does not follow that they were not learning their trade by association with the bishop and his professionals. Béthisy de Mézières, bishop of Uzès from 1779, ran his diocese with four *grands vicaires*, all nobles; he had two in charge of the rural parishes, one of the town parishes and all charitable initiatives, the other of the seminary, retreats, *conférences ecclésiastiques*, missions, and all the monasteries—they came to a weekly staff meeting at 9 a.m. every Wednesday.[74] The apprenticeship served by many bishops was real. Indeed, circumstances like a frequently absent bishop or one in poor health sometimes pushed them into performing episcopal duties long before they got dioceses of their own. Thus François d'Andigné went to Dax in 1733 after ten years running Luçon as vicar-general, and Urbain de Hercé went to Dol in 1767 after being in charge at Nantes for thirteen years. The picture of the aristocratic *grand vicaire* idling away his years of waiting is untrue to human nature. These were active young men anxious to distinguish themselves. La Fare, who became bishop of Nancy in October 1787, had been a *grand vicaire* at Dijon under a distant relative, and here he became *syndic* of the diocese (that is, in charge of clerical taxation and correspondence with the agents-general in Paris), a member of the local Académie des sciences, arts et belles-lettres (succeeding Voltaire), dean of the Sainte-Chapelle of Dijon, a deputy to the Assembly General of the Clergy, *élu général du Clergé des États de Bourgogne* (that is, one of the committee running the affairs of the province in the intervals of the triennial meetings of the estates), and was summoned to Paris in 1787 as one of the Notables—quite an accumulation of distinctions and responsibilities for a man in his early thirties.[75]

The average time spent as a *grand vicaire* before promotion to the episcopate was ten years, not enough in circumstance or time span to gain pastoral insight, but adequate to master the details of administration and command. There is every reason to suppose that most of them took the business of learning seriously, whether from vocation, pride, or (except for the sons of the very greatest families) prudence, for the Crown took pastoral considerations seriously, and with vacancies occurring at the rate of only six to four a year, many candidates were going to be disappointed.

8

THE BISHOPS: WORLDLY GREATNESS

I

What sort of men were brought to the bishoprics by the operation of royal choice and these aristocratic vocations? They had poise and a social viability enabling them to look impressive and act forcefully in their great office, and the system ensured they were reasonably learned and trained in diocesan administration. Anticlericals censured the favouritism by which they were appointed, and watched them narrowly to detect the vices typical of their aristo-cratic origins—they were generally accused of slackness about residence in favour of a life-style centred in the capital and Versailles, of haughtiness and spendthrift display, and, in snide allegations rather than circumstantial accusations, of sexual adventures in breach of their oath of celibacy and ordinary Christian duty.

One of the most obvious obligations of a pastor was to reside in the midst of his flock. The Council of Trent had defined an absence of more than three months without good cause as mortal sin, and authorized metropolitans to act against offenders. Royal declarations and edicts had reaffirmed the prescriptions of canon law, the edict of 1695 ordering the parlements to watch for absentees and report them to the *chancelier*, whose sanction would be the confiscation of temporalities. The law was clear, and there was machinery to enforce it, but it was not obeyed. 'I know of dioceses more . . . presbyterian than Scotland,' said D'Argenson in 1748, though he gave only one example of episcopal absence.[1] But a multitude of illustrations was forthcoming in 1764, when the parlement of Paris, acting in the spirit of the edict of 1695, published a list of prelates currently living in Paris with their addresses: about a quarter of the Gallican episcopate was there.[2] Two years later, without giving any figures, the papal nuncio reported that there were always too many bishops in the capital—they came to intrigue for better sees, he said, or to enjoy society.[3] In 1784, Louis XVI issued a circular, through

Breteuil, the new minister for the Maison du Roi, instructing the bishops to seek permission before absenting themselves from their dioceses. The abbé de Veri complained against this infringement of protocol, for this was really a matter for the *chancelier*; even so, he agreed that urgent action was needed, as no fewer than sixty bishops were renting houses in Paris.[4] As the wits were accustomed to observe, the Gallican Church could act quickly in a crisis, a quorum of bishops always being available for an emergency meeting at a few hours' notice. The *cahiers* of 1789 reflect the common opinion: 51 per cent of the *bailliage* meetings of the Tiers État, 38 per cent of the nobles, and 24 per cent of the clergy complain of episcopal non-residence.

There are a few examples throughout the century of absentees so blatant that they no longer scandalize, since they are vocationless prelates, given rank and emoluments in the Church for purely secular reasons, like Saint-Albin at Cambrai and—the most notorious case of all—Cardinal Polignac, diplomat, member of the three great Parisian academies, a handsome figure adorning high society, who died in 1741, archbishop of Auch for fifteen years without ever having been there. There were others, supposed to be in real command of their dioceses, whose absences were so frequent or prolonged as to be inexcusable by any standards. There was Jacques de Grasse, who died without sacraments in 1782, having run his diocese of Angers for twenty-four years chiefly from his Parisian lodgings. The story goes that after a long journey from Paris the day before, he stayed in bed and refused to conduct an ordination—until turned out by M. Emery, the austere superior of the seminary: 'a stay in Paris which does not appear to have been necessary and which ought to have finished earlier does not constitute a valid excuse; the clergy will not understand such a dereliction of duty'.[5] Louis-Jacques de Chapt de Rastignac, a well-loved archbishop of Tours for eighteen years, suddenly changed when disappointed in his hope of promotion to the see of Paris, and became an 'absentee monarch' for the next nine years.[6] There are numerous cases of bishops not normally given to absence, who had not hastened to take up their duties after they were consecrated, having family affairs to settle and preparations to make. An extreme example was Le Tonnelier de Breteuil, appointed to Rennes in October 1723, consecrated only in July 1725, and making his entry into his episcopal city on 7 June 1726; before 8 December, he was back in Versailles.[7] This custom of initial delay went on until the end of the century. In the early days of the Revolution, in 1790, Carcassonne still waited to catch a glimpse of its chief pastor, consecrated in October 1788, and in January 1791, when the bishops were on the verge of being displaced, Valence had not seen the prelate consecrated to serve the diocese fifteen months before.[8] If one adds to these two invisible men two established bishops who were also absent from Embrun and Saint-Brieuc[9] (one for the last three years, the other for five), they form an odd group of characters, presumably of political sense if not of religious conviction, who stayed away from their posts of responsibility when the whole future of the nation was being decided. The standard period of delay for taking over a see was something like a year. This was the period of waiting imposed on their expectant flocks by Jean de Caulet,[10] punctilious and miserly, going to Grenoble (1725–7); by the haughty Montmorency-Laval[11] going to Metz (1761–2); Christophe de Beaumont, pious, charitable, and intolerant, going to his first see of Bayonne (1741–3); Boisgelin, administrator and reformer, going to his first see of Lavaur (1764–5); and Jacques d'Audibert de Lussan,[12] a dedicated pastor, going to Bordeaux (1744–5). With their various virtues and vices, they seemed to regard this length of time as defensible.

While half the *cahiers* of the Tiers État condemned episcopal absenteeism, only a quarter of those of the clergy did so. It may be significant also that the clerical editors of the *Nouvelles ecclésiastiques*,[13] keeping a baleful eye on the conduct of all in authority in the Church, found no more than nine cases between 1769 and 1790. It could be that informed opinion about episcopal duties distinguished between necessary and self-indulgent absences. By canon law an ecclesiastic was entitled to take time off to visit his family, and by royal policy, bishops were planted away from their homes. Members of the Académie would feel they had to attend at least some meetings, and they had to be present when it was their turn to give a panegyric. Peers would be urged by their lay fellows to attend the parlement of Paris to defend the rights of their order. The minister of the *feuille* had to be at Versailles, and the ambassador to the Holy See (often a bishop) at Rome. Election by the ecclesiastical province as a deputy to the Assembly General of the Clergy was an obligation to be fulfilled, just as invitations from provincial estates to go on deputations to Versailles could hardly be refused. And even prelates who were not presidents of diocesan or provincial estates had sometimes to go to the centre of affairs when their people needed an advocate to ask for tax remissions or other favours. It could be time-consuming—two sojourns of a year each at Paris to get a subsidy for dredging the harbour at Fréjus.[14] Such was the nature of the social

238 The Religious Establishment

order that serving the royal family in affairs of conscience or ceremonial was a duty outranking all others, and at any one time as many
as a dozen bishops might be chaplains at Court. Nicolas de Saulx-
Tavannes, the most genial of pastors, was promoted to Rouen, the
most responsible see in France, in 1734; three years later he became
chaplain to the queen, who insisted he accompany her everywhere.
By the standards of the day he was singularly honoured: on any
rational view, the last twenty years of his life were wasted.

No doubt the excuse of necessary business was often misused,
whether by the inflation of a small issue or by lingering over an
important one. Jean de Caulet of Grenoble spent a long time in Paris
prosecuting a lawsuit worth little more than 1,000 livres a year to
his episcopal income, blandly excusing his conduct to Fleury by saying: 'a bishop discredited (presumably by losing a legal battle) is a
bishop rendered useless'. Boisgelin,[15] justifiably an absentee during
frequent negotiations with the government on behalf of the estates
of Provence, had his private apartments and chapel in the mansion
of the comtesse de Grammont near Versailles, and was able to attend
the Academy fifty times in fourteen years. The argument of necessity had become elastic. The intense focusing of political life at
Versailles and of civilization and culture at Paris constituted a powerful attraction, a lure to draw the ambitious, the sociable, and the
intellectually sophisticated. The only way to defeat the temptation,
Le Camus decided, was to cease all correspondence with the centre,
asking no news and receiving none, cutting himself off amidst his
mountains. Massillon yielded to the temptations of Academy and
political involvement after his consecration, spending twenty
months in Paris and only six in his diocese of Clermont. Then he
made the break. Apart from a Court funeral sermon in 1723, he
remained in the Auvergne for the twenty-one years still left to him.[16]

The anticlerical stereotype of a bishop of the *ancien régime*
included a mistress, and if no candidate for the post could plausibly
be named, often enough a niece or widowed sister-in-law living in
the palace would be put in the category of suspects. Like most
stereotypes, this one throve on a few startling examples. The
Regency—that period of astonishing immorality among the great—
provided the most blatant cases of vocationless characters favoured
from the centre of power, who were contemptuous alike of religious
obligations and public opinion. There was Dubois, whose most
respectable liaison was with Mme de Tencin, ex-nun, novelist, and
'political whore' of the period; Saint-Albin, the regent's bastard,
whose mistress was to be the famous Mme O'Brien de Lismore,

coveted by the king;[17] and Phélypeaux, bishop of Lodève—he lived openly with women, says Saint-Simon, and boasted he did not believe in God, and 'all this was forgiven him for his name was Phélypeaux'.[18] There was also the sad case of the unbalanced abbé de Beauvilliers, named bishop of Beauvais in 1713, spending his first five years as a penitential anchorite, then falling in love with a woman and living as her inseparable companion. In the end he was forced to resign, compensated with an abbey, and finally interned in the monastery of Cîteaux.[19] Outrageous cases like these are hard to find later, though anticlerical sniping went on. D'Argenson in 1750 has a story of a bishop of Troyes giving a dubious lady a pair of earrings made from an altar ornament, and of a hoax letter from a 'widow' to the bishop of Chartres which led him to endow an allowance for her illegitimate child—'les histoires galantes sur les évêques les déshonorent à perpétuité'.[20] Even so, in 1766 the papal nuncio praised the bishops in his secret report as 'for the most part of good morals and praiseworthy conduct'.[21] In fact, what liaisons there were, were discreet, even if well known, as Jarente's with Mlle Guimard. The successor to the Regency stereotype-makers was Cardinal Rohan, bishop of Strasbourg, whose handsome, elegant figure glittered disastrously for Church and State through the reign of Louis XVI.[22] All Paris knew him, prouder of his cordon bleu than of his pectoral cross, striding between the ranks of his liveried lackeys, driving off to his mistress in the Chaussée d'Antin, the leafy suburb where the courtiers and bankers built houses for their secret pleasures. In 1782, he was shamed by association with his brother, who went bankrupt for a vast sum, bringing ruin to hundreds of minor creditors; in 1783, he himself was investigated by the parlement over shady transactions with the property of hospitals which he held in trust as chief chaplain to the king; in 1785, disguised as a musketeer, he met a woman he thought was the queen in a wood near Versailles, and was conned into buying a one-and-a-half-million-livres diamond necklace which vanished—as 'Cardinal Collier', he was tried before the parlement for treasonable culpability.

This is an example of a butterfly *grand seigneur* ensconced unworthily in ecclesiastical office, expected by all to live in mindless worldliness and not disappointing them. In other cases where anti-clerical gossip alleges furtive misbehaviour, it is not easy to find convincing evidence. There were plenty of vague general smears. A courtesan specializing in masochism says she has had the honour of whipping the highest ranks of the clergy, magistracy, and finance;[23]

a bishop gives a lift to a notorious brothel-keeper when her cab is damaged in a collision with his carriage—this does him great honour, since most of his colleagues would have known her and avoided becoming ridiculous.[24] *La Chasteté du clergé dévoilée* (1790), when all inhibitions were lifted from the pens of journalists, produced information, supposedly from the police files, about delinquent clergy, but only one out of about 200 bishops in the period covered was included. The police had said that the carriages of Jarente and Loménie de Brienne were driven too fast to be tailed, and the editors remarked that the bishops naturally would not be found out because they misbehaved at home, without needing to frequent the bordels. The *cahiers* of 1789 complain of the worldliness of bishops, but do not allege sexual immorality against any specific individual. The accusations of pamphleteers, when capable of being verified, look shaky. The story about the wife of the coachman of the comte d'Artois was ascribed to the bishop of Meaux, then transferred to his colleague of Chartres; a story which could well be true of the new bishop of Pamiers was told of his predecessor, who died in 1786 at the age of 84. For long, Conzié of Arras was supposed to have fought a duel for the affections of his mistress, disarming his opponent; rather disappointingly, it turns out to have been a fabrication.[25]

Looking at all episcopal sin, sexual and other, and making a grand total of the guilty men, the chief inquisitors of the day, puritanical or anticlerical, did not find a great deal to report.[26] Between 1760 and 1790, the *Nouvelles ecclésiastiques* found twenty sinners and five saints; of the newsletters, Bachaumont's censure 28 of the 130 prelates of 1789, and Lescure's have reservations about 36, the most extreme being another allegation of a duel—against an angry husband. Perhaps a dozen of the generation of 1789 were unworthy of their high office, and of these half a dozen were scandalous figures to boot. A special case deserving of sympathy is La Font de Savine of Viviers,[27] of brilliant talents but unstable character, giving lavish entertainments yet dreaming of a life of Rousseauistic simplicity, neglecting to say mass for months and leaving his valet to read the breviary for him, then falling into fits of devotion and spending days on his knees. The others of the six were vocationless *grands seigneurs*. Dillon, archbishop of Narbonne,[28] lived most of the year at his château of Hautefontaine near Paris, where there were balls, concerts, and hunting thrice a week. 'No swearing today,' he told his guests when the worthy bishop of Montpellier paid a visit. It was a household, said his niece in later years, 'where the rules of religion were daily violated'. Even so, he was most attentive to his duties as a secular administrator. Little can be said on behalf of the 'Cardinal Collier' and his cousin, Prince Ferdinand de Rohan-Guéménée of Cambrai, who lived in Paris leaving his suffragan, Millancourt, bishop of 'Aymeles', to run his diocese, or of Montmorency-Laval of Metz, spending his time in local high society and with the officers of the garrison, and too proud to speak to his parochial clergy. The sixth member of the scandalous group is unique in his total cynicism, playing the system with remorseless self-interest, without respect for the office of bishop or pride in exercising it. Talleyrand[29] was consecrated to the see of Autun on 16 January 1789. His story at the time and subsequently was that his family forced him into the Church: 'I am lame, a younger son, there is no way of escaping my destiny.' But probably he was a willing accomplice, driven by ambition; after all, he would go to the chapel of the Sorbonne to dream before the tomb of Richelieu. A career as *grand vicaire* to his uncle, the archbishop of Reims, and a brilliant tour of office as agent-general of the clergy provided solid qualifications, though promotion came slowly because of the hostility of the queen and a dearth of vacancies. There was never a pretence at a moral life, only a judicious discretion in gambling in closed clubs and liaisons, well known but never flaunted. With the Estates General approaching, Talleyrand was determined to be elected a deputy—the times being what they were, this was the only way to move into the loftiest political circles. The election campaign of the new bishop of Autun among his clergy was a masterpiece of diplomacy and hypocrisy.[30] An unctuous pastoral letter told how he was moved by the last moment of happiness of his dying father at the news of his promotion, how in a retreat he had decided to devote himself to his diocese—he was a 'public man' now, and public men have no rights, only duties; he praised the curés for succouring the poor during the harsh months of winter, and begged for their prayers; like St Paul writing to the Romans, he had a great longing to come to them. And on 12 March he did indeed arrive in his episcopal city. During the next twenty days he was seen frequenting churches and walking in the garden reading his breviary; he had his clergy to dinner, with Lenten fish brought daily on the stage-coach from Lyon, and he urged them to profit by the practice of mental prayer. On a reforming programme including the defence of church property, he was elected on 2 April. On Easter Day ten days later he left Autun without appearing at the cathedral services, and never came there again except in 1802, when his carriage broke down as he was passing through on diplomatic business.

Few bishops were scandalous figures, but an aura of worldliness hung around many more of them, lending credence to gossip. Even those who were frugal in their private lives lived in a splendid décor, and there were others, those who were often found in Paris, who had an aristocratic disdain for affecting to be better than they were, extending to an inclination to brinkmanship, refusing to conform to conventional suppositions about their role. Boisgelin expressed the irresponsible theme in verse:

> Et moy, j'ay le plaisir qu'a tout homme d'Église,
> Quand, ne pouvant pécher, au moins il scandalise.

While praising the conduct of the majority, the nuncio regretted that 'the severity of the observance of the canonical rules' was declining among them; the aged archbishop of Reims, he said, was 'a man of exemplary sanctity', yet he lived 'suivant l'usage d'ici et de la Cour'—true to his vocation, but not a man set apart, fitting in easily with the world of the courtiers.[31] 'In high society,' said Mercier twenty years later, 'you do not meet exaggerated characters . . . the magistrate, the bishop, the soldier, the financier, the courtier seem to have annexed the traits of each other's characters. There is no dominant colour, only nuances.'[32] The evolution of episcopal portraits from the seventeenth century shows a succession of generations following the prevailing fashion, without insistence on their status as churchmen.[33] They go along with lay society in abandoning the beard, then, under Louis XIV, they reduce the moustache to a thin line, then they become clean-shaven. They wear the everyday habits of their ecclesiastical rank, but not their mitres, and they display the coat of arms of their family, adorning it with the episcopal hat (with three tassels, rising to four for an archbishop and five for a cardinal). The memoir writers enjoyed collecting stories[34] showing them mixed up in comparatively blameless but incongruous pleasures—putting on a firework display at which a cardinal's hat was blown off, attending a ballet of animals (in this case leaving before the vulgar spectacle was completed). The Church's unreasonable ban on the theatre was breaking down, and in a box reserved for them at Mme de Montesson's private performances, Brienne, Champion de Cicé, Dillon, Talleyrand, and a few others could be found; two bishops are noted as attending a dubious play put on in secret in Trudaine's salon.[35] So too with the traditional canons prohibiting hunting. There had always been prelates devoted to the chase, with their dogs for chaplains, as Mme de Sévigné said.[36] They were fewer in the eighteenth century, though Grimaldi of Le Mans became notorious for thundering on horseback on a Sunday through a village procession of the Virgin. In a revealing witticism, Dillon replied to Louis XVI's complaint that he hunted himself but forbade the pastime to his clergy: 'Sire, my vices come from my ancestry, my curés' vices are their own.'[37] High birth, he is saying, confers immunity from the constraints imposed upon ordinary people, even if they arise from the laws of the Church.

These men were proud, a pride giving a curious, almost blatant insouciance to their failure to live up to their state as representatives of the mission of Christianity. But with the pride of their race came independence, courage, and generosity. When, against their worldly greatness, is set their activity as 'fathers in God', we can see how the vices coming to them from their ancestry were counterbalanced by the virtues.

II

To maintain his life-style and perform his duties, a bishop had to organize the collection of revenues—of the see and from his abbeys —from a variety of sources. From the start, he would need some expert *homme de confiance*, possibly coming from his family estates, to survey the position and advise him, and he would probably end up by employing one or more local capitalists as 'farmers' doing the collecting, whether on a fixed lease or for a percentage. Two contrasting dioceses illustrate the scope of possible problems. The vast riches of Strasbourg[38] were drawn from land—the domain and château of Saverne, estates, vineyards, huge tracts of forest, mining rights, and isolated farms in places well outside the diocesan boundaries; by contrast, Auch, also rich, drew only 6 per cent of its revenue from land; 94 per cent came from tithes in hundreds of parishes. The income of Toulouse and Cahors was predominantly from tithes, Embrun entirely so. Another source of income, sometimes associated with land ownership, sometimes not, was feudal dues. Quimper drew 20,000 livres from such seigneurial incidents as against only 8,000 livres from tithes and 4,000 livres from land.[39] Paris was the beneficiary of profits flowing in from the network of archaic feudal units which underlay the bustling scene of urban redevelopment and suburban expansion. In 1674, the archbishop had been deprived of his temporal jurisdiction in twenty-five seigneuries covering 500 streets, but he had received compensation and had the fiefs of Grange-Batelière and Poissy and the duchy of Saint-Cloud.[40]

Along with ancient levies, some bishops also presided over ventures of the modern kind: iron foundries brought profits to Evreux and Langres, and the most productive foundry in Brittany, at Paimpont, was jointly owned by the bishop of Saint-Pol-de-Léon and six noblemen.[41] Great possessions provided continual occasions for churchmen to incur odium, and they always constituted a problem of conscience—as the Jansenist Colbert of Montpellier put it, refusing to follow worldly men in their methods meant prejudicing the rights of one's successors.[42] Most bishops did the obvious thing, and left it all to their estate agents.

The initial expenses in becoming a bishop were considerable. Vestments, mitre, and ring were costly, and even an everyday habit would run to 300 livres or so—and they were required in black, in red, and in purple.[43] The bulls from Rome—unless as a concession they were gratis—had to be paid for. There was no relationship between the revenues of the see and the charges: Autun paid twice its annual income, and Strasbourg paid a tenth. At the installation in the royal chapel, the *suisses* and the musicians shared out 500 livres, even if the ceremony was transferred elsewhere.[44] Then the episcopal palace had to be furnished, the general procedure being to make an offer for the furniture of the previous incumbent. Negotiations with the heirs could be difficult. At Alet, in August 1764, billstickers and drummers toured the town announcing the sale, and offers and counter-offers succeeded until, in March 1765, Mgr de Chantérac, the new man, bought it all, library included, for 41,900 livres, 10 sols, 3 deniers (an exact sum indeed!).[45] Talleyrand, going to Autun in 1789, bought his predecessor's effects; when dunned for the money in September 1790, he coolly replied: 'the times we live in and present circumstances as well as the uncertainty of the future are obsessing everyone's minds—it is impossible to occupy oneself with personal affairs'.[46] There would be more trouble with the heirs over repairs. It was not just the palace and the buildings on the estates, there were also the towers and chancels of the churches in the parishes where the see owned the tithes. The bishop taking over at Dax in 1733 had lawsuits before the local *sénéchaussée* and the parlements of Pau and Bordeaux until, in the end, there was arbitration by the bishop of Lescar, and 6,000 livres was handed over.[47] At Dol in 1767, the income of the see was 18,000 livres, and the repairs stood at 55,000 livres. The situation of the poor see of Glandève in 1771 was so hopeless that the king stepped in and paid for the repairs, as neither the bishop who had just retired through ill health nor his successor could ever have settled the bill.[48] One of the resounding lawsuits of the century was Cardinal de Polignac versus the heirs of the previous archbishop of Auch but one, who had died in 1712 leaving 170,000 livres to the poor, 12,000 livres to the cathedral for a silver statue of St Augustine and nothing for repairs. According to the estimate, these stood at 400,000 livres. The Grand Conseil heard the case, Polignac in attendance every day in full episcopal regalia. He lost, and the court ordered the confiscation of a third of his revenues annually to pay off the debt.[49]

Once a bishop's revenues were coming in smoothly and he had cleared the initial debts he had incurred, his family would expect him to assist its poorer members. Certainly, those with no establishment of their own might come and live in the palace. Orphaned nieces and nephews were taken in, unmarried or widowed sisters or nieces would come, taking over the supervision of the household, sometimes usefully and winning local praise for charitable works as well.[50] Or there could be scandal. Mme Dusage, niece of Cordorcet, bishop of Auxerre, had her portrait painted with a ridiculous hairstyle featuring a ship in full sail, and shouted from her window at passers-by, soldiers included, inviting them to come up and see if it did her justice.[51] There were occasions when a major financial contribution was needed, the obvious ones being a dowry for a young woman or the purchasing of command of a regiment for a young man. At a dinner party in 1787 the marquis de Bouillé was declaiming against the clergy when the archbishop of Narbonne reminded him that his uncle, the bishop of Autun, had bought him his regiment. 'Un arrangement de famille': 'yes, an arrangement by which he paid everything.'[52] According to severe moralists, only money coming from the family could be applied to family needs, but the general view was that contributions from ecclesiastical income were in order during the donor's lifetime—legacies were a different matter. 'You know my principles,' said Boisgelin, archbishop of Aix, 'be rich to be useful, be rich without costing the State anything.'[53] By being useful, he meant giving his two sisters 300,000 livres each as a dowry, at the expense of the Church.

A bishop had to employ a numerous staff. Tronson, the austere head of the seminary of Saint-Sulpice, in 1683 was asked to prescribe what expenditures were morally justifiable to figure in episcopal accounts. His reply was puritanical.[54] A bishop could spend his private fortune on pleasures, provided he was generous to the poor and there was no display; he must not use revenues coming to him from the Church. He was not entitled to entertain the great—say, the magistrates of the parlement. If he wanted to win respect, let him give alms. Nor was he entitled to employ musicians: if he wanted recreations, there were 'walks and conversations with a few people of learning and piety'. Yet, along with this impractical rigorism, numerous servants are listed as indispensable. At the top of the hierarchy were the chaplain, the 'gentleman secretary', and the *maître d'hôtel*; then there was a surgeon, five lackeys for the bishop, and one for the secretary, two *valets de chambre* and an extra one for the *maître d'hôtel*, a cook, a turnspit, and two kitchen boys, a cellar man, a furniture maintenance carpenter, an odd-job boy, a stable man, and an unspecified number of grooms. The minimum list has obvious omissions, like gardeners, outside maintenance men, and, as seen in the bishop of Alet's inventory of 1763, a porter and a seamstress (*couturière-lingère*). Nor has Tronson allowed for caretakers in residences other than the palace.

The main residence of a bishop was in his episcopal city, probably alongside the cathedral, and there was almost always a country house, from two to nine leagues away, where he would, like as not, spend the hotter months of the year, from Easter to All Saints' Day. The bishops of Clermont and Tarbes had rural châteaux with panoramic views of distant mountains; the archbishop of Albi could relax in the gardens and orangery of the Petit Lude away from the vast, grim, thirteenth-century fortress which was his residence in town. For the see of Carcassonne there was the country retreat at Vallelier, surrounded by rectangular sheets of water and fountains; for Rouen the château de Gaillon with a fine billiard-room and a chapel as big as a church; for Rennes the manor-house at Bruz; for Besançon the château de Guy; for Dol the château des Ormes; mansions at Andard for Angers, at Noslon for Sens, at Germiny l'Évêque for Meaux; the bishops of Strasbourg had the vast palace out at Saverne. The bishops of Alet had no country seat, but they were accustomed to move in summer to a separate lodging rented from the canons—it was on the south of the cathedral with views across the river to the mountains. The archbishop of Paris spent most of his time away from the stench and throngs of the capital at his château of Conflans set in superb gardens designed by Le Nôtre, its fountains kept playing by a hydraulic machine pumping in the water across a wooden bridge of three arches.[55] A very great prelate could maintain—probably rent—a town lodging in Paris, though none were as splendid as the hôtel de Rohan of the bishops of Strasbourg, adorned with landscapes by Boucher and its vast stables surmounted by Le Lorrain's bas-relief of the horses of Apollo.

The eighteenth-century bishops were great builders. Brand-new palaces in the elegant classical style went up at Lodève, Alais, Viviers, Dol, Carcassonne, Agen, Bordeaux, Lombez, Coutances, Belley, and Saint-Papoul, and there were embellishments and improvements almost everywhere. Enormous sums were expended. Mgr de Salignac de la Mothe Fénelon of Lombez died in 1787, heavily in debt because of his outlay on stones and mortar, and in 1790 the see of Carcassonne was still paying interest of 30,000 livres a year on sums borrowed by Mgr de Bézon to erect a new palace in place of the towers in the old *cité* which had housed his sixty-nine predecessors.[56] The country houses were also rebuilt or embellished anew. Having restored his town residence, Cardinal de Luynes in 1759 practically demolished the château of Nolson to add suites of rooms in the modern style, then went on to do the same at his manor-house of Brienon.[57] Another cardinal, Choiseul of Besançon, spent a million livres on the château de Guy; another, Rohan of Strasbourg, rebuilt Saverne on a scale which afforded (so it was said) 700 beds for the guests who came to his hunting parties. Cardinal Bissy, Bossuet's successor at Meaux, did not do much at Germiny l'Évêque, but he replaced the iron railings so the new ones could be crowned with a cardinal's hat, like the enamelled one he had erected near the altar in the cathedral.[58] The last bishop of the diocese before the Revolution adorned the gardens behind these cardinal-hatted railings with figurines of bagpipe players, dancing swains, and nymphs, 'bought in the faubourg Saint-Antoine at Paris', said a critical tourist, 'and seeming to me unworthy of the country house of a bishop'. Stories of aristocrats using their influence to get roads rerouted to improve the amenities of their country seats abound in eighteenth-century France, and the anecdotes include some churchmen. The archbishop of Rouen[59] got the lane leading to the village of Gaillon diverted away from his kitchen garden, and the bishop of Mende intrigued to get improved access to his château, and found himself censured by Necker and the archbishops of Bordeaux and Toulouse, and having to give an account of his doings to the provincial estates of Haute Guienne.[60]

The 'building mania' has been censured as a spendthrift hobby unsuitable for churchmen. Yet zealous, pastorally minded prelates indulged in it as well as the worldly ones—Jean-Georges Souillac at Lodève, Cardinal de Luynes at Sens, François Renaud de Villeneuve Forcaliqueiret at Viviers, Gabriel Cortois de Quincey at Belley, Charles Lefèvre de Quesnoy at Coutances. There were worse ways of laying out a sizeable income than in building for posterity and using the best available architectural and artistic talent to adorn the episcopal city. Many a town in France is indebted to the good taste of these eighteenth-century prelates whose handsome buildings now house the *mairie*, the prefecture, the museum, or the archives. Since medieval buildings had been converted in the sixteenth century for more social living, enough time had elapsed for major repairs and improvements to be needed again (unless the work had been done already in the seventeenth century, as at Aix). The palace at Rennes[61] was constricted between the cathedral and two narrow streets, having no outlook and only a tiny courtyard and a sunless little garden. Not surprisingly, Mgr Bareau de Girac in 1770 moved to the abbatial mansion of a suppressed abbey nearby, set in the midst of spacious grounds, and adapted it for himself and his staff. When Souillac took over at Lodève in 1732, there was no episcopal residence, as the Protestants had destroyed it long ago—he expended his own fortune in building another.[62] The château of Saverne had been burnt down—that was why Rohan had to rebuild it, though he was not compelled to do so in such a sumptuous fashion.[63] At Lombez, La Mothe Fénelon had not much choice about going into debt, for his five-storey palace with its tottering spire was becoming dangerous and had to be demolished.[64] Charles Lefèvre de Quesnoy, doctor of the Sorbonne, was a sober prelate who had been vicar-general of the diocese of Coutances for twelve years before succeeding to the bishopric in 1757. A few expensive years later he was at his ease in his new palace—the chapel walls decorated with gilded bronzes, his library resplendent with tapestries and rich bindings, his bedroom in crimson velvet and gold fringings and adorned with pictures of Our Lady, allegories of the four seasons, and his own recently painted portrait. He was proud of his building achievements: he had, he said, provided work for those who needed it, rather than 'feeding the idle'.[65] In the context of his time it was a valid argument: people expected their bishop to spend his wealth locally—provided he did this, only bilious anticlericals would have grudged him his splendour. With one proviso: as a cliché of the Gallican lawyers had it, 'the wealth of the Church is the patrimony of the poor'—a bishop must give generously to the material needs of his flock.

III

Aristocratic privilege, allied to reasonable abilities and good fortune, gained promotion to a bishopric, and episcopal office, once gained, was a passport to additional distinctions, privilege leading to more privileges.

Peculiar honours and resounding titles went with certain sees—to rule at Strasbourg, Metz, or Cambrai was to be a prince of the Holy Roman Empire with the dignity of 'altesse sérénissime', at least until 1754, when the princes of the blood royal protested and got the title suppressed within the French territories.[66] Six bishoprics conferred peerages on their holders—Reims, Laon, and Langres with the status of 'duc', Beauvais, Châlons, and Noyon with that of 'comte'. In a similar category came the archbishop of Paris, though with a different justification, being a 'conseiller d'honneur né', a distinction he shared with the abbot of Cluny.[67] These eight ecclesiastics, together with the princes of the blood royal and the thirty-two lay ducs with peerage status had the right to sit in the parlement of Paris when they chose to do so, and to have their lawsuits judged there (though the bishop of Beauvais faced challenges on his claim from the magistrates of his local *présidial*).[68] The peerage bishops, proud of their distinctions, made common cause with the lay peers to defend them; more especially, the three episcopal ducs were solid with the thirty-two others. In September 1715, during a wrangle in the parlement after the death of Louis XIV, the archbishop of Reims was put up by his colleagues to make a protest to the regent; to his chagrin he realized afterwards that he had inadvertently conceded a point in his discourse, calling Orléans 'Monseigneur', while a peer of France should merely say 'Monsieur'.[69] When the *premier président* of the parlement refused to take off his hat when asking the ducs for their opinions (in the trial of the duc de la Force in 1721), the archbishop of Reims held a meeting in his Parisian lodgings to try to invalidate the whole proceedings.[70] At the ball for the marriage of Marie Antoinette some derogation to the precedence of the ducal peers was proposed (for diplomatic reasons to placate pretensions of courtiers from Vienna); the bishop of Noyon was chosen to take a protest to Versailles.[71] Sometimes the ecclesiastical peers ran into dilemmas peculiar to their standing as churchmen—how, for example, did they stand when a cardinal claimed to come before the peers at a meeting of the Royal Council?—and if that cardinal was Dubois?[72] The right to have lawsuits exclusively heard before the parlement had potential disadvantages. In 1731, the magistrates were proposing to call the peers to join them in trying the bishop of Laon for a fanatical pastoral letter. Was it wise to claim the right to be tried by a court of bishops alone, waiving the peerage privilege?[73] It made tactical sense in the circumstances, but it would be undermining an immunity from ecclesiastical process which might be useful on other occasions.

Under the *ancien régime*, the great were as proud of undeserved honours as of those they had merited—titles and decorations served as a confirmation of the splendour of their lineage and their high standing in royal favour. A prelate with claims to intellectuality, or who was well enough connected to become a court chaplain or tutor to royal children, would consider he had a claim to belong to the Academy, and would begin appropriate intrigues. 'This ambition to be of the Academy is very strange in a great lord,' said Piron in 1749, 'but I find it almost scandalous in a bishop.'[74] In this year, Paul-Albert de Luynes, who had ruled the see of Bayeux for the last fourteen years and was destined to greater things still in Church and at Court, was pushed by the royal advisers in preference to Voltaire. Apparently, the archbishop of Narbonne had been asked to allow his name to go forward, but had refused to stand against such a distinguished man of letters. Boyer, bishop of Mirepoix, who was running the royal patronage, was blamed for the whole affair. 'The Academy, the King, and the public,' said Voltaire, 'destined me to succeed Cardinal Fleury as one of the 40. Boyer was against it, and at last, after ten weeks' search, he found a prelate to fill the place of a prelate, in conformity to the ecclesiastical canons.'[75] Thirteen years later, the retired bishop of Limoges, Jean-Gilles de Coetlosquet, was elevated to the ranks of the immortals before Diderot. In a sense, these elections were demonstrations of the established social order, putting religious belief before scepticism. Duclos, the permanent secretary of the Academy, had a difficult time balancing between his friends the philosophes and the *dévots* and courtiers who accused him of plotting against religion, hence his famous *coup* in the election of 1763, when he, D'Alembert, and two others of the irreligious party illegally retained their black balls to prove that they had not voted against a churchman, the abbé de Radonvilliers.

Connoisseurs of literary curiosities rejoiced when the *éloge* of a dead academician or of a newly elected one had to be given by a member of the opposite party. Archbishop Languet of Sens, obliged to welcome Nivelle de la Chaussée, the sentimental dramatist, praised his plays for reading only, not for actual performances, when actors and actresses might be the occasion for erotic imaginings in the minds of the audience.[76] When, later on, he had to receive Marivaux, he reflected on his shortcomings, style included. Surely Marianne is more interesting, said the wits, than the prelate's heroine, Marguerite-Marie Alacoque.[77] Eleven years later, in 1754, Gresset, welcoming D'Alembert, levelled the score by satirical observations on the episcopate in referring to the achievements of the previous holder of the chair, the bishop of Vence. The temper of the times changed, however, and Archbishop Boisgelin, elected in 1776, gave an oration worthy of a philosophe, exhorting churchmen to study science and literature to defend religion, and praising republicanism, for a Cicero would be impossible under a monarchy.[78]

As princes of the Empire, as peers in the parlement, and as members of the Academy, some bishops achieved national standing; all of them, however, were splendidly predominant within the walls of their episcopal city. A new bishop was not consecrated in his diocesan cathedral, but in the royal chapel at Versailles or, sometimes, in the chapel of the Sulpicians at Issy. Before he went to his episcopal city, he had been consecrated by representatives of his fellow bishops to be one of their number, and had taken the oath of allegiance to the king, and the oath to obey the Pope. Thus he came to his people as the king's man, accepted by the hierarchy of the Church. His reception in his new home was marked by ceremonies symbolizing both his elevation as the representative of the Crown and of the universal Church, and also of his acceptance into a tightly knit, hierarchical local society, where all had their due place and, in their different ranks, their peculiar privileges. The representatives of all corporations and interests came to render deference to their new pastor—but with the implication he must recognize and respect their rights.

The municipal officers would be the first to present themselves (though local custom might allow some of the clergy to get in a brief gesture before them). At Paris, the archbishop had to stage for a night at the abbey of Saint-Victoire before entering town; here he was met by the *prévôt des marchands* and the aldermen.[79] At Grenoble, on the preliminary day, the clergy would come to the episcopal palace in the morning and the *consuls* of the town in the afternoon; that night, the sky was red with bonfires paid for by the municipality. The *jurats* of Bordeaux went out to the harbour of Blaye to greet their new prelate, then sailed down the estuary with him in the *maison navale*, a specially commissioned vessel decorated with damask, silks, and tapestries. (In 1781, to save money, they all came in from Blaye in an ordinary brigantine.) Everywhere, the seigneurs who held fiefs in town would present themselves to offer fealty and to escort the bishop into his cathedral—in Paris, they had the right leg bared in token of homage. In return, they had their perquisites, like the option to take away a piece of silver from the ensuing banquet. An archbishop of Auch prevented the baron de Montaut from collecting his souvenir, and ran into a lawsuit costing him 5,000 livres damages.[80] The second day of the observances at Grenoble was marked by the successive arrival of all the officers of the minor courts of justice and representatives of the notaries and *procureurs*, deputations from the parlement and the *chambre des comptes* (these specially honoured, as the bishop went out to meet them as they descended from their carriages), the officers of the artillery school, and the administrators of the *hôpital général*. On the day of the actual installation, the dean and canons and the guilds and confraternities escorted the bishop, with the *consuls* carrying the canopy held over his head. On the following day, in the chapter house, the canons took their oath of fidelity one by one, and were rewarded by a dinner that night in the palace.[81]

These courtesies, deferential but hinting at latent tensions, foreshadowed the future relations of bishop and municipality. A town expected its prelate to represent the interests of the citizens against the intendant, the provincial governor, the taxation officials, and the courtiers at Versailles; they would petition him to intervene, and generally he would do so.[82] A resident bishop would meet with approval, even if slack in performing his duties, for he would be spending money and providing employment locally. There was anger in Fréjus when Mgr du Bellay (1739–60) transferred his residence to Draguignan, and when Mgr de Bausset (1766–91) proposed to move the seminary also. Luckily, both prelates felt guilty, and encouraged by his predecessor from retirement in Paris, Mgr de Bausset moved back to Fréjus and won a bonus of applause by persuading the government to give funds for dredging the harbour.[83] The *consuls* of Carcassonne were gratified that their bishop was building a new palace in the lower town, but not when they discovered they might have to pay for repairs to the old one—they succeeded in evading the obligation.[84]

Whether present or absent, almost every bishop inherited conflicts with his municipality arising from his ancient status of seigneur of the town and 'haut, moyen et bas justicier'. In this capacity, he might have the right to levy archaic dues, like those on the measuring scoops for selling grain at the market, piercing doors and

windows in the old city walls, while he might have the outright
ownership of the ramparts with their potentially valuable building
sites.[85] Equally contentious were rights to confirm mayor and aldermen in their offices or even to appoint some of them, or to sit,
whether in person or by deputy, on the town council, perhaps
taking the chair. At Albi, an episcopal officer presided over the
conseil politique (the six *consuls*) and the *conseil renforcé* (the *consuls* and
twenty-four oligarchically elected representatives).[86] At Béziers, the
bishop named two of the *consuls*, and his *viguier* intervened in council
meetings.[87] At Mende, he named all the *consuls* and various other
officers, a range of powers angrily described by the citizens in
January 1789 as 'feudal anarchy allowed to subsist by Richelieu
because it favoured his creature, bishop de Marillac'. Half the aldermen of Cambrai had been named by the archbishop; the right had
lapsed, but when Léopold-Charles de Choiseul arrived in 1766, he
got letters patent restoring it by the influence of his brother, the
royal minister. Once the fortunes of politics had removed his
powerful influence at Versailles, the municipality demanded the
restoration of its independence. These sorts of feuds could go on and
on as a matter of routine. But some were settled amicably. In 1746,
the archbishop and city of Reims suspended their rivalry to combine
to defeat the government's plan for a new system of representation
on the municipal council—each side stood to lose privileges.[88] The
consuls of Nîmes in 1779 withdrew their opposition to the bishop
sitting on their council, and he reciprocated by buying pumps for the
fire brigade and paying a dole to unemployed workers—he was
recorded officially as having 'conferred innumerable benefits on the
town'.[89] A wrangle at Beziers about the right to supervise the taking
of oaths by officials was ended by getting the intendant to mediate,
'recognizing that nothing is more disagreeable for the community
than being in dispute with its bishop'. Mgr Armand-Claude de
Nicolai, who had proposed the mediation, said he 'regretted going
to law against his people', and cemented the new happy relations by
refraining from exercising his right to send an officer to preside over
the council—his *viguier* never attended again.[90]

These feuds are not properly interpreted as power struggles. A
prelate who wanted his way in the affairs of a town could work
through influence in high places: he did not need to be involved in
the mêlée at council meetings. What was at stake was honour and
precedence. So too with disputes with that splendid lofty figure the
provincial military governor and with the rather ordinary *lieutenant
du roi* of the city—about the way a seat faced in the cathedral, the

right to be consulted on the date fixed for a Te Deum.[91] Bordeaux was a scene of disobliging measures (including the hiring of a flute-player to follow the archbishop everywhere, drawing attention to the company he kept) until in 1775 the prelate and the military governor made their *Traité de conventions de politesse et d'honnêteté.*[92] There were similar clashes between the palace and the local law courts. In 1726, the parlement of Brittany censured its *premier président* because he made a visit to the new bishop instead of waiting for the installation—he had 'compromised the dignity of parlement'. Three years later, after various quarrels, the magistrates scored off their bishop by rushing out of church after a Te Deum to light the bonfires before he could get out to wield the torch.[93] In 1743, the judges of the *présidial* at Auch showed their opinion of their Father in God by refusing to kneel at his benediction at the feast of the Assumption. 'A genoux là bas', cried Mgr de Montillet, and he took litigation right up to the Royal Council to ensure future compliance.[94] What in a later age looks like expensive and trivial one-upmanship, under the *ancien régime* was an expression of the ethos of the social order, held together by tradition, hierarchy, and deference, real and effective only because everyone was determined to retain his due place in it, whatever scandal or litigation ensued.

IV

In his memoirs, Talleyrand divided bishops into 'the very pious', 'the administrative specialists', and 'the worldly'. He himself belonged to the last two categories. The phraseology he used was common currency in the later years of the *ancien régime*. The term 'évêque administrateur' had become a cliché of discourse, used as a censure. 'An administrative bishop', said a pamphleteer, 'is a sort of hybrid, half sacred, half profane, who, under the livery of sanctity, exercises a philosophic apostolate, whose object is to purge France of all defects of government; he is a man inspired by the spirit of public philanthropy, aiming to demonstrate that in the last resort the sole religion of the State is the pursuit of the general happiness.'[95] Earlier, Le Franc de Pompignan, the virtuous bishop of Puy (later archbishop of Vienne), had described the 'prélats administrateurs' as a new phenomenon, a danger to the Church; later on, he himself was to accept a major administrative and political role.[96] In 1783, the bishop of Lombez said it was important to keep these dubious characters out of the great sees: he hoped La Luzerne would not be promoted from

Langres to Auch because 'he is a man of fashionable theories (*un homme à système*), one of our administrative bishops of the school of the philosophes'.[97]

Though both anticlericals and churchmen cried shame at men of God absorbed in worldly administration, the ruler of a diocese had always had secular duties to perform. This was evident in the number of public welfare enquiries involved in episcopal visitation tours, in the duty of chairing the committees running hospitals and other charitable institutions, and occasionally in taking the lead in enforcing government legislation. The royal declaration of 1776 ordering the closure of unhygienic cemeteries would never have been effective without the bishops intervening with ordonnances interdicting so many of the old urban burial grounds.[98] These predominantly secular duties simplified the problem of vocation for young men of the right social standing who wished to gain distinction and remuneration in the service of the State. Ordination was one option among the others. Turgot, who studied at the Sorbonne with Champion de Cicé, gave way to scruples which others found easy to push out of the conscious mind, and abandoned an ecclesiastical career; he was unable, he said, 'to resign myself to wearing a mask all my life' (and was also hopelessly in love with a charming beauty). Champion de Cicé became a leading administrative prelate, and Turgot intendant of Limoges. When complaints arose about the *évêque administrateur*,[99] it was not because the phenomenon was new, but because attitudes were changing. There was a growing awareness of the incongruity of the traditional alliance between sacred and secular. The ideas of the Enlightenment, the vortex from which the gales of reform were blowing, were a strange blend of quasi-Christian humanism and anticlericalism. The pious suspected prelates who adopted them, however selectively, and the philosophes had a vested interest in keeping this complex of ideas as their own monopoly.

Administratively, France fell into two very different areas. In rather more than two-thirds of the kingdom, the division into *généralités* and rule by intendants had taken over from the old traditional organization. In the remaining third, the provinces in the South and along the frontiers, provincial estates survived, levying taxation to meet the demands of the Crown and to pay for local needs. These estates were ramshackle bodies with traditional membership, varying from place to place, but always on oligarchical lines. Their clerical representatives were from the upper ranks of the hierarchy. In the Cambrésis, it was the bishop, six deputies of the metropolitan chapter, seven of the other chapters, and three abbots; in Burgundy, the bishops, the dean, and one canon from each chapter, and the heads of the most important abbeys; in the Mâconnais, the bishop, a representative of the cathedral chapter, and another of the noble canons of Saint-Pierre, and the abbots of Cluny and of two other great monasteries (a delegation of parish priests could attend at the *chambre du clergé* of Mâcon, but they were not allowed to vote). The nine bishops of Brittany, a canon of each of their cathedrals and the thirty-seven abbots of monasteries attended the estates of Brittany; in Languedoc the twenty-three bishops only, and in Provence the three bishops.

The part played by nobles (sometimes defined as 'nobles holding fiefs') varied from place to place. Of the many entitled to attend in the Cambrésis, only about a dozen did so, while in Brittany, a horde of penurious squires turned up, lured by the expectation of free drink when authority sought their votes; in Languedoc only twenty-three could attend, and in Provence, two. The representatives of the Third Estate, the commoners, were all aldermen or other members of the oligarchies ruling the towns. There was no representation of the countryside and the ordinary urban population. However, contrary to the general ethos of society, the structure and voting procedures of the most important estates gave a certain independence, or, indeed, priority to the commons. In Brittany, there were three chambers, and vote was by order. In the Mâconnais, each of the three chambers sent a representative to sit in the *chambre des élus triennaux*, in which the important business was transacted, and if it was a matter of taxation, the representative of the Third Estate had the casting vote. The estates of Béarn were unique in having only two houses, the clergy and nobles sitting together in one, leaving the commons in the other free to press their independent policies. The twenty-three bishops and the equal number of nobles of Languedoc sat in a common assembly with the forty-six deputies of the commons, and the vote was by head—united, the commons could not be defeated. In Provence, the three bishops and two nobles were similarly outweighed. The nobles of Provence intrigued to change the balance of power, and in October 1787 persuaded the government to re-establish the medieval form of the estates in which the aristocracy enjoyed numerical predominance. The parlement of Aix ordered the citizens to illuminate their houses in rejoicing, an astonishing example of the blindness of the privileged classes on the eve of the Revolution.

All these provincial assemblies were under episcopal presidency.

An exception up to 1766 was the Cambrésis,[100] and to mark their displeasure, the archbishops of Cambrai for long had ostentatiously stayed away. Then came Léopold Charles de Choiseul, strong in the backing of his brother the minister, and he obtained letters patent entitling him to take the chair at both the general assembly and the standing executive committee. The estates of Foix were under the bishop of Pamiers, of Bigorre under the bishop of Tarbes, of Béarn under the bishop of Lescar (or, in his absence, his colleague of Oloron), of the Gévauden under the bishop of Mende, of Artois under the bishop of Arras. The assemblies of the extensive province of Burgundy were presided over by the bishop of Autun, not without challenges to his authority, for his colleague of Chalon-sur-Saône had claims, and when Dijon became an episcopal see, there was a third competitor in the field.[101] And the presidential role was essentially political, very obvious at Mâcon; here the prelate was rarely seen at the *chambre du clergé*, but always took the chair at the dominating *chambre des élus*, where, except in taxation matters, he enjoyed the casting vote.[102] The estates of Brittany were tumultuous rebellious assemblies, and the Crown expected the bishops to manipulate votes for government policy. This made the task of the bishop of Rennes, normally in the presidential chair, a miserable one. Succeeding a prelate who had got himself translated to another see in despair, Bareau de Girac from 1770 ran the estates with general approval, but only because he took the side of the province against the royal officials—once he turned to the side of the Court, his position became hopeless: the only way for royal business to pass, it was said, was for the bishop of Rennes to pretend to be against it.[103] In Provence, the archbishop of Aix, provided he was conciliatory, could run the province from his chairman's position by wooing the votes of the dominant commons. The deliberations in Languedoc were directed by the archbishop of Narbonne or, in his absence, the archbishop of Toulouse; when appointing to the latter see, the king's advisers looked for someone who could handle the business of the estates and in due course proceed to Narbonne and inherit the presidency.[104]

Languedoc was peculiar in having numerous political assemblies operating individually in broad financial subordination to the estates. The vast province was divided into twenty-three 'civil dioceses', roughly, but not exactly, coinciding with the ecclesiastical units; in each, there was an assembly, the *assiette*. Immediately after the estates concluded their annual session, these *assiettes* met in each episcopal city under the direction of their bishops; each had a standing committee (the *comité de direction*) with the bishop in the chair, and through this organization he could run the affairs of the secular diocese, with the proviso that in matters financial, the decisions had to be verified by the estates of Languedoc. Thus the prelates of the province—and more especially those who ruled in the important dioceses of Narbonne, Toulouse, Lodève, Lavaur, Agde, Uzès, Saint-Pons, and Albi—had major secular responsibilities, and when the king had to fill one of these bishoprics, he had to look for candidates of proven administrative ability. From the king's point of view, the role of the presiding bishop in the estates of the various provinces was to ensure that the subsidies to the central government were duly voted; seen from the side of the provinces, he had the duty of intervening at Versailles to moderate the royal demands. On becoming archbishop of Aix in 1770, Boisgelin[105] got the estates of Provence to make him their standing representative in Paris—he welcomed the excuse to be so often in the capital, but his first foray there was certainly profitable, sending back a decree of the Royal Council remitting 150,000 livres on the province's payment to the salt tax. The estates commissioned half a dozen paintings by Vanloo as a tribute of gratitude. Later, he got the government to reduce its subsidy demands by the amount the province had already given as a loan to help in the Seven Years War, and he obtained a grant to meet two-thirds of the cost of a new Palais de Justice in Aix. When in 1782, the *intendant de la marine* at Toulon set up a bakery in the arsenal to cut the profits of the bakers in town, the archbishop rushed off to Court on behalf of his needy and kneading constituents. The cultivation of influence at Versailles by their bishops also served the people of Mâcon well, for without it they would have lost their estates altogether. The powerful estates of Burgundy were bent on absorbing minor assemblies around the periphery of their province; the comté de Charollais lost its independence in this way in 1751, and the Mâconnais was scheduled to be next. Bishop Henri de Valras, already successful in obtaining a reduction in the government's taxation demands, now obtained a promise that the estates of the Mâconnais would remain for his own lifetime. He died in 1763, but his successor, Gabriel-François Moreau, stayed on in Paris negotiating until the Burgundian plotters were again thwarted.[106]

No doubt many bishops enjoyed these involvements in high politics and the opportunity to linger in Parisian society; yet there were probably as many who preferred the quietness of provincial life or were zealous to concentrate on pastoral duties, and found jolting up by coach to the capital a burden. Witness the misadventures of

Urbain de Hercé of Dol, dragged out of his pious and comfortable routine by the estates of Brittany to be the mouthpiece of Breton grievances at Versailles. He was there in 1773 protesting against infractions of provincial liberties and excessive taxation, and two years later he read to the Court a memorandum against the oppressive conscription to the militia doing coastguard service. In 1782 he was back to register protests about taxation. Four years after, he presided over the estates in the absence of the bishop of Rennes, and was rewarded by the king with an abbey *in commendam*, which did nothing to soften his courageous outspokenness. Indeed, in the same year he was back at Versailles, and in January 1788 he appeared before the king with a Breton deputation to protest against the edict giving a very limited toleration to Protestants. 'The arches of the sanctuary are shaken,' he thundered—a great monarch like Constantine, Theodosius, or Charlemagne would have called a national council on an issue of this importance. He was exiled to his diocese, but was back at Court in July denouncing the royal measures of discipline against the parlement of Rennes—'edicts flatly contrary to our rights . . . registered by military force without the consent of the estates, the magistrates exiled, the courts rendered idle, the Temple of Justice profaned'.[107] He got back to his palace just in time for Christmas. The Breton nobles spoke of their bishops as pliable agents of royal absolutism, yet they were glad to push one forward to face royal displeasure by expressing their grievances at Versailles.[108]

What credit should go to the president of the executive committee of a local authority for improvements made during his tenure of office? This was a time when the enlightened classes were enthusiastic for public works, whether improvements to communications to facilitate trade and the movement of grain in times of shortage, or beautifying cities with prestigious architecture. Some of the bishops received praise for what was done under their chairmanships—Mgr de Bonneval, the last bishop of Pamiers, for road building in the Pyrenees, Mgr de Fumel for driving boulevards and avenues through the medieval walled city of Lodève, Loménie de Brienne of Toulouse for the digging of the canal du Midi, Boisgelin of Aix for the Malemort–Terrasson canal. A bishop of Castres built roads through difficult mountain country, introduced the potato ten years before Parmentier recommended it, and set up a cotton factory; a bishop of Sisteron devised irrigation schemes ('the fathers curse me but the children will bless me'); at Fréjus, it was the calling in of engineers to drain the marshes; at Agde, the promotion of the silk industry; at Saint-Pons, the bishop had the nursery for mulberry trees (for free distribution) set up near his country house—'so I can keep an eye on it'. Loménie de Brienne at Toulouse became famous throughout Europe for his remarkable 'philosophic' pastoral letter of 1774 to the farmers of his countryside in a time of cattle plague. He explained how the disease had originated in untanned hides imported from Guadalupe through Bayonne, ordered the killing of diseased animals, promising compensation from the estates (and, indeed, partly from himself), and forbade the old custom of bringing the herds together to be blessed by the parish priest—precautions, not prayer, would bring the infection to an end. This circular was published in the *Journal politique*, and was widely read in France and beyond.[109]

The trouble with fame of this kind, however, was that tax payers, expecially those who were not gaining prestige or profit from the innovations, were reluctant to pay for them. In Languedoc in 1789 the nobles complained, 'it is the bishops who settle public taxation, and they do not bear the burden of it', and a pamphleteer asked what good were all the fine roads of the province, 'more use to the prelates in their six-horse carriages than to the peasants with their carts'. 'You are not men,' the diatribe concluded, 'not citizens, but slaves of the archbishop of Narbonne.'[110] In Provence, the anger of the commons against the revival of the old form of the estates was boundless. Archbishop Boisgelin, who originally promoted this reactionary *coup*, now changed tack and asked for a doubling of the representatives of the Third Estate. The government refused, and it looked as though the selection of deputies to the approaching Estates General of the nation might fall into the hands of the privileged classes dominating the revised form of the provincial estates. The idea was swept away in a storm of popular discontent. Boisgelin, now swimming strongly with the tide, announced the desire of his clergy to surrender their taxation privileges.[111] Cardinal Bernis, archbishop of Albi, for long had been away from these tumults, living in splendour in Rome as French ambassador. But in the old days when he had presided over the estates of the Albigeois, he had made a remarkable statement of concern for the peasant majority unrepresented by anybody anywhere. 'The price of a single feast where boredom reigns,' he said, 'would feed a family of peasants for a year.' To tax these poor people, who have no property but their labour, to pay for the adornment of the province, would be 'sacrilegious theft'. 'Gentlemen, as Christians we are all brothers, as men we are friends, members of the same citizen body.'[112]

Archbishop Boisgelin regarded himself as 'the first Minister of Provence'. Why should he not go further? Given proven ability and favour at Court, anything was possible. There was a tradition of ecclesiastical diplomats—d'Estrées, Forbin-Janson, Polignac. They were fewer after Louis XIV, but there were two glittering examples. At Vienna, Rohan upheld French grandeur with outrageous ostentation, winning the favour of all the ladies except the two who would matter to him—the Empress and her daughter Marie Antoinette. In the last twenty years of the *ancien régime*, Bernis, archbishop of Albi, was at Rome, 'keeping the inn of France at the crossroads of Europe', rejoicing in seeing the cardinals flocking in to enjoy his ice-cream and in brilliant negotiations to settle minutiae— when the Revolution came, his procrastination and reactionary prejudices were to usher his king to disaster. But it was possible to rise higher than embassies. France had never been so great as when it was ruled by cardinals—Richelieu, Mazarin, and Fleury. They had been strong and subtle, and (though it was treasonable to say so) they had avoided the war-like excesses of Louis XIV which brought the country to starvation. Dubois was in the series of political cardinals, but he did not count in the same way; he had been an upstart who accumulated prestigious ecclesiastical ranks to atone for being the son of an apothecary. When the façade of absolutism cracked and Louis XVI began his experiments towards introducing an element of consent into government with the Notables and the Provincial Assemblies, Boisgelin, Champion de Cicé, and Loménie de Brienne pushed themselves forward in the role of administrative bishops willing to use their acquired skills in leading France into a new era of liberal monarchy. Brienne, who was said to have had these great ambitions from the start, 'étudiant la théologie comme un Hibernois pour être évêque et les *Mémoires du cardinal Retz* pour être homme d'État', was the one who arrived to play the role of a Richelieu, a Mazarin, or a Fleury—too late for France, for events were out of control; too late for himself, for he was already beyond enjoying power, tormented with eczema and pulmonary consumption, coughing blood. A bishop—Richelieu—had built up the absolutism of the monarchy, and a bishop finally presided over its approaching dissolution.

9

THE BISHOPS: FATHERS IN GOD

I

To fulfil his pastoral duties effectively, a bishop needed to know his diocese. The traditional aid to understanding and investigation was the diocesan *pouillé*, the annotated list of benefices. Such documents were notorious for their inaccuracy, though in the eighteenth century there were greater efforts at updating; at Aix, new editions were prepared in 1708, 1730, 1768, and 1781.[1] Good maps also became available. The French Academy produced a superb engraved map of the *généralité* of Paris in 1678; from this, a version covering the diocese was extracted. Soon afterwards came a map of the diocese of Coutances by Hariette de la Pagerie, and Bossuet commissioned one for Meaux in 1698—it included the basic patterns of relief, afforestation, and cultivation, the boundaries of parishes, rural deaneries, and archdeaconries, with symbols showing roadside calvaries and the sites of the ruined Protestant chapels. Eight years later Cardinal Noailles commissioned a Parisian revision from the geographer Besson; at the same time, the bishop of Le Mans sent a technically expert priest and one of his archdeacons to make a cartographical survey of his diocese. Their final production was broadly accurate, except for the area around Laval, where the inhabitants gave false data as they thought they were being assessed for taxation. Cartographers now did brisk business, Delisle (dd. 1720), the most famous of them, compiling maps for several dioceses.[2] In 1732, the bishop of Lisieux adopted the system which was to become the common practice of all cartographers, ecclesiastical and secular, asking the curés to co-operate in measurements and listing topographical details, thus circumventing the duplicity of the laity. Towards the end of the *ancien régime*, prelates with a bent for administration, some zealous pastors, some zealous only for efficiency, adopted the use of such questionnaires to their clergy to collect information for a diocesan dossier for easy reference.[3] This was done by Loménie de Brienne at Toulouse (1763), Champion de Cicé at Rodez (1770), Rohan-Guéménée at Bordeaux (1772),

Talleyrand-Périgord as coadjutor at Reims (1774), Rosset de Fleury at Cambrai (1778), Gain-Montagnac at Tarbes (1783), and Le Tonnelier de Breteuil at Montauban about the same time, and, in a most detailed fashion, by Eustache-Antoine d'Osmond at Comminges (1786). These might be simple enquiries, as at Cambrai, where they constituted a census of the number of communicants and the total number of inhabitants; or they could be comprehensive, perhaps unreasonably so. At Tarbes, there were many questions, but the form was simple, the curés having to fill in the blanks. Champion de Cicé showed his secular and humanitarian preoccupations in wanting to know especially about hospitals, schools, midwives, crops, trades, and economic resources; Osmond had a questionnaire of eight large pages, which irritated the curés, especially as they knew that the covert aim was to find out exact details of income for the purposes of clerical taxation. Some gave testy answers: about the extent of the parish—'You'd have to ask a geographer', about the total of the surplice fees (the *casuel*)—'Just work it out from my reply on the numbers of births, marriages and deaths'. Le Tonnelier de Breteuil was proud of the dossier he compiled, and had it bound in red morocco along with a couple of maps, and kept it in a pouch of purple silk embossed with his coat of arms.[4] Loménie de Brienne left his as it was—it filled seven volumes.

II

A bishop's relations with the people of his diocese was necessarily mainly indirect, through the parochial clergy whose pastoral labours he supervised. But there were two ways by which he was in direct contact with the laity: through his pastoral letters (*mandements*) and his visitation tours.

Every bishop, even an absentee, was expected to edify his diocesans quite frequently with a pastoral epistle, perhaps ordering his curés to read it to the faithful, perhaps leaving it to them to quote and summarize. Invariably, there was one for the beginning of Lent, awaited by all, not because of the eloquence of its call to penitence, but as defining what exemptions were to be granted to the fasting regulations. Eggs would normally be authorized, and in bad weather other foods would be taken off the prohibited list to make up for shortages. A pastoral letter would herald the calling of a synod, the issue of new liturgical books, a new catechism, or the publication of synodal statutes. In times of plague, drought, or storm, there would be calls for penitence to turn away God's wrath, and as time went on, among the catalogue of sins drawing down divine punishment, the spate of writings advocating scepticism and unbelief would receive a special censure. When Rome proclaimed a year of jubilee, the bishop would define the dates and details of the observances, and exhort to repentance and confession on the way to a good communion as against mere outward conformity with the jubilee requirements. For royal marriages, births, and deaths, the chief pastor of the diocese would express the loyal sentiments of his flock and urge all to join the Court in its mourning or celebration. When Louis XV died, in addition to patriotic rhetoric and reflections on the transitory nature of human grandeur, there were *mandements* insinuating fears for that womanizing monarch's eternal salvation. In time of war, in response to the king's request, calls for prayers for victory would be issued, and if victory came, a Te Deum of thanksgiving would be ordered in all the great churches. From mid-century, the episcopate began to use the pastoral letter as a vehicle to make public its corporate feeling on the dangers threatening the Church.[5] Archbishop Christophe de Beaumont's attack on the parlements in September 1756 evoked similar letters from sixteen of his episcopal colleagues, and there were other adherences to his renewed attack in October 1763, though three independent-minded Gallicans broke ranks and denounced it. The Assembly of Clergy's complaints against the rising literature of unbelief were taken up and elaborated in diocesan circulars, and from 1765, after the queen's appeal to the Assembly to promote the cult of the Sacré-Cœur, numbers of pastorals authorized and encouraged the devotion, Bishop Fumel of Lodève providing the prototype, which others copied or paraphrased.

Mandements were composed in orotund prose reinforced with the standard pious clichés which created the 'unction' approved by some and ridiculed by others, and their argument was supported by an array of learning—scriptural texts, the opinions of the Fathers, decisions of Councils, prescriptions of royal legislation. Not surprisingly, bishops called on their expert theologians to help with the drafting. The abbé Couet, a *grand vicaire* of Paris, was so pleased with an effort he wrote on behalf of Archbishop Noailles that he sent a copy to Voltaire, receiving *Mariamne* in return: a pastoral and a tragedy, said Voltaire, combining to provide the world with comedy.[6] 'Have you read my *mandement*?' 'Et vous, Monseigneur?'[7] The authorship of pastoral letters was a never-failing subject of jest. Mgr should teach his secretary logic, for what he has produced 'is as stupid as if he had written it himself'.[8] An improved variant was to ascribe the sacred eloquence to some dubious literary hack. La Motte was supposed to have penned Tencin's denunciations of the Jansenist bishop Soanen. 'A remarkable fact,' said Voltaire, 'an archbishop condemns a bishop and it is an author of operas and comedies who pens the archbishop's censures.'[9] Pious folk collected pastoral letters to furnish arguments for the true faith against incredulity, and the wits sought them for their involuntary humour. Their archaic phraseology gave an agreeably comic flavour to the zoological distinction of aquatic creatures into flesh, fowl, and fish for Lenten purposes offered by a worthy bishop of Agde;[10] to the bishop of Marseille's denunciation of the clergy who attended the city's pleasure dome, the 'Wauxhall';[11] to Cardinal Rohan's pastoral from prison when he was under arrest for his shady activities in the diamond necklace scandal, comparing himself to 'St Paul in fetters'.[12] Equally collectable for connoisseurs was the 'philosophical' pastoral letter of Loménie de Brienne vetoing a pious practice on the principles of the Enlightenment: farmers were forbidden to bring their beasts together for benediction in a time of cattle plague, regarding the limiting of the spread of infection as more important than intercessions for divine intervention. The eighteenth century was the great age of pamphleteering, and the bishops' pastorals counted among their number. It was, said Marais in 1732, 'le siècle du papier et le siècle des mandements'.[13]

III

According to the Council of Trent, the bishop or his delegate was required to visit every parish at least every two years, but preferably annually.[14] Monasteries were to be exempt, being subject to their own visitations. A declaration of Louis XIV in 1696 had gone further than the Council, overriding the monastic claim to exemption. No doubt, as the Fathers of Trent had said, the aim of the episcopal tours of inspection was to extirpate heresy, maintain ecclesiastical discipline, and edify the faithful; royal legislation, especially a declaration of 1695, added specific points of secular importance: to examine the accounts of churchwardens, assess the adequacy of the curé's lodging, see to the decency of the cemetery, rectify errors in parish registers, and review the local schools, hospitals, and charities. The bishops were 'fathers in God', but so far as the State was concerned, they were also 'administrative inspectors'. A visitation to perform these duties was organized as the bishop thought fit, but the secular courts were prepared to intervene to protect the rights of the lower clergy and the laity. This could happen anywhere by the invocation of the *appel comme d'abus*, and in the jurisprudence of the parlement of Brittany, a group of parishes could not be convoked to a common meeting—the bishop of Léon was prevented from resorting to this economical method in 1735.[15]

The episcopal power of visitation could be delegated. In huge dioceses like Bourges and Rouen, this was inevitable, and in areas of difficult terrain or in seasons of bad weather, a bishop of advancing years or in poor health could advisedly send others to do the riding and walking. 'In addition to episcopal grace', said Le Camus of Grenoble, 'a mountain bishop needs the surefootedness of a chamois.' The last bishop of Dié, Mgr Plan des Augiers, visited from 1756 to 1778, preserving the record of his journeys in twelve *cahiers*. Not surprisingly, he gave up after these twenty-two years of peregrination, for away from the old Roman road Valence– Dié–Gap, his parishes were accessible only by bridle-paths he traversed by horse or mule.[16] A young man might enjoy such adventures. In the 1730s Mgr La Motte of Amiens was tramping the lanes of his diocese. 'I do not think that a four-horse carriage can ever give so great a pleasure as the freedom of the open road from which I so often profited,' he said in later years.[17] How an older man reacted is reflected in a letter of Souillac of Lodève in September 1735, after getting back to his fireside at night exhausted:

My legs, the muscles having been so severely punished, punished me in their turn. I had been obliged to go down the hill on foot by paths full of rocks and stones; add to that all the preaching, the detailed work of the inspections, the weight of the vestments, especially the heavy cope, not to mention the cross and mitre, which I had to walk in, sometimes over long distances, in a procession over broken paving stones.[18]

And in any case, bishops had duties to take them away from their dioceses and administrative responsibilities which at times were all-absorbing. There always had been compelling reasons to delegate, and this was being done in more organized fashion in the eighteenth century. Though the archdeacons sometimes carried on with their traditional role, more and more the prelates were handing over the visitation duties to their *grands vicaires* and to the rural deans, the latter probably the most efficient of all, in close touch with the local problems of the parishes on which they reported. So a general assessment of pastoral visitations must take account of the many taking place under delegated authority, with the certainty that the documentary record of many of these enquiries has long been lost.

For some dioceses our information is fragmentary.[19] The bishop of Lombez was on tour in 1764, 1777, and 1780, of Sarlat in 1737, 1753, and 1764; a single *tournée* is recorded for Tulle. For Condom, there are no archival minutes, but a letter of Alexandre-César d'Auteroche shows that he conducted a *tournée* in 1765. At Auch, the archbishop visited in 1754; we know, however, of one of his *archiprêtres* active in every parish of his rural jurisdiction annually from 1731 to 1742. Local annalists record with relish forays by their bishops and the ensuing alarms and confusions—incidents which otherwise we would not have heard about.[20] The pattern of the episcopate of Charles-Maurice Le Tellier at Reims (1671–1710) is of a certain number of inspections of his own, but the continuous routine being kept going by the rural deans; even so, the local record shows the archbishop coming six times to the hamlet of Etrépigny in twelve years—true, the curé was Meslier, posthumously to become notorious for his atheism, yet this was not known in his life-time, and the Fathers, Malebranche, and Fénelon on his shelves proved his respectability.[21] Clearly, more visitations must have been taking place all over the country without ever being recorded.

A few scandalous prelates were little concerned with what went on in their dioceses, leading to complaints from their curés, not about being left alone, something most of them greatly desired, but because (unless there was a suffragan) there were few confirma-tions.[22] A Grimaldi who once, when driven to it, laid hands on 4,570 candidates in a single session, and a cardinal de Gesvres who did three visitations in forty years and held a confirmation at his palace once a decade were pastors whose flocks had only heard of their existence by hearsay, and, as the joke had it, were like the disciples in Acts 'who had not so much as heard if there be a Holy Ghost'. Yet significantly, visitations went on, whether episcopally conducted or by delegates, even when the head of the diocese was notorious for slackness or worldliness. Cambrai[23] was neglected after the death of Fénelon, and from 1716 to 1721, absentee prelates ruled. The next appointment was Charles de Saint-Albin, the loose-living illegiti-mate son of the regent, only 24 years of age. For two and a half years he postponed his arrival, but once he reached his episcopal city, he went out at once on a pastoral inspection, winning golden opinions by giving a threadbare old curé a pension of 100 livres. Cardinal Tencin of tarnished reputation, archbishop of Lyon at the end of his days, Mgr de Vauréal of Rennes, 'the handsomest man of his time' and active in the royal diplomatic service, Talaru de Chalmazel of Coutances, charitable but morally ambiguous, are all found visiting their parishes.[24] Others, neglecting the duty themselves, organized others to do it. There is evidence of the archdeacons and a canon conducting major inspections at least during the last ten years of Jarente's absentee episcopate at Orléans; Loménie de Brienne, constantly engaged in high government business, had his five vicars-general looking after every detail of pastoral administration in Toulouse. In 1767, Louis-André de Grimaldi, a byword for indifference to religious observances, arrived in Le Mans and organized his diocese into 'départements', each under a *grand vicaire*; they ruled, complained a curé, 'in little despotic empires—no reference to the bishop possible; he lived in inaccessible grandeur'.[25] Translated to Noyon in 1778, he inherited a system of delegation from his predecessor Charles de Broglie: a busy archdeacon visited continually, and he was left to continue his labours.[26]

By contrast, there were bishops, more numerous than the idle and the professional delegators, who regarded visitation as their inescapable duty and, sometimes, their pleasure. Early in the century there were fanatical workers like Le Peletier, who covered the whole diocese of Angers from 1693 to 1694, then went methodically around again in the next twelve years; his system was to lodge for a week in one place and go out from it to inspect a parish every day.[27] There was Charles Frézeau de la Frézetière, a tough ex-soldier, who stormed round 600 parishes of the diocese of La Rochelle in eight years.[28] Massillon began a general visitation of Clermont in 1721, taking nine years to complete, then another in 1730 taking five years, then in 1738 his third and last.[29] The diocese of Orléans, later to be so neglected by Jarente, was comprehensively covered under Fleuriau d'Armenonville (1706–33) by his *grand vicaire* Nicolas-Joseph de Paris; then as bishop himself Paris carried on all through his rule over the next twenty years (1733–53).[30] A bustling archdeacon had looked after Soissons for fifteen years until the arrival of Fitz-James in 1739—for the next twenty-five years he and the three archdeacons were continually active.[31] Much the same happened at Saint-Pol-de-Léon, where *grands vicaires* had done all the inspections for a decade, until La Marche arrived in 1772, and for the next eighteen years went out to the parishes every year himself.[32] Aristocrats of the highest lineage did not spare themselves. Cardinal de Luynes, in an episcopal career spanning three-quarters of the century, visited at Bayonne, then at Sens; the two brothers La Rochefoucauld were active at Beauvais and Saintes in the 1780s.[33] Juigné at Châlons-sur-

Marne travelled round all his parishes in his first eight years, then in 1772 began a second tour, this time sending a circular to his curés saying that all he would need was shelter—he was bringing cooks and provisions and invited them to dine with him. When translated to Paris, he could not continue such a demanding routine, but in his first year we find him inspecting the royal parish at Versailles.[34] Some zealous bishops were still pursuing their itineraries in extreme old age. La Motte of Amiens (1734–74) covered his whole diocese every five years, and at 85 was still carrying on. Baüyn of Uzès in 1774 issued a pastoral letter to say he was beginning his fourth general visitation at the age of 75, and listed twenty-six points on which he would require information. Jean de Dousset at Belley (1712–45) kept going until crippled by age and illness. Olivier Ségonde Kervilio completed eleven *tournées* of Tréguier in twenty-eight years, doing his last visitation in 1729 at the age of 86; his successor from 1731 completed ten tours in a dozen years, then collapsed exhausted in 1741, though two years later he was trying again.[35]

In some dioceses, the bishop's activity was intermittent. Jean de Caulet,[36] who ruled at Grenoble from 1725 to 1771, began with vigour, visiting sixty-nine parishes in 1728, fifty-two in the following year, then a gap while he attended the Assembly of Clergy in Paris, then ninety-six parishes in 1732 and seventy-six in 1733. At that point he stopped, and did not hold another general visitation until 1757. Perhaps, having familiarized himself with every hamlet in his mountainous diocese, he decided he would now administer from the centre, which was not unreasonable. La Rochelle was inspected by its bishop from 1729 to 1740; he then fell ill and did not go on tour for his remaining twenty-seven years.[37] Paris had a gap of sixty years after the death of Noailles, though there were archidiaconal tours of inspection. The pattern would change abruptly when a fervent bishop succeeded a slack one. At Alet yearly activity began when Charles de la Cropte de Chantérac took over (1763–89).[38] Gaspard de Jouffroy-Gonsans, succeeding Grimaldi at Le Mans in 1778, declared that he intended to visit every parish—'it is the only way to obtain the close union between pastor and flock . . . so much to be desired'. When he went to Fougerolles, no bishop had been there since 1744; at Landivy he confirmed 1,600 from four parishes amid a huge crowd 'who, within living memory, had never seen the bishop in this place'.[39]

There are other dioceses where the record of episcopal visitation is continuous for long periods.[40] The tiny dioceses of Senez and Orange were visited by their bishops all through the century. So too at Alais and Nîmes. On 6 March 1734, François d'Andigné entered Dax to be installed, and he began his first visitations on 21 November in winter weather. From then onwards, in his reign and under his two successors, the diocese was constantly visited up to the Revolution. The record is also extensive in Fréjus (to 1781), Vence (to 1779), and Grasse (to 1759). The big sees of Bordeaux, Langres, Montpellier, and Châlons were models of the working of the system throughout the century.[41] At Bordeaux, there was a change of emphasis in 1769, for after forty years' rule by prelates who regarded visitation, as one of them said, as 'their indispensable duty', under Rohan-Guéménée and Champion de Cicé *grands vicaires* took over, though there was a major archiepiscopal tour in 1787. Langres, visited from 1734 to 1789 by Mgr de Montmorin and Mgr de La Luzerne, was the scene of a not entirely successful experiment in 1741, an attempt to organize an independent assessment of the efficacy of the visitations by filtering the reports through a committee of experienced priests, the *bureau du gouvernement spirituel du diocèse*.[42] The severity and continuity of the visitations in the diocese of Montpellier were intensified by the tensions of the great ecclesiastical quarrel of the century. Colbert, as befitted the austere leader of the Jansenist cause, went everywhere in person; his successor, the ruthlessly orthodox Berger de Charancy (1738–48), followed his example—out of pastoral enthusiasm, rivalry with the achievements of his predecessor, and to smoke out Jansenists entrenched in the parishes. Raymond de Durfort (1766–74) delegated a far-ranging visitation policy to others, though he is found going to thirteen parishes himself in the course of the years 1769–71. Joseph-François de Malide (1774–90) kept the system going, but joined in frequently himself—there are records of his presence in 115 parishes.[43]

IV

'The 18th century was a great epoch for pastoral visitations.'[44] This was so, not only because of their frequency and continuity in many areas, but because the processes were becoming more sophisticated—organized delegation to vicars-general and rural deans, more attention to preliminary enquiries, to the dignity of the proceedings, to the follow-up for enforcement. In broad outline, there was a standard procedure built up through the years.[45] It was well known what documents had to be produced (in Clermont the diocesan *Rituel* listed them)—the inventory of possessions, the title-deeds to the property of the foundation, the accounts of the churchwardens, the confraternities, chapels, and hospitals, and the letters of priesthood of the clergy together with the warrants of their nomination to office, their authorization to preach, and, if absent from duty, a medical certificate. By the end of seventeenth century, it was established that the curé must also produce a filled-in copy of the diocesan questionnaire. Like so many pastoral innovations, the idea had come from Charles Borromeo, and the Assembly of the Clergy of France in 1579 had elaborated a list of questions along his lines; there was also a more detailed list in the treatise of the Italian monk Bartolomeo Gavanti. The circulation of a solemn pro forma to all the parishes came in at Clermont in 1620 and was rapidly adopted everywhere; soon it was printed, and the printed form was universal in the eighteenth century, although it came late to Limoges in 1730. In outline, the run of questions had become fixed, though additions and amendments were made from time to time. In the diocese of Clermont,[46] everything was unchanged from 1636 to 1789, except that an omission was made in deference to the ideas of the Enlightenment: the demand to name 'sorcerers, fortune-tellers—male and female—and others who weave spells' was dropped. In the diocese of Châlons-sur-Marne[47] in the early eighteenth century questions were added concerning parishioners who failed to perform their Easter duty and the 'dominant vices' of the population; at mid-century there were further additions asking about the provision of sermons and catechism classes, and whether steps were needed to deal with characters who frequented wine bars during the hours of divine service. Bordeaux began the century with thirty questions, soon dropping the one asking for details of the 'spiritual life' of the parish as a subject more suitable for private discussion between the priest and his bishop. In 1731, however, Mgr François Casaubon de Maniban sponsored a new model based on Italian practice,[48] with seventy paragraphs with their various subheadings making a total of 500 items, a document which, Mgr Louis d'Audibert de Lussan (1734–69) refined. No doubt there came a point when the multiplication of questions became self-defeating. Curé Nicolas Dumont of Villers-devant-le-Thour (500 communicants) told the archbishop of Reims in 1774, concerning the 'qualities and vices' of his parishioners: 'le caractère des habitants de Villers est à peu près celui des autres hommes'.[49]

There was a great deal to do on a visitation, so the bishop needed assistants. Bareau de Girac who, like all the bishops of Rennes in the century, rarely visited, when he did turn out, went in style—

coachman, outrider, lackey, *valet de chambre*, cook, a notary, and two priests. But the standard minimum formula was to take the domestic chaplain and a *grand vicaire*. Thus in 1748 the folk of Aubais in the diocese of Nîmes gathered to greet their prelate as he arrived with his vicar-general in a barouche drawn by two black mules, and the chaplain riding alongside on a white one.[50] The director of the seminary might be taken—he would probably have the advantage of personal knowledge of the parish priest in his earlier days.[51] The bishop of Mâcon in 1745–6 made an unusual addition to his party, one more characteristic of the seventeenth than the eighteenth century, taking the *promoteur* of his *officialité*, presumably a sinister gesture, as if offenders against morals were being noted down for prosecution.[52] According to the area and its dangers, whether of terrain or lawless inhabitants, a servant or more would be needed, a coachman, a groom, a lackey. These could be a nuisance. When the bishop of Agde was at Bouzigues in 1773, the town failed to give his retainers their tip, so they seized the *dais* (the canopy to shield the bishop, proudly carried in procession on its four poles by the churchwardens and two leading citizens). These, rather than miss their hour of glory, handed over the money.[53] A precisely similar episode over the 'pourboire au dais' is noted at Saint-Jeanret early in the century.[54] Characteristically of the age, the parishioners were subjected to an inspection at their own expense. The *pourboire* to the servants was part of a more general bill for entertainment—the notables of a little town borrowing 395 livres to make a splash,[55] those of a village modestly laying out 36 livres, recouped by a tax on farm animals, ten sols on a 'big beast', five on a pig, and two on a sheep.[56] There might be a fee, a *droit de procuration*, to be paid in lieu of entertainment, probably very small, 15 livres or so, the joint responsibility of clergy and laity.[57] The administrative assembly at Nîmes, the *assiette*, was accustomed to vote the bishop a lump sum to cover all the parishes at the beginning of his *tournée*—2,000 livres was given in 1787.[58]

In the seventeenth century, a bishop might well have been accompanied by a Jesuit or member of some other religious order as his preacher; the practice was dropped in the eighteenth century, though the bishop occasionally gave a sermon himself, not always being entirely comprehensible to rural congregations. Cardinal de Luynes once denounced the philosophes. 'You stupid girl,' said a mother to her daughter, 'falling asleep instead of listening to Monseigneur and learning about the lives of Saint Voltaire and Saint Rousseau.'[59] More often, the bishop was satisfied with celebrating a pontifical mass, perhaps with the offer of an indulgence to those who communicated. And he would hold a confirmation; peasants and their families from all around would gather, so a crowd of 500 or so was not unusual.[60] La Motte, bishop of Amiens, even when he was old, prolonged proceedings by interrogating candidates personally, 'resisting', as he said, 'the parents who are jealous when they see children of the same age accepted in preference to their own'.[61]

This would be embarrassing to some, but the dreaded moment for all came when the inquisitors began to inspect the church, the vicarage, and the cemetery. If the camouflage was seen through, the community would have to pay for repairs and improvements. A close scrutiny of the liturgical equipment[62] was sure to reveal faults which everyone had come to live with through usage, or put up with through parsimony—chalices, ciboriums, and pyxes to be regilded, tabernacles to be adorned and their locks repaired, the stoppers of the bottles for consecrated oil to be fitted properly, pictures to be cleaned, missing pages in the service-books replaced. Bishop La Motte always looked in the linen chest, for if the corporals used in the communion were grubby, 'to a believer in the Real Presence . . . this is worse than heresy, it is impiety'. He also specialized in the reverence due to the baptismal font; it was to be railed off, and the lid must be pyramidal, not flat, lest women attending divine service should seat their babies on it.[63] In some respects, however, a visitation might be welcome to curé and people, enabling them to bring the great to order and end the tyranny of their portentous pews obstructing the aisles.[64] The offenders, seigneurs (and sometimes the churchwardens themselves), could ignore ordinary complaints, but the bishop could order the sawing off of a foot or two and, indeed, total demolition if the documentation of the right to possess a pew was not forthcoming. A particularly searching enquiry was conducted at the church of Saint-Michel at Draguignan on 26 April 1763, by the bishop of Fréjus.[65] He ordered various pews to be shortened; the font was to be moved, since, where it was, 'little children are being exposed to draughts'; the five side altars would be interdicted unless 'within a month, counting from today' their pictures and steps were repaired. From these practical matters he moved to the local liturgical calendar, reducing the excessive use of the Holy Sacrament in processions and benedictions, forbidding nocturnal assemblies in the church, prescribing the exclusive use of the Roman rite, and requiring a low mass to be said after the Sunday high mass so that infirm people could attend. Then he dealt with the whole system of confraternities drawing the faithful away from the ordinary services in the parish church. The Pénitents survived, but were forbidden to frequent their chapels in the Easter fortnight or to have burials there; the other confraternities were reduced to three in number (the Holy Sacrament, the Rosary, and the Souls in Purgatory), and these were put under the control of the churchwardens and the sacristan.

Some adornments of the church might meet with disapproval as lacking in taste or conventional pious sentiment. The late seventeenth and early eighteenth centuries had been a time to get rid of dubious images—a St George looking like Perseus rescuing Andromeda, a Mary Magdalen in her finery as a courtesan.[66] Yet others had survived to catch the censorious eye later on—'a deformed and indecent statue' of Our Lady, a life-sized figure of a bucolic-looking Christ riding on an ass into Jerusalem, an image of St Martin on an unconvincing horse. An order to remove such objects would be made, always with the instruction to bury them in the churchyard—having been objects of piety to an earlier, naïve generation, they could not be reduced to secular firewood. A critical eye, wary of superstition, would be cast over relics. If the documents of authentication were inadequate and the stories concerning the saint were not edifying or reasonable, the bishop might order the removal of the fragmentary remains, or he might mercifully concede that an immemorial connection or the devotion of the parishioners could serve in lieu of formal correctness.[67] If the decision was removal, the bishop was well advised not to announce it until he was safely back in his palace; in 1721, Massillon opened the reliquary of the patron saint of one of his parishes, and was besieged in the sacristy by a mob and had his coach windows broken as he fled.[68]

Parishioners used every artifice to delay having to make repairs to the vicarage. Visitation time was the curé's opportunity to get authority on his side. If he convinced the bishop, the whole matter would be put to the intendant, who had the power to order a parish to hold a meeting to fix a rate to pay the building contractor—though, as a hard-headed layman, he was not likely to enforce an excessive degree of comfort at public expense.[69] By the edict of April 1695, the parishioners were also obliged to maintain the cemetery, especially the walls and gates.[70] In the first three-quarters of the century, when the great were buried inside the church and the rank and file piled in the *fosse commune* until it was filled, the graveyard was not the lonely spot for poetic reverie it subsequently became— cattle grazed, children played, men engaged in games of boule and hands of cards, and washing was hung out to dry. Reforming bishops objected to these profane activities, and if the church-wardens had not had the foresight to round up the beasts, expel the intruders, and hide the washing, episcopal censures would come their way. Far from wishing to make the burial ground an umbrageous romantic place, however, the bishops tended to order the sawing down of such trees as there were, since they gave shade to the gossips and the gamblers. By mid-century, a new consideration arose, a concern with hygiene, and the bishop of Saint-Papoul, anticipating the action of the government, interdicted a cemetery 'à cause de l'odeur'. A royal declaration of March 1776 banned burials in the churches, and ordered the setting up of new cemeteries in places where the old one had become a pestilential danger to the nearby inhabitants. In towns (though rarely in the countryside) this meant the reluctant parishioners might have to buy new land, hire a mason to wall it, and in addition still have to maintain the walls of the old graveyard for fifteen years—a heavy expense. Thus a new and sombre thunder-cloud hung over their heads at visitation time; if they failed to obey the royal orders or complied parsimoniously and nominally, they were sure to be brought to book when the inquisitors returned.

It was the curé's turn to tremble when the registers of the *état-civil* were called for—the records of births, marriages, and deaths.[71] The system ought to have been foolproof with copies of entries sent to the *greffe*, the record office of the nearest royal jurisdiction. In fact, the parish priests often did not bother to make these returns, and the idle officials did not bother to ask for them. In the parish, the register could be lost, damaged by fire or drips from a leaking roof, or gnawed by rats; through idleness, illness, or old age, some curés failed to fill them in anyway. In these circumstances, the best that could be done was to set in motion the process of individual declarations by which the record could be reconstituted.

This inspection over, the curé could breathe again and conduct his chief pastor to see the charitable institutions of the parish.[72] Was the schoolhouse big enough? Was there a schoolmaster, and was he properly paid? Was he competent? He might well be tested on the spot for numeracy and literacy. The midwife would be sent for. Had she qualifications, and if not medical ones, had she at least taken the ecclesiastical oath of her profession? If the parish had a *procureur des pauvres* or charitable bureau, the accounts would be checked, and if there was a hospital, it would be inspected. Here the bishop had the right to investigate, but he was on the borderline of his powers to issue orders; if things were wrong, he would have to invoke the secular authorities. There is a grim letter of Champion de Cicé, bishop of Rodez, to Necker in August 1780 describing the *maison de force* of Castelgaillard,[73] a sort of prison for vagabonds and beggars under the control of the intendant of Montauban. There were 200 men and women in a place built for 50, lying on rotting straw left unchanged for seven months, the living moving into the dirty sleeping places vacated by those who died; the surgeon was ignorant, and the gaoler brutal. The one redeeming feature was that in the course of the last year forty prisoners had escaped. For such an inspection, the bishop would ask some medical expert to join him. Mgr de Barral, bishop of Castres, indeed, was always accompanied by Dr Icard, the expert on inoculation against smallpox. By episcopal ordinance (perhaps of doubtful validity) he had declared this treatment obligatory on all children of his diocese, and those who were unwary enough to be around at visitation time were duly caught and given their 25 per cent chance to live longer.

The climax of a visitation was when the people were asked about the conduct of their curé, and he in turn was asked about theirs; normally, there were separate interrogations.[74] The tension was often less than might have been supposed, partly because from about 1730 the official assumption (unlike that of the seventeenth century) was that the clergy would be living moral lives, and partly because of the unspoken concordat between priest and parish to rub along together without getting into trouble with authority. Was the curé present at all the services? Did he give sermons, take catechisms, visit the sick, behave morally? Mostly, the parishioners expressed satisfaction, except over practical matters—he was asking for excessive improvements to the presbytery, he had taken possession of the churchwardens' accounts and would not return them. In Brittany, the parish elected two *témoins synodaux* as spokesmen, a system to throw up professional complainants. In the diocese of Tréguier they were hard put to find examples of sexual misdemeanours or violence, but they specialized in reporting drunkenness, with picturesque details of children fleeing from catechism and marriages held up for the taking of liquid refreshment. The curé who turned up drunk at visitation time at least had no defence to the charge. The bishop of Dol turned savagely on one malicious witness: 'I can see you are a *mauvais sujet*; think of your death, it is nearer than you imagine'—the man and his wife died within the week.[75]

When interrogated in his turn, the curé generally took care not to get others, or himself, into difficulties: 'Assez content'; 'Répond qu'il n'a pas lieu de s'en plaindre'; no one misses Easter Day, but ordinary Sundays are not so good—'répond qu'ils pourraient mieux l'observer'. If he wanted change, he would hope that authority would impose it without revealing where the proposal came from— like getting rid of the old *rituel* for conjuring away hailstones from the crops, the people being much attached to it and blaming the curé when it failed. He was unlikely to give the bishop the actual names of immoral parishioners—unless it was some ne'er-do-well whom nobody loved. In the eighteenth century, the emphasis of the questions changed to fit the reality of the answers likely to be given—the names of 'public sinners' were not asked for, but rather 'the dominant vices' of the community.[76] Some bishops, however, in the backwaters of the country, managed to carry on in the old rigorous ways. In Tréguier, the *promoteur* went round on the visitations, and held a sort of preliminary hearing of the ecclesiastical court on the spot for couples living in sin and applicants for judicial separation or marriage dispensations. In 1739, the bishop of Grasse banned dancing on the square in the shadow of the village cross: 'Christians should blush to resort to such divertissements before the symbol of our redemption.' Soanen, the Jansenist prelate of Senez, forbade parents to sleep along with their children or to have boys and girls in the same bed, and anathematized dancing and various folk observances of rural carnivals. But lay society was reacting against these archaic attempts to police morality by visitation ordinances. The parlement of Rennes in 1748 and the parlement of Rouen in 1768 suppressed pastoral letters of bishops because they included the usual questions about the morals of parishioners in their visitation programme.[77] By then, in most parishes, these enquiries were just a formality. What did survive, however, and indeed, became more important in the eighteenth century, was an old feature of the visitation which was very acceptable to the thought of the Enlightenment: the intervention of the bishop to reconcile feuds and wind up lawsuits by compromise.[78] Mostly, the episcopal arbitration, once offered, was successful. The bishop of Alet noted with surprise in his record of a visitation at Caudier in 1785 that he had failed to bring a lawsuit to an end.[79]

The findings of the bishop were recorded in the minutes of the visitation, and in the eighteenth century it became customary to issue separate ordinances specifically requiring the curé and parishioners to act, or exhorting the civil authorities (the intendant and the magistrates) to co-operate. *Grands vicaires* could also issue such injunctions, since they had full episcopal power by delegation; other clerics carrying out a visitation had to send the *procès-verbal* to the bishop, who would take action for enforcement. Given the bishop's power to discipline the clergy and to close churches by interdict, obedience was usually given, though in matters requiring the intervention of the civil authorities (like major repairs or police action against the keepers of wine bars) the episcopal complaint might receive only a nominal satisfaction. The best way to ensure compliance to ordinances was for visitations to be frequent. Thus the churchwardens of Saint-Julien de Courville, who were found neglecting their parish accounts by a visitation of 1755, were brought to book when the suffragan bishop of Reims arrived on another tour of inspection four years later and found they had still not managed to produce a record of their expenditure.[80] On rare occasions, a very strict bishop would follow up his visitation with a *contre-visite* a few months later. In September 1784 the bishop of Tulle published his visitation ordinances concerning various parishes he had covered in the summer and autumn months, saying he was allowing three months' grace for all concerned to put things in order; in February of the following year a vicar-general (the dean of the cathedral) went round on a tour of verification. This was unfortunate for the people of Lagarde, who had failed to put right the plank floor of their cloister, for the new inspection of their church revealed a need for some roof repairs which the bishop had missed.[81]

The eighteenth century had been a great epoch of episcopal visitation, but it was the last. The instrument was effective for dealing with outrageous scandals—clergy living in concubinage or riot, over-mighty laymen tyrannizing over the church; it was an excessive parade of authority to deal with minor cases. Life was becoming more civilized, and the conduct of churchmen more respectable. The seminaries had ensured that the clergy knew their professional duties, episcopal oversight and public opinion had brought them to conform to strict rules of conduct; catechism classes had given even the most ignorant laymen a concept of basic Christian duty. Coercing the laity into morality by clerical intervention had become an impossible dream—far from co-operating, the law courts would prevent it.[82] The printed pro formas filled in by the curés became an end in themselves, a substitute for the actual visitation; the bishop could stay at his headquarters with the basic file they provided and have the information cross-checked against the regular reports of the rural deans, coming in more reliably as communications improved. Pious critics of eighteenth-century religion have complained of the growing formalization of the visitation, its concentration on detailed 'practical' affairs. Truth to tell, the visitation was suitable only for dealing with the practical. If the fostering of spiritual needs and progress is the main duty of the bishop, it needs to take place in entirely different and non-inquisitorial circumstances—in long private conversations with individual priests or in clerical discussion groups, in sermons delivered on confirmation tours, and friendly visits totally unconnected with the search for shortcomings.

V

The formal method for a bishop to meet and direct his clergy was to assemble them in a diocesan synod; here, matters of common interest could be discussed, and the bishop could embody the findings—or impose his own—in statutes and ordinances. At Coutances, in 1744, a synod was convened to consider the *Rituel* newly drawn up by the diocesan liturgiologists. The curés, 300 of them, poured into town. There were few absentees, for the fine for remissness was stiff—3 to 5 livres to the poor. On the morning, the bishop took his place in the chapel of Saint-Lô in the cathedral; he was flanked by the archdeacons and rural deans, who had come up early to have preliminary discussions. One by one, the curés presented themselves in the episcopal presence. In the afternoon, the full synod met to consider the *Rituel*. It was approved, and very shortly afterwards was published. At two synods in earlier years the subjects considered (as revealed in the subsequently published ordinances) had concerned penitential discipline; in 1724, the necessity of having a confessional box in the church and hearing all confessions there, not elsewhere, was affirmed; in 1727, there was a review of the *cas réservés*—that is, sins too grave to be remitted by the curé on his own authority. Later, in 1761, the bishop reminded the synod of the rules prohibiting curés from employing young women as housekeepers and from drinking in wine bars. All this had been said before in earlier editions of the diocesan statutes, but copies of them had become rare, so those particular clauses needed to be reaffirmed.[83]

As in the diocese of Coutances, so also in that of Lodève, synods were frequent in the first half of the eighteenth century. In 1745, the bishop, having prepared a revised edition of the diocesan statutes, called a general synod, inviting all ecclesiastics who had cure of souls—not only the curés, but also the cathedral canons and the monks of the two Benedictine abbeys. In the morning, there was communion, a sermon, and prayer, ending with the *Libera* and the *De Profundis*. In the afternoon, all assembled at the episcopal palace for discussions which carried on into the following day, ending with a universal profession of the faith as laid down by the Council of Trent. By local custom, the synod ought to have elected the clergy's representatives on the diocesan bureau for assessment of clerical taxation, but in fact the bishop named them, and his choice was ratified (his successor was to exercise the same initiative at the synod of 1751). Forthwith, the *Statuts synodaux du diocèse de Lodève renouvelés et publiés dans le synod* were published, so swiftly that it was unreasonable to suppose that the two days of debate had made any difference. The volume bore the imprint of the bishop's Jansenist sympathies, excommunicating parishioners absent from mass for three consecutive Sundays, their sin solemnly listed as being on the *cas réservés*. As for lukewarm priests, the episcopal pastoral letter of the preface declared crudely that Christ was 'prêt à vomir de sa bouche tout prêtre qui ne paraît ni bien ni mauvais'.[84]

The calling of a synod was at the bishop's absolute discretion:[85] if he did not choose to call one—as at Montpellier from 1700 to 1724 and Auch from 1698 to 1727—there would be a gap in the series of meetings. There were none in the diocese of Nantes all century, and only three in that of Rennes after 1711—contrasting with frequent meetings convoked by the bishops of Saint-Malo and Dol. In the present state of our knowledge we cannot plot the incidence of synodal assemblies over the various dioceses, but it is sure that from mid-century they were dying out. At Lodève, they became infrequent. At Coutances, the numbers attending declined. From 1674 to 1712, of those invited, 70 per cent came; in a year of numerous absentees, like 1710, it was because of very bad weather. From 1726 to 1738, only 40 per cent of the parish priests turned up. Thereafter, synods faded out. The diocesan calendar still gave the dates for the meetings (in 1789 it was 28–9 April), but these were fossilized entries no longer observed. The *cahier* of the clergy of the *bailliage* of the Cotentin (which included the greater part of the dioceses of Coutances and Avranches) regretted the passing of the synods, and asked to have them back again. According to the regulations of the diocese of Paris, three separate synods were to meet annually. One was of the curés of the city and suburbs, under the presidency of the *official*, one of the rural curés under their archdeacons, and one of the whole diocese under the bishop himself. In fact, the last synod of the whole diocese was held in 1673, when a set of statutes was published.[86] Only the gatherings of capital and suburbs continued. The sixty curés attended well, the average number of absentees being a dozen. Their meeting of 1727 called on the bishop to summon the whole diocese (this was to protest against the bull *Unigenitus*), but the request was refused. When, in 1786, Archbishop Le Clerc de Juigné imposed a new *Rituel* it was never considered in synod; as a result, the canons of Notre-Dame refused to use it.[87]

One reason for the decline of synods was the rising temper of independence among the parish priests. The Jansenists encouraged the tendency; as they saw it, a bishop ought to convoke his curés at regular intervals, accepting their right to share in his authority and be co-regents of the diocese. The days of statutes going through on the nod were ended.[88] At Saint-Malo and Luçon in 1769 there were protests against the publication of new statutes in defiance of the will of the assembled clergy; at Rouen in 1783 there were complaints against the archbishop and his 'court of Zelanti'; at Rodez in the following year there were protests against 'dictation' from on high. If this was to be the new temper of synods, not surprisingly the bishops hesitated to hold meetings and invite challenges to their authority.

Yet, if this was their motive, they were being short-sighted; times were changing, and by judicious use of discussion in synod they could have transformed their relations with their clergy. Le Clerc de Juigné, who failed to revive the old general synod of Paris when he went there as archbishop, as bishop of Châlons-sur-Marne, from 1764, held synods in 1765 and 1766.[89] He forbore from hectoring his clergy about their conduct, merely reminding them to dress properly in cassocks, take care in making entries in their parish registers, and to refrain from hunting. He mentioned a few points about ceremonies which were far from obvious and where misconceptions could arise. The exposition of the Holy Sacrament was in order for the patronal festival, but not for the Sunday of the octave; there was no fee to the officiant at the funeral of a curé except the dead man's breviary; sin is officially possible only when a young person reaches the age of 7, a point to be borne in mind in any sermon at the funeral of a child; when several marriages are celebrated together, the final benediction must be given separately to each couple. And he invited his curés to let him have comments as to changes needed in a proposed new edition of the *Rituel*. There was nothing to offend the pride of the curés here, and, in a minor way, they were being treated as colleagues. A striking demonstration of episcopal solidarity with the lower clergy was given by Bishop La Luzerne of Langres when he held a long synod, from 27 August to 3 September 1783, the purpose being to consider the inadequacy of the *congrue*, the official salary for vicaires and non-tithe-holding

New. Seeing the curés were at this time also required to come to synods and to an annual retreat, they must have felt themselves too enthusiastically supervised. In the diocese of Bordeaux,[94] the rural deans (there called *vicaires forains*) presided over the seven monthly *conférences* (*assemblées foraines*); they had to send to the archbishop an account of each meeting and attend collectively twice a year at the palace to give an account of their stewardship. The *assemblées* met in a different parish for each session, the local parish priest having to produce a meal for his colleagues, for which each paid 15 sols. There was low mass, high mass, a procession to the cemetery, and a sermon before lunch (eaten in silence while extracts from the New Testament were read). Then in the afternoon the *Veni Creator* and prayers, followed by four half-hour discussion periods (on a chapter of the Bible, on ecclesiastical duties, on moral theology, and on actual difficulties individuals had recently encountered in the con fessional). Absentees were punished by having to send in writte answers to the questions at the *conférence* they had missed.

Similar edifying sessions were prescribed for their clergy b reforming bishops in other dioceses. At Autun,[95] early in the centur the curés were ordered to assemble twice a year for discussions in t presence of their bishop and come to another two meetings in th local *archiprêtrés* under the rural dean. The synodal ordonnancesf Carcassonne of 1713 impose fines for absence from the mont *conférences*, the third offence involving a suspension of two mor from clerical duties on weekdays. The bishop circulated advice to clergy at their meetings on commercial problems in the confessio judiciously balancing between the rights of masters and emplo and advising on measures to take concerning issues of non-payn and defaulting creditors—a subject on which he was an expert, b a splendid aristocrat who had run up huge debts.[96] The syn statutes of Amiens in 1736 ordered each rural dean to ho 'chapter' of his parish priests twice a year.[97] In the diocese of S the archbishop circulated an annual list of discussion questions, there was complaint when the new prelate, arriving in 1753 them at a more demanding intellectual level.[98]

Reports of *conférences* in the diocese of Coutances sugg different atmosphere.[99] True, the formalities were there. Abse were fined on a diocesan scale fixed in 1730, the discussions serious, and the secretary forwarded the minutes to the bishop the curés were very willing to go—indeed, their meetings had b in the mid-seventeenth century, with voluntary assemblies taken over by the bishop and formalized. In the eighteenth cer for a while, meetings were fortnightly, though they finally became monthly. Some curés chose to attend in more than one rural deanery, and exempt curés (that is, those under the cathedral chapter, one in an enclave belonging to another diocese, and one in an independent *commanderie* of the Order of Malta) turned up to nearby meetings. The *conférences* had a cheerful communal spirit; a patron saint was nominated and duly honoured, masses were said for dead comrades, officers were democratically elected, and the whole gathering referred to itself as a 'republic'. This was a confraternity and a trade union as well as an officially sponsored discussion group. No doubt the Coutances evidence is a clue to what went on in other dioceses behind the official record; however severely a bishop might try to regiment the gatherings, there was a lot of good fellowship, renewal of friendships from seminary days, exchange of gossip and, indeed, of grievances. According to an embittered Jansenist curé of Poitou, they all had far too good a time. 'I seek out the society of persons of merit,' he sanctimoniously declared, 'as for those noisy gatherings where, under the name of *conférences* they assemble only to indulge in shameful and sometimes criminal excesses, I not only never liked them, but the first time I went to one I said quietly to myself—this will be the last.'[100]

Like the synods, the *conférences* began to decline, though there seems to have been a revival towards the end of the *ancien régime*: they began again in Toulouse in 1768 and in Lisieux in 1775.[101] Theological discussion month after month or quarterly would grow boring, and the curés, rising in social status, income, and educational qualifications, were becoming more sociable among themselves in informal ways, meeting to give lunch parties or to vie in the composition of verses and epigrams, or going off to some of the lay *sociétés de pensée* which were rising everywhere. If they wanted theological wrangles, they would have them privately among their friends, not in gatherings under episcopal supervision. Perhaps the growth of a radical temper among the parish priests disinclined the bishops to sponsor opportunities for the airing of dangerous opinions.

Indeed, the bishops were now inclining to favour yet another type of clerical meeting, one directed not to intellectual improvement, but to renewing and deepening the spiritual life of the individual by withdrawing for a few days into the seminary for prayerful exercises and silent contemplation away from the hassle of parochial business. According to a pious handbook of 1750,[102] the custom was established in a number of dioceses; according to another of 1770, in all of them.[103] Some bishops attempted to coerce their clergy to attend by withholding their power to hear confessions if they did not turn up at a retreat,[104] say, every two years; this had been the rule at Rennes and later at Dol.[105] Others encouraged them by keeping down the charge for board and lodging; at Le Mans in 1780 it was only 12 livres for nine days, and at Rouen about the same time it was entirely free.[106] The threats were a device of a bygone era, and the incentives did not work well. The rule in the dioceses of Amiens and Lisieux was a retreat every three years; in 1768, the bishop of Amiens complained that few curés and vicaires obeyed, 'even though it's only for a short time and not expensive'; in 1773, some of the curés of Lisieux went to the parlement by *appel comme d'abus* to have the obligation declared illegal.[107] The use of seminaries as places of discipline had given them sinister connotations, and the silence of retreat precluded the good fellowship which the *conférences* afforded. The curés, more and more imbued with the conviction of their independent status in the Church, were not happy to have their devotional lives policed as if they were monks obliged to pray by rote.

VII

Two factors conditioned the direct contacts and relationship between a bishop and his individual parish priests: one was the independent status of the curés, the other was their social inferiority.

While the bishop had power to discipline his clergy, this was only within the limits imposed by public opinion and the ever-watchful law courts with their procedure of the *appel comme d'abus*. The curés mostly did not need to fear their bishop; nor, for the most part, were they dependent on his favour. Except in a limited number of dioceses, the bishop had few parochial benefices to bestow, and his power to veto an appointment was limited and rarely used, for this could be done only on the ground of immorality, needing solid evidence to stand up before the secular magistrates, who were sure to be invoked. Nor had a bishop much chance to offer promotion to a better parish, and thus win support by fostering a lively anticipation of benefits to come. Even when a parish was in his gift, his plans for filling it might be thwarted by the operation of the 'resignation in favour', and by definition this right was most likely to be exercised in the important well-paid cures, those most worth having.

The prelates of a few dioceses were lucky. The archbishop of

Auch had more than four-fifths of the livings in his gift. Bordeaux, Tarbes, Saintes, Lodève, and Paris provided their rulers with the influence going with about half the appointments. But it was rare for more than a third of the parishes to depend on their chief pastor. This was the proportion at Alet. At Coutances, it was only 30 out of 489, 5 out of 145 at Saint-Pol-de-Léon, 12 out of 204 at Nîmes, 15 out of 213 at Strasbourg, 135 out of 1,460 at Rouen. The city of Paris,[108] as distinct from the whole diocese, is an example of the weakness of the archbishop's control; the patronage structure reveals one of the reasons why the clergy could so often be recklessly independent. Of the fifty-seven parishes, chapters appointed to sixteen, abbeys to thirteen, the University of Paris to three, the superior of Saint-Lazare to two, and one each were in the gift of the Grand Aumônier of France, the Grand Prieur of the Temple, the Order of Malta, the Oratory, and two of the curés. The archbishop had only seventeen parishes, and five of these were minuscule, only twenty to forty houses in each. Sainte-Marine had 'all 15 parishioners churchwardens', and only continued in existence, the story went, because the curé had the right to marry pregnant girls without their parents' consent, using wedding-rings made of straw. Of the nine huge populous parishes, only Saint-Paul, Saint-Germain-l'Auxerrois, and Saint-Eustache were in episcopal patronage; the others, Saint-Côme, Saint-Nicolas-des-Champs, Saint-Laurent, Saint-Étienne-du-Mont, Saint-Gervais, and Saint-Sulpice were outside the archbishop's gift. It was all very well to expect an archbishop to extirpate Jansenism: even if he could get rid of a curé, he had little control over who would become his successor.

The line between aristocrat and commoner ran clear through the Church of France, the offices of great emolument and distinction being monopolized by nobles. Closely examined, the line is blurred, for some families, especially those 'living nobly', were difficult to place, and some offices, like canonries, might be held by priests of differing social origins, depending on the need to have a sprinkling of efficient or learned practitioners appointed on merit. But so far as bishops are concerned, they were all on one side of the line, they were aristocrats: the curés were on the other, commoners (exceptions are so few that they can be ignored). From their youth, the bishops had expected to reach their great office because of their lineage; the curés knew that, however efficient or learned they were, they could never achieve elevation to the episcopate. The collaborators chosen by the bishop to run his diocese, the *grands vicaires*, were aristocrats, serving an apprenticeship to qualify for a mitre.

True, a prelate organizing to ensure his own peace of mind would do well to have a *grand vicaire* among the others who was an expert and not on the promotion ladder, some director of a seminary, a canon grown white-haired in pastoral duties. Mostly, however, the *grands vicaires* belonged to the bishop's own class and social circle. The dividing line was sharp, and the curés naturally resented it.

Yet the resentment, at least earlier in the century, should not be exaggerated. There was a fund of deference in society, and a sense of hierarchy in the Church working towards an acceptance of things as they were. And there was a respectable argument for aristocratic leadership: the head of a diocese had to be ready to outface the great to get justice for his people and his clergy. The curé of La Tour-Saint-Gélin in the diocese of Tours was harassed by his parishioners, led by the local seigneur, over tithes and payments for certain masses. In June 1777 a letter from his archbishop, Mgr de Conzié, arrived: 'Do not fear the threats made to you—insist on payment for your masses. If they raise a dispute in this matter, I will defend you. The same with your tithe; if they refuse to pay . . . whatever repugnance you have to start a lawsuit, I order you to do so, and I will be responsible for whatever legal means you have to employ.'[109] On Maundy Thursday 1779 the curé received from his archbishop a copy of the judgment of the parlement of Paris vindicating his case; no doubt he was glad to have an influential nobleman as his master. But progressively throughout the century, the curés, led by an intelligent and fiery minority, became more and more hostile to the subversion of the principle of the brotherhood of the ministry involved in the aristocratic monopoly. 'It is notorious . . . that the order of curés is totally excluded from the rewards your majesty bestows,' said one of their *cahiers* in 1789; 'it is an outrage, an injustice—we are disinherited.'[110]

Quite apart from the social gulf between them, there were good reasons why personal contact of a fulfilling sort between bishops and curés was limited. The sheer number of parishes in the bigger dioceses and the accumulation of courtly, secular and ecclesiastical administrative duties in many more left little time available for individual interviews. Also, the ethos of the hierarchical system tended to make all the opportunities for personal contact into formal, official occasions. In the synod, and at the visitation, the parish priest was, as it were, on parade, under test; even in the discussions of the *conférences* he was treated, often enough, as an examination candidate submitting his answers. It took a bishop of a particularly understanding and friendly nature to break through the obstacles of birth and the trammels of the system. Some followed the example of Fénelon and admitted curés to their table as occasion arose, even if it meant halting conversations about the price of pigs last market-day.[111] There were paradoxes: lack of fervour did not always go with aloofness, and virtue did not necessarily mean affability. Irreligious characters like Grimaldi and lazy ones like Couet du Vivier de Lorry were charming in personal intercourse when anyone managed to see them, while conscientious prelates like Thémines and Christophe de Beaumont never entertained their clergy. What was disastrous to relationships was not so much worldliness, but aristocratic *hauteur*. Boisgelin of Aix, a good administrator and an effective diocesan, was never likely to win the hearts of the men he described in a private letter as 'coarse, scruffy, ignorant; you'd have to be a lover of pestilential odours to enjoy the society of these mediators between heaven and earth'.[112] Montmorency-Laval, bishop of Metz from 1760, was a veritable caricature of obsessive pride—setting up a chapter for noble ladies, transforming his cathedral into a sanctuary for exclusively noble canons, entertaining army officers and nobles in his country château at Frascati, with never a thought of his lower clergy. As one of them said, 'his cold disdainful reserve withered the very hearts of the curés who dared approach him'. There was an inn on the road outside his park gates which did a good trade in providing meals for the curés who had come up to see him and needed refreshment before the long ride home.[113]

VIII

Bishops were judged, above all else, by their generosity to the poor. They intervened to try to protect their people from excessive taxation. 'If the pastors do not tell you about the misery of their flocks, who ever will?' wrote Massillon to Fleury.[114] They were acting as the voice of those who were allowed no voice of their own—as a bishop of Montauban said sardonically, denouncing the capitation tax, the poor have no say in what they have to pay, 'since people of wealth and consideration are normally at the head of public affairs'.[115] They were also watchful to ensure that the poor were not deprived of any of their traditional perquisites. When the maréchal de Richelieu, inveterate theatre-goer and seducer of ballet dancers, persuaded Louis XV to divert the poor-rate levied on theatre tickets to the adornment of the Opéra and the Comédie, archbishop Christophe de Beaumont stormed to Versailles to have the decision reversed.[116] The public expected these gestures, but they also expected the bishops to be forthcoming in their personal almsgiving. Local annalists knew exactly what sums they gave—one bishop of Nîmes gave donations totalling 43,000 livres to the Miséricorde over a period of five years, and his successor had a standing subscription of 300 livres a month.[117] Every act of meanness would be recorded, as the bishop of Grenoble giving only 12 livres a year to the collection for the hospital and, after a year of absence, having the gall to say 'he had given his alms in Paris'.[118] A curé would put a lapidary observation in his parish register: 'his liberality consisted in giving his zeal to God and nothing to men'. The Jansenist *Nouvelles ecclésiastiques* had its watch-dogs everywhere, and would make an ironical comment: 'by a perfection more than evangelical, neither his right hand nor his left know anything about his alms'.[119] But it seems that most bishops attempted to do their duty, though many fitted it in uneasily with maintaining their episcopal splendour and supporting members of their family. Some did a great deal more than any possible duty, having a strict rule of almsgiving verging on the prodigal, or giving recklessly with aristocratic indifference to accountancy. Every 30 December Mgr du Tillet of Orange checked his financial position, and on 1 January gave all the surplus to his curés for distribution to the needy.[120] Christophe de Beaumont, the archbishop of Paris who did so much harm to religion by his intolerance, gave away two-thirds of his vast income: at his death, more than 1,000 ecclesiastics and 500 nuns or women who had found refuge in convents were found to be his pensioners.[121] When he won half a million livres in a lawsuit, he gave it to Mme Necker, Protestant though she was, for her work for hospitals. His successor at Paris, Juigné, gave 100,000 livres a year, and handed over a great capital sum for rebuilding the *hôtel-Dieu* after it was destroyed by fire. Cardinal Dominique de la Rochefoucauld, with the revenues of the archbishopric of Rouen and the abbey of Cluny at his disposal, was spendthrift both on display and on charity, so much so that when he fled from France during the Revolution, he had to borrow for the journey.[122] At Dol, with its limited income, Urbain d'Hercé laid out his generosity with precise, patriarchal supervision. He lived simply, having his sister for housekeeper and refusing to put his servants into livery. Some of his savings he doled out to parishes and hospitals, some went on feeding his seminarists at his table, but the most part went in accordance with his principle that the poor do not need workhouses or medical attention but simply plenty of bread, meat, and wine. He subsidized the nuns of La Sagesse to run a daily soup kitchen, and always went there in person (or sent his sister or his brother, his vicar-general) to sample the cooking. On the Monday before Ash Wednesday the soup was replaced with a feast in the palace courtyard, followed by dancing.[123] His contemporary, the bishop of Alet, was another believer in hot broth, and the poor came daily to his palace with their bowls. There were others of the same generous disposition, like La Motte of Amiens (who told a convent of nuns, 'Never forget, what is given to you has been refused to the poor') and François-Renaud de Villeneuve of Montpellier, whose funeral in 1765 was interrupted by the throng struggling for relics of their 'saint'.[124]

A bishop, even one whose charities were routinely modest or thoughtlessly intermittent, in a crisis had to live up to his station and its duties, demonstrably so. A murrain strikes the herds—the bishop buys '7,000 horned cattle' as free replacements, or he offers to pay compensation to the farmers who are being ordered to destroy their diseased animals. In a famine he distributes 1,000 loaves every Sunday, or gives a sum of money, stands guarantor for a municipal loan to bring in grain from overseas, or contracts to feed so many hundred poor. The palace might be turned into a hospital in time of plague, or thrown open as a shelter for refugees from floods.[125] In desperate emergencies, there were bishops who sold their possessions and ran into debt. When the powder magazine at Abbeville blew up wreaking devastation all around, La Motte of Amiens sold even the altar silver of his chapel, and Henri-François Desnos auctioned his dinner plate in the severe winter of 1782–3. These are individuals from whom such gestures might have been expected, but there was also Bernis, worldly diplomat rather than pastor, who borrowed 150,000 livres for the victims of the great inundation at Albi in 1766.[126] In the terrible winter of 1788–9, stories come from every diocese about episcopal leadership in relief. Juigné at Paris sold his silver, gave 300,000 livres, then borrowed another 400,000 on the credit of his brother the marquis.[127] Palaces elsewhere were thrown open, bonfires kept blazing in their courtyards, food distributions made, large sums given and loaned to municipalities, hospitals, and *bureaux de charité*. The bishops recognized the obligation of overwhelming need, even if they were slow to react to everyday deprivations. Never had the old episcopate of France appeared so generous as on the eve of its ruin.

In times of great danger, the chief pastor of a diocese was expected not only to be ready to help the victims afterwards, but to be present sharing the risks. This spirit is epitomized in the conduct of Belsunce, the prickly and intolerant bishop of Marseille, in the great plague of 1720.[128] On 25 May, the *Grand Saint-Antoine* sailed into harbour with a cargo of bales of cotton from the Levant; in them lurked the fleas carrying the plague. Once the dreaded tumours were diagnosed, the prosperous citizens, about 10,000 of them, fled to their country retreats. At the end of July, flight was no longer possible, for the parlement of Aix ordered the closure of all exits from the city. A cordon of soldiers shot or clubbed to death those who tried to break through. By August 400 a day were dying: by the beginning of September, 1,000. The *corbeaux* (mostly galley-slaves) who carted the bodies away to mass graves had a life expectancy of two days. Few ventured out into the corpse-strewn streets. Doctors went round wearing hideous parrot-head masks filled with antiseptic perfumes, their bodies totally swathed in waxed canvas robes, fending off passers-by and dogs with ten-foot poles. Belsunce made his palace into a hospital, and went out daily with three confessors and his household staff, giving alms and organizing the administration of the last rites. It was no longer possible to obtain absolution in the churches, as their porches were stacked high with corpses. Almost every day, the bishop lost one of his confessors; when forty had died, he feared that he himself might perish without the sacraments. On 14 September he had to move to the mansion of the chief magistrate, since it was impossible to get in and out of his palace without clambering over rotting bodies half-eaten by dogs. He did not use his carriage: the only time he rode anywhere, it was said, was when he sat beside the drivers of the carts carrying the corpses to the burial pits. On 1 November, with half the inhabitants dead, the plague was abating rapidly, and the bishop walked barefoot to the church of Saint-Ferréol and preached; on 31 December he processed round the ramparts overlooking the desolate city. The plague was over. Belsunce was a hero, and his enemies accused him of being self-consciously so. But he refused the proffered rewards of translation to better bishoprics. He had not deserted his people when the pestilence walked by noonday; he would not go now for enhanced prestige and emoluments.

In the towns, with so many narrow streets, wooden houses, piles of rubbish, and trade and industrial premises crowded in among the inhabitants, and the houses in the richer quarters stuffed with stocks of grain and fuel, fire was an ever-present hazard. At the end of the *ancien régime*, bishops were active in setting up *bureaux de secours*: the curés collected funds to form their reserves, and after an outbreak of fire the leading citizens on the committee assessed the damage and decided what level of compensation was possible—the bishop would normally add to it himself. But he was expected to do more. When the alarm was given, it was his duty to turn out: unless the Capuchins or other mendicants had organized themselves as the fire brigade, there would be no professional expertise available, and not every city had gone to the expense of buying pumps. It was a question of forming a bucket chain, knocking down burning roofs and walls, and setting guards against looters. When a conflagration was out of control, the grim decision to demolish neighbouring houses to make a fire break might have to be taken. Leadership was needed, and exhortations to courage.[129] In the inferno that destroyed the whole centre of Rennes in December 1720, the soldiers of the garrison and townspeople were standing in despair; the bishop, the intendant, and a few leading citizens donned leather jackets and clogs to make symbolic efforts to beat out the flames as an example. On 30 December 1784, at a fire in Orange, Mgr du Tillet joined the bucket chain (and later made good all the losses suffered). Three bishops at least are recorded as heroes. Jarente, the morally dubious courtier who held the *feuille des bénéfices* during the ministry of Choiseul, had earlier, as bishop of Digne, led a fire-fighting foray. Juigné at Châlons performed a rescue at the risk of his life. When a child was shouting for help from a blazing building, Mgr d'Apchon of Dijon called on the bystanders to help, offering 100 louis as a reward. This was 2,000 livres, four times the annual wage of a skilled artisan, but there were no takers. So the bishop rushed in and brought out the child himself. It was a splendidly aristocratic performance. He demonstrated the valour of his class, but it was not for him to soil his hands with a menial heroic task if the lower orders would do it for money.

There was a general inquest into a bishop's fulfilment of his duty to the poor when the content of his last will and testament became known. During his life, there had been the conflicting demands of obligations to family and obligations to charity—now there was a final revelation where the priority lay. According to Le Camus, bishop of Grenoble, famous for pastoral zeal and tolerance to Huguenots, the laws of the Church required a bishop to give back to his family what he had received from it, and to the Church and to the poor whatever he had saved from his ecclesiastical revenues. In accordance with this principle he left his immense private fortune of over 1,000,000 livres to his two brothers and nephews and nieces; this left only 50,000 livres for other legacies, though in mitigation Le Camus noted that in his lifetime he had given 472,000 livres for ecclesiastical objects, mainly in repairs to his palace and country house.[130] A later bishop of Grenoble, Jean de Caulet, who died in 1771, left virtually everything, including his magnificent library, to his nephew the marquis de Grammont; the town hospital received only 1,000 livres. The city raised a subscription to buy the library, and the marquis did the decent thing and let it go at the cut price of 40,000 livres.[131] Another great family man was Cardinal Tencin, who left everything to his sister. The rectors of the hospital of Lyon threw on to the junk heap the marble bust of their late archbishop which they had commissioned in the hope of enlisting his gratitude.[132] Dubois, the minister of the regent, had built up an annual income which Saint-Simon estimated to have totalled 1,500,000 livres a year (including his bribes from England). His vast inheritance descended to his nephew, a canon, who gave it all to the poor, retaining only a sum of money to pay for a marble tomb for his uncle in the church of Saint-Honoré (the sculptor, perhaps maliciously, showed Dubois turned away from the altar, looking suspiciously towards the door).[133]

But Le Camus, in the interest of family, had distorted the 'laws of the Church'. They did not recommend the giving of a private fortune back to the family; they simply allowed it. The true ideal, the one which would ensure the psalmist's 'peace at the last', was to prefer the poor, to prefer them even to worthy ecclesiastical objects. Fléchier and Fénelon, who helped their nephews during life, made it clear to them that they could not expect anything by inheritance.[134] The examples of bishops who died nepotists to the last are outweighed by those who preferred pious works and the poor to the interests of their heirs. 'The *bureau des pauvres* is my universal legatee. I ask, indeed I order, that I be given a simple pauper's burial,' declared a bishop of Beauvais. An archbishop of Rouen forbade all adornments and armorial bearings on his tomb, and left all he possessed to his seminary of Saint-Louis, the refuge for the aged and infirm priests of his diocese.[135] A bishop of Châlons left 180,000 livres, only 10,000 of it to his relatives.[136] Of the rulers of the see of Lombez, Cône Roger, dying in 1710 at the age of 95, left everything to the hospital and the seminary. Charles de Maupeou, dying in 1751, left little, but all to the hospital. Jacques Richier de Cérisy, dying twenty years later, had made a judiciously balanced testament: relatives got 24,000 livres, his executor 3,000 livres; masses for his soul to the tune of 300 livres were ordered; his servants got 5,800; convents of nuns 6,900; the chapters of Rouen and Lombez 3,500 each; the cathedral 3,000 for ornaments; the schools of his diocese 2,000; the poor of his native place 1,600; the poor of Lombez 4,200; with a sum of 300 for such paupers as walked in his funeral procession. It was a suitable will for a Christian of the century: not too much on masses, fair to the relatives but not pampering them, reasonable to both ecclesiastical institutions and the poor. Perhaps, by the standards of the Enlightenment, there should have been more to the servants—Cardinal Charles-Antoine de la Roche-Aymon, archbishop of Reims, who left virtually everything to hospitals, was criticized for leaving only a year's wages to his staff. Alas! what Richier de Cérisy had not considered was his solvency. As so often happened, when his effects were realized, there was not enough money available, and all the legacies had to be halved.

No doubt one day historians will make a statistical analysis of all the testamentary dispositions of the bishops throughout the century. The final picture will be revealing, a comparative demonstration of how relatives, servants, pious works, ecclesiastical foundations and the poor were treated. Even so, conclusions as to the character and piety of individuals will not be easy to draw. Other disparate factors will have to be weighed. It was a precept of the casuists, especially the Jansenists, that almsgiving during life was more effective for salvation than distributions after death, so what had already been given must be set alongside the last gifts of all. For some, family obligations were overwhelming, for others, unimportant or already fulfilled. Some episcopal revenues were large, some very limited. And human nature is full of paradoxes. What of Cardinal de Gesvres, archbishop of Bourges, a notorious miser who for long had lived as a recluse, indifferent to what happened in his diocese? In 1744, at the age of 88 he died, leaving a huge fortune, including 293,000 livres cash in his coffers, and a store of gold. His will specified that it was all to go, in the first place, to fulfil his repairing obligations, then to endow the seminary and hospital, while his library was bequeathed to Saint-Germain-des-Prés. His relatives were to have his silver plate—nothing more.[137]

A minority of bishops had a saintly attitude towards wealth, being generous and charitable in the extreme. By contrast, a minority was generous only to immediate family. The majority between accepted their incomes and all the extras of pensions and abbeys, however excessive, without self-questioning, as their bounded right, and they spent profusely, whether in palace building, display, supporting relatives, or in charity; in a crisis, they would make spectacular charitable contributions. They did not doubt their own right to monopolize the great offices of the Church, and only late in the century did they take serious notice of the idea that they ought to pay ordinary taxation. They did not identify with the demand of the

rising middle classes for careers open to talent and taxation fairly
imposed on all. When they proclaimed the egalitarian commonplaces of gospel eloquence, as they did in sermons and pastorals, their
favourite idea was the need to sympathize with those who had no
property but their labour, nothing to sustain them but the sweat of
their brows. They believed in their own privileges, and counterbalanced this complacency by taking up the cause of the disinherited. Theirs was an aristocratic attitude to wealth, tempered
with Christian idealism, but motivated more by pride. In the early
days of the Revolution, when ecclesiastical wealth was under universal scrutiny, a few of the bishops, the saints, were willing to
abandon the greater part of it. In a pastoral of 7 March 1789 Tillet
proposed ordinary taxation for all and the confiscation of two-thirds
of the revenues of bishoprics and abbeys for five years to avoid any
increase of tax burdens on the people. Men are equal, he said; 'we
have the same Father in heaven, we are all descended from the same
family tree, the same sun lights our path, we all descend equally into
the tomb and we all appear before the same Judge'. Most of his
colleagues, without such dramatic renunciations, refused to fight for
their revenues: when they finally challenged the National Assembly,
it was on an issue of principle, the right of the Church to be consulted about changes in its government. No doubt there was an
element of instinctive tactical thinking in their conduct, but it
corresponds to their aristocratic attitude to wealth: they accepted
money without shame and spent it without restraint, but they were
too proud to haggle about it.

PARISHES

I

By the eighteenth century, the parish boundaries of France had ceased to correspond to social realities and pastoral needs—in so far as they had ever done so. In towns, the population was illogically distributed. The migration of labour into a peripheral urban area had inflated one parish of Angers to 11,000 inhabitants, and one of Nantes to 25,000, whereas some of the others in these two cities had only a few hundred.[1] In Paris, Saint-Gervais, Saint-Merry, Saint-Paul, and Saint-Côme each had between 20,000 and 30,000 communicants; Saint-Étienne-du-Mont had 80,000, and Saint-Sulpice 90,000; by contrast, Saint-Opportune had 120, and Saint-Jean-de-Latran a few dozen.[2] There were great disparities in the extent of rural parishes. Though by law ten houses was the minimum, there were still official parishes in 1789 consisting of one or two houses alongside the presbytery;[3] some consisted of a mere hamlet and its fields; some were huge. A writer in the *Mercure géographique* in 1678 described examples in Brittany measuring five leagues by four, containing numbers of villages and twenty or more chapels apart from the main church. 'Each of these parishes has the aspect of a little province,' he says; 'the inhabitants speak of them as if they were separate and individual *pays*. Just as we talk of provinces, saying "in Brittany", "in Anjou", they say "in Quarantoy", "in Guer", "in Pimpoint".'[4]

Disparities in population and area were not the only illogicalities. Parish churches were rarely conveniently central—they might be on the very circumference. Perhaps two would stand right next to each other, as at Sablé, where the churches of Saint-Martin and of Notre-Dame were at opposite ends of a bridge over the river, with disputes about the ownership of the bridge and about sermons being interrupted by the peals of alien bells.[5] Boundaries zigzagged and curved. Here and there a parish had an enclave in the middle of another. In Paris, Saint-Étienne-du-Mont had enclaves at the Luxembourg and the Hôtel de Cluny, and Saint-Merry had the chapel of Jean-

Baptiste-de-Belleville, three kilometres away. The first accurate ecclesiastical map of the capital, drawn up on the orders of the archbishop in 1786, was said to reveal 'une mosaïque invraisemblable'.[6] Here, the explanation was that the boundaries were those of the medieval seigneuries of ecclesiastical institutions: distance had not hampered rent collecting as it did pastoral ministrations. But there could be more elevated explanations, as at Moulins, where the parish of Saint-Bonnet outside the walls had jurisdiction over a chapel and the houses around it in town, because in 1635 the curé had ventured there to minister to the plague-stricken.[7] In some places, the borderline between parishes was in dispute. In others, a dispute had been settled by the device of the '*alternatif*': a farm or hamlet would come under one curé in one year and under the other the next. Of the 274 parishes in the archdeaconry of Autun, thirty-eight had alternating areas on their boundaries—two had as many as six each, and in a few cases the rotation was among three parishes rather than two. Take-over date (generally on the feast of St Michael on 29 September or of St Martin on 11 November) was a time of pastoral confusion. In 1689, the curés alleged serious long-term effects, the folk concerned being 'like lost souls, without religion or fear of God'.[8] Another sort of alternation, less deadly to souls but vexing to bishops, was that of parishes oscillating between dioceses—as between Limoges and Périgueux.[9] Another variant of these cumbrous compromises was the system found in Normandy, of having more than one curé ruling in a parish. There is an example of three of them, each with his own sector to administer, with the supreme authority rotating at fortnightly intervals. In a parish under the bishop of Lisieux, there were four coequal parish priests, and the general statistics of that diocese showed the—at first sight—mysterious figures of 489 parishes and 522 curés.[10] Old disputes had been settled by creating a legacy of confusion for the future.

In some rural areas, traditional boundaries took no account of the difficulties of the terrain: curés might have to visit their people across marshes, ravines, or rivers. In those days of sudden floods and ill-repaired bridges, a river was regarded as the most sinister obstacle; a *cahier* of 1789 from Périgord, proposing reorganization, asked 'that no parish should extend to the far side of a river, for crossing is an inevitable cause of fatal accidents, whether to the pastors or to the parishioners'.[11] Another source of confusion was the way in which secular boundaries sometimes cut across ecclesiastical ones. The parish of La Tour Saint-Gélin was partly in the province of Touraine and partly in Poitou, with all its inhabitants claiming they were in

Poitou, as the *gabelle*, the odious salt tax, did not operate there.[12] The intendancy of Montauban was unique in that its 1,411 parishes and 1,179 village communities were separate entities, with the added complication that communities sometimes overlapped each other. The extreme cases at the ends of the spectrum were a parish which included seventeen communities as against a community including sixteen parishes. In 1782, an attempt was made to put all administrative business into the pattern of the parochial units, but with little success. Two years later, the intendant confessed that he was still baffled.[13] Not all these cross-divisions were inherited from distant times. In 1784–5, in their war against smuggling, the Farmers General of the taxes built a wall round Paris linking up the gates where customs duties were levied, cheerfully bisecting various parishes as they did so.[14]

Ecclesiastical reformers lamented the chaotic parochial structure, more especially in the towns, and exercised their ingenuity in plans for unions and separations. Sometimes they succeeded. In Paris, eight new parishes, mainly peripheral, were created in the seventeenth century, and three in the eighteenth.[15] There were two new creations in the diocese of Nîmes in 1772–3, and two in that of Boulogne in 1787.[16] But these were piecemeal tinkerings, the best that could be done in the circumstances. It was difficult to find new endowments. As ever, tithe owners would resist new burdens, and curés on modest incomes would rather stay overworked than be rescued by a reform that left them underpaid. When the bishop of Bayonne in 1776 ordered the separation of two villages which for long had coexisted uneasily within one parish, he felt constrained to add the proviso that the ruling would not come into effect until the pension of 600 livres paid by the curé to his predecessor was extinguished.[17] Local demands for reform would be countered by local objections to new expenditure. Though the bishop was not obliged to wait on anyone's consent, he had to hold a legal enquiry *de commodo et incommodo*, at which evidence was presented by interested parties.[18] The bishop of Oloron held such an enquiry in 1745 to consider the application of the hamlet of Sarrance, site of a prestigious pilgrim sanctuary, to be separated from the parish of Bedous. He decided that a new church must be built at Sarrance, and the intendant ordered a local levy of 3 livres a barrel of wine for twelve years to help to pay for it. The innkeepers were enraged, the owner of the proposed site refused to sell it, and the architect produced impossible plans. In the end, in 1760, the new church of Sarrance was consecrated, with the ruling that the curé of Bedous was to send a vicaire there to officiate, but that Easter communions and weddings were to be confined to the parish church. This system was unpopular, and in 1780 the inhabitants of Sarrance again asked to have a curé of their own. Another investigation *de commodo et incommodo* ensued, the petitioners having to pay more than 300 livres in expenses to a vicar-general, a legal official, and a clerk. The bishop decided to create the new parish, its pastor to be paid by the deduction of 500 livres a year from the tithes of Bedous. The curé refused to pay, and appealed to the secular courts, alleging that the whole independence movement at Sarrance had been inspired by the local family of Castéra plotting to create a new benefice which, in fact, had fallen to one of its sons. But by 1785, the incumbent of Bedous had lost his case, and the new parish became a reality at his expense.[19] A longer battle, lasting for more than a century, was waged to create the new parish of Boutonnet on the outskirts of Montpellier. The people of this village, it was argued in 1650, were in danger of dying without the sacraments, since they were far distant from the parish church and the city gates were locked at night. The cathedral chapter of Saint-Pierre held up progress until 1750, when a pastoral visitation by the bishop revealed that the population, recorded as 500 at an enquiry in 1687, had reached 1,500. At this point, the chapter gave way, but the seigneur took over the opposition role, as the site proposed for the new church was outside his seigneurie. Another site was chosen, but the cathedral chapter rejected it. And so it went on, until the revolutionary reorganization of the Church, when the new parish was created by annexing the chapel of the Récollets for general worship.[20] It took the Revolution, confiscating ecclesiastical property, abolishing tithes, instituting State salaries for the clergy, and replacing the rights of patrons by election, to make the redrawing of the old parochial boundaries possible.

II

By a deduction from the main technical terms in use, one might imagine that the parish in eighteenth-century France had a logical and effective administrative structure. There was the *assemblée générale* (the parish council, as it were), which was the final authority. It might well have an inner committee meeting more frequently, the *bureau ordinaire*. The executive officer was the *marguillier* (church-warden); his task was to pay the bills incurred in keeping the church and its services going, and to collect and administer the revenues of the parish, legally embodied in a corporate institution, the *fabrique* (vestry). This broad picture has its validity, but the detailed reality almost defies description by its complexity.

The responsibility of the assembly was defined by Potier de la Germondaye in his *Introduction au gouvernement des paroisses* (1777). (He uses the term 'général' for the assembly, as that was the customary title in Brittany, the province with which he was especially concerned.) 'Temporal government', he says, 'has as its objective the administration of the property and revenues of the *fabrique*, repairs to the church, the provision of vestments, books and sacred vases, and of all that is necessary for the celebration of divine service. This government is confided to the *général* of the parish.'[21] 'Général' and 'assemblée générale' have a democratic ring, but the trend of the century, especially in the towns, was to exclude ordinary people. Guyot's legal dictionary says that the general assembly (to be held twice a year) should consist only of 'persons of consideration'— nobles, judicial officers, *avocats*, ex-churchwardens, the solid citizens who are in charge of distributions to the poor, and notables (defined as inhabitants paying from 12 to 15 livres a year to the *taille* or the *capitation* taxes).[22]

He based his enumeration on formal decisions of the parliament of Paris for parishes in Orléans and in Nogent-sur-Marne in 1762 and 1763. He could equally have cited Angers, where the municipal officers, troubled by a caucus of the lower orders in their official parish of Saint-Michel du Tertre, obtained a 'wise regulation' of the parlement of Paris to exclude them. In 1766, the parish of Saint-Julien followed suit in adopting this oligarchical constitution, and by an ordinance of 1786, the parlement made it general for the whole of Anjou.[23] Early in the century, the magistrates of Brittany had limited the *général* to seventeen members, all legal officers and notables,[24] and those of Toulouse had imposed similar limitations later.[25] Even so, in some places, there were well-attended meetings. A town parish might boast many of the great within its boundaries; on 5 April 1778 at Saint-Gervais in Paris there were fifty-five present, including two *présidents* and two *conseillers* of the parlement, one of the *chambre des comptes*, three marquises, two counts, seven army officers, six *avocats*, nine doctors, one merchant, and d'Hozier, the court genealogist.[26] Conversely, in rural France a tendency to democratic attendance remained, if only because peasant villages could not throw up the galaxy of official talent which the regulations of the parlements prescribed.

Questions of eligibility to attend were complicated, because there

were two other kinds of assembly in addition to that of the ecclesiastical parish; often enough, no distinction of any kind was made, but
sometimes they were separate. In the village, the *grands jours* of the
seigneurie might still be held, called together by the lord's legal
officer; here, regulations about chimney sweeping and fire precautions were announced, and dates were prescribed for the beginning
of harvesting, and appointments made to communal jobs like
cowherd and goatherd. In many places in Burgundy, this meeting
was separate from that of the ecclesiastical parish—a churchwarden,
for example, would be described as having been elected 'à l'issue des
grands jours'—that is, immediately after the seigneurial assembly had
ended.[27] It was this separation of assemblies which one Bertrand was
appealing to in 1738 in a dispute in the village of Pouilly (seventy-
six houses). He accused the seigneurial legal officer of 'surprising' the
assembly by introducing a proposal to finance improvements to a
chapel, since, properly speaking, such a matter ought only to have
been raised at an assembly held in the church. He was fined 10 livres
for 'contempt', increased to 15 when he said 'Metté vingt'.[28] The
other kind of assembly was one of all the inhabitants—the sort of
gathering Sully had in mind when, early in the seventeenth century,
he ordered the planting of two elm trees near church doors to give
shade to its deliberations.[29] In Angers, the municipality called for
meetings in the parishes to review the names of candidates for
municipal office, to elect deputies to attend at the town hall when
the new officers were installed, and to give an opinion on proposals
for innovations which would affect the pockets of citizens, like the
installation of street lamps or the founding of an orphanage.[30] In the
North, around Cambrai and Lille, custom excluded the curé from
any part in these gatherings.[31] In Lille, he was also excluded from the
magistracy, and in 1699 the city fathers went so far as to try to prevent him concerning himself with official charity—'the curés ought
to apply themselves principally to know the consciences of their
parishioners rather than enquiring about their temporal necessities'.[32]
In the diocese of Tarbes, the *assemblée générale* was the common
gathering for the affairs of both the ecclesiastical parish and the
community, and hence all householders were entitled to attend.[33]
Elsewhere in the countryside the numbers present were sometimes
high enough to show that the concept of wide involvement carried
on; more especially there was a presumption that all householders
could attend in matters involving the levy of a heavy rate.

　Assemblies everywhere tend to do detailed work through committees, and, generally in parishes of some importance, the device of

using a *bureau ordinaire* was becoming more frequent in the eighteenth century.[34] The parlement of Paris, at the request of various
parishes, issued *arrêts* of authorization—for Saint-Jean-en-Grève in
1737, for Saint-Germain-en-Laye in 1739, for Nemours in 1763; the
parlement of Rouen did the same for its whole area of jurisdiction
in 1751. The usual formula for membership was the curé, the
churchwardens and ex-wardens, and, in country areas, the seigneur.
Meetings were generally to be fortnightly. In 1774, the curé of
Givry-sur-Aine replied to a questionnaire of his bishop concerning
the *bureau de fabrique*. Attending, he said, were himself, the warden
in office, and three ex-wardens; the other parishioners did not want
to come to the meetings (he implies that they could), but if a difficult
decision was to be made, 'we ask those from whom we expect good
advice and they come along'.[35] Regulations published by the
government on 25 June 1787 proposed to systematize this arrangement and to get rid of lingering elements of democracy in the composition of the assemblies. The *assemblée générale* was to consist of the
inhabitants paying at least 10 livres in taxation, and it was to set up
a *conseil* of from three to nine members, with the curé and seigneur
being there *ex officio*.[36]

In the parish assembly the curé had the place of honour and signed
first, but the chief *marguillier* presided and had the casting vote.[37] The
parish priest was not supposed to write the minutes or to have
custody of them; if he made a proposal, he had to retire while it was
discussed,[38] and meetings were to be held in the church or some
other official place, and not in the presbytery.[39] Manifestly, in poor
and illiterate communities, these rules were unlikely to be observed.
The assembly was supposed to elect the churchwardens and officers
to take charge of poor relief, and to appoint sacristans and schoolmasters; it approved the accounts and any unusual expenditure, and
accepted foundation masses (provided the curé also agreed). The
wardens or the *bureau* dealt with seating, burials, leases, invitations to
visiting preachers, and other detailed matters.[40] From 1759 to 1782
the assembly of Saint-Pierre de Montsort in the province of Maine
voted money to supplement the miserable yield of collections to
support the vicaire and pay fees to visiting preachers, took over the
repairs to the choir from the curé in return for his seating fees, suppressed pews and introduced chairs, arranged for paving the church
floor and having the bell recast, and argued with the curé over
church furnishings and the salaries of the sacristan and the vergers.
This was a parish with well-attended meetings, as many as fifty
people recorded as present on one occasion, and dissentients allowed

to record their opposition: 'Je signe le présent, qui est que je m'oppose.'[41]

As we might imagine, discussion tended to centre on how to avoid spending money. The parish of Notre-Dame de Vitré, where the people were particularly mean towards their clergy, was confronted in 1776 with an expensive problem. The new curé, Béchu, was a giant, and no rochet or surplice in the sacristy would fit him. Gloomily, the *général* resigned itself to buying new ones, but imposed economy by ruling that linen would henceforward be provided for Sundays and high festivals only. Béchu scored by moving elsewhere two years later. The assembly tried to persuade him to buy the new vestments at current prices; if not, there was nothing for it but to have them made into surplices for choirboys.[42]

III

Every parish had a churchwarden responsible for the administration of its corporate property and revenues and for paying the costs of maintaining the church and its liturgical observances out of the proceeds. There might be from one to four wardens, but the actual handling of the money was always the responsibility of a single one of them. In theory, the parish assembly elected the wardens,[43] but where the assembly was not an oligarchy already, the right to vote was usually limited to 'notables' and higher taxpayers. Sometimes the *bureau* appointed, sometimes the outgoing man nominated his successor, sometimes the seigneur of the place had the dominant voice;[44] there were places where the curé said who it would be and that was an end to it.[45] In the diocese of Tarbes, the municipal officers, the *consuls*, succeeded to the wardenship when their tour of secular duty was over; the parlement of Toulouse wanted to make this a general rule within the area of its jurisdiction, but at least one bishop (Mirepoix) forbade it.[46] Given the method of selection and the desirability of literacy, numeracy, and solvency, churchwardens were taken from the more prosperous reaches of society; in towns, notaries, *procureurs*, and merchants are often found. The Parisian parish of Saint-Leu-Saint-Gilles always had four wardens in office, one a magistrate and three from the bourgeoisie, and there was a specific rule that no one exercising a mechanical art was eligible.[47] The financial status of the *marguilliers* of Saint-Médard may be deduced from the custom which constrained them to give a gift of 200 livres to the church on their retirement; the new pulpit installed in 1718 was paid for by six such contributions.[48] By contrast, in poverty-stricken rural areas the parish was lucky to find anyone remotely qualified to serve. If there was such a person, he might well hold office for life in default of a replacement. There were places where a single individual, for meagre fees, was cleaner, organ-blower, bell-ringer, gardener, and grave-digger, and was saddled with the responsibility of *marguillier* as well.[49] In the Auvergne, these comprehensive duties were not infrequently allotted to a woman— a *bailleresse*—until in 1768 the parlement of Paris forbade the practice.[50]

A churchwarden undertook a time-consuming job fraught with financial perils: a sensible man would try to evade it. When Louis XIV put up offices for sale, this was one for which he found no takers.[51] With the usual injustice of the *ancien régime*, nobles were exempt, though in great town parishes like Saint-Gervais at Paris they might condescend to accept the title of *marguillier d'honneur* and give aloof and dignified protection.[52] Exempt too were soldiers, *avocats*, and the holders of certain official posts. Anyone who had served as *marguillier comptable* (financially responsible warden) was entitled to refuse to accept a further term of office, even if he had moved to another parish.[53] Assemblies would resort to legal summonses to compel some recalcitrant citizen to serve, while the nominated victim would try to escape by producing medical certificates[54] or purchasing an office conferring exemption. The *général* of a Breton parish bitterly minuted of such a draft-dodger that he was far from being the most meritorious candidate and that they assumed that 'le sieur Lorin ne s'est pas trouvé digne de servir à l'église'.[55]

On the other hand, there were those who volunteered to be churchwardens—a few out of piety or public spirit, but most out of pride. To walk immediately after the clergy in processions, often preceding even the officers of justice, to appoint lay employees like vergers, choristers, *suisses*, and ringers, to name Lent and Advent preachers, draw up the roster of inhabitants for presenting the *pain bénit*, to talk about leases and investments with local bigwigs—all this made a man important and affirmed that he had arrived.[56] This was the decisive stage in the ascension of a *coq du village*: 'having been the accounting warden (*trésorier*), he's immediately named as *syndic* (the chief lay representative of the village); then he crowns his pate with an ample wig, swells proudly in his pew, argues over sacristy matters, persuading himself that the nave belongs to him more than to other parishioners, because he pays more than others towards its repairs'.[57]

A *marguillier* needed the consent of an assembly to spend more than a limited sum (generally 10 livres).[58] Cash and valuables were kept in a box in the sacristy with two or three locks: the warden, the curé, and, maybe, the seigneur's legal official kept the keys. These arrangements were well known to thieves, so any considerable sum in hand would be loaned out among solvent parishioners rather than hoarded. In 1776, the parlement of Rennes ordered parishes to have a man bedded down in the sacristy at night, ready to ring the bells if he was awoken by intruders. Accounts were supposed to be rendered to the assembly and, if notice was given, to the bishop or archdeacon when they came on visitation. Satisfactory records of receipts and expenditure were hard to come by. 'What I collected I put into a single pocket and when I paid out I took it from the same pocket'—an effective system which did not lend itself to documentation. A parish might put up with financial informalities if there was no one else capable of taking over, but if there were ex-wardens who had successfully given an account of their stewardship in the past, they would be sure to lead the clamour in the assembly for the 'verification' of their successors' accounts.[59] So too if parishioners had noticed any frivolous expenditure: *marguilliers* were not granted any entertainment allowance for 'collations and bottles'.

Relations between churchwardens and parish priests were better than might have been expected, perhaps because the lawyers had drawn the boundaries between spiritual and secular in parochial affairs with a fair degree of precision. The administration of the revenues of the *fabrique* was 'a purely lay and temporal affair'.[60] So too was the allocation of seating in the nave. Church furnishings were generally controlled by the laity; a curé, for example, could not exchange an old crucifix for a new one without permission.[61] On the other hand, the content of the liturgical services was the curé's affair; Saint-Germain-l'Auxerrois was unique in having the churchwardens prescribing the prayers to be said when the Holy Sacrament was exposed in a particular ciborium.[62] In some dioceses, there was disagreement about the *marguillier*'s oath on taking office, the synod ruling that it was to be said in the presence of the curé, the Gallican lawyers denouncing the practice.[63]

There were also disputes about the appointment and disciplining of the minor functionaries who assisted at the liturgical offices—sacking a choirboy or a verger could be a sensational affair in the depths of provincial France.[64] The tough tanners and tilers of the Parisian parish of Saint-Médard, deprived of their Jansenist curé, waged war against his successor, more particularly refusing to pay for

the *suisse* he had appointed to precede him in processions and protect him from insult. The churchwardens took the affair to the
Grand Conseil and won, and when a royal *lettre de cachet* reversed the
verdict, they went back to the Grand Conseil again.[65] The other
great cause of disagreement was the control of charitable distributions. The tensions found in many parishes are evident on a bigger
scale at Saint-Gervais in Paris from 1761, when the curé François
Feu died at the age of 90 after a reign of over sixty years. The
churchwardens were then free to speak out and demand the
appointment of a *trésorier des pauvres*. Up to then, the curé had dominated the pious lady who ran the general charitable fund and the
committee in charge of aid to poor families, while keeping in
his own hands the giving of alms to the 'pauvres honteux', the
respectable folk who did not wish anyone to know of their plight.
To ensure his control, Feu had abstracted from the parish archives
the documents concerning the legacies and other funds available for
charity. 'There will be general surprise', said his will, 'at finding in
my files a number of contracts in favour of the poor . . . Precautions
to safeguard their interests are good. God will enlighten my successor on this point, which is delicate.' His successor, indeed, carried
on as before. The wardens challenged the legality of the 'so-called
charitable assembly' he defiantly called in April 1773. The whole dispute went to the parlement, ending in 1780 with the curé being
awarded 2,000 livres legal costs against the parish.[66] There was a
growing desire among the laity to have a greater say in parochial
affairs—at least, so it seemed to the archbishop of Paris, who in 1772
complained to the Assembly of Clergy about the *marguilliers* who
ousted curés from their rights in the distribution of alms and in
the nomination of ecclesiastics to employment in churches. 'Such a
manner of proceeding', he said, 'is imperceptibly building up the lay
and secular power in the temporal administration of parishes upon
the ruins of ecclesiastical authority.'[67]

IV

The property and revenues of a parish church were corporately
embodied in the *fabrique*. This was an independent body, protected
by the law courts from the interference of bishops[68] and, like the
clergy, exempt from ordinary taxation, but paying dues levied on the
acquisition of new property.[69] Revenue came from diverse sources.
There would be small parcels of land—meadows, fields, enclosures,

houses—acquired higgledy-piggledy over the years from pious legacies.[70] Money bequeathed to pay for masses would be loaned out or invested with the Clergy of France. In some places, the curé had to hand over to the *fabrique* a portion of his tithe levies.[71] The pious made gifts in kind—a piglet or some flax; a lady would hand over a silk dress to make a new chasuble.[72] Collections[73] taken at church services or at the door yielded miserable sums, except where, as in Paris, Mercier saw pretty girls taking round the plate preceded by the *suisse* insistently banging his pike butt on the floor.[74] Door to door collecting, which yielded more, needed legal permission. The *troncs*, the offertory boxes in churches, were prominently displayed but brought in little, so that in some parishes the wardens did not bother to open them for years. Whatever could be put up for sale was sold—nuts or fruit growing in the cemetery, worn linen, posts of honour in confraternities, candle wax left over after ceremonies.[75] The *fabrique* owned 'ornaments' which were hired out to families for funerals—20 sols for silver candlesticks to take to the house and other small sums for candelabra on the altar, a black pall to cover the coffin, 'noms de Jésus' and 'têtes de mort'. There were special fees to pay for a burial space within the church building, and lesser fees for places outside, separate from the common burial pit.[76]

The living, like the dead, had to pay differential fees for their accommodation. Rents were charged for private pews, and chairs were hired out, usually through a contractor. The law looked after the interests of the poor, since the contractor had to leave standing room for those who were not his clients, and he was forbidden to charge for the parish mass on Sunday mornings.[77] In country places, seating revenue would be small, since pews were not expensive (maybe 3 livres entry fee and an annual payment of 3 sous a place), and few would wish to pay for a chair. In important town parishes, however, the income might be considerable, from 800 livres in the richest parish of Angers to 18,000 livres in a major Parisian one like Saint-Merry.[78] Official pews were limited to the *seigneur haut justicier* and the patron and, in a city, to the municipal officers in the parish where the town hall was situated (they were entitled to have the mayoral accommodation painted blue and adorned with fleurs-de-lis). Otherwise, the churchwardens disposed entirely of pew space; when a life concessionaire died, they were entitled—nay, obliged—to auction the amenity, though in the event of a tied bid, the heirs ought to have precedence.[79] In theory, there was no priority for nobles. The writer of a legal treatise applauded the system of the highest bidder: 'if people have to fight it out with hard cash, the

Church profits thereby, and he who is defeated by money alone will not consider himself vanquished so far as his honour is concerned.'[80] In practice, such philosophical resignation to defeat was rare. In 1727, the duc d'Uzès was trying to evict the municipal officers from their pew in the cathedral and put his own arms and livery upon it; in 1729 a wine-grower of Cormeilles sued the wardens for a pew which, he said, had always gone along with the house he had just purchased.[81] Frauds over payment were frequent. Families would rent pew space, then quietly expand it; others brazenly moved in without authorization, and might even rent to others the privilege they had usurped; others engraved fictitious names on the wood-work to evade payment, or moved the whole contraption out when payment time came round, then moved it back afterwards.[82]

Abuses of this sort, and the rising tide of sentimentality and theoretical egalitarianism, helped to make pews unpopular, but there was a more decisive argument against them: if the space was turned over to a contractor to hire out chairs, the income could be doubled.[83] In the royal parish of Notre-Dame at Versailles, in 1749, chairs yielded 8,000 livres, pews 1,143 livres, and as the latter belonged to some of the greatest in the land, change seemed impossible. But in 1753, the king authorized a reform of ruthless illegality, and on the night of 9–10 July the pews were carted away. 'Je ne comprends rien de cette destruction,' complained the duc de Luynes who had been paying 50 livres a year for his privilege. The parish did well, financially at least, out of the change; in 1778, the chairs yielded 13,000 livres.[84] The parish of Saint-Leu-Saint-Gilles in Paris followed suit a year later, once more with a nocturnal clearance. Only a stealthy *fait accompli* could avoid the lamentations and obstructions of influential families with their lackeys and attendant lawyers' clerks and notaries.[85]

Normally, the income from endowments and seating, charges for the 'ornaments' and for burials, and the yield of collections and boxes and pious donations sufficed to pay the expenses of the liturgical offices. Candles, books, linen, and vestments were needed; in some places the tithe owner had obligations in these respects, though the churchwardens were not always able to enforce them. The chief expense, however, would be the payment of employees. In those days of ecclesiastical wealth, no one performed an ecclesiastical function without being paid for it. Calculations were made with some precision: in 1735 the *porte-bannière* of Saint-Merry at Paris had his yearly wage raised from 4 livres, 10 sols, to 9 livres, because the new banner was heavier than the old.[86] A wealthy town parish would

employ a swarm of officials. The chief would be the sacristan, probably an ecclesiastic. In charge of the altar silver (depositing caution
money against loss or damage) and of the registers, and exercising
general oversight, sacristans were notoriously self-important. The
parish of Toussaint in Rennes had one who was too superior to
decorate the altars himself, a task which he delegated to his servant;
he ruled the church with a rod of iron, and demonstrated his power
by deliberately locking the churchwarden in the vestry.[87] Vergers
(*bedeaux, bâtonniers, massiers*) wore black gowns when on duty, and
bore wands of office when escorting the faithful to their places in
church and handbells when escorting them on their last journey to
the cemetery; they took round notices of parish assemblies and
morsels of the *pain bénit* to distinguished citizens; they might have
sweeping and ringing obligations and act as agents for the hire of
chairs, as well as such other duties as their contracts might prescribe
('mettre les draps mortuaires à sécher dans le cimetière' being a
curious instance).[88] The archetypal verger was at once pompous and
decrepit, since he was likely to hang on in office as long as his legs
would support him. By contrast, the *suisse* had to be a fine upstand-
ing figure, his uniform and halberd giving him a military air—the
suisse of Saint-Eustache became a general in the revolutionary
armies.[89] The bell-ringers, the *corbeaux* who bore the dead to their
graves, and the *fossoyeurs* who dug them were typecast in a different
fashion, as being addicted to alcoholic refreshment; the ringers had
to slake their thirst, the bearers clearly needed cheering up, and the
diggers qualified under both headings. Organists were a superior
category of employee, though they were rarely generously paid—
hence the common complaint that they wore out the instrument in
supplementing their income by teaching children to play and allowing unqualified adults to experiment, 'useless characters who fool
around with the keyboard and the bellows, stir up a great cloud of
dust and ruin the stops'.[90] As an alternative to an organist, a parish
might hire a player of the serpent, apparently an effective instrument
for leading the congregation in the simple singing of the Kyrie,
Gloria, Credo, Sanctus, and Agnus Dei. Or maybe, there would be
a choir. At Saint-Martin in Rennes the men were paid a mere 3
livres a year, at Sainte-Croix in Nantes, 50 livres. For this higher
wage they would have to be well turned out, 'frisé et poudré', be
punctual, open the doors for ecclesiastics, and undertake never to go
out in the streets in their surplices. Choirboys, in theory at least,
were subjected to an even stricter discipline.

The lay employees of parish churches deserve their own sociological study. Though churchwardens were inclined to economize and appoint the least demanding applicant, certain families—as so often happened in eighteenth-century France—managed to corner these modest offices. A verger would be succeeded by his son or son-in-law, and children and grandchildren would be taken on as choirboys, thurifers, cross-bearers, and banner-carriers. These arrangements suited a conservative social order, and kept traditional liturgical observances and other routines going smoothly. Not everyone would know how to remove the stains of spitting and to put a gloss on marble paving. When the parishioners of Helfaut in 1753 laid blue and white marble slabs in their sanctuary, the wife of the verger was sent to Saint-Omer to find out the secret (on condition of a small gratuity) from the *suisse* of the cathedral.[91] Hereditary succession avoided the scandal of ex-employees of the Church falling into destitution in their declining years. When the *suisse* of Saint-Merry grew old, the wardens gave 200 livres to his son-in-law to pay his fees to become a master cobbler, on condition that he provided a home for his father-in-law and stood in for him when he was not well enough to perform his duties.[92] Nepotism took the place of retirement pensions.

This picture of swarming ecclesiastical employees in their cosy dynasties applies only to the big and wealthy town parishes, of course. In a poor rural parish one omni-competent person would ring the bells, dig the graves, clean the church, preside at its ceremonies; he might also be schoolmaster (or his wife schoolmistress). Where all were poor and ignorant, he might also be constrained to act as churchwarden as well, charged with the care of largely non-existent monies. But where the finances extended to paying extra bodies, they would surely be taken on. This was a labour-intensive society, with many people on the margin of survival, scraping together a living by odd jobs and makeshifts; the church had a duty to provide as many opportunities as possible. It was a society too where one of the major signs of success was conspicuous waste in the employment of numerous retainers: the parish church had its dignity to maintain, as much as any nobleman surrounded by his lackeys.

V

With its ordinary incomings and ordinary outgoings, a parish would carry on in approximate equilibrium, but rarely were there reserves in hand to meet a financial crisis. More especially, desperate

measures had to be taken when a major repair to the church building was required. While the tithe owner was responsible for the
chancel, the parishioners had to repair the nave (except in Flanders
and Artois where the tithe paid everything, and in Roussillon
where it contributed nothing). Short of some extraordinary source
of revenue, like getting permission to fell timber on communal
property or to confiscate the enclosures of those who had
encroached on it,[93] a rate would have to be levied. The bishop,
probably alerted by a visitation report, would issue an ordinance for
repairs; if this was ignored, he could close the building by interdict
as well as calling on the lay magistrates to intervene. Tension was
likely to arise between the curé and his flock: he would have to be
vigilant to ensure no corners were being cut in the repairing plans,
and sometimes he was also actively campaigning for improvements
to be incorporated into it—this would be resisted with grim determination.[94] The intendant had to be informed, as he gave permission
for the financial levy; his *subdélégué* would make an inspection and
supervise the auction of the contract in three sessions spaced at
intervals of three weeks.[95] All these proceedings were regarded with
dismay by the parishioners. Either they would turn up and raise
every possible objection, or they would stay away altogether,
leaving the intendant to proceed by arbitrary fiat against a solid wall
of non-co-operation.[96] Tight-fisted, suspicious, and unwilling to
commit themselves to corporate civil responsibility,[97] the peasants
did their best to avoid paying—hence, most country churches were
left in poor repair by a conspiracy of evasion. Visitation reports early
in the century retail stories of unpaved floors, tottering walls, and
intruding animals—dogs, maybe, making off with the bones of the
faithful from the tombs in the aisles.[98] In 1738, a curé of the diocese
of Saintes nearly died from the bite of an adder which had nested
in his tabernacle.[99] Conditions improved, but gradually. In mid-
century, fifty parishes of the diocese of Boulogne had no sacristies,
and in others, what passed for one was too damp to be used: 'on
est obligé de se revêtir à la vue du peuple, rien de plus indécent'.[100]
Even in the 1780s, reports of picturesque dilapidation are still found.
In one parish in Brittany, to stop the rats eating the altar cloths,
wooden covers had to be made with spaces for cats to circulate.[101] In
a church in Burgundy, most of the windows were broken, the door
did not fit, the roof leaked, and the communion rail was sagging.[102]
Neglect of repairs sometimes created a danger to life and limb. In
1756, a report on a country church said that 'most of the inhabitants
stay away from mass and the offices because they are afraid of being

engulfed in a collapse'. In the North, at the church of Saint-Nicolas in Braine, in April 1787, a beam of the framework of the tower fell close to the confessional, and the vicaire, a woman penitent, and the notary Petiteau who was waiting his turn to be shriven narrowly escaped being crushed.[103]

Such dangerous incidents were not unknown in cities, even in churches which were rich and famous. In 1739, chunks of plaster, big enough to be lethal, were falling from the ceiling of the Parisian church of the Madeleine, and six years later, creaks and groans in the high altar of Saint-Merry showed the supports worm-eaten, and the whole structure, statues, reliquary, and suspended tabernacle could have fallen at any minute.[104] There were casualties at Mâcon in 1759 in a wild rush for safety when the roof beams of the cathedral began cracking.[105] To be a regular worshipper in one of the six parishes of Besançon required fortitude.[106] The church of Saint-Donat, closed as unsafe in 1688, stood as a crumbling warning, until in 1769 it had to be demolished. On 25 February 1729, the spire of the cathedral fell, flattening two bays of the apse. In the following year, the church of Sainte-Brigitte was pulled down. The year after, the city council ordered the parishioners of the Madeleine to move their services to the chapel of the Cordeliers; the wisdom of the decision was demonstrated fifteen years later when the tower of their old church collapsed. It was as well they had not transferred to the precincts of the other friary in the town, since in 1752 the roof of the chapel of the Jacobins caved in. The parishioners of Saint-Jean-Baptiste, better organized than most, anticipated disaster, and repaired their tower in 1745–6, and on the eve of the Revolution were collecting money for a reconstruction of the entire building. Through long neglect, the splendid central church of Saint-Pierre, scene of all the municipal ceremonies, was in a parlous state; in 1727 the intendant reported it to be 'ready to collapse, perhaps at the very moment when this is least expected'. As this was the official parish, and Besançon was a garrison town, the local people expected help from the government, and they were, in fact, granted the sealing fees from the four so-called *chancelleries* of Franche Comté. The intendant wished to elaborate the reconstruction project, buying up houses to provide a new site for the church, and leaving a vast square for military parades. At 5 p.m. on 23 August 1729, a high-powered conference was held at the presbytery; the duc de Levy, the provincial governor, was there, the *premier président* of the parlement, the lieutenant-general of police, two municipal councillors, the curé, the churchwarden, two ex-wardens, the professor of law at the uni-

versity, and an *avocat*. The intendant undertook to compel the house
owners to sell at a valuation, and he offered financial help (in fact,
the Royal Council sent 22,000 livres). Even so, the parishioners
established their point: they could not legally be constrained to pay
for the enlargement of a public square. This was the responsibility of
the municipality, and in 1732 the intendant ordered the city fathers
to buy up the houses as a matter of public utility. The contract for
rebuilding the church was let at the huge sum of 156,699 livres, and
on 5 July 1732 the archbishop consecrated the foundation-stone
with pomp. Not everyone was satisfied. The three chaplains of
Saint-Pierre complained that the new edifice would be too small,
and offered 8,000 livres towards its enlargement, which offer, they
said, was refused 'with invectives, arrogance and scorn'. By contrast,
the municipality complained that it would be too large, and that
the alignment of the façade was not parallel to the town hall. The
parishioners complained of the cost; at an assembly in March 1741,
presided over by the intendant in person, their rate was set at 8,000
livres a year for the next twenty years. In fact, ten years and 80,000
livres later, the work stopped with the walls twenty-five feet high.
Nothing more was done until 1770, when three successive parish
assemblies were held in the town hall, reaching an agreement to pay
10,000 livres annually for the next six years. In 1772, work was suspended again on the king's order. An architectural competition held
by the academy of Besançon had thrown up new ideas, including an
even bigger square with a statue of the monarch in the centre, and
the parishioners of Saint-Pierre to be moved elsewhere—say, to the
collegiate church of Saint-Paul. The municipality liked the idea of
robbing Peter to transfer to Paul—or to the chapel of the Carmelites
or the Benedictines: 'if we can clear a useful public square in place
of a useless parish church, the opportunity must not be missed'. The
parishioners replied that Saint-Paul was near the barracks, and
therefore unsuited to the attendance of young women and children,
while the streets leading to the Carmelites and Benedictines
were impassable in winter. The archbishop agreed with them, and
promised to persuade the government to sanction the financing of
the completion of the new church of Saint-Pierre by a lottery (this
was refused, since the state lotteries would suffer by competition). In
1779, with a new curé, a new archbishop, and a new Minister of
War pushing for action, the rebuilding began again. The parish, in
January 1785, agreed to borrow 30,000 livres and to tax itself at 8,000
livres annually for the next twelve years. Alas! in the following year,
with the work nearing completion, a committee of architects,

masons, and master carpenters declared the foundations insecure and the roof beams of dubious timber: the whole structure, they said, was dangerous. No doubt their minds were conditioned by the past history of church architecture in Besançon; time has vindicated the maligned building contractor, since his work survived intact into the twentieth century.

In spite of the reluctance of the mass of inhabitants to pay for propping up their parish churches, the eighteenth century, especially the latter half, was an age of restoration, improvement, and new building.[107] The authorities were becoming insistent in enforcing the old edict of 1661 concerning church repairs, and the growing sophistication of society was reflected in the desire of churchwardens in richer parishes to make a name for themselves by innovations in the current fashion, while the generosity of wealthy individuals could make up for the thrifty hostility of the majority—though it is true that wealthy benefactors were most often found in the more opulent parishes and their contributions were directed more to the creation of new splendours than to maintaining the old. But in a crisis, an aristocratic parishioner was expected to demonstrate his superiority by conspicuous giving. When the church of Bolbec had to be rebuilt after a fire in 1772, the duc de Charost was prominent in choosing an architect and exhorting to action, though when he gave only 10,000 livres of the 60,000 required, the parishioners were disillusioned. About the same time, the *premier président* of the parlement of Rouen presented the village near his country mansion with a brand-new church in elegant brick: with mixed motives and vastly more publicity, Voltaire had done the same for the parishioners of his estate. In country churches we hear of panelling, wainscot, gilding, paving, porches, and sacristies added, a roof of brick instead of the old timber, newly fashionable plastering and whitewashing, new altar-pieces in the ornate baroque style of the early century, and the new sobriety and elegance of the reign of Louis XVI.[108] The twelve churchwardens of Notre-Dame of Versailles, in attempting to give superior adornment to their church as befitted its royal connections, got into a famous lawsuit: their ornate new clock, costing more than 30,000 livres, would not go, but the parlement of Paris ordered payment in full to the maker—as if the chief purpose was to preach to the congregation about mortality, with the ability to tell the actual time a bonus.[109] In the great Parisian churches, the wardens spent lavishly. At Saint-Merry[110] the pews were thrown out (in a nocturnal foray to pre-empt objections), and the floor richly paved; the worm-eaten altar was replaced

by a new one by the Slodtz brothers at the enormous price of 85,000
livres, and an even more expensive pulpit commissioned from
Michel Slodtz (in 1753, the contract was to represent Error and
Paganism overthrown amid the débris of pagodas, idols, and books;
six years later, the ideas of the Enlightenment had had their effect,
and the design was changed to a figure of Religion escorted by two
angels with laurel wreaths). In the first half of the century Paris was
agog with stories of the scandalous excesses of Languet, the curé of
Saint-Sulpice, in raising money for the rebuilding of his church
(including confiscating a piece of tableware wherever he dined to be
melted down for his silver statue of the Virgin). 'He even managed
to extract a subscription from the Pope,' said the wits, recording the
laying of the foundation-stone of the new altar by the nuncio—in
the end, the vast income from the royal lottery paid for the completion of the façade and the towers.[111]

A particular amenity of the church which could impose heavy and
unexpected expenditure was the bell, or peal of bells; there was
always a danger of a crack in the metal. The tithe owner might have
to maintain the tower, but the *fabrique* was responsible for the bell,
the timber framework supporting it, and the rope.[112] This was not
unreasonable, for while bishops liked to issue ordinances against
'profane ringing', the bells were as much a lay institution as an ecclesiastical one. They pealed for military victories, royal occasions, and
local celebrations. In times of invasion, fire, or other danger, they
rang as a tocsin, and in areas favourable to smuggling as a warning
that the customs officials were coming.[113] At the approach of
thunderstorms, they were rung to ward off the dangerous lightning
strike; the parlement of Paris, duly informed of the new discoveries
about electricity, banned the practice in 1784.[114] Younger and more
light-hearted parishioners liked to ascend the belfry to ring on
festive occasions like the eve of St John's Day, All Saints, or
Christmas—sometimes officially rewarded with bread and cheese or
black pudding (*boudin*)[115] and sometimes unofficially fortified with
strong drink. But for the sober respectable inhabitants, the less the
bells rang the better: they were easily damaged, and costly to replace.
This was one of the uncovenanted expenses of untoward celebrations. When Louis XVI went on solemn progress through
Normandy in June 1787, and the 200 bells of Rouen were swung *en
branle*, the most famous of them all, the 'Georges d'Amboise', 40,000
livres in weight, was cracked beyond redemption.[116] In October
1716 the parish assembly of Saint-Martin of the Breton town of
Vitré looked back sadly on the activities of the 'gens de bonne

volonté' who for 'le seul plaisir de sonner' had rung some extra peals; thanks to their zeal, one of the bells was cracked, and the *fabrique* was already in debt.[117] Frequent ringing might do more than break the bell—the tower itself might suffer damage. So argued the city fathers of Metz in 1745, hoping to persuade the cathedral to cease ringing the big 'Marie' (installed in a tower whose repairs were a municipal responsibility). The treasurer of the chapter tested the vibrations with 'a goblet full of red liquid'; none was spilt, so the canons decided to carry on as before, 'considering the fine effect that this bell produces'.[118]

When a recasting was necessary, every effort was made to find a patron who would spare the parish the expenditure. Affluent curés, 'seduced by the thought of passing on to posterity their names engraved on bronze', often made a gift to their church in this way.[119] When the new bell was blessed—'baptized' in popular parlance—a 'godfather' and 'godmother' were chosen from wealthy parishioners of the neighbourhood; for example, the parish of Avernay in 1729 had the marquis de Lhéry, commander of the garrison at Reims, and the abbess of the local abbey.[120] The sponsors would make a solid gift to the church; the curé and parish in return would give them gloves and sweetmeats, have their Christian names and coats of arms engraved on the bell, and, maybe, an entry in the parish register would record their right to 'the glorious title of benefactor of humanity'.[121] The parishes of Notre-Dame and of Saint-Louis at Versailles and that of Fontainebleau could hope to have the king and queen or other members of the royal family; their gifts would be a roll of cloth of gold (to drape the bell and make vestments after-wards, possibly worth as much as 25,000 livres) and a sum of money, from 300 to 600 livres.[122] The assembly of Saint-Martin at Vitré was dumbfounded when the local seigneur and his wife refused to act as godparents; to put pseudo-obsequious pressure on them, it sent the bell-founder to call and 'ask for their instructions' concerning their coat of arms which the bell was scheduled to bear.[123]

The *fabrique* was determined to get value for money when a recasting was necessary. There would be a strict contract, by which the bell was to be taken down, weighed, recast (with a specific price for any extra metal that was needed), a final exact weight would be specified, the tone would have to be harmonized with the other bells, and finally there would be the rehanging. The parish of Saint-Pierre of Montsort got all this for 120 livres;[124] another Angevin parish got a smaller bell recast by a travelling expert from Lorraine for 80 livres 4 sols, including the extra metal.[125] When the big bell

of Saint-Jeannet in Provence had to be renewed in 1766 as a result
of the activities of 'une troupe d'enfants qui sonnèrent plus qu'à
l'ordinaire', the churchwardens economized by having an old
cauldron, used by a confraternity to cook beans for charity soup,
incorporated in the melting. It was a mistake, and the work had
to be done again.[126] (Presumably the cauldron was copper; the
eighteenth-century formula for bell metal was fifty parts pure
copper, ten to twelve parts pewter or tin, and one part antimony.[127])
Things could go wrong: the process was dicey, and the bell-founders
were, often enough, wandering adventurers with dubious credentials.[128] The parish of Helfaut had to have the same bell recast in
1750, 1770, and 1781 at a cost of about 1,000 livres a time.[129] At
Saint-Jean de Luz the mould collapsed at the pouring, and a second
founder had to be engaged to give a verdict on who was to blame
and how to rescue the situation.[130] The great abbey of Chelles could
afford to employ the best, yet in 1752, when the recasting of the first
and third bells was complete, they were found to be greatly under-
weight and out of harmony; the founder, owing more by penalty
clauses than was due to him, fled far from the province.[131] The air
above the cities of France was full of the reverberation and
tintinnabulation of a fanciful diversity of peals, recalling some to
pious reflection, but worrying all by the thought of yet another levy
on the pockets of householders.

Repairs to the presbytery were a lesser burden than repairs to the
church, but an even more fertile source of acrimony.[132] Paradoxically, by being extended to cover every contingency, the legal
regulations had multiplied occasions for litigation. Royal edicts laid
down a minimum accommodation, but what amenities ought to be
included in the definition of each room? The curé had to do the
running repairs, and the parish the major ones; what if neglect of the
former brought on a big bill for the latter? If no house was provided,
or if the available house was uninhabitable during reconstruction,
the curé had to be paid a lodging allowance of 60 livres a year (40 if
there were fewer than 100 families in his care); if repairs would cost
over 500 livres, the parish could ask to have the building demolished
and simply pay the annual sum. Since such lodging payments always
fell into arrears, curés generally insisted on a house, and normally got
one. If the parish priest wanted a barn or stables, he had to pay for
them himself. In 1749, a parish in the diocese of Reims added a barn
to its vicarage, by mistake, in ignorance of the law; the wardens tried
to persuade the curé to contribute, but he refused; the parish therefore put the barn up for auction; nobody wanted it, so the curé

bought it for a mere 318 livres.[133] If an incumbent improved his presbytery at his own expense, the addition would ultimately become a repairing burden to his flock; hence, the intendant had to approve all new plans. In 1782, the intendant of Tours fined a curé 2,000 livres for spending 10,000 livres of his own money on unauthorized additions.[134] While the law clearly made the parish responsible for the presbytery, the laity occasionally suggested that an affluent cleric had at least a moral obligation not to insist on the letter of his rights; those who were learned could cite a decision of the Council of Rouen in 1231[135] and the continuing jurisprudence of the province of Flanders to support the argument.[136]

Given such opportunities for dispute and reproach, vicarage repairs were an inevitable focus for local anticlericalism. Once the curé mentioned his leaking roof or creaking beams in the parish assembly, a cloud of gloom and ill will descended. The inhabitants might refuse to discuss the matter, and fail to turn up at subsequent meetings;[137] they might argue that neglect of running repairs had caused the trouble or, conversely, that the presbytery was an oasis of comfort in the midst of their own miserable hovels, and needed nothing doing to it. If the curé resorted to the law, his parishioners might engage him for years in guerrilla warfare in the courts; it took the abbé Laugier thirteen years—from 1721 to 1734—to get a new presbytery from his parishioners of Saint-Jeannet, and in the end he also extracted 468 livres lodging allowance and the costs of his litigation.[138] In 1669, the parlement of Paris ordered a village in the diocese of Autun to pay the penal sum of 220 livres a year so long as there was no vicarage; the stubborn inhabitants were still paying in 1739.[139] With luck, a curé might be successful in invoking the arbitrary power of the intendant against the inhabitants, as at Bouzigues on the southern coast in 1770, where the community was peremptorily ordered to do 2,650 livres of repairs (decently, the curé voluntarily forwent 900 worth).[140] But generally, royal officials tended to be unsympathetic. 'The curés all want to be lodged like seigneurs,' complained a *subdélégué* in the second half of the century.[141] 'The curés ask too much,' said an intendant; 'in consequence I propose in future not to agree to anything beyond what is indispensable.'[142] The law courts and the Royal Council were strict about running repairs: unless a curé could demonstrate that he had been up to date with the 'réparations locatives', he had little chance of winning his case over the 'grosses réparations'. In the last resort, when a contract for doing the repairs had finally been made, the angry parishioners might threaten reprisals against the builders' men, or riot to keep them away from the decaying vicarage which was causing so much expense.[143]

Since running repairs were so important at law, an incumbent who was solicitous of the interests of his heirs would either do the work and keep evidence that he had done so, or—better still—make a contract with the churchwardens to pay a yearly sum (say, 30 livres) on condition the parish took over from him the 'réparations locatives'.[144] When a benefice holder died, his successor did well to call in surveyors and have an official list of dilapidations prepared, ready to go to law against the heirs. Meanwhile, the parish would ensure that seals were put on the dead man's furniture and his savings kept in legal custody until the responsibility for the repairs had been settled. In 1772, the curé of Belle-Isle in the diocese of Vannes died. His nephew and heir, a parish priest in the diocese of Le Mans, offered a lump sum to put the vicarage to rights. The wary parishioners were not to be bought off (it could be that a local contractor was hoping to overcharge a 'foreigner'). The nephew took the matter before the parlement of Rennes and finally got possession of his inheritance in 1775; he had a lump sum in cash, but the sale of the furniture barely covered his legal expenses.[145] With the injustice characteristic of the *ancien régime*, a vicarage of minimum standard had to be maintained, irrespective of the number of parishioners, their wealth, and the size of the endowments. The people would have wished, if other things had been equal, to see their priest well housed, and curés disliked being a burden—hence the ruthlessness of all concerned when an outsider arrived to claim a clerical inheritance.

The government of France, expert at centralizing power, was equally skilful at devolving financial liabilities. Parishioners, taxed for the State and tithed for the Church, were also responsible for the upkeep of church buildings and presbyteries. They did their duty under duress or with gloomy acquiescence, but they would go to any lengths to avoid an increase in the burden. Thus, when schemes of parochial reform were mooted, the universal clamour was for the cheapest variant. If a parish was to be divided, only the most essential and rudimentary new buildings were to be provided; if a union was proposed, the church and vicarage cheapest to maintain must be preserved, not the most convenient or prestigious. When Church and State progress majestically forward in harmony, on every side human nature furtively seeks escape routes and hiding-places, to avoid being implicated in their costly splendour.

THE CURÉS: SOCIAL ORIGINS, INCOMES, MENTALITY

1 *Social Origins*

In many areas of France, the curés were local men, born and bred in the diocese. Of the 273 parish priests of the diocese of Bologne in 1725, we know the place of origin of 268; only twenty-eight had come from outside, and ten of these were from the neighbouring diocese of Amiens.[1] Of the 730 ecclesiastics who answered the questionnaire of the archbishop of Reims in 1774, no fewer than 644 said they had been born under his jurisdiction;[2] Le Mans was such another diocese where the clergy were locally recruited.[3] In the dioceses of Beauvais,[4] Bazas, Lisieux,[5] Dol, Rennes, and Saint-Malo, about 25 per cent of the curés (or recteurs) were 'foreigners'; most of these, however, were foreigners from near at hand—the influx to serve under the three Breton bishops was mostly from other areas of Brittany, while of the fifty-nine outsiders of Lisieux, all but eight came from Normandy, no fewer than twenty-two of them from the single diocese of Bayeux.[6] This 'natural' pattern of local men occupying local benefices could only operate, of course, where ecclesiastical vocations were maintained at a reasonably high level, as they were in Normandy (source of one-eighth of the recruitment of the whole country) and the Massif Central (source of one-tenth). By contrast, there were signs of a decline in clerical vocations in the Loire Valley, Berry, the Orléanais, and much of the South.[7] Vocations also came in patterns which might vary sharply between one comparatively small locality and another; the bishop of Boulogne, for example, knew that his supply of priests came from around his episcopal city and the town of Saint-Pol, and not around Calais;[8] the bishop of Strasbourg knew that his was in central Alsace,[9] just as the bishop of La Rochelle would look towards the Mauges and the Gatine areas (though recruitment was evening up through-out the eighteenth century).[10] Depending on how these local patterns of vocations fitted into the official boundaries of ecclesiastical jurisdiction, contrasting situations in neighbouring dioceses were created: thus Valence always had candidates for its vacant posts and a surplus which was exported to help the contiguous diocese of Dié, usually in difficulties.[11] A small diocese lacking solid catchment areas for vocations was vulnerable, and it was not necessarily a sign of pastoral neglect if it became dependent on outsiders—as in Lodève in 1735, when thirty-two of the fifty-seven parishes had an imported curé.[12] These dissimilarities between clerical recruitment areas have been described as 'self-reinforcing', on the ground that where there were few vocations, parishes would be served by incoming priests of a lower calibre, lacking a knowledge of local dialect and custom, and thus incapable of eliciting more vocations from their flocks.[13] Yet things could and did change. So often, the patrons of livings— bishops, seigneurs, chapters, monasteries—were local persons and institutions, subject to the solicitations and pressures of neighbours, and therefore inclined to local men if they could be found. The practice of 'resignation in favour' worked in the same direction. A reforming bishop pushing for recruits and the teaching of a well-organized seminary would have their effect, and in the worldly and family context in which, so often, vocations were formed, discussions about locally available vacancies would in time create the will to fill them. In the mid-seventeenth century, half the priests ordained in the diocese of Vannes came from outside; by 1789, nearly nine out of every ten recteurs were local men.[14] In the diocese of Strasbourg, half the clergy in 1680 came from outside Haute-Alsace; in 1700, the situation was much the same, there being only fifty-one Alsatians among the 127 curés whose place of origin is known to us; by 1720, eight out of ten were Alsatians, and by 1760 virtually all of them. There had been a great onrush of vocations: the clergy 'multiply so strongly', complained a *grand vicaire* to the bishop in 1740, 'that I do not know where I can place them'.[15] At the beginning of the eighteenth century, the 213 parishes in the diocese of Gap were understaffed, but by 1760 there were too many priests for the employment available; by the 1780s, vocations had declined again, so that vicaires were brought in from Embrun, one of the dioceses like Valence which had a supply of priests for export.[16]

In the two areas, the city of Paris and the diocese of Bordeaux, where an influx of clergy from outside was most evident, there were special circumstances. In Paris, of the priests who took the oath to the Civil Constitution of the Clergy in January 1791 and gave their diocese of origin, two-thirds came from outside, especially from Normandy, that great reservoir of vocations.[17] The capital was a centre to which clerics came for education and where they stayed because of opportunity, and this immigration of churchmen corresponded to what was happening in lay society. Paris lived and expanded by drawing in its population from the provinces: marriage contracts in the faubourg Saint-Antoine and elsewhere show that 40 per cent of the bridegrooms were provincials by origin. According to the ecclesiastical census of 1772 in the diocese of Bordeaux, a third of the curés and half of the vicaires came from outside[18]—we may guess that the difference between these two fractions represents the degree of favouritism in promotion given to local men. It can be seen clearly in the town of Bordeaux itself, where the office of curé or vicaire was much sought after—nine of the fifteen curés were born in the city, two in other places in the diocese, and, indeed, there was only one who was entirely without local connections, while of the twenty-seven vicaires in town, sixteen were born there, and four in other places in the diocese—the rest had become 'naturalized', as it were, by serving elsewhere under the archbishop's jurisdiction before being promoted to a parish in his episcopal city.[19] One reason, no doubt, for the failure of the diocese to produce sufficient vocations was that the town itself, one of the great commercial centres of France, afforded a wider variety of lay careers for intelligent young men than the other provincial centres. Another reason was the dearth of attractive rural cures. There were so many parishes in the Landes so sunk in misery and poverty that only the most dedicated or desperate priests would have wished to go there. In 1731 the curé of Lamothe wrote to his archbishop saying that the clergy all around him wanted to leave, 'preferring serving as a vicaire elsewhere rather than being a curé in a place where you are too poor to pay a farm worker, where in winter you are cut off by floods and in danger of drowning whenever you go out, and where in the fine weather you are devoured by flies'.[20] Focused on its port, the Bordeaux diocese had the chance to import clergy from overseas as well as across its land boundaries: 15 in every 100 of its immigrant vicaires came from Ireland.[21]

In the Church, as everywhere in society, nobles gravitated towards well-paid and dignified offices—including the limited number of parochial cures that qualified for this description. The proportion of nobles among the secular clergy was small, perhaps 1 per cent overall,[22] and it was declining throughout the century. But in some areas, the average was greatly exceeded: 18 per cent in the diocese of Tréguier,[23] 15 per cent in that of Aix,[24] 5–10 per cent in Tarbes,[25] 6–12 per cent in Vannes (falling to 2 per cent after 1740),[26]

4 per cent in Lisieux,[27] 2 per cent in Reims.[28] The figures are highest where there were numerous families of poor nobles of the sword whose younger sons had little to inherit and only the Church and the army for a career. Normally one would expect to find nobles in the better sort of canonries, but parishes with a substantial income could also attract high birth. When reconstruction in Alsace greatly increased the value of a number of parochial benefices, the sons of some of the best families in the province came forward to possess them.[29] In Burgundy, Brazey-en-Plaine was one of those odd, lucrative cures where the priest was on the *congrue*, but had a substantial income from surplice-fees and pious foundations; in 1773, Pierre-Claude Perrot, 'écuyer, bachelier en droit, prêtre', son of a magistrate of the chambre des comptes of Dijon, resigned his canonry in the church of Saint-Jean in that city to possess it.[30] For almost a century, the rich cure of La Haye-Pesnel in Normandy was held by a succession of noblemen until in 1759 the monopoly collapsed and a peasant's son who had been vicaire there for twenty years was appointed—and the presbytery changed its appearance from a château to a farmhouse.[31] One would guess that there were attractions in the parish of Fontenay-le-Comte when we find it held in the second half of the eighteenth century by M. de Rémigioux, écuyer, seigneur de la Grégouillière.[32] And perhaps the most splendid parish in the whole kingdom was that of Saint-Sulpice in Paris, ruled from 1748 to 1778 by Jean Dulau d'Allemans, the son of a marquis.[33] Down in the South, in the diocese of Lescar, the Tristan family, *jurats* of the town of Pau, held the lucrative cure of Gan in family possession, as if it was yet another of their fiefs or vineyards. After forty years as curé, Henri de Tristan resigned in 1721 to his nephew Arnaud, who forthwith resigned to his brother Daniel, who remained in Paris for eight years before he actually undertook the duties. Thereafter, portly, witty, resplendent with gold snuff-box and gold-topped cane, and in wigs sent specially from Paris, he presided over his parish, hobnobbing with the bishop and the intendant, and attending the sessions of the estates of Béarn arrayed in his *veste de noblesse*.[34] In the diocese of Tréguier (18 per cent nobles in the ranks of the secular clergy), there were a dozen rich cures with incomes ranging from 2,400 livres to 4,000; these were held chiefly by nobles, the other parochial benefices, mostly poor, going to commoners.[35] In 1764, the necrology of the diocese published the names of priests who were nobles above those who were commoners. 'If they'd made a necrology at Rome in the year of the death of Saint Peter and Saint Paul,' a disgruntled curé wrote to the superior of the

seminary of Vannes, 'and if they'd put Paul first because he was a nobleman, the Christians would have been scandalized. They revered Peter the prisoner more than Paul the *gentilhomme*.'[36]

This did not mean that noble curés were admitted to office by the bishops without assessment of their worthiness. Marie-Hubert-Lénor d'Imbleval was refused the living of Saint-Germain-de-Clairefeuille by a *vicaire général* of the bishop of Lisieux in 1764, even though he had been a canon and a curé elsewhere;[37] Canon de Luzarches was turned down for the rich double parish of Saint-Laurent with Notre-Dame de Recouvrance at Orléans after doing a year's special study for an examination which he failed—though a cynic might point out that he was asked very elementary questions, and that after an appeal to the archbishop of Paris and a new examination, he finally succeeded.[38] By contrast, there were some nobles who accepted humble parish offices that might have gone to anyone. Charles-Sextus Ventré de la Touloubre, allied to the Vintimilles, the princes of Monaco, was a vicaire in various parishes of the diocese of Paris before becoming curé of Bièvres in 1789;[39] and the abbé D'Espouy, son of the *chevalier* of that name, was *archiprêtre* and curé of the miserably poor parish of Saint-Paul d'Oueil in the diocese of Comminges; as the vicarage was in ruins, he lived fifteen minutes' ride away in his château.[40] Probably, such aristocrats were as effective pastorally as most of their contemporaries, even if they were accustomed to make their flocks call them 'M. l'abbé' instead of 'M. le curé'.[41] The *cahier* of the village of Fougerolles accuses Jean-Baptiste Ouvrard de la Haye of being a hard man where tithes were concerned (he was on the fringe of the *noblesse*: his father owned three seigneuries, a brother was a magistrate in a *bailliage* court, and an uncle an *avocat* pleading before the parlement of Paris). With his comfortable revenue, his seven horses in the stables, and his ostentatious coat of arms in the church, he was proud and, maybe, harsh; but he employed extra vicaires at his own expense, and in the terrible winter of 1788 he maintained the poor by paying them (children included) for building a terrace and planting it with lime trees at the end of his rectory garden.[42] He was acting as nobles generally did, living ostentatiously with no sign of a social conscience in ordinary times, but generous in a crisis.

Though there were few nobles in the parochial ministry, their presence is evidence of the great dignity of the office of curé in popular esteem. The sons of affluent commoners might consider that the status compensated for the shortcomings of income. A coal, iron, and corn merchant of Saint-Florent-le-Vieil exhorted his son to weigh well the profits of the business before seeking ordination: 'Tu pourras amasser du bien dans mon commerce.' But Claude Robin's heart was set on the role of leadership the parochial office conferred—in 1752, he even permuted a canonry, after only six months' tenure, to become curé of Saint-Pierre at Angers.[43] Among the lesser bourgeoisie, there was a perpetual quest for 'notability', hence the expensive, ineradicable determination to buy office from the Crown, whether in a minor law court or tax office, or as a 'registrar' or 'controller' of something or other. A son safely in the Church served the same purpose, as well as guaranteeing his own future. Of the sons of an apothecary of Libourne, one followed the law and made his son, in his turn, a *conseiller* of the *présidial* and, in 1743, *maire*; the other became a country curé nearby—the family had done well for itself.[44] 'Often, in our milieu', said Thibaudeau, 'you choose between the Church and the law courts.' With embarrassing frankness, the abbé Baston describes his own decision. 'I had to choose one of three states of life: the Church, Medicine and the Bar. Well, wrangling wearied me, hence, no Bar. Illnesses scared me—hence, no Medicine. That left the Church.'[45] At the end of the *ancien régime*, there were signs that the rewards of parochial benefices were coming to be regarded as too meagre for the sons of the bourgeoisie, especially in an area of economic decline like Brittany, where families were feeling the pinch. In 1784–5 the bishop of Rennes drew up a memorandum on the decline of vocations in his episcopal city: 'the fathers of well-off families who can't hope to put their sons into canonries or the more considerable benefices, take care to discourage them from embarking on a long and expensive course of study and a career in which they'll have to live on a mere 200 livres for several years awaiting a parochial cure which might only give them 500 or 600'.[46] The same tendency was noted in the town of Nantes. In the neighbouring dioceses of Saint-Malo and Saint-Brieuc, however, there was a rise in sacerdotal recruitment—but it was from less well-off families. Here is a hint of the new nature of clerical recruitment which would prevail in the nineteenth century—from poorer classes of society, corresponding to the decline in the income and status of the curés.

Further down the social scale, below the bracket of lower bourgeoisie and the corresponding peasant group of self-sufficient farmers, among those who were respectable though without pretensions to notability, the security and dignity of the parochial ministry were the utmost boundaries of a father's ambition for his son. 'What are you going to do with the boy?' someone asks an artisan whose

son is at *collège*. 'Ah! we'll see, he must begin by learning a bit of
Latin; he can then take the cassock.' 'You are dedicating him to the
ecclesiastical state?' 'Certainly, it's the best job there is; *Dominus
vobiscum* never wanted for bread.'[47] But not all who aspired to the
authority to pronounce the clerical blessing could get there. A boy
had to be both clever and lucky to get the necessary education free
of charge, and in any case the years of schooling and study were a
loss of earning capacity to the family. And the clerical 'title', something like 100 livres of guaranteed yearly income, had to be found.
For the mass of peasants (day-labourers or possessing only enough
land to earn a bare subsistence) and for poor artisans and manual
workers in towns, the prospect of a son in the ecclesiastical state was
a distant one. These people could not afford to have a vocation. In
1780, the bishop of Saint-Pol-de-Léon complained that he was
short of clergy because vocations were declining among the more
prosperous families, and he could not think of a way to supplement
'the lack of resources of the parents whose children seek the ecclesiastical state, a disposition which we now find only among the most
indigent classes'.[48] There are no day-labourers or *haricotiers* among
the curés, says the historian of the Beauvais area—they are all from
the milieu of shopkeepers, the literate classes, and the small peasant
farmers.[49] The historian of the peasants of Burgundy notes the exclusion from the ministry of most of the subjects of his study; the
clergy come from the ranks of the *petite bourgeoisie* and the better-off
rural families.[50] A boy from a poor family sometimes broke through
the barriers set by indigence by coming to notice as clever and
receiving a bursary or help from a patron; his clerical title might be
made up by help from pious well-wishers, subscriptions from relatives, the gift of a benefice, or the bishop agreeing to waive the
obligation. The chances were better in the towns—more schools,
the possibility of employment as a choirboy or server, more clergy
and pious ladies who might be inclined to acts of charity. The best
leg-up of all for the poor aspirant to orders was to have someone in
the family who had already beaten the odds and achieved ecclesiastical office or connections. Antoine Plassard, who became curé of
Saint-Vincent at Mâcon in 1746, was the son of an artisan; his
chance had come as a choirboy in the church of Saint-Pierre where
his uncle was an assistant priest.[51] The abbé Jallet, curé of Chérigné
in Poitou, the tenth child of a gardener and only 5 years old when
his father died, would never have been heard of had not his maternal uncle, the curé of Nanteuil, taken him in and educated him.[52]
Bernier, a brilliant young man who became a vicaire at Angers in

1787, the son of a weaver of Daon-sur-Mayenne, owed everything to the fact that his mother was a schoolmistress and his father the local sacristan.[53]

A conspectus of the range of society from which the parochial clergy were recruited is seen in the curés of the town of Angers at the end of the *ancien régime* (they would be a more respectable group than the average, because of the requirement of a university degree for a benefice in a 'walled town'). Huchelou des Roches's father was a *conseiller de la Prévoté*, and his mother bore a name highly respected in the Angevin magistracy; Robin was the son of a wholesale merchant in a little market town; Boumard came from a family of agricultural middlemen who farmed scattered properties of ecclesiastical landlords; Bernier was the son of a country weaver; Gruget was one of the numerous children of a hard-pressed saddle maker.[54] In social status they ran from the minor 'robe' and officials to merchants, estate managers, and farmers, down to artisans.

These generalizations from examples are confirmed by the available statistics on a wider scale, though as these concern either all secular priests at a given time or candidates presenting themselves for ordination over a period, they do not reflect the composition of the parochial ministry exactly. Sons of distinguished families would usually, given the opportunity, choose to go to canonries in the better-endowed chapters, or to one of the odd offices in state employment or the legal profession which fell to ecclesiastics. Some priests became tutors or chaplains, while the unambitious might choose to remain as *habitués*, earning small fees by saying foundation masses. Probably, when we have general statistics of the class origin of the secular priesthood, we ought to assume that rather fewer from the top and bottom of the social range we are dealing with found their way into the parochial ministry.

Thanks to the bureaucrats of the Revolution drawing up lists of clergy (for taking oaths of loyalty or qualifying for pensions—or for exile or the guillotine), we can sometimes make a statistical generalization for the whole country without waiting for the exhaustive accumulation of local detail. Forty per cent of the priests of France in 1790 had been born in a town (defined as possessing at least 2,000 inhabitants).[55] There were great contrasts between dioceses, however; urban recruitment accounted for 10 per cent of the vocations of the diocese of Nantes, and for 78 per cent of those of the diocese of Orléans. Rural recruitment predominated in the mountain areas (Alps, Pyrenees, and the Massif Central), and also in Normandy, Brittany, the Boulonnais, and Bas-Poitou. It is important to remember, however, that the distinction between town and country in eighteenth-century France did not usually follow the boundary lines which historians like to draw between social groups; so many urban dwellers owned or managed country property, so many of the richer sort alternated between town and country houses, so many notaries and other sorts of lawyers lived in the countryside gathering feudal rents or managing the affairs of absentee landlords, so many peasants plied trades and were involved in cottage industries. In the diocese of Vannes,[56] half the vocations were those of the sons of *laboureurs*—that is, the better-off peasants who ploughed their own acres and had fully enough to live on. But very few of the other half came from the urban milieu. Artisans and shopkeeping families in the towns provided only 3–7 per cent of the ordinands (rising to 11 per cent in 1740); 7–10 per cent of the ordinands were sons of artisans and merchants living in villages and the countryside; 20–26 per cent were technically 'bourgeois' but chiefly from the rural bourgeoisie of notaries, seigneurial judges, and the like. If we are looking for priests with a 'peasant' mentality (a doubtful concept to isolate, as so many professional and urban people were closely in touch with rural affairs), the significant statistics are those of the *laboureurs*: 75 per cent in the diocese of Coutances, 61 per cent in Tréguier, 50 per cent in Vannes, 48 per cent in Boulogne, 25 per cent in Gap, 22 per cent in Lisieux, 19 per cent in Reims and 9 per cent in Luçon.[57]

Four of these dioceses have recently been studied in detail. For that of Boulogne[58] we know, roughly, the social standing of the families of 326 ordinands throughout the century (two-thirds of the total). After the *laboureurs* (157), it is the merchants of the three main towns of Boulogne, Calais, and Saint-Pol who produce the most vocations (52); next come the artisans of town and country— farriers, cobblers, bakers, tailors, etc. (37); there are 15 legal and official types (7 notaries, 2 *avocats*, 4 *procureurs*, 2 *greffiers*), and lower down are 3 surgeons, 5 innkeepers, and 4 cooks. There are no fisher-men or sailors, and only five families of the poorer peasantry. In the diocese of Reims,[59] the *laboureurs* provided only one-fifth of the vocations, merchants one-third, *officiers* one-fifth, and a twentieth from schoolmasters and the medical profession. Artisans provided a higher figure than elsewhere (16 per cent), because Reims was a centre of cloth manufacture.[60] In the diocese of Lisieux, the *laboureurs* account for 21 per cent of the vocations, as against a large bourgeois recruitment—54 per cent merchants and another 20 per cent from a congeries of highly respectable groups (those 'living nobly' 4.5 per cent; *rentiers* 3 per cent; *officiers* 8 per cent; legal, medical, and professional 4.5 per cent). There were few artisans, only 4 per cent.[61] The impression gained from the figures of professions, trades, and contemporary classifications like 'notable', 'rentier', 'officier' should be verified, when possible, on the simpler, harsher scale of actual riches. We know that 71 per cent of the titles for ordination in the diocese of Lisieux and 87.5 per cent of those of Boulogne were paid up by the families of the ordinands—the others needed help of various kinds. Timothy Tackett's remarkable study of clerical recruitment in the diocese of Gap has improved on this sort of analysis.[62] From the rolls of the capitation tax he has drawn up an index showing the percentage of heads of household in each community assessed for tax at a lower rate than that of each priest's family. The results demonstrate that the ordinands came from the 'economic élite' of their respective communities; more than half came from families in the upper 15 per cent of taxpayers, and more than three-quarters from the upper 30 per cent. During the century, there was a shift in vocations from the south to the north of the diocese, and from bourgeois to peasant milieux. This does not affect the rule that vocations come from the more prosperous; as bourgeois ordinands became fewer, the rise in grain prices in Dauphiné from 1740 lifted more peasant families of the valley of the Drac in the north into the income bracket which favoured clerical vocations. Idealists may regret that the ministry of the Church had become the preserve of the respectable class of society, but it was the inevitable result of the work of the Catholic reformers. An educated clergy had to be paid for.

II *Income*

Concerning sources of income, the curés fell into two broad categories. In about a third of the parishes of France, the principal tithes were collected by a bishop, chapter, monastery, or seigneur, and the tithe owner paid the curé a fixed salary, the so-called *portion congrue*. The other two-thirds of the parish priests collected their own tithes, and these, together with whatever lands went with the benefice, were their main source of income. In some areas, these lands were extensive. In the Sarthe[63] (the diocese of Le Mans) no fewer than half the curés had ten or more hectares (this was the acreage which could maintain a peasant family of six, in a good year, assuming two-thirds of the area was left fallow); one in every ten had thirty or more hectares, and one in every thirty had fifty hectares or more. But the curés here were lucky; such extensive landholding was rare. Even so, almost everywhere, those who had an acre or two in addition to their garden were numerous, and to have something, however small in extent, was valuable—a resource for fruit and vegetables, chickens and eggs, grazing for a horse, an opportunity for pig keeping. There were, too, curés from the richer sort of families who inherited land, while those who accumulated savings might buy property as an investment.[64] The landed endowment of a parochial cure, where it existed, usually consisted of scattered fragments, subject to obligations (like foundation masses) and by custom rented out cheaply to local people: a curé was not likely to draw anything like the standard return which a private owner could have hoped for. The laity watched narrowly to keep the privileges of clerical agriculturalists to a minimum.[65] Exemption from the *aides* (internal customs duties on drink) applied only to wine produced on their actual benefices, and only when sold in bulk, while free entry through the *octroi* barriers at the gates of towns was granted only for foodstuffs for their personal consumption. In provinces of *taille réelle*, the laity tried hard to find evidence that the land exploited by the clergy had been originally owned by laymen, and thus subject to land tax; in Languedoc, where there was no limitation of date, and antiquity carried no prescription, such enquiries often ranged far back, with the enthusiastic co-operation of the Cour des Aides of Montpellier. In areas of *taille personnelle* (most of France), the curé's exemption was for a limited area, and only if he tilled the land himself—otherwise, his tenant had to pay the tax.[66] Hence, there were all sorts of agreements on the borderline of fraud between curés and the peasants who undertook to cultivate their acres, while the rest of the village, anxious to spread the burden of the *taille* on as many households as possible, was ruthlessly vigilant against them.

The curé landowner was certainly in touch with the life of his peasant parishioners. Too much so, occasionally, as when the wife of Pierre Perrachon put a sheep and a goat into the sown cornfield of the curé of Saint-Point, threatened him with a stick, and told the concourse of delighted spectators about his failure to find a 'p—' in the village and his resort to one at Mâcon.[67] The letters of curé Jacques Lorieul of the diocese of Lisieux are full of rural technicalities: the weather, the price of corn, ideas of agricultural improvement, a mare that cost 110 livres, the two cows calving, so there was milk to rear two pigs at a clear profit of 25 livres each, the butter safely stored for winter, and the surplus sold for 70 livres.[68] A pig also

figures prominently in the correspondence of curé Barbotin writing
back to his parish from the meeting of the Estates General at
Versailles in 1789: bought to kill in December, the animal died,
amidst the lamentations of his servant Catherine. Don't forget, he
says, to cover the jasmine, the myrtles, and the little orange tree at
the first sign of bad weather in October. At another time he is wanting to be sure the tulip bulbs are stored in their boxes; at another he
is ordering the cutting of the bleached linen into bed sheets, leaving
enough for Catherine to make herself a shift; sell the grain, he says,
to local people only, but for cash down unless we really know the
buyer.[69] No doubt, tenants often fell out with their clerical landlords—none the less, theirs was a relationship affording opportunities for generosity on the one hand and reciprocal good nature on
the other. The curé of Rémalard in the diocese of Chartres in 1767
rented a house to a barber-wig maker for a nominal sum of money,
two sugar loaves each of four livres weight, four bottles of brandy, a
wig of ordinary quality once a year, and a free shave twice a week.[70]
One hopes their frequent meetings were enlivened by the gossip and
badinage usually associated with barbers' shops.

   For most curés, tithe was the main source of income—more
important than the lands of the benefice. It was commonly said
that a tithe-owning priest was to be envied as compared with those
miserably dependent on the *congrue*: this was generally, but not
always the case, for tithes could yield anything from 10,000 livres a
year and more to 300 and less. Often, what appeared to be enormously rich tithing benefices were not so in reality. For one thing,
the curé had to be an effective man of business before all that was
due to him was collected. The incumbent of Saint-Pierre d'Eyraud
boasted in 1790 that he had been drawing 3,000 livres a year from
half the tithe of his parish, whereas the other half, belonging to the
chapter of Périgueux, yielded only 1,555 livres.[71] Sometimes,
Christian charity or, failing that, mere self-preservation would indicate the inadvisability of being too efficient. There were so many
legal pitfalls concerning different kinds of tithe and complicated divisions of the produce between tithe owners; a curé did well to take
what he could get without controversy, rather than stirring up ill
will and engaging in costly lawsuits. A parish priest in the diocese of
Lyon described how his claim to a particular tithe might one day be
contested, 'which would be disastrous for the benefice, that is why
I conduct myself on this subject with the greatest kindness, and turn
a blind eye to a lot of things'.[72] By law, even a very small tithe had
to be gathered by an accredited agent, a *chercheur de dixmes*, who

would claim a sheaf in every two dozen for his pains.[73] Collecting on a bigger scale meant hiring carts, horses, day-labourers, threshers—this might run away with a tenth or even a fifth or a quarter of the income.[74] One or two vicaires might have to be paid from the proceeds. There was, too, the obligation to repair the chancel of the parish church, possibly including an expensive tower or spire. When reformers complained of the inequalities in the remuneration of ministers, the curés, some with fat tithes, replied by drawing attention to their outgoings. One with a modest 1,712 livres in tithe paid 350 to a vicaire, and gave compulsory alms of 16½ bushels of barley to the poor.[75] Another with 2,050, said he paid a vicaire, and maintained two horses (his parish being extensive in area); in August, to collect his tithe, he hired four more horses and five men; he had to pay for repairs to his barn, winepress, and stables, and to subscribe a quarter (he had this proportion of the parish tithe) of the repairs to the choir, 'which is exposed to extraordinary gales of wind'—he also gave alms to 400 poor.[76] Another, with the splendid figure of 8,300 livres from lands and tithe, had only 3,937 left after paying expenses and the salary of two vicaires.[77] On the other side, we should remember the fringe benefits which come the way of those who deal in indispensable commodities: no doubt the curé and his household took out as much as possible for their own subsistence before the official calculations of income began.

We have considered elsewhere the complexities of the tithe system and the legal entanglements which ensued. Sometimes, curé would be set against curé, with lay society relishing the impropriety of the conflict. In May 1731, the wealthy and aristocratic curé of Gan in Béarn wrote to his neighbour, the abbé Pessarton, doctor of theology and curé of Rébénac, a letter which at least had the merit of abjuring hypocrisy.

I am grateful for the charity which prompts you to remind me that zeal for the house of God and the salvation of souls ought to be the unique solicitude inspiring a pastor who is charged with the oversight of the faithful. I will do all that is within me, *Monsieur*, to profit from your salutary exhortations, by conserving the flock that is committed to my care and vigilance and, if possible, augmenting its numbers. But setting aside for the moment the question of the glory of God, let us drop the mask, let us speak without disguise, using the language of truth. The spirit of all the letters which you have done me the honour to write to me, tends only to one single objective—to deprive me, under a lofty pretext, of the *novales* (tithes on new crops) of 14 or 15 houses in (the hamlet of) Haut-le-Gan, upon which you claim to have acquired a right dating from a mythical

concordat which was made—if you are to be believed—in the Year of
Grace 1711, between the bishop of Oloron, the late Mgr de Mesplas
bishop of Lescar, and my late uncle.[78]

Curés in poorer circumstances could not afford to be so suave: in
1750 we find the *prieur-curé* of Vienne-la-Ville turning out, shotgun
under arm and accompanied by his housekeeper, the schoolmaster
and a few 'armed men', to repel the tithe collectors of the neighbouring parish.[79]

Disputes of curés with their flocks were legion. When to collect,
how, what measures to use, the introduction of new crops, the
changing of areas of cultivation—almost anything could lead to a
lawsuit, and even the most irenical of pastors, willing to sacrifice his
own income, had to remember that he was responsible for the
interests of his successors. In an extreme gesture, one parish priest
refused absolution to recalcitrant parishioners at Eastertide, leading
to further resort to the courts for abuse of ecclesiastical power.[80] On
the other side violence brooded. In a parish in Normandy, where
there was a dispute over the straw of the tithe, the peasants near the
vicarage marked their geese with a special sign so they could shoot
those of the curé when they strayed on to their land;[81] in a parish
near Puy de Dôme, after mediation by the *subdélégué* over payments
on sheep had broken down, the horsemen of the *maréchaussée* who
were sent in to coerce the inhabitants (by the cost of their billeting)
had to flee for their lives.[82] Sometimes a curé was faced by a cynical
alliance of seigneur and peasants refusing to pay, or the inhabitants
leagued together to defeat him on a test case. The picture was
unedifying; as Voltaire sardonically pointed out to the bishop of
Annecy when the curé of Moens, near Ferney, won a tithe suit
against his parishioners before the parlement of Dijon, Protestant
pastors did not go to law against their people.[83]

In the *cahiers* of 1789, the peasants occasionally take their chance
to censure the rapacity of their curé; he appropriates the straw which
is essential for their manure;[84] his men throw the sheaves around to
choose the biggest, and in so doing shake out some of the grain;[85] he
comes round meanly in person checking the number of new-born
calves.[86]

Of the fifth of the parish *cahiers* which propose the abolition or
buying off of tithe, and the two-fifths wanting a reform of the
system, most are concerned with tithes usurped by bishops, chapters,
and monasteries: it would be a different matter if the curé, living in
the place and responsible for its poor, was drawing all the income.[87]

This is what so many of them imply: even then, the parish priest's share of the harvest would always have been the subject of grumbling. 'These tithes', said the *cahier* of the parish of Thouai in Périgord, 'by their very nature compel us to look on our pastors, who are our friends and the consolers of our sorrows, as persons hostile to us, and expose them to the risk of being regarded as members of the class which oppresses the common people.'[88]

A tithe-owning curé might happen to be poor; the curés on the *congrue*, however, were officially so—unless they had fortuitous supplementary sources of income. The word *congrue*[89] was derived from an old adjective meaning 'expressed in exact terms': it had nothing to do with 'congruous', and it was certainly never congruous with the cost of living. Since the end of the sixteenth century, the king had fixed the amount which the holders of the great tithe had to give to their 'perpetual vicars'. In 1686, the figure was put at 300 livres a year, a small sum, but by the edict the *congruistes* also had a right to the *dîmes novales*, the 'new tithes' on wastelands brought under cultivation, and on crops newly introduced into the area (these were becoming important—the cultivation of maize, potatoes, beet, and tobacco was spreading). By a declaration of 17 May 1768, the government raised the payment to 500 livres, which was said to be the average price of 25 *setiers* of wheat; a sustained rise in grain prices was to lead to a further increase in the *congrue*. Counterbalancing the generosity, however, the declaration transferred the *novales* (including those the curés were already levying) to the holders of the great tithe. Perhaps this could be justified on grounds of administrative convenience, but it looked very much as though the higher clergy had foreseen how the expansion and diversification of agriculture was going to make the *novales* a gold-mine in the future. Grain prices did indeed rise. 'Le cas prévu', said the curés of Aurillac in Auvergne in May 1780, 'c'est-à-dire l'augmentation considérable dans le prix des graines est arrivé.'[90] A leisurely five years later, the abbés Talleyrand and Boisgelin, agents of the clergy, reported to the General Assembly of the Clergy of France in favour of a *congrue* of 700 livres, which was established by the edict of 2 December 1786.

Most *congruistes*, we may assume, drew the salary officially prescribed, but by no means all did so: eighteenth-century France was a patchwork of traditional agreements and exceptions. We find wretched priests who accepted less in consideration of a scrap of land which the tithe holder transferred to them.[91] In 1789, of twenty-four *congruistes* in the area around Rennes, at least seven were being underpaid,[92] and in the poverty-stricken Mauges area of Anjou most were drawing only 500–600 livres,[93] well short of the official figure—probably, the tithe holder was incapable of paying the full amount in many cases. Royal edicts fixing the *congrue* did not apply to the numerous parishes dependent on the Order of Malta; according to the knights, this was fair, since the Order paid the clerical taxation on its benefices, waived visitation fees, and, through its provincial chapters, was willing to vote special grants to needy incumbents.[94] If the instance of the curé of Pomerol, near Bordeaux, is typical, these special grants were a fable. The *congrue* here was 200 livres, raised to 300 in 1758 (the local *commandeur* of the Order drew 2,800 from the tithes of the parish). The curé who died in 1734 left verses complaining of his melancholy diet:

> Sans pain, sans vin de dîme
> Il vit d'une sardine

His successor, according to the magistrates of Libourne, who appealed on his behalf to the *commandeur*, lived solely on bread and water—they gave a certificate to this effect.[95] On the other hand, some *congruistes* drew more than their official salary. This might be the case when the curé was rendering some special services to his tithe owner, or because the latter was inclined to be generous. Thus, there were two curés at Chelles, ministering to their flocks in the shadow of the great abbey: one was quite well off from his lands and an annual grain payment from the nuns for saying their masses, and the other had 160 livres extra from leases over and above his 700 livres *congrue*.[96] When the Crown acquired the duchy of Châteauroux in 1741, the Conseil d'État awarded minor additions, ranging from 15 livres to 134, to the clergy of the seventeen parishes involved.[97] More usually, the *congruiste* who was getting more was benefiting from some old local agreement—on such a ground, the courts refused to allow the abbey of Eu to bring down one of its curés from his traditional 800 livres to the 500 of the 1768 edict.[98] By a series of 'transactions' with their canons, the thirty *vicaires perpétuels* of the chapter of Périgueux by 1790 had pushed their salaries well above the official 700 livres; according to their declarations in that year they were drawing on the average 1,354 each, which was only 313 short of the average for all the curés of the diocese.[99]

About 30 per cent of the curés of France were in receipt of the *congrue*. The figure, however, conceals wide local diversities. In seventeen of the larger dioceses for which exact figures are conveniently available,[100] there was a total of 7,694 parishes, and in 2,754 of them the priest was on the *congrue*. But in four of these dioceses, such unlucky salaried curés constituted a small minority—in Coutances (22 out of 295), Saint-Pol-de-Léon (9 of 120), Metz (30 of 397). The standard proportion of a third is found, roughly, in the huge dioceses of Bourges (222 of 792) and Limoges (209 of 868), and in Auch (74 of 262); the proportion is rather lower in Paris (137 of 470), Bordeaux (98 of 282), Reims (99 of 418), Rennes (38 of 142), and Oloron (47 of 149). In the remaining five dioceses, *congruistes* are over half the total—Clermont (410 of 800), Rodez (293 of 465), Tarbes (188 of 298), Gap (146 of 214), with Vienne having an almost exclusively salaried ministry (400 of 430). Just as areas of vast ecclesiastical property holding were the pacemakers for the accelerating movement of anticlerical envy among the laity, so too the regions where the *congrue* predominated tended to play a role of leadership in clerical discontent. In the latter years of the *ancien régime* Dauphiné was a centre of the agitation of the lower clergy: the percentage of *congruistes* in the seven dioceses of that province, as recorded by the Clergy of France in 1760, was: Vienne 93 per cent, Valence 41 per cent, Dié 61 per cent, Saint-Paul-Trois-Châteaux 74 per cent, Embrun 80 per cent, Grenoble 92 per cent, Gap 68 per cent.[101]

Whenever and wherever the *congruistes* complained, they were conscious of the solid backing of their parishioners. It was a general local interest to have the produce of the village fields sold to local people, and profits locally made used to provide employment and poor relief near at home. In a presentation of their case in 1755, the curés of Nîmes[102] begin by citing the standard arguments from inside the ecclesiastical structure: 'the tithe belongs to the curés by common law; its passing into other hands is a usurpation'; ecclesiastical revenues are held by those who do not do the work, 'most often they are cold spectators of the tribulations of the Church whose revenues they have monopolized'; the good of religion and the decencies of distributive justice demand reform. Then they go on to say that lay society is with them, 'the voice of the people', who have an interest in ensuring that their contributions are spent locally and provide the sort of wage to attract able clergy into the parochial office. A lay pamphleteer of 1786 did a precise calculation; suppress monasteries and chapters, confiscate their tithes, and share them out among the parish priests, and each curé would have an income of 1,428 livres, double the figure of the official *congrue* newly prescribed in that very year.[103]

All parish priests, whether tithe owners or *congruistes*, were

entitled to the income from the *casuel*, the surplice-fees for the performance of the occasional offices. A very small parish would not
yield much; in 1756, the curé of Épinay near Paris complained that
his thirty families provided him with only two funerals a year and a
marriage in every three or four. In two neighbouring parishes, with
incomes of over 1,000 livres a year, the *casuel* contributed 100 to
each; in another, nothing at all.[104] But in Gemeaux, a populous
village in Burgundy where the tithe yielded 600 to 700 livres, the
occasional offices brought 1,000 to 2,000 (the folk were generous
here; everyone joined in putting an offering for the celebrant on the
patten used in the nuptial mass).[105] There were town parishes where
the *casuel* was virtually the whole of the revenue—La Trinité at
Cherbourg (1,100 livres),[106] Saint-Gervais (8,000)[107] and Saint-Leu-
Saint-Gilles (3,900) at Paris.[108] The curé could not hope, of course,
to keep such large sums exclusively for himself, since he had to
provide for the minor ecclesiastics who helped him—unless, like the
curé of the cathedral at Bordeaux, he maintained his standard of
living by spending his entire time baptizing, marrying, and burying.[109]

The *casuel* was hated by the laity.[110] They had already paid for the
services of the clergy, they argued, through the tithe. Any extra
offering for the pastor should be purely voluntary, and so it had been
until custom hardened into obligation towards the end of the sixteenth century. At weddings amid the general hilarity and show-off
expenditure, an extra payment among the others could be handed
over with reasonable cheerfulness, but there was universal dissatis-
faction at the charges for funerals. It was intolerable that these sad
occasions should be a source of profit to the pastor of the flock. 'Is
it not sufficiently distressing for us to lose our relatives?' asked a
cahier of 1789; 'must the memory of our sorrows be renewed by a
bill for surplice-fees which is even more burdensome to us than the
crushing weight of official taxation?'[111]

Some of the diocesan tables of fees (drawn up by the bishops in
accordance with Louis XIV's edict of 1695) made concessions to the
Christian and common-sense principle that the tariff should take
into account the ability of a particular family to pay. The Autun
ordinance, which remained in force from 1706 to 1789, divided the
population into four classes, though their payments were not very
steeply differentiated, as the nobles, *avocats*, doctors, and *rentiers* of
the first class had to pay only double the fees imposed on the servants, day-labourers, and *menu peuple* of the fourth.[112] The Amiens
tariff of 1744[113] left baptisms free of charge (as was universal), and

charged ordinary folk 15 sols for *fiançailles* (ceremony of engagement to be married), with 1 livre, 5 sols, for the richer sort; the calling of banns cost 3 or 5 livres, and the nuptial benediction and mass was 1 livre, 4 sols, or 3 livres, 15 sols. As against these graded charges for supposedly equal access to the offices of the Church, funerals were differentiated according to the magnificence of the ceremonies on offer. An ordinary funeral cost 2 livres; there were four more expensive ones, culminating in a 'service très solennel à neuf leçons, vigiles à neuf leçons, convoi, enterrement, grandes commendations' at 12 livres, 15 sols, with extra charges if more than one priest attended, and for acolytes, cross-bearers, and so on.[114] Some of the occasional offices were optional, and the very poor, maybe, would have to do without them—the blessing of the nuptial bed at 10 sols plus 5 for the clerk and 3 for the attendant choirboy; blessing new houses at 10 sols, or beehives at 5.[115] This deprivation of spiritual and picturesque adjuncts to family life imposed on the poor was most grimly evident at the funeral of a child. An infant could be buried drably for 12 sols, but to have a mass of the Holy Angels, with white stole and the message of assured salvation, cost 2 livres, 5 sols, the price of three days' labour amid sheaves and furrows.[116]

A few curés tried to institute more sharply differentiated surplice-fees in their parishes to ease the burden on the poor.[117] One, in the diocese of Boulogne, tried the opposite tack, and to rescue them from humiliation, insisted on having the same service for all, in spiritual equality; this was unpopular, for the poor liked to see displays put on by their superiors.[118] Another curé tried to persuade the village to pay a fixed annual composition which would cover all households.[119] But more and more parish priests found it impossible to levy any sort of surplice-fees; some of their people were too poor to pay them, and all of them were recalcitrant. In 1728, a curé of Normandy described his parish: 150 households, two-thirds of the bread-winners being poor fishermen, and the State levying 800 livres a year in taxation—he could ask nothing, *'casuel néant'*.[120] A parish priest wrote to the bishop of Grenoble in 1765 asking permission to retire to a religious community, so weary was he of struggling to exist on the *congrue*—as for the surplice-fees, he said, 'l'humanité répugne à tirer d'eux les moindres émoluments'.[121] Three of the replies of curés to the bishop of Comminges's comprehensive questionnaire of 1786 refer to fees of 100 livres or over (786, 400 shared with the vicaires, and 100), but for the most part, the sums are derisory, and some curés flatly state that it is out of the question to levy anything at all. 'Only a priest without heart or compassion

could do so'; 'Surplice-fees are no longer customary'; 'Lost entirely';
'For long extinct'; 'Practically destroyed'; 'nil, nil, nil'; 'It is an
honorarium which will soon be remembered only as a name'; 'An
odious and execrable word'; 'What profit can you draw from the
casuel in a parish where the curé himself has to pay for the candles
for a funeral?'; 'The dead are a surcharge on the curé'.[122]

When Church property was confiscated during the Revolution,
the curés had to make declarations of their income. Since they were
to be paid a basic rate and, if they had drawn more than this under
the *ancien régime*, half the excess (excluding from the calculation the
proceeds of the *casuel*), their statements naturally do not err on the
low side. These declarations reveal a further source of income which
some parish priests had enjoyed—a source not fully discussed in
earlier controversies about clerical poverty. Every tonsured ecclesiastic was technically qualified to hold benefices without cure of souls,
and those who were well connected accumulated a fair revenue in
this way. Some of these, of course, were curés. A priest who was
particularly learned or efficient might be favoured by interested
patrons with gifts of chapels or priories, and with these to support
him, might be persuaded to stay in some strategic parish even if its
income was small. Of the seventeen curés of Angers,[123] four enjoyed
1,000 livres or more from such extra benefices. One, the curé of
Saint-Aignan, a tiny parish in the centre of town, drew practically
nothing by virtue of his parochial office, but had 1,500 livres from
eight chapels. The curé of Sainte-Croix, with a basic income of 400
livres, was the titular of three chapels bringing in half as much again.
Just as bishops were fortified by grants of abbeys *in commendam* by the
Crown, so too the more favoured (and generally more able) curés
had their supplementary resources.

Like everyone who was of respectable status in eighteenth-
century France, the curés had their perquisites of office. In richer
parishes, the offerings at the main mass of Easter might reach a fair
figure—in the Breton countryside, said a report of 1781, they were
scandalously solicited: 'a verger or choirman follows the recteur or
curé who is administering the communion, and cries "Payez vos
deniers pascaux! Pay your Easter dues!" Then everyone hastens to
fumble in his clothing, most often in an indecent fashion, to get
money out of his pocket or his purse to put on the collection
plate.'[124] In some places, farmers who owned plough animals gave
the curé one or two sheaves each on condition he read the Passion
narrative daily 'from the feast of the Invention of the Holy Cross to
the feast of its Exaltation'.[125] There were small payments for saying

foundation masses (about one livre for a low mass and three times as much for the nine lessons, commendation, and high mass).[126] Perhaps there would be the candle ends left after the ceremonies of the First Communion and of Candlemas (not on other days, these belonged to the churchwardens).[127] Gifts dedicated on the high altar were supposedly the curé's, but not those on the minor ones.[128] Pious ladies might leave some contribution to the comfort of their pastor behind them in the confessional, and learned priests in university towns might draw fees for examining theses in the Faculty of Theology.[129] Some curés also managed to insist on the continuance of 'folkloric' levies which most people in the eighteenth century were now refusing to render—a tribute of eggs from the boys and girls making their First Communion, or of flax by those who attended mass on the day of Sainte-Barbe.[130]

In this complex, archaic social order, perquisites were offset by uncovenanted obligations—the many things the pastor had to pay for because there was no one else to do so. There were no retirement pensions; a parish priest who resigned contracted with his successor for a pension, normally a third of the income of the benefice. Bad harvests might be as disastrous for the priest as for the peasant parishioners. Just as his income fell, there would be more poor to be rescued from starvation, and if a pauper died, like as not, it would be the curé who paid for the shroud and the necessary minimum of four candles. A *casuel* of 8,000 and 1,200 livres in house rents made the curé of Saint-Gervais in Paris seemingly rich, but he complained that inescapable good works took away half his revenue—300 livres and 80 livres lodging allowance to maintain a priest at Pont-aux-Choux for catechisms; 100 for classes to educate young clerics; gratuities coming to 500 to assistant clergy for attending the offices of the church; lodgings for them, 1,000; to poor families, about 500; unpredictable sums to parish schools, and 54 to the Dames de la Charité who went visiting in the slums. 'I wanted to shake off this latter burden,' he naïvely recorded in 1762, 'but the universal outcry (*le soulèvement général*) obliged me to submit to it.'[131]

The difficulty of assessing the necessary outgoings of a curé is matched by the difficulty of finding out exactly what he had coming in originally. So often, the income was a composite affair. In his memoirs, curé Ducastel describes how by 1785 he had at last been awarded one of the plums of ecclesiastical preferment, the living of Marolles-les-Braults—6,500 livres from tithes farmed out, 350 from tithes in kind, a *métairie* (a farm leased on a crop-sharing basis) worth 922, an enclosure bringing in 260, and a field worth 126, assorted other lands worth 600, *casuel* and foundation masses worth 500.[132] Had he not told us all this, it is probable that some branch or other of his earnings would have been as impenetrable to the historian as it probably was to the diocesan bureau that assessed taxation. Contemporary attempts to state a global sum by the addition of disparate earnings were approximations, and loaded at that. The diocesan *pouillé*, the published list of benefices, always quoted much too low a figure, reflecting the amount the incumbents reluctantly admitted to be theirs in the face of overwhelming evidence. Conversely, the declarations of 1790, seeing it was a question of extracting the maximum salary from the government, were pushed as high as credulity would allow. The pension obtained by a resigning curé is probably the best guide of all; it would be a third of the total income, a figure arrived at after negotiation in which the new man had investigated the accounts to keep the figure down and the old one had used every argument to inflate it. In the diocese of Lisieux, the evidence from retirement pensions tends to add 25 per cent to the published figures of benefice income.[133] Even then, in a particular case, we may be mistaken. A candidate may have been willing to pay at a high rate because he knew his predecessor had not long to live, or because of affection for him, or because of sheer desperation to get the parish; the retiring curé may have been willing to accept less than his due because he was resigning to a close friend or relative, or to build up a good relationship—and in any case, the value of any extra benefices without cure of souls would not have entered into the calculation. In interpreting official figures of income without the aid of account-books or resignation pensions, the rule must be to increase the amount by at least a quarter, but with one proviso. The very lowest figures are more likely to be accurate. Everyone knew how much the *congrue* was, and there were few opportunities to augment it. Where the product of land or tithes was minute, there was little scope for improvement, and the priests who spent their lives in the poorest parishes were those who lacked the influence which obtained supplementary benefices. The curés who were officially poor were probably really so; those who were higher up the scale were richer than was given out, and progressively so as we ascend the published tabulations of incomes.

Another 'rule' of analysis for clerical revenues is: in spite of continual fluctuations, the rich curés will remain rich, and the poor ones poor. Where the land is productive and agriculture progressive, the income of the parish priest will share in the general prosperity—his acres will produce more, his leases go up, his tithes increase, his people will be more able to pay his surplice-fees, the money from foundations and pious gifts will increase, the priories and chapels nearest at hand to provide supplementary benefices will be more productive. If a curé was comparatively well-off under Louis XIII, it was likely that his successor would be so under Louis XV.[134] There was, then, an established geography of clerical incomes. The pattern varied in different parts of the country. Towards the end of the *ancien régime* there were few parish priests with less than 700 livres in Anjou (the Mauges area excepted), in the Sarthe, in the dioceses of Quimper, Nancy, and Metz.[135] By contrast, probably half the curés of the dioceses of Bordeaux, Dijon, Autun, Nîmes, Reims, Clermont, Rodez, Tarbes, and Gap did not rise much over the 700 mark.[136] This was principally because of the *congrue*, but not entirely so: of the 336 parishes of Bordeaux, 149 were in the poorest category, and there were only 98 *congruistes*.[137] In every diocese there were a few splendidly lucrative cures, the distant object of everyone's ambition: 4,000 livres seems to have been the point at which envy became universal.[138] In six areas for which comprehensive figures are available, the solid figure of 3,000 livres or above is found in a proportion of 1 : 7 in the most favoured, and 1 : 27 in the least favoured, with various intermediate ratios in the others.[139] Bordeaux, with its mass of poor incumbents, had twenty curés who drew over 3,000 livres, with two of them enjoying over 10,000. Most curés had an income of something between the 700 of the poor and the 3,000 of the prosperous; many between 700 and 1,200, fewer between 1,200 and 2,800, fewer still between 2,000 and 3,000. Everywhere there were illogicalities and inequalities. The richest curé of Anjou had over 7,000 livres, the poorest just over 400. A country rural dean of the diocese of Le Mans cites the incomes of the parishes of his deanery as five at 700 livres, nine at 700–1,000, seven at 1,000–2,000, and three over 2,000.[140] The curés of Saint-Sulpice and Saint-Eustache at Paris, said Mercier, drew more than some provincial bishops;[141] but some of the smaller parishes of the capital were just above the *congrue* level. In this comparison the weight of duties and the scale of income have some relationship, but this was unusual. A curé in the town of Dijon[142] with 400 communicants had an income rather larger than that of two colleagues who each had ten times the number, and in the countryside nearby a priest with a tiny flock had five times the income of another who served four times the population. These injustices, theoretically indefensible, did not cause as much bitterness as might be imagined. Social standing and influence and, less certainly, learning and ability, brought promotion to the richer benefices, while supplementary chapels, which in some cases added to the inequality, in others helped to rectify it. Envy was, no doubt, a universal passion, but the arrangements of the Church reflected the unjust arrangements of the social order, so that, revolutionary spirits apart, most curés' realistic expectations were realistically catered for.

It was an eighteenth-century commonplace—parishioners, reforming ecclesiastics, philosophes, and anticlericals all echoed it— that the curés were not given their fair share of the wealth of the Church, and that many of them were underpaid.[143] This was true of the priests who received the bare *congrue* or less. According to two modern historians of the rural population,[144] 500 livres (700 after the 1786 edict) was a more than living wage, and this is undeniable in comparison with the mass of the peasantry. It was more than double the amount a novelist assumed would keep a wounded soldier— board, lodging, and medical attention.[145] But it was not enough to enable a curé to discharge his duties with dignity and to give alms to the needy. The curé who saved enough from his *congrue* to have his tombstone inscribed with a last protest, 'Dionisius Boutinot, Vixit Pauper, et Pauper mortuus est', was telling the sober truth.[146] A *congruiste* of Dauphiné filled in the details, describing himself as wearing coarse, ragged clothing, living on black bread, vegetables, milk, nuts, and 'a few scraps of bacon', with no possibility of entertaining respectable parishioners who called on him, or of helping the deserving poor.[147] Maybe he exaggerated; even so, the numerous contemporary estimates of an appropriate income for a curé ran a good deal higher than 500 or 700 livres. Early in the century, the abbé de Saint-Pierre thought these 'officers of morality' should have a minimum of 1,200.[148] In their *cahiers*, the favourite figure for the clergy to ask is 1,500 (exactly what was proposed by the Tiers État at Auch and Angoulême).[149] In the National Assembly in June 1790 the abbé de Marolles, demonstrating his patriotic austerity, pared the figure down to 1,040,[150] and the Assembly, trying to be fair but not extravagant, decided to give a basic 1,200 livres plus half the extra income individuals had earned under the *ancien régime*. This was not a bad figure; a canon of Saint-Omer in 1781 said he could live well and keep two servants on 1,200 livres,[151] though a country curé at the time argued for a minimum of double this amount.[152] (These estimates and proposals all concerned net income, without any expenses concerning agricultural production or tithe collection.) It all depended, of course, on what sort of dignity a curé was supposed to maintain. While poor folk dressed in the motley cast-off clothing of the better sort, or in threadbare family heirlooms, a curé had to be respectably turned out, and new clothing was expensive. One of them said he needed 12 livres a year for three pairs of shoes, 15 for three pairs of stockings, 8 for three shirts, 6 for gaiters and as much for a hat, 10 for clerical bands and neckwear and handkerchiefs—add two pairs of breeches yearly, a new cloak and a short cassock every three years, and wear and tear on the long cassock worn in church, and 100 livres a year was required.[153] A servant was indispensable and, in most parishes, a horse. In difficult terrain, two servants and two horses were needed, for in bad weather or at night, through swamp or on precipitous tracks, the curé needed a man riding with him and someone left at home to guard the presbytery from thieves.[154] Local prices varied. Clerical estimates of the cost of a servant ran from 60 to 200 livres (probably the former figure does not include food and clothing),[155] and of a horse from 100 to 200 livres (the latter figure no doubt includes the cost of an eventual replacement).[156] The curés of Orléans in 1773 put together a complete list of necessary expenses: food and wine, 600 livres; wood and candles, 200; dress and furnishings, 200; books and surplice, 60; horse, 100; a servant, 60; repairs, 30; spending money, 80; alms to the sick, 50—with a few other items, like clerical taxation, they reached a total of 1,340 livres. Four years earlier a curé of the diocese of Nantes had made an almost identical estimate, though pushed up to 1,800 livres because he asked for two servants and two horses.[157]

Bearing in mind what lay society expected of a curé, 1,500 livres seems a comfortable, reasonable income. Most parish priests got less. A tiny minority lived in grinding poverty, and about a quarter[158] of the total had half the desirable figure, which gave them a standard of living above the mass of the peasantry, but short of the necessary dignity of their office. Perhaps a third had more than 1,500, with some at the top of the scale enjoying real affluence. Since promotion recognized both ability and influence, the system, with all its injustices, tended to fulfil social expectations. What was resented by all the curés, however, was the grip of monasteries, chapters, and bishops on the tithes and lands of the Church, and when they complained, they knew lay society was solidly behind them. Their discontent was intensified by theological and legal theories exalting the role of the parish priest, combined with the humanitarian and utilitarian propaganda of the Enlightenment. When the *novales* were confiscated by the edict of 1768 and the news spread in the dioceses that the upper clergy were not paying their fair share of clerical taxation, resentment hardened into revolt. It was not just a question of an improved standard of living and distributive justice, it was also a struggle for status, and for a level of income that would make the more effective performance of professional duties possible, while reducing envious passions among the clergy themselves and improving social and charitable relations with parishioners. It was not often that those who wanted to be paid more could cite such unexceptionable social and religious arguments for their case.

III *Mentality*

Collet's *Traité des devoirs d'un Pasteur* (1758) lists the recommended composition of a parish priest's library.[159] Though the actual titles are updated, the span of coverage is that established in similar lists by three generations of reforming bishops.[160] The central items were the decrees and the catechism of the Council of Trent and the Bible. Collet proposed the newly published edition of the Council by the abbé du Petitchâteau, which had the advantage of annotations saying which points had been accepted in France and which not. Since, in these difficult days, women (no doubt Jansenistically inclined) study the 'petites notes' of M. de Saci in a design to embarrass their clergy with questions about the Scriptures, he recommended two or three solid biblical commentaries; not that a curé needs to know the details of Hebrew musical instruments—sufficient to study the sacred history in so far as it conveys moral lessons, and the Psalms, the Wisdom books, and the Prophets as evocative preludes to the New Testament. Another principal heading concerns the manuals of casuistry necessary for the guidance of souls in the confessional. In place of St Charles Borromeo, the old stand-by, Collet lists the dictionary of Pontas, the *Résolutions* of M. de la Paluelle, and the *Conférences* of Paris and Angers. A curé must also be knowledgeable in ecclesiastical law and in some branches of civil law—thus Fleury, Héricourt, and La Combe should be on his shelves—and he would do well also to make enquiries about the customary law of his particular province. For controversy with Protestants—a subject other lists were not much concerned with—there are authoritative authors (especially Bossuet), though Collet advised against going into too much detail about subjects like Purgatory: 'Keep to the promises of Christ to the Church because this fundamental point settles all the others.' Finally, there is spiritual reading. Strangely, Collet does not follow the usual custom of including St Thomas à Kempis and St François de Sales. Instead, he has Charles Demia,

Tronson, Massillon, Opstraet, Abelly, Boudon on prayer, and Père le Brun's explanation of the ceremonies of the mass. As usual in these bibliographies, he proposes whatever lives of the saints are conveniently available, and to these he adds a pious biography more relevant to the experience of ordinary people, *La Vie de Jacques Cochois, ou le bon laquais* (1696). The emphasis throughout is on what might be called 'applied theology'. The curé must know the rules the Church has prescribed and the details of ecclesiastical law; he must be able to explain difficulties in the Bible and to rehearse the arguments against heretics; he must deal effectively with moral problems in the confessional; while cultivating his own interior priestly life, he must also be versed in a spirituality adapted to composing sermons in which exhortation plays a more important part than explanation.

How many curés bought the books reformers so enthusiastically prescribed for them? At the end of the reign of Louis XIV, a priest with as many as a dozen volumes was a rarity in the west of France.[161] In the diocese of La Rochelle (worse than most, it is true), a single book on law, another on casuistry, a catechism, and a few sermon manuals were regarded as adequate—some priests did not even possess a New Testament.[162] Throughout the eighteenth century, a few rural curés can be found, financially hard up and with no pretensions to learning, whose ambitions had not strayed above this low, minimum level. A report of 1790 speaks of some as satisfied with an *ABC*, a catechism, a psalter, 'et quelques rares autres bouquins'; though, more optimistically, a similar report for another area gave the composition of the standard book shelf as the breviary, the proceedings of the Council of Trent, the synodical ordinances of the diocese, the theological *summa* of Collet or of Habert, some works of meditation and sermons, a handbook on tithe law, the *Mercure* for the news, and a cookery book.[163] Curés in towns were usually better provided; at the beginning of the century, a parish priest in the diocese of Paris was likely to own at least a hundred volumes.[164] Everywhere, in both town and country, there was rapid progress in the eighteenth century. In the West, of forty-five curés whose book holdings for the years 1725–30 are listed, thirty-three had at least twenty titles, and nineteen had over a hundred; after 1760, a similar sample suggests that three-quarters of the secular clergy had passed the 100 mark.[165] At the end of the *ancien régime* there were curés (their cases no doubt illustrating the happy coincidence of the solid learning of the incumbent and the substantial tithes of the benefice) who had impressive libraries—a Breton recteur with 1,225 books (at a time when the bishop of Nantes had only 78),[166] a curé of Sens who fled during the Revolution, leaving 2,170 volumes behind him.[167] Though we hear occasionally of Diderot's *Encyclopédie*, of works of Voltaire, essays on newly fashionable scientific experiments, and the like, the contents of these clerical libraries are rarely eclectic; most of the books are 'religious' and, indeed, figure generally on the Counter-Reformation lists—the Bible, casuistry and moral theology, liturgy, pastoralia, and devotion predominating.

Since the shelves of the parish priests contained so little about science, geography, secular history, or contemporary literary and philosophical debates, we might infer that the new specialized ecclesiastical culture and the new culture of lay society were diverging far apart.[168] Churchmen had broken free from the tyranny of the Latin literature of their college days, and become professional students of moral and pastoral theology; in the process, they were losing touch with the educated laity.

There is broad truth in this generalization, but reservations need to be made. It is only when books become comparatively inexpensive that a personal collection provides the historian with a guide to the mentality of the owner. A curé generally had enough to do to pay for his basic professional library—the solid volumes for reference and pastoral purposes which impressed the bishop or the archdeacon at visitation time. But no doubt, in his friendly contacts with the educated laity and in visits to the *cabinet littéraire* or lending library of his local town, he would come across more lively reading than the tomes solemnly listed as on his shelves when the testamentary executor came round after his funeral. We must distinguish too between being well read and being well informed. Curés who read few of the works of the Enlightenment often knew their content and purpose, none the less, from the literary journalism of the day. The standard reading for a curé who was a severe moralist and theologian, said one of the wits, is 'La Gazette et les Saints-Pères'—the *Gazette* and the ancient Fathers.[169]

There were two practical subjects on which society expected the clergy to use their reading for the general benefit—medicine and agriculture. Generally, doctors and surgeons were concentrated in towns, country areas being poorly served with professional medical advice. Apart from a few tips in the almanacs, the leaflets hawked by pedlars showed little interest in matters of health;[170] it seemed that the peasants relied on their old traditional remedies, or on advice from some local worthy, more especially from their parish priest.[171]

It was the curé's task to read from the pulpit the proclamations of the intendant concerning precautions to be taken in times of epidemic, and he would be in charge of the distribution of the medicines officially provided—'the peasant would put them in his soup and think them sweeter than honey because they cost nothing'.[172] 'Healing the body and the soul', one curé declared, 'are two ministries which the pastors ought to exercise simultaneously,' and another described himself as having been 'apostle, judge, surgeon, and doctor' to his people for thirty-four years.[173] Occasionally, we hear of a parson who had become a specialist. In 1775, four curés meeting in Le Mans had a theological argument so heated that one of them collapsed and died—the local chronicle laments that he was the only one in town who could treat maladies of the eyes.[174] Mostly, however, the role of the parochial minister was to be a general practitioner, and as such he was more closely in touch with the lives, and more particularly the deaths, of his people than we can easily imagine today.

As cultivating land, leasing it to others, or as tithe owners, country curés were knowledgeable about farming. They were expected to be, for this was an improving century, and the priest had a duty to read up on the latest agricultural improvements in the gazettes or government pamphlets and to pass on the advice to his peasant neighbours. In 1763, Duhamel du Monceau, the chief theoretician of agricultural reform, paid tribute to the clergy. 'A country curé, once the duties of his office have been completed, always has a certain amount of leisure. Many of them think that the best employment they can make of it is to instruct their parishioners in the useful practices which they have found set out in reliable books about agriculture.'[175] The royal societies of agriculture which sprang up in the second half of the century usually had a parish priest or two on their membership lists (along with more dilettante monks and canons), and the intendants were accustomed to ask the parish clergy for information or advice when there was an epidemic among the cattle or a plague of insects devouring the crops.[176] The abbé Froger, who ruled the parish of Mayer in the diocese of Le Mans and was a member of the Agricultural Society of Tours, in 1769 published his *Instructions d'agriculture et d'économie pour les habitans de la campagne*, a volume calculated to teach country folk to read, to improve their agricultural methods, and to reform their morals simultaneously. Hard work was his gospel: he urged the peasants not to spend too much time on devotional practices, but to please God by enthusiastically fulfilling the penance they had inherited from the curse on Adam; the sweat of their brows, he pointed out, would also make them rich.[177] Less dourly, he urged generosity to servants and kindness to children. Clearly he had read Rousseau, recommending breast-feeding, frequent changes of nappies, and loose, comfortable clothing for infants—and when they grew older, they were not to be frightened with stories about ghosts or witches.[178] By contrast, Louis-François Norbert de Pressac de la Chagnaye, curé of Saint-Gaudent in the Vienne, was a technical expert rather than a moralist; he published the results of his investigations into the medicinal properties of herbs, and denounced the wastefulness of common pasture and land left fallow—and won the gold medal of the Parisian Society of Agriculture in 1789.[179] Félix Armand, curé of Saint-Martin-en-Lys in the diocese of Alet, who introduced the potato to his parishioners, also gave them an easier road to market; he surveyed (by having himself lowered on a rope into the gorges) and directed the construction of the track to Quibajon, which reduced the journey time of muleteers from twelve hours to one. Later, he came to the notice of Napoleon: 'a pity he's a priest, I'd have made him a general'.[180] These practical activities were what the men of the Enlightenment expected of their clergy. When the bishop of Amiens sent young aspirants for parochial benefices to work in a mill to learn the latest techniques, a Parisian gazetteer applauded the spectacle of their black coats dusted with flour, evidence of time better spent than in 'theological speculation'.[181]

Another practical service which lay society expected of the curé—supposing he was sufficiently lettered—was to teach young people Latin, thus opening their way to places in the Church or the medical or legal professions. 'M. le curé continues zealously to teach Latin to nine or ten young people, and in so doing fulfils the wishes of Mgr the archbishop,' say the minutes of a ruri-decanal visitation in Normandy in 1775.[182] A surgeon's son near Perpignan, destined by his family for the medical profession, remembered how he was sent to the worthy curé of Canet, and within three years, he was translating Virgil.[183] This was one of the manifold uses of a relative in holy orders; thus Jean-Joseph Mounier of Grenoble, the future politician, was dragooned into literacy by the curé of Rives, an uncle he remembered as 'a severe, choleric pedagogue'.[184]

Some parish priests, holders of doctorates and men of serious learning, found a sphere for themselves in the faculties of theology of their local universities, attending the formal disputations for the examination of theses and the unplanned disputes which were the normal way the faculties were governed. 'Give me my money back and I'll hand in my doctorate', curé Robin of Angers was wont to cry when losing his temper at such meetings.[185] Pierre Buquet of Caen[186] even contrived to run the parish of Saint-Sauveur-du-Marché along with being librarian of the university, though there were those who disapproved of this demanding plurality. The more ambitious of the learned sought fame by publication. The two most distinguished theologians of the century, Cotelle de la Blandinière, author of the *Conférences* of Angers, and Bergier, author of the famous *Dictionnaire de théologie dogmatique*, came from the ranks of the curés, though in due course they were whisked off to prestigious canonries, the first to the cathedral of Blois, the second to Notre-Dame at Paris.[187] Less seriously learned figures found inspiration in their parishes for contributions to apologetics. Husson, a curé of the diocese of Toul, challenged Rousseau's confession of faith of the 'vicaire savoyard' with his *La Confession de foi d'un curé Lorrain* (sound, but too difficult for ordinary folk, said a colleague[188]), and Bernière in the diocese of Le Mans demonstrated the falsity of all non-Christian religions from the beginning of time in his *Élève de la raison et de la foi* (1771).[189]

For the most part, however, parish priests inspired with the passion for authorship preferred history to theology—more especially, local history. Among many minor antiquaries in the diocese of Angers there was one more significant figure, Rangeard, curé of Andard, the luminary of the local academy, who struggled to write the definitive history of Anjou, though he was manœuvred out of completing it by the dog-in-the-manger Benedictines of Saint-Maur. There was also curé Robin, who specialized in archaeology, tracing the line of the old Roman road and finally proving, to his own satisfaction, that his church of Saint-Pierre was senior in foundation to the cathedral. In every diocese[190] they had their counterparts—mostly less able—collectors of genealogical information or curious historical anecdotes, readers of papers about their antiquarian discoveries to local academies. According to some austere critics, a priest in the pastoral office ought to apply himself to higher things: to these, curé Robin gave the appropriate reply:

It was nearly always the . . . pastors of the people . . . the priests of the various nations, who transmitted to us the history of the most celebrated epochs and the most interesting events; and as for the time I spend, my writings are to me what social engagements are to others—they are my tric-trac, my games of draughts, my hands at cards.[191]

Even if he did not have ambitions as a historian, a curé still regarded himself as the repository of local traditions. After all, he kept the registers of births, marriages, and deaths. The curé of Souppes, near Montargis, made an index to these volumes from 1622 to his own day in the 1740s, so his parishioners could look up their ancestors and their family alliances. 'People want to know from whom they are descended,' he said, 'who their parents are and to have the evidence that they have been born in legitimate wedlock and are members of the Catholic faith, to know what became of their ancestors . . . and where their mortal dust reposes, and to see the names of the successive generations set down in these hallowed records.'[192] (Curé Froger knew of a more utilitarian reason for his parishioners to keep up with their parish registers: they would be ready to claim any inheritance which fell due to them.[193]) Historians are particularly grateful to the clergy who used their registers as a convenient place to record the significant events of their times. 'The 9 January 1709 it froze so hard that the sown grain was destroyed. The vines froze to the very roots . . . grain sold at 7 livres a measure and barley at 12.'[194] The weather, floods, thunderbolts, and hailstones are general in these chronicles. Robin, curé of Saint-Pierre of Angers, tells of the mild winter of 1758–9, 'like a continual spring', of the savage duration of the winter of 1766, when 'on Ash Wednesday, 12 February, we were still going to see the skaters on the meadow of Saint-Serge', and the great freeze of 1788–9, when carts and horses crossed the ice on the river, and of the following thaw, when the curé himself had to use a bridge of planks to get home after celebrating midnight mass on Christmas Eve.[195] Sometimes, the registers tell of the tribulations of famine—and sometimes, the hardships are daringly ascribed to government mismanagement. The outcome of a lawsuit might be recorded, one conducted by the parish priest himself, or perhaps by others. In 1726, a curé gleefully notes how the parlement of Dijon found in favour of his bishop against a league of eight senior curés embattled against the episcopal plan of reform.[196] Another specializes on catastrophe—a wolf terrorizes the parish in 1748, and an earthquake follows seven years later (a minor tremor radiating out from the great Lisbon disaster). 'Manus Dei fecit hoc ad correctionem nostram'[197]—something like this was the standard comment. Or some figure from the great world outside flashes like a meteor across the dull provincial sky: as in 1777, an Angevin tells how the Emperor Joseph II, brother of the queen, passed by, pausing only to change horses.[198] Or the great events of national life might suddenly irrupt into the local torpor; curé Robin tells how the news of the fall of the Bastille reached Angers, how there was a rush to the town hall to demand the formation of a militia, while the duc de Brissac, the military commander, dared not go out of his lodgings to inspect his troops.[199] One of the most assiduous of these clerical chroniclers is the naïve Antoine Plassard, curé of Saint-Vincent of Mâcon, who made a record of notable occurrences in his city from 1744 to 1767. Among those passing through was the Turkish ambassador, the artillery going to the war in Italy, and prisoners coming back from it, a chain-gang on the way to the Mediterranean galleys, a triumphal procession of friars displaying the emancipated slaves they had ransomed from the Barbary corsairs, and another of converted Chinese, and an alarming fairground 'satyr', no doubt an orang-utan. He records the death of a nobleman, and on the same line, 'the mortality among farm animals has been general this year'. There was a man who murdered his wife and was broken on the wheel before a prodigious crowd, a dog poisoner who was never caught, an ancient citizen who was fêted when he reached 104 until it was realized that he was using his father's birth certificate, a Capuchin preacher at the Carmelites who was too fat to get into the pulpit, and the picnic on an island in the lake given by M. de Lamartine at which three people were drowned when the boat overturned—a curious mid-eighteenth-century association between a Lamartine and 'le lac'.[200]

From gossipy entries in parish registers to journalism was a short step. At Troyes in 1776, when the disapproval of polite society drove the satirical *Éphémérides Troyennes* out of business, the respectable *Almanach de la ville de Troyes* which replaced it had the curé of Saint-Savine as co-editor.[201] A more lively publication of these latter years of the *ancien régime* was *L'Improvisateur* of Louis Sallentin, curé of Mouy in the diocese of Beauvais—Talleyrand is said to have enjoyed dipping into its pages. (More than once, the author warned his readers to be cautious about matrimony, but this did not stop him, in November 1793, at the age of 48, from marrying the young exnun who was the popular society of Clermont's goddess of liberty.[202]) Unless there was a royal postmaster living nearby,[203] the country priest would be the first man to turn to for the news, whether of war or of politics, or of the cultural achievements of the Enlightenment. If a Montgolfier balloon passed over, he would explain to the terrified peasants what it was,[204] and if he incautiously went on to declare that 'the whole thing is folly, because it will never be possible to travel through the air as on the water',[205] who can blame him? When an eclipse was expected to cause difficulties in the holding of divine service, the bishop's staff would send round a circular, and a curé with superior scientific knowledge might have a chance to show off to his parishioners that he knew better than a panicky *grand vicaire*.[206] From artificial respiration to recent techniques in midwifery, from electric shocks to mesmerism, the curé would be the local expert on matters scientific. No doubt a few of them took up scientific experiments as a hobby, after the fashion of the day—though whether the working model of the universe according to Ptolemy constructed by the curé of Viroflay in 1755 for the edification of the eldest son of the dauphin was science more than classical studies and craftsmanship is hard to say.[207]

Though freemasonry was under the ban of the Church, curés are found as members of lodges; they are not, however, as numerous as monks and canons. Whether a parish priest joined probably depended more than anything else on the attitude of his diocesan bishop. The bishop of Luçon being strict, the curé of Sables d'Olonne refused to say mass at the inauguration ceremonies of his local lodge. In 1770, the curé of Lunéville, under orders of the bishop of Toul, refused to say a requiem for the soul of a parishioner who was a mason—until the secular courts ordered him to do so.[208] By contrast, we find a parish priest prominent in the lodge of Montreuil-sur-Mer, and another in that of Alençon,[209] and the pastor of Chatellerault holding a solemn mass annually on St John's Day for the masonic fraternity, to which they came with drums, violins, and candles (until in 1753 the bishop of Poitiers intervened).[210] In country places, it was the clergy who had heard of Voltaire and Rousseau, and maybe approved of them, even if they misspelt their names in comments in their registers.[211] Of forty subscribers to the *Encyclopédie* on two lists in Périgord, twenty-four were curés, and of 253 subscribers on a list for Franche Comté there were nine country curés along with nine canons of Besançon.[212] Considering how few parish priests had incomes large enough to justify such a purchase, the number is significant. La Gorce's old-fashioned comment on these progressive, well-read clergy of the *ancien régime* as 'enlightened and blind . . . lacking any sense of the (dangers) of the future and closing their eyes in case they saw too much'[213] misunderstands the relations between the Church and society. The better-educated curés who acted as intellectual middlemen distinguished between literary merit and progressive ideas on the one hand and anticlerical propaganda and irreligious speculation on the other. In their own way, they condemned 'prejudices' and 'systems', and looked forward to the triumph of a respectable and conformist Enlightenment.[214] True, there were two parish priests who achieved notoriety as total unbelievers, and contributed to the clandestine manuscripts which circulated in the first half of the century—Meslier, who left behind him the atheistical testament so relished by Voltaire, and Guillaume, who made a learned study of the 'three impostors', Moses, Jesus, and Muhammad. Meslier wrote with bitter revolutionary zeal, but Guillaume, apparently, for distraction. 'A poor country curé, bored and like the ungrateful deer which eats the vine which conceals it from the hounds, he amused himself by writing a treatise to fit the title of the legendary one about which there had been so many rumours, the *De Tribus impostoribus*.'[215] The sceptical abbé in the camp of the philosophes is a common eighteenth-century phenomenon, but these are probably the only ones to be drawn from the ranks of the curés.

Inevitably, the parochial ministry added its routine quota to the official poetry of the century, the *éloges* of famous men or local worthies, celebrations of national occasions, odes to distinguished visitors—as also to the solemn theologizing versification typified in curé Charles-Hubert Saint-Just's *L'Athéisme détruit . . . ou l'homme évadé* and *Zo-andro-Théodicié, ou le système de la Nature*.[216] The critical comments on the government which were slipped into parish registers might also find expression in bitter verses, as in those of curé Légiste of Pomerol on the death of Louis XIV; an insomniac who wrote in bed to keep boredom at bay, he also produced Christmas carols, madrigals, and satires on monks and canons.[217] A crude lyricism is found in Jean-Claude Peyrot's *Poésies diverses, patoises et françaises* (1774) and *Les Quatre Saisons, ou les Géorgiques patoises* (1781), realistically depicting peasant life in the Rouergue, where his parish was situated. Though his verses were enlivened by burlesque details, the *Mercure de France* complained of him counting sheep one by one and spending whole pages on a fly or a blade of grass.[218] What the *Mercure* preferred from its curé contributors was pastoral verse in a moralizing vein on the innocence of the golden age and the vanity of riches; Jean-Jacques Rousseau copied some of these down with approval.[219] Most satisfying of all, though most ephemeral, were the light-hearted poems of curés on social occasions—an ode in praise of tobacco dedicated to a *grand vicaire* who enjoyed his snuff[220] and the invitations to dinner written in verse by the confraternity of country clergy to which Marmontel was lucky enough to be invited. 'Happy society of poets,' he said, 'where no one was envious, no one was difficult to please; where each was as satisfied with himself as with others, as if the circle had been wholly composed of Horaces and Anacreons.'[221]

To go beyond occasional verse or antiquarian discussions and produce a novel or a tragedy was a dangerous venture. This was to
move up into a different league and attract the notice of the wits and
reviewers of the capital. J.-J. Gautier, curé of Lande-de-Goult, got
away with it. With 1,500 livres a year, only sixty households to care
for, and his only link with civilization a track impassable to carriages,
he lived a comfortable, lonely existence, which he enlivened by trips
to the masonic lodge at Alençon and by writing. His *Essai sur les
mœurs champêtres* (1787) was an idyllic picture of the life and leisure
of a country parson; next came a pamphlet defending the right of his
parishioners to collect wood from the Crown lands nearby; and then
his *Jean le Noir ou le misanthrope* (1789), a picaresque novel imitating
Voltaire. Provincial society applauded his publications, and, his
ecclesiastical vocation abandoned, he finished up directing the
chief establishment of secondary education at Alençon after the
Revolution.[222] Curé Petit of Mont-Chauvet in Normandy was not
so lucky. His was another tiny parish, with no one to talk to but the
schoolmaster, who was 'only a peasant dressed in black' anyway. So
he wrote his tragedy *David et Bethsabée*, published at Rouen in 1754.
In the preface he explained why he had not put the bath-tub scene
on stage, and to those who said his style resembled Corneille's, he
replied that this was not because of any plagiarism on his part.
Unfortunately, just as he was working on his second literary venture,
a madrigal of 700 verses on his farm labourer putting his serving-girl
in the family way, he met Diderot, who wickedly invited him to
read his tragedy to a gathering of the philosophes at d'Holbach's,
which he did portentously amid scenes of desperately stifled hilarity.
Rousseau told him they were making a fool of him, but, undeterred,
he published a second tragedy, *Balthazar*, saying in the preface that
if Racine had not been willing to try again after a flop, he would
never have written *Phèdre*; and he vanishes from history promising
to write a third—'I am young, and I am courageous'.[223]

For every curé whose literary and intellectual ambitions are
known to us, there must have been many others whose aspirations
remain unrecorded, or, if recorded, have now been forgotten, and
many more still whose horizons were limited to the performance of
their pastoral duties and the enjoyment of such sociability and status
as their parish afforded. Yet an impressionistic survey of the activities of a few is a pointer to the outlook of the whole class. In close
touch with the ordinary life of their people through land, tithes, and
fees on the one hand and, by contrast, charitable works on the other,
the curés were also medical, legal, and agricultural advisers, educa-

tionalists, counsellors of families, custodians of local traditions and chroniclers of contemporary events, memorialists of occasions of public rejoicing or mourning, disseminators of news, official and unofficial, and of selective and censored information about the writings of the Enlightenment. The Counter-Reformation had revolutionized the education of the clergy, but the results were not what zealous reformers had expected. Instead of priests solidly grounded in the Scriptures, the Fathers and the masters of spirituality, knowledgeable in theology and skilled in the casuistry of the confessional, redoubtable controversialists against Protestants and unbelievers, preachers who would exalt ecclesiastical discipline and conformity, a race of socially active, well-informed, and picturesquely individualistic local leaders had been turned out. To be 'in the world, not of it' is an impossible ideal. The instrument is always affected by the material it works on.

> My nature is subdu'd
> To what it works in, like the dyer's hand;
> Pity me then, and wish I were renewed.

12

THE 'BON CURÉ'

I

Upon my word of honour, and speaking the simple truth, I say that if I was to be born again, or if my youth could be renewed like that of the eagle, I would never be anything other than a country curé—ministering to the smallest of hamlets—which I would prefer to all the prelacies in the universe . . . Shall we never see the dawn of the happy day which will bring back the golden age of the Church, when the office of the country parish priest will be held in the high esteem which it merits?[1]

So said Jean-Pierre Camus, bishop of Belley, in 1642, a churchman exalting the pastoral office in the spirit of the Catholic reformers, and a novelist echoing the literary tradition which magnified 'le bon prêtre', the reconciler of family feuds, the rescuer of star-crossed lovers, the moralistic commentator on the injustices of an unfeeling world.

Eighteenth-century deists and philosophes inherited this tradition, and praised the worthy parish priest—though with a difference. Rousseau's Savoyard vicaire[2] yearned for a parish of his own, where he would share the poverty of his people and reconcile them to their lot; he would look after Protestants equally with Catholics, never attempting to convert them, and would teach the ideals of the gospels without too much concern about the narrower precepts of the Church. 'Je ne trouve rien de si beau que d'être curé. Un bon curé est un ministre de bonté comme un bon magistrat est un ministre de justice.' To the philosophes, a real-life curé was an appropriate butt for ridicule: Diderot was merciless about the curé of La Chevrette's all-too expressive nose,[3] about 'le petit Croque-Dieu de Sussy',[4] and the Norman parish priest who published an unfortunate tragedy about Bathsheba;[5] while Voltaire enjoyed the comic enthronement of the curé of Courdimanche by a country house party tricked out in paper hats and moustaches of soot.[6] But in theory and officially, in the writings of the philosophes, the kindly country curé was awarded enthusiastic praise. There was, however, one proviso: he had to be useful, advising his people on law, medicine, and agriculture, and, said Voltaire sardonically, making sure that they kept on working in the fields on saints' days.[7] The same prescription for the good parish priest is given in La Chalotais's *Essai d'éducation nationale* (1763); being useful as a doctor, surveyor, and arbiter of disputes is what is required, not 'bad Latin, useless scholasticism and theological quarrels'.[8] Rousseau was not so crudely utilitarian, though he wanted his parish priest to concentrate on teaching moral conduct, not doctrine. 'I agree that you must teach them all the nonsense in the Catechism,' he told a friend who had just been appointed to a parish, 'provided that you teach them also to believe in God and to love virtue. Make them Christians, since you have to, but do not forget the more important, indispensable duty of making them honest folk.'[9] Nearer to the harsh and humdrum realities of peasant life, Restif de la Bretonne was more inclined to consider Christian belief as useful in a parish priest, though he conceded it was not essential. One of his heroes, Antoine Foudriat, curé of Saci, 'had all the moral virtues which make an *honnête homme*'; he was a perceptive adviser to families and a courageous defender of his people, winning a lawsuit for them against their oppressive seigneur. 'What was lacking in this pastor? . . . He was not a Christian . . . His brilliant imagination, his unfailing good taste, his sophisticated insight—all this inclined him, not towards an appreciation of Christianity, but rather to distance himself from it.' He was a materialist, a pantheist. 'Dieu ne fut pour lui que la Nature', and the religion which he taught officially was to him an unsociable faith which condemned pleasure and devalued intelligence. By contrast, Edmé-Nicolas, Restif's half-brother, curé of Courgis near Chablis, spent a great deal of time meditating on the Scriptures and the story of revelation, rising at three in the morning to do so; he said his mass at seven o'clock, then stayed in church kneeling at the altar, available to those who wished to come for advice. He was 'the father of all his parishioners, the arbiter of their differences, the consoler and helper of the sick'. He lived on a third of his 1,500 livres income, and gave the rest away. In winter, he arranged for loans of grain from the richer folk to the poorer, setting the example himself. Every week he visited every household; he organized free schools, and went in person into the fields to teach children who were obliged to go out to work. When his parish was swept by a great fire in 1749, he wrote letters and went off preaching to gather subscriptions for rebuilding the houses. When the bishop offered him a better living, he refused to move. His parishioners had one complaint against him: his sermons were too long.[10]

From a stock literary character, *le bon curé* had become a hero of the Enlightenment: his activities were a standing criticism of the rich and idle upper clergy, and a proclamation of the ideal of utilitarian, secular benevolence. The spiritual writers of the Counter-Reformation approved of the same practical achievements, but put them in a loftier, other-worldly context. Charles Demia's *Trésor clerical* (1694) described parish priests as 'les Sacrificateurs et adorateurs de la divine Majesté pour les Paroissiens'; at the altar, they represent all their people in offering sacrifice and adoration to God.[11] The ceremonies for the installation of a curé emphasized this role of sacerdotal representation of the whole worshipping community: taking holy water and aspersing all present, kneeling before the crucifix, praying before the high altar and kissing it, opening the missal and reading from it, adoring the Holy Sacrament, intoning the Te Deum, giving the benediction with the Sacrament held aloft before returning it to the tabernacle, visiting the baptismal font, and ringing the bell as a signal for the ringers to embark on a full peal—all this as a prelude to the practical business of visiting the vicarage and having the local apostolic notary read the act of taking possession to the assembled people at the main door of the church.[12] A law-book describes this representational role another way, looking westwards down the nave, as it were, instead of eastwards to the altar: the curé leads the faithful on their journey towards eternal life by ensuring that they fulfil all the precepts of revealed religion, more especially the reception of the sacraments. The State recognized this leadership function for its own purposes, since in administering the sacraments the curé 'assures and records the legal existence of all citizens'. Thus, 'in the eyes of both statesmen and Christians, the rank and office of curé cannot be other than infinitely respectable'.[13]

The dignity of the curé was enhanced by his security of tenure—perhaps we should say, all curés properly so called were secure. A *desservant*—a priest put in by the bishop to run a parish in a vacancy—could be dismissed.[14] The curés royaux of Alsace, holding benefices set up by the Crown in Protestant areas, were named by the royal intendant, invested by the bishop, and, if need be, removed by him.[15] There were also the so-called prieurs-curés, for the most part canons regular of the Order of Sainte-Geneviève (63 of the 400 parishes of the diocese of Angers were theirs, 60 of the 767 of the archdiocese of Sens, and most of those of the diocese of Uzés[16]). The triennial chapters of Sainte-Geneviève examined the evidence of superiors and visitors and drew up a list of priests suited for parochial office; once appointed, they were likely to remain, though they could be revoked by the head of their Order, provided he could demonstrate 'just cause' and had the agreement of his 'assistants' and the consent of the diocesan bishop. In the course of a Parisian dispute in 1747, a Jansenist parish priest ridiculed a prieur-curé as lacking in true authority—'since your abbot, in concert with M. the archbishop, can dismiss you at will, you are not a proper titular'.[17] As this gibe shows, the curés were proud of their security and independence. The machinations of the espiscopally dominated Assembly of the Clergy in 1682 and 1700 to abolish the parson's freehold failed. In theory, the ecclesiastical court of the diocese, the *officialité*, could hear a case against a scandalous curé and sentence him to confinement in a monastery; in practice, the secular courts were likely to overturn the sentence at the slightest hint of doubtful procedures. When, in the 1770s, the inhabitants of Marbaix appealed to the archbishop of Cambrai to get rid of curé Jean Philippe Denise, whose eccentricities were making worship impossible (he would say mass only in the afternoons, and when he did so, it was 'in a ridiculous and indecent manner'; he cursed the children at catechisms, and showed his backside to a complaining parishioner), the procedures were long-drawn-out and hesitant. In 1776, a coadjutor was appointed to take the main services, but after years of struggle, he found it impossible to carry on in face of the interruptions of Denise. So in January 1788, the *promoteur* of the diocese appointed a distinguished parish priest to conduct an investigation, and depositions were taken from twenty witnesses. In July, the *official*—he was an archdeacon and a canon of Cambrai—heard all the evidence again in person, together with some extra witnesses, and interrogated Denise himself for five days in August. The file was then handed to Deprez, professor of canon and civil law in the University of Douai, who advised the *official* that he had omitted to read certain legal warnings to Denise at the first interrogation. So the whole process started again on 3 September. Then, on 8 and 9 November, Denise and the witnesses were brought into confrontation. At last, it was possible to think of passing sentence, and the *promoteur* proposed six years' confinement in a monastery, with the recitation of the penitential psalms on Fridays. Professor Deprez declared the penitential provisions inappropriate for one who was mentally deranged, and drew the *official*'s attention to the need to have two graduates at law conjoined with him for passing judgment. On Christmas Eve 1788, the *official* held a final interrogation assisted by two luminaries of the parlement of Flanders, a *conseiller-clerc* (a magistrate who was also an ecclesiastic) and an *avocat*, and sentence was pronounced. It had taken twelve years to push poor crazy Denise into a monastery, and in February 1791, the municipality of Marbaix was panic-stricken at the thought that under the new order in France he would be let out to haunt their parish services once again.[18] Since legal procedures were so cumbersome, the only effective way for a bishop to get rid of a parish priest was to apply to the Crown to use the arbitrary device of a *lettre de cachet*.[19] Such an intervention, if granted, could be cruel enough; a litigious curé of the diocese of Saint-Dié was locked up by his bishop in various ecclesiastical internment centres from 1780 to 1789—at the *maison de force* of Maréville, the gaolers told him that he had been sentenced to an extra two years' imprisonment 'immediately after the dinner which ought to have been followed by his release'.[20] It was not easy, however, to get a *lettre de cachet*, the resort to it was unpopular, the intendant and his officials made careful enquiries before the Minister signed the order, and the law courts were watchful to strike a blow against oppressive prelates; it took the archbishop of Bordeaux three years to get rid of the outrageous curé of Saint-Bonnet, who, Sacrament in hand, had denounced a distinguished citizen whose tenants had refused to cart the vicarage firewood.[21] What a bishop could do more easily to discipline a parish priest was to invoke the royal edicts of 1695 and 1698, and send him for three months to a seminary. Even so, there were strict rules about procedures, and the secular magistrates could intervene by the process of *appel comme d'abus*; the law-books cite several cases of bishops being condemned to paying costs and damages for misuse of their powers.[22]

A curé enjoyed great independence in the exercise of his spiritual role. The mere fact of holding letters of appointment entitled him to hear confessions, preach, catechize, administer the last rites, and baptize within his parish. With some exceptions (exempt monasteries, emergencies, and so on) these were exclusive rights which others needed permission to exercise, and they were rights which were jealously guarded. Mostly, it was a question of defending them against the encroachments of monasteries, chapters, and the clergy of other parishes. The son of a courtier born in the parish of Saint-Roch was to be baptized in the royal chapel at Versailles by a great prelate: there was nothing for it but to have the curé of Notre-Dame of Versailles and the curé of Saint-Roch both present, important and arrayed in white stoles.[23] On his deathbed Cardinal Fleury confessed to a monk, but after solemn discussion, it was decided that only the parish priest of Fontainebleau could bring him the viaticum.[24] The archbishop of Paris's palace dominated the tiny parish of Sainte-Marine, but there was a grave legal scandal in 1732 when a priest other than the curé gave the episcopal *valet de chambre* the last rites.[25] Some monasteries had exemptions; even so, their servants had to be confessed, shriven, and buried by the parish priest.[26] If it was the bishop who trespassed on the powers of the parochial clergy, the law courts would intervene. Thus, in 1756, the curés of Auxerre routed their bishop, who was trying to claim the power to license them to catechize.[27] What a bishop could do was to prevent a curé from hearing confessions or preaching outside his parish, though an express individual prohibition had to be issued.[28] Since (curés within their own boundaries excepted) preaching and confessing needed episcopal warrant, the bishop in practice had a veto on the appointments of vicaires—a curé's theoretical right to choose his collaborators was not of much use unless they were granted powers from on high.[29] In short, a bishop could pin down an unsatisfactory parish priest (or one with whom he was in feud) within the duties of his own parish, keeping him out of the pastoral life of the rest of the diocese[30] and depriving him of vicaires. But to do more, and more especially to get rid of him, was difficult indeed.

Security of tenure and the consciousness of their standing in the local community encouraged the curés to proud independence. Inevitably, some were obsequious to aristocratic prelates; equally, some were truculent. A Breton recteur in 1778, accepting a proposal for arbitration put forward by his bishop, gratuitously observed, 'Je l'ai fait uniquement par religion et non en vue de vous obliger.'[31] Obviously, a parish priest with a large income and a large congregation was a man of importance. In Paris, there was a concentration of such clergy; they were, said a lawyer in 1757, 'universally esteemed and respected . . . celebrated in all the kingdom by their capacity, their talents and their education, so that to say "He is a curé of Paris" is equivalent to delivering a formal encomium on a man'.[32] These were the clergy described by an envious Jansenist in 1789 as elevating themselves above their fellows in the provinces 'by the distance between heaven above and earth beneath'.[33] Truth to tell, however, provincial curés tended to be just as proud. To the Parisian who was standing on his dignity as the pastor of the church of Saint-Médard, a provincial colleague from the archdiocese of Sens replied, 'Monsieur, it's the curé of Rocheplatte who is speaking to you. I think one is as good as the other.'[34] In 1750, the priest of the miserable hamlet of Chênhutte in Anjou went on a trip to Paris and a pilgrimage to Rome. To the footman who tried to exclude him from the royal dining-room at Versailles he protested, 'I am one of the king's men, I am a curé of his dominions, and I desire the honour of seeing him dine'—and he stayed to examine the gold plate and sample the dessert. At Rome, he declared openly that he would rather rule the parish of Chênhutte than be Pope.[35] The revolt of the lower clergy at the end of the *ancien régime* was less a protest of the harassed and browbeaten than of the proud, demanding further recognition of their status.

II

The second half of the seventeenth century and the first two decades of the eighteenth saw the moral reformation of the parochial clergy of France. 'If you compare the clergy in 1724 with those of the beginning of the seventeenth century', writes the historian of the diocese of La Rochelle, 'you see . . . that the Catholic reform had fashioned a new style of *bon prêtre*, which represents at once a socio-logical type, a spiritual ideal and a pastoral programme.'[36] Instead of exalting the priestly office in the abstract, the dignity of the priest-hood was tied to the pastoral function and the responsibility for souls. The grinding poverty which had degraded so many parish priests was alleviated, and educational standards were transformed. (In more than one diocese, the links between clerical poverty and ignorance and dubious morality is evident in the visitation returns.[37]) As civilization advanced, the laity became more demanding: parishioners who had joked about their clergy's affairs with women and complained only about their financial exactions had tended to get the pastors they deserved.[38] Educated church-goers no longer regarded the priest as the mechanical performer of the sacramental actions: they looked to him for advice and example. The improve-ment is evident everywhere. Between 1622 and 1695, the boorish priests who did not even know the formula of absolution vanished from the countryside around Paris, and literate professionals took their place.[39] Complaints of concubinage had been numerous in the diocese of Autun in the mid-seventeenth century; but there are only half a dozen known cases in the eighteenth; the dubious curés of the episcopal town of Autun in 1689 had given way to excellent pastors forty years later.[40] Drunkenness was common in the diocese of Tréguier at the end of the reign of Louis XIV—toping in the sacristy, collapsing at catechisms, charging a bottle of eau-de-vie as the price of absolution: it was rare in the late eighteenth century.[41]

In the first half of the seventeenth century, the list of parish priests of the diocese of La Rochelle at any one time would include 10–25 per cent who had been under censure; in 1724, the figure was 5 per cent. The number of sexual offences remained much the same; it was drinking and brawling that were declining.[42] In a rural deanery near Rouen in 1682, a dozen out of the forty-seven clergy were noted as unsatisfactory (true, this was chiefly because of their ruthless litigation over tithes); after 1736, few clergy of the diocese of Rouen merited censure.[43] In 1682, of the 182 curés of the diocese of Strasbourg, 32 had been before the *officialité* at one time or another (a recent case was one who had melted down the *trésor* of his church to make ornaments for his mistress). Counting others who had been disciplined by archdeacons and rural deans, probably a quarter of the clergy were unsatisfactory. The chief offence was sexual misconduct—generally going to bed with the housekeeper on cold winter nights or when drunk. A report of 1697 said that all but twenty of the clergy were inadequate, and that none of them ever opened a book. But in the eighteenth century, most curés were well educated and well behaved. Between 1701 and 1720, there were fifteen sexual offences censured, nine between 1721 and 1740, and only four between 1741 and 1760.[44] Statistics from other places for the eighteenth century are equally reassuring. Of the 450 priests of the diocese of Quimper (263 of them ruling parishes), only half a dozen were removed from their charges in the last thirty years of the *ancien régime*.[45] In the 130 parishes of the Grand Vicariate of Pontoise, there were twenty-five disciplinary cases between 1680 and 1770; in 90 parishes around Dijon, there were a dozen cases between 1731 and 1789.[46] The secretary of the bishop of Toul, in notes he compiled on the parish priests of the diocese in 1773, put down three-quarters of them as good men; of the less impressive minority, the only ones whose offences approached scandal were a nobleman who did not know the language of his flock, and five accused of sexual misdemeanours—of these, one cleared himself before the law courts, and one was vouched for as being a faithful pastor notwithstanding.[47] The bishop of Nîmes's 'observations' of 1775 on the discipline of his clergy referred to their hunting, their application for dispensations to have under-age housekeepers, their abbreviation of catechisms and homilies, unauthorized absences, and wearing lay attire when travelling; he does not refer to more serious offences, and the only breach of the rules which was common was failure to attend the *conférences*, the bishop's improving discussion groups.[48] A similar set of notes drawn up by a vicar-general of the diocese of Valence in 1789 covering 277 clergy (100 being curés) contains hardly any cases of serious censure.[49]

Inevitably, among 30,000 parish clergy there would be some black sheep. In 1727, the *vicaire perpétuel* of La Coste in Provence was sentenced to be hanged for 'spiritual incest', seducing a female penitent;[50] in 1757, the curé of Ludres was condemned by the sovereign court of Lorraine to be burned for sodomy (he made an edifying speech to the parishioners before his execution, and pilgrimages were organized to the site of his execution).[51] Journalists never failed to report a sexual scandal; it was satisfying to find a cleric who added extra names to his baptismal registers and cuckolded the men he married.[52] Village gossips were always on the watch. If their curé was walking in the dusk with a woman, sure enough, it would be possible to say that 'plusieurs personnes les ont vu s'embrasser'.[53] A whisper of an ambiguous proposition in the confessional was hard to rebut; if the housekeeper at the presbytery became pregnant, the priest was the first suspect. A story from the diocese of Orléans told how one curé was blatantly cheerful at the news: 'that means a little *benedicamus* to act as server at my masses'.[54]

Any sign of affinity between a priest and a female parishioner, however innocent, would be noted—and, no doubt, the romantic abbé Pollin was not the only celebrant who sighed after a girl who attended his masses, yet never dared to speak to her.[55] If an incumbent was ruthless about his financial dues, his parishioners might be inclined to mention their suspicions in other respects at visitation time; as in 1783, the people of Bertincourt (Cambrai) accused curé Robert Coplo of dubious sexual relations, and 'il exige des droits insolites et exorbitants'.[56] Anticlericals found it easier to make dark hints in general terms than to give specific examples. The *cahier* of Vihiers says, 'there are many virtuous curés, but even these will concede that they certainly have colleagues who are not. Ask in country places and the folk will tell you things about the morals of many of their pastors that we dare not set down here.'[57] Occasionally, some scandalous story would come to light, when episcopal sanctions were taken and the offender was exiled to the seminary; in the diocese of Quimper, in 1757, a recteur was disciplined for his 'commerce très scandaleux avec la fille d'un marchand de sardines', and in 1785, a priest was revealed as having had an affair with the wife of a septuagenarian, while another felt it wise to flee from his parish and join the navy.[58] Yet, what is striking is the contrast between the very few formal accusations of sexual misconduct and the general enthusiasm to speculate, spy out, or joke about the possibilities. It seems that this was a matter in which the clergy knew they were being tested, and discipline was maintained.

That a cleric should compensate for his enforced celibacy by moderate addiction to some other pleasure was popularly approved; indeed, a curé was supposed to be a sociable character, and refusing a proffered glass could cause offence.[59] Occasionally, however, parishioners would delate their pastor at visitation time if he was a real drunkard or, maybe, if he tippled and they had financial grievances against him, making them more aware of his other failings. The curé whose legs gave way under him at the altar, another who wassailed continually, 'even after midnight', another who in an inebriated rage at vespers broke the processional cross on the back of an intruding dog were duly reported.[60] As for the character of the diocese of Autun who turned up tipsy at the synodal meeting of the clergy, he had indeed volunteered for the bread and water and the penitential psalms.[61] Bishops tended to be strict about drunkenness: the curé of the diocese of Sens who in 1770, under the influence, chanted the Pascal anthem at a funeral was fined 60 livres by the diocesan court and sent for two years to a seminary (though it is true that when summoned before the archbishop, he had over-fortified himself with restoratives beforehand).[62]

The vices of the country curé tended to be those of the peasants among whom he lived and whose agricultural labours he so often shared: over-indulgence at festivals or in rare times of abundance, going out hunting[63] in defiance of diocesan ordinances, coarse jesting, appearing at fairs, horse-trading and pig dealing, frauding and jostling with the scruffiest, perhaps even lending money at usurious rates.[64] An individual with peasant preoccupations yet vested with authority spiritual and temporal was subject to dangerous temptations—hence, sometimes, threats of refusal of communion to enforce payment of dues, and high-handed interventions to serve worldly ends. In the parish of Cirgues in the suburbs of Clermont, Mathieu Geneix, a graduate of the University of Paris, coveted the house and garden of old Payard as a site for a new vicarage. To evict him, he got his parishioners to divert a massive sluice of drain water into the cemetery, and to break down Payard's wall so that it swept on knee deep into his property. Whether it was divine retribution for this design on Naboth's vineyard, or simply ignorance of hydrostatics, he contrived to flood his church as well, and to ruin the 'sacred well of Abraham' which was its unique feature.[65] The violence and malice which often characterized peasant feuds were sometimes evident in the conduct of the pastor—ringing the bells in triumphal peals when an enemy left the parish, heaping cinders on to another who unsuspectingly presented himself at the altar rails during the Ash Wednesday ceremonies, turning out with a club or even a gun to lead a cohort of supporters (generally including the sacristan, schoolmaster, and the housekeeper with her broom) in a tithe war.[66] The militia fire at pigeons, interrupting a baptism—the curé rushes out, seizes a musket, and knocks down its owner. A vicaire wins at cards and punches his unlucky adversary because he insists on signing his note of indebtedness as 'argent de jeu'.[67] Half a dozen peasants put on a Christmas farce, *La Vie des trois roys*; the recteur judges it to be sacrilegious, goes down with his shotgun, and orders them to desist—Herod draws his sabre and is knocked flat by the priest with his gun butt, and the angry audience attack the presbytery.[68] These are the sort of incidents that enliven rural chronicles. Voltaire got a good deal of anticlerical mileage out of the curé of Moens's puritanical attempt to maintain morality by collecting a posse of parishioners from the local wine bar to chastise three young men who had gone to spend the night with a widow of bad reputation. The Sage of Ferney professed to be surprised when the neighbouring parish priests backed up their bellicose colleague: 'they claim they have a judicial right to beat their parishioners with sticks as granted by the First Lateran Council'.[69] What Voltaire does not emphasize is that the curé of Moens had the support of his people—he had only to call at the cabaret to be able to recruit his team of vigilantes. As often as not, a priest involved in affrays and subterfuges was collaborating with his parishioners rather than acting against them. Villages near the internal customs boundaries often engaged in smuggling, and it was not unknown for parish priests to cross over with a load, or to hide sacks of salt or boxes of tobacco in sacristies or behind altars.[70] Or, if not in actual collusion, they might conform to what was expected of them and do their best for smugglers on the run—maybe ring the bell as a tocsin to alert the countryside to the presence of enforcement officers,[71] or give shelter to fugitives. The dramatist Sedaine had a story of a curé who took provisions to two starving smugglers hiding in his confessional; he was given money for his poor-box and a roll of cloth, but died of remorse three weeks later.[72]

Examples of dubious curés become fewer as the century progresses, and the gossip about them comes to concern foibles, eccentricities, and pardonable self-indulgences, rather than vices. Slackness in dress, unbuttoned cassocks and the like (as befitted men without wives) was common.[73] Risqué jesting offended sensitive parishioners. 'He was renowned for his administrative skill, his wisdom and his morals,' says Cournot of his curé in Franche Comté, 'but that did not exclude from his conversation a certain Gallic wantonness (*certaines gaillardises gauloises*) which shocked us'.[74] Over-familiarity with liturgical observances led to irreverent incidents which, perhaps, gave more cause for amusement than censure, like curé Robin of Angers interrupting his sermon to give instructions about a leg of mutton for his supper that evening.[75] These were haphazard, unsqueamish days, and anticlericals could always take a solemn, reverent line to justify their censures. 'Curé Flollet and his vicaire both have a dog', says one censorious village official, 'which they take with them to the church. The dogs urinate against the pews and the altar, and even in the holy water stoup at the entrance to the chancel.'[76] Marmontel recounts a Limousin story of the curé at mass hearing the hunting dogs baying when they started the hare.

'Briffaut y est-il?'
'Oui, monsieur le curé.'
'En ce cas-là, le lièvre est f . . . . . Lavabo inter innocentes Manus meas.'[77]

A similar story of a conversation at mass is told of Pierre Guyart, curé of Lélanne, learned and lame, who translated all the works of Horace, did battle royal in the courts for a neighbouring village against its seigneur, and maintained the six orphan children of one of his nieces.

'Introibo ad altari Dei. Ta mère a-t-elle filé ma chanvre?'
'Nenni, M. le curé.'
'Tu lui diras qu'elle est une bougre de paresseuse.'
'Oh, pour ça, M. le curé, nenni, elle me battrai.'
'Si tu ne lui dis pas, je te rosserai: ainsi choisis et va ton train.'
'Ad Deum . . .'[78]

Another subject for amused and not too censorious gossip was the inclination of the clergy to be good trenchermen. Piron, a seigneurial official in the village of Aubais, chronicled enviously the gastronomic exploits of his curé. The *fermier* of the lands of the marquis gave a party in 1749, after which none of the guests ate for two days and the parish priest for even longer. Another prosperous citizen gave a collation in 1752 with 'lofty pyramids of meringues . . . very delicate, melting in the mouth'; 'the ladies, and principally the gentlemen of the clergy, did the most execution'. The next year the curé himself gave a dinner: pâté, turkey, two shoulders of lamb, a rabbit, and a salad, which seemed all the more gluttonous as Piron was not invited.[79] Occasionally, at the end of the *ancien régime*, we hear of clerical dining clubs: when it was his turn, Yves Besnard introduced his less sophisticated and poorer colleagues to the delights of having liqueurs with their coffee.[80] The curé of Lande-Fleurie was so pleased with himself after giving such an entertainment that he entered the menu (turbot, sole, and smaller fish) in his baptismal register: 'It is good that posterity should know we fared well and that wine was not lacking.'[81] His naïve pride suggests that this was a rare indulgence.

III

Parishioners did not wish their priest to be an austere man, and they would turn an indulgent eye on his little luxuries. What they expected from him was geniality and helpfulness and, to those who were poor, generosity. Generally, their expectations were fulfilled. Curés tended to live long,[82] and as often as not, stayed in the same parish. Over the years they got to know their people intimately. Their principal duty, it was universally agreed, was to visit their flocks, whatever the weather and the difficulties of the terrain. 'Autant de pas, autant de casse-cou', one curé told his bishop; it would take 'several hours', he said, to get to a shepherd who fell ill up in the summer pastures in the hills. There are places, said another, where in bad weather you have to pick your way on foot, not forgetting to make the sign of the cross and an act of contrition before venturing.[83] Conversely, members of the parish continually had to visit their curé. He officiated at births, deaths, and marriages, giving congratulations, consolation, and advice as required, and he had the official duty of recording these family events, together with the names of witnesses, details of trade or profession, of dispensations for consanguinity and so on.[84] Great was the expense and tribulation of establishing a new set of records if an inefficient or senile curé had neglected his duty.[85] These were documents of the utmost importance 'to the republic', said the standard legal handbook, 'and to establish the status of individuals and to maintain the peace of mind of families'.[86] The curé's signature was needed on all sorts of other documents. For some charitable distributions, those presenting themselves needed authentication of their need.[87] A nice story circulated in Paris in 1777 about an old man who used a certificate of poverty issued by the curé of Saint-Roch to get bread for his dog; when the fraud was detected, the curé sportingly paid himself to maintain the faithful hound.[88] Peasants who had been ruined by fire, flood, hail, theft, or fraud would ask their parish priest for *la pique*—their hard-luck story formally written down and signed as an authorization to go round begging. Chimney-sweeps and pedlars liked to carry one, forged if necessary, for use if trade was slack.[89] Sea bathing was supposedly efficacious to cure the bite of a mad dog, and victims begged their way to the coast, fortified by clerical attestations.[90] Some certificates were splendidly formal, issued by the bishop himself on the recommendation of the parochial clergy. 'Christophe de Beaumont, duc de Saint-Cloud, peer of France, Commander of the Order of the Saint-Esprit, *Proviseur* of the Sorbonne . . . archbishop of Paris, having reviewed the certificate of *le sieur* Brunet, a curé of our diocese . . .' and so on, allowing a named individual whose house had been burned down to beg for two months around Paris.[91] Those who, because of a supposed infirmity, were allowed to eat meat in Lent, sent down to the butcher's a document from the curé confirming that their case had been established. The wretched peasant who was nominated to collect the *taille*, the main land tax, was responsible to the government for the money owed by defaulters, but with a note from the parish priest he could recover the sum from the next year's assessment.[92] Certificates of good morals were required to be able to practise as a midwife and, indeed, were often asked for by employers. Thérèse, Rousseau's old mistress, had to have one before she could draw the pension awarded to her by the National Assembly in December 1790.[93] There was a story of two asses which bit each other, leading to a court case between their owners in which one of the parties turned up with the curé's certificate of previous good conduct for his animal.[94] A wet nurse applying to foster an orphan baby for one of the great hospitals had to arrive furnished with the attestation of her parish priest (giving name, husband's name and profession, moral standing of the family, age, health, number of children and date of birth of the last one), and a further clerical signature was required before she could draw her first payment.[95] When wolves plagued a district, it was customary for the intendant to offer a reward for every one killed; bounty hunters had to take the ears to the curé who would exchange them for the necessary certificate.[96]

In rural France, the presbytery was the main point of contact for the village with the outside world. Just as passing vagabonds knocked at the door for alms, so respectable travellers who could not find an inn would call there for refuge—customs or taxation officials who would be unwelcome elsewhere, a doctor coming over a long distance to give a consultation, a notary coming to draw up a contract, a honeymoon couple whose coach had lost a wheel (and were given dinner, a bed for the night, and the loan of the curé's horse the next day to get back to civilization).[97] At La Balme near Lyon, where there was a sacred grotto, the incumbent continually had the better sort of pilgrims calling for refreshments; 'on ne peut faire autrement que de les recevoir', he said, though he was glad to get to know some influential city people.[98] Government officials applied to the parochial clergy for statistical information—the numbers of vagrants, for example.[99] In 1770, the intendant of the Auvergne asked them to help him to produce a census of children; a rumour that they were to be kidnapped and sent to colonize Corsica led to threats of murder and arson if the parish priests sent in their returns.[100] When compiling his famous geographical dictionary, the abbé d'Expilly tried, with indifferent success, to get the clergy to supply him with demographical data from their registers, and in some dioceses, notably Lisieux, Bayeux, and Narbonne, the bishops allied with the scientists in an attempt to persuade the clergy to fill in geographical questionnaires and to take compass bearings for map-making projects.[101] In times of plague, the curé going round anointing the dying with drips of consecrated oil on the end of a long stick,[102] was the sole channel of communication to advise the outside authorities of the needs of the entrapped inhabitants. Had Turgot lasted longer in office, he might have systematized the role of the curés as government agents—when he had been intendant of Limoges, he said, he regarded them as his natural *subdélégués*.

Whether from spiritual contacts, official ones, or purely from sociability, the curé knew everyone within his boundaries—except in some of the teeming parishes in the great cities. Perhaps he kept an annotated register of his flock as prescribed by St Charles Borromeo, who had wanted an index of those capable of giving alms, those who could co-operate with information, the few suitable to be trained to form a spiritual élite, and, on the other hand, the recalcitrant sinners. In the second half of the seventeenth century the *Rituels* of at least a dozen dioceses ordered the keeping of such a register or notebook, and at least eight other dioceses followed suit in the eighteenth century. There was a difficulty, however, for the whole concept was suspect to the laity: in 1673, the bishop of Agen was taken to law before the parlement of Toulouse by the municipal officers of his episcopal town (abetted by the canons of the cathedral)—this sort of record, they said, 'threatened the repose, tranquillity and honour of families'. Certainly, if an index of sinners fell into the wrong hands, an action for defamation would arise; this was why one *Rituel*, in 1751, prescribed the use of cipher. Probably most curés regarded the keeping of such formal records as useless systematization, wasting time and in doubtful taste—few of these 'livres d'états des âmes' have survived.[103] In any case, whether he knew the people concerned or not, the curé would be the first to know of anyone in trouble. A village girl gets pregnant: he comes round to protect her from the wrath of her parents and, if necessary, to find her an alternative refuge.[104] If there are other girls in the family, he checks on the parental discipline.[105] The daughter of a magistrate of Grenoble is betrayed by the son of a newly rich official; her parish priest gets a respectable matron and a midwife to look after her, and extracts certificates of paternity and a promise to maintain the child from the seducer (a future member of the National Convention and a terrorist).[106] A girl being pushed unwillingly into a convent does well to appeal for help in her parish confessional.[107] A writer on politically sensitive subjects has documents he wants to put away safely: Mme d'Houdetot tells Jean-Jacques that the curé of Deuil will take charge of them with great discretion.[108] The daughter of a poor noble in the provinces has to write business letters to a rich *fermier général* in the capital: her parish priest composes them so skilfully for her that she is called to Paris with a view to marriage.[109] A young and pretty widow is entangled in legal difficulties, and an older widowed farmer with seven children who lives nearby is just the influential man she needs to protect her; the curé virtually orders him to marry her, and he never regrets it.[110] At Le Mans, a rich young man sends flowers and verses to the daughter of a *trésorier de France*; alas, a fall as a child has left him with an absurdly flattened nose, and he does not dare to propose—but the parish priest is at hand and puts the question for him.[111]

IV

In rural France, it was important for the curé to have good relations with the seigneur, both for his own comfort, and for the benefit of his people. 'The curé and the seigneur ought to be allies for the edification of the people,' said a solemn legal handbook.[112] No doubt, if only for worldly reasons, both parties had much to gain from such an alliance, and there were curés who did what they were told and lords of the manor who attended church services and listened attentively to sermons to set a good example. But within the very church building itself there were established occasions for quarrels, given that this was a society where precedence and inherited rights were cherished and only the poor were shy of litigation. 'If jurisprudence had not set limits to the ambition of men,' said a lawyer, 'everyone who was anyone in the parish would claim honorific recognition within the church'[113]—that is, the so-called 'droits honorifiques' or the 'honneurs de l'Église'. These privileges were accorded only to the patron and to the seigneur[114] (the two, not infrequently, were the same person). The patron presented to the benefice; he was also in a unique position in that, if he had fallen on hard times, he could demand alms as of right from the revenues of the church, getting something back of what his ancestors had given; he also had the right to be received in procession by the clergy (there was a procession for the seigneur only if he had the rank of prince). The comparative standing of patrons and seigneurs was debated by the lawyers: the former had obviously given most to the parish, but the latter, it was argued, represented the Crown.[115] But, broadly speaking, both had the right to the honours of the church, and the language of jurisprudence tended to use the heading of 'seigneur' to subsume both of them.

The curé wafted incense towards the seigneur at long range from the altar steps at mass, and at close range at vespers—provided always the clerks wearing surplices were incensed first, the lord was in his official pew, the calendar showed an incense day according to the diocesan *Rituel*, and it was not one of the special parochial days when the Holy Sacrament was exposed on the altar.[116] Needless to say, the courts had ensured that a parish priest who obtained permission to take over an incense day for an additional exposition of the Sacrament—whether as a pious innovation or as a manœuvre against secular authority—would have to render the duty to the seigneur on the following Sunday.[117] Another so-called major honour was the right to a seigneurial pew; but if this structure hampered the performance of divine service, the ecclesiastical authorities could move it—though the circumstances would always be a matter of argument; certainly, a curé was advised to wait until the archdeacon or bishop authorized this drastic action.[118] Another major honour was that the seigneur and his wife were to be recommended by name, and their children collectively, to the prayers of the congregation;[119] whether this was done with sincere feeling and the right inflection of voice was difficult to embody in legal rulings. The death of the lord was the occasion for his family to demand a special honorific recognition. The bell had to be tolled, possibly for a very long time. The coat of arms of the dead man could also be displayed, repeated round the building on a black band of paper or cloth—the so-called *litre funèbre*—or the heirs might even demand that the whole band be painted directly on to the walls.[120] The corpse would be buried in the sanctuary, possibly in a family vault; this privilege was retained for patrons, seigneurs, and curés only, in the hygienic legislation of 1776.[121] Aspersion with holy water was counted a 'minor' honour. A theologian argued that in this respect, 'with the exception of the bishop, everyone counts as *peuple* in their relation to the celebrant'.[122] Seigneurs disagreed,[123] taking the view that they ought to precede minor clerics who happened to wear surplices and might well be their gardeners or servants. The law was ambiguous, and as the curé could score by splashing holy water with excessive liberality, actions were as liable to contrary interpretations as the law itself. Another minor honour was precedence in the reception of the *pain bénit* distributed at the end of mass. One legal authority joined the theologians in saying there should be no recognition of ranks here, all being equal, as at the Eucharist, of which the *pain bénit* was the symbol.[124] Another, however, laid down the order of priority: clerks in surplices, the patron and his family, the seigneur and his, then all the faithful—though the churchwardens were not obliged to seek out the great in their private pews.[125]

These standard honours of the church, codified by decisions of the law courts, were without prejudice to other rights which might have been inherited. A *cahier* of 1789 from Provence complains of a ceremony of homage still exacted from the whole community: 'You see the curé on one side, and on the other more than 300 property owners, led by the *consuls* . . . taking liege homage on their knees, and bare headed.'[126] In Burgundy, at Bretenières, Bernard Garnier de Terreneuve, ex-captain of grenadiers, in addition to the usual honours, was entitled to have a churchwarden call on him to remind him of the hour of mass, and when he and his lady entered the church, 'all the parishioners must rise and salute them'.[127] In the church of Auxerre, the marquis de Chastellux was entitled to attend divine service in surplice and sword, plumed hat and spurs, with two dogs on the leash and a bird of prey on his wrist, 'and where he sits, there is a ring to tie up the dogs and a perch for the bird'. It is said, a diarist of 1722 records, that the marquis comes once a year to exercise his right lest it lapse—'cela est fort extraordinaire'.[128]

There were three reasons, said the curé of Saint-Denoual in the diocese of Saint-Brieuc, why a parish priest ought to be on good terms with his local seigneur. On principle, the representative of the founder of the church should be respected, while the parish and, more particularly, its poor continually need assistance (he himself had been given wood for rebuilding his church and 100 livres to buy seed-corn for the indigent after the dearth of 1768). Thirdly—a self-regarding reason—once the peasants see you are out of favour with the great, they will cheerfully make difficulties for you.[129] Another curé added a fourth reason of an entirely opposite nature. Around him were poor and illiterate nobles, prepared to marry a daughter to one of their farm labourers in lieu of wages, who came to the presbytery after church, accompanied by their families, to get a square meal in the name of their ancestors; they deserved to be treated generously by the clergy.[130] Supposing, however, that the lord of the manor were rich enough and well disposed, the curé had much to gain. He would have an ally in his charitable work; in the last years of the *ancien régime*, the marquis de Fayolle in Poitou was persuaded by his parish priest to found a charity workshop and to sell his stock of grain at low prices, 'imitating the conduct of Joseph when he was in charge of feeding the land of Egypt'.[131] Repairs to the presbytery might be done free of charge, and the church building improved. 'Ask what you will for the repair of your cure and I'll do it,' said a capitalist who had just leased a seigneurie; and he pulled down the ugly old church which masked the view from the château and built a new one (according to an English traveller, the gilded Christ in it was given the seigneur's features). True, this was Voltaire,[132] putting up his façade of sardonic respectability, though after all, he was merely demonstrating that he knew what was expected of him. On occasion, the curé would be invited to the château to dine. Collet's treatise on the duties of a pastor specifically warns against maintaining a diplomatic silence in face of the seigneur's luxurious living, 'so you can have a place marked down as yours at his table and the honour of joining the company of Mme la Comtesse'.[133] The marquis de Ferrières often had the curé of Poligny-en-Mirebalais to dinner; being a cultivated nobleman and engaged in writing a book on theism, he was glad to exchange ideas with a well-read ecclesiastic of a Jansenist turn of mind.[134] Another noble of Poitou, César de Marans, an army officer who was far from well off, had to put up with the parish priest at his table occasionally because his wife and mother-in-law would persecute him otherwise. On 11 January 1790 he noted in his diary, 'the recteur is coming to dine with us, Madame is deploying all her graciousness'.[135] Though the chapel of the château (where there was one) might be regarded by the parish clergy as a threat to their pastoral monopoly, the chaplain of the seigneur could be of assistance to them. At Aubais in the diocese of Nîmes, the chaplain was a great preacher, whether in standard French or in patois, a specialist at haunting the congregation with menaces of judgement in Advent.[136] Dubois de Fosseux, secretary of the academy of Arras at the end of the *ancien régime*, seems to have been the ideal seigneur so far as the clergy were concerned. He rebuilt the church of Fosseux, extracting 2,000 livres from the tithe owner, the abbess of Etrun, and lending the rest of the money himself. He would send the *Année littéraire* and the *Mercure de France* across to the presbytery when he had finished with them (Swift's 'gazettes sent gratis down and franked, for which the patron's duly thanked'), and frequently invited the curé to dinner. His charity was lavish, and curé Delebarre would send him a note if it was excessive: 'I've no need for soup this week'; 'as for the meat, it's not all distributed yet'. In winter, Dubois de Fosseux spent his time in his house at Arras, where he was a churchwarden of Sainte-Croix; the abbé Poche, who was the parish priest there and called himself 'votre curé d'hiver', enjoyed his friendship, receiving invitations to go out to the château of Fosseux in summer, and getting his shopping done for him when the great man was in Paris.[137]

In return for dinners, repairs, and charitable contributions, what could the curé offer? Through his daily contact with the peasants, he could smooth over difficulties—get agreement, for example, that a chaotic feast, 'vulgarly called *la Trippe*', need no longer be given by the lord, but could be bought off for an annual payment of 45 livres.[138] When the abbé Delebarre took over the parish in 1780, Dubois de Fosseux, who was often away on business and fulfilling cultural and literary engagements in Arras, took the opportunity of making him his home correspondent, sending regular letters describing how things were going in the village and on the estate.[139] The curé of Rémaugis in Picardy, who succeeded his uncle in office in 1783, was a trained lawyer who was taken by the marquis de Mailly as his estate agent for the lands around the village; continually pressed by the dowager marquise in Paris to send more money, and accused by the marquis of softness towards the peasants, he carried on for ten years until he was dismissed and left undisturbed in the fulfilment of his pastoral duties.[140] If the nobleman's family was pious and the parish priest was skilled in spiritual direction, there would be more respectable reasons for his being welcome at the château. With his eye for the wry practicalities of his ministry, curé Gautier cited the value of the confessional in persuading the lady of the manor to accord due marital rights to her henpecked husband, 'who never ceases to admire the powerful eloquence of his curé who brings about such a great transformation'.[141]

When curé and seigneur were at loggerheads, the lawyers rubbed their hands. Ringing the bells for forty days on the death of the lord or his lady seems excessive, but in 1743 the parlement of Toulouse settled a lawsuit by ordering this—and the covering of an ancestral bust in the church with the parish funeral pall (except when it was being used for another funeral, and in Holy Week and at Easter).[142] The courts had to decide whether the holy water sprinkler was to be presented to the seigneur so that he could asperge himself, or whether the clergy should do it for him; the latter was the right answer, leading to lawsuits about raps on the knuckles inflicted by this holy instrument, the spoiling of a new wig, and the soaking of guests.[143] Without permission, a lord would extend his pew as his family or finances expanded, making the route to the altar circuitous; without due warning, an angry curé would take an axe to a venerable seigneurial chair.[144] In 1733, the bishop of Autun enjoined the inhabitants of Arnay-le-Duc to demolish the pew of their seigneur— and he was the duke of Lorraine.[145] In 1775, the inhabitants of Villedieu-les-Poêles and their priest threw out the pew of the local *commandeur* of the Order of Malta and those of his officers, and set up a fine churchwarden's bench in their place.[146] One ingenious curé solved the problem of an offensive pew without wrecking it by filling the chapel where it was situated with barrels.[147] Sometimes, the intercessions for the lord's family were rendered with less than convincing sincerity; more directly insulting, the seigneur might be subjected to unflattering observations in the homily at mass.[148] The curé of Bonneville in 1774 read from the altar the documents of his lawsuit against the seigneurial family, describing its members as 'stupid clots' and 'comics'.[149] In 1756, the purchaser of the seigneurie of La Marte in Haute-Provence was welcomed to his new parish by the priest with fighting words—'No! I receive you as Augustin Pellicot, a merchant trading to Spain, and I'll never recognize you as the master of La Marte'.[150]

Both sides in these disputes had their pride. Even a charitable action by the lord could meet with disapproval if the curé's role as intermediary with the poor was not recognized. Stanislas de Clermont Tonnerre, taking over the seigneurie of Champlâtreux in the 1780s, unthinkingly got the old men of the parish to elect three of their number to distribute his alms of bread and meat; even though the curé nominated the poor families who received this largesse, he was displeased. 'Ce mode convient à la paroisse et déplut à M. le curé.'[151] Sophisticated nobles at feud with the clergy could quietly vanish from church services and hear mass in their private chapel (though bishops insisted that parishioners must not attend and that the lord and his family should make their Easter duty with the parish).[152] Rustic nobles would show their displeasure without finesse. In 1778 one is recorded as wearing his hat in church, whistling all the way as he walked to his seat in the chancel, and dis-tracting the congregation by doing conjuring tricks.[153] Bad relation-ships might culminate in blows. We hear of an aged nobleman com-plaining of being bullied, and of a curé who set his dog on a *commandeur* of the Order of Malta, and conversely, of a parish priest hit with the butt of a musket, and another beaten up by the Negro lackey of the lady of the manor.[154] Some curés on principle had no time for nobles of any sort. 'They obstinately insist on treating the Third Estate like a race of slaves and beasts of burden,' said one; 'pastors ought not to keep company with nobles, their natural enemies,' said another.[155] Jean Roux, the parish priest of La Balme (the pilgrim sanctuary near Lyon), in 1769 recorded: 'How happy the curé will be after the death of M. de Boulieu! . . . Thank the Lord it will be the end of his race.' Five years later, the longed-for event occurred. 'Ah! how good it is to have the seigneur in the next world: he's at rest and so am I.'[156]

In 1789, complaints against the aristocracy became universal. A Norman curé called for the end of the 'servitude' of holy water and incense, a worldly annexation of honours due to God alone, and 'the cause of a multitude of ruinous and scandalous lawsuits'.[157] Another in Avranches denounced the local seigneur from the pulpit as an opponent of national regeneration, 'who has nothing of the man but the name'.[158] Nearby, in the Norman *bocage*, the peasants, in the July tumults, forced Mme de Grieu d'Enneval to give up the 3,000 livres costs she had won in a lawsuit over a pew.[159] The marquis de Villette wrote an open letter to his notary renouncing his feudal dues and declaring: 'No more masses at the château! Convert the foundation to benefit the poor, and we will attend the mass of the community. Sign on my behalf a renunciation of my pew, of holy water and, above all, of incense, an impertinent usage, an *ultramondaine* [sic] pantomime.'[160] But in some places, old habits of deference died hard. Municipalities in 1790 and 1791 were protesting against parish priests who continued to give individual aspersion with holy water to 'ci-devant seigneurs', and on 18 September 1792 a complaint was made that notables and *ci-devant* officers of seigneurial justice were having the *pain bénit* presented to them 'in distinguished morsels on an individual plate'.[161]

V

There was a popular feeling that the seigneur ought to be generous to the poor in the lands where he was gathering feudal dues and incidents, but all too often, the expectation went for naught, the lord of the manor being more concerned in saving up to spend his winters among the élite society of the nearest major town. But the curé's obligation to the poor was inescapable. They were his special responsibility: 'Giving alms is a duty of the rich, but for the curé it is a rigorous obligation. Whatever he takes from his benefice to spend upon himself beyond what is necessary, he is taking it from the poor.'[162] Beggars came to the door of the presbytery expecting alms as of right. 'I have to give daily hospitality to passers-by of every kind,' said a priest whose parish was at a crossroads.[163] Another was so poor, he said, that his parishioners expected nothing from him, but not so those from outside: 'strangers, not knowing the situation, believe that, as my house is a presbytery, they have the right to insist on help, and if they don't get it there are oaths, blasphemies, curses, and menaces of arson'.[164] As the bishop of Avranches said in the same year (1786), the more prosperous peasants should be grateful that their clergy divert dangerous visitors from their doors, the beggars who begin with supplications but end with threats; 'someone has to give them bread and soup . . . and it's the curés who provide it'.[165] The incumbents of the bigger Parisian parishes had substantial incomes and huge numbers of poor, to whom they were correspondingly generous—in personal terms, over and above the institutional charities, lay collections, and so on which existed in so many places.[166] In the dearth of 1725, Languet de Gergy of Saint-Sulpice sold his furniture to feed his parishioners (his ability to extract subscriptions from the rich was notorious: he made them support a muslin factory to provide employment, and when invited out to dine, he would take away the silver from his place to be incorporated in a statue of the Virgin he was planning—'Notre-Dame de vieille vaisselle').[167] In the 1770s curé Cochin of Saint-Jacques was also running a factory making linen; it promoted employment, and the product was made into shirts for the aged, 'having them first worn by the young people so that the material would be softened by usage'.[168] At the same time, the curé of the Madeleine was giving

3,000 livres a year of his own money to the poor.[169] When Élie de Beaumont, the celebrated barrister and publicist, in January 1778 sent eight partridges to the presbytery of Saint-Nicolas 'for the poor', the reply was devastating:

I suppose you think that I have inherited the ability of our divine Lord to multiply loaves and fishes . . . I have 20,000 poor . . . and I know of no anatomist who could perform the dissection necessary for a share-out . . . Reserve your delicate taste and refinement for your literary productions, and be more straightforwardly generous in your charitable offerings.[170]

In the countryside, when a family fell on bad times, a loan, a gift of seed-corn, or other alms would be likely to be forthcoming from the curé.[171] The peasant *cahiers* of 1789, even those tinged with anti-clerical bitterness, generally sing the praises of the parish priests— 'consolers of the miseries of the people', 'humble and virtuous ecclesiastics living in our midst and sharing our hardships'; 'if only their incomes could be raised to a level which corresponded to the generosity of their instincts'.[172] These sentiments reflect the memories of the recent conduct of the parochial clergy during the harsh winters of the last years of the *ancien régime*. In 1785–6, the recteur of Theix provided employment for the poor by paying them to repair two bridges: had he been the actual tithe owner, he told the intendant, he would have been able to do more.[173] The curé of Ailly-le-Haut-Clocher spent his patrimonial income of 800 livres a year entirely on feeding the hungry who flocked in from all around, especially from Abbeville, to take advantage of his generosity.[174] In the spring of 1787, in the Breton parish of Berné, plague arrived on top of hunger as a scourge of the inhabitants; 'the only man in the parish who is generous and a friend of humanity', said the local surgeon, 'is their pastor'; he had sold his table silver and was living only on rye bread so that he could help others.[175] Jallet, curé of Chérigné, was finding 24 livres a week himself to add to the contributions of a few richer parishioners to maintain the poor, and when he went up as a deputy to the Estates General, he gave all his stock of grain away.[176]

In crises of a different kind—some parochial lawsuit against a seigneur or other influential person, the curé was expected to give leadership, maybe to go off to the distant town for long sojourns with lawyers. When plague drew near, it was the clergy above all who had to stay in place when others fled; when other sorts of danger threatened, their people would look to them for leadership, heroism even. In the 1780s we hear of a curé of the Châlons area fording a river in flood sixteen times to carry infirm parishioners to safety,[177] and another of Lorraine who was lowered into a collapsing well to rescue a trapped bricklayer (he offered a reward first of all to anyone who would do it, and when there were no takers, went down himself).[178] From the later years of Louis XIV comes the remarkable story of the curé of a coastal village taking command when the English fleet loomed on the horizon, threatening invasion; he lined up the armed coastguards on the beach, and behind them had all the inhabitants, women and girls included, wearing red hats, and some mounted on horses, donkeys, and cows—giving the appearance, from a distance, of a force of infantry and cavalry.[179]

These of course are exceptional incidents—but they illustrate an atmosphere of relationships very different from the manifold tales of arguments about tithe or surplice-fees. In everyday contacts, in any case, a curé tended to have genial, albeit businesslike, relations with his people. Witness curé Barbotin's letters from the Estates General at Versailles to the priest who was looking after his parish in his absence. 'I haven't paid for the wood I bought from Jean-Baptiste Devaney. He owes me money and I owe him. I am persuaded that he is not well off. If you can give him a few écus, that would be fine.' 'There is no need to ask for a receipt from honest folk.' 'I must set an example in paying my debts.' Then, apropos of a small sum owed to him (Barbotin is not sure just how much it is): 'If he pays, accept it; if not, do not press him, because he can't be well off.'[180] Another glimpse of friendly relationships comes in an obituary notice in a parish register concerning a curé who had refurnished his church (which had been 'a real stable of Bethlehem'), and set up a fund to provide milk for children and to award an annual prize for 'wisdom and virtue' to a girl elected by the parish.

He fell ill at Fresney where he had gone to see his family, on 1 December 1780. Immediately he set off back to his parish . . . On arrival, knowing that he was dying, he solemnly received the sacraments on the fifth of the month, and died on the ninth at six in the evening, loved and regretted by all his people and especially by his successor, who had always been his friend.[181]

Another entry in a register gives a glimpse of an ancient, worthy curé in high serious mood:

Today, 8 June 1762, having taken possession of this parish on 8 June 1712, for 50 years I have lived and live still without trouble and in peace with all men. But I have every reason to fear the terrible judgements of God who has confided to me, over so long a period, the care of thousands of souls—

a perilous task. *Pasce oves meas!* He will demand a rigorous account of them from me. *Itaque miseremi mei vos saltem, amice mei, et orate.*[182]

We do well not to forget that the diverse and picturesque concourse of the curés of the *ancien régime*, however worldly or rumbustious some of them seem, consists of men who knew that they lived in the shadow of judgement.

13

COLLABORATORS OF THE CURÉ

I *Life at the Presbytery—the housekeeper*

Most curés were ill housed. The reason was simple: the parish had to provide the presbytery and do the major repairs, and the inhabitants were never willing to part with money. Royal ordinances specified what the minimum accommodation must be. In 1695, it was two rooms with fireplaces, a kitchen, barn, cellar, and stable; in 1776, this was improved to the standard kitchen, stable, barn, and cellar, a bedroom with a little 'cabinet', a study, and another room suitable for hospitality.[1] In bigger towns, the law was better observed than elsewhere; there were more parishioners, often, to pay the rates; there were more respectable people who had to be entertained; and ecclesiastical authority was nearer at hand to see that decency was maintained. In Angers, a parlour, a dining-room, and two to five other rooms with fireplaces are found.[2] In the limited number of country parishes where the curé drew fat tithes, his house was likely to correspond to his affluence, since successive generations of incumbents would have had the means to improve and extend at their own expense. At Chauffailles in the diocese of Mâcon, where from 1728 onwards for thirty years the curé had paid for a rebuilding programme, there was a walled garden, a 'pretty courtyard enclosed with walls and a gateway' with a brand-new barn and stable on one side, while the house had a vestibule with a decorated ceiling, a dining-room and a study, both panelled, and a stone staircase leading up to 'two handsome rooms, excellent accommodation', with two small bedrooms alongside them.[3] But in any case, even the most agreeable country vicarage was likely to resemble a farmhouse rather than a mansion. The one at Clohars-Carnoët in Brittany was supposed to be attractive, but this was chiefly because it offered barn, stable, dovecote, pigsty, winepress, bakery, and two cellars, one for wine and one for cider, all in good order.[4] In the poorer rural areas and in parishes with a small population, the curé often lived in something approaching squalor. The inhabitants would never agree that this was the case, of course; many were so much worse off than he was, and the few who were better off would have to pay a substantial rate if his house was to be improved. The curé of Flaxien in the diocese of Belley appealed to the intendant to enforce a rebuilding; he had, he said, no more than a kitchen, cellar, bedroom, and small study, with half the roof consisting of thatch in a dangerous condition. A small committee of the more important citizens, however, reported that he had one 'spacious, splendid room', together with three smaller ones—a study, a bedroom, and a spare room—'le tout en fort bon état'. The *subdélégué* reporting to the intendant complained that 'these gentlemen, the curés, all want to be lodged like seigneurs'.[5] Whatever the truth of the matter, one doubts that phrase 'all in good order'. Curés continually complained that their parishioners refused to concern themselves with the vicarage until it was actually falling down. 'My house lets in everything except light,' said one, and he went on to describe how one of his parish registers had been totally eaten by rats.[6] Another wrote a comic poem about the frogs which had taken up residence in the pools in his sitting-room, and how he had to keep moving his bed around to avoid drips from the ceiling.[7]

In 1786, the parish clergy of the diocese of Comminges had to report to their bishop just how they were lodged; making allowance for their natural bias and the fact that this was a poor diocese, their replies are revealing. Few were precise about their available space; one had eight rooms, four had two up and two down, one had two rooms, and one had a single chamber only. But some gave picturesque descriptions of their misery. 'I am in danger of being buried in the ruins of the old seigneurial castle.' 'A very simple presbytery: one room and a lean-to with a wooden roof and no walls; no means of locking up, and adjoining the cemetery; it's a house isolated from all others, where I have the dead as my only neighbours.' 'The presbytery of Cazeneuve is . . . uninhabitable—without a chimney, propped between two very old houses and in continual danger of collapse and, although it is on high ground, it's mainly subterranean, like a bottle that is immersed in a bucket of water to cool the wine.' Thus, the curé has to live elsewhere, at Saint-Elix, his subordinate church, 'the only place where he was able to find a room fourteen paces wide and eighteen paces long, and even so, having to keep his firewood, wine, grain and horse in eight different sheds'. 'The presbytery is a sewer and in a very bad state, badly situated and dangerously unhealthy because of damp.' 'The presbytery is much dilapidated, perched on a rock exposed to the storms—no comfort here; no stable, no hen-house, no garden; in a word, uninhabitable.'[8] These were among the worst cases, of course. The total statistics which came in to the bishop's office showed that sixty-four vicarages were in good repair (eleven having been rebuilt by parishes and six by the curés out of their own pockets), sixty needed major repair (of which half a dozen needed total reconstruction), and eleven were uninhabitable. There were, in addition, twenty-one pastors who simply had no house at all and lodged where they could (one had a single room in a house occupied by two families, 'which causes all sorts of unpleasantness'[9]).

In the official prescription of accommodation in a presbytery, nothing was provided for the housekeeper; if she lived in, she might well have to sleep in the kitchen. Some curés were looked after by a female relative. A family which made sacrifices to get a son into the priesthood expected some reciprocity; a widowed mother, an aunt, a sister[10] needed a home, just as a celibate priest needed a housekeeper—and the two necessities sometimes conveniently coincided. Orphaned nieces were a special problem; the wills of curés frequently include provision for them,[11] and Restif has a moving story about a parish priest who saved for years to accumulate dowries for two of them, then gave all the money to his parishioners to rescue them from starvation after a terrible fire.[12] When a niece came to live at the presbytery, there was lively interest in the village: maybe she was given to good works, or perhaps just embarrassingly ultra-pious; maybe she got pregnant or married some riotous husband[13]—or was she a niece at all? There was always scope for gossip.

But whether the housekeeper of the curé was a relative or—as was more likely—not, she was one of the most intriguing figures in the chronicles and mythology of rural France. Every diocese had its stern synodal statute devised to prevent young women from taking up this prestigious office—at least 40 years of age was a common formula, some even said 50.[14] Bishops tended to interpret the rules strictly; a relaxation granted because aged parents were present, as chaperones as it were, would be withdrawn when they died, and priests who were of advanced years themselves could rarely hope for indulgence, 'as if age ever took away concupiscence'.[15] Yet the rules were frequently infringed, often because it was simply impossible to find a suitable person within them. There were heavy farmyard chores[16] to do, as well as cooking and cleaning; the place had to be protected from insistent beggars and sinister prowlers;[17] there were messages to carry, often at a distance; and it was important for the housekeeper to get around the village gossiping, partly to report back about which way public opinion was moving,[18] and partly to drop appropriate hints in prosperous households about current needs in the presbytery. If he could afford it, a curé also needed a manservant, a *valet*[19] to do repairs, gather the tithes, thrash the grain, dig the garden, and groom the horse, and if this all-purpose handyman had a young wife who did the vicarage housekeeping, what could be more reasonable? If the age rule were strictly observed, the position might soon be reached when the curé was burdened with an ancient *gouvernante* who had to have a young maidservant to help her, whose labours she would grumpily supervise from her permanent chair at the fireside, from whence she would talk endlessly to all callers of 'the cows, of the vicaire, of the hens and of God, of the rosary and of werewolves, of the virtue of the scapulary against fevers and agues, and of apparitions of the dead, muttering an occasional enlivening chorus learned from some stupid mission preacher'.[20]

Gossip about the clergy jumping into bed with their housekeepers was inevitable and (as we have argued) largely unjustified in the eighteenth century, except in backward and isolated areas. Even so, relations between curés and their *gouvernantes* were necessarily close and often friendly; there were consultations about local problems, discussions about the advisability of accepting some preferred new benefice.[21] Curé Barbotin at the Estates General often thought of his Catherine and her husband back at home; he was concerned for her comfort, amused at her foibles, alarmed at her illness, and when the Revolution confiscated half his income, he promised to continue to support them: 'as long as I have bread to eat, I'll try to keep both of them'.[22] Direct questions about sexual morality, yes or no, are not the best way to understand these subtle relationships. Curé Jacques-Joseph Besse of Saint-Aubin (Avesnes) explained, long afterwards, to an investigating papal official, why he had married his housekeeper during the Revolution. She had served him for twenty-four years, refusing offers of marriage on the assumption that he would provide for her in her old age. Having a little land of his own, which he could not legally settle upon her unless she was his wife, he had married her. 'She was justified in relying on the uprightness of my heart!' He claimed that he had lived chastely before his marriage, but he could not help thinking that the rule of celibacy for the clergy was a mistaken one—and he wished things had been otherwise for him all those years ago.[23] This is a story about a long friendship, not to be frowned upon by the austere, or what is worse, treated with a wry Clochemerlian tolerance.

II *The vicaires*

As a rule of thumb in eighteenth-century pastoral calculations, the curé of a rural parish with 500 communicants needed a vicaire to help him.[24] There were other factors involved, of course: the extent and difficulty of the terrain, the availability of masses at the chapels of monasteries, seigneurs, or confraternities, the presence of *prêtres habitués* or tonsured clerks to give assistance, the age and health of the incumbent himself. A town parish was different: a compact population of three times the size could be served by a single pastor.[25] So far as a reasonable equation of population with clerical manpower was concerned, the traditional boundaries of parishes were often absurd, but the allocation of assistant clergy frequently helped to remedy the imbalance. Of the dozen town parishes of Angers, three tiny ones were served by the curé alone, and a fourth had a vicaire only because of the duties connected with the perpetual adoration of the Holy Sacrament at its altar. Six parishes had two vicaires each, and there were two others which were specially favoured with more. One was the splendid official parish of Saint-Michel du Tertre, in whose church the mayors had their pew and where the walls were lined with the tombs of the Angevin magistracy, and in whose narrow streets, amidst numerous dwelling-houses, the prison and most of the tennis-courts, billiard-saloons, gaming-houses, and inns of the city were found; here were four vicaires. There was also the huge working-class parish of La Trinité, with its 11,000 population, which had five.[26] For different reasons, the curé of Antibes in the diocese of Grasse had been allowed the same high number of assistants; though there were only 4,500 inhabitants, there was a large military garrison permanently stationed there, and the Crown, which collected the local tithes, was disposed to be generous in making provision for a peculiarly difficult pastoral situation.[27] In the huge parishes of Paris, curés presided over confraternities of bustling, ambitious vicaires as well as a multitude of *prêtres habitués*. Maybe they would operate as a team, as at Saint-Laurent, where the eccentric and charitable abbé Cottrell, a hypochondriac who never ventured outside in winter and was perpetually shouting 'Fermez-moi cette porte!', left one of his staff to arrange the complicated duty rosters;[28] maybe they would be allocated to particular districts, as in 1739 the curé of Saint-Germain-l'Auxerrois broke up his empire into nine sectors, each to be pastorally directed by one of the vicaires.[29] Often, such delegation of duties followed naturally from the geography of the parish, as at

Notre-Dame of Alençon, where the two vicaires were stationed at each of the two dependent churches.[30]

Ask in any parish, and almost everywhere curé and people would say how welcome a vicaire would be to give a helping hand—provided they did not have to pay for him. Usually, the tithe owner was responsible for the salary—that is, the curé himself or, if he was on the *congrue*, the person or institution which actually held the great tithes. There was an official *congrue* laid down for a vicaire: 150 livres, raised to 200 in 1768, to 250 in 1778, to 300 in 1784. The inhabitants, who might have to pay something if the tithe could not cover the cost, were in any case legally responsible for finding lodgings (though not furniture) for their vicaire;[31] in practice, they tended to expect the parish priest to put him up in the presbytery. Since a vicariate was not a benefice, the holder, strictly speaking, had to be in possession of the clerical 'title', which meant an extra 100 livres or so in addition to the *congrue*. Thus, towards the end of the *ancien régime*, one might assume that a vicaire with his free lodgings and *congrue* was securely above the poverty line, though far from well-off.

Having said this, we must remember that, as usual in eighteenth-century France, there were almost as many exceptions to the rule as examples confirming it. Sometimes, a parish contrived to have a vicaire without being able to offer the official salary; a mere pittance, backed up by permission to cultivate a piece of the common land, perhaps, or a fee for acting as village schoolmaster.[32] On the other hand, there might be something over and above the general *congrue*. A common ingredient in a salary, or a supplement to it, was an annual offering, often in kind, with the vicaire going from door to door to collect it. In Brittany, where the parlement had forbidden this embarrassing exercise, there were parishes where a local rate was levied in lieu, others where a few pious families came forward with voluntary donations, and mean ones where no supplement at all was offered.[33] Sometimes, an old custom or the proceeds of a legacy helped out—a tribute of butter as a reward for performing some monthly liturgical observance in one place,[34] a substantial fund yielding no less than 600 livres a year to the lucky vicaire in another.[35] The parish of Linselles in the diocese of Tournai got along comfortably with a vicaire who drew 335 livres a year from the local seigneur for acting as his chaplain, the community doing no more than adding a small supplement for saying a low mass every Sunday. But in 1742, the bishop refused to allow the doubling-up of seigneurial chaplain and vicaire to continue; the community, unwilling to add to its charges, hired a Capuchin cheaply to say the low masses; the angry curé got the bishop to ban the Capuchin from celebrating—and so it went on to 1750, when all was settled at the expense of the tithe owner.[36]

Here indeed was the general difficulty in obtaining a vicaire when one was needed: it was a new burden on the tithe owner, and he was unlikely to pay up cheerfully. Witness, for example, a battle of claim and counter-claim which took place in the early eighteenth century between the parish of Vaulx and the canons of Saint-Géry of Cambrai over the inhabitants' demand for a vicaire to serve the dependent chapel of Vraucourt. The parishioners said that some of them had to walk half a league to church, the canons said a quarter (and surely it was not reasonable to take into account everyone who was foolish enough to build a house on the fringes of the parish). Some people had to cross a dangerous stream; the canons asked why they did not build better bridges, and denied that anyone had ever died without the sacraments because of floods. The area is subject to warfare; if so, replied the canons, everyone runs away, so no clergy are needed. The curé said he needed help in hearing confessions; the canons agreed, seeing that he was away from the place half the time and was principally engaged in mending clocks. (Merely a hobby, replied the curé.) Finally, the archbishop's commissioners arrived, accompanied by a professional surveyor and an assistant to carry his instruments—the parish was measured out, and it was solemnly ruled that Vaulx and Vraucourt were so close together that a vicaire was not necessary, so the canons saved their money.[37] The diocesan ruling might not be the end of the matter; there were curés who went up to the parlement or even beyond to the Royal Council to extract a *congrue* to pay an assistant. When François-Antoine Drogy, doctor of the Sorbonne and a son of a minor family of the robe, took over the parish of Saint-Nicolas at Coutances in 1773, he found himself with 6,000 parishioners and only one vicaire, whom he had to pay himself out of a total income of 1,622 livres (*congrue*, surplice-fees, and foundation masses all included). He needed four helpers, let alone one, he told the bishop. Since he insisted on his point, the orders finally came down from Bayeux for the holding of the usual enquiry into 'the extent of the parish, the size of the population, and the difficulty of the roads'. When it appeared that the tithe-owning prelate was not likely to pay (there was a flaw in Drogy's case—there were fourteen *prêtres habitués* in his parish), he wrote around to his colleagues asking for advice. Gervais de la Prise, curé of Saint-Pierre of Caen, it turned out, was already suing the bishop before the parlement of Paris for just such a grievance. Wiser heads suggested a petition, backed by a few other parish priests, to the Assembly General of the Clergy, suggesting that some of the funds that maintained the *habitués* should be confiscated and turned from the support of 'drones' to the payment of genuine vicaires.[38]

According to handbooks of spirituality, the vicariate was a period of apprenticeship to pastoral expertise and the building-up of the interior life of prayer; according to the legal ones, it was an interval of manœuvre and intrigue to obtain a permanent benefice. Influence and contacts were important; indeed a newly ordained priest without them might not even find a suitable place as a vicaire for a while. Living at home or with friends he would say masses at 12 sols a time or walk in funeral processions at a rather higher fee, and preach the two or three sermons he had off by heart in parishes willing to offer him the proceeds of the collection. Out of this meagre income (it is the memoirs of the abbé Lesage, a priest of the diocese of Saint-Brieuc at the end of the *ancien régime*, which recount these details[39]), his first expenditure was to provide himself with the basic equipment of the wage-earning ecclesiastic, a watch, an umbrella, a good-quality long cassock, and a collection of cribs of sermon notes. Finally, a parochial vacancy would come his way—maybe just a *vicariat de tolérance* (helping out temporarily) or, much more satisfactory, a *vicariat fondé*, an established post.[40] Since the ultimate object was promotion, and a degree of subservience was inevitable, it was best (said a cheerfully cynical curé giving advice to junior clergy) to avoid taking up service under a young parish priest; he was likely to be proud and a hard taskmaster, and to have an old mother or aunt or young niece coming to live with him, so many unpredictable womenfolk to be humoured and placated. Failing an uncle or a friend of the family, look for some old parish priest with no relatives who has fallen out with his parishioners—just the man to leave you independently in charge and to nominate you as his successor when he decides to resign and take his pension.[41]

Vicaires moved around. Some posts were much more attractive than others—a better salary, more agreeable society, better chances of promotion. An assistant priest who made his mark as a pastor or a preacher, or who was well connected, would get his own parish quickly; one who was something of a failure might think it wise to start again somewhere else—indeed, he might be encouraged to do so. In the village of Aubais, in 1748, the abbé David left after four years, having accidentally shot the local surgeon in the leg when they were out hunting; the abbé Favre, a sentimental preacher beloved of the ladies, was called to higher things; Père de la Croix, a monk, arrived in 1757, but moved within the year to become an army chaplain; his successor, Clément, departed even more rapidly, being virtually hooted out of the church by the congregation.[42] Since only about half the rural parishes had a vicaire, the overall proportion of rural benefices to applicants was not unfavourable (from the massive documentation put together in the investigations of 1790, it seems that 20,500 vicaires were waiting for the deaths or resignations of 39,000 curés[43]). Thus, while much would depend upon circumstances and local supply and demand, promotion to a parish of one's own was not likely to be delayed more than ten years.[44] In 1766, a vicaire of Orléans wrote some comic verses addressed to his bishop (did he send them?), pronouncing himself ripe for becoming a parochial curé ('I am an expert at funerals,' he said; 'when I bury them, they don't come back'); he had been a subordinate for seven years, and clearly regarded this as over the average.[45] Even so, in every diocese we find priests who were stranded for ever in the vicariate. Some, it is true, might not aspire to go further. To be a senior vicaire in one of the great Parisian parishes was to be an ecclesiastic of some distinction—like the rotund abbé Jay, premier vicaire of Saint-Barthélémy as Mme Roland remembered him: severe of mien and a man of business, with a private income, two brothers successful notaries living nearby, and a horse-faced, aristocratic female relative running his household and laying on lavish dinners and agreeable parties at tric-trac.[46] Or there were the eccentrics deaf to the call of ambition—perhaps through innate diffidence or disciplined humility, or even through aristocratic pride. Chateaubriand never forgot how, as a boy, he was given an écu wrapped in a dirty piece of paper by his relative the abbé de Chateaubriand de la Guéronde—hefty, red-faced, with an unkempt wig, torn cassock, dirty shoes, holed stockings, plodding along with his big stick and muttering his matins; he was just a vicaire, but he had blown up the prince de Condé for insulting him by the offer of a tutorship in a ducal household.[47] But mostly, the unpromoted vicaire was a melancholy failure. Even if, over long years, he settled happily locally, what if a thrusting new curé arrived and sacked him?[48] And what happened when he was too old to carry on? A curé could always resign and keep a third of his income, but there was no such resort for the aged vicaire. Well-meaning bishops tried to set up institutions to receive them, but how could a parochial pastor settle down, in the company of fellow geriatrics, to 'a monastic type of life, meals only in the refectory, having to attend choir and sing the psalms, in a house in which there was a superior over him and porters in charge at the gates? He'd rather beg or starve.'[49]

III *The* prêtres habitués

Though the Church in France was like a hierarchical pyramid, with some footholds for ability and many more for birth and influence to assist ambitious climbers to work their way upwards, the analogy needs modification. At every level of the crumbling traditional monument there were horizontal side-tracks and devious openings and passages, leading to comfortable chambers, sunny niches, and convenient ledges, places where the modest, the unspiritual, or the ruthlessly ascetic cleric might decide to rest a while, or even to stay in perpetuity. Just as there were great aristocrats who were content with the unearned income of an abbey *in commendam* without hankering after a bishopric, so there were ordinary priests (large numbers of them—one estimate runs as high as 10,000[50]) content to live on the margins of the parochial structure, enjoying—for good or bad reasons—their leisure and independence. 'Immediately after his ordination,' it was said of one of these, 'he returned to his village and occupied himself with manual labour, digging the garden, chopping wood, scything grass, churning the milk, content to repeat his daily office every evening and to say a mass every Sunday in a private chapel.'[51] Curé Gauthier the essayist knew such a one—a big, leather-jacketed peasant type, spending all the week on his farm and giving no help to the curé except that he came in to say the early mass on Sunday mornings.[52] Others, perhaps with some private means or some small benefice without cure of souls, or maybe dependent entirely on what could be scraped together from ecclesiastical fees, hung around a particular church earning small sums from saying masses, helping in various ceremonies or undertaking some duties like those of sacristan. In the archdiocese of Besançon they were called *vicaires domestiques*, as distinguished from the genuine *vicaires canoniques*; elsewhere they went by the names of *obitiers, choristes, chapelains fondés, prêtres libres, familiers*, and, the most general name, *prêtres habitués*.

The big parishes of Paris were haunts of these supernumerary clergy. In the preliminary elections to the Estates General of 1789, in the fifty-two parishes of the capital, 600 'parish clergy' voted; there were 23 at Saint-Merry, 36 at Saint-Germain-l'Auxerrois, 62 at Saint-Nicolas-du-Chardonnet, 72 at Saint-Eustache, and 85 at

Saint-Roch. At Saint-Étienne-du-Mont there were 173, but this is a figure of a rather different kind, as it includes many academic teachers and students in holy orders.[53] Alternatively, an idea of the number of priests around in the capital can be gained by looking at the expense accounts of distinguished funerals. At Saint-Sulpice on 15 November 1785, the coffin of an aristocratic lady was accompanied by the curé, a vicaire, 'le vicaire des convois', 'le confesseur en robe et gants', and sixty other ecclesiastics, all paid for attending.[54] In the city of Bordeaux at the end of the *ancien régime* there were 77 priests belonging to the *sociétés de bénéficiers* which existed in eight parishes, and another 44 *prêtres habitués* (all these in priests' orders: there were also 108 deacons and subdeacons, sacrists, and tonsured clerks).[55] It was not always ancient foundations and legacies which provided the funds to maintain this pool of supplementary ecclesiastical labour. Versailles was a new town with a convent of Récollets, but no abbeys or collegiate churches and only one ancient parish; here, the royal parish of Notre-Dame (founded in 1682) had thirty priests available, the aristocratic parish of Saint-Louis (founded in 1754) had twenty-five, while Saint-Symphorien (founded in the late Middle Ages), which served the working-class population, had only four.[56] In some places, more especially in Brittany, there were towns and bigger villages which hired supernumerary priests, called *prêtres de chœur*; a vacancy was announced with the other notices at Sunday mass; candidates had to present a certificate of good morals, and were tested for vocal musical ability, and the winner would be appointed to office by the parish council.[57] Depending on the amount of surplice-fees available, they might earn from 30 livres a year in a rural place to up to 250 in a town, though not all towns were profitable places—only about 50 livres was available in Coutances or Cherbourg, and at Alençon it was said that their income would barely pay for the laundry of their surplices.[58]

    An unbeneficed hanger-on was very much an ecclesiastical dogsbody; there were, however, certain *prêtres habitués* who held modestly dignified formal offices in their local church, living corporately in a sort of 'college' (probably presided over by the curé, just as a dean presided over a cathedral chapter), enjoying a recognized place in society and an income from some ancient foundation. Usually, the original founder had laid down the conditions of eligibility for membership; probably it was necessary to have been born in the town or in the actual parish, or to have parents of local lineage, or even to be 'founder's kin'. Such privileged little corporations were the *prêtres filleuls* and the *communalistes* found in various

churches in the dioceses of Saint-Flour and Limoges and, more especially, Clermont (129 communities there);[59] so also were the forty or
so communities of *mépartistes* in the dioceses of Autun, Mâcon,
Langres, Chalon-sur-Saône, and Dijon (there were five in the city of
Dijon itself).[60] There were also sixty colleges of priests under the
name of *familiarités* in Franche Comté,[61] and the *enfants prêtres* of
Mirecourt in Lorraine.[62] Cournot tells how his grandfather transferred his practice of notary to the little town of Gray in Franche
Comté specifically to ensure that his sons would qualify, if they so
desired, for such an ecclesiastical sinecure.[63] A family man had to be
far-sighted; a young priest who became one of the *filleuls* of Saint-
Gervais in Paris obtained entrance only after a long lawsuit—parishioners had priority for entrance, but he had been born prematurely,
while his mother was making a social call outside the boundaries. He
was lucky, won his case, and enjoyed 200 livres a year for life.[64] The
members of the communities naturally wished to limit the number
of entrants so as to leave more money for each of them in the distributions from the common fund. In 1752, the nine *filleuls* of
Montaigut (whose income was very low) sent a legal officer, a
huissier, to their curé to warn him formally that there were young
clerics of dubious qualifications seeking the priesthood solely to get
access to the revenues of their guild: let him not give any of them
attestations of good morals or certificates of belonging to the parish
until formal announcements had been made in church, so that
challenges could be made against them.[65]

In theory, a college of priests attached to a parish ought to have
been a boon to the curé: in practice, many parish priests did not find
this to be the case, and most would have wished to replace them
with proper vicaires. At the church of Saint-Pierre in Caen, there
were twelve *habitués* earning no less than 500 livres a year each;
resplendent in grey cloaks, they gave themselves the airs of canons.
At the beginning of the century, the curé went to law to try to
confiscate two of their places for vicaires; they always say they help
me, he complained, but when you ask one to preach, he has a sore
throat; to visit the sick, and he has an attack of cramp; to take a
catechism, and a fit of diarrhoea strikes him just when the class is
about to begin, and they are everlastingly away visiting sick relatives.
The bishop of Bayeux tried in vain to reform them. They remained,
said the curé in 1787, 'a swarm of useless and idle drones who eat
the honey of the bees'.[66] Nearby in Caen was the parish of Saint-
Nicolas with 10,000 population and only one vicaire; the four *obitiers*
and two other supernumerary priests were of little use, said the curé

in 1785. 'Only one occupies himself with pastoral duties. The others, being independent, spend their time in sheer idleness, or in forming cabals to defeat my best efforts, stirring up the parishioners and sounding the alarm at the least thing that displeases them.'[67] In the diocese of Clermont, where communities of *filleuls* flourished more than anywhere else, curés struggled continually against them; a parish priest on the *congrue* was sometimes financially worse off than they were, and one who was a newcomer found them entrenched with popular support, for they were by definition members of local families. In 1724, Bishop Massillon issued an ordinance against these 'idle priests who regard themselves as masters of the churches and . . . expend all their zeal in denying to the curés the rights which are essential to their office'; accordingly, he laid down rules giving curés and vicaires precedence at all ceremonies, and prescribing fines on *filleuls* for every absence from masses, vespers, and processions. In 1764, a later bishop of Clermont tightened these rules and imposed an examination for admission to the communities, in which the curé would have the decisive voice.[68] Occasionally, disputes between parish priests and corporations of *habitués* came up before the parlements, with varying outcomes, for the instinct of the magistrates to favour the pastoral ministry sometimes clashed with their devotion to ancient custom. The most successful case for the curés was one of 1766, when the parlement of Lorraine cracked down on the *enfants prêtres* of Mirecourt, subordinating them to the parish clergy, and even denying them corporate status.[69]

From the curé's point of view, the usefulness of a community of *habitués* depended very much on the degree of control he could exercise over its members. In the vast parish of Saint-Gervais in Paris, where sixty of them (freely recruited, though preference was given to candidates born within the parish) lived together in a sort of seminary under central discipline, they were indispensable. Curé François Feu, who resigned in 1699, left his substantial fortune to help to maintain them. During the reign of his nephew, namesake, and successor, however, the value of the investments maintaining the community collapsed, and the new man arriving in 1762 was in despair at having only thirty priests, inadequately paid at that, to keep going the manifold parochial activities.[70] But to control subordinates who had independent sources of income and could not be dismissed was difficult. The curé of Sainte-Feyre (diocese of Clermont) had a college of priests of which he was the head (enjoying a double share in their distributions), and they were formally his vicaires, doing ordinary parish duties. Even so, he was not happy with such permanently established and influential collaborators, and in 1723, 1735, and 1748 he went to law, unsuccessfully, to try to suppress their foundation.[71] In the little town of Ille in Roussillon, the curé seemed to have triumphed in 1736 when he got the ecclesiastical courts to order the local community of priests to provide him with two vicaires; in fact, by 1765, everyone wanted the end of the arrangement, for pastoral authority had disintegrated and the parish complained of having three heads instead of one.[72]

Ecclesiastical reformers looked coldly on footloose priests outside the official command structure, and the trend of the late seventeenth century was to replace *habitués* with vicaires wherever possible. In the diocese of La Rochelle there had been 110 *habitués* and 175 vicaires in 1648; by 1724 there were fewer than a dozen *habitués* and about 200 vicaires.[73] (These figures suggest that it was easier to get rid of abuses than to find the money for improvements.) The eighteenth century saw the decline of most of the colleges and communities of supernumerary priests—whether as a result of the hostility of the curés, the rigour of new regulations imposed by bishops, the decline of revenues by maladministration, or because of changes in the attitude of public opinion towards sinecures and clerical idleness. We have seen how the curé of Saint-Gervais lost half of his team of assistants. Most of the *mépartistes* of the diocese of Autun were gone by mid-century.[74] At Ille, the college which had thirty-one priests in 1732 was down to twenty-three in 1763;[75] at Sainte-Feyre, the income which had once maintained twenty priests was divided among eight in 1700, among two or three in 1750, until by 1790 there was only one to share with the curé.[76] In the first half of the century the *filleuls* of Notre-Dame of Aurillac were sixty-strong; by 1789 the number of their 'prebends' was halved, and some were unfilled.[77] At Treignac-sur-Vézéré in the Limousin the *prêtres filleuls* who had sixteen members in the mid-seventeenth century were down to three in 1700, and survived to 1789 with only one or two members.[78] The sixteen places of the *société de bénéficiers* of the parish of Saint-Michel in Bordeaux were mostly empty by the end of the *ancien régime*.[79] These were all communities in towns (albeit some of them were very small ones—2,000 inhabitants constituted a 'town' by the standards of the *ancien régime*); in other words, in the more sophisticated places where opinion was hardening against abuses. In the rural isolation of Raulhac-en-Caulades, however, the old ways were undisturbed, and in 1789 there was a community of eleven priests, all born in the parish and sons of fathers born there, sharing nearly 4,500 livres a year among themselves, adding to the income of their sinecure by commercial or agricultural work, and meeting from time to time to dine together—and, no doubt, to toast their generous fifteenth-century founder.[80]

The suppression of the colleges of the *prêtres habitués* by the Constituent Assembly in August 1790 was an inevitable reform: the Revolution did what bishops had been trying to do for more than a century. The chief result was that respectable, middling sort of families in provincial towns lost a comfortable resort of modest sinecures, and had to push their sons into the new bureaucracy. The Church was rid of a system which had encouraged dubious vocations, though it was also one which had provided opportunities for eccentric individuals to express themselves, sometimes with advantage to religion or society. The *prêtres habitués* ranged from peasant farmers, shopkeepers, idle young men who lived at home, and tired old men with private incomes who enjoyed the consideration accorded to ecclesiastics; to acolytes, sacristans, chaplains, and all the minor functionaries who kept the ceremonial life of the bigger churches going; to confessors, spiritual guides, and preachers; to students, tutors, scholars, and publicists. François de Chaffault, an *habitué* of Saint-Gervais, who made a will in 1714 leaving money to pay forty fellow priests ('only 40', he said modestly)[81] to walk in his funeral procession, had done well for himself by becoming chaplain to the duchesse d'Orléans. Pierre-Antoine Textoris of a solid family of Aurillac, which had often held municipal office, was a *prêtre filleul* there, and a tutor in a noble family and chaplain to a convent of nuns.[82] Michel-Claude Guibert of Dieppe, the son of an artisan, was ordained in 1721, and spent the rest of his days as an *habitué* of the church of Saint-Rémy, drawing a meagre 40 livres a year which he made up to 200 by saying masses and acting as chaplain to two local charitable institutions. In a long, laborious lifetime (he died in 1784 at the age of 87) he wrote a massive chronicle of the history of Dieppe, which earned him election to the academy of Rouen and nomination as a notable of his native town.[83] It does not become a fellow historian to complain too much of the abusive system which gave leisure for research and writing to a colleague and predecessor in the great tradition which we serve.

14

CANONS AND CHAPTERS

I

There were 130 cathedrals in France, one for each diocese. Strictly speaking, there were 131, for the diocese of Sisteron had two, the collegiate church of Forcalquier having the title of 'con-cathédrale'; in its choir there was an episcopal throne, and a new bishop had to come to the church to repeat his solemn entry and his oath.[1] There were lawsuits, but the parlement of Aix maintained the canons of Forcalquier in their rights. Most of the cathedrals were in towns of over 2,000 inhabitants; perhaps fifteen were in smaller places—Saint-Lizier in the Pyrenees was a hamlet, Vaison an encampment in a Gallo-Roman ruin. The diocese of Glandève had no cathedral in its episcopal town, a flood having swept it away, so there was a miserable substitute in the tiny town of Entrevaux. Rennes presented the unusual spectacle of a chapter without a church, as the cathedral had been destroyed in the great fire of 1720; rebuilding was proceeding intermittently, but by the Revolution the new walls were only five feet high.

The diocesan chapters were not the only collegiate churches: there were at least 500 others.[2] Some were rich and splendid, like Saint-Honoré in Paris and Saint-Martin in Tours, others were little more than seigneurial chapels founded to pray for the souls of the lords of some estate; between these extremes there were all sorts of variants. Because of the distribution of dioceses, the cathedrals were mainly in the South, while the other collegiate churches were concentrated in the richer North, above the Bordeaux–Valence line. Half of them were in places with over 2,000 inhabitants, though there were larger towns entirely without them—Le Havre, Dieppe, Fécamp, and, much larger still, over 20,000, Caen, Versailles, and Brest. A quarter of the collegiate churches were in episcopal cities: Lyon had eight, Soissons six (for only 8,000 people), Le Mans and Angers four, Reims and Marseille three, Paris thirteen. The cathedrals naturally claimed pre-eminence. Their chapters, they held, were 'the synod of the diocese' and the *de jure* council of the bishop.

By the eighteenth century, the bishops had become too powerful to be subjected to compulsory advice; even so, the cathedral would be a focus for diocesan affairs through the activities of individual canons—archdeacons, *grands vicaires*, the *official*, and the *promoteur*. And in a vacancy of the see, its chapter took over the administration of the diocese, holding synods, issuing pastoral letters, consecrating the holy oils, absolving reserved cases, supervising the ecclesiastical court, and (though this was disputed) instituting to benefices. The other chapters of the town, however, would make a point of not being too deferential. They had their corporate pride, and such singularities and distinctions as they possessed would be flaunted against their colleagues at the cathedral. A classic feud was seen in the diocese of Cambrai,[3] the chapters of Saint-Géry and Sainte-Croix against the metropolitan chapter over representation in the provincial estates. In 1786, a coalition of the two minor chapters with the abbots of great monasteries, the provincial nobles, and Court interests around Calonne obtained a royal ruling depriving the cathedral of its privileged position, so the metropolitan canons shook the dust of the estates of the Cambrésis off their feet and attended no more. In some episcopal cities, the cathedral's claim to dominate rang hollow in face of the sheer riches and splendour of a rival. In Bordeaux, Saint-Seurin was on a level with the metropolitan church, as was Saint-Sernin in Toulouse. The canons of Saint-Honoré in Paris were much richer than those of Notre-Dame. In Tours,[4] Saint-Martin eclipsed the cathedral; the king himself had the supreme title of 'abbé', and princes of the blood and dukes were honorary canons; the fifty-one prebendal stalls and the eleven for dignitaries attracted vast incomes, and the minor clergy of the foundation, benefice holders, and *prêtres habitués* were 271 in number, one-sixth of the total of priests in the entire archdiocese.

There was no fixed number of canons for the chapter of a collegiate church, and not even an agreed optimum number. Of the cathedrals, adding dignitaries to the total, there were 93 at Chartres, 84 at Laon, 62 at Tours, 50 at Autun and Auxerre, 49 at Le Mans, 40 at Clermont, 32 at Lyon, and fewer than 30 at Angers, Alet, Tarbes, Boulogne, and Strasbourg. In a provincial town with three or four collegiate churches, the streets of the old city could see the coming and going of something like a hundred canons—at Reims,[5] Notre-Dame had 73, Saint-Symphorien 22, Saint-Timothée 13, Saint-Balsamie 13. By contrast, in the small dioceses of the South, there were cathedrals where there were hardly enough clergy to keep the liturgical services going, and the bishop had to call in curés from the countryside to make up the numbers when he officiated pontifically.[6] The cathedral of Agde was an exception, having substantial endowments, and therefore able to employ 68 ecclesiastics, a third of them priests—in a diocese where there were only 25 curés and 15 vicaires.[7]

There were vast disparities between chapters in the level of canonical incomes, though it is difficult to give precise figures; these were not available to outsiders at the time, and have proved elusive since. The total revenue of the foundation is not always a guide to what individuals drew, since the number of stalls and the responsibilities of the chapter have to be taken into account. There were good years and bad years, depending on the harvest, efficiency of land management, the accidents governing feudal dues, and the outcome of lawsuits. A canon might rise in income as he grew more senior, and deans and dignitaries drew supplements, sometimes double. Figures put forward in the second half of the century for canonical incomes in the cathedrals show Metz, Nîmes, and Bordeaux at 5,000 livres and more; Uzès, Nancy, Tarbes, and Angers at 3,000; Reims, Langres, Périgueux, Agen, Saint-Brieuc, and Amiens between 2,000 and 3,000; Sarlat and Bazas at about 1,500; Sens and Rennes at 700 to 900. Quimper and Autun were poor foundations with a sharp differentiation of income internally, the junior canons scraping along miserably until they went up a few rungs on the ladder of seniority. In some of the tiny dioceses of the South, there were cathedrals with more debts than income, so canons at Gap, Digne, Rieux, and Glandève got virtually nothing.[8]

There were similar wide diversities in incomes in the other collegiate churches. At Saint-Honoré in Paris, Saint-Martin at Tours, and Saint-Caprais at Agen the rewards were far above those offered in most cathedrals. Many, without having such wealth, nevertheless provided a comfortable life-style. Such a foundation was the church at Ecouis, a little town in Normandy.[9] The twelve canons each had a little house with a garden, grouped together in an enclosure cut off from the world by a high wall and from the church by several ranks of lime trees; none of their prebends yielded less than 2,000 livres a year, and the dean drew double. They said the services, looked after the parish, met in chapter every Wednesday and Friday, and were the leaders of local society. On similar incomes, the canons of Saint-Sauveur at Metz lived a dignified existence in an urban milieu. In the province of Guienne, there were rural canons whose incomes were less than those of the poorest parish priests on the *congrue*—not surprisingly, at Génissac and Villandraut they were to be unanimous in supporting the revolutionary church settlement—they did not regret the passing of the old ecclesiastical order.[10] In the diocese of Autun, the prebends of Avenay yielded 1,000 livres a year, while at Aigueperse and La Pré-sous-Arcy the canons no longer drew any remuneration. They had virtually ceased to perform any duties, except that at La Pré-sous-Arcy they met to celebrate a high mass on the great feast-days—that is, until 1757, when their penniless foundation was suppressed.[11]

Collegiate churches too poor to keep their liturgical offices going, with their canons wandering the countryside to earn a living, were anathema to reforming bishops, while the revenues of some of the others might have been employed more usefully elsewhere in the Church. Suppression, however, was not easy. Pensions had to be allotted to the chapter members, and arrangements made for the pastoral care of local people and the continuance of the masses for the souls of founders and benefactors. While the canons might be happy to be pensioned off, the laity of the place might object, out of conservatism, fear of the obligations of repairing the church, the drying up of income for local tradesmen, and the loss of sinecures for their children. The obligatory legal procedures of *de commodo et incommodo* gave all interested parties a chance to state their opposition, and the episcopal decree of suppression needed letters patent of the king registered in the parlement of the relevant jurisdiction to be effective. A less contentious way of proceeding was to leave the foundation extant but to suppress some of the prebends. Thus the archbishop of Sens, in a campaign to bring order among his collegiate churches between 1759 and 1778, ended two of them altogether, took a post of dignitary and three canonries from another, eleven canonical stalls from another, and seventeen chapels attached to the foundation from another.[12] A chapter might itself appeal to the king to allow a reduction in the number of prebends, or to leave one of them empty for a term of years to pay for some unusual expenditure, say, on the organ.

From the point of view of a chapter, however, the ideal remedy for poverty was a 'union', an extra benefice without cure of souls absorbed into the foundation, and petitions would be made to the king, the bishop, or, if there was one, a lay patron to ask for such a prize.[13] It was difficult, for all the *collèges*, seminaries, and hospitals were competing for similar annexations. More difficult still, for entirely different reasons, were prospects of union of a more sweeping kind, the merger of two chapters. The canons on either side would insist on getting a good bargain, financially, or in honorific distinctions and precedences. Willy-nilly, there had to be an amalgamation at Montauban in 1739, for the cathedral of Saint-Martin and the collegiate church of Saint-Etienne had been destroyed by the Protestants in the Wars of Religion, and the king had paid for building a single church for both of them.[14] Susceptibilities were allayed by making it a federal union, each group retaining its own *mense* (property and income), with the provost of Saint-Martin the head of the united chapter and the dean of Saint-Etienne next in seniority, the balance being evened by making the sacristan of Saint-Etienne the *ex officio* curé of the town parish. Another successful union took place at Le Mans in 1743, the two royal collegiate foundations there amalgamating, Saint-Pierre de la Cour absorbing the Sainte-Chapelle du Gué de Maulny.[15] On 11 February the clergy of the two churches processed together in copes, transferring the reserved Sacrament permanently from the one church to the other, singing as they went, 'Ecce quam bonum et quam jucundum, habitare fratres in unum'. It was indeed good and joyful, though it had taken three years of tight negotiations. For success, the chapters to be united needed to be in the same town, thus minimizing local protests, and have ample resources to pool, or, failing that, be able to balance superior riches on one side against superior distinction on the other—in the way daughters of financiers were married off to sons of nobles. In accordance with these rules, in 1744 two unions to bolster the revenues of metropolitan chapters were agreed: Isle-Barbe joined the cathedral of Lyon,[16] and Saint-Germain-l'Auxerrois joined Notre-Dame of Paris. For the most celebrated church in the land, Notre-Dame was poor, its canons drawing barely 2,500 livres a year, while at Saint-Germain-l'Auxerrois it was three times this. It took eight years of argument, the churchwardens of the parish of Saint-Germain and representatives of the university leading the opposition. In the end, two royal councillors negotiated a compromise, by which canonries would be extinguished as their holders died, up to the point when all the prebends afforded a suitably large income—by 1789, a canon of Notre-Dame had 7,000 livres.[17]

By contrast with these successes, the archbishop of Sens ran into insurmountable obstacles when he tried to unite the collegiate churches of Bray and Val de Provins to his cathedral.[18] The pastoral benefits were manifest: the metropole was under-endowed, and priests were needed to transfer to the pastoral ministry. From 1756 to 1770 negotiations went on, the inhabitants of Bray and Provins raising a clamour—money would move away from town and be spent elsewhere, and fewer priests would be available to help in their parishes. But the final rock of shipwreck proved to be the intransigence of the intended beneficiaries, the canons of Sens. By the proposed merger, the dignitaries of the two alien foundations would assume places in the choir subordinate, it is true, to the metropolitan dignitaries, but in advance of ordinary canons—this, they said, was 'revolting'. The archbishop sardonically replied that their pride had cost them 450 livres a year each, a 50 per cent rise of income thrown away.

Reform was slow, and all that could be done in the short term was to reduce anomalies and scandals. So, throughout the century, something over 600 chapters remained, containing perhaps 12,000 canons, a few very rich, many comfortably off, some living a meagre and threadbare existence. Given the hierarchical nature of the social order, the kind of appointments to the various canonries, rich and poor, may easily be predicted. A study of the incomes of the members of the twelve chapters of Guienne (including the extra benefices they held, along with the emoluments of their stalls) shows how the inegalitarian logic of the system operated: 'the canon conserves . . . a level comparable to that of the social group from which he derives'.[19]

II

A candidate for a stall in a particular collegiate church would scrutinize the canons in place, and wonder who would be the first to be called to higher things, in this world or the next. 'It is time for fortune to take an interest in my affairs,' wrote the abbé Siéyès, 'appearances are not favourable at the moment—all the canons are in marvellous good health.'[20] If chance seemed to beckon, he had to make enquiries to find where the power of appointment was vested, and this might vary according to which stall was involved and at what time of the year the vacancy occurred. Power to nominate might lie with the king, the bishop, the chapter, or outside persons or institutions, lay or ecclesiastical. If the chapter was the authority, nomination might be by election, by the holder of a particular prebend or, more likely, by the canon on duty, the 'canon of the week'—variously known as the 'chanoine hebdomadier', the 'chanoine en aigle', the 'chanoine en semaine de chape', the 'tournaire', or the 'semanier'. Quite often, there was a system of alternating appointment: for example, the king might appoint in certain months, and the chapter in others; or the division might come between canonries conferring seats on the left of the choir and those on the right, or there might be a simple turn for turn. Since Nancy[21] was a diocese newly created in 1771, one might assume that the arrangements for its cathedral were those officially regarded as best— equal sharing between king and chapter, but with royal patronage for the office of dean and chapter election for the canon *écolâtre* in charge of teaching and education. Troyes and Sarlat had all canons episcopally appointed, Notre-Dame of Paris all but two; at Autun, all the stalls, the dean's included, went by capitular election; at Alet and Bazas bishop and chapter appointed in alternation. Among minor collegiate churches there were many where collation was made by the bishop on the presentation of a noble family; in the diocese of Bazas the twelve canons of La Réole, the twelve of Uzeste, and the ten of Casteljalux were seigneurially appointed. The variant possibilities may be illustrated from the diocese of Metz.[22] Saint-Sauveur had a provost, the nominal head, appointed by the Crown, an elected dean, and eleven canons chosen in half the year by the king and in the other half by the canon of the week. At Saint-Pierre le Grand, the provost was a royal nominee, and, once in office, he appointed the canons as vacancies occurred. The chapter of Gorce was established in the church and with the endowments of the old Benedictine abbey, and thus, for historical reasons, the canons were nominated by the commendatory abbot (in 1789, this was the papal nuncio Pamphili). At Mars-la-Tour the provost and the four canons held stalls under the patronage of the owners of neighbouring seigneuries.

Everywhere there was a patchwork diversity which time and custom had established. Yet even this was not the end of the story: there were various general legal rules in favour of privileged patrons or candidates qualifying for special priority, and these rules could intervene and override—there were the rights of the Crown and magistrates of parlement enforceable in certain contingencies, the months allocated to graduates, and the possibilities of permutation or resignation in favour.

In the quest for a canonry, the most important advantage was to have a relative already ensconced in the chapter. He might influence his colleagues in an election or, better still, confer a stall on his own authority if he was *en semaine* when the vacancy occurred.[23] More certainly however, the appointment would come from a resignation in favour—there seem to have been more of these for canonries than for parochial cures. Nepveu de la Manouillière, of a noble family of the province of Maine, had three relatives who were canons of Le

Mans, and in 1759, when he was 27, one of them resigned in his favour.[24] Observing the chapter from within, he records similar resignations in 1760, 1768, 1772 (the deanery), and 1776, and two permutations (1760, 1784). The 1776 appointment he recounts with disapproving relish. The abbé Savanne became a canon, even though, as the son of a bankrupt tanner, he was not welcome to the chapter. Canon Roger resigned his stall to him on condition of the usual pension and of an additional one from a rich and lonely widow, Mme de Nouans, who had taken up with Savanne and, indeed, paid him an allowance ('since she is horribly ugly, she has to pay dearly to get anyone to befriend her'). Eight years later she died, and Savanne inherited her fortune, which put him one up on his grudging and haughty colleagues. There were places where the transmission of stalls by resignation was so common that dynasties formed and a whole foundation consisted of closely connected local families—as at the cathedrals of Autun and Clermont and the collegiate churches of Draguignan, Beaucaire, and Chérolles.[25] The system was abusive, but not without advantage to the Church, as Massillon recognized when he took Jean-Baptiste de Champflour, who had inherited his canonry from one relative and the provostship from another, as his *grand vicaire*.[26] A man wielding great local influence could be useful to his bishop.

In some cases, merit alone won a stall: the bishop might want a collaborator to help with writing sermons and pastoral letters, look after diocesan legal or financial business, conduct visitations, perhaps as a *grand vicaire*; the chapter itself might want an expert theologian, a preacher, an expert on music. For most appointments, however, influence was the key, though exercised in diverse ways, whether at Versailles or locally, within the chapter or in the networks of family connections outside it. The broad general effect followed from the nature of the social order: well-endowed and prestigious chapters filled with nobles, and the deans and provosts of moderately important collegial churches tended to be noble also.

In the case of twenty-one chapters (in 1789) the system of preference to the aristocracy was systematized into monopoly—stalls were exclusively reserved for nobles. Those who enjoyed this privilege were not shamefaced about it; provincial families kept complaining that there were not more, and occasionally the king promoted an existing collegiate institution into the exclusive category. When the new diocese of Saint-Claude was created, the monks of the abbey of Saint-Pierre became canons of a 'noble' cathedral; in 1751 the bishop of Marseille made the old abbey of Saint-Victor into a collegiate church reserved for ancient families of Provence; in 1776 and 1777, the cathedrals of Toul and Metz were ennobled, though in the case of Metz, commoners with university degrees could still aspire to ten of the prebends, the five offices of dignitary and the twenty-eight other prebends being closed to them. Normally, four generations of nobility on both father's and mother's side were required; Besançon, where eight quarters were stipulated, had an escape clause admitting the sons of the more recently ennobled, provided they held a doctorate of theology or canon law. The genealogical documents (the *preuves*) had to be produced, and a defect would disqualify. Thus the abbé de Tencin was excluded from the chapter of Saint-Jean at Lyon; he gloated later when he went back there as archbishop: 'Lapidem quem reprobaverunt aedificantes, hic factus est in caput anguli'; a quick-witted canon capped the quotation with the next verse of the psalm, and honours were even: 'A Domino factum est istud; et est mirabile in oculis nostris.'[27] Aristocratic families arranging a marriage with a bride of the new nobility had to weigh the size of the dowry against the shortfall in genealogical qualifications to get privileged canonries for the sons. The disagreeable maréchal de Broglie used to reproach his wife because their marriage 'had closed the doors of the great chapters against the children'. 'The only doors I have closed to them are the doors of the poorhouse', she would reply.[28] When the comte de Horn was to be broken on the wheel for murder, Saint-Simon tried to get the penalty changed to beheading, not from merciful sentiments, but because 'the infamy would exclude the three following generations from any noble chapter'.[29]

Among these exclusive foundations, there was a hierarchy of splendour. Mende, Vienne, Saint-Dié, Bar-le-Duc, and Brioude were open to long genealogies without great supporting influence, while Besançon, Lyon, and Strasbourg were for the very great. The canons of Besançon, resplendent in violet cassocks and ermine-lined mantles, were rich; those of Saint-Jean of Lyon by comparison were poor (except for the abbeys they held *in commendam*, of course), but they were compensated by peculiar distinctions: the title of 'comte', the right to wear a mitre when officiating on feast-days, and, from 1745, membership of an order rejoicing in wearing an eight-pointed gold and enamel cross, the image of St John the Baptist in the centre and fleurs-de-lis and coronets radiating from it.[30] But Strasbourg stood high above all rivals. Its canons were princes of France or Germany, or at least counts of the Holy Roman Empire. In 1789, there were three Rohan, four Hohenlohe, one Croÿ, one

La Trémoille, two Trocheser, six Koenigsegs, and four Salm—names famous throughout Europe.[31]

Outside the charmed circle of the 'noble' chapters, aristocratic churchmen by preference sought a place in the greater cathedrals. At Angers in 1789,[32] the dean and eleven canons were nobles, two from the city itself, the rest from Anjou, Brittany, the Vendée, and Normandy. Their families were of solid provincial standing, sending sons into the Church, the Army, and the Law. Only two canons were commoners, one the son of a tanner, one the former schoolmaster of the choirboys. Three other stalls provided an income for absentees; two were in the royal household—a minor clerk in the chapel at Versailles and a tutor to the pages of the Grande Écurie du Roi; the third stall had been annexed by the rector of the University of Paris using a peculiar professorial right, a procedure some regarded as sharp practice. In the cathedral of Chartres,[33] with ninety stalls to fill, half the canons were nobles (47 per cent from 1750 to 1759), and of the commoners, half were doctors of the Sorbonne, some mostly concerned with university business in Paris, some running the diocese for the bishop. A curé of the town described the feud between the two parties:

one composed of men of high birth, the other of commoners, doctors or at least, learned, who had got their canonries either by the operation of the months reserved for graduates or because they were needed for their learning or their usefulness. These two parties are at continual war, the one side armed with disdain, the other with arguments. What sad effects the distinctions between men cause—or, rather, their folly . . . Happily, blood has never been shed. From time to time, though, common interest and corporate feeling unite all the canons, nobles and commoners.

Falling short of the distinction and income of Angers and Chartres, the cathedral of Saint-André at Bordeaux and the rival church of Saint-Seurin had a lesser proportion of nobles, a quarter at the end of the *ancien régime*.[34] The magistrates of the parlement and the merchant patricians sought better things for their sons.

'Every little town', said Montesquieu, 'has one or two chapters with small revenues . . . and from 10 to 20 or 30 places; if these places were more considerable, the nobility would be interested in them—being the only idle corporation in the kingdom, needing property other than its own to maintain itself.'[35] Two qualifications need to be made to this broadly true generalization. Nobles would be interested in the office of dean, with its double emoluments and priority of esteem. In Angers, there were five chapters altogether, and in 1789 all the deans were of high birth. Also, in a province like Périgueux, where there were many penurious noble houses, candidates of long lineage might compete for even unimportant posts. Otherwise, the poor foundations were staffed by the sons of notaries, *avocats* and other lawyers, officials, merchants, and tradesmen. The bourgeoisie, like the aristocracy, had its sinecures; the more influential a middle-class family, the higher in the ecclesiastical scale of affluence and distinction its sons were likely to be found.

Influence was what counted, but it could only be exercised on behalf of candidates with the appropriate qualifications—or who were on the way to getting them. By ecclesiastical law, it was possible to hold a canonry and go no further in orders than the tonsure, but in the eighteenth century, very few held back from major orders, as to do so meant incurring the disapproval of the bishop and of colleagues and exclusion from the choir and a voice in chapter.[36] Nor was it possible any longer to take over a stall at an early age, or at least, to do this required untoward social pressure; in the two chapters of Bordeaux during the eighteenth century only six became canons before the age of 18, all of great families, four being of the nobility of the robe. Nine out of every ten canons of these two foundations were above the age of 20 when appointed, and the subdiaconate leading to the priesthood was necessary before emoluments could be drawn. Canons of cathedrals were often doctors of theology; half of those of the two great chapters of Bordeaux held this degree, while in the lesser collegiates most held the *maîtrise* or the *baccalauréat*. It was mostly the middling and lower bourgeoisie of town and countryside which could afford to educate its sons to this standard, and had contacts sufficient to warrant the hope that by doing so, it would be able to place them agreeably.

Only a fifth of the canons of the twelve chapters of Guienne moved on, and then rarely to higher promotions. A few applicants may have hoped to stage for a while until superior promotion came, but most were simply in search of an establishment for life, possibly one already noted by their family as appropriate and, with reasonable good fortune, obtainable.

III

Canons were following a career prescribed for them by family and society, their progress facilitated by influence—so much is easy to document. The inner spiritual yearning, the response to the divine

call, the desire to serve religion and the Church, remain, for most of
them, their individual secret. Perhaps they tended to be less idealis-
tic in their vocation than the curés, given their generally greater
income and less demanding pastoral obligations. In the second half
of the seventeenth century one of them asked himself in verse what
his motivation had been:

> Eus-tu d'autres motifs que ceux de la fortune
> Et ne la pris-tu pas, animé du plaisir
> D'avoir mieux de quoy vivre, avec plus de loisir?[37]

The only test he could apply was to examine his own conduct,
putting out of his mind how he came by his canonry, and asking
only what use he was making of it. For most churchmen of the past,
this is the only test of vocation available to the historian.

By the eighteenth century, the conduct of most canons was
respectable—gone were the scandal and indecorum associated with
their name in earlier ages. True, there were occasional *déboires* to
rejoice the anticlerical gossips—leaving for England with a nun,
raping the bell-ringer's daughter, installing a lady in a house in the
country[38]—but sexual lapses were rare, and only flight would save
the serious offender from destitution of office and imprisonment in
a house of penitential discipline. As with monasteries, so too the
collegiate churches in out-of-the-way places could slide into misconduct through lack of supervision: the provost of Bourbon-Lancy
sold the lead from the seigneurial coffins and the metal of the bells,
and allowed his housekeeper to make skirts from old altar linen.[39]
The clergy of Notre-Dame de la Fosse at Guémené-Guincamp in
Brittany were so ill remunerated that they had to wander round
seeking supplementary employment in local chapels; consequently,
the chapter could not keep an eye on all its members, and in the end
asked the bishop of Vannes to evict the abbé Thibaut, habitually
drunk during divine service.[40] The typical sins of canons were less
dramatic than those. A list of comic book titles circulating in Reims
in 1758, probably written by a young canon of the cathedral, had the
dean down as author of 'How to take off a calotte' (an ecclesiastical
hat), and two of his colleagues as offering 'Detachment from the
goods of this world' and 'How to speak about religion without
having any'[41]—implying preoccupation with trivialities, worldliness,
and hypocrisy as the shortcomings of chapter members. Almost
everywhere the best-documented failings were slackness and
irreverence in the performance of the liturgical offices. There are
picturesque examples, but it is dangerous to generalize from them.

Bernard-Laurent Soumille, one of the minor clergy of Villeneuve, near Avignon, noted the lapses of the canons in his journal: 8 February 1737, they stayed late at dinner in the Benedictine monastery, so a minor clerk had to say the offices; 2 August 1757, there were no canons in the choir, only the dean and four assistant priests; 9 May 1769, only a single canon turned out for the Rogation procession, the morning being misty. Yet these are the only examples he found over thirty years, and of them he says 'chose extraordinaire', 'I have never seen anything like it'.[42]

Our knowledge of the failings of canons is well documented, because chapters collectively took measures to put things right. Here, a canon is noted in the registers for going hunting, there for wearing a red coat under his surplice for a wager, somewhere else for clearing his head at mass by taking a pinch of snuff.[43] In 1777, all was not well at Notre-Dame du Val in the town of Provins: one canon had falsified a register, another only attends matins in the first half of the year, and the dean cannot come to services because of a nervous illness—'that may be so, but it is all his own fault . . . with his daily indulgence in good cheer'.[44] We know all this because canon Brunet, in charge of chapter discipline, called on the bishop to intervene. In 1781, Canon Bexon wrote to his colleagues of the Sainte-Chapelle in Paris exhorting them to desist from irreverent conduct, 'talking to each other loudly and freely during the divine office . . . sustained conversations, prolonged dialogues . . . with an air of facility, indeed of gaiety, even of petulance . . . making it obvious the subject is profane'.[45] Cathedral chapters were generally decorous, being better organized and proud of their splendid display and music; they were also under the censorious eyes of the towns-folk, and if the bishop was strict and resident, under episcopal scrutiny as well. Fitz-James, bishop of Soissons, hearing that only four or five canons were going on the customary procession from the cathedral to the church of Saint-Crépin for the first vespers of the parochial feast, at the last chime of the bell joined in himself—there was a wild rush of the canons from their houses, so that thirty or more were present when the march reached its destination.[46]

If there was a besetting sin of canons, it was pride. In their intro-verted collegiate life they had resounding feuds with each other, like the dispute between the *trésorier* and the *chantre* of the Sainte-Chapelle in 1607, which provided the plot for Boileau's *Le Lutrin*. But more often it was a corporate pride, a pride turning against the whole outside world—bishop, curés, municipality, and other chapters. When a canon was installed, he presented a cope to the sacristy, endowed an anniversary mass, and gave tips to chapter employees; it marked the beginning of an allegiance, probably for life, to the institution with which he identified more and more as the years went by. Canons lived longer than most classes of society, most clergy even. In the two chapters of Bordeaux, where the average life expectancy was 65, in 1790, out of forty-six, thirty-one were over 50 years of age, and eleven were over 70. Old men grow set in their ways, cling to their distinctions, more and more take refuge in the life of the closed corporate society in which their lot has been cast. The daily ceremonial routine and the recurrence of processions and dignified observances instilled into the mind the importance of precedence and status, of privileges to be maintained out of piety for past generations, and in the interests of those to come after. There was a continual concern to prove and celebrate the antiquity of the foundation, the provenance and efficacy of the relics, the splendour of the architecture and music.

After pride, the next most insidious temptation was sloth.

> Les chanoines vermeils et brillants de santé
> S'engraissent d'une longue et sainte oisiveté,

said Boileau. His picture of canons in bed during matins and leaving minor clerks to sing the office while they dined was no longer true in the eighteenth century, but the accusations continued. Curé Meslier used the same phrase as Boileau: 'holy idleness'. It was a continual complaint of the curés that canons were well paid for doing little. Truth was, there was more to be done than was commonly supposed, and a great deal more that could usefully be done, though not obligatory. A canon's life-style was what he chose to make it.

IV

Canons had an obligation to reside. When first appointed, they had to keep residence for a fixed period (*la rigoureuse*), generally for eight months, to qualify for future payments. Thereafter, each foundation had its particular requirement, there being no necessary uniformity. The legitimacy of this diversity of regulations was confirmed in a lawsuit of 1749.[47] Five of the canons of Dreux decided to tighten up their rule and extend the minimum annual period to nine months; the other four objected and invoked the law. The courts ruled canonries to be temporal benefices, not subject to the laws of the

Church, and exempt from episcopal intervention except when the morals of an individual or the decency of the liturgical offices were in question; the obligations of residence were such as were laid down by the rules of the foundation, and the secular judges would interpret them. There were a few places where the rules were lax: the high and mighty canons of Strasbourg had to reside for a mere three months. In most places, the rule was six months. At the cathedral of Sens, it was stricter: six months qualified to receive the *gros fruits*, in the case of this penurious chapter, a mere 60 livres, staying on for a total of nine months qualified for the *grandes distributions*, about 600 livres.

Inevitably, some canons evaded the regulations. Court chaplains had an official right to enjoy an income without appearing to collect it, and men of great families whose influence overawed the chapter an unofficial one. A celebrated case was Pezé de Courtalvert[48] of an illustrious noble family of Maine, who died in 1771 at the age of 91, a canon of Nantes for fifty years while residing all the while in Paris (but did he in fact draw an income?—he also had two rich abbeys). Most canons, however, at least those in reputable foundations, were constrained to obey the rules: if they failed to keep residence, they drew no income. Nor was it possible to alleviate the burden of residence by missing the occasional service. A register was kept recording who was present on each occasion, sometimes with two entries, the one at the end to catch any who slipped away early. There was a tariff of fines for absences so noted, with extra to pay for great feast-days and a surcharge on officers with greater incomes. And 'absence' was defined: it began at the Gloria of the *Venite* at matins, and of the first psalm at vespers, and at the last Kyrie of mass. The registers bear witness to the sort of excuse needed to win an exemption.[49] 'M. Tardif, being in ill health, will not be fined (*picqué*) if he does not attend matins this winter'; a medical certificate accompanies permission to go to a thermal station to bathe for a skin eruption; two or three months are granted to an applicant who wishes 'to breathe the air of his native place'. Aristocratic birth did not exempt: even at Strasbourg a prince came in person to make application, even though as a court chaplain he might have stayed away with impunity. Nor did spiritual duties out of town: a preacher from Autun, much in demand in Paris, lost his *gros fruits* because he was away too long. The prevailing strictness is seen in the debate among the cathedrals of Normandy[50] on the question of absence for university study in the case of canons appointed (legally but abusively) before ordination. Avranches wished to know what the others did, firstly about dispensation from the *rigoureuse*, and secondly, once the *rigoureuse* was completed, did the absentee student just get the *gros fruits*, or was he allowed a share in the distributions as well? Evreux and Coutances allowed exemption from the *rigoureuse*, the others not (strictness on this point was probably general, for even the noble chapter of Lyon was unyielding here[51]). As to sharing in the distributions, Sées gave nothing, Bayeux said it all depended on circumstances, Lisieux allowed a proportion of the annual allowance of grain, Rouen gave a fixed 500 livres, Avranches only 100. All agreed on one point: if the favoured individual did not get ordained, he must be evicted from his canonry and, if possible, compelled to restore whatever income he had drawn.

A canon was expected to attend chapter meetings. Twice a year, there would be a general chapter, theoretically compulsory for all, whether in residence or not. A solemn mass of the Holy Spirit would open proceedings, followed by a sermon of exhortation behind closed doors, with the public excluded. The minor clergy would appear one by one for praise or blame, and the sittings would continue for two or three days, drawing up regulations on matters which had arisen during the past six months. Thereafter, there were the routine chapter meetings attended by those in residence, sometimes once a week, more often twice. In a crisis, there would be a special emergency meeting, with the canons summoned by the pealing of the great bell. At Rouen, the chapter assembled for its regular sessions no fewer than three times a week, and, according to one of its members, the discussions were exemplary—'in 12 years . . . I never heard a disobliging word'.[52]

The liturgical round of the great collegiate churches consisted of the seven daily offices and high mass, with low masses shared out among canons and minor clerks. Strictly followed, this programme would have broken up the day to the point of preventing many other activities. In practice, however, the offices were usually grouped into three sessions: perhaps mass, matins, lauds, and prime between 4 and 6 a.m., tierce, none, and high mass beginning at 9 a.m., and vespers and compline at 2.30 p.m. Though convenient, this could still mean spending five or six hours a day in the cathedral, probably telescoping into about four, since amalgamation tends to mean abbreviation. The comfort of chapter life was greatly affected by the hour at which the first service was set. Matins at 6 a.m., as at Nancy, was a routine hardship, while set at 3 a.m. (and 1.30 in Lent and Advent) as at Clermont, it was a severe one. There was an oath dating back to 1367 at Notre-Dame of Paris, to attend matins at midnight;[53] there was no dispensation from the obligation, not even for illness or for the *chanoines jubilés* (over 50 years of age) who were excused the daylight offices. These nocturnal forays were bleak, so the canons wore their nightcaps, looking (as one of them remarked) 'like characters in a theatrical farce', though they left them behind on Christmas Eve, when the faithful crowded in to greet the Nativity.[54] Whether by night or by day, four to five hours was a long time to spend in a vast church in winter: rheumatism was the canons' occupational disease.

In addition to the daily round, attendance was required on special occasions, especially at processions. Some would be ordered by the bishop at times of national rejoicing or penitence and to intercede for favourable weather. At Angers[55] there were general processions of all churches on St Mark's Day, Palm Sunday, Ascension Day, and Corpus Christi, while the cathedral had its own observances on the first Sunday of the month and on nineteen other special days throughout the year. Other liturgical observances when the full attendance of available canons was required were those arising from the fraternal alliances of churches. The cathedrals of Le Mans and Angers were in such a 'society of prayer', and both had agreements with others outside France, Angers with Compostela, Le Mans with Paderborn. The minor chapters of Angers had their humbler alliances: Saint-Pierre with Saint-Maurille, and Saint-Laud and Saint-Martin with each other and with Saint-Pierre de la Cour of Le Mans. The obligations of these capitular confraternities included sending representatives to patronal festivals and attending certain joint processions; when news of the death of a canon of the other chapter arrived, the vespers of the dead were recited, and on the following day a requiem was celebrated.

At the ceremonies of processions and high festivals the canons were the cynosure of every eye, so much capitular time was spent discussing the details of dress, music, and choreography. Timings would be changed, processional routes altered, precautions laid down to prevent confusion; a note would be made in the registers even if such a conjunction of events would not recur until thirty years afterwards. The eclipse of the sun on 1 April 1764 did not catch the canons of France unawares. In the South, they could be proud of having put the service times forward to escape the darkness, but in the North, the eclipse turned out to be a mere passing shadow, and those who set out in procession armed with candles were chagrined to find they had made themselves ridiculous.[56] There were strict rules for dress, whether in the stalls or in the processions. There was a summer and a winter habit; in most collegiate churches the black cassock was the foundation garment, with the *aumusse* covering the shoulders in summer (a sort of hood lined with fur or grey or red material); in winter, there would be the *rochet* (an embroidered surplice with narrow sleeves), and over it the *chape* (a long black sleeveless garment, perhaps with trimmings of fur, silk, or velvet). For outdoor ceremonies, the standard dress would be enfolded in the *camail* (a hooded cloak of black cloth lined with crimson satin). The old ecclesiastical ban on wigs had been collapsing from the early years of the century, so a powdered *perruque* surmounted by the *bonnet carré* (the black box hat) would complete the canonical splendour. Each liturgical occasion had its prescribed variant of dress, and there was scope for quarrels between those who stood by tradition and others who wanted to change to something more colourful or prestigious. The canons of Notre-Dame of Paris[57] were accustomed to put aside their purple summer cassocks and change to cold weather habit at All Saints; so if there was a celebration of national rejoicing after that date, they would attend the Te Deum in black cassocks and capes. The older men were against change; the younger wanted to use the summer colour. Thanks to the king describing their appearance at the celebration for the birth of the dauphin (December 1781) as 'werewolves' and the discovery of a seventeenth-century precedent in the archives, the younger men prevailed, and at the next Te Deum they were all resplendent in purple. At Le Mans, the quarrel over dress was one chapter against another. The canons of Saint-Pierre de la Cour, already enjoying special finery for feast-days by royal *brevet*, in 1782 voted themselves into a new splendour for ordinary days, black velvet (silk in summer) with red buttons and laces. Inconsolable at this gesture of sartorial one-upmanship, the canons of the cathedral complained bitterly.

At some time in his career, a canon would have to take on administrative duties for his chapter—supervising the collection of rents, feudal dues, and tithes; drawing up accounts, paying over clerical taxation; prosecuting the inevitable lawsuits; negotiating with contractors over repairs and improvements; inventorying furniture and church ornaments. These affairs were time-consuming, not only because of the complexities of property holding, but also because they involved questions of public relations. Everywhere it was a story of tithe strikes, rent evasions, opposition to seigneurial justice by innkeepers, local notables or municipal authorities, wrangles with the heirs over the *lods et ventes* paid on houses when the owner died. The obviously efficient method of coping was to have a single practical expert and leave everything to him. In poor provincial chapters this was normal—a single *trésorier* who drew extra emoluments for his pains. Even so, there always had to be two separate allocations of property and resources: the *mense capitulaire* for the maintenance of the church, the paying of the choir, employees, and the liturgical expenses, and the *mense canonicale*, to pay the canons. These departments might well be under separate control. In some very poor foundations there was no choir and no staff beyond an all-purpose verger, and the *mense capitulaire*, probably called by the less imposing name of *fabrique*, had little revenue, sometimes none at all. Before Saint-Pierre de la Cour in Le Mans simplified its procedures in 1775, there had been three departments of revenue, not two: the *office de l'argenterie* for repairs, music, services, and clerical taxation; the *office des anniversaires*, paying the minor clergy, sacristan, and the fees for masses; and the *gros des prébendes mise en partition*, and within this office two separate groups of estates, one to pay each canon his *gros fruits*, the other providing the distribution for daily attendance at services. In the cathedral at Chartres,[58] the chapter collectively named the lay *fermiers* gathering the income of the *mense capitulaire*, and the rest of the property was divided into twenty-three prebends, each with possessions spread over the province of Beauce. Each prebend was allocated to a group of canons (averaging four each), the members having to hold the *régence* in turn for a year, naming the bailiffs and clerks, and with the obligation to tour round the property on personal inspections. Everywhere there were lawsuits: the chapter at Digne was bankrupted by them. The courts were leisurely and the law complex; a chapter did well to appoint one of its members to run all the litigation, a task in the cathedral of Langres falling to Didier-Pierre Diderot, brother of the *philosophe*. A literary connection like this brings the notice of history, and Didier-Pierre has deserved notoriety as intolerant; he should also be remembered, however, as efficient, austere, and recklessly charitable.[59]

Among the canon administrators, there was a special category of those concerned with helping the bishop to run the diocese. In the cathedral there would be the archdeacons, perhaps in place despite the bishop, or perhaps his welcome collaborators. There would be some of the *grands vicaires*, since they often acquired a canonry to provide for their establishment; the bishop was also likely to choose the *official* and the *promoteur* of his ecclesiastical court from the chapter members, or, if choosing them from outside, would look out for a canonry to reward them. During the vacancy of a see, often prolonged for a year or two owing to the leisurely way in which newly appointed prelates moved to take up their duties, the cathedral chapter ran the diocese. This meant appointing four canons as administrators, whether from the existing *grands vicaires* or others, and discussing a new range of affairs in chapter meetings. Since one perennial item of business, the search for ways and means to resist episcopal encroachments, would for the time being fall into abeyance, perhaps the average duration of debate was not too far exceeded.

According to the abbé Baston, canon of Rouen, 'the canonical life, when its duties are properly performed, absorbs the greater part of the day'.[60] A doctor of the Sorbonne and devoted to scholarly pursuits, he naturally put first in his list of possible duties preaching and teaching—in particular, training young men for the ministry of the Church. By royal edicts, renewed by Louis XIV in 1695, every cathedral had to reserve a prebend for a *théologal*, who was to preach every Sunday and give three lectures a week on the Scriptures. The rule was observed, with varying results. In one cathedral the canon *théologal* received presentations of table silver from his colleagues for his moving Lent and Advent courses; in another, the canons found his sermons unbearable (perhaps because the bishop had forced his appointment on them), and in face of their hostility, he hired a Capuchin to deputize in the pulpit.[61] Some cathedrals had another official post, the *écolâtre*, with responsibilities for education in the city or the diocese; at Notre-Dame in Paris he had the duty of inspecting the elementary schools of the capital.[62] In some provincial collegiate churches there would be an endowment called a *prestimoni*, the canon holding it receiving extra income for teaching local children.[63] In a university town, there would be chapter members active in the Faculty of Theology, some attending as doctors exercising their right to join in the examination of theses, others holders of chairs and giving lectures—professorial remuneration was so low that ecclesiastical benefices like canonries were needed to survive. In the cathedral of Angers a succession of such learned figures produced that vast compendium of rigidly orthodox theology, the *Conférences d'Angers*. These *conférences* were delivered as actual lectures; then, from 1703, publication began, reaching twenty-four volumes by 1758. The last in the line of the authors was Cotelle de la Blandinière, who in 1780 was given a pension by the Assembly of Clergy for his services. By then, he had moved from Angers to Blois, where he was a canon and archdeacon. From there, in 1785, at the age of 78, he added four new volumes defending the rights of bishops against the rising tide of agitation among the parish clergy.

A canon against the curés—this was to be expected, for chapters were under attack as appropriators of revenues which could have been better used to support the parochial ministry. Yet some canons were fully occupied in the pastoral ministry, whether holding the office of curé as an obligation of their stall, or elected to the office by their chapter, or informally, taking on the duties by preference or to gain an additional income.[64] At Bray, Brienon, and Saint-Julien-du-Sault in the diocese of Sens, the chapter ran the parish. In the diocese of Autun, there were three poor foundations where the dean was curé with one or two canons around him, while the rest were away eking out a living doing pastoral duties in the countryside. The parishes of Saint-Martin and Saint-Gengulf in Metz had a canon as their *ex officio* parish priest. So too at Paris at Saint-Merry, Saint-Sépulchre, Saint-Benoît, and Saint-Etienne-des-Gués, churches at once collegiate and parochial, where the cure of souls was the responsibility of the *chanoine chéficier*. The sacrist of Saint-Etienne of Montauban was curé; he was not one of the nine canons, but was much richer than any of them, with a lodging allowance and large surplice-fees on top of a canonical income. At Draguignan, the 6,000 inhabitants attended the church of Notre-Dame-et-Saint-Michel, with the curé as head of the chapter, having under him a *capiscol*, four canons, and two chaplains. Did he really rule the chapter? It appeared so, especially after the bishop's ruling of 1735 that he, and not the canon of the week, was entitled to administer the last sacraments to all members of the foundation. Even if there were no formal ties with a parish, a chapter was, in any case, a pool of talent from which help could come by invitation of the curé—to conduct missions and retreats, for example. Or an invitation might come from the laity, for confraternities and guilds chose ecclesiastics to conduct their liturgical services, and bringing in a canon as *prieur* would fortify the members with the presence of a local celebrity.

There was also the hearing of confessions, a duty high on Baston's list. These were the days when numerous clergy were required to man the confessionals, not only to help out in the parishes, but also to hear the frequent and obligatory confessions of nuns, the inmates of hospitals and workhouses, and schoolboys in the *collèges*. Canons as well as friars might be involved in these duties, though it was more usual for them to be invited to fulfil a more prestigious role as the *supérieur ecclésiastique* of a monastery, nunnery, or charitable institution. This office did not involve being the chaplain, confessor, or visitor (though any of these duties might be combined with it), but acting as a liaison officer with the bishop, and as an adviser and protector. Canon Moranges of the cathedral of Clermont was such a superior to two convents of nuns; Bishop Massillon praised his 'douceur et modération', and when he died, invited his brother, another canon, to succeed him.[65] The abbé Blain had held a stall in the cathedral of Rouen, resigned to become a curé, then got back into a canonry again, feeling 'more attracted to the life of prayer and contemplation'. Even so, he became adviser to the Sœurs du Sacré-Cœur at Ernemont six leagues out of town, the Hospitalières de Saint-François near at hand, and the Frères des Écoles Chrétiennes.[66] There can never be a history of the office of *supérieur ecclésiastique*, but it was significant in interlocking the tiny closed worlds of the religious communities of provincial towns, rendering them susceptible to undemonstrative guidance and capable of forming a common opinion on questions of the day in times of crisis.

There are two other entries on Baston's list of optional tasks: one, writing, is obvious; the other may sound incongruous. 'Several sit as judges in the magistrates' courts,' he says. These were the *conseillers-clercs*, clerics highly qualified in the law who had bought magisterial office and were useful to the tribunals for cases involving canon law and ecclesiastical issues. In every parlement there were a few of them, very often combining the office conveniently with a canonry; there were the colleagues of Baston in Rouen and there were others in Toulouse, Bordeaux, and Paris. Here, in the parlement of Paris, was one who won nation-wide fame, the abbé Pucelle, short of stature, purple and choleric of countenance, a fearless denouncer of the encroachments of the Crown. Others served in the hierarchy of courts next below the parlements, the *bailliages*, *présidiaux*, and *sénéchaussées*. In the *présidial* of Quimper was Canon Reymond, in trouble with the bishop in 1776 because he was president of the masonic lodge where his fellow magistrates foregathered.[67] At Villefranche, an ornament of the *sénéchaussée* court was Canon Dominique Roland (brother in law to the future heroine of the Girondins); not only that, but he won election to the local academy, was chaplain to the *hôpital général*, and the precentor of his church[68]—one canon at least who could not be described as idle.

Every major chapter could boast of one or two members who achieved fame, at least locally, as writers and modest intellectuals. Numerous canons engaged in antiquarian pottering, generally collecting anecdotes about their foundation or local affairs; the chapter archives would take them this far, but their libraries mostly lacked the books to move on to wider themes, and few canons had substantial private collections. A few serious attempts to write history were made. The abbé Montjoie of Notre-Dame, a *conseiller-clerc* at the parlement, published his *Curiosités de l'Église de Paris* in 1763; Du Temps, of Bordeaux, produced a survey of all the great benefices of the country in *Le Clergé de France* (1774), and a life of that hammer of the armies of Louis XIV, John, Duke of Marlborough; another from Bordeaux, Dubignon, in 1778 gave the world two volumes of *Considérations sur l'origine et les révolutions du gouvernement des Romains*, suitably critical of tyrants, since they were 'the fruit of solitude and unhappiness', written during eighteen months in the Bastille and three years of exile resulting from a quarrel with the bishop of Arras.[69] We hear of a specialist in oriental languages at Besançon, a promoter of a cure for paralysis by electric shocks at Sens, an inventor of a technique for reclaiming the *landes* by terracing with hurdles and planting pine trees at Bordeaux, and of versifiers both in Latin and French, including one who wrote 728 alexandrines on an intrepid journey on horseback by a canonical colleague all the twelve miles from Carrouges to Alençon.[70]

Some gained minor celebrity on the margins of the Enlightenment. At the end of the seventeenth century, Claude Nicaise of the Sainte-Chapelle of Dijon was a correspondent of all the scholars and wits of Europe, 'l'agent général de la république des lettres'.[71] About the same time Jules Bellet of Bordeaux published his novel of adventure, *Relation curieuse des voyages du sieur Montauban, capitaine des Flibustiers* (1698), and for thirty years more continued to pour out verses, studies on biology and climatology, speculations on the souls of animals, the nature of angels, fauns and satyrs in the Bible, and a practical treatise on the use of the divining rod. Canon Talbert of Besançon beat Rousseau for the Academy of Dijon prize: he described how inequality came with the Fall, yet still had to be accepted, 'quae sunt, a Deo ordinata sunt'—though religion will help us to bear it. The abbé Gaudet published four volumes on *L'Harmonie générale du Christianisme et de la raison* (1766), and about this time the abbé Trublet of Saint-Malo had taken over the role once filled by Claude Nicaise, and was the universal correspondent of the Republic of Letters.[72] At the end of the *ancien régime* there were three outstanding canonical intellectuals in Paris. Bergier, the theologian, was at Notre-Dame; so too was Mazéas, whose work on logic and mathematics won him election to the Royal Society of London and the Academy of Berlin. At the Sainte-Chapelle was Bexon, master of many languages, a technical publicist on agricultural methods, the writer of a history of Lorraine, and a major collaborator of Buffon, who encouraged his researches, appropriated

them, and made no acknowledgement. Bexon's achievements, however, got him promotion within the Sainte-Chapelle to the dignity
of *grand chantre*. It was here in 1784 that he opened a crate of
mineralogical specimens and died through inhaling their poisonous
dust, a martyr to science.[73]

Historical research was an excuse to get chapter permission to
escape to Paris. At the beginning of 1789, Canon Lépine of
Périgueux was there, working with the Benedictines of Saint-
Germain-des-Prés during the day on the history of his province, and
spending his nights at the theatre, even in Lent. He was given to
good cheer, and had a figure to match. 'Take care not to add a name
to the martyrology,' wrote a colleague; 'all that is needed is for the
poissardes to take one look at you and decide that you are the cause of
the high price of bread.'[74] Pascal Fenel de Darguy of Sens died in
1753, having had many a leave of absence from his chapter and grants
from the archbishop and diocese to live in Paris and work on local
history—he left a stack of notes and had not written a line. Typically
of academic researchers, rather than being grateful, he resented
having to do ordinary canonical duties: 'to compose history you need
a more tranquil life-style, and chapter business wastes all my time'.
Truth was, he mainly occupied himself competing for essay prizes,
hoping to win election to the Academy of Inscriptions.[75]

Another constant visitor to Paris was Canon Le Gouz of the
Sainte-Chapelle of Dijon.[76] At home, he said, people thought of him
as wearing brocaded coats at the salons of duchesses, playing cards
with the wives of farmers-general, and drinking champagne with
opera girls. Yet his activities were blameless—to him the capital was
a place for cultured ease and spiritual uplift. He listened to all the
great preachers, sought out the churches with the finest music,
wandered the quays browsing at bookstalls, and daily read a page of
Latin, Greek, and Hebrew to keep up his linguistic skills. One of his
favourite authors was Quesnel, whose Jansenist severities he found
'beautiful . . . you would have to be made of bronze not to be
moved'. Even more he loved the Scriptures; beside them, all other
writings were merely 'tittle-tattle', insubstantial nourishment,
'whipped cream'.

V

In a labour-intensive society devoted to ostentation, the ceremonies of the great churches were supported by a horde of minor ecclesiastics and lay employees, making their meagre living and enjoying their minor prestige on the fringes of a religion of outward show. At Bordeaux, Clermont, Orléans, Bourges, Saint-Martin of Tours, and elsewhere, at the summit of the hierarchy of this clerical underworld were the *chanoines semi-prébendés*. They were not real canons, being excluded from chapter meetings; they were paid little and worked hard, having to attend all the services. Everywhere, their ambition was to gain admission to the chapter, and nowhere did they succeed. Three tried at Clermont, in 1761, to manœuvre their way to recognition by insisting that, as 'canons', they could stay in their stalls to sing instead of going down to join the men of the choir. The chapter censured them, but did not punish them otherwise, since their leader had 'worn out his eyesight working in the library', and the other two were in poor health. Six years later, they revolted again; the parlement of Paris found against them, except that, in future, they were not to be insulted by being called 'the canon's serfs'.[77]

Below the *semi-prébendés* the *bas chœur* began. This consisted of ecclesiastics, mostly priests, who were permanently employed on salaries of from 300 to 600 livres a year—they would be called *chapelains hebdomadaires*, *prébendiers mineurs*, *prêtres bénéficiers*, or some such title. In a small place, there would be only four or so, in larger ones a dozen to thirty. Though all had to be available to sing the offices, walk in processions, do pastoral work, or whatever else was needed, some had specific offices and duties. At Notre-Dame[78] one was a *chevicier*, who had to sleep in the church as the night-duty priest, another a sacristan of masses, and a third the sacristan of the chapelle de la Vierge. The cathedral of Toulouse had two groups of clergy paid under collective endowments (four *prébendiers de la douzaine* and ten *prébendiers du vingt-quatre*—of which four were cantors and two epistle readers) and fourteen other *prébendiers* who were salaried independently. Care of the relics, of the ornaments for certain altars, of the functions taking place in a particular chapel, the oversight of a confraternity, keeping minutes of chapter meetings, or registers of attendances at services—these were tasks for which someone had to be given specific responsibility. There was never difficulty in filling the posts in the *bas chœur*, for every great church also had a pool of *prêtres habitués*, making a living by saying masses, walking in funeral processions, and doing other ecclesiastical odd jobs for which fees were forthcoming. They tended to consist of the very old and the very young, the old trying to survive with dignity in their retirement, the young hoping for promotion to *chapelain hebdomadaire*, or the grant of some small chapel in the foundation, or some lucky offer from outside. Some places had an endowed confraternity for the benefit of these *prêtres habitués*, as at the cathedral of Bordeaux, where there was the *Treizaine de Notre-Dame*, a group recruiting by co-option and paying small allowances to its members.[79]

The securely beneficed *chapelains hebdomadaires* came from the ranks of promoted choirmen and instrumentalists, ex-choirboys educated up to holy orders, sons of modest local families happy to have found a niche and intending to sojourn there for life, and, by contrast, young priests with ambition hoping to find contacts, possibly among the canons, to forward their careers. Those who chose to live and die in these minor posts were not necessarily untalented: they may have just wanted an undemanding existence. Bernard-Laurent Soumille,[80] *prêtre bénéficier* of Villeneuve, was a mathematician who published two treatises applying the calculus of probabilities to games of chance, another on an agricultural machine and how to work it, and another on his own invention of a hydraulic device. In his journal, he recounts the doings of his canons without envy; perhaps, having begun as a shepherd-boy and come to the notice of a kindly ecclesiastic by carving the alphabet on a tree, he felt lucky to have risen so far.

Not all the clergy of the *bas chœur* were so self-effacing. They battled for precedence among themselves and collectively to impose their claims upon their canons. At Villeneuve, they wanted the right to accompany the chapter to meet visiting bishops, and if this was not allowed, they would not go at all.[81] From 1767 to 1771, the canons of Toulouse were at law before the parlement against their senior *prébendier*,[82] while those of Dax were prosecuting similar cases before the parlement of Bordeaux, one being rather sinister, an affair of false keys to the sacristy cupboard. In 1783, an arbitration ended the Dax feud, leaving the canons supreme, though *prébendiers* who were dissatisfied were to be entitled to retire with generous life pensions of 600 livres a year.[83] As ever, these sorts of disputes were enlivened with comic and sacrilegious incidents. In 1745, the parlement of Paris ruled that *prêtres habitués* at Saint-Merry should be allowed to sit in the lower reaches of the stalls if there was room. In 1754, Canon Moussinet, enraged to see one of them exercising his right and sitting immediately below, 'smote him with a breviary in-quarto several times and in divers fashions, and using insulting terms. *D'où scandale!*'[84] Moussinet, a canon of thirty-four years' standing, belonged to the Jansenists, and was the covert banker of their funds—but austere religious allegiance did not incline him to for-bearance where the rights of his chapter were concerned.

A great church also had a multitude of lay employees. The material possessions of the chapter were in the oversight of lawyers, registrars, bailiffs, collectors, and the like, little concerned with the liturgical life of the place, though often seen around on their legal and financial business. The maintenance of the fabric employed many others. Local tradesmen would be given the official title of capitular architect, mason, glazier, goldsmith, jeweller, clock-winder; major repairs would mean resort to contractors. Other laymen were employed to play their pompous role in the ceremonies of the church. Notre-Dame of Paris had three *suisses*, six vergers, five *francs sergents* and six *huissiers* (these latter two categories were probably employed chiefly in policing the cathedral square and keeping order in the court room of the feudal jurisdiction). Vergers were not equal: they had precedences and peculiar titles, various ornamented staves, chains, badges, and gowns. Some were specialists at outdoor proces-sions: Saint-Martin at Tours had a *pauvre de Saint-Martin* marching in all of them, a symbolic beggar, as it were, awaiting the saint's proverbial largesse.[85] Then there were the bell-ringers, sweepers, cleaners, and dog-catchers. It is difficult to know how their schedules of work were organized. Le Mans had a *sergent* who supervised everything from the bell-ringing to the chapter prison, appointing appropriate staff; he bought the office for a down payment of 1,400 livres, so presumably it was profitable—perhaps the sum was a sort of caution money. When he died in 1770, the canons did not replace him, but appointed a *suisse* and three vergers directly, at salaries of 300 livres each.[86] As was usually the case with ecclesiastical institu-tions, the lay employees lingered on long after their days of effective service were over. Vergers were proverbially tottering and venerable figures. When Church property was sold in the Revolution, there were many unimportant people who regretted the loss of their modest employment and status in the wasteful ostentatious days before the invention of liberty.

VI

The great chapters of France had clients and influence, but few real friends. In the cities, the townsfolk were ambivalent in their attitude. They were glad to see revenues sucked in from the countryside to be spent to the profit of urban tradesmen. In Chartres, about one in twenty of the 13,000 inhabitants directly or indirectly drew a living from the cathedral; when three deputies were elected by the commons to the Estates General of 1789, they were all *baillis*, legal and financial agents of the canons. But great possessions and privilege drew hatred. During the Revolution, Siéyès risked his liberal reputation to defend Church property, urging the Assembly to resist 'the bourgeois jealousy which torments the inhabitants of little towns against M. *le chanoine* and M. *le bénéficier*'. As a canon of Chartres, he knew. 'Here', writes the historian of the foundation, 'it seems that all the opposition to the abuses of the *ancien régime* had crystallized in concentration upon the cathedral chapter, regarded as the symbol of parasitism.'[87] Half the canons were nobles, and of the total, nobles and commoners together, two-thirds came from outside the province. The aristocracy was pushing ahead in preferment by virtue of birth, and foreigners were drawing incomes which might have gone to deserving local families. It was not easy for these newcomers to win acceptance in town, though the Herculean abbé Mitouflet, who could carry two sacks of grain at arm's length, was the toast of the wine bars. And this alien chapter controlled other posts coveted by local people, 213 parochial cures and 83 chapels of the diocese being in its patronage. As in so many places, there were disputes with the municipality over seigneurial jurisdictions and the nomination of aldermen. But envy was the undercurrent in society which swept on the tide of anticlerical feeling. As the notaries of the city observed in 1784 in one of their disputes with the chapter, they were 'citizens with limited incomes, fathers of families . . . working hard to maintain and educate their children', while against them were 'eighty benefice holders, rich without working for it, bachelors without dependants, indifferent to other people'.

Most cathedrals exercised a feudal superiority in parts of the episcopal city. By virtue of the rights of the fief, the chapter would exact *lods et ventes*, a charge of about a fifteenth of the price when a house within the jurisdiction was sold. The area directly adjacent to the church was usually under seigneurial control in a more direct sense, with the chapter exercising police powers to the exclusion of the civic authorities. Ordinances directing householders to clean the street outside their doors or to have their chimneys swept (to avoid fire hazards), everyday matters if emanating from the secular authorities, suddenly became tyrannical when issued by churchmen.[88] The fief of Saint-Seurin at Bordeaux was a *sauveté*, a sanctuary, a refuge for artisans escaping the yoke of the guilds, for criminals and prostitutes in flight from the municipal police, and entrepreneurs setting up fearful establishments in defiance of city regulations—tanneries, slaughterhouses, foundries, and even a gunpowder magazine. There were many complaints, including some from citizens who censured the spoil-sport canons for refusing to allow the traditional bull race to crash through their streets. The municipality, in alliance with the intendant, worked continually and, finally and belatedly, successfully, to subject the *sauveté* to the ordinary police.[89] Chapter property within the urban boundaries often enough occasioned disputes about eligibility to local taxation. The city of Béziers had been at law against the cathedral of Saint-Nazaire since the time of Saint Louis over such a question, in some years the costs running away with half the municipal budget. The case was before the *cour des aides* of Montpellier and the Royal Council in the 1770s; then the bishop mediated and, having failed, in 1778 called in his father, a distinguished lawyer, to devise a compromise. At this point, the documentation ends, though probably not the lawsuit.[90] Fairs and markets posed problems to relationships, for the square in front of the cathedral was generally the ideal location, and it was not always obvious who was entitled to authorize the market and to collect dues from the stall holders. In 1770, the law had to be invoked at Metz, for the city aldermen encouraged trading in the Place Saint-Etienne, and the canons had just paid for paving it.

Everywhere, there were quarrels about protocol and precedence. At Tréguier,[91] prominent citizens claimed the right to have the great bell of the cathedral tolled for family funerals, but they were reluctant to pay the 80 livres ringing fee. The mayor expected the celebrant at the high mass on Palm Sunday to come down to his pew and present him with a palm frond, and at the feast of the Purification with a candle—gestures resented by canonical pride and arguably incompatible with a high theological view of the Sacrament. What was the order of precedence in the Corpus Christi procession? The municipal oligarchy could not be denied its splendid pew in the nave, but was it entitled to have its coat of arms proudly emblazoned on it? In a society obsessed with rank and status, every provincial town had these running feuds. Expensive though they were, they had less effect on personal relationships than might be supposed—in a peculiar sense the participants saw themselves as putting on a comedy for public entertainment: self-affirming display by conspicuous waste through litigation. Yet they had their effect on the popular concept of religion, continually treating it as a pattern of formal observances, an everyday affair without mystical overtones.

Cathedral chapters were proud corporations. Just as they did battle with municipalities, so they would fight against bishops and any other churchmen whose pretensions exceeded, even fractionally, the rights which precedent gave them. Any ecclesiastic coming into their precincts, however lofty his station and solemn his mission, had to conform to the rules of the foundation. The bishop of Soissons, arriving at Reims in 1721 to conduct the funeral of the late archbishop, found he had to take an oath to the church of Reims before he was allowed to officiate.[92] When there was a royal visit to Notre-Dame, the canons lay in wait to repel the claims of chaplains from Versailles. The young king came in 1721 to give thanks for his recovery from illness; 'il y avait une dispute ecclésiastique', said a Parisian diarist, 'ce qui ne manque jamais d'arriver'—the *premier aumônier du roi* was there to say mass, but the canons excluded him from the high altar. The regent was called on for a ruling, and he transferred the mass to the chapelle de la Vierge. This was the arrangement enforced in 1743 when the dauphin came, and when his wife came four years later. On this latter occasion, the ecclesiastics of the Court brought bread, wine, and candles to the chapel, but the canons would not allow them to be used—it was their prerogative to furnish all the materials for a Eucharist in their church.[93]

When the ceremonies involved the diocesan bishop, the situation might be different, for he had certain rights which could not be gainsaid. While a cathedral was independent of ordinary episcopal jurisdiction, being directly under the Holy See, the bishop was entitled to have the last word on certain occasions and issues.[94] His approval was needed for major changes in the building and its seating arrangements, and burials could not be made in tombs in the chancel without his permission; he could nominate Lenten preachers, and prescribe the ceremonies for ordinations, the consecration of the sacred oils, and meetings of the diocesan synod. If there was a controversy about foundation masses, relics, or miracles, an episcopal ruling would settle the matter. A conciliatory bishop would consult his chapter about arrangements in its church, but a disobliging one could bustle through, enforcing his rights. Yet precedent could not cover every eventuality, so a prelate riding roughshod over his canons might take a fall in the law courts. As chief pastor, he might claim to adjust the time of services to make them more convenient for the laity, but at Rieux, the attempt led to litigation right up to the parlement and the Royal Council.[95] At Notre-Dame in Paris there were only seven days in the year when the archbishop had the right to officiate in the choir without chapter permission. He had not asked for it for the high mass of the jubilee of April 1751, so the sacristans refused him the communion plate; after a wrangle, he gave an undertaking that the occasion would not constitute a precedent, and the mass began two hours later.[96] A bishop was entitled to be saluted by the thurifer when the incense was swung and to have acolytes carrying candles before him; in 1722, the canons of Nîmes enquired of their colleagues at Carcassonne about the limits of these privileges—was he entitled to remain seated while being wafted with incense, was he allowed to put his coat of arms on the candlesticks? No, came the reply.[97] The archbishop of Rouen who swept down the aisle with a train-bearer carrying the tail of his robe was innovating—the dean in person forcibly pulled the robe away.[98] If a new edition of the breviary came out without consultation, the cathedral might refuse to use it, as happened at Lyon in 1774, because the minor changes inconvenienced those canons who said the responses by heart.[99] A chapter could not control the ceremonies for consecrating the sacred oils, but what if the whole prestigious ceremony was moved away to the seminary chapel? This breach with tradition occurred at Le Mans in 1760, the bishop alleging the handicap of his rheumatism. 'There were several extraordinary chapters held over this affair,' noted one of the canons, though in the end, the idea of a lawsuit was abandoned—after all, the prelate was 81 years of age, and his excuse was convincing.[100]

There were places where bishop and cathedral chapter became locked into a permanent feud. The canons of Saint-Maurice of Angers feared Mgr Jacques de Grasse without respecting him; they were super-orthodox, anti-Jansenist, and full of zeal, whereas he was a tough, unspiritual Gallican and Jesuit-hater, who neglected his diocese to live in Paris. On his rare forays into the cathedral, he ignored the canons' rules about dress, and when he issued pastoral letters, he did not consult them, and omitted to call them 'frères'. The chapter scored by neglecting to repair the gutters cascading water on to the leaking palace roof, and the bishop arranged for an increase in clerical taxation to fall on his inconsiderate neighbours (taxation to which he himself was a notorious defaulter). In 1760 and 1769, he rounded off the vendetta by allying with his parish priests to defeat the chapter on questions concerning the authorization of confraternities and representation on the municipal council.[101] At Lombez, early in the century, there was an accumulation of miserable disputes—about the provost's claim to a chair in the sanctuary, the episcopal dykes draining water away from the chapter's mill, the election of officials, the right to light the municipal bonfire on St John's Eve, and about the shadow cast by a wall. Later in the century there was a different kind of confrontation, with the bishop trying to reform the too-comfortable canons. In his Christmas allocution to them on 23 December 1782, Mgr Salignac de La Mothe Fénelon accused them of malicious gossip, even in the sacristy and when the sacred vestments were worn, and of sheer idleness. He begged them to engage in edifying reading or, even, just study profane history, and offered to lend them books.[102]

Yet estrangement was not always bitter. Lawsuits about precedence and privileges were the common coin of relationships in French society, and did not preclude an appreciation of their comic quality or co-operation on other matters. The seventeenth century had been the age of the great battles of bishops against chapters; their eighteenth-century disputes were skirmishes on the margins of power. Because the Crown had adopted the episcopate as an instrument of domination and direction, the cathedrals had lost any effective right to be institutions of counsel and co-administration in the dioceses. Indeed, this was one of the reasons for the genial torpor reigning in many a cathedral close: 'confined to a secondary role, the canons were driven to find solace in the agreeable idleness of a life without challenges'.[103] Some bishops liked that kind of existence too, and were not disposed to stir up trouble at their very palace gates. In Angers, Couet du Vivier de Lorry, idle but sympathetic, soon effaced the memories of Jacques de Grasse's bristling hostility. Grimaldi, worldly and genial, came to Le Mans in 1767; he encouraged his canons to adopt a more splendid ceremonial dress and to beautify their church, and he often came to celebrate there, and welcomed them to dine at his table.[104] As 1789 approached, the demands of the parish priests for a say in the government of the Church became vociferous, and bishops and canons drew together in a conservative alliance; their rivalry had been a luxury of privilege, to be abandoned when both sides were threatened from below.

The quarrels of chapters with bishops and municipal officers were conducted within the established order of things: the canons were censured, but not so as to challenge their *raison d'être*, their right to exist. This radical criticism came into the debate because of their intensifying feud with the parish clergy, and lay society was glad to annex the arguments overheard in the course of clerical disagreements. Those who had to work hard for their living, whether in the pastoral ministry or in the everyday toil of society, were instinctively united in suspicion of members of corporations enjoying the inestimable boon of leisure. 'Aquets messieurs lous chanoines . . . biben comme dos princes et n'a d'autres penes que de canta queque litanie,' said the Bordeaux fishwives. Their life, said curé Meslier, is 'la perfection de la sainte-oisiveté'.[105] Canons were well paid for doing nothing but sing responses: with this utilitarian criticism agreed on, what was needed was a demonstration that this easy mode of life was not of divine institution, and was not necessary to the Church.

The parish priests envied the canons of the great foundations their wealth, the splendour of their ceremonies, the multitude of assistant clergy they had orbiting around their ministrations. Some curés had cause, not only for generalized envy, but for specific resentment when a chapter was the *curé primitif* of their parish.[106] This meant that the chapter paid them a dole by way of salary, and exercised honorific rights within the parish church which were vexatious to the pride of both priest and people—notably, sending a representative to celebrate the high mass of Christmas, Easter, Pentecost, All Saints, and the patronal festival. There was a variant type of humiliating dependence when the parish shared the church building with the chapter. In these cases, it was general to find the canons monopolizing the high altar, the stalls, and the great peal of bells, while the curés celebrated and preached in bleak naves or inglorious side chapels, their offices announced by the tintinnabulation of an inferior bell. There were disputes and lawsuits, and from this milieu of strife arose the pamphlet attacks on canons which were to have so much effect on public opinion. These writings combined the rehearsal of particular grievances with the ecclesiology of the Richerist theologians to press the cause of the curés, part of a growing movement of clerical unrest in the eighteenth century.

Auxerre became a centre of agitation in the late 1760s, when 'letters' were published on the dignity of the curés as against the canons.[107] A few years later, the controversy was renewed by Canon Frappier, who made an astonishing challenge to the old jurisprudence of France, alleging the cathedral to be 'la Paroisse des paroisses', a church in which all townspeople were entitled to make their Easter communion, bypassing their parish of residence, and the dean to be the 'archiprêtre' enjoying powers over the curés. Curé

Saloman of Saint-Regnobert replied in his *Lettres d'un Auxerrois à M. Frappier, chanoine de l'église cathédrale* (1779).[108] He had looked up Frappier's learned references; most were incorrectly cited, and some were sheer invention—let him confine himself to his task of supervising the cathedral repairs, something requiring none of the qualities of the historian. The curés were instituted by Christ himself; they are responsible only to the bishop, not to the dean, and all the pastoral functions are theirs by right. They alone can administer the last sacraments to their parishioners, marry them, bury them, and, in cases of emergency, authenticate their last testaments in the presence of two witnesses. The canons cannot perform these duties, even for their own bell-ringers. 'What is a canon? A man of retreat, of prayer, of study . . . How glorious for canons thus to be associated with the functions of the Angels! . . . But with all this, they are not Pastors in the Church . . . nor are they charged with the direction of its affairs.'

The same arguments were put forward from Angers, where the churches of Saint-Pierre, Saint-Maurille, Saint-Laud, and Saint-Martin were in dual occupancy, with chapters lording it over parishes. The story of their disputes was publicized, locally, then finally nationally, by the abbé Robin, the bellicose and eccentric curé of Saint-Pierre. The money he inherited from his father, a wholesale merchant, gave him funds to prosecute lawsuits, and in achieving his doctorate at the University of Angers, he had accumulated sufficient learning to embark on researches into provincial history—to his own satisfaction, they proved that the curés of the town had the right to be called 'cardinals', the natural councillors of the bishop, and were entitled to accompany him when he celebrated pontifically. Not surprisingly, the parish priest of Saint-Pierre was the senior 'cardinal' of them all. For forty years curé Robin battled against his chapter: over his right to an honorary canonry, to take the funerals of relatives of canons, over the building of a house for the parish sacristan, the ownership of the title-deeds to the cemetery, the parish right of way through the sacristy, the ownership of a ciborium, and the control of a confraternity—a story he recounted in a volume of 200 pages published in 1785. Having set his tribulations in the context of the Richerist arguments about the superiority of the parish priests, he recommended the abolition of most of the chapters of the land—not all of them, for he was not declaring them useless: 'nothing so sanctifying as psalm singing'.

'Chapters are simple gatherings of hermits who continually try to aggrandize themselves . . . the status of a canon is a private one, with the sole aim of sanctifying those who embrace it.' This was the condemnation of the two chapters of the city of Bordeaux launched by the fifteen curés of the place in 1778.[109] By contrast, they argued that their own status was one of usefulness to others: they were 'dedicated to the service of the faithful, the public and society'. The chapters replied feebly, saying they were 'the mother churches', claiming their privileges from tradition, irrespective of the question of usefulness. In Chartres, a similar debate took place with greater asperity in 1789.[110] Curé Pierre-Nicolas Tabourier accused the cathedral of usurping property truly belonging to the parish clergy, and imposing its 'aristocratic' domination on a Church that was in origin 'republican'. An *avocat*, Janvier de Flainville, joined in with a call for immediate practical measures: the suppression of numerous canonries in the eighteen chapters of the diocese to improve the wages of the parish clergy—'12 canons less means the enrichment of 50 curés'.

The effect of these agitations was to leave the canons friendless in the crisis of revolutionary times. Smaller and poorer foundations in the countryside enjoyed some local tolerance, especially if they did parochial duties; but the great chapters in the towns were the subject of comprehensive censure, and it was in the towns that a politically effective public opinion was formulated. The king's government was encouraged, almost compelled, to weight the voting system for electing clerical deputies to the Estates General against the canons and in favour of the curés. In their protests, the chapters revealed how out of touch they were: they argued that, being 'distinguished corporations', they should be given power as against 'isolated individuals', and that since bishops, chapters, and great benefice holders had, collectively, twice the wealth of the curés, they should have commensurate voting rights[111]—in short, a new injustice to compound the old. To no avail—only ten canons were elected.

15

THE GREAT CHAPTERS:
ARCHITECTURE AND MUSIC

I

For long the cathedrals and great collegiates had been churches belonging to the canons, in that it was here they said their obligatory daily offices, and belonging to the people, in so far as they were a congeries of chapels and shrines devoted to the cult of saints and the observances of confraternities, sites for prestigious burials, and places of popular resort for secular purposes. In the seventeenth century there was a clerical take-over, the canons downgrading popular usages and looking on their churches as settings for triumphalist liturgical services. The principal role of the people was to be worshippers under ecclesiastical direction. In the monasteries, the round of daily offices was still directed to the improvement of the spiritual health of the clerks who performed them; in the collegiate churches, the edification of the worshipping laity was becoming the primary aim—here, they would find the pomp and dignity lacking in their parishes. As the canons of Bordeaux, writing in self-justification to the National Assembly in 1789, declared, 'le ministère habituel d'un chapitre est de présenter journellement au peuple le spectacle du culte public dans sa plénitude'. In public statements at about the same time they described their cathedral as 'a Gate to Heaven for the whole diocese' and their high mass as 'the daily sacrifice of the town and diocese'.[1]

Translated into practice, this meant sophisticated music and, especially at high mass, elaborate ritual and displays of rich vestments. The splendour of the worship of the great churches of France in the eighteenth century has rarely been surpassed. True, there were wrangles, insults, jostling for precedence, to add a note of comic incongruity. But this was the price paid for employing such a multitude of clergy and, on the many occasions of national and civic celebration, drawing a packed congregation of those who counted—provincial governors, military officers, municipal aldermen, magistrates of the law courts, notables, guildsmen, members of confraternities. 'It is astonishing that men bring their love of distinctions to the very steps of the altars—practically all treatises on this matter begin with this reflection,' says the standard law dictionary of the century; 'but those who have the right to these public honours must have them recognized in the churches, since under our constitution the people has no opportunity of gathering together elsewhere.'[2] So, sacred ground as it was, rank and standing in the hierarchy of society were maintained, and if it meant fisticuffs and lawsuits, so be it.

But whatever the intrusive incidents, the cadre of worship was dramatic, its choreography precise and measured, the vestments glittering, the display of gold and silver ornaments and reliquaries opulent. Picturesque traditional ceremonies survived to diversify standard routines. At Saint-Martin of Tours, the celebrant at high mass made his confession at the tomb of the saint while the choir sang the introit, and at the offertory, the deacon and subdeacon brought the bread and wine in procession to the altar, preceded by a verger with staff, two choirboys with candles, and two thurifers arrayed in copes. At matins on Easter Day at Angers, two ecclesiastics in dalmatics wearing gloves and red hats represented the mourning women and approached the long white curtains symbolic of the 'sepulchre'; the gospel words were read, and from the 'tomb' emerged the 'angels', two chaplains in copes bearing silver-mounted ostrich eggs and singing 'Alleluia, Resurrexit Dominus'; the choir responded 'Deo gratias, Alleluia', and the organ swept into the Te Deum. There were similar enactments on Easter Day at Troyes. Not all antique observances survived, for the eighteenth century was all the while imposing its sense of decency and order, expurgating versicles and ceremonies which might excite the mockery of the sophisticated. At Chartres in 1700, the chapter ended the installation of a 'boy bishop' on Holy Innocents' Day; in 1765, the release of a pigeon during the liturgy of Pentecost was abandoned—organizing the pigeon-man and keeping him sober had proved difficult, and the fluttering distracted the choirboys.[3] Then, alas, in 1784, the reformers suppressed the wearing of wreaths of flowers by the choir during the octave of Corpus Christi and the following Sundays to St John the Baptist's Day. Abandoning the flowers was unimaginative austerity, but most changes were judicious, so the traditional and the new were agreeably blended, the sombre vividness of medieval copes allied to the pale pastel colours and gold thread of the modern chasubles, the lofty gothic arches overhead, the gilded magnificence of the baroque high altars, and the rococo encased walnut of the pulpits below. It is in the context of this liturgical splendour combining old ceremonies with the new emphases of Counter-Reformation spirituality that the architectural demolitions and additions of the eighteenth-century canons should be evaluated.

II

'Vandalisme' was a word coined by Grégoire in a report to the Convention on 31 August 1794 (14 Fructidor, Year III) recommending official protection for the Roman inscriptions of Gaul. Then, and subsequently, it was used to censure the cultural devastation wreaked by the French Revolution, whether motivated by anti-clericalism, hatred of aristocracy and monarchy, or by expedients to serve the war effort. By extension, it is used by art historians in love with the Middle Ages to describe the ruthless modification of their churches by the canons of the *ancien régime*—'le vandalisme embel-lisseur des chanoines'.[4] This is welcome to historians of the left, who relish the myth of monks and canons, blinded by their 'intransigent classicism',[5] waging a campaign to destroy the monuments of the Middle Ages—the argument *tu quoque* offered in mitigation of the crimes of the revolutionaries. In fact, these clerics of the old France, whatever demolitions were their responsibility, were far from being intransigent followers of a fashion or haters of things medieval. They were connoisseurs, aware of the nuances of competing artistic styles and (what is rarely conceded to them) churchmen with a spiritual and theological preoccupation with the ways in which art can serve religious ends.

True, they had in their minds a stereotype, evolved in the seventeenth century, of what a new-style church should look like, a concept sharply differing from the Gothic of the cathedrals they had inherited. Mansart's chapel of the Invalides embodies the ideal—the arching dome, the vast free-standing columns of the interior supporting a far-projecting entablature, and a high altar in black marble modelled on Bernini's baldachin in St Peter's at Rome. It was an amalgam of classical and baroque, according with the pervasive principle of the age, 'le bon goût'. On 6 September 1764, Parisians had the chance to see the definitive Enlightenment neo-classical version of the French style when the king laid the foundation-stone of the new church of the abbey of Sainte-Geneviève.[6] Soufflot, the architect, had on display a painted plaster model of the project: a cross-shaped building with four equal arms, lighted by forty-two large windows, a central dome under which the reliquary of the saint would repose, and an altar with a colossal *gloire* of angels set in one of the arms, and, outside, a vast colonnade. The central dome brought echoes of Byzantium, the Renaissance, and the baroque, and showed a rejoicing in technical expertise, an expertise that was incomplete, for in 1776 cracks began to appear in Soufflot's unfinished masterpiece. Since the continuing proceeds of the public lottery were to pay the bills, the architect planned a lavish interior, adorned with works from the chisels of Coustou and Houdon and the brushes of every distinguished metropolitan painter. The fame of the splendid building project resounded in the provinces. When the chief engineer for the province of Burgundy designed a new church for the little town of Givry in 1778, it was Soufflot's plan reduced to miniature.[7]

Yet, while the men of the eighteenth century had their peculiar ideal of ecclesiastical architecture, they were not blind to alternatives. In the arts, the Enlightenment proclaimed simple luminous principles while indulging in complex, eclectic, and exotic realizations. For architecture, Blondel's *Cours d'architecture* (1675–8) gave them their basic doctrine: to follow nature and reason, not fantasy. But they debated endlessly about what was natural and, even, what was reasonable. Were Gothic interiors 'natural' because (as was wrongly supposed) they tried to reproduce the effect of avenues of immense trees reaching skywards? Must columns be cylindrical because nature made nothing square? According to Blondel, the orders of architecture were permanently valid because derived from the proportions of the human body; the abbé Laugier, distrusting this abstract analogy, said they had been devised to show off exterior façades in sunlit climates.[8] The Quarrel of the Ancients and Moderns shook Blondel's dictum of seeking inspiration in classical antiquity and the Renaissance; it became a commonplace to say that the past could not bind the present—what progress could there be in the arts if everything had to be done by imitation? The canons of the eighteenth century were not trapped in classicism and the rules of Blondel. If they had in their minds a single directing principle, it was elegantly expressed by Voltaire:

> Simple en était la noble architecture,
> Chaque ornement en sa place arrêté
> Y semblait mis par la nécessité,
> L'art s'y cachait sous l'air de la nature,
> L'œil satisfait embrassait sa structure,
> Jamais surpris et toujours enchanté.[9]

This was how reason and nature worked in harmony: the utmost exercise of human ingenuity in detail creating a whole which appeared inevitable and hence, in a special sense, 'natural'.

Cathedral chapters did not instruct their architects with the gilded dome of the Invalides or the colonnade of Sainte-Geneviève in mind; nor were the architects single-minded enthusiasts for the modern idiom they had adopted. Astonishingly confident in their own sureness of artistic touch, they were nevertheless at one with the intellectual fashion of their age, which was discovering the splendour of the Middle Ages.[10] The Benedictines of Saint-Maur lauded the diligence of the monastic chroniclers, La Curne de Sainte Palaye the magnanimity of chivalry, the comte de Tressan the romance of the troubadours, and architects admitted the beauties of the Gothic style. In 1741, Soufflot produced a *Mémoire sur l'architecture gothique* for the Académie des Beaux-Arts of Lyon. He condemned the 'bizarre and chimerical ornaments of the Goths',[11] and regretted their excessive enthusiasm for sheer height and vertical lines; yet they were masters of light and shade, and erected buildings full of unexpected vistas and ravishing surprises. In 1775, the architectural theorist Laugier declared Gothic to be the best available style for churches: 'behind the mass of grotesque ornamentation which mars the effect, you sense a compelling, indefinable atmosphere of grandeur and majesty'.[12] An architect of Bordeaux in 1776 distinguished the intellectual appeal of the fashionable new architecture from the spiritual appeal of the medieval. 'By their prodigious height, our Gothic churches offer beauties missing from Saint-Sulpice, Saint-Roch and modern buildings in the Greek style. These, our intellect approves, but it is in the Gothic churches that our soul is moved and freed from bondage.'[13] There was praise, though always with a reservation, concerning the 'ornements'. They destroyed coherence, Montesquieu said: 'the confusion of ornaments fatigues . . . a Gothic building is a kind of enigma.'[14] Others found a lack of sophistication and propriety in the details themselves. A journalist in 1765 agreed that Gothic was splendid, but rejected it all the same, since 'its daring and lightness appear inseparable from its bad taste'.[15] Cochin the engraver, defending his friend Soufflot's plan for Sainte-Geneviève in 1770, explained why the Gothic style was not acceptable—'le mauvais goût des ornements'.[16] Through most of the century, this standard criticism prevailed. Yet by the 1780s, the climate of opinion was changing as the mood of pre-romantic reverie became fashionable. 'Medieval' ruins and tombs became features of the 'English garden', and at the Salon of 1785 artists were exhibiting paintings of mysterious Gothic interiors. 'A veritable Gothic revival'[17] was beginning. It was a tragedy that the revolutionary and Napoleonic era, inspired by Pompeii and Herculaneum, turned to the grim classicism of power and the style of ancient Rome.

The canons did not reject the architectural heritage of the Middle Ages. Repairs were made with a sense of the importance of avoiding incongruities. The cathedrals of Blois and Toulouse and the abbey church of Saint-Etienne at Caen were restored in the late seventeenth century in their original Gothic style, as was Strasbourg after the fire of 1759, and here, in the 1770s, additions along the outer walls for shops were done in an elaborate archaic pastiche. If accident destroyed a church, the rebuilding was likely to be a recreation of the past.[18] This happened at the abbey of Corbie, spires included, from 1701 to 1730, and at the abbey of Poissy, under the supervision of the king's architect, Robert de Cotte. The question of new style or old was fought out at Orléans, where the Huguenots had destroyed the cathedral.[19] Robert de Cotte repaired the skeleton of the portico in Gothic, but submitted a neo-Greek design for the nave, and there were some who looked forward to a fashionable imitation of the dome of the Invalides. But the canons and some influential citizens led by Bishop Fleuriau d'Armenonville in 1708 successfully appealed for royal consent to a plan in the original style by a local architect, Guillaume Hénault. It was his avowed aim to 'unite the Gothic to the Antique', and in this spirit Robert de Cotte refined the design before the rebuilding began.[20] It went on through the century, not without controversy, for under Trouard as architect, from 1769, there was danger of collapse, since the medieval techniques of thrusting heavy masses skywards had been only imperfectly mastered. The work was completed early in the nineteenth century, an uninspiring example of the Gothic revival devised before due time, in the era of the Enlightenment.

The canons appreciated the majesty and religious feeling of their Gothic heritage, but they were unhappy about 'le mauvais goût des ornements'. They wished to banish what was crude or grotesque and, even more importantly, what was superstitious, for theological as well as aesthetic considerations were involved. Burial vaults in churches were expressions of a naïve conviction that proximity to the altars could confer a priority on the Day of Resurrection, and they represented assertions of family pride as against Christian equality, so there was a bias towards getting rid of 'the gilded tombs of frail and sinful mortals'[21]—though this did not prevent the erection of some splendid eighteenth-century mausoleums with dramatic allegorical force. These grounds of challenge would not, of course, affect the tomb of Lazarus at Autun; but the canons destroyed it, partly because its twelfth-century design in the form of a church struck them as 'd'un gothique bâtard et de mauvais goût', but also because they were embarrassed at the story—how Lazarus, Martha, and Mary had sailed to Marseille, then travelled northwards. Superstition should be banished from the ornamentation of churches, and sound scholarship should prevail. Statues and paintings ought to conform to a proper understanding of biblical times (the disciples at the Last Supper should be reclining, not sitting, for example).[22] Pagan influences should be rejected: no nudes, no monsters, nothing 'capricious'. In this the Christian critics were saying much the same as Diderot from his unbelieving vantage-point: the infant Christ should not be Cupid minus wings, John the Baptist Ulysses in a sheepskin, Jesus a 'muscular bandit' like Hercules.[23] And Diderot and everyone else were quick to laugh if female saints had an aura of erotic charm.[24] The Last Judgement, a favourite subject on the western façades of churches, could be relied on to provide nudes and naïvetés and be all too literal—hence the fate of these sculptured assizes at Saint-Germain-l'Auxerrois, Notre-Dame, Angers, and Autun.

But theology intervened to do more than sanitize and exclude: it provided the driving principle for change, one which coincided neatly with the Voltairean ideal of noble simplicity and unity:

> Chaque ornement en sa place arrêté
> Y semblait mis par la nécessité . . .

This would come about when every detail led the eye to the devotional heart of Christian worship. In Counter-Reformation spirituality, devotion was brought to a central focus, away from the cults of minor saints and provincial traditions: God comes to earth, and the worshipping congregation comes together at the altar, in the Eucharist. The centre of the church must be the high altar, to be made overwhelmingly splendid in the fashion coming from Rome, with marble columns, a great baldachin, and a golden *gloire* of cloud-borne angels. This was the centre to which a new perspective would lead, uninterrupted by rood-screens, tombs, memorials, and clutters of statuary—the eye would rather be led up to it by delicately wrought grilles and polished marble floors. Down these vistas, the sunlight would stream, through new clear glass if necessary, suggesting a belief that was luminously reasonable, as against the mystery of the dim religious light.

A rich Benedictine abbey like Saint-Nicaise of Reims, with no one to please but its own inmates, could embark on these changes in a comprehensive programme. In 1772, when it was completed, Dom Philbert Leauté described what had been achieved.[25] The wooden medieval altar had been replaced with a new one in marble and bronze. The choir and the sanctuary leading up to it had been paved with red, grey, black, and white marble, so that a pattern of cubes was seen whichever way one looked at it. The windows had been reglazed in white glass, creating 'a wonderful effect'; then, since 'un vilain jubé gothique' interrupted 'the beautiful prospect of such elegant architecture', it had been demolished, together with the twelve-foot walls around the choir, which were replaced with grilles of wrought iron. Finally, from 1760 to 1765, new stalls and panelling were fitted.

Changes of this kind carried through by a brashly self-confident generation were bound to result in archaeological tragedies. At Sens, the Carolingian gold reredos was sent to the Royal Mint, and the altar where St Louis had married his queen was destroyed;[26] at Rouen the tombs of Richard Cœur de Lion and Charles V vanished, and the chapel in the episcopal palace where Joan of Arc was tried was rebuilt, albeit elegantly;[27] at Angers, the tomb of Duke René, hero of the province, and of his lady was evicted from the chancel, while tapestries of the fourteenth and fifteenth centuries were sold;[28] at Autun the tomb of Lazarus went; at Auxerre the gigantic statue of St Christopher was felled.[29]

Yet listing these disasters in an undifferentiated catalogue of crime is unjust. Changes were usually carried out piecemeal, over an extended period, beginning with the installation or, at least, the planning of a splendid new altar. The Slodtz brothers, at a cost of half a million livres, gave Soissons its new high altar with the great *gloire* towering over it; Servandoni, the architect of Saint-Sulpice, designed the Roman-type baldachin for Sens; when the fashion for the baroque was declining, in 1786, Sées built a severely classical altar with columns.[30] At Angers, the process of change began in 1699 with moving forward the altar in isolation, 'à la romaine', with handsome new paving leading up to it. Then, in 1757, the great baldachin on red marble columns was erected, with a flurry of cherubim supporting a gilded orb and crown. High mass at these altars was to be the focal point of Christian worship and the centre of architectural unity of the church, to which all perspectives tended. The parishioners of Saint-Étienne-du-Mont in Paris got rid of the rood-screen in 1740— it was, they said, 'a bridge whose presence interrupts the view of our Holy Mysteries'.[31] Five years later, the clergy of Saint-Germain-l'Auxerrois followed the same argument: the mass should not be concealed, but be 'a spectacle for the faithful'. Astonishingly, the prior of Saint-Denis dared to propose to the king the removal of the royal tombs in his abbey church. They are unsightly, he said, some of the effigies lacking hands and their crowns damaged. The new black and white marble paving could not be laid 'avec toute la symétrie de l'art' so long as they encumbered the floor; they impeded processions, and they made it impossible to see the celebrant at the altar.[32] The last was the strongest argument: a sweeping perspective was needed.

This was why the medieval rood-screens were doomed. At Reims, Beauvais, Angers, Bourges, Sens, Chartres, Puy-en-Velay, Tours, Limoges—indeed, almost everywhere—they were removed. There were degrees of ruthlessness in the operation: the canons of Chartres had the whole structure dismantled and the stones pounded into gravel to level the floor, except those adorned with bas-reliefs, which were incorporated into the paving; the bishop of Limoges ensured that his chapter rebuilt everything as it had been against the wall at the back of the nave. The canons of Amiens destroyed their screen, but refused to sacrifice their high-backed stalls to the view, since they were exquisitely carved, as if from fine wax. In some places the medieval work was replaced with a more delicately constructed barrier, one which broke up the view without obliterating it—a grille of ironwork in acanthus designs at Rieux, a row of Ionic pillars at Sens. A defence of rood-screens, *Dissertation sur les jubés*, had been published in 1688, an appeal to the quaint liturgical traditions of the Gallican Church: in their niches, arches, and pulpits, anointings, abjurations, and preachings had taken place, and soloists had been stationed there to alternate responses with the choir.[33] These precedents, referring to observances preceding the focusing of worship on the high altar, were little heeded. When some of the canons of Rouen fought against the majority of their colleagues in an attempt to preserve the old rood-screen, they argued from aesthetic and religious congruity, not from ancient practice.[34] The proposed replacement, they said, with its arches and Ionic columns, would clash with the Gothic surroundings; furthermore, the new project involved irreverence to the Holy Sacrament, since the tabernacle was to be housed in the pedestal of a statue. They were outvoted; the stone saints and Virgin were sold off to parish churches, and the new colonnade went up, consisting of six marble shafts of antique workmanship, plundered long ago from the ruins of Leptis Magna in North Africa.

The clear glass in the abbey of Saint-Nicaise had created 'a wonderful effect'. But this was not an innovation to be introduced lightly, since excessive sunlight could be an embarrassment—one parish church making the change had to buy curtains to keep the nave cool in summer. Most removals of stained glass were limited exercises. A damaged window might be glazed in clear, because replacement stained glass was hard to find; Pierre Le Vieil's *Traité pratique et historique de la peinture sur verre* was an advertisement for himself as the only successful practitioner of the art in Paris. If the scene depicted was theologically suspect or 'indecent', there was all the more reason to abandon it. Bernini had shown the way to direct the fall of light to intensify the impact of the sculptured dream, but few in France had followed him. Yet, if a new artistic masterpiece was installed, it would need illumination—clear glass was put in individual windows at Strasbourg and Notre-Dame in Paris to make the most of fashionable mausoleums by Pigalle. Above all, light had to be focused on the new high altars. Chartres from 1763 to 1789 was the supreme example. The fine range of sixteenth-century statuary round the choir was preserved and augmented; the thirteenth-century screen was replaced by a grille; the nearby pillars were encased in marble and stucco; and Bridan was commissioned to carve a colossal Assumption and bas-reliefs to frame the new altar of marble and gilded bronze. To show off this dramatic new liturgical centre-point, the stained glass of six of the famous windows was removed.[35]

The ideal of unity hymned by Voltaire and Blondel's doctrine of the 'bel ensemble' ran disastrously to seed in the second half of the century. Blondel's treatise had shown an incomprehension of the value, to both eye and imagination, of the sight of the natural building materials and their finish and graining: 'the nature of the materials ought not to matter; the beauty of the masses, the proportion of the parts and the unity of the whole are the first considerations.'[36] This sounds well until translated into practical terms as plaster and whitewash. Experts on these processes from Italy toured France, and at Metz, Meaux, Chartres, Angers, and various other places found cathedral chapters willing to hire them to complete the 'bel ensemble', obliterating the pattern of the stonework, engulfing ancient frescos, knocking off gargoyles and projections, and walling up niches and embrasures. Instead of the ornamental clutter distracting from the majesty of Gothic, there was now a modern fashion to degrade its splendour by a superficial contrivance. A process beginning intelligently with the building of splendid new baroque high

altars finished up with unselective and damaging innovation which
had lost any vestige of aesthetic or theological justification.

The architectural history of Notre-Dame in Paris reflects the
differing motives intervening for change, whether improving or
vandalizing. There was a revolutionary transformation early on,
based on the idea of the centrality of the altar, followed by a period
of repair and innovative restoration, then, finally, another of destructive incidents. From 1699 to 1725, under the direction of Robert de
Cotte, a new high altar was built, and the rood-screen, the sculptured walls surrounding the choir, and various medieval tombs were
swept away. Magnificent new choir-stalls in ornate woodwork (paid
for by Canon La Poste) were substituted for the old; there were
fifty-two high stalls and twenty-six low ones, their backs decorated
with bas-reliefs and the pillars between the seats carved in foliated
scrolls and the instruments of the Passion. Statues of the Virgin and
of Louis XIII and Louis XIV were commissioned from Coustou and
Coysevoix, to go at the east end. Under Cardinal Noailles as archbishop, the keynote was restoration, mostly at his expense. The
southern rose window with Christ surrounded by saints, apostles,
and the wise and foolish virgins was repaired and modified. The
decrepit chapels of St Martin and St Anne were knocked into one
under the invocation of St Louis, made resplendent in the modern
style with a marble altar and two marble statues. Austere as he was,
Noailles had his share of aristocratic pride, and the new chapel
became his family burial vault. In 1741–3, Le Vieil drastically
replaced some of the stained glass with clear. Thereafter the changes
were episodic and destructive, getting rid of excesses of an
unfashionable past. At Soufflot's instance the central pillar and statue
of Christ were removed from the porch, ostensibly to allow canopies
carried in procession to enter more easily.[37] In 1786, the colossal
statue of St Christopher (ridiculed by the wits as 'un roi Gothique')
was destroyed; the canons, facing the complaints of simple folk, pre-
tended that a heavy beam from the scaffolding of a repairing operation had fallen on it. In 1787, capitals of columns and gargoyles
which had become loose were knocked off and not replaced.[38]

The educated consensus of the day was with the canons in their
ruthless programme of modernization. Mercier complained, not of
the destruction of Gothic features, but of the clear glass and bright
daylight. He had loved promenading in the shadows, trembling with
solemn thoughts when the bells thundered in the gloom—the
canons had ended 'that imposing obscurity' which arouses religious
emotions. But this was in 1782, and he was reflecting the new mood

of pre-romantic reverie; the men of the Enlightenment preferred to think of the divine as manifested in glittering light, not in twilight melancholy. To them, religious awe arose from the sight of the lofty grandeur of the Gothic framework. A French exile in Rome, devotee of neo-classicism as he was, took Notre-Dame as the perfection of spirituality in architecture, with its 'unshakable mass' allied to 'daring' and 'lightness' of construction.[39] It was the aspect of their inheritance which the eighteenth-century canons admired and, in their self-confident and reckless way, assumed they were enhancing.

III

The splendour of the liturgical offices required music, and the great chapters laid out large sums, in some cases as much as a quarter of the income of the foundation, on maintaining a choir backed up by the organ and half a dozen or more musical instruments. The routine minimum music for the daily offices remained the traditional Gregorian chant (the notation in black lozenges on four lines and spaces), sung in unison without accompaniment.[40] Dr Burney found this at Lyon, where the canons and choirboys sang together 'without organs or books', and he thought it was the usual weekday practice in most places.[41] In fact, however, monodic plainsong was coming to be reserved for days of penitence—fauxbourdon and polyphony were taking over.[42] In the seventeenth century, the canons of Sisteron, under a statutory obligation to be proficient in the 'ars musica', had won a lawsuit defining this as plainsong, since, said their lawyers, the four-part singing only began in the fifteenth century. But times had brought changes, and this legal judgement had since been reversed. On Sundays and, sometimes, weekdays, the offices, especially vespers and compline, were diversified by the addition of motets, while at Benediction there would be a motet and the brief psalm *Laudate Dominum omnes gentes* as an epilogue.[43] At high mass, there were full settings, including the Kyrie, Gloria, Credo, Sanctus, Agnus Dei, and Benedictus, and motets might be added after the Epistle and during the Offertory and the Consecration. Though some of the congregation attended principally to enjoy the music, the structure of the sacramental rite at least dominated the presentation. The churches did not follow the Royal Chapel in making the music an end in itself: the daily mass at Versailles was a low mass with a motet of a quarter of an hour or more running on until the beginning of the Consecration, then a brief motet during the Elevation and Post Communion, the whole choir finally joining in singing the *Domine salvum* for the preservation of the king.[44] It was 'a musically elaborate, but liturgically minimal, service'.[45] In addition to the continual liturgical round, every church had its traditional musical requirements for special occasions and seasons. Something original would be expected from the choir for the feast of the patron saint. In times of national danger the psalm *Deus judicium* would be sung, in times of rejoicing, a Te Deum.[46] The season of Lent required a certain austerity in the music, but it provided haunting candle-lit performances of *Tenebrae* with two or three voices. At Christmas, there were carols, perhaps locally composed ones, depicting each guild and community in town bringing picturesquely characteristic offerings to the manger; in Toulouse, the young men of the city wrote new ones every year, competing for the honour of theirs being chosen by the canons for performance by the cathedral choir.[47]

A great deal of music was required, and the *maître de musique* had to provide it. The choirmaster of a cathedral today chooses scores from a huge fund of ready-made, perfected music, taking an eclectic view over a whole range of differing styles and periods, from the elaborate naïveté and spontaneous lyricism of earlier ages to the formalities and brilliance of the grand styles, classical, baroque, romantic, modernist, experimental. The range of music available in eighteenth-century France was inevitably more limited. There were plainsong and traditional settings for psalmody and standard responses—the fauxbourdon accompaniment of Lassus and of Jean de Bournonville for the Gregorian chant had been in print since the early seventeenth century. The Parisian firm of Ballard published music, sometimes traditional (as in 1707, ten masses by Lassus), sometimes new, by French composers.[48] In the 1680s, by order of Louis XIV, it printed fifty motets by Lully and other composers of the Royal Chapel. Posthumous publication made the works of others available; when Michel-Richard de Lalande died in 1726, his widow published his forty motets, the glory of the newer music of Versailles.[49] There was also a good deal of manuscript material available. Chapters encouraged their *maîtres de musique* to deposit copies of their scores in the archives; an ex-choirboy who had risen to eminence would send a few of his pieces as a tribute of gratitude for the education he had received. In 1782, François Giroust, *surintendant de la musique du roi*, gave the chapter of Orléans manuscript copies of a dozen Magnificats in memory of his happy days as *maître de musique* there. A director of provincial music would not lightly make his materials available to rivals and plagiarists, but he would be glad to gain fame by publishing a few choice items, and his canons, not loath to become renowned by association, would vote him a 'gratification' in recognition. Some of their compositions touched greatness—like Gilles's requiem with its haunting splendour.[50] These *maîtres de chapelle* of the old France, said Prunières, deserve to be the subject of a major monograph rescuing them from oblivion—they lived in their distant provinces, yet they were rivals of Campra and Rameau, who had themselves shared their provincial life-style before being drawn to Paris and the Opera.[51]

Yet, while there was material available for direct use or adaptation, the canons of a great French church would choose their *maître de musique*, not only as choir trainer and conductor, but as composer, and they expected that his own works would be the mainstay of his repertoire. No doubt he would simplify or adapt from some of the examples from Paris and Versailles and plagiarize here and there, but his pieces would bear the imprint of his own craftsmanship, and be written to fit the resources available to him. The congregations of that day listened to the music of their church in a different fashion from those of our century. The writer of the score would be known to them, and he would be using the idioms of the current fashion. As they listened, they were at once more involved and more critical, more confident in their own judgement, yet more limited in their expectations than we are.

A *maître de musique* needed many qualities, but the indispensable one was the ability to compose. When filling a vacancy, the chapter of Chartres would invite a prospective candidate to come, expenses paid, to stay for a week. On the Sunday, he would put on the music for the services, and then spend the remaining time setting given passages of devotional writing to music.[52] The scores he produced would be examined by a committee of canons and their advisers. If a candidate was unable to come, the chapter, as a concession, might allow him to send a selection of his musical compositions for the committee's consideration. The church of Saint-Séverin at Bordeaux locked up its candidates for several days composing music for given proses then sent the finished efforts to Paris for review by experts.[53] In 1786, Notre-Dame of Paris systematized these sorts of tests into a formal competition, in which J.-F. Lesueur defeated the *maîtres de musique* of Arras, Meaux, Tours, and Orléans. The triumph went to his head, and he did not have a long reign. After making some startling innovations, he announced to the chapter that he was going to London to audition there; in fact, he never did set off for

England, but was away long enough for the chapter to decide to dismiss him (though one of the canons gave him lodging in his country house, where he settled down to write operas).[54]

The candidates in these competitions were not unknown to the chapters beforehand. Vacancies were advertised by sending personal letters to reputable *maîtres de musique* of other churches encouraging them to apply. The canons watched the progress of promising choir boys, encouraging them to write compositions for performance by the choir: these might be so impressive that promotion could come direct from senior boy, as happened to Louis Fromental at Rouen in 1728, on the strength of his six motets with full orchestration.[55] In other cases, when a boy's voice broke, he would be kept on as an instrumentalist or clerk in the *bas chœur* until he was ripe to take over. This was how Henri Hardouin became *maître* at Reims. After serving as a choirboy, he was given a place among the minor clergy with the income of a chapel to support him; in December 1748 he was ordained subdeacon, and in the following year, at the age of 22, he took charge of the music. Liège backed up the career of a promising boy in a similar fashion, sending him to Rome to study in 1728, giving him a benefice when he came back in 1731, so that he was available for final promotion seven years later.[56] A chapter might also keep in touch with an ex-choirboy who had gone elsewhere and won fame, then in due course appeal to his local connections and loyalties to urge him to return. The canons of the cathedral of Sainte-Croix of Orléans had followed the career of Charles Hérissé after he left in 1758 to become *maître de chapelle* at Meaux; they knew of his gold medal in the competition of 1770 for a motet for unaccompanied voices and of his mass for the patronal festival of his church, much talked of in Paris.[57] In 1776, they moved to capture him with 2,500 livres a year and a canonry *semi-prébendé*; when, eleven years later, Notre-Dame of Paris issued an invitation, they kept him by the award of a generous retirement pension.

Since there was keen competition for their services, the *maîtres de musique* were inclined to move frequently—there was always some better financial offer, some more prestigious choir to conduct, some more agreeable place to live, some disagreeable circumstance to escape from, or some whim to gratify. Chartres, rich and splendid, found it easy to poach established musicians, but difficult to keep them. After fifteen years' stability to 1722, there was a two-year tenure, followed by a major competition in 1724, with candidates from the cathedrals of Evreux, Le Mans, Orléans, Mantes, Cambrai, Saint-Quentin, Coutances, and Langres.[58] The man from Langres was appointed, but never came (he heard that he was the favourite for the succession at Notre-Dame in Paris). So the canons settled for the man from Evreux. After three years, he was offered Rouen, accepted, but changed his mind and stayed. When he died in 1731, a former choirboy of Chartres who had risen to direct the music at Orléans succeeded, but for him it was only a stepping-stone to Notre-Dame in Paris. When he left three years later, the canons appointed Dulac from Tours; he stayed for three years, then decided he preferred Tours after all. The *maître de musique* of Verdun came, but could not control the boys and was dismissed, though this did not prevent him from progressing to fame at Saint-Germain-l'Auxerrois and Notre-Dame. The next appointment, from Dijon, was also disastrous, and he was sent packing, not only ignominiously, but with a royal *lettre de cachet* excluding him from the diocese. Dulac changed his mind again, and was persuaded to return; four years later, in 1753, he was off to Rouen. A search among the churches of Paris turned up a replacement from Saint-Jean-en-Grève who proved hopelessly idle. There was another competition in 1756, and three ex-choirboys of Chartres, all *maîtres de musique* in other cathedrals, applied. Demongeot was chosen, and he presented the canons with a manuscript collection of his masses as a gesture of gratitude for the start in life they had given him. Five years later, Notre-Dame of Paris, that menace to the musical ambitions of provincial chapters, stole him away. Stability finally came with Lalande from Soissons. He stayed for twenty-four years, tormented with illness towards the end—when the Corpus Christi procession toured the city, he had himself carried round so that he could conduct at each 'station'. He died in 1785, and the canons, who had long foreseen the vacancy, were ready to bring in the *maître de musique* from Evreux.

If Chartres with its wealth could not achieve continuity, what chance had the poorer chapters? At Troyes, the canons paid too little, and expected too much. At mid-century, they dismissed one *maître de musique* because he got married, 'par décence pour l'église'.[59] The next one, brought from Sainte-Radegonde of Poitiers, lasted two years. Deroussy came from Sées, but the canons were outraged at his Te Deum for the birth of the dauphin; he failed to compose a complete musical setting, and had some of the verses 'sung in *chant sur le livre*', 'au lieu de faire exécuter de la grande musique'. He was dismissed; others were tried; none was satisfactory; so Deroussy was reinstated. His successor resigned in 1761 after only a year in office, chagrined at having had to make an apology to one of the canons for some gesture of insolence. The chapter resolved to train a replacement, and sent one of the minor clerks to Paris to study music; no sooner was he back than he married. The same expedient was tried again; the abbé Duval returned from Paris, was ordained priest, and took over the music. His ordination had disqualified him from marriage, but qualified him for ecclesiastical promotion, and he left to become a canon at Dôle. Confusion followed. A candidate from Rouen was rejected because he demanded a higher salary. The *maître de musique* of Evreux made no such demand and was appointed; immediately he arrived, he made an increase of salary a condition of staying. Three months later, in June 1788, he refused to live in the *maîtrise*, and was forthwith dismissed. The old chapter declined to its fall with a subdeacon arriving from Paris to take over a collapsing choir.

What inducements could a chapter offer to persuade a man to stay? Given an appropriate person who had taken holy orders, he might be offered a canonry. Troyes, Meaux, and Bazas resorted to this guarantee of permanency; by this means Bazas kept Jean Maurin for fifty-one years.[60] The canons of Reims, having had a fright when Chartres tried to tempt Hardouin away, made sure they kept him by giving supplements to his income. His basic salary of 1,500 livres and free board and lodging were augmented by 'gratifications', including payments when he published collections of masses. In 1756 they gave him a second chapel (worth 200 livres) and in 1779 a third (245 livres), and in 1776 they made him a canon of Saint-Balsamie (500 livres), a chapter in town whose prebends were in their gift.[61] As the years went by, however, a musician in the post at Reims would be less and less likely to leave, for here, once in a generation, the most prestigious musical celebration of all took place, the coronation. True, Hardouin came off second-best in the negotiations with the *chapelle du roi*, for on the Sunday when Louis XVI was crowned, the mass was the composition of Giroux, the royal *maître de musique*, who conducted in person, and the Te Deum was to a setting by Rebel, the *surintendant de la musique du roi*. However, at the vespers of the preceding Saturday, the choir of Reims was allowed to sing the psalms antiphonally with the choir from Versailles, and on the following Saturday, at the vespers when the king was installed as the Grand Master of the Ordre du Saint-Esprit, Hardouin and his musicians had the monopoly.

Chartres, a rich, huge chapter full of feuds and unpopular with the laity, could not keep its directors of music—probably, they found it difficult to integrate with local society. By contrast, Angers, a small chapter, happily united and meshed with the social life of the town, kept its musicians because they found recognition and struck roots in the place. Bachelier, appointed shortly after leaving the choir school, stayed for forty-eight years, and left only because he was given a canonry in the neighbouring church of Saint-Pierre. Three successors followed in fifteen years, then Voillement, brought from Troyes, stayed to the Revolution. The local newspaper praised his style, declaring him to have 'a place among the most distinguished composers of church music';[62] his advice and co-operation were sought for every musical occasion, and the amateur musicians of the town came to the cathedral to form an orchestra when he celebrated the first mass after his ordination in 1785. Three years later, Notre-Dame of Paris called him, setting him above forty-seven rivals (so it was said), but the adulation and companionship he had found in Angers and the guarantee of a retiring pension of 800 livres at the age of 50 sufficed to convince him that the grandeurs of the capital were overrated. Recognition and friendship probably did more to retain the services of a *maître de musique* than straightforward financial inducements, but, if there was a more prestigious choir to conduct and greater musical scope, the temptation to move became almost irresistible. That is why music was a migratory profession in eighteenth-century France.

IV

The number of choirboys employed by the great churches was comparatively small: ten was the standard formula, as at Reims, Angers, and Chartres; in Paris there were twelve at Notre-Dame, and eight at the Sainte-Chapelle; there were six at Bordeaux and Coutances. The quality of the voices was superb. Candidates were legion, and the search for outstanding talent relentless. For children of peasants, artisans, and lower-middle-class people, there was no better opportunity for a start in life; for parents, no greater pride than to see a son walking the street to the cathedral, resplendent in red cassock and black biretta (at Chartres), or in white cassock like the pope with purple cap and red cape (at Angers). Chapters combed the parishes of their dioceses, following up every rumoured discovery of perfect tone and timbre—raw, untutored quality was what mattered, for the most intensive training would be given. At Troyes, the *maître de musique* was allowed time off to tour the villages, and in 1774 the canons decided to have advertisements read at sermon time at mass in all the churches of the town for the six weeks before the examination. At Chartres, the *maître de musique* not only went round the parishes, but also kept up a wide correspondence, including writing to his colleagues running the music of other cathedrals and to the *musiciens du roi* at Versailles. This network of contacts was effective: in the eight years before mid-century, six boys were brought in from Paris and a few from further afield. It was a two-way traffic, for musicians from Versailles were sent to spy out outstanding talent in the provinces, and it was not easy to resist an invitation—or, indeed, an order—to move to the Royal Chapel.[63] The final decision at Chartres was made at an audition in the presence of the whole chapter. The boys arrived, escorted by their parents or their parish priest (travel expenses paid), and the winners were appointed for a year's probationary period, the chapter making a formal contract with the family. This involved leaving home and taking up residence, if all went well, for something like ten years, in the choir school (variously termed the *maîtrise*, the *psalette*, or, at Reims, the *Maison au Pélican*). (Ten years may seem long, but voices broke later in those days.) Such was the rivalry between chapters that the office of choirboy was one of the few worthwhile employments in eighteenth-century France which was awarded exclusively on the basis of ability, though a testimonial from, say, the duchesse de Choiseul, could make a difference if other things were equal.[64]

The boys were well cared for. The chapter would appoint representatives to exercise oversight: at Tours, it was the two canons living in the house facing the *psalette* with windows overlooking the playground; at Reims, the annually elected *chanoine maître de la prébende des enfants de chœur*; at Chartres, a committee of three canons; at Troyes, two with a third added if major decisions had to be taken. The *maître de musique* was required to live in the choir school and be responsible for the running of the place, with a couple of women servants to cook and clean. If he neglected his duties, the canon superiors would act quickly, as at Troyes in 1782, when they hired seminarists to take over. The accommodation would be spartan but spacious, much better than the boys could have hoped for at home. An inventory at Troyes shows a dormitory with eight beds, a study with a wooden table and benches and an altar with a white cloth, flowers, and brass candlesticks, together with a kitchen and two other rooms. The food was remarkable for an age when the poor so often went hungry and so rarely ate meat; one contract with parents specifies bread, meat, and wine at every meal. There was generous medical attention. At Toulouse in 1735, two boys with ringworm were sent twice a week in a sedan chair to the hospital for treatment, and wigs were purchased for them to hide the deformity; at Troyes in 1738, when a boy was sent home with an infectious disease, a doctor was commissioned to pay visits, and an allowance was made to his mother to provide meat to make 'beef tea'.

Choirboys received a thorough education, specialist, but not narrow. Latin, French, and catechism were taught by a *maître de grammaire*; at Chartres in 1780 this was a well-paid office—1,125 livres with an extra 200 for doubling up as 'épistolier' and fees for masses, a total income which many a curé would envy. The musical training extended far beyond reading music, voice production, and accurate singing; expert tutors were brought in to teach the boys to play instruments, the serpent, bassoon, double bass, and the newer-fashioned violin, perhaps with the proviso that the instrument would be theirs eventually. Harmony, counterpoint, and orchestration were taught, and the boys were encouraged to produce original compositions. They could submit a motet, or even a complete mass, to the chapter for performance on a feast-day; if accepted, there was the honour of celebrity on the occasion and a gratuity voted by the canons, perhaps 20 or 30 livres. At Chartres, a boy on leaving had a right to read a Latin oration to the chapter asking permission to have a final motet performed and to be allowed to conduct it—a request usually granted.

When a choirboy's voice broke, the chapter saw to his future. There was a 'trousseau' of clothing and a leaving payment, a basic sum with extras—accumulated fees for having sung in endowed services, or for general meritorious conduct. At Notre-Dame of Paris and the great parish of Saint-Eustache and at Chartres, the total was regularly 300 livres or more, at Toulouse and Troyes half as much. Apprenticeship fees were paid, and contracts with employers arranged. A superior performer might be invited to stay on as an instrumentalist, or the post might be offered as a means of temporary support until it was possible to seek audition as a choirman. Those who chose an ecclesiastical career would have some or all of their seminary expenses paid; the cathedral of Coutances had an endowment providing six scholarships (*bourses*) at the Collège d'Harcourt in Paris. Outstanding musical talent could win astonishingly rapid promotion. In 1727, Louis Fromental, senior boy at Rouen, presented his canons with half a dozen motets with full orchestral score: in the following year they appointed him their *maître de musique*.[65] Bernard Jumentier left Chartres at the age of 18 to take charge of the music at Senlis. After a few months he fell ill;

the canons of Chartres, who had already paid his travelling expenses, welcomed him back and maintained him until he recovered, when he went off to be *maître de musique* at Saint-Malo, later moving up to Coutances.

Given their good prospects and their superior lot among their contemporaries, choirboys worked hard and behaved well. The sanction of expulsion was rarely needed: a consistently 'mutinous and proud' individual, after being given a second chance, might have to go, so too the senior boy involved in 'un épouvantable scandale dans la maîtrise'. Even so, a chapter might offer to arrange an apprenticeship and give a small maintenance allowance on condition of attending catechism classes. Another sanction, less severe, was to withhold payment of some customary gift. In 1786, the Sainte-Chapelle cancelled the Easter pocket-money because of irreverence during the services, and on two occasions refrained from adding supplementary extras to the leaving grants of boys who had contrived to have masses of their composition performed without the permission of the chapter. But punishments were rare. The canons accepted the inevitability of a measure of original sin, and put up with a moderate degree of laughter, whispering, and 'the circulation of manuscript works whose content is unknown to the chapter'[66]—had they been confiscated, no doubt by now they would be given in a footnote to some study of the clandestine literature of the Enlightenment.

In return for their generosity, the canons required the utmost diligence. The day of a choirboy was packed with regimented activity, though perhaps no more so than was the lot of the pupils in the *collèges*. At Reims, prayers were said at 6 a.m., then there was the procession to the cathedral in cassocks, surplices, and hats, with cloaks in cold weather. Matins and lauds were then sung antiphonally, with the choir divided into two sections. Breakfast was at 7 a.m., then a music practice for the two masses following; after the masses, classroom work till noon. Dinner and a recreational break all took place in an hour. Then an hour's practice for vespers, sung at 2 p.m.; then classes until 7 p.m., with a short break for a snack. Supper and recreation occupied the hour from 7 p.m. to 8 p.m., followed by prayers with the singing of versicles. Thereafter, bed, though some might be allowed to stay up to copy music. There was a mid-week relaxation of this austere curriculum—a free afternoon on the Tuesday and a supervised walk after vespers on the Wednesday. At Coutances, Toulouse, and Notre-Dame of Paris the programme of a choirboy's life was equally stern (indeed, at

Coutances, everything began earlier, at 4 a.m. in summer and 5 p.m. in winter). There was hardly any home leave, though every church had its occasions of holiday celebration—a feast or an excursion. Notre-Dame had its annual day trip to Saint-Denis and another to Meudon, and Archbishop de Juigné added a third by his summer invitations to his palace and gardens at Conflans.

No doubt in the *maîtrise*, as in French society generally, the official regulations were much sterner than actual practice, with plenty of that collusive idleness between masters and pupils which can make school-days so agreeable. And the daily round of the liturgical offices was not as boring as might be thought. The music was continually varied, and everyone's turn came to sing a solo. There were ceremonial duties—carrying the processional cross or candles in their silver sconces, wielding the snuffer, swinging the incense (there would be a practice incense boat in the *maîtrise*), parading round the church or outside in processions, joining in a foray from the choir-stalls to chant a motet at the tomb of the founder, making an informal pilgrimage to sing a May carol at the bishop's palace. Churches had their seasonal observances, with the boys playing picturesque roles. In Holy Week at Chartres, after *Tenebrae*, they accompanied two canons to the altar and sang 'miserere nobis' as the canons intoned the Kyrie, and at 'factus obediens usque ad mortem', a single boy replied 'mortem crucis', then all lay prostrate on the paving stones until the dean gave the signal to leave by striking three times on his stall. On Holy Saturday at Troyes, after compline, the litanies of the Sacred Name of Jesus were sung by two boys kneeling in the aisle, the full choir in the stalls accompanying in faux-bourdon; then there was a procession, and after in the vestry there was 20 sous for every boy for his 'Easter breakfast'. There was an abundance of such quaint rituals, often supported by an endowment to provide pocket-money or a feast. There was rivalry to be chosen for the posts of honour and intrigues to avoid the boring ones, basking in praise when things went well and taking refuge in wry 'in jokes' when some would-be reverent observance ended in disaster. Though the work was hard and the hours long, life was always interesting for the choirboys of the *ancien régime*.

A choirboy whose voice broke well, retaining force and purity of tone, might well aspire to a career as a professional singer. His chapter might give him a grant to study music in Paris in lieu of paying for an apprenticeship, but it was not easy to move directly into the world of opera and the theatre; the staging-point post would have to be a period as a choirman in one of the great churches. Other boys, with an ecclesiastical career in mind, might follow the same path and serve as a church musician while studying. And in any case, to be a choirman was a career in itself. At Angers, a *psalteur* could expect to earn 900 livres a year, with the possibility of a house provided. At Chartres in 1791, the salaries were said to run from 1,000 to 1,400 livres; since this was at a time when applicants for government pensions tended to inflate their returns, no doubt the figure included fees for singing anniversary masses, and also extras from the foundation of 'Saint-Piat', a sort of prebend applied to supporting the musical side of the cathedral's activities. Employment was usually for life, with income continued in sickness and old age.[67] At the Sainte-Chapelle in Paris there was no concept of retirement, for when a choirman aged 67 asked for 'vétérance' so that he could miss matins, the canons refused on the grounds that there was no precedent; however, they agreed to let him stay in bed in the early morning and mark him down as present. The same concession was made, seventeen years later, to another weary applicant. Ecclesiastical employment had its constraints, of course. The canons would not allow their singers to perform in secular concerts unless the repertoire was dignified and had religious overtones. At Troyes, choirmen were supposed to present a *billet* four times a year certifying they had received communion; in 1783, the canons decided to enforce the rule against those who had grown negligent.[68] Everywhere, chapters had the right to impose fines for breaches of discipline. The registers at Angers show deductions from salaries for unconventional dress in church, insolence to a canon, absence from matins, slipping off to the vestry before the end of the service, and for causing scandal by 'des conversations inutiles, souvent prolongées, même à haute voix, et par leurs rires immodérés', a nice formula used in 1772 and regarded as so appropriate that it was copied into the record when fines were imposed again three years later.[69]

The number of choirmen, like the number of boys, was comparatively small—sixteen at Chartres, ten at Bordeaux, in very small places only four. There was a great pool of talent to choose from, especially from former choirboys already trained to musical expertise. But there was difficulty in recruiting good voices in the high register—Toulouse, which at one time had one bass, two tenors, and three countertenors, was a remarkable exception.[70] In 1749 a canon of Troyes wrote from Paris to one of his colleagues: he had found a tenor, and it was urgent to get him, as the bishop of Meaux was making offers. He was an ex-opera singer, retired on an inadequate pension. Somehow, and not very suitably, he had managed to get ordained as a priest; his life was blameless, but he lacked intelligence and could not sight-read—he could only sing things he had studied the night before.[71] Nevertheless, his voice was strong and soaring. Seeing there was a demand for their services, the choirmen of the great churches constituted a mobile profession; outstanding talent always got better offers from outside, and tended to move round until local circumstances and friendships brought equilibrium. Some good performers did not accept contracts tying them down, but made themselves available for hire. In 1777, the *maître de musique* of Reims was looking for a tenor for a special occasion; he failed, but managed to get two good bass voices to come from Soissons. For major occasions, like the memorial service on the death of Louis XV, the Sainte-Chapelle of Paris would hire a dozen extra singers. The ecclesiastical musical world, in which everybody knew everyone else, constituted a sort of confraternity. A wandering singer of any quality was likely to be welcomed to join in the liturgical services while he was in town and be voted a gratuity by the canons when leaving, while a famous performer who was passing would offer to give a solo without reward—a nice question for the canons to decide: was he too distinguished to be offered an honorarium?

V

The development of French church music of the Enlightenment towards complexity, sophistication, and virtuosity owed something to sheer technological progress. From the beginning of the seventeenth century, there was a remarkable improvement in the precision and tone of musical instruments. The serpent, said to have been invented in 1590, was a development from various types of horn, bent to be shorter and more manageable, and was used to provide a heavy, rather raucous bass undercurrent. Cathedrals, which normally had two of them, had to look for senior choirboys well endowed with 'vent' and 'estomac' capable of blowing them. Le Cerf de Viéville, writing in 1705, described the serpent as 'privileged', since it was established in the churches by long usage.[72] Together with the organ (to keep the voices 'steady'), it had come to be regarded as the only allowable accompaniment for services 'around the altar'; then, he said, about twenty years earlier, strings had come in, being introduced into Notre-Dame of Paris by Campra. Even so, there were usually only two or three bass fiddles and a rather larger number of violins. As he wrote, all constraints had been abandoned in the

Royal Chapel at Versailles. At the baptism of the dauphin thirty-
seven years earlier, the full orchestra of the Chambre and the
trumpets and drums of the military establishment had been added to
the chapel instrumentalists.[73] A provincial visitor to Versailles in 1699
was surprised to hear oboes and flutes dominating the cadences of
the violins; however, he said, the effect was deeply religious: 'ils ne
servirent qu'à m'élever le cœur vers Dieu'. With the example of
the Royal Court and religious concerts in Paris shaping educated
opinion, the idea that only certain instruments could be 'religious'
faded. When the clarinet came from Saxony to the Opéra in mid-
century, the greater churches adopted it soon afterwards.[74] As the
canons of Notre-Dame said in 1786, when hiring a professional
orchestra to support their music on solemn feast-days: 'Why must
we have only reedy bassoons and lugubrious violins? By what
fatality do the most melodious instruments come under an especial
anathema?'[75] There was always the problem of expense, however.
The cost of a full orchestra every day, or even every Sunday, would
have been prohibitive.

The organ, always the indispensable accompaniment in churches,
in the course of the seventeenth century had been improved into an
instrument of rich and varied scope—there had been an increase in
the number of manuals, the multiplication of reed-stops, the widen-
ing of the boundaries of resonance into a sonorous timbre, the
multiplying of the facilities for embellishment in counterpoint and
complex cadences. This elaboration of function was matched by
proud display on the organ case: a show of flowers, cherubs, wreaths,
fiery-crested urns, musical instruments, palm trees, St Cecilia with
her spinet, and King David with his harp. In the seventeenth century
the style of high fashion was white and gold, as in the royal chapel
at Versailles, the Sainte-Chapelle and Notre-Dame at Paris, though
later the richness of the natural wood was preferred to emphasize
the delicacy of the carving.[76] Either way, it was a search for a visual
pleasure to prefigure the charm of the music.

The seventeenth century had its great organ-builders; early, there
was Valeran de Héman, who gave Rouen the splendid instrument
on which Jean Titelouze, the composer, trained a whole school of
church organists, and later, there was Alexandre Thierry who constructed the king's organ at Versailles.[77] In addition to the big names,
in every little town there were workmen who could at least do
repairs, and from their families came the great *facteurs d'orgues* of the
eighteenth century: Clicquot, Dallery, Cavaillé. Clicquot, whose
great individual achievements were the organs of Saint-Gervais

(1760), Saint-Sulpice (1781), and Poitiers (1790), did most of his other work in partnership with Charles Dallery, who had learned his trade from an uncle, a cooper of Amiens, who had exchanged the skills of barrel hooping for the mechanics of music. Together, Clicquot and Dallery built or repaired the instruments of Notre-Dame, Saint-Nicolas-des-Champs, Saint-Merry, and the Sainte-Chapelle, as well as doing numerous repairs—at the Royal Chapel and, in 1766, at the parish church of Versailles, where the organ had never been the same since 1730, when a thunderbolt had perforated the pipes with a multitude of little holes.[78] In the provinces, the Dupont family maintained the organs of the great churches of Lorraine. The area round Toulouse was the circuit of the Dominican friar Joseph Cavaillé and his assistant Frère Isnard—they rebuilt the cathedral organ, and repaired those of the parishes all around. Jean d'Angeville came to Angers from Paris in 1738 at the invitation of the chapter of Saint-Pierre; after working for this church, he was given the contract for renewing the cathedral instrument, and thereafter stayed in Anjou.[79] In like manner the Micot family, father and son, came from Paris to Bordeaux at the invitation of the canons of Saint-Seurin and then stayed on. The finest organ in town, however, was not their work—this was at the abbey of Sainte-Croix, completed in mid-century by one of its monks, the famous Dom Bedos, whose treatise, *L'Art du facteur d'orgues* (1766), became the indispensable handbook of contemporary expertise.[80]

Great *facteurs* were invited: lesser ones travelled round seeking commissions. Chapters and churchwardens examined their testimonials and made enquiries before signing a contract, but while doubts tormented their thrifty minds, if their church was bereft of music, there was a bias towards seizing the opportunity. In 1722 at Saint-Jean-de-Luz on the Spanish frontier, the notables committed 4,800 livres seeing that 'un entrepreneur horganiste estranger se trouve sur les lieux', and in 1755, another 1,500 livres because 'un facteur d'orgue de reputation est sur le lieu'.[81] When the work was finished, an expert would be called in to certify it; in 1722, the organist of the cathedral of Troyes earned a fee of 54 livres for going out to Ervy to make such a check.[82] The churchwardens of Saint-Jean-de-Luz made a mistake in 1722, for within eight years they had to call in an expert from far-away Paris to find out what was wrong, and on his recommendation brought in a *facteur* from the capital at a fee of 3,000 livres. The canons and parishioners of Saint-Michel of Draguignan in 1717 signed up an Italian who took their instrument to pieces then fled; seven years later they paid 2,000 livres to an expert from Marseille to put it together again.[83] The chapter of the cathedral of Orléans flatly refused to pay Adeline of Langres, for they had his repairs assessed by their own musicians and by the *maître de musique* and organist of Saint-Aignan and the organist of Saint-Paul, and they were united in condemnation.[84] The verdict of such a high-powered 'jury' (as the term went) had to be accepted. The wretched *facteur d'orgue* had to struggle on making readjustments, hoping he would not go bankrupt in the process—though he might try to shift the blame on to the conditions in which he had to work. The organist of the cathedral of Perpignan rejected the repairs made to a village organ; according to the *facteur*, the faults were the result of 'les déprédations des rats qui avaient gâté son ouvrage'.[85]

Organ playing, like organ building, was usually a family profession. Given the technicalities of the instrument and the difficulty of access, to become an accomplished performer needed the patronage of an established one: thus, Louis-Claude Daquin, the prodigy of the century, who played before Louis XIV in 1700 at the age of 6, was trained up to greatness by Louis Marchand of the Royal Chapel. A chapter might select a promising choirboy and send him to Paris for expert tuition, as the canons of Amiens did in 1780. Usually, however, skill was transmitted within the family circle. Organists, even if they took minor orders, generally stopped short of the subdiaconate and the obligation of celibacy; they married, and naturally wished to pass on their profitable expertise to their sons—and sometimes, their daughters.[86] Or there would be a nephew anxious to join the profession. Pierre-Claude Fourqueray, the son of an organist, came to Notre-Dame in 1761, and when he died eleven years later, his place was taken by his 27-year-old nephew, Nicolas Séjan. A father would negotiate to get his son appointed to some nearby church; Bainville, of the cathedral of Saint-Maurice at Angers, in 1773 suggested this to the canons of Saint-Pierre, offering to come over himself to play on great occasions—the young man, however, preferred to take his chance in Paris. Jean-Philippe Rameau, the future maestro of French opera, whose father was organist of the cathedral of Dijon, also chose to adventure on his own account; he played the violin with a travelling opera troupe, took employment as a church organist at Avignon and Clermont, then succeeded his father at Dijon briefly, before going back to Clermont by way of Lyon.[87] The canons of Clermont hoped to confine his wandering genius by a nine-year contract, but he haunted them with such barbarous music that they had to let him go to his destiny in Paris. In more conventional families, the young man would stay on as coadjutor, as it were, at the keyboard, in due course inheriting the succession. Louis Siret played for the cathedral of Troyes for fifty-one years, and on his death his son Nicolas took over for another half-century. Nicolas died in 1754, and was succeeded by the Joly brothers; after thirty years one of them was replaced by his son in the condominium. In Paris, centred on the church of Saint-Gervais, there was the resplendent Couperin dynasty. In the seventeenth century, Louis and Charles followed one another, with François their brother playing in other churches.[88] In 1685, at the age of 17, François II, the most famous of them all, took the inheritance. His father had died six years earlier, and the churchwardens paid Lalande to be *locum tenens* until the youngster grew up. Nicolas, a half-cousin of Couperin 'the Great', succeeded at Saint-Gervais in 1733. When he died fifteen years later, the succession fell to his son, Armand-Louis Couperin, who combined the duties with those at the churches of Sainte-Marguerite, Saint-Barthélemy, Saint-Merry, Saint-Jean-en-Grève, the Carmes-Billette, and the Sainte-Chapelle, with the addition, from 1755, of Notre-Dame; all the while he was also taking his turn, over a quarter of the year, at the Royal Chapel. One after the other, his two sons followed him at Saint-Gervais and the cathedral.

Armand-Louis Couperin was able to hold his collection of seven musical pluralities by playing himself in each church on its most important festivals and sending his wife and sons to deputize at others. This was a common practice. Guillaume-Antoine Calvière, a national celebrity praised in verses in the *Mercure*, reigned at Notre-Dame from 1730 to 1755, along with the Sainte-Chapelle, Saint-Germain-des-Prés, Sainte-Marguerite, and, from 1738, the Royal Chapel. The same practice is found in the provinces. The Joly brothers at Troyes, assisted by their sons and one of the wives, played for the cathedral and three parish churches, accumulating small fees and tied up in tricky contracts specifying when and where the two experts should play in person. The chapel at Versailles was an exclusive engagement, but here there were four organists, each in office for a quarter of the year, and free to play elsewhere at any other time. After the death of Calvière, Notre-Dame adopted the same system, simultaneously appointing Drouard de Bousset and Daquin (both of the Royal Chapel), Solange, and Armand-Louis Couperin. When Bousset died in 1760, Balbastre was brought in, fresh from his scandalous triumph of drawing such crowds to the midnight mass of Christmas at Saint-Roch that the archbishop had barred him from performing on this occasion in future.[89] Thanks to its adoption of fourfold appointments, from 1760 to 1772, the cathedral of Paris enjoyed the services of the two most sophisticated virtuosos of the century, vying with each other in their periods of duty, Daquin and Balbastre.

What was the role of the organ in church services? From contracts of the late seventeenth century it seems that it was commonly omitted from the weekday music of Lent and Advent, from Holy Innocents' Day, and a few other saints' days, but was necessary for all Sundays and major festivals.[90] Then, the organist was required to contribute at first and second vespers, matins, lauds, the evening *salut* and compline, and at high mass. For the mass, the instructions might be detailed, mentioning the Kyrie, Gloria, Sanctus, Benedictus, Agnus Dei, and the psalm *Domine salvum* (the patriotic addition for the safety and honour of the king). For the Elevation and Communion, an improvisation might be required as a devotional background, hence the warning that the tone must be one of solemnity. At the offices sung in plainsong, he was expected to subordinate his playing to the voices; he must not drown the chant, though he could 'alternate' with the choir and contribute 'interludes'. This is what Dr Burney found on his tour of France: the serpent was the essential accompaniment to the chant, the 'crutch for the voices to lean on', and the organ was used principally to play the melody before it was sung.[91] But what connoisseurs came to hear were the motets diversifying the offices with their elaborate harmonies and embellishments, and the Kyries, Glorias, and other set pieces of the masses, and here the organ might be used as the dominant or exclusive accompaniment. The two masses for organ by Couperin 'the Great', one for a parish, one for a convent, are masterpieces of virtuosity, 'to show off the instrument and the skill of the player', arabesques and dialogues of brilliant descriptive music anticipating Berlioz and Liszt.[92]

For church organists, the supreme moment came when they could improvise. Their skill became legendary. There were stories of contrivances to make an organ half-dismantled for repair sound complete, of panic caused by the tumultuous rendering of a battle scene, of the imitation of the song of a nightingale so convincing that vergers were sent to the upper galleries to expel the intruding bird. According to Mercier, the Parisian organists played ariettas and sarabands at the Elevation at mass, and at the Te Deum and vespers, hunting songs, minuets, sentimental airs, and rigadoons.[93] There is whimsical exaggeration here, and a hint of the journalistic predisposition to poses of moral rigorism. But outrageously brilliant improvisation was what the public wanted; there was no more popular musical occasion in the capital than Daquin or Balbastre performing fantastic variations on the tunes of old carols—a Christmas custom which had begun with Lalande in the chapel at Versailles. Great players were surrounded by the incense of hero worship. A parodist of La Bruyère's 'characters' describes them as they could be seen and heard in the churches of Paris.[94] 'Benoît' with his cloak slung negligently over his shoulder and his vast-brimmed hat, his playing thunderous and decorative, but lacking in delicacy; he bows low to his audience expecting an encore—he regards no praise as too fulsome. 'Célestin' goes to the organ loft as to a sanctuary where none but the perfect can enter, and when he comes down among the throng, it is with eyes raised to heaven and voice choking with emotion: 'Oh cher ami, merci!' Praise of his performance is not enough, you must 'understand' it. Then there is the modern organist admired by the great public, 'Rapido-Prestout', the acrobat of the keyboards, the inventor of novelties. Alas! why can we not exchange them all for 'Cromatius', forbidding in mien, playing only noble and majestic music?

French musicologists have seen the exhibitionist dexterity of these organists of the *ancien régime* as evidence of the decadence of the discipline, with the mastery passing to the Protestant North.[95] Perhaps this amounts to saying little more than that in Germany the instrument was developed to be capable of a wider range, and that France produced no Johann Sebastian Bach. With the advent of the Revolution and its crude propagandist insistence on military and patriotic themes, decadence—if such it was—became collapse. Balbastre finished up playing improvisations on the 'Marseillaise' and the 'Ça ira' at Notre-Dame, but at least, by doing so, he rescued the organ from demolition by the de-Christianizers.

VI

What was the nature of the music which the canons so lavishly subsidized? Did they have an ideal and seek to impose it, or did their musicians produce a dominant style which they accepted? Or was there an evolution of style going on progressively, shaped by the musicians under pressures from canons, other patrons, and educated opinion generally?

The rules of the Church reflected the traditional puritanical fear of the excessive passion aroused by music and of the worldly pleasure it gave its hearers. A papal circular in 1749 repeated the terms of the decree of Innocent XII of 1692 limiting music at mass to introit, gradual, offertory, Gloria, and Credo, and if anything more was added (for example, at the Elevation), it must be sober, perhaps a hymn of St Thomas Aquinas.[96] 'Fastidious repetitions' and 'confusions of voices' were banned. If there was instrumental music, it must be solemn, not theatrical; drums, trumpets, oboes, flutes, and harps were forbidden. Some of these rules for decorum had support from opinion in Europe. Dr Burney defined church music as 'grave and scientific compositions for voices only, of which the excellence consists more in good harmony, learned modulation and fugues upon ingenious and sober subjects than in light airs and turbulent accompaniments'.[97] But the whole tendency of the eighteenth century was towards throwing off those constraints. As Voltaire observed gleefully, 'Church music—it is a search for the pleasures of the senses in the observances of a religion established to fight against them.'[98]

What was happening in music, as in the arts generally, might be described, though over-dramatically, in an analogy borrowed from Spengler. The eighteenth century to Spengler was the mellow autumn of the West, an indefensible proposition outside his cyclical theory of history. But there was an autumn, one of vivid sunset splendour, the beginning of the end of the 1,300-year-old Christian culture of Europe. The arts were gaining their total independence, completing their emergence from the cocoon of religion which had formed and nourished them. Yet the organic connection still existed, and religion, in a sense, became worldly to accommodate the inspirations of the artists who served it. In music, looked at from one side, the relationship shows the world of secular music as parasitic. It was the ex-choirboys, church organists, and instrumentalists (and their children) who became the basses and tenors and conductors and musicians of the Opéra, the writers of the scores like Philidor, Grétry, and Rameau, the directors of the Royal Chapel like Lalande and Campra.[99] 'All the singers who have achieved any fame,' wrote Portalis to Napoleon in 1805, 'received their musical education in the *maîtrises*; in those days there were no other institutions to teach vocal music—not only did these old choir schools do the task well, but as everyone knew, there was no possible alternative.'[100] Nor was there when he wrote: the music for the Emperor's coronation was devised by two *maîtres de musique* of the *ancien régime*.

The churches provided the world with its musicians, and the world, by a reverse traffic, set its imprint upon the music of the churches, for better or for worse, according to the assumptions and prejudices of the critical listener. Among severe moralists, there remained lingering doubts about music for God's service being produced by worldly men and unbelievers. But by the eighteenth century, the civilized concept that superior artistic achievement in itself belongs to the divine inspiration running through creation[101] had more than half won acceptance. Certainly, it was rare for the life-style of a composer to be taken as a disqualification for his music. Secure in the favour of Louis XIV, Lully wrote the *grands motets* of the Royal Chapel, though well known to qualify, by membership of a ring of sodomists, for execution by burning.[102] André Campra's geriatric bohemian adventures were not in the reckoning when music was needed to grace the laying of the foundation-stone of the new altar of Saint-Sulpice by the papal nuncio in 1732.[103]

But what of the day-to-day performers? Were they allowed to combine their sacred duties with forays into the world, playing music to stir the passions, singing songs of profane amours? In 1734, the bishop of Montpellier urged the canons of his cathedral not to allow 'the musicians of the temple of the Lord to sing the praises of his Enemy in the place of his abode', that is, in a secular concert-hall.[104] Most chapters, however, would allow their choirmen and instrumentalists to accept outside engagements provided the repertoire was broadly concerned with religious themes. The cathedral of Saint-André at Bordeaux dismissed its German organist Franz Beck because he conducted in the theatre—the rival chapter of Saint-Seurin promptly signed him on as choirmaster.

The converse problem arose when outside professionals were hired to strengthen the church music on important occasions. Often, it was possible to do so without scandal, for singers from other churches might be available, as well as former choirmen who had left ecclesiastical service but came back occasionally to earn a supplementary income. It was different, however, when talent was hired from the theatrical world. The ecclesiastical ban on actors did not apply to opera singers, for they belonged to an institution under royal patronage.[105] Nevertheless, the logic of their immunity was not accepted by the strictest of moralists. The audience at a theatrical performance felt the thrill of passion, without having to bear its severe and salutary consequences.[106] The Sorbonne in 1693 expressed specific reservations where opera was concerned. In the inevitable love intrigue of the plot, temptation lurks—in the words, often enhanced by declamation, and in the appearance and gestures of the singers—while the music sweeps us away on a tide of unthinking emotion.[107] Yet, even as the doctors of theology made their pro-

nouncements, the courtiers and the rich of Paris were flocking to the
convents of the Feuillants and Théatins to hear *Tenebrae* sung by
soloists of the Opéra, men and women.[108] Because they haven't
added dancing as yet, asked La Bruyère, must we call the spectacle
an office of the Church?[109] At the Jesuit church of Saint-Louis, the
psalms of vespers were sung by professionals in fashionable town
dress—the writer of a comparison of French and Italian music at
the beginning of the century said that new arrivals at the Opéra
regarded the invitation to Saint-Louis as their indispensable initiation
ceremony.[110] Throughout the century, the tradition of sophisticated
performances of *Tenebrae* continued at the abbey of Longchamps
(except for a period when the archbishop of Paris banned them).[111]
But the great collegiate churches of Paris, in spite of their rivalry, did
not yield to the temptation of hiring professionals of the stage—that
is, until Lesueur became *maître de musique* of Notre-Dame in 1786.
He persuaded the chapter to bring in singers from the Opéra and a
full orchestra for the four principal feasts of the calendar. The cathedral was crowded, but some of the canons panicked when the complaints of the devout came in.[112] In their deliberations, they finally
decided to keep on the orchestra—indeed, the vote of money for
the instrumentalists was doubled—but to discontinue having the
opera singers.

Anyone employed by a church was liable to be dismissed for
immorality—if it was known. Where outstanding talent was concerned, it was not necessary to be officious and inquisitorial.[113] As for
church musicians being eaten up by pride, 'gaining fame . . . before
the altars in the presence of Jesus Christ who lived a humble and
inconspicuous life',[114] as one strict moralist said, no one cared about
it; nor was there much support for the complaint that the cost of the
music was excessive when so many were poor and the Church had
other responsibilities. Truth was, church-goers rejoiced to hear displays of ostentatious virtuosity and sophisticated contests for excellence, and canons spent as much as they could afford to keep their
church's musical reputation ahead of that of all their rivals.

The imprint of the world was set upon church music by the ambitions and ingenuities of the musicians, coupled with the operation of
social and cultural pressures. High society and sophisticated taste in
eighteenth-century France were dominated by two milieux, 'la
Cour et la Ville', the royal court at Versailles, and the capital, Paris.
This was so with church music, as with so much else. The dominant
influence in fashion was the royal chapel at Versailles. It had unique
resources. In mid-century, in addition to the organ, there was an

orchestra of fifty, which could be reinforced by other instrumental-ists from the king's *musique de la chambre*.[115] There were thirty chap-lains to sing the priestly parts of the offices, doing so in a rotation around the calendar, and another four who were experts reserved for the masses at the great festivals. The choirboys were double the number at most of the great cathedrals—twenty of them. The chapel *coutumier* allows us to glimpse them off duty, allowed to play skittles, boule, and quoits but not to skate, fight, throw stones or snowballs, and doomed to instant expulsion if found writing on walls.[116] There were fifty-two men, nicknamed 'Grille Boudins', since one of them was caught toasting a sausage on the incense burner during mass.[117] The shortage of high tenors was overcome by sending promising singers to be trained at the Opéra, and by importing castrati from Naples.[118] The chapel calendar was divided into four quarters, each with a different *maître de musique* in charge. The office, prestigious and allowing the holder to enjoy employment in one of the major churches of Paris for three-quarters of the year, was sought after by leading musicians from the churches of the provinces; when there was a vacancy, they presented themselves at Versailles to compete, being locked up in solitary confinement for six days, producing original compositions. They were expected to conform to, and enhance, the existing tradition of court music, hence one quarter of the year was 'le quartier des morts' devoted to performing the music of former composers of the Royal Chapel.

The *motet à grand chœur* which came to prevail at Versailles had reached its definitive form with Lully—vocal parts in infinite com-plexity, sometimes with double choirs responding to each other, solos, duets, and trios with orchestral accompaniment, recitative and declamation accompanied by organ and bass strings.[119] It was unabashedly theatrical music, written by a libertine, yet touched by surges of deep religious feeling. The motets and the gigantic Te Deum with drums and trumpets represent only one aspect of Lully's genius.[120] His Elevations for one or two voices, *De Profundis*, *O Lacrimae*, and *Miserere* are moving—Mme de Sévigné said of the *Miserere* there could be 'no other music in heaven'.[121] The tradition of the *grand motet* created by Lully was taken over and refined by Lalande; after his death in 1726 the court of Louis XV made the Tuesday of every week a Lalande day, devoted to his composi-tions.[122] His widow published his forty finest motets, tremendous set pieces with their battery of five-part singers and the orchestra sweep-ing on beyond the themes of the choir, violins rising in counterpoint above the voices.

The theatrical colour and uninhibited resort to operatic devices which characterized the music of the Royal Chapel owed something to Italian influences, mediated through two of the fashionable churches of Paris. Towards the end of the seventeenth century, Paolo Lorenzani, an ultramontane musical adventurer, excluded from Versailles by the jealousy of Lully, became *maître de musique* of the Théatins, while Marc-Antoine Charpentier, an imitator and rival of Lully and a disciple of Carissimi, ruled at the Jesuits.[123] Visitors returning from Rome had brought back glowing accounts of the dramatic performances of the massed choirs hired by the French embassy to celebrate the annual feast of St Louis;[124] polite society could now hear the Italian style every day at home. The Opéra was another meeting-place for the syncretism of national styles, and its effect on church music was evident in the religious music of Campra. In 1694 he left Notre-Dame to write for the theatre, and twenty-nine years later he left the Opéra to become a *maître de musique* at the Royal Chapel, and there for ten years he added to the tradition of the *grand motet* of Lully and Lalande elements of drama and pathos as in the Italian mode.

All the while a dispute resounded between connoisseurs enamoured of Italy and patriots loyal to France. To both sides, it was more than a rivalry between musicians over questions of style. At the stage of the 'Querelle des Bouffons' in 1752–4, one writer set French against Italian as talent versus nature, vehemence versus naïveté, ornament versus the truth in its purity. If there was a philosophical question at stake, it concerned the original derivation of music—is it a rational principle of nature, or is it the spontaneous language of the emotions?[125] The antithesis was artificial and ended in absurdity: Rameau's *boutade* that he could set the *Gazette d'Hollande* to music, and Rousseau's solemn assertion that only simple song, without harmony or instruments, is legitimate.[126] The controversy was tangential to church music, except in so far as the validation of emotional expression was concerned. 'Church music ought to be expressive' said a writer in 1725; 'the passions of opera are cold when compared to those depicted in our church music.'[127] His words are a pointer to the fallacy of attempting to divide music, ecclesiastical and secular, into sharply differentiated compartments: the feelings of love, pathos, tragedy, and hope, inseparable from our human condition, are all we have as guides to these sentiments as offered to God. In this sense, the 'Italians' in the quarrel were offering the musicians grounds for a greater freedom of expression. Yet, while the theorists argued about the two rational styles, the musicians themselves were engaged in the more prosaic activity of borrowing whatever attracted them in the compositions of their rivals. In the preface to his book of cantatas (1708), André Campra said he had tried to combine 'the delicacy of French music and the vivacity of the Italian'.[128] So too François Couperin in *Les Goûts réunis* (1724)—he proposed to imitate the best modes of both schools.[129]

Seeing that on the great ecclesiastical feasts and penitential days of the Church secular music was inappropriate, if not illegal, high society in Paris had grown used to enjoying religious music on these occasions, performed with worldly éclat. There were Christmas carols at the duchesse du Maine's, devoutly sung, though concluding with verses likening the bright eyes of the hostess to the star of Bethlehem;[130] mass every Sunday in the chapel of the wife of the farmer-general La Popelinière, when Gossec played the violin and Rameau improvised on the organ;[131] the *Miserere* of Lalande and motets by Mondonville sung in Pompadour's salon on Holy Saturday and Easter Day, with the royal mistress one of the voices.[132] This idea of religious music as entertainment was systematized for the theatre-going public of Paris by the foundation of the *Concert spirituel* in 1725. At first, performances were confined to Holy Week when the theatres were shut, but soon they were extended to all major ecclesiastical festivals and to all the days from Palm Sunday to Low Sunday. The entrance fee was four livres, affordable to all but the ordinary majority, and there were seats for 800 in the audience. Like the Royal Chapel, the *Concert spirituel* drew in talent from the churches—a bass from the choir of Lille who came and stayed on to write for the theatre, a choirboy of the Sainte-Chapelle who played the violin and finally became *surintendant de la musique du Roi*.[133] In 1766 the organizers of the concert offered a gold medal for a setting for *Super flumina Babylonis*, and, faced with two brilliant entries, awarded an extra one; both were won by Giroust, who was thus tempted from the *maîtrise* of Orléans to Paris and the Court.[134]

Parisians flocked to the concerts to hear the productions of the highly developed religious music of the French school, the glory of the chapel of Versailles. Apart from Pergolesi, practically all the music was by French composers, mostly of the century, Lalande, Gilles, Gossec, and Mondonville being the favourites.[135] It was staged without inhibition, from the start using the full range of professional talent available. At the second concert there was a motet by Couperin with full orchestra, sung by the tall and graceful Mlle Antier of the Opéra, with violin and flute sonatas. In 1728, Courbois's *Omnes gentes plaudite manibus* crashed out with an accom-

paniment of trumpets and cymbals.[136] The linkage with the style of
Versailles was accentuated when Mondonville, one of the royal
maîtres de musique, became director of the concerts from 1755. With
him, the repertoire of the *grands motets* (at which he himself excelled)
was diversified by the introduction of the oratorio. Originating in
Rome, the genre in France had begun with Charpentier—in 1703
it was defined as 'a species of sacred opera'. But there were few
examples before mid-century—the idea of telling a story in vocal
and orchestral form had been largely confined to the cantata, usually
on a mythological theme with an idealized love interest, the genre
of 'the embarkation for Cythère'.[137] Mondonville's *Les Israëlites à la
montagne d'Horeb* in 1758 marked the inauguration of the oratorio as
a fashionable form. In the following years oratorios figured as major
items in many a *Concert spirituel*—the biblical incident presented over
half an hour or so, the words in French, and the resources of the
Opéra, the Royal Chapel, and the choirs of Parisian churches
enlisted to make a sweeping dramatic performance.[138] The fashion
was relished by the musicians as an opportunity for displays of
virtuosity, and by the public, especially those who agreed with
D'Alembert's philistine verdict that 'toute musique qui ne peint rien
n'est que du bruit'.[139] The worldly nature of the nominally religious
themes of the *Concert spirituel* seemed to be reaffirmed when Gossec
became director in 1773, for he had risen (from the inevitable choir
school) as master of the music of La Popelinière and the prince de
Conti. Yet his religious compositions are sincere and convincing.
Religion and the arts were going their separate ways, but it was still
possible for musicians to turn from vividly secular subjects and the
passionate emotions of the human condition to the rarefied yearnings of religion with unselfconscious mastery.

The music of the Royal Chapel and the *Concert spirituel* was the
ruling style of the Church of France. Only wealthy chapters had
the resources to perform these tremendous motets, masses, and Te
Deums, and then only on special occasions. But the *maître de musique*
could put on the many pieces not requiring a sizeable orchestra—
motets and masses for voices only, Elevations, *Misereres*, and
Tenebrae; they adapted others, pillaged some, and in their own compositions emulated them all. Echoes of Lully, Lalande, Campra,
Charpentier, and Mondonville were heard in many a provincial
cathedral, recognized by those of the congregation who could afford
to winter in Parisian society. Musicologists have censured the loss of
true religious feeling in the 'great vocal and orchestral frescos'[140] and
the abandonment of liturgical prayers for para-liturgical exercises of

musical virtuosity.[141] Yet is true religious feeling an absolute ever the same? Who can be sure what devices of art and music evoke it, whether in the past or in varying social and cultural milieux today? A pious canon of Dijon thought Mondonville's motets at the *Concert spirituel* 'superior to everything I ever heard in later music',[142] without a hint of censure on grounds of worldliness; and an English visitor to Saint-Germain-l'Auxerrois in 1776 was touched to the heart: 'I heard them chanting the service, which I think the finest and most sublime devotional music in the world. I was fixed fast in a fit of devotion.'[143]

16

MONASTIC WEALTH AND THE
SOCIAL ORDER

I

You can never cross the Pont Neuf without seeing a monk, a white horse, and a whore, ran the proverb—which was hard luck on the two ladies who stood there and saw the first two but could not find the third.[1] The assumption was that, wherever one turned, a monk would be in view—or if not a monk, a nun. Voltaire's sardonic examples of the characteristic features of the civilization of his day included them: 'man will always be what he is now; this does not mean to say, however, that there will always be fine cities, cannons firing shot of 24 lbs weight, comic operas and convents of nuns'.[2] Members of the religious Orders in their habits of black, white, brown, and grey were a feature of the scene in the streets, and everyone had a monk or a nun among their relatives. Profession in the monastic life was an obvious possibility, duly weighed by families reflecting on how they could find an establishment for their sons and, more particularly, for their daughters.

Thanks to the inventories of the Revolution and the pension registers afterwards, a reasonable estimate of total numbers in 1789 can be given: 26,000 monks and 56,000 nuns.[3] Thus, religious were more numerous than parish clergy, for there were something like 60,000 curés and vicaires. The distribution of monasteries over the country was uneven; there was a concentration of monks in the borderlands of Artois, Hainault, Flanders, and Lorraine, and in Basse-Provence and Basse-Languedoc, and comparatively few in most of central France. Paris, however, was an exception, for here there were 900 monks in thirty-eight houses and 2,500 nuns in a hundred houses, about one person in religious life for every 300 inhabitants of the capital. The vast network of monastic establishments all over France was partly the legacy of the pious founders of the Middle Ages, and partly the recent creation of the zeal of seventeenth-century reformers. Of the hundred houses of women in Paris, only eight were created before the seventeenth century, and only eight from the century's end to the French Revolution. In the diocese of La Rochelle, in 1648 there were 130–80 nuns in seven houses; in 1724 there were 430 in twenty-two houses. The new foundations concentrated on education and caring for the sick and the poor. Of the seven convents of La Rochelle in 1648, all were 'cloistered', separated from secular life, and five were devoted to contemplation; of the twenty-two three-quarters of a century later, only eleven were 'cloistered', and only seven contemplative.[4] For the most part, in the eighteenth century the education of boys was in the hands of the Jesuits, Oratorians, Doctrinaires, Lazarists, Frères des Écoles Chrétiennes, and of girls in the hands of the Ursulines, nuns of the Visitation, and other 'new' congregations. The Filles de la Charité, founded by St Vincent de Paul in 1633, had spread everywhere, devoting their lives to the care of the sick with unparalleled dedication. These new and active congregations were immune from the decline in monastic recruitment which took place in the second half of the eighteenth century. Indeed, for those concerned with nursing and the education of the children of the poor, this was a golden age of new foundations.[5]

The wealth of the monasteries had been accumulated in the Middle Ages. The great institutions which had served the development of civilization in those distant days and had grown rich in the process, by now were mostly resting in the shade, leaving the new foundations to endure the toil and heat of the day. There were exceptions both ways, but this was the general picture. Pressures operating in the eighteenth century helped to ensure that the rich grew richer and the poor were kept down. Landed property conferred a security which even maladministration could not entirely undermine. The tendency was for agricultural rents to rise; this was true of tithe also, and it was the medieval foundations generally which enjoyed it. The pattern was uneven: in the diocese of Sens the income of one abbey quadrupled, while that of another remained stationary. Yet the general tendency was firm. The revenues of Sainte-Croix of Bordeaux tripled between 1730 and 1790. Saint-Aubin of Angers had a steady, small rise from 1720 to 1760, then 'an extraordinary explosion of land rent', amounting to a doubling in the next thirty years.[6] And, given landed possessions, it was often possible to devise some new method of exploitation. The monks of Sainte-Croix, always in debt, set up a rope factory and three sugar refineries, and, like the Cistercians of Beaune and the Antonists of Bar, they developed their wine trade, exporting their *vin blanc* to the Muslim Levant in bottles labelled 'eau minérale de

Sainte-Croix'.[7] The Discalced Carmelites of the rue de Vaugiraud in Paris owned a strip of urban land on which they built five mansions, leasing them out at about 7,000 livres a year each.[8] In 1723, the Benedictines of Liesses, realizing that the iron masters of Hainault were in a ring to keep down the price of the wood they bought from the abbey, set up furnaces themselves. Poor Dom Gérard had to stay in Paris for three years directing the lawsuits which ensued, distributing cheeses, snuff-boxes, and cash (and once a whole wild boar) as presents. 'To me the town is a prison and solitude is paradise,' he wrote, and he died there before he knew his case was won.[9] The Cistercians of Silvanes took advantage of the thermal springs on their lands to set up a hotel and two bathing places, getting Dr Malrieu in 1722 to certify their waters as 'containing chlorine, iron and sulphur, suitable for delicate, emaciated and weak persons, invalids and all those suffering from melancholy'.[10] And in emergencies, like a collapsing building, it was possible to ask royal permission to have a felling of timber.[11]

It was different with the newer institutions whose income was not safely derived from land. Disaster befell many of them in 1720 with the bursting of the bubble of Law's Scheme. The borrowers, whether institutions or individuals, on whose payments of interest so many communities depended, rushed to pay off their debts in paper. The estates of Brittany did so, and ruined two convents of nuns in Rennes.[12] The abbess of Gomerfontaine, making an entry in her registers in December 1721, attached one of the worthless banknotes of Law as a warning to her successors.[13] The royal edict of Mortmain in August 1749, banning religious institutions from increasing their holdings of land, hedged in the newer monasteries from acquisitions which might have guaranteed their future; the same edict also limited monastic investment to the loans floated by the government, the Clergy of France, dioceses, towns, and provincial estates, and on these, the interest was 5 per cent, lowered to 4 per cent in 1760. Enquiries in some dioceses in the 1720s revealed the grinding poverty to which so many of the convents of nuns were subjected— as in the diocese of Autun, where the bishop reported that twelve of his eighteen houses were running at a loss, and two more were just breaking even.[14] In 1727, the Royal Council set up a Commission de secours to rescue poor houses, but it seems to have been more inclined to propose suppressions than to provide financial help.

Reliable figures for incomes of religious houses are hard to establish. The religious and their superiors always had reasons to conceal affluence, and sometimes poverty as well. In 1727, the Dominicans of Bordeaux, hoping for royal help, said they had a deficit of 3,000 livres a year; faced with a threat of suppression, they discovered a 6,000 livres surplus.[15] Some apparently brave rent rolls had heavy charges to meet, like repairs to churches in parishes where tithe was levied and payments of the *congrue* to dependent curés. Even so, lack of precision does not invalidate broad comparisons, and everywhere we see a yawning divide between the rich and the poor houses.

In the diocese of Metz there was a massive concentration of wealth in the four great abbeys of the Congregation of Saint-Vanne, two Cistercian abbeys, a house of Chartreux, another of Prémontrés, a house of canonesses, and the abbey of Benedictine nuns of Saint-Glossinde; outside this charmed circle, the monastic scene was one of subsistence revenues running down to sheer penury.[16] In the diocese of Quimper, seven abbeys of men averaged 28,000 livres each, one of nuns had 5,000, and all the other houses were about 1,000 livres or less.[17] The contrast was stark in the monasteries crowded together in a provincial town. In Angers, the landed estates coming down from the Middle Ages were held by three Benedictine abbeys of Saint-Maur and by Ronceray, a haven for nuns of aristocratic lineage. The canons regular of the abbey of Toussaint had pretensions to grandeur which their income hardly warranted, and the Benedictine house of Lesvière was bankrupt. Of the seven houses of mendicants, four managed austerely, while the Récollets, Capuchins, and Minims were literally beggars. The Lazarists (preaching missions) and the Oratorians (running the *collège*) had arrived in the seventeenth century and had little endowment, and the Frères des Écoles Chrétiennes, invaluable teachers, had come only in 1741. Twelve Orders of women had established their convents since 1600, and of these, only the Ursulines were well off, having got their investments in land. The sisters caring for the sick, impotent, and penniless in three huge charitable institutions were short of resources (though some medieval endowments had fallen to the *hôtel-Dieu*). Seven of the twelve convents had been ruined by Law's Scheme in 1720, and struggled thereafter to survive; two (one for converted Protestant girls, now a hostel, and another of fallen women) never really became solvent again.[18]

The monasteries were wealthy—riches disproportionately divided as between individual Orders and houses, with little relation to social usefulness or service to religion, excessive in comparison with the income available to support the parochial ministry, and constituting an absurd proportion of the resources of the nation. Great riches create envy, and their misuse gives excuse for confiscation. By the eighteenth century, in a quiet way this had already happened; a comprehensive system to redistribute monastic income had come into being, a system operated by the Crown in the interests of the aristocracy.

II

By the Concordat with Rome of 1516, the king named the abbots of most of the regular abbeys of men in his kingdom. Exceptions were the seven houses which were the headquarters of their Order, as were Cîteaux and Grandmont, the four chief Cistercian daughter-houses, and Sainte-Geneviève at Paris, whose right to elect was confirmed by letters patent in 1626.[19] Also, up to 1764, the Benedictines of Saint-Maur made triennial elections to five major abbeys, but in that year the parlement of Paris overturned their right and transferred the nominations to the Crown. In Hainault, Flanders, Artois, the Cambrésis, and Alsace, provinces incorporated in metropolitan France after the Concordat, election by the monks remained the rule.[20] On very rare occasions, the king, by arbitrary fiat, imposed a cardinal or a prince of the blood royal on one of them; in these cases, the parlement and estates of Flanders insisted that the bulls of appointment contain the phrase, 'for this time only and without constituting a precedent'. Any election by the monks was supervised by a royal commissioner, who had the power to exclude individuals from voting if they were not French subjects, and the king's final warrant of confirmation was required. A cardinal appointed to an abbey whose headship was theoretically reserved to a monk had no power in the affairs of the whole Order;[21] priories in France depending on monasteries in the Low Countries were not at the Crown's disposal, but those in the Low Countries depending on French houses were. But an accumulation of legal rulings had defined most of the cases, and on the *feuille des bénéfices* at Versailles there were something like 815 abbeys and 280 priories for the aristocracy to intrigue for, and quite a number of others if those of small value are included.[22]

Usually, the king appointed an ecclesiastic who was not a monk— an *abbé commendataire*, holding the abbacy *in commendam*, that is, having the title and the revenue without being qualified to perform the duties. By the canonical rules,[23] the person nominated had to be at least 23 years of age and accept the obligation to proceed to priestly orders within a year; he must recite the offices of the breviary daily and wear clerical dress. These rules were ignored. All an *abbé commendataire* needed by way of qualification was to have become technically an ecclesiastic by being tonsured—a lock of his hair snipped off by the bishop at any time from the age of 7. Once tonsured, it was possible to hold benefices which did not involve the cure of souls, without any question of an obligation to celibacy or restriction of profession (though once an ecclesiastical benefice was obtained, it was not possible to bear arms without either renouncing it or obtaining a papal dispensation). Run-of-the-mill applicants for an abbey would improve their chances of getting one—or at least one that was fairly rich—if they proceeded to the priesthood, taking 'les derniers engagements'.[24] But influential candidates were awarded vast abbatial incomes on the strength of the tonsure alone, without pretence of any other tincture of religion.

The richest abbeys went to the great aristocrats. The *Almanach royal* for 1789 records their names, families more prestigious than most of those listed as holding bishoprics: Tilly, d'Estrées, La Rochefoucauld, Rohan, Vintimille, Chabannes, Crillon, Montesquieu. There was no question of the rules prohibiting the accumulation of benefices applying—a courtier would look back nostalgically at the thrill of having begun his accumulation, 'my first abbey'.[25] True, if some huge benefice came along, it became only decent to surrender a few minor ones. When he was young and well thought of at Court because his two brothers had just distinguished themselves on the battlefield, the abbé de Broglie was given the abbey of Vaux-de-Cernay with 7,500 livres. Two years later, in 1714, another (worth 13,000 livres) came his way. Then, after being agent of the Clergy of France from 1710 to 1720, he was rewarded with another worth 30,000 livres.[26] The story went that he had recommended a certain wine to the regent and sent him a present of 300 bottles. After estimating the costs of the original purchase, storage, and transport, Orléans said, 'the total is just right: the abbey of Mont-Saint-Michel'. Twenty years afterwards, to the astonishment of the courtiers, the abbé retired from society to live in his abbatial mansion at Vaux-de-Cernay, where he daily attended the offices of the monks. Had he been converted, or was he just saving to pay his debts? Vaux-de-Cernay was only six leagues from Versailles, so he would not lack for sophisticated company. Broglie was a priest and a doctor of theology, a churchman who preferred not to be tied down in a bishopric. A better—indeed, the classical—example of an unspiritual aristocrat waxing rich on ecclesiastical funds is his contemporary, Louis de Bourbon Condé, comte de Clermont, son of the prince de Condé and Mlle Nantes, daughter of Louis XIV and Mme de Montespan. With such a lineage, bulls for abbatial appointments rained on his once-tonsured locks—Bec, Saint-Claude, Marmoutier, Saint-Nicolas-des-Champs, and two others by the age of 13, and one more to top up at the age of 23. He surrendered three of these when the immense revenues of Saint-Germain-des-Prés came to him in 1737.[27] Rumour had it that he now had 300,000 livres a year, though in fact he had more than double this. Authorized by the Pope to bear arms without renouncing his benefices, he played the general in the French armies. Galloping back from the rout of Crefeld, he met the officer in charge of the baggage train. 'Have you seen any fugitives?' 'Non, Monseigneur, vous êtes le premier.' His harem in Paris was recruited principally from the Opéra; Mlle Carmago was succeeded by Mlle Le Duc, notorious for her parade down the Bois de Boulogne in Holy Week, glittering with diamonds and in a blue and gold carriage drawn by six tiny horses. The nearest he came to performing an ecclesiastical function was to build a marble mausoleum for his pet monkey McCarthy.

Vast revenues drew high-born and scandalous applicants. But for the most part, the system worked more decently. Bishops were always awarded supplementary income, those from the poorer dioceses because they needed them, those from the richer because they were from the great aristocratic families which expected unlimited largesse. In a distribution of ten abbeys in April 1745, Louis XV gave four to bishops, two to canons, two to *grands vicaires*, one to the French representative at Rome, and one to an ecclesiastical courtier.[28] According to the examples chosen, the system was a realistic redistribution of monastic revenues for the benefit of the wider church, or a pool of undeserved sinecures for the aristocracy. In the second half of the century, of the three Benedictine abbeys of Angers, the richest, Saint-Aubin, was held by the bishop of Sées, whose see provided an inadequate income; Saint-Serge was a perquisite of the bishop of Angers, who was in the middle-income episcopal range; and Saint-Nicolas was one of several benefices held by the abbé de Mostuejouls, a court chaplain. The Mostuejouls illustrate the way in which aristocratic families provided for themselves by decorous inroads into ecclesiastical wealth: the eldest son inherited the estate, the second son was a chaplain at Versailles, the third was a canon of the exclusively noble chapter of Saint-Julien de Brioude, and a daughter was a noble canoness of Remiremont.[29] The abbé François-Xavier Talbert, *grand vicaire* of Lescars, won a dozen academy prizes for essays and poetry, including the Academy of Dijon award on the origin of inequality (he suppressed his printed version when he read Rousseau's). Yet he was so poor that he had to sell his prize medals to survive. Who, then, could begrudge him the income from the priory of the Mont-aux-Malades at Rouen, leaving him free to follow his vocation as a preacher, which took him twice to Paris to deliver the prestigious panegyric of Saint-Louis before the Academy?[30] By contrast, who could defend the abbatial revenues of Saint-Vaast in Flanders going to Rohan, bishop of the wealthy see of Strasbourg and *grand aumônier* to the king? They came to 52,000 livres a year when he took over, and he went to law and got much more. Yet in 1749, the broad acres of Saint-Vaast, accumulated over more than a thousand years, found no aristocrat willing to be abbot, and Dom Vigor de Briois, one of the monks, took over. It was because the lofty spire of the abbey church, long tottering, had finally collapsed in February 1741, demolishing the roof of the chancel. Repairs, the responsibility of the abbot, would cost 2,800,000 livres. Dom Briois died in 1780, having restored the church and reorganized the monastic revenues. Another Rohan took over the role of titular abbot, now that it was profitable again.[31]

It was an illustration of the power of the aristocratic grip on the State that the king so generally gave away, by the *commende*, so much of the revenues of the abbeys of his kingdom, for he had other means of confiscating monastic wealth which operated in parallel and could easily have been extended. Just as, by the *régale*, the Crown drew the revenues of bishoprics during vacancies, in the same way, appointment to an abbey could be suspended, putting the abbot's income, as the phrase went, 'aux économats'. Thus in 1745, it was agreed to put several abbeys *aux économats* to pay for the rebuilding of the parish church of Saint-Louis at Versailles, and in 1750, the 50,000 livres a year of the abbey of Ligny was annexed for repairs to other parish churches.[32] The king's faithful subjects throughout the realm kept asking him for a share of this windfall income for useful projects. Thus, the University of Angers in 1762 applied for extra endowments for a *collège* to replace that of the Jesuits of La Flèche, asking the king to 'grant, for a fixed number of years, priories and other benefices which are under the *économat* or which might come under it—this would be sufficient to fulfil the object we propose'.[33] Abbeys also had to pay an annual tax, the *droit d'oblat* for the maintenance of the old soldiers in the Invalides.[34] Originally, an *oblat* was a royal pensioner granted the right of free residence in a monastery, and a few superannuated campaigners are still found enjoying this privilege as late as the mid-eighteenth century. But for the most part, the tax had replaced the obligation of direct hospitality. As the boundaries of France extended, so the tax followed to other monasteries, being imposed on those of Lorraine in 1768. This was the year in which the levy was raised to 300 livres a year on institutions with incomes of over 2,000 (75 livres a year on those of under 1,000). It was a trivial fee for rich foundations, but onerous for poor ones. The king was also entitled to grant a pension to be levied on the income of a nominated religious house. Occasionally, the money was directed to a respectable ecclesiastical use, like Saint-Vaast having to furnish 3,000 livres a year to a convent of nuns in Tournai. More often, it was a matter of conferring personal favours, with the aristocracy ever watchful to pounce for the lion's share. The duc de Luynes kept noting in his diary the awards as they became known at Versailles:[35] the monks of Saint-Amand elect a new abbot, but the king takes the opportunity to slap 38,000 livres worth of extra pensions on their house in addition to the old ones; the abbé de Castries gets a Cistercian abbey, but 7,000 of his 20,000 livres revenue is already appropriated for pensions; a converted Swedish nobleman living in Rome is given 6,000 a year from Saint-Germain-des-Prés; M. de Saint-André for long has had a pension on an abbey in Flanders, yet he does not belong to any order of chivalry—how can he be regarded as sufficiently distinguished to qualify? The king's will was sufficient to guarantee the worthiness of the recipients to have the money of the Church, a guarantee that was not transferable. Thus the law-books rejoiced in the case of Charles Gabrielli, aged 11, in 1765 given a pension of 1,500 livres on a priory; being hard up, he sold it to a lady who wanted an investment income; but the monastery refused to pay her; the affair went up through the courts to the parlement, which cancelled the transaction as simony.[36]

Another, more drastic way in which monastic wealth was diverted to other uses was by 'union des bénéfices'.[37] There were safeguards: an enquiry *de commodo et incommodo* with the appearance of the interested parties, royal letters patent to be registered, and if the cure of souls was involved, the diocesan bishop to be asked for his consent. On the other hand, if the government was carrying on a programme of reform, the necessity for a 'union' was taken for granted, and the king could act by arbitrary fiat. If a new diocese was planned, the first thing was to look for an abbey church for the cathedral and its buildings for an episcopal palace.[38] A bishop in a poor see could expect an abbey *in commendam* to see him through, but he might also try to unite one of his abbeys to the see in perpetuity for the benefit of his successors. He could also try for a union to bolster the income of his seminary or some other diocesan institution. But it was not easy to override vested rights. In 1781, the archbishop of Lyon got the priory of Savignieu (Forez) for the Oratorian *collège* at Montbrison, but the holder of the *commende* had to keep his revenues for life.[39] Massillon at Clermont tried for years to get the Benedictine abbey of Ébreuil for a seminary, putting in his nephew as abbot, a Trojan horse within the defences; he failed, but his successor made the building into a hospital when the number of monks fell to four.[40] A union might involve the suppression of the monastic house concerned, or it might just be the abbot's revenue that was taken over—as at the abbey of Saint-Jean at Laon, where the abbatial manse was given in 1756 to the new chapel being built at the École Militaire.[41] Generally speaking, unions were devised to put monastic wealth to a better use, whether within the Church or on its margins; but aristocratic greed being what it was, it was not impossible for a useful institution to be wound up to finance a sinecure.[42]

A commendatory abbot generally contrived to get half and often more of the revenues of the institution on which he was imposed. Reports submitted by the monastic houses of Normandy between 1723 and 1727 show the immensely rich abbey of Fécamp yielding 140,000 livres a year to its abbot and 138,840 to the community, while typical submissions from more ordinary houses show figures of 30,000 to the holder of the *commende* and 10,000 to the monks, ranging down to 10,000 as against 1,200. There are few examples of the community retaining the larger share, and there are complaints from some of the priors that they are being penalized by the unrealistic assumption that an allocation of 350 livres per head per year is enough for monks to live on.[43] Voltaire, who had a specialist anticlerical line in crocodile tears, professed to lament 'the fearful lot of a monk whose house is rich', since he will continually compare his own 'misery' to the 'opulence' of the abbot and the officials, and enviously curse the day he took his vows.[44] In fact, the monks in many of the great abbeys lived in some splendour, and Voltaire was the first to notice it. Even so, it is true that the *commende* did reduce some houses to penury and compelled them to limit their intake. In most monasteries, there was an established threefold division of revenues,[45] the abbot and the monks each having a share, and a further allocation to the *tiers lot*, which covered the *charges*—that is, repairs and a whole diversity of routine expenditure. The division might be traditional, or agreed by negotiation (*partage à l'amiable*); at

any time however, one of the parties could go to the law courts
asking for a *partage judiciare*. This possibility helped to bring about an
equilibrium, the side which was doing best out of present arrangements making concessions to avoid the hazards of a major redistribution. From the monks' point of view, the best arrangement was to
persuade their abbot to accept a fixed pension and leave the administration to them—after all, they had the local knowledge to extract
the best terms from farmers and building contractors. Under the
Regency, the abbé Du Bos was given the abbey of Notre-Dame de
Ressons (Rouen); he had the abbot's share and control of the *tiers
lot*, but for a quiet life he gave it all up for a guaranteed 2,000 livres
a year.[46] On the other hand, an abbot, if he could arrange for the care
of the administrative details, was likely to extract more if he kept the
tiers lot in his own hands or, indeed, kept everything. The Maurists
of the abbey of Ferrières accepted a fixed annual sum of 9,000 livres,
on which they lived reasonably well, but their abbot was pocketing
three times as much in a good year and shamefully neglected their
buildings.[47] When a *partage* took place, or adjustments were made to
it, there were a multitude of legal precautions the monks had to take.
Under certain conditions, lands allocated to their 'claustral offices',
like cellarer, were exempt from the *partage*—if they could establish
the documentation to prove the case; it was up to them to push into
the *tiers lot* as many things as possible—the library, the porters'
wages, clerical taxation, hospitality, as well as repairs, and the repairs
needed to be defined, whether 'minor' or 'maintenance' or 'major',
preferably all of them. Otherwise, they would receive letters like the
one sent by the archbishop of Aix to his abbey of Montmorel in
1741, refusing to be responsible 'for all the panes of glass broken by
neglect, for paving a church that never has been paved, and for
rebuilding buildings burned down, not by fire from heaven, but by
your imprudence'.[48] And there was the problem of keeping the
holder of the *commende* to his contractual obligations. On the death
or resignation of a titular, like as not there would be a backlog of
neglected repairs, possibly even going back to his predecessor—not
just the monastery buildings, but farmhouses, wells, mills, aqueducts,
winepresses, and local churches all over the estates.[49] If the bill came
to too much, the heirs would renounce the inheritance. The new
man coming into the abbacy *in commendam* would have to weigh up
the gamble: he had to manage to live long enough to begin to scrape
up a profit from an estate in dilapidation.[50] The monks had the consolation, such as it was, of knowing that it was the new abbot who
had to pursue the litigation against his predecessor or the heirs, but

this did not seal the leak in their dormitory roof or prevent the revenue of the estates from declining. The good Maurists of Ferrières, having jogged along for thirty years on their 9,000 livres a year from the distant chaplain to the duc d'Orléans, in 1780 were faced with the imminent collapse of their buildings; their new abbot, the bishop of Pamiers, had to arrange for demolitions and raise a large mortgage.[51]

A commendatory abbot might go and live in his benefice. When Huet resigned the bishopric of Avranches in 1699, the Court gave him Fontenay, and he soon had his nephew there putting the abbatial mansion in order, right down to having the fountains playing and reliable locks on the cellar doors.[52] Or perhaps he would make his abbatial mansion a hostel for retired priests, or a country resort for his holidays. But mostly, he was an absentee. The hard-up Benedictines of Saint-Gildas of Rhuys in Brittany, accustomed to never seeing their nominal head, had long ago incorporated his house into their living quarters—great was their chagrin when, in 1740, the abbé de Villeneuve announced that he wanted to occupy it; they had to build him a new one.[53] But continued absence did not make an abbot any the less determined to maximize his income. If he allowed the monks to administer the property in consideration of a pension, it would be by a lease for a limited term, to be put up in line with increases in agricultural rents at the renewal. If the monks would not pay more, there would be threats of the law and the *partage judiciaire*. Sometimes, a succession of abbots went along quietly, with their incomes being gradually increased by agreement. François-Charles de Béringhen d'Armainvilliers agreed with the Maurists of Sainte-Croix of Bordeaux in 1713 for 7,000 livres; Montmorency-Laval in 1743 improved the figure to 9,000. Growing dissatisfied, in 1754, he asked for the *partage*, but proceedings at law were inconclusive, and he resigned the abbey when he became bishop of Metz in 1760. Buisson de Beauteville, bishop of Alais, agreed a new lease, increased in 1770 to 10,400 livres a year. Two more abbots followed, and under the second, a *vicaire général* of Rouen, a *partage* was conceded by mutual agreement in 1787; it was never carried out.[54] By contrast, there was often great acrimony. Claude de Saint-Simon at the age of 20, in 1716, got the abbey of Saint-Pierre at Jumièges; he promptly broke the old agreement dating back to 1545, and demanded payment for every tree cut down since that time, struck the cellarer with his cane, and forced him and the prior to take refuge in other Benedictine houses; he insisted that the abbey dig deep into its capital to build a splendid new dormitory adorned with his coat of arms; as a result, the community had to reduce its numbers, leaving the new building half empty.[55] Still, there were worse cases of exactions: there are examples of poor houses being forced to close altogether.[56]

The incidence of monastic wealth was so unjust that it was impossible to argue against the principle of redistribution. According to good churchmen like the abbé Fleury, the ecclesiastical historian, the most appropriate use for the vast monastic surpluses was to make better provision for the secular clergy. In so far as the *commende* did this and contributed to pastoral efficiency, even austere Jansenists approved of it, plurality of benefices included. The stern Jansenist bishop of Agde, who died in 1702, asked pardon in his last testament for having two abbeys: he had prayed for grace to surrender them, but never had, for he made good use of the revenues, and did not wish to let them fall into less scrupulous hands.[57] But the *commende* was used essentially to provide for the aristocracy, to give supplementary incomes to members of great families, whether or not in high ecclesiastical office, and to provide respectable support for the younger sons of provincial nobles. As such, local opinion condemned it, since money which should have been spent where it was earned, for the benefit of trade or to provide alms to the poor, was siphoned off and spent elsewhere, more particularly in Paris.[58] And more and more, the sheer unfairness of the aristocratic grip on the wealth of the country rankled. In 1773, a pamphlet, *De l'usage qu'il conviendroit de faire du revenu des abbayes qui sont en commende*, proposed the abolition of the whole system: let the monks run their own estates, and let the king oblige them to pay pensions to maintain poor clergy, hospitals, seminaries, and good works of every kind.[59] Here spoke the charitable and egalitarian sentimentality of the latter years of the *ancien régime*. Yet the opposing theory of the rights of the nobility continued to flourish—not those of the great aristocrats, which were indefensible—but those of the hard-up provincial nobles, especially in areas where the customary law prescribed the division of heritages, resulting in families of ancient lineage inexorably slipping downwards into the ranks of the peasantry. To rescue them, Cardinal Fleury had thought of turning over the income of Saint-Germain-des-Prés to form a cadet school. Barbier heard the news and, cynical and envious bourgeois as he was, welcomed it: he accepted that provincial nobles needed help to educate their children.[60] Another cardinal, Bernis, looking back on how important to him had been his admission to the noble chapter of Lyon, reflected how, had he been a royal minister longer, he would have taken a good deal of monastic revenues to found more noble chapters, both of men and of women—and he would have ensured better endowments for canonries for the old nobility as against the new, to free them from the necessity of accepting marriages with rich commoners.[61] The archbishop of Reims in 1787 wanted all communities of monks in his diocese to sacrifice an annual sum in perpetuity to provide for the sons of poor nobles—giving them places in *collèges* and cadet schools and settlement grants for a start in life—and the houses of nuns were to make similar sacrifices for the daughters. 'The nobility, according to the constitution of the State', he said, 'has not the resources of the bourgeoisie or the people.'[62] It was a remarkable statement, on the very eve of the Revolution, of the divine right of a social class to be subsidized to maintain its status.

III

An abbot holding by the *commende* could take solemn possession of his church,[63] kiss the altar, sit in the highest stall, be presented with holy water, and wafted with incense—and, if in priestly orders, could even wear a pectoral cross; not that these privileges were ever exercised by the vast majority of Crown appointees. But he was legally prohibited from having anything to do with the internal discipline of the monastery: this was in the charge of a claustral prior elected by the monks (though some bishops who held a *commende* in their own diocese tried to claim the right to appoint).[64] There was, however, one Order, half-monastic, half-chivalric, whose vast income was monopolized by the sons of the aristocracy in a different fashion—by taking the vows and performing the obligations, in this case, the duty of waging war against the infidel.

The knights of St John of Jerusalem, a crusading Order of Hospitallers dating from the end of the eleventh century, had their headquarters at Malta, their base for warfare against the Turks and the Barbary corsairs.[65] The king of France regarded them as under his protection, and as providing a training school for his navy; their estates all over the country also furnished incomes and pensions for his naval officers. However, the Order of Malta, commonly so called, was jealous of its international status.[66] Of the seven *langues* (or *nations*) into which it was divided, three were French (Provence, Auvergne, and 'France'), but the other four were Italy, Germany, Castille, and Aragon. Of the three grand masters elected from 1734 to 1775, two were Spaniards and one Portuguese, and when a

Frenchman was elected in 1775, he was Emmanuel de Rohan, who was not *persona grata* at Versailles, since he served the duke of Parma, his father having fled from France after being involved in the Breton conspiracy of 1720. The lands of the Order in France, with their accompanying feudal dues and ecclesiastical tithes, were divided among 263 *commanderies*; these were grouped into *grands prieurés*, and these in their turn were units within the three *langues*. By contract, State and ecclesiastical taxation were paid by lump sums on favourable terms, coming to less than 200,000 livres a year, and half a million had to go annually to headquarters in Malta. This left five and a half million livres to reward the knights who rose to occupy the *commanderies*.

To become a *chevalier de Malte* required a minimum of four quarters of nobility on both the paternal and maternal side. There were exceptions, though they were few. It was possible to join, without proofs of nobility, as a *servant d'armes* and be promoted for distinguished services. Such a one, an exception in every way, was the French artist Favray, who was invited to Malta in 1744 to decorate churches and paint portraits, and rather more than thirty years later was made a knight by grand master Rohan. Towards the end of the *ancien régime*, wealth also came to make a difference, and old families accustomed to providing for their sons in the *commanderies* complained of the newly ennobled creeping in.[67] A young aristocrat might join the Order as a page of the grand master at the age of 12 or, more usually, wait to the age of 17 or 18 and go to Malta as a *caravaniste*. Each *langue* had its *auberge*, all fine seventeenth-century buildings, and here the young men lived a collegiate existence, playing billiards, fighting duels, and swaggering in cafés in their uniform of white breeches and red coats with yellow facings, occasionally being called out for forays at sea in the galleys. Finally, with splendid ceremonies, came investiture as a knight of the Order of St John of Jerusalem. The vow of celibacy was optional. The silver and enamel cross of the Order, worn round the neck on a ribbon of black watered silk, had three branches for the majority of knights who chose to preserve the right to marry; for the austere minority it had four branches and a white cross sewn on to the coat on the left-hand side.[68] The idea of a gallant crusader who had renounced the pleasures of the world was one to haunt the imagination of the age of *sensibilité*. The chevalier d'Anceny who kills Valmont in the duel in the denouement of the *Liaisons dangereuses* goes back to Malta to observe his vows, live separated from the world, and try to forget. And in real life there was the romantic story of the chevalier de

Boufflers, vowed to celibacy, who in 1778, at the age of 40, met Eléonore, comtesse de Sabran, a love that endured.[69]

Five years after investiture, a chevalier was eligible for a *commanderie* in his own *langue*. This could come eventually by seniority, or by promotion, depending on the grand master, the local *grand prieur*, and on influences from Versailles. *Commanderies* varied greatly in income. In the *prieuré* of Saint-Gilles in the *langue* of Provence, there were fifty-five of them with an average income of 18,500 livres each, but while Valence was worth 26,000, Valdrôme was farmed, in 1782, for a mere 4,800—hence, it was usually occupied by a *servant d'armes*. Every five years or so, a visitation was supposed to be made, a 'visite d'améliorissement' to test if the knight in occupation was worthy to be moved to a more lucrative post. But promotion tended to come slowly. Gaillard d'Agoult was at Poël-Laval in Dauphiné from 1748 to 1780 with revenues which rose little higher than 8,000 a year before he was offered the *commanderie* of Beaulieu with more than double the income.[70] The knights had the reputation of being harsh landlords. This was partly because most of them collected two sets of impositions which were often levied by different people—feudal dues and ecclesiastical tithe, and partly because nobles tended to be more exigent than monks of the religious Orders proper. Gaillard d'Agoult, with one-third of his revenues in tithe and one-third in seigneurial incidents, was in perpetual dispute with the inhabitants of Dieulefit (half of them being Protestants), and two other communities where he administered property joined with them to oppose him in lawsuits. His was a poor *commanderie*, but the bailli de Mirabeau (father of the revolutionary), who enjoyed 60,000 livres a year from Sainte-Eulalie, levied *champart* at one sheaf in every four to seven, tithe at one in ten, and the *prémice* at one in six—or so his peasants told the traveller Richeprey.[71] So much for 'l'ami des hommes'.

Gaillard d'Agoult had a great uncle who was *grand prieur* of Saint-Gilles and a brother who was a *commandeur* at Valence. This was typical: seafaring families of the nobility looked to the Order of Malta to support their sons in their naval careers. It was natural for the reforming abbé de Saint-Pierre to include in his project for 'perpetual peace' a scheme for a European fleet to burn out the North African pirates, for he had two brothers and a cousin who were squadron commanders in the Mediterranean.[72] Pierre André de Suffren followed two paternal uncles to Malta, served in both the Maltese galleys and the French navy, and at his death was drawing 58,000 livres income from his three *commanderies*.[73] These and other *chevaliers de Malte* form a picturesque gallery of adventurers—living dissolutely on their *commanderies* or bombarding the ports of Algiers and Tunis, writing from their ships to Rousseau or defending Voltaire in a literary society, languishing in the Bastille for verses describing Mme de Pompadour as a 'bloodsucker', taking up botany, and proposing the colonization of Guiana.[74] The marquis d'Éguilles, the future champion of the Jesuits before the parlement of Aix, was a *caravaniste* at Malta in his youth, and jumped ship in Sicily in a fit of pious fervour, attempting to join a local house of friars.[75] Claude de Rouvray de Saint-Simon (nephew of the writer of the memoirs) began as an Augustinian friar, fled to England and married, then got into the Order of Malta (against all the rules), was the hero of a naval engagement, became a *grand prieur* and the possessor of four *commanderies* and ended up as a diplomat.[76] Thus, a crusading Order devoted originally to driving the infidels from Jerusalem became the support of the life-style of French noble families and a major contributor to the efficiency of the French navy. And to draw an income as a *commandeur* or a *grand prieur* did not preclude a chevalier from holding the revenues of an abbey *in commendam* as well. A call for public prayers addressed to all the *langue* of France resounded with sonorous titles which are also attributions of sources of income. 'Jean-Philippe, Chevalier d'Orléans, Grandee of Spain, Great Cross of the Order of Jerusalem, Grand Prieur of France, General of the galleys of the King, Lieutenant-General of the Seas of the Levant, Commendatory Abbot of the abbey of Saint-Pierre d'Auvilay . . .'[77] He was fitting out his flagship and maintaining his state from the endowments bestowed on the Church in the pious Middle Ages.

IV

It was even more difficult for the poorer nobles to provide for their daughters than for their sons. A young man could join the army, taking the *brevet* of lieutenant and hoping to rise to lieutenant-colonel or even to *maréchal de camp*, the highest of the genuine fighting ranks. There was also the navy, preferably by way of the Order of Malta. Though trade was banned by the so-called law of *dérogéance*, it was possible to manage the estates or the finances of some great man. Marriage, judiciously arranged, could create a comfortable establishment, trading rank for dowry. And there was always the Church, possibly going no further than the tonsure and the *commende*. The girls had nowhere to turn but marriage, and the difficulty here was that a dowry had to be given, not received. Otherwise, the Church was the indispensable resource, and this meant taking religious vows. But, for a favoured minority, by definition from the more distinguished families which needed the help least, there was a less demanding way of gaining support from ecclesiastical revenues. All over France, but particularly in Lorraine, Franche Comté, Alsace, Hainault, Flanders, and Brabant, there were chapters of noble canonesses, providing staging-points where girls could await the arrival of eligible men and, failing a suitable match, could stay on for the rest of their lives. Though there were some differences in their rules, a standard pattern was: an abbess with two or three dignitaries, all taking the vow of chastity, and *chanoinesses prébendées* holding stalls, who vowed to obey the statutes of the house but did not accept the obligation of chastity and could leave whenever they desired. These ladies had the right to name a 'niece' or 'coadjutrice', who would come and live there intermittently and eventually, if both parties so desired, inherit the prebendal stall. Such a chapter was, said the *Dictionnaire de Trévoux*, 'rather a seminary or a respectable retreat for girls awaiting marriage than one for those engaged in the service of God'. They have no duties, said a lawyer sardonically, but to sing the office of Our Lady, 'an occupation which has nothing difficult about it except monotony'. However, he did not disapprove. 'Today', he added, 'these chapters are regarded as more useful establishments and more reasonable ones than the greater part of other religious institutions.'[78]

To gain admission, at least four quarters of nobility on both sides of the family were required. There was a formal examination of documents: Mme de Genlis tells how, at the age of 7, on her way to be installed as a canoness of Alix, she had to wait a fortnight at Lyon until the check was completed.[79] The genealogist's verification was expensive, though once the certificate was obtained, successive children could all make use of it: of the Chateaubriands, Lucile became a canoness of l'Argentière, then of Remiremont, on the strength of the family's *preuves*; then both her brothers took the opportunity to exercise the right of being presented to the king at Court, and one of them used the documentation to join the Order of Malta (in September 1789, too late to be of use to him).[80] Even when the proofs of nobility were established, a place in a noble chapter was hard to find. The search began early, and if a girl reached the age of 12 without a promise, the father would begin to despair.[81] More than influence was normally required: it was impor-tant to find a canoness in office to act as sponsor to a 'niece' and eventually pass on the prebendal stall. At Épinal in Lorraine, Gabrielle de Spada was pushed in by ducal nomination in 1729 at the age of 15, and was named as abbess by the duke in 1735 (with a papal brief of authorization, for the canonical age was 30). When she died in 1784, she had insinuated no fewer than five of her relatives into the chapter.[82] Her successor, promoted from canoness, was Mme d'Argenteuil, and she brought in her actual niece, aged 14, to occupy the stall she was vacating. Looking back after the Revolution on these golden days of privilege, the niece gave the standard aristocratic explanation: her grandfather and her two maternal uncles were killed in battle—'the Church nourished, in the shelter of its altars, a small number of daughters of the most distinguished families which had shed their blood for the fatherland'.[83]

There could be no question of subjecting chapters of noble canonesses to monastic discipline: all the pressures of polite society would be exercised against it. When the bishop of Grenoble early in the century tried to reform the chapter of Montfleury, the nobles of the province protested:

The decent liberty which the aforesaid ladies have enjoyed up to the present has always been a powerful attraction to persuade girls to renounce the world and retire to this house . . . They would never think of entering it if it was as frightful as the bishop of Grenoble prescribes by his ordinance, which would cause a notable prejudice to all the noble families of the province.[84]

Thus, life in these oases of quasi-ecclesiastical calm tended to be comfortable. In a few, there was scandal or rumours of scandal. The abbey of Sainte-Marie de Saint-Jean-le-Grand in the suburbs of Autun, where the inmates took no vows and came and went as they pleased, was notorious; Sainte-Marie de Saint-Andoche in the middle of town was similarly disorganized, but was more respectable, ever since the shock administered by the bishop in 1679, when he threw out trouble-makers and walled up the gates.[85] Two chapters in the diocese of Metz claimed to be exclusively under the jurisdiction of the Pope and continually engaged their bishop in litigation, until the king finally forbade them to fill any vacancies.[86] But scandal was the exception. If, in Franche Comté, Migette went on to 1789 without either community life or canonical rule, Baume-les-Dames, Notre-Dame de Battant, and Château-Chalon were decorous.[87]

Overwhelming pride and excessive comfort were the only charges which a severe moralist could make against most houses. It was, indeed, a splendid destiny to be abbess of Remiremont, by virtue of office a princess of the Holy Roman Empire, administering a revenue of over 300,000 livres, exercising jurisdiction in more than seventy-five towns and villages, patron of a hundred livings (on her death all these churches had to toll their bells for twenty-four days without stopping).[88] And it was, indeed, an unforgettable memory for a teenage girl awaiting marriage, to be installed as a canoness of Alix, received in the choir by the ladies in black silk and voluminous cloaks fringed with ermine, then proceeding to one's own house in the semicircle of gardens around the abbatial mansion, and savouring the title of 'countess'.[89] Mme de Chastenay recorded how she was received at Épinal in 1785. The twenty-one ladies preceded by the band of the garrison came to her aunt's house to fetch her. Then, in church, the questions: 'What do you seek, my daughter?' 'The bread and wine of Saint Goëry, to serve God and the Holy Virgin.' Then the biscuit and the wine, the arraying with the blue sash with its pendant cross, the ermine embroidered cloak and the black veil, with the singing of the Te Deum. Thereafter, for four or five days, nothing but balls and celebrations. Contemporaries relished the incongruity of girls playing the ecclesiastic. They noted the sister of the princesse de Montauban, Mme de Béthizy, a 'pretty canoness of Poussay', going out hunting with a musket (she fell, and it killed her), and Charlotte, sister of Président de Brosses of the parlement of Dijon at Neuville-les-Dames, 'a certain little canoness, lively and jaunty, who does not look as if she passes her time with her breviary'.[90]

Never had the French nobility schemed more ruthlessly to profit from the accident of birth than in its autumnal years, when privilege was withering into discredit. Of all their entrepreneurial efforts to annex the patrimony of the Gallican Church, the most effective was the institution of chapters of canonesses. Priests on subsistence wages said the liturgical offices, and the ladies (abbesses and dignitaries excepted) could spend most of the year elsewhere in the social whirl, looking for husbands. The royal government, which ought to have been channelling ecclesiastical surpluses to charity and education, was more concerned to satisfy aristocratic greed, and made a virtue of directing more church funds to the canonesses, as if it was a salutary reform. Neuville-les-Dames in the diocese of Belley shook off the control of the abbey of Cluny in 1710, keeping some of its lands, accumulated various priories, and in 1786 was given half the income of the abbey of Tournis; Louis XV had meanwhile conferred on the ladies the title of 'countess'.[91] In the diocese of Metz, a new

chapter of ladies was founded in 1762 by annexing two old
Benedictine foundations, the first abbess appointed being the sister
of the royal minister Choiseul.[92] When the hospitaller Order of
Saint-André-de-Viennois was suppressed in 1782, the canonesses
of Vienne got its property, circumventing a plot to annex it by
the Order of Malta.[93] About this time, Pierre-Louis de la
Rochefoucauld, bishop of Saintes, backed by the local nobles, established a chapter of canonesses in his episcopal town, annexing the
abbey of Benedictine nuns of Notre-Dame-hors-les-murs for the
purpose. But he had reckoned without the formidable abbess, Mme
de Parabère, daughter of the regent by his most famous mistress; by
1789 she had got the king to cancel his permission, and had the bells
of her church rung for twelve hours in celebration.[94] In the same
year, another noble chapter of women was created in the diocese of
Saint-Flour from the abbey of Saint-Pierre de Blesle, which was
already a foundation of nuns of exclusively distinguished birth, with
the income of other benefices added.[95] The destruction of the privileges of the nobility and the closure of the monasteries were at hand,
but the aristocratic pursuit of ecclesiastical money went on to the
very end.

V

Abbeys and priories of women did not come under the Concordat,
but the king had quietly arrogated to himself the right to appoint to
great houses; in ineffectual protest, the Roman Daterie sent provisions omitting the reference to royal nomination and saving face by
stating, imaginatively, that the nuns had elected in secret ballot by a
two-thirds majority. Because of their limited revenues, most convents of nuns were outside the scope of the royal interest, so their
superiors were elected or, according to varying traditions, nominated by bishops or by lay or ecclesiastical patrons. The Crown also
exempted the Annonciades and certain other houses from its
assumed right of appointment.[96] What interested the king and the
courtiers of Versailles was, above all, the disposal of the splendid
abbeys of France, with their broad acres and proud buildings. For
example, there was Avenay, owning extensive vineyards in the wine
country round Reims; from their profits, the church and monastery,
destroyed in the fire of 1754, were rebuilt within six years. There
was Notre-Dame de Jouarre, 'Jouarre-la-Noble, Jouarre-la-Riche';
one farm, seven plantations of woods, and a quarry were exploited

directly, sixteen farms and many meadows were leased out and extensive tithes collected, yielding an income of 2,000 livres for every nun in residence.[97] Fontevrault, with even more extensive estates, employed a *sénéchal*, a *procureur fiscal*, and a *greffier* solely to collect its feudal dues, and one employee to levy tolls on barges passing through Saumur on the River Loire. Louis XV made the abbey even richer, exempting it and its farmers from all taxation as a reward for its nuns having brought up four of his young daughters.

Such proud and wealthy foundations were inevitably given an abbess from one of the great aristocratic families at Court. The normal rules which governed the pattern of life of nuns did not apply to these ladies. They changed the Order to which they belonged to take promotion, they would move from the headship of one house to another supposedly more distinguished, and not infrequently—normally by the device of coadjutorship—arranged for a relative to succeed them. Whether as aristocrats, nuns, or human types, these remarkable ladies deserve the attention of historians and demographers. They tended to live to a great age, and since they were sometimes very young when appointed, their reign could be prodigiously long. At Notre-Dame de Perrigne[98] in the province of Maine, Renée de Beaumanoir came to rule in 1691, transferring from the Order of Fontevrault. Her niece, Eléonore de Morell d'Aubigny, succeeded her, and was in office for nearly forty years, dying at the age of 78. Anne-Madeleine de Girard de la Chaume then ruled for twenty-seven years, dying at the age of 82. When the eccentric daughter of the regent resigned the abbey of Chelles in 1734, Anne de Clermont Gersen de Chartre followed, and was still in office fifty-five years later when the Revolution began.[99] An even longer reign was that of Charlotte-Julie de Boufflers, daughter of the *maréchal*, who at the age of 22 succeeded her aunt at Avenay in 1720, and fifty-six years later resigned in favour of a noble lady who had been held up for long as subprior in the royal abbey of Saint-Paul under the rule of her sister.[100] 'Jouarre-la-Riche', after being held successively by three ladies of the Rohan clan, fell out of the family grip when a niece destined to succeed died suddenly, and in 1738 Catherine-Henriette de Montmorin de Saint-Hérem became abbess; she was still there, aged 90 and thinking of retiring, when the Revolution came.[101] Hers was a family with a particular vocation to serve the Gallican Church, conjoined with the inclination to administer its property. Twenty-eight years earlier, after the death of her mother, her widowed father had become bishop of Aire. Her brother Gilbert succeeded to his bishopric and then in 1733 was translated to the richer one of Langres. Catherine and her elder sister Louise-Claire had meanwhile become nuns in the abbey of Clavas (Lozère) under their aunt as abbess. Louise-Claire succeeded at Clavas, then moved on three times to the abbatial manses of more distinguished houses, and finally in 1742 got the greatest prize of all, Fontevrault; here, her brother, the bishop of Langres, installed her.[102] Catherine became abbess of Cherenton (Cher) in 1737, and a year later moved up to the splendours of Jouarre. Here, in 1753, her sister from Fontevrault, grievously ill, came to join her for the last two months of her life. To this family, as for others, having an aunt or other relative in the office of abbess, acting as an initial protector and sponsor, was important. Witness the ill luck—temporary as it turned out—of Anne-Eléonore-Marie de Béthun d'Orval, who was put in an abbey under her aunt's care from the age of 3 and was professed at 16. When her aunt left to rule elsewhere, her fellow nuns persecuted her for ten years, until she went off to her sister, the abbess of Saint-Pierre of Reims; after fourteen years there, she herself became an abbess, and went to rule the Benedictines of Notre-Dame du Val de Gif.[103]

For good and for ill, the exercise of power came early to these lofty aristocratic ladies; perhaps its satisfactions helped to prolong their days. Their estates were well run and their farmers held to strict accountability. Their alms were limited—the doctor of Chelles was paid more than the poor of the village received in charity. Yet, true daughters of *grands seigneurs*, they ran their communities into debt if the maintenance of status demanded conspicuous expenditure. Their curés were kept in due subordination; no share of the monastic wealth came to augment their often meagre allowances, and they had to render attendance at processions and liturgical offices, which demonstrated the superiority of the nuns. Anyone, however exalted, who challenged the abbey's rights would be resisted in the law courts. Early on in the Regency, the abbess of Fontevrault waged a battle against the secular courts to try to prevent them judging the case of a nun accused of arson; the secular judges won, luckily for the nun, who was proved innocent, while her abbess had been intending to inflict life imprisonment on bread and water.[104] Then there was a dispute with the officers of the department of Eaux et Forêts of Poitou over the felling of some timber; then a lawsuit of thirteen years' duration against the duc de Châtillon over dues he exacted on sheep at the market (lost in the end because Richard the Lion-Heart was proved to have been on crusade at the date when he was supposed to have granted the exemption). Then another battle against the comte de Montsoreau, involving the papal documents giving him the right to go through the abbey premises every Easter Monday to visit the tomb of one of his ancestors.

An aristocratic lady established in the rule of an abbey did not regard herself as having forsaken the world: there would be coffee drinking and giving dinner parties for local notables and distinguished callers from the social round of Paris and Versailles. Gossip writers sometimes alleged sexual adventures, but the accusations were rare and lost nothing in the telling.[105] More often, complaints concerned excessive contributions to the maintenance of relatives. Sisters or sisters-in-law who came to the abbey to retire after the death of their husbands were one thing, young men of the family were another.[106] Life for the nuns of Notre-Dame d'Yerres (in the diocese of Versailles) under the last two abbesses was disrupted by worldly nephews, and at Willancourt near Abbeville, Mme de Bron gave accommodation to the chevalier La Barre, who had unsuitable friends and collected dangerous books—as his trial and condemnation to death revealed to the whole of France.[107] One of the scandals, though a touching one, under the Regency was the spectacle of the ex-*garde des sceaux* D'Argenson, in disgrace at Court, living in retirement at the convent of La Madeleine du Trainel in the faubourg Saint-Antoine, in the company of the abbess, Gilberte-Françoise Véri d'Arbonze de Villemont, his former mistress. Jesting with the novices and endless conversations with his old flame were his only pleasures—he was 'le sacristan de la Madeleine'.[108] Scandal could only go so far; except for the very greatest, a royal *lettre de cachet* would bring an end to it—as in 1773, when the abbess of L'Abbaye Blanche at Mortain was sent under police escort to the abbey of Clairet (Nogent-le-Rotrou). She had travelled around the countryside running up debts and brought herself to public notice.[109] Generally, life in the great abbeys was decorous, but it was always comfortable and, when income allowed, sometimes luxurious. There was splendour at Chelles under the regent's daughter, until she was converted, asked pardon of her nuns, and finally left her greatness to die in a Paris convent. Fontevrault gave a three-day hunting and picnic party every 1 September for the anniversary of its abbess, Sophie Gillette de Pardaillon d'Eperon.[110] At Jouarre, Mme de Montmorin de Saint-Hérem had her own *maître d'hôtel*, coachman, postilion, lackeys, chamber maids, and other servants; her nuns dined well, and drank wine brought from Champagne, and this after 1755 in a fine new refectory she built by demolishing the seventh-century cell of Sainte-Felchilde, the first abbess. It was a worldly existence, yet Mme de Montmorin, as her nuns called her, wore a hair shirt under her silks. The great nobles looked with satisfaction on the provision available for their daughters, and the lesser nobles on the lesser provision for theirs in less distinguished houses. The rest of society could not be expected to have their enthusiasm. What reflections arose among the inhabitants of Rest-sous-Montsoreau when they found that Fontevrault had had a ditch specially dug to prevent them exercising their right of felling an oak sapling for a maypole in the abbey woods, or among those of the villages on the banks of the Loire when they saw the boat go past flying the abbey flag, bringing the coffee and other colonial luxuries tax-free from Nantes?[111]

VI

Montalembert described the *commende* as the 'leprosy' of the monastic Orders. This is the indignation of a clerical historian of the nineteenth century—the monks with their sincere vocations, on the one hand, and the aristocratic outsiders filching their revenues, on the other. But the nobles—and, indeed, others lower in the social scale in their turn—were gaining the use of monastic wealth, not only by annexation, but also by infiltration, by taking monastic vows and thereby finding an assured maintenance and niche in society. Like everything else in eighteenth-century France, the process operated along hierarchical lines. The monastic vocation was not general: it was to a particular Order, and there were vast differences in lifestyle. A Benedictine monk would live a collegiate life in one of the great abbeys, dining on fish and poultry, taking relaxation at cards or concerts of music, going on an annual holiday with a horse and an allowance provided; a Capuchin friar, wearing the white hood of poverty ('a mushroom on a dunghill'), went round begging. It looks as though vocations of the Benedictine kind came from higher classes in society than those of the Capuchin kind. But until we have studies of recruitment, establishing the status of families by reference to the rolls of the capitation tax, it will be difficult to be more precise about the male religious Orders. As it happens, however, we can go some way to categorizing the houses of women by drawing inferences from the working of the system of the 'dowry'.

Dowries, forbidden by the Lateran Council of 1215 and the Council of Trent, were authorized in France by the royal declaration of 28 April 1693, which limited them to houses of Orders founded since 1600, except when the bishop allowed them because of the difficult financial position of a particular community.[112] Maximum figures, whether for lump sum payments, annual subscriptions, or gifts of furniture were also specified—limits which were usually ignored. The amounts normally required were well known, being published in the almanacs, though in negotiations between the convent bursar and the family, rebates might be granted, especially in the case of a candidate who had exceptional qualifications or important social connections. A *contrat de religion* was signed at the taking of the habit, coming into force on the day of profession two years later. The presumptive heirs had to agree, and sometimes all the nuns would vote on the admission and sign the contract.[113]

The payment of dowries could be a great burden to families. An ecclesiastic of Nantes who negotiated for a year before agreeing to pay 100 livres on behalf of his niece had a message for her inserted with the documents: 'let her remember her poor uncle who generously sacrifices his bare necessities for the good of her salvation'.[114] A country nobleman who was already paying 345 livres a year to the Ursulines of Lamballe for the support of his two aunts and another 150 for his sister, had to find a lump sum of 33,000 livres to get his daughter in—all he could do was borrow it. A good lady of Lamballe helped him by paying for the banquet which, by custom, he had to give to the nuns on the day of the profession. Another provincial noble, in Périgord, told his daughter that she would have to renounce her manifest vocation: 'for long my second daughter has been asking me to be allowed to become a nun, but I will never be in a position to be able to pay her dowry. Yet how happy I'd be if I could see one of my daughters settled for life in a convent.'[115] In times of economic hardship like the latter years of the reign of Louis XIV, recruitment to the Ursulines of Tarbes dried up—families could not afford the 2,300 livres which was their tariff.[116] The system carried on, unreformed, right to the Revolution. 'It is a crying abuse', said a *cahier* of 1789 from Périgord, 'that communities of women have got permission to exact heavy gifts in the form of dowries . . . which have become ruinous to families.'[117] In addition to the main charge, the indictment went on, they ask for the furniture of a room, the provision of robes and linen, a fee for the sacristy, and an admission banquet for the nuns, so that there are families still paying off debts to convents contracted eighty years ago.

A dowry of 1,000 livres in 1768 was exactly double what a royal edict had first prescribed as the annual salary of a parish priest, and more than three times the sum which a novelist quoted as enough to provide a wounded soldier with board, lodging, and medical attention for a year.[118] Ordinary peasant and artisan families could not afford such sums, so their daughters could only go into the few convents which asked no dowry, or if a special concession was made, for example, to a girl with a good singing voice; otherwise, the nearest they could get was to join a religious house as an unprofessed lay servant. The great abbeys were an aristocratic preserve, the ordinary convents a bourgeois one. An orator to the academy of Angers in 1770 put the situation with naïvely brutal frankness—the reason for the existence of so many religious houses in the town was 'to provide decent and honourable retreats for that numerous portion of the nation which is too well-bred to degrade itself by doing the humble tasks to which lack of income seems to condemn it'.[119]

Convents diverged widely in the amounts of money they demanded, and families had to place their daughters on the dowry scale at the points which they could afford. In Paris, the Cistercian Dames de Panthémont, whose nuns were all of noble birth and whose work was the education of girls of distinguished families, prescribed 7,000–8,000 livres. In this same bracket were the Bénédictines de la Présentation and the Ursulines (both keeping schools for daughters of the rich), the Carmelites of the Marais *quartier* (their other house in the faubourg Saint-Jacques charged less), Port-Royal, the Dames de l'Assomption of the rue Saint-Honoré, and the noble Dames du Saint-Sépulcre. A whole series of others followed. At the middle range were the Filles de Saint-Agnès, who took no permanent vows and taught the children of the poor in the *quartier* of the Halles—they charged 2,000 livres. And at the bottom of the scale came three convents which did not insist on a dowry at all: the Filles de Saint-Thomas de Villeneuve looking after prostitutes in their house of the Bon Pasteur, the Filles de la Croix, and the Bénédictines du Val-de-Grâce. In the houses of women in Angers at the end of the *ancien régime* we can see how hierarchy was recognized by everyone. The wealthy abbey of Ronceray was, in its own definition, 'for the poor noble ladies of Anjou and Maine'. It is doubtful if any were poor, but their aristocratic credentials had to be impeccable—only one girl from the town itself had ranked high enough to gain entry to its dignified splendours. For the outstanding families of local fame, the Visitation was the first choice, both for the education of daughters and for their final establishment as nuns. When little Sophie de Milscent began her school-days there in 1781, two of her aunts were members of the community, and she remembered how one of them waylaid the visiting bishop to give him a proud recital of their family genealogy. The Ursulines, both for schooling and for the monastic profession, came next in order. This completed the charmed circle: the rest of the convents came a good deal lower, though even the Bon Pasteur, a home for fallen women, asked a 1,000 livres dowry from its novices.

Parents of the appropriate social groups expected one or more of their daughters to become nuns as a matter of family policy. Providing a dowry for a suitable marriage was vastly more expensive than finding a monastic one; it was important to preserve the inheritance intact for the eldest male heir; they did not want to have too many grown-up children staying perpetually at home; they were concerned to give their daughters an assured status in life, and a secure refuge against the day when death broke up the family unit.[120] These motives, of course, did not preclude others: the desire to see their daughters usefully occupied, to preserve their virtue, and to foster their piety. The question inevitably arises: to what degree and in what forms was persuasion—or even compulsion—used? How often did children voluntarily desire for themselves what others desired for them? What was the spiritual content of vocations, the sense of responding to a divine call, as against complying with the mores and exigencies of society?

Novelists relished the theme of the forced vocation, dramatic and affording a chance to moralize—'to show fathers and mothers that they ought always to leave their children free to choose their own way of life', as the tragic story of *La Religieuse malgré elle* demonstrated.[121] There were three beautiful Tencin girls: two married without affection to escape the cloister; the youngest, Claudine-Alexandrine, forced to take vows, recorded her protest before notaries, and fought until she got a papal rescript releasing her; she then made up for lost time in a career of political, literary and erotic adventures under the Regency. There were no such consolations for Mlle de Brun, forced into the Madelonnettes of La Flèche by her father the marquis after her elopement with Henri de Mirabel in 1732. She was released from her vows when her father died fourteen years later and Henri de Mirabel came back, a hero, from the Emperor's war against the Turks. But she would not marry him, and died, sick and lonely, long afterwards, in the days of Napoleon.[122]

Crude compulsion of this kind was rare. Parents who pushed their children into convents were matched by others who enjoyed the company of their daughters and wished to keep them out. In 1747 and 1760 there were fathers and mothers applying to the court of the

Châtelet for legal injunctions to prevent their daughters from taking vows,[123] and in 1760 the marquise de Mirabeau refused to be present when her third girl was professed in the convent of Montargis.[124] Ecclesiastics who were friends of the family might sing the praises of the monastic state, but they were just as likely to give warnings against worldly or sentimental motivation. The marquise de Créquy remembered with gratitude how her aunt, an abbess, and her uncle, a bishop, backed her determination to stay in the world.[125] The procedures for admission to the religious life gave opportunities for refusal. At a preliminary enquiry, a novice had to state that her parents had not 'forced her, pressured her or solicited her'. At the vesture, when the decisive question was asked, a public refusal could be given; 'I want the key of the convent gate,' one courageous young woman is said to have replied.[126] At the final profession, there was still a possibility of refusal, though admittedly remote. And even when solemn vows were taken, there were five years within which protest could be made alleging coercion, longer, if the 'violence' had continued.[127] In the first instance, the bishop's legal registrar and the superior of the religious house sat together to study the objections; if they rejected them, the secular courts could intervene by *appel comme d'abus*.[128] In the view of the lawyers, the presumption was in favour of the applicant, for God does not want unwilling subjects, monasteries ought not to want unsatisfactory inmates, and, as for the family, inheritance problems are no more difficult than those presented when a man presumed dead returns from overseas.[129] The law-books give startling illustrations of the anti-monastic attitude of the courts—all concerning monks rather than nuns, perhaps because complaints from women were rare and their allegations less sensational. If constraint was proved, the verdict was severe on those who had exercised it. In 1769, the parlement of Paris fined a merchant and condemned him to pay 10,000 livres damages to his son, and confiscated the money he had given to a religious house for its co-operation. Even in apparently hopeless cases, the courts would rescue an individual on a technical formality. In 1763, the Grand Conseil awarded 30,000 livres compensation to the wife of an ex-Cistercian monk who had been arrested for fleeing from his Order and died in prison; there was also an equally heavy fine on the abbot of Clairvaux.[130] Ten years later, the parlement of Bordeaux released a friar from vows he had taken twenty-five years earlier. In both cases, the pretext was the unsatisfactory state of the registers of the original profession. Forcing an unwilling subject into a monastery was not as easy as novelists supposed. At the Revolution, when the doors of the religious houses were thrown open, the nuns generally wished to maintain their vocation. Making allowances for the difficulty of women deciding to start new lives, their loyalty suggests that they were in their convents willingly. Under Napoleon, 356 married nuns applied to Cardinal Caprara to have their status recognized. Of these, seventy said they had never had a true vocation, and of these fifty-five alleged family pressures, direct in the form of beatings and deprivation, indirect in wrangles over property and from the burden of sheer poverty. Though these were obvious excuses to put forward, comparatively few made use of them.[131]

Forced vocations were rare; even so, there was a general assumption among contemporaries that veiled pressures within the family operated. But it was a business not of compulsion, but of social conditioning. Girls, especially those who were plain or belonging to the group of one in every five marked by smallpox, or who knew that little or no dowry was available for them, had to make a realistic calculation of their chances of marrying and ask what the alternatives might be. Cardinal Bernis tells how his two sisters were destined for the cloister; the elder, who was beautiful, was rescued by the marquis de Narbonne-Pelet, who took her without a dowry; the younger, 'not good-looking, just good-hearted', refused to become a nun so long as her father insisted, then became one voluntarily.[132] With the dowry crucial and the class system rigid, disappointment in love was frequent, and for the sad in heart, the cloister was a refuge. This was where the star-crossed lovers in Mme de Tencin's novels ended. This simple theme achieved a degree of sophistication through the growing interest in the tragic story of Héloïse and Abélard—reading their letters in Bussy-Rabutin's translation and weeping over Colardeau's famous poem.[133] The abbé Prévost, whose romantic imaginings always had a rough, earthy foundation, warned young people against such sacrificial follies: 'when the mists of desire clear, you will find yourself alone, disconsolate, without help from God or man'. Sometimes, the family was responsible for a child choosing the religious vocation, not because of actual promptings, but simply because the parents' vices made life at home insupportable—a daughter fleeing from the threat of sexual abuse, a son fleeing from violence and cruelty.[134] Or a girl would become a nun when the family broke up after the death of a father, as happened with a daughter of Melfort, the Jacobite exile, and of André-Michel Ramsay, the Scottish adventurer.[135]

Going into a religious house was, often enough, going among friends, joining sisters and aunts and acquaintances who were there

already. A girl who had attended school under the nuns might wish
to stay on with the teachers she had known and trusted. It was not
just family pressure which counted, but family tradition. In 1691, at
the age of 12, the eldest daughter of the duc de Beauvilliers went to
the convent of Montargis, and stayed on there as a nun. Six of her
sisters followed, at ages ranging from 5 to 2, and all, like her, eventually took lifelong vows. An eighth girl of the family was also
educated at Montargis, but left to marry her cousin, the duc de
Mortemart; she had two daughters who were sent to the same
convent to be educated, and they both died there as nuns in mid-
century.[136] Those whose birth qualified them for entrance to prestigious abbeys might have to go far from home, but ordinary candidates for the religious life would be going to a nearby institution,
well known locally and with a web of friendly contacts, even in
Orders which had strict seclusion. Only in heartless families (generally the very great) were children in monasteries forgotten. Adrian
de Bertier, marquis de Pinsaguel, had one daughter married and
three in a convent; when he died in 1752, his will left 40 livres to
each of the three nuns, 'not to be paid to their superior, but to my
daughters', and when his wife the marquise died four months later,
life annuities of 20 livres each came to them. Families thought in
terms not so much of getting rid of children, as of finding them an
establishment for life corresponding to the family dignity.

    If it was a question of edging a son or daughter towards the
religious life, parents could always find an ecclesiastic who would act
as persuader, one of those 'accapareurs de conscience' with head on
side and lowered eyes whom Mme Roland remembered with revulsion.[137] Theological treatises still put the celibate state above the
married, and the contemplative life above the active. A learned
Dominican drew an astonishingly selfish conclusion from these
premisses and from the law of self-preservation: go into the religious
life, he said, because it offers the maximum chance of salvation;
'assure your own happiness before working for that of a third party,
where this can be done without injustice'.[138] An argument more in
tune with eighteenth-century opinion was the appeal to duty to
Church and to society. It was hardly one to win recruits to the male
religious Orders, since men had so many opportunities to serve in
the secular clergy and in the world in general, but it did apply to
women, whose chief opportunity to serve the Church and, indeed,
society through teaching and nursing, lay in religious houses. With
this in mind, churchmen discussing the vocation of nuns sometimes
got to the point when it seemed more natural to them for a girl to

choose the religious rather than family life—to stay in the world was the course requiring an explanation. There is a revealing statement in a handbook of spiritual direction of 1750. If a confessor finds a novice who has joined a religious community for wrong reasons, or even has been forced in, he must not attempt to get her out. There must be a delay, to see if she may have, after all, a real vocation: 'it must not be assumed [she] is not called, for God uses various methods to direct us to our destiny'. In such a case, the nuns would exercise their utmost persuasion. One may doubt the novelist who said they did so 'like soldiers finding a sort of consolation in getting themselves companions in their misery',[139] and also doubt the tales of their exercising compulsion, though there are examples of touting for money from families anxious to have a daughter brought to take the veil.[140] But there were plenty of arguments—not always elevated ones: the dangers of childbirth, the harassments of family life, the useful work to be done, the danger of 'shipwreck at the hour of death'.[141] And attitude was more important than argument, and for that we ought to turn to Marivaux's imaginative insight. The nuns were kind; they called the novice's doubts 'temptations'; they flattered her, and led her on until she became 'an uncomprehending spectator' of her irrevocable engagement.[142] The collective will of a friendly community could be persuasive, and the end proposed, the ceremonies of vesture and profession, were picturesque and moving—the candles, the chanting, the thrill of being the cynosure of every eye, the farewells to the family, the crawling under the funeral pall before the Te Deum thundered out; their uncompromising finality appealed to youth as a gesture of self-affirmation, and their sombre undertones were haunting, exercising an attraction Diderot understood, according with the 'profound melancholy' which accompanied the awakening of sexual desire.

The monasteries of France in the eighteenth century show a peculiar equilibrium between spiritual inspiration and social needs. The aristocracy gained for its children the use of the great wealth which had accumulated in ancient institutions, whether by blatant annexation as in the *commende* or by infiltration as in the great abbeys of women. Lower down the social scale, the bourgeoisie was equally anxious to place its children. For boys, the opportunity was one of many; for girls, the convents were indispensable establishments to provide security and an outlet for useful activity, and the middle classes contributed by their dowries to keep the system going.

Yet what is true as a general sociological description does not explain away the genuine spirituality of vocations. There were some startling renunciations of the world, and a great deal of dedication and devotion within the cadre of social conditioning. Spiritual inspirations do not exist in a void. 'Can molten gold be carried from place to place in anything but crucibles of iron and steel?' asked Friedrich Naumann, himself an exponent of charismatic religion. This chapter has been concerned with the base metal crucible, which the historian can describe with more evidence to hand than is available for the molten gold. Yet the gold was there.

17

THE RELIGIOUS VOCATION AND
SOCIAL USEFULNESS: MEN

I

A wealthy monastery was a centre of consumption and expenditure. This was the argument used by municipal authorities when protesting against commendatory abbots annexing half the income and spending it far away. Certainly, a great abbey provided employment. This was more especially so in a century when there was lavish architectural reconstruction. In some places, a 'school' of artists and craftsmen gathered around the long-continued building works, their favourite themes and technical devices being evident in the churches and châteaux of the neighbouring countryside. The number of permanent servants, if funds allowed, was sure to be excessive. The eight monks of the Cistercian abbey of Pereigne in 1789 had two cooks, a baker, two porters, a brazier, a gardener, two cowherds, a boy to look after the guest-house, three women (housekeeper, sewing maid, and dairy maid), and an archivist with legal qualifications.[1] At this time the Grande Chartreuse had 100 monks and 300 servants. 'When the religious houses in France are suppressed,' said a visitor, 'this one will have to be left, because it is indispensable to support the surrounding countryside.'[2] One of the reasons for the multiplication of servants was the comfortable tradition that local families ought to be offered places for their children, not necessarily within the limits of sheer utility. It was a substitute for almsgiving. When the government found it had German immigrants on its hands (brought in to colonize Cayenne but never sent), it circulated the abbeys of Brittany to ask the monks to stretch their payrolls and find places for them.[3] Another reason for the numerous servants was the custom of keeping on old retainers beyond their usefulness. At the Cistercian abbey of Morimond in its latter years, the nine servants had been there for an average time of twenty-five years, and in this century, when medical experts and economists supposed a working man would be worn out by the age of 50, six of them were over 60 years of age.[4]

Anticlericals gave the monks little credit for their easy-going attitude to their employees: by the mercantilist principles of the day, it was drones subsidizing subsidiary drones. It was also an anticlerical commonplace to describe the monasteries as stingy with their almsgiving. This was the general view of the peasants on the estates on which rich abbeys collected rents, feudal dues, or tithes. An enquiry of 1775[5] in the Toulouse area showed the abbey of Saint-Sernin as giving only 30 livres annually to one of the parishes where it collected tithe, and 35 to another (true, there was also another 35, being the interest on a sum bequeathed to the poor by a former abbot). The abbey of Moissac, enjoying a half share of a tithe of 3,600 livres in one of its parishes, was accustomed to give from 15 to 21 annually. Curés, often too poor to give to charity themselves, led their people in complaints.[6] These cases are typical of many, but there were exceptions. The tax expert Richeprey,[7] investigating in the South, found a Cistercian house giving back as much as it received from a feudal rent, though in an uncritical fashion—distributions at Christmas and Easter at a flat rate to everyone above 14 years of age irrespective of need. There were some canons regular nearby who also gave generous alms in such a haphazard fashion that the bishop of Rodez proposed to compel them to reform their undiscriminating largesse. One of his curés wrote to him in alarm, with a warning that the people had come to depend on these handouts—'if *Votre Grandeur* proposes changes, I supplicate you to give me a warning, so I can flee as fast as I can from the fury that will be kindled; it's all very well to say that the authorities will repress disturbances—in the first uprising nothing will be respected, and whatever else happens, I'll be the unhappy victim.' As a general rule, it was the parish in which a monastery was situated which received significant charity, and the ones further away which were neglected.[8] The village of Mézidan, with a house of the Congrégation de France (Génovéfains) in its midst owing five-sixths of the land, declared in 1790 that it had become entirely dependent on the canons regular, who employed six men directly, and provided the sick and the poor with food, clothing, firewood, and medicines; now that the monastery was being suppressed, the parishioners 'are reduced to the greatest misery'.[9]

Even if they tended to show indifference to everyday poverty, it was characteristic of monks (as also of bishops) to react with remarkable generosity in crises of famine or other natural disasters—finding accommodation for a family whose house had been burned down, giving food and seed-corn when the crops had been flattened by hail, lending money to borrowers who might not be able to return it, selling grain at low prices in time of starvation.[10] There are plenty of stories of attacks on rural monasteries in the 'Grande Peur' of 1789, but 3,000 peasants formed a cordon round the abbey of Arrouaise in Artois to protect the supplies of grain which the monks were selling cheaply from being pillaged by alien marauders.[11]

Monasteries were expected to provide hospitality to travellers. The great abbeys welcomed fulfilling the obligation so far as visitors of quality were concerned. Towards the end of the century, the son of a duke records enjoying 'excellent fish' at one of them; Chateaubriand remembered a dinner of 'eggs, carp and an enormous pike'; the English traveller Wraxall boasted of 'a dinner of great elegance'.[12] The Cistercian abbey of Saint-Sulpice at Bugey, on a snow-swept ridge with only sullen peasants[13] for neighbours amid the mountain desolation, to the uninitiated might have been expected to be a meagre place to dine, but Brillat Savarin, a dedicated gastronome, was delighted to go there—he had a small amateur orchestra, and the monks invited him to provide the music for mass and vespers on St Bernard's Day. The musicians arrived in time to breakfast on vast chines of ham and veal and 'a paté as large as a church'; they dined on a variety of delicately cooked meats and vegetables, supported by liqueurs and coffee ('clear, aromatic and wonderfully hot'), and ended the day with mulled eau-de-vie, a speciality of the cellarer, brought into the refectory in procession to the cheers of the assembled monks.[14] Earlier, John Breval at Cîteaux had found the guest master hospitable and reluctant to let him go; the monastic estates, said Breval, 'were never failing Resources for game and fish, and their cellars fill'd with the best Growths of Burgundy from their own vineyards; Guests of the greatest condition shall never catch them unprepared'.[15] The best families of Nîmes and Montpellier came to regard the Cistercian abbey of Franquevaux as a holiday resort, spending a week or two in this agreeable 'lieu de villégiature'.[16] When exiled to provincial towns by royal command, magistrates of the parlement of Paris would apply to the more comfortable monasteries for accommodation, though they might have to buy their meals from an outside *traiteur*.[17] When the great wished to escape from court, their families and friends, and the places where they were known, they would seek apartments in a religious house—a noble fleeing from the reproaches of the heirs he had disinherited, a converted *roué* trying to rehabilitate himself, a courtier withdrawing from the world to prepare for death.[18] Ladies more frequently sought refuge in houses of nuns, but the same resource could be useful, whether to a spiritual or a worldly end, for men who could afford it.

What happened to less respectable folk who arrived at the gates of a monastery? It was impossible to entertain every vagabond, though the austere *pères* of Sept-Fons 'made bread and soup available to all who presented themselves'. The Carthusians, equally dedicated, had a policy of helping travellers after enquiry into their circumstances. At their house of Boserville in Lorraine,[19] between January 1788 and March 1789 they gave 6,524 livres in alms, including money to a shipwrecked Italian sailor, a Frenchman returning to Liège from Naples, a soldier begging his way to Gascony, and a larger sum of 62 livres to 'a marquis who had fallen into destitution'. The 'unknown man apparently about 70 years of age with grey hair and rotting teeth' who died on his way to the Carthusian house of Notre-Dame de la Verne in 1777 had been directed there by the local peasants with a boy to guide him.[20] But most great abbeys limited their charity to a regular dole of bread without enquiry into the circumstances of recipients, though in some places a certificate of indigence from the curé was required, thus confining the benefit to local people. Documentation concerning the provisional continuance of customary alms when monasteries were being closed in 1790 gives some idea of the amount of charity being offered. In the North, the abbey of Vicoigne distributed 56 big loaves a fortnight and 400 small ones, and 200 herrings on Good Fridays; another abbey gave 15 large loaves every Sunday.[21] More substantially, Fécamp provided bread to the value of 15,000 livres a year, and there were similar doles at Fontevraud, Saint-Wandrille, Jumièges, and Bec.[22] The poor would assemble to collect their portions at fixed times; the Benedictines of Paray-le-Monial rang their great bell on three days in the week and every day in Lent and Advent to convoke them.[23] These indiscriminate hand-outs met with no favour from the men of the Enlightenment. As the *cahier* of Honfleur said, 'the day of distribution is a holiday, the worker puts down his spade and his axe and reposes in the bosom of sloth'.[24] Complaints of this kind against the Benedictines of Lessay in Normandy came to the ear of the government, and the king ordered the ending of the bread doles and the diverting of the expenditure (one-fifteenth of the total income of the monks) to the deserving poor of the parishes where the abbey owned property.[25]

No doubt some monks took vows out of a desire for a life of idleness. But for many more, this anticlerical formula represents a halftruth: they wanted to lead a leisured existence with freedom to pursue their own interests, not easy in a society where tradition, hierarchy, and family constrained individuality. Thus, a monastery would contribute to local life according to the idiosyncratic inspirations of its members. Antiquaries in search of curious historical or archaeological details and intellectuals savouring the debates of provincial academies would profit from the neighbourhood of some abbey, more especially one of the Congrégation de Saint-Maur or that of Saint-Vanne; so too would enthusiasts for the new sentimental egalitarianism finding expression in the masonic lodges, and the political gossips who met to read the newspapers at booksellers' counters and in cafés. Being much concerned with the cultivation of their estates, there were monks who became agricultural experts, contributing to the deliberations of the agricultural societies of the 1770s and 1780s—like Dom Leronge, author of the *Principes du cultivateur*; Dom Le Gendre, who experimented with sowing different kinds of grain; and Dom Wartel, exponent of deep manuring.[26] Vine growers were indebted to the intelligent husbandry of the abbeys. Dom Pierre Pérignon, bursar of Saint-Pierre d'Hautvilliers for forty-seven years (he died in 1715), made various discoveries, not least of which was the formula for perfecting champagne.[27] The monastic zeal for book collecting and cataloguing soon turned to the new fashion for surveys of scientific information, and it became common for rich abbeys to have their natural history collections; the one at Clairvaux was surprisingly up to date when inventoried in 1791, containing specimens of tungsten (only discovered in 1780) and molybdenum (isolated in 1782).[28] Some of the religious made a name for themselves in engineering and invention. The great waterworks at Marly, the pumps for the Jardin des Plantes, and the fire hydrants for the Palais Royal were designed by the Carmelite Sébastien Truchet (dd. 1729), as well as pieces of medical equipment—artificial arms and hearing aids.[29] A contemporary Augustinian friar devised the machine to lift the floor of the Opéra to the height of the stage, thus providing a level dance arena for the *bal de l'Opéra*.[30] In 1747 André Féry, a Minim of Reims, following the engineering tradition of his Order, published his *Dissertation sur le projet qu'on forme de donner des eaux à la ville de Reims*. A canon of the city gave the money to realize the project, and two years later the hydraulic machine began lifting water to the top of a sixty-foot tower; by 1753, fountains were playing in the centre of town.[31] A design (never realized) of the amateur inventor the Cistercian Dom Ganthey was praised by the Academy of Sciences in 1783: he proposed to institute a speedy postal service by attaching packets of letters to arrows fired from post office to post office by powerful mechanical bows.[32] More usefully, Noel, a Benedictine of Reims, perfected the technique of grinding spectacle lenses; Louis XV had him brought to Saint-Germain-des-Prés to construct a superior microscope for the royal apartments at Versailles.[33] The world had infiltrated the cloisters, but the monks were integrated into the life of the world. The gap between what Christian moralists wrote about the monastic vocation and that vocation in practice had never been greater, yet the contrast was not entirely to the discredit of those who took their vows in accordance with the routine assumptions and expectations of their families and society.

II

A man suffering from stones in the urinary tract or captured at sea by the Barbary corsairs would look more favourably on the religious than most of his contemporaries. The Frères de Saint-Jean-de-Dieu ran the best hospitals in France, with the most skilful surgeons, including the chief expert on the extraction of stones, while the ransoming of Christian slaves of the North African coast was organized and financed by the Trinitaires and the Order of Notre-Dame-de-la-Merci. The members of these three Orders won unstinted praise from Voltaire, especially those who risked their lives and freedom in the bazaars and slave markets of Algiers, Tunis, and Morocco. 'Les religieux de la rédemption des captifs sont la plus belle institution monastique,' he wrote.[34] His praises should be extended to the Lazarist house in Algiers and the Franciscan convents in Marrakesh and Meknes.[35] Considered by the criteria of fervour and regularity, the Trinitaires[36] (also called Mathurins after their founder, Jean de Matha) and the religious of La-Merci came low in the table of respectability. They were both international organizations dating from the thirteenth century, but their French establishments had never come under effective control, whether from Rome or from their own chief houses in Paris, which, indeed, were as undisciplined as any. Many of the eighty houses of Mathurins were tenanted by only one or two individuals (out of the total of 300), who did parish work and took life easy. La-Merci,[37] with only sixteen houses, all very poor, was condemned to suppression by the Commission des réguliers though no one seemed interested in enforcing the sentence.[38] But if they were drifting into decadence, these two Orders really did raise ransom money, and considerable sums. The

Trinitaires made annual payments to Algiers of about 100,000 livres; they also worked in Tunis, Tripoli, Smyrna, Constantinople, Egypt, and Persia.[39] Their budget for 1729 showed receipts of 274,559 livres and ransom payments of 235,803. At the head of their fund raising was the *procureur général des captifs*, elected by the national chapter general. He appointed laymen to take charge of the various collecting areas (with the title of *commissaires généraux des quêtes*), and these *commissaires* found local wardens (*marguilliers*) who organized collections and sold mementos and badges, especially scapulars—ordinary ones very cheap, and the gold and silver embroidered ones at 20 sous.[40] A parish might have a confraternity of 'la Rédemption', whose members, in consideration of their collection efforts, were entitled to wear the white surtout with the red and blue cross of the Order. To avoid clashes with the similar activities of La-Merci, the government had divided France into spheres of influence, with the smaller Order having the eastern frontier and the South.[41] On occasion bishops would issue pastoral letters exhorting the faithful to generosity: in 1754 it was to build a chapel in the slave barracks at Algiers, where the old buildings were being demolished; in 1756 it was to ransom 200 slaves from Morocco, the bishop of Le Mans describing them as hungry, vermin-ridden, 'toiling under a sky of bronze', and in danger of being tortured into apostasy.[42] Since the Dey had made this transaction a condition of concluding a treaty with France, the king paid for fifty releases, the Assembly of Clergy voted 200,000 livres,[43] and the monks found the rest—not easy, for the cost ran at 3,000 to 4,000 a head.

The ransoming process had been reduced to routine, but it was precarious.[44] The religious, who had chapels in all the slave barracks, were in touch with the captives and decided which cases could most usefully be followed up. They had to put the money into Mexican or Sevillian piastres, or in goods like tea, or even bring Turkish galley-slaves for exchange, having to buy them at Malta or Leghorn, the king of France not being inclined to let them have his. The usual bribes and the Dey's 10 per cent cut had to be arranged. In emergency, monks had to become hostages for the completion of a deal. And their lives could always be endangered by some warlike incident at sea, some false move by the other Order, or the forays of some 'Scarlet Pimpernel' like Père Jehannot. The king was not generous. Even when ransoming 300 of his soldiers (in 1785) by direct negotiation through his consul at Algiers, he extracted 443,000 livres of the ransom of 639,000 from the two religious Orders. The wealthy knights of Malta were as mean, allowing two of their officers to languish as slaves from 1708 to 1715, hoping to push the monks into paying.[45] Protestant captives were not allowed the benefit of Catholic collections, but if their own churches put up the funds, the Mathurins would act for them. So too for the Americans: Jefferson in 1787 found that the Order could do a deal at a tenth of the price the Dey of Algiers was asking in formal diplomatic negotiations.[46]

When the returning ransom ships reached Marseille, there were celebrations, then the monks and their liberated captives proceeded northwards, repeating their triumphal observances in various towns, ending up in Paris. These were the occasions when the local confraternities basked in public esteem and their major collections were taken. The ceremonies were traditional, following the same pattern ever since the mid-seventeenth century. In Paris in 1641 the processions defiled through the streets from 23 to 26 May with drums and trumpets sounding—soldiers, the city watch, the brethren of the confraternity of Notre-Dame-de-Bonne-Delivrance barefoot and carrying candles, the Mathurin fathers in their white robes with the red and blue cross on the front, with palms in their hands, the former captives bearing the banner of the Order, escorted by children dressed as angels. On 26 May, after receiving communion at the hands of the general of the Order, the captives were finally sent home, furnished with a certificate and money for the journey. With occasional variations, these ceremonies were repeated in the eighteenth century, the heart of the symbolism (derived from the banner of the Mathurins) centring on the 'angels' leading the liberated Christian slaves—sometimes dressed in rags, revealing their sunburnt and lacerated backs—the festoons of ribbons held by the children representing their former fetters. If the royal family had contributed to their release, some of them would have to go in procession at Versailles, from the parish church to the royal chapel.[47] A problem for the monks was that their cast of actors might be depleted by ungrateful individuals sneaking off home during the northward progress. In 1717, a knight of Malta whose freedom had been purchased by 12,000 livres from the Trinitaires and 10,000 from La-Merci refused to process as soon as he set foot in Marseille. He was summoned by a formal legal injunction, but it seemed that the courts could not oblige him. At least, however, the legal process has left us his name, Louis de Castellan d'Esparron.[48] Since the ranks would be well thinned by the time Paris was reached, how could the monks demonstrate to the public how many rescues they had made? An anticlerical diarist at the end of the *ancien régime* accused them of hiring substitutes, 'men from the suburbs who play the same masquerade every year'. Captives, whether real or suppositious, and some of the religious yielded to the temptation of the drink they were offered on their triumphal march, occasioning frequent stops while they were sobered up.[49] To the Parisians, who had never known the fear of being pursued by the galleys of the Barbary corsairs, it was comic entertainment.

The Frères de la Charité de Saint-Jean-de-Dieu[50] came to France at the beginning of the seventeenth century (having been founded in Portugal two centuries earlier). By 1789 they had 355 brothers running thirty-six hospitals, with a total of 3,181 beds. Most of their houses had reasonable endowments, and a few were rich. Thus, at Paris their central hospital and noviciate had 180,000 livres a year, Charenton had 128,000, and their small convalescent home 16,000, which was enough for its sixteen beds. To maximize income, some of the establishments specialized in taking soldiers and sailors as patients—in particular, there were 215 at the Isle of Ré and 1,200 at Brest. The king paid, but he got a good bargain: the vast naval hospital at Brest had been run by private contractors at 5 livres a head; when the brothers took over, the tariff dropped to 20 sous. Charenton had fifteen beds providing treatment for workers injured in the local stone quarries, while the money came from the fees paid for 100 internees in the prison wing. In the hospitals which were well off, the brothers set standards of medical care unknown elsewhere. In their central hospital at Paris, sixty brothers, eight doctors and surgeons, and twenty-four lay servants looked after 200 patients —a very favourable ratio. The sick were one to a bed, each having slippers, dressing-gown, chamber-pot, urine bottle, water flask, and cup alongside, and they enjoyed good meals, ending with beef tea and calf's-foot jelly after supper. They were spread over six spacious wards, each with its altar surmounted by a picture—one was by Rubens, another by Le Brun. The curious visitor could watch the procession of thanksgiving after dinner, proceeding from the ward altar with cross and candles, aspersing the patients with holy water to the chanting of the *De profundis*: perhaps he would be allowed to see an operation conducted by one of the best surgeons of the day, whether hired layman or brother. Of the brothers, Frère Cosme was the most famous. Son and grandson of provincial surgeons, he had begun as a Feuillant novice, then transferred. His speciality was the stone, for which he invented an alternative operation for certain cases, one which did not need an incision.[51] Stories of his fearsome dexterity and eccentricities were legion: removing a stone of 26 ounces, four times as big as any before; interrupted by the wife of the maréchal de Muy so that the stone broke fatally under the slipping pincers;[52] seated in the choir opposite his parish priest, the curé speculating on how soon he would be able to say the requiem over the surgeon, and the surgeon wondering when he would get the curé's body for dissection.[53] His fanaticism to practise on corpses led to Diderot's tale: he was disconsolate when a man expected to die recovered—'mon cadavre!' he lamented, and was pacified only when they found him another one.[54]

Serving the king could bring the Frères de Saint-Jean-de-Dieu into unpleasant places—as to the four military hospitals in San Domingo.[55] True, they had privileges, including the ownership of several plantations, and they had a Negro labour force to man the wards. But in this place of steamy heat, mosquitoes, and 'putrid exhalations', clergy of every kind succumbed to worldly tempta-tions—the authorities regarded even the Capuchins as useless. Of the garrison of 7,000, up to 2,000 might be in hospital at one time, and the soldiers were drunken, insubordinate patients. The brothers pressed the governor to cut alcohol supplies and encourage orange juice; the governor accused the brothers of treating their patients with cold contempt, even though 'as religious and as doctors and surgeons they have a double obligation to serve the sick'.[56] The model Parisian hospital was filled with respectable patients, for it required influence to gain admission—hence the suavity and sym-pathy of the nursing staff, an attitude not found in the sweating, brutalized wards of San Domingo.

The prison run by the Frères de Saint-Jean-de-Dieu at Charenton was one of a number of such *maisons de force* kept by religious Orders at the behest of the king. Although the prisoners were incarcerated by royal order, it was normally at the request of their families. Of the 1,287 *lettres de cachet* issued in Provence from 1745 to 1789, 1,052 had been solicited by relatives, while 67 were at the instance of the ecclesiastical authorities.[57] The register of a *maison de force* would record the reasons, as at Charenton on 4 July 1789, the recording brother noted the arrival from the Bastille of the 'comte de Sade', a royal prisoner from 1777 on the application of his family, the law courts having found him not guilty of poisoning and sodomy, but known to be a libertine and insane.[58] (Unfortunately, the marquis de Sade's correspondence does not give an impression of the place; he says he got little exercise and became fat, and was glad to get out on the following Good Friday.[59]) In 1790, the National Assembly, moved by a storm of liberal protest against *lettres de cachet*, decreed a census of the establishments where victims of these arbitrary orders were detained. The list included ten royal fortresses, like the Pierre-en-Scize at Lyon and the Château d'If of later Monte Cristo fame; there were eight houses of Cordeliers, three of the Écoles Chrétiennes, and four others. There were also eleven convents and thirteen establishments under lay administration listed for women. These were far from being all the religious houses used from time to time as places of internment, but the Assembly had probably been given a comprehensive list of those most formally organized for the purpose.[60] One of the motives for the action of the legislators had been indignation at the recital of terrible conditions at Charenton, including confinement in dark cells fifty feet underground. Inspectors from the municipality went there, and reported the horror stories to be unfounded. The prison was in two departments: one where the inmates lived in agreeable apartments and moved around freely in spacious gardens against a background of idyllic scenery, another for the confinement of dangerous lunatics, who were kept behind bars. But there were no subterranean cells, the food was good, and there were frequent changes of linen, 'whose good quality astounded us'. The brothers humoured their prisoners, held long conversations with them, and cooked their favourite dishes; according to the inspectors, the place was an advertisement for true Christianity. It was honest praise, for the same inspectors reported a certain harshness of the nuns of the nearby Val d'Osne towards the four mad women in their charge.[61]

As was usually the case with institutions of the *ancien régime*, some *maisons de force* were humane and well organized, some abysmally crude and inefficient—the presence or absence of a secure income and an effective chain of command making the difference. It was a rule that a prisoner got the treatment corresponding to the maintenance grant which was being paid for him. At the Cordeliers of Caen, lunatics at 150–250 livres fared meagrely; libertines subsidized to the tune of 300 or more could eat with the monks, and at 450 and above could have a private room. The Cordeliers of Limoges specialized in confining erring ecclesiastics, an unhappy place, as the payments on their behalf were small.[62] The chevalier de la Musse, put into the Frères de Saint-Jean-de-Dieu at Pontorson at the age of 71 to stop him marrying a prostitute, the son of a farmer-general in a monastery at Nancy for a scandalous publication, the son of another farmer-general in Saint-Lazare, then at Mont Saint-Michel, for defying his father, the abbé d'Espagnac at the Barnabites of Montargis ('une espèce de maison de correction et comme un séminaire') for financial speculation—these were offenders from the monied classes, and their lot was an easy one.[63]

Yet there were *maisons de force* which, irrespective of income, fell into scandal. At Mont-Saint-Michel, the religious, 'sovereign despots on their rock', would not allow local officials to enter to check on the welfare of the prisoners. This was not because dark cruelties were being perpetrated—the great wooden cage and the oubliettes of the Middle Ages were empty, gaped at by shuddering tourists.[64] The fault of the place was laxity, the gaolers joining with the prisoners in loose living. A young nobleman confined for debauchery laughed at his mother, who had sent him there: 'She thought she was putting me among saints whose good . . . example would operate my conversion. She was absolutely mistaken. It was with the religious that I got drunk, in the refectory, or in my room, to which they brought wine night and day to drink with me.'[65] There was no such revelry at the Cordelier house of Saint-Pierre de Canon in Provence,[66] where negligence and ill will ruled. The *gardien* was a drunkard, the bursar could not read, and the chaplain had affairs with peasant women, while the prison was in the hands of an outside contractor whose only object was profit. The detainees were dressed in rags and slept on straw, their staple food was soup and stale bread, and they were flogged for misbehaviour. The contractors paid an annual fee, which went to the Cordeliers of Marseille, a source of revenue which dried up when inspectors arrived in 1767 to investigate complaints. Institutions of the *ancien régime* tended to be run on a perverse application of the principle of the greatest good of the greatest number, irrespective of the welfare of their inmates. Thus at Saint-Pierre de Canon, where families got rid of disreputable relatives, the Cordeliers had a rural corner where useless friars could be posted, together with a small annual income for their provincialate, a local contractor provided employment and lined his own pockets—if lunatics and libertines suffered, perhaps it was what they deserved.

III

The nobles and bourgeois of eighteenth-century France were educated in *collèges* run by institutes founded under the influence of the Counter-Reformation: the Jesuits, the creation of Ignatius Loyola in 1534: the Pères de la Doctrine Chrétienne established in the Comtat Venaissin in 1592 by César de Bus, then spreading to France and Italy; the Oratorians, founded by Bérulle in 1611 on the model of the Italian Oratory of Philip Neri; and the Lazarists of Vincent de Paul, dating from 1625. Until their suppression, the Jesuits were the dominant educational force, running 151 *collèges* with numerous teachers.[67] Next came the Oratorians, with 72 *collèges* and 800 or so staff, with their centre of gravity in Anjou and Touraine; then the Doctrinaires, with 60 *collèges* and about 500 staff, their main sphere of action being the South. The Lazarists had 83 establishments, but these were mainly seminaries and centres for the preaching of missions.

In small country places there were other *collèges* staffed by secular priests hired by the municipal authorities. At Saint-Gaudens, there were three of these masters and—a luxurious extra—a professor of philosophy paid by the provincial estates of Nébousan. The number of these 'secular' schools increased greatly as a result of the expulsion of the Jesuits. By the edict of 27 February 1763, the vacated institutions were to be directed by boards of governors, the diocesan bishop to preside, and the members to be the *premier président* and *procureur général* of the local parlement, the two chief municipal officers, two co-opted notables, and the headmaster of the school.[68] The boards would hire teachers by inspecting certificates of degrees, competitive examination, or review of testimonials. Practically all the masters appointed by the system were clergy. In some places, the system would not work, partly because the lay governors insisted on pushing their own fancy educational ideas on teachers who had no time to implement them. 'Education is a matter in which the imagination can roam and everyone can draw up schemes for it,' said the bishop of Langres sardonically, 'and the bourgeoisie, who have nothing else to administer, are infinitely jealous to run that of the *collèges*.'[69] When lay control collapsed, the towns had to call upon the established ecclesiastical teaching institutes and forgo their opportunities for interfering. At Lyon,[70] from the start, the practised Oratorians were invited to take over to replace the Jesuits, and in the following years Tournon, Arras, Béthune, Tours, Agen, and finally, in 1786, Autun followed suit. A dozen *collèges* fell to the Doctrinaires. But efficient teachers were in short supply. The Oratorians accepted these apparently splendid new opportunities only with reluctance—they lacked numbers to expand effectively. At Lyon, where the Jesuits had stationed eighty-five priests, they could never muster more than sixteen replacements, and parents complained of over-large classes and superficial teaching.

The Oratorians and the Doctrinaires[71] did not take monastic vows: they remained secular clerics attached to their institute by *vœux simples*, temporary obligations. As the century progressed, more and more of the Oratorians chose to hold back from proceeding to the priesthood; at the end of the *ancien régime* the proportion of the *pères* to the *confrères* was one to six. From mid-century, the same process was operating among the Doctrinaires—they moved more slowly to the priesthood: 'on est toujours à temps de s'engager pour la vie'.[72] At their general chapter of 1776, the Doctrinaires abolished vows altogether, replacing them with a simple promise, a change welcomed unanimously in France, though rejected in Italy. Recruitment to both institutes was principally from the *moyenne bourgeoisie*.[73] While among the secular clergy generally, there was a strong minority—a quarter to a third—of ordination recruits from the sons of artisans (generally *maîtres*, not ordinary journeymen) and the more prosperous peasants, in the two teaching institutions there were virtually no representatives of artisan or peasant families up to mid-century, and few afterwards. Sons of merchants, doctors, surgeons, apothecaries, notaries, and bureaucrats were numerous, and as much as a third of the total consisted of sons of nobles of the robe and other magistrates and royal *officiers*, with the aristocracy of the parlements preferring the Oratory. These were men from well-off families who chose a demanding vocation, but with the intention of fulfilling it in comfort. Their teaching duties were arduous, and they would attend mass on Sundays and saints' days and attend prayers every morning and evening (the Doctrinaires abolished this latter obligation in 1783). Yet they retained their private incomes (under some supervision) and, perhaps, drew the profits from some ecclesiastical sinecure; they had their own furniture, fires—servants even—and moved freely in society, dining with the best local families and dressing elegantly, sometimes ostentatiously. One of the pupils of the Oratorians at Angers remembered Père Limonas, hair curled and powdered, frock-coat open to reveal the trim legs (set off in silk stockings) which were his pride: he was given to witticisms, and was prepared to accept an excuse for laziness if presented with a *bon mot*.[74] And no doubt the schoolboys of Nantes long remembered their professor of physics, Père Mouchet, who, to the accompaniment of cheers and salvoes, went up in a hot-air balloon on the evening of 14 June 1784, vanishing over the horizon and coming down an hour later near Chinon.[75] As France became a hive of political speculation in the last years before the Revolution, the place to go for news was an Oratorian *collège*. At Dieppe they took *L'Esprit des Journaux*, the *Gazette de Leyde*, and the *Mercure* (sharing the cost with two prominent citizens), to which in 1788 they added the

Courrier de l'Europe and the *Année littéraire*.[76] An administrative official of Nantes in January of that year complained that the masters of the *collège* were more concerned with the news from Paris than with their teaching: 'always promenading around in society, the hours they are obliged to spend in their class-rooms are sheer boredom to them'.[77] Unlike those pillars of papal orthodoxy, the Jesuits and the Lazarists, the Doctrinaires and the Oratorians were deeply marked by Jansenism. In 1725, 20 per cent of the members in each of these institutes were appellants against *Unigenitus*.[78] They were harassed into outward submission by royal commissioners vetting the attendance at general chapters and by bishops closing *collèges* and banning individuals from teaching. Defying authority on a point of conscience can be a first step towards political liberalism. Both institutes were open to the political ideas of the Enlightenment—it was Oratorian thinkers at the end of the seventeenth century who had proclaimed the equality of men in the state of nature and declared the power of kings to originate in delegation from the people, and not directly from God. These progressive schoolmasters welcomed the collapse of royal absolutism in 1789, the Doctrinaires proudly proclaiming, 'nous sommes citoyens avant d'être instituteurs'. Their support for the new order was evident in the numerous recruits they provided for the constitutional Church. When the destructive tide of revolution ebbed, they were leaders in the creation of a new educational system and in the restoration of provincial cultural life. Strange mutations can happen to ideals. It has always been a psychological problem to understand the minds of the ex-Oratorian terrorists. Billaud Varenne is easiest to comprehend, since he had left teaching and become a lawyer (though he always admired his old colleagues, and wanted national education to be put into their charge).[79] But Joseph Lebon, who taught Latin diligently at Beaune and gave half his exiguous salary to buy books for poor students, and Fouché at Arras, knowing Massillon's sermons by heart and half in love with Charlotte Robespierre—how did they come to degrade their sentimental egalitarianism into anti-Christian masquerades and wholesale massacres?[80]

In 1789, there were about 48,000 pupils in the various *collèges*, that is, one in fifty-two of the boys aged from 8 to 18.[81] The vast majority came from the families of the upper and middling bourgeoisie. At big centres of population like Lyon, there would be numerous representatives of nobles of the sword and of the robe.[82] At the fashionable Oratorian *collège* of Juilly, there were prestigious names: Adrien Duport, Alexandre de Beauharnais, Bonald, Louis de Narbonne,

Hérault de Séchelles, the Baron Clootz, and the two sons of Laborde, the court banker.[83] At Angers, where half the intake was from families of merchants and master artisans, there was a strong counter-balancing minority (36 per cent) of the sons of the municipal oligarchy and magistrates of the *présidial*. Much the same at Lille, magistrates and municipal officers providing 30 per cent.[84]

At the other end of the social scale, most ordinary families could not hope to send a son to a *collège*. *Bourses*—exhibitions—were not numerous, and many were reserved for pupils proceeding to an ecclesiastical career. The *collèges*, lacking endowments, were dependent on municipalities (and sometimes provincial estates) for funds. There were examples of generosity, for, after all, the governing hierarchy of towns tended to consist of 'old boys'—paying the salary of the masters at Toulon and Marseille when the bishop closed the classrooms, and at Le Mans paying enough to enable free pupils to be taken.[85] But often, the schoolmasters had to operate on a shoe-string budget. At Forcalquier in Provence in 1769, only a single teacher was left to take all the classes, the town having ended its financial aid because it objected to the bishop exercising his right to appoint the masters. The Doctrinaires at Gimont in 1758 and at Lectoure in 1770 had to go on strike to get their salaries.[86] The Oratorians of Angers in 1770 had an income of only 2,148 livres to pay nine teachers and five servants; at the same time debts forced their house at Saumur to close its boarding wing, and at Soissons to consider closing altogether.[87] Free places for all candidates of real merit was the ideal of both the institutes, but in practice, a *collège* had to charge fees running from 400 to 700 livres. And in any case, even a free place was not much good to a family living beyond walking distance of the classrooms; relatives in town or some patron, probably an ecclesiastic, who would offer free lodgings were needed. The sons of artisans who got through to secondary education all went into the Church, and so did the sons of most of the merchants. Peasants' representatives were few, except in tiny *collèges* in the remote countryside. If there was a substantial rural recruitment (as at Le Mans, where it was 15 per cent), it was the sons of the richer peasants, the *laboureurs*.[88] The financial standing of a family also tended to determine the length of the course of schooling. In theory, a pupil attended from the age of 7 to 14, starting at the 'fifth class', then on a year at a time to the 'second' at the age of 10, then 'rhetoric' and 'rhetoric renewed' and 'logic' and 'logic renewed'. In practice, except for the sons of richer families or boys going on to an ecclesiastical career, it was common to leave after completing the 'second'. By contrast, if their parents could afford it, some less able pupils might stay on, repeating an unsatisfactory year; it was not unusual to find young men of 19 still hanging round as students.[89]

In certain respects, it was impossible to treat rich pupils as equal to poor ones. In establishments with boarders, the rich would demand a room with a fire and, perhaps, a servant in attendance. When theatrical performances were staged, the heroic parts would have to go to sons of distinguished families—and in any case it was their parents who could afford to provide splendid costumes. But equality was observed in the classroom, where the competitive spirit was fostered by rivalry for class placings, by prize givings, public recitals of rhetorical compositions and Latin verses, and the upholding of theses. In these ways, a line was drawn between pupils on grounds of merit alone. Dulaure's guide-book to Paris in 1787 described the competitions in rhetoric at Juilly at six-weekly intervals as designed to show 'it is not riches or wealth, but only merit and talents which deserve consideration'.[90] This bridging of class barriers was a conscious aim of the Oratorians. When constrained to run military academies, they declared their intention to mix pupils doing ordinary courses with those on the military side, 'thus stifling the haughtiness which young nobles are all too easily disposed to confuse with elevation of soul, and induce them to consider from a just point of view all orders in society'.[91] In the last pre-revolutionary generation it became a commonplace to say that the educational system of the *collèges* had ended the external differences between nobles and richer commoners. 'The sons of merchants and bourgeois', said Restif de la Bretonne in 1773, 'have as polished an exterior as the great because they are brought up like them.'[92] Why, then, should privilege subsist? 'The old order made a crucial error,' said Danton.

I was educated by it as an exhibitioner at the Collège du Plessis. I studied with great nobles who lived with me on equal terms. My studies once finished, I had nothing . . . My former comrades turned their backs on me. The Revolution came. I—and all those like me—we threw ourselves into it. The *ancien régime* drove us to it by giving us a good education without opening any opportunity for our talents.[93]

The education given in the *collèges* was not 'religious' in broad intent, though each day was set in a religious cadre. At Juilly in 1720, there were prayers at 6 a.m., supper and evening prayer at 8.45 p.m.; everything between was study and classes, with little time off for recreation.[94] In the lay *collèges* which succeeded the Jesuit institutions, there was hardly any relaxation in the pattern of observances: prayers and half an hour's Bible study beginning at 6 a.m., mass at 10.30 a.m., evening prayers at 8.45 p.m. It was formal religion, part of the unquestioned social order.[95] True, in Rennes after the Jesuits, there were traditional survivals regarded as overstepping the boundaries of devotions appropriate for schoolboys. At the annual prize giving, the successful pupils processed through the city behind their teachers, did seven 'stations' in the seven chapels of the Jacobins, heard a sermon, then were regaled with strawberries and wine and were allowed to fill their pockets with apples, finishing with a visit to the chapel of the Virgin, to prostrate themselves before her statue. 'We—professing as we did a passionate enthusiasm for the eighteenth century—were sunk deep in the Middle Ages,' said Moreau de Jonnes.[96]

The daily religious routine was the structure holding together the introverted world of the *collège*. Within this closed social unit the hours of work were long, and periods of recreation were few; holidays were limited—perhaps one day a week and two weeks in summer. Ordinary life was shut out. The claustrophobic atmosphere was intensified by the nature of the instruction (at least in the early decades of the century). The materials on which the mind was exercised came from a vanished civilization, studied through the medium of a dead language, one, moreover, approached mainly in the form of extracts judiciously selected. There were no opportunities to range curiously in the classical epoch, turning up, no doubt, scandalous incidents, dangerous arguments, erotic verse. The artificiality of the proceedings was defended by vaguely, though not very obviously, religious arguments: the need to know the language of the liturgy and of the officially available version of the Bible, the edifying nature of the moral and patriotic incidents of pagan antiquity, the value of studying a conspectus of the utmost perfection to which natural religion can attain, to gain a point of departure for an appreciation of the blessings of the Christian revelation.[97] Besides, a degree of abstraction from everyday reality was useful to keep concupiscence out of the mind (a consideration annexed by reformers who wanted more time given to mathematics). Oddly, the more obvious argument of our day emphasizing the training of the mind by the study of a demanding subject, whatever its factual content, was little used, except in the cliché 'Latin leads to anything' used by old-fashioned fathers arguing with sons who could not see why they should flog through Latin grammar and write essays on the remorse of Nero or verses on the virtue of magnanimity.

From the end of the seventeenth century, change was in the air. It was implicit in the proposals for the education of royal pupils devised by Bossuet and Fénelon, in Locke's proposal to bring the Latin classics to life by the use of interlinear translations, in Rollin's *Traité des études* (1726) giving translation and commentary priority over theme and composition. The Quarrel of Ancients and Moderns, with the Moderns prevailing, brought into competitive focus the glories of seventeenth-century French literature: Racine equalled the Greek tragedians, and Molière was superior to the Roman comic playwrights. French had become the intellectual tongue of the civilized world, a language other nations had to learn—why should the youth of France spend its time learning a different one? From the abbé Fleury's *Choix des études* (1686), the idea was abroad that the classical languages were useless, except it might be a snobbish conversational gambit to remark how easily Greek can be forgotten.

The Oratorians were the first to put the new ideas into effect. They had two allegiances which drew them towards innovation. One was their sympathy with the Jansenist cause. Port-Royal had used simplified Latin grammars written in French, a new departure breaking with the myth of the school as a re-creation of a patrician assembly in ancient Rome. The other allegiance was to Cartesianism—this brought them under the censure of the University of Paris and of Louis XIV. The prohibition against teaching Cartesianism was not, as Mme de Sévigné supposed, damaging to them, at least in the long term. For one thing, the philosophical fashion changed, and the Oratorians with it; the cosmology of Descartes was replaced by Newton's, and his epistemology by Locke's and Condillac's. For another, the lesson that clarity of thought was the cardinal intellectual virtue had been assimilated, and could not be forgotten. What the official ban did was to strengthen the Oratorian tradition of resistance to authority. In another fashion, they followed Descartes, who, as a friend of Bérulle and a native of Anjou, their heartland, was their cult figure. He had written, not in Latin, but in French, to appeal to the ladies and to those who 'use their pure and natural reason' rather than relying on 'old books'. Why should not French educationalists do the same? Lamy, an Oratorian of Cartesian persuasion, in his *Entretiens sur les sciences* (1684), complained of the obscurantist education he had endured, taught as if his head was tied up in a sack, and whipped if he went in the wrong direction. He wished to dethrone Latin, its versification, dictation, and themes, and the Aristotelian scholasticism which seemed to be its natural accompaniment, and pleaded for the study of the sciences, especially mathematics and geometry. In a manuscript proposal of 1720, Père Hoobigant wanted to exchange Latin for French, his new key discipline to be, not mathematics, but history. True, he favoured working from translations of Plutarch and classical historians, and wanted more poetry to sharpen the imagination, inevitably blunted by the factual examples of history.

From the beginning of the seventeenth century, the Oratory taught Latin through French grammars, and gave translation priority over the composition of themes. By mid-century, French was dominant. At Troyes, of the forty-five essays read by the class of rhetoric from 1765 to 1766, only four were in Latin, and from 1757 all the theses of logic and physics were in French. It was a great thing for a boy to take home his thesis bound and adorned with the arms of the Oratory (two angels bearing a crown of thorns and a palm with an inscription to Jesus and Mary); the privilege was available to more of them now that the language barrier was down. The current of intellectual fashion was turning towards history—the Maurists and their researches, popular histories of France by Président Hénault and various Jesuits, Bossuet and, in a different fashion, Voltaire, making the sweep of universal history a theme for the imagination. The demand was for a study of events relevant to the eighteenth century, and a great deal of modern history came into the curriculum of the *collèges*. This turning to the 'real' and away from the artificial environment constructed out of sanitized fragments of classical antiquity also prompted the study of the sciences. The abbé Coyer's *Plan d'éducation publique* of 1770 was concerned with 'things'—the pattern of lines in geometry, maps, globes, machines, skeletons, plants, animals. After 1770 the proportion of time devoted to the sciences within the philosophy course rose from a third to a half and kept on increasing, more especially because the custom developed of leaving the philosophy in Latin and teaching the mathematics, physics, and astronomy in French.

The Doctrinaires were following the same path as the Oratorians. From the end of the seventeenth century, they made French the main language of teaching—after 1770, exclusively. By that time their set authors included Corneille, Boileau, La Fontaine, Gresset, J.-B. Rousseau (not Jean-Jacques), and Voltaire. Then, belatedly, Racine came in; no doubt his tragedies had been held back because of their intense undertow of sexuality. History and geography became central subjects. In 1771 the Doctrinaires were denounced by the University of Paris; they had abandoned Latin themes and versification, logic and metaphysics, it was said, putting in their place a heterogeneous jumble of history, geography, and other superficial and interesting subjects—they had sold out to the philosophes. The Doctrinaires accepted this as the ultimate accolade, though they proffered defensive reservations about Latin. Perhaps more than the Oratorians, the Pères de la Doctrine Chrétienne taught 'citizenship', the fashionable word which was to link the sentimentality of the *ancien régime* to the severities of the Revolution. They emphasized morality rather than dogma, focusing on the concept of 'vocation', the fulfilment of the duties of one's station, the most corrupting sin of all being idleness. Their philosophy of society was summed up in the *Traité d'éducation civile, morale et religieuse* (1789) of Père Corbin, the principal of their *collège* at La Flèche, a study of Christian vocation in its obligations towards the State, society, and the property and persons of fellow citizens.[98]

More closely examined, the reform of the syllabuses of the *collèges* was not as radical as the University of Paris and other angry traditionalists supposed. Not all the new subjects were regarded as entirely respectable: the visitor of the Oratorians calling at the *collège* of Condom in 1784 said that 'mercenaries' could be hired to teach the light-hearted subjects, with the actual members of the institute limiting themselves to 'scientific and Christian education'.[99] The Maurists at Sorèz, defending themselves against the University of Paris, said that it was only the stupid pupils who were excused Latin, the others having to do it for four hours a day. The Doctrinaires in 1789 were still using many extracts from Latin authors, even if studying them through the French language. Their favourite was Cicero; there was never any use of Seneca or Tacitus. No doubt these exclusions were for moral reasons, just as the Oratorians, advanced as they were, as late as 1776 and 1785 banned theatrical productions, a prohibition which most *collèges* ignored. Moral instruction was ruthlessly imposed on any sort of entertaining reading. Père Grozelier of the Oratory published fables in 1760 and 1768 to enliven the classroom—the 'enfant gâté' who was cruel to a sheep got a broken leg, and another maltreating a cat lost an eye; another, given to gluttony, perished miserably, having mistaken arsenic for sugar.[100] There was a rush to study history, but it was history in the old providentialist vein. The principal of the *collège* of Lille, the abbé Lefian, ordered by the committee of management in 1772 to reform the syllabus, pronounced history to be central, 'the ruler of men'; therefore, he said, we must study sacred history first of all, then go on to demonstrate 'how God gives his aid to nations that are just'.[101] In 1789, the

Doctrinaires at Aix taught their sixth class from Erasmus, La Fontaine, and Racine's *Phèdre*; they had a course on natural history (this year's subject being birds), and they taught some French history. Even so, they had plenty of dogma from Fleury's catechism; they covered the Old Testament from creation to Judges; they had a special theme from the New Testament in the early life of Jesus; and their national history was organized as a theme of apologetics, a quarry of evidence to demonstrate the working of God's judgements.[102] At the end of the *ancien régime* the old and the new jostled together in the teaching of the *collèges*—an education ostensibly given by churchmen for Christian ends, yet generally regarded by families as being 'moral' in intention rather than specifically Christian, and all the while being quietly secularized from within.

IV

The *collèges* provided a civilized basic education for pupils who were born to status and office, without too much nonsense about merit, and for those of lower social classes who hoped to rise through the Church or the lower reaches of the legal profession. What they did not offer was technical or vocational training; the method and content of their teaching were evolving, but too slowly to forestall the rise of competition. Well-off parents who distrusted the *collèges*, whether as too ruthless, too religious, or as lacking in practical usefulness, could resort to other schools which were multiplying at the end of the *ancien régime*, the *pensionnats*. A guide-book to Paris of 1787 listed no fewer than three in the grande rue de Passy alone, charging fees like 450 livres from the age of 4 to 10, and 700 from 10 onwards.[103] Some establishments of this kind were down-market, like the one Mercier attended, run by 'le père Tocquet', a portly figure in scarlet coat and black velvet breeches, a great wielder of the rod, and a fine singer who performed at the parish offices of Saint-Germain-l'Auxerrois. 'Père' was unusual, probably ironical; 'abbé' was the general title, but in either case, these managers of schools were—nominally, at least—ecclesiastics. Some establishments claimed to be select. 'Although this pensionnat', says the prospectus of the abbé Liébault at Dijon in 1776, 'is singularly suited to young noblemen who are destined for a military career, we nevertheless admit the sons of bourgeois and merchants.'[104] In the local newspaper he proclaimed a syllabus of languages, sciences, arts, mathematics (useful for war), dancing, fencing, riding, with Greek optional—for

600 livres a year, rising to 800 after the age of 10. The abbé Hazard, more exclusive still, made no concessions to the middle classes: he opened a school at Nanterre for nobles only—too often, he said, they have to go into a military career having been educated like bourgeois.[105] He was starting his venture at an unpropitious time— February 1789. The most lavish academy of all was probably the abbé Choquart's in Paris. Hugh Elliot, who was there with his brother and their tutor from England, describes how the school celebrated the feast of St Louis in 1765, the boys in their blue and silver uniforms engaged in Prussian drill and military manœuvres all day, then performing in a ballet at night in the illuminated gardens, with opera singers and fireworks to complete the entertainment.[106]

As these establishments proliferated, they poached pupils from the *collèges*. The University of Angers tried to get a municipal regulation limiting the number of *pensionnats* in town to eight, to rescue the Collège d'Anjou from decline. Similar measures at Nantes failed, and by 1788 the boarding-house of the Oratorians there was half empty.[107] In 1777, the abbé de Massannes, after twenty years' teaching in Sorèz, 'giving lessons on the whole range of human knowledge to the élite youth there', came to Grenoble and opened a *pensionnat* which had 100 pupils within a year. In despair, the *collège* had to open a house for boarders in competition, call in new teachers, and institute a reform of the curriculum.[108]

The *pensionnats* gave vocationally oriented education to the sons of families which could afford to pay substantial fees. There was, however, an institution of this name which also gave highly specialist instruction, but as a remarkable philanthropic gesture—the abbé de l'Épée's *pensionnat* in Paris for deaf and dumb children. A Portuguese Jew in Bordeaux had invented an ingenious method of teaching them; he was pensioned by the Crown and by his own Jewish community, but was not able to put his scheme into large-scale practice. This was done by Épée, who put his inheritance into creating a school for the deaf and dumb in Paris. It became famous, was visited by noble ladies, bishops, the papal nuncio, the Emperor Joseph II, and Gustavus III of Sweden, and finally received an annual grant from the king, and was given accommodation in an empty monastery. Épée's disciples went out to set up similar establishments in Vienna, Rome, and Angers. Archbishop Champion de Cicé sent the abbé Sicard to Paris to learn the teaching methods; he returned and set up an institute at Bordeaux, though before long he went back to Paris to take over the main house. Here was an example of religion combining with the Enlightenment concept of philanthropy to produce an organization in which the thrill of putting a new 'scientific' discovery into practice was allied to the moral satisfaction of helping a disadvantaged class.

Some of the new *pensionnats* were angling for customers from traditional military families. Warfare was becoming more technical, and in mid-century the government set up a new structure for training military cadets. There were two specialist schools—of artillery and engineering—and a central École Militaire in Paris offering 500 places to the sons of nobles. This central school was confided first of all to the Prêtres de la Mission; predictably, they proved too rigorous in imposing the observances of religion, so three doctors of the Sorbonne were called in to supervise the teaching.[109] The professors who served under them were nearly all ecclesiastics, but they were not allowed to adopt the style of 'abbé'. Berthelin, who taught mathematics, complained of the deprivation, for he was indeed 'an honorary canon of Saint-Denis at Douai'.[110] The arrival of the comte de Saint-Germain as Minister of War led to further expansion. He had risen as a mercenary in foreign service; he knew better than anyone how the face of warfare was changing; and he was determined to professionalize training. Under his reform, a cadet had to go for five years to one of twelve new academies in the provinces; then, at the age of from 13 to 15, he would move up to the École Militaire in Paris; thereafter, he would be sent either to the Artillery or to the Engineering School, or directly to his regiment. By 1785, these twelve new provincial academies had 2,775 cadets. A quarter of these were paid for by the king; of those paying for themselves, half were of noble birth.[111]

These academies were all run by religious Orders: six by the Benedictines of Saint-Maur, three by the Oratorians, one by the Minims, one by the canons regular of Notre-Sauveur, one by the Doctrinaires. The government's advisers had a field-day devising a syllabus, the abbé Batteux drawing up fifty-eight volumes which, fortunately, were ignored. The Maurists had already been experimenting with a new scheme of modern subjects, more especially Dom Victor Fougeras, prior of the abbey of Sorèze. Now, with a teaching unit of twenty-four monks and twenty lay associates, he was given the opportunity of setting up one of the provincial military academies.[112] Latin and Greek became optional, while modern languages, mathematics, French history up to contemporary times, music, and gymnastics became core subjects. Molière was declared to be a superior writer of comedy to Aristophanes, and extracts from Voltaire's *Henriade* were set texts. There was the inevitable religious instruction and practice: compulsory daily services, Fleury's *Caté-chisme historique*, and the study of sacred history from the Old Testament to the sixth century. In these military schools, more than in others, the imposition of religious routines was counter-productive. At Brienne, run by the Minims, the pupils placed bets on how long each friar would take to say the daily mass; some unpopular ones took twenty minutes, but Père Châtaux won approval by omitting the Credo and Gloria and finishing in five. The usual disputes between religious and their parish priest for pastoral oversight of the rites of passage took place, the curé of Brienne winning a legal ruling to have the boys compelled to make their First Communion in his church. The first one to be sent was the Corsican cadet Bonaparte.[113]

V

On the margins between the bourgeoisie on the one hand and peasants and artisans on the other was a whole class of ambitious families wanting a good education of a vocational kind for their children. What was on offer in the *collèges* and *pensionnats* was not suitable; nor could they afford it. At the same time, among enlightened churchmen there was an awareness that the imposition of religious routines in schools needed a new philosophy of Christian instruction to achieve dispositions more inward than mere conformity. In a paradoxical fashion, movement towards these two objectives was achieved by a new foundation, the Frères des Écoles Chrétiennes[114]—paradoxical because the original inspiration had a different orientation, and because the Frères allied ideas of the Enlightenment with reactionary attitudes of an intolerant kind. Jean-Baptiste de La Salle, their founder, was a saint in the mould of Rancé of La Trappe. An aristocrat, destined for an easy life off ecclesiastical revenues, a canon of Reims at the abusive age of 16, he was converted, gave up his canonry and his private fortune, and in 1648 formed a brotherhood to educate the children of the very poor. It was to be a ruthlessly religious education—attendance at mass daily, a period of recollection of God's presence in the course of every lesson, half an hour of religious instruction every day and one and a half hours on Sundays. His brethren were to be uncompromisingly orthodox, giving total obedience to the Pope and set in flint-like opposition to Jansenism. By 1700, the Frères des Écoles Chrétiennes were running elementary schools in five towns.

In the years following, up to his death in 1719, La Salle diversified the activities of his followers by organizing Sunday classes for adults in more advanced subjects, by giving technical training in seamanship to boys in Calais, and by setting up a boarding-school for the sons of middle-class tradesmen in Rouen, with a curriculum suited to their needs. Eventually, these departures from the original aim became the Frères' claim to educational originality and influence in society. There was a choice, in founding a new institute, between the usual permanent vows of monks and the 'simple', temporary vows taken by the Oratorians, and La Salle ingeniously combined the two systems in a way which at once encouraged recruitment while discouraging faint-hearted vocations. Up to the age of 25, a brother took renewable vows, after which time he could choose either to undertake the lifelong obligation (provided he had already served for three years) or to stay in the provisional status, retaining his freedom to leave. In fact, this freedom was frequently used: of the twenty-six postulants coming into the noviciate of Saint-Yon in 1720, fourteen eventually departed from the institute; of those of 1740, eighteen out of twenty-six left; of 1748, twenty-three out of thirty-three; of 1760, ten out of seventeen.[115] There was no assumption that piety was enough to make a teacher; a brother was never sent to a school to teach until he himself had been instructed in educational techniques.

The *petites écoles*, the free elementary schools—the original purpose of the institute—proliferated up to mid-century. An invitation would come from a diocesan bishop (always a strictly orthodox one), an investigator would be sent down from headquarters, and he would ensure that financial support was guaranteed—generally in the form of a fixed salary for each teacher; then a task force of qualified teachers would arrive, a house of residence would be set up for them, and from it they would go out to teach in schools in the adjoining parishes—four schools in Arras, for example, five in Tours. By 1747, the Frères des Écoles Chrétiennes had put down roots in eighty locations, with a total of about 800 teachers working; by 1779, they had a hundred residences and were teaching 30,000 pupils. By now, expansion was virtually over, though Loménie de Brienne brought them belatedly to Toulouse, confiscating monastic revenues for the purpose—the opening date was, inauspiciously, March 1789.

In some places the Frères elaborated their elementary schools to undertake the teaching of vocational specialities, such as hydrography at Vannes and Nantes and commerce at Boulogne—thus drawing to their classes children from families of higher social standing than would normally have been interested. However, the major technical training for careers—in navigation, horticulture, surveying, accounting, in shop, office, and government service which was to become the speciality of the Frères—was given in their *pensionnats*, boarding-schools, at Angers, Saint-Yon, Saint-Omer, Marseille, Maréville (Lorraine), Montpellier, Mirepoix, Nantes, and Reims. Three more *pensionnats* were opened later. These establishments had to be self-financing. Municipalities, dominated by the upper classes, were old boys' associations of the local *collège*, and they lacked enthusiasm for rival institutions bringing superior education to the lower orders. The central government would help only on its own terms, and what the king's ministers required were prisons, with reliable gaolers to take care of special offenders—*maisons de force*. Three of the *pensionnats* took up this unpleasing work as a sideline to the school, in this way gaining an income and official favour. This combination of roles proved disastrous for Maréville. The delinquent population rose to 500, more than double the number of pupils, and the school was disrupted from 1778 to 1783 by extensive building work. Finally, given an inefficient superior, in 1789 the place was described as fit only for closure. The other two *pensionnats* doubling up as *maisons de force* also suffered, though less grievously. There was a major prison revolt at Saint-Yon in 1774. Earlier, at Angers, 'writings, arms, ropes and files were smuggled in and riots ensued, several brothers being victims . . . and perishing from the ill-treatment they suffered'. Although a wealthy family might pay as much as 1,000 livres a year to have a member confined, most contributed less, and the king's standard payment was 100, so the profits were not great, and school fees still had to be charged, as in the other *pensionnats*. Usually, parents were asked to pay 400 livres together with twelve changes of linen; only a family which had risen as far as the lower middle class could afford this.

There was no shortage of applicants. Mathematics with trigonometry, algebra, and geometry, book keeping and commercial law and practice, horticulture, the maintenance of machinery, calligraphy, surveying, and other practical disciplines made it an eminently useful syllabus. Latin was banned; grammar was ruthlessly hammered in, but without going on to the frills of rhetoric. Teaching did not consist of long expositions, but in crisp questions and answers, and in doing things, rather than knowing how to do them. In the textbooks, the commonplaces of the old educational methods were kept as adornments, while the substance of the instruction was newly presented. Thus, the explanation of how to turn from adding, subtracting, multiplying, and dividing to fractions was well founded psychologically—slowly, step by step, retaining confidence all the while; this was balanced by the old clichés in praise of mathematics— Archimedes outwitting the besiegers by his calculations, St Jerome declaring numbers to have mystical powers, and the parables of the unjust steward and the talents demonstrating the importance of learning to add up bills and calculate interest.

A student in a *pensionnat* was subject to a regime of fanatical orthodoxy: not a suspect volume in the library, the daily routine including prayer, meditation, mass, litanies of the Child Jesus and the rosary before breakfast, self-examination, the *De Profundis* and the Angelus before dinner, and litanies of the Passion and St Joseph afterwards, with catechism at 6 p.m. taught from a version which, in spite of the commercial speciality of the teaching, flatly condemned loans at interest.

Yet, in spite of these rigours, there was a new spirit in the teaching, ultimately derived from Locke and Fénelon and, perhaps, from Rollin. It was set out in La Salle's *Conduite des écoles*, published in 1720, the year after his death, and refined and augmented by Frère Agathon, the greatest of the superior-generals, in his *Les Douze Vertus d'un bon maître, par M. de la Salle* (1785). These twelve virtues included some surprising ones, certainly by the standards of the day: silence, humility, and generosity. Relationships with pupils were to be friendly. There were to be no beatings. Punishment should strike at pride, by imposing a period on the dunce's stool or relegation to the bottom of the class. In impossible cases, a refractory pupil should be sent home. There were to be no satirical observations, no discouraging words, no sneaking to parents—at the most say, 'could do better'. A teacher was not just a distributor and imposer of information, but must have thought out the reasons behind every commonplace proposition, and devised ways to make his subject interesting. Allegiance to Christian principles and beliefs would come to children by slow, indirect processes; their instructors should use the method already familiar in prayer and meditation: first, inculcate the truth, then explain it, then seek to give it vital force in the soul.

There is always a gap between educational ideals and what actually happens in the classroom, and the sheer rigour of the cadre of religious routines accorded ill with La Salle's almost Rousseauistic theory of sympathetic relationships with the children. So the Frères were not welcome everywhere. Upper-class citizens who sent their sons to the *collèges* scorned an intolerant organization educating children of the lower orders above their station; some bishops, whether because of their tolerant disposition or their Gallicanism, did not want them in their dioceses; some families complained of an excessive discipline exercised by mental pressures: the Jansenist *Nouvelles ecclésiastiques* kept up a running commentary on every fanatical incident or moral lapse which occurred in their establishments. The Frères des Écoles Chrétiennes were an ambivalent organization, the last creation in France of the uncompromising Counter-Reformation, and the appropriator of Enlightenment ideals into the ecclesiastically dominated educational system of the country.

18

THE RELIGIOUS VOCATION AND SOCIAL USEFULNESS: WOMEN

I

The work of educating children and caring for the sick and the poor in eighteenth-century France was performed, almost exclusively, by monastic and quasi-monastic institutions founded since the year 1500. Immense endowments had fallen to the monasteries in the Middle Ages, but the new inspirations to a wider social and religious service had, mostly, passed these houses by. The Orders which had arrived earliest had retired to the shade, and the later arrivals bore the burden and heat of the day, without hope of receiving the traditional equal penny.

The newer congregations and institutes, so often lacking in endowment, had to resort to continual shifts to keep going—charging for the services they rendered, or resorting to methods of raising money not always compatible with the highest monastic ideals. Convents of nuns faced especial difficulties, since they did not have the resorts of male communities of going out begging, undertaking parish duties, earning fees for saying masses and preaching. So they had to be calculating about the dowries novices brought with them, let out rooms to old ladies as boarders, make things for sale— tapestries, chair covers, sweets, cakes, liqueurs, medicines—and coax free consultations from doctors and lawyers and delay the payment of tradesmen's bills for years on end. If they managed to make investments, it was generally in *rentes*, contracts of loan bringing in a regular income of interest; under Law's Scheme, the sensational financial experiment of the Regency (1718–20), borrowers rushed to repay their debts in the depreciating paper which was compulsory tender, bringing many a convent to ruin.

In 1727, the government took action to deal with the chaos caused by the bankruptcies. A Commission de secours of four prelates and four *maîtres des requêtes* instituted a sweeping enquiry. The nuns faced a dilemma when furnishing information, for while disclosure of their poverty might bring assistance, it was more likely to result in a decree of suppression, or of union with another house. The many communities where pockets of Jansenist influence were found (the Cistercian and Benedictine convents, and those of the Annonciades, the Calvairiennes, the Visitandines, the Carmelites, and the Ursulines) were particularly alarmed, for the bishops might take their chance to root out the weeds of heretical influence in their dioceses. In fact, the bishops avoided drastic action because of the danger of stirring up lay protests; the disaffected nuns were quietly disposed of by exile to other communities and deprivation of the sacraments, a story of suffering which went unnoticed except in the pages of the *Nouvelles ecclésiastiques*. When it came to the crunch, no one wanted to face the local unpopularity which a ruthless reform would have incurred. Like the Commission des réguliers which forty years later enquired into the monasteries of men, the Commission de secours filled the archives with statistics and did little. Over a long period, fifty houses of Ursulines received a *lettre de cachet* forbidding the reception of novices (fifteen because of Jansenism), but in the end only twenty were suppressed—out of a total of 400. The multitude of poverty-stricken communities of women struggled on, most regaining a precarious solvency.

II

Girls of the upper classes were all educated by nuns, families sending them into different convents according to their position in the social hierarchy, with the fees charged acting as a regulator. In Paris, there were forty-three houses of nuns devoted to such educational work.[1] The daughters of the highest aristocracy would gather at the Abbaye-aux-Bois, rue de Sèvres. A family choosing the maximum tariff with a couple of women attendants might pay as much as 30,000 livres a year. Actresses from the Comédie-Française and dancers and singers from the Opéra paid regular visits to give instruction in the theatrical graces, and the pupils performed sophisticated ballets and plays. Girls from families of the robe and high finance were found in the Dames de Sainte-Marie, rue Jacques, a severely disciplined academy. Noble but not quite so rich girls and those of distinguished bourgeois status would aspire to the Dames de Panthémont, rue de Grenelle, at 800 livres a year, with an extra 200 to be admitted to the table of the abbess and a further 300 for the services of a *femme de chambre*.[2] There were similar fees at La Madeleine de Traisnel, rue de Charonne, the abbaye Saint-

Antoine, Port-Royal, and the Bénédictines du Saint-Sacrement, rue Cassette.

In expensive boarding establishments such as these, girls stayed until a husband was found for them. Mercier ridiculed the dramatists who put on stage young men making their 'declaration' to the girl they adored. 'Nothing could be falser and further from the practice of society . . . No one makes love to young ladies. They are shut up in convents until the day of their marriage. No one sees them alone.' The same, he adds, in bourgeois households with the daughters at home—they are never seen apart from their mothers. Protestations of love can be made only to *grisettes*, the pretty shop girls on their weekend off. Mercier was exaggerating: convent supervision was not as fierce, and young people not so lacking in ingenuity, as he implies. True, the high aristocracy, determined to clinch advantageous alliances in their select circle, tended to ignore the wishes of their daughters; a marriage might be hastened on, even though the bride was not of age to consummate it—in this case, she would go back to her convent after the ceremony, as happened in 1778 when Mlle de Choiseul and, later, Mlle de Bourbonne returned to the Abbaye-aux-Bois,[3] where, no doubt, they cut a splendid figure among the other envious *pensionnaires*. Lower down the social scale, and more and more throughout the century, there was a recognition by families of a daughter's right to be consulted and consent. As marriageable age approached, the convent school slipped unobtrusively into becoming a marriage agency, and the nuns, abandoning their traditional role of persuaders towards a religious vocation, moved into the role of advisers in worldly or sentimental choices. Occasionally, a young woman would be transferred by her family from her convent school to another sort of convent acting as a 'finishing school' to await her suitors, as Mirabeau's beautiful 13-year-old sister was moved from the house of the Benedictine nuns of Montargis to that run by nuns of Dominican allegiance. 'What is charming about this monastery', said her notorious brother, 'is that it is not in the least religious, and numerous ladies retire here for an agreeable social life.'[4] The marriage-agency role might be blatant; Barbier tells a grim story of young men crowding to a Parisian convent to meet an ugly girl supposed to have 30,000 livres a year— all the result of a cruel practical joke. There could, however, be something touching about the brides-for-sale system. In 1775 the comtesse de Brionne asked the abbess of Panthémont to find a wife for her friend, M. de Saint-Péravy, a magistrate of the parlement. The abbess addressed her *pensionnaires*: 'There is a gentleman with

40,000 livres a year and holder of a distinguished office who wants to marry one of you. I warn you he is not much to look at but he has a beautiful disposition.' The rich girls scoffed and a shy and pretty poor one was sure no one would want her; within a few days she was Mme de Saint-Péravy.[5] As a matrimonial agency, the system worked well enough, since everyone understood the rules. A rich planter in Guadeloupe, not finding suitable men on the island for his daughter, naturally sent her to a convent in France—at Bordeaux. Here, a relative advised her on how to make her choice: do not be impatient to escape the cloister; do not see one suitor too often, lest you get too attached to him too early; remember that the public will be judging your conduct as you make your choice.[6] So in the end, though it might be difficult, a young woman had her choice, or at least a liberty to refuse. A few, in the end, decided against marriage altogether, and without taking vows, stayed on comfortably as *pensionnaires* all their lives.[7]

There was speculation among watchers of protocol when the little daughters of Louis XV were to be sent to school, Cardinal Fleury insisting this must be done to avoid the expense of maintaining a separate household for them at Versailles. The Court rejected the gilded Parisian academies for daughters of the high aristocracy, and ensured that the 'filles de France' were kept aloof in their unique rank, taking little heed of their educational prospects, and none of their happiness. Aged 5, 4, 2, and 1 (a baby in arms), they were packed off to the abbey of Fontevrault eighty leagues away. Marie Adélaïde, aged 7, was lucky. Coached in a piteously worded entreaty, she threw herself at the king's feet and was excused from exile. In their seven years at Fontevrault, one of the girls barely managed to complete learning the alphabet, and another had a nervous breakdown from having to go to confession in the vault serving as the convent's burial place. The pious queen never went to visit them.[8]

Paradoxically, the king's daughters were ill brought up, while a superb, but severe education was available for girls at the one school which was a royal foundation, paid for by royal gifts and compulsory levies on other monasteries decreed by the Crown. Under the influence of Mme de Maintenon, Louis XIV had founded 'la communauté royale de Saint-Louis de Saint-Cyr' to educate 250 girls from poor noble families which had served the nation in war. The Dames de Saint-Louis began as a lay institute taking temporary vows, but in 1692 their vows were made permanent, and the community became a regular monastery under the rule of St Augustine.

The girls were at Saint-Cyr from the ages of 7 to 12, and could stay on until they were 20. They were dressed in severe uniforms; their days were full of classes and religious exercises; they were never allowed to go home; and their parents could come to see them only four times a year, and always in the presence of a nun. Under this strict regime, they were taught a great deal of practical expertise, more especially the art of household management, and it was a lament among country noblemen looking for diligent wives that the nuns so often persuaded their charges to stay in the religious life.[9] The 'filles de France' would have done a great deal better there than among the sycophantic and inefficient splendours of Fontevrault.

As in Paris, so on a lesser scale in the other towns, there was a hierarchy of convents educating fee-paying girls. Some nuns ran a formal school as their main activity—at the abbey of Saint-Georges at Rennes, the terms were 230 livres a year, sheets and towels not included, with the abbess guaranteeing personal attention to her pupils.[10] Others took boarders occasionally, according to their incli-nation and financial necessities. Strictly, the Visitandines were not supposed to teach; François de Sales had wished them to devote their lives to contemplation, though a particular convent might take in three or four girls who were known to have a precocious vocation to the monastic state. The daily routine prescribed by the Order was two meals a day, at 10 a.m. and 6 p.m., the first preceded by public confession of faults and eaten in silence (except on the eve of the Epiphany); there were two hours' recreation, all the rest of the time being spent in reciting the offices, spiritual reading, prayer, and meditation.[11] Within the intensity of this contemplative life, the Visitandine cult of the Sacred Heart of Jesus was born. But as time went on, the proviso allowing the taking of pupils considered to have the beginnings of a vocation to the cloister became the gate-way for some of the nuns in some houses to become school-mistresses. Convents of the Visitation were all autonomous, with no central direction to prevent them from following their own inclina-tions. The rules, in a way, facilitated the change, for François de Sales, to accommodate ladies of a delicate constitution, had abolished the night offices and prescribed a period of rest of two hours at noon: the routine of liturgical observances was not all-absorbing. The nuns were practically all from families of great distinction, and within their family circles there was always pressure to find places for girls to be educated under the charge of persons of their own station in life, in whose society they could safely grow up to marriageable age. It is remarkable how often a house of Visitandines had boarders who

were nieces of nuns in the same establishment.[12] Educational activities also ensured recruitment. An analysis of the careers of the 403
Visitandines mentioned in the circular letters of the various houses
from 1667 to 1789 shows how half of them had begun their connection with the Order as schoolgirls in its care: these convents for
ladies of the highest social class were self-perpetuating.

In some houses, educational activities were a sideline to the contemplative life, taking a few girls on grounds of family relationship or
potential vocation. In the diocese of Autun, at Moulins, Charolles,
Paray-le-Monial, and Autun itself, the number of boarders at any
one time was between seven and fourteen, a limited number, short
of being a school. At Moulins, the implication that the little girls
were presumed to be going to take the veil was emphasized by
making them wear the habit of the Order, a resort to a parade of
pious intention which did not please all parents.[13] On the other hand,
a particular house might decide to move into education as its
principal activity. At Angers, more than thirty boarders were taken,
all from aristocratic or leading bourgeois families.[14] As befitted their
station in life, the girls were taught singing, dancing, acting, and the
social graces; the annual play was a social occasion for Angevin high
society, and if some of the girls had to dress as men to complete
the cast, no one minded—except the Jansenists, of course. The
Visitandines' line on girls taking male parts did not include doubts
about transvestism: what was to be avoided was amorous intrigue.
Thus, in their convent at Beaune, when they drew lots for a play to
celebrate the birthday of their mother superior, they rejoiced when
the verdict fell on the *Mort de César*, an all-male heroic piece without
sexual overtones. There remained the problem of a prologue to mark
the occasion, and one of the nuns wrote to her cousin, Mme du
Châtelet, who persuaded her lover, Voltaire, to write what was
required, done in twenty minutes flat as he stood in the corner of the
chimney-piece. It was an orthodox effusion, the philosophe asking
the sisters to pray for him 'to the Master of all our imaginings'.[15]

By contrast with the Visitandines, the Ursulines were an Order
specifically devoted to education.[16] Angela Merici, their Italian
founder, had organized them as celibate schoolmistresses living in
their own homes, and Charles Borromeo had brought them into
community life under the modified rule of St Augustine. Pontifical
bulls (as to the Ursulines of Toulouse in 1615) had praised them as a
bulwark against heretics, and defined their duties as giving free education to girls, to include reading, writing, and needlework, though
with the primary object of inspiring them to religious ardour. In the

battle against heresy, they indeed played their part when Louis XIV's persecution forced Protestant girls of prominent families into convents for education. The bitter-sweet cruelty of persuasion which followed is unpleasant to imagine. On occasion it worked, and girls stayed on to take the veil: there was the strange case of Marguerite de Labouetière, who on her wedding-day fled to take refuge for ever in the Ursuline convent of Orthez, where her enforced school-days had been spent. As for free schooling, most houses made an effort to give some elementary instruction to the poor, but their essential role came to be the running of fee-paying boarding-schools. In towns where there was straight competition, the Visitandines, or the Clarisses, were likely to attract the most prestigious pupils; even so, the Ursulines stood high socially. At Rouen, a third of the intake came from families of nobles of the sword or of the robe. Even the snobbish girls at the Visitation of Angers were constrained to concede that the Ursuline school was 'exactly the same as ours, only less well run'.

'Increasing religious ardour', as prescribed by the papal directives, was a difficult formula to implement. Certainly, an Ursuline house took entire possession of a girl's life, reducing her connections with home to a minimum. The regulations of Paris in 1651 and 1705 allow no holidays: at Dijon, the vacation was a month. If the parents lived locally, they could visit their children in the convent parlour, or meetings at home would be allowed, though never staying overnight. The girls rose at 6 a.m. and attended a daily mass; on Sundays they also had the rosary, the office of the Virgin, the seven penitential psalms, and litanies of the saints; on Christmas Day they attended three masses. On the Friday of the week after Corpus Christi, there were religious celebrations all day, for this was the day to commemorate the visions of the Sacred Heart to Marguerite Marie Alacoque at Paray-le-Monial in 1673 and 1674. The nuns were adept at devising picturesque little ceremonies: the usage of the white veil for the First Communion is an Ursuline invention. The convent library would have the *Imitation*, St François de Sales's *Introduction*, and a few Jesuit works of spirituality, while the Order printed various handbooks of devotion for the use of its boarders, one of the favourite exercises being the renewal of baptismal promises. Catechism courses were held twice a day, at Angers all through the century from the same dog-eared notebooks dating from 1700. The nuns prepared 'abridgements' of Christian doctrine for use in teaching, generally using a quadripartite division: the Creed, the Pater Noster, the Ten Commandments, and the sacraments as the guide to the four dispositions leading to salvation—faith, hope, charity, and the doing of good works. Classes began and ended with prayer, and all who passed by the crucifix on the classroom wall paused to bow. How deep and affecting was the inner experience behind the accumulation of observances? According to an angry Jansenist, the Christian life was being 'reduced to a few external practices which they ally with the maxims of the world'.[17] Yet the magnetism to draw so many girls to choose the monastic vocation was there, and it was commonly said, whether in praise or blame, that convent education made a permanent imprint on those who were brought up in its religious regimentation.

Ursuline education was adaptable to local circumstances. There were 400 houses, each independent, with the sisters electing their mother superior annually. There was no imposition of syllabuses from central direction, and the bishops, who had the official disciplinary oversight, were little concerned with teaching programmes. Houses even drew up their own catechisms, or chose them from among those produced in various dioceses, and if there was a leaven of Jansenism in the place, there were some powerful examples from the pens of Jansenist theologians available. Convents had their educational specialities. All taught needlework, but Angers became a centre of rich embroidery from the time the first needlewoman of the queen arrived from Versailles to make her profession. In many places, the sisters made a great deal of local history and stories of the saints of the province, and they had a growing interest in the wider field of Church history and in the secular history of France. News of Ursulines working abroad—like Marie de l'Incarnation in Canada—encouraged them to add the reading of the Jesuit *Relations* to the curriculum. For its day, the Parisian rule-book was enlightened in its educational methodology. Like the Jesuits, the Ursulines were to organize their classes in competing groups, though of twelve instead of ten, *dizainières* instead of *décurions*. The teacher was 'to speak little but ask many questions', encouraging the pupils to 'move from . . . the known to the unknown'. The way to break into a new subject was to treat it 'historically', tracing its development. The peculiar difficulty of being supposed to offer free education, yet actually charging for it, was reflected in the calculated ambiguity with which teachers were directed to 'treat rich and poor pupils alike, but not to put girls of distinguished families near to the poor and dirty ones'. The regulations also had a puritanical paragraph forbidding 'indecent games, such as comedies and dances'. In the interests of a lively upper-class education, this prohibition was ignored. There were limits, of course; there was a great scandal in the late seventeenth century when an Ursuline convent near Grenoble put on a performance of *Tartuffe* in the choir of the chapel.[18] But 'speech-days' with sketches, ballets, pastorals, and burlesques written by the nuns and featuring local characters were universal. The rules were strict, the practice cheerfully individualistic. This being so, the quality of the education depended even more than is usually the case on the quality of the teachers. The Ursulines were recruited from the social groups, like the nobles of the robe, where intellectual families abounded. Among their number were a granddaughter of Malherbe, two sisters of Ménage, three aunts of Fénelon, a daughter of Jean Racine, the sister of Diderot (she was prouder of her brother the canon than of the philosophe), the sister of Buffon, and two aunts of Lamartine. As a result of the undercurrent of Jansenism in the Order, many of the sisters read historical and controversial books with serious attention—they knew their Nicole, Pascal, Bossuet, and the pulpit orators of the reign of Louis XIV. 'She made herself very proficient at teaching by the enlightenment she drew from prayer and the reading of good books,' said the obituary notice of one of the ladies of the Parisian house of Saint-Jacques. In the context of the times, it was as good a way of teacher training as any.

The Ursulines were the biggest teaching order of women, but there were innumerable other convents of various allegiances scattered over the country, offering paying places for girls. The quality of the education varied, and families, unless they had precise local knowledge, made enquiries. A Carmelite friar in Paris replied to anxious parents: do not send your daughter to the nuns of Compiègne, 'they go in for silly ceremonies, they shear the girls' hair and give them ridiculous pet names'; send her rather to the abbey of Sainte-Austreberthe.[19] To what extent did this diversity of schools really fulfil the expectations of the public? According to Molière, the object of the education of girls was twofold: character formation, to ensure moral conduct, and training in household management.[20] Defenders of convent education were eloquent about moral purpose. 'What use are so many convents?' asks the sceptic. An orator at the Academy of Angers in 1770 replied: 'What use are they? ungrateful men. To rear for you good mothers of families, chaste and loyal spouses, vigilant housewives, women who are virtuous citizens. Can the sweet voice of Nature be heard amid the tumult and worldliness of your own homes . . .' and so on.[21] Yet, granting the priority of moral formation, should household management set the boundaries of feminine intellectual endeavour? It was as if, Mme de

Lambert complained, 'girls were a species apart, to be left in isolation, without any thought of the fact that they comprise half of the population . . . and that by them, families either rise or go down to destruction'.[22] Late in the century there were a few campaigners for total equality for women, Riballier and Condorcet in particular. But the main current of liberal feeling, from Fénelon to Rousseau, was to give equal rights, but not to equal things. Girls should be regarded as of equal importance to boys, though they should be trained essentially as wives and mothers and—a potentially far-ranging admission—as educators of the next generation of citizens. This meant that it was less the deficiencies of the content of feminine education which were challenged, as the very idea of the convent as the setting for the educational process. The eighteenth century saw a remarkable change in the status of women, associated less with the theoretical idea of equality than with their more effective contribution to the work of the world as civilization and economic life advanced and diversified, and with the discovery of the supreme value of 'femininity'—'a decisive mutation in the history of civilization'.[23]

In the context of this new view of women, the writers of the Enlightenment made a predictable attack on convent education. Girls, it was said, were deprived of knowledge of the real world. They emerge like cave-dwellers blinded when they step into the sunshine, said Fénelon. The man who presents himself at the convent grille on a reconnaissance for a marriage partner, even if he looks like a monkey, is welcomed as a deliverer—the view of Voltaire.[24] Grimm was savagely dismissive: according to him, girls are taught nothing of true virtue, honour or decency, for what they learn of these things is unconnected with reality; they are forced into the arms of a husband they do not love and subjected to his ruthless sexual demands; by reaction, they then throw off all the decencies themselves. Having been locked up without pleasure, said a great lady, they rush to seize it once it comes within their grasp: 'une fille qui n'a rien vu, se meurt de tout voir à la fois'.[25] These accusations (not all compatible one with another) invert the moral argument for convent education. The enclosed life is meant to inculcate Christian morality; in fact, it merely creates an ignorance of the world which encourages immorality. Both churchmen and philosophes talked of these matters with unimaginative solemnity, the first exaggerating the strictness of convent education and its benefits, the second exaggerating its unworldliness. Girls (and, for that matter, nuns) were neither so punctilious in pious observances nor so clueless about the facts of life as was supposed. Humourless commentators on education do not understand how children are resourceful enough to outwit the system and how they contrive to educate each other.

III

The communities of women devoted to education felt an uneasy obligation to make no distinction between rich and poor families. In practice, discrimination was inevitable, since the rich insisted on it, and the poor could not pay the fees. The Ursulines ought to have dispensed free education to all, but in the diocese of Autun, their communities charging minimum fees to poorer families (120 livres in 1720) found they were incurring a running deficit—and such a fee excluded half the population anyway.[26] So the general practice was to have a fee-paying school to which a few ordinary children were admitted free for reading and writing lessons. At Angers, the Ursulines claimed to teach such a free class of sixty: according to their enemies, the true figure was nearer twenty.[27] At Quimperlé, though it was hard to make ends meet, they took some peasant girls into their classes at no charge. Marie-Anne de Kervénozael, the aristocratic prioress, was a woman of principle; she refused to admit rich ladies as paying guests, even though her brother the marquis was dipping into his own fortune to save her house from bankruptcy, and in 1740 she roundly condemned those of her nuns who were using disparaging words to their penurious pupils and driving them away. In education, she said, peasants count as much as nobles.[28]

As a rule, however, the nuns who took lifelong vows and accepted the full obligation of the cloistered life were chiefly concerned with educating the daughters of fee-paying families.[29] Free education was given by the many new 'secular' institutes which arose in the seventeenth century, composed of dedicated women who took only 'simple' (temporary) vows, or no vows at all. There were varying degrees of formality in organization. Some women volunteering for teaching became tertiaries, members of the 'Third Order' of one of the existing older congregations—Dominicans, Capuchins, Récollets, Eudistes, and so on. The Carmelites of the diocese of Vannes drew up rules in 1670 for entry to this confraternity of service: to be over 30 years of age, unmarried, and enjoying economic independence—this necessarily limited recruits to reasonably well-off families.[30] There was no question of withdrawing from worldly affairs, though there was a rule to avoid the riotous celebrations accompanying weddings and baptisms unless the happy event concerned relatives. By the eighteenth century, numerous parishes of the diocese had Carmelite schoolmistresses, and some had a Dominican tertiary.

Most of the schoolmistresses, however, came from the new foundations which proliferated from 1660 onwards. These teaching institutes went by the names of 'Sœurs grises', 'Dames régentes', 'Filles de la Charité', 'Béates', or other names derived from those of their founders, or under the invocation of the names of Jesus, Our Lady, and various saints, and associated by designation with the particular towns in which they had originated.[31] The process continued in the eighteenth century. The Sœurs d'Ernemont[32] and the Sœurs de Saint-Paul of Chartres at the end of the seventeenth century were followed by the Filles de Saint-Paul at Tréguier (started in 1699, statutes drawn up in 1727),[33] the Congrégation de la Sagesse of Saint-Laurent-sur-Sèvre (1703), the Filles du Saint-Esprit of Plérin (1706), the Congrégation de la Providence of Evreux (1714), the Sœurs du Bon Sauveur of Caen (combining, not entirely incongruously, teaching children and prison visiting), the Institut des Sœurs de l'École of Toul (1720), the Sœurs de la Doctrine Chrétienne of Nancy, called the 'Vatelottes' after Canon Vatelot, their founder (1752). After the mid-century, innovation slackened, but in 1762 Jean-Martin Moye, a retired missionary from China, founded the Filles de la Providence in Lorraine, an inspirational group with little formal structure, to teach in rural parishes.[34] About the same time, the bishop of Langres, disappointed by the sloth of his three houses of Ursulines, decided to attach lay women, taking only annual vows, to one of them. The experiment succeeded, and by 1789 the educational work of all three houses was run by the sisters with informal vows.[35]

In contrast to what was happening in Orders where the nuns took solemn perpetual vows, recruitment to these congregations of temporary allegiance flourished in the eighteenth century. The Sœurs de Saint-Paul, founded in 1694 by a curé, and moving into Chartres to run a school and hospital in 1708, had fifteen houses by 1727 and fifty in 1780.[36] The best years for the Sœurs d'Ernemont were after 1750; for the Filles de la Providence of Rouen, 1730–9 and after 1760. The great expansion of the Filles de la Sagesse of Saint-Laurent-sur-Sèvre came after 1730, and, indeed, was still going on throughout the Revolution, in spite of the horrors of the Vendean civil war in the countryside which they served. In 1760, recruitment to such congregations constituted 11 per cent of women entering religious life in France: in 1789 it was 21 per cent.[37]

The proliferation of these new organizations to educate the children of the poor (and sometimes to nurse the sick as well) was possible because of a surge of vocations, a fruit of the inspiration of the piety of the Church of the Counter-Reformation and of a transformation of social relationships with the advance of civilization. Women of the aristocracy, once married, enjoyed great freedom; those of bourgeois families helped their husbands in shop and counting-house, and ran the business if their partner died. But women of lower social classes had few opportunities for working independently with recognized status. With the new foundations came their breakthrough. The initial impetus for recruitment and organization came, often, from zealous parish priests seconded by pious aristocratic ladies. In this way, the Congrégation de la Providence of Evreux began about 1700.[38] Curé Duvivier of the village of Caër set up a school with his sister Justine as the teacher; then came a legacy from a great lady of a family of the robe, another from an abbé, another from the curé of Thevray. Bishops, aware of the importance of a religious education for the mothers of the future, gave support, especially in Protestant areas. 'The education of girls', said the bishop of Dax about the crypto-Calvinist population of Orthez, 'is the only method we have of bringing the people to the true faith.'[39] Some prelates, weary of the multiplication of formal nunneries, wanted teachers with a minimum of institutional fuss and amenable to the direction of the parish priests; as the bishop of Cahors said in 1673, 'pious girls and widows' could do useful work and 'banish for ever from those who run such Christian schools all desire to form their own religious institutions and convents, as has sometimes happened'.[40]

Though formality and regulation were kept to a minimum, the drive of some formidable lady (generally of aristocratic family) at the centre often ensured continuity. Similarly, the setting up of a central 'seminary' to train the teachers (a device often used) would ensure high standards and a corresponding welcome in the parishes. Both factors were evident in the successful expansion of the Dames de Saint-Maur.[41] They began in the seventeenth century as the Filles maîtresses des écoles charitables du Saint-Enfant-Jésus, and in 1678 set up their seminary in Paris in the rue Saint-Maur. When Louis XIV revoked the edict of Nantes, there was a demand in the southern dioceses for teachers for the 'converted' Protestant girls, and twenty-seven new foundations were made there from 1681 to 1689. In 1719, the Rouen community became separate, under the title of the Sœurs de la Providence, while the main branch centred at Paris called itself the Dames de Saint-Maur. From 1719 to 1761 Catherine de Bossedon, of the high nobility of Auvergne, was superior, presiding over further expansion and outwitting the bureaucracy which denied her institute letters patent by passing on the property by private testament to individuals. At the Revolution, there were fifty-six schools with 500–600 sisters teaching in them.

The standard combination of founders—a curé and an aristocratic lady—was matched by another: the charismatic Christian propagandist and the lady who was his spiritual friend, like François de Sales and Jeanne de Chantal, Vincent de Paul and Louise de Marillac. The Filles de la Sagesse owed their origin to such an alliance. The organization of mission preachers set up by Louis-Marie Grignon de Montfort would never have been accompanied by an institute of women teachers and nurses but for the quiet persistence of Marie-Louise Trichet (Sœur Marie-Louise de Jésus), who carried on after her mentor's disorganized ventures at Poitiers and La Rochelle had foundered, and after his death in 1716 lived on for forty more years perfecting the work of his dreams.[42]

Numerous schools were run as a sideline by congregations whose primary duty was to nurse the sick. The Filles de la Charité of Vincent de Paul ran classes in annexes to municipal hospitals. In Paris, in twenty-five parishes they had houses as bases for sisters fulfilling the dual role of nurses and teachers. In Lorraine, the Congrégation de Saint-Charles had forty-six establishments of this kind. In the countryside, the resident sister of a teaching institute was expected to be a social worker in every sense of the word. A curé, rejoicing in the decision of the Filles de Notre-Dame to set up a school in his parish, listed the benefits he expected from the arrival of the sisters: they would 'help the poor, learn how to do (surgical) bleeding, study medicines and know how to make them, instruct poor children free of charge, teaching them not only to read and write but also the principles of religion, as well as how to work at a trade appropriate to their station in life, so they can subsequently earn their living'.[43] Since many of the men of the province spend half the year away from home as migratory labourers, he added, the education of girls was doubly important, as in the end, it was the mothers acting alone who brought up the children.

If the fulminations of bishops against mixed education had been effective, the sisters would have taught only girls, but in practice, only fanatical curés insisted on the rules. In his synodal charge of 1747, the bishop of Lectoure said his parish priests had assured him of the impossibility of realistically organizing the segregation of the sexes, so he could only hope that they would at least ensure 'that the boys do not place themselves promiscuously among the girls'.[44] For most children, attendance at school was of brief duration. According to the educational theorists of the day, children of the poor should not begin until the age of 7 or 8, and by then they were almost ready for apprenticeship or work in the fields. The Parisian parish of Saint-Étienne-du-Mont[45] was unusual in its regulation specifying two years, but this was only for those who showed signs of progress, otherwise six months was the limit; and the full curriculum was ambitious, including the reading of Latin as well as French. The emphasis of the schools was on 'moral' development, with many religious observances—the sign of the cross, prayers, catechism, attendance at mass, and learning to serve at the altar. Discipline and routine were the keynotes, not the cultivation of the imagination; as the abbé de Saint-Pierre defined education, it was 'to bring about the happiness of mankind by the inculcation of indispensable habits'. The regulations of schools and handbooks like Crousez's *Traité de l'éducation des enfants* (1722) show how reading was taught: it was a matter of being able to recite passages and learn them by heart. The content would be explained to the children to retain their interest, but teasing out the meaning for themselves was secondary; first, they would learn the passage, then they would go on to the recognition of individual letters, then individual words, then put the words together. Later in the century reformers tried to humanize the system, proposing to begin by teaching a vocabulary of 300 words, then proceeding to reading as essentially understanding; there were also experiments with manual aides to memory, like arranging alphabetical cards or setting type on toy printing presses.[46] Such luxuries were not for ordinary pupils. The typical school was stuck in the rut of a primitive methodology. This was inevitable, for classes were huge, sometimes a hundred strong. The sister from the religious institute would preside, making forays for testing, while a dozen or so *récitateurs*, chosen from the most forward pupils, would teach small groups. The air would be full of the drone of these different units monotonously chanting their lines.

In many places, especially in the towns, the sisters would economize on reading and writing time to teach girls a trade—spinning, or weaving. In Paris, the Filles de Sainte-Geneviève did something of everything—taught in schools, nursed the sick, conducted devotional meetings for women, and ran a *chambre de travail* to train girls for their first job. The Filles de la Providence of the capital taught orphans to make tapestries and ornate embroideries, including some commissioned by the palace of Versailles.[47] In Lyon, the ladies of a lay association, the Tiers Ordre féminin de la Trinité, had as their aim 'to teach manufacturing work to girls who have no dowry to get themselves a husband or to gain entry to a nunnery, so enabling them to subsist and keep them from the dire necessity which might bring their innocence to shipwreck'.[48]

On Sundays, the sisters would be called to the parish church to take catechism classes. The regulations of the Dames de Saint-Maur prescribed question-and-answer sessions to encourage children to 'generous emulation', with their parents invited to attend to add solemnity to the rivalry. As for the sisters themselves, they were 'forbidden to give themselves airs as preachers'.[49] Another, more interesting duty was incumbent on the Sœurs d'écoles of Châlons-sur-Marne; they were to go in their formal grey dresses to the *veillées*, the evening social gatherings of women, where sewing and knitting were accompanied by gossip and folk-tales—if possible, they were to introduce catechism competitions and the singing of pious canticles.[50] As ever under the *ancien régime*, a place had to be found for social misfits in religious institutions, however incongruously. In Angers, the house of La Providence at one time was charging a fee of 200 livres to one family for teaching their daughter sewing, to another for looking after a mad girl and to another for looking after a kleptomaniac. Or, at the other end of the scale, an institute might be required by the government to move into more sophisticated teaching and set up a boarding-school. In 1775, the king transferred the revenues of a suppressed house of Cordeliers to the Dames de Saint-Maur, to enable them to set up an academy for daughters of impoverished nobles' families around Toulouse—it ended up with eighteen sisters and twenty servants looking after a hundred girls—even so, there was a free class for the daughters of ordinary people.[51]

Some of the educational institutes remained small. The Migamionnes, founded in the Parisian parish of Saint-Nicolas-du-Chardonnet, expanded to no more than four parishes in the nearby countryside. The Sœurs de Sainte-Anne (Saumur), the Sœurs de l'Enfant Jésus (Reims), and the Sœurs de la Croix (Lavaur) had from fifty to a hundred teachers; the Sœurs de la Chapelle-Riboul (Evron) had eighty-nine schools and more schoolmistresses; the Sœurs de la Doctrine Chrétienne (Metz) and the Filles de la Charité (Nevers) had more; and the Filles de la Sagesse in their heyday had 941 schools. In some dioceses, women hastened to take the opportunity of this new kind of religious and social service; in others, where the practices of church life and devotion were lukewarm, vocations were few. It was not easy for enterprising bishops or ambitious superiors of institutes to switch teachers into the barren areas, for local knowledge was important, and in many places familiarity with the patois was indispensable. About 1780, in the diocese of Tarbes only 3 per cent of the parishes had a significant number of girls in their schools; in the dioceses of Albi, Castres, and Lavaur, the figure was 6 per cent; in Arles, 60 per cent. The variations in these figures were chiefly—though not entirely—due to the incidence of vocations to teaching duties.[52]

Girls had the best chance of becoming literate in the towns.[53] In Grenoble, there were five free schools for them, with four convents also taking external pupils; in Paris, there were innumerable elementary schools—the canon-precentor of Notre-Dame had inspection rights in 334 of them, 167 reserved for girls. In some cities— Clermont, Riom, Moulins, Aurillac, Puy, and Lyon—there were more elementary places for girls than for boys. The classes in towns were often large, so the number of women in the various teaching institutes must be multiplied by a large factor to estimate the number of children taught. As the duration of a pupil's school career tended to be brief, there was a rapid turnover—many received some education, albeit superficial. And the sum total of the modest instruction available is not exhausted by a survey of the teaching sisters. Parishes hired lay teachers, men and women (though at starvation rates of pay); curés and vicaires taught children of favoured families, or boys and girls who seemed promising candidates for a religious vocation; elder sisters back from service in urban households and tired old uncles back from the wars passed on the rudiments of literacy they had picked up. The old assumption that the vast majority of girls of the poorer classes received no formal education was an unjustified deduction from the contrast between the numbers of women who could sign their names as compared with men. Writing was not put high on the list of feminine educational priorities; moral and religious instruction, sewing and other handicrafts, and reading of simple pious manuals and folk-tales were the essentials, and in these respects, the sisters of the new institutes served them well.

IV

Schoolgirls were not the only boarders accepted by convents; if the nuns had sufficient accommodation, they might let it out to ladies seeking a retirement home or a refuge.[54] It was a way to make money—perhaps the nuns would build a special annexe for boarders, or adapt the mansion of the abbess if it was spacious. At Rennes, almost all the communities of women were in this business. The Carmelites, whose rule forbade *pensionnaires*, with an income of only 4,000 livres could not afford to obey it, and by 1789 were drawing 10,000 a year from forty paying guests. By taking a rich boarder in the seventeenth century, the Ursulines had added to their enclosure an attractive house; the contract specified that Mme du Chastellier de la Thébaudais who gave it had to have her private parlour, a space in the garden to grow flowers, oranges from the orangery, and the right to name a novice to be accepted without a dowry. The Calvairiennes, who made a similar contract about the same time, found it a disastrous bargain, for the lady had huge debts, and as her heirs, the nuns were liable; in 1780 they were still being sued by creditors.

A lady who took rooms in a convent might be doing so for temporary convenience, as during the months her husband was away with his regiment, or for a period of retreat, perhaps to recover after a bereavement.[55] Or it might be for a space of meditation before a major event in her life—girls sometimes went in for a few weeks before their First Communion.[56] A long lease on an apartment might be part of a plan to economize, as with the widowed duchesse de Choiseul trying to pay off her husband's debts, or the marquise de Créqui saving up for her children.[57] A permanent lease was a standard resort of ladies wanting a refuge in old age or, at the end of a stormy life, seeking a period of detachment to prepare for death.[58] Taking residence in a particular convent might be a device to achieve social cachet, hence the applications to get into the Parisian house of l'Assomption when Mlle Alexandrine, Mme de Pompadour's daughter, went there.[59] A lady pursued by malicious gossip might become a monastic boarder to pre-empt a veneer of respectability, like the princesse de Talmont going to the nuns of Saint-Joseph in the rue Saint-Dominique while she carried on a prestigious liaison.[60] A maltreated wife awaiting the parlement's decree of separation was supposed to keep a low profile while proceedings lasted; the Filles de l'Union Chrétienne, rue Saint-Denis, specialized in exercising discretion in these cases.[61] More dramatically, the mistress of some great nobleman might retire to break off the affair, as Mlle Ménard in flight from the duc de Chaulnes. M. de Sartine, the lieutenant of police, got the abbé Duguet to negotiate a place for her and her daughter in the Cordelières of the rue l'Oursine. He did this by pretending she was a relative; she left after a fortnight, and the good abbé looked ridiculous.[62] The mother of M. Prévot called on Mlle Basse, a dancer at the Opéra, and pleaded with her to abdicate her hold over her son so that he could make an advantageous marriage: the girl generously retired to a convent to leave her lover free.[63]

There was a strange underworld of relationships in the life of boarding-houses. The paying guests could fall out with the nuns or with each other, perhaps dragging the nuns into their quarrels. Such bitterness arose in a community at Fécamp in 1738 that the house was banned from taking more *pensionnaires*, and one of them, Mme Diggs, an Englishwoman, was expelled.[64] There were special difficulties when the paying guests were there reluctantly, banished from the world by a royal *lettre de cachet*. The king rarely paid the fees, the family asking for the reclusion order being responsible. The four houses at Paris usually used by the authorities for this purpose occasionally refused to accept 'des personnes trop décriées', insisting on a direct order from the archbishop before they would comply.[65] There were mysteries. Who was 'Milady' in the Benedictine abbey at Pontoise (a house of English nuns of noble lineage). She had been sent there, willingly, by a *lettre de cachet* requested by the great Soubise family, and she wrote unrevealing letters of brooding melancholy.[66] Parents would use the royal authority to discipline an erring daughter, it could be, unjustly—Marie de Massol was released from the Ursulines of Châtillon because the nuns took her part. Catherine de Beauzeville was not so lucky: she was incarcerated in 1747, took unwilling vows six years later, and in 1789 was still trying to get free.[67] There was a standard legal procedure for dealing with an adulterous wife. She was put in a convent for two years wearing secular dress, during which time her husband could recall her. If not, she had to stay for life, observing the rules like a nun, without being one, though if her husband died, she could get out if someone wanted to marry her.[68] The comte de Choiseul-Stainville, who had married a girl twenty-five years his junior, put up with her gallantries until she began an affair with an actor who had been a *garçon perruquier*. As she was setting off to a fancy-dress ball, she was bundled into a carriage and sent to the Filles de Sainte-Marie at Nancy, never to emerge, her fortune sequestrated for her two daughters.[69] Protestant husbands envied Catholics this grim resource for establishing domestic peace: in 1789 the consistories of Alsace asked for the restoration of their old right to pronounce divorces, 'since they have not the convents available for the confinement of women who are adulterous or lacking in circumspection'.[70] Lacking in circumspection—clearly there could be reasons other than adultery, for example, spendthrift folly. Indeed, there was a presumption that a woman separated from her husband ought to withdraw from society. On this ground, Louis XVI ordered the princesse de Monaco into a religious house: 'quand une femme ne vit pas avec son mari, elle ne doit pas vivre dans le monde'.[71] In the lawless days of the Regency, a retreat into seclusion might be in the woman's best interests. There was a guard of fifty soldiers at the monastery of Port-Royal in Paris in 1723 when the princesse de Conti was boarding there, lest the prince should try to kidnap her. He was wanting to force her to sign a deed of separation by which she would live in a convent for four years (moving to a different house if there was a fire or an outbreak of smallpox), but with the obligation to come back home if the couple's two sons died, staying for long enough to provide another heir.[72] These sorts of social arrangements provided novelists with convenient tragic denouements. 'Mme d'Archenes is still in a convent, where she was sent for having incurred the resentment of a man in high office and for having brought disgrace upon her husband.'[73] Mme de Tourval, betrayed, dies in the same religious house and in the very room where she had slept as a schoolgirl.[74] Real life could be stranger than fiction, as the adventures of the Mirabeau family showed. The marquis, the so-called 'Ami des Hommes', with a wife, daughter, and son incarcerated at the same time, broke a record: 'vous avez donc entrepris de peupler les couvents?' And Sophie de Malroy, marquise de Monnier, thrown into a nunnery by her injured husband, found consolation with the son (the revolutionary Mirabeau), who settled in her room, disguised sometimes as a nun and sometimes as a gardener. When the death of the Président de Monnier released her, she chose to live in a house at the monastery gates, conducting a liaison with the lieutenant of the local police, and finally committing suicide after sending a farewell letter to her old lover as he sat in the National Assembly, where the debates were in progress which would leave no convents available to house unwilling guests, and end the royal power to send them.[75]

V

The institutions caring for the sick, the infirm, the poor, the homeless, and orphans in eighteenth-century France were the comparatively recent creation of the zeal of Counter-Reformation piety, seconded by the power of the royal government. They were mainly in the towns, for throughout the seventeenth and most of the eighteenth century, the bias of State organization was towards centralization, and the endowments of so many of the rural charitable foundations of the Middle Ages were confiscated for the big urban establishments. Yet some of the local 'hospitals' in villages and tiny market towns survived: in 1789, of the 2,189 organizations listed under this name in an official enquiry, a quarter had fewer than ten beds. Some were well run. At Avallon (population 4,311) three *économes* with only informal vows of religion were in charge of a ward with twenty-four beds; the old endowments yielding 5,000 livres a year were ample. The governing committee was proud of its nursing sisters, and in 1781 provided them with uniforms: brown and dark blue, with round hats, a black silk neckerchief and a pectoral cross.[76] At Saint-Cales in the province of Maine, four sisters, not belonging to any Order, were on renewable three-year contracts under a governing body of the mayor, the curé, the prior of the nearby monastery, and two elected notables.[77] But places removed from the critical scrutiny of a wider public tended to inefficiency. The 2,000 inhabitants of Trets had 'ignorant artisans' as the recteurs of their hospital, and these officials misappropriated the funds or lent them to each other free of interest.[78] The traveller Richeprey found the hospital of Marcilhac a veritable 'stable', and the sight of the three straw palliasses made him feel ill.[79] In mitigation of such horror stories, it should be said that the beds of country hospitals were not normally occupied by sick persons, for the nurses preferred to treat their patients at home.[80] The institution would shelter pilgrims, indigent travellers, and homeless folk. A dictionary of 1680 defined 'hospital' as 'a place to which the poor who do not have means to live retire, and where a particular care is taken of their souls'.[81] The care of souls was important: the chapel attached to the filthy room at Marcilhac was in good order and well decorated.

By 1700, every sizeable town in France had two major charitable institutions: the *hôtel-Dieu* and the *hôpital général*. The first was a hospital in our sense, with wards where the sick were under medical care; the second was a multi-purpose building—almshouse, workhouse, orphanage, staging-point for poor travellers, prison for incorrigible vagabonds. Very often, the *hôtel-Dieu* was the successor to a medieval foundation, while the *hôpital général* was a recent creation. Just after the mid-seventeenth century, the puritanical group of upper-class zealots, the Compagnie du Saint-Sacrement, had set up a prototype in Paris, and in 1662 a royal decree ordered every town to follow suit. This order was reinforced by the preaching of Jesuits sent round as government emissaries: they would conduct a three-day mission, then urge the municipality to set up an 'hôpital à la capucine', that is, without endowments, in the hope that benefactors would be forthcoming.[82] There was a divergence between the aims of the king and the hopes of his preachers. The latter were concerned for the welfare of the poor: the object of the royal decree was to round up beggars and 'instruct them in the ways of piety', thereby preventing crime and providing recruits for the army, the navy, and the colonies.

The structure of charitable organization in the towns, being dependent on the vagaries of individual generosity, was inevitably a patchwork, yet there was a common pattern. At Aix-en-Provence, a metropolis of Church and Law, the old foundations of Saint-Lazare for lepers and Saint-Eutrope for the dropsical were gone, and by the end of the sixteenth century the scene was dominated by the *hôtel-Dieu* (1519) and La Miséricorde (1591), an association of great ladies distributing alms to the 'pauvres honteux'—respectable folk who had fallen on hard times. Later on came the *hôpital général*, called La Charité, the Petit Bethléem for orphans, La Pureté to help poor girls preserve their virginity, and committees concerned with prison visiting and legal aid.[83] At Montpellier, with 30,000 inhabitants, about the same size as Aix, though with a manufacturing suburb alongside the splendid façades marking the headquarters of an intendancy and a bishopric, the main institutions were the same.[84] In the mid-century, the *hôtel-Dieu* had 200 patients, and the *hôpital général* over 700 inmates, as well as a clientele dependent on its food distributions outside the gates. La Miséricorde, an exclusive club recruited by co-option from the wives of the intendant, military governor, magistrates of the *cour des aides*, and others who were very rich, directed activities which elsewhere might have been independent—a manufactory to put the poor to work, the Bon Pasteur for prostitutes, schools, prison visiting, the provision of dowries for poor girls, and medical attention at home. Outside this nexus, there was an institution found in only a few cities—a military hospital for venereal disease. In Paris, as befitted its size, the standard institutions were bigger than elsewhere.[85] The *hôpital général* was a complex of ten buildings, including the grim Salpêtrière for erring or lunatic women, the Bicêtre for madmen, and the vast sad Enfants Trouvés for abandoned children. In place of a Miséricorde, there was the Grand Bureau des Pauvres, attended by magistrates of the *parlement* and high officials; individual parishes had their charitable committees linked to it. There were many smaller foundations, like the Hospice des Quinze-Vingts, a refuge for 300 blind 'brothers', who were a familiar sight outside churches, with their copper fleur-de-lis badges and collecting boxes, four houses of the Frères Hôpitaliers de Saint-Jean-de-Dieu, and the various parish charities, like the old folks' home founded in the mid-eighteenth century by curé Cochin of Saint-Jacques-du-Haut-Pas out of his private fortune.

The jurists did not regard the hospitals as ecclesiastical institutions, but as secular foundations in the position of minors under the tutelage of the government.[86] In 1505 the parlement of Paris ousted the canons of Notre-Dame from control of the *hôtel-Dieu* and substituted lay administrators. In 1579 a royal ordinance excluded ecclesiastics and nobles from hospital boards. Something of a change was made in 1698, for Louis XIV then decreed a mixed régime for any new foundations, the mayor, an alderman, the chief judicial officer of the place, and elected representatives of the inhabitants were to be joined by a single parish priest and have the bishop as president— honour to the clergy, but lay control. The letters patent setting up a hospital at Versailles in 1720 embodied the same principle in a rather different formula. The archbishop of Paris and the curé were to be in charge of the spiritual, while all temporal affairs would be run by the military governor, the *bailli*, the *procureur du roi*, and three elected inhabitants.[87] This pressure towards uniformity and lay control did not prevail everywhere. In remote areas hospitals would be run as they had always been, even by the local feudal seigneur. The *hôtel-Dieu* in Chartres remained under the control of the cathedral chapter. At Lisle-Noé the chapter of Auch had built a hospital and continued to own it—though it had the buildings knocked down in 1727, and the local community, after fifty years of litigation, compelled the canons to rebuild it. At Orléans, the three canons and six laymen on the board of the *hôtel-Dieu* were locked in disputes over precedence.[88] But the usual pattern in the bigger towns conformed to royal ordinances: control by a lay body with the bishop presiding. There might be another ecclesiastic or two among the administrators (for example, a representative of the cathedral chapter as one of the great local corporations), but this could not alter the lay dominance. For the most part, the *cahiers* of 1789 are not concerned with questions of hospital management (though the Tiers of Paris made the anticlerical point strongly), but many of them proposed the diversion of monastic wealth for their maintenance.[89] The general eighteenth-century view of the hospitals was that they were lay institutions, but the Church had the duty, whether by direct contribution or by exhorting the faithful to generosity, to raise money for them.

Most charitable institutions had wholly inadequate endowments. A town faced desperate problems in maintaining its *hôpital général*—being new, it had continually to be sustained by new funds. The work done by inmates was a limited resource, generally inefficiently done, and if efficiently, arousing the wrath of the local workers who resented the competition. Orphans sent out to work in the fields by some rural institutions were welcome to local farmers, but if they succeeded by dint of deft fingers and long hours at weaving silk or knitting woollen stockings, the local guildsmen would organize opposition.[90] Municipal contributions were grudging, though a small percentage might be given from the *octroi* on foodstuffs entering the city gates, or a levy on theatre tickets, or the profits of selling meat in Lent (to those who had medical certificates). Charitable gifts and legacies were a major resource, though variable and tending to decline.[91] At Aix-en-Provence, from 1710 to 1770, the annual collection fell from 4,000 to 1,000 livres, and from bequests in 80 per cent of the wills, the figure fell to 30 per cent. In Montpellier, half the wills in 1740–1 gave legacies to the *hôpital général*, and in 1782–6 only a quarter. People were switching their gifts to the Miséricorde.[92] La Charité at Lyon had a system of enforced generosity by appealing to pride in a way approaching blackmail. On co-option as a recteur, a gift of 4,000 livres was due and an interest-free loan of 10,000, while the *trésorier*, the most prestigious figure of all, was expected to lend vast sums—which were never repaid. From 1776 to 1784, three held office and lost sums ranging from half a million to well over two million.[93] For a while, it was impossible to find a successor, and the citizen who eventually took over was bankrupted. In most places, the diocesan bishop was generous, though the well-intentioned craft of the recteurs at Lyon failed to penetrate the thick skin of their archbishop (Tencin, of Council of Embrun notoriety). They commissioned a marble bust from Coustou to be his memorial, but when he died, everything was left to his married sister. The bust was thrown on a rubbish heap, and rescued from a shop sometime later with the nose missing.

Everywhere, debts accumulated. In 1760 the *hôtel-Dieu* of Marseille[94] owed 3,500,000 livres, and the like institution at

Toulouse faced a bill for 700,000 livres interest, with only 196,000 available. Similar crises of debt occurred in Aix and many other places. Three years later the *hôtel-Dieu* of Autun was closed altogether, and its nuns pensioned off.[95] The creditors were mostly middling and little people who had invested their savings in return for a retirement income. The law courts intervened to compel municipalities to subsidize their collapsing institutions, but the activities of hospitals had to be curtailed, and the creditors suffered savage cuts in their annuities. Government policy and public opinion switched course. There was an end to annexing small charitable endowments to the big urban institutions; indeed, some such confiscations were reversed. Free food distributions were wound up. Private generosity turned to supporting the *miséricordes* and *bureaux de charité* dispensing help at home to the poor who could be identified as deserving.[96] The Enlightenment saw a switch from 'charité' to 'bienfaisance', a change in ideological approach, no doubt, but triggered by the spectacular and tragic bankruptcies of the 1760s.

VI

The 'hospitals' of every kind were run by women dedicated to the religious life. Some had vocations without formal engagements, as at La Charité at Lyon where the staff were recruited from the widows and orphans who came there for refuge. Others took permanent vows to care for the sick without belonging to any religious Order, as at Saint-Cales; here, the four ladies were engaged on short-term contracts, yet their families none the less had to provide them with dowries (including furniture, uniforms, and table silver) as if they were ordinary nuns.[97] There were numerous religious Orders to care for the sick, mostly founded in the seventeenth century—the Filles de la Charité de Saint-Vincent de Paul, the Sœurs de l'Annonciation, the Sœurs grises du Tiers Ordre de Saint-François, and sisterhoods under the invocation of Saint-Louis, Saint-Thomas de Villeneuve, Saint-Charles de Nancy, Saint-Maurice de Chartres, Sainte-Marthe, and Saint-Joseph. Small local initiatives could still arise in the eighteenth century, like Jeanne Delanoue's Servantes des Pauvres de la Providence de Saumur.[98] All had their peculiar ethos deriving from the rule of their founder. Some had educational work or the administering of outdoor charity as well as nursing on their charter. Some took temporary vows, some permanent, and the daily

ies of work and prayer varied. The sisters of Saint-Joseph took including vows, and by their constitution of 1686 fulfilled a complete round of liturgical offices; they made three visits a day to the wards, but the actual care of the sick was in the hands of the 'sœurs domestiques' (who had no voice in chapter) and the paid servants under them. By contrast, the sisters of Sainte-Marthe took only temporary vows, and looked after the sick themselves; there was a dispute in 1695 when an attempt was made to push them up to gentility, with daily devotions to take them out of constant attendance in the wards, and their families required to pay dowries of 1,500 livres for entrance to profession.[99]

The biggest nursing order of all was the Filles de la Charité de Saint-Vincent de Paul, the Order which broke through the practice of keeping nuns cloistered from the world. They took 'simple vows', voluntarily renewed annually, lived in 'houses', not 'convents', and were ruled not by 'superiors', but by 'sœurs servantes'. Their time was not spent in liturgical observances or in exercises of mortification; they offered silent individual prayer twice a day, otherwise they worked to respond to the cry of the poor, 'leaving God for God'. There was no question of their finding a niche near home and family, like so many nuns; for after central training in Paris, they were not allowed to serve in their own region. Thus Sœur Marguerite who in 1779 became head of the new hospital built by the bishop of Dax had qualified at the Paris noviciate twenty years earlier, followed by eight different postings, triangulating France from Pau to Autun to Brest; when stationed at Fontainebleau, she had become famous when chosen by Marie Antoinette to nurse Mlle de Fleury through the smallpox.[100] The Filles de la Charité had an exacting and in some ways lonely existence, but within their community they were well looked after. The food was good, the dress allowance reasonable, and in old age and infirmity they were made comfortable. Recruitment was from the lower-class majority, but from the élite within it. Voltaire,[101] who praised them unstintingly, thought, probably mistakenly, that many girls from distinguished families joined; a visitor to the *hôtel-Dieu* of Besançon described the sisters as 'well born (*bien nées*) and well educated'.[102] This was the impression they gave. But whatever their background, there was no doubt about their sterling character. 'A sister of charity', writes Colin Jones, their historian, 'was patient, saintly, laborious, discreet, committed—and tough.'[103]

By 1700, these dedicated women had taken control of 200 institutions, and expansion was continuing. 'One of the greatest predicaments in administering this community', said its governing sister in Paris in 1769, 'is to know how it can manage not to agree to the most energetic solicitations that are made nearly every day for new establishments.'[104] By preference, the Filles de la Charité would take over the *hôtel-Dieu* in a town, though sometimes they were constrained to accept the direction of the *hôpital général*, in which case they might stipulate that care of infants, the aged, and vagabonds would not be their responsibility, except in cases of illness—a limitation which in practice could rarely be enforced. The keynote of their organization was strong and simple central control, allied to informality and individual initiative below. Headquarters in Paris drew up a detailed contract with the municipality when a hospital was taken over. On the one hand, the sisters would accept obligations to keep a register of admissions, make an annual audit on St John's Eve, account for the drugs, perhaps look after the bakery, laundry, and livestock or even, in an *hôpital général*, supervise the work of the orphans. On the other hand, their individual dress allowances (about 80 livres in the 1780s) were guaranteed; they were assured of absolute control over the servants and of freedom from responsibility for lodging the chaplains or doing their laundry; and they would have the right of deciding who could be admitted as a patient—the doctors would check for venereal disease, but not rule on eligibility. Posting orders also came from Paris, each sister being moved every five years or so, and the *sœurs servantes* every eight or ten. The superior of the Congrégation de la Mission, the male foundation of Saint-Vincent de Paul, appointed confessors and nominated visitors; if occasion demanded, he would use his influence at Versailles to defend the sisters against local attempts to whittle down their rights. In a society where sinecures, inefficiency, and privilege were rampant, and hampered every government proposal to help the poor, the Filles de la Charité showed how selfless devotion and clear-headed organization could make a difference.

Conditions in an *hôtel-Dieu* were grim. Budgets were tight in comparison with ever growing needs. Everyone knew that patients ought to be one to a bed: in practice, it had to be two or three, with mattresses on the floor and in the corridors as well. Given the overcrowding, surgical operations, terrifying affairs in this age before anaesthetics, might take place in view, or at least within earshot, of the next batch of victims. Infections were general, and every scratch tended to become gangrenous. The mortality rate was high. In the *hôtel-Dieu* of Paris, one in every four entering left on the mortuary cart. But it is a myth that hospitals everywhere were death-traps.[105]

At Montpellier in the 1780s, deaths were at the rate of one in ten; it had been double a century earlier, so things were improving. Statistics need interpretation, however. From 1740 to 1785, the overall mortality figure for Nîmes was 11.7 per cent; however, this total is 'improved' by the fact that roughly a quarter of the admissions were soldiers, whose mortality rate was only 2–5 per cent, and that others swelling the total number of patients were vagabonds from outside the city, mostly younger people taking refuge, not because they were ill, but because they were starving. The various groups of nursing sisters had a common policy in refusing to accept anyone suffering from venereal disease, on moral grounds as well as because of the danger of infection, and anyone suffering from smallpox, because it was a killer impossible to contain. Some also rejected pregnant women. This was not so at Paris—here, in the year 1757, the maternity ward was responsible for 1,508 deliveries.[106] While in theory, through their contracts and their protests, the sisters would try to keep an *hôtel-Dieu* a hospital of the modern kind for the treatment of the sick exclusively, in practice they might have to put up with intruders. At Nîmes, beggars took refuge; at Montpellier, from 1770 to 1786 the *hôtel-Dieu* had to accept them by order of the intendant, who by government policy had to intern vagabonds somewhere; in crises of famine, a tide of starving humanity surged into every place where there was hope of support. In the grim winter of 1789, 30,000 of them swamped the resources of the *hôtel-Dieu* of Paris, camping in the courtyards, hopeless in their misery.[107]

Lunatics, who were not so much treated for illness as chained up or locked behind grilles or in cells, were not a suitable clientele; but where else could they be accommodated? At Paris, within the general orbit of the *hôtel-Dieu*, there were specific institutions for them. In the Salpêtrière, madwomen were chained or confined in airless, low-ceilinged rooms, five to a bed; at the Bicêtre, soldiers handed out food to the madmen at the point of the bayonet. In provincial towns, there was sometimes an establishment also called a *bicêtre*, a multi-purpose sink for the misfits who would cause disruption in hospitals proper. Alongside the *hôtel-Dieu* at Alençon there was one of them, described by a visitor as accommodating 'madmen, dangerous characters, abandoned children, criminals whose crimes cannot be documented by enough evidence for a trial, but about whom there is a moral certainty, and debauchees'.[108] Failing a *bicêtre*, however, lunatics would have to be confined in one of the existing hospital-type institutions. A man ran berserk at Montpellier in 1713, killing his wife and setting fire to their house. This led to an agreement to build twelve cells for madmen in the *hôtel-Dieu*, financed partly by the institution itself, partly by the bishop, and partly by the municipality and its police bureau.[109] Three years later a tenth sister was appointed to the staff to look after the new department and take charge of the wine-cellar, a joint task in which one duty may have provided some compensation for having to do the other. By 1789, the number of cells had risen to twenty-five, six belonging to the diocese (which had the right to nominate candidates for confinement) and six to the municipality and the police.

It was scarcely possible for sisters, however dedicated, to do all the chores of a hospital, though in small country places they might have to do so. At Montpellier in 1779, the *sœur servante* exercised general supervision, kept the registers, inventoried and stored the personal possessions of the patients, and ran some profit-making ventures, including selling the effects of the deceased and the bran extracted from the flour. Two sisters ran the pharmacy, three the kitchen, one the bakery, two the laundry, one the wine-cellar and the madhouse, and each of the remaining six was in charge of a ward. The wards and the other departments all had their lay auxiliaries—men as gaolers for the lunatics and doing the heavy portering, women as cleaners and assistant nurses. The *hôtel-Dieu* at Paris, run by the Sœurs Augustines, was a masterpiece of large-scale organization. As it existed before the great fire of 1772, there were seven lay doctors and one master surgeon, with thirteen other surgeons also coming in occasionally without pay. The department for bulk buying of corn, wood, and other commodities, the bakery, the kitchen (with ten cooks), and the *sommellerie* for buying and storing wine were all in lay hands. The 140 sisters had under them *emballeurs* (sweepers and porters), *garçons*, and women *servantes*. The mother superior herself and her deputy, with three other sisters, supervised the storehouse where the linen and dresses of the sisters were kept, and where jams, delicacies, and soap for the use of the patients were made. The entrance lodge with two sisters (assisted by two janitors) checked comings and goings and visitors to the sick. The laundry was a huge affair. In the Grande Lavanderie four sisters supervised thirty-six lay helpers. Eight thousand sheets had to be taken to the river, then back to be boiled in coppers, then to the river again, then up to the roof for drying, a continually repeated operation taking five days. Work in the Petite Lavanderie—the most revolting jobs in the hospital, for here the contaminated bandages were washed—was done by eight women and twelve boys directed by two sisters. Another department with three sisters and their helpers mended and stored the shirts of the patients, and went round weekly to change them; they also supervised the annual refilling of the mattresses, which took three months. The most agreeable post to hold was that of one of the two specialists in the pharmacy. The twenty-one wards were grouped into ten *offices*, each in charge of a sister called the *cheftaine*, elected for a three-year period to be in charge of the ward sisters and their teams of auxiliaries. At night, a force of fifteen sisters came in to relieve them all as *veilleresses*. These night nurses had keys for the side door leading to the Petit Pont, and through it sent out the bodies of the sick who had died that day; *emballeurs* pulled them on a cart, and, preceded by a priest in surplice with a server with bell and lantern, they went out into the night.

The *hôpital général* was a portmanteau institution combining in one a workhouse, reformatory, prison, old people's home, crèche, orphanage, hospice for travellers, and a bureau for outdoor relief. It might also include cells for lunatics and a surgery ward. From the mid-seventeenth century, government policy concerning vagabonds and beggars was 'enfermement', shutting up. It was a police measure to stop the tides of misery from surging dangerously around the towns, allied to the mercantilist rule of having no idlers in the commonwealth, and the drive of the Compagnie du Saint-Sacrement to regiment the poor into the observances of religion. In 1718, there was an overall plan to stage rootless and shiftless people in the *hôpitaux généraux* until they could be transported overseas to the Mississippi—but the colonists would not have them.[110] In 1724, a royal declaration ordered the incarceration of the unemployed, defined as those who had been given a fortnight to find work and had failed to do so. This was absurd—there was simply nowhere to put them all. In 1767, the government tried a new policy, setting up new institutions, *dépôts de mendicité*; later on, it was charity work-shops, *ateliers de charité*.[111] These workshops were flooded with applicants within a few months of opening. Any charitable refuge in eighteenth-century France, once established, was sure to be used by everyone in authority to clear the streets of nuisances, criminals and lunatics included. This had been the fate of the *hôpitaux généraux*, hopelessly underfunded, chaotic unpredictable places. It is obvious why the Filles de la Charité and the other nursing sisters did not wish to run them, and also why they so often had to do so, since nobody else would.

The range of the *hôpital général* was from the very old to the very young. Not all old people could hope to gain admission. At Lyon, the conditions were: to have lived in the town continuously for ten years, to be 70 years of age or over, and in possession of a certificate of indigence from the curé.[112] Some of the old people were supported by contributions from relatives or from former employers, and depending on the amount paid, conditions might be correspondingly better than were generally available. But it was the very young who took up the most space and presented the greatest problem. The eighteenth century, the age of the evolution of a new, affectionate attitude towards children, was also the age of abandoned infants. A modern estimate for the whole country in the single year 1784 is 50,000. It was an urban phenomenon. In Bordeaux there were 300 waifs left annually in charge of the municipality early in the century, rising to 600 later on.[113] In Paris there were 1,738 in 1700, 3,150 in 1740 (this was a fifth of all births in the capital), and 6,419 in 1776 (this was a third). At Metz in this latter year, a winter of sheer starvation, there were 900, an even greater proportion of total births than in the capital. 'Within a century all children will be without fathers and mothers,' observed a contemporary, extrapolating the figures.[114] Most of the abandoned victims were illegitimate, and probably half their mothers were girls in domestic service, a prey in their loneliness to seducers or to male members of the family exercising the 'droit de cuissage'. In years of economic disaster, however, desperate families would place their legitimate babies in municipal care, often leaving identification tokens in the hope of reclaiming them. If they did so and could afford it, they might be asked to pay a search fee and maintenance.[115] Jean-Jacques Rousseau, the prophet of sympathetic understanding of children, abandoned his five without distinguishing marks—he was ashamed of Thérèse, his ignorant mistress, and did not see how he could go on writing his masterpieces surrounded by squalling brats. In a prize essay of 1780, the abbé de Malvaux observed, darkly, that the provision of refuges for children was an invitation to get rid of them: 'l'hospice des Enfants Trouvés est le tombeau de l'amour maternel'.

Yet refuges there had to be, and in most places it was the all-purpose *hôpital général*. Paris—as also Nîmes[116] and Bordeaux—was exceptional in having a specialist foundling hospital, though it was in alliance with the great *hôtel-Dieu* in its various ramifications. The Enfants Trouvés of Paris, founded by royal edict in 1670, was a vast place. In addition to the 3,000 (rising to 6,000) babies coming in annually from the city itself, another 2,000 or so were carted in from the provinces, from as far afield as Angers. The procedure, here as elsewhere, was to send out the babies as soon as possible to wet-nurses in the countryside. Most of the children died quickly:

only one or two out of ten survived. In a poor state to begin with, probably starving or disease-ridden, they had to face a long trip out to their wet-nurses—the foster mothers in the nearer villages were pre-empted by bourgeois families of the town. Those carried from Angers to Paris had an even more dangerous preliminary ride, in charge of carriers who got the same fee for a dead body as a living one. And there were plenty of sinister mercenary wet-nurses caring only to draw the fee. Contemporaries lamented this tragic mortality, whether from sympathy with suffering or from the mercantilist belief in the importance of an increasing population. Yet the system worked only because death was its accomplice. As a nursing sister of the Enfants Trouvés of Paris told a visiting Genevan doctor: we must be glad the children are going to eternal happiness and not wish for them to live longer, 'because the revenues would not be sufficient to feed them all'.[117]

What happened to the survivors? At the age of 5 or so, they came back to the *hôpital général* (in Paris to the terrible Salpêtrière). Since they might be kept there for anything up to a dozen years, they would crowd the institution: at Montpellier, in mid-century, of the 600–750 inmates, two-thirds were children. These orphans spent their days sewing or spinning and, by all accounts, under a heartless discipline, alleviated only by excursions to parade the streets with billboards or to walk in the funeral processions of the rich, thus earning a fee towards their keep.[118] No wonder the Filles de la Charité were reluctant to have the running of orphanages imposed on them. At the age of 18, or possibly earlier, the young people were sent out to apprenticeship, domestic service, or casual labour (in coastal areas boys could go to sea)—or simply to become beggars and vagrants, thus qualifying to return to the crowded dormitories of the *hôpital-général* in a different capacity.

To complete the heterogeneous incongruity of life in an *hôpital général*, the gatherings of vagabonds, old people, helpless babies, and mobile orphans might be diversified by a special wing or corridor for prostitutes and other fallen women—though most often there was a house of correction for them. Originally, the government rule had been that prostitutes must be committed to the *hôpital général* nearest to the place of their arrest. The judicial regulations were codified in 1684, with a savage additional penalty to protect soldiers from the pox: a prostitute found within two leagues of a military camp would be condemned to nose slitting before imprisonment in the *hôpital général*. The concern of the government was to protect the public, rather than to reform the sinner—this was left to religious inspirations. In 1657, the Sœurs de Notre-Dame de Charité du Refuge were founded—a branch of the congregation of women already set up at Caen by Jean Eudes; its members took an additional fourth vow, to care for fallen women. About the same time came the Madelonnettes in Paris, Rouen, and Bordeaux. Then—the most significant development of all—in 1686, Mme de Combe, a converted Dutch Protestant, established, in Paris, the first house of the Bon Pasteur. She made astonishing demands on the sisters she persuaded to join her—they were to share the work equally with the girls, perform the same penances, and observe the almost perpetual silence of the rest of the inmates. It was an experiment in suffering shared, the just joining the unjust in their humiliation. This inspiration proved too demanding, and it was abandoned in the institutions under the invocation of 'the Good Shepherd' which were subsequently founded in many provincial towns. The initiative in setting up a house of the Bon Pasteur normally came from the wives of the leading citizens—leagued together in the Miséricorde, they would find a suitable building and recruit staff, possibly by calling in an existing religious Order. At Montpellier, they did this and more, for by their contacts and vigilance they identified the ladies of the night and for some years were responsible for more detentions than the *bureau de police* itself.[119] It was not just pharisaical delation; often they paid the fees to maintain a girl in whom they had taken an interest. In other places, the municipality itself took the lead, or an individual acting alone—as Mme Pugin at Rennes, to the wrath of her heirs.[120]

At the same time as refuges to reform prostitutes were being set up, preventive institutions were being founded, houses of safety for girls subjected to temptation. There were two in Lyon, both dating from the mid-seventeenth century, founded by members of the severely devout Compagnie du Saint-Sacrement and their wives. The Filles Pénitentes accepted fallen girls of good family, whether at the request of the parents or the girls themselves; after twelve years of repentance, they could be professed as sisters. La Providence was for the poor, for girls whose virtue was in danger because of sheer starvation. They were taken in until a job, probably as a domestic servant, could be found for them.[121] At Marseille there was another house of La Providence, but the annual fee was 195 livres—as the regulations not surprisingly stated, 'only girls of a status above that of the artisan class are admitted'.[122]

There had always been two aspects to society's view of prostitutes: they were lost sheep to be led back to the fold—the Bon Pasteur idea—and they were criminals to be locked up and disciplined. In

the course of the eighteenth century, the latter concept was winning. At Montpellier, charitable contributions to the Bon Pasteur,
which had once been half the revenues, fell to 3 per cent, while
charitably sponsored detentions fell from a quarter of the total to 2
per cent. Prostitutes came to be classed as criminals, serving a formal
sentence of three to five years, whether they repented or not. Their
first weeks were spent in a punishment cell; thereafter they had to
work gainfully, under strict discipline, though well fed and well
housed. Life was much the same at the Recluses of Lyon under the
Sœurs de Saint-Joseph—here, the prostitutes served a two-year
sentence in prison cells, working at sewing shirts for the army. The
corresponding institution in Paris was the fearsome Salpêtrière, a vast
building formerly a saltpetre factory, and now a place of confinement for women. A visitor in 1787[123] described how a dozen
sisters of Sainte-Catherine (no doubt with numerous auxiliaries)
ruled over 2,400 *filles de joie* clad in shapeless sacks, herded together
for eight hours a day on rows of backless seats, eternally sewing, then
sleeping at night in tightly packed, low-ceilinged dormitories. If dis-
obedient, they were punished by being pushed in with the senile and
insane. In better conditions were kept *pensionnaires* confined at the
expense of their families and prisoners of the Crown (including
Mme de la Motte, notorious for having impersonated the queen in
the diamond necklace affair). There were also the good-time girls
who had incurred the wrath of some powerful protector to whom
they had been disloyal. In kennels behind an iron grille madwomen
were chained, deep in filth. Under the *ancien régime* charity or family
subscriptions had to maintain all the social institutions: only for the
rare individual case did the king's government pay.

In all the charitable institutions, the routines of religion were
enforced. The chaplain was an indispensable member of staff: the
hospital of Saint-André at Bordeaux had three of them, as against
four physicians and two surgeons.[124] The doctors themselves, in
theory at least, were under strict religious obligations. Those who
took their degrees at Paris had to swear to defend the Catholic, apostolic, and Roman religion 'usque ad effusionem sanguinis'.[125] By a
royal declaration of 1712, on the second day of a serious illness, the
doctor had to warn the patient of the duty of confession, and if he
refused, call in the parish priest. Apart from the *hôtel-Dieu* at Paris,
hospitals had a religious test for entry. At the *hôpital général* of
Orléans a *billet* of confession had to be produced within a fortnight,
otherwise the fare was bread and water.[126] The ceremony of admission at Montpellier consisted of an interview by the board of

management, shaving of the head, and confession. At La Charité of Lyon, an entrant began with a month of instruction: duties to God, the obligations of religious practice, the obedience due to the recteurs, reverence due to the memory of benefactors, the necessity to live in peace and work hard. Applicants for outdoor relief had to produce a certificate from their curé that they knew the principal articles of the faith, and ecclesiastics went round with one of the recteurs annually to check that they had not forgotten them.[127] There might be a rule for monthly communion; at Fougères, this could be enforced only by the chaplain calling in the constables (*archers*) to march the poor to the altar, 'most of them being so depraved and idle that he cannot oblige them to do their duty'.[128] The institutional life of orphan children was a monotonous catalogue of work and piety. In the *hôpital général* of Orléans the boys in the dormitory of Saint-Louis and the girls in that of Sainte-Agnès were awoken at 5 or 5.30 a.m. for prayer, mass, and breakfast, then three hours' work with half an hour off for catechism; there was silence at dinner to listen to the 'spiritual reading', then prayers and half an hour's recreation. Then six hours' work with a catechism break, supper at 6.30 p.m., half an hour's recreation, then off to bed preceded by the Angelus, Pater, Ave, prayers for benefactors, the *De Profundis*, and *In Manus tuas Domine*. There was no contact with the world except when getting outside the walls for street sweeping, carrying advertisement boards, or walking in funeral processions (thus getting a fee for the institution).[129] The Comité de Mendicité of the Constituent Assembly of 1790 was to wax angry at the exclusion of non-Catholics, 'as if charitable help should not be given to all, whatever their creed', and ironic about the pious precociousness of children who knew all about funerals and church services and could explain how the way for Christ had been prepared by the patriarchs and prophets.[130] The Revolution abolished the insupportable religious obligations attached to charity; also, in spite of grandiose schemes on paper, it abolished most of the charity as well.

The nursing sisters in an *hôtel-Dieu* would let no one forget that they were in charge. They insisted on supervising the meals, and, said the medical experts, overfed the patients. They would not allow any interference with the pharmacy and the supply of drugs; they monopolized the right to admit the sick and give them the good news that they could go; they defended the privacy of the sick 'pour ménager l'amour propre des pauvres', excluding students and curious visitors from the wards.[131] In Montpellier, they would not allow the doctors to take corpses away for dissection, on the ground that this offended the susceptibilities of local people; clinical researches had to be conducted in the morgues of prisons, the military hospital, and the Protestant one.[132] As the medical profession in the second half of the century developed an interest in precise observations to build up case histories, tensions between the doctors and the nursing sisters increased: in 1788, relations in the *hôtel-Dieu* of Paris reached crisis point, and the bureau of administration had to intervene.[133] The great Desault wanted his surgical patients two in a bed instead of four, while the sisters pointed out that this would halve the number which could be treated: he put on his anatomical lessons at times disrupting meals and visiting hours; also—a perennial problem—the sisters wanted the surgeon's apprentices excluded from the women's wards, where they flirted with the *servantes* and better-looking patients, and indulged in licentious discourses among themselves.

Other difficulties for the nursing sisters arose from the interventions of the lay administrators. The notables and oligarchs who held office in towns were proverbially self-important and parsimonious, and while they or their predecessors had been anxious to get the good ladies to take the sick off their hands, they were never happy with the stiff contracts they had signed. At Caen, the administrators tried to get rid of the Filles de la Madeleine altogether—'ces femmes inutiles, incapables, dépensières'—and habitually let their salaries fall into arrears.[134] Things were different at Nantes, the contract being so strict that the sisters did as they pleased and ran their house deep into debt. The bureau at Montpellier would not agree to their *sœur servante* taking time off to act as an inspector of hospitals in other towns, and refused to pay wages to young recruits still in training. In 1718 and 1723, authoritarian intervention from Versailles defeated the laymen, but in 1785, they scored a victory and had the *sœur servante* dismissed.[135] The Hôpital-Mage (the name of the *hôtel-Dieu*) at Béziers was a scene of guerrilla warfare in which the Dames de la Charité de Notre-Dame proved the most ingenious tacticians: orders from the bureau about admissions were ignored, new recruits were accepted without the customary dowry, thus diminishing the revenues, the archives were hidden from inspection, and meetings of the administrators with the nurses fixed at awkward times.[136] When Louis XV set up the Infirmerie Royale at Versailles for his servants and bodyguards, he naturally called on the Filles de la Charité to take charge (there were four of them in 1721, twenty-two in 1789). There was no management committee here; the royal institution was under the rule of a single administrator, the military governor.

In 1787, the maréchal de Rouchy wanted more discipline; the sisters were 'to sweep out the wards twice a day' in person. They are 'servants of the poor', said this crusty old soldier—besides, Mme Louise, the king's daughter, had done sweeping duties at the Carmelites. And he was not going to let the Filles have their contractual half-bottle of wine a day—'I don't drink any more myself'. It ended with the wine staying as before and the sisters undertaking 'to ensure that the wards are swept out', not necessarily doing it themselves.[137] When complaints of dubious conduct are made against hospital sisters, the source is—almost always—disgruntled municipal officers, wanting more for their money and less money to pay.[138] In one place they accused the sisters of treating rich bourgeois in preference to the poor, in another of taking in soldiers rather than local people because the government paid 13 sous a day for military men; or they were charging a small fee for the preferential treatment of a single bed and a private chamber-pot. At Provins, the sisters had a fine garden adorned with 'immodest statues' and a marquee in which they held garden parties and, in the house, a billiard-table. It all adds up to: the sisters had to earn money to keep their hospitals going, and they sometimes organized for themselves the relaxation they deserved.

THE COMMISSION DES RÉGULIERS

I *The Commission*

The Jesuits, useful to both Church and State, had been disbanded—
what then of the other religious Orders? The deliberations of the
Assembly of Clergy of 1765 were overshadowed by this question.
The bishops present knew of examples of misapplied wealth and lax
conduct in their dioceses, and two specific questions giving cause for
immediate concern were raised. One was the abuse of the translation
ad laxiorum, easily available from the Roman bureaucracy, allowing
a monk to transfer to a less rigorous Order and, skilfully used, a
device for escaping the cloister and slipping quietly into lay society.
The other was the proliferation of lawsuits of monks against their
superiors by use of the *appel comme d'abus*. In a famous case of 1760,
the parlement of Paris had overturned a sentence of three years'
imprisonment passed by the general of the Prémontrés on one of his
canons regular, awarding a pension on the revenues of an abbey as
damages.[1] A report to the Assembly listed lawsuits pending within six
different Orders, the Benedictines of Saint-Maur having three *appels
comme d'abus* before three different parlements.[2] Anything bringing
in the secular magistrates was dangerous: litigation before the parlement of Paris had led to the suppression of the Society of Jesus.

It was important to do something and to be seen to be doing it.
The Assembly therefore accepted a proposal from Loménie de
Brienne, archbishop of Toulouse, to ask the Pope, through the king,
to name a commission of enquiry and reform. Brienne was acting in
concert with Choiseul, Louis XV's anticlerical minister, and must
have known that the court of Versailles would not allow Rome to
exercise such authority over the Gallican Church. Nor would the
parlement of Paris. The magistrates vetoed recourse to the Pope, and
insisted on lay members being appointed to the commission as well
as ecclesiastics. On 31 July 1766 a royal order set up the Commission
des réguliers. The members were to be the archbishops of Reims,
Arles, Bourges, Narbonne, and Toulouse (zealots like the archbishops of Paris and Tours being excluded), and, as lay commis-

sioners, four luminaries of the great legal families of France, with six *avocats* and four theologians as technical advisers. Loménie de Brienne was rapporteur and in charge of all the business. Men of piety distrusted Brienne, but even from the narrowly ecclesiastical point of view, he was an excellent choice. A prelate with little in the way of Christian belief and devoured by ambition, he was concerned to promote the interests of the Church as an institution, and he was an indefatigable worker. 'He is ambitious,' said the abbé Véri, 'but in his eyes ambition is best furthered by duties zealously performed.'[3] Nothing could be done in eighteenth-century France without the conciliation of vested interests, and he was an arch-manipulator.

The files of the Commission accumulated denunciations.[4] Curés —though surprisingly few of them—complained of the honorific rights of the great abbeys in their parishes, and of the contrast between monastic wealth and their own poverty. Laymen volunteered picturesque delations, like the story of Dom Villemur of Saramon returning to his monastery 'dressed like a sailor' because the skirts of his cassock had been cut off by an angry citizen who caught him philandering with his sister. Local authorities admitted their interest in the confiscation of monastic property: the Cordeliers of Châteaudun are irreproachable, said the municipality, but there are only three of them, and their house would make a barracks for the garrison.[5] Rank-and-file monks and their superiors also told their conflicting stories.

But the reports that mattered came from the bishops responding to a questionnaire from Brienne in August 1766. Whether from idleness or conscientious objection, thirty did not reply. The bishops of Brittany sent a collective letter expressing reservations: 'in a destructive century like ours, one cannot be too careful to respect the rights of property and the intentions of founders'. Six older bishops said as little as possible, suspecting the use to which their answers would be put. Of the others, some waxed eloquent, the best-informed, incisive criticisms coming from worldly prelates like Jacques de Grasse of Angers, who for years had refused to pay his share of clerical taxation and spent most of his time in Paris. The bishops had their idiosyncratic bias. As aristocrats, they did not see the *commende* as the abuse it was; the archbishop of Reims, president of the Commission, and Brienne, its chief executive, drew as much income from abbeys held *in commendam* as they did from their episcopal sees. Their chief concern was to extend their jurisdiction to the regular as well as the secular clergy; in our dioceses, said one of them, there are 'as many little individual dioceses as there are monasteries, in which the bishop has no right of access for inspection'. Their chief criterion for approval was usefulness to the parishes; a fairly common observation was to praise a particular monastic house for its regularity, but to note its irrelevance to the needs of the pastoral ministry. They had an interest to promote suppressions to release income and buildings which could be used for diocesan projects. Though their reports give circumstantial details, they do not seem to be based on the formal procedure of *de commodo et incommodo* used by the jurisprudence of the day; their facts had not been verified by adversarial procedures. They were reporting what was said in the upper-class circles in which they moved or coming to them through their vicars-general, archdeacons, and curés. Even so, as representatives of the pastoral mission of the Church, the bishops' views were important, and their practical proposals for reform were realistic: they wished to close thinly populated houses and to raise the age for taking monastic vows—changes which the Commission was to implement.

Generalizations about monastic life in a particular country and century are likely to be falsified by the inevitably unequal distribution of evidence. Orders with a practical role in Church and society have a history; those dedicated to contemplation and prayer in the silence of the cloister have no history to speak of, unless things go wrong. The bishop of Bayeux praised the Trappists, the Chartreux, and the nuns of Sainte-Claire and of the Carmelite Order as austerely conforming to their ideals—what else was there for him or anyone else to say?[6] To describe French monasticism in the eighteenth century from the papers of an inquisitorial commission compounds the injustice, for behind so many complaints lie legacies of the past and pressures of local circumstance, while reformers naturally work from the formal concept of the monastic ideal rather than from a view of actual vocations in their accepted social context. In what follows, an impressionistic view of the diversity of monastic institutions will be given, broadening out in the case of some Orders into an account with the circumstantial detail which is needed to temper criticism with sympathy.

II *The Chartreux (Carthusians) and Grandmontins*

According to the files of the Commission,[7] there were 26,674 monks in France (this does not include lay brothers, possibly 8,000 of them). The mendicant Orders furnished half the total (14,388), the Benedictines one-fifth (4,647), the canons regular one-sixth (3,521).

Of the remaining groups the Carthusians were the most numerous (1,004). This left a few others with a limited number of houses, thinly populated—La-Merci, Grandmont, the Servites, the Barnabites, the Brigittines, and the Théatins.

Of these smaller Orders, two—the Carthusians and the Grandmontins—had originated as refuges for men who wished to follow the lonely disciplines of the hermit's life. The sixty-six houses of the Carthusians were beyond reproach. The bishops praised them, the only reservation coming from one who thought they were too fervent: their regime of absolute silence (except for saying the offices) was impossible for human nature to bear; they became prematurely aged, and their sanity was undermined.[8] The account-books of their house at Boserville in Lorraine show no wine or meat, no luxuries except tobacco and seed to feed cage-birds, and a dark entry 'for the carriage of a package of hair shirts from Lyon, 10 livres'.[9] An English traveller describes their house in Paris, the cells around a grassy quadrangle, each with a hatch for the delivery of meals and a private walled garden on the other side. Mercier forgot his journalistic irreverence when he visited this quiet spot: 'The trees are humble and bowed like the monks who salute you without looking at you; here is the noviciate of eternity.'[10]

Without being poor, the Carthusians kept the rules of eremetical discipline; by contrast, Grandmont, originally a fraternity of hermits forbidden to own property or deal in worldly affairs, had become a monastic Order like any other. From the start, the Commission seems to have had in mind the suppression of its thirty houses and the pensioning off of their 114 inmates, who were said to spend their days hunting and fishing. The accusation does not square with petitions from the villages around the mother-house of Grandmont in the diocese of Limoges, which talked of charitable contributions of 20,000 livres a year, and priests being sent out to help with parish duties and teach in schools. Essentially, two things were wrong with the Order.[11] First, the superior-general, Abbot René-Pierre François de la Guerinière, who died in 1744, had burdened his communities with crushing debts by embarking on an ostentatious building programme; at the mother-house, he had pulled down almost everything, including the medieval church, and rebuilt in the modern style, and at Paris he had enlarged the Collège Mignon, intending to make it a centre of learning. When Dom Mondain, simple and unworldly in spite of his name, became head of the Order in 1748, he had to fight Dom Vitecoq, the *procureur général* in charge of the finances and director of the Paris reconstruction project, to try to enforce economies. Nine years of litigation followed, with Vitecoq backed by the University and Parlement and Mondain by the Crown. Finally, in 1755, a general chapter accepted retrenchment, but the huge debts remained.

The second disastrous factor was the decline of Grandmontin recruitment. There were only forty-two monks in eight houses in the Strict Observance and seventy-two in twenty-two houses in the Common Observance. Behind the back of his superior-general, Dom Razat, the new *procureur général* of the finances, recommended to Loménie de Brienne the disbandment of the Order with pensions for himself and his colleagues, since they had not the numbers to keep going, and the faction fighting at general chapters would prevent any agreement on reform. The nineteenth-century historian of Grandmont calls this treachery; as between debts and depopulation, perhaps it was just realism. Dom Nicod, vicar-general of the Strict Observance, recommended suppressing four out of the eight houses to gain a reasonable quorum in the surviving ones. The question was not likely to be examined impartially, for D'Argentré, the bishop of Limoges, had the ear of the Commission and was pressing for the confiscation of the property of the mother-house for the benefit of his diocese. He was engaged in building a new episcopal palace, and the ill-disposed suggested it was this, and not concern for his parishes, which was inspiring his quest for supplementary funds.

III *The Mendicants*

The mendicants constituted more than half the total of male religious, and the Franciscans more than half the total of mendicants (1,001 houses with 8,870 inmates).

Of the five main Franciscan branches, three met with episcopal approval. The Picpus friars (the Tierçaires de Saint-François, called Picpus from the name of the village where their principal house was situated), a small group numbering 494 and running sixteen houses, were engaged in the care of lunatics—in their establishment at Saint-Omer they had no fewer than 200 of them. This dismal task made them indispensable. Then there were the Récollets, the result of a reform which arose in France at the beginning of the seventeenth century (222 houses with 2,491 friars). The bishops gave them an overwhelming vote of confidence, thirty-three for, and only three against.[12] Such criticisms as there were could be reversed and interpreted as reluctant praise. Many friars were from humble origins, 'peasants driven into religion by necessity and hunger', it was said. They specialized in the work of chaplains to the army and the navy, and those doing so were recalcitrant to ecclesiastical authority and affected an air of unspiritual toughness. The friars at Bergerac, where half the population was Calvinist, were censured for their tolerance, educating the children without trying to convert them to Catholicism and giving out 'certificates of Catholicity' (to obtain employment or admission to a hospital) without making an inquisition into details of belief. The majority of bishops praised the Récollets as active in the parochial ministry and welcome to the people, being 'well educated', 'peaceful', and 'laborious'. From within the Order itself the reports of the provincials and submissions from the rank and file do not suggest the tensions evident in the other mendicant Orders. A few scandals came to light, though one might forgive the *gardien* of the friary at Sainte-Foy his silk dressing-gown and house in the country, since he was a famous preacher and moved in high society.[13] 'We are not angels,' wrote the head of the Orléans province, 'but no abuse of any consequence has as yet arisen among us.' And he pointed out—an important consideration when passing judgement on mendicants—that those who are obliged to live by the collecting box are thereby involved in the rough-and-tumble of lay society, and are subject to continual temptations.[14]

The third group winning approval were the Capuchins, who had separated from the rest of the Franciscans by the reform which began in Italy in 1529. They were the biggest mendicant organization in France, having 3,497 friars in 418 establishments grouped in fourteen provinces covering the whole country. Sixty-five bishops praised them. Only five complained, saying their begging was a nuisance, they were ignorant, and competed with the curés for the allegiance of their parishioners. True enough, there were complaints about the continual rattle of collecting boxes, and the popular word for an obscurantist pious diatribe was a 'capucinade'. But behind the proverbial ridicule, the Capuchins had won a place in the affections of the people. In their white habits with pointed cowls, sandals, and obligatory beards, they were picturesque figures. 'Ils ont le don de fasciner.' As beggars, they acquired the arts of insinuation, appearing at the gates of a seigneur silent, with downcast eyes, at the door of a parish priest with modest deference, and calling at a farmhouse with the utmost affability.

He pats the dog, calls back the children who are running away, familiarizes them with his long beard and gives them pious images; he offers great compliments to the mistress of the house, and enters into discussions with the farmer in which he appears almost learned; you'd imagine that he had not come to ask for anything, but his request is forestalled, they offer him something and he accepts benignly.[15]

Partly by inclination, partly to alleviate their poverty, the Capuchins volunteered for parish work. Their house of Sollies near Toulon was typical: miserably poor, as the inventory of their battered furniture shows, they kept going from 350 livres a year for acting as vicaires in the parish of Saint-Michel, a smaller fee for a chaplaincy in a country mansion, and the municipality doing their repairs on condition of being allowed to use their buildings as a staging-point for conscripts to the coastguard service.[16] As Paris expanded, a new parish in the Chaussé d'Antin was needed, so the government moved the Capuchins of the rue Saint-Honoré to run it, building them a new friary.[17] Learned Capuchins specialized as preachers of Lent and Advent sermons, and the less learned in conducting evangelical missions, allying pastoral solicitude with hell-fire declamation. In time of plague, the friars were expected to risk their lives in the danger zone to help the dying and hear their confessions.[18] In popular mythology a cudgel-swinging Capuchin was the recognized exponent of muscular Christianity; the friar who knocked out a pistol-carrying highwayman was living up to the public image.[19] In most towns, the Capuchins were the fire brigade. The Parisian diarists record their exploits; one of Restif de la Bretonne's journalistic set pieces describes them effecting a hazardous rescue.[20] At the conflagration at the fair of Saint-Germain in 1763, soldiers formed a cordon to keep out looters, the seminarists of Saint-Sulpice rescued private possessions, and the Capuchins 'flew to the spot (the expression is no exaggeration) where peril and charity beckoned them, we saw them in teams, cowl over head, robes hitched up to the knees, carrying buckets, dragging their water pumps, rushing to seek danger and to perish as martyrs to their . . . love for their fellow citizens'.[21] More than other regulars, they were regarded as useful, and in a variety of activities. Père Antoine, Mme de Genlis remembered, was chaplain to the château, reading pious literature to the family after dinner; he ran the parish when the curé was away, and 'had shown his valour in several fires'.[22]

There was trouble in the Capuchin camp, however: corruption at the top, evident in the complaints of the rank and file which came in to the commissioners. The *gardiens* of the individual houses rigged the elections of the provincial superiors, and these superiors rigged the appointments of the *gardiens*. Thus secure in their despotic authority by 'ruse and cabal', they could live worldly lives at the top of the pyramid of mendicity and poverty. Intriguers aspiring to posts of command worked hard to ingratiate themselves with those who held them. An anonymous friar of Lyon described the mentality:

Men . . . brought up to be ploughmen or shop assistants join an Order where they pass their early years in extreme poverty under superiors who live comfortably, but treat them with a harshness no decent man would use towards a servant; they swear to themselves that they will go to any lengths to escape from their unhappy state, and they can contrive this all the more easily because official places are not awarded either by seniority or merit.[23]

This combination of despotism and self-indulgence at the top was characteristic, in greater or lesser degree, of most of the mendicant Orders. Just as aristocratic churchmen intrigued for the bishoprics reserved to their class, the bishop of Toul declared in a frank comparison, so, too, plebeians of the mendicant Orders strove to become 'provincials' and 'dominants'.[24] It was so with the Cordeliers. These were the original branch of the Franciscan tree, called 'Cordelier' in France because of the knotted cord of their girdles. There were two groups, the Observants (288 houses, 2,077 friars) and the Conventuals (57 houses, 311 friars). Thirty-nine bishops approved of the Observants, with twenty against; only six approved of the Conventuals, with fourteen against. Yet, whatever else was wrong with the Cordeliers, they certainly co-operated in the pastoral ministry. In the ports they did specialist work with seafaring families.[25] They volunteered to go to Protestant areas where it was difficult to find curés willing to face hostile parishioners. The bishop of Cahors praised their 'indefatigable zeal . . . I'd be in serious difficulties without them.' Complaints from the rank and file, however, tell the same story of corruption at the top as with the Capuchins. The dominants of the provinces of Aquitaine, Franche Comté, Touraine, and Provence are accused of 'despotism' and of accepting bribes from families to allow entry to the Order of army deserters and drunkards. Since they virtually appointed their own successors, the three-year term of office did not limit their depredations—all they needed were a few accomplices to keep the rotation going. Nineteen friars of Provence revealed how Père Julian, their retired dominant, had done well for himself, now living in his house in the country and owning another nearby for two girls 'he passes off as his nieces'. Others had doubts about the accounts of the four friars of the Commissariat of the Holy Land, who collected alms for the guardians of the Holy Sepulchre. There were also a few picturesque scandals in individual houses: the Cordeliers of Alise-Sainte-Reine drinking, womanizing, and playing cards all night to the outrage of the pilgrims who came to their shrine, the students in the Grand Couvent at Paris who indulged in drinking bouts and fisticuffs when the friars were away preaching their Lent and Advent courses.[26] These were not typical, but they were signs of a lack of inspection and oversight, which the discredited dominants could not hope to exercise.

The history of the mendicants had been one of periods of declining ideals followed by periods of regeneration by the separation of new, reformed observances from the old. Inevitably, the effects of the reform would fade, but there was always a residue of improvement preserved. It had been so with the Franciscans: the Capuchins and the Récollets of 1768 were better than the Cordeliers, and within the Cordeliers the Observants were better than the Conventuals.

This was equally true of the Augustinian and the Carmelite friars,[27] each group having its reformed offshoot. The Grands Augustins (with 123 houses and 844 inmates) had their stricter colleagues, the so-called Petits Pères (34 houses, 323 inmates). As against the Grands Carmes (129 houses, 1,194 inmates) there were the Carmes déchaussés—the 'discalced Carmelites'—who had separated to follow a more severe rule at the end of the sixteenth century (62 houses, 750 inmates). The limited number of comments made by the bishops about the two reformed observances, the Petits Pères and the Carmes déchaussés, were favourable. But their attitude was very different to the larger, unreformed branches. The Grands Augustins had fifteen bishops against, and only eleven for; the Grands Carmes were approved by twenty-two bishops, with those in Protestant areas being enthusiastic, but there were eleven against. In both cases, the rank and file were feuding with their superiors—the almost universal flaw in the mendicant Orders. The dominants ruling the provinces kept themselves (or each other) in office, and, ruling abusively, they lacked the moral authority to exercise discipline. The Toulouse province of the Grands Carmes had been under Père Sérapion for forty years, while the friary at Albi fell into ruin and the buildings at Béziers were rented out for shops, with the friars in both places living in town and doing what they pleased. In the Grands Augustins the divisions between rulers and ruled were exacerbated by the favours shown from on high to the aristocracy of doctors of theology, who received greater dress allowances and were excused from some of the rules of austerity. The moral accusations against the seven provincials were also more serious than in other Orders. Some were said to grow rich by trading and taking bribes for accepting novices, and, as for one of them, 'his mistress is known by all the province'. These accusations came from below, and were countered by accusations of insubordination; neither side should be implicitly believed in details, though the bitter divisions between them are clear.

In none of the mendicant Orders was election rigging developed to a finer art than with the Minims,[28] the friars who owed their origin to the other St Francis, Francis of Paola, in the fifteenth century. Yet to all appearances, their constitution was democratic, the local superiors (*correcteurs*) being elected and ruling for only a single year, and the provincials being elected by the deputies to the general chapter, with their term of office strictly triennial. This egalitarian system was subverted, however, by the operation of little groups who monopolized the office of provincial by rotating in power: in the provinces of Lorraine and Aquitaine, two brothers played this game over long periods. The election of the deputies to general chapter was manipulated. In houses where the friars showed independence, their opposition was overcome either by declaring the place a 'vicariate' (in which case the provincial had the right of naming the *correcteur* over the head of the community) or by adding to the nominal roll the names of friars from other houses, which entitled them to vote, though they never came into residence.

Yet the effect of these practices was less disastrous than in other Orders. Twenty-two bishops gave the Minims their approval, and the twelve who had reservations were complaining about atypical houses in which discipline had collapsed. Apart from the Trappists, the Minims had the most severe rule of all the monastic Orders. Eggs and cheese, as well as meat and fish, were excluded from their diet—they lived on bread, water, and vegetables. Their routine of daily devotions, sung without musical ornamentation with slow, strict concentration on meaning, was carried on in a perpetual Lent. To join them required a more than conventional vocation. Hence, their generally good conduct—and also their declining numbers. Many of their 153 houses (they had 975 friars) were already scheduled for closure before the Commission des réguliers met. Another factor—paradoxically perhaps—worked to preserve the Minims from decadence: their ownership of property.[29] Fees for saying masses and for burial in their chapels, the profits of annuities, and property rents kept them solvent, though modestly so. They were preserved from the temptations of wealth, on the one hand, and from those of the rough-and-tumble of continual begging, on the other. This conferred a freedom, not only to observe their routines of prayer, but also to indulge in scholarly pursuits—at the end of the seventeenth century the Order had Mersenne the mathematician and polymath, Maignen the engineer, Plumer the zoologist, and other scientific writers. A third factor helping to preserve standards among the Minims was their associated Third Order of pious laymen, who met in their chapels and bound themselves to a strict rule of life, including the famous penance of standing with arms outstretched every Friday for the space of five Paters and five Ave Marias, to share the agony of the cross. They were, said Père Antoine Masson, the 'kingdom of God in its discipline established here on earth'.[30] As such, they provided a continual example, an ever-watching lay censorship on the monks who were charged with their spiritual oversight.

The Dominicans—the 'Black Friars' so called from the black mantle they wore over their white habits, or, in France, the 'Jacobins', from their principal house in Paris in the rue Saint-Jacques—fared worst of all the mendicants in the episcopal assize: thirty-seven bishops condemned them, and of the twenty-eight who approved, some were lukewarm. The severity of the indictment owed something to the suspicion that the Black Friars (1,432 of them in 179 houses) retained a continuing allegiance to Jansenist opinions; hence they were described as 'republicans', 'infected with the spirit of revolt which for long they have shown against all legitimate authority'. Their institute, said one bishop, is 'a serpent which we have nourished in our bosom'. But in other ways, apart from doctrinal remissness, they were a threat to the orderly administration of dioceses, for the free and easy nature of their organization encouraged eccentricity and indiscipline.

The law of corporate poverty imposed by St Dominic in the thirteenth century had been revoked in 1475. Thereafter, the various houses had come by endowments, enough to involve them in worldly affairs, but not enough to allow them the independence and scope which a comfortable income might have provided. The Dominican answer to the pressures of poverty was an unusual one. Trappists dug, Capuchins begged, but the Black Friars paid their way as individuals, whether by bringing with them a personal pension furnished by their family, or by earning money, principally from fees for their sermons (after all, preaching was the chief duty of their institute). From their *pécule*, invested with some theoretical supervision from their superiors, they contributed to their meals and other communal expenses. At Angers[31] in 1737, the prior ruled that those who gave as much as 100 livres would be entitled to an extra pair of shoes and four pounds of candles a year more than the others. In the following year, a friar loaned the house 533 livres to pay off its debts. Later on, another friar died, and the community inherited his investment income of 55 livres a year. There was a nice—and disputatious—balance between the corporate life and individual independence. When the new buildings at Angers were completed in 1769, the friars chose their rooms in order of seniority, and the furniture was pooled for re-allocation. Thereafter, individuals were responsible for maintaining their own window-glass and keys and for providing their own firewood, though the house would provide a communal fireplace for those who needed it.

Informal arrangements of this kind undermined discipline.[32] Visitation reports speak of tonsures too small and hair too long and curled and powdered, of highly polished shoes and fancy leather hats, with accompanying attitudes of 'impudence', and conversation in 'disdainful terms' airing the sentiments of sceptical 'philosophy'. Those who were in nominal authority proved incapable of imposing reforms. Some priors and provincial officials did well for themselves: there are stories of their mirrors and marble-topped tables, carriages and junketings, while in nearby priories the inmates are reduced to collecting their drinking water in chamber-pots from leaks in the roof and staying in bed while their breeches are mended. As was their wont, the doctors of theology claimed privileges, ranging from exemptions from the daily offices to a monopoly, along with the priors, of acting as deputies to provincial chapters. As in all the mendicant Orders, there was no effective central direction over the ten Dominican provinces of France. The general in Rome, by special permission of the French court and the parlement, enjoyed exclusive power over the Paris noviciate, and it was a model of decent conduct. The visitation reports about the state of the other houses went to him, but what could he do? The Gallican liberties prevented him from intervening. When the Commission des réguliers met, the Roman general was being sued before the parlement of Toulouse by one of his provincials and in 1766 the court declared his decrees to be invalid in France unless confirmed by royal letters patent registered at law.[33] When in 1774 the government yielded on the issue of principle and called in the general to reform the college of the rue Saint-Jacques, it was with so many reservations that nothing effective was done.[34]

The Dominicans were unlucky. By the standard contemporary tests of monastic discipline, they were decadent. But if their establishments are accepted for what they really were, boarding-houses for preachers, confessors, and students, their local, non-monastic usefulness can be recognized. The Black Friars preached a great deal (they had to), and made an unregimented contribution to the life of the Church. The prior and the four Jacobins at Grasse were described by their enemies as running a gambling school, but when, in 1771, orders for the suppression of their house arrived, the mayor wrote in their defence. Their conduct is edifying, he said, and their masses 'provide us with a second parish'; they are all of honourable families of the town, 'finding there a comfortable and decent refuge without getting out of touch with their families and their native locality'.[35] A consideration of the activity of individuals goes some way to mitigating the severity of visitation reports. Amid the scandalous confusions of the house of the rue Saint-Honoré, Père Charles-Louis Richard, the librarian, published four volumes of sermons, six volumes of a *Dictionnaire universel des sciences ecclésiastiques* and sixty-three other tomes; the four Black Friars at Vitré were described by the parishioners as indispensable because of their exactitude in saying the offices, their care for the sick and the poor, and 'their elegant, moving, frequent and continuous preaching'.[36]

IV *The Canons Regular*

The bishops might have been expected to be tolerant of the seven branches of the Augustinian canons regular, since their main task was to man parochial cures. Yet approval was given to only two branches, the reformed Augustinians of Chancelade (six houses, 173 canons) and the canons of Saint-Antoine, the Antonins (thirty-eight houses, 242 canons). The abbey of Chancelade in Périgord,[37] with its five dependencies, had kept the right to elect its own abbot, and was fairly rich. It was therefore independent in running its own affairs, and had resources enough to undertake scholarly projects, especially in the writing of provincial history. As a result, young men of good families and intellectual inclinations were glad to join. From 1762, there was a further incentive, as the abbey branched out into superior journalism, founding the *Éphémérides du Citoyen*, a publication to which Mirabeau and Dupont de Nemours were to contribute. The Antonins were another small group (indeed, some of their houses were now deserted), but they too were able to attract recruits from notable families. The bishop of Belley was delighted with their seminary and their work in the parishes. Only one of his colleagues was critical, and he had to be inventive to find a grievance: they were not fulfilling their original purpose 'to care for the indigent sick afflicted by a malady very little known today'— which made it hardly surprising that they were doing something different. The Congrégation de Notre-Sauveur (seventeen houses and 169 canons, all in Lorraine) was detested by the bishops, but their assessment cannot be trusted—nowhere else was there such a lively nest of Jansenists.

This left four other branches of canons regular under condemnation: the forty-nine houses of those directly under diocesan authority, the Prémontrés (fifty-two houses of the Old Observance and forty of the Reformed), the Trinitaires (seventy-four houses of the Old Observance and seven of the Reformed), and the Génovéfains, or Congrégation de France (106 houses). Altogether, these four branches totalled about 3,000 canons. There were individual exceptions to the general allegations of decadence: notably all seven establishments of the reformed Trinitaires, the so-called *déchaussés*. There would have been more if the bishops had enquired more closely and been fair. Truth was, far from appreciating this particular monastic contribution to parish work, many of them objected to it. To be both a canon regular and a curé, it was argued, is to fulfil neither duty satisfactorily. 'They think they are independent of bishops because they are regulars, and independent of their monastic superiors because they are curés.'[38] Many young men who join the canons regular of Sainte-Geneviève, said the bishop of Orléans, are lacking in ability and deficient in morals, seeking a back-door entrance to the ranks of the parochial ministry, where they have independence and an assured income.

This was a libel, coming ill from a courtier of dubious morals. The Genovéfains had to study for seven years—two of literature, two of philosophy, and three of theology. Those who desired the pastoral ministry had then to teach for two years in a seminary and complete five years in priestly orders; thereafter, on consideration of reports from superiors and visitors, the triennial general chapter could put the candidate on the list for appointment to one of the 600 parishes in the gift of the congregation.[39] Yet only six bishops approved of their seminaries and parish work, while nineteen were dissatisfied. The real reason is not far to seek—the canons regular were not amenable to diocesan discipline. A *prieur-curé* was secure in his tenure; only the abbot, acting with the consent of both his council and the bishop and able to prove 'just cause' could revoke his title. Even so, while secure, he was under no obligation, for he could leave the pastoral vocation to teach or administer in a house of his Order. The Genovéfains regarded themselves as gentlemen-monks. They were resplendent in their white cassocks and well-creased cambric surplices, and the decrees of general chapters show how they affected silver watches and snuff-boxes, hair-powder, and shining buckles, and how they moved too freely in society. There were some strict houses, but most were inclined to comfort and sociability, which suited well-off families who liked the idea of establishing their sons in religious clubs rather than monasteries.[40] The congregation was in debt, yet insolvency did not seem to affect this superior life-style. Young men seeking a career in scholarship would join without a religious vocation, drawn to the Parisian abbey of Sainte-Geneviève with its prestigious library of over 100,000 volumes—like Mongez, elected to the Académie des Inscriptions at the age of 38, and Barthélemy Mercier, the librarian. Unmoved by the spectacle of St Augustine trampling on heresies depicted on the library dome, others of the canons regular of Paris ventured into dangerous speculation: there was Pingré, the astronomer, both a Jansenist and a freemason; Joseph Barre, who wrote anonymously in favour of Protestants; and Pierre François Courayer, who published various works in 1723 and 1726 to prove Anglican orders valid and in the end fled to England and obtained a sinecure in the Anglican Church.[41]

The bishops were alarmed by this sort of learning. The scholarly activities of the Prémontrés were also under suspicion. They published a great deal[42] on history, music, campanology, poetry, chronology, liturgiology, and casuistry; after twenty years' work, one of them produced a 'dictionary of the origin of all things'. These were mostly unexceptionable books, but what of Remacle Lissoir, the head of an abbey, who in 1766 published an attack on papal claims in the vein of Febronius? Later on there was J.-B.-A. Hédouin, who issued an appreciative study of the subversive writings of the abbé Raynal, and was rescued from dire consequences only by the heroic conduct of a relative, Captain Hédouin de Pons Luden, already in jail for libertinage, who wrote to the police claiming authorship. Independence, a free and easy life-style, and opinions ranging from Jansenism to sympathy with Protestants and philosophes ensured the condemnation of the Genovéfains and the Prémontrés, their work in the parishes largely forgotten.

V *The Anciens Bénédictins, Cluny and Cîteaux*

The great Benedictine family had 660 houses and about 6,000 monks. Of the seventy monasteries of the Anciens Bénédictins, the bishops approved of eighteen, condemned twenty-six and gave no verdict on the other twenty-six. Two broad conclusions may be inferred from the Commission's enquiry into these houses of the Old Observance. First, the prevailing temper in clerical and lay society was a major factor in maintaining or undermining monastic morale, for the houses where the rule was decently—sometimes fervently—observed were in the pious northern boundary zone, the dioceses of Arras, Boulogne, Cambrai, Saint-Omer, Tournai, and Ypres. Secondly, the rule tended to fall into abeyance and the monks slink off into a quasi-lay existence in houses with few inmates. There were exceptions either way: Troarn, in the diocese of Bayeux, was one of the few abbeys described as utterly scandalous, and it had fourteen monks, while the prior of Saint-Sever (Coutances) was proud of his tiny community, three of the four having previously served in the parochial ministry, and the other as a chaplain to the East India Company in Senegal. And small communities sunk in decadence could be engaging in their worldliness. One prior, with only three monks, admitted that they lived a 'purely secular life', and wondered why their house was permitted to survive. The prior of Chemillé (the diocese of Angers) said that he and his three monks each had a little house in which they lived privately, though they fasted and recited the offices.

Is our way of life an abuse? I would not be certain. All I will say, Monseigneur, is that I am edified by the conduct of my brethren. In truth, our duties are not burdensome, being indistinguishable from those of secular canons. We were instructed in these duties as novices, and we fulfil them. If they had been more onerous, perhaps we would not have under-taken them and our vocations would have been different.

This is revealing: taking vows was not forsaking the world in entire self-dedication; it was entering into a contractual relationship to hold an ecclesiastical sinecure on certain conditions. The ultimate logic of the idea was seen at Maurs (Aurillac), where the buildings had collapsed long ago and only the vestiges of the foundations remained. The twelve monks lived at home like secular priests, and, as their prior said, 'they support their families who, without them, would be in abject poverty'.

Brienne thought these old Benedictine houses ought to be

grouped together with the eleven houses of the so-called Exempts under the rule of a general chapter. But would this have improved them? The Exempts already had their chapter meetings to rule them, and the bishops condemned seven of their abbeys and approved only one.

The bishops who gave positive approval to only a quarter of the monasteries of the Anciens Bénédictins and the Exempts gave their warrant to even fewer of the Cluniac branch, sixteen houses out of eighty-eight. True, some escaped without notice, and of those condemned, few met with such severe and circumstantial censures as the bishop of Rodez directed against Sévérac and the bishop of Mâcon against Charlieu. In the first, the four monks put the parish clergy in fear of their lives and endangered the chastity of the local girls; in the second, there were female servants and every night, after the prior retired to bed, the brethren ran a gambling school. The great abbeys were decorous and proudly expending their wealth in splendid building programmes.[43] At Cluny itself, the head of the Order, the solemn routines of liturgical life rolled on, while all around new conventual buildings were being erected, their severe classical façades adorned with balconies and stair rails in cast iron designed by Frère Placide. At Saint-Martin-des-Champs in Paris, construction went on under the direction of the architect Soufflot the younger, nephew of the great one.[44] Here was the research centre of the order, where its history was being compiled by a team under Dom Claude Baudinot—nearly a thousand manuscript volumes of copies of documents were accumulated. It was not entirely disinterested history, for the general chapter of 1716 had resolved to print the basic charters 'serving to sustain the cause of the Strict Observance against the attacks of the commendatory abbot of Cluny'.[45]

This resolution is a pointer to the feuds which made the order incapable of reforming itself. Cluny was always held *in commendam* by a prelate of the court aristocracy, who would sometimes exercise his right to preside over general chapters and would sometimes interfere with the internal business of monasteries, which was not his right at all. The monks were not united against the incursions of their abbots. There were two observances, the 'old' (fifty houses with 296 monks) and the 'strict' (thirty-eight houses with 333 monks). The first tended to let the abbot have his way, the second to battle against him and his 'violation of our most sacred maxims'. Each observance had seven *définiteurs* at the triennial general chapters; they met separately for business concerning their own affairs and jointly for common interests.[46] When Louis XIV annexed

Franche Comté in 1684, he united the Benedictine houses of the province to Cluny, with a *définiteur* to represent them in the general chapter. From the start, the new arrival aligned himself with the old observance, which left the abbot's party dominant. This might have been the moment for the commendatory abbot, Cardinal Bouillon, to press home his advantage decisively, but he quarrelled with the king, who prevented him from subverting the right of the *définiteurs* to appoint the priors of monasteries.

In this continuing quarrel, neither side would allow the other to take the initiative in making major changes; nor would they agree to anyone else doing so. In 1730 a papal brief appointed Cardinal Bissy, archbishop of Rouen, as apostolic commissioner to reform Cluny; the commendatory abbot, Henri Oswald de la Tour d'Auvergne, archbishop of Vienne, refused to co-operate. Nothing was done, though twenty-two years later the lay magistrates of the Grand Council issued a regulation to keep priors of houses in order—they had to have permission from the abbot of Cluny to be away for more than a month, and if they went to Paris, they had to lodge in one of three named institutions. The Commission des réguliers in its turn was reticent about making proposals for action, leaving decisions to the abbot, Dominique de la Rochefoucauld, archbishop of Rouen— a sure formula for immobility.[47]

The Cluniacs had become an independent branch of the Benedictine family over eight centuries ago; the Cistercians had followed them to independence rather less than two centuries later. Both Orders were wracked with debilitating internal divisions. Strife between Cîteaux and its first four daughter-houses (each with the attendant train of the monasteries it had founded) was almost as old as the Order itself.[48] During the reign of Louis XIV, the abbot-general (a genuine abbot, not a commendatory one), ruling from Cîteaux, was backed in his authoritarian designs by the authoritarian king, and achieved a dominance over the proto-abbots of La Ferté, Pontigny, Morimond, and Clairvaux which continued after the great monarch died. General chapters were no longer called, so what little was done was done despotically, while the constraints which a common opinion might have exercised against abuses in individual houses were absent. The proto-abbots had two possible manœuvres for edging themselves out of their position of inferiority. According to their argument, the final authority in the Order should be vested in the steering committee, the *Definitorum*, on which they had a majority. By an old papal ruling, the abbot-general named four members, and the proto-abbots named five—though of these five only four could actually sit, for the abbot-general could exercise a veto against any one of them, a nice refinement of electoral procedure invented by the court of Rome; the abbot-general could easily be outvoted, but he need not put up with harassment by the most extreme of his enemies. However, the dominance of the *Definitorum* was never conceded at Cîteaux, where it was considered to be a 'subsidiary tribunal' capable of executive action only on matters specifically referred to it by a general chapter.

The other line of attack for the proto-abbots was to insist on the calling of the supposedly triennial general chapter. This would give them a forum in which to air their grievances, but the trouble was, they were not likely to win a vote. Half the Cistercian houses which had survived the Reformation were outside France, and the contingent of abbots coming from Germany voted solidly for authority. The Germans had political leverage: they could intrigue with the Austrian ambassador in Paris, and hold over the French court the threat of a schism in the Order, rejecting the generalship of a Frenchman. When, finally, in 1738, a general chapter did meet, the votes of the foreign abbots ensured the reaffirmation of the abbot of Cîteaux's authority.

There was an election for a new abbot-general in 1748. It was a glittering office to hold, conferring entitlement to a seat in the parlement of Dijon and in the provincial estates of Burgundy.[49] Anticlericals made the usual allegations of bribery by the various candidates.[50] Victory went to François Trouvé, a doctor of the Sorbonne and a man of character, of bourgeois origin and only 37 years of age. Sensing possible weakness, the proto-abbots renewed their claims, and finally, in 1760, took their case to the Grand Conseil. In the following year, the court gave its ruling: decisions of Trouvé taken without due consultation were illegal.[51] The issue came before the general chapter of 1765, the Germans once again swinging the vote to reject the proto-abbots' argument that final authority must rest with the *Definitorum*. The proto-abbots walked out and appealed to the king; the abbot-general went to the parlement of Dijon, where the magistrates reaffirmed his authority, a finding influenced by the lawyers of the German abbots, who declared that they would not attend assemblies of the Order if they were to be subject to a 'despotic committee'. So, when the Commission des réguliers met, the Cistercians were in chaos.

It would have been well if, as some had proposed, the Cistercian Order had split up, with each proto-abbot becoming independent, with his own general chapter to direct him. Smaller groupings were less prone to divisions, and more amenable to discipline. A break-away of this kind had taken place at the end of the sixteenth century, when the Feuillants had escaped from the control of Cîteaux. Their twelve houses in France (and their equal number in Italy) were a manageable group under coherent direction, and even the censorious bishops found no fault with them, though they still asked their usual questions about usefulness. But the vast main complex of Cistercian monasteries (288 of them) was too big, and the confusions of the government of the Order prevented the monks from reforming themselves, whether by authoritarian dictation or by communal inspiration.

The results were evident in the files of the Commission des réguliers.[52] Of the fifty bishops recording an opinion, eighteen praised the Order, thirty-six condemned it, and six were neutral. Few houses received the unreserved praise bestowed by the bishop of Lavaur on La Rode: there were only six monks, but they served in parishes, gave alms, provided employment, and had such a high reputation that the sons of the nobility were glad to join them. Praise, when it was given, tended to be qualified. The bishop of Agen said that the monks' conduct was 'fairly good . . . but they are useless'. Some houses were said to have nothing in their favour but their alms and the employment they provided. One was generous in times of disaster, another was custodian of the fragment of the Holy Shroud, and the local people made a living from the pilgrims who came to revere it. Of the four abbeys of his diocese, the bishop of Châlons-sur-Marne said, they recite the offices with dignity, give limited hospitality, and, above all, provide work—'that is the use they are and this usefulness is genuine'.

Great constructors of palaces themselves, the bishops did not complain of the building programmes of the richer Cistercian establishments. They ought to have done so, for there was a wasteful failure of central oversight. The abbey of Châlis was allowed to run up an astonishing debt of a million livres on its extension programme, an amount which could never be repaid, and led to bankruptcy and closure. Meanwhile the fabric of the Collège de Saint-Bernard at Paris was decaying all through the century. The great Gothic hall and the fourteenth-century church (adorned with the high altar salvaged from Port-Royal-des-Champs when Louis XIV demolished it) echoed empty, as a handful of students struggled through an exacting curriculum in the few viable rooms. Even selling the garden to speculators setting up a cattle market in 1772 barely paid off half the collegiate debt.[53]

There were many Cistercian houses with few inmates. The average was eight per house; 191 monasteries had nine monks or fewer, and of these, forty-four had three or less. Only thirty-seven had ten monks or more, the biggest being Cîteaux (60), Clairvaux (54), and Morimond (30). Smaller institutions were always in danger of slipping into the life of lay society, especially when they were in the depths of the countryside. The bishop of Poitiers accused the monks of the six priories in his diocese of doing nothing but ride around supervising their property. The archbishop of Bourges had eleven houses with only thirty-three monks in all of them together. He saw no hope of increasing their number, as the only recruits coming forward were 'of low birth and ignorant'—the idea that the uneducated mass of people might be a good recruiting ground for the cloisters never struck this great aristocrat. Only one house had a library, the others having merely their choir-books and lives of St Bernard; when not supervising their tenants, the monks read 'old gazettes and newspapers'. Of his four abbeys, each with only five or six monks in it, the bishop of Angers declared they did nothing but sing the offices, go hunting, and play cards with the locals. These reports generally stop short of total condemnation as scandalous; only one house in ten was accused of either neglect of duty or immorality. The general impression is of a lack of fervour and only a marginal contribution to the life of the Church.[54]

There were a few Cistercian houses which were astonishing exceptions, places where ruthless austerity, far beyond any rational interpretation of the rule, reigned supreme. In every case, the trans-formation was the achievement of a charismatic abbot. Orval[55] in the Low Countries was reformed by Charles de Bentzeradt (dd. 1707), but his task was made easy by the secret inspiration of the place, which was Jansenist. Here was one of the covert refuges for disciples of Quesnel and an *entrepôt* for the importation of Jansenist books. When a papal representative made a visitation in 1725, no fewer than twelve monks had to flee lest they were recognized. Orval was rich—so did not need to make the compromises with the world which poverty engenders—but disciplined; so the riches did not corrupt, though there was a splendid building programme. The abbey of Sept-Fons[56] in the diocese of Autun was reformed by Dom Eustache de Beaufort in a long reign which lasted from 1656 to 1707. A mixture of almost feminine tenderness and grim severity (he wept if he had to send a novice away, but put a sardonic thrust into the obituary notice of an old colleague), he had that strange personal magnetism which has the power to draw men to the ways of complete self-sacrifice. Throughout the eighteenth century, the harshness of the régime, with its perpetual silence, was proverbial: a father with noisy children would set them to play the game of 'aux pères de Sept-Fons' where everything was done by gestures. Yet there was no lack of recruits, and many had to be turned away: from 1701 to 1722, of 461 postulants or novices, only 99 were accepted for final profession.[57]

Orval, Sept-Fons, and a few other monasteries—Laigle, Verneuil, and Soligny—were also reformed in imitation of (though without coming into dependence upon) the most famous and grimly austere house of them all, La Trappe, in the diocese of Sées in Normandy. Here, from 1664 to his death in 1700, Armand-Jean de Rancé had ruled.[58] A scholar, courtier, dilettante churchman, and absentee holder of rich benefices, he had been converted by the death of Mme de Montbazon, a warning of the transience of earthly things. From commendatory abbot of La Trappe, he transformed himself into the regular one. The way of life which he imposed was designed to annihilate every pleasure, of both the body and the mind. The brethren lived in perpetual silence, doing arduous work in the fields and singing the offices with slow measured deliberation. Study was banned. They slept on straw mattresses placed on boards. Meat, fish, eggs, and seasonings such as thyme or garlic were excluded from their diet, the one meal of the day coming from the range of roots, beans, lentils, cereals, fruit, nuts, and black bread. Rancé was not a fanatic. His way was destined only for the few who had a special vocation to it, and the hardships were not meaningful except as being necessary to direct the mind solely to God: 'Dieu ne veut point de partage'. Dom Chabon, a later abbot of La Trappe, spoke of monks as 'successors of the martyrs . . . irreproachable witnesses . . . guardian angels of the world by the fervour of their prayer . . . models to the human race by the saintliness of their lives'.[59] Rancé would have seen dangers of pride lurking in this proclamation, for he was haunted by the shadow of the *amour propre* which feeds upon self-abasement. He would have been gratified by the men of the eighteenth century who regarded his foundation with contempt, denouncing useless austerities, anti-social renunciation of fatherland and family.[60] What would have alarmed him was the procession of fashionable courtiers who came to spend a night or two at his monastery, and the pilgrims who flocked— between 4,000 and 5,000 of them every year—to gape at the wild surroundings and the silent figures in their white habits, sleeves sweeping the ground, and shudder at the sight of the cells without light or fire, adorned with a skull and pictures of deathbeds and hell.[61]

The severe regime cut short the life span of those who accepted its rigours.[62] Yet, like Sept-Fons, La Trappe had no dearth of applicants: towards the end of the century, it was said that of the fifty novices who joined every year, only four or five were taken.[63] Visitors found it a frightening place, but serene. Revolutionary officials interviewing the monks noted how they appeared to be happy: 'with the exception of five or six, who seemed to be of limited intelligence, the monks are men of strong and well-balanced personality, not weakened by their fasts and austerities . . . It seemed to us they loved their state in the depths of their hearts.'[64]

VI *The Congregations of Saint-Vanne and Saint-Maur*

The Congrégation de Saint-Vanne was founded at the beginning of the seventeenth century, and it eventually drew into its orbit forty-nine of the old Benedictine houses, all in the provinces of Champagne, Lorraine, and Franche Comté. They were better-populated monasteries than most, for the total of monks in 1765 was over 600. The fourteen bishops of the dioceses where these houses were found faced a dilemma when they made their reports. The Vannists for the most part were Jansenists, yet—or because of the fact—their conduct was hard to fault. The episcopal reports, which covered thirty-six houses, described the monks as morally irreproachable, but deplored their mental attitudes. 'Their studies are perverted . . . they teach "Quesnelism",' said the bishop of Toul. 'It is much to be desired that they become more submissive to the bishops and the laws of the Church,' said the bishop of Verdun.

It was a learned congregation. Dom Calmet, the indefatigable biblical commentator, renowned for his learning and notorious for his naïveté, was one of theirs. His devotion to scholarship extended to inviting Voltaire to study at his abbey of Senones, and at the age of 80 climbing ladders to get down volumes for him; his reward was to have his commentaries plundered for dubious anecdotes to discredit the Scriptures and to have unpleasant suggestions made about his motives for writing about them.[65] There was Dom Sinsart, controversialist against Protestants and an expert on the topography of Hell; Dom Petitdidier, who had once given refuge to Quesnel, but ended up writing anti-Jansenist polemics; Dom Chardon, banned from teaching by the general chapter of 1730 because of his opposition to *Unigenitus*, who published a famous six-volume history of the sacraments fifteen years later.[66] As time went on, the Jansenist writers were silenced, but their *frondeur* spirit lived on in the brothers Cajot, Dom Charles writing a learned study of the Benedictines to recommend their suppression, and Dom Joseph publishing 'a critical history of monastic cowls', ridiculing the habit and those who wore it, himself included.[67]

Special problems arose in a congregation with a tradition of devotion to scholarship. One concerned the government of houses where so many of the inmates were absorbed in their own researches. Dom Sébastien Dieudonné wrote a snide report to Loménie de Brienne in 1774,[68] complaining of how superiors and *procureurs* were left to rule as they pleased, so they travelled round agreeably under pretext of looking after the estates and awarded themselves handsome suites of apartments, habits of fine cloth, and fancy snuff-boxes. (It is remarkable how often snuff-boxes figure in the inventories of misdemeanours in allegations of monastic decadence.) Brienne took this seriously, and feared the rise of 'a vicious aristocracy'. Another problem was the degree of allowable comfort. Reformers held up their hands in horror at the thought of monks with fireplaces in their cells. Dom Ignace de Courcelle pointed out the fallacy of freezing to be holy—if monks gathered round the communal fire, they would gossip and cabal, rather than concentrating on their studies. Even so, concessions to scholars by way of comfort or absence from the choir offices inevitably had the effect of separating them from the rest of the confraternity, a division and breach of community feeling which was to bedevil the most learned congregation of them all, the Benedictines of Saint-Maur.

The Congrégation de Saint-Maur was founded in 1618, in accordance with Gallican prejudice, as a purely French federation. When papal bulls of authorization were issued in 1621, five houses belonged to it; by 1667 there were 161, by 1766, 191—containing a total of 2,456 monks.[69] At the general chapter of 1684, a programme of research and publication, including every aspect of monastic history and editions of the Greek and Latin Fathers, was adopted. Thus, the great Maurist historical enterprise began. The monks received an extensive basic education: two years of classics, two of philosophy, three of theology, and another of 'recollection'. During their studies they were observed by their priors, who reported outstanding talent to the superior-general, who made the final choice of those who were to devote their lives to scholarship. Each established scholar named an assistant (as Mabillon co-opted Dom Germain and after him Dom Ruinart), and as their enterprise proceeded, they could call on the various houses of the congregation for help in locating manuscripts, transcription and translation, indexing, and handling the other chores leading to publication.

Was a lifetime of research a suitable occupation for monks? Rancé, abbot of La Trappe, denounced the idea as an infiltration of worldliness into the cloister. From Saint-Germain-des-Prés, the headquarters of the Maurists, came Jean Mabillon's[70] famous reply, the *Traité des études monastiques* (1691). A Jansenist by intellectual inclination and austerity of life, but not by partisanship, Mabillon distrusted theological studies in the scholastic vein as 'base chicanery'; as for philosophy, Christianity has abridged its subject-matter by 'settling definitively the final end of man and the methods which will bring us to it', leaving only themes for inconclusive wrangling. 'The disputes will go on for ever and men will remain the same, always in error and uncertainty.' So monks must concentrate their studies on the Bible, the Councils, the Fathers, and the developing history of the Church. These were necessary investigations in which certainty could be achieved. Erudition would lead to truth, and truth to charity, thus 'forming in us and others the new man whose likeness was revealed to us in the person of our Saviour'. The controversy was not all it seemed: Rancé had the art of using erudition while concealing it, and Mabillon would have followed learning even if its spiritual advantages had been proved non-existent.

When Mabillon died in 1707, the principles of Maurist research had been established.[71] His *De liturgica gallica* (1685) had made liturgiologists aware of the processes of development and adaptation which had layered over the practices of primitive antiquity: he showed, for example, how the custom of administering extreme unction after the last sacrament rather than before was a thirteenth-century innovation with superstitious overtones. His six volumes of the lives of the Benedictine saints were serene and reverent expositions of verifiable truth, scorning hagiography. And the greatest achievement of all was the *De re diplomatica* (1681), which created the science of authenticating and dating charters and other manuscripts; the many volumes of documents he edited were examples of its application.

Mabillon's work at Saint-Germain-des-Prés was carried on by Bernard de Montfaucon,[72] a soldier-turned-monk who, with military discipline, worked thirteen hours a day, accumulating a knowledge of six ancient and three modern languages, and publishing forty-four vast surveys—in folios—of the monuments of antiquity and of the early centuries of France, a catalogue of European manuscripts, and a pioneering work on Greek palaeography. Around him gathered a band of collaborators, united in scholarly endeavour, even though they differed on 'les affaires du temps', Montfaucon and Dom Martin being hostile to the Jansenists, while Dom Bouquet, who began the *Recueil des historiens des Gaules*, was an appellant and re-appellant. They held a learned discussion group attended by intellectuals from outside the congregation, including Rollin, the Jansenist recteur of the university; Père Tournemine, the editor of the Jesuit *Mémoires de Trévoux*; and Canon Gédoyn of Notre-Dame, author of dilettante essays on 'the urbanity of the Romans' and 'the pleasures of the table among the ancient Greeks'. In 1713, the abbey began to build a new library for its scholars with a gallery extension in the cloister to house manuscripts. Its fame attracted substantial acquisitions—bequests from bishops and magistrates of the parlement and the books of the abbey of Corbie and the chapter of Saint-Maur-des-Fossés (the secular canons here accepting money and a golden monstrance for their chapel in exchange).

Up to the Revolution, the Maurists produced more than 800 volumes: catalogues of manuscripts, descriptions of ancient monuments, collections of source material, grammars (Dom Guérin's Hebrew grammar leading to a splendidly acerbic dispute with canon Masclef of Amiens over the necessity of the Masoretic points[73]), and editions of the Fathers, some of which remained standard texts until our own century. They also turned to French history in a spirit not only of religion, but of patriotism, 'to illustrate the glory of France, to encourage the present generation to emulation lest the race degenerate'. From their indefatigable pens came the early volumes of the *Gallia Christiana*, the *Recueil des historiens des Gaules et de la France*, and, above all, the *Histoire littéraire de la France*, a project 'the mere idea of which makes slothful humanity tremble'. Exceptionally, it was produced, not at Paris, but at Le Mans, for Dom Rivet, its originator, was excluded from the capital as a Jansenist. When he died in 1749, the first eight volumes were in print, and Poncet, Colomb, and Duclou, still working from Le Mans, continued the next four.

In the course of the seventeenth century, the history of half a dozen French abbeys had been written. With Mabillon, the project was advanced by the systematic ransacking of the provincial archives. He himself travelled widely, searching and inspiring others to search, and his assistant, Dom Claude Estiennot, wandered everywhere, expanding the enquiries. One of their successors was Dom Jacques Boyer,[74] who from 1710 to 1714 was riding along the Pyrenees and the southern margins; his journal records some good dinners he enjoyed and the astonishing spectacle of the charter-house of the abbey of Obezine, all the manuscripts missing and a cluster of 300 bats on the ceiling, their dung on the floor a foot deep. The Maurist research tours went on throughout the century, and local antiquaries dropped their pens in despair in face of the competition of the Benedictine machine exhaustively accumulating every scrap of evidence. 'There can be no limit', wrote a canon of Paris in his memoirs, 'to the achievements of those who are so clever and industrious and who always have 400,000 crowns available in their coffers. This was said long ago about the congregation of Saint-Maur.'[75]

Meanwhile, each province had been allotted an official historian. The first to publish was Dom Lobineau on Brittany. A team of five researchers had worked for seven years before him; the first draft was put together at the abbey of Saint-Vincent in Le Mans; and the final version was polished by experts at Saint-Germain-des-Prés; it was presented—a volume of narrative and another of supporting documents—to the estates of Brittany in 1707. Historians being a prickly tribe the world over, there were controversies. From Le Mans, Dom Liron attacked the account of the early invasions of the province; what he said was sound sense, but he was denouncing phantom errors derived from the sight of an earlier version never put into circulation. The Rohan family, which had nagged Lobineau to constrain him to put in their legendary ancestor King Conan, were enraged to find him omitted, and tried to dissuade the estates of Brittany from paying the expenses of publication. Dom Morice, who took over on Lobineau's death in 1727, proved more amenable, and Conan rode again. 'Even if it was demonstrably false, which I do not admit,' wrote Rohan, bishop of Strasbourg, to Morice about the spurious charter on which the claim was grounded, 'it is not for you to say so, still less to prove it, on the contrary, it is fitting for us to defend it as far as it can be.'[76] It was not just the revenues of the abbeys which the aristocracy claimed to appropriate, but also the consciences of the monastic historians.

The estates of Languedoc,[77] burning to catch up with the Bretons, tried to persuade Lobineau to take over their history; he refused, though he sent a memorandum detailing his methodology. The work was done—five volumes by mid-century—by Dom Vaissète and Dom de Vic, the first being a Jansenist, protected against persecution by his collaborator, who was a supporter of *Unigenitus*. But if zeal for research could be a bond of union, it could also be divisive: just as Liron had attacked Lobineau, so Dom Marchard attacked the two historians of Languedoc, ridiculing their prospectus and publishing a rival one of his own, an unfriendly manœuvre among colleagues, which had the covert support of the superior-general. When the general chapter met in 1737, it had before it the first two volumes of the Languedoc history, Morice's revision of Lobineau's Brittany, and the manuscript of the first volume of a history of Burgundy. The meeting decided to press on, concentrating on Normandy, Touraine, Anjou, Maine, Gascony, and Dauphiné, provinces where there were numerous houses of the congregation, and as far as possible appointing local monks as the historiographers.

Yet the research drive was losing impetus. In 1746 Dom Morice wrote to a fellow monk at the abbey of Saint-Florent in Saumur: 'our rulers are vastly indifferent to what has up to now been the glory of the congregation; it is useless to talk to them about our provincial histories'. Sixteen years later another Maurist complained of the abandonment of the history of the province of Berry, researchers being in short supply as a result of 'the crass ignorance and idleness of the recruits who are now joining us'.[78] Even so, the government saw the congregation as its hope for the fulfilment of the plan of the royal historiographer Moreau to create a national archival depository by bringing in collections from all over the country. The general chapter of 1766 agreed to help, declaring: 'we are proud to be called Frenchmen, we wish to be useful to our country'. The work would be put in hand by twelve monks at Saint-Germain-des-Prés and another twelve at the Blancs-Manteaux, all dispensed from the night offices and other duties, with the right to call on help from auxiliaries in the provincial monasteries; for its part, the government promised to pay 1,200 livres annually for each historian seconded to the task. A committee was set up to meet weekly at Saint-Germain-des-Prés under Moreau. The project ran to 1787, when it merged into another of Moreau's creations, a 'Society of French History'. Yet, as organization became formalized, effectiveness declined. There were never more than eighteen historians available for the archival project, and they could not shake off the writing assignments they had already undertaken. The urgency faded from the provincial history ventures. The research teams amassed notes (299 volumes survive for Picardy), but failed to press on to publication. There was a deal of quiet torpid scholarship with no evident public achievement, like Dom de Gennes's fantastically detailed nine-volume catalogue of the 25,000 volumes at the library at Le Mans.[79] (A typical librarian, when the monks proposed to take some of the books away when the Revolution ousted them, he rushed off to give the keys to the municipality, to keep the collections intact.) Dom Rousseau, taking over the history of Champagne at the abbey of Saint-Rémy in Reims from 1752, failed to put his mass of accumulated materials in order; while Dom Housseau, coming in about the same time to direct the four historians working on Anjou, Touraine, and Maine, succeeded in frightening off local historians with rival schemes and in gathering a cartload of notes, but never published a line.[80] Even so, when in 1787 the government asked the superior-general for a list of the works on French history which his monks had produced in the last 150 years, the total was impressive—more than 200.[81]

The erudite productions of the Maurists were to win more approval from the generations of historians who succeeded them than from their own contemporaries. The Enlightenment wanted lively and readable history pointing a humanistic moral. 'The madness to get into print is an epidemic plague which continues unabated,' wrote Voltaire; 'the indefatigable and ponderous Benedictines have just published ten volumes of their *Histoire littéraire de la France*—I won't read them.'[82] In the second half of the century, Dom Colomb complained of the lack of interest in the succeeding volumes of the series: 'a work like ours is not to the taste of our century, it is too serious'. 'Frivolous literature stifles erudition,' wrote another monk; 'people want to read only books that are amusing.'[83] The congregation published the Fathers and monastic history at its own expense, but expected the provinces to pay the historians who wrote their secular chronicles, and laymen in France were notoriously stingy towards clerics—not surprisingly, considering the spectacle of ecclesiastical wealth so ill-distributed. In 1720, Dom Lobineau wrote to the mayor of Nantes saying he was no longer being paid, so he was laying down his pen; henceforward he would do only the duties of his 'office de moine moinant de moinerie'.[84] In 1770, Turgot, the intendant of Limoges, wanted his provincial history written, provided the archbishop of Rouen gave Dom Col a benefice to support his researches.[85] Six years later, Sénac de Meilhan, intendant of Hainault, declared that Dom Bévys would get nothing more than free accommodation in monasteries which were willing to put him up. The province would give nothing, though once a history appeared in print, a 'gratification' might be forthcoming. 'I have seen in several provinces similar enterprises which produced no results, and the most part of the monks who addressed themselves to the task did so with no aim other than to travel and escape for a while from the rule of their monasteries.'[86] Detractors of the Maurists drew attention to the disproportion between the total numbers in the congregation and the limited number of genuine scholars: according to a seventeenth-century critic, 'scarcely forty of them'. This was a strict count of actual writers, not taking into the reckoning researchers, indexers, and other auxiliaries; including all these, there would have been, say, 200.[87] In the mid-eighteenth century the congregation was about 2,500 strong, so the famous works of erudition were the production of a minority. But there were many others who, from the secular and utilitarian point of view, were usefully employed, whether as teachers or administrators, in the *collèges* established in thirty of the abbeys—schools very like those run by the Jesuits and other religious Orders, though the original aim had been to be severely selective, and take only the sons of the nobility.[88] In 1776, when the royal government set up a dozen military academies to improve the quality of candidates for commissions in the army, no fewer than five of these institutions were entrusted to the Maurists. It was partly a question of where spacious buildings and grounds were available, and partly a recognition of the Benedictines' willingness to experiment with a modernized curriculum adapted to practical ends, for the general chapter of 1759 had agreed to make Latin an optional subject and to teach it without the composition of themes and verses, and with a minimum of grammar. The great Benedictine military academies at Sorèze (diocese of Lavaur), Pontlevoy (Blois), and Beaumont (Lisieux) became famous, concentrating on history, geography, modern languages, music, gymnastics, fencing, and riding, with the performance of plays and ballets as a standard recreation. By 1788, Sorèze had forty-six monks engaged in teaching, with numerous lay auxiliaries, and there were 400 boarders. 'What would Saint Benedict say', asked a scandalized academic of the University of Paris, 'if he could come back and see a prize-giving there, with drums and bugles, drill and dancing?' Dom Ferlus made a reply which, in its frank acceptance of Enlightenment values, contrasts sharply with Mabillon's answer to Rancé a century earlier:

If our founder returned to earth, he would begin by looking for us in desert places. Then, finding them now cultivated and populated, with towns in place of rocks and forests and men in place of wild beasts, he would acclaim us as his disciples. He would say, 'Oh my children . . . you have enlarged the work whose foundations I laid, you have spread literacy and enlightenment, you have brought about an educational revolution.'[89]

Monks not engaged in education or teaching—about half the congregation—were left to get on with what Lobineau had contemptuously called 'moinant de moinerie', saying the day and night offices, training the novices, looking after the aged, managing the corporate possessions, and running the domestic affairs of the various houses, dispensing hospitality and contributing to local activities, ecclesiastical and secular, as individuals felt inclined. When we catch glimpses of the life they led, even in unsympathetic observations by anticlericals, it seems to have been generally decorous, though often lacking in fervour, and always comfortable. With revenues rising from the late seventeenth century, the great abbeys spent their surplus on rebuilding programmes.[90] Amid trim formal gardens, neo-classical façades in harmonious local stone arose (there was none of the baroque and rococo exhibitionism of the South German and Italian abbeys). Long ago dormitories had been abandoned, and the individual cells which were built exceeded the modest dimensions officially prescribed. From the beginning of the century, they were being fitted with fireplaces, and new chimney-stacks arose along the skylines of the abbeys. Recruitment did not keep pace with building programmes, and by 1789, in many houses an individual monk had two rooms, and priors sometimes three. There were fine staircases, vestibules, galleries for promenading, and panelled reception rooms for recreation and entertaining. Monks dressed well, their standard habits well tailored, worn with black silk stockings and elegant shoes; they enjoyed hands at cards, games of billiards and tric-trac, and attended concerts and soirées. They dined well, even if the fasts were technically observed, and sometimes they evaded the fasting rules by posting themselves for a while to the infirmary table. The Jansenist Chevalier de Folard,[91] visiting Saint-Germain-des-Prés to receive help with his writing on Polybius, enjoyed intellectual conversation from 11 a.m. to 1 p.m., followed by a dinner which still had not reached the stage of coffee by 5 p.m. (Our knowledge of monastic cuisine comes from laymen who enjoyed the hospitality, then made puritanical remarks about it afterwards.) This was life in an agreeable religious club. 'If I am on the road to heaven,' wrote one of its members, 'I find the carriage very comfortable.'[92]

Though the vows of the Benedictines did not exclude reasonable comforts, they ought to have imposed discipline, and this was lacking in the eighteenth century. The *Unigenitus* quarrel brought strife and bitterness into the life of the community. Most of the Maurists sympathized with the Jansenist cause. Their studies of Church history in the centuries before papal claims were formulated inclined them to Gallicanism, as also their pride at being a purely French congregation. They had quarrelled with the Jesuits over the editing of the works of St Augustine, and there were recurrent aggravations over royal warrants annexing Benedictine priories to bolster the revenues of Jesuit houses. By 1713, intrigues and counter-intrigues in Rome had reached the point that the Pope urged Louis XIV to suppress the congregation altogether.[93] This was an astonishing proposal to put to a Gallican ruler; even so, in his last two years, the ageing king cracked down on the Maurists: a few were imprisoned (one fled to Canada, and one to Holland, to escape this fate[94]); others were exiled to the provinces; and three priors were deposed. Orders were issued to deploy some of the researchers to write in favour of *Unigenitus* (the monks evaded the command by ironically declaring their unwillingness to infringe the prior rights of the better-qualified Jesuits). During the brief thaw under the Regency, most of the monks in most of the abbeys signed the appeal to a General Council (Saint-Nicaise at Reims being a notable exception). At Saint-Germain-des-Prés, the only abstention was by Dom Coustant, a Jansenist, but just about to publish a book on the decretals which he wished to dedicate to the Pope. At the general chapter of 1720, Dom Denis de Sainte-Marthe, an appellant, was elected as superior-general. Then came the years of repression. Chapters were dominated by royal commissioners who excluded Jansenists and dictated the voting; appellants were kept out of official posts, excluded from monastic benefices, and sent off to isolated provincial abbeys. In 1763, of the 193 superiors of houses elected by the general chapter, only one or two were appellants.[95] The Jansenists, silenced, kept in touch with one another through clandestine correspondence.

Repression was effective, but its side-effects were disastrous. Priors imposed on houses received no respect, feuds abounded, and in the poisoned atmosphere latent vices of character emerged, revealing masochistic fanatics, servile hypocrites, boasters, and informers. As the commissioners of the great monastic enquiry of 1765 put it, on the one side were 'Jansenists who pride themselves on their regularity to accredit their party', and on the other, 'Constitutionals who affect submission to the Bull to dispense themselves from the observances'. To the commissioners, most of the monks were unsatisfactory, and of the others, a very few were 'saints', but they were 'isolated and without influence', while rather more were 'upright in their lives but negligent and lacking in fervour'.[96] In this same year when the Commission des réguliers was set up, the state of the congregation came to public notice in a resounding dispute over 'mitigations'.[97] On 15 June, twenty-eight monks of Saint-Germain-des-Prés (all except the prior and two others) petitioned the king for changes in rules and organization, and circulated their request to the other houses asking for adhesions. Their proposals were at once realistic and high-minded. They wanted to bring back free elections, both for officers in individual abbeys and for representatives from the six provinces to the general chapter. They also wished to rationalize arrangements by setting aside certain named houses for specialist tasks: two to receive novices, one for teaching canon law, one for learned languages, one for retired scholars, with Saint-Germain-des-Prés and the Blancs-Manteaux remaining as the centres of erudition. In each province, they proposed to turn one abbey into a seminar where a few young nobles would be given a theological education. Learning was to be encouraged by sending monks to study in the universities of Paris and of Reims, and by setting up a special committee to allot funds for research. As for 'mitigations', all they asked was to return to the old Benedictine monastic dress, to limit fasting to Lent, Advent, and three days a week at other seasons, and to make bedtime and getting up time two hours later, saying matins earlier, to avoid the nocturnal pilgrimage to chapel. A few vexatious trivialities were to be abandoned, like the prescription of an exact contour for the tonsure or the obligation to hold the cup in both hands when drinking. There was nothing in their petition against the spirit of St Benedict. 'Better a less severe rule with general conformity than a severe one ill observed' sums up their object.[98] The twenty-eight signatories included most of the established scholars—the editors of the *Gallia Christiana* and the other great collections and the writers of the provincial histories. As scholars, they were already exempt from matins and other time-consuming routines; they wished to get monastic communities together, themselves included, for the saying of all the offices.

Alas! with the incautious exaggeration of academic polemicists, they presented their case in a form calculated to arouse opposition and misrepresentation. They denounced 'despotism', thus alarming all in authority, and they referred to the 'minute practices' and 'pointless austerities' which 'keep away recruits from the nobility', giving the impression that they merely wished to make life easier for themselves. Their petition raised an outcry. The archbishop of Paris got the king to forbid Saint-Germain-des-Prés asking the houses for support. The superior-general sent round a circular denouncing this 'work of darkness', this 'yearning for the flesh-pots of Egypt. We must praise the Lord more especially in the silence of the night,' he said, 'when all nature seems buried in oblivion of its Creator.' He also forwarded a protest to the king, which 800 monks joined in signing. Some signed twice, and others came back from the dead to add their names. With the Commission des réguliers investigating discipline and some abbeys in danger of suppression, this was no time to conceal one's zeal under a bushel. The Blancs-Manteaux, jealous of the priority given to Saint-Germain-des-Prés more than a century ago, joined in the attack. Midnight psalmody, they said, was a practice of the earliest Christians, as attested by Pliny, and Peter the Venerable had described monks who break abstinence as crows, wolves, and bears. Three years later, long after the proposal for mitigations had been withdrawn, they were still thundering self-righteously against this apostasy.[99] The rank and file of monks seem to have agreed with one of the more temperate censures levelled against the petitioners by their superior-general—they were trying to make the congregation 'a society of men of letters, free and almost independent'. Most monks, not being concerned with scholarly activity, wished life to go on as usual. This meant supporting a régime of austerity which in practice they would ignore: as Tocqueville said, here was the essence of the *ancien régime*: 'règle rigide, pratique molle'. The defeat of the 'mitigations' was a victory for orthodoxy and unreality.

By now, the bitter divisions inherited from the Jansenist quarrel were ingrained and permanent, even as the original issues were coming to be forgotten. The general chapter at Saint-Denis in 1766 told the Commission des réguliers that the principal 'abuse' was 'the spirit of independence' which set the rank and file against authority—as the deputies to the chapter were heads of houses, the observation was predictable. The Commission itself thought the fault lay with the superiors.[100] By their thriftless inefficiency, they had allowed the congregation to run up a debt of nine million—so much for their right to rule. As for relations with their monks, they were too harsh to make the rule loved and too lax in their own conduct to make it respected.

Against the spectacle of decadence and feuding in the Congregation of Saint-Maur should be set the worthiness of so many individuals. They should be judged not by the monastic ideal as represented in pious handbooks and the sermons addressed to them at their profession, but by the notion of 'my station and its duties' which their families and society expected of them. There were the learned heroes of the Jansenist cause:[101] Dom Gesvres, who died at the age of 48, worn out by working fourteen hours a day in defence of the theology of Antoine Arnauld; Dom Gerberon, exile in

Holland, prisoner in the fortress of Vincennes, and writer of a vast number of polemics, the list of them occupying twenty-four pages in the *Histoire littéraire* of the congregation; Dom Massuet, who produced a digest of the Greek Fathers whose writings supported predestination; Dom Martienay, who published his translation of the New Testament in defiance of the censors; Dom Coustant, who never received visitors, never used a fire, and whose only relaxation from learning was an annual five days' walking tour. Their lives were austere; but austerity was not a Jansenist monopoly—Dom Charles de l'Hostallerie, superior-general from 1714 to 1720, ate sparingly, drank only water, devoted himself to prayer, and passed his final year of retirement at the age of 80 in teaching his servant to read.[102]

As the Jansenist propagandists died off or were silenced, the historical researchers dominated the work of the congregation. No others achieved the greatness of Mabillon and Montfaucon, but there were many who rivalled them in exactitude of conduct and indefatigable industry. Some come alive to us in their correspondence—above all, Dom Lobineau. Angular and legalistic, as befitted a descendant of an old legal family of Rennes, offering good value and demanding good money for it, with a sardonic wit which did not exclude self-mockery (as over his disastrous donkey ride on a Breton beach), given to wine and overwork, he toiled on, striving to complete his quota of writing before fate thrust him down 'into that damned worm-hole by which we have to go to Paradise'. And whatever sins he may have had to account for, obsequiousness to the great was not one of them, as the anger of the Rohan family bore witness. His older contemporary, Dom Denys Briant, another Breton, provides an interesting contrast, being a historian *malgré lui*, 'leafing through old books which so often tell me nothing, seeking out the names of the abbots no one cares about, amid an impenetrable confusion of old papers'. This research he hated; his real interest was in accumulating ideas to compose the definitive treatise on moral philosophy, 'how to live and how to die', a work which he never completed.[103]

The tradition of scholarship continued to produce dedicated characters right up to the Revolution, like Jean-Pierre Deforis,[104] who edited the works of Bossuet, not without controversy. He died heroically on 25 June 1794, standing on the platform of the guillotine, insisting on going last under the blade so that he could exhort the younger victims to fortitude. But in the last generation of the *ancien régime*, a new kind of learning became fashionable in the congregation, in the form of the contributions to controversy and competitions of wit which characterized the provincial culture of the Enlightenment. Such were the satires, odes, and essays which won Dom Maugier[105] so many prizes of the Academy of Caen, and the disquisitions on electricity, mesmerism, the physiological problem of the 'fluide nerveux', and the proof that republicanism was the best form of government which made Dom Gourdin the oracle of the academy of Rouen.[106] There was a Maurist who died in 1763 as prior of the minor benefice of Gennes, who published more than any of them, and in his own right was a major figure of the literature of the Enlightenment. From the first he had been unsure of his call to the monastic life. A priest and working in Saint-Germain-des-Prés on the *Gallia Christiana*, he knew his vocation was gone: 'my books were my faithful friends, but like me, they were dead'. In his cell he wrote the four volumes of the *Mémoires d'un homme de qualité*, a novel in which he described his superior-general and colleagues under the guise of the monks of the Escurial. He fled to England, came back, and was absolved and reintegrated into the congregation, remaining nominally a member even when chaplain to the Prince de Conti. All the while his hallucinatory imagination moved on, creating worlds which to him were more substantial than everyday reality.[107]

Those who publish, whether *Manon Lescaut*, like the abbé Prévost, or the *Histoire de Bretagne*, like Dom Lobineau, survive in historical memory; so too do many of those who indulge in intrigue and faction fights. But information is lacking about the ordinary majority who, with how strong a vocation we know not, joined in the natural course of things and led uneventful lives. Dom Benoît de Monceau d'Anvoile,[108] of a noble family, joined the Maurists with two of his brothers, ruled four houses successfully as prior, then in 1717, at the early age of 48, retired to Saint-Denis, where he ran the business affairs of the abbey; five years later he died, heroically ministering to the sick in an outbreak of smallpox. Others had more modest careers. Dom Benoît Dassac[109] followed his elder brother into the congregation, looked after the novices at Grasse, then became sub-prior at Avignon. Until the Revolution, nothing more startling is recorded in his journal than the cutting down of meals to a single course during the harsh winter of 1788–9 so as to be able to give more to the poor. Dom Pierre Chastelain, son of a cooper at Reims, joined the Maurists there and towards the end of his life succeeded in getting posted back to end his days in familiar surroundings. He had a few troubles because of his Jansenist connections, but nothing more serious than a malicious librarian locking up some books he needed. The brightest pages of his record concern the four days' holiday the abbey of Saint-Denis allowed him in 1733, at the age of 24. With a fellow monk and a small allowance of pocket-money, he spent a night at the Cordeliers of Noisy, saw the Trianon and the menagerie at Versailles, and the famous water-pumping machine at Marly, dined on the last day at Saint-Germain-des-Prés, and got back 'in a cart that charges five *sous* a seat to Saint-Denis in time for compline, very pleased to have seen such fine things. *Sic transit Gloria mundi.*'[110]

The young in their naïveté can scorn the glories of the world and believe that they will continue to do so. The abbé Prévost knew from the start the fickleness and ambiguity of vocation. Shortly after he was professed, he wrote:

I know the weakness of my heart, and I understand how important it is for my peace not to apply myself to sterile studies which will leave my heart dry and enfeebled. If I want to be happy in religion, I must conserve in all its force the inspiration of the grace which brought me to it. I know only too well—I realize it daily—how far I can sink if I lose the great rule from sight for a single moment, or even if I look with the least complaisance on certain images which all too often intrude into my mind.[111]

As with the individual, so too with the institution itself, the inspiration of grace faded as the monasteries became integrated into the social order, with the monastic vocation an ordinary way of life along with all the others.

VII *The Achievements of the Commission*

The working of the Commission des réguliers and the limited nature of its achievements is an illustration of the impossibility of radical reform under the *ancien régime*. As often, there was a change of ministry: in 1770, Brienne's backer, Choiseul, fell from power. The parlements, defending liberty as they saw it, stood by to protect the monks from arbitrary interventions; letters patent registered by the law courts were needed for the setting up of a monastic Order in France, so the magistrates considered themselves entitled to exercise a watching brief over them. Soon they were declaring the Commission 'an illegal tribunal', concerned with 'destroying rather than reforming'. The general assemblies of the clergy were a forum for episcopal complaint. The Pope was dissatisfied, and resort to extreme courses of action would have driven him to refuse the bulls of reform or suppression which—in the end—he usually conceded. Some Orders had foreign generals stationed in Rome, jealous of their rights and objecting to proposed changes in France because of their international implications. Other Orders, with their higher command in France, had foreign dependencies inaccessible to coercion from Versailles, their abbots threatening to secede if their interests were infringed. And above all, there was the play of aristocratic influence at court and of agitation by local notables in the provinces. Influence ruled much of what was done in eighteenth-century France, and dictated a great deal of what could not be done.

To end disputes between monks and their superiors and to adjust the rules, whether towards severity or towards mitigation, Brienne proposed to revise the existing monastic constitutions. He wished to promote 'democracy' by having more ordinary monks elected as conventuals at general chapters, to have superiors holding office for only limited periods, and to tie up provincials by compelling them to consult a committee of assessors, a 'définitoire'. He proceeded by authoritarian means, despatching royal commissioners (usually two, generally bishops) to the meetings of general chapters, if necessary arming them with *lettres de cachet* to exclude potential opponents. These authoritarian measures prevailed with seven congregations. Reforms in a 'democratic' direction were imposed on the Génovéfains, the Trinitaires, Picpus, and the Grands Carmes. Some mitigations were allowed to the Récollets, but none to Picpus; the separate Orders of the Trinitaires were united, and the provinces of Picpus increased from four to six for convenience of administration. Saint-Vanne did not need constitutional change, for its general chapters already had an equal number of elected monks and priors voting; certain games (*jeux*) were allowed as 'better than useless conversation', and priors holding independent benefices had to surrender their income to their monastery. By contrast, Saint-Maur was a prime example of 'despotism', with general chapters composed only of superiors. New rules therefore added twelve conventuals to the thirty-three existing ones, and superiors were limited to a reign of seven years. But it was not long before all the old feuding broke out again. General chapters continued to be scenes of chaos and of bleak authoritarian intervention. The royal commissioners at the meeting of 1778 reported the six provinces to be acting like independent congregations competing against each other for offices and power. In 1783, the parlement of Paris made the opposite complaint about the extraordinary chapter held at Saint-Denis: the prelates attending as commissioners in the king's name had used *lettres de cachet* to dragoon the voters into fraudulent unanimity. The Maurists, said the magistrates, 'will soon be just an incoherent assembly of individuals, strangers to one another'. In the following year, a lay observer complained of the lawsuits against abbots and priors which were bringing some houses to the brink of insolvency. The superior-general himself, in March 1788, wrote despairingly to the government. The education of novices was being neglected, since those who ought to teach them were more concerned with intrigues to draw them into partisan allegiances, while honest men were no longer prepared to accept office and responsibility, given the impossibility of doing any good. 'C'en est fait de la Congrégation de Saint-Maur,' he said; 'it's all up with the congregation if the reign of anarchy goes on much longer.'[112]

Other congregations refused changes, or delayed them. Monks whose conduct was irreproachable and who were not divided proved impregnable: the Feuillants, Chancelade, and the Carthusians retained their existing organization unchanged. Brienne accepted the rule of a general for life in the Congregation of Le Sauveur; its monks were austere and Jansenist—far be it from him to give them a *définitoire* as a discussion forum for their dying heresy. Cluny, left to its commendatory abbot, the archbishop of Rouen, did not have a new constitution approved in Rome until May 1789.

Cîteaux had 'foreign' houses, which helped to prevent change. The feud between the abbot-general and the proto-abbots had brought the Order near to ruin; the Commission decided to bring dissension to an end by a new and definitive constitution. Two royal commissioners (the bishop of Senlis and the intendant of the province of Burgundy) attended the general chapter of 1768[113] to compel action. A committee was set up to draft new statutes, but it was chosen to reflect the balance of the assembly, which was thirty-one for the general and twenty-three for the proto-abbots. So it was a committee of five, dividing three against two, though the representatives of the minority, the abbots of Chaloche and La Trappe were tough characters. Predictably, there were two rival projects presented to the general chapter of 1771. Royal policy was indecisive; Versailles was pressed towards the side of the proto-abbots by the bishop of Senlis, the papal nuncio, and Mme Louise, the king's pious daughter, and towards the abbot-general's side by Mercy d'Argenteau, the Austrian ambassador. After wrangling for a month, the longest meeting ever, the representatives dispersed with nothing decided. The deadlock was insuperable so long as the Germans came, but at the general chapter of 1783 there were only four, since the anticlerical Emperor Joseph II had refused travel permits to the rest. So, by twenty-one votes to fifteen, a royal decree proclaiming a new constitution was accepted. The *Definitorum* would be the supreme authority, its decisions binding unless overturned by a unanimous vote of the general chapter. These chapters would meet triennially at fixed dates without the need for formal summons, and the proto-abbots were to have authority over their affiliated abbeys independent of general headquarters at Cîteaux.

At the next assembly in 1786, with the defeated abbot-general and the victorious proto-abbots at last working in harmony, a belated programme of reform was agreed. It was decided to go along with the times and win public approval by running free boarding-schools for the 'sons of nobles and poor but deserving commoners'. The abbey of Morimond opened such a school for twenty boys in the very same year,[114] and other abbots announced their preparations. The Order resolved to pay off the debts of the Collège de Saint-Bernard in Paris and put the buildings in order to house a central seminary to train monks as teachers. Men of the Enlightenment wondered why something like this had not been done a century ago.

The generals of the Capuchins, the Dominicans, and the Discalced Carmelites held up reforms. The Capuchins were ruled from Rome by a Frenchman, P. Aimé de Lamballe; his letter of protest was given by Mme Louise, the king's Carmelite daughter, to her father when he visited her convent. The Spanish general of the Grands Augustins raised no overt difficulties, but he may have pulled strings behind the scenes, for Rome never approved the 1772 revision. The Commission wished to unite the two observances of the Cordeliers and make the rule of life stricter; the friars outwitted the reformers by agreeing at once to a union in which the practices of the lax observance were preserved, a change promptly accepted by the Franciscan Pope Clement XIV in 1771.

Some Orders were suppressed. In almost every case the monks wanted to go, and Brienne encouraged them with the offer of generous pensions, as he said, 'making bridges of gold for whoever wishes to give up his rights'. The canons of Saint-Ruf had already asked for a bull of secularization in 1760, and the Brigittins (only two houses in existence) in 1762. From 1742, the Servites de Marie had been forbidden to take novices, and now had only fourteen priests, all old. The canons of Saint-Antoine voted their own demise. The Commission delayed implementing it in the hope (vain, as it turned out) of keeping their property for ecclesiastical use—it went to the Order of Malta. There were only 168 Célestins, and all except eight wanted to be secularized. The rule of 1670 had not been observed within living memory, they said, and the vows which they had taken were to the comfortable way of life which they had seen. Their Italian general opposed them, and it was not until 1776 that they began drawing their generous pensions. The argument of the Célestins—that the *status quo* was the implied condition of the vows they had taken—was respectable by the standards of the day; the fervent Camaldolese also used it. Faced with an order to unite their six houses into one, they decided to abandon the monastic life altogether, since their 'peace of mind' amid familiar companions and in familiar surroundings would be lost.

Loménie de Brienne ruthlessly made sure that this same argument for leaving their monasteries was forced upon the monks of Grand-mont. Attending as royal commissioner at their general chapter of 1768, he ruled that only those monks who undertook to go back to the original rule of the twelfth century would be allowed to stay. This meant a diet of bread and vegetables and a life in silence. Recruitment was cut off by banning the taking of novices, and the bishops were instructed to close houses as they fell empty, allocating pensions to the monks and appropriating the rest of the property for diocesan works. But there were legal formalities which could be invoked as barriers against arbitrary action, and old Dom Mondain quickly learned how to make use of them. Not until his death in 1787 was the bishop of Limoges able to take over the mother-house, having lost a lot of money in legal fees during the intervening years. The episcopal palace was completed, while the abbey of Grandmont was demolished, the lead from the roof and the enamels from the altars sold, and the manuscripts disposed of by weight for use as wrapping paper.[115]

By contrast, the Order of La-Merci, with only 120 monks, raised no legal objections, but authorized its nineteen houses to negotiate with the local bishops for suppression. Even so, there were difficulties with the foreign general and the king of Spain, so that in 1788, seven houses were still in existence. The Benedictine congre-gation so-called of the Exempts (eleven houses and sixty-eight monks) refused to change its statutes or to name houses for suppres-sion, so royal letters patent were issued to pension them off (which the parlement suspended to allow the general chapter to vote its own end). It was discovered that two of their abbeys had no buildings, the monks simply living at home and drawing their money.[116]

The winding up of small and moribund Orders was not much more than a tidying-up operation on the margins of the monastic

problem. The Commission hoped to achieve more by the suppression of individual houses. The criterion for the decision was to be a
new rule of 'conventuality': the minimum number in a house which
was part of a congregation was to be ten, and fifteen in isolated ones.
Merely to keep the liturgical offices going and to administer the
property would need as many, and small numbers encouraged
somnolent conspiracies of idleness, and facilitated absorption into the
secular world outside the gates. This was a fact of observation, but
churchmen challenged the limitation on grounds of theology, canon
law, tradition, and utility.[117] 'Where two or three are gathered
together, there I am in the midst,' Jesus had said. Some rural areas
would be deprived of spiritual support, and with a plenteous harvest
the labourers would be few. Early councils of the Gallican Church
had defined conventuality as consisting in six monks, or even three.
The wishes of founders were being ignored; so too were the wishes
of the present generation, for by the strict legal procedures for an
'alienation' of ecclesiastical property, the local inhabitants and the
monks ought to be consulted, and the agreement of the bishop
and of the Roman Curia obtained. What would happen to the
employees of a suppressed house, to those who relied on its alms, to
travellers who expected hospitality in difficult terrain?

Enforcing conventuality was not easy. Saint-Vanne and the
Feuillants, for good reasons, and the Cistercians, for bad ones,
escaped unscathed. Cluny suffered little until 1787–8, when a final
revival of the reforming impulse caused the closure of the forty-four
houses of the old observance. The story of the suppressions among
the Anciens Bénédictins (37) and in Saint-Maur (only 21 out of 191
houses) is a revelation of the operation of the web of influences
over provincial France. There were petitions to preserve pilgrimage
sites and famous relics, orders from parlements prohibiting action,
bishops wanting to retain help in parishes, and parishes wanting to
retain schoolmasters, peasants revolting with sticks and muskets,
intrigues by duchesses, marshals of France, and magistrates. The
abbey of Troarn survived in spite of the vote of all its monks to
leave; Brienne wrote to the bishop of Bayeux to say that he could
not find where the opposition came from. Significantly, when an
abbey was suppressed and its revenues diverted to worthy diocesan
projects, the commendatory abbot still continued to draw his
abusive revenues; real abbots and priors could be evicted, but the
absentee, nominal ones had their pensions for life.

The canons regular suffered little, since the king insisted that the
parochial cures they served must all be maintained. Only fifteen

houses of Génovéfains were closed, fifteen of the Augustinians, one of Prémontrés and none of Chancelade. The Trinitaires lost sixteen establishments; the official total was double this, but half of these were empty already. Mostly the mendicants were allowed to keep their tiny groups of friars scattered over the land, since the bishops required their help in the parishes. The Récollets lost about a hundred friaries, but many of them were virtually empty already. The Cordeliers lost only 51 out of 345, the Capuchins only 22 out of 451. The Discalced Carmelites preserved all but four of their sixty-two establishments by acting quickly and drafting their members around to fill depleted contingents. The Grands Carmes with only 67 friars and 129 houses to maintain seemed in a hopeless position, but they lost only 22 establishments—Mme Louise, the king's daughter, was a Carmelite nun.

Even the worldly Dominicans lost only 20 friaries out of 179. When it came to the crunch, their preachers were needed. But the careless life-style in their friaries continued. A report of 1778 on the Parisian house on the rue Saint-Honoré spoke of 'dissipation and worldliness; everyone arrogates to himself the liberty to act as he thinks good'. Across in the rue Saint-Jacques a prior specially installed by a commission of reform was writing to the general in Rome asking to be released; the place, he said, 'is less a monastic community than a boarding-house where practically everyone is concerned with his own affairs'.[118] A new prior was sent, and was confronted by a rival prior illegally elected by the community. And both these Parisian houses were virtually bankrupt. The *collège* in the rue Saint-Jacques was in terminal disrepair, the chapel having been closed eight years ago as dangerous. The prior thanked Providence for the crumbling façade when mobs began to search other monasteries for hoarded food supplies—they did not trouble the obviously penurious Jacobins. In this same revolutionary year the other Parisian house (in the rue Saint-Honoré) sold its silver to keep solvent, and rented out its refectory to the Club Breton, later to be called the Jacobin Club. 'Thus, for 200 francs had been created the most terrible and powerful instrument of the Revolution,' wrote Lenôtre.

The Commission's most effective interventions were embodied in two royal edicts which could have been issued without any preliminary investigations, by the sole light of nature. The first, in March 1768, made a change which was much applauded by lay society. The age for taking monastic vows was raised from 16 for both sexes to 21 for men and 18 for women. As Joly de Fleury insisted, it was impossible to marry without parental consent before the age of 25, or to proceed to holy orders before 22. Celibacy, he said, is against nature, therefore extra years are required for mature consideration. The second edict, that of February 1773, was a Gallican document designed to increase the powers of bishops over the monasteries in their dioceses, and to codify the powers they had already.[119] A monastery could not accept foundation masses or sponsor a lay confraternity, and a monk could not be ordained, preach, or hear confessions without formal diocesan permission. Houses not under a general chapter were to be under episcopal tulelage, requiring approvals for their elections of priors, administrators of property, and masters of novices. In these and all other houses the bishop was authorized to intervene to suppress scandal, provided he gave the monks six months' warning and then conducted his visitation in person. Foreign generals could continue to exercise their jurisdiction, but not from Rome: the case had to be heard in France, and the verdict needed validation by royal letters patent.

The Assembly General of the clergy of France had no grievances against the edict of 1773, but it regarded that of 1768 on the age of taking vows as disastrous. There was an immediate gap in the flow of vocations, and once this mathematical hiatus ended, the psychological effect continued, for in the five years between 16 and 21 young men could so easily decide to follow worldly ambitions and affections. According to the archbishop of Arles, the trend of declining vocations predicted the end of all the mendicant Orders within forty years and of all the others after another thirty. The protests of the assemblies of clergy in 1770, 1772, 1775, and 1780 helped to bring the Commission des réguliers to an end. In 1780, it was transformed into a committee with a different name and limited powers, and Brienne left the scene. The proposed reform had achieved little, but had stirred up lay opinion, intensifying doubts about the usefulness of monks and whetting desires to appropriate monastic property.

20

VOCATION AND THE ART OF
OBTAINING A BENEFICE

I

'Before the foundation of seminaries', said Godeau, bishop of Grasse in the mid-seventeenth century, 'the doctrine of the divine vocation to the ecclesiastical state was practically unknown.'[1] He was using the word 'doctrine' in the technical sense of an officially formulated statement of belief; vocation—the thing in itself—was evident everywhere in the Old and New Testaments, whether it was the calling of Israel as a nation and the Pauline election of the people of God to salvation, or the special calling of individuals to service— Abraham, Samuel, the prophets, Jesus himself, and his disciples. The problem with the individual vocation was: how to authenticate it. The onlooker might be sceptical, and the person called would wonder how to be certain—has God spoken to me in a dream, or did I dream God spoke to me? With the advent of the seminary, it became important to have criteria to judge authenticity, if only to help and encourage the candidates for ordination. Antoine Godeau, learned, dwarf-like, with an ear for poetry and (in his younger days) an eye for women, visiting and reforming his mountain diocese, was a realist about the sort of clergy the Counter-Reformation needed. He did not want readers of Plato and Aristotle, but men who knew their New Testament and were expert at giving advice in the confessional; and they must have conviction. 'In a seminary,' he wrote, 'the matter to which particular attention must be paid is the testing of the vocation of the young clerics.'[2] In his *Discours de la vocation ecclésiastique* (1651), he laid down the questions to be asked, codifying the ideas current in the first half of the century. A candidate for ordination must ask himself, he said: 'Am I living a moral life?' 'Are my intentions pure?' 'Do I possess the requisite ability?' 'Am I praying to God daily to help me to remain unswervingly loyal to the ecclesiastical profession in the depths of my mind?'[3]

With elaborations, these questions formed the basis for later discussions of vocation. Louis Habert (1708) made more specific the tests for purity of intention—they were to include a disinclination to pursue the things of this world, a devotion to the discipline of the Church, and zeal for the glory of God. 'Discipline'—in Habert and in Sevoy's *Devoirs ecclésiastiques* (1763) there was a greater emphasis on objective tests imposed by the Church. A vocation is justified if the confessor approves it, the bishop accepts it, and the testimony of the people confirms it—though this testimony is unadventurously defined as 'evidence of a good reputation'.[4] While the casuists were ruthless in condemnation of anyone who actually sought promotion in the Church, they emphasized that when the Church in its wisdom offered high office, it ought not to be refused. Humility, fear, distrust of the worldly manœuvres of relatives, were not adequate motives for refusing a bishopric; indeed, there was an obligation to accept when 'the Pope or another legitimate superior orders'.[5]

To us, something seems lacking in these analyses: what of sheer 'attraction', the impulse in the soul, the hearing of God's voice— 'Magister adest et vocat te'? But we should not judge the eighteenth-century idea of vocation in the context of our own social order, in which the Church is a marginal community, and in the light of more complex ideas of psychological motivation reached through recent controversies.[6] Given the ordinariness of a career in the Church, and the rewards which such a career might offer, stern moralists at the end of the seventeenth and the beginning of the eighteenth centuries were inclined to reject 'attraction' as a dangerous concept. M. Olier (in a treatise posthumously published in 1675) and Louis Habert saw a sentimental attraction to the ecclesiastical life and the ardent desire for priestly office as dangerous; they could well be superficial, or arise from 'interest'. Later, however, the eighteenth century's rehabilitation of 'happiness' and its reconciliation of the human desire for self-fulfilment with the will of God for man seem to have had their effect, in a cautious way, on the idea of ecclesiastical vocation. This is evident in Sevoy, and in the anonymous *Conduite des âmes dans la voie du salut* (1750), where it is stated that 'L'inclination est la principale marque de la vocation de Dieu'. Given the requisite qualities and being in a state of grace and under the direction of ecclesiastical authority, a man was free to follow his impulses.

Maybe so, but one thing was certain to all the casuists and spiritual writers. A man must not seek any sort of comfort or pre-eminence from his vocation to the ministry; nor was he allowed to procure advantages of any kind for his family and friends. It was wrong to apply for a position of dignity and honour, even if worthy of it; as for rewards, a priest should ask only for enough to live on decently (*l'honnête subsistance*).[7] Relatives were not to be supported from an income derived from ecclesiastical sources; the most that was allowed was the giving of a very small sum to fathers or mothers to preserve them from utter destitution. If the sight of aged parents in poverty was too harrowing, a cleric must move away from them, lest he be tempted to liberality.[8] Whatever promotion came along, it must be freely offered, never solicited, even indirectly. Hence Tronson's subtle grounds of reproach to Fénelon when he became tutor to the duc de Bourgogne—sophisticated self-interest lurks behind our conviction that we are disinterested: we do not seek to exercise influence, but we remove obstacles; we do not solicit the great, but we take care to show ourselves to them in the best light; 'no one can be entirely certain that he has not called himself', instead of waiting for the calling of God.[9]

This was the ideal of an ecclesiastical vocation as the theologians defined it and as it was taught in the seminaries—a vocation based on the honest conviction (after all advice was taken) that one's life was pure, one's intentions disinterested, and one's abilities adequate; a vocation sustained by prayer for lifelong steadfastness, emphasizing allegiance to the Church, and, indeed, closely supervised by ecclesiastical authority; a vocation within which all worldly desires, including even affection for parents, were virtually annihilated. The object of this chapter is to test the theoretical ideal by looking at sources other than ecclesiastical, principally at the handbooks of the lawyers, and to see what had to be done in practice to get ordained and established in a benefice.

II

The first step on the way to a clerical career was the taking of the tonsure. According to the Council of Trent, 7 was the minimum age, though French bishops were inclined to set a rather later time.[10] Confirmation was usually a prerequisite, but not, apparently, First Communion.[11] No spiritual power or office was conferred by the tonsure ceremony—which consisted of little more than the snipping off of a lock of hair—and no clerical obligations were undertaken.[12] The essential point was: the tonsure admitted its recipient to the order of the clergy, and made possible the holding of benefices (provided no cure of souls was involved). Next came the four minor orders (porter, lector, exorcist, acolyte); again, no indelible clerical character was conferred, and the way back to a lay vocation remained open.[13] The decisive commitment came with admission to the subdiaconate, for which the minimum age was 21 (or, according to some ecclesiastical lawyers, 22). At this stage, a vow of perpetual chastity was taken, and a sort of banns were called in church before-hand, asking if the candidate had made some previous promise of marriage.[14] A year later, promotion to the diaconate was allowable, and at the age of 25, ordination to the priesthood. Before admission to the subdiaconate, the candidate had to demonstrate that he would not become a burden to the Church which he was undertaking to serve in perpetuity: hence the necessity for a 'clerical title'. This meant that he had to prove the possession of a permanent income, whether from his patrimony or from a benefice. In the diocese of Paris, 150 livres[15] annually was required; it was less—80 to 100, in the provinces.

A family of the poorer sort would have to reflect on ways and means—possibly all clubbing together—to produce the necessary capital; it was roughly about the amount which would be required to buy a minor judicial office.[16] A father making provision for his sons in his will might lay aside a sum to pay fees at a seminary and a 'pension sacerdotale' for any who might choose to seek ordination; this was done by a bourgeois of Nantes, Carrier, and one of the sons was the future terrorist, the inventor of the infamous *noyades*.[17] A clerical title was supposed to be inalienable, but in practice, a clause was sometimes inserted in the contract specifying that the endow-ment would revert to the family once a benefice of a suitable income had been acquired.[18] The contract, formally drawn up by a notary, would be witnessed by three or four persons, who engaged to make good, out of their own pockets, any deficiency in the property or other investments which were meant to yield the income of the 'title'.[19] The whole document had to be read out in Church on three successive Sundays, at the time of calling marriage banns and giving notices. The formula of publication ended with: 'If anyone knows that the possessions enumerated in the aforesaid contract are not of the value therein declared, or that they are not in full ownership quit of all other obligations, or that they do not belong [to the donor], let him so declare to me that all occasion of fraud may be avoided.'[20] Occasionally, there would be an objection: Père Coudrin, later to become famous for his austere spirituality, found his right to proceed to the subdiaconate challenged by creditors of his father, a pious man whose zeal to further his son's vocation was not matched by strict accountability in the affairs of the market-place.[21] A certificate that the contract had been published unopposed was required, along with the standard attestation of faith and morals, when a candidate for the subdiaconate presented himself to his bishop.

In addition to ordination *sub titulo patrimonii* or *sub titulo beneficii* there was a third way—*sub titulo paupertatis*.[22] A monk who had taken a vow of poverty could be so accepted, and the privilege was extended to the 'prêtres hibernois', the miserable Irish clerics who hung around so many towns doing odd jobs in churches and hiring themselves out to families to walk in funeral processions. The fact was: the bishop was the judge of who could be ordained, irrespective of all other considerations. When Fleury was bishop of the tiny, poverty-stricken diocese of Fréjus, he made up the numbers of his clergy by ordaining some whose title was 'la mense commune'—he would see to their support, provided they were at his disposal to be sent to take parish services.[23] Or a bishop might bestow the subdiaconate on someone with the understanding that a benefice would be following soon—probably the job of vicaire in some grim rural parish. One such cleric in November 1790 wrote to the Constituent Assembly asking that priests of this sort be not overlooked in the awarding of pensions now that Church property was to be sold. He himself had come in this way in 1788, 'sub titulo ab ordinario approbando'; this was Joseph Le Bon, the future terrorist.[24]

Long before ordination, the search for benefices had begun—something to support a course of study, to contribute towards the clerical 'title,' and to form a supplement to income in the longer-term future. France was full of 'chapels', 'prebends', and 'priories', minor benefices without care of souls, available to ecclesiastics once they had received the tonsure. These *bénéfices simples*, reformers always said, should be secularized or abolished;[25] indeed, search was made among them for income that could be confiscated whenever a new seminary, hospital, or *collège* was founded. Local officials (consulted, as the law prescribed, about these 'unions') were torn between the desire to accumulate endowments for a public amenity and regret at the prospect of supplements to the incomes of their sons being lost. Some 'chapels' had minor duties attached to them, like teaching Latin to local children; others were outright sinecures, like the one that the prince de Beauvau gave to a young theological student, son of his business manager.[26] Even sinecures, however, needed a certain amount of work put into them to collect and improve their revenue; repairs were an eternal problem, litigation was always a possibility, and research among old charters to safeguard rents and dues was a necessary precaution.[27] A curé, M. Marquis-Ducastel, has left a record of his father's unavailing attempts to get

him a benefice to pay for his seminary and university education. The
father, a minor official on the staff of the dauphin at Versailles,
pondered long on how best to enlist the aid of the great prince he
served. Finally he wrote to him, and the dauphin sent the petition
to Cardinal de La Rochefoucauld, who held the royal *feuille des
bénéfices*. Success seemed certain, but eight days later, on 29 April
1757, the cardinal died. A hard-up student in his seminary, Marquis-
Ducastel became friendly with a young man who gave up his ecclesiastical vocation and turned over to him a chapel in the jurisdiction
of the cathedral of Mâcon. Alas! its income turned out to be
exiguous, and he found himself in the ridiculous position of having
a useless benefice which he dared not surrender, as there was a
considerable bill for repairs which would have to be settled before
handing over to a successor. At Versailles, his father was still trying.
Long ago, he had been kind to a lackey, who had now become
secretary to a duke who was a friend of the archbishop of Paris. A
word passed along this chain of influence, and the archbishop came
up with an exhibition of 500 livres a year in one of the colleges of
the University of Paris. But the previous holder of this substantial
bourse had embarked on a lawsuit against the head of the college,
who refused to pay a sou to the new exhibitioner while the dispute
lasted. So Marquis-Ducastel completed his theological education
without subsidy: it was left to him to try to make it up to his parents
later.[28] After ordination to the priesthood, the search for supplementary benefices went on; vicaires and curés pursued chapels and
priories as before. In the rural deanery of Évron in the diocese of Le
Mans, a parish priest listed in his diary the opportunities he came
across; he recorded forty-four chapels, with incomes ranging from
10 to 500 livres, their average income being 102.[29] During the
Revolution, when Church property was confiscated and pensions
were arranged for the clergy, allotting a basic sum together with half
the income which had been derived from supplementary benefices,
the true story of the incomes of the curés under the *ancien régime*
began to appear. Some had been better off than their complaints had
implied. In the town of Angers,[30] the curé of Saint-Jacques had a
single extra benefice worth a mere 100 livres. But his confrère at
Saint-Aignan, whose living yielded only a derisory income, had
eight chapels bringing in 1,500 livres annually. Three other city
curés had extras totalling over 1,000 livres each. At least two vicaires,
both from well-known families, had begun their accumulation of
chapels; less well-connected ecclesiastics might have to wait for forty
years for something to turn up—if at all.

Furnished with an ecclesiastical income, a clerk might stop short of ordination and become a footloose abbé adventuring on the fringes of the Parisian literary bohemia or, more respectably, acting as a tutor in a noble household. If he became ordained, he might still do these sorts of things or, more prosaically, stay at home as a *prêtre habitué*, with his name inscribed on the list of those eligible to receive fees for helping at the offices of his church. More ambitiously and usefully, he might become a vicaire, serving an apprenticeship under a curé until he was ripe for promotion to a parish of his own. Perhaps, with appropriate influence, he might hope to annex a canonry in some local collegiate church. How long must he wait? Anything from a couple of years to a lifetime, depending on family connections, friendships, contacts, and luck. The great objective was to attract the notice of a patron. Concerning promotion to the office of curé, it might be supposed that the bishop would be the best judge of the worthiness of a vicaire, and some bishops had ample patronage at their disposal. This was so in Brittany.[31] In the South, rather more than half the parishes of the diocese of Tarbes had the bishop as collator, and rather less than half those of Agen; the archbishop of Auch disposed of seventeen out of every twenty livings, and the archbishop of Bordeaux of three out of every five. But some bishops had very little to give. Those of Alsace were ill provided, the bishop of Metz, for example, with 600 parishes under his jurisdiction had only 50 to which he nominated the incumbent—and these included some which came his way as abbot of Saint-Arnould. Of 234 parishes of the see of Dijon, the chief pastor appointed to only 47; in Angers to 102 out of 400; in Bourges, to 134 out of 802; in Coutances, to 30 out of 489; in the vast diocese of Rouen, to 135 out of 1,460. In many dioceses, a vicaire bent on promotion would do better to look towards a chapter, more especially a cathedral; the metropolitan church of Besançon had 24 parishes, Langres 8, Autun 26, Angers 60. In the diocese of Bourges, the cathedral and the chapters together exercised patronage in 144 parishes, seven more than the bishop. Contacts with great abbeys and their dependent priories were even more valuable; of the 802 parishes of Bourges, 344 belonged to monastic foundations. The abbot of Cluny nominated to 35 parishes in the diocese of Autun, the abbey of Saint-Martin to 11, and other monasteries to 36 more. Two abbeys of Dijon had 46 parishes; five monastic institutions of Angers had 99.

All in all, the great majority of parochial livings in France were in the gift of ecclesiastical persons and institutions. There were, however, some lay patrons—few in most dioceses,[32] but many in

Normandy and Alsace; in the diocese of Coutances, 215 parishes out of 489 had a lay collator; in that of Metz, 170 out of 600. The Law and the Gallican liberties protected these lay patrons: they did not lose their right of presentation, as ecclesiastics sometimes did, by the exercise of 'prevention' (except after a long interval), the 'expectations of graduates', and the 'papal months'.[33] Nor had the diocesan bishop much control over their presentations, since if he declared their candidates unworthy, they could go to the metropolitan, or to another bishop, to ask for institution, as well as appeal to the parlements.[34] The high-water mark of the magistrates' defence of lay patronage came with a judgment of 1774 declaring that a Jew who had bought a seigneurie was entitled to take with his purchase the seigneur's right of nominating canons in the local collegiate foundation.[35] (True, this was a deliberately provocative verdict; the numerous Protestant seigneurs of Alsace retained their rights of presenting to livings, but had to exercise it through a Catholic delegate.) Among the lay patrons of the land, the Crown was the chief. By the Concordat, the Pope had granted the king the right to name to the 'consistorial benefices', that is, the bishoprics and the abbacies *in commendam* of the 1,092 great abbeys; along with these went 552 priories. There were, too, stalls in collegiate churches which had been founded by monarchs in the Middle Ages—the Sainte-Chapelle in Paris and its sister church in Bourges. Also, certain prebends had come to the Crown as successors to the rights of individual seigneurs, or by papal concessions allowing the king to alternate with canons of a chapter in filling its vacant places, as at Nîmes.[36] But the Crown also had some humble parishes in its gift—as many as 137 in the diocese of Bourges, though this was exceptional. In addition, the king was sometimes entitled to appropriate a patron's turn to appoint as a sort of dignified perquisite on special occasions; these windfalls will be considered later. All in all, the Crown possessed a great deal of varied ecclesiastical patronage—not just the bishoprics and the commendatory abbacies which aristocratic families angled for at Versailles, but canonries, parochial livings, and minor benefices without cure of souls. Most of these were awarded by the prelate who held the royal *feuille des bénéfices*—hence the scene described by a pamphleteer in the antechamber of Marbeuf, bishop of Autun, minister of the *feuille* at the end of the *ancien régime*:

A bizarre collection of monks, abbés, curés, soldiers, women. They all want bread. 'Pension, abbey!' Monseigneur has promises and consolation for everyone. 'M. le chevalier . . . these are hard times, but do not get impatient, all will be arranged.' 'M. le curé you know my intentions; use them as a pillow for your repose, and believe me, the moment of happy awakening is not far away. I foresee . . . yes, go along, do not worry.' 'My dear abbé, you are angry, so am I; the queen is getting hold of everything, I am master of nothing. But leave it to me, I have my plan. Good day, be discreet, and rely on me.'

No doubt the insistence of the applicants matched the cynicism of their reception.[37]

III

So far, we have considered benefices solely as they were in the gift of their patrons: the whole pattern was complex, but it was pre-dictable, and the earnest benefice-hunter could map out the field with some assurance. But over this pattern of predictable patronage was superimposed a whole web of incidental rights capable of ousting the ordinary collator on particular occasions. The Crown, for example, in addition to its patronage of the ordinary kind, had certain opportunities of privileged intervention. When a bishopric was vacant, benefices in episcopal patronage could be filled at royal discretion. When a new bishop was consecrated (or translated), the king could nominate a cleric, by the so-called *brevet de serment de fidélité*, to be given the first vacant stall in the cathedral. There were two similar *brevets* which the Crown could issue; one was on the occasion of the monarch's accession, the *brevet de joyeux avènement*, and the other when the king entered in person into certain churches, the *brevet de joyeuse entrée*.[38] These nominations were resented, bishops and cathedral chapters trying their best to defeat the royal intruders by presenting them with a *fait accompli*. At six o'clock on the morning of 7 January 1732, a canon of Montpellier died. At seven o'clock the bishop named one of his own *protégés*, a doctor of the Sorbonne. At eight o'clock, too late for the moment, the abbé Morel arrived, flourishing his *brevet de joyeux avènement*. A month passed, then the senior *gradué nommé* arrived, and as he had put down his name formally on the official waiting-list, he had priority for appointment in the graduate month of January, and the doctor of the Sorbonne was evicted. But Morel, the royal nominee, won in the end.[39] Another splendid race to take possession occurred at Sisteron on 11 January 1728. At nine o'clock at night, a canon died. The chapter met at once to circumvent Balthasar Barle de Curban, a vicar-general of the diocese, who was known to have a *brevet de joyeux avènement*. At 10.30 p.m., M. de Réal, captain of infantry, maternal uncle of Barle de Curban, arrived, accompanied by a royal notary and an apostolic notary and witnesses, and bearing copies of the *brevet* to serve on the chapter. After a tumult, at 11.30 p.m., the chapter elected its own candidate, and the canons went off to bed. But Barle de Curban beat them eventually—the king could not so easily be flouted.[40]

Like the Crown, magistrates of the parlement of Paris enjoyed a right of intervention in the award of benefices. This was by the so-called *droit d'indult*,[41] conceded by feeble Popes in the days of the Avignon schism. Then, there had been a dozen magistrates to enjoy the privilege: in the eighteenth century there were 352.[42] A *conseiller* of the parlement who sought a benefice for a friend (as Turgot did for the abbé Morellet) would put his name down (through the chancellor) with some ecclesiastical patron, who would thereby be obliged to hand over the next vacant benefice in his gift.[43] There were strict rules. Each magistrate could exercise the indult only once, and a particular collator could be subjected to such a requisition only once (if the patron was an institution, such as a chapter, once in the lifetime of the reigning monarch). The benefice had to be worth 600 livres or more, and the candidate had to be properly qualified to hold it. There were arguments as to whether the *droit d'indult* ran in provinces united to the Crown after the original bulls granting it; it certainly did not apply in Flanders and Artois, and it was much disputed in Brittany. But given compliance to all the rules, the indult was a powerful document indeed, overriding the rights of patrons and prevailing even over a royal *brevet de joyeux avènement*.

There were certain vacancies in benefices of the Gallican Church which fell as windfalls to the Pope. If a benefice holder died in the city of Rome or within two days' journey of it, the Pope could appoint his successor (though benefices in royal or lay nomination or which were elective were excluded from this provision, which operated almost exclusively at the expense of ecclesiastical patrons).[44] In the provinces of France which were united to the Crown after the Concordat of 1516, there were certain months of the year in which ecclesiastical patrons had to yield their right of appointment to the Pope; again, this did not apply to the rights of the Crown or of laymen.[45] In dioceses on the eastern frontier, in lands which had been under the old Germanic Concordat, most of the papal rights to appoint to benefices had been lost, surrendered to the French

Crown by various indults in the seventeenth century.[46] In Brittany, half the papal entitlement had been lost, but for a different reason, since, to encourage the bishops to reside in their dioceses, the Popes had allowed them to take over some of their 'apostolic months', provided always that there was not a single day of absence in any month in which an appointment was made (unless it was demonstrably for the urgent business of the king or the good of the Church). Arrangements of this kind left plenty of scope for litigation. A bishop who was a cardinal was exempt from the papal 'alternative' by right, not by grace. So too, according to the Gallican lawyers, was the collator of a Breton benefice who lived in the central area of France subject to the Concordat—a more doubtful proposition.[47] Just when did a month end? Officially at midnight, and this, said the standard law dictionary, was to be fixed by reference to the first chime of the public clock of the place where the benefice was situated; if there was no such clock, 'recourse must be had to the testimony of those who are experts in the interpretation of the course of the stars or of the crowing of the cock'.[48] Precise information was also required about the time when a Pope died, for then, all the rules of the Roman chancellery lapsed, and ordinary collators in the provinces of France could appoint to benefices until a new pontiff was elected.[49] It was not easy, then, for the Popes to reward French ecclesiastics for loyalty to the Roman cause. But it was done. In the memoirs of Le Gendre, a canon of Notre-Dame of Paris at the end of the seventeenth century, we read how Dr Gaillaud, a zealot for the bull *Unigenitus*, got himself a lucrative sinecure in Brittany this way.[50] Père Timothée de la Flèche tells how a canonry at Vannes was his for the asking, since it fell vacant in one of the months reserved for the Pope, but how he recommended some other priest of unimpeachable orthodoxy, to the edification of the town and the wrath of the bishop.[51]

For the encouragement of learning, and to raise intellectual standards among the clergy, there were rules giving preference to graduates for appointment to benefices. In theory, all curés in 'walled towns' and all dignitaries of cathedrals must have university qualifications.[52] In practice, in cathedrals only the canons holding the offices of *théologale* and of *pénitencier* had to be graduates; as for walled towns (defined as those which had walls standing in the fifteenth and sixteenth centuries), the simple *maîtrise ès arts*, with two years' university study, sufficed.[53] There was also a rule which was supposed to ensure that a third of all parishes in the patronage of ecclesiastics (lay patrons were exempt) had a scholarly curé. To this end, vacancies falling in the months of January, April, July, and October were reserved for graduates. Two of these months, April and October, were 'mois de faveur', when the patron chose as he pleased from whatever graduates were available (*gradués simples*). January and July were 'mois de rigueur', when the senior graduate of all those who had formally put themselves on the waiting-list (the *gradués nommés*) had to be appointed. In 1745, a royal declaration amended the law concerning the 'rigorous months'; in January and July the patron was to be allowed a modest margin of personal preference, provided always no applicant of lower status was promoted over a more distinguished one.[54] The order to be observed was: first, doctors of theology; second, the holders of master's degrees who had been academic teachers for at least seven years (*professeurs septenaires*);[55] third, the doctors of faculties other than theology; then *licenciés* and *bacheliers* (with those whose theses had been on theological topics preferred). If more than one graduate of a particular academic category was listed, the patron's choice determined between them.

No doubt these regulations improved the intellectual content of sermons: they certainly sharpened the wits and lined the purses of the lawyers. Once a graduate had aligned his sights on a particular benefice, a check had to be made to be sure that the 'expectation' really applied to it. Generally, in provinces united to the Crown after 1516, graduates did not enjoy special favours, but clever lawyers could find exceptions.[56] The collator had to have more than two benefices at his disposal; if not, he was exempt from requisition.[57] The graduate's own case had to be carefully organized, so that no flaws were evident. Benefices already held had to be manipulated for the record, lest disqualification arose from being too well provided (*rempli*).[58] The rules prescribed a minimum time to be spent at the university for each degree (ten years for a doctorate of theology, and so on); this was a favourite subject for investigation by *dévolutaires*, the bounty hunters of the Church, who hoped to be rewarded for making a delation of irregularities. A canon of Lyon, one of the splendid aristocratic 'chanoines-comtes', lost the dignity of *chamarier* in his great foundation because a colleague revealed that his doctorate from the University of Valence had been obtained without residence.[59] To become a *gradué nommé*, your legal representative had to give notice of your degrees and titles (baptismal extract, letters of tonsure, letters of ordination, diplomas of degrees, certificate of the duration of university courses) to the collator whose benefice was targeted—notification to be renewed annually at the end of Lent. When the actual vacancy occurred, formal requisition had to be made, and all the documents deposited at the diocesan registry. The slightest defect or omission nullified the application.[60] Entangling reluctant patrons in the web of graduate priorities was not an easy process, and could be an unedifying one. And so many of the degrees solemnly recorded in the dossiers of candidates were virtually worthless. The abbé Paul-Louis de Mondran was admitted to the *maîtrise ès arts* at Toulouse in 1751; after three years' idleness, he reflected, an examination lasting twenty minutes, and the payment of a fee, four pistoles, he had obtained 'a fine parchment . . . I was a graduate, *ergo*, invited by the Concordat to put in for benefices in the four months reserved for us'.[61] And what an affair it was waiting, and hoping for the benefice holder to die in the right month! The abbé Raguenet, says a Parisian diarist in 1723, committed suicide on the first day of February, having postponed the deed throughout January to ensure that his rich priory was left in the gift of the archbishop of Vienne rather than falling to a graduate.[62] In January 1721, Jansenists had gathered round the deathbed of M. Bouret, curé of Saint-Paul, trying to persuade him to resign the parish to a fellow Jansenist, lest it fall into the hands of M. de Châlon, the senior graduate applicant, a fervent supporter of the bull *Unigenitus*. Bouret refused. 'It does not befit me', he said, 'who am about to be judged before God not many days hence, to criticize the morals or doctrine of my brother. The Providence of God is great, and it will dispose things as pleases Him.' So it was: he survived until 2 February, out of the graduate month of January, and Châlon was disappointed.[63] Sometimes, a graduate had long to wait. On 27 July 1762, a canon of Le Mans died, and his stall fell to Jacques Loppé de Mesnil, the oldest graduate of the diocese. He was 61 years of age, and had waited for thirty-seven years. On 6 May 1765, canon Loppé de Mesnil died in his turn, without having had time to remedy his lifelong penury. 'As he had no fortune,' a fellow canon records, 'he was buried with only the second-class display of candles.'[64]

Another device for awarding benefices according to merit was to settle the conflicting claims of anxious vicaires for parishes of their own by examination. A bishop was always free to institute such a system of selection, as the prelate of Le Mans did in 1783. Graduates who had served as vicaires for six years and non-graduates who had served for eight were eligible to try. Thirty-three candidates came to the seminary one day and wrote papers from 8 a.m. to 3 p.m.; a dozen qualified, and were promised the next vacant parishes. A canon noted in his diary that the experiment would not last: the bishop had too few cures at his disposal to reward all the successful examinees.[65] This was a competition, putting the candidates in order of merit. There was a different way of proceeding: a bishop could tighten up his rules for testing the worthiness of priests who were put forward by patrons, subjecting them to a 'pass' examination to qualify. In the diocese of Bâle (which had some French parishes) the examination *pro cura* lasted a whole week, spent in the seminary. (There was an unusual system of marking; 'O' was *insigniter*, which was top; running down to 4½, *vix mediocriter*, and to 6, *nihil*, presumably consigning the candidate to outer darkness.[66])

In certain dioceses, there was a more general system of examination for the office of curé. According to the Council of Trent, the rights of patrons were to be transferred to the Pope for eight months of the year, on the understanding that vacancies occurring then would be filled strictly by merit. The decrees of Trent had not been accepted by the French monarchy, but they ran in the peripheral provinces which had conformed to them before being brought into union with the Crown.[67] As was usual, it was only benefices in the patronage of ecclesiastics which were subject to this reforming pre-emption, though there were exceptions. In the dioceses of Toul, Nancy, and Saint-Dié (the complication of the separating of these dioceses did not affect the system), a cure in the gift of an ecclesiastical patron which fell vacant in the months of January, February, April, May, July, August, October, or November was awarded to the winner of a competition held in the episcopal town within twenty days. The dossier of the victor was sent to Rome, from whence, in about two months' time, bulls of appointment would arrive—the parlement of Nancy checked these before granting permission to take over the temporalities.[68] In the diocese of Cambrai, there was an annual examination in Scripture, dogma, moral theology, preaching, and Gregorian chant, open to vicaires who had served at least three years in the diocese.[69] There were similar arrangements in the province of Roussillon, in Gex, Bugey, and Volromey, in the diocese of Tournai, and in Flanders and Artois.[70] In the diocese of Arras, the system left some latitude of choice to the patron: a priest who was admitted to examination on the certificate of his curé and rural dean, and passed in doctrine, moral theology, the administration of the sacraments, the conduct of ceremonies, sermon writing, and chanting, was put on the *feuille du concours*, which was sent to the patron, who chose one from those who had qualified.[71] In Brittany, the eight papal months were reduced to four, since Rome rewarded bishops who kept residence by allowing them to present to cures in the 'alternative months'. In the four 'apostolic months' retained by the Pope, benefices were awarded on the results of an examination held in Rome (or at least, assessed there). In 1740, however, the bishops of Brittany asked Pope Benedict XIV to allow them, for convenience sake, to take over the examination; this was granted by the bull *In apostolicae potestatis plenitudine*, registered by the parlement at Rennes in February 1741. A royal declaration drew up the rules in detail: six examiners, two at least being graduates; candidates must have been vicaires within the province, for a minimum of two years in the actual diocese, or of four years in one of the others; they must know the language, French or Breton, commonly spoken in the parish to which they sought appointment; the examination to consist of three written answers, a viva voce interrogation and the composition of a homily on a passage of Scripture.[72] There were fears about the fairness of the marking in dioceses where the Jansenist battle had raged. Bishop Fagon, a promoter of the doctrines of Quesnel, held the first examination in the diocese of Vannes in August 1741. There were twenty-one candidates competing for three vacancies, submitting solid essays in Latin to a high-powered jury of two vicars-general, one dignitary of the cathedral, the superior of the seminary, an expert theologian, and the incumbent of a city parish. All members of the jury (except one, and he did not attend) were Jansenistically inclined. Even so, the verdict seems to have been honest: three moderates were appointed.[73] Fagon died on 16 February 1742, and the cathedral chapter, in charge during the vacancy, put Archdeacon Dondel, an ally of the Jesuits, in charge of a new jury, with other members to match. At the examination of August 1742, twenty-five candidates competed for two livings (one rich). Severely orthodox supporters of the bull *Unigenitus* topped the list. Yet for the most part, the examiners seem to have been conscientious. Charles-Jean de Bertin, bishop of Vannes from 1746 to 1755, presided at all examinations in person (except in 1751 when the business of the Clergy of France called him to Paris).[74] In the diocese of Dol, there were no fewer than four fixed examinations annually, on the first day (if not a major feast) of March, June, September, and December.[75] Not surprisingly, it was universally said that parish priests were of higher quality in those areas where appointment was by competitive assessment. There were hard cases, of course—worthy vicaires who lacked the quickness of wit to dash off plausible answers presenting themselves again and again to the humiliation of failure. A curé of Lorraine noted in his journal, in 1782, how fate had been unkind to a vicaire of his acquaintance. 'M. Colvis d'Averaille, s'est présenté au concours pour la dix-neuvième fois, mais, sur le point de répondre, il a eu une extinction de voix.'[76] Perhaps, of his nineteen attempts, this was the only one when they asked him a question to which he knew the answer.

Churchmen and ecclesiastical institutions could, then, lose their right to appoint to a benefice on a particular occasion in various ways—the issue of a royal *brevet* of, say, *joyeux avènement*, a magistrate using his indult, the requisition of a graduate in an appropriate month, the papal entitlement in certain provinces to the 'apostolic months'. But the most frequently used legal device which clipped the patron's prerogative was the right of the titular of a benefice to resign to a cleric of his own choosing. The 'resignation in favour' had to be approved at Rome, but by the Gallican liberties, the application to the Pope was purely formal: no delay, let alone a refusal, was allowed.[77] As might be expected, since ecclesiastical superiors had little control over such resignations, the rules were strict. Bishoprics and other consistorial benefices and those in lay patronage could not be handed on by such agreements. Deathbed transfers were forbidden. If the resigning cleric had been in poor health and he died within twenty days of his signature, the benefice was vacant in the usual way, though if the attestations attached to the legal instruments of the transaction proved him to have been in perfect health when he signed, the transfer stood.[78] The son of a doctor who treated a *résignant* could not be the beneficiary, though oddly enough, by a decision of 1777, the parlement of Paris seemed to agree that a confessor could be.[79] The procuration which was sent to Rome had to be drawn up in the presence of two notaries (or one and two other witnesses), and all the documents had to be registered by the diocesan *greffier des insinuations ecclésiastiques*.[80] The law gave ample protection to the resigning cleric, affording him various grounds for revocation—undue pressure, recovery of health, and so on. This power of revocation, variously called the right of *regrès* or *regrets* (with contrasting, but equally plausible, etymological derivations) could be irresponsibly used with exasperating consequences. In the diocese of Nîmes in 1739, the aged curé of Villevielle resigned, but when his successor arrived from another diocese, did not like the look of him, so stayed on for ten years, when he finally resigned in favour of someone else.[81] In 1774, in another parish of Nîmes, Antoine Valette, feeling ill, resigned to his nephew, a neighbouring vicaire. Somewhat recovered, he revoked, and the nephew had to make do with a less agreeable parish ceded to him by another *résignant*. Five years later, Valette's health had declined again, so he

permuted cures with his nephew.[82] No doubt, behind the changing
medical verdicts lies some history of family relationships to compli-
cate the explanation. Another case, in the diocese of Sens, about the
same time, has sombre undertones. The curé of Saint-Sulpice de
Moulon fled when a serving-girl who had killed her illegitimate
child accused him of having seduced her; as he departed, he resigned
his cure to an acquaintance. On the scaffold, the girl withdrew her
accusation, and since the new incumbent of the parish unsportingly
refused to withdraw, the unlucky curé used the proceedings by *regrès*
to try to get back into his vicarage.[83] There were also rules to protect the incoming benefice holder, or rather, to prevent him from
striking a bargain tainted with simony. The *résignant* was not to be
given a pension unless he had served for a minimum of fourteen
years (or was in failing health); the sum must not be more than a
third of the revenues; and if the benefice was a parish on the *congrue*,
no pension was allowed at all.[84] Once the pension was agreed, however, it was sacrosanct: the titular who failed to meet his obligations
to his predecessor incurred automatic excommunication thirty days
after falling into default.[85]

According to the standard eighteenth-century dictionary of canon
law, resignations in favour were so common that they were no
longer regarded as an abuse, provided the 'formalities inimical to
simony and fraud' were observed.[86] How many benefices changed
hands in this fashion? The records of the diocese of Lisieux suggest
that one in five of the parish priests throughout the eighteenth
century named his own successor.[87] In some dioceses, the proportion
was higher. Certainly, resignation in favour was a general phenomenon, one which anticlericals seized on to cry scandal. There
were anecdotes of benefices changing hands during drinking bouts:

> When Esau sold his birthright,
> it was because he hungered,
> When he signed away his cure,
> he'd dined before he blundered.[88]

There were tales of monstrous pensions illegally accorded to persuade incumbents to hand over; Mme du Deffand tells of a vicaire
of Saint-Sulpice who agreed to pay his curé 15,000 livres a year for
the succession.[89] In another Parisian parish, the agreement was for a
pension of 2,500 livres to the heirs of the dying curé—which was
dubiously allowable.[90] In 1718, Romain de la Forest, holder of a
prebend in the cathedral of Strasbourg, was going round after dark
to visit potential candidates for his stall, bearing his accounts with

him as the basis of a sort of auction.[91] There was plenty of litigation. There was a lawsuit lasting six years after the curé of La Madeleine in Paris resigned to his nephew in 1732.[92] In 1783, the cathedral chapter of Saint-Flour appointed a new curé to its parish of Ternes, acting promptly, eight hours after the old one died. Fourteen months later, another claimant appeared, flourishing the resignation of the previous holder, accepted at Rome on the very day of his death. Another lengthy lawsuit ensued.[93]

But the essential abuse—and, paradoxically, the redeeming grace—of the resignation in favour was that it was the instrument used by families to obtain places in the ministry of the Church for their sons. 'People regard benefices as a patrimony', sighed Fleury, the great Church historian, 'that can be given by personal prefer- ence, and to which relatives have more right than others.'[94] 'A benefice', said a curé, 'is a piece of real property that ought not to be allowed to go out of the family.'[95] Christophe La Come resigned his living to a nephew in 1764, and went off to be a canon of Lescar; he moved again in 1778, in his turn succeeding an uncle.[96] Pierre Thuin, of a Parisian merchant family, had the good fortune to be tutor to the son of an influential man; his former pupil, rising in the Church ahead of him, resigned to him a canonry at Montereau, then in 1790 passed on to him the rich cure of Dontilly.[97] This was the way things were done. Certain desirable benefices were annexed more or less permanently. Eleven of the incumbents of parishes in the diocese of Auch in 1729 had the same name as their predecessors in 1672.[98] Two parishes of the diocese of La Rochelle were in the hands of the same family all through the seventeenth and eighteenth centuries; there were two parishes of this kind in the diocese of Autun.[99] It was a noble eccentricity when Joseph Chevassu, curé of Rousses in the Jura mountains, in 1743 put his parish at the disposal of the bishop, 'even though he had ecclesiastical nephews of great merit'.[100] Rousses was a harsh place, where snow lay all the year round. Had it been less forbidding, family pressures might have overcome pious scruples. Not surprisingly, it was the most lucrative benefices which changed hands by resignation. A family would cling to a rich prize, once one of its members had been lucky in the lottery. Besides, large incomes provided the larger pensions, enough for a retired ecclesiastic to live on in comfort. It was said of the parish of Andrezal-en-Brie, ten miles from Paris, with its income of 1,200 livres, that it was 'an excellent morsel', so much so that the canons who held the patronage could never exercise it unless the curé died suddenly.[101] Henry de Tristan enjoyed the cure of Gan, the richest in

Béarn, for forty years. Belatedly, in 1721, he decided to resign it to a nephew, and as the family nominee was in Paris, gave it to another nephew as a bridgeman, who, a year later, resigned to his brother. It was a risky procedure, challenged by a *dévolutaire*; but once the long lawsuit was won, Daniel de Tristan held office for twenty-three years.[102] Another parish with a substantial income was Saint-Merry in Paris. Curé Jean Vivant resigned it to his nephew Louis Métra in 1717. In 1744, on the day Métra died, the chapter of Notre-Dame hastened to appoint his successor, Artaud, brother of one of the canons. In 1757, Artaud became bishop of Cavaillon in the papal enclave of the comté Venaisson, his native country, so he resigned the parish to his nephew for a pension of 2,000 livres. The nephew, Donzeaud de Saint-Pons, died in 1773, and the chapter of Notre-Dame appointed the abbé de Vienne. Then appeared Louis Esprit Viennet, a curé from the distant diocese of Narbonne, smugly displaying the resignation documents of Donzeaud, duly countersigned by the Pope on the very day the old curé had died. Viennet took over the parish, and from his newly enhanced income was able to provide for his brother and give his three sisters dowries of 3,000 livres each.[103]

Bishops were angry to find the best livings in their nominal gift so rarely available to reward their most deserving clergy. They also regretted that a curé who was paying a pension to his predecessor had so much less left to give to the poor. On these grounds, the bishop of Le Mans did his best to stop resignations in favour. His tactics, he said, in a letter of 1784,[104] were to enforce strictly the rules governing pensions: anyone with less than fourteen years' service was disqualified. In 1785, when the richest cure in his diocese went by resignation to the abbé Bonnouvrier, his wrath knew no bounds, and with no justification he refused the worthy abbé the necessary attestation of faith and morals. In the end, the bishop had to withdraw from his untenable position; Bonnouvrier moved in and proved an excellent pastor—and he was able to help his poverty-stricken family: his mother, a bankrupt innkeeper, and his two sisters, seamstresses, who came to live with him, and he provided occasional refuge for his brothers, itinerant cooks, who were often out of employment.[105]

Like some other abuses of the *ancien régime*, the resignation in favour had much to be said for it in the overall social context. Favour, influence, family contacts, and intrigue ruled almost universally in appointments, even in the Church, and it might be supposed that a curé nominating his own successor was as likely to care for the interests of his parishioners as the usual patron—unless, maybe, this was some austere reforming bishop. The candidates a curé favoured—generally a nephew or a vicaire, occasionally a friend from seminary days, or a neighbour in a less favoured parish—were as likely to be reliable pastors as others brought from further afield, and they would have the advantage of knowing the local scene. There is an edifying story of François Feu, the Jansenist curé of Saint-Gervais in Paris, who in 1699 resigned into the hands of his archbishop, judging his nephew, at 28, too young to succeed him. The archbishop promptly appointed the nephew, François Feu II, to the parish, where he reigned in the odour of sanctity for sixty-two years.[106] No doubt there were many examples of a nephew brought up and trained in the hope of succeeding to a particular parish, carrying on the good work of his uncle. In the countryside, parishioners tended to be suspicious of outsiders and to prefer to carry on—grumbling, maybe—with someone they had come to appreciate. And peasants well understood the system of handing over to a relative—the younger people taking over the farm after making a contract with their parents to support them for the rest of their days.[107] From the point of view of the curé, what alternative was there? A parish priest growing old and feeble was in a difficult position: few dioceses had arrangements to care for him in his retirement, and by its very nature, the exercise of a celibate and authoritarian ministry would have left him with few close relatives and with friendships that stopped short of intimacy. Yet the only world he would know would be his parish. He could stumble on ineffectively as curé (a cynical parish priest said, postpone your resignation as long as you can, for once you do so, no one will court you—if your younger clergy have expectations, they will run your parish for you and even bring your chamber-pot).[108] Or, he could put some relative or friend into the vicarage, take a pension from him and potter round doing a few sacerdotal chores amid familiar faces for the rest of his days. And if the benefice stayed in the family, continuing to provide dowries for virtuous nieces and a refuge for ailing mothers and aunts, what was the harm in that?

IV

There was a further complexity in French benefice law: where there was dispute and confusion, an application might have to be taken before the court of Rome. In any case, the papal chancellery was concerned when dispensations were required before a candidate could qualify, and after an appointment had been made, lack of such authorization might be made a ground for eviction. Dispensation would be required for receiving holy orders below the fixed minimum age—22 for the subdiaconate, 23 for the diaconate, and 25 for the priesthood; similarly, for obtaining benefices—7 for one without cure of souls, 10 for an ordinary canonry, and 14 for a stall in a cathedral. There were also certain disqualifications for ordination which the Pope could overrule—bodily mutilation, illegitimate birth, and, in the case of a widower, a history of two marriages. In all these cases, dispensation would normally be forthcoming, but it would have to be applied for in Rome or at Avignon.[109] All resignations of ecclesiastics involving the transfer of the benefice to some other person, whether *in favorem*, with or without a pension, or an exchange, or *causa concordiae*, to settle a dispute with appropriate financial arrangements, had to be certified by the papal bureaucracy. Provided there was no defect in the application, there was nothing the officials in Rome could do to prevent these transactions going through (the parlements saw to that[110]), but the rigmarole had to be complied with all the same, and the procuration *ad resignandum*, sent by courier from France, circulated to the departments of the 'Concessum', the 'Consens', the 'de Missis', the 'little dates', the first and second 'Revisors', the 'Registry', and the 'Chancellery'.[111] Rome was also involved in the affairs of French benefices by the operation of the rules favouring *prévention*. These were calculated to penalize the negligence of collators. If there was undue delay in making an appointment, the Pope could issue provisions awarding the benefice to whatever French applicant presented himself.[112] The rules for the exercise of prevention were strictly drawn. The benefice must be genuinely vacant, and enough time must have elapsed for the news to have reached Rome by ordinary courier. Lay patrons had a full four months' grace (six months in Normandy) before their rights lapsed. Benefices in the collation of cardinals, consistorial benefices, those subject to the 'alternative' papal months, those under requisition by indult of the parlement of Paris, and the elective dignitaries of collegiate churches were exempt from Roman intervention. If the Pope and a bishop conferred the same benefice simultaneously, the ordinary's nomination prevailed.[113] Subject to these exceptions and safeguards, benefice hunters had a fine field for their operations. Given a negligent collator or an official candidate who was complacent, a pirate might get in first at Rome or Avignon and bear off the spoils. These operators in the art of prevention were not the most dedicated of ecclesiastics, but they were models of respectability compared with another sort of applicant at the Roman Curia, the *dévolutaires*. By the rule of *dévolut*,[114] an informer who could demonstrate that a benefice had been irregularly obtained was entitled to papal provisions transferring it to him—or at least, providing him with a prima-facie case to ask the royal tribunals to put him in possession. Bishoprics, abbacies, and benefices in lay patronage were exempt from such challenges; so too was an ecclesiastic who had held undisturbed possession for three years, except when his offence had been simony or fraud. *Dévolutaires* were universally hated and despised; the law-books describe them as 'odious', as 'pirates'. According to the Clergy of France, by very definition, they must be as bad as the ecclesiastics they displaced.[115] The courts required from them a deposit of 500 livres to guarantee any costs to which they might be condemned if they failed, a sum which was raised, in 1776, to 1,200 at the instance of the Assembly of the Clergy.[116] Generally, a benefice holder who was evicted by a *dévolutaire* was not a heretic, a pluralist, or guilty of simony, misconduct, or marriage; most often, it was a question of some error in legal title, some omission of protocol—for after all, these minor careless accidents were the easiest things to prove.[117]

In all these affairs of resignations, preventions, and devolutions, the Roman Curia had little scope for the exercise of judgement. By the Gallican liberties, the Pope was obliged to agree to the requisition of a benefice by a French ecclesiastic, provided it was put forward in due form; what is more, the consent had to be given the very day the application was received (even though half a dozen officials reviewed the documents). 'Date retenue, grâce accordée' was the formula.[118] The date was vital. Not infrequently, two candidates were after the same benefice, and other things being equal, it was first come, first served. Since simultaneous applications were regarded as cancelling each other, and since the Roman bureaucracy kept these transactions secret, it was sound policy to pay for the reservation of several dates, in the hope of hitting on the first clear one. This race for dates was complicated by the existence of a Daterie in the Vice-legation of Avignon[119] as an alternative resort for papal provisions for the neighbouring ecclesiastical provinces of Arles, Vienne, and Embrun. Thus, no amount of spying at either centre of papal officialdom could guarantee that no rival date buyer was on the trail. At Avignon, the registers recorded not only the day on which an application was made (as at Rome), but also the hour and minute,[120] so candidates there ran no danger of cancelling each other's applications. Also, by a not entirely logical rule, the exact time was taken as superior to the day pure and simple—an unjust advantage enjoyed by Avignon which the Assembly of the Clergy persuaded the king to cancel by a declaration issued in 1748.

The strict formalities of the Roman system (not unconnected with collecting fees) were paralleled by equally strict regulations on the French side. All applications for provisions, dispensations, and graces from Rome (though not from Avignon) had to go through the *banquiers expéditionnaires*, liaison agents.[121] Legislation of the second half of the seventeenth century prescribed that these officials must be laymen, at least 25 years of age, not servants or employees of ecclesiastics, sworn to strict secrecy, and forbidden to use extra-ordinary couriers to favour particular clients. There were twenty of these *banquiers expéditionnaires* in Paris, four in Lyon, three each in Toulouse and Bordeaux, and so on in the other parlement cities.[122] An ecclesiastic might be resident himself in Rome or Avignon, have friends there, have some ally willing to ride breakneck to get there—all to no avail, since no arrangement was legal unless it was recorded in the registers of the *banquiers* and verified by their signatures.[123] Their registers would show how, at a precise date after the benefice really fell vacant, the application was sent off—the name of the courier and the time of his departure were recorded. The documents brought back from Rome must have the signatures of two *banquiers* on the back, the name of the Roman agents, and the date of final delivery in France.[124] If the papal bureaucrats cancelled some clause or other in the French application, the *banquiers* could certify that the grace could be obtained only in this form, and their signature sufficed to reinstate the clause in question so far as the French courts were concerned.[125]

Legal pitfalls yawned on every side of the unwary candidate for Roman graces. When should dates reserved at the Daterie be trans-ferred (at a stiff extra fee) to the permanent registers, bearing in mind that the officials burned all other records at yearly intervals?[126] In Brittany and other provinces outside the Concordat, the system of reserving dates did not apply, yet in Provence the custom of making a reservation at Avignon had arisen—did one follow the rule, or the custom?[127] The Roman chancellery began the year on 25 March, while the chamber began it on 25 December.[128] Rescripts of the court of Rome concerning private individuals were free from the formalities of publication required for briefs on public affairs—except in Artois, Flanders, Franche Comté, and Provence, where *lettres d'attache* from the magistrates were required.[129] And everywhere in France the Roman provisions had to be followed up with the visa of the diocesan bishop, which included a certificate of having been examined and found capable, and a mandate authorizing taking possession. If the bishop refused his visa, legal representations had to be made to him to extract a written statement of his reasons—to be used in an appeal to the metropolitan archbishop and to the parlement.[130] And when all documentation was complete and the take-over took place, the local curé must be asked to publish the event at mass or in an assembly of inhabitants, with the names of four reputable witnesses recorded. A move into a benefice without all these formalities made the careless ecclesiastic into an *intrus*, automatically disqualified from holding it, and open to eviction by the *dévolut* or prevention at Rome by some jealous rival.[131] Let no one therefore venture on the benefice quest without having an apostolic notary (*notaire apostolique*) engaged, a lawyer who knew all the niceties of the trade of the *banquiers expéditionnaires* and of the bureaucrats at Rome and Avignon, as well as the jurisprudence of the parlements.

No doubt there were many uncontroversial and reputable sets of provisions forwarded from Rome to worthy French ecclesiastics as a matter of routine. But the writers of law-books, the diarists, and anticlericals generally relished the comic and outrageous cases. Above all, everyone hated the *dévolutaires*, and longed for their downfall. Marais tells a story of the scandalous ousting of a Jansenist from a priory by an orthodox adventurer.[132] Barbier gloats over the parlement throwing out the abbé Baudry for simony, yet refusing to let the *dévolutaire*, his old tutor, profit by his delation.[133] The law-books applauded the monk with a defective title who quickly permuted his benefice to outwit his accuser; they approved also of the archbishop of Vienne who delayed granting a visa to a *dévolutaire* just long enough to allow a second bounty hunter to oust him on grounds of the delay in taking possession.[134] Where prevention was concerned, jurists loved to record how rivals took up astronomical numbers of dates in Rome; there were cases of 500 to 600 duly paid for before one outflanked the other. In 1772, a dispute over a priory in the Vexin ended in a draw, each claimant having taken up eighty-five dates, which, it so happened, exactly cancelled out.[135] The *prévôté*, the highest dignity in the cathedral of Auch, vacant in March 1742, was annexed by the abbé Palerue by Roman provisions dated 27 May, beating the archbishop's nominee by four days; but the archbishop's man won, since Palerue's date had also been taken by the abbé d'Orvalle (doubtfully, as the Roman registers did not show it, but the parlement was glad of an excuse to oust a 'pirate').[136] In 1749, the archbishop of Arles gave the priory of Charlotte-la-Petite in the diocese of Sens to a canon of Vannes—this grant was null, for the priory ought to have gone to a regular priest, not a secular. Three days after, the *grand vicaire* of the archbishop gave it to Dom le Prévôt—this was null because no one is entitled to usurp the episcopal prerogative. The abbé Chaumont, who had reserved 150 dates in Rome, thought he was home and dry, but he had not reckoned with the abbé Marion, who had taken up 372. In the end, the parlement awarded the priory to le Prévôt: at least he was properly qualified to hold it.[137] One confrontation of this kind is well known through having aroused Diderot's ironical and unfraternal contempt: the five years of to-ing and fro-ing to Rome by the agents of Didier Pierre Diderot, secretary of the bishop of Langres and brother of the *philosophe*, on the one hand, and the chevalier de Piolanc, a tonsured clerk of the Order of Malta, on the other. In the end, in 1757, the abbé Diderot got the priory after paying the 1,200 livres legal expenses of his rival, and accepting responsibility for repairs—all this for a benefice worth only 458 a year.[138]

One device available to operators by prevention was to guess the day on which a failing benefice holder would die, add on the standard time it took for news to get to Rome, then reserve a strategic run of dates around the crucial point. If this fraud was detected—the crime of *de impetrantibus Beneficia viventium*—the penalty was total disqualification.[139] Another device was to conceal the death of the benefice holder while the application to succeed him was speeding to Rome in the courier's saddle-bag; if found out, the crime involved excommunication by canon law as well as penalties by state law. Royal magistrates were entitled to make a search for ecclesiastics in poor health who had not been seen around recently; relatives, servants, and nurses were under orders to have the church bells rung immediately a benefice holder died, while bell-ringers were constrained to answer their call, even in the middle of the night. If suspicions of fraud were subsequently raised, an exhumation might be held to see if the corpse had been pickled in brine or otherwise artificially preserved.[140] These legislative precautions seem to have been effective, for in the eighteenth century the crime of 'recèlement du corps mort d'un bénéficier' was rare; the standard law dictionary found only one good example to quote—a commendatory priory of Le Mans, obtained in 1750 on the strength of forty-five dates reserved by one Bernard, lost by him to one Correard who convicted him of 'recèlement', then lost by Correard because the abbé Gobier had been lurking all the while in the wings with a better date up his sleeve.[141] In 1785, the dean of a great Parisian foundation died on a holiday in Montpellier, which left the way open for a rush to Avignon by one of the local clergy. The archbishop of Arles then made his famous protest to the Assembly General of the Clergy:

One of the most distinguished chapters of the kingdom lives in the fear that it will soon have as its dean an unknown character who happened to ask for and obtain provisions in the court of Rome a few days before the chapter elected. What mysteries of iniquity would appear to the light of day if we were allowed to ransack the registers of the *banquiers expédition-naires*?

He therefore asked for a month's delay before prevention could be allowed to operate.[142] Some of the *cahiers* of the clergy in 1789 echo this demand: two ask for a month's delay, one for two months', and another wanted to end applications to Rome altogether.[143]

V

An aspirant for the office of curé, consulting his local almanac, would be able to list a diversity of patrons to be courted—bishops, chapters, abbeys, laymen. Within each ecclesiastical institution there might well be complex arrangements for making appointments to livings, and it was important to know just how they worked. Some senior ecclesiastic of the diocese might be acting on behalf of an absentee commendatory abbot; some particular monastic official—a cellarer or a treasurer—might have peculiar rights. In a cathedral, the holder of a certain prebend would sometimes control a living, or the whole chapter might elect, or the canon in residence at the time of the vacancy would be in charge. Or there might be, for some parishes, a system of rotating choices. The University of Paris, for example, exercised its patronage in the parish of Saint-André des Arts in a pattern of seven turns: the Faculties of Theology, Law, and Medicine, then each of the four 'Nations' of the Faculty of Arts, 'France', 'Normandy', 'Germany', and 'Picardy'.[144]

Having completed his list of local patrons, the earnest benefice hunter then had to reflect upon possible accidents and interventions—those he might organize himself, or those that might be engineered against him. Was a *brevet* from the Crown or an indult from a magistrate a possibility? He might not have the standing to get one himself, but he could be ousted, after all his expenditure of time and money, by someone more influential. Should he register as a *gradué nommé*, and if so, with what patron or patrons? If, unexpectedly, something fell vacant in the appropriate month, what about coming forward as a *gradué simple*? Some neighbouring ecclesiastic had gone off on a pilgrimage to Rome; was it worth covering the remote possibility that he would fall mortally ill near to the Eternal City? Of the patrons near at hand, was any likely to be slow in making a nomination? If so, his candidate might be beaten by the exercise of 'prevention'. Was there a benefice holder who had got into office by dubious means or with defective qualifications, and therefore vulnerable to deposition by invoking the *dévolut* against him? And above all, there was the question, 'What friends have I who might offer me a resignation in favour?' This was the best bet of all. The very existence of the possibility helped to prevent the parochial ministry from becoming subservient to the great holders of patronage. A vicaire's best policy was to keep in with the local curés and with his own ecclesiastical uncles and other relatives. Whatever manœuvres the aspirant to a parochial charge embarked on, one thing was certain: speed was essential. The patron, or whoever was supposed to influence the patron, might make a promise to someone else, or a rival might get in an early application to Rome or Avignon. Possession was nine-tenths of the law. Immediately a curé died, there was a rush of applications for his benefice, with supporting letters from influential backers.[145]

'The curé of Dolgueville is dangerously ill: the priests of Épinal have been on the watch, and they are paying solicitous social calls on the chapter of Épinal, which is the patron of this good benefice.'[146] 'The Parish of Crouaï, which your brother was wanting for one of his protégés, is not vacant just yet: the curé is still alive. Mgr the duc d'Orléans also asked for it, thinking the curé was dead.'[147] These reports are typical. It was a standard ploy of applicants to anticipate the medical verdict and to transform grievous illness into death when asking a patron for his nomination. In 1781, the bishop of Le Mans condemned this 'ambitious practice'; he would refuse to promise a living to anyone, he declared in a diocesan circular, until he received an assurance from the local rural dean that the curé in question was well and truly dead.[148]

The picture of the way benefices were obtained in eighteenth-century France as given in the law-books is an unedifying one, far removed from the pious clichés of the theological treatises on 'vocation'. One is tempted to regard the whole process of favouritism, family interest, and chicanery as totally worldly and unspiritual. True enough, there were those whose vocation to the ecclesiastical state was simply a vocation to draw an easily earned income. It was the only profession, said a cynic at the beginning of the eighteenth century, which made its members rich instantaneously. 'A man gets up in the morning a chaplain or a mediocre abbé, and goes to bed a wealthy benefice-holder.'[149] Marmontel, seeking a literary career, took the tonsure to placate his family, who were trying to force him into a trade, and later, he even proposed to go on to ordination.[150] The abbé Pollin, in 1792, when over-frank admissions were welcomed by revolutionary officialdom, confessed that his vocation had been settled by a consideration of 'the delicacy of my health, my natural laziness which I cannot vanquish', and 'a secret attraction towards the first Order in the State, its majesty, and the distinction which it conferred upon its members'.[151] Vergniaud, the future Girondin, studied theology at Paris because his father at Limoges had gone bankrupt. He left his seminary in disillusionment, but was willing to go back if it was the only way to earn a decent living. 'If I thought that the ecclesiastical state would provide me with the existence that I cannot obtain through any other profession, I'd take it up again,' he wrote to his brother-in-law on 1 January 1780, 'and don't think that this would be by inconstancy: I took it up the first time without knowing what I was doing, I left because I didn't like it, and I'd only take it up again out of necessity.' His chief contact in the Church was an uncle, prior of a Cistercian monastery, who had made his way as a monk after serving as a soldier. The shrewd old prior discouraged his nephew's self-interested vocation: 'One priest in the same family is enough,' he declared, and Vergniaud became a successful *avocat* at Bordeaux.[152] Sometimes, an individual was manœuvred into a sense of vocation by his family, who pushed him into the ministry of the Church because there was no other way of providing for him. This was the accusation commonly made by the austere authors of handbooks of spirituality. A boy is physically unfit or deficient in intelligence—'fathers then usually imitate Cain, offering to Jesus Christ the worst of their children as candidates for the ecclesiastical condition'.[153] Or, it might simply be a younger son who was got rid of, to leave the inheritance intact for the eldest.

A child is destined for the ecclesiastical state from his mother's womb. The family is not well off, and it is numerous. He is not the eldest or, if he is, he has no talent for a worldly career. Uncle dear has a canonry which has been in the family, as if by inheritance, for more than a century . . . That settles it, his vocation is decided. He is taught parrot-wise what the tonsure means so that he can receive it just as soon as they can hoodwink the bishop about his motives. The first *bénéfice simple* that falls vacant will go to him, and pray God that they do not procure it by simony. You say that taking the tonsure and accepting a benefice is not a commitment. True—except that it is a commitment concerning his parents' eternal salvation.[154]

Undeniably, a worldly attitude to an ecclesiastical career predominated, but the austere censures of spiritual men and cynical admissions by unspiritual ones do not fairly reflect the atmosphere in which the decision to seek ordination was made. Religion then was so woven into all the affairs of ordinary life that it could hardly be regarded as an aspect of human thought and action which could be considered in isolation, in its own right. The assumptions behind the social complex are revealed in the games of children. 'If a mission is preached', said a novelist, 'all the children play at processions; if a regiment marches through, they all do drill.'[155] André Chénier, who was to become a poet and a priest-hater later, described how he had played at 'chapels':

I said mass, I preached: they listened to me and made the sign of the cross. And when, in the evening, at *salut*, by the light of 100 tiny candles, after many genuflexions and anthems, I elevated a toy 'Host' made of lead, my old nurse took her bonnet off and my aunt Juliette and her friends knelt down.[156]

In the eyes of most families, the choice of the ministry of the Church was an ordinary everyday matter, one of those commonplace reasonable decisions that did not need an explanation. An ecclesiastical career was self-justifying. This remained so, often, for those who came to have doubts about revelation. Rousseau was not the only one who did not see why intellectual reservations should withhold a young man from accepting a useful office of moral direction in the community. The standard logical progression in which the question of vocation would be approached today—Do I really believe? Am I willing to commit myself? Am I prepared to separate myself from the world?—did not prevail in the eighteenth-century mind. Ordination, like marriage, was 'arranged'—not necessarily in a bad sense of the word—within the family context. The Church provided places for so many sons of lower and middling bourgeois families who would otherwise have had no fortune, as well as offering the only opportunity for betterment to the clever sons of the poor. The Roland family of Thizy-en-Beaujolais—the father being a magistrate of the *bailliage* court and the mother from a poor noble family—had two sons in secular careers; one, Jean-Marie, became Minister of the Interior in the revolutionary government in 1792. The four other sons were ecclesiastics in comfortable situations. Planning was needed to make such successful provision for one's children.[157] A notary who settled in Gay in 1745 knew what he was doing: his sons, if he had any, would be eligible for places in the chapter there or in the *familiarité* of the priests who earned fees for helping at the parish church; this was a family that looked back with satisfaction to an ancestor who had one son inheriting the farm, one a curé, and six in monastic life—'they couldn't have organized things better if it had been a question of maintaining intact the lands of a duchy'.[158]

The family obligation worked both ways: the successful churchman would look after his aged parents and the lame ducks of the family. The abbé Brendel, professor in the seminary of Strasbourg at the end of the *ancien régime*, supported his 90-year-old father, a sister who had been left with seven children, and a nephew completing his studies.[159] When Mme de Grange Berthelot died in 1787, her four daughters had nowhere to go. Their brother, a canon of Le Mans, came fifty leagues to collect them in a broken-down old cabriolet, and walked all the way back on foot ahead of them to save expense. Another prebendary of Le Mans died: 'he leaves behind him a niece and a nephew who have lost everything.'[160] We have followed the tribulations of Marquis-Ducastel whose education cost his parents so much. Finally, he took a dogsbody job with the curé of Saint-Laurent in Paris: 'c'est que je cessai par là d'être à charge à ma famille'. The dauphin died in 1765, thus putting an end to another intrigue of his father to win him promotion. But in the following year, the bishop of Vannes sent for him to assist in the work of his *officialité* (the ecclesiastical court of the diocese). Why? His uncle, the curé of Belle-Île, had shown heroism five years before when the English had bombarded that port, and a vicar-general of the bishop, visiting Paris, had noted the efficient way in which Marquis-Ducastel ran routine parish business for the hypochondriacal curé of Saint-Laurent. Promptly, Marquis-Ducastel's father and mother came to Vannes to join him, and rejoiced when the commendatory abbot of Évron gave him the rich cure of Sainte-Suzanne in the diocese of Le Mans. What a rush there was for the new curé mounted on a hired horse, to take possession, lest some rival forestall him by prevention at the court of Rome! At last, Marquis-Ducastel reflected, 'I can provide a comfortable existence for my parents'. Alas! on 11 September 1771, his father, aged 67, painfully afflicted by the 'stone', died, having had only a few months to enjoy his son's new status and enhanced income.[161]

Looking back from his comfortable canonical stall in the cathedral of Rouen, the abbé Baston reflected on the chain of circumstances that had made his modest fortune possible. Son of the collector of municipal taxes at Pont-Audemar—an office of some standing, but small income—and the eldest of eleven children, he was lucky to attract the interest of a priest who ran a little private boarding-school; he thus learned Latin. His mother scoured Rouen to try to find someone who would contribute towards fees at *collège* and seminary. A prosperous canon who had the reputation of 'liking to make priests' failed her. Mme X, who had been helped by Baston's father to make a marriage of affection, said she could have obtained one of the exhibitions financed by the duc d'Orléans, had he been of noble birth: 'without *noblesse*—solid noble standing—the thing can't be done'. The marquise de X said: pass the hat round among your relatives—'you get him ordained priest, then I'll get him a rich living'. She was over 60. His mother left, expressing the hope that she'd live long enough to fulfil her promise. Finally, an old seam-stress gave him free lodgings in town on condition he did some errands; and, belatedly, another canon chipped in with a contribu-tion. At 17, he took the tonsure. 'It's not irrevocable,' he mused; 'even so, it is an engagement, a weight unreflectively placed on the scales on the opposite side to liberty'—'but I thought I could assume the ecclesiastical state with the same indifference as anyone else, not having the least tincture of what they call vocation.' He regretted not being able to go to the theatre, however. Then came five happy years of study at the seminary of Saint-Sulpice in Paris. He was allowed home for two months in each year—'feted by everybody. They all said I looked "very well" in the *petit collet*.' The best houses invited him; the curé put him on the *feuille des gagnants de l'office*, those who were paid for attending certain services in church; and a cleric who had stayed in minor orders told him how to know which services these were by the way in which the bells were rung. Then came the great, serious decision—should he become a sub-deacon? Two considerations encouraged him to do so: he had no interest in women, and he would be able to help his family. 'It certainly came into my mind that, as a priest, I would be able to help my respectable parents in their old age; surely religion would not condemn such a warm natural sentiment (*un sentiment si cher à la nature*).' He never regretted it, and after twelve years of teaching in seminaries and *collèges*, he became a canon of Rouen in 1778.[162]

'Pray to the Lord that in his majesty he will deign to shed upon me some rays of his beneficent light, without which study and toil are but grain sown on stony ground,' wrote a young theological student, the abbé Coudrin, to his father in 1786. Three years later, he was exhorting all his family to be edifying in their conversation and 'to say nothing but . . . what has the odour of sanctity'. He also exhorted his father, ruined in a lawsuit, to accept suffering in a religious spirit, while, by contrast, he himself was 'so happy to be right with God that I cannot prevent myself speaking of it'.[163] All this is most unlike our canon of Rouen's straightforward choice of a useful career with an assured income which would help his parents, but there are those who would not regard the comparison as unfavourable to Baston. How can the historian assess the 'vocations' of the past? In actual language and in secret thoughts, our minds work in clichés: we are conditioned by our social and religious environment to ascribe to ourselves not only avowable motives, but those that we can formulate intelligibly and convincingly. In an age when service in the ministry of the Church was at once a useful and, often enough, a well-paid career, and also a matter of spiritual and sacrificial decision, a man was not obliged to force the two things apart so that he could assess them for conscience' sake. To live means deciding, and decisions are normally made not by looking at all the evidence, but by looking at sufficient to produce the conviction that leads to action. Ordinations, like the marriages of the century, were arranged in the family context, but just as the world of arranged marriages had its detours of romance and vagaries of individual choice and could lead to lifelong devotion, so, too, the highest inspirations of spirituality could flourish amid the conformities and pressures arising from family interests. By our standards, there is something wrong with Canon Baston's scholarly complacency and the abbé Coudrin's fanatical insensitivity. The task of the historian is to set both within the cadre of the assumptions of the age so that we can at least accord them sympathetic understanding.

ABBÉS

I

'Abbé' originally meant abbot, the ruler of a monastery, and the term was extended to cover the nominal churchmen who, by virtue of the tonsure as the minimum qualification, held abbatial revenues *in commendam*.[1] There was a certain incongruity in using the word for a beneficiary of monastic income otherwise totally outside the life of the cloister: it would take six months, said Montesquieu, for a visitor from India or China to understand 'ce que c'est qu'un abbé commendataire qui bat le pavé de Paris'. There were other ecclesiastical benefices—priories, chapels, foundations—resembling the titular headships of abbeys in having no cure of souls and no duties to perform and capable of being enjoyed by *tonsurés*; by a further extension, the term 'abbé' was applied to their holders. Finally, by a quirk of semantic evolution, a word covering clerics living off the Church without working for it widened in meaning to become an honorific form of address for canons, curés, and all other ecclesiastics short of the rank of bishop, provided they were not monks or friars. The process was complete by the end of the seventeenth century. The Jansenist society of Port-Royal still used 'abbé' in its distant, original sense of the ruler of a monastic house,[2] but it was an archaic, strait-laced usage.

The ceremony of the tonsure signified, said a solemn liturgiologist, separation from the laity and renunciation of the world, a demonstration of the willingness to wear the crown of thorns, to suffer with Christ.[3] Often, the candidate being tonsured was very young, perhaps 9 or 10 years of age; it would have been unreasonable to expect him to grasp these lofty implications. His family was moving him into position to obtain an ecclesiastical income if he turned out to be willing; as the opera singer Sophie Arnould said in 1790 about her grown-up son by a great nobleman, 'we made him an abbé because we had sufficient influence to contrive the little fellow's fortune (in this state of life we'd have made him Pope—or, anyway, a holder of a big benefice). But heaven ruled otherwise . . . he is a soldier'.[4] Just short of the age of 13, Diderot's family had him tonsured; an uncle was supposed to be resigning a canonry in his favour, but died too soon—'eighteen hundred livres income lost', complained his father. All the same, the adolescent wore ecclesiastical dress for two years, and had a crisis of religious devotion, before realizing his unsuitability.[5] The same family policy, however, encouraged his brother into orders, becoming a sincere and intolerant archdeacon. Among those who were older, some had already chosen to proceed to the ministry of the Church, and would reflect seriously on the meaning of the ceremony. But many others would take the tonsure as a staging-point, moving into the status, and possibly an income, without knowing what opportunities would present themselves or what their sentiments would be in a few years' time. An illegitimate boy, of good family and recognized by his father, but with no hope of inheriting, paid for as a permanent boarder at the Collège de Lisieux in Paris, naturally took the tonsure and the distinctive dress going with it. However, it turned out that there was no need for Jacques Delille to seek a career in the Church; he won all the scholastic prizes, became an academic teacher, and with his translation of the *Georgics* in 1769 achieved financial security and membership of the Academy—the poet of nature and the darling of the salons at the end of the *ancien régime*.[6] François de Neufchâteau, whose precocious brilliance earned him election to the academy of Dijon at the age of 15, was tonsured because the bishop of Toul, hoping to recruit his talent, became his patron, 'the respectable benefactor I will never forget'. Soon he realized the clerical life was not for him, and left the seminary.[7] Another case was Marmontel, a tonsured prize-winner of the academy of Toulouse. Without wealth or influence to promote a career, he finally decided to ask for ordination, but his archbishop turned him down, saying (Marmontel records), 'I was just a gay young abbé, quite taken up with poetry, paying my court to the ladies and writing pastorals and songs for them—nay, sometimes at dusk I went to the public promenades to take the air with pretty girls.'[8] These three had socially conditioned provisional vocations, Delille for want of an alternative, François de Neufchâteau conforming to flattering episcopal patronage, Marmontel moving towards reluctant commitment to a profession, but compelled to face the superficiality of his sentiments by a stern prelate. Rightly for all of them, their tonsure took them no further in the Church.

As against these young men of ability with provisional vocations, there were other *tonsurés*, who from the start had no shred of vocation but simply wanted the qualification to hold a benefice without cure of souls, no work involved. For these, the relevant words of their initiation ceremony were those of the psalm: 'the Lord himself is the portion of mine inheritance and my cup; thou shalt maintain my lot. The lot is fallen to me in a fair ground: Yea, I have a goodly heritage.' Given the mores of the day, taking the tonsure without vocation may be allowed, but going on to the priesthood was cynical. Chamfort would not stoop to it: for a time he wore the clerical *petit collet* of the abbé, but he told the principal of the Collège des Grassins that he would never be ordained, 'liking repose, philosophy, women and honour too much'.[9] By contrast to this scrupulosity, the abbé Pollin in his autobiography (1792) confessed naïvely, in the manner of his idol Rousseau, how he became a priest for a livelihood, intrigued to try to get office as a minor chaplain at Versailles, then reverted to the status of abbé when he fell in love, 'au pied des autels', with a girl attending his mass.[10] Such vocation as he had was worldly, and the sight of a girl ended it, and he became one of the abbés by default, drop-outs from the established clergy, secular or regular.

Another variant of this category of abbé consisted of those who had the status as the aftermath of a failed vocation; they had joined a religious Order, gone through the noviciate and, possibly, further, then obtained their release. The late age for final profession in the Jesuits made a return to lay society more evidently available to their recruits, and some of them, well educated, experienced in writing and teaching, made their mark in the Parisian milieux of scholarship and literature. 'You are fortunate in having been [a Jesuit],' wrote a friend to Desfontaines, 'and fortunate in having left them; you have retained the inimitable characteristics and attributes which have made you so well-known in the world.'[11] Desfontaines always recognized his debt: the Jesuits, he said, had taught him to study, to reason, to argue, and to satirize, 'l'honneur que lui font ses ouvrages rejaillit sur eux'. Marsy left because of a homosexual relationship with an aristocratic pupil, and La Motte because he seduced a female penitent; but most parted amicably with their Institute.[12] Some— Olivet, the exponent of Ciceronian scepticism; Fraguier, of the Academy and the *Journal des Savants*; Gédoyn, Le Mascrier, Millot, Le Grand d'Aussy, and Grosier pursued scholarly activities away from the constraints of claustral discipline; others followed their poetic muse, as Gresset did, or embarked on journalism, controversy, and the precarious career of authorship—Fréron, Desfontaines, Lambert, Raynal, La Touche, and La Porte.[13] Except for La Touche,

who denounced his former colleagues as fanatics, all showed respect
and a certain affection for the teachers and the system which had
formed them. Raynal exempted the Society of Jesus from his anticlerical censures; La Motte continued to take the Jesuit side against
the Jansenists; and even the disreputable Lambert's novel, *Anecdotes
jésuitiques* (1740), the story of the amorous adventures of a renegade,
showed admiration for the rebarbative discipline which was only for
the few. Fréron, who resigned from the Society early in his teaching
career (perhaps because his escapade at the theatre in lay dress got
him banished to the provinces), was looked after by two ex-Jesuits
when he came to Paris to earn his living by his pen: the abbé
Boismorand gave him lodgings and introduced him to Desfontaines,
who employed him on his literary journal, *Observations sur les écrits
modernes*. The vocation of Desfontaines, said an admirer, was to
'guard the gates of the *Temple du Goût* to prevent the invasion of
ignorance or pseudo-wit', and this mission he passed on to Fréron,
who fulfilled it with irony and critical insight in the pages of his
Année littéraire.[14]

Considering the diversity of its membership, and the gulf between
actuality and terminology, contemporaries found the category of
'abbé' hard to define.[15] The *Encyclopédie* simply says 'the superior of
a monastery of monks established at an Abbey', being 'a title derived
from the Hebrew for father (Syriac *abba*)'. The article goes on to give
the history of the institution, including the rise of the *commende*.
There is nothing about the swarm of abbés on the contemporary
scene, and no censure, unless it be the irony of noting how the bulls
of appointment still include the archaic provisions conferring spiritual jurisdiction over the monks and the obligation of proceeding
from the tonsure to holy orders in due course. Given that the
Encyclopédie faced a threat of suppression, the early pages of the first
volume were hardly the place for anticlerical irony or reflections on
the greed of the aristocracy. Guyot's vast repertory of jurisprudence
and Durand de Maillaine's dictionary of canon law had articles of a
similar sort, without sardonic undertones, unless it be in pointing out
how a commendatory abbot can take possession of his church with
book, holy water, and incense like a regular one. Bergier's theological dictionary does not complain about the abuses of the system
except to say that the 'best-regulated dioceses' do not accept candidates for the tonsure under the age of 14. (An example could have
been the diocese of Paris under Noailles: in his synod of 1697 he had
laid down a minimum age of 15, with a certificate from the curé that
the candidate had been essaying his vocation for six months under

supervision.[16]) Indeed, Bergier defends the *commende* as an ever present resource (as appointments fall vacant) for the king to make grants for schemes of 'public utility' or to pension useful servants— there is no reference to the scandal of the dispositions actually made. These were definitions in terms of the vast old traditional edifice, ignoring the interest groups operating within and around it, adapting and plundering. A novelist in 1739 describes the abbés as 'having the rank of those who have none, and the profession of those who do not propose to work at one'[17]—they were a motley crew, moving in to annex funds lying around to reward the performance of a ritual gesture of allegiance. According to another eighteenth-century description, 'the abbé does not enjoy a position in life (*état*), but simply wears a costume'.[18] This covers not only those lucky enough to get a benefice, but also those who were tonsured and adopted clerical garb while waiting for Fortune to smile on them, or simply to gain standing and consideration. This came with the dress. Canon Baston, who received the tonsure in 1760, tells how he forthwith donned the ecclesiastical habit and went round calling on his relatives, being surprised to find with what respect they now treated him.[19] When in Venice, Grossley adopted the dress for this reason, and to be able to turn out respectably without having to buy expensive clothes.[20]

A standard costume had evolved among the abbés, distinguishing them from monks and the pastoral clergy (though canons and curés on holiday might borrow it). Instead of, or supplementary to, the broad *rabat* ('bands') was the *petit collet*, a white collar of linen or lace, and instead of the cassock there was a short coat, generally brown in colour, with gold buttons. The ensemble would be surmounted by a wig.[21] True, the law of the Church banned the *perruque*, citing Tertullian, 'non amat falsum auctor veritatis'; but the abbés of the mid-seventeenth century broke through the prohibition, the other clergy following. In 1685 even the severe Tronson of Saint-Sulpice conceded wigs might be worn, though only in rare circumstances when celebrating mass, and always provided the bishop had given permission and the false hair was short.[22] Thereafter, two sorts of churchmen took up the fashion. There were the bald, concealing their handicap or just trying to keep warm, and if they were serious-minded (or affectedly scrupulous), having a hole in the middle to simulate a tonsure, perhaps with a fill-in of flesh-coloured silk or pigskin ('an unclean animal rejected from the sacrifices of antiquity', said a censorious Jansenist). The other class of wig wearers were the modish and frivolous, hiding their tonsure or lack of it. For abbés, the fashion was a wig of short hair, powdered and crowned with a recognizably ecclesiastical hat. Up to the end of the seventeenth century, it was the calotte, a round, shiny, black skull-cap, but from then onwards it became the standard wear of a doctor of theology, while the abbés turned to the three- or four-cornered *bonnet carré*.[23] According to Mercier, by the end of the *ancien régime* in Paris, they had dispensed with both *collet* and *rabat* and let the short 'Prussian' coat and the hat indicate their clerical status, while the wig would be 'impertinently curled'. There would be accompanying affectations, a favourite being the flaunting of a snuff-box.[24]

Some of these vocationless benefice holders stayed at home and did nothing. The *cahier* of the Tiers of Saint-Sulpice de Roumagnac in Périgord, in 1789, complaining of abbés, divided them into two types: one, with a considerable income, would go off to the city to live 'en homme du siècle'; the other, with a small income, would stay at home—'il végète dans sa famille'.[25] Cournot described 'mon oncle l'abbé':

an amiable and courteous man, a connaisseur of books, interested especially in literary curiosities, though without great expertise, writing verses in Latin and French and, even, publishing a few of them. While still a boy, he was already called 'l'abbé' because he had been tonsured in the customary way to enjoy a tiny benefice (I believe it had an income of 200 livres) depending on the patronage of a friend of the family, and because he had a singularly beautiful voice which was presumed to give him prospects in a clerical career. Of vocation, that was all he had, and he readily agreed this was so. The ecclesiastical state had seemed to him the means to have a more agreeable and comfortable existence.[26]

Occasionally, provincial abbés like Cournot's uncle emerged from leisured anonymity to read papers at the local academy—on some archaeological find, a curiosity of classical antiquity like the Amazons, an amateur scientific speculation, as on perpetual motion. At Besançon, an abbé, having failed to gain election to the academy, founded his own 'Société littéraire et militaire' (it was a garrison town), but was defeated by the jealous academicians, who obtained a royal *lettre de cachet* against him. An idyllic non-achieving or dilettante life-style like this depended on having a niche with well-off relations. Down-at-heel clerics without such a base eked out a subsistence doing small jobs around churches, like walking in funeral processions or keeping vigil over the corpse the night before the funeral.[27] In the end, said another *cahier* of 1789, 'they wander round in indigence and die at the Bicêtre'.[28] A sad case in the 1770s was an abbé of Saint-Malo grown old in poverty, excluded from office by his Jansenism; the bishop met him in the street and took him to dinner—he abandoned the resistance of a lifetime, and signed the Formulary.[29] The provincial abbés, whether well-beneficed, comfortable with their relatives, or miserably threadbare, for the most part escape the historical record. But there were those who ventured forth into the secular world, especially in Paris, and made contributions to literature, invention, and intellectual progress, to teaching and administration, and to the chronicle of scandal and the gaiety of the nation.

A particular group of abbés should be set aside from the rest: the aristocrats of old families who enjoyed huge incomes from the spoils of the great abbeys, pensions on the revenues of bishoprics, and the like; Blondel's *Des hommes tels qu'ils sont et doivent être* (1758) provided a name for them—those with at least 25,000 livres a year from ecclesiastical sinecures are 'abbés de cour'.[30] The most outrageous example of the century was Louis de Bourbon-Condé, who drew the abbatial income of Bec, Marmoutier, Saint-Claude, and Saint-Germain-des-Prés, each enough to furnish a life-style of the utmost luxury. Some *abbés de cour* did indeed frequent Versailles, making the life of a courtier their career. There was the abbé de Broglie,[31] raw-boned, tall, scruffily dressed, and outrageously witty, a familiar of Louis XV, to whom he retailed scandalous anecdotes, and of the queen and her pious circle, because he entertained them with sanitized ones. He drew the abbatial revenues of Mont-Saint-Michel, and apart from a 'retreat' every year in the sea air of his monastic domain, he never left the Court. While promoting the military careers of his brother and nephews, he asked for nothing for himself—he was, said Hénault, 'an intriguer without ambition and indecent with irreproachable morals'. In the following reign, the abbé de Véri was continually at Versailles, knowing everyone and observing everything.[32] He could have been a bishop, having studied at the Sorbonne and served as a *grand vicaire* at Bourges, but he chose to accept a prestigious legal office at Rome, one well known to attract the gift of benefices. After ten years he had over 100,000 livres of ecclesiastical income, and established himself at Court, advising the ministers, all the while realizing that disaster lay ahead, and confiding 'republican' sentiments to his journal—the king was just 'l'homme d'affaires de la nation'. He liked to think he could influence events, and encouraged Turgot towards reform, and discouraged Marie Antoinette from frivolity. But his only real success was in helping to ensure that Louis XV received the last sacraments before it was too late: he pressed Mme du Barry to leave Versailles, letting her and the king think it was revokable, and Mme Adélaïde and the archbishop of Paris assume it was definitive.

Other *abbés de cour* had the entrée to Versailles, but used it infrequently, having found more interesting things to do. The abbé de Dangeau, subject of a contemptuous notice by Saint-Simon when he died in 1723 at the age of 80, had bought the office of *lecteur* to have status at court if he wished to go there, but preferred living at ease in his 'joli prieuré' in agreeable countryside near Paris.[33] Scholarly activity was the vocation of the abbé de Bignon of the Académie Française and the Académie des Sciences, royal censor and librarian, editor of the *Journal des Savants*, enjoying 55,000 livres a year from two abbeys, as befitted the nephew of a chancelier of France.[34] So too, but in seclusion, was the abbé de Marolles immersed in his books in his apartment in the faubourg Saint-Germain or in his abbatial mansion in Touraine. The abbé de Radonvilliers, a former secretary to the embassy in Rome, came to Court as Latin tutor to the future Louis XVI, but his chief interest was in translating the ancient authors and compiling a guide to learning languages by the 'direct' method.[35] In spite of the scandal of a duel in his youth, the abbé de Voisenon could have hoped to be a bishop if, in Turgot's phrase, he had been 'willing to wear a mask for the rest of his life'; but he had been realistic about his suitability to lead the people of God: 'comment veut-on que je les conduise, lorsque j'ai tant de peine à me conduire moi-même?'[36] So he turned to monastic revenues, the writing of plays and novels, and the society of the actresses of the Comédie-Italienne. These and other sons of great aristocratic families stood apart from the common run of abbés: their share of monastic plunder was so much greater.

At the margin of the class of the *abbés de cour* were others, lacking the high birth which made the abbatial revenues of the great foundations available, but by their talents enjoying Court favour and in line for sinecures, the editorship of official journals, and the holding of canonries with permission not to reside. These, a sort of fluctuating artificial aristocracy at the summit of the 'republic of letters', will be considered later. Not entirely distinct from them was another class of abbé, prosperous and distinguished, the grandees of the University of Paris. Early in the century there was the abbé Renaudot, professor of Oriental languages, translator of the narratives of Muslim travellers to China, member of the Académie, and editor of the *Gazette de France*—he did not need to publish for profit. Batteux the aesthetician, a professor in the Collège de Navarre, had influential connections which got him into the Academy and appointed to devise the new syllabus for the École Militaire; he was well off, witness his 500 livres every year to the curé of the parish for the poor.[37] Nollet was an internationally renowned expounder of Newton's cosmology and of the wonders of electricity, dukes and duchesses and foreign royalty attending the Collège de Navarre to see his demonstrations, and he lectured at the artillery school at La Fère and the school of military engineering at Mézières.[38] Pluquet, writer of essays on fatalism and on luxury, in confutation of the philosophes, was a professor at the Collège de France, a former *grand vicaire* of Albi, and drew the income of a canonry at Cambrai. These academics moved in a lofty milieu far above the multitude of abbés who were Grub Street hacks, journalists, and the like; they had their professorial dignity to maintain, and one of them, the abbé Sigorne, fell into disgrace for publishing light-hearted trifles, 'unworthy of his profession and habit'.[39]

In the novels, correspondence, and memoirs of the age, there was a stereotype of the footloose, vocationless abbé involved in dubious adventures. It was a creation of public opinion hostile to a privileged class. Serious clergy and devout laymen saw the abbés as parasites on the Church, their income unearned and their leisure blameworthy. The mass of folk who had to work for their living envied them: law clerks, errand-boys, and porters whistled at them on the streets and in the theatres. Besides, whenever a secular cleric came to notice by a crime or a folly, he was commonly reported as an 'abbé', without reference to his standing as, say, a canon or a vicaire. The abbé de Moncrif, locked up in the Bastille, then in the fortress of Vincennes in the mid-eighteenth century, for an accumulation of mis-demeanours—claiming descent from Scottish royalty, boasting of knowing State secrets, running up huge debts, seducing a girl com-mitted to his charge, causing riots in the various monastic houses where his family had him confined—was a doctor of theology and of canon and civil law, and dean of the cathedral of Autun, yet it was not as a doctor or a dean that he was censured, but as an abbé.[40]

There were a few wearers of the *petit collet* who brought intelli-gence to the enterprises of the Parisian underworld. In 1749, the abbé de Flers was hanged in the Place de Grève for forging lottery tickets; he refused the ministrations of the attendant confessor, and clung to the ladder complaining that they would not accept his money to buy a pardon.[41] Four years later, the abbé Abbadie was broken on the wheel for a confidence trick leading to the attempted murder of a jeweller.[42] In 1760, the abbé de la Coste was sent to the galleys for life for another lottery fraud.[43] These were not penniless adventurers: Flers had an income of 10,000 livres from inheritance and benefices; Abbadie was a canon of a minor chapter in Bordeaux (though the judicial writ for his execution concealed the fact); while La Coste had been the 'homme de confiance' of the farmer-general La Riche de la Pouplinière, and had just negotiated his master's marriage to a girl in Toulouse whose fame as a beauty and a musician had inspired the old financier to seek simultaneous gratification for his two ruling passions. The forgery tradition carried on: when the Revolution printed the *assignats* as currency, the biggest-scale counterfeiter was another marginal churchman, and the police spy who informed on him was an ex-abbé already notorious for having stolen the silver from the garrison chapel when the mob stormed the Bastille.[44]

These were unusual cases; criminality did not figure in the stereotype of the dubious abbé, though sexual licence did.[45] Outrageous examples come from the dissolute age of the Regency. In the 'Société du Temple' (the Temple being an enclave immune from police intervention), the abbé de Chaulieu held court, 'a smug, libidinous, parasitic old reprobate . . . a disgrace to his cloth and to society'.[46] With him were two other nominal clerics pilloried in Saint-Simon's rogues' gallery: the fat and gluttonous Courtin, 'who took orders because of sloth and debauchery', and Servien, who publicly ridiculed the cult of deference to Louis XIV, 'was still a debauchee at the age of 65', and died 'surprised' in the company of a male dancer of the Opéra.[47] These were imitators of the old *libertin* tradition, without its intellectual awareness and irony, finding justification only in the commonplaces of Chaulieu's elegant verse. After Servien's death, the most notorious sodomist in Paris was the ex-Jesuit, the abbé Desfontaines,[48] an indefatigable translator from Latin, English, and Italian, a prolific commentator on the theatrical and literary scene, and the historian of Paris, Portugal, and the dukes of Brittany. Among his contemporaries were a group of rich and dissolute abbés haunting the theatrical world. Voisenon, the Court aristocrat, held an abbey and a priory bringing him 30,000 livres a year. Asthmatic, little, and simian, yet effervescent and charming, he was described by Grétry as 'much in society, where his smiling expression masked the signs of death . . . employing in his remarks to the ladies all the roses of love and the most amiable gallantry'.[49] His scope as a writer was wide, his style epigrammatic, the content insubstantial, his comic invention tedious; he wrote plays and religious oratorios, a *conte* teaching the vanity of pleasures, and an obscene fable on the vicissitudes of characters changed by wicked fairies into animals and chamber-pots, 'l'ordure mise en calem-bours'.[50] Aunillon was a lesser noble who had been envoy at The Hague before settling down as the 'curé of the Comédie'.[51] La Garde was a secretary to Pompadour and organizer of fêtes at Versailles, writing verses for royal occasions, theatrical criticism, reviews of exhibitions of paintings, as well as novels, the most successful being the *Mémoires d'une jeune demoiselle de province pendant son séjour à Paris* (1739). Another protégé of Pompadour and tutor to her brother was Leblanc, son of a prison warder, come to Paris from the provinces, a playwright, a popularizer of English cultural ideas, and, in later life, a correspondent of Buffon.[52] All four were in the police reports for their mistresses from the Opéra and the theatre, Aunillon with special mention of his venereal disease, Voisenon for his *ménage à trois* with Mme Favart, and Leblanc for his penchant for three in a bed. Other abbés of the alcove figured in the chronicle of scandal of the reign of Louis XV: a composer of erotic fables who was a boon companion in debauchery of the maréchal d'Estrées, the librarian of a royal prince dying of pox, two reckless characters who dared to be lovers of wives of magistrates of the parlement,[53] and—less culpably—the son of a duke and ambassador running off to Italy to marry a jeweller's daughter.[54] The type of dissipated abbé was well established, hence a young man new to the streets of Paris was not surprised when propositioned by one, 'an effeminate character with the face of a satyr';[55] hence too the joke in the *Encyclopédie* about the abbé who was so alarmed at the news of the falling population of France that 'he devoted a day a week to propagation'. Abbés of great families sowing their wild oats before moving on to become *grands vicaires* occasionally came to the notice of the police of Paris; but, by the reign of Louis XVI, sexual escapades had become a disqualifi-cation for promotion in the Church, and even in the days of the Regency they could be a disadvantage; Orléans warned his illegiti-mate son, in the presence of the outraged bishop of Soissons, to avoid womanizing as an abbé and wait until he had been safely awarded his mitre.[56]

The great found the wearers of the *petit collet*, with their entrée to polite society and, often, their verbal facility, useful to forward their designs—sometimes sinister ones; there was the hunchback employed by the duchesse de Bouillon to administer a potion to the actress Adrienne Lecouvreur to make her fall out of love with the maréchal de Saxe,[57] and the vicious pamphleteer hired by the enemies of Marie Antoinette to write the *Lever de l'aurore* against her.[58] By contrast, there was the heroic plotter who revealed to the

Jesuits Choiseul's hostile designs against them, and had to flee, escaping to England by holding a pistol to the head of a captain of a sailing boat.[59] Accused of conspiracy, though guilty only of naïveté, was the son of an intendant of Bordeaux sent to the Bastille for verses against the king—no one had told him how the police opened letters.[60] Another subversive versifier was the abbé Bon, tutor to the son of the duc de Chaulnes, who produced bitter lines on the subservience of the government to England in expelling the Pretender at the peace of 1748: 'tout est vil, Roi, ministre, maîtresse'. He kept them to himself, except for Turgot, who told the abbé Sigorgne of the University, who dictated them to his class. For his remaining years, Bon lived in terror, hiding in refuges provided by friends of Sorbonne days (after all, another poet on the same subject spent three years in the iron cage at Mont-Saint-Michel).[61] Other abbés made a name by eccentricity. One, a gambler, threatened God with the betrayal of a divine secret if he lost the next throw, and when he did, announced: 'There is no Purgatory'. An Irishman borrowed money to promote his career, then used it to go to Turkey to become a Muslim. A libertine collected papal medals; an egalitarian fanatic told the duchesse d'Harcourt that he was as well-born as her husband, being the son of a 'maréchal ferrant' (farrier), while the duke was the son of a 'maréchal de France' (field marshal). Another, an earnest patriot, concerned about the failure of the royal pair to produce an heir to the throne, pressed a paper into the hand of Louis XVI recommending a particular position to improve the chances of conception.[62]

   Socially viable by education, status, and formal costume, abbés of the respectable sort were welcome in polite society. The sons of noble families needed tutors, and almost always these were ecclesiastics. Most parents would consider a modicum of religious instruction was necessary, though not all, for Saint-Simon tells of a magistrate of the parlement of Paris and his wife who wanted 'a tutor who had no religion, and who on principle would bring up their son carefully ensuring he did not have any'.[63] Even so, there were abbés to fit this unusual requirement. By contrast, the princesse de Rohan-Guémené wanted a serious theologian for her two sons. Mallet, later to be a professor of theology in the University of Paris, was appointed, but soon left; the princess was haughty and irregular in paying, and one of the sons was spoilt and unteachable—the future Cardinal Rohan, of diamond necklace notoriety.[64] So often, aristocrats had little time to spend with their children, and they would require the tutor to live continually with his charge and, maybe, in the end accompany him to the university, on the grand tour, and, at least in one case, on the battlefield.[65] Enquiries would be made as to character and religion—the abbé Du Parquet of the marquis de Sade's imaginings would never have qualified. Good salaries were offered. Morellet, as tutor to the son of Chaumont de La Galaizière, chancellor to King Stanislas of Lorraine, received maintenance, lodging, and 1,000 livres a year as he accompanied the young man during his studies in Paris and on a tour of Italy.[66] If the employer had contacts with patrons of benefices, ecclesiastical revenues might augment the stipend. The abbé Belley, tutor to a daughter of the regent, had an apartment at the Palais Royal, 400 livres salary, and a priory worth 900 livres a year.[67] The rewards for educating the son of Prince Ferdinand of Parma (the boy, through his mother, being a grandson of Louis XV) were splendid—Condillac was made for life by the appointment, his salary of 8,000 livres a year continuing as a pension, while the king of France gave him an abbey in the diocese of Toul with a similar income.[68] For a personable young man, the costume of abbé led to contacts, and contacts to offers of employment. In 1738 a young abbé of Nantes decided to throw over his parents' expectations and go to Paris to join the royal bodyguard. Once there, he found he could not afford to serve the necessary apprenticeship of two years as an unpaid supernumerary; but he stayed on, retaining his ecclesiastical dress, 'which will give me an entrée to society and a sort of standing'; social engagements followed, and the duc de Richelieu got him taken on as tutor to the sons of the duc d'Aumont.[69] Two noblemen have left lively portraits of the abbés who gave them their manifestly good education. The baron de Frénilly tells of M. Giraudet, who hated being regarded as an ecclesiastic and being called 'M. l'abbé', and was so ashamed of his position as tutor that, when walking with his pupil, he would cross the street to avoid being recognized.[70] By contrast, the prince de Ligne remembered the abbé Verdier as the only teacher he ever had who believed in God, a man of piety, like the best sort of country curé.[71] An absence of vocation is not to be assumed, even when it was not necessary.

Being a tutor gave the opportunity to join in the life of a great household, with the possibility of rising to high office within it. There was an engaging example at the court of Lorraine, where the wit in residence was the dapper little abbé Porquet, who had gone there as tutor to the second son of King Stanislas by his mistress Mme de Boufflers, and stayed on as chaplain and social ornament, though only after a year's probation to enable him to make up his mind to believe in God.[72] After educating the young duc de Penthièvre, the son of the comtesse de Toulouse, the abbé Quesnel was rewarded with a charming retreat in the Tuileries garden, and spent his days as a companion to the countess—when he took her invitations round to her lady-friends, his stock joke was to urge them to bring their husbands, as 'without him you would be bored and you'd be a bore yourself'. For the learned, there were posts as librarians and archivists with great aristocrats like the comte de Saint-Florentin and the duc d'Orléans, or as a keeper of the royal collections of books, coins, and medals. The king's library in the first half of the century was newly catalogued by Sallier, professor of Hebrew at the Collège Royal, member of the Académie des Inscriptions, the Académie Française, and the Royal Society of London.[73] Or learning might be encouraged by a household sinecure. Vertot, who died in his apartments in the Palais Royal in 1735, had written the histories of the 'revolutions' of the Roman Republic, of Portugal and Sweden, and the story of the knights of Malta, in a flowing style untramelled by lust for accuracy (he refused to correct his manuscript of the siege of Malta: 'mon siège est fait'); he had been a friar and a curé, but had finally achieved leisure for learning in the office of *secrétaire des commandements* to the duchesse d'Orléans. For abbés with administrative talents, there were supervisory appointments, keeping accounts, directing the servants, running the estates. Before settling down to preside over his licentious circle in the Temple, Chaulieu had run the household of the duc de Vendôme, feathering his own nest while doing so, according to Saint-Simon, and brazening it out when detected.[74] During the Regency, Law, the financier, had Coetlogeon as his 'âme damnée', and rewarded him with an estate bought with the notorious *billets* before their value collapsed. Having gone on to the subdiaconate, Coetlogeon had incurred the obligation of celibacy, preventing him from retiring there with a wife— until he got a dispensation from Rome enabling him to marry his mistress.[75] At that time, the household of Cardinal Rohan was run by the abbé de Ravenes, who could be seen 'going round the corridors and apartments finding dust everywhere and lamenting the state of the furniture'.[76] In 1725, the entourage of the cardinal was joined by another nominal ecclesiastic, Huber, tiny, deformed, agreeable, and witty, a convert from Protestantism, brother of the Marie Huber who wrote works of spirituality overthrowing grim, unethical notions of Hell. He went on to join the staff of a financier and become the agent of the farmers-general in America, negotiating for direct supplies of tobacco, and then in London, making a contract on their behalf, at the same time engaging in industrial espionage on textile machinery. When he died in 1744, he left his carriage and pair and the bulk of his fortune to La Tour, the Court painter, together with legacies to good causes, without enough money to pay them.[77] The abbé de Villemont, secretary to the prince de Croÿ, was sent to Turin to negotiate a marriage with a princess of the lineage of Carignan, a mission doomed to failure, for the family restricted its alliances to sovereign houses.[78] The great Orléans dynasty employed abbés to direct its affairs; in 1761, Breteuil was *chancelier* to the duke, and refused to allow his master to give Collé, the dramatist, a sinecure as one of his 'secretaries'. When Collé was given a less prestigious appointment, it was another abbé, Omelanne, who welcomed him when he arrived at the Palais Royal to take up his nominal duties.[79] At the end of the *ancien régime*, the chaotic finances of the then duc d'Orléans (Égalité) were run by the abbé de Limon, while Mme de Genlis looked after social events, and Choderlos de Laclos conducted political intrigues.[80] Lower down the social scale, in bourgeois establishments, abbés would find a niche as administrative assistants. In many houses in Paris, said Mercier, they enjoyed the title of 'friend' and supervised the household, helped the master with his business affairs, and chatted with his wife at her *toilette*.[81] In humbler milieux they insinuated themselves with impressive talk and worldly-wise advice, like Anatole France's Jérôme, l'abbé Coignard, always welcome at the fireside and to a free meal at the sign of *La Reine Pédauque*.

II

Numerous publications came from the abbés, some using the leisure afforded by their sinecures, others striving to make a living by their pens. One day it may be possible to hazard a generalization about their multifarious writings, detecting a contribution of a specific kind to the thought of the Enlightenment, one corresponding to their ambiguous station between Church and world. This essay, however, goes no further than attempting an impressionistic view of the marginal churchmen who sought fame—or mere survival—in the harsh and brilliant Parisian literary milieu.

There is a problem of categorization. Anyone who had been tonsured could call himself 'abbé', perhaps ceasing to do so later on, or even formally renouncing the status; others might call him 'abbé', whether in accordance with present facts or harking back to the past, or merely in irony. Taking examples from the ex-Jesuits, scandalous figures like Raynal and Desfontaines were always so called, and Desfontaines wore the costume, at least sometimes—'quel homme pour un tel habit!', exclaimed Piron. Marsy, disgraced as he was, did not abandon the *petit collet*; Fréron wrote savagely against him

> Revêtu du manteau d'abbé
> Laisse là ton honneur flambé!

For his own part, Fréron called himself 'abbé' for the first seven years after leaving the Jesuits, until he started living with his niece in 1748, marrying her two years later. Similarly, Gresset renounced the ecclesiastical connection when he got married. As with the ex-Jesuits, so with the other abbés on the literary scene. Some kept the title all their days, hoping for a benefice; Coyer, endlessly composing treatises on subjects of public utility, expected that the Church, in which he had proceeded to priestly orders, would reward him; not so, his last will and testament is bitter—'I give nothing to the Church which has given nothing to me'.[82] Others abandoned the *petit collet*, yet their friends continued to intrigue to try to get ecclesiastical revenues for them (as did Marmontel's allies in high places).

A further complexity arises because canons and curés in formal pastoral office might spend their leisure in writing for publication, and figure as abbés on their title-pages (these, professionals in the Church, but amateurs in the republic of letters, ought to be excluded—when their standing can be identified). Even so, there were holders of benefices supposedly with cure of souls who were dispensed from residence and simply drew the emoluments—abbés indeed. Of those we meet in the literary world, Expilly had an inconsiderable canonry in the Midi, and Dubos had a considerable one in his native town of Beauvais—in the last ten years of his life he visited it twice. He scored smugly both ways when discussing his absenteeism: the chapter, he said, was guilty of 'cowardly indulgence' in breaking the rules, but all the same, his own merit 'put him above them'.[83] Batteux, a professor at the Collège de Navarre in Paris, was a canon of Reims, but did not reside there, having won a three-year-long lawsuit against the chapter to establish his right to absence.[84] Trublet drew the income of prebends at Nantes and Saint-Malo while occupying all his days in Parisian literary circles; however, he did go to stay in Saint-Malo from 1750 to 1753, and he retired there at the end of his life, from 1765 to 1770, in spite of frail health attending all the offices, leaning on the shoulder of his servant.[85] Towards the end of the century the abbés Gérard and

Maydieu published successful moralizing novels; one was a canon of Saint-Louis-du-Louvre, the other of a provincial chapter—did they do the duties? Numerous nominal churchmen moved in the end into the formal ecclesiastical establishment: there were Mallet and Yvon of the *Encyclopédie*, and Prades too, though his benefices were outside France. A tutor to the sons of the duc de Clermont-Tonnerre moved on to teach at the École Militaire, then became a curé, and finally, during the Revolution, was elected a constitutional bishop. Or the movement might be the other way. Vertot, the historian, had once been a curé. Outhier, who accompanied Maupertuis to Lapland, was a canon of both Bayeux and Arles; but, accused of seducing a penitent, he fled to Avignon, and earned his living by writing for the local *Courier*. The archetypal abbé, always so called, is Prévost, master of the novelist's art of interpreting the passions; yet, in his productive years he was a Benedictine monk, in and out of his Order twice, a soldier, an adventurer in exile, and chaplain to the prince de Conti. In his last years he was indeed an abbé, with no ecclesiastical duties, his benefices providing a comfortable house, a cook, a lackey, and 'a good-looking housekeeper', the great novels behind him, his literary reputation secure, and cherishing the unfulfilled design of writing a work of religious apologetics in his declining days.[86]

Fortunately, the distinction between abbés as nominal churchmen and those of the ecclesiastical establishment hardly needs to be drawn in the case of editors, journalists, translators, playwrights, and novelists. Most of them manifestly fall into the first category, and precision about status is rarely necessary. But where writings on the margins of religious apologetics are considered, it is useful to separate the ministers of the Church committed and commissioned to defend it from those who wrote for a living and properly belong to the republic of letters. It would be valuable, too, to divide the literary abbés into Christian believers and others. But the status of many will remain ambiguous. It is a sad comment on the mores of the age that the distinction between simple *tonsurés* and those who proceeded to the priesthood does not necessarily help. The abandonment of aspirations to an ecclesiastical career or loss of faith may have come after ordination, or ordination may have been sought because the richer benefices tended to be reserved for those who accepted the (supposedly) ultimate commitment. Saint-Pierre, the sardonic conformist; Raynal, the sceptical anticlerical; Voisenon, Aunillon, and La Garde, the lechers; Desfontaines, the sodomist, were in holy orders.[87] Condillac proceeded quite naturally to the priesthood, while his brother Mably stayed in minor orders. Pellegrin was a hack playwright, but he composed hymns, carols, metrical psalms, and scriptural canticles, and he was proud of his ordination—'prêtre, poète et provençal', he boasted. No doubt the acid test of vocation would be the dutiful saying of mass (except that the hard-up might volunteer to acquit foundations for the fees). By this criterion, Pellegrin qualifies, for he said mass until Archbishop Noailles banned him because of his theatrical connections. Prévost, however, is excluded; the prince de Conti, offering him the post of chaplain, gave the warning that he never attended mass—'Monseigneur, I never say it'. But for most abbés, there is no evidence. Breaking the rules of the priestly life does not mean that belief is lacking. Deduction from publications is hazardous, unless religion is attacked in an unbelieving spirit. A writer was not bound to take the official line of the clerical hierarchy; certainly, the literary abbés tended to advocate toleration. Works reflecting the haunted or enthusiastic deism of the age do not exclude the underlying acceptance of revelation: a man is not obliged to state everything he believes when composing a book to sell. Behaving carelessly, yet intending to finish in the allegiance implied in the original tonsure, is an understandable attitude for those with a living to make in a morally dangerous milieu—the dyer's hand betrays his trade, but not his inmost thoughts. Desfontaines, given to unnatural vice and bitter feuding, had the Jesuits Segaut and Berthier at his deathbed: 'he died a good Christian, fortified by the Sacraments of our Mother the Church,' and edified his weeping friends 'with deeply religious protestations'.[88]

A convenient starting-point in considering the literary abbés is one where contemporary opinion has passed down to us the categorization—there was a stereotype of the age, 'the abbé philosophe', routinely denounced by serious churchmen. Though the denunciation was a commonplace, those who were effective writers accepted into the confraternity of the philosophes were comparatively few. There was Saint-Pierre, the optimistic, improving rationalist, deviser of proposals for utilitarian government and international order; Terrasson, whose *Séthos* (1731) exalted the efficacy of humanistic morality; Morellet, who wrote on theological subjects for the *Encyclopédie* with the detachment he would use for reviewing the doctrines of Muslims or Brahmins; Mably, the Rousseauistic 'republican' vaunting the austerity and equality of Sparta and ancient Rome; Raynal, cataloguing the cruelties of fanaticism and prophesying the decline of Christianity through deism to atheism; Condillac, drawing all thought and reasoning from the prompting of the senses; Marmontel, the apostle of toleration and hedonism. Perhaps only Raynal, ex-priest and ex-Jesuit, was a hater of religion; and even then, some of his savage observations were written for him by Diderot and other gleeful mischief makers. (And how serious were his extreme poses? In 1791, at the age of 78, he threw away his popularity with the new order, and went to Paris to denounce all the works of the Revolution.) The rest, if not deists, at least took a conventional attitude towards religion. Saint-Pierre recommended insincere conformity to the religion of one's own country; he died with the last sacraments, though telling his curé afterwards it was only a concession to decorum.[89] According to Grimm, Terrasson died without the sacraments, though he made a deathbed confession to a priest all the same (with the famous asides to his housekeeper for verification).[90] During his life, he had always worn the costume of an abbé (he was a *tonsuré*, not a priest). Except to clerical readers panicking at the idea of deism as a sufficiently effective promoter of morality, his Egyptian prince devising a universal code of conduct was harmless, and his account of ancient Egypt was safely packaged in the learned solemnity appropriate for the professor of Greek philosophy at the Collège Royal and author of a critical discourse on the *Iliad*.[91] Mably, a *tonsuré*, avoided attacks on the Church, a natural policy for a writer whose political views could be regarded as extreme; his brother, Condillac, had studied theology for eight years before proceeding to priestly orders, and his morals and religion were formally certified before his tutorship with the reigning house of Parma was confirmed; as for his philosophical writings, he hoped they would establish the proof of the existence of God, at least as the celestial clock maker.[92] After his early bid for ordination, Marmontel no longer used the title of abbé, except during the four years he spent as a tutor in the household of a farmer-general; thereafter he lived without religion (according to a malicious acquaintance, he had forgotten the words of the Creed), but in his later years he pontificated as if he had always been on the side of the angels. Morellet was a campaigner for toleration, ironically compiling a *Manuel des Inquisiteurs* (1762), but he had completed four years' theology at the Sorbonne, and he never renounced his title of abbé or his Catholic allegiance; in d'Holbach's atheistic circle he stood out as a deist. Mme Necker described him as a man 'of candour and probity . . . with enough religion to suspect there may be a God and to avow the fact sometimes to friends he knows are discreet and won't give him away'.[93]

These seven are clearly philosophes, by contemporary acceptance and subsequent agreement. More nominal churchmen could be included in the group, depending on the criteria chosen for its definition.[94] For reformist social opinions, there is the abbé Coyer, the utilitarian opponent of aristocratic and ecclesiastical privilege, also the abbé Badeau, the physiocrat, who had just enough religion to be given a deanery in Poland, but not enough to prevent him ogling the ladies at the Opera in Warsaw.[95] No doubt a sceptical and critical attitude to religion is one of the criteria; indeed, with obsessive emphasis, the *Dictionnaire de Trévoux* defined the philosophes as 'ces prétendus esprits forts'. In this respect the abbé Dulaurens would qualify with *Le Compère Mathieu* (1766), not because it is scabrous, but because it ridicules Christianity. Surely, however, something more than irreverence and anticlericalism is needed: a positive, shared ideology, however difficult to define, a self-conscious sense of mission. There are bound to be marginal cases, admirers or hangers-on who in the last resort were not really accepted as full members of the club. The case of the abbé de Prades was to show how risky it could be to manœuvre between the religious establishment and its sceptical critics; it was possible to gain a reputation and a living by brinkmanship, but it was also possible to be disowned by both sides.

Until the solemn determination to eradicate abuses took over during the last generation before the Revolution, *écrasez l'infâme* was less typical of the warfare of 'ces prétendus esprits forts' against religion than the contriving of entrapments into untenable positions and public ridicule. One was the affair of the thesis of the abbé de Prades in 1751–2. The story as fixed in the mind of the public by the philosophes had Prades writing it with unbelieving collaborators, putting it forward, as Helvétius said, as a dove sent out from the ark to see if the ocean of prejudices had abated. The writing being hard to decipher, the candidate read extracts to the chief examiner over dinner, and was certified as qualifying 'entre la poire et le fromage'.[96] The truth of the matter was otherwise.[97] Prades, of a noble family of the Midi, had hopes of a genuinely ecclesiastical career, and was being considered for a canonry at Montauban. He had translated Huet's Latin defence of the Scriptures against Hobbes and Spinoza into French, and his first three theses at the Sorbonne, the *tentative*, the *sorbonique*, and the *mineur* were praised by the examiners as effective presentations of the 'proofs of religion'. The final thesis, agreeably entitled 'Jerusalem coelesti', had to be printed and distributed to all the doctors before the oral examination, and as time was short, Dr Hooke had a hurried meeting with Prades, instructed him to change three expressions, and allowed publication. Thereafter, eight doctors in a day-long *soutenance* passed the thesis (true, it was printed in type so small that the faint-hearted might have been discouraged from attentive perusal). Concerning the Bible, the candidate's opinions were conservative: he said that the Pentateuch was entirely by Moses, the ark was a literal reality and all the animals could have boarded it, and the events of the life of Christ were predicted in the Old Testament. The only derogation from the Scriptures was the acceptance of Chinese chronology as correcting the time span commonly deduced from Genesis.[98] Though Prades believed in toleration, he made no concessions to the idea in the thesis, where he affirmed the right of the exponents of the true religion to establish their faith in Oriental countries. The Chinese annals apart, the complaints against the thesis concerned atmosphere and emphasis. The Latin was Ciceronian, not ecclesiastical (a style the archbishop of Paris called 'obscure and shocking'); the Fathers were cited only infrequently; the proofs of deism were more cogently put than those of revelation (except in a Barthian theology, surely this is inevitable); though Christ's miracles were affirmed as proofs of his mission, they were cavalierly compared with pagan ones, and the fulfilment of prophecy was taken as superior evidence (as with the ark, the critics suspected difficult propositions were being blandly affirmed, to invite ridicule); equality among men was proclaimed to be in accordance with reason (a cliché of theological discourse, but a convenient allegation to alarm the civil authorities).

The attack on Prades began with two Jansenistically inclined doctors putting forward two objections to the award of the degree. First, the Chinese chronology; the Jesuits had been the impresarios introducing Chinese civilization to the West, and here was a complaint to bring in all their enemies in defence of the Scriptures. Second, Prades was a contributor to the *Encyclopédie*. Together with the abbé Yvon he had just produced the article 'Certitude' for volume ii, a blameless piece approved by the professors of the Collège de Navarre, but all the same inexcusable as written for editors whose design was supposed to be the propagation of doubts about religion. The thesis also echoed ideas in the preface to the first volume of the *Encyclopédie*, notably in accepting Locke's epistemology. There was enough here to bring in the parlement of Paris; and facing the wrath of the magistrates, the Faculty of Theology, after eleven stormy sessions, cravenly condemned the thesis by a vote of 105 out of the 146 doctors present (21 January 1752). The archbishop of Paris weighed in with a pastoral letter, a Roman condemnation was fulminated on 22 March, and on 7 February the Royal Council suppressed the first two volumes of the *Encyclopédie*. Far from there having been a philosophic hoax against the theologians, it looks as if there was a disorganized effort by enemies of the philosophes to stop the *Encyclopédie*, with Prades a genuine apologist for religion clumsily trying to contrive arguments acceptable to the Enlightenment. All the same, the affair finished up as a triumph for the philosophes, Diderot taking the opportunity for a powerful diatribe he craftily tacked on to the 'apology' Prades issued from exile in Berlin, and Voltaire and others wrote comic pieces on the Sorbonne. True, the first two volumes of the *Encyclopédie* were suspended for the moment, but with a maximum of publicity, and the Sorbonne was covered with ridicule.

Another triumph of the opponents of the Church came when Marmontel, an undoubted philosophe and once an abbé aspiring to ordination, published his *Bélisaire* in 1767, notable for a forceful chapter on toleration. The Sorbonne issued a condemnation, a reactionary fulmination the doctors regretted almost as soon as they released it. They were out of tune with the age, and had gone further than the defence of Catholicism required, incurring hostile criticism from all sides. In fact, they deserved a certain sympathy, for they had been unsure and divided, and while they argued, the printing press clattered on, so the book was on the streets before they had time to devise a more sophisticated demurrer. The higher clergy had been anxious to avoid a confrontation, for while they wanted to preserve the formulas of Catholic monopoly, they were aware of the inevitability of concessions in practice. The message of *Bélisaire*[99] was reform by an enlightened ruler, Marmontel having lost faith in his earlier hope of a 'creeping virtue' spreading from a solid bourgeois culture to improve the morals of the rest of society. It was important not to have intolerance prominent on the list of evils to be eradicated by the new-look monarchy which the philosophes were asking for—the future was to show, indeed, that the conversion of the king and his closest advisers to liberal sentiments would enable the Protestants to break through the clergy's monopoly of presiding over births, marriages, and deaths. The archbishop of Paris invited Marmontel to a conference with a group of doctors of theology at his country house at Conflans, and the bishops of Noyon and Autun made a separate effort to influence him.[100] Their attempts to persuade him to retract failed; the public rushed to buy the book to a total, prodigious for the time, of 40,000 copies; and the Sorbonne issued ineffective statements in self-exculpation.

While few *tonsurés* were publishing members of the philosophic élite, many were admirers or clients, not necessarily sharing in sceptical opinions, but basking in the acquaintance of literary lions,[101] seeking their advice or recommendation, publishing minor works in their shadow, and popularizing their ideas. Amid the extensive literature evoked by *L'Esprit des Lois*, the first refutation was by an abbé, while two others issued commentaries explaining and approving. They were effective journalists parasitic on greatness; there was, however, another churchman who had anticipated Montesquieu and provided him with a key idea which he annexed, simplified, and adorned with epigram. In 1743, the abbé Espiard, of a family of the *noblesse de robe* of Besançon, published in three volumes *Essais sur le génie et le caractère des nations*.[102] Montesquieu took over his aphorism, 'le climat est, de toutes les causes, la plus universelle, la plus puissante', and, dispensing with the abbé's cautious insistence on the complex of other factors combining to create a natural environment, elaborated brilliantly on the more limited theme. Espiard's work passed almost unnoticed, and when he published a revised edition in 1752, he was blamed for plagiarizing Montesquieu, who had published in 1748 with all the éclat of apparent originality. On the lower slopes of Parnassus, where stentorian voices and broad shoulders were aids to promote victories of the Enlightenment, abbés could be recruited to support the philosophic cause. When the philosophes mounted their attack on Fréron in 1760, by staging the *Écossaise*, with Diderot in person directing the claque of 'the printers, booksellers and their errand boys', he was assisted by two battered abbés of the literary bohemia leading their battalions to boo and cheer, one at the back of the theatre, and the other at the front as 'strategic reserve'.[103] There were others who did odd jobs for Voltaire on the business side, organizing money transfers, passing on manuscripts to publishers. It was the abbé Cordier de Saint-Firmin who presented him to the masonic lodge of the Neuf-Sœurs to be an apprentice member, and the abbés Millot and de Boismont who were the only clergy who attended when he was received in triumph at the Academy (of the latter, D'Alembert observed that he had none of the attributes of a priest save the eligibility to hold benefices). Some of Rousseau's most devoted admirers were found among the wearers of the *petit collet*, whether recognizing themselves in his 'Savoyard vicaire', or trying to put the theories of *Émile* into practice when tutoring the sons of the nobility.

A conspectus of abbés moving on the margins of the philosophic movement, and their diversity of attitudes and allegiances, can be seen in the contributors to the *Encyclopédie*.[104] Of the eleven church-men, seven may be classed as abbés—that is, omitting two ex-Jesuits and one ex-Oratorian who left their Institutes in their early twenties and the curé who wrote the article on 'eau-de-vie'. For a time, one of the major theological contributors, Mallet, had been a parish priest, and at the end of his life he was awarded a canonry; but most of his active years were spent as a literary abbé and a professor. He was a Christian believer, censored by Voltaire for his article affirming the reality of 'Hell', though praised for his enthusiasm for religious toleration. The abbé Pestres earned his living by tutoring the sons of bankers and businessmen; he became suspect because he shared lodgings with Prades and Yvon, though in fact he wrote his contri-butions on philosophical topics with the avowed aim of 'upholding the morals and religion of J. C., our Legislator and also our God'. Sauvages spent most of his life in minor orders, but in 1771, at the age of 61, he was ordained priest and showed himself a zealous pastor. La Chapelle, a brilliant mathematician, a Fellow of the Royal Society of London and for forty years a royal censor of publications, had been a devout Christian, but lost his faith in middle age. From then on he indulged in agreeable eccentricities. In 1765 he invented a cork life-jacket, and entertained Parisians by demonstrating it in the Seine (when the king came to see, the current swept him away just before the royal party arrived). Seven years later, he published a manual on the art of ventriloquism, suggesting that it explained the pagan oracles and, maybe, some of the Christian ones. The historian Lenglet du Fresnoy, a doctor of theology of the Sorbonne, main-tained a façade of religious belief while being a free-thinker, having to take out religious insurance to cover his suspect political opinions.[105] On several occasions he was imprisoned in the Bastille, and in 1751, four years before he died, the police described him as 'a dangerous man . . . who could overthrow a kingdom'. The two friends, Prades and Yvon, both priests, have long been taken as the archetypal 'abbés philosophes', as distinct from the respectable clerical contributors to the *Encyclopédie*, who were 'flags to cover the contraband'.[106] They were, in fact, ambiguous figures. The outcry against the notorious thesis of Prades was not justified by its actual content; he always maintained he was orthodox in religion, and finished up accepted as such by the Pope and the University of Paris and holding benefices in Eastern Europe. Even in his comfortable exile there were question marks over him:[107] how did he win so much in an uncharacteristic venture into gambling? Did he spy for France against his protector Frederick the Great? (No, but he would not write accounts of Prussian victories against a French army in which his uncle, brother, and nephew served.) Yvon, like Prades, claimed to be writing in defence of religion: he excluded atheists from his pleas for toleration; he backed the condemnation of *Émile* by the archbishop of Paris, and after a lifetime of penury, ended up a benefice holder of the diocese of Tours, a canon of Coutances, and historiographer to the comte d'Artois. Believers and unbelievers of various hues, the ecclesiastics of the *Encyclopédie* seem to have had one thing in common: their acceptance of religious toleration. One might guess this was a fairly general trait among the literary abbés; certainly, when pamphleteers were urging the government of Louis XVI towards the liberal edict of 1787, two of the most effective, Guidi and Besoigne, were wearers of the *petit collet*.

There were disadvantages in alliance with the philosophes. Prades prospered on the income of benefices; but in a distant, colder climate, Diderot unsportingly added a section of extreme opinions to his 'apology', and Voltaire, far from showing gratitude to one who had been persecuted for the cause, was quick to accept the tale of his treachery to his Prussian protector. The corresponding advantages, however, were favourable reviews, invitations to certain salons, and the pulling of strings in high places—say, enlisting support from Mme de Pompadour. Churchmen conforming to the shibboleths of the Enlightenment might go far enough in brink-manship to be granted the philosophic accolade of a chair in the Academy; this was how the historian, the abbé Millot, was elected in 1778.[108] Conversely, the abbé Trublet was kept out because of his apologies for Christianity, until the *dévot* party at Court took up his cause and circumvented the ban. Yet he remained a friend of Voltaire and Helvétius, as did the abbé Pluquet (a professor at the Collège de France) after his defence of orthodoxy in his *Examen du fatalisme* (1757). In matters religious, feuds within the republic of letters tended to be single-issue affairs, not personal and lasting, though many a reckless blow was struck and misrepresentation and ridicule were standard weapons.

The philosophes had their inner ring and outer circle, but most of the literary abbés were in neither, writing without sceptical over-tones, unless some daring flourish occurred to them, or there was an accidental slip into a prevailing fashion. Their object was to earn a living. Those with contacts and influence would angle for nomina-tion to one of the government posts in the literary world, managerial offices in the republic of letters. There were appointments as official censors, with a salary of 6,000 livres, the right to be dispensed from the obligation of residence in benefices like canonries where it was normally required, and the intangible deference accorded to those with power to hinder publication. By the same token, it was possible to incur odium—the abbé Riballier, unpopular with the philosophes for his severity, contrived to fall out with the pious as well, by banning a biography of a general of the Capuchins because of its naïve acceptance of edifying anecdotes. The editorship of government-sponsored journals was more lucrative still—10,000 livres a year for the *Gazette de France*.[109] The abbé Arnauld, author of articles on the philosophy of the Etruscans, Greek tragedy, Roman eloquence, and Italian poetry, had the dauphin and Choiseul promoting his interests, was elevated to the Academy, and made director of the Foreign Ministry's *Gazette littéraire de l'Europe*, and when it folded, of the *Gazette de France*.

There were also sinecures at Court, not prestigious enough for great aristocrats, but suitable for literary men. Mme de Pompadour tried to get the abbé Leblanc elevated to the Academy in 1748; she failed, but ensured he was compensated by the office of *historiographe des bâtiments du Roi*.[110] The abbé Robin, who published a collection of the lives of great Christians in 1787 and another of great women the year after and settled down to write a history of the Estates General, was *secrétaire de la vénerie* of the comte d'Artois.[111] Two abbés patronized by Choiseul were given sinecures of this kind—men of solid learning, Le Grand d'Aussy and Barthélemy. The former, an ex-Jesuit and a collaborator in the medieval researches of La Curne de Sainte-Palaye, had earned his living by tutoring the sons of financiers until, in 1770, Choiseul, who was on the verge of leaving office, made him *secrétaire de la Direction de l'École Militaire*; from this secure base he published highly readable works on the margins of scholarship, old fables retold, a *Histoire de la vie privée des Français* and the *Voyages d'Auvergne*.[112] Jean-Jacques Barthélemy,[113] of the Académie des Inscriptions, curator of the Cabinet des Médailles, orientalist, classical scholar, and numismatist, was given another nominal secretarial office, that of the Gardes Suisses at Versailles, at 15,000 livres a year. He was a scholar of Christian convictions, for when Bausset, bishop of Béziers, sent for him to be his *grand vicaire*, Barthélemy, though in despair at the prospect of leaving the world of learning, offered to go if the bishop felt it was his duty; fortunately, Mgr de Bausset did not accept the 'sacrifice'. After thirty years' research, accumulating 20,000 *fiches* of quotations, in 1780, the abbé published his masterpiece, *Les Voyages du jeune Anacharsis en Grèce*, a fictional account of a young Scythian wandering over

Greece between 363 and 337 BC, meeting everyone and seeing everything recorded in the author's bank of quotations. The four volumes were well received by the intellectuals, because of the interest in classical antiquity aroused by the excavations at Herculaneum and Pompei, and by the wider public, because of the revolutionary political ferment of the day—here was a celebration of the supreme cultural achievements of the human spirit in a civilization ruled by 'les mœurs républicaines'. Versailles had its conventions about sinecures: they went to the high-born irrespective of merit, and to others through contacts, with merit borne in mind, but sheer sycophancy did not qualify. Hence the discomfiture of a certain abbé Petity, 'auteur obscur de plusieurs mauvais livres', who in 1775 went to the palace to present his two-volume study *La Sagesse de Louis XVI*; the king was tempted to throw it in his face, and Turgot banned the journals from reviewing it.[114]

In this age of enthusiasm for scientific experiment and invention, one way of coming to the notice of the Court—or, failing the Court, the Académie des Sciences—was to make useful discoveries. Abbés who published on mathematical subjects were invited by the Academy to go on prestigious expeditions—to Lapland to measure the width of a degree of latitude near the Pole, to observe the transit of Venus in Siberia in 1761 and in California in 1769, to the Cape of Good Hope in 1780 to report on the stars of the southern hemisphere. (From information gathered on his Siberian trip, the abbé Chappe d'Auteroche published a travel book on Russia, denouncing the dead hand of despotism, and thus arousing the wrath of Catherine II, who had grown used to the flattery of the philosophes.)[115] The invention of a diving suit and of a visual telegraph brought recognition from the Court, and of a bronze talking head from the sightseeing public in Paris. Even quicker profits were made by the two abbés who charged three livres a head for spectators to come into their enclosure in the Luxembourg gardens to see their ascent in a Montgolfière balloon; it took fire before take-off, to the rage of the crowd, especially when they found that the promoters had decamped with the takings.[116] When Turgot was minister, substantial rewards came to the nominal churchmen who produced handbooks on wine-making, silk production, the cultivation of beetroot, and the rectifying of hail damage. But ecclesiastical revenues were hard to come by when it was a question of merit without an immediate utilitarian contribution and unbuttressed by influential connections. Expilly, who compiled the monumental *Dictionnaire des Gaules et de la France* (6 vols., 1762–70) based on questionnaires filled in by local inhabitants, mostly the curés, waited long for government bounty, and when it came, it was meagre.[117] Nollet's invention of a device for projecting images earned him a present of books from the queen, but Boyer of the *feuille des bénéfices* refused to make an ecclesiastical sinecure available, 'the research not being of such a nature as to be recompensed from the property of the Church'. (Later experiments, making a chain of monks leap in the air by an electric shock and a study of the generative process by putting condoms on frogs, were even less eligible for ecclesiastical funding.)[118] Another devotee of experimental science turned down by Boyer was the abbé de Saint-Elier, naturalist and vivisectionist. His brother, the mathematician Maupertuis, put him forward for a benefice, and was told that 'the property of the Church ought to belong to those who serve it; if the abbé de Saint-Elier wishes to qualify, let him work for the salvation of souls, instead of amusing himself by mutilating cats'. However, influence intervened in the form of a letter from Frederick II of Prussia to the king, and a monastic sinecure had to be conferred. The abbé then gave further proof of his unworthiness by publishing a treatise anticipating La Mettrie in making men into machines, as well as warning women not to breast-feed children, advice capable of doing more harm than his philosophical rejection of moral responsibility.[119]

Life could be hard without a benefice, a sinecure, or a patron. For those who had to write saleable books or starve and who lacked the inspiration to produce works of the imagination, useful resorts were translation and compilation. Masterpieces of classical antiquity brought only modest profits, except to Jacques Delille; it was better to offer translations from newly fashionable English works (Desfontaines did well out of *Gulliver's Travels*, *Joseph Andrews*, and the *Essay on Man*). As for compilation, this was the century of encyclopedias, with the public avid for packaged information. From the abbés came dictionaries, whether conventional or of languages, neologisms, or technical terms, of notable French women and contemporary poets, of books classified for recommended reading. They also turned out anthologies—of fraud stories and of ghostly visitations, of jokes and epigrams, of extracts concerning matters of controversy or the religious Orders, of the writings of Rousseau and other luminaries, travellers' tales, literary anecdotes, and military ones. Plagiarism was the order of the day—reducing the *Encyclopédie* to five volumes for easy reference, reprinting an illustrated Dutch compendium of the religious ceremonies of all nations (taking out the sardonic references to Catholicism of the original Protestant editors), producing a manual of military science lifting the information from the handbooks of the Prussian army (this was the abbé Raynal's device to get a subvention out of the Foreign Office in his earlier, penurious days). To encourage sales, the trick was to assure the public that they were making an investment on the way to becoming a well-informed and witty conversationalist, and to choose intriguing titles—like 'arrows from Apollo's quiver', 'impostors unmasked', *Almanach astronomique, géographique et qui plus est, véritable*[120]—and if the adjective 'curious' could be introduced, its ambiguous nuances would extend the range of potential buyers still further. The master of the compiler's art was the ex-Jesuit, the abbé Joseph Delaporte (1713–79),[121] who always had a volume at the press, yet found time to pour out expert reviews of plays, ballets, exhibitions of paintings, and books of every kind.[122] According to Grimm, he produced a reference work every week and enjoyed 6,000 livres a year—a comic exaggeration of output, but an underestimation of earnings. Though he had the best-stocked mind in Paris, he saw (as his play *L'Antiquaire* demonstrated) the comic side of the mania for information which gave him his living, and he regretted that his trade of purveyor of ephemera doomed him to remain a 'commoner' in the world of literature, disqualifying him from election to the aristocracy of the Academy.

While translating, editing, and compilation were natural resorts for the abbés adventuring into the republic of letters, it might seem unlikely that they would seek a living in writing for the theatre. Yet one in fifty of the plays put on in Paris during the century came from their pens.[123] Perhaps some training in the casuistry of the confessional had promoted an interest in the working of the passions, and in an age when actors spoke in a formalized declamatory style, stints of composing sermons for sale had given some of them a flair for the language of the stage. Not that the subjects of their plots bore much affinity with their erstwhile ecclesiastical vocation: Aunillon, Allainval, and Voisenon wrote frivolous comedies with titles like *Les Amants déguisés* (1728), *Le Mari curieux* (1731) and *La Coquette fixée* (1746), and another abbé, an adventurer from the provinces, Pierre Rousseau, succeeded to their speciality of amorous intrigue—calling himself 'Rousseau de Toulouse' to be distinguished from Jean-Jacques of Geneva, thereby causing more laughter than any of his farcical situations.[124] Pellegrin, the widest-ranging of all the tonsured playwrights, scored his greatest successes in tragedy, especially when he turned from the heroes of antique Greece and Rome to the exotic fringes, with Artaxerxes and Bajazet. The abbé Leblanc also recognized the appeal of settings in the cruel and colourful confines of Asia, and his *Aben Saïd*, with its background of Persia under the successors of Genghis Khan, won applause from Voltaire and earned him 1,000 livres, a large sum for the day.[125] Perhaps abbés of the tragic stage should have turned more often to the Old Testament for themes of violence and pathos, following the way shown by the abbé Boyer's *Judith* (1695), which reduced the ladies to tears but not the men, except one who wept for Holofernes.[126] Aubert's *Mort d'Abel* (1765) did well, and Pellegrin's *Jephthe* (1732) was printed in four editions within the year, with five more to follow; while Voisenon's greatest triumphs were his oratorios on the *Madness of Saul* and the *Israelites on Mount Horeb*; he was less concerned with the severities engraved on the tablets of stone than with the thunder and lightning, and Mondonville composed suitably dramatic music.

III

A phalanx of formal apologists for Christianity replied for the establishment to the attacks of the sceptics and anticlericals of the Enlightenment; these are not counted here as abbés. Bergier, Nonnotte, Guénée, Barruel, Dom Calmet, Gros de Besplas, and the others were more tolerant, and had more common ground with their opponents than has been supposed. On points of logic and scholarly precision, they often had the better of the argument; but they could not repel the assaults on the weakest points in their defences—the concept of eternal punishment in Hell, the literal veracity of the Scriptures and miracles overturning the laws of Nature; and they lacked the extrovert talent to reply in kind to the wits and ironists operating against them.

It is not necessarily a disadvantage for an apologist to be dependent on his book sales for a living: those literary abbés who rallied to the defence of Christianity at least had the trick of being lively and readable. A few took the way of defending the faith not by joining the garrison in the ill-sited defences, but by sorties from the citadel to harass the enemy. Fréron's[127] guerrilla raids threatened the enormous reputation enjoyed by Voltaire and the deference accorded to the coterie arrogating to themselves the title of 'philosophe'. Against them he set his idol, Boileau, and the doctrines of classicism and, contrastingly, the example of Shakespeare, Young, Richardson, Prévost, and Rousseau, who recognized the spark of the divine in the doings of men and had deep resources of sympathy. '*Candide* excites laughter,' he said, 'but leaves despair in the heart.' Combining acceptance of the Enlightenment with 'a virulent conservatism',[128] courageous to endure every insult, his standing enhanced by his choice of lay status independent of the Church and its rewards, Fréron was the philosophes' most dangerous adversary. He swayed opinion not only by his triumphs, but in his defeats, for the persecution unleashed against him by scurrilous innuendo and influence on the government revealed for all to see a strain of malice and injustice in his would-be high-minded foes.

There was only one Fréron, but his school of counter-attack was joined, in 1757, by a rumbustious abbé who struck a notable blow against the philosophes, as it were by accident. This was Odet Giry de Saint-Cyr, who in the *Mercure de France* warned against the 'Cacouacs', a tribe waging war with a venomous poison in their tongues and by weaving illusionist spells. His pedestrian comic invention would soon have been forgotten, but his legendary tribe was brought to vivid life by an account of a voyage to their land published two months later by Moreau—lawyer, historian, and royal pensioner—embarking on satire in the cause of religion and political conservatism. Coded into his account of the illusions conjured up by the Cacouacs were references to Diderot's materialism, Voltaire's scepticism, and Rousseau's egalitarianism, tied together in a single subversive design. The abbé de Saint-Cyr tried to reclaim his property by publishing a 'catechism and manual of casuistry for the use of the Cacouacs'; but it was Moreau who won the applause of the public and the glory of inflicting a rare defeat on the philosophic confraternity.[129]

In contrast to these adversarial tactics, the abbé Pluche had been annexationist, taking the most evocative ideas of the age and combining them to present a world-view in harmony with Christian belief. His naïve and glowing *Spectacle de la Nature* (1736) was a bestseller: Mornet found more copies in eighteenth-century libraries than any other work save Buffon's natural history. At once a glorification of scientific enquiry and a precursor of Rousseauistic deism, it is the work of a Christian believer—indeed, of a principled Jansenist, who lost his teaching post for refusing to take the Formulary. His preferred argument for supporting the faith is minimalist, irrefutable because not presenting a target area: the Church is one of those institutions we accept as given, imposing themselves by 'l'éclat de leur notoriété'.[130] With Jansenist severity, he insists on the Fall and the curse of unremitting toil laid upon mankind, yet he subscribes to the optimism of the Enlightenment, for God has counterbalanced the curse with the gift of sociability.[131] At the same time Pluche was writing, the Jesuits were emulating his design to make apologetics readable by presenting the sacred drama of redemption as an epic tale, and in so doing had fallen foul of ecclesiastical authority. In 1753 the abbé La Baume followed by publishing a sequel to Milton, *La Christiade, ou le Paradis reconquis*. It came to its crisis when Christ, triumphant over death, visits Hell. 'Adam, where art thou?' The question that struck fear in Eden after the first transgression is now an offer of reconciliation: 4,000 years of penitence are over. Unmoved, the parlement of Paris condemned the epic as treating the gospel mysteries too familiarly.

Less obviously, and for the intellectual minority, apologetical issues were involved in one of the more rarefied controversies of the century—concerning aesthetics. Three of the literary abbés were involved; indeed, as a formal discipline, aesthetics was their creation. As befitted such an Olympian subject, they were not professional authors with an eye on the market, but scholars of sophistication, well provided with ecclesiastical benefices and enjoying an entrée to high society; they were respectful to the Church, and one of them, Trublet, was a zealous and committed apologist. There was already a controversy concerning the concept of beauty, whether as an absolute or as existing in the mind of the beholder,[132] and the abbé Dubos, an intellectual of universal scope, diverted it into new and more enlightening courses. Under Louis XIV and the Regency he had been a diplomat, rewarded with a pension, an abbey, and a canonry where he did not reside, and thereafter he wrote on archaeology, numismatics, Homer, the contrasting virtues of the Ancients and Moderns, and finally, in later life, produced a voluminous history of the origins of the French monarchy.[133] In 1719, soon after his diplomatic career ended, he published his *Réflexions critiques sur la poésie et la peinture*. There were abbés who were connoisseurs of the visual arts (Louis Gougenot, consultant on the composition of monuments to Pigalle, and Saint-Non, a familiar of Fragonard and Hubert Robert);[134] Dubos did not have their expertise, but he was widely read and a knowledgeable reviewer of theatrical performances.[135] His *Réflexions critiques* was concerned, not with artistic techniques, but with mental attitudes: looking into the mind, he detected a 'sixth sense' by which beauty was recognized. In the classical tradition, he took beauty as objectively given, and he excluded reason from challenging the findings of the sixth sense— faced with its verdict, 'reason tells us not to reason'. A deficiency in this sense is like blindness, an affliction incurable by thought or application. These principles were modified by two other literary abbés, Trublet and Batteux, who sensed a lurking danger to Christianity; for what if religious feeling and devotion are similarly inspired, say, by a 'seventh sense', with some men for ever blind, incapable of conversion? Trublet rehabilitated reason in a supporting role, allowing education to play a part in developing aesthetic appreciation and, by analogy, in religious conviction; Batteux, in *Les Beaux-Arts réduits à un même principe* (1747), described the intelligence as seeing things according to their essence (that is, he makes reason all-embracing), and *goût* as seeing things in their relationship to us, bringing inspiration. Though aesthetics moved on into greater subtleties, the abbés had founded the discipline, especially Dubos. D'Alembert's *éloge* indicated dissent from Dubos' conclusions, but admitted his influence: 'il a le mérite de faire beaucoup penser . . . il a répandu la semance qui a fait naître les idées'.[136] Apart from this courteous hat doffing, there seems almost to have been a conspiracy to ignore Dubos. For all his learning, he lacked style; his presentation was formless, repetitive, and boring. Batteux, the *Encyclopédie*, and Diderot annexed his themes without acknowledgement, an author not to be praised but plagiarized.

A further theme favoured by the abbés—and this was a popular one—was the working of the mind in matters of conscience. Some wrote as apologists for Christianity, some as advocates of deism: all were high-minded, but it could not be denied that this was a lucrative genre; there was a market for improving books on moral issues—a fashion established by the end of the reign of Louis XIV, when the abbé Jean Richard's voluminous *Discours moraux* had earned him eight times what Molière got for *Tartuffe* and fifty times what Claude Fleury got for the first volume of his ecclesiastical history.[137] Some of their writing provided an entertaining reworking for lay amusement of the dour manuals of the confessional. Between 1741 and 1767 four of them published treatises, and another a novel, to wean their readers from the selfish pursuit of pleasure: separate the true pleasures from the false, recognize those pleasures recommended to us by the obligations of society, do not pursue enjoyment obsessively to hide the inner void behind personal gratification. Chaudon,[138] compiler of a successful *Dictionnaire anti-philosophique* (1767), produced a solemn work in the tradition of reconciling Christianity with worldly *savoir-faire*, *L'Homme du monde éclairé* (1774). Inclining rather to the arguments of the Enlightenment were Sauri's *La Morale du citoyen du monde, ou la morale de la raison* and Duval Pirrau's *Code de la raison*.[139] In them, Christian morality was equated with the dictates of reason, with the unavoidable implication that even if revelation was abandoned, the moral code would remain intact.[140]

From discussion of morality in general, the literary abbés inevitably moved into the long-running controversy over whether works of the imagination, particularly novels, ought to have a moral content. The Jesuit *Mémoires de Trévoux* continually expressed the case for constraints, pugnaciously summed up in 1736 in an oration by Père Porée: the unfettered working of the imagination can threaten morals and be aesthetically disastrous, overthrowing the classical ideal of 'a controlled reworking of nature'.[141] The abbés who joined in the controversy were sufficiently influenced by the notion to hedge their approval of the novel with conditions. The most liberal was Granet, who in 1730 declared that the 'only rule' was 'to please and to amuse', though he insisted on realism of plot and setting—no need to moralize, but foster no illusions, present things as they really are.[142] The test of a novel for Desfontaines was to ask if it presented 'un tableau de la vie humaine', though anything dangerous to religion must be excluded.[143] According to Leblanc, the fault of romances was their all-too-frequent superficiality, and he unchivalrously blamed the ladies for creating the demand for frivolous literature. The reactionary clerical line was taken by the abbé Jaquin, in his *Entretiens sur les romans, ouvrage moral et critique* (1758); it was wrong to present a picture of manners without adding criticism, and he complained especially of romances implying marriage to be the 'self-giving of hearts', independent of 'vain ceremonies', an attack on Prévost's *Cleveland* and Rousseau's *Nouvelle Héloïse*. Further solemnities came from the abbé Chasles in 1785, in his *Timanti*,[144] denouncing authors who rise in the world by writing without serious purpose; he rose himself in consequence, for the archbishop of Tours rewarded him with a canonry. Two examples of the serious purpose which Chasles was demanding had just been published by churchmen, masterpieces of didactic fiction, best-selling and saccharine: Gérard's *Le Comte de Valmont ou les égarements de la raison* (1774), and Maydieu's *Histoire de la vertueuse portugaise, ou le modèle des femmes chrétiennes* (1779). They used the current vogue of *sensibilité* to recommend Christian doctrine and morality, though perhaps they involuntarily contributed to the evolution of fashion towards sentimental deism.

The intellectual warfare between the Christian apologists and the philosophes, in spite of its complexities, is straightforward to chronicle; but almost insuperable difficulties arise concerning an

allied, but less tangible, issue in the literature of the Enlightenment—how to define the relationship of traditional Christianity to
the tide of Rousseauism which swept on to the cult of 'sensibilité' at
the end of the *ancien régime*. Directly or deviously, all the roads of the
century lead to this destination, innumerable writers being involved
in the creation of an optimistic deism incorporating the magic and
wonder of nature and excluding the darkness of sin and the harsh
necessity of redemption. Did the abbés play a significant role,
whether by tacitly limiting apologetical arguments to the more
defensible frontiers of belief, or by airing religious convictions allied
to scepticism about revelation, or, like Delille,[145] according respect
to the old convictions but reserving enthusiasm for the new? An
impressionistic sketch of the eighteenth-century abbés can do no
more than pose the question. It could be that it is from the *sensibilité*
of those years and its associated 'culte des tombeaux'[146] that the
'religion populaire' of today arises, a creedless hope of reunion
beyond the grave, a lingering residue of an abandoned Christianity,
all that is left to cling to in the shadow of death. Perhaps the abbés,
masters of the art of balancing between Church and world, played a
part in shaping this last decadent compromise of all.

Everywhere in the towns of eighteenth-century France, wearers
of the *petit collet* and the *bonnet carré* were to be seen, sauntering in
the streets, showing off in salons and provincial academies, leading
claques in the theatres or at ease in the boxes, tutoring the sons of
the rich, administering households, their exploits enlivening the
newsletters and figuring in novels, their names on the title-pages of
books, successful or remaindered. They were a unique phenomenon
on the margins of a Church whose dominance over men's minds
faltered even as its power in social relationships remained, whose
wealth was out of proportion to its needs and in contradiction to its
ideals, which was so completely absorbed into the life of the nation
that vocation to its service was a routine. The abbés were utterly
diverse in their activities, a disparate group defying generalization;
their common defining characteristics were eligibility to wear a
costume and assume a title and to qualify for an ecclesiastical income
without duties to perform. Their cloth gained them a modicum of
consideration, though they thereby made the cloth of others, the
serious clergy, less respected. Their presence blurred the boundaries
between Church and world. A composite picture derived from
examples over the space of three generations makes them look
more interesting than they were; so many whose doings were not
recorded were provincial nonentities or Parisian failures. But a

collage of the more noteworthy figures at least gives a fair reflection of the impression the abbés made on public opinion. They provided amusement, inspired gossip, brokered ideas, and could be useful; but taken together, they constituted an abuse, a picturesque excrescence on society too expensive to be allowed continued maintenance as the nation slid towards bankruptcy. By their accepted status as drones, they were an incitement to anticlericals to propose the confiscation of the ecclesiastical wealth so many of them so cheerfully misappropriated.

NOTES

CHAPTER I

With the permission of the Clarendon Press I have used my chapter from *Christian Authority: Essays in Honour of Henry Chadwick*, ed. G. L. Evans (1988), as the first section here.

1. Blue coats, white breeches, red stockings, red facings on waistcoats, white belts ('Les Gardes Françaises à Versailles', *Rev. Versailles* (1915), 10). Other details in Claude Manceron, *Les Hommes de la liberté* (2 vols., 1972), i. 208, and P. de Nolhac, *La Reine Marie-Antoinette* (1948), 97–102.
2. The abbé J.-A. de Véri, *Journal*, ed. J. de Witte (2 vols., n.d.), i. 68. Cf. Mme du Deffand to the duchesse de Choiseul, 25 Feb. 1772. *Correspondance complète de Mme du Deffand avec la duchesse de Choiseul, l'abbé Barthélemy et M. Craufort*, ed. Sainte-Aulaire (3 vols., 1880), ii. 138.
3. J. Gog, *A Reims, le sacre des rois de France* (1980), 95.
4. The maréchal de Croÿ, *Journal 1718–1784*, ed. le vicomte de Grouchy and P. Cottin (4 vols., 1906), iii. 173.
5. L. S. Greenbaum, *Talleyrand Statesman-Priest* (1970), 18.
6. *Mémoires du prince de Talleyrand*, ed. the duc de Broglie (5 vols., 1891–2), i. 24. Otherwise, just the vague 'tout était amour! tout était fêtes!'
7. Account in the *Correspondance secrète*, conveniently given in A. Chéruel, *Dictionnaire historique des institutions, mœurs et coutumes de la France* (2 vols., 1855), ii. 1118.
8. Ibid. 1119.
9. See H. Jadart (ed.), 'Journal anonyme', *Trav. Acad. nat. Reims* (1902), 269–315. For description of the sacred object and for its final fate, G. Laurent, 'Le Conventionnel Rühl à Reims: la destruction de la Sainte Ampoule', *Ann. hist. Rév. fr.* (1926), 26.
10. Full wording in Chéruel, *Dictionnaire*, ii. 1119.
11. Gog, *A Reims*, 65.
12. Croÿ, *Journal*, iii. 184; A. N. Duchesne, 'Relation d'un voyage à Reims à l'occasion du Sacre', *Trav. Acad. nat. Reims* (1902), 48.
13. Chéruel, *Dictionnaire*, ii. 1120. The archaic titles had been annexed to the Crown, and the king nominated the six relatives who were to bear them (*Encyclopédie, ou dictionnaire raisonné des Sciences, des Arts et des Métiers*, xiv (1765), 476, s.v. 'Sacre'). The sardonic comment is Manceron's, *Les Hommes*, 215.
14. In fact, a crown made in the late twelfth century for a queen. An identical one for the king had been stolen.
15. H. Destainville, 'La Jeunesse de Danton', *Ann. hist. Rév. fr.* (1928), 427–8.

16. Nolhac, *Marie-Antoinette*, 102; Duchesne, 'Relation', 47; Croÿ, *Journal*, iii. 188.

17. Marie-Antoinette, in *Correspondance secrète entre Marie-Thérèse et le Cte de Mercy-Argenteau avec les lettres de Marie-Thérèse et Marie-Antoinette*, ed. A. d'Arneth and M. A. Geffroy (3 vols., 1875), ii. 343. For the queen's tears etc. see Mercy d'Argenteau's letter, p. 346.

18. F. Masson, *Le Cardinal de Bernis depuis son ministère, 1758–94* (1884), 193 n.

19. Manceron, *Les Hommes*, 223–5.

20. Croÿ, *Journal*, iii. 203–5.

21. Liturgy given in full in Gog, *A Reims*, 61–88.

22. Chéruel, *Dictionnaire*, ii. 1120.

23. M. Bloch, *Les Rois thaumaturges*, trans. J. E. Anderson, *The Royal Touch* (1973), 126–8.

24. J.-J. Chifflet, *Tractatus de sancta Ampulla Remensi*, cited by Gog, *A Reims*, 20. For others, see J. W. Merrick, *The Desacralization of the French Monarchy in the 18th Century* (1990), 21.

25. Letter of 18 June 1740 to Frederick II, in *Corresp.* x (1954), 161 (letter 2110).

26. B. Plongeron, *Théologie et politique au siècle des lumières, 1770–1820* (1973), 64–5.

27. For a defence of the royal power see E. Regnault, *Dissertation touchant le pouvoir accordé aux Rois de France de guérir les Escroüelles, accompagnée de preuves touchant la vérité de la Sainte Ampoule* (1722). Regnault was a canon of Saint-Symphorien of Reims.

28. Bloch, *Les Rois*, 224. See also Voltaire, *Mœurs*, introduction. No less a celebrity than Jansenius had pointed out that the curing of king's evil demonstrated only God's gifts, not a king's right to rule. Balaam's ass had prophesied, but had no right to dominate other animals: R. E. Mousnier, *The Institutions of France under the Absolute Monarchy, 1598–1789*, i, trans. B. Pearce (1974), 675.

29. Luynes, i. 116–17, 154, 426. Barbier, iii. 167. For Louis XV's statement that he did not exercise his healing power because he was not in a state of grace see Merrick, *Desacralization*, 19.

30. Durand de Maillane, *Dictionnaire de droit canonique et de pratique bénéficiale*, 3rd edn. (1776), v. 225, s.v. 'Sacre'.

31. D'Aguesseau (H.-F. Chancelier), *Essai d'une institution du droit public*, ed. L. Rigaud (1955), 123.

32. *Encyclopédie*, xiv. 476.

33. K. M. Baker, 'French Political Thought at the Accession of Louis XVI', *J. Mod. Hist.* (1978), 279–81. For Baker's view of the background, the 'new political culture' arising at the end of the *ancien régime*, see his 'On the Problem of the Ideological Origins of the French Revolution', in D. La Capra and S. L. Kaplan (eds.), *Modern European Intellectual History* (1982), 197–219.

34. *Correspondance secrète*, in Chéruel, *Dictionnaire*, ii. 1120.

35. D. Bien, 'Catholic Magistrates and Protestant Marriage', *Fr. Hist. St.* (1962), 409–25. For the neat legal arguments used, see Guyot, iii, 318–39.

36. D. Dakin, *Turgot* (1939), 217–21.

37. M. C. Peronnet, 'Les Assemblées du Clergé de France sous le règne de Louis XVI, 1775–1788', *Ann. hist. Rév. Fr.* (1962), 29, 31.

38. Ch. Robert, *Urbain de Hercé, dernier évêque de Dol* (1900), 162–3, 183.
39. R. A. Schneider, *The Ceremonial City: Toulouse Observed, 1738–80* (1995), 161–5. For the more general picture, Schneider cites M. Fogel, *Les Cérémonies de l'information dans la France du XVIᵉ au XVIIIᵉ siècle* (1989).
40. For these events in Paris see Barbier, ii. 77, 49–54; iii. 547, 551; Marais, i. 477, 499–500; Barbier, ii. 366–8.
41. A. Delahante, *Une Famille de finance au XVIIIᵉ siècle* (2 vols., 1881), i. 197.
42. A. Bernard, *Le Sermon au XVIIIᵉ siècle, 1715–89* (1901), 276–7.
43. Merrick, *Desacralization*, 125.
44. *Sur les devoirs des Rois*, Palm Sunday, 1662, in *Sermons* (9 vols., 1772), vii. 220–55.
45. A. Sicard, *L'Ancien Clergé de France: les évêques avant la Révolution* (1912), 185.
46. Oath in full in Masson, *Le Cardinal de Bernis*, 37.
47. Guyot, xiv. 254.
48. *Sermon sur les écueils de la piété des grands* (Petit Carême), Massillon, *Œuvres* (14 vols., 1822) vi. 151–76.
49. Cited by A. Mathiez, *Rome et le clergé français sous la Constituante* (1911), 460.
50. Plongeron, *Théologie*, 64–5.
51. Ibid. 115–19.
52. P. Quesnel, *La Discipline de l'Église tirée du Nouveau Testament* (1689), and idem, *La Souveraineté des Rois défendue contre l'Histoire Latine de Melchior Leydecker* (1704), in R. Taveneaux, *Jansénisme et politique* (1965), 124–33.
53. *P.V. Ass.* vii. 1886 (1745).
54. Bossuet, *Politique tirée des propres paroles de l'Écriture Sainte*, ed. J. Lebrun (1967), p. i.
55. Bossuet, *Œuvres Oratoires*, ed. J. Lebarq (6 vols., 1921), iv. 356. Cf. *Politique*, viii (i).
56. Mousnier, *Institutions*, 312–31.
57. J. Rogister, 'The Crisis of 1753–4 in France and the Debate on the Nature of the Monarchy and of the Fundamental Laws', in R. Vierhaus (ed.), *Herrschaftsverträge, Wahlkapitulationen, Fundamentalgesetze* (1977), 105–20. Cf. the gifts of ecclesiastical ornaments the king had to give to the chapter of Reims and to the tomb of Charlemagne at Aix-la-Chapelle: Papillon de la Ferté, *Journal, 1756–80*, ed. E. Boysse (1887), 383–5.
58. M. Antoine, *Le Conseil du Roi sous la règne de Louis XV* (1970), 7–8.
59. Ibid., 15–17.
60. R. Bickart, *Les Parlements et la notion de souveraineté nationale au XVIIIᵉ siècle* (1932), is devoted to this theme.
61. Baker, 'French Political Thought', 279–83.
62. R. L. Herbert, *David, Voltaire, Brutus and the French Revolution: An Essay in Art and Politics* (1972), 15–61, 71–4.
63. L. Voyer de Boutigny (1682), cited by H. Leclerq, *Histoire de la Régence* (3 vols., 1921), vol. i, p. xvi.
64. Marais, iv. 288.
65. D'Aguesseau, *Mémoire* (1718), in J. Carreyre, *Le Jansénisme durant la Régence* (3 vols., 1929–33), ii. 41.
66. Gerbier (*avocat*), cited by L. M. Raison, 'Le Jansénisme à Rennes', *Ann. Bretagne* (1941), 255–6.
67. Guyot, ix. 302.

68. Mousnier, *Institutions*, 315.
69. Gerbier, cited by Raison, 'Le Jansénisme'.
70. Guyot, lxiv. 5–14.
71. The argument that First Estate means 'the Church' rather than 'the Clergy' was not discussed outside clerical circles.
72. Guyot, xi. 290–1; xlvii. 187–92.
73. Père H. Griffet, *Mémoires pour servir à l'histoire de Louis, Dauphin de France* (2 vols., 1777), i. 124–6.
74. *P.V. Ass.* viii/2. 421 (1765).
75. Ibid.
76. Ibid., 425–6.
77. Dom Rémi Carré, *Recueil curieux et édifiant, sur les cloches de l'Église, avec les cérémonies de leur bénédiction* (1759), 67–8.
78. *P.V. Ass.* viii/2. 429.
79. D. Van Kley, 'Church, State and the Ideological Origins of the French Revolution: The Debate over the General Assembly of the Gallican Clergy in 1765', *J. Mod. Hist.* (1979), 629–51.
80. *P.V. Ass.* viii/1. 102–7.
81. Ibid., viii/2. 2313 (1775).
82. J.-M. Goulemot, *Discours, histoire et révolution* (1975), 259–70.
83. Cited by G. Weulersse, *Les Physiocrates* (1931), 311.
84. Maugard, *Remarques sur la noblesse dédiées aux assemblées provinciales* (1787), cited by Y. Durand, *Les Fermiers Généraux au XVIIIe siècle* (1971), 227.
85. *Journal de l'Assemblée des Notables de 1787 par le comte de Brienne, et Loménie de Brienne, archevêque de Toulouse*, ed. P. Chevallier (1960), 149.

CHAPTER 2

1. Guyot, iv. 60–2.
2. Ibid. x. 365.
3. Luynes, xi. 389; iv. 84; viii. 437, 440, 137; iii. 298; v. 288; E. Lavaquery, *Le Cardinal de Boisgelin* (2 vols., 1920), i. 316; Mme du Hausset, *The Private Memoirs of Louis XV* (Eng. trans. 1895), 20–1; the maréchal de Croÿ, *Journal, 1718–84*, ed. the vicomte de Grouchy and P. Cottin (4 vols., 1906), i. 439–40.
4. The actual office gave revenues of 14,400 livres, of which 6,000 was as a commander of the Ordre du Saint-Esprit (Guyot, iv. 62). He named chaplains of regiments, and had the hospital of the Quinze-Vingts and the convent of the Assumption under his jurisdiction (Luynes, vi. 260).
5. A. Sicard, *L'Ancien Clergé de France: les évêques avant la Révolution* (1912), 209–13.
6. Georgel, *Mémoires pour servir à l'histoire de la fin du 18e siècle* (6 vols., 1820), ii. 5–6, 11–18.
7. Sicard, *L'Ancien Clergé*, 209–15.
8. Luynes, ii. 410–12; iv. 100; viii. 469.
9. L. Bassette, *Jean de Caulet, évêque de Grenoble* (1946), 16–17. Cf. *Mémoires de la duchesse de Brancas*, ed. E. Asse (1890): 'La chapelle du Roi était, pour les jeunes ecclésiastiques, une autre espèce de séminaire qui les préparait à entrer dans le monde, comme les mousquetaires en étaient une pour ceux

qui se destinaient au service.'

10. F. Masson, *Le Cardinal de Bernis depuis son ministère, 1758–94* (1884), 426.
11. Luynes, iii. 423; vii. 298. For the importance of the office see Saint-Simon (Pléiade), iii. 447–8.
12. J. Levron, *La Vie quotidienne à la Cour de Versailles* (1965), 40–53, 135. Saint-Simon's account (iv. 1081–92) of Louis XIV's religious observances in his pious later years differs somewhat.
13. Luynes, i. 228–31; iv. 114.
14. Ibid. i. 235; iv. 115.
15. Ibid. i. 345; iv. 116–17; vi. 405; ix. 77.
16. Mme de Campan, *Mémoires* (2 vols., 1822), i. 316.
17. Luynes, iii. 367; iv. 13; vii. 283.
18. Ibid. i. 427–8; vii. 276.
19. Strictly, the rules of the Lazarists forbade any of their members to take episcopal rank.
20. E. Houth, *Versailles, la paroisse royale* (1962), 36–8, 46, 59, 63, 111–14, 138. Similar figures from the archbishop's visitation of 1784: 45,000 parishioners, 14 priests (A. Joly, 'La Paroisse de Notre-Dame de Versailles pendant la Révolution', *Rev. Versailles* (1973–5), 33).
21. Saint-Simon, iv. 1094.
22. Luynes, ii. 176; M. Leroy, 'Une Visite à l'église Notre-Dame de Versailles', *Rev. Versailles* (1912), 215.
23. Houth, *Versailles*, 42–4. He was also there for a Te Deum on 4 Sept.
24. Luynes, v. 458.
25. Ibid. xiii. 2. The last *fête-Dieu* at the parish with the Court present was on 11 June 1789. The procession for the opening of the Estates General started here, 4 May 1789 (*Gazette de France*, 12 May 1789).
26. Y. Bezard, 'L'Assistance à Versailles sous l'ancien régime', *Rev. Versailles* (1919), 67–80, 242–51.
27. P. Bienvenue, 'La Manufacture royale de dentelles et de blondes établie pour l'instruction des enfants pauvres de Versailles', *Rev. Versailles* (1954), 18.
28. C. Kunstler, *La Vie quotidienne sous la Régence* (1960), 185.
29. Signing himself 'curé' (E. Mennet de Goutel, 'L'Exposition de Marie-Antoinette à la bibliothèque de Versailles', *Rev. Versailles* (1929), 107). See also the list of baptisms, weddings, and funerals of the royal family, and the families of Orléans, Condé, Conti, Bourbon, Maine, and Penthièvre in L.-A. Gatin, 'Les Anciens Registres de l'état civil de Versailles', *Rev. Versailles* (1913), 27–31.
30. P. de Nolhac, *Louis XV et Marie Leczinski* (1922), 80.
31. Saint-Simon, iii. 845.
32. Luynes, iii. 208.
33. Ibid. xi. 399–402.
34. P. Fromageot, 'La Mort et les obsèques de Mme de Pompadour', *Rev. Versailles* (1902), 275–87; M. Tourneux, 'Un Mot célèbre qui n'a jamais été prononcé', *Rev. Versailles* (1903), 25–6.
35. The queen went to Paris, Sept. 1728, to Notre-Dame and Sainte-Geneviève to pray for a male heir (Nolhac, *Louis XV et Marie Leczinski*, 143–7).
36. Saint-Simon, iii. 644.
37. Luynes, viii. 361–3.

38. Saint-Simon, vii. 262–4.
39. Luynes, i. 228; vi. 213; vii. 277; viii. 167–70. (For duchesses claiming the monopoly of parasols at the Corpus Christi procession, see v. 35.)
40. Luynes, vii. 358–9; xi. 411.
41. Ibid. i. 436–7; ii. 3.
42. Ibid. vi. 138–9.
43. Guyot, xv. 295–6. *P.V. Ass.* vi. 1769–75 (1723). Other clashes: ibid. vi. 1493, 1169, 1232–4.
44. Luynes, vii. 51–2.
45. Ibid. ix. 74 n.
46. Ibid. ix. 73.
47. Ibid. i. 111–12.
48. Ibid. vii. 357.
49. 'Les Obsèques de Louis XIV et de Louis XV', *Rev. Versailles* (1907), 70–3. Cf. the plot of bishops to get better chairs at the dauphin's funeral in 1712 (Saint-Simon, iii. 1190–1).
50. Saint-Simon (Pléiade), iv. 531.
51. Luynes, i. 107–8.
52. E. Oroux, *Histoire ecclésiastique de la Cour de France* (2 vols., 1777), ii. 633–4.
53. François-Joachim de Pierre, cardinal de Bernis, *Mémoires et lettres*, ed. F. Masson (2 vols., 1878), i. 45.
54. Sicard, *L'Ancien Clergé*, 209.
55. A. Bernard, *Le Sermon au XVIIIᵉ siècle, 1715–89* (1901), 42–3.
56. Ibid. 119.
57. Ibid. 120; Luynes, v. 53.
58. Luynes, iii. 129; iv. 88; xiii. 148; xvi. 354. See also iv. 15; xi. 392; xiv. 405–6, and D'Argenson, viii. 265–6.
59. Luynes, iv. 114.
60. Ibid. iv. 263–4.
61. Ibid. xi. 392.
62. Ibid. viii. 21–2. (For a canon of Sens who had not prepared an alternative, see vii. 139.)
63. Ibid. ix. 7.
64. Ibid. iv. 15.
65. Barbier, ii. 456–7.
66. D'Argenson, vi. 370, 378 (Mar. 1751).
67. Ibid. viii. 265–6; Luynes, xiii. 228.
68. Luynes, xiv. 405–6.
69. E. and J. de Goncourt, *La du Barry* (1880), 178.
70. J. Levron, *Un Libertin fastueux, le maréchal de Richelieu* (1971), 383–5.
71. A. Rosne, *M. de Beauvais, évêque de Senez, 1731–1790* (1883), 35–7.
72. Bachaumont, vii. 114 (7 Feb. 1774).
73. J. Truchet, *La Prédication de Bossuet* (2 vols., 1960), ii. 219–21.
74. Ibid. ii. 223.
75. P. Girault de Coursac, *L'Éducation d'un Roi. Louis XVI* (1972), 252–3.
76. Métra, vi. 181–2 (23 Apr. 1778). (Voltaire was in Paris, and the abbé de Beauregard had attacked him in his Lenten sermons (ibid. vi. 183).)
77. Sicard, *L'Ancien Clergé*, 209.
78. Luynes, ii. 227.

79. G. Minois, *Le Confesseur du roi* (1988), 493–7.
80. Ibid. 508.
81. According to Hardy, *Mes loisirs*, ed. M. Tourneux and M. Vitrac (1912), 7, the Jesuits helped his father, a grocer of the faubourg Saint-Antoine, when he went bankrupt, then promoted his own ecclesiastical career by taking him on as a sacristan. For the story that the Jesuits even wanted to have the dauphin's *valet de chambre* as one of theirs, see 'Mémoires de Marc-Antoine Thierry, baron du ville d'Auray', *Rev. Versailles* (1908), 84.
82. R. Roux, 'L'Abbé Madier archiprêtre de Paris, confesseur de Mesdames, 1725–1799', *Rev. Versailles* (1924), 21–39.
83. Montesquieu, *Lettres persanes*, letter 107, ed. L. Versini (1995), 215. The two powers are rivals under a young king, allies under an old.
84. J. Sareil, *Les Tencin: histoire d'une famille au XVIIIᵉ siècle* (1969), 362–5.
85. Bernis, *Mémoires*, ii. 70–1. For Desmaretz's appointment in 1753 see E. Regnault, *Christophe de Beaumont, archevêque de Paris, 1703–81* (2 vols., 1882), i. 247–8.
86. Girault de Coursac, *L'Éducation*, 214–15; Minois, *Le Confesseur*, 511–15.
87. See L. Dussieux, *Le Château de Versailles* (2 vols., 1881), ii. 108–12, and L. Deshàirs, 'Documents inédits sur la chapelle du château de Versailles, 1689–1772', *Rev. Versailles* (1905), 241–62.
88. Deshàirs, 'Documents', 261–2.
89. La Bruyère, *Les Caractères*, viii. 74, ed. R. Barthes (1965), 240.
90. Luynes, v. 95 (June 1743).
91. Ch. Hirschauer, 'Les Premières Expériences aérostatiques à Versailles', *Rev. Versailles* (1916), 39–40.
92. Bachaumont, xiii. 251–2 (12 Jan. 1779). Taken as a plot to hint that Louis XVI was not the father by G. Walter, *Le Comte de Provence* (1950), 97.
93. P. de Nolhac, *Marie-Antoinette, Dauphine* (1896), 102; A. N. Duchesne, 'Relation d'un voyage à Reims à l'occasion du Sacre de Louis XVI', *Trav. Acad. nat. Reims* (1902), 47.
94. J. Flammermont, *La Journée du 14 Juillet 1789* (1892), pp. clxxv–vi.
95. Ascribed to Mme de Lafayette.
96. F. Evrard, 'Les Mœurs à Versailles sous Louis XVI', *Rev. Versailles* (1928), 95–204.
97. Mme de Campan, *Mémoires*, i. 12–13.
98. P. de Nolhac, *Louis XV à Versailles* (1934), 19–28.
99. L. Madelin, *Le Crépuscule de la monarchie* (1936), 112.
100. Cited by G. Poisson, *M. de Saint-Simon* (1973), 187.
101. Y. Coirault, *L'Optique de Saint-Simon* (1965), 302, 465–6, 576–7. For the injustice to Le Tellier, see P. Bliard, *Les Mémoires de Saint-Simon et le père le Tellier* (1891).
102. Mme du Hausset, *Private Memoirs*, 42.
103. Croÿ, *Journal*, i. 353.
104. J. N. Dufort, comte de Cheverny, *Mémoires sur les règnes de Louis XV et Louis XVI* (2 vols., 1886), i. 173 (date *c*.1755).
105. Mme du Hausset, *Private Memoirs*, 44.
106. Levron, *La Vie quotidienne*, 132.
107. See J. McManners, *Death and the Enlightenment* (1981), for the qualifications made by the theologians.

108. Croÿ, *Journal*, iii. 88, 109.
109. If gossip is to be believed, Louis insisted that the teenage girls he kept in his harem at the Parc aux Cerfs, attend mass, and say their prayers before going to bed with him ([J. L. Soulavie], *Mémoires historiques et anecdotes de la cour de France pendant la faveur de la marquise de Pompadour* (1802), 237–8).
110. Nolhac, *Marie-Antoinette*, 323, says his last Easter duty was in 1736. Luynes, however (i. 350), says in 1737 that the king's custom is to communicate five times yearly.
111. Croÿ, *Journal*, iii. 97.
112. Luynes, vi. 47–8, 85.
113. Croÿ, *Journal*, i. 366; Dufort, *Mémoires*, i. 182, 188.
114. D'Argenson, ix. 196–8; Luynes, xv. 324–5; Croÿ, *Journal*, iii. 335–8.
115. G. Desnoiresterres, *Voltaire et la société française au XVIIIe siècle*, 2nd edn. (8 vols., 1867–76), v. 196–7.
116. E. and J. de Goncourt, *Mme de Pompadour* (1888), 124. Soubise called on her husband to warn him not to.
117. Croÿ, *Journal*, ii. 137.
118. Luynes, i. 113–14; vi. p. iii; x. 19. D'Argenson, viii. 77 (19 July 1753).
119. D'Argenson, vii. 16–17.
120. Luynes, vi. 419; vii. 91. Girault de Coursac, *L'Éducation*, 19–20.
121. E. and J. de Goncourt, *Marie-Antoinette* (1875), 34–5.
122. Luynes, xi. 423. Cf. Mme de Campan, *Mémoires*, i. 29.
123. Girault de Coursac, *L'Éducation*, 33; D'Argenson, vii. 100–1, 130, 179–80.
124. [J. L. Soulavie], *Mémoires historiques et politiques du règne de Louis XVI* (6 vols., 1801).
125. Ph. Mansel, *Louis XVIII* (1981), 12.
126. Police report of 1765 that du Barry slept with her daily but also farmed her out to the great, on this particular day to the maréchal de Richelieu and the marquis de Villeroy (cited by M. Mansergh, 'The Revolution of 1771' (Oxford Ph.D. thesis, 1973), 90–100).
127. Walter, *Le Comte de Provence*, 15–16.
128. Campan, *Mémoires*, i. 336 ff.; Nolhac, *Marie-Antoinette*, 323–5; E. and J. de Goncourt, *La du Barry*, 1–2.
129. Nolhac, *Marie-Antoinette*, 326.
130. Croÿ, *Journal*, iii. 100–1.
131. Nolhac, *Marie-Antoinette*, 328.
132. Croÿ, *Journal*, iii. 104.
133. Sicard, *L'Ancien Clergé*, 202.
134. *Lettre de Voltaire à M. de Beauvais, évêque de Senez*, in App. X of A. de Coulanges, *La Chaire française au 18e siècle* (1901), 524.
135. R. Metz, *La Monarchie française et la provision des bénéfices ecclésiastiques en Alsace, 1648–1789* (1947), 65 ff. The Crown collected the revenues of these benefices in the vacancies (ten months was the limit of vacancy, and once a nomination was made, only one-third of the revenue was appropriated until the taking of possession). There was a bureau, the Œconomats, of six *conseillers d'État* and four *maîtres des requêtes* to handle these revenues—they went to pension converted Protestants and to support new parishes in which the king had an interest (e.g. Saint-Louis at Versailles). See Luynes, xvi. 472–3 (June 1758).

136. See Ch. 20 below.
137. *Relation de la Cour de France en 1690, par Ézéchiel Spanheim, envoyé . . . de Brandenbourg*, ed. M. Ch. Schefer (Soc. de l'histoire de France, 1882), 278–9.
138. M. Antoine, *Le Conseil du Roi sous le règne de Louis XV* (1970), 61.
139. Dom H. Leclercq, *Histoire de la Régence* (3 vols., 1921), i. 403.
140. Métra, vi. 199–200 (1778).
141. Bernis, *Mémoires et lettres*, i. 40.
142. Marais, i. 36–7, 49–51.
143. Bernis, *Mémoires*, Masson's Introduction, i. p. xxvii.
144. E. Appolis, *Le Jansénisme dans le diocèse de Lodève* (1952), 72–3.
145. Luynes, xi. 3 (Jan. 1751).
146. Bernis, *Mémoires*, i. 73–4.
147. Ibid. i. 81; Luynes, vii. 269–70: Sicard, *L'Ancien Clergé*, 496.
148. D'Argenson, iv. 213. (Cf. the Jansenist Pavie de Fourquevaux, *Catéchisme historique et dogmatique* (1768), iii. 259–60; cited by Appolis, *Le Jansénisme*, 239.)
149. D'Argenson, iv. 214.
150. Bernis, *Mémoires*, i. 81–2. For his severity—refusing a bishopric to the nephew of a bishop because of a madrigal—see C. Collé, *J. hist.* (1911), 193–4.
151. Letter to Tercier, 3 Feb. 1764, in *Correspondance secrète inédite de Louis XV sur la politique étrangère*, ed. E. Boutaric (2 vols., 1866), i. 311–12.
152. To the duchesse de Choiseul, 25 Feb. 1772: *Correspondance complète de Mme du Deffand avec la duchesse de Choiseul*, ed. M. de Sainte-Aulaire (3 vols., 1877), ii. 138.
153. P. Vial, 'L'Église de France vue par le nonce en 1766', *Cahiers hist.* (1963), 109.
154. Louis d'Illiers, *Deux prélates de l'ancien régime: les Jarente* (1948), 29–32.
155. Ibid. 32.
156. Sicard, *L'Ancien Clergé*, 508 n.
157. To the duchesse de Choiseul, 25 Feb. 1772 (cf. n. 152).
158. J.-A. de Véri, *Journal*, ed. J. de Witte (2 vols., n.d.), ii. 68–9.
159. Ch. Monternot, *Yves-Alex. de Marbeuf, . . . archevêque de Lyon, 1734–99* (1911), 11–19.
160. Bachaumont, xxii. 296–7 (May 1783). The abbé de Bourbon, son of Mlle de Romans, wandered in Italy and died at Naples in 1787.
161. Métra, v. 261–2 (11 Nov. 1777).
162. Mme de Campan, *Mémoires*, i. 237 (a secret agreement at Court to keep all priories for nobles; she was censured by Vermond because she obtained a priory for a curé).
163. D'Argenson, iv. 213; viii. 453.
164. Vial, 'L'Église', 109.
165. F. de Saint-Just, *Témoins de quatre siècles* (1962), 194.
166. *Lettres de Turgot à la duchesse d'Enville, 1764–74, 1777–80*, ed. J. Rowet (Travaux de la Faculté de Philosophie et des Lettres de l'Université Catholique de Louvain, 1976), 148.
167. Voltaire, *Corresp.* lxxxi. 139–40 (Mar. 1772).
168. The baron A. de Maricourt, 'Lettres de l'abbé Le Gouz au baron de Gémeaux', *Rev. quest. hist.* (1914), 120–1.

169. A Sicard, *La Nomination aux bénéfices ecclésiastiques avant 1789* (1896), 12.

CHAPTER 3

1. H. Doniol, *Le Comte de Vergennes et F. M. Hennin* (1898), 89–90.
2. *Éloge de Reinhard*, cited by F. Masson, *Le Cardinal de Bernis, la suppression des Jésuites* (1884), i. p. xi.
3. François-Joachim de Pierre, cardinal de Bernis, *Mémoires et lettres*, ed. F. Masson (2 vols., 1878), ii. 88.
4. His reports in A. de Saint-Priest, *Histoire de la chute des jésuites* (1846), app. V.
5. Bernis, *Mémoires*, i. 77.
6. The abbé J.-A. de Véri, *Journal*, ed. J. de Witte (2 vols., n.d.), i. 2–3, 5–8, 33, 37.
7. For these two see Bernis, *Mémoires*, Masson's notes at i. 275, 171.
8. Guyot, ix. 252–9; J. F. Bluche, *L'Origine des magistrats du Parlement de Paris au XVIIIe siècle, 1715–71* (1956), 58, 61, 96–7, 194–5, 218, 221–4, 361, 367–8; G. Desnoiresterres, *Voltaire et la société française au XVIIIe siècle*, 2nd edn. (8 vols., 1867–76), vii. 388–90; B. de Lacombe, *La Résistance janséniste: l'abbé Nigon de Berty, 1704–77* (1948). A new study of the *conseillers-clercs* has just appeared: W. Doyle, 'Secular Simony: The Clergy and the Sale of Offices in 18th-Century France', in N. Aston (ed.), *Religious Change in Europe, 1650–1914* (1997), 135–47.
9. A. Tuetey, *Répertoire général des sources manuscrites de l'histoire de Paris pendant la Révolution* (11 vols., 1890–1914), i. 296, 328.
10. J. McManners, *Death and the Enlightenment* (1981), 381–9.
11. Mme de Sévigné, *Lettres*, ed. G. Gailly (3 vols., Pléiade, 1953), i. 573 (20 June 1672).
12. F. de Dainville, *La Géographie des humanistes* (1940), 257–8.
13. M.-C. Varachaud, 'La Formation des aumôniers de la Marine du Roi Soleil', *Rev. hist. Église Fr.* (1994), 65–83.
14. Guyot, iv. 65.
15. M. Giraud, 'La Crise de conscience et l'autorité à la fin du règne de Louis XIV', *Ann.* (1952), 294–7.
16. A. Carré, 'Notes sur l'histoire de la médecine du travail et l'ergomanie dans la marine', *Rev. hist. écon. sociale* (1969), 271–3; A. Cabantous and J. Messiaen, *Gens de mer à Dunkerque aux XVIIe et XVIIIe siècles* (1979), 31–8.
17. P. M. Conlon, *Jean-François Bion et sa relation des tourments soufferts par les forçats Protestants* (1960), 14, 25, 18, 86–7.
18. A. Cabantous, *Le Ciel dans la mer: Christianisme et civilisation maritime, XVIe–XIXe siècle* (1990), 222–3, 234–5. For the Irish seminary at Nantes see C. Berthelot du Chesnay, *Les Prêtres Séculiers en Haute-Bretagne au XVIIIe siècle* (1974), 169–71.
19. Ibid., 236–7.
20. Guyot, iv. 64.
21. Marriages conducted by army chaplains were suspect (L. Châtellier, *Tradition chrétienne et renouveau catholique dans les cadres de l'ancien diocèse de Strasbourg, 1650–1770* (1981), 253).
22. A. Babeau, *La Vie militaire sous l'ancien régime,* i: *Les Soldats* (1889), 225.

23. A. Redier and G. Hénocque, *Les Aumôniers militaires français* (1940), 124–8, basic for all this section.

24. E. Regnault, *Christophe de Beaumont, archevêque de Paris, 1703–81* (2 vols., 1882), ii. 336; F. Masson, *Le Cardinal de Bernis depuis son ministère* (1884), 342.

25. *Les Invalides: trois siècles d'histoire* (Musée de l'Armée, 1974), 163–5, 176, 191–4, 197, 210–11.

26. See J.-P. Bois, *Les Anciens Soldats dans la société française au XVIIIe siècle* (1990).

27. Germain Brice, *Description nouvelle de la ville de Paris* (3 vols., 1713), cited in *Les Invalides*, 211. For another testimony to the 'sincere piety of these defenders of the fatherland', by the abbé Hébert, 'Dix jours à Paris, 1791', ed. J.-A. des Retours, *Rev. quest. hist.* (1937), 70.

28. A. Corvisier, *L'Armée française de la fin du XVIIIe siècle au ministère de Choiseul: le soldat* (2 vols., 1964), ii. 866.

29. François de Chennevières, *Détails militaires dont la connaissance est nécessaire aux officiers* (4 vols., 1742), ii. 147; cited by Redier and Hénocque, *Les Aumôniers*, 126.

30. Babeau, *La Vie militaire*, i. 227; A. Corvisier, 'La Mort du soldat depuis la fin du Moyen Âge', *Rev. hist.* (1975), 10.

31. Corvisier, *L'Armée française*, ii. 865–7.

32. J. Godefroy, 'Dom Chardon', *Rev. Mabillon* (1944), 82–3.

33. J.-M. Alliot, *Le Clergé de Versailles pendant la Révolution* (1912), 30–1.

34. 'Le Journal de guerre de M. Nicolas Segretier', ed. 'P.G.', *Bull. Soc. Orléanais*, NS 1 (1959), 170–6. For another chaplain see G. Robert, 'La Vie d'un aumônier militaire au 18e siècle', *Rev. hist. armée* (1972), 23–37.

35. Bachaumont, xxi. 156–7 (Oct. 1782).

36. J. Gaudemet, 'Législation canonique et attitudes séculaires à l'égard du lien matrimonial au XVIIe siècle', *XVIIe Siècle* (1974), 15–24.

37. B. Plongeron, *Théologie et politique au siècle des lumières, 1770–1820* (1973), 200–16.

38. Ibid. 211.

39. Ibid. 225–34.

40. M. Marion, *Dictionnaire des institutions de la France aux XVIIe et XVIIIe siècles* (2 vols., 1923), i. 215.

41. J. Brunet, *Le Parfait Notaire apostolique*, rev. Durand de Maillane, rev. edn. (2 vols., 1775), i. 215.

42. A. Dupuy, 'La Collégiale de Notre-Dame de la Fosse', *Ann. Bretagne* (1889–90), 604. The resentment of the curés was evident when the intendant asked them for population statistics in 1785. They referred him to the *greffe* where they had to deposit copies of their registers (C. Berthelot du Chesnay, *Les Prêtres séculiers en Haute-Bretagne* (1974), 550).

43. A duty of curés, according to one who did not do so himself (J. Salvini, 'Clergé rural en Haut-Poitou à la veille de la Révolution', *Bull. Soc. Ouest* (1957–8), 240).

44. L. Cahen, 'La Question de l'état civil à Paris au 18e siècle', *Rév. fr.* (1909), 193–202.

45. D. Diderot, *Correspondance*, ed. G. Roth and J. Varloot (16 vols., 1955–70), viii. 212 (Nov. 1768).

46. Dupy, 'La Collégiale', 476.

47. C. L. Chassin, *Les Cahiers des curés* (1921), 180.

48. M. Delamare, *Traité de la Police* (4 vols., 1722), i. 287.

49. Ibid. i. 240, 221–2.

50. O. Christin, 'Sur la condamnation du blasphème (XVIe–XVIIe siècles)', *Rev. hist. Église Fr.* (1994), 43–65. See also A. Cabantous, 'Du blasphème au blasphémateur', in P. Dartevelle (ed.), *Blasphèmes et libertés* (1993), 11–31.

51. N. Rateneau, 'Les Peines capitales et corporelles en France sous l'ancien régime', *Ann. internat. crim.* (1963), 303.

52. F. Hildesheimer, 'La Répression du blasphème au XVIIIe siècle', *Mentalités* (1989), 70.

53. Guyot, vi. 210.

54. Ibid. vi. 209.

55. E. Appolis, *Le Jansénisme dans le diocèse de Lodève au XVIIIe siècle* (1952), 200.

56. McManners, *Death*, ch. 11.

57. P. Rétat et al., *L'Attentat de Damiens: discours sur l'événement au XVIIIe siècle*, Centre d'Études du XVIIIe siècle, Univ. Lyon, 2 (1979); Barbier, ii. 421 (29 Aug. 1733). At this time, Barbier says, such a theft in a church would have been punished with a flogging only.

58. Guyot, lvii. 145.

59. J. P. Gutton, *La Société et les pauvres: l'exemple de la généralité de Lyon, 1534–1789* (1971), 202.

60. O. H. Hufton, *The Poor of Eighteenth-Century France, 1750–1789* (1974), 251. For two sentences of perpetual slavery on the galleys for blasphemy, see R. Demogue, 'La Criminalité . . . en Champagne', *Trav. Acad. nat. Reims* (1904), 137.

61. Dom Pierre Chastelain, *Journal, 1709–1782*, ed. M. Jadert (1902), year 1725.

62. T. J. Schmitt, *L'Organisation ecclésiastique et la pratique religieuse dans l'archidiaconé d'Autun de 1650 à 1750* (1957), p. lxxxiii.

63. G. Bouchard, *Le Village immobile: Sennely-en-Sologne au XVIIIe siècle* (1972), 278.

64. Barbier, i. 95 (Dec. 1720). The soldier was executed by burning.

65. L. Baloche, *L'Église Saint-Merry de Paris* (2 vols., 1911), i. 488.

66. P. Chevallier, *La Première Profanation du temple maçonnique, ou Louis XV et la Fraternité, 1737–1755* (1968), 52.

67. Guyot, lvii. 144–5.

68. S. T. McCloy, *The Humanitarian Movement in 18th-Century France* (1937), 174.

69. Guyot, lvii. 144–5; there were burnings for sacrilege at Mende in 1787 and at Montpellier in 1789 (Hufton, *Poor*, 251). Did the parlements and the other 'sovereign courts' tend to a greater strictness than inferior courts? This was the case in Lorraine in the early eighteenth century (A. Logette, 'La Peine capitale devant la cour souveraine de Lorraine et Barrois à la fin du règne de Louis XIV', *XVIIe Siècle* (1980), 14).

70. A. Dinaux, 'Sacrilège à Lille en 1713', *Archives historiques et littéraires du nord de la France et du midi de la Belgique*, 2e sér. 5 (1844), 82–5.

71. Montesquieu, *L'Esprit des Lois*, xxvi. 8 (Pléiade (2 vols., 1951), ii. 758).

72. Ibid. xii. 4 (Pléiade, ii. 433).

73. Voltaire, 'Blasphème', in *Dictionnaire philosophique*, in *Œuvres*, xvii. 3.

74. Voltaire, *Prix de la justice et de l'humanité*, in *Œuvres*, xxx. 554.

75. Guyot, vi. 210.

76. McManners, *Death*, 375.

77. M. Chassaigne, *Le Procès du Chevalier de la Barre* (1920), 154–5.
78. Ibid. 41.
79. Ibid. 181.
80. Martial-Levé, *Louis-François-Gabriel d'Orléans de la Motte, évêque d'Amiens, 1683–1774* (1962), 130.
81. Voltaire, *Relation de la mort du Chevalier de La Barre*, in *Œuvres*, xxv. 503–6.
82. Voltaire, *Prix de la justice*, in *Œuvres*, xxx. 556.
83. Voltaire, *Relation de la mort*, in *Œuvres*, xxv. 542–5.
84. J.-B. Thiers, *Traité des jeux et des divertissements qui peuvent être permis, ou qui doivent être défendus aux chrétiens* (1686), 413.
85. Guyot, xxiv. 526–31.
86. P. Crousaz-Crétet, *Paris sous Louis XIV* (2 vols. 1922–3), ii. 237; A. Rébillon, 'Recherches sur les anciennes corporations . . . de Rennes', *Ann. Bretagne* (1902–3), 424.
87. Y. Brisset de Morcour, *La Police séculière des dimanches et fêtes dans l'ancienne France* (1938), 84.
88. Ibid. 78–84.
89. Ibid. 69–70.
90. Restif de la Bretonne, *L'École des Pères* (3 vols. 1776).
91. Guyot, xxiv. 526–33.
92. Brisset de Morcour, *La Police*, 71.
93. P. Wolff, *Histoire de Toulouse* (1974), 360.
94. P. de Saint-Jacob, *Documents relatifs à la communauté villageoise en Bourgogne* (1962), 60–1.
95. F. Baqué and A. Rouquette, *Un Village du littoral au cours des siècles: Bouziques* (1960), 121–2.
96. Brisset de Morcour, *La Police*, 60.
97. Ibid. 61–7.
98. J.-B. Lyonnet, *Histoire de Mgr d'Aviau-du-Bois-de-Sanzay, archevêque de Vienne et de Bordeaux* (2 vols. 1847), i. 129.
99. R. Mandrou, *De la culture populaire aux 17e et 18e siècles* (1964), 126.
100. Reports that Sunday is observed in country areas: Bouchard, *Sennely*, 288–9; J. Déchelette, 'Visites pastorales des archiprêtrés de Charlieu par Mgr De Lort de Sérignan de Valras, évêque de Mâcon, 1745–64', *Ann. Acad. Mâcon* 3e ser., 6 (1901), 422. Reports that it is not: Hubrecht, 'La Région, Sedanaise à la veille de la Révolution', *Ann. hist. Rév. fr.* (1936), 324.
101. J. de Viguerie, 'Les Missions intérieures des Doctrinaires Toulousains au début du XVIIIe siècle: un missionnaire, le père Jean-Baptiste Badou', *Rev. hist.* (1969), 48.
102. J. Delumeau, *Histoire du diocèse de Rennes* (1979), 128.
103. M. C. Péronnet, *Les Évêques de l'ancienne France* (2 vols., 1977), ii. 779–80.
104. Thomas Bentley, *Journal of a Visit to Paris, 1776*, ed. P. France (1977), 34–5. Cf. Voltaire on the gloom of the English Sunday, *Lettres philosophiques*, 6e lettre in *Mélanges* (Pléiade, 1901), 17.
105. H. C. Payne, *The Philosophes and the People* (1976), 122.
106. Voltaire, *Œuvres*, xxviii. 312.
107. The abbé C. I. C. Saint-Pierre, *Œuvres* (7 vols. 1735–41), vi. 73–5.
108. A. Sicard, *Les Études classiques avant la Révolution* (1887), 265.
109. H. Grange, *Les Idées de Necker* (1974), 193–4.

110. Marion, *Dictionnaire*, i. 72.

111. M. Marais, iv. 7.

112. Luynes, xiii. 183 (Mar. 1754).

113. Ibid. xi. 59 (Feb. 1751).

114. Guyot, vii. 435.

115. D'Argenson, viii. 394.

116. M. Fosseyeux, 'Le Cardinal de Noailles et l'administration du diocèse de Paris', *Rev. hist.* (1913), 267.

117. Guyot, vii. 437.

118. R. Laprune, *Histoire religieuse de Montier-sur-Saulx* (1969), ii. 47.

119. C. Port, *Inventaire analytique des archives anciennes de la Mairie d'Angers* (1861), 274–5.

120. G. Cormary, *Loménis de Brienne à Toulouse, 1763–1788* (1935), 14.

121. Voltaire, 'Carême', in *Dictionnaire philosophique*, in *Œuvres*, xviii. 53–4.

122. Guyot, vii. 433.

123. G. Avenel, *Anarcharsis Cloots* (2 vols., 1865), i. 10–11.

124. Voltaire, *Requête à tous les magistrats* (1770), in *Œuvres*, xviii. 342–5.

125. Grimm, viii. 33–4. Cf. Bachaumont on the abbé Georgel's composition for the Lenten pastoral of the Court, xxxi. 201–3.

126. M. Vallery-Radot, *Un Administrateur ecclésiastique à la fin de l'ancien régime: le Cardinal de Luynes, archevêque de Sens (1753–88)* (1966), 50.

127. Cited by A. Monod, *De Pascal à Chateaubriand: les défenseurs français du Christianisme de 1670 à 1802* (1916), 214.

128. G. Maugras, *La Fin d'une société: le duc de Lauzan et la cour intime de Louis XV* (1895), 17.

129. Getting butter sent up from Brittany to Paris, a basket of twelve 'pots' every week. Letter of 13 Jan. 1787 in A. Le Moy, *Le XVIIIᵉ siècle breton . . . correspondance inédite de M. M. de Robian et de la Bellangerais, 1765–91* (n.d.), 253.

130. Mme de Campan, *Mémoires sur la vie de Marie Antoinette*, ed. F. Barrière (1886), 28–9.

131. Voltaire, *Corresp.*, lxxiii. 86 (27 Sept. 1769).

132. Ibid. xxix. 183 (22 Apr. 1756).

133. M. Bouchard, *De l'humanisme à l'Encyclopédie: essai sur l'évolution des esprits dans la bourgeoisie bourguignonne sous les règnes de Louis XIV et Louis XV* (1929), 62.

134. A. Bernard, *Le Sermon au XVIIIᵉ siècle, 1715–89* (1901), 78.

135. Yves Besnard, *Souvenirs d'un nonagénaire*, ed. C. Port (2 vols., 1880), i. 196.

136. L.-S. Mercier, *Tableau de Paris*, new edn. (12 vols., 1782–8), v. 213.

137. Ch. Collas, *Saint-Louis d'Antin et son territoire* (1932), 53; Bachaumont, ix. 52–3 (24 Feb. 1776).

138. Thiery, *Guide des amateurs et des étrangers à Paris* (2 vols., 1787), i. 25.

139. Bachaumont, iii. 324 (30 Mar. 1768).

140. Ibid. vii. 134 (4 Apr. 1774); Métra, i. 313–16 (15 Apr. 1775).

141. Britsch, *La Jeunesse de Philippe-Égalité* (1926), 392; Bachaumont, xv. 15 (Mar. 1780).

142. Bachaumont, xxv. 56–7 (30 Apr. 1787).

143. J. Dupâquier, 'Sur la population française aux 17ᵉ et 18ᵉ siècles', *Rev. hist.* (1968), 70–2. There are innumerable references in the literature of demography to the Lenten low.

144. Guyot, iii. 198.
145. A. Forrest, *Society and Politics in Revolutionary Bordeaux* (1975), 13.
146. L. de Loménie, *Beaumarchais et son temps* (2 vols., 1880), ii. 67–9.
147. Guyot, i. 442.
148. F. Duine, 'Les Généraux des paroisses Bretonnes—Saint-Martin de Vitré', *Ann. Bretagne* (1907–8), 16–17. Some *cahiers* of 1789 asked for the charge for private notices to be limited to one sol (E. Dupont, 'La Condition des paysans dans la sénéchaussée de Rennes d'après les cahiers', *Ann. Bretagne* (1900–1), 59). For announcing stolen horses, see R. Plessix, 'Les *Affiches* du Mans, 1787', *Bull. Soc. Sarthe* (1973–4), 241.
149. A. Mathiez, *La Lecture des décrets au prône* (1907), 36–9.
150. Ibid.
151. *P.V. Ass.* viii. 2 (1775), 2390–2.
152. P. de la Gorce, *Histoire religieuse de la Révolution française* (3 vols., 1909), i. 379–80.
153. Guyot, xl. 209–26.
154. *Le Parfait Notaire apostolique*, i. 689.
155. A. Schaer, *Le Clergé paroissial catholique en Haute-Alsace sous l'ancien régime, 1648–1789* (1966), 203.
156. For an effective one, T. Leuridan, *Histoire de Linselles* (1883), 214 (in 1740, diocese of Tournai). In some areas, where there was a Mafia-like code of silence, the *monitoire* might give an informer a feeling of respectability (Y. Castan, *Honnêteté et relations sociales en Languedoc, 1715–80* (1974), 94–5).
157. J. McManners, *French Ecclesiastical Society under the Ancien Régime: A Study of Angers* (1960), 21.
158. J. Meyer, *La Noblesse bretonne au XVIIIᵉ siècle* (2 vols., 1966), i. 569.
159. T. Tackett, *Priest and Parish in 18th-Century France* (1977), 212–13. The cases in O. Hufton, 'Le Paysan et la loi en France au XVIIIᵉ siècle', *Ann.* (1983), 695–6.
160. P. Gosset, 'Scandales littéraires rémois au xviiiᵉ siècle,' *Nouv. Rev. Champagne et Brie* (1936), 88–9; McManners, *Angers*, 21; G. Walter, *Hébert et le Père Duchesne* (1946), 16.
161. M. Forestier, 'Une Exécution manquée', *Ann. Bourgogne* (1960), 60.
162. G. Aubry, *La Juridiction criminelle du Châtelet* (1971), 30.
163. E. G. Léonard, *Mon Village sous Louis XV* (1941), 335–6.
164. Roualt (curé), *Traité des monitoires* (1740), 149.
165. A. Coquerel, *Jean Calas et sa famille* (1869), 91–2.
166. Voltaire, *Lettre d'un membre du conseil de Zurich* (1767), in *Œuvres*, xxvi. 106.
167. Duine, 'Les généraux', 12.
168. Chassin, *Les Cahiers des curés*, 194–5; Marion, *Dictionnaire*, i. 583.
169. Cit. A. Babeau, *Le Village sous l'ancien régime* (1883), 128.

CHAPTER 4

1. Ph. Sagnac, *La Formation de la société française moderne* (2 vols., 1945–6), i. 32.
2. G. Frêche, *Toulouse et la région Midi-Pyrénées au siècle des Lumières* (1975), 531.
3. G. Lizerand, *Le Régime rural de l'ancienne France* (1942), 173–5.
4. Barbier, iii. 208.

5. P. de la Gorce, *Histoire religieuse de la Révolution française* (5 vols., 1909–23), i. 10.

6. A. Rébillon, 'La Situation économique du clergé à la fin de l'ancien régime', *Rév. fr.* (1929), 328–30.

7. G. Lefebvre, 'The Evolution of Peasant Society', in E. M. Acomb and Brown (eds.), *French Society and Culture* (1961), 44.

8. P. Wolff, *Histoire de Toulouse* (1974), 316; A. Thouroude, *La Vente des biens nationaux particulièrement dans le District de Revel* (thèse droit, Toulouse, 1912), 110–15; A. Guillon, 'La Vente des biens nationaux dans l'ancienne commune de Fougerai', *Ann. Bretagne* (1908–9), 338–9.

9. G. Lefebvre, 'Recherches relatives à la répartition de la propriété et de l'exploitation foncière à la fin de l'ancien régime', *Rev. hist. mod. contemp.* (1928), 110.

10. J. Lestocquoy, *Le Diocèse d'Arras* (1949), 173.

11. T. Bentley, *Journal of a Visit to Paris in 1776*, ed. P. France (1972), 25–6.

12. C.-G. Porée, 'La Vente des biens nationaux dans le district de Sens', *Rév. fr.* (1914), 88.

13. A. Meynier, 'La Terre et le paysan de la Révolution à l'Empire', *Rév. fr.* (1936), 126.

14. D. Dakin, *Turgot and the Ancien Régime* (1939).

15. Lefebvre, 'Recherches', and Meynier, 'La Terre'.

16. A. Degert, 'La Propriété ecclésiastique dans le Gers à la veille de la Révolution', *Rev. Gascogne* (1913), 267.

17. J. Bascou, 'Les Paysans de Béarn en 1789', *Ann. hist. Rév. fr.* (1940), 12.

18. A. Rébillon, *Ann. Bretagne* (1910–11), 463.

19. C. Port, *La Vendée angevine* (2 vols., 1888), ii. 1–21.

20. Lizerand, *Le Régime rural*, 172–4.

21. J. Loutchisky, 'Régime agraire et populations agricoles dans les environs de Paris à la veille de la Révolution', *Rev. hist. mod. contemp.* (1933), 106–12.

22. R. H. Andrews, *Les Paysans des Mauges au XVIIIe siècle* (1935), 15–17. A more sophisticated calculation comes to almost exactly the same conclusion: clergy 5.1 per cent, nobles 59.8 per cent, peasants 17.2 per cent (C. Tilly, *The Vendée* (1964), 74).

23. G. Michaux, 'Les Abbayes Bénédictines de Metz à la veille de la Révolution', *Ann. Est* (1979), 259.

24. M. Vallery-Radot, *Un Administrateur ecclésiastique à la fin de l'ancien régime: le cardinal de Luynes, archévêque de Sens* (1966), 159.

25. P. Goubert, 'Disparités de l'ancienne France rurale', *Cahiers hist.* (1967), 58–9.

26. Ch. Girault, *Les Biens de l'église dans la Sarthe à la fin du XVIIIe siècle* (1953), 359.

27. R. Caisso, *La Vente des biens nationaux de première origine dans le district de Tours* (1967), 38.

28. Girault, *Les Biens*, 358–71. The *cahiers* say that these capitalist *fermiers* treat their subtenants 'comme des nègres qui ne doivent travailler que pour les enrichir'.

29. O. H. Hufton, *The Poor of 18th-Century France* (1974), chs. 3 and 4.

30. G. Lecarpentier, 'La Propriété foncière du clergé et la vente des biens ecclésiastiques dans la Seine-Inférieure', *Rev. hist.* (1901), 73–5.

31. Girault, *Les Biens*, 376.

32. Caisso, *Tours*, 42.

33. M. Chamboux, *Les Paysans dans la Creuse à la fin de l'ancien régime* (1955), 26.

34. G. Lefebvre, *Questions agraires au temps de la Terreur* (1932), 61.

35. M. M. Kovelevsky, *La France économique et sociale à la veille de la Révolution* (2 vols., 1909–11), i. 12.

36. C. Bournisien, 'La Vente des biens nationaux', *Rev. hist.* (1909), 39. But see Caisso, *Tours*, 51. Basing estimated prices on the leases was to forget that the *fermier* also had to make a profit.

37. Bournisien, 'La Vente', 39. For communities claiming an immemorial right to cultivate the curé's land see L. Châtellier, *Tradition chrétienne et renouveau catholique dans l'ancien diocèse de Strasbourg, 1650–1770* (1981), 116.

38. F. D. Mathieu, *L'Ancien Régime dans la province de Lorraine et Barrois* (1879), 324–5.

39. J. McManners, *French Ecclesiastical Society under the Ancien Régime: A Study of Angers* (1960), 115–16.

40. M. Marion, *Histoire financière de la France depuis 1715* (2 vols., 1933), ii. 43.

41. Lefebvre, *Questions agraires*, 81.

42. G. Robert, 'La Seigneurie de Givry-sur-Aisne', *Trav. Acad. nat. Reims* (1913), 307–8.

43. G. Lefebvre, *Les Paysans du Nord pendant la Révolution française* (1924), 264.

44. L. Fournier, 'Les Paysans de l'ancien régime en Picardie', *Rév. fr.* (1884), 185–6.

45. M. Marion, *Dictionnaire des institutions de la France au XVIIᵉ et XVIIIᵉ siècles* (2 vols., 1923), i. 31.

46. Alexis de Tocqueville, *L'Ancien régime et la Révolution* (1856), ch. 11.

47. Girault, *Les Biens*, 374–7.

48. F. Rozier, *Démonstration élémentaire de botanique* (2 vols., 1766; 3 vols., 1789); *De la Fermentation des vins, et de la meilleure manière de faire l'eau-de-vie* (1770); *Traité sur la meilleure manière de cultiver la navette* (1776); *Mémoire sur la culture du chanvre* (1787); *Cours complet d'agriculture . . . et de médecine rurale et vétérinaire* (9 vols., 1781–96).

49. L. Froger, *Institutions d'agriculture et d'économie pour les habitans de la campagne* (1769), 16.

50. O. Festy, *L'Agriculture pendant la Révolution française: l'utilisation des jachères, 1789–1795* (1950), 92.

51. The abbé de Commerell, *Mémoire sur l'amélioration de l'agriculture par la suppression des jachères* (1788); *Instruction sur la culture, l'usage et les avantages de la betterave champêtre* (1786, 1788), and other essays on the cultivation of 'la racine de disette' and the 'chou à faucher' in 1786 and 1789.

52. François de la Rochefoucauld, *Voyages en France*, ed. J. Marchand (1933), 123. Cf. Arthur Young, *Travels in France during the years 1787, 1788, and 1789* (1792), 2 Aug. 1789 (ed. T. Okey (1934), 183).

53. F. Cognel, *La Vie parisienne sous Louis XVI* (1882), 5.

54. Fr. Crouzet, R. Pijassou, and J.-P. Poussou, in F. G. Pariset (ed.), *Bordeaux au XVIIIᵉ siècle* (1968), 160.

55. Ibid. 181.

56. A. Chaulac, *Histoire de l'abbaye de Sainte-Croix*, Archives de la France monastique (1910), 284.

57. B. Gille, *Les Forges françaises en 1772* (1960), 41–66, 98–9, 154–9.

58. J. Peter, 'Un Curieux Procès du XVIIIe siècle, 1723–6', *Rev. Nord* (1937), 243–59.

59. R. Dauvergne, *Les Résidences du maréchal de Croÿ, 1718–84* (1950), 56.

60. J.-F.-H. de Richeprey, *Journal des voyages en Haute-Guienne*, ed. H. Guilhamon (1952), 240–1.

61. E. Préclin, 'La Situation ecclésiastique et religieuse de la Franche Comté à la veille de la Révolution', *Bull. Féd. Socs. Franche Comté* (1955), 19–20; J. Faivre, 'Le Bas-clergé franc-comtois au milieu du XVIIIe siècle', *Ann. rév.* (1914), 10.

62. E. Appolis, *Le Diocèse civil de Lodève* (1951), 48–50, 64–66.

63. J. Savina, *Le Clergé de Cornouaille à la fin de l'ancien régime et sa convocation aux États-Généraux* (1926), 27.

64. M. Fosseyeux, 'Le Cardinal de Noailles et l'administration du diocèse de Paris', *Rev. hist.* (1913), 44, 272–3; *Le Gendre, chanoine de Notre-Dame, Mémoires*, ed. M. Roux (1863), 126–8. For the revenue in 1746, N. Ravitch, *Sword and Mitre: Government and Episcopate in France and England in the Age of Aristocracy* (1960), 219.

65. A. Soboul, 'La Révolution française et la féodalité', *Rev. hist.* (1968), 53.

66. G. Laurent, *Reims et la région rémoise à la veille de la Révolution* (1930), pp. vii–x. For the bishop of Beauvais as comte and *haut justicier* see P. Goubert, *Familles marchandes sous l'ancien régime: les Danse et les Motte, de Beauvais* (1959), p. ii.

67. McManners, *Angers*, 97–8, 64–7.

68. R. Métivier, *Les Anciennes Institutions judiciaires de l'Anjou* (1851), 5–10.

69. Rébillon, 'La Situation économique', 341.

70. A. Soboul, 'De la pratique des terriers à la veille de la Révolution', *Ann.* (1964), 1063.

71. Richeprey, *Journal*, 69–70.

72. Lefebvre, *Paysans du Nord*, 159.

73. J. Chétail, 'Pierre Louis de Leyssin, archevêque d'Embrun', *Bull. Acad. Delp.* (1958–9), 96–9.

74. Richeprey, *Journal*, 60–70.

75. Laurent, *Reims*, pp. xlvii–xlviii, lxxiv–lxxx, 108–9.

76. L. Trénard, 'La Crise sociale lyonnaise à la veille de la Révolution', *Rev. hist. mod. contemp.* (1955), 26.

77. McManners, *Angers*, 116.

78. G. Hubrecht, 'La Région sedanaise à la veille de la Révolution', *Ann. hist. Rév. fr.* (1937), 19–49.

79. Lizerand, *Le Régime rural*, 176.

80. J. Q. C. Mackrell, *The Attack on Feudalism in 18th-Century France* (1973), 6, 33, 119.

81. H. Sée, 'Les Classes rurales en Bretagne du XVIe siècle à la Révolution', *Ann. Bretagne* (1905), 15–25; L. Dubreuil, 'L'Usement de quevaise dans le domaine de Penlan, évêché de Tréguier', *Ann. Bretagne* (1961), 403.

82. L. Barbedette, 'La Terre de Luxeuil à la veille de la Révolution', *Ann. hist. Rév. fr.* (1927), 157–9.

83. Voltaire, *Précis du siècle de Louis XV*, in *Œuvres*, 427.

84. G. Demante, *Étude sur les gens de condition mainmortable en France au XVIIIe siècle* (1894), 20, 31–2.

85. Voltaire, *La Voix du curé*, in *Œuvres*, xviii. 567–74. Other references in Voltaire on this subject in G. Desnoiresterres, *Voltaire et la société française au XVIIIe siècle*, 2nd edn. (8 vols., 1867–76), vii. 479.

86. Demante, *Étude*, 39–49.

87. Marion, *Dictionnaire*, i. 508–9.

88. G.-L. Chassin, *L'Église et les derniers serfs* (1880), 113.

89. Ibid. 263.

90. Barbedette, 'Luxeuil', 159.

91. Ph. Sagnac, *La Révolution et le concept de la propriété, 1789–1804* (1946), 35 ff.

92. Guyot, ii. 74–5.

93. Durand de Maillaine, *Dictionnaire de droit canonique et de pratique bénéficiale* (2 vols., 1776), i. 127.

94. G. de la Véronne, 'Une Aliénation de biens ecclésiastiques', *Rev. quest. hist.* (1914), 490–4.

95. R. Tallegrain, *Du Temporel des bénéfices ecclésiastiques sous l'ancien régime* (1909), 87–9.

96. Maillaine, *Dictionnaire*, i. 150.

97. F.-A. Isambert, *Recueil des anciennes lois françaises* (29 vols., 1822–33), xxii. 226–35, and interpretive declaration in 1762 at 323–8.

98. McManners, *Angers*, 119.

99. D'Argenson, vi. 46 (24 Sept. 1749).

100. L. Antoine, *Le Conseil du roi sous le règne de Louis XV* (1970), 465.

101. S. T. McCloy, *Government Assistance in 18th-Century France* (1946), 377.

102. E. Vaillé, *Histoire générale des Postes françaises* (6 vols., 1953), v. 232.

103. F. Braesch, *La Commune du dix août, 1792* (1911), 869.

104. C. Carrière, M. Courdurié, and F. Rebuffat, *Marseille, ville morte: la peste de 1720*, ed. Courdurié (1968), 27–9; R. Forster, *The Nobility of Toulouse in the 18th Century* (1960), 22; E. Esmonin, 'Un Recensement de la population de Grenoble en 1725', *Cahiers hist.* (1957), 266; A. Babeau, *Histoire de Troyes pendant la Révolution* (1873), 6; Laurent, *Reims*, p. lxviii; G. Aubert, 'La Révolution à Douai', *Ann. hist. Rév. fr.* (1935), 316; E. Palanque, *Le Diocèse d'Aix-en-Provence* (1975), 124–6.

105. N. Wraxall, *A Tour through the Western, Southern and Interior Provinces of France* (3 vols., 1777), ii. 198.

106. E. Charpentier, 'La Loge maçonnique de Montreuil-sur-Mer, 1761–1809', *Rév. fr.* (1894), 533.

107. P. Tartat, *Avallon au XVIIIe siècle* (2 vols., 1951–3), i. 34–42.

108. F. Le Lay, *Histoire de la ville et communauté de Pontivy* (1911), 13, 16, 18, 35–8.

109. Descriptions of the town in Arthur Young, *Travels in France*, and in Legrand d'Aussy, *Voyage fait en Auvergne en 1787 et 1788*.

110. L. and G. Trénard, *Belley*, Histoire des diocèses de France (1978), 108–9.

111. A. Babeau, *La Ville sous l'ancien régime* (2 vols., 1884), ii. 102–29; generally, see J.-C. Perrot, 'Rapports sociaux et villes au XVIIIe siècle', *Ann.* (1968), 252 ff.

112. McManners, *Angers*, 117–28.

113. E. Martin, 'La Population de la ville de Vannes au début et à la fin du XVIIIe siècle', *Ann. Bretagne* (1921–3), 613.

114. P. Chevallier, *Loménie de Brienne et l'ordre monastique, 1766–89* (2 vols., 1959–60), i. 83–4.

115. M. Bouchard, *De l'humanisme à l'Encyclopédie: essai sur l'évolution des esprits dans la bourgeoisie bourguignonne sous les règnes de Louis XIV et Louis XV* (1929), 6–7; D. Ligou, 'Population, citoyens actifs et élections à Dijon, 1790–1', in *Actes du 88ᵉ Congrès des Sociétés savantes* (Clermont-Ferrand, 1963) (1964), 243–7; M. Garden, 'Niveaux de fortune à Dijon', *Cahiers hist.* (1964), 140.

116. Cognel, *La Vie parisienne*, 75.

117. McManners, *Angers*, 253.

118. O. Hufton, *Bayeux in the Late 18th Century* (1967), 40.

119. H. Prentout, 'Les Tableaux de 1790 en réponse à l'enquête du Comité de mendicité, Calvados', *Rév. fr.* (1907), 425–6.

120. J. McManners, *Death and the Enlightenment* (1981), ch. 10.

121. McManners, *Angers*, 120.

122. J. Thibaut-Payen, *Les Morts, l'Église et l'État dans le ressort du Parlement de Paris aux XVIIᵉ et XVIIIᵉ siècles* (1977), 375, 379–81, 396.

123. e.g. the article 'Biens d'Église' in the *Dictionnaire philosophique* (1764).

124. Montesquieu, *Lettres persanes*, letter 117, in *Œuvres complètes*, ed. R. Caillois (2 vols., 1951), i. 305–7; *L'Esprit des lois*, xxv. 5, ibid. ii. 740–1.

125. J. A. Clarke, 'Turgot's Critique of Perpetual Endowments', *Fr. Hist. St.* (1963–4), 495–501.

126. Étienne Mignot, *Traité des droits de l'État et du prince sur les biens possédés par le Clergé* (6 vols., 1755–7) (Bibl. Nat. 8° Ld4 2831); id., *Histoire du démêlé de Henri II, roi d'Angleterre, avec Thomas Becket, archevêque de Cantorbéry* (1756) (Bibl. Nat. 8° NF. 43). For his Jansenism see P. Feret, *La Faculté de Théologie de Paris et ses docteurs les plus célèbres* (7 vols., 1900–10), vii. 49–50.

127. Bachaumont, vi. 148–51 (13 Aug. 1770).

128. Métra, v. 281–7 (Nov. 1777).

129. I am grateful to Cambridge University Press for permission to use my essay in *History, Society and the Churches: Essays in Honour of Owen Chadwick* (1985), 147–68.

130. H. Marion, *La Dîme ecclésiastique en France au 18ᵉ siècle et sa suppression* (1912), 116.

131. Arthur Young, *Travels*, Fr. trans. H. Sée (3 vols., 1931), with excellent notes, iii. 1038.

132. P. Gagnol, *La Dîme ecclésiastique en France* (1910), 137–51; M. Marion, *Dictionnaire*, i. 174.

133. A. Poitrineau, *La Vie rurale en Basse-Auvergne au XVIIIᵉ siècle, 1726–1789* (2 vols., 1965), i. 351.

134. Lefebvre, *Paysans du Nord*, 108.

135. Gagnol, *La Dîme ecclésiastique*, 151–3.

136. Appolis, *Lodève*, 124–5; Poitrineau, *Basse-Auvergne*, i. 353.

137. Appolis, *Lodève*, 124–5.

138. Gagnol, *La Dîme ecclésiastique*, 35–9; Marion, *Dictionnaire*, i. 174.

139. Potier de la Germondaye, *Introduction au gouvernement des paroisses suivant la jurisprudence du Parlement de Bretagne* (1777), 146–8.

140. M. Faucheux, *Un Ancien Droit ecclésiastique perçu en Bas-Poitou: le boisselage*, (1953), 19–21, 44, 57, 63, 66; J. Deharge, *La Bas-Poitou à la veille de la Révolution* (1963), 102.

141. Appolis, *Lodève*, 126; Sée, 'Les Classes rurales', 507.

142. Voltaire, *Dictionnaire philosophique*, 'Impôt', *Œuvres*, xix. 444.
143. F. Caussy, 'Voltaire et ses curés. Lettres sur les dîmes', *Rev. hist.* (1909), 254–6, 619–35. (His parish priest was not the one in the tithe dispute.)
144. Guyot, xix. 509–17. L. Michel, 'La Dîme et les revenus du clergé d'Anjou à la fin de l'ancien régime', *Ann. Bretagne* (1979), 570.
145. See Ch. 50 below.
146. Hubrecht, 'La Région sedanaise', 33.
147. Mathieu, *Lorraine et Barrois*, 140.
148. Frêche, *Toulouse*, 521.
149. Marion, *La Dîme*, 20.
150. Girault, *Les Biens*, 379.
151. Guyot, xix. 429–32.
152. Laurent, *Reims*, pp. cclxiv–cclxviii.
153. Michel, 'La Dîme', 572.
154. F. Évard, 'Les Dîmes dans le parc de Versailles', *Rév. fr.* (1928), 115.
155. E. Le Roy Ladurie, *Les Paysans de Languedoc* (1966), 480.
156. Frêche, *Toulouse*, 527–30.
157. J. Rives, *Dîme et société dans l'archidiocèse d'Auch au XVIIIe siècle* (1976), 57–60.
158. Michel, 'La Dîme', 571.
159. Gagnol, *La Dîme ecclésiastique*, 124–5.
160. Poitrineau, *Basse-Auvergne*, i. 352.
161. A. Saramon (ed.), *Les Paroisses du diocèse de Comminges en 1786* (1968), 23.
162. R. Laprune, 'Histoire religieuse de Montiers-sur-Saulx' (5 vols., dupl. thesis, Bibl. Nat. 4° Lk7 58305 (1–5), 1967), i. 25–6.
163. Gagnol, *La Dîme ecclésiastique*, 86–9.
164. Marion, *La Dîme*, 76–7.
165. M. Pialès, *Traité des réparations* (4 vols., 1762), ii. 22.
166. A. Playoust-Chaussis, *La Vie religieuse dans le diocèse de Boulogne au XVIIIe siècle* (1976), 60.
167. Marion, *La Dîme*, 154–5.
168. Ibid. 148.
169. Guyot, x. 50.
170. Évard, 'Versailles', 122–3.
171. Pialès, *Traité*, ii. 133, 191–210.
172. Guyot, xi. 112–27.
173. Marion, *La Dîme*, 73.
174. Gagnol, *La Dîme ecclésiastique*, 113.
175. Ibid. 114–15.
176. E. Sol, *La Vie en Quercy à l'époque moderne (le mouvement économique)* (1948), 99.
177. Gagnol, *La Dîme ecclésiastique*, 15.
178. C. Bloch, *L'Assistance et l'État en France à la veille de la Révolution* (1908), 273–6.
179. Laurent, *Reims*, pp. ccxlv–ccxlvii.
180. Marion, *La Dîme*, 35–8.
181. Poitrineau, *Basse-Auvergne*, i, 352.
182. Évard, 'Versailles', 58–9.
183. P. de Saint-Jacob, *Les Paysans de la Bourgogne du nord au dernier siècle de l'ancien régime* (1960), 271.

184. P. de Saint-Jacob, *Documents relatifs à la communauté villageoise en Bourgogne* (1962), 146–8.
185. Gagnol, *La Dîme ecclésiastique*, 128; Marion, *La Dîme*, 97.
186. Trénard, *Belley*, 114.
187. Marion, *La Dîme*, 144.
188. Guyot, xix. 404–7.
189. G. Coolen, *Helfaut: essai sur l'administration d'une paroisse sous l'ancien régime*, Méms. Soc. Morinie, 37 (1939), 24.
190. P. de Vaissière, *Curés de campagne de l'ancienne France* (1933), 88–9.
191. G. Guillot and A. Amic, 'Le Dernier Abbé de la Ferté-sur-Grosne', *Rev. Mabillon* (1907), 367–9.
192. Voltaire, *Corresp.* rev. edn. (1971), 299–30, 312 (nos. D7996 of 25 Dec. 1758 and D8011 of 29 Oct. 1758). When the curé got into a fracas, Voltaire got his revenge by stirring up a legal inquiry (F. Caussy, *Voltaire, seigneur de village* (1912), 53–6).
193. P. Lemarchand, 'Journal d'un curé de campagne au 18ᵉ siècle', *Bull. méms. Soc. Côtes-du-Nord* (1960), 63–4.
194. Restif de la Bretonne, *La Vie de mon père*, in *Œuvres*, ed. M. Bachelin (9 vols., 1930–2), iv. 81.
195. V. Gourdet, 'Saint-Hilaire-de-Briouze', *Bull. Soc. Orne*, 13 (1894), 78–9.
196. Guyot, xix. 421–6, and for what follows.
197. Marion, *La Dîme*, 48–53.
198. G. Weulersse, *Le Mouvement Physiocratique en France de 1756 à 1770* (2 vols., 1910), i. 462. See ii. 185–6, where it is said that most dioceses had accepted.
199. J. Rives, 'Dîme et défrichements en Gascogne et Quercy au XVIIIᵉ siècle', *Ann. Midi* (1980), 57–66.
200. P. de Vaissière, *Gentilshommes campagnards de l'ancienne France* (1928), 356–7.
201. Marion, *La Dîme*, 112–13.
202. Sée, 'Les Classes rurales', 506–7.
203. Marion, *La Dîme*, 10–13; Gagnol, *La Dîme ecclésiastique*, 49–50.
204. Richeprey, *Journal*, 300.
205. P. Goubert, *Beauvais et le Beauvaisis de 1600 à 1730* (2 vols., 1960), i. 180.
206. L. Ampoulange, *Le Clergé et la convocation aux États Généraux de 1789 dans la sénéchaussée principale de Périgord* (1912), 47–9.
207. Lizerand, *Le Régime rural*, 175. Cf. register of the commune of Artiguelouve, 'Une Commune rurale des Pyrénées au début de la Révolution', *Rev. hist.* (1889), 97.
208. Marion, *La Dîme*, 117–22.
209. Duhamel du Monceau, *Éléments d'agriculture* (2 vols., 1763), i. 200.
210. Châtellier, *Tradition chrétienne*, 287.
211. F. Mourlot, 'La Convocation des États Généraux de 1789 dans le bailliage de Vire', *Rév. fr.* 31 (1896), 421.
212. Lefebvre, *Paysans du Nord*, 112.
213. Hubrecht, 'La Région sedanaise', 33–4; Girault, *Les Biens*, 318.
214. Gagnol, *La Dîme ecclésiastique*, 122.
215. *Vie de M. Marquis-Ducastel, doyen rural d'Évron et du Sonnois*, ed. E. Pichon (1873), 57–8.
216. *Journal d'un curé de campagne au XVIIIᵉ siècle*, ed. M. Platelle (1965), 88.
217. P. Viard, 'La Dîme en France au 17ᵉ siècle', *Rev. hist.* (1927), 243.

218. Guyot, xix. 399–400; L. F. Dejouy, *Principes et usages concernant les dixmes* (1761), 4.
219. Guyot, xlvii. 162–7.
220. Montesquieu, *L'Esprit des Lois*, xxxi. 12, in *Œuvres complètes* (Pléiade, 2 vols., 1966), ii. 960–2.
221. Voltaire, *Dictionnaire philosophique*, 'Curé de campagne', in *Œuvres*, xviii. 303–5.
222. J.-A. de Véri, *Journal*, ed. J. de Witte (2 vols., n.d.), i. 255–6.
223. Weulersse, *Le Mouvement physiocratique*, i. 454–5.
224. E. Lavaquerie, *Le Cardinal de Boisgelin, 1732–1804* (2 vols., 1920), i. 230–1.
225. Marion, *Dictionnaire*, i. 175.
226. Marion, *La Dîme*, 141–3. In fact, so far as the great were concerned— bishops and chapters—the parlement was often inclined to favour them (Frêche, *Toulouse*, 539–40).
227. A. Degert, 'Les Assemblées provinciales du Clergé Gascon', *Rev. Gascogne* (1925), 87–184.
228. Saramon (ed.), *Les Paroisses*, 66.
229. Rives, *Dîme et société*, 147–56.
230. Marion, *La Dîme*, 140–1.
231. Saint-Jacob, *Bourgogne*, 374–6.
232. It was then resolved that arrangements for buying off tithe would be made. Earlier proposals would have made tithe a permanent tax, see [G.-F.-R. Molé, *avocat*], *Vœu d'un citoyen pour la conversion des dîmes en un impôt territorial qui sera perçu au profit de l'État* (1788). For the injustice to *métayers* involved in this gift to landowners see S. Aberdam, 'La Révolution et les luttes des métayers', *Études rurales*, 59 (1975), 73 ff.
233. Condorcet (M. J. A. N. marquis de), *Sur les Assemblées provinciales*, in *Œuvres*, ed. M. L. S. Caritat *et al.* (21 vols. 1804), viii. 160. The fluctuations in the yield of tithe are being studied as an indicator of agricultural progress (E. Le Roy Ladurie and J. Goy, *Les Fluctuations du produit de la dîme. Conjoncture décimale et domaniale de la fin du Moyen Âge au XVIIIᵉ siècle* (1972)). For the eighteenth century, the findings are: around Toulouse and Bordeaux and along the Pyrenees, the tithe yield was rising slowly, but there was no improvement in Brittany (summary in E. Le Roy Ladurie and J. Goy, 'La Dîme et le reste, XIVᵉ–XVIIIᵉ siècles', *Rev. hist.* (1978), 123–38; but the whole thesis of growth is denied by M. Morineau, in *Les Faux-semblants d'un démarrage économique: agriculture et démographie en France au XVIIIᵉ siècle* (1971); see also 'La Dîme et l'enjeu', *Ann. hist. Rév. fr.* (1980), 162–80). In some areas, the rise of population must have cancelled out any improvement of living standards which might have been expected from the increased yield of agriculture, in contrast to the extra income which ecclesiastical institutions received from the tithe; it would be interesting to know if these were areas of more intense rural anticlericalism. But at the moment the whole subject bristles with difficulties and disagreements.

CHAPTER 5

1. *P.V. Ass.* i, Préface.
2. M. C. Peronnet, *Les Évêques de l'ancienne France* (2 vols., Univ. Lille III, 1977), ii. 732. For the early history of the assemblies, see L. Serbat, *Les Assemblées du Clergé de France, origines, organisation, développement* (1906), and P. Blet, *Le Clergé de France et la Monarchie. Études sur les Assemblées du Clergé de 1615 à 1666* (2 vols., 1957).
3. The abbé Dangeau (1693), in F. de Dainville, *Cartes anciennes de l'église de France* (1956), 282–91.
4. A. Cans, *La Contribution du Clergé de France à l'impôt, 1689–1715* (1910), 75–6.
5. G. Lepointe, *L'Organisation politique et financière du Clergé de France sous le règne de Louis XV* (1923).
6. Luynes, xiv. 177 (June 1755).
7. M. Marion, *Histoire financière de la France depuis 1715*, i (1914), 131.
8. Lepointe, *L'Organisation politique*, 7.
9. A. Cans, *L'Organisation financière du Clergé de France à l'époque de Louis XIV* (1910), 197.
10. Guyot, vii. 45.
11. Up to 1719 there were provincial *receveurs* also, acting as intermediaries. These were unnecessary officials created by the Crown merely to have jobs to sell; they were abolished in 1719.
12. Lepointe, *L'Organisation politique*, 106.
13. V. Dufour, 'État du diocèse de Paris en 1789', *Bull. Com. Paris*, 1 (1883), 329.
14. J. McManners, *French Ecclesiastical Society under the Ancien Régime: A Study of Angers* (1960), 191.
15. [M. Jousse], *Traité de la juridiction des Officiaux et autres juges d'église, tant en matière civile que criminelle* (1769), 457–8.
16. *P.V. Ass.* vii. 2062–7. Cf. the dispute at Chalon-sur-Saône, 1726–40, ibid. vi. 1720–1.
17. Ibid. vi., p. viii; viii 2. 2512.
18. According to Jousse, *Traité*, 46, Pau should be added.
19. McManners, *Angers*, 190.
20. A. Degert, 'Les Assemblées provinciales du clergé Gascon', *Rev. Gascogne* (1924), 174, 63, 177, 210, 214; 20 (1925), 81–5, 89, 183, 187–8.
21. Peronnet, *Les Évêques*, ii. 741–4.
22. P. Guillaume, *Essai sur la vie religieuse dans l'Orléanais de 1789 à 1801* (3 fasc., 1958), i. 9. Things were worse at the end of the seventeenth century. One deputy from the province of Aix was a boy under the charge of his tutor (*Mémoires de l'abbé Le Gendre, chanoine de Notre Dame*, ed. M. Roux (1863), 99–100).
23. *P.V. Ass.* viii 2. 2615–36.
24. Peronnet, *Les Évêques*, ii. 748–56.
25. Luynes, vi. 294, 304 (1745).
26. Peronnet, *Les Évêques*, 734, 726.
27. J. Boswell, *Life of Johnson* (6 vols., 1901), iii. 234. In 1775 the *receveur général* claimed 132,000 livres in costs and fees.
28. J. F. Bosher, *French Finances, 1770–1795* (1970), 165–93. *P.V. Ass.*, vii.

92–158, 331–70. Ogier, the *receveur*, had lost them 471,776 livres, 6 deniers.

29. E. Besnier, *Les Agents généraux du Clergé de France, spécialement de 1780 à 1785* (1939), 16593.

30. M. Antoine, *Le Conseil du roi sous le règne de Louis XV* (1970), 239. See also J. Coudy, *Les Moyens d'action de l'ordre du Clergé au conseil du Roi* (1956).

31. *P.V. Ass.* vii. 1853.

32. Ibid. viii/1. 109–12.

33. Ibid. vi. 1356–66. Additional room added in 1725, ibid. (vii. 61).

34. Ibid. viii/2. 1765, 2601–2 (1775).

35. L. S. Greenbaum, 'Talleyrand as agent-général', *Cath. Hist. Rev.* (1963), 475.

36. Besnier, *Les Agents généraux*, 76–132.

37. Ibid. 57.

38. Ch. Robert, *Urbain de Hercé, dernier évêque et comte de Dol* (1900), 76–7.

39. Guillaume, *Essai*, i. 11–12.

40. Guyot, ii. 547–9.

41. *P.V. Ass.* viii/2. 1328–30.

42. Ibid. viii/1. 952–7.

43. Ibid. viii/2. 1331–3. Similar cases: viii/2. 1336, 1566–75.

44. Ibid. vii. 1307, 1439 (1735); vii. 1675–81 (1740); vii. 1785–6, 1834–6 (1742); vii. 2007–9 (1745); viii/1. 327–30 (1750); viii/1. 505–14 (1750); viii/1. 828, 1705 (1760); viii/2. 1308, 1311 (1765); viii/2. 2590–3 (1770–5).

45. Cans, *L'Organisation financière*, 189.

46. T. J. Schmitt, *L'Organisation ecclésiastique et la pratique religieuse dans l'archidiaconé d'Autun de 1650 à 1750* (1957), 150.

47. *P.V. Ass.* vi. 1749–50 (1723); vii. 1181–9 (1730); vii. 1464–5 (1739); vii. 1740 (1752); vii. 2073–5 (1745); vii/1. 375–90 (1750).

48. Lepointe, *L'Organisation politique*, 243–6.

49. *P.V. Ass.* viii/1. 536–7 (1755).

50. Ibid. vii. 412–13 (1725); vii. 778 (1726); vii. 1766–9 (1740); viii/1 527 (1755).

51. Ibid. viii/1. 525, 529 (1755).

52. Ibid. viii/1. 851–6 (1760). The full story of the new system is at viii/2. 1790 ff. (1770).

53. Ibid. vii. 1842 (1742); viii/1. 71–8 (1747); viii/1. 392–3 (1750); Grenoble alone, viii/2. 2462–3 (1775); Provence alone, viii/1. 673 (1758); viii/2. 2434 (1775).

54. Ibid. viii/1. 79–82 (1747); viii/2. 1086 (1762).

55. Ibid. vii. 1450–4 (1735).

56. Rodez case of 1772, ibid. viii/2. 2574–8 (1775).

57. Ibid. viii/2. 1423–9, 1515–23 (1765).

58. Ibid. viii/2. 2347–51 (1775).

59. Ibid. vii. 1115 (1730); viii/2. 1075 (1762).

60. Ibid. vii. 454–6 (1725).

61. Ibid. vii. 1082–99 (1730).

62. Ibid. viii/1. 102–11 (1752).

63. Ibid. vii. 2016–23 (1745); viii/1. 339–45 (1750); viii/1. 675 (1758); viii/2. 2219 (1775).

64. Ibid. viii/1. 405–7 (1750).

65. Ibid. viii/2. 2527–44.

66. Ibid. viii/2. 2527–44.

67. Ibid. vii. 1691–1706 (1740). Other cases at vii. 186–90 (1726), 433–5 (1725).

68. Ibid. viii/2. 2374–6 (1775). Cf. vi. 1223–7 (1711).

69. Ibid. vii. 1110 (1730); viii/2. 1078 (1762).

70. Ibid. vi. 1123–6 (1710); vi. 1218–19 (1711); vi. 1466 (1715); vi. 1703–7 (1723); vii. 426, 478–9 (1725); vii. 1463 (1735); vii. 1717–18, 1724–5, 1727–8 (1740); vii. 2027–31 (1745); viii/1. 706–7 (1758); viii/2. 2319–20 (1775).

71. Ibid. viii/2. 1053 (1762); viii/2. 1961–2011 (1772); viii/2. 2241–60 (1775).

72. Ibid. vi. 597 (1700).

73. Ibid. vii. 415–18 (1725); vii. 1063–73 (1730).

74. Ibid. viii/2. 1394–7 (1765). For the argument that the Assembly was a sort of 'Concile National' see J. M. Gres-Gayer, *Théologie et pouvoir en Sorbonne: la Faculté de Théologie de Paris et la Bulle Unigenitus* (1991), 188, citing Ellies Du Pin, *Traité de la puissance ecclésiastique et temporelle* (1707).

75. *P.V. Ass.* vi. 315–16, 345–7 (1700).

76. Ibid. vi. 1243 (1713–14).

77. Ibid. vii. 23–4 (1725).

78. Ibid. vi. 842 (1705); viii/2. 1441–2 (1765); vii. 476–7 (1725); vii. 1490 (1735); viii/2. 1448 (1765).

79. For what follows, see Lepointe, *L'Organisation politique*, and Marion, *Histoire financière*.

80. *P.V. Ass.* vii. 1–4, 65, 81–9, 577, 614–15.

81. A 'despotic' speech: Luynes, x. 425 (22 May 1750).

82. V. Durand, *Les Évêques au XVIIIe siècle en Languedoc* (1907), 68–72.

83. Luynes, x. 463.

84. L. Bassette, *Jean de Caulet, évêque de Grenoble, 1693–1771* (1946), 167.

85. D'Argenson, vi. 145.

86. A. Mathiez, 'Les Philosophes et le pouvoir au milieu du XVIIIe siècle', *Ann. hist. Rév. fr.* (1935), 1.

87. Voltaire, *Extrait du décret de la sacrée Congrégation de l'Inquisition de Rome*, in *Œuvres*, xxiii. 463.

88. D'Argenson, vi. 166, 280, 391, 23.

89. *P.V. Ass.* viii/2. 1123, 1169, show both clergy and king recognizing that there had been 'few examples of such a delay'.

90. J. McManners, *The French Revolution and the Church* (1970), 3.

91. Luynes, vi. 292–3; iii. 193–9.

92. *P.V. de l'Assemblée générale extraordinaire du Clergé de l'année 1782* (1783), 17, 34, 333, 99–101, 146, 131–2, 297, 86–7, 261–2. On the 'bourses de jetons' see C. Florange, *Les Assemblées du Clergé de France avant 1789 et leurs jetons commémoratifs* (1927).

93. Marion, *Histoire financière*, i. 40.

94. A. Guth, 'Les Impositions du clergé d'Alsace', *Arch. Église Alsace* (1956), 164–201; (1958), 120–89; (1959), 152–78.

95. M. Fosseyeux, 'Le Cardinal de Noailles et l'administration du diocèse de Paris', *Rev. hist.* (1914).

96. H. Antoine, 'Recherches sur la paroisse et sur l'église de Saint-Pierre-de-Montsort', *Rev. Maine*, 6 (1879), 183–4.

97. René-Pierre Nepveu de la Manoullière, *Mémoires*, ed. G. Esnault (3 vols., 1877–9), i. 51.

98. See J. Marchal, *Le Droit d'oblat* (1955).

99. McManners, *Angers*, 193–4.

100. Guyot, i. 282–7. For its enforcement, Antoine, *Le Conseil du roi*, 507. For the following examples, *P.V. Ass.* viii. 1129–36, 1296, 1458.

101. Durand de Maillane, *Dictionnaire de droit canonique et de pratique bénéficiale* (1776), 150.

102. *P.V. Ass.* vii. 1719 (1740).

103. Guyot, iv. 467.

104. *P.V. Ass.* viii/1. 674 (1758).

105. Ibid. vii. 1139 (1742); viii/2. 2039 (1772).

106. J.-A. de Véri, *Journal*, ed. J. de Witte (2 vols., n.d.), ii. 339.

107. Lepointe, *L'Organisation politique*, corrects a lot of older estimates here.

108. Bosher, *French Finances*, 128.

109. Cited by E. Lavaquery, *Le Cardinal de Boisgelin, 1732–1804* (2 vols., 1920), i. 216–17.

110. Véri, *Journal*, ii. 330–9.

111. R. Chevallier, 'Les Revenus des bénéfices ecclésiastiques au 18ᵉ siècle', *Bull. Soc. hist. mod.* (1921).

112. E. Sévestre, *Les Idées gallicanes et royalistes du haut clergé . . . la correspondance de Pierre-Augustin Godert de Belbeuf, évêque d'Avranches, 1762–1803* (1917), 58–63.

113. J. Letaconnoux, 'Le Régime de la corvée en Bretagne', *Ann. Bretagne* (1906–7), 604.

114. M. Pialès, *Traité des Collations* (1753), pp. i–viii; Guyot, vi. 71–6.

115. Cerfvol, *Du Droit du souverain sur les bien fonds du clergé et des moines* (1770), cited by C. Bloch, *L'Assistance et l'État en France à la veille de la Révolution* (1908), 372.

116. Guyot, i. 143.

117. Ibid. xxx. 162.

118. Ibid. i. 140.

119. Cans, *La Contribution*, 8–10.

120. Barbier, iv. 469–70.

121. R. Tattegrain, *Du Temporel des bénéfices ecclésiastiques sous l'ancien régime* (1909), 56–7; for the eighteenth century see M. Laubry, *Traité des unions* (1778), 159.

122. [J.-L. Brunet, rev. Durand de Maillane], *Le Parfait Notaire apostolique*, rev. edn. (2 vols., 1775), ii. 2–3.

123. Guyot, xxx. 140.

124. Ibid. 147.

125. Ibid. i. 139.

126. Cans, *La Contribution*, i. 139.

127. Guyot, i. 139.

128. *Très humbles Remontrances présentéés au Roi par l'assemblée générale du clergé de Bourgogne*, in Luynes, x. 469–70; D'Argenson, vi. 162–3.

129. Guyot, xvii. 160–9.

130. They pay 'quasi-rien', says Le Gendre (*Mémoires*, ed. M. Roux (1863), 43) in 1690.

131. McManners, *Angers*, 206.

132. E. Préclin, 'La Situation ecclésiastique et religieuse de la Franche Comté à la

veille de la Révolution', *Bull. Féd. Franche Comté* (1955), 3–27; L. Bourgain, 'La Contribution du clergé à l'impôt sous la monarchie française', *Rev. quest. hist.* (1890), 103.

133. McManners, *Angers*, 201.

134. J. Savina, *Le Clergé de Cornouaille à la fin de l'ancien régime et sa convocation aux États Généraux* (1926), 101.

135. *Procès-verbal de l'assemblée générale du clergé de France . . . en l'année 1782* (1783), 99–101, 104, 141–6, 219–21, 307–11.

136. Ibid. 225–78. For the history of the dispute, *Mémoires du prince de Talleyrand*, ed. the duc de Broglie (5 vols., 1891), i. 21, and *Précis . . . des matières contenues dans la Nouvelle Collection des P.V. des Ass. Gén. du . . . Clergé* (1780), 1129–59.

137. *P.V. Ass.* viii/1. 352–5.

138. Ibid. viii/2. 2292.

139. *Mémoires pour le Clergé de France dans l'affaire des foi et hommages, et réponses de l'inspecteur du domaine* (1785) (Bibl. Nat. Fo. L⁵d529), 73, 133, 249–96, 9–59.

CHAPTER 6

1. See H. Marion, *Dictionnaire des institutions de la France aux XVIIᵉ et XVIIIᵉ siècles* (2 vols., 1923), i. 177 ff., and F. de Dainville, *Cartes anciennes de l'Église de France* (1956).

2. F.-J. Casta, *Le Diocèse d'Ajaccio* (1974).

3. The bishop, driven out by the infidels, followed a duke of Nevers to France, and was given the administration of the hospital there (Luynes, xiii. 236).

4. M. Vovelle, *Piété baroque et déchristianisation en Provence au XVIIIᵉ siècle* (1973), 436.

5. J. Chétail, 'Notice sur les limites du diocèse de Glandève et son dernier évêque', *Actes 86ᵉ Congrès national des Sociétés savantes: Montpellier, 1961* (1962), 27–8.

6. No map of the dioceses as a whole was available before 1790, though individual dioceses and provinces had theirs (J. Dubois, 'La Carte des diocèses de France avant la Révolution', *Ann.* (1945), 681–6).

7. Ch. Berthelot du Chesnay, 'Le Clergé diocésain français et les registres des insinuations ecclésiastiques', *Rev. hist. mod. contemp.* (1963), 261–2.

8. Ch. Robert, *Urbain de Hercé, dernier évêque et comte de Dol* (1900), 14–15.

9. A. Brette, 'Papiers et correspondance du prince Emmanuel de Salm-Salm', *Rev. hist.* (1899), 67.

10. F. Glasson, 'Le Rôle politique du Conseil Souverain d'Alsace', *Rev. hist.* (1900), 37–8.

11. A. Schaer, *Le Clergé paroissial catholique en Haute-Alsace sous l'ancien régime, 1648–1789* (1966), pp. v–viii; A. Guth, 'Les Impositions du clergé d'Alsace', *Arch. Église Alsace* (1956), 163.

12. G. Gatherot, 'Gobel, évêque constitutionnel de Paris', *Rev. quest. hist.* (1909), 493–9.

13. R. Collier, *La Vie en Haute Provence de 1600 à 1850* (1973), 322–4.

14. D. Andreis, 'Le Rôle du Sénat de Nice, 1614–1792', *Nice historique* (1973), 25–49; L. and G. Trénard, *Histoire des diocèses de France: Belley* (1978), 114–15,

126; A. Bergier, *Des Libertés de l'Église savoyarde, 17ᵉ–18ᵉ siècle* (thèse droit, Paris, 1942).

15. J. Chétail, 'La *Réduction* du temporel de Mgr Caulet, évêque de Grenoble', *Cahiers hist.* (1960), 417–20.

16. V. Durand, *État religieux des trois diocèses de Nîmes, d'Uzès et d'Alais à la fin de l'ancien régime* (1909), 6; Th. Puntous, *Un Diocèse civil de Languedoc: les États particuliers du diocèse de Toulouse aux XVIIᵉ et XVIIIᵉ siècles* (1909), 37–61, 107.

17. L. Ampoulange, *Le Clergé et sa convocation aux États-Généraux de 1789 dans la sénéchaussée principale de Périgord* (1912), 30.

18. G. Stivil, *Le Régime administratif du Roussillon* (1927), 41–2.

19. See J.-F. Soulet, *Tradition et réformes religieuses dans les Pyrénées centrales au XVIIᵉ siècle* (1974).

20. T. J. Schmitt, *L'Organisation ecclésiastique et la pratique religieuse dans l'archidiaconé d'Autun de 1650 à 1750* (1957), 4.

21. For the proposal to unite Digne and Senez see L. Ventre. 'L'Ancien Diocèse de Senez', *Bull. Soc. Basses-Alpes* (1930), 23 ff. On the legal requirements, Guyot, xix. 241–2; lxii. 87–91.

22. J. Gallerand, 'L'Érection de l'évêché de Blois', *Rev. hist. Église Fr.* (1956), 184–201.

23. R. Sauzet, *Contre-réforme et réforme catholique en Bas-Languedoc: le diocèse de Nîmes au XVIIᵉ siècle* (1979), 45–8.

24. G. Dumary, 'Les Évêques de Dijon', *Mêms. Comm. Côte-d'Or,* 12 (1899–90), 2–11.

25. B. Hours, 'La Création du diocèse de Saint-Claude', *Rev. hist. Église Fr.* (1984), 322.

26. E. Martin, *Histoire des diocèses de Toul, de Nancy et de Saint-Dié* (3 vols., 1900–3), ii. 386–625; iii. 6–7, 15–18, 24–37. For problems of organization in the diocese of Nancy, see *Répertoire des visites pastorales de la France (anciens diocèses),* ed. D. Julia and M. Venard, iii, (1983), 243. See also Roussel, 'L'Érection de l'évêché de Saint-Dié', *Bull. Soc. phil. vosgienne* (1932).

27. M. Braure, *Lille et la Flandre wallonne au XVIIIᵉ siècle* (2 vols., 1932), ii. 619.

28. L. Welter, 'Projet de l'érection d'un évêché de Moulins, 1787–90', *Bull. Auvergne* (1944), 73–82. Comment in E. Champion, *Rév. fr.* (1888), 591–2.

29. V. Durand, *Le Jansénisme au XVIIIᵉ siècle et Joachim Colbert* (1907), 312–13.

30. A. Cans, *L'Organisation financière du Clergé de France à l'époque de Louis XIV* (1901), 69 n.

31. *Mémoires de l'abbé Le Gendre, chanoine de Notre Dame,* ed. M. Roux (1863), 296.

32. M. Jousse, *Traité de la juridiction des officiaux* (1769), 35, 52, 57; Guyot, ii. 551.

33. A. Degert, 'L'Ancien Diocèse d'Aire', *Rev. Gascogne* (1907), 177–8.

34. François-Joachim, cardinal de Bernis, *Mémoires et lettres,* ed. F. Masson (2 vols., 1878), ii. 57–8; Jousse, *Traité,* 454–5; M.-L. Rostagnet-Latreille, 'Le Primat des Gaules et Louis XIV', *Cahiers hist.* (1958), 155.

35. *Mémoires de Le Gendre,* 313.

36. E. Regnault, *Christophe de Beaumont, archevêque de Paris, 1763–81* (2 vols., 1882), i. 437; for Saint-Sulpice see the Duc de Croÿ, *Journal, 1718–84,* ed. the vicomte de Grouchy and P. Cottin (4 vols., 1906), ii. 190–1; he was a parishioner.

37. M. C. Peronnet, *Les Évêques de l'ancienne France* (2 vols., 1977), ii. 744 ff.

38. Dainville, *Cartes*, 191.

39. For Reims see G. Laurent, *Reims et la région rémoise à la veille de la Révolution* (1930), pp. clxxii–iii; for Quimper, J. Savina, *Le Clergé de Cornouaille à la fin de l'ancien régime* (1926), 7; for Paris, L. Longon, 'L'Ancien Diocèse de Paris et ses subdivisions', *Bull. Com. Paris*, 1 (1883), 16–17.

40. Schmitt, *L'Organisation*, 1, 2, 5.

41. [J.-L. Brunet, rev. Durand de Maillane] *Le Parfait Notaire apostolique* (2 vols., 1775), i. 641–3.

42. P.-T. Durand de Maillane, *Dictionnaire de droit canonique et de pratique bénéficiale* (2 vols., 1776), i. 207.

43. Berthelot du Chesnay, 'Le Clergé', 248–50. (There were 20 sols to the livre.)

44. Potier de la Germondaye, *Introduction au gouvernement des paroisses* (1777), 62.

45. Dom P. Piolin, *L'Église du Mans durant la Révolution* (4 vols., 1868), i. 454.

46. Potier de la Germondaye, *Introduction*, 61.

47. L. Marcel, *Le Frère de Diderot* (1913), 119–20.

48. A. Playoust-Chaussis, *La Vie religieuse dans le diocèse de Boulogne au XVIIIᵉ siècle, 1725–90* (1976), 134–6.

49. *Répertoire des visites pastorales*, iii. 226–32.

50. G. Viard, 'Les Visites pastorales dans l'ancien diocèse de Langres', *Rev. hist. Église Fr.* (1977), 253–70.

51. *Répertoire des visites*, iv (1985), 478.

52. Berthelot du Chesnay, 'Le Clergé', 247.

53. Peronnet, *Les Évêques*, ii. 744.

54. Schmitt, *L'Organisation*, 5–6.

55. Berthelot du Chesnay, 'Le Clergé', 247.

56. Jousse, *Traité*, 366–8. For Saintes, L. Audiat, *Deux victimes des Septembriseurs, Pierre-Louis de la Rochefoucauld, dernier évêque de Saintes, et son frère, évêque de Beauvais* (1897).

57. J. Grente and O. Havard, *Villedieu-les-Poêles: sa commanderie, sa bourgeoisie, ses métiers* (2 vols., 1898), i. 241–2.

58. Jousse, *Traité*, 117–20.

59. Guyot, xliii. 239–40.

60. Durand, *État religieux*, 18.

61. Berthelot du Chesnay, 'Le Clergé', 242.

62. Brémond d'Ars Migré, *Un Collaborateur de Buffon: l'abbé Bexon* (1936), 33–4.

63. Jousse, *Traité*, 124–6.

64. V. Dufour, 'État du diocèse de Paris en 1789', *Bull. Comm. Paris*, 1 (1883), 48–53.

65. Jousse, *Traité*, 224–68.

66. Ibid. 251–87.

67. Guyot, xi. 243 ff.

68. R. Phillips, *Family Breakdown in 18th-Century France: Divorce in Rouen 1792–1803* (1980), 4–7; A. Lottin, 'Vie et mort du couple . . . dans le Nord de la France aux XVIIᵉ et XVIIIᵉ siècles', *XVIIᵉ siècle* (1974), 65–8. For Cambrai, Guyot, xliii. 267–9. The *officialité* of Strasbourg had only 144 applicants from 1685 to 1719, two-thirds of them being women: 48 applications were granted (L. Châtellier, *Tradition chrétienne et renouveau catholique dans les cadres de l'ancien diocèse de Strasbourg, 1650–1770* (1981), 251).

69. V. Durand, *Les Évêques au XVIIIᵉ siècle en Languedoc* (1907), 190.

70. M. Briffaut, 'Incident tumultueux dans l'église de Saint-Géry en 1758', *Méms. Soc. Cambrai* (1970), 215–24.

71. Barbier, ii. 71–2 (July 1729).

72. P. L. Varaigne, 'Justice royale et justice ecclésiastique au XVIIIe siècle', *Rev. Soc. Villiers-sur-Marne*, 22e ann., NS 2 (1969–70), 7–12.

73. B. Plongeron, *La Vie quotidienne du clergé français au XVIIIe siècle* (1974), 65–8; René-Pierre Nepveu de la Manoullière, *Mémoires*, G. Esnault ed. (3 vols., 1877–9), ii. 87; G. Doublet, *Le Jansénisme dans l'ancien diocèse de Vence* (1901), 290–1.

74. The basic authority is A. Degert, *Histoire des séminaires français* (2 vols., 1912). Also indispensable is G. Bonnenfant, *Les Séminaires normands du XVIe au XVIIIe siècle* (1915).

75. Bonnenfant, *Les Séminaires normands*, 156–8, 182, 167, 173, 199, 288–9.

76. Ibid. 393–7, 334.

77. Degert, *Histoire*, ii. 347–8.

78. Ibid. ii. 458–505.

79. Ibid. ii. 508–10. Toulouse had three seminaries (Lazarist, Oratorian, and Jesuit); there was also an Irish one (Cl. Tournier, *Histoire des séminaires toulousains* (1942)).

80. P. R. Harris, *Douai College Documents, 1639–1794* (1992), 148–9.

81. P. Boyle, *The Irish College in Paris, 1578–1901* (1901).

82. C. Mooney, *The Irish Franciscans in France* (1964).

83. H. Fleming, OP, *The Undoing of the Friars of Ireland: A Study of the Noviciate Question in the 18th Century* (1972), 109–16, 191.

84. The view as angrily described by the bishop of Ossory (ibid. 115).

85. *P.V. Ass.* vii. 1753 (23 Aug. 1740).

86. Degert, *Histoire*, ii. 337–8, 346. There is a life of Claude-François Pouillart by le Floch (1904).

87. J. Ferté, *La Vie religieuse dans les campagnes parisiennes, 1622–95* (1962), 161–70.

88. L. Dantin, *François de Gain-Montagnac évêque de Tarbes, 1782–1801* (1908), 25–8.

89. P.-D. Bernier, *Essai sur le tiers état rural: les paysans de Basse-Normandie au XVIIIe siècle* (1891), 233–4.

90. Bonnenfant, *Les Séminaires normands*, 368–73.

91. Ch. Robert, *Urbain de Hercé*, 57, 94.

92. One year for ordination at Auch (J. Bénac, 'Le Séminaire d'Auch', *Rev. Gascogne* (1907), 216–38).

93. J. Charrier, *Histoire religieuse du département de la Nièvre* (2 vols., 1936), i. 12.

94. J. Daranatz, 'Les Ordinations sacerdotales du diocèse de Bayonne au XVIIIe siècle', *Bull. Soc. Bayonne* (1931), 143.

95. F.-G. Pariset (ed.), *Bordeaux au XVIIIe siècle* (1968), 132.

96. 'Mémoires inédits de M. Lebay, curé de Veules, 1761–1834', *La Semaine religieuse de Rouen*, 10 (1876), 460 ff.

97. J. Leflon, *M. Emery* (2 vols., 1943), i. 33; J. Delumeau, *Le Diocèse de Rennes* (1979), 135; Degert, *Histoire*, ii. 19; Bonnenfant, *Les Séminaires normands*, 410.

98. Reminiscences of his early days by Cardinal Fesch, Napoleon's uncle (A. Latreille, *Napoléon et le Saint-Siège* (1935), 47).

99. F. Lebrun (ed.), *Histoire des catholiques en France du XVe siècle à nos jours* (1980), 151–2.

100. Bonnenfant, *Les Séminaires normands*, 264, 391, 379; Degert, *Histoire*, ii. 512; F. D. Mathieu, *L'Ancien Régime en Lorraine et Barrois* (1879), 335–6; A. H. Van der Weil, *Paul-Louis de Mondran, un chanoine homme d'esprit* (1944), 13.

101. J.-J. Gautier, *Essai sur les mœurs champêtres* (1787), ed. X. Rousseau (1935), 21–2.

102. The abbé Dinouart, in A. Bernard, *Le Sermon au XVIIIe siècle, 1715–89* (1901), 369.

103. P. Sage, *Le Bon Prêtre dans la littérature française d'Amadis de Gaule au Génie du Christianisme* (1951), 148 n.

104. R. Darricau, *La Formation des professeurs de séminaire au début du XVIIIe siècle d'après un directoire de M. Jean Bonnet* (1966), 4–12.

105. Detail in Degert, *Histoire*, ii. 148–300.

106. A. Degert, 'L'Enseignement de l'histoire dans les anciens séminaires français', *Rev. quest. hist.* (1910), 125–9.

107. Van der Weil, *Paul-Louis de Mondran*, 11.

108. Ch. Berthelot du Chesnay, 'Études ecclésiastiques et formation du clergé en Bretagne au XVIIIe siècle', *Ann. Bretagne* (1976), 659.

109. Y. Poulet and J. Roubert, 'Les Assemblées secrètes des XVIIe et XVIIIe siècles en relation avec l'Aa de Lyon', *Divus Thomas* (1967), 165–92.

110. The Lazarists took lifelong vows, but they were 'vows simple'—they could withdraw (J. W. Carver, *Napoleon and the Lazarists* (1974), 74–5).

111. Leflon, *M. Emery*, i. 11.

CHAPTER 7

1. R. Darricau, 'Louis XIV et le Saint-Siège: les indults de nomination aux bénéfices consistoriaux', *Bull. litt. ecclés.* (1905), 16–34, 107–31. Durtelle de Saint-Sauveur, *Les Pays d'obédience dans l'ancienne France* (1908).

2. Recorded by the abbé de Dangeau in 1690 (in F. de Dainville, *Cartes anciennes de l'Église de France* (1956), 280–1).

3. L. S. Greenbaum, 'Ten Priests in Search of a Mitre: How Talleyrand became a Bishop', *Cath. Hist. Rev.* (1964), 305–7.

4. J. Blampignon, *L'Épiscopat de Massillon* (1884), 32–4.

5. L. Tronson, *Correspondance*, ed. L. Bertrand (3 vols., 1904), iii. 389–90; Mme de Sévigné, *Lettres*, ed. Gérard-Gailly (3 vols., 1995), ii. 813. Even if the six nominated but not yet consecrated bishops she refers to are added, the number falls short of Nicea.

6. G. Namer, *L'Abbé Le Roy et ses amis* (1964), 58.

7. All this section is based on the indispensable work of M.-C. Peronnet, *Les Évêques de l'ancienne France* (2 vols., 1977).

8. J. Godel, 'Le Cardinal des montagnes: Etienne le Camus, évêque de Grenoble, 1671–1707', *Actes Colloque le Camus, Grenoble, 1971* (1974), 24.

9. Luynes, viii. 208–9.

10. Peronnet (*Les Évêques*, i. 154–9) takes the strict line about *preuves*, and counts these two as *roturiers*. This is what the genealogists would have said, but it does not accord with eighteenth-century social usage.

11. Pioneer work here by N. Ravitch, *Sword and Mitre: Government and Episcopate in France and England in the Age of Aristocracy* (1966).

12. Peronnet, *Les Évêques*, i. 580.

13. Marais, i. 145–6.

14. A. Rosne, *M. de Beauvais, évêque de Senez, 1731–90* (1883), 13–41. For the miserable diocese, M. Vovelle, *Piété baroque et déchristianisation en Provence au XVIIIᵉ siècle* (1973), 463 ff.

15. P. Feret, *La Faculté de Théologie de Paris et ses docteurs les plus célèbres* (7 vols., 1909), vii. 358.

16. Examples in the Oxford thesis of Dr Nigel Aston, 'The Politics of the French Episcopate, 1786–91' (1985).

17. Ch. Robert, *Urbain de Hercé* (1900), 14–15; L. Alloing, *Le Diocèse de Belley* (1938), 276–7.

18. Peronnet, *Les Évêques*, i. 347–9.

19. Ibid. i. 576–7.

20. C. Bianchi, 'L'Application de la constitution civile du clergé dans l'ancien diocèse de Grasse', *Ann. Soc. Cannes* (1951–4), 98.

21. J. Eich, *Histoire religieuse du département de la Moselle pendant la Révolution* (1964), i. 4.

22. J. Loth, *Histoire du cardinal de la Rochefoucauld et du diocèse de Rouen* (1893), 24.

23. J. Carreyre, *Le Jansénisme durant la Régence* (3 vols., 1929–33), iii. 369.

24. Peronnet, *Les Évêques*, i. 612 ff.

25. E. Appolis, *Le Diocèse civil de Lodève au milieu du XVIIIᵉ siècle* (1951), 72–3; C. Cézérai, 'A propos de la nomination de Mgr de Latour-Dupuis à l'évêché d'Auch', *Rev. Gascogne* (1903), 357.

26. E. Sévestre, *Les Idées gallicanes et royalistes du haut clergé. Pierre-Augustin Godart de Belbeuf, évêque d'Avranches, 1762–1803* (1917), 44–5.

27. J. Meyer, *La Noblesse bretonne au XVIIIᵉ siècle* (2 vols., 1966), ii. 1101–3. Only one Breton succeeded to the see of Rennes between 1642 and 1789 (J. Delumeau, *Le Diocèse de Rennes* (1979), 131–2).

28. Luynes, vii. 381–2.

29. Peronnet, *Les Évêques*, i. 337.

30. François-Joachim, cardinal de Bernis, *Mémoires et lettres*, ed. F. Masson (2 vols., 1878), ii. 211–13, 218–19.

31. T. Tackett, *Priest and Parish in 18th-Century France, 1750–91* (1977), 30.

32. N.-J. Chaline, *Rouen-Le Havre* (Histoire des diocèses de France) (1976), 127–8.

33. A. Sicard, *L'Ancien Clergé de France: les évêques avant la Révolution*, 5th edn. (1912), 279; Luynes, x. 350, xiii. 387–8.

34. H. Lancelin, *Histoire du diocèse de Cambrai* (1946), 248.

35. Peronnet, *Les Évêques*, i. 353.

36. *Dictionnaire portatif des cas de conscience*, 2nd edn. (2 vols., Lyon, 1761), i. 421.

37. Tronson, *Correspondance*, iii. 301.

38. R. Daon, *Conduite des âmes dans la voie du salut* (1750).

39. *Dictionnaire portatif*, i. 422.

40. L. de Sambucy Saint-Estève, *Vie de Mgr de Beauvais, ancien évêque de Senez* (1843), 55.

41. Cited by Ravitch, *Sword and Mitre*, 118–19 (though the preacher added that the Gallican Church was burdened with prelates 'without learning or virtue').

42. Voltaire, *Instruction pastorale de l'humble évêque d'Alétopolis* (1763), in *Œuvres*, xxv. 2 ff; P. Sage, *Le 'Bon prêtre' dans la littérature française* (1951), 379.

43. J. F. Marmontel, 'La Mauvaise Mère', in *Contes Moraux* (3 vols., 1765), ii. 101.

44. P. de Vaissière, *Gentilshommes campagnards de l'ancienne France* (1903), 372. (Cf. G. Gilot and A. Amic, 'Le Dernier Abbé de la Ferté-sur-Grosse', *Rev. Mabillon* (1907), 239 ff.)

45. M. Vallery-Radot, *Un Administrateur ecclésiastique à la fin de l'ancien régime: le cardinal de Luynes, archevêque de Sens, 1753–88* (1966), 12–13.

46. G. Vavasseur, 'L'Abbé Souquet de Latour', *Bull. Soc. Orne* (1895), 309–38; C. de Lacroix, *Souvenirs du comte de Montgaillard*, cited by Fabre de Massaguel, *L'École de Sorèze de 1758 au 19 fructidor, an IV* (1958), 155.

47. Chateaubriand, *Mémoires d'outre-tombe*, ed. M. Levaillant and G. Moutinier (2 vols., 1958), i. 135, 203.

48. *Mémoires du duc des Cars* (2 vols., 1890), i. 8.

49. J. Perrin, *Le Cardinal de Loménie de Brienne, archevêque de Sens* (1896), 3–6.

50. P. Coste, *Le Grand Saint du grand siècle: M. Vincent* (3 vols., 1932), ii. 426.

51. Sévestre, *Les Idées*, 29–45.

52. E. Lavaquery, *Le Cardinal de Boisgelin, 1732–1804* (2 vols., 1920), i. 24, 31, 41.

53. F. Lorin, 'Les Trois Derniers Abbés de Vaux-de-Cerney', *Méms. Soc. Rambouillet* (1913), 445.

54. L. Audiat, *Deux victimes des Septembriseurs, Pierre-Louis de la Rochefoucauld, dernier évêque de Saintes, et son frère, évêque de Beauvais* (1897), 178 ff.

55. V. Dubaret, 'Notice historique sur les évêques d'Oloron, 506–1792', *Bull. Soc. Pau*, 2ᵉ sér. 17 (1881–2).

56. A. Degert, 'L'Ancien Diocèse d'Aire', *Rev. Gascogne* (1907), 119–69.

57. Ch. Monternot, *Yves-Alexandre de Marbeuf . . . archevêque de Lyon, 1734–99* (1911), 2.

58. P. Parfouru, *Les Comptes d'un évêque et les anciens manoirs épiscopaux de Rennes et de Bruz au XVIIIᵉ siècle* (1895), 6.

59. L. W. B. Brockliss, *French Higher Education in the 17th and 18th Centuries* (1987), 236. Details of the examination in J.-J. Pialès, *Traité des gradués* (6 vols., 1757), i. 432–8.

60. Alloing, *Le Diocèse de Belley*, 274.

61. The king could send letters asking for dispensation from theses (Feret, *La Faculté*, vi. 44).

62. *Mémoires de l'abbé Baston, chanoine de Rouen*, ed. J. Loth and C. Verger (3 vols., 1897) i. 101–2.

63. Feret, *La Faculté*, vi. 194–6.

64. Baston, *Mémoires*, i 115–18.

65. Tronson, *Correspondance*, i. p. ix, ii. 143, iii. 158, 200–1, 257–8, 305; J. Ferté, *La Vie religieuse dans les campagnes parisiennes, 1622–95* (1962), 154.

66. P. Boissard, *Issy, le séminaire et la communauté de Saint-Sulpice* (1942), 19–34.

67. Talleyrand, *Mémoires*, ed. the duc de Broglie (5 vols., 1891–2), i. 22.

68. J. Leflon, *M. Emery* (2 vols., 1943), i. 115 ff.

69. Baston, *Mémoires*, i. 119.

70. Cited by P. Pisani, *L'Église de Paris et la Révolution* (4 vols., 1908–11), i. 65–6.

71. C. Laplatte, *Le Diocèse de Coutances* (1942), 47; Degert, 'L'Ancien Diocèse

d'Aire', 221–2; P. Pérez and S. Daugé, 'Nomenclature des prêtres et religieux de la famille de Daignon de Sendat', *Bull. Soc. Gers* (1932), 280–1.

72. Eich, *Histoire religieuse*, i. 15–16.

73. Fr. de la Rochefoucauld, *Voyages en France*, ed. J. Marchand (1933), 12–13; A. Degert, 'Un Vicaire-général aérostatier', *Rev. Gascogne* (1903), 373–4.

74. V. Durand, *État religieux des trois diocèses de Nîmes, d'Uzès et d'Alais à la fin de l'ancien régime* (1909), 36.

75. See Bernard de Brye, *Un évêque d'ancien régime à l'épreuve de la Révolution: le cardinal A.L.M. de la Fare* (1985).

CHAPTER 8

1. D'Argenson, v. 246–8.

2. A. Sicard, *L'Ancien Clergé de France: les évêques avant la Révolution*, 5th edn. (1912), 306.

3. P. Vial, 'L'Église de France vue par le nonce en 1766', *Cahiers hist.* (1963), 112.

4. The Véri MSS, *cahier* 128, arch. dép. Drôme, cited by J. Hardman, 'Ministerial Politics from the Accession of Louis XVI to the Assembly of Notables' (Oxford thesis, 1972).

5. J. Leflon, *M. Emery* (2 vols., 1943), i. 39.

6. D'Argenson, v. 246–8.

7. P. Parfouru, *Les Comptes d'un évêque et les anciens manoirs épiscopaux au XVIIIe siècle* (1895), 11–12.

8. F. Baboin, 'L'Application de la Constitution Civile du Clergé dans la Drôme', *Rév. fr.* (1899), 228.

9. C. Port, *La Vendée angevine* (2 vols., 1888), i. 153. Dr Nigel Aston tells me he was being treated by doctors in Paris.

10. L. Bassette, *Jean de Caulet, évêque de Grenoble, 1725–71* (1946), 38–43.

11. J. Eich, *Histoire religieuse du département de la Moselle pendant la Révolution* (2 vols., 1964), i. 11.

12. L. Desgraves and J.-P. Poussou, in F.-G. Pariset (ed.), *Bordeaux au XVIIIe siècle* (1968), 122–4.

13. M. C. Peronnet, *Les Évêques de l'ancienne France* (2 vols., 1977), ii. 966–8.

14. H. Espitalier, *Les Évêques de Fréjus* (1898), 225–6.

15. E. Lavaquery, *Le Cardinal de Boisgelin, 1732–1804* (2 vols., 1920), i. 258.

16. J. Blampignon, *L'Épiscopat de Massillon* (1884), 38.

17. D'Argenson, v. 379 (Feb. 1749).

18. E. Appolis, *Le Jansénisme à Lodève* (1952), 14–16.

19. G. Lizerand, *Le Duc de Beauvillier, 1648–1714* (1933), 308–10; G. Poisson, *M. de Saint-Simon* (1973), 245–6.

20. D'Argenson, vi. 282, viii. 398–9.

21. Vial, 'L'Église', 110.

22. Moreau de Jonnès, 'Mémoires', *Rév. fr.* (1890), 34–5; J. Flammermont, 'La Banqueroute Rohan-Guémené', *Rév. fr.* (1898), 140–7; Ch. Collas, *Saint-Louis d'Antin* (1932), 47; H. Carré, *La Noblesse de France et l'opinion publique au XVIIIe siècle* (1920), 258–9.

23. According to Doppet's solemn *Traité du fouet et de ses effets sur le physique de*

l'amour (1788), 31, cited by R. Mauzi, *L'Idée du bonheur au XVIIIe siècle* (1960), 427–8.

24. J.-A. Dulaure, *La Vie privée des ecclésiastiques qui n'ont point prêté leur serment sur la Constitution civile du clergé* (1791), 81–3.

25. M. G. Coolen, 'Le Duel de Mgr de Conzié', *Bull. Soc. Morinie* (1938), 46–61.

26. For all that follows, masterly analysis in Peronnet, *Les Évêques*, ii. 1013–20.

27. See S. Brugal, *Le Schisme constitutionnel dans l'Ardèche: Lafont-Savine, évêque jureur de Viviers* (1889).

28. G. Maugras, *Lauzun and the Court of Marie-Antoinette* (E.T. 1896), 369–76; the marquise de la Tour-du-Pin, *Journal d'une femme de cinquante ans, 1778–1815* (2 vols., 1913), i. 3, 27, 29, 30.

29. L. S. Greenbaum, *Talleyrand, Statesman Priest. The Agent General of the Clergy and the Church of France at the End of the Old Régime* (1970); and id., 'Ten Priests in Search of a Mitre: How Talleyrand became a Bishop', *Cath. Hist. Rev.* (1964), 307–31.

30. B. de Lacombe, *Talleyrand évêque d'Autun* (1903), 75–118.

31. Vial, 'L'Église', 108.

32. E. S. Mercier, *Tableau de Paris*, new edn. (12 vols., 1782–8), iv. 110. The 1st edn. was 1781.

33. Péronnet, *Les Évêques*, ii. 1006–8.

34. Luynes, iii. 321 (Feb. 1741); *Correspondance complète de la marquise du Deffand*, ed. M. de Lescure (2 vols., 1865), i. 273–4.

35. Bachaumont, x. 172 (Mar. 1778), x. 186 (Apr.).

36. Mme de Sévigné, *Lettres*, ed. Gérard-Gailly (3 vols., 1953), ii. 465 (6 Oct. 1679).

37. Sicard, *L'Ancien Clergé*, 101–3.

38. L. Châtellier, *Tradition chrétienne et renouveau catholique dans les cadres de l'ancien diocèse de Strasbourg, 1650–1770* (1981), 56–8.

39. J. Savina, *Le Clergé de Cornouaille à la fin de l'ancien régime et sa convocation aux États-Généraux de 1789* (1926), 27.

40. M. Fosseyeux, 'Le Cardinal de Noailles et l'administration du diocèse de Paris', *Rev. hist.* (1913), 44–6, 272–3; *Mémoires de l'abbé Le Gendre, chanoine de Notre-Dame*, ed. M. Roux (1863), 126–8.

41. B. Gille, *Les Forges françaises en 1777* (1960), 91, 99, 157–8.

42. V. Durand, *Les Évêques au XVIIIe siècle en Languedoc* (1907), 3.

43. Deffand, *Correspondance*, ii. 522–3 (3 Jan. 1776).

44. Luynes, iii. 99, vii. 451.

45. L. Charpentier, 'Un Inventaire épiscopal à Alet en 1764', *Méms. Soc. Carcassonne* (1904), 3–40.

46. Ch. Monternot, *Yves-Alexandre de Marbeuf . . . archevêque de Lyon, 1734–99* (1911), 47.

47. A. Degert, *Histoire des évêques de Dax* (1903), 379.

48. Ch. Robert, *Urbain de Hercé* (1900), 83–4; J. Chétail, 'Notice sur le diocèse de Glandève', *Actes 86e Congrès national des Sociétés savantes; Montpellier* (1961), 25.

49. Luynes, i. 140, 150; J.-J. Pialès, *Traité des réparations* (4 vols., 1762), ii. 459.

50. *Vie de M. Marquis-Ducastel, curé de Sainte-Suzanne*, ed. F. Pichon (1873), 36–9; A. Vidal, *L'Ancien Diocèse d'Albi* (1913), 54–7.

51. E. Esmonin, 'La Société grenobloise au temps de Louis XV d'après les

Miscellanea de Letourneau', in *Études sur la France des XVIIe et XVIIIe siècles* (1964), 490.

52. Bachaumont, xxxiv. 239–40.
53. Lavaquery, *Boisgelin*, i. 183.
54. L. Tronson, *Correspondance*, ed. L. Bertrand (3 vols., 1904), iii. 88–93.
55. J.-A. Dulaure, *Nouvelle Description de Paris* (2 vols., 1787), i. 127.
56. Sicard, *L'Ancien Clergé*, 80–1.
57. M. Vallery-Radot, *Un Administrateur ecclésiastique à la fin de l'ancien régime: le cardinal de Luynes, archevêque de Sens, 1753–88* (1966), 21–3.
58. 'Un Pèlerinage à la campagne et à la cathédrale de Bossuet en 1775', *Méms. Acad. nat. de Caen* (1899), 20.
59. Luynes, vii. 38.
60. J.-F.-H. de Richeprey, *Journal des voyages en Haute-Guienne*, ed. H. Guilhamon (1952), 78.
61. Parfouru, *Les Comptes*, 40–4.
62. E. Appolis, *Le Diocèse civil de Lodève* (1951), 244–5.
63. Sicard, *L'Ancien Clergé*, 98.
64. G. Couarraze, *Lombez, évêché rural, 1317–1861* (1973), 212.
65. E. Vivier, 'La Condition du clergé séculier dans le diocèse de Coutances au XVIIIe siècle', *Ann. Normandie* (1952), 3–4.
66. Guyot, ii. 369. See also R. Metz, *La Monarchie française et la provision des bénéfices ecclésiastiques en Alsace, 1648–1789* (1947), 43, 65 ff.
67. F. Bluche, *Les Magistrats du Parlement de Paris au XVIIIe siècle* (1960), 49.
68. P. Goubert, *Beauvais et le Beauvaisis de 1600 à 1730* (2 vols., 1960), i. 283–9.
69. Marais, i. 159–60.
70. Ibid. ii. 89.
71. F.-X.-J. Droz, *Histoire du règne de Louis XVI* (3 vols., 1839–42), i. 120.
72. Guyot, *Traité des droits . . . annexés en France à chaque dignité* (4 vols., 1787), ii. 138 ff.
73. Marais, iv. 281–4.
74. Piron, *Lettres*, ed. E. Lavaquery (1920), 31–2.
75. Th. Besterman, *Voltaire* (1965), 558.
76. J. McManners, *Abbés and Actresses: The Church and the Theatrical Profession in 18th-Century France*, Zaharoff Lecture (1986), 12–13.
77. Piron, *Lettres*, 32.
78. Lavaquery, *Boisgelin*, 258.
79. Sicard, *L'Ancien Clergé*, 60 ff.
80. P. Tallez, 'Mgr Claude-Marc Antoine d'Apochon, archevêque d'Auch', *Rev. Gascogne* (1926), 220–4.
81. Bassette, *Jean de Caulet*, 43–6.
82. e.g. Christophe de Beaumont when bishop of Bayonne (E. Regnault, *Christophe de Beaumont, archevêque de Paris, 1763–81* (2 vols., 1882), i. 78–83).
83. Espitalier, *Les Évêques*, 198–270.
84. A. Babeau, *La Ville sous l'ancien régime* (2 vols., 1889), i. 23.
85. e.g. Appolis, *Le Diocèse civil de Lodève*, 33, 48–53, 66, 72, 76, 82, 108.
86. F. Masson, *Le Cardinal de Bernis depuis son ministère, 1758–94* (1884), 42–3.
87. Sicard, *L'Ancien Clergé*, 74.
88. E. Laurent, *Reims et la région rémoise à la veille de la Révolution* (1930), pp. xx–xxiv.

89. Durand, *Les Évêques*, 25, 49, 50.
90. E. Laurès, *La Municipalité de Béziers à la fin de l'ancien régime* (1926), 18, 45–7, 50.
91. Bassette, *Jean de Caulet*, 126; Guyot, ix. 297–8.
92. Desgraves and Poussou, in Pariset (ed.), *Bordeaux*, 129.
93. A. Le Moy, *Le Parlement de Bretagne et le pouvoir royal au XVIIIe siècle* (1909), 14–15.
94. J. Pandellé, 'Une Grande Figure épiscopale, Jean-François de Montillet', *Rev. Gascogne* (1937), 113–16.
95. *Lettres secrètes sur l'état actuel de la religion et du clergé*, in Métra, xiii. 366.
96. Sicard, *L'Ancien Clergé*, 75.
97. C. Cézérac, 'A propos de la nomination de Mgr de Latour-Dupin à l'archevêché d'Auch, 1783', *Rev. Gascogne* (1903), 357.
98. J. Thibaut-Payen, *Les Morts, l'Église et l'État dans le ressort du Parlement de Paris aux XVIIe et XVIIIe siècles* (1977), 334–5.
99. On the exaggerations in the outcry about administrative bishops see F. Dumont, 'Les Prélats administrateurs au XVIIIe siècle', in *Études d'histoire et du droit canonique dédiées à Gabriel Le Bras* (1965), 513 ff.
100. M.-R. Vilette, *Les États-Généraux du Cambrésis de 1677 à 1790* (thesis, Lille, 1950), 44–70.
101. T. J. Schmitt, *L'Organisation ecclésiastique et la pratique religieuse dans l'archidiaconé d'Autun de 1650 à 1750* (1957), 7; Sicard, *L'Ancien Clergé*, 203.
102. J. Roussot, *Le Mâconnais* (1937), 111–24.
103. Savina, *Le Clergé*, 18–19.
104. Luynes, iii. 74 (Nov. 1739).
105. Lavaquery, *Boisgelin*, i. 130–5, 150–2.
106. Roussot, *Le Mâconnais*, 189–90, 195–6.
107. Robert, *Urbain de Hercé*, 128, 153, 162–3, 195, 215.
108. J. Meyer, *La Noblesse bretonne au XVIIIe siècle* (2 vols., 1966), ii. 1101. For their part the bishops did not conceal their contempt for the drunken conduct of the nobles (ibid. ii. 1081; A. Le Moy, *Le XVIIIe Siècle breton: correspondance . . . de M.M. de Robien et de la Bellangerais, 1769–91* (1931), 180).
109. G. Cormary, *Loménie de Brienne à Toulouse, 1763–88* (1935), 86 ff.
110. Durand, *Les Évêques*, 80–1.
111. Lavaquery, *Boisgelin*, 340–77.
112. Masson, *Le Cardinal de Bernis*, 61–2.

CHAPTER 9

1. R. J. Palanque, *Le Diocèse d'Aix en Provence* (1975), 123.
2. F. de Dainville, *Cartes anciennes de l'Église de France* (1956), 52–7.
3. For Reims, G. Hubrecht, 'Les Droits seigneuriaux dans la région sedanaise', *Nouv. Rev. Champagne et Brie* (1936), 35–49. For Cambrai, P. Bourgard, 'Dénombrement de la population du Cambrésis', in M. Lachiver *et al.* (eds.), *Hommage à Marcel Reinhard* (1973), 73. For Tarbes, L. Dantin, *François de Gain Montagnac, évêque de Tarbes, 1782–1801* (1908), 22. For Comminges, A. Sarramon, *Les Paroisses du diocèse de Comminges en 1786* (1987), 13–15.

4. C. Daur, 'L'État du diocèse de Montauban à la fin de l'ancien régime', *Rev. quest. hist.* (1914), 495–7.
5. M. C. Peronnet, *Les Évêques de l'ancienne France* (2 vols., 1977), i. 945–60.
6. Voltaire, *Correspondance*, ed. Th. Besterman, i. 322 (Aug. 1725).
7. Grimm, vi. 456–7 (Jan. 1760).
8. J. Dautry, 'Sébastien Lacroix', *Ann. hist. Rév. fr.* (1933), 50.
9. Voltaire, *Écrivains français du siècle de Louis XIV*, in *Œuvres*, xiv. 89.
10. G. Cholvy, *Le Diocèse de Montpellier* (1976), 161–2.
11. Bachaumont, vii. 81–2 (Nov. 1773).
12. J. Droz, *Histoire du règne de Louis XVI* (3 vols., 1839), i. 447.
13. Marais, iv. 428 (Oct. 1732).
14. Details in R. Suadeau, *L'Évêque inspecteur administratif sous la monarchie absolue* (2 vols., 1940), i. 7–17.
15. Potier de la Germondaye, *Introduction au gouvernement des paroisses* (1777), 66.
16. J. Lovié, 'La Vie paroissiale dans le diocèse de Dié à la fin de l'ancien régime', *Bull. Soc. Drôme* (1931–2), 358 ff.
17. Martial-Levé, *Louis-François-Gabriel d'Orléans de la Motte, évêque d'Amiens, 1683–1774* (1902), 18.
18. E. Appolis, 'Entre jansénistes et constitutionnaires', *Ann.* (1951), 160.
19. R. Darricau and B. Peyrous, 'Les Visites pastorales dans le Midi aquitain: bilan d'une enquête', *Ann. Midi* (1977), 398. See also the same two authors, 'Les Visites pastorales des évêques d'Aire et des évêques de Dax', *Bull. Soc. Borda* (1977), 107–21, and 'Les Visites pastorales des évêques de Bazas', *Cahiers Bazadais* (1977), 3–15.
20. M. A. Coulandres, 'Journal de Bernard-Laurent Soumille', *Mems. Soc. Alais* (1879), 157; L. Boisse, 'Les Chapelles anciennes de Grange-Gontard', *Bull. Soc. Drôme* (1931–2), 118–22; M.-C. Guibert, *Mémoires pour servir à l'histoire de la ville de Dieppe*, ed. M. Hardy (2 vols., 1878), i. 97.
21. M. Dommanget, *Le Curé Meslier* (1965), 33–8, 62.
22. A. Sicard, *L'Ancien Clergé de France: les évêques avant la Révolution* (1912 edn.), 360–70. Another case in M. Riollet, 'Le Journal d'un curé de campagne, 1768–90', *Rev. Lyon* (1911). Grimaldi's successor at Le Mans immediately set out on a confirmation tour (A. Durand, *Une Paroisse mayennaise: Fougerolles sous la Révolution, 1789–1800* (1960), 130).
23. H. Lancelin, *Histoire du diocèse de Cambrai* (1946), 237–42; L. G. Trénard, 'Les Visites pastorales dans le diocèse de Cambrai', *Rev. Nord* (1970), 473.
24. A. Kleinclausz, *Histoire de Lyon* (1948), i. 196; Raison, 'Le Jansénisme à Rennes', *Ann. Bretagne* (1940), 186–7; C. Laplatte, *Le Diocèse de Coutances* (1942), 44.
25. R.-P. Nepveu de la Manoullière, *Mémoires*, ed. G. Esnault (3 vols., 1877–9), ii. 60.
26. D. Julia and M. Vénard (gen. eds.), *Répertoire des visites pastorales de la France (anciens diocèses)*, iii (1983), 300–5.
27. F. Lebrun, *Le Diocèse d'Angers* (1981), 128.
28. L. Pérouas, *Le Diocèse de la Rochelle de 1648 à 1724: sociologie et pastorale* (1964).
29. J. Blampignon, *L'Épiscopat de Massillon* (1884), 39–44, 55–60.
30. Julia and Vénard (eds.), *Répertoire*, iii. 326–32.
31. Ibid. iv (1985), 366–76.
32. Ibid. iv. 211 ff.

33. M. Vallery-Radot, *Un Administrateur ecclésiastique à la fin de l'ancien régime: le cardinal de Luynes* (1966), 25, 103; L. Audiat, *Deux victimes des Septembriseurs, Pierre-Louis de la Rochefoucauld, dernier évêque de Saintes, et son frère, évêque de Beauvais* (1897), 21, 35; P. Pisani, *L'Église de Paris et la Révolution* (4 vols., 1908–11), i. 79.

34. E. Houth, *Versailles, la paroisse royale* (1962), 64–5; A. Kwantan, 'Antoine Elénore-Léon Le Clerc de Juigné, évêque de Châlons, 1764–82', *Méms. Soc. Marne* (1973), 168.

35. Martial-Levé, *Louis-François-Gabriel*, 37, 38; V. Durand, *État religieux des trois diocèses de Nîmes, d'Uzès et d'Alais à la fin de l'ancien régime* (1909), 45; L. Alloing, *Le Diocèse de Belley* (1938), 274; G. Minois, 'Les Visites épiscopales du diocèse de Tréguier, 1700–80', *Méms. Soc. Côtes-du-Nord* (1978), 18.

36. L. Bassette, *Jean de Caulet, évêque de Grenoble, 1725–71* (1946), 123.

37. Pérouas, *Le Diocèse de la Rochelle*, 353–4.

38. J.-T. Lasserre, *Recherches historiques sur la ville d'Alet et son ancien diocèse* (1877), 192–3.

39. Durand, *Fougerolles*, 130; *Vie de M. Marquis-Ducastel, curé de Sainte-Suzanne*, ed. F. Pichon (1873), 99–100.

40. The following examples in M.-H. Froeschlé-Chopard, 'Les Visites pastorales de Provence orientale', *Rev. hist. Église Fr.* (1977), 273–4; S. Bonnet, *Notice biographique sur Guillaume-Louis du Tillet, évêque d'Orange* (1880), 45; A. Degert, *Histoire des évêques de Dax* (1900), 379; H. Espitalier, 'Les Évêques de Fréjus', *Bull. Soc. Draguignan* (1898–9), 188–9, 192, 197, 220, 241, and 'Pouillé historique, 1743', ibid. (1869), 360; M.-H. Froeschlé-Chopard, *La Religion populaire en Provence orientale au XVIIIe siècle* (1980), 37–8.

41. F.-G. Pariset (ed.), *Bordeaux au XVIIIe siècle* (1968), 127; E. Alain, 'Un Grand Diocèse d'autrefois', *Rev. quest. hist.* (1894), 513–18; M. Bordes, *Contribution à l'étude de l'enseignement et de la vie intellectuelle dans les pays de l'intendance d'Auch au XVIIIe siècle* (1958), 21–2; G. Le Bras, 'L'État religieux et moral du diocèse de Châlons au dernier siècle de l'ancien régime', *Nouv. Rev. Champagne et Brie* (1935), 162–4.

42. G. Viard, 'Les Visites pastorales dans l'ancien diocèse de Langres', *Rev. hist. Église Fr.* (1977), 234–70.

43. Julia and Vénard (eds.), *Répertoire*, iii. 222–42.

44. Darricau and Peyrous, 'Les Visites', 389.

45. Suadeau, *L'Évêque*, i. 136.

46. Ibid. i. 107.

47. Le Bras, 'L'État religieux', 165–6.

48. B. Peyrous, 'La Vie religieuse dans le pays Bordelais: les visites pastorales durant le XVIIIe siècle', *L'Information hist.* (1975), 73–4; R. Darricau, 'Les Formulaires des visites pastorales dans l'archidiocèse de Bordeaux, 1600–1789', *Bull. Soc. Guyenne* (1968), 131–49.

49. H. Jadart, *Nicolas Dumont, curé de Villers-devant-le-Thour* (1885), 35.

50. E. G. Léonard, *Mon Village sous Louis XV* (1941), 236.

51. C. Laplatte, *Le Diocèse de Coutances* (1942), 46.

52. J. Déchelette, 'Les Visites pastorales des archiprêtrés de Charlieu et du Rousset par Mgr de Lort de Sérignan de Valras, évêque de Mâcon', *Ann. Acad. Mâcon*, 3e sér. iii (1898), 446–9.

53. F. Baqué and A. Rouquette, *Un Village: Bouziges* (1960), 145–6.

54. Halaussère, *L'Évolution d'un village frontalier de Provence: Saint-Jeanret* (1909), 333–6.
55. J.-F. Soulet, *Tradition et réformes religieuses dans les Pyrénées centrales au XVIIᵉ siècle: Le diocèse de Tarbes de 1602 à 1716* (1974).
56. Boisse, 'Les Chapelles', 122.
57. Suadeau, *L'Évêque*, i. 126–7.
58. Durand, *État religieux*, 46.
59. Vallery-Radot, *Un Administrateur ecclésiastique*, 104.
60. e.g., at Lormont in 1766 (F. Lemoing, *Ermites et reclus du diocèse de Bordeaux* (1953), 80).
61. Martial-Levé, *Louis-François-Gabriel*, 73.
62. Déchelette, 'Les Visites', 449–53.
63. Martial-Levé, *Louis-François-Gabriel*, 49–50.
64. 'Visites pastorales dans les Hauts de Gironde aux XVIIᵉ et XVIIIᵉ siècles', *Cahiers Vitrezais* (1975), 35, 46; Vallery-Radot, *Un Administrateur ecclésiastique*, 109.
65. R. Poulle, *Histoire de l'église paroissiale de Notre-Dame et Saint-Michel à Draguignan* (1865), 360–5.
66. T. J. Schmitt, *L'Organisation ecclésiastique et la pratique religieuse dans l'archidiaconé d'Autun de 1650 à 1750* (1957), 112; A. Schaer, *Le Clergé paroissial catholique en Haute-Alsace sous l'ancien régime, 1648–1789* (1960), 44–7.
67. P. Cattin, 'La Visite pastorale de Mgr Claude de Saint-Georges en 1700', *Bull. Belley* (1973), 40, 63–6.
68. Blampignon, *Massillon*, 42–3.
69. Kwanten, 'Antoine-Léon', 170–1.
70. J. McManners, *Death and the Enlightenment* (1981), ch. 10.
71. Suadeau, *L'Évêque*, i. 49–57; Maugis, 'L'enquête du Parlement sur la tenue des registres de l'état civil', *Rev. hist. droit fr.* (1922), 637.
72. Suadeau, *L'Évêque*, i. 56–7; E. Houth, *Versailles, la paroisse royale* (1962), 644.
73. J.-F.-H. de Richeprey, *Journal des voyages en Haute-Guienne*, ed. H. Guilhamon (1952), 96–7.
74. Froeschlé-Chopard, 'Les Visites', 282–8; Minois, 'Les Visites', 19; Déchelette, 'Les Visites', *Ann. Acad. Mâcon* (1898) 468–587, (1899) 576, (1900) 47, 422, 448, (1902) 322, 355–6.
75. Ch. Robert, *Urbain de Hercé* (1900), 45–9.
76. M. Vénard and D. Julia, 'Le Répertoire des visites pastorales', *Rev. hist. Église Fr.* (1977), 232–3.
77. Peronnet, *Les Évêques*, i. 934.
78. Pérouas, *Le Diocèse de la Rochelle*, 372.
79. Lasserre, *Recherches historiques*, 193.
80. A. Frézet, 'Guillaume Desmarets, curé de Courville, 1682–1765', *Nouv. Rev. Champagne et Brie* (1936), 185–6.
81. Suadeau, *L'Évêque*, i. 34. A 'contre-visite' by the archbishop of Auch in person in 1745, in J. Pandellé, 'Une Grande Figure épiscopale, Jean-François de Montillet', *Rev. Gascogne* (1937), 177–8.
82. Peronnet, *Les Évêques*, i. 935.
83. J.-M. Gouesse, 'Synodes et conférences ecclésiastiques dans le diocèse de Coutances aux XVIIᵉ et XVIIIᵉ siècles', *Ann. Normandie* (1974), 37–66.
84. E. Appolis, 'Les Assemblées spirituelles du clergé dans un diocèse de France

aux XVIIe et XVIIIe siècles', in *Liber Memorialis Antonio Era*, International Commission for the History of Representative and Parliamentary Institutions, 26 (1963), 212–20.

85. W. R. V. Brade, *The Diocesan Synod, being some Chapters from the Treatise by Pope Benedict XIV* (1926), 32.

86. J. Ferté, *La Vie religieuse dans les campagnes parisiennes, 1622–95* (1962), 26–7.

87. P.-D. Bernier, 'Les Synodes du diocèse de Paris de 1715 à 1790', in *Études d'histoire du droit canonique dédie à Gabriel Le Bras* (2 vols., 1965), i. 33–40.

88. Peronnet, *Les Évêques*, i. 924. Case of an *appel comme d'abus* against a bishop's synodal ordinances in 1726 (Schmitt, *L'Organisation*, 9).

89. Kwanten, 'Antoine-Léon', 163–7.

90. L. Marcel, *Le Frère de Diderot* (1913), 120–30.

91. Peronnet, *Les Évêques*, i. 922–3.

92. F. Lebrun, *Histoire des catholiques en France du XVe siècle à nos jours* (1981), 153.

93. Appolis, 'Les Assemblées spirituelles', 221–6.

94. Allain, 'Un Grand Diocèse', 513–19.

95. Schmitt, *L'Organisation*, 36–7.

96. L. Charpentier, *Un Évêque de l'ancien régime: Louis Joseph de Grignan, 1650– 1722* (1899), 80–4.

97. J.-M. Mioland (ed.), *Actes de l'Église d'Amiens: recueil de tous les documents relatifs à la discipline du diocèse, 811–1849* (2 vols., 1849), i. 346.

98. Vallery-Radot, *Un Administrateur ecclésiastique*, 346.

99. Gouesse, 'Synodes', 37–66.

100. The marquis de Ferrières, *Théisme* (1790), cited by L. Salvini, 'Le Clergé rural en Haut-Poitou à la veille de la Révolution', *Bull. Soc. Ouest* (1957–8), 250.

101. Peronnet, *Les Évêques*, i. 925.

102. R. Daon, *La Conduite des âmes dans la voie du salut* (1750), 343. The first edition was 1738.

103. F.-H. Sevoy, *Devoirs ecclésiastiques* (3 vols., 1770), i. pp. iii–v.

104. Daon, *Conduite des âmes*, p. xxvi.

105. Robert, *Urbain de Hercé*, 43.

106. Nepveu de la Manoullière, *Mémoires*, i. 359; J. Loth, *Le Cardinal de la Rochefoucauld, archevêque de Rouen* (1893), 50.

107. *Mémoires de l'abbé Baston, chanoine de Rouen*, ed. J. Loth and C. Verger (3 vols., 1897–8), i. 234–7.

108. V. Dufour, 'L'État du diocèse de Paris en 1789', *Bull. Com. Paris* (1883), 194– 432.

109. E. Millet, 'La Tour Saint-Gélin, vicissitudes d'un curé au XVIIIe siècle', *Les Amis du vieux Chinon, Bulletin* (1912), 349.

110. Sicard, *L'Ancien Clergé*, 349.

111. e.g. Urbain de Hercé, bishop of Dol.

112. E. Lavaquery, *Le Cardinal de Boisgelin, 1732–1804* (2 vols., 1920), i. 192.

113. J. Eich, *Histoire religieuse du département de la Moselle pendant la Révolution* (2 vols., 1964), i. 12–13.

114. Blampignon, *Massillon*, 162.

115. V. Durand, *Les Évêques au XVIIIe siècle en Languedoc* (1907), 62–5; S. Pillorget, *Provence historique* (1967), 253–5.

116. Luynes, xi. 37 (Feb. 1751).

117. Durand, *État religieux*, 8, 31.

118. E. Esmonin, 'La Société grenobloise au temps de Louis XV d'après les *Miscellanea* de Letourneau', in his *Études sur la France des XVIIe et XVIIIe siècles* (1964), 482–3.

119. J. Charrier, *Histoire du Jansénisme dans le diocèse de Nevers* (1920), 38–40.

120. S. Bonnet, *Notice biographique sur Guillaume-Louis du Tillet, évêque d'Orange* (1880), 41.

121. See Sicard, *L'Ancien Clergé*, 386, 415.

122. Loth, *Le Cardinal*, 83, 118–19.

123. Robert, *Urbain de Hercé*, 115–16.

124. Levé, *Louis-François-Gabriel*, 132; M. Bruyère, *Le Cardinal de Cabrières, 1820–1921* (1926), 89.

125. Curé A. Plassard, 'Journal', ed. J. Joachim, *Ann. Acad. Mâcon* (1954–5), 101; *Rev. Gascogne* (1927), 39–44; Richeprey, *Journal*, 93; L. Pingaud, *Les Saulx-Tavannes* (1876), 265 (in Rouen, 1740–1).

126. Sicard, *L'Ancien Clergé*, 387–9.

127. Pisani, *L'Église de Paris*, i. 80.

128. Th. Bérengier, 'Journal du maître d'hôtel de Mgr Belsunce durant la peste de Marseille', *Rev. quest. hist.* (1878), 567–76. See also McManners, *Death*, 43 ff.

129. From Sicard, *L'Ancien Clergé*, except for Rennes (in S. T. McCloy, *Government Assistance in 18th-Century France* (1946), 88).

130. E. Esmonin, 'La Fortune du cardinal Le Camus', in his *Études sur la France des XVIIe et XVIIIe siècles* (1964), 391–2.

131. P. Vaillant, 'La Fondation de la bibliothèque de Grenoble', *Cahiers hist.* (1963), 286.

132. G. Armigon, *Banquiers des pauvres* (n.d.), 83–8.

133. Saint-Simon (Pléiade), vii. 325–6.

134. Sicard, *L'Ancien Clergé*, 377–9.

135. Pingaud, *Les Saulx-Tavannes*, 269.

136. Luynes, xiii. 116.

137. Ibid. vi. 139–41 (Nov. 1744).

CHAPTER 10

1. McManners, *French Ecclesiastical Society under the Ancien Régime: A Study of Angers* (1960), 130; J. Meyer, *La Noblesse bretonne au XVIIIe siècle* (2 vols., 1966), ii. 1151.

2. P. Pisani, *L'Église de Paris et la Révolution* (4 vols., 1908), i. 3–14. See also the grading of the 52 parishes of Paris by the number of priests (Saint-Eustache 80, Saint-Nicolas-des-Champs and Saint-Roch 60 etc.) in D. Garrioch, *Neighbourhood and Community in Paris, 1740–90* (1986), 153.

3. A. Babeau, *Le Village sous l'ancien régime*, 3rd edn. (1882), 115–16; E. Champion, *La France d'après les cahiers* (1921 edn.), 185.

4. F. de Dainville, *Cartes anciennes de l'Église de France* (1956), 195.

5. E. Chevrier, 'Notice sur les églises de Sablé', *Rev. Maine* (1876), 415–16.

6. A. Friedmann, 'Les Circonscriptions paroissiales de Paris avant la Révolution', *L'Année canonique* (1960), 33–40.

7. T. J. Schmitt, *L'Organisation ecclésiastique et la pratique religieuse dans l'archidiaconé d'Autun de 1650 à 1750* (1957), 104.

8. Ibid. 101–2, 261.

9. Dainville, *Cartes anciennes*, 196.

10. Ch. Berthelot du Chesnay, 'Le Clergé diocésain . . . au XVIIIᵉ siècle et les registres des insinuations ecclésiastiques', *Rev. hist. mod. contemp.* (1963), 244; E. Sévestre, *L'Organisation du clergé . . . corresp. du curé de Saint-Nicolas de Coutances, 1784–8* (1911), 189.

11. L. Ampoulange, *Le Clergé et la convocation des États Généraux dans la sénéchaussée principale de Périgord* (1912), 65–6.

12. E. Millet, 'La Tour Saint-Gélin: vicissitudes d'un curé au XVIIIᵉ siècle', *Amis Chinon* (1957–8), 27.

13. J.-F.-H. de Richeprey, *Journal des voyages en Haute-Guienne*, ed. H. Guilhamon (1952), 44.

14. M. Reinhard, *Paris pendant la Révolution* (dupl. Sorbonne lectures, n.d.), i. 26.

15. Ibid., i. 205.

16. V. Durand, *État religieux des trois diocèses de Nîmes, d'Uzès et d'Alais à la fin de l'ancien régime* (1909), 88–9; A. Playoust-Chaussis, *La Vie religieuse dans le diocèse de Boulogne au XVIIIᵉ siècle, 1725–90* (1976), 50–2.

17. J. Daranatz, 'Les Ordinations sacerdotales du diocèse de Bayonne au XVIIIᵉ siècle', *Bull. Soc. Bayonne*, NS 7 (1931), 363–5.

18. Guyot, xvi. 635–7.

19. V. Dubaret, *Études d'histoire locale et religieuse* (2 vols., 1889–92), ii. 190–230.

20. X. Azéma, 'Évangélisation populaire sous l'ancien régime: le faubourg Boutonnet à Montpellier', *Ann. Midi* (1970), 399–408.

21. Potier de la Germondaye, *Introduction au gouvernement des paroisses* (1777), 1.

22. Guyot, xliv. 414–15.

23. McManners, *Angers*, 152–3.

24. A. Dupuy, 'L'Administration municipale de Bretagne au XVIIIᵉ siècle', *Ann. Bretagne* (1887–8), 560–1.

25. E. Lafforgue, *Histoires des Fabriques des églises de Tarbes sous l'ancien régime* (1923), 61, 64, 87.

26. L. Brochard, *Saint-Gervais: histoire de la paroisse* (1950), 242–3.

27. P. de Saint-Jacob, *Documents relatifs à la communauté villageoise en Bourgogne* (1962), 148.

28. Ibid. 51–3.

29. Babeau, *Le Village*, 31–45.

30. McManners, *Angers*, 153–4.

31. G. Lefebvre, *Les Paysans du Nord et la Révolution Française* (1924), 320; A. Babeau, *La Ville sous l'ancien régime* (2 vols., 1884), i. 35.

32. A. Lottin, 'Mémoire des Curez de la ville de Lille . . . contre le magistrat . . .', *Rev. Nord* (1971), 25.

33. Lafforgue, *Histoire*, 64. In Brittany, in small places with no municipal officers, the *général* was said to be responsible for the rights and duties of all citizens (F. Duine, 'Les Généraux des paroisses Bretonnes', *Ann. Bretagne* (1907–8), 4).

34. Following Guyot, xliv. 413–14, and Lafforgue, *Histoire*, 57–9.

35. G. Robert, 'La Seigneurie de Givry-sur-Aisne', *Trav. Acad. nat. Reims*, 133 (1913), 364–5.

36. Babeau, *Le Village*, 28–30, 55.

37. Guyot, xliv. 415.

38. Dupuy, 'L'Administration' (1887–8), 577.

39. Guyot, xliv. 415. In Brittany, discussion was in Breton, but the transcription of the resolutions was in French (D. Bernard, 'Le Breton dans les actes publics', *Ann. Bretagne* (1921–3), 23–49).

40. Guyot, xliv. 416.

41. H. Antoine, 'Recherches sur la paroisse . . . Saint-Pierre de Montsort', *Rev. Maine*, 6 (1879), 175–80.

42. Dupuy, 'L'Administration', *Ann. Bretagne* (1889–90), 665–6.

43. M. Marion, *Dictionnaire des institutions de la France aux XVIIe et XVIIIe siècles* (2 vols., 1923), i. 363, 229; Lafforgue, *Histoire*, 14–20; J. Boyreau, *Le Village en France au XVIIIe siècle* (1955), 99–102.

44. Saint-Jacob, *Documents*, 148.

45. Lafforgue, *Histoire*, 15–16.

46. Ibid.

47. M. Vimont, *Histoire de l'église et de la paroisse Saint-Leu-Saint-Gilles à Paris* (1932), 101.

48. M. Brongniart, *La Paroisse Saint-Médard* (1951), 65.

49. Saint-Jacob, *Documents*, 121, 148.

50. Babeau, *Le Village*, 134; Schmitt, *L'Organisation*, 119.

51. Babeau, *Le Village*, 133–4.

52. L. Brochard, *Saint-Gervais, histoire de la paroisse* (1950), 242. Cf. Potier de la Germondaye, *Introduction*, pt. 3, 1.

53. Dupuy, 'L'Administration', *Ann. Bretagne* (1887–8), 572–3.

54. E. Houth, *Versailles, la paroisse royale* (1962), 119.

55. Dupuy, 'L'Administration', 573.

56. Guyot, xxxix. 139–49, 13.

57. J.-J. Gautier, *Essai sur les mœurs champêtres* (1787), ed. X. Rousseau (1935), 15.

58. For what follows, Lafforgue, *Histoire*, 25, 47–53, 56; Babeau, *Le Village*, 136–40; A. Dupuy, 'L'Administration', *Ann. Bretagne* (1887–8), 57–121; (1889–90), 184–5; Duine, 'Les Généraux', 9.

59. McManners, *Angers*, 156–7.

60. La Poix de Fréminville, *Dictionnaire de la police*, cited by Babeau, *Le Village*, 141.

61. Boyreau, *Le Village*, 115.

62. A. Lesort, 'Particularité liturgique de la paroisse Saint-Germain-l'Auxerrois', *Bull. Soc. Paris* (1942–3), 14–15.

63. Lafforgue, *Histoire*, 17.

64. Ibid. 28.

65. Barbier, ii. 250–1; Marais, iv. 358–61.

66. Brochard, *Saint-Gervais*, 159, 162, 227–8, 230–2, 242–3, 288, 296–7, 300.

67. Lafforgue, *Histoire*, 29.

68. G. Minois, 'La Situation matérielle des paroisses du diocèse de Tréguier dans la première moitié du XVIIIe siècle d'après les visites pastorales', *Ann. Bretagne* (1977), 44.

69. Guyot, xxiv. 283–4.

70. Lafforgue, *Histoire*, 96–9; L. Froger, 'De l'organisation et de l'administration des fabriques au diocèse du Mans', *Rev. quest. hist.* 63 (1898), 406. The parish of Rémalard had eight meadows, one piece of arable land, and its principal confraternity had a meadow, a field, and nine houses (M. Lecoq, 'La Vie paysanne dans un coin du Perche', *Ann. hist. Rév. fr.* (1949), 62).

71. Froger, 'De l'organisation', 423.

72. Dupuy, 'L'Administration', *Ann. Bretagne* (1889–90), 182.

73. Ibid. 177–80.

74. L.-S. Mercier, *Tableau de Paris*, new edn. (12 vols., 1782–8), ii. 87–9.

75. Dupuy, 'L'Administration', 171–2.

76. J. McManners, *Death and the Enlightenment* (1981), ch. 9.

77. Guyot, viii. 396–7.

78. Lecoq, 'La Vie paysanne', 42; McManners, *Angers*, 153; C. Baloche, *L'Église Saint-Merry de Paris: histoire de la paroisse et de la collégiale, 700–1910* (2 vols., 1911), i. 566. Cf. 5,400 livres in Saint-Leu-Saint-Giles (Vimont, *Histoire*, 87) and 13,000 in the royal parish of Notre-Dame at Versailles (Houth, *Versailles*, 131).

79. Guyot, v. 48–53; Isambert, *Recueil des anciennes lois françaises* (29 vols., 1822–33), xx. 504.

80. M. Maréchal and M. J. A. Serieux, *Traité des droits honorifiques des patrons et des seigneurs dans les églises* (2 vols., 1772), i. 77.

81. Guyot, v. 50–4. In another case, a notary gets back his pew after threatening litigation (A. Pioger, 'Thorigné-le-Reneaulme au XVIIIe siècle', *Bull. Soc. Sarthe* (1973–4), 98–9).

82. Dupuy, 'L'Administration', *Ann. Bretagne* (1889–90), 160–5; *Vie de M. Marquis-Ducastel*, ed. F. Pichon (1873), 86–8.

83. Dupuy, 'L'Administration', 166–7.

84. Houth, *Versailles*, 131; Luynes, xiii. 11–12.

85. Vimont, *Histoire*, 87.

86. Baloche, *L'Église Saint-Merry*, i. 515.

87. Dupuy, 'L'Administration', *Ann. Bretagne* (1887–8), 586.

88. Ibid. 594–8.

89. G. Bouchard, *Prieur de la Côte d'Or* (1940), 179.

90. Dupuy, 'L'Administration', 592–3.

91. G. Coolen, *Helfaut: essai sur l'administration d'une paroisse sous l'ancien régime*, Méms Soc. Morinie (1939), 76.

92. Baloche, *L'Église Saint-Merry*, i. 300.

93. Babeau, *Le Village*, 101–2; Saint-Jacob, *Documents*, 153.

94. Legal position in J.-J. Pialès, *Traité des réparations* (2 vols., 1762), i. 215–43; La Poix de Fréminville, *Traité général du gouvernement des biens des communautés d'habitans des . . . paroisses* (1760).

95. Babeau, *Le Village*, 47.

96. Saint-Jacob, *Documents*, 134.

97. As, for example, in law enforcement.

98. 'Visites pastorales dans les Hauts de Gironde aux XVIIe et XVIIIe siècles', *Cahiers Vitrezais* (1975), 31–2; P. Caffin, 'La Visite pastorale de Mgr Charles de Saint-Georges en 1700', *Bull. Belley*, 49 (1974), 28.

99. Marion, *Dictionnaire*, i. 175.

100. Playoust-Chaussis, *La Vie religieuse*, 53–4.

101. Dupuy, 'L'Administration', *Ann. Bretagne* (1889–90), 668.

102. Saint-Jacob, *Documents*, 152.

103. F. Baqué and A. Rouquette, *Un Village du littoral au cours des siècles: Bouzigues* (1960), 137; A. Hawtin, 'Le Testament d'un Prémontré en 1792', *Rev. Nord* (1962), 304.

104. A. Krieger and L. Ruffin, *La Madeleine* (1937), 50.
105. Ch. Joathan, 'Le Journal inédit d'un curé de Saint-Vincent de Mâcon au XVIIIe siècle', *Ann. Acad. Mâcon* (1954–5), 104.
106. L. Ledeur, 'La Difficile Reconstruction de l'église Saint-Pierre: un problème d'urbanisme à Besançon au XVIIIe siècle', *Méms. Soc. Doubs*, 13 (1971), 1–43.
107. M. Vénard, 'Les Églises paroissiales, XV–XVIIIe siècles', *Rev. hist. Église Fr.* (1987), 7–39.
108. P. Maloubier-Tournier, 'Les Rétables du XVIIe et du XVIIIe siècle en Ille-et-Vilaine', *Ann. Bretagne* (1962), 93–137.
109. L. Lery, 'Une Visite à l'église Notre-Dame de Versailles', *Rev. Versailles* (1912), 219–20.
110. Baloche, *L'Église Saint-Merry*, i. 537, 541, 571–3.
111. Barbier, ii. 140–1 (Dec. 1730), 333 (Aug. 1732); C. Hamel, *Saint-Sulpice* (1900), 176–86.
112. Guyot, xi. 323.
113. In a case of 1717, the intendant punished the village by putting it to the expense of 'having the bells taken down and flogged by the public executioner' (Babeau, *Le Village*, 118).
114. Ibid. 117–18; H. Carré, *Recueil curieux et édifiant sur les cloches de l'Église, avec les cérémonies de leur bénédiction* (1757), 29.
115. P. Dop, 'L'Église de Saint-Jean-de-Luz', *Bull. Soc. Bayonne* (1932), 404.
116. M. Yvart, 'La Vie d'un écolier au séminaire Saint-Nicaise et au collège royal de Rouen de 1786 à 1792: Eloi Pigré', *Rev. Socs. Haute-Normandie*, 3e trim. (1957), 37. The weight in Carré, *Recueil*, 4.
117. Duine, 'Les Généraux', 477.
118. J. B. Pelt, *Études sur la cathédrale de Metz* (1853), 264.
119. R. Charles, 'Les Chroniques de la paroisse et du collège de Courdemanche au Maine', *Rev. Maine*, i (1876), 298–9.
120. L. Paris, *Histoire de l'abbaye d'Avenay*, i (1879), 497–8.
121. F. Duine, 'Guipel: les communes rurales en Bretagne', *Ann. Bretagne* (1924–5), 260–1; René-Pierre Nepveu de la Manouillère, *Mémoires*, ed. G. Esnault (3 vols., 1877–9), i. 326–7.
122. Houth, *Versailles*, 37, 57, 69–70; Luynes, xiv. 339, vii. 100–2, 175.
123. Duine, 'Les Généraux', 484–5.
124. Antoine, 'Recherches', 182.
125. M. L. Legros, 'Le Fessier et "Son Bérus", 1764–91', *Rev. Anjou* (1916), 190.
126. J. E. Malaussène, *Saint-Jeannet: l'évolution d'un village frontalier de Provence* (1969), 336.
127. Carré, *Recueil*, 314.
128. e.g., at Saint-Jeannet, the first bell-founder was from Piedmont, the second a German from Lorraine.
129. Coolen, *Helfaut*, 64.
130. Dop, 'Saint-Jean-de-Luz', 404.
131. C. Torchet, *Histoire de l'abbaye royale de Notre-Dame de Chelles* (2 vols., 1881), ii. 182.
132. See Pialès, *Traité*; Guyot, xlvi. 565–6, liv. 7.
133. M. Louis, *Trav. Acad. nat. Reims* (1902), 199–200.
134. Ch. Girault, *Les Biens d'église dans la Sarthe à la fin du XVIIIe siècle* (1953), 377.
135. Guyot, xlvi. 565.

136. Ibid.
137. Pierre de Vaissière, *Curés de campagne de l'ancienne France* (1933), 178–86.
138. Malaussène, *Saint-Jeannet*, 331–6.
139. Schmitt, *L'Organisation*, 135.
140. Baqué and Rouquette, *Bouzigues*, 143.
141. L. de Montfalcon, 'Querelle autour d'un presbytère à Flaxie au XVIIIᵉ siècle', *Bull. Belley* (1966), 35.
142. A. Kwantan, 'Antoine-Elénore-Léon Le Clerc de Juigné, évêque de Châlons (1764–82)', *Méms. Soc. Marne* (1973), 171.
143. P. de Saint-Jacob, *Les Paysans du Bourgogne du nord au dernier siècle de l'ancien régime* (1960), 533.
144. Dupuy, 'L'Administration', *Ann. Bretagne* (1887–8), 578–80.
145. Marquis-Ducastel, *La Vie*, 704.

CHAPTER 11

1. A. Playoust-Chaussis, *La Vie religieuse dans le diocèse de Boulogne au XVIIIᵉ siècle, 1725–1790* (1976), 153.
2. E. Buchez, 'Le Clergé paroissial du diocèse de Reims d'après l'enquête de 1774', *Trav. Acad. nat. Reims* (1911), 128.
3. Dom P. Piolin, *L'Église du Mans durant la Révolution* (4 vols., 1868), i. 4.
4. P. Goubert, *Beauvais et le Beauvaisis de 1600 à 1730* (2 vols., 1960), i. 198.
5. D. Julia, 'Le Clergé paroissial du diocèse de Reims à la fin du XVIIIᵉ siècle', *Rev. hist. mod. contemp.* (1966), 195–216.
6. Ch. Berthelot du Chesnay, 'Le Clergé diocésain français au XVIIIᵉ siècle et les registres des insinuations ecclésiastiques', *Rev. hist. mod. contemp.* (1963), 263.
7. T. Tackett and Ch. Langlois, 'Ecclesiastical Structures and Clerical Geography on the Eve of the French Revolution', *Fr. Hist. St.* (1978–80), 364.
8. Playoust-Chaussis, *La Vie religieuse*, 142.
9. L. Châtellier, *Tradition chrétienne et renouveau catholique dans l'ancien diocèse de Strasbourg* (1981), 379.
10. L. Pérouas, *Le Diocèse de La Rochelle de 1648 à 1724: sociologie et pastorale* (1964), 200, 444.
11. J. de Font-Réaulx, 'Études administratives et financières du diocèse de Valence', *Bull. Soc. Drôme* (1931–2), 277.
12. E. Appolis, *Le Jansénisme dans le diocèse de Lodève au XVIIIᵉ siècle* (1932), 83.
13. Tackett and Langlois, 'Ecclesiastical Structures', 369.
14. T. J. A. Le Goff, *Vannes and its Region: A Study of Town and Country in Eighteenth-Century France* (1981), 251–3.
15. Châtellier, *Tradition chrétienne*, 373–9.
16. T. Tackett, 'Le Clergé de l'archidiocèse d'Embrun à la fin de l'ancien régime', *Ann. Midi* (1976), 181–3.
17. M. Reinhard, *Paris pendant la Révolution française* (dupl.), fasc. i. 38–9.
18. B. Guillemin, *Le Diocèse de Bordeaux* (1979), 151–3, 197.
19. F. G. Pariset (ed.), *Bordeaux au XVIIIᵉ siècle* (1968), 131. The town of Metz shows a similar recruitment: of twenty-nine curés and vicaires, twelve were

born in the town itself (J. Eich, *Histoire religieuse du département de la Moselle pendant la Révolution* (2 vols., 1964), i. 22–4).

20. Cited by B. Peyrous, reporting on his thesis, in *L'Information hist.* (1975), 76.

21. Ph. Loupès, 'Le Clergé paroissial du diocèse de Bordeaux d'après la grande enquête de 1772', *Ann. Midi* (1971), 21. See also Loupès' 'Les Ecclésiastiques Irlandais dans le diocèse de Bordeaux sous l'ancien régime', *Rev. Bordeaux* (1974), 181–200.

22. T. Tackett, 'L'Histoire sociale du clergé diocésain dans la France du XVIIIᵉ siècle', *Rev. hist. mod. contemp.* (1979), 211.

23. G. Minois, 'Les Vocations sacerdotales dans le diocèse de Tréguier au XVIIIᵉ siècle', *Ann. Bretagne* (1979), 52.

24. J. R. Palanque (ed.), *Le Diocèse d'Aix-en-Provence* (1975), 97.

25. J. F. Soulet, *Tradition et réformes religieuses dans les Pyrénées centrales au XVIIᵉ siècle* (1974), 120–7.

26. Le Goff, *Vannes*, 250.

27. Berthelot du Chesnay, 'Le Clergé diocésain', 48–9.

28. D. Julia, 'Le Clergé paroissial', 199.

29. Châtellier, *Tradition chrétienne*, 378–82.

30. J. Richard, 'L'Élaboration d'un cahier de doléances: Pierre-Claude Perrot, curé de Brazey-en-Plaine', *Ann. Bourgogne* (1960), 10.

31. E. Vivier, 'La Condition du clergé séculier', *Ann. Normandie* (1952), 15–23.

32. P. Boucher, *Charles Cochon de Lapparent* (n.d.), 15.

33. C. Hamel, *Histoire de l'église de Saint-Sulpice* (1900), 161–212.

34. V. Lespy, *Un Curé béarnais au 18ᵉ siècle: correspondance de l'abbé Tristan* (1879), 1–39.

35. A. Leveille, 'Les Revenus du clergé breton avant la Révolution', *Rev. quest. hist.* (1912), 467.

36. J. Meyer, *La Noblesse bretonne au XVIIIᵉ siècle* (2 vols., 1966), ii. 1107.

37. The vicomte de Motey, 'Saint-Germain-de-Clairefeuille', *Bull. Soc. Orne* (1894), 200–1.

38. C. Marcilhacy, *Le Diocèse d'Orléans au milieu de XIXᵉ siècle, les hommes et leurs mentalités* (1964), 432.

39. J.-M. Alliot, *Le Clergé de Versailles pendant la Révolution française* (1913), 41.

40. A. Sarramon (ed.), *Les Paroisses du diocèse de Comminges en 1786* (1968), 334–5.

41. J.-J. Gautier, curé, *Essai sur les mœurs champêtres* (1787), ed. X. Rousseau (1935), 33.

42. A. Durand, *Une Paroisse mayennaise: Fougerolles sous la Révolution, 1789–1800* (1960), 121–7.

43. J. McManners, *French Ecclesiastical Society under the Ancien Régime: A Study of Angers* (1960), 135, 186.

44. H. de Sarrau, 'Un Poète libournais inconnu, l'abbé Léglise, curé de Pomerol', *Rev. Libournais* (1961), 106.

45. L'abbé Baston, *Mémoires*, ed. S. Loth and C. Verger (3 vols., 1897), i. 53.

46. C. Berthelot du Chesnay, *Les Prêtres Séculiers en Haute-Bretagne au XVIIIᵉ siècle* (1974), 52–4.

47. Verlac, *Nouveau Plan pour toutes les classes* (1789), cited by A. Sicard, *Les Études classiques avant la Révolution* (1887), 325–6.

48. Meyer, *La Noblesse*, ii. 1151. For the same recruiting problem in the nearby

diocese of Quimper see J. Savina, *Le Clergé de Cornouaille à la fin de l'ancien régime et sa convocation aux États-Généraux* (1926), 38.

49. Goubert, *Beauvais*, i. 199–200.

50. P. de Saint-Jacob, *Les Paysans de la Bourgogne du nord au dernier siècle de l'ancien régime* (1960), 532–3.

51. Ch. Joathan, 'Le Journal inédit d'un curé de Saint-Vincent de Mâcon au XVIIIᵉ siècle', *Ann. Acad. Mâcon* (1954–5), 7.

52. 'Trois Lettres inédites de l'abbé Jallet', *Ann. hist. Rév. fr.* (1950), 326; G. Tardy, *Notice sur l'abbé J. Jallet* (1882), 2–4.

53. McManners, *Angers*, 135–6.

54. Ibid.

55. Tackett and Langlois, 'Ecclesiastical Structures', 352–70.

56. Le Goff, *Vannes*, 250–4.

57. For Coutances, H. Nédelec, summarized in *Rev. hist. droit fr.* (1962), 500. For Tréguier, Minois, 'Les Vocations sacerdotales', 52.

58. Playoust-Chaussis, *La Vie religieuse*, 149–52.

59. Julia, 'Le Clergé paroissial', 200. The administrative and liberal professions provided one out of every nine in the diocese of Viviers (J. Charay, *Petite histoire de l'église diocésaine de Viviers* (1977), 160–1).

60. Cf. the cloth makers of Lodève (Appolis, *Le Jansénisme*, 834).

61. Berthelot du Chesnay, 'Le Clergé diocésain', 256–7.

62. T. Tackett, *Priest and Parish in Eighteenth-Century France: A Political and Social Study of the Curés in a Diocese of Dauphiné, 1750–1791* (1977), 59–67.

63. Ch. Girault, *Les Biens d'église dans la Sarthe à la fin du XVIIIᵉ siècle* (1953), 374–5. Note: the livre was 20 sous or sols, and there were 12 deniers in each. The pistole was 10 livres commonly. The écu was an actual coin whose value varied up to 1762, but thereafter was fixed at 6 livres. The louis was a gold coin originally worth 10 livres, but had risen to 36 by 1718; finally, in 1720, it was fixed at 36.

64. Saint-Jacob, *Les Paysans*, 534–5. For France generally, J. Loutchisky, *L'État des classes agricoles en France à la veille de la Révolution* (1911), 22.

65. P. de Vaissière, *Curés de campagne de l'ancienne France* (1933), 143–50, 109–14.

66. The Assembly General of the Clergy took up this issue in 1745, and in 1747 a royal declaration stated that the *taille* fell on the *fermier*'s own profits alone. But in fact, this remission was not observed.

67. L. Lex, 'Histoire de Saint-Point', *Ann. Acad. Mâcon*, 3ᵉ Sér. 3 (1898), 307–9. The law courts had awarded the possession of the field to the curé, over-riding her claim.

68. J. Rombault, 'Un Curé de campagne au 18ᵉ siècle', *Bull. Soc. Orne*, 12 (1893), 21–32.

69. Curé Barbotin, *Lettres*, ed. A. Aulard (1910), 18, 40, 19, 65, 13–14, 70.

70. M. Lecoq, 'La Vie paysanne dans un coin du Perche', *Ann. hist. Rév. fr.* (1949), 67.

71. G. Mandou, 'Les Revenus des vicaires perpétuels du chapitre de Périgueux au XVIIIᵉ siècle', *Ann. Midi* (1980), 50.

72. H. M. Riollet, 'Le Journal d'un curé de campagne, 1768–1790', *Rev. Lyon* (1911), 283.

73. Vaissière, *Curés*, 128.

74. P. Gagnol, *La Dîme ecclésiastique en France* (1910), 124–5.

75. F. Duine, 'Les Communes rurales en Bretagne: Guipel', *Ann. Bretagne* (1924–5), 243.

76. G. Roches, 'La Commune des Rieux (Manche) pendant la Révolution', *Rév. fr.* (1914), 339–40.

77. Durand, *Fougerolles*, 17. Cf. a parish with 2,450 livres income has to pay 750, the salary of two vicaires; see F. Lemeunier, 'Bazouges', *Province du Maine* (1978), 51.

78. Lespy (ed.), *Un Curé béarnais*, 36.

79. G. Robert, 'Le Prieuré de Saint-Thomas en Argonne', *Nouv. Rev. Champagne et Brie* (1936), 246.

80. E. Millet, 'La Tour Saint-Gélin: vicissitudes d'un curé au XVIIIe siècle', *Amis Chinon* (1957–9), 27–32.

81. P.-D. Bernier, *Essai sur le tiers état rural ou les paysans de Basse-Normandie au XVIIIe siècle* (1891), 120–1.

82. Gagnol, *La Dîme ecclésiastique*, 159.

83. G. Desnoiresterres, *Voltaire et la société française au XVIIIe siècle*, 2nd edn. (8 vols., 1867–76), vi. 43–4.

84. See above, ch. 4 (Tithe).

85. Durand, *Fougerolles*, 14.

86. F. D. Mathieu, *L'Ancien Régime dans la province de Lorraine et Barrois* (1879), 196.

87. Gagnol, *La Dîme ecclésiastique*, 162–9.

88. L. Ampoulange, *Le Clergé et la convocation aux États Généraux de 1789 dans la sénéchaussée principale de Périgord* (1912), 51–2.

89. Vaissière, *Curés*, 159–75.

90. Ibid. 169–70.

91. P. Perceveaux, 'La Portion congrue: aumône ou minimum vital? Notes sur les conditions de vie du bas clergé en Valromey aux 17e et 18e siècles', *Bull. Belley* (1967), 89. Cf. an agreement of the curé with the inhabitants of Mornay in H. Cottin, *La Liquidation des biens du clergé à Is-sur-Tille* (1911), 37.

92. P. Janvier, 'Histoire religieuse du district de Rennes sous la Constituante', *Ann. Bretagne* (1908–9), 352.

93. R. H. Andrews, *Les Paysans des Mauges au 18e siècle* (1935), 180.

94. H. Marion, *Dictionnaire des insitutions de la France aux XVIIe et XVIIIe siècles* (2 vols., 1923), i. 412.

95. Sarrau, 'Un Poète libournais', 109–13, also *Rev. Libournais* (1961), (1972), 65–9.

96. C. Torchet, *Histoire de l'abbaye royale de Notre-Dame de Chelles* (2 vols., 1889), ii. 218–19.

97. E. Hubert, *Inventaire sommaire des archives départementales de l'Indre*, Sér. A, Apanage du comte d'Artois (1901), 143–4.

98. Ch. Berthelot du Chesnay, 'Le Clergé diocésain', 251.

99. Mandou, 'Les Revenus'. (They used the *novales* as a lever.)

100. Vaissière, *Curés*, 76; H. Marion, *La Dîme ecclésiastique en France au 18e siècle et sa suppression* (1912), *passim*, give general figures. Add E. Sévestre, *L'Organisation du clergé paroissial à la veille de la Révolution. Correspondance du curé de Saint-Nicolas de Coutances, 1784–88* (1911), 14; Tackett, *Priest and Parish*, 120; Eich, *Histoire religieuse*, i. 44–5; T. J. Schmitt, *L'Organisation ecclésiastique et la pratique religieuse dans l'archidiaconé d'Autun de 1650 à 1750* (1957), 144.

101. Tackett cites the figures in A. Nat. G[8] 499–516 as published by Ch. Léouzon Le Duc, 'La Fortune du clergé sous l'ancien régime', *Journal des économistes*, 4e sér. 15 (1881), 228–30.

102. Vaissière, *Curés*, 220 ff.

103. E. Lavaquery, *Le Cardinal de Boisgelin, 1732–1804* (2 vols., 1920), i. 225.

104. J.-P. Desaive, 'Clergé rural et documents fiscaux. Les revenus et charges des prêtres de campagne au nord-est de Paris, d'après les enquêtes fiscales des XVIIe et XVIIIe siècles', *Rev. hist. mod. contemp.* (1970), 941–52.

105. A. Huguenin, *Un Village bourguignon sous l'ancien régime* (1893), 43.

106. Berthelot du Chesnay, 'Le Clergé diocésain', 250.

107. L. Brochard, *Saint-Gervais, histoire de la paroisse* (1950), 170.

108. M. Vimont, *Histoire de l'Église et de la paroisse Saint-Leu-Saint-Gilles à Paris* (1932).

109. F. de Saint-Just, *Témoins de quatre siècles* (1962), 183.

110. J. McManners, *Death and the Enlightenment* (1981), 281–4 (quoted in various places in this para.).

111. G. Hardy, 'L'Anticléricalisme paysan', *Ann. rév.* (1912), 607–8.

112. Schmitt, *L'Organisation*, 146.

113. J.-M. Mioland (ed.), *Actes de l'Église d'Amiens: recueil de tous les documents relatifs à la discipline du diocèse, 811–1849* (2 vols., 1849), i. 367–72.

114. Details from the Parisian table of fees in C. Baloche, *L'Église Saint-Merry de Paris: histoire de la paroisse et de la collégiale, 700–1910* (2 vols., 1911), i. 445–6.

115. E. Préclin, 'La Situation ecclésiastique et religieuse de la Franche Comté à la veille de la Révolution', *Bull. Féd. Franche Comté* (1955), 10.

116. McManners, *Death*, 284.

117. Préclin, 'La Situation ecclésiastique', 10.

118. Playoust-Chaussis, *La Vie religieuse*, 279.

119. E.-G. Léonard, *Mon village sous Louis XV* (1941), 83–4.

120. Gagnol, *La Dîme ecclésiastique*, 100.

121. E. Esmonin, 'La Société grenobloise au temps de Louis XV d'après les Miscellanea de Letourneau', in his *Études sur la France des XVIIe et XVIIIe siècles* (1964), 485–7.

122. Sarramon (ed.), *Les Paroisses*, 21, 60, 90, 126, 128, 138, 302, 307, 331, 332.

123. McManners, *Angers*, 139–41.

124. A. Dupuy, 'L'Administration municipale de Bretagne au 18e siècle', *Ann. Bretagne* (1887–8), 580–1.

125. J. Déchelette, 'Visites Pastorales des archiprêtrés de Charlieu par Mgr De Lort de Sérignan de Valras, évêque de Mâcon, 1745–64', *Ann. Acad. Mâcon*, 3e sér. 3 (1898), 474; 5 (1900), 442.

126. C. Lafforgue, 'Charges et revenus d'un curé de campagne en 1790', *Rev. Gascogne* (1905), 278–81.

127. M. Jousse, *Temporel et spirituel des paroisses* (1769), 79.

128. Dupuy, 'L'Administration' (1889–90), 180–1.

129. McManners, *Angers*, 141.

130. Cottin, *La Liquidation*, 51.

131. Brochard, *Saint-Gervais*, 307, 298.

132. *La Vie de M. Marquis-Ducastel*, ed. F. Pichon (1873), 129.

133. Borthelot du Chesnay, *Les prêtes séculiers*, 259.

134. Desaive, 'Clergé rural', 940–3.

135. L. Michel, 'La Dîme et les revenus du clergé d'Anjou à la fin de l'ancien régime', *Ann. Bretagne* (1979), 576–7; Savina, *Le Clergé de Cornouaille*, 44–5; Mathieu, *L'Ancien Régime, passim*; Eich, *Histoire religieuse*, i. 44–5.

136. G. Dumay, 'Pouillé du diocèse de Dijon', *Méms. Comm. Côte-d'Or* (1889–95), 81–100. V. Durand, *État religieux des trois diocèses de Nîmes, d'Uzès et d'Alais à la fin de l'ancien régime* (1909), 111–12.

137. E. Allain, 'Un Grand Diocèse d'autrefois', *Rev. quest. hist.* (1894), 531–4.

138. R.-P. Nepveu de la Manoullière, *Mémoires*, ed. G. Esnault (3 vols., 1877–9), i. 333. (He thought his benefice the richest in the diocese—but see one at 10,122 livres, in Piolin, *L'Église du Mans*, i. 5.)

139. Rennes 22 : 143; Anjou 23 : 328; Bordeaux 20 : 336; Metz 14 : 397; Quimper 6 : 171; the Sarthe 59 : 444.

140. Marquis-Ducastel, *La Vie*, 102–8.

141. P. de Crousaz-Crétet, *Paris sous Louis XVI* (2 vols., 1922), ii. 11.

142. Dumay, 'Pouillé', 81–100.

143. See Ch. 50, sect. III. Even a standard legal handbook joins in: M. Pialès, *Traité des réparations* (3 vols., 1761), ii. 258.

144. Goubert, *Beauvais*, 202–3; Saint-Jacob, *Bourgogne*, 531.

145. Diderot, *Jacques le fataliste*, in *Œuvres* (Pléiade, 1935), 33. How to be happy in the simple life, with a bed, table, a few chairs, and simple food in a non-expensive area—200 livres is needed, says Paradis de Raymondi, *Traité de la morale et du bonheur* (1784), cited by R. Mauzi, *L'Idée du bonheur dans la littérature et la pensée françaises au XVIIIᵉ siècle* (1960), 177. Voltaire's 'quarante écus' is 240 livres.

146. F. Bridoux, *Histoire religieuse du département de Seine-et-Marne pendant la Révolution* (2 vols., 1953), i. 42.

147. Lavaquery, *Boisgelin*, i. 226–7.

148. *Œuvres* (1734), xvi. 80, cited by P. Sage, *Le Bon Prêtre dans la littérature française d'Amadis de Gaule au Génie du Christianisme* (1951), 203–4.

149. Gagnol, *La Dîme ecclésiastique*, 104. In the Mauges, they asked 1,200–2,500 livres (Andrews, *Les Paysans des Mauges*, 180).

150. *Moniteur*, 169 (17 June 1790), 690.

151. *Mémoires* of the abbé Fabry, cited by G. Lefebvre, *Ann. hist. Rév. fr.* (1935), 70.

152. M. Jusselin, *Recherches sur les cahiers de 1789 en Eure-et-Loir: paroisse de Saint-Germain-les-Alluyes, cahiers des curés* (1934), 58–9.

153. J. Leuffour, 'L'Édict de 1768 et le clergé du diocèse d'Auch', *Rev. Gascogne* (1903), 489–90.

154. Ibid.

155. Diocese of Auch, 200 livres; curés of Nantes, 400 livres for a farm worker and a cook; L. E. Pouchet, *Traité sur la fabrication des étoffes* (1788), 7, says that in the pays de Caux a woman servant costs 80 livres plus the cost of her food (cited by J. Marchand (ed.), *Voyages en France de François de la Rochefoucauld, 1781–83* (1933), 48–9).

156. Auch and Nantes, 200; Orléans, 100.

157. Vaissière, *Curés*, 216–18.

158. Assuming the 30 per cent on the *congrue* comes down to 25 per cent when 'extras' are considered.

159. P. Collet (prêtre de la Congrégation de la Mission), *Traité des devoirs d'un Pasteur* (1758), 32–68.

160. See the lists of the Congrégation académique de Molsheim (omitting Jesuit works after 1770), in Châtellier, *Tradition chrétienne*, 389–91. For the bishop of Agde's list of 1673, very Jansenist, see X. Azéma, *Un Prélat janséniste, Louis Foucquet, évêque et comte de Agde, 1656–1702* (1963), 87. Lists of the bishops of Autun in Schmitt, *L'Organisation*, 132–3. For the diocese of Bâle in 1716, see A. Schaer, *Le Clergé paroissial catholique en Haute-Alsace sous l'ancien régime, 1648–1789* (1966), 158.

161. J. Quéniart, *Culture et société dans la France de l'Ouest au XVIIIᵉ siècle* (1978), 112–16. From here to ibid. 224 the information is essential for this paragraph.

162. Pérouas, *Le Diocèse de La Rochelle*, 203.

163. L. Salvini, 'Le Clergé rural en Haut-Poitou à la veille de la Révolution', *Bull. Soc. Ouest* (1957–8), 249. (For the little reading of the curés of the diocèse of Lodève *c.*1735 see Appolis, *Le Jansénisme*, 84.) A. Babeau, *La Vie rurale dans l'ancienne France* (1883), 158 (citing Gazier's *Lettres à Grégoire*, 146).

164. H. J. Martin, *Livre, pouvoir et société à Paris au 17ᵉ siècle, 1598–1701* (1969), 927.

165. Quéniart, *Culture*, 193–221. For a vicaire, not well off, who in 1789 had 105 books, see Berthelot du Chesnay, *Les Prêtres Séculiers*, 557. For a focused view on a single town see Quéniart, 'Les Bibliothèques ecclésiastiques à Rennes au XVᵉ siècle', *Rev. hist. Église Fr.* (1997), 203–14.

166. Meyer, *La Noblesse bretonne*, ii. 1160–1.

167. Bridoux, *Histoire religieuse*, i. 39.

168. Quéniart, *Culture*, 224.

169. La Louptière, *Poésies* (1768), i. 203, cited by Babeau, *La Vie rurale*, 276.

170. W. Coleman, 'The People's Health: Medical Themes in 18th-Century French Popular Literature', *Bull. Hist. Med.* (1977), 65–8.

171. In what follows, I am using my *Death*, 27–8.

172. Report of 1786 in Bernier, *Essai*, 146–7.

173. Salvini, 'Le Clergé rural', 259, 238; A. Brette, 'Les Dépenses des assemblées électorales en 1789', *Rév. fr.* (1897), 113.

174. Nepveu de la Manoullière, *Mémoires*, i. 223.

175. Duhamel du Monceau, *Éléments d'agriculture* (2 vols., 1763), i. p. x.

176. A. Rigaudière, 'La Haute-Auvergne face à l'agriculture nouvelle au XVIIIᵉ siècle', in *Études d'histoire économique rurale au XVIIIᵉ siècle*, Trav. Fac. Droit Paris, 6, 47; Duhamel de Monceau and Tillet, *Hist. d'un insecte qui dévore les grains de l'Angoumois avec les moyens que l'on peut employer pour le détruire* (1762), 9, cited by Eich, *Histoire religieuse*, i. 24–5. For curés in Societies of Agriculture—at Alençon, two curés, one monk, the intendant and eighteen laymen; at Falaise, one curé, two monks, twenty-four laymen (H.-L. de la Sicotière, 'La Société royale de la généralité d'Alençon', *Bull. Soc. Orne*, 13 (1894), 488–93).

177. L. Froger, *Instructions d'agriculture et d'économie pour les habitans de la campagne* (1769), 6–11.

178. Ibid. 248–59, 223–40.

179. E. Salliard, *Trois petits constitutionnels de province, les frères Pressac de Civray, 1789–1815* (1922).

180. J.-T. Lasserre, *Recherches historiques sur la ville d'Alet et son ancien diocèse* (1877), 355–7.

181. Bachaumont, xxi. 147–9 (21 Oct. 1782).

182. G. Bonnenfant, *Les Séminaires normands du XVIᵉ au XVIIIᵉ siècle* (1915), 241.

183. 'Cassanyes et ses mémoires inédits, 1758–1843', *Rév. fr.* (1888), 968.

184. F. Vermale, 'La Jeunesse de Mounier', *Ann. hist. Rév. fr.* (1939), 3.

185. McManners, *Angers*, 188.

186. Y. Leblanc, 'Pierre Buquet, bibliothécaire de l'Université de Caen et curé de Saint-Sauveur du Marché', *Bull. Soc. Normandie* (1956), 640.

187. For Cotelle de la Blandinière, see McManners, *Angers*, 199–200. Bergier, curé of Flangebouche, then principal of the *collège* of Besançon, 1767; then canon of Notre-Dame (A. Sicard, *L'Ancien Clergé de France: les évêques avant la Révolution*, 5th edn. (1912), 398–9).

188. J.-M. Ory, 'Les Curés du diocèse de Toul en 1733, d'après les notes de l'abbé Chatrian, secrétaire de l'évêque', *Ann. Est* (1977), 39.

189. 'Les Affiches du Mans', *Bull. Soc. Sarthe* (1973–4), 251.

190. McManners, *Angers*, 44–56. Others elsewhere, e.g. Dr Charles Trignan, curé of Digoville, diocese of Coutances (P. Feret, *La Faculté de Théologie de Paris et ses docteurs les plus célèbres* (7 vols., 1909–10), vii. 152); Pierre Lespine, curé of Montagnac-la-Crempse (L. de Lanzac de Laborie, 'La Révolution à Périgord . . . d'après les notes et correspondance de l'abbé Lespine', *Rev. quest. hist.* (1895), 97).

191. McManners, *Angers*, 56.

192. P. Gache, 'Curés et registres paroissiaux de Souppes au XVIIIᵉ siècle', *Bull. Soc. Montargis*, 3e ser. 43 (1978), 74. Date 1740.

193. Froger, *Instructions*, 243–4.

194. S. Dontenvîde, 'Les Crises démographiques à Charlieu, 1690–1720', *Cahiers hist.* (1969), 125.

195. McManners, *Angers*, 150.

196. 'Travaux et recherches', *Ann. Bourgogne* (1962), 71.

197. A. Dupuy and Charvot, 'Journal d'un curé de campagne, 1712–1765', *Ann. Bretagne* (1889–90), 407.

198. C. Port, *Inventaire analytique des archives anciennes de la Mairie d'Angers* (1861), 270–1.

199. McManners, *Angers*, 150.

200. Joathan, 'Le Journal inédit', 98–104.

201. Ricommard, *La Lieutenance générale de police à Troyes au XVIIIᵉ siècle* (1934), 143.

202. L. Dautheuil, 'Louis Sallentin, 1746–1821, curé de Mouy, puis membre du Directoire du District de Clermont', *Comptes Clermont-en-Beauvaisis* (1957–9), 28–44.

203. See E. Vaillé, *Histoire générale des Postes françaises* (6 vols., 1949–55), vi. 222–75.

204. Bachaumont, xxiii. 131 (29 Aug. 1783).

205. Jean Roux, curé of la Balne, near Lyon (Riollet, 'Le Journal', 302).

206. De Lamarre, curé of Saint-Denoual, in P. Lemarchand, 'Journal d'un curé de campagne au XVIIIᵉ siècle', *Bull. méms. Côtes-du-Nord* (1960), 54–97.

207. *Mercure de France* (1755), cited by P. Girault de Coursac, *L'Éducation d'un roi: Louis XVI* (1972), 37.

208. A. Lantoine, *Histoire de la franc-maçonnerie française: la franc-maçonnerie dans l'État* (1935), reviewed by G. Lefebvre, *Ann. hist. Rév. fr.* (1936), 175.

209. L. Charpentier, 'La Loge maçonnique de Montreuil-sur-Mer, 1761–1809', *Rév. fr.* (1895–6), 536–7; J.-J. Gautier, *Essai sur les mœurs champêtres*, ed. X. Rousseau (1935, orig. pub. 1787), pp. iii–x.

210. Ch. Gérin, 'Les Francs-maçons et la maçonnerie française au XVIIIe siècle', *Rev. quest. hist.* (1875), 553.
211. R. Pomeau, *La Religion de Voltaire* (1956), 434; Riollet, 'Le Journal', 298–91.
212. P. de La Gorce, *Histoire religieuse de la Révolution française* (5 vols., 1924–34), i. 25; R. Darnton, *The Business of Enlightenment: A Publishing History of the Encyclopédie, 1775–1800* (1979), 293.
213. La Gorce, *Histoire*, i. 64.
214. See my comments in *Angers*, 37–45.
215. The marquis de Mirabeau, cited by I. O. Wade, *The Clandestine Organization and Diffusion of Philosophic Ideas in France from 1700 to 1750* (1938), 23. For Meslier see below, ch. 50.
216. Saint-Just, *Témoins*, 195–8.
217. Sarrau, 'Un Poète libournais', *Rev. hist. arch. du Libournais* (1961), 105–14, (1962), 65–71, 115–21, (1963), 15–21.
218. E. Guitton, *Jacques Delille, 1731–1813, et la poésie de la nature* (1976), 365–6.
219. P.-M. Masson, *La Religion de Rousseau* (3 vols., 1916), i. 103–4.
220. J. Lestrade, 'Les Poésies de M. Bordages', *Rev. Gascogne* (1903), 127. (Curé of Estancarbon, diocese of Comminges.)
221. J. F. Marmontel, *Mémoires*, ed. J. Renwick (2 vols., 1972), i. 48. He was staying with the curé of Saint-Bonet after his father died.
222. Gautier, *Essai*, pp. iii–x.
223. Grimm, iii. 60–3, 71 (Aug. 1755). A. Wilson, *Diderot: The Testing Years* (1972), 182.

CHAPTER 12

1. P. Sage, *Le Bon Prêtre dans la littérature française d'Amadis de Gaule au Génie du Christianisme* (1951), 113–14.
2. Rousseau, *Émile*, in *Œuvres complètes* (Pléiade, 1964), iv. 629.
3. Diderot, *Lettres à Sophie Volland*, ed. A. Babelon (2 vols., 1948), ii. 109–10 (30 Sept. 1760).
4. R. Hubert, *D'Holbach et ses amis* (1928), 59.
5. See p. 356.
6. Voltaire, *Corresp.*, i. 336–7.
7. Voltaire, 'Catéchisme du curé', in *Dictionnaire philosophique, Œuvres*, xviii. 80.
8. L.-R. de Caradeuc de la Chalotais, *Essai d'éducation nationale* (1763), 145–6.
9. Rousseau, *Correspondance*, ed. Th. Dufour (1924), i. 291–2 (Aug.–Sept. 1749).
10. Restif de la Bretonne, *La Vie de mon père*, in *Œuvres*, ed. M. Bachelin (9 vols., 1930–2), iv. 95–8, 174–80.
11. Ch. Demia, *Trésor clérical, ou conduites pour acquérir et conserver la sainteté ecclésiastique* (1694).
12. Document in H. M. Legros, 'Assassinat du curé de Gesves-le-Gandelain', *Rev. Anjou* (1920), 185.
13. Guyot, xvi. 563–4.
14. C. Berthelot du Chesnay, 'Le Clergé diocésain français au XVIIIe siècle et les registres des insinuations ecclésiastiques', *Rev. hist. mod. contemp.* (1963), 245.

15. A. Schaer, *Le Clergé paroissial catholique en Haute-Alsace sous l'ancien régime, 1648–1789* (1966), 77.

16. Berthelot du Chesnay, 'Le Clergé diocésain', 244; J. McManners, *French Ecclesiastical Society under the Ancien Régime: A Study of Angers* (1960), 226; M. Vallery-Radot, *Un Administrateur ecclésiastique . . . le cardinal de Luynes, archevêque de Sens, 1753–88* (1966), 84–5; F. de Dainville, *Cartes anciennes de l'Église de France* (1956), 197. In the archdiocese of Sens there were sixty canons regular, twelve *prémontrés*, four *frères prêcheurs*, and one Lazarist.

17. P. Furet, *L'Abbaye de Sainte-Geneviève* (2 vols., 1883), ii. 774–5.

18. M. Chartier, 'Un Procès à l'officialité de Cambrai en 1788', *Rev. Nord* (1965), 295–300.

19. e.g., P. Gaffarel, 'Les Lettres de cachet en Provence', *Rev. hist.* (1914), 14–15. The curés referred to in n. 45 were removed by *lettres de cachet.*

20. E. Martin, *Histoire des diocèses de Toul, de Nancy et de Saint-Dié* (3 vols., 1900–3), iii. 58; F. D. Mathieu, *L'Ancien Régime dans la province de Lorraine et Barrois* (1879), 121–3.

21. L. Audiat, *Deux victimes des Septembriseurs: Pierre-Louis de la Rochefoucauld, dernier évêque de Saintes, et son frère, évêque de Beauvais* (1897), 50–4. For the intendant, see Ch. Berthelot du Chesnay, *Les Prêtres séculiers en Haute-Bretagne au XVIIIe siècle* (1984), 443–6.

22. Guyot, xvi. 610–11; M. Jousse, *Traité de la juridiction . . . des Officiaux et autres juges d'église, tant en matière civile que criminelle* (1769), 397. Complaints against the bishops' power of imprisoning in a seminary in the *cahiers* of the curés of Beauvais and of Bigorre (E. Champion, *La France d'après les cahiers* (1921), 89).

23. Luynes, iv. 217–19 (Sept. 1742).

24. Ibid. ii. 255.

25. Barbier, ii. 286–7 (June 1732).

26. Guyot, xvi. 605–6.

27. Ibid. 593.

28. Ibid. ii. 479–80, xvi. 600–3.

29. Complex legal situation: synodal statutes of a particular diocese might make a difference to the findings of the courts (Guyot, lxiii. 251–65, xvi. 594–7).

30. The bishop was also the judge of the legitimacy of the cause which would allow a curé to be absent from the parish (Guyot, xvi. 588, 592).

31. J. Savina, *Le Clergé de Cornouaille à la fin de l'ancien régime et sa convocation aux États-Généraux* (1920), 59–60.

32. M. Pialès, *Traité des gradués* (2 vols., 1757), i. 211. In 1766, the papal nuncio reports that the curés of Paris were excellent (P. Vial (ed.), 'L'Église de France vue par le nonce en 1766', *Cahiers hist.*, viii (1963), 113–14).

33. A. Aulard (ed.), 'Relation sommaire . . . de ce qui s'est passé dans l'Assemblée du clergé de Paris intra muros', *Rév. fr.* (1894), 75.

34. A. Mousset, *L'Étrange Histoire des convulsionnaires de Saint-Médard* (1953), 91.

35. McManners, *Angers*, 184.

36. L. Pérouas, *Le Diocèse de La Rochelle de 1648 à 1724: sociologie et pastorale* (1964), 452.

37. T. J. Schmitt, *L'Organisation ecclésiastique et la pratique religieuse dans l'archidiaconé d'Autun de 1650 à 1750* (1957), 134; Mme H.-L. Rostagnet, 'Les Visites pastorales de Mgr Camille de Neufville dans le diocèse de Lyon au XVIIe siècle, 1654–1662', *Cahiers hist.* (1960), 271–5.

38. As in various cases 1691–1700 in the diocese of Cambrai. See G. Deregnaucourt, 'Scandale et religion au XVIIe siècle: aspects de l'image du prêtre dans les campagnes cambrésiennes', *Rev. Nord* (1976), 451–61.

39. J. Ferté, *La Vie religieuse dans les campagnes parisiennes, 1622–95* (1962), 187.

40. Schmitt, *L'Organisation*, 140–1.

41. G. Minois, 'Les Visites épiscopales dans le diocèse de Tréguier de 1700 à 1750', *Méms. Soc. Côtes-du-Nord* (1978), 19–20.

42. Pérouas *La Rochelle*, 449–51.

43. M. Join-Lambert, 'Pratique religieuse dans le diocèse de Rouen de 1707 à 1787', *Ann. Normandie* (1953), 250–60 (1955), 39.

44. L. Châtellier, *Tradition chrétienne et renouveau catholique dans l'ancien diocèse de Strasbourg, 1650–1770* (1981), 172–80, 388–9.

45. Savina, *Le Clergé*, 60–3. Of the forty-six *lettres de cachet* issued against secular priests in the five dioceses of Haute-Bretagne from 1735 to 1788, only ten were for sexual offences, fifteen for drunkenness, seven for violence (Berthelot du Chesnay, *Les Prêtres séculiers*, 455).

46. Pierre de Vaissière, *Curés de campagne de l'ancienne France* (1933), 230.

47. J.-M. Ory, 'Les Curés du diocèse de Toul en 1773, d'après les notes de l'abbé Chatrian, secrétaire de l'évêque', *Ann. Est* (1979), 33–8, 43, 45, 48, 51, 53, 58–9, 62–3.

48. V. Durand, *État religieux des trois diocèses de Nimes, d'Uzès et d'Alais à la fin de l'ancien régime* (1909), 115–17.

49. J. de Font-Réaulx, 'Études administratives et financières du diocèse de Valence', *Bull. Soc. Drôme* (1931–2), 276.

50. R. Collier, *La Vie en Haute-Provence de 1600 à 1850* (1973), 360.

51. E. Martin, *Histoire*, ii. 346–7.

52. Métra, xv. 72–3 (Aug. 1783); cf. Bachaumont, xxxii. 3–4 (28 Apr. 1786); Voltaire, *Corresp.* xlii. 226 (July 1760).

53. G. Hardy, 'L'Anticléricalisme paysan dans une province française avant 1789', *Ann. rév.* (1912), 613. Cf. J. Faivre, 'Le Bas-clergé Franc-Comtois au milieu du 18e siècle', *Ann. rév.* (1914), 1–7, arguing on limited evidence, that the *bon curé* is a legend.

54. C. Marcilhacy, *Le Diocèse d'Orléans au milieu du XIXe siècle* (1964), 432.

55. A. Monglond, *Le Préromantisme français* (2 vols., 1930), ii. 319.

56. L. Trénard, 'Les Visites pastorales dans le diocèse de Cambrai', *Rev. Nord* (1976), 473.

57. C. Port, *La Vendée angevine* (2 vols., 1888), i. 62.

58. Savina, *Le Clergé*, 60–3.

59. Schaer, *Le Clergé*, 221.

60. Schmitt, *L'Organisation*, 131; J. Lovie, 'La Vie paroissiale dans le diocèse de Die à la fin de l'ancien régime', *Bull. Soc. Drôme* (1941–2), 376, 378.

61. Schmitt, *L'Organisation*, 130.

62. Vallery-Radot, *Un Administrateur ecclésiastique*, 87.

63. J. Eich, *Histoire religieuse du département de la Moselle pendant la Révolution* (2 vols., 1964), i. 27; Durand, *État religieux*, 115–17; F.-Y. Besnard, *Souvenirs d'un nonagénaire*, ed. C. Port (2 vols., 1880), i. 285.

64. Faivre, 'Le Bas-clergé', 10; E. Préclin, 'La Situation ecclésiastique . . . de la Franche-Comté à la veille de la Révolution', *Bull. Féd. Franche Comté* (1955), 19–20.

65. P. Belne, 'Démêlés du curé de Saint-Cirgues de Clermont avec un de ses paroissiens, 1764–9', *Bull. Auvergne* (1961), 25–32.
66. Hardy, 'L'Anticléricalisme', 616.
67. Ibid. 610; Faivre, 'Le Bas-clergé', 3.
68. T. J. A. Le Goff, *Vannes and its Region: A Study of Town and Country in 18th-Century France* (1981), 263.
69. Voltaire, *Corresp.* xlv. 9 (3 Jan. 1761), 30 (12 Jan.), 92–3 (29 Jan.); xlvi. 300–1.
70. O. H. Hufton, *The Poor of Eighteenth-Century France, 1750–1789* (1974), 292–6.
71. G. Gautier, 'La Contrebande du sel en Bretagne', *Méms. Soc. Bretagne* (1957), 105–82.
72. E. Guieysse-Frère, *Sedaine: ses protecteurs et ses amis* (n.d.), 123–4.
73. J.-M. Mioland (ed.), *Actes de l'Église d'Amiens* (2 vols., 1849), i. 134, 216–17, 444, 452, 479, 526.
74. *Souvenirs d'A. Cournot, 1760–1860*, ed. E. P. Bottinelli (1912), 210.
75. McManners, *Angers*, 144.
76. Schaer, *Le Clergé*, 23 (date 1771).
77. Marmontel to Beaumarchais, cited by L. de Loménie, *Beaumarchais et son temps* (2 vols., 1880), ii. 34–5.
78. F. Guérin, 'Un Original Curé de campagne au XVIIIᵉ siècle', *Bull. Soc. Meuse* (1972), 115–27.
79. E. G. Léonard, *Mon village sous Louis XV* (1941), 149, 151.
80. F.-G. Pariset (ed.), *Bordeaux au XVIIIᵉ siècle* (1968), 133; Monglond, *Le Préromantisme*, ii. 308–9; Besnard, *Souvenirs*, i. 295, 311–12.
81. C. Port, *Dictionnaire historique, géographique et biographique de Maine et Loire* (3 vols., 1878), i. 446. This was in 1764.
82. In the diocese of Vannes, the average age in 1789 was 57. In that of Bordeaux, 83 per cent were over 40 years of age, and 23 per cent over 60. In that of Reims, two-thirds were between 40 and 59 years of age; here, curé du Chesne of L'Echelles resigned in 1769 at the age of 105, and in 1774 he was still living with his successor, 'hearing the confessions of those who wished to address themselves to him' (Ph. Loupès, 'Le Clergé paroissial du diocèse de Bordeaux d'après la grande enquête de 1772', *Ann. Midi* (1971), 5–24; E. Bouchez, 'Le Clergé paroissial du diocèse de Reims d'après l'enquête de 1774', *Trav. Acad. nat. Reims* (1911), 128). For Vannes, see Le Goff, *Vannes*, 259.
83. A. Sarramon (ed.), *Les Paroisses du diocèse de Comminges en 1786* (1968), 16, 411, 71, 343.
84. A. Zink, *Azereix: la vie d'une communauté rurale à la fin du XVIIIᵉ siècle* (1969), 26–30, for details.
85. J. Boyreau, *Le Village en France au XVIIIᵉ siècle* (1955), 122; Schaer, *Le Clergé*, 266–7; M. M. Legros, 'Le Fessier et son Bérus, 1761–1791', *Rev. Anjou* (1916), 26.
86. [J.-L. Brunet, rev. Durand de Maillane], *Le Parfait Notaire apostolique* (2 vols., 1775), i. p. vii.
87. T. J. Schmitt, *L'Assistance dans l'archidiaconé d'Autun au XVIIᵉ et XVIIIᵉ siècles* (1952), 323; S. T. McCloy, *Government Assistance in 18th-century France* (1946), 303; J. P. Gutton, *La Société et les pauvres: l'exemple de la généralité de Lyon, 1534–1789* (1971), 194.

88. Métra, v. 5–6 (1777).

89. Hufton, *Poor*, 83–4.

90. McManners, *Angers*, 146.

91. L. Lallemand, *De l'organisation de la bienfaisance publique et privée dans les campagnes au XVIIIe siècle* (1895), 16.

92. J. Villain, *Le Recouvrement des impôts directs sous l'ancien régime* (1952), 48.

93. Monglond, *Le Préromantisme*, ii. 56.

94. J. A. Dulaure, *Nouvelle Description de Paris* (1787), ii. 257.

95. L. Lallemand, *Un chapître de l'histoire des Enfants trouvés: la Maison de la Couche à Paris, XVIIe–XVIIIe siècles* (1889), 54–5.

96. D. Dakin, *Turgot and the Ancien Régime* (1939), 58–9.

97. J.-J. Gautier, *Essai sur les mœurs champêtres*, ed. X. Rousseau (1935), 43–4; M. de Broc, 'Une Famille de province au XVIIIe siècle', *Bull. Soc. Orne* (1890), 195–200.

98. M. Riollet, 'Le Journal d'un curé de campagne, 1768–1790', *Rev. Lyon* (1911), 286, 298.

99. J. Buvat, *Journal de la Régence*, ed. E. Campardon (2 vols., 1865), ii. 92.

100. E. Esmonin, *Études sur la France des XVIIe et XVIIIe siècles* (1964), 253, 297.

101. Dainville, *Cartes anciennes*, 62–91.

102. P. Collet, *Traité des devoirs d'un pasteur* (1758), 91–114.

103. L. Michard and G. Couton, 'Les Livres d'états des âmes', *Rev. hist. Église Fr.* (1981), 261–9.

104. J. A. T. Dinouart, *Abrégé de l'embryologie sacrée* (1766), 200–2.

105. E. Barbotin, *Lettres de l'abbé Barbotin, député à l'Assemblée Constituante*, ed. A. Aulard (1910), 54.

106. G. Lenôtre, *Vieilles maisons, vieux papiers* (1930), 31–4.

107. See the plot of La Harpe's *Mélanie*.

108. Rousseau, *Correspondance*, iii. 299 (3 Mar. 1758).

109. The fermier général La Pouplinière was dissatisfied when he met her—so gave her a dowry of 130,000 livres and married her to an officer of the *gardes suisses* (Mme de Genlis, *Mémoires* (2 vols., 1825), i. 81–2).

110. Restif de la Bretonne, *La Vie de mon père*, pt. 2, bk. 3. For the wise curé in another novel, F. C. Green, *La Peinture des mœurs de la bonne société dans le roman français de 1715 à 1761* (1924), 121.

111. M. de Broc, 'Une famille' (consists of the memoirs of Michel Le Prince, 1737–1815).

112. M. Maréchal, rev. M. J. A. Serieux, *Traité des droits honorifiques des patrons et seigneurs dans les Eglises* (2 vols., 1772), i. 37.

113. P.-J. Guyot, *Observations sur le droit des patrons* (1751), 15.

114. P.-J. Guyot, *Dictionnaire*, xxi. 271. He says *seigneur haut justicier*—there were, in fact, many complexities in definition (265–6).

115. Ibid. xxi. 296–310. (As against Maréchal, who is for the patrons—because, says Guyot, he was a patron himself in various churches.)

116. Ibid. xxi. 342–4.

117. Guyot, *Observations*, 329–30.

118. Guyot, *Dictionnaire*, xxi. 369–70; id., *Observations*, 279, 387–8; Maréchal, *Traité*, i. 73–6.

119. Guyot, *Dictionnaire*, xlviii. 5; id., *Observations*, 240 ff., 331.

120. Guyot, *Observations*, 153, 161, 232.

121. McManners, *Angers*, 311.
122. Collet, *Traité*, 39.
123. Guyot, *Observations*, 350–61; id., *Dictionnaire*, xxi. 346–60.
124. Maréchal, *Traité*, i. 287–9.
125. Guyot, *Observations*, 373; id., *Dictionnaire*, xi. 301.
126. Champion, *La France*, 140–1.
127. P. de Saint-Jacob, *Les Paysans de la Bourgogne du nord au dernier siècle de l'ancien régime* (1960), 248.
128. Barbier, i. 190 (Feb. 1722).
129. P. Le Marchand, 'Journal d'un curé de campagne au XVIIIe siècle', *Soc. Côtes-du-Nord: Bull. et Mém.* (1960), 75–89.
130. Gautier, *Essai*, 13–14, 44.
131. J. Salvini, 'Le Clergé rural en Haut-Poitou à la veille de la Révolution', *Bull. Soc. Ouest* (1957–8), 240.
132. G. Desnoiresterres, *Voltaire et la société française au XVIIIe siècle*, 2nd edn. (8 vols., 1867–76), vi. 132, 65, 119.
133. Collet, *Traité*, 148.
134. Salvini, 'Le Clergé rural', 245–8. Ferrières says so in his *Théisme* (2 vols., 1790).
135. P. Massé, *Varennes et ses maîtres, 1779–1842* (1956), 62.
136. Léonard, *Mon village*, 82, 88.
137. L. N. Berthe, *Dubois de Fosseux, secrétaire de l'Académie d'Arras, 1785–92* (1969), 82–7.
138. H. Beauchet-Filleau, *Pièces inédites . . . concernant le Poitou* (2 fasc., n.d.), i. 16–19.
139. L. N. Berthe, 'La Fin de l'ancien régime à Fosseux, d'après les lettres du curé au seigneur', *Mélanges sc. relig.* (1955), 51–8.
140. E. Bouley, 'Nobles et paysans Picards à la fin de l'ancien régime', *Rev. hist. mod. contemp.* (1969), 606–10.
141. Gautier, *Essai*, 11.
142. Guyot, *Dictionnaire*, xi. 325.
143. Vaissière, *Curés*, 295–9; Guyot, xxi. 266–7; H. Carré, *La Noblesse de France et l'opinion publique au XVIIIe siècle* (1920), 317–18.
144. Vaissière, *Curés*, 294.
145. Marais, iv. 516 (16 Aug. 1733).
146. J. Grente and O. Havard, *Villedieu-les-Poêles: sa commanderie, sa bourgeoisie, ses métiers* (2 vols., 1898), i. 244.
147. Guyot, xxi. 266–7.
148. Ibid.
149. Carré, *La Noblesse*, 318.
150. Collier, *La Vie en Haute-Provence*, 87.
151. Ch. du Bus, *Stanislas de Clermont-Tonnerre et l'échec de la révolution monarchique 1757–1792* (1931), 39.
152. J. Camoreyt, 'Une Lettre de Mgr de Montillet', *Rev. Gascogne* (1927), 226–7.
153. Vaissière, *Curés*, 301–2.
154. Schmitt, *L'Organisation*, 136; Riollet, 'Le Journal', 290; Carré, *La Noblesse*, 318; Vaissière, *Curés*, 303.
155. Carré, *La Noblesse*, 317.
156. Riollet, 'Le Journal', 283–90.

157. C. Hippeau, *Les Cahiers de 1789 en Normandie* (2 vols., 1869), i. 148.

158. J. Bindet, *L'Évêque constitutionnel de la Manche, François Bécherel, 1732–1802* (1934), 12.

159. G. LeFebvre, *La Grande Peur de 1789* (1932), 123.

160. Carré, *La Noblesse*, 399–400.

161. A. Aulard, 'La Féodalité sous la Révolution', *Rév. fr.* (1913), 112.

162. Le Monnier (1778), cited by Sage, 288.

163. Sarramon (ed.), *Les Paroisses*, 23, 26.

164. P. Gagnol, *La Dîme ecclésiastique en France* (1910), 101.

165. E. Sévestre, *Les Idées gallicanes et royalistes du haut clergé . . . d'après la correspondance de Pierre-Augustin Godert de Belbeuf, évêque d'Avranches, 1762–1803* (1917). Letter of 18 Jan. 1786.

166. Praise of the charity of the curés of Paris in [Seguier de Saint-Brisson], *Lettre à Philopémas, ou réflexions sur le régime des pauvres* (1764), cited by P. M. Masson, *La Religion de Rousseau* (3 vols., 1916), iii. 65.

167. Grimm, iii. 416 (Sept. 1757); see also Luynes, ix. 126 (Nov. 1748), and C. Hamel, *Histoire de l'église de Saint-Sulpice* (1900), 169.

168. *Journal de Paris*, 3 Dec. 1777, cited by Masson, *La Religion*, iii. 208–9.

169. A. Krieger and L. Raffin, *La Madeleine* (1937), 57–8.

170. Bachaumont, xi. 73–5 (28 Jan. 1778).

171. Saint-Jacob, *Bourgogne*, 534.

172. E. Dupont, 'La condition des paysans dans la sénéchaussée de Rennes d'après les cahiers des paroisses', *Ann. Bretagne* (1900–1), 59; 58; G. Hubrecht, 'La Région sedanaise à la veille de la Révolution', *Ann. hist. Rév. fr.* (1937), 129–32; id. '*Cahier* of Tiers of Verdun', *Rév. fr.* (1900), 452; Port, *La Vendée angevine*, 61–2, 105.

173. Le Goff, *Vannes*, 261–2.

174. F. Clérembray, 'Le Comté d'Eu au moment de la convocation des États Généraux de 1789', *Rév. fr.* (1894), 144.

175. A. Dupuy, 'Les Épidémies en Bretagne au XVIIIᵉ siècle', *Ann. Bretagne* (1886–7), 28.

176. Salvini, 'Le Clergé rural', 238; A. Brette, 'Une Lettre de l'abbé Jallet à Necker', *Rév. fr.* (1893), 83.

177. McCloy, *Government Assistance*, 78–9.

178. Gilbert van de Louw, *Baculard d'Arnaud, romancier ou vulgarisateur* (1972), 71.

179. A. Corvisier, *L'Armée française de la fin du XVIIᵉ siècle au ministère de Choiseul*, 2 vols. (1964), i. 105–6.

180. Barbotin, *Lettres*, 18–19, 71, 83, 70.

181. E. Chevrier, 'Notice sur les églises de Sable', *Rev. Maine* (1876), 403–6.

182. A. Dupuy and Charvot, 'Journal d'un curé de campagne, 1712–1765', *Ann. Bretagne* (1889–1907), 407.

CHAPTER 13

1. J.-J. Pialès, *Traité des réparations* (3 vols., 1762), ii. 10; E. and L. Delonca, *Un Village en Roussillon* (1947), 234.

2. J. McManners, *French Ecclesiastical Society under the Ancien Régime: A Study of Angers* (1960), 141–2.

3. J. Déchelette, 'Visites pastorales des archiprêtres de Charlieu par Mgr De Lort de Sérignan de Valras, évêque de Mâcon, 1745–64', *Ann. Acad. Mâcon*, 3ᵉ sér. iii (1898), 522–3.

4. J. Savina, *Le Clergé de Cornouaille à la fin de l'ancien régime et sa convocation aux États-Généraux* (1926), 41.

5. L. de Montfalcon, 'Querelle autour d'un presbytère à Flaxien au XVIIIᵉ siècle', *Bull. Belley* (1965), 29, 36.

6. J. Charrier, *Histoire religieuse du département de la Nièvre pendant la Révolution* (2 vols., 1920), i. 19.

7. P. Feret, *L'Abbaye de Sainte-Geneviève et la Congrégation de France* (2 vols., 1883), ii. 261–8.

8. A. Sarramon (ed.), *Les Paroisses du diocèse de Comminges en 1786* (1968), 269, 147, 228, 296, 346.

9. Ibid. 374.

10. Comic observations about a curé's sister, very fat and always sacking the servants (E.-G. Léonard, *Mon Village sous Louis XV* (1941), 81–3).

11. e.g. G. Coolen, *Helfaut: essai sur l'administration d'une paroisse sous l'ancien régime* (1939), 85; A. Frézet, 'Guillaume Desmarets, curé de Courville, 1682–1765', *Nouv. Rev. Champagne et Brie* (1936), 186.

12. They saved and made up the dowries to him later, Restif de la Bretonne tells us (*Vie de mon père*). The curé was Foudriat's predecessor.

13. Stories in J. A. Dulaure, *Nouvelle Description de Paris* (2 vols., 1787), ii. 26–34, and in C. du Povey, 'Un Épisode sensationnel de la vie de l'abbé Torné exhumé des casiers d'un greffe', *Ann. rév.* (1913), 127. (Both took place in 1766.)

14. T. J. Schmitt, *L'Organisation ecclésiastique et la pratique religieuse dans l'archidiaconé d'Autun de 1650 à 1750* (1957), 128; M. Vallery-Radot, *Un Administrateur ecclésiastique . . . le cardinal de Luynes, archevêque de Sens, 1753–88* (1966), 55.

15. A. Playoust-Chaussis, *La Vie religieuse dans le diocèse de Boulogne . . . 1725–90* (1976), 180.

16. As the curés of Le Mans argue in synod (A. Babeau, *La Vie rurale dans l'ancienne France* (1883), 160). Cf. V. Durand, *L'État religieux des trois diocèses de Nîmes, d'Uzès et d'Alais à la fin de l'ancien régime* (1909), 115–17 (Nîmes).

17. e.g. Sarramon (ed.), *Les Paroisses*, 201, 219.

18. J.-J. Gautier, *Essai sur les mœurs champêtres*, ed. X. Rousseau (1935, orig. pub. 1787), 47.

19. P. de Vaissière, *Curés de campagne de l'ancienne France* (1933), 117–24. The advantage of a job with the curé was that it might be used to avoid militia service.

20. Verses of Poisson de la Chabeaussière in L. Johanet, *Bull. Soc. Orléanais* (1942), 286.

21. See the abbé A. Prévost, *L'Ordre moral*, in *Œuvres* (39 vols. 1810–16), xxxix. 3–5, 153, 156.

22. Curé E. Barbotin, *Lettres*, ed. A. Aulard (1910), 36, 46, 79, 85–6.

23. M. Chartier, 'A travers les papiers Caprara', *Rev. Nord* (1921), 121 ff.

24. L. Dantin, *Le Diocèse de Tarbes* (1908), 33.

25. McManners, *Angers*, 132. The clergy of Anjou in 1760 said the optimum size for a compact town parish was 3,000 souls.

26. Ibid. 131–2.

27. E. Sévestre, *L'Organisation du clergé paroissial à la veille de la Révolution: correspondance du curé de Saint-Nicolas de Coutances, 1784–88* (1911), 113.

28. *Vie de M. Marquis-Ducastel*, ed. F. Pichon (1873), 27–8 (date 1763).

29. M. Baurit and J. Hillairet, *Saint-Germain-l'Auxerrois* (1955), 103. (The parish where Boucher was buried, where Danton was married.)

30. Alençon, population 18,000 (Sévestre, *L'Organisation*, 113).

31. Guyot, xlvi. 558–9.

32. Payment of 72 livres only (P. Perceveaux, 'La Portion congrue: aumône ou minimum vital? Notes sur les conditions de vie du bas clergé en Valromey aux 17ᵉ et 18ᵉ siècles', *Bull. Belley* (1967), 88). Plot of common land, H. Cottin, *La Liquidation des biens du clergé à Is-sur-Tille* (1911), 36, 41.

33. A. Dupuy, 'L'Administration municipale en Bretagne', *Ann. Bretagne* (1887–8), 579–80.

34. P. de Saint-Jacob, *Documents relatifs à la communauté villageoise en Bourgogne* (1962), 144–6. In 1749 the inhabitants refused to go on paying it.

35. Ch. Berthelot du Chesnay, 'Le Clergé diocésain français au XVIIIᵉ siècle et les registres des insinuations ecclésiastiques', *Rev. hist. mod. contemp.* (1963), 253.

36. T. Leuridan, *Histoire de Linselles* (1883), 143–50.

37. R. Desreumaux, 'À propos d'un arpentage au 18ᵉ siècle, Vaux-Vraucourt, Pas-de-Calais', *Ensemble d'Écoles supérieures et des Facultés catholiques, Lille* (1977), 227–35.

38. Sévestre, *L'Organisation*, 7–8, 14, 55–78.

39. A. Laveille, 'Les Revenus du clergé breton avant la Révolution', *Rev. quest. hist.* (1912), 462–3.

40. E. Bouchez, 'Le Clergé paroissial du diocèse de Reims d'après l'enquête de 1774', *Trav. Acad. nat. Reims* (1911), 282–6.

41. Gautier, *Essai*, 27.

42. Léonard, *Mon village*, 84–9.

43. T. Tackett and Cl. Langlois, 'Ecclesiastical Structures and Clerical Geography on the Eve of the French Revolution', *Fr. Hist. St.* (1980), 715–45.

44. In the diocese of Vannes, the average waiting time was eight years; in that of Bordeaux half the vicaires had achieved their ambition within eight years, and nearly all the others in a further four years. In the town of Bordeaux, where the parishes were regarded as superior, the average wait was ten years from ordination.

45. Le Maire, 'Le Placet d'un vicaire . . . 1760', *Bull. Soc. Orléanais* (1943), 440–58.

46. Mme Roland, *Lettres*, NS, ed. Cl. Perroud (2 vols., 1913–15), ii. 83.

47. Chateaubriand, *Mémoires d'outre-tombe*, ed. M. Levaillant (2 vols., 1947), i. 86.

48. In April 1790 this fate befell a vicaire who had served in a parish for twenty-two years and was the support of his aged parents (Sévestre, *L'Organisation*, 26).

49. Gautier, *Essai*, 30. Cf. J. Charrier, *Claude Fauchet* (1909), 51. In a funeral oration Fauchet praises the archbishop of Bourges for closing such a home for aged clergy and giving them pensions instead. 'Men who are used to long years of freedom must not, at the end of their days, be subjected to a monastic discipline nor, old themselves, be limited to the company of the old.'

50. R. Mousnier, Sorbonne lecture course, duplicated (n.d.), 54.

51. P. D. Bernier, *Paysans de Basse-Normandie* (1891), 104–8.

52. Gautier, *Essai*, 25–6.

53. P. Pisani, *L'Église de Paris et la Révolution* (4 vols., 1908), i. 29–33.

54. 'Obsèques d'une grande dame à Saint-Sulpice à Paris', *Bul. Com. Nîmes* (1959), 33.

55. F.-G. Pariset (ed.), *Bordeaux au XVIIIe siècle* (1968), 131.

56. J.-M. Alliot, *Le Clergé de Versailles pendant la Révolution française* (1913), 47–8.

57. Dupuy, 'L'Administration', 586–9.

58. Sévestre, *L'Organisation*, 27–8.

59. R. Suadeau, *L'Évêque inspecteur administratif sous la monarchie absolue* (2 vols., 1940), ii. 66–7; Guyot, xiii. 196; L. Welter, 'Les Communautés de prêtres dans le diocèse de Clermont du XIIIe au XVIIIe siècle', *Rev. hist. Église Fr.* (1949), 9.

60. Schmitt, *L'Organisation*, 25–7.

61. E. Préclin, 'La Situation ecclésiastique . . . de la Franche Comté à la veille de la Révolution', *Bull. Féd. Franche Comté* (1955), 8–9.

62. Guyot, xxv. 201.

63. A. Cournot, *Souvenirs, 1760–1806*, ed. E. P. Bottinelli (1913), 9.

64. Semonsons, 'Communautés des prêtres à Cambraille', *Bull. Auvergne* (1959), 100–1.

65. Ibid. 101–10.

66. Sévestre, *L'Organisation*, 29–30, 61–2.

67. Ibid. 55.

68. Suadeau, *L'Évêque*, i. 70, ii. 8–10, 14–18.

69. Guyot, xiii. 197–9, 202.

70. L. Brochard, *Saint-Gervais, histoire de la paroisse* (1950), 156–6, 210, 299.

71. H. Manissadjan, 'La Communauté des prêtres de l'église de Sainte-Feyre', *Cahiers hist.* (1957), 227, 240.

72. Delonca and Delonca, *Un Village*, 234–5.

73. L. Pérouas, *Le Diocèse de La Rochelle de 1648 à 1724: sociologie et pastorale* (1964), 129, 445–6.

74. Schmitt, *L'Organisation*, 25.

75. Delonca and Delonca, *Un Village*, 234.

76. Manissadjan, 'Saint-Feyre', 240.

77. G. de Léotoing d'Anjouy, 'La Communauté des prêtres-filleuls de l'église Notre-Dame d'Aurillac', *Rev. Haute-Auvergne* (1952), 287–301.

78. J. Vinatier, *Histoire générale de Treignac-sur-Vézéré* (2 vols., 1974), ii. 34–6.

79. Pariset (ed.), *Bordeaux*, 131.

80. 'Une Paroisse rurale sous l'ancien régime: Raulhac-en-Caulades', *Rev. quest hist.* (1905), 210–17.

81. Brochard, *Saint-Gervais*, 285–6.

82. His journal is in the communal archives—see Léotoing d'Anjouy, 'Notre-Dame d'Aurillac', 455.

83. M.-C. Guibert, *Mémoires pour servir à l'histoire de la ville de Dieppe*, ed. M. Hardy (2 vols., 1878), pp. vii–xxi.

CHAPTER 14

1. Guyot, xii. 70–3.
2. Indispensable reading is Ph. Loupès, *Chapitres et chanoines de Guyenne aux XVIIe et XVIIIe siècles* (1985), ranging wider than its title.
3. M.-R. Vilette, *Les États-Généraux du Cambrésis de 1677 à 1790* (thèse droit, Lille, 1950), 86–126.
4. E. Jarry, 'Le Chapitre de Saint-Martin de Tours aux XVIIe et XVIIIe siècles', *Rev. hist. Église Fr.* (1961), 119–20.
5. G. Laurent, *Reims et la région rémoise à la veille de la Révolution* (1930), pp. xiv–xv. More details in *L'Église et les chapîtres de Reims avant 1790, par l'abbé Bauny*, published in *Le Bibliophile rémigeois* (1881), e.g. on incomes, p. 36.
6. M. Laubry, *Traité des unions* (1778), 93.
7. G. Cholvy, *Le diocèse de Montpellier* (1970), 163.
8. R. Collier, *La Vie en Haute-Provence de 1600 à 1800* (1973), 104, 184, 364.
9. L. É. Bellivière, *Jacobins du village: un bourg de Normandie pendant la Révolution* (1943), 16–18.
10. Loupès, *Chapitres*, 423.
11. T. J. Schmitt, *L'Organisation ecclésiastique et la pratique religieuse dans l'archidiaconé d'Autun de 1650 à 1750* (1957), p. xiii.
12. M. Vallery-Radot, *Un Administrateur ecclésiastique à la fin de l'ancien régime: le cardinal de Luynes, archevêque de Sens, 1753–88* (1966), 118–29.
13. A. Dupuy, 'La Collégiale de Notre-Dame de la Fosse', *Ann. Bretagne* (1888–9), 429–83. The Guéméné family were the patrons.
14. C. Daux, 'État du diocèse de Montauban à la fin de l'ancien régime', *Rev. quest. hist.* (1914), 499–500.
15. J. Denais, 'La Sainte-Chapelle royale du Gué de Maulny', *Rev. Maine* (1892), 379–99.
16. Laubry, *Traité*, 109–10.
17. See J. Meuret, *Le Chapitre de Notre-Dame de Paris en 1790* (1903), and E. Delmas, *Essai historique sur le chapitre de Saint-Germain l'Auxerrois* (1905).
18. Vallery-Radot, *Un Administrateur ecclésiastique*, 129–39.
19. Loupès, *Chapitres*, 298.
20. P. Bastid, *Siéyès et sa pensée* (1939), 39. For interesting details, N. Aston, 'The Abbé Siéyès before 1789: The Progress of a Clerical Careerist', *J. Ren. Mod. St.* (1989), 41–52.
21. F. D. Mathieu, *L'Ancien régime en Lorraine et Barrois* (1879), 130–1.
22. J. Eich, *Histoire religieuse du département de la Moselle pendant la Révolution* (2 vols., 1964), i. 118–19.
23. The appointment of a 23-year-old at Lombez before he had even proceeded to the subdiaconate, in J. Clermont, 'Louis Aygobère, 1765–1842, chanoine de Lombez', *Rev. Gascogne* (1936), 75–9.
24. R.-P. Nepveu de Manoullière, *Mémoires*, ed. G. Esnault (3 vols., 1877–9), i. pp. ix, 7, 10, 79, 140, 234–5; ii. 91, 106–7.
25. R. Poulle, *Histoire de l'église paroissiale de Notre-Dame et Saint-Michel à Draguignan* (1865), 372–3; Schmitt, *L'Organisation*, 12–13; A. V. Durand, *L'État religieux des trois diocèses de Nîmes, d'Uzès et d'Alais à la fin de l'ancien régime* (1909), 58–9.
26. J. Blampignon, *L'Épiscopat de Massillon* (1884), 23, 28.

27. E. Regnault, *Christophe de Beaumont, archevêque de Paris, 1763–81* (2 vols., 1882), i. 72–3 (he was a canon of Lyon at the time).
28. J. Meyer, *La Noblesse bretonne au XVIIIᵉ siècle* (2 vols., 1966), ii. 878.
29. C. Van der Cruysse, *La Mort dans les mémoires de Saint-Simon* (1981), 249.
30. François-Joachim, cardinal de Bernis, *Mémoires et Lettres*, ed. F. Masson (2 vols., 1878), i. 122–3 n.
31. R. Reuss, *La Cathédrale de Strasbourg pendant la Révolution* (1885), 2–5.
32. J. McManners, *French Ecclesiastical Society under the Ancien Régime: A Study of Angers* (1960), ch. 4.
33. M. Vovelle, 'Un des plus grands chapitres de France à la fin de l'ancien régime: le chapitre cathédral de Chartres', *Actes 85ᵉ Congrès national des Sociétés Savantes, Section d'histoire moderne et contemporaine, 1960* (1961), 236–62; M.-M.-J. Compère, summary of thesis in *Bill. Soc. Eure-et-Loire* (1968), 28–32.
34. Loupès, *Chapitres*, 237–9.
35. Montesquieu, *Pensées*, in *Œuvres*, ed. H. Masson (3 vols., 1955), ii. 63.
36. Loupès, *Chapitres*, 224, 229, 277–8, 327.
37. Cited, ibid. 247.
38. Marais, ii. 191 (Sept. 1721); C. Marcilhacy, *Le Diocèse d'Orléans au milieu du XIXᵉ siècle* (1964), 432; McManners, *Angers*, 61; A. Playoust-Chaussis, *La Vie religieuse dans le diocèse de Boulogne au XVIIIᵉ siècle, 1725–90* (1976), 69. A few more cases in Bachaumont, xxviii. 229 (1785), xxvii. 157 (1774), xxxiv. 11 (1787), xxxi. 164 (1768).
39. E. Violet, 'Quatre Plaisantes Affaires judiciaires au XVIIIᵉ siècle', *B.S.A.A.T.* (1958), cited in *Ann. Bourgogne* (1962), 69.
40. Dupuy, 'La Collégiale', 469–70.
41. P. Gosset, 'Scandales littéraires rémois au XVIIIᵉ siècle', *Nouv. Rev. Champagne et Brie* (1936), 88–95.
42. Bernard-Laurent Soumille, 'Journal', ed. M. A. Coulondres, *Méms. Soc. Alais* (1879), 131, 153, 197.
43. G. Doublet, *Le Chapitre abbatial de Foix sous Louis XIV* (1890), 6–7; Deschamps de la Rivière, 'Un Braconnier dans le chapitre de Saint-Pierre de la Cour', *Bull. Soc. Sarthe* (1901–2), 277; J. Contrasty, *Histoire de la cité de Rieux-Volvestre et de ses évêques* (1936), 310.
44. Vallery-Radot, *Un Administrateur ecclésiastique*, 142–3.
45. Bremond d'Ars-Migré, *Un Collaborateur de Buffon: l'abbé Bexon* (1936), 183.
46. Dom P. Chastelain, *Journal*, ed. M. Jadert (1902), 89.
47. Guyot, xlv. 111–12.
48. Nepveu de la Manoullière, *Mémoires*, i. 115.
49. The following from Mathieu, *Lorraine*, 132; Doublet, *Foix*, 5; Luynes, ix. 16; Schmitt, *L'Organisation*, 16.
50. G. Bonnenfant, *Les Séminaires normands du XVIᵉ au XVIIIᵉ siècle* (1915), 430–3.
51. Regnault, *Christophe de Beaumont*, i. 32–5.
52. L'Abbé Baston, *Mémoires*, ed. J. Loth and C. Verger (3 vols., 1879), i. 271.
53. V. Dufour, 'État du diocèse de Paris en 1789', *Bull. Com. Paris*, 1 (1883), 41–2.
54. A. H. Van der Weil, *Paul-Louis Mondran, 1734–95, un chanoine homme d'esprit* (1942), 93–5.

55. McManners, *Angers*, ch. 2.
56. Soumille, 'Journal', 178; McManners, *Angers*, 24.
57. Bachaumont, xviii. 172–3 (1781).
58. Vovelle, 'Chartres', 256–8.
59. Marcel, *Le Frère de Diderot* (1913), 73.
60. Baston, *Mémoires*, i. 269.
61. McManners, *Angers*, 63; Schmitt, *L'Organisation*, 16.
62. Cl. Joly, *Traité historique des écoles épiscopales et ecclésiastiques* (1673). Joly was a canon of Notre-Dame of Paris.
63. L. Paris, *Histoire de l'abbaye d'Avenay* (2 vols., 1879), i. 18–19.
64. For the examples following: Vallery-Radot, *Un Administrateur ecclésiastique*, 85; E. Préclin, 'La Situation ecclésiastique de Franche-Comté à la veille de la Révolution', *Bull. Féd. Franche-Comté* (1955), 8; Schmitt, *L'Organisation*, p. xiv; Eich, *Histoire*, i. 20; P. de Crousaz-Crétet, *Paris sous Louis XIV* (2 vols., 1922), ii. 7; Daux, 'État du diocèse de Montauban', 500–1; Poulle, *Histoire*, 234–58.
65. Blampignon, *Massillon*, 281.
66. A. Faure, 'J.-B. Blain, chanoine de Rouen', *Rev. Socs. Haute Normandie* (1959), 39–42.
67. J. Savina, *Le Clergé de Cornouaille à la fin de l'ancien régime et sa convocation aux États-Généraux de 1789* (1926), 22–7.
68. Cl. Perroud, 'Une Entrée épiscopale en 1791', *Rév. fr.* (1896), 164.
69. Bachaumont, xix. 75 (Jan. 1778). For reclaiming the *landes*, ibid. xix. 239.
70. H.-L. de la Sicotière, 'La Société royale de la généralité d'Alençon', *Bull. Soc. Orne* (1894), 503.
71. A. Barnes, *Jean Leclerc et la république des lettres* (1938), 191–2.
72. For Trublet see the chapter on 'Abbés'.
73. Bremond d'Ars-Migré, 38, 75–82, 176–7, 181, 189.
74. Loupès, *Chapitres*, 312.
75. E. Chartraire, 'Trois recueils de la correspondance des abbés Fenel avec l'abbé Lebeuf et autres', *Bull. Soc. Sens* (1927), 118–26. The other abbé Fenel was his brother and the dean of his chapter.
76. The baron A. de Maricourt, 'Lettres de l'abbé Le Gouz', *Rev. quest. hist.* (1914), 96–126.
77. L. Welter, 'Le Chapitre cathédral de Clermont: sa constitution, ses privilèges', *Rev. hist. Église Fr.* (1955), 7–20.
78. Dufour, 'État', 34.
79. Loupès, *Chapitres*, 177–8.
80. Soumille, 'Journal', 124–9, 208.
81. Ibid., 141, 186.
82. Van der Weil, *Mondran*, 35–7.
83. A. Degert, *Histoire des évêques de Dax* (1903), 416.
84. C. Baloche, *L'Église Saint-Merry de Paris* (2 vols., 1911), i. 519, 548.
85. Jarry, 'Saint-Martin de Tours', 121.
86. Nepveu de la Manoullière, *Mémoires*, 101, 112.
87. Vovelle, 'Chapitres', 235 ff.
88. McManners, *Angers*, 57, 116.
89. M. Lhéritier, *L'Intendant Tourny, 1695–1760* (2 vols., 1920), ii. 94–5.
90. E. Laurès, *La Municipalité de Béziers à la fin de l'ancien régime* (1926), 144–7;

for Metz see J. B. Pelt, *Études sur la cathédrale de Metz* (1853), 334.

91. P. de la Haye, *Histoire de Tréguier, ville épiscopale* (1927), 287–8.

92. J. Carreyre, *Le Jansénisme durant la Régence* (3 vols., 1929–33), pp. xx, 218.

93. Barbier, i. 152; Luynes, v. 29–30, viii. 252–3 (June 1743, June 1747).

94. Guyot, ix. 420–62, and, generally, Ducasse, *Traité des droits et des obligations des églises cathédrales* (1706).

95. Contrasty, *Rieux-Volvestre*, 350–3.

96. D'Argenson, vi. 396.

97. L. Charpentier, *Un Évêque de l'ancien régime: Louis-Joseph de Grignon, 1670–1722* (1899), 130–8.

98. L. Pingaud, *Les Saulx-Tavannes* (1876), 267.

99. Bachaumont, vii. 144–5.

100. Letter of Dom Jean Colomb, 30 Mar. 1760, *Rev. Maine* (1877), 236–7; Nepveu de la Manoullière, *Mémoires*, i. 6–7, 53.

101. McManners, *Angers*, 178–9.

102. G. Courraze, *Lombez, évêché rural, 1312–1801* (1973), 135–9, 210–11.

103. G. Viard, 'Le Chapitre de Langres' (thesis), cited by Loupès, *Chapitres*, 365.

104. Nepveu de la Manoullière, *Mémoires*, 63–101.

105. M. Dommanget, *Le Curé Meslier* (1965), 283.

106. For a detailed account of this trouble in Angers, see McManners, *Angers* 162–89. The lawyers usually favoured the rights of the curés (Laubry, *Traité*, 86–7).

107. Summed up in *Lettres à un ami sur la dignité des curés et des chanoines* (1770) (Bibli. nat. F 6361), pp. v, 4, 113.

108. Bib. nat. LK3 114, pp. iv, vi, 3, 12, 19, 56, 143.

109. Loupès, *Chapitres*, 384–5.

110. Vovelle, 'Chapitres', 260–2.

111. Loupès, *Chapitres*, 403–5; J. Loth, *Histoire du cardinal de la Rochefoucauld et du diocèse de Rouen pendant la Révolution* (1893), 134–5.

CHAPTER 15

1. Ph. Loupès, *Chapitres et chanoines de Guyenne aux XVIIe et XVIIIe siècles* (1985), 58.

2. Guyot, xxi. 264–5.

3. J. McManners, *French Ecclesiastical Society under the Ancien Régime: A Study of Angers* (1960), 14; Clerval, *L'Ancienne Maîtrise de Notre-Dame de Chartres* (1899), 171, 186, 195.

4. L. Réau, *Histoire du vandalisme: les monuments détruits de l'art français* (2 vols., 1989), i. 13–14.

5. E. Champion, 'J.-J. Rousseau et le vandalisme révolutionnaire', *Rév. fr.* (1908), 163.

6. P. Feret, *L'Abbaye de Sainte-Geneviève* (2 vols., 1883), ii. 40–6; N. Jacquin, 'Louis XV pose la première pierre de la nouvelle église de Sainte-Geneviève', *La Montagne Sainte-Geneviève* (Mar. 1973), 58–61.

7. H. Tavernier, 'Gauthey, ingénieur en chef de la province de Bourgogne au XVIIIe siècle', *Méms. Acad. Lyon*, 3e sér. 9 (1907), 226–7.

8. M.-A. Laugier, *Observations sur l'architecture* (1765), 84.

Notes to pages 437–42

9. Voltaire, *Le Temple du goût* (1733), ed. E. Carcassonne (1938), 70.

10. R. Lanson, *Le Goût du Moyen Âge en France au XVIIIe siècle* (1926), 7–39; M. Jacoubet, *Le Genre troubadour et les origines du romantisme: La Curne de Sainte-Palaye* (1929); L. Gossman, *Medievalism and the Ideologies of the Enlightenment . . . La Curne de Sainte-Palaye* (1968).

11. J. Mondain Monval, *Soufflot, sa vie, son œuvre, son esthétique* (1918), 43, 431.

12. M.-A. Laugier, *Essai sur l'architecture* (1755), 173. Ten years later, he said 'Gothic' was best for interiors, 'Greek' for exteriors (*Observations*, 116–17).

13. Réau, *Histoire*, i. 110.

14. Montesquieu, *Essai sur le goût*, cited by Réau, *Histoire*, 111.

15. Grimm, v. 349–50 (Aug. 1765).

16. Cochin, *Doutes . . . d'un marguillier de la paroisse de Saint-Etienne du Mont sur le problème proposé par M. Patte, architecte* (1770), cited by Mondain Monval, *Soufflot*, 431.

17. F. Pupil, 'L'Architecture médiévale religieuse dans l'iconographie de l'époque révolutionnaire', in *Pratiques religieuses, Mentalités, Spiritualités. Actes du Colloque bicentenaire de la Révolution, Chantilly, 1986* (1988), 695.

18. J. Lestocquoy, 'La Persistance du style gothique aux XVIIe et XVIIIe siècles', *Rev. Nord* (1938), 103 ff.

19. M. Lévi, *Inventaire des papiers de Robert de Cotte, premier architecte du Roi, 1656–1735* (1906), p. xxvii.

20. G. Chénesseau, 'Un Essai d'alliance du *gothique* de l'*antique* par un architecte Orléanais au XVIIIe siècle', *Bull. Soc. Orléanais* (1936), 36–8. See also his *Sainte-Croix d'Orléans, histoire d'une cathédrale gothique rééditée par les Bourbons, 1599–1829* (1921).

21. J. McManners, *Death and the Enlightenment* (1981), 305–6.

22. Laugier, *Essai* (1755), 156; J. Seznec, *Essais sur Diderot et l'antiquité* (1957), 113.

23. Diderot, *Salons*, ed. J. Seznec and J. Adhémar (4 vols., 1957–67), iii. 315–16, i. 244.

24. Grimm (Dec. 1752), cf. N. Wraxall, *A Tour through the Western, Southern and Interior Provinces of France* (3 vols., 1777), ii. 195.

25. Dom G. Givelet, 'L'Église abbatiale de Saint-Niçaise de Reims', *Trav. Acad. nat. Reims* (1897), 129–45.

26. J. Corblet, *Histoire dogmatique, liturgique et archéologique du sacrement de l'Eucharistie* (2 vols., 1886), i. 129.

27. L. Pingaud, *Les Saulx Tavannes* (1876), 267.

28. McManners, *Angers*, 35.

29. A. Babeau, *La Ville sous l'ancien régime* (2 vols., 1884), ii. 129–30.

30. For these, see Réau, *Histoire*. Up to then, no one had listened to J.-B. Thiers's arguments for a simple dome on classical columns as being the decoration over the first recognizable Christian altars (*Dissertations ecclésiastiques* (2 vols., 1688), ii. 39–60).

31. Réau, *Histoire*, 119–24.

32. 'Les Tombes royales de Saint-Denis à la fin du XVIIIe siècle', *Le Cabinet historique*, 22 (1876), 2–12.

33. J.-B. Thiers, *Dissertation sur les jubés* (1688), 29–40, 146. For Amiens see Laugier, *Observations*, 139–40. For Rieux, J. Contrasty, *Histoire de Rieux-Volvestre* (1930), 347.

34. Langlois, *Notes historiques . . . sur les jubés de l'Église métropolitaine de Rouen: Précis analytique* (1851), 244 ff.

35. Guide Bleu, *Île de France* (1968), 256–7.

36. F. Blondel, *Cours d'architecture* (1683), 236.

37. R. Farcy, *Les Travaux de Soufflot à Notre-Dame* (1930).

38. A. H. Van der Weil, *Paul-Louis Mondran, 1734–95, un chanoine homme d'esprit* (1942), 135.

39. Séroux d'Agincourt, a retired farmer-general (Y. Durand, *Les Fermiers Généraux au XVIIIᵉ siècle* (1971), 512–20). Also F. S. Mercier, *Tableau de Paris*, new edn. (12 vols., 1782–8), i. 240.

40. Some of the chant books used were of great antiquity, especially the big bound copies for the lectern.

41. Dr Charles Burney, *A Musical Tour of France and Italy*, ed. P. A. Scholes (2 vols., 1959), i. 5, 37.

42. D. Launay, in *The New Oxford History of Music* (10 vols., 1975), vol. 5: *Opera and Church Music, 1630–1750*, ed. A. Lewis and N. Fortune (1975), 418.

43. H. Carré, *Recueil curieux et édifiant sur les cloches de l'Église* (1757), 47–8.

44. M. Benoît, *Versailles et les musiciens du roi, 1661–1733* (1971), 46.

45. H. E. Smither, *A History of the Oratorio* (3 vols., 1977), i. 418.

46. Carré, *Recueil*.

47. Grimault, *Noëls angevins* (1876), cited by C. Port, *Dictionnaire hist. géog. biogr. de Maine-et-Loire* (3 vols., 1878), iii. 234; Van der Weil, *Mondran*, 16–17.

48. D. Launay and N. Dufourcq, in *New Oxford History of Music*, v. 418–20, 443.

49. A. Cellier, 'Les Motets de Michel-Richard de Lalande', *Rev. mus.* (1946), 20–3. It is estimated that over 1,000 *grands motets* from 1683 to 1789 have survived, mostly gathering dust in libraries (Ph. Beaussant, *Rameau de A à Z* (1982), 219). A Benedictine of Le Mans in 1719 wrote to Paris for music for motets—voices with bass accompaniment (W. P. Denis, *Rev. Mabillon* (1910), 521).

50. Jean Gilles, 1668–1705. His requiem was used for the funerals of Rameau and of Louis XV. See *The New Grove Dictionary of Music and Musicians*, S. Sadie (ed.) (20 vols., 1980), vii. 378–9. For Giroust see J. Brosset, *François Giroust, 1737–91* (1911), 14.

51. H. Prunières, review in *Rev. mus.* (1960), 566.

52. Clerval, *L'Ancienne Maîtrise*, 81–92.

53. Loupès, *Chapitres*, 169–70.

54. Van der Weil, *Mondran*, 57, 148–9.

55. *La Revue des maîtres de chapelle et musiciens de la Métropole de Rouen* (1850), 221.

56. F. J. Fétis, *Biographie universelle des musiciens* (8 vols., 1800–5), iv. 210.

57. J. Brosset, *Charles Hérissé, chanoine honoraire de l'Église d'Orléans, maître de chapelle de la cathédrale, 1737–1817* (1904), 9–18.

58. Clerval, *L'Ancienne Maîtrise*, 90–104. Cf. Coutances; in the first half of the century, two appointments from Paris, one from Caen, one from Marseille (J. Toussaint, *Feuilles détachées de l'histoire de Coutances—la maîtrise de la cathédrale* (1967), 12–131).

59. A. Prévost, 'Histoire de la maîtrise de la cathédrale de Troyes, *Mém. Soc. Aube*, 3ᵉ sér. 42 (1905), 258–65. There was no positive rule against marriage for someone who had not reached the subdiaconate. Toulouse appointed a married man in 1723 (R. Machard, 'Les Musiciens de la cathédrale Saint-

Étienne de Toulouse, 1682–1790', *Ann. Midi* (1976), 302. Concerning Deroussy, his crime may have been more than idleness. The *chant sur le livre*, said the abbé Lebeuf in 1729, 'is not singing at sight what the open book presents to view; it is to compose on the notes that are printed in the book harmonies corresponding to these notes'. He adds that the bass singers follow the book while the tenors improvise descants. There were variants and complexities, set forth in Henri Madin's *Traité du contrepoint simple ou du chant sur le livre* (1742). Madin, while appreciating the fantasy and 'joyful discord', admits there can be a collapse into confusion. For this reason, and from a distrust of unpredictable ornamentation, some French churches banned the genre—described later, in 1838, by La Fage, as 'that baroque and indecorous harmony'. See J. Prim, 'Chant sur le livre in French Churches in the Eighteenth Century', *JAMS* (1961), 37–49; and for the earlier history, Margaret Bent's erudite '*Resfacta* and *Cantare Super Librum*', *JAMS* (1984), 371–91.

60. Fétis, *Biographie*, v. 446; M. Brenet, 'Sébastien de Brossard', *Méms. Soc. Paris* (1896), 105–6.

61. J. Leflon, *Henri Hardouin et la musique du chapitre de Reims au XVIIIᵉ siècle* (1933), 42, 52, 57.

62. C. Port, *Les Artistes angevins* (1881), 10–11; McManners, *Angers*, 28–9.

63. Benoît, *Versailles*, 245–6, 372.

64. O. Marcault, *Le Diocèse de Tours* (3 vols., 1918), ii. 579.

65. *Rouen*, 22.

66. Loupès, *Chapitres*, 181.

67. M. Brenet, *Les Musiciens de la Sainte-Chapelle du Palais* (1910), 309–10.

68. Prévost, 'Histoire . . . de Troyes', 349.

69. McManners, *Angers*, 30.

70. Machard, 'Les Musiciens . . . de Toulouse', 303–5.

71. Prévost, 'Histoire . . . de Troyes'; for Reims below, Leflon, *Hardouin*, 53.

72. Le Cerf de Viéville, *Comparaison de la musique italienne et de la musique française* (1705), 178.

73. Benoît, *Versailles*, 60–1, 48.

74. Garault, 'Instruments d'amour', *Rev. mus.* (1927), 105; A. Prévost, 'Instruments de musique', *Méms. Soc. Aube*, 3ᵉ sér. 41 (1904), 194–210.

75. Van der Weil, *Mondran*, 145–6.

76. B. Gérard and R. Machard, *La Grande Orgue et les organistes de Notre-Dame de Paris* (1980), 11.

77. N. Dufourcq, 'Coup d'œil sur l'histoire de la facture d'orgues', *Rev. mus.* (1929), 113–19, and id. 'L'Orgue de la chapelle de Versailles', *Rev. mus.* (1934), 288–9. See generally, P. de Fleury, *Dictionnaire biographique des facteurs d'orgues nés ou ayant travaillé en France* (1926).

78. E. Houth, *Versailles, la paroisse royale* (1962).

79. Port, *Les Artistes angevins*, 115. For the Dupont family, Fétis, *Biographie*, iii. 81.

80. A. Chaulieu, *Histoire de l'abbaye de Sainte-Croix* (1910), 201.

81. P. Dop, 'L'Église de Saint-Jean-de-Luz', *Bull. Soc. Bayonne* (1932), 395–8, 424–5.

82. Prévost, 'Instruments', 177.

83. R. Poulle, *Histoire de l'église paroissiale de Notre-Dame et Saint-Michel à Draguignan* (1865), 424–30.

84. J. Brosset, *L'Orgue et les organistes de l'Église Saint-Paul d'Orléans* (1909), 9–10.
85. E. and L. Delonca, *Un Village en Roussillon* (1947), 258.
86. Some of the great organists had female relatives who acted as 'stand-ins'—Armand-Louis Couperin's daughter, Calvière's sister, Bainville's wife.
87. D. H. Foster, *Jean-Philippe Rameau: A Guide to Research* (1989), 5–6. The anecdote about the Clermont contract originates with Maret, *Éloge historique de M. Rameau* (1766), who cites the secretary of the local academy as his source. More certainly, it is told of Rameau's brother. C. Girdlestone, *Jean-Philippe Rameau* (1957), accepts both stories. If one brother used the trick, why not the other in imitation?
88. W. Mellers, *François Couperin and the French Classical Tradition* (1957), 4–5; J. Tiersot, *Les Couperin* (1926), 115–18.
89. Gérard and Machard, *La Grande Orgue*, 30.
90. N. Dufourcq, 'De l'emploi du temps des organistes parisiens sous les règnes de Louis XIII et Louis XIV', *Rev. mus.* (1955), 35–8.
91. Burney, *Musical Tour*, i. 6, 15.
92. A. Tessier, 'Les Messes d'orgue de Couperin', *Rev. mus.* (1924), 37–47; N. Dufourcq, 'Les Grandes Formes de la musique d'orgue', *Rev. mus.* (1937), 89–91.
93. Mercier, *Tableau de Paris*, ii. 81.
94. G. Servais, 'Quelques organistes du grand siècle', *Rev. mus.* (1922), 198–200.
95. Dufourcq, 'Coup d'œil', 118–20.
96. P. C. C. Bogaerts, *Études sur les livres choraux qui ont servi de base dans la publication des livres de chant Grégorien édités à Malines* (1855), 118–20.
97. Cited in *New Oxford History of Music*, 288–9.
98. Voltaire, 'Sottisier', in *Œuvres*, xxxii. 577.
99. G. E. Bonnet, 'L'Œuvre de Philidor', *Rev. mus.* (1921), 226; G. de Froidcourt, *Correspondance générale de Grétry* (1962), 21. Other examples in Fétis, *Biographie*, i. 168, 387, 473; ii. 40, 172, 405, 456; iii. 10, 31, 200, 442, 451; iv. 91, 438–9; v. 170, 256, 265, 438; vi. 55–6, 333, 490–1; vii. 3, 92, 109, 337, 341. For the seventeenth century, Th. Gérold, *L'Art du chant en France au XVIIe siècle* (thesis, Strasbourg, 1921), pp. xi, 189.
100. Cit. Marcault, *Tours*, ii. 286.
101. See the discussion from Couturier and Maritain in J. McManners, *The Oxford Illustrated History of Christianity* (1990), 13. For the assimilation of the music of church and theatre so that all music was 'profane', see J.-M. Duhamel, *La Musique dans la ville de Lully à Rameau* (1994), 254–63.
102. R. H. F. Scott, *Jean-Baptiste Lully* (1973), 65–7, 100–5.
103. L. de la Laurencie, 'André Campra, musicien profane', *Rev. mus.* (1913), 152, 195. See also his article on Campra's church music in *Recueil de la Société Internationale de Musique* (1909), 159 ff.
104. *Nouvelles ecclésiastiques*, 14 July 1734.
105. J. McManners, *Abbés and Actresses: The Church and the Theatrical Profession in 18th-Century France*, Zaharoff Lecture (1986), 3.
106. C. Kintzler, *Poétique de l'Opéra français de Corneille à Rousseau* (1991), 107–8.
107. A. B. Oliver, *The Encyclopedists as Critics of Music* (1947), 6–7.
108. M. Busson, *La Religion des classiques* (1948), 17.
109. La Bruyère, *Les Caractères*, xiv (19), ed. P. Kuentze (1969), 207.
110. L. Blond, *La Maison professe des Jésuites* (1956), 114.

111. E. Regnault, *Christophe de Beaumont, archevêque de Paris* (2 vols., 1882), i. 256. In 1721 the singers of the king's music sang a *Miserere* by Lalande at *Tenebrae* in the chapel of the Temple (Marais, ii. 118, 9 Apr.).

112. Van der Weil, *Mondran*, 137–46.

113. See the view of the church-goers of Saint-Merry about an organist, in opposition to their curé (C. Baloche, *L'Église Saint-Merry de Paris* (1911), 544–9).

114. *Des Églises et des temples chrétiens* (1706).

115. They took over the Te Deum entirely in Aug. 1752 (Luynes, xii. 101–2). For their organization, M. Benoît, *Musique de cour, chapelle, chambre, écurie, 1661–1733, Documents* (1971). For special occasions, the orchestra could be reinforced by the military drums and trumpets of the *écurie* (twelve trumpets, six oboes, fifes, and drums). The regiments of the palace guard also had trumpets (Benoît, *Versailles*, 48, 51–2).

116. F. Raugel, 'La Musique à la chapelle du château de Versailles sous Louis XV', *XVIIᵉ Siècle* (1957), 21–3.

117. Luynes, xiii. 390–1.

118. Ibid., vi. 436–7, vii. 280. A list of 1702 shows six Italian castrati and three French *hauts*. Strong high male voices were important to keep the boys firm in difficult passages.

119. Raugel, 'Versailles', 20.

120. Conducting the Te Deum with massed choirs in the church of the Feuillants on 8 Jan. 1687 killed him (gangrene from the conducting pole striking his foot).

121. She heard it at the funeral of Chancelier Séguier.

122. Luynes, vii. 9.

123. H. Prunières, *New History of Music* (E. T.), 97–112, 278. (Also influences from Saint-André des Arts.)

124. 'Arcangelo Corelli à Saint-Louis-des-Français à Rome', *Rev. mus.* (1922), 25–6. In Paris, St Louis was celebrated by the Académie royale de Musique in the garden of the Tuileries (G. Sadler, 'A Letter from Claude-François Rameau', *Music & Letters* (1978), 143–4.

125. E. Fubini, *The History of Music Aesthetics*, trans. F. M. Habwill (1962), 201–9.

126. For the link between Rousseau's view and his conviction of the decadence of society see A. Whittall, 'Rousseau and the Scope of Opera', *Music & Letters* (1964), 308.

127. S. Bonnet, *Histoire de la musique* (1725), cited in *New Oxford History of Music*, v. 288.

128. D. Tunley, *The 18th-Century French Cantata* (1974), 89.

129. F. Couperin, *Les Goûts réunis*, preface.

130. Marais, iv. 458.

131. Mme de Genlis, *Mémoires* (2 vols., 1825), i. 78 (1760).

132. Luynes, vii. 280 (1746); ix. 9 (1748).

133. Fétis, *Biographie*, i. 172. M. Pincherle, 'Le Peintre violiniste ou les aventures de l'abbé Robineau', *Rev. mus.* (1925), 232–9. He painted the portrait of the future George IV of England.

134. Brosset, *François Giroust*, 8.

135. C. Pierre, *Histoire du Concert spirituel* (1975), 220–2.

136. R. Viollier, 'Jean-Joseph Mouret', *Rev. mus.* (1938), 20–1.

137. Tunley, *French Cantata*, 29, 31, 72–89.

138. Smither, *Oratorio*, iii. 539–42.
139. E. Haeringer, *L'Esthétique de l'opéra en France au temps de Jean-Philippe Rameau* (1990), 23.
140. N. Dufourcq, *La Musique religieuse française de 1660 à 1781* (1954), 109–10.
141. Some written by Racine (L. Boulay, *Les Cantiques spirituels de Racine mis en musique au XVIIIᵉ siècle* (1957), 79–92.
142. The baron A. de Maricourt, 'Lettres de l'abbé le Gouz', *Rev. quest. hist.* (1914), 30–1.
143. Thomas Bentley, *Journal of a Visit to Paris, 1776*, ed. P. France (1977).

CHAPTER 16

1. S. R. N. Chamfort, *Maximes et anecdotes*, with preface by A. Camus (1963), 63.
2. Voltaire, *Essai sur les mœurs*, in *Œuvres*, xi. 21.
3. C. Langlois and T. Tackett, in F. Lebrun (ed.), *Histoire des catholiques en France du XVᵉ siècle à nos jours* (1980), 216–17.
4. L. Pérouas, *Le Diocèse de la Rochelle de 1648 à 1724: sociologie et pastorale* (1964), 187–9, 432–45.
5. Cl. Langlois, *Catholicisme au féminin: les congrégations françaises à supérieure générale au XIXᵉ siècle* (1984), 136–8.
6. M. Vallery-Radot, *Un Administrateur ecclésiastique à la fin de l'ancien régime: le cardinal de Luynes, archevêque de Sens, 1753–88* (1966), 159; A. Chaulieu, *Histoire de l'abbaye de Sainte-Croix* (1910), 285; P. Goubert, 'Disparités de l'ancienne France rurale', *Cahiers hist.* (1967), 58.
7. Chaulieu, *Sainte-Croix*, 284. For Beaune, Fr. de la Rochefoucauld, *Voyages en France*, ed. J. Marchand (1933), 123.
8. R. Dauvergne, *Les Résidences du maréchal de Croÿ, 1718–84* (1950), 56.
9. J. Peter, 'Un Curieux Procès: l'abbaye de Liesses contre les maîtres de forges de Hainault', *Rev. Nord* (1937), 243–59.
10. J.-F.-H. de Richeprey, *Journal des voyages en Haute-Guienne*, ed. H. Guilhamon (1952), 240–1.
11. J.-J. Pialès, *Traité des réparations* (4 vols., 1762), i. 371 ff.
12. B. Pocquet du Haut-Jussé, 'La Vie temporelle des communautés de femmes au XVIIᵉ et au XVIIIᵉ siècle', *Ann. Bretagne* (1917), 540.
13. The baron A. de Maricourt and A. Briard, 'Une Abbaye de femmes au XVIIIᵉ siècle: Gomerfontaine', *Rev. quest. hist.* (1907), 25–7.
14. T. J. Schmitt, *L'Organisation ecclésiastique et la pratique religieuse dans l'archidia-coné d'Autun de 1650 à 1750* (1957), 86–91.
15. L. Desgraves and J.-P. Poussou, 'La Vie religieuse', in F.-G. Pariset (ed.), *Bordeaux au XVIIIᵉ siècle* (1968), 136.
16. J. Eich, *Histoire religieuse du département de la Moselle pendant la Révolution* (2 vols., 1964), i. 38–40; C. Michaux, 'Les Abbayes bénédictines de Metz à la veille de la Révolution', *Ann. Est* (1979), 257–70.
17. J. Savina, *Le Clergé de Cornouaille à la fin de l'ancien régime et sa convocation aux États-Généraux de 1789* (1926), 32.
18. J. McManners, *French Ecclesiastical Society under the Ancien Régime: A Study of Angers* (1960), ch. 5.

19. Guyot, i. 12, 16–17; xii. 358–404.

20. C. Pfister, 'Extrait d'un mémoire sur l'Alsace', *Rev. hist.* (1916), 85; J. Marchal, 'Remacle Lissoir', *Ann. Est* (1967), 29–30.

21. François-Joachim, cardinal de Bernis, *Mémoires et Lettres*, ed. F. Masson (2 vols., 1875), ii. 308, 326; G. Lizerand, *Le Duc de Beauvillier, 1648–1714* (1933), 83–4.

22. J. Thomas, *Le Concordat de 1516* (3 vols., 1910), ii. 73, 359.

23. Guyot, i. 41–7, xii. 402–4.

24. A. Sicard, *L'Ancien Clergé de France: les évêques avant la Révolution*, 5th edn. (1912), 22.

25. L'Abbé de Véri, *Journal*, ed. J. de Witte (2 vols., n.d.), i. 3.

26. Marais, ii. 61; the duc de Broglie, *Le Secret du roi: correspondance secrète de Louis XV et ses agents diplomatiques* (2 vols., 1886), i. 458–68.

27. Luynes, i. 324–5, 375; Barbier, iii. 69–70, 89, 341.

28. Luynes, vi. 403–4.

29. McManners, *Angers*, 76.

30. P.-L. Langlois, *Histoire du prieuré du Mont-aux-Malades-lès-Rouen, 1120–1820* (1951), 320–3.

31. A. de Cardevacque and A. Terninck, *L'Abbaye de Saint-Vaast* (3 vols., 1865–8), i. 47–8, ii. 57–69.

32. Luynes, vi. 402–3; D'Argenson, vi. 272; Pialès, *Traité*, iv. 4.

33. B. Bois, *La Vie scolaire et les créations intellectuelles en Anjou, 1789–99* (1929), 40.

34. J. Marchal, *Le Droit d'oblat* (1955), 234–53.

35. Luynes, xiii. 215, 406; i. 252, 324.

36. Guyot, lviii. 465–6.

37. Ibid. lxii. 349–87.

38. J. Gallerand, 'L'Érection de l'évêché de Blois, 1697', *Rev. hist. Église Fr.* (1956), 175–201.

39. A. Broutin, *Histoire du couvent de Montbrison avant 1793* (2 vols., 1874), ii. 65–70.

40. J. Blampignon, *L'Épiscopat de Massillon* (1884), 194–5.

41. R. Laulan, 'Aperçu sur les finances de l'École Royale Militaire, 1751–88', *Actès 86ᵉ Congrès National des Sociétés Savantes: Montpellier 1961* (1962), 228–32.

42. M. Cornereau, 'Les Hôpitaux du Saint-Esprit et de Notre-Dame de la Charité à Dijon', *Méms. Comm. Côte-d'Or* 12 (1889–95), 272.

43. P.-D. Bernier, *Essai sur le tiers état rural ou les paysans de Basse-Normandie au XVIIIᵉ siècle* (1891), 85–9.

44. Voltaire, 'Biens d'Église', in *Dictionnaire philosophique*, in *Œuvres* (50 vols., Firmin Didot, 1843), vii. 261–4. This entry is omitted from modern critical editions.

45. Pialès, *Traité*, iii for details, esp. 359–60.

46. A. Lombard, *L'Abbé Dubos* (1913), 163–4.

47. E. Jarossy, *Histoire de l'abbaye de Ferrières en Gâtinais* (1901), 426–7.

48. L. Deries, *La Vie monastique en Normandie* (1937), 49.

49. L. Côte, *Histoire du prieuré Clunisien de Souvigny* (1942), 276–81.

50. Luynes, xiv. 12; McManners, *Angers*, 77.

51. Jarossy, *Gâtinais*, 421–4.

52. See 'Lettres inédites de P.-D. Huet à son neveu', *Méms. Acad. nat. Caen*

(1900), 133–65; Deries, *Normandie*, 71–3.

53. Pialès, *Traité*, i. 268.

54. Chaulieu, *Sainte-Croix*, 238 ff.

55. J. Loth (ed.), *Histoire de l'abbaye royale de Saint-Pierre de Jumièges par un religieux de la Congrégation de Saint-Maur* (3 vols., 1885), iii. 201–3.

56. Deries, *Normandie*, 243–8; E. Goiffon, *Monographies paroissiales: paroisses de l'archiprêtré de Nîmes* (1898), 277–8.

57. X. Azéma, *Un Prélat janséniste: Louis Foucquet, évêque et comte d'Agde, 1656–1702* (1963), 131.

58. e.g. C. Hippeau, *Les Cahiers de 1789 en Normandie* (2 vols., 1869), i. 55.

59. Bachaumont, vii. 44–6 (Aug. 1773).

60. Barbier, iii. 89 (1737).

61. Bernis, *Mémoires*, i. 125.

62. Dom P. Denis, 'Un Projet . . . de Mgr Talleyrand-Périgord, archevêque de Rouen, 1787', *Trav. Acad. nat. Reims* (1910), 261–7.

63. Guyot, i. 41–2.

64. Deries, *Normandie*, 61–71.

65. See C.-É. Engel, *L'Ordre de Malte en Méditerranée, 1530–1798* (1957).

66. In 1789, to try to avert the confiscation of its lands in France, the Order threatened to hand over Malta to a foreign power (G. Saumade, 'La Révolution française et l'Ordre international de Malte', *Rév. fr.* (1937), 249).

67. G. Gangneux, 'Société nobiliaire et l'Ordre de Malte', *Cahiers hist.* (1975), 358–9.

68. Luynes, iv. 23–4.

69. G. Maugras, *Delphine de Sabran, marquise de Custine* (1912), 46.

70. G. Gangneux, 'Une Commanderie de l'Ordre de Malte aux XVIIe et XVIIIe siècles', *Cahiers hist.* (1962), 355–78.

71. Richeprey, *Journal*, 139–42.

72. A. Guelloni, 'L'Évolution de l'idée internationale dans les écrits de l'abbé de Saint-Pierre', in A. Viala and H. Labriolle (eds.), *La Régence, Colloque Aix-en-Provence, 1968* (1970), 333.

73. R. Cavalière, 'Le Bailli de Suffren', *Ann. Malte* (1962), 101–2.

74. Engel, *L'Ordre de Malte*, 292–3, 122, 175, 287.

75. A. Bouyal d'Arnaud, 'Un Gentilhomme provençal au 18e siècle', *Rev. hist. mod. contemp.* (1955), 59–60.

76. Engel, *L'Ordre de Malte*, 122.

77. Luynes, vii. 167–8.

78. Guyot, ix. 135.

79. Mme de Genlis, *Mémoires* (2 vols., 1825), i. 14–15.

80. Chateaubriand, *Mémoires d'outre-tombe* (Pléiade, 2 vols., 1955), i. 16.

81. Ch. du Bus, *Stanislas de Clermont-Tonnerre et l'échec de la révolution monarchique, 1757–1792* (1931), 23.

82. F. Boquilon, 'Gabrielle de Spada, abbesse d'Épinal, 1738–84', *Ann. Est* (1980), 243–56.

83. Mme de Chastenay, *Mémoires 1771–1815*, ed. A. Roderot (2 vols., 1896), i. 50–69.

84. P.-M. Masson, *Mme de Tencin* (1909), 7 n.

85. T. J. Schmitt, *L'Assistance dans l'archidiaconé d'Autun aux XVIIe et XVIIIe siècles* (1952), pp. xxix, 60.

86. Luynes, vi. 82 (1744).
87. E. Préclin, 'La Situation ecclésiastique . . . de la Franche Comté à la veille de la Révolution', *Bull. Féd. Franche Comté* (1955), 17–18.
88. F. D. Mathieu, *L'Ancien Régime en Lorraine et Barrois* (1879), 70–1.
89. Mme de Genlis, *Mémoires*, i. 14–18, 50.
90. Luynes, iv. 125 (1742); Président de Brosses, *Lettres à Ch. C. Loppin de Gemeaux* (1929), 41.
91. L. Trénard, *Le Diocèse de Belley* (1978), 116 ff.
92. Eich, *Histoire religieuse*, i. 20.
93. F. Masson, *Le Cardinal de Bernis depuis son ministère, 1758–94* (1884), 417–20.
94. L. Audiat, *Deux victimes des Septembriseurs: Pierre-Louis de la Rochefoucauld, dernier évêque de Saintes et son frère, évêque de Beauvais* (1897), 69–74.
95. L. Welter, 'Une Tentative pour redonner prospérité à l'abbaye de Saint-Pierre de Blesle', *Bull. Auvergne* (1945), 123–35.
96. Durand de Maillaine, *Dictionnaire de droit canonique* (4 vols., 1776), i. 30–1; Guyot, i. 12.
97. 'M. B.', 'Contribution à l'histoire de l'abbaye de Jouarre', *Rev. Mabillon* (1933), 47.
98. G.-M. Oury, 'Abbesse et moniales de Notre-Dame de Perrigne aux XVIIe et XVIIIe siècles', *Province du Maine* (1978), 315.
99. See C. Torchet, *Histoire de l'abbaye royale de Notre Dame de Chelles* (2 vols., 1889).
100. L. Paris, *Histoire de l'abbaye d'Avenay* (2 vols., 1879), i. 460–87; ii. 1.
101. See Dom Y. Chaussy *et al.*, *L'Abbaye royale de Notre Dame de Jouarre* (2 vols., 1961), ii. 312–45.
102. See S. Poignant, *L'Abbaye de Fontevrault et les filles de Louis XV* (1966).
103. J.-M. Alliot, *Histoire de l'abbaye . . . de Notre-Dame du Val de Gif* (1892), 235–6.
104. J. Levron, *Amours et drames du passé* (1976), 193–215.
105. La marquise du Deffand, *Correspondance complète*, ed. M. de Lescure (1865), p. ix; Bachaumont, vii. 36–7 (5 Aug. 1773).
106. Canon Uzureau, 'La Maréchale d'Aubeterre', in *Andegaviana* (1927), 145; J.-M. Alliot, *Histoire de l'abbaye de Notre-Dame d'Yerres* (1899), 276–9.
107. See M. Chassaigne, *Le Procès du chevalier de la Barre* (1920).
108. Marais, i. 163–4, 272, 320; Saint-Simon, xi. 310; Barbier, i. 42.
109. Deries, *Normandie*, 194.
110. F.-Y. Besnard, *Souvenirs d'un nonagénaire*, ed. C. Port (2 vols., 1880), i. 258 ff., 322–7.
111. Poignant, *Fontevrault*, 109–10, 116–17.
112. Guyot, xx. 488–97.
113. Paris, *Avenay*, i. 523.
114. Pocquet du Haut-Jussé, 'La Vie temporelle', 342–3.
115. P. de Vaissière, *Gentilshommes campagnards de l'ancienne France* (1925), 379–80.
116. J.-F. Soulet, *Traditions et réformes religieuses dans les Pyrénées centrales au XVIIe siècle* (1974), 212–13.
117. L. Ampoulange, *Le Clergé et la convocation aux États Généraux de 1789 dans la sénéchaussée principale de Périgord* (1912), 101–2.
118. Diderot, *Jacques le fataliste*, in *Œuvres* (1935), 333.
119. McManners, *Angers*, 93; cf. L. Pérouas, 'Les Religieuses dans le pays

Creusois', *Cahiers hist.* (1979), 24.

120. D'Argenson, vi. 31; J. Bouchary, *Les Compagnies financières à Paris à la fin du XVIIIe siècle* (3 vols., 1940), i. 12.

121. By Brunet de Bru (1720). See F. C. Green, *La Peinture des mœurs de la bonne société dans le roman français de 1715 à 1761* (1924), 92–6.

122. L. Pingaud, *Les Saulx-Tavannes* (1876), 292–305. For Mme de Tencin see P. M. Masson, *Mme de Tencin*, and J. Sareil, *Les Tencin* (1969).

123. Guyot, xlix. 81–2; E. Regnault, *Christophe de Beaumont, archevêque de Paris, 1763–81* (2 vols., 1882), i. 429–30.

124. L. de Loménie, *La Comtesse de Rochefort et ses amis* (1879), 190–2.

125. M. Cousin (ed.), *Souvenirs de la marquise de Créquy*, 2nd edn. (1865), 29.

126. Paris, *Avenay*, i. 489–90.

127. Guyot, xlix. 99–101, 110–11.

128. A nun released in 1750 (P. de la Haye, *Histoire de Tréguier, ville épiscopale* (1977), 272).

129. Guyot, lxiv. 63–6.

130. Ibid. xlix. 79–86, lxiv. 52–3.

131. R. Graham, 'The Married Nuns before Cardinal Caprara', in *Pratiques religieuses en l'Europe révolutionnaire. Colloque* (1986), 324–5.

132. Bernis, *Mémoires*, i. 5.

133. C. Charrier, *Héloïse dans l'histoire et dans la légende* (1933); R. Shackleton, 'The Cloister Theme in French Preromanticism', in N. Moore *et al.* (eds.), *The French Mind: Studies in Honour of Gustave Rudler* (1952), 173–7; A. Prévost, *Mémoires et aventures d'un homme de qualité*.

134. A. Mathiez, 'Les Prêtres révolutionnaires devant le cardinal Caprara', *Ann. hist. Rév. fr.* (1926), 8.

135. A. Chérel, *Un Aventurier religieux: André-Michel Ramsay* (1928), 63.

136. J. Verbier, 'Les Demoiselles de Beauvilliers à Montargis', *Bull. Soc. Montargis*, 3e sér., 47 (1979), 11–12.

137. Mme Roland (Marie-Jeanne Philipon), *Mémoires*, ed. Cl. Perroud (2 vols., 1905), ii. 69–70.

138. C.-L. Richard, *Dissertation sur les vœux en général et sur les vœux des religieux* (1771), 50.

139. Brunet de Brou (Green, *La Peinture*, 99).

140. e.g. Pingaud, *Les Saulx-Tavannes*, 294.

141. J. B. Bergier, *Histoire de la communauté des prêtres missionnaires de Beaupré* (1853), 198.

142. Marivaux, *La Vie de Marianne ou les aventures de Mme la comtesse de XX* (1736), ed. M. Gilot (1978), 402–3.

CHAPTER 17

1. G. Fleury, 'L'Abbaye cistercienne de Pereigne, 1145–1790', *Rev. Maine* (1878), 50.

2. Fr. de la Rochefoucauld, *Voyages en France, 1781–3*, ed. J. Marchand (1923), 157–9.

3. L. Vignols, 'Les Émigrants allemands cantonnés en Bretagne, 1763–6', *Bull. méms. Soc. Ille-et-Vilaine* (1894), 34; J. Mathorez, *Les Étrangers en France sous*

l'ancien régime (2 vols., 1919), ii. 151.

4. J. Salmon, *Morimond: les derniers jours de l'abbaye* (1961), 24–7.

5. 'L'Assistance publique au XVIIIe siècle: l'enquête de 1775 dans le diocèse civil de Toulouse', *Rév. fr.* (1917), 157–64.

6. e.g. J. Meyer, *La Noblesse bretonne au XVIIIe siècle* (2 vols., 1966), ii. 1108.

7. J.-F.-H. de Richeprey, *Journal des voyages en Haute-Guienne*, ed. M. Guilhamon (1952), 103–4, 51–2.

8. e.g. 2,400 livres in one parish, 60 in another (G. Lefebvre, *Les Paysans du Nord pendant la Révolution française* (2 vols., 1924), i. 294).

9. H. Prentout, 'Les Tableaux de 1790 en réponse à l'enquête du Comité de Mendicité (Calvados)', *Rév. fr.* (1907), 426.

10. L. Lallemand, *De l'organisation de la bienfaisance dans les campagnes au XVIIIe siècle* (1893), 36–7; Lefebvre, *Les Paysans du Nord*, 36–7.

11. L. Jacob, 'La Grande Peur en Artois', *Ann. hist. Rév. fr.* (1936), 140–1.

12. La Rochefoucauld, *Voyages*, 51; Chateaubriand, *Mémoires d'outre-tombe* (2 vols., 1955), i. 85; N. Wraxall, *A Tour through the Western, Southern and Interior Provinces of France* (3 vols., 1777), ii. 242–3.

13. They sacked the abbey in 1789 (see A. Faure, 'L'Abbaye de Saint-Sulpice en Bugey', *Le Bugey* (1971–4), 517 ff.).

14. G. Macdonogh, *Brillat-Savarin, the Judge and his Stomach* (1992), 39–40 (a book throwing entertaining light on an aspect of French history neglected by solemn professionals).

15. J. Breval, *Remarks on Several Parts of Europe* (2 vols, 1738), ii. 50.

16. V. Durand, *État religieux des trois diocèses de Nîmes, d'Uzès et d'Alais à la fin de l'ancien régime* (1909), 153–4.

17. J. F. Bluche, *Les Magistrats du Parlement de Paris au XVIIIe siècle, 1715–71* (1960), 346–7.

18. Marais, iii. 39 (1723); Loaisel de Tréogate, *Dolbreuse* (1783), cited by A. Monglond, *Le Préromantisme français* (2 vols., 1930; new edn., 1965), i. 81–2; J. McManners, *Death and the Enlightenment* (1981), 224–5.

19. F. D. Mathieu, *L'Ancien Régime en Lorraine et Barrois* (1879), 91–4.

20. M. Dubois, 'Documents . . . la Chartreuse de Notre-Dame de La Verne', *Rev. Mabillon* (1933), 131.

21. G. Lefebvre, *La Grande Peur* (1932), 294.

22. O. H. Hufton, *The Poor of 18th Century France, 1750–89* (1974), 125.

23. T. J. Schmitt, *L'Assistance dans l'archidiaconé d'Autun aux XVIIe et XVIIIe siècles* (1952), 323.

24. Lefebvre, *La Grande Peur*, 16.

25. L. Deries, *La Vie monastique en Normandie* (1933), 42, 59, 61–2; Lallemand, *De l'organisation*, 37.

26. J. Dehergne, *Le Bas Poitou à la veille de la Révolution* (1963), 107; Duhamel du Monceau, *Éléments d'agriculture* (2 vols., 1763), i. 251; L. Bertre, 'Moulins à blé et moulins à huile', *Rev. Nord* (1959), 164–5.

27. R. Gandilhon, *La Naissance du champagne: Dom Pérignon* (1968), 245, 92, 100; G. Laurent, *Reims et la région rémoise à la veille de la Révolution* (1930), p. ccxx.

28. E. Maury, 'L'Inventaire du cabinet d'histoire naturelle de l'abbaye de Clairvaux', *Ann. hist. Rév. fr.* (1924), 567.

29. E. Lery, 'Le Père Sébastien Truchet et ses travaux à Versailles et à Marly', *Rev. Versailles* (1929), 220–30. For monks as architects see F. Machelart,

'Religieux architectes en Cambrésis aux XVIIe et XVIIIe siècles', *Rev. Nord* (1980), 415–27.

30. Marais, i. 481.
31. G. Laurent and G. Boussinecq, *Histoire de Reims* (2 vols., 1933), ii. 170–5.
32. Bachaumont, xxi. 23–4 (18 July 1782).
33. Luynes, x. 51 (1751).
34. Voltaire, *Dictionnaire philosophique*, in *Œuvres*, xvii. 117.
35. C. Serpas, 'Les Esclaves chrétiens au Maroc', *Bull. hist. Prot. fr.* (1930), 243.
36. P. Delandres, *L'Ordre des Trinitaires pour le rachat des captifs* (2 vols., 1903), i. 124, 287; Guyot, xlii. 213.
37. See G. Lambert, *L'Œuvre de la rédemption des captifs à Toulon* (1882).
38. P. Chevallier, *Loménie de Brienne et l'Ordre monastique, 1766–89* (2 vols., 1959–61), i. 97.
39. H. de Gramont, 'Études algériennes', *Rev. hist.* (1885), 11.
40. Deslandres, *L'Ordre des Trinitaires*, i. 343–51.
41. L. Vignols, 'La Piraterie sur l'Atlantique au XVIIIe siècle', *Ann. Bretagne* (1889–90), 228.
42. Martial-Levé, *Louis-François-Gabriel d'Orléans de la Motte, évêque d'Amiens, 1683–1774* (1962), 143–4.
43. *P.V. Ass.* viii (2), cols. 1595–7.
44. See Vignols, 'La Piraterie', 231–3; Deslandres, *L'Ordre des Trinitaires*, i. 379–88, 406–7; Gramont, 'Études algériennes', 22–5; L. Pingaud, 'Les Captifs à Alger au XVIIIe siècle', *Rev. hist.* (1880), 335.
45. C.-E. Engel, *L'Ordre de Malte en Méditerranée, 1530–1798* (1957), 169–71.
46. J. G. Lydon, 'Thomas Jefferson and the Mathurins', *Cath. Hist. Rev.* (1963), 192–202.
47. Deslandres, *L'Ordre des Trinitaires*, i. 396.
48. Lambert, *L'Œuvre*, 82.
49. Moreau de Jonnes, 'Mémoires', ed. F.-A. Aulard, *Rév. fr.* (1890), 363; Bachaumont, xxx. 24 (Oct. 1785). For accounts of processions see S. Moreau-Rendu, *Les Captifs libérés: les Trinitaires de Saint-Mathurin à Paris* (1974); account of Le Chevalier, *avocat* of Rouen, in *La Semaine religieuse de Rouen* (1876), 629–30; A. Plassard, 'Journal', *Ann. Acad. Mâcon* (1954–5), 102; 'Notes et souvenirs d'Antoine Sabatier', *Bull. Lyon* (1922), 161–2.
50. E. Lequay, *Études historiques de l'Ordre de la Charité de Saint-Jean-de-Dieu et ses établissements en France* (1854), 33–4, 42–8, 54–5, 61, 111.
51. J. T. Murphy, *The History of Urology* (1972), 111–20.
52. Métra, ii. 197–8 (1775).
53. J.-B. Rousseau, *Œuvres*, ed. A. de La Tour (1869), 381 (epigram 17).
54. Diderot, *Correspondance*, ed. G. Roth and J. Varloot (16 vols., 1955–70), v. 197 (1765).
55. M. Giraud, 'Crise de conscience et d'autorité à la fin du règne de Louis XIV', *Ann.* (1952), 228–32.
56. C. Frostin, 'Les *Enfants perdus* de l'État, ou la condition militaire à Saint-Domingue au XVIIIe siècle', *Ann. Bretagne* (1973), 328–35.
57. F. X. Emmanuelli, 'Ordres du roi et lettres de cachet en Provence', *Rev. hist.* (1974), 358.
58. G. Lely, *Vie du Marquis de Sade* (2 vols., 1957), ii. 347–8.
59. Marquis de Sade, *Correspondance inédite*, ed. P. Bourdin (1926), 264.

60. G. Vauthier, 'La Maison du Charenton en 1790', *Ann. hist. Rév. fr.* (1926), 264–6.

61. Ibid. 267–70. In fairness to the nuns, it should be noted that they themselves led lives of grim severity—with an income of only 150 livres a head and penitential scourging every Friday and many other days (J. Jobin, 'Le Prieuré du Val d'Osne à Charenton, 1700–93', *Bull. Com. Paris* (1883), 105–37).

62. Ch. Gérin, 'Les Monastères franciscains et la Commission des réguliers', *Rev. quest. hist.* (1895), 95.

63. Deries, *Normandie*, 297–8; P. Grosclaude, *Malesherbes, témoin et interprète de son temps* (1961), 35; Y. Durand, *Les Fermiers Généraux au XVIIIᵉ siècle* (1971), 589–90; P. Chevallier (ed.), *Journal de l'Assemblée des Notables* (1960), 51.

64. Wraxall, *Tour*, ii. 213–15 (in 1777).

65. Deries, *Normandie*, 97–104.

66. Emmanuelli, 'Ordres', 358–64; G. Gaffarel, 'Les Lettres de cachet en Provence', *Rev. hist.* (1914), 5–19.

67. For the Jesuits, see below, ch. 42.

68. P. Ricordel, 'Le Collège de Rennes après le départ des Jésuites, 1762–1803'. *Ann. Bretagne* (1936–7), 108.

69. A. Sicard, *Les Études classiques avant la Révolution* (1887), 413.

70. M. Garden, *Lyon et les Lyonnais au XVIIIᵉ siècle* (1970), 371.

71. Maillard, *L'Oratoire d'Angers au XVIIIᵉ siècle* (n.d.), 116–19; Jean de Viguerie, *Une Œuvre d'éducation sous l'ancien régime: les Pères de la Doctrine Chrétienne en France et en Italie, 1592–1792* (1970), 153–8, 276.

72. Viguerie, *Une Œuvre*, 270.

73. Ibid. 222–33.

74. Y. Besnard, *Souvenirs d'un nonagénaire*, ed. C. Port (2 vols., 1880), i. 102–3.

75. Canon Uzureau, 'Les Ballons en Anjou', *L'Anjou hist.* (1901–2), 30.

76. A. Queinot, 'Les Dieppois et la presse périodique à la fin du 18ᵉ siècle', *Ann. hist. Rév. fr.* (1938), 55.

77. A. Martin, 'Les Chambres littéraires de Nantes et la préparation de la Révolution', *Ann. Bretagne* (1926), 349.

78. 20 per cent of Doctrinaires, 19.8 of Oratorians (Viguerie, *Une Œuvre*, 425).

79. G. Guillaume, *Billaud Varenne* (1969), 4–24. His brother had been astonished when he joined the Oratory in the first place (Billaud Varenne, *Mémoires et Correspondance*, ed. A. Begis (1893), 4–5.

80. See L. Jacob, *Joseph Lebon* (2 vols., 1933), and L. Madelin, *Fouché* (1900).

81. R. Chartier, M.-M. Compère, and D. Julia, *L'Éducation en France du XVIᵉ au XVIIIᵉ siècle* (1976), 194–6.

82. M. Garden, 'Pédagogie et parents d'élèves au collège de La Trinité, Lyon, 1763–92', *Cahiers hist.* (1969), 308.

83. E. Dard, *Hérault de Séchelles, 1759–94* (1907), 20. For the Labordes, see J.-A. Dulaure, *Nouvelle Description de Paris* (2 vols., 1787), ii. 5.

84. Maillard, *L'Oratoire*, 108–10; P. Marchand, 'Le Collège de Lille', *L'Information hist.* (1975), 164.

85. A. Brun, 'Un Collège d'Oratoriens au XVIIIᵉ siècle', *Rev. hist. Église Fr.* (1949), 207–9; Lallemand, *De l'organisation*, 70–1.

86. R. Collier, *La Vie en Haute-Provence, 1600–1850* (1973), 463.

87. Lallemand, *De l'organisation*, 41–3, 55, 68, 103, 105–6.

88. Maillard, *L'Oratoire*, 108–10.

89. F. de Dainville, 'Les Effectifs des collèges et scolarité aux 17ᵉ et 18ᵉ siècles', *Population* (1955), 455–88.

90. Dulaure, *Paris*, ii. 3.

91. Lallemand, *De l'organisation*, 194.

92. Restif de la Bretonne, *La Femme dans les trois états* (1775), in *Œuvres*, ed. M. Bachelin, iii. 153.

93. Mallet du Pan, *Mémoires et correspondance*, ed. A. Sayous (2 vols., 1851), ii. 491–2.

94. P. Haudrière, 'Mémoire' (1720), in *L'Information hist.* (1975), 200–1.

95. A. Franklin, *La Vie privée . . . les collèges* (1892), 220–1.

96. Moreau de Jonnes, 'Mémoires', 456–7.

97. G. Snyders, *La Pédagogie en France aux XVIIᵉ et XVIIIᵉ siècles* (1965), 60–4.

98. Chartier *et al.*, *L'Éducation*, 216–17.

99. Snyders, *La Pédagogie*, 413–14.

100. See G. Saillant, *La Fable en France* (1912).

101. P. Marchand, 'L'Enseignement de l'histoire et de la géographie au collège de Lille, 1765–1791', *Rev. Nord* (1968), 351–6.

102. J. Leflon, *Eugène de Mazenod* (2 vols., 1957), i. 67, 76.

103. M. Thiery, *Guide des amateurs et étrangers voyageurs à Paris* (2 vols., 1787), i. 8–10.

104. G. Bouchard, *Prieur de la Côte d'Or* (1948), 21.

105. A. Babeau, *La Vie militaire sous l'ancien régime* (2 vols., 1890), i. 72.

106. The Countess of Minto, *A Memoir of the Right Hon. Hugh Elliot* (1868), 4–6.

107. Maillard, *L'Oratoire*, 101; Lallemand, *De l'organisation*, 62–4.

108. W. Frijhoff and D. Julia, 'Deux pensionnats', *Cahiers hist.* (1970), 107–10.

109. Babeau, *La Vie militaire*, ii. 59.

110. Corresp. Acad. Anjou, 4 Dec. 1758 (Bibliothèque Municipale, Angers MS 611 (56 ff.)).

111. Chartier *et al.*, *L'Éducation*, 220–2; E. G. Léonard, *L'Armée au 18ᵉ siècle* (1958), 247.

112. J. Fabre de Massaguel, *L'École de Sorèze de 1758 au 19 Fructidor, an IV* (1958), 42–128.

113. A. Chuquet, *La Jeunesse de Napoléon* (3 vols., 1897–9), i. 114.

114. Definitive history by G. Rigault, *Histoire générale de l'Institut des Frères des Écoles Chrétiennes* (9 vols., 1937–53), i and ii.

115. Ibid. i. 292.

CHAPTER 18

1. H. Carré, *La Noblesse de France et l'opinion publique au 18ᵉ siècle* (1920), 197–8.

2. E. and J. de Goncourt, *La Femme au 18ᵉ siècle* (1862), 17.

3. C. Kunstler, *La Vie quotidienne sous Louis XVI* (1950), 272.

4. L. de Loménie, *Les Mirabeau* (5 vols., 1891), iii. 125.

5. Carré, *La Noblesse*, 183.

6. W. Doyle, *The Parlement of Bordeaux* (1973), 117.

7. L. Paris, *Histoire de l'abbaye d'Avenay* (2 vols., 1875), i. 513.

8. See S. Poignant, *L'Abbaye de Fontevrault et les filles de Louis XV* (1966).

9. R. Chartier, M.-M. Compère, and D. Julia, *L'Éducation en France du XVIᵉ au*

XVIIIᵉ siècle (1976), 242–3; J. A. Dulaure, *Nouvelle Description de Paris* (2 vols., 1787), i. 143.

10. A. Le Moy, 'La Grande Prêtresse', *Ann. Bretagne* (1932–3), 77.

11. E. Catta, *La Vie d'un monastère sous l'ancien régime: La Visitation Sainte-Marie de Nantes, 1630–1792* (1954), 110–18.

12. Chartier *et al.*, *L'Éducation*, 236.

13. T. J. Schmitt, *L'Assistance dans l'archidiaconé d'Autun aux XVIIᵉ et XVIIIᵉ siècles* (1952), 80–2.

14. J. McManners, *French Ecclesiastical Society under the Ancien Régime: A Study of Angers* (1960), 92–3.

15. G. Desnoiresterres, *Voltaire et la société française au XVIIIᵉ siècle*, 2nd edn. (8 vols., 1867–76), iii. 791–2.

16. Definitive history by Chantal Gueudré, *Les Monastères d'Ursulines sous l'ancien régime* (1960), being vol. ii of her *Histoire de l'Ordre des Ursulines en France*.

17. *Nouvelles ecclésiastiques*, 16 Jan. 1789.

18. E. Maxfield-Millar, 'Le "Tartuffe" joué par les religieuses', *Rev. hist. du théâtre* (1972), 383–5.

19. Fr. de Saint-Just, *Témoins de quatre siècles* (1962), 166.

20. Molière, *Les Femmes Savantes*.

21. McManners, *Angers*, 97.

22. Mme de Lambert, *Avis d'une mère à sa fille*, in A. Chérel, *Fénelon au XVIIIᵉ siècle, 1715–1820* (1917), 317.

23. Gusdorf, in P. Hoffmann, *La Femme dans la pensée des Lumières* (1978), 12. See also E. Jacobs (ed.), *Women and Society in 18th-Century France* (1979). Further bibliography in J. McManners, *Death and the Enlightenment* (1981), ch. 13.

24. Voltaire, *Dialogue de l'éducation d'une fille* (1765), in *Œuvres*, xxiv. 285.

25. L. Versini, *Laclos et la tradition: essai sur les sources et la technique des 'Liaisons dangereuses'* (1968), 553.

26. Schmitt, *L'Assistance*, 83.

27. McManners, *Angers*, 97.

28. Gueudré, *Les Monastères d'Ursulines*, ii. 116, 379, 392.

29. An exception, the Congrégation de Notre-Dame in Lorraine (M.-E. Aubry, 'La congrégation de Notre-Dame de Nancy et l'éducation des filles aux XVIIᵉ et XVIIIᵉ siècles', *Ann. Est* (1974), 76–96).

30. Cl. Langlois and P. Wagret, *Structures religieuses et célibat féminin au XIXᵉ siècle* (1972), 14–63. See also Th. Perrée, *Le Tiers Ordre de Notre-Dame du Mont Carmel d'Avranches* (1965).

31. Ch. Molette, *Guide des sources de l'histoire des Congrégations féminines françaises de vie active* (1974).

32. J.-P. Latrobe, 'Contribution à l'enseignement au XVIIIᵉ siècle: les écoles des Sœurs d'Ernemont', *Cahiers hist. enseign.* (1978), 4–86.

33. Pierre de la Haye, *Histoire de Tréguier, ville épiscopale* (1977), 258–9.

34. G. Tavard, *Jean-Martin Moye, mystique et missionnaire* (1978).

35. Gueudré, *Les Monastères d'Ursulines*, ii. 201–3.

36. J. Vaudon, *Histoire générale de la Communauté des Filles de Saint-Paul de Chartres* (4 vols., 1922–31).

37. Cl. Langlois, *Catholicisme au féminin: les congrégations françaises à supérieure générale au XIXᵉ siècle* (1984), 101–2, 139–42.

38. Cl. Langlois, *Histoire de la congrégation de la Providence d'Evreux* (2 vols., 1901).

39. J. Perrel, 'Les Écoles de filles dans la France d'ancien régime', in D. N. Baker and P. J. Harrigan (eds.), *The Making of Frenchmen: Current Directions in the History of Education in France, 1679–1979* (1980), 77.
40. Chartier *et al.*, *L'Éducation*, 239.
41. R. P. H. de Grèzes, *Histoire de l'Institut des écoles charitables du Saint-Enfant Jésus, dit de Saint-Maur, 1700–1877* (n.d.), 27–39.
42. Sr. Paul-Marie de Jésus, *Mère Marie-Louise de Jésus, première fille de la Sagesse, 1641–1759* (1947).
43. Perrel, 'Les Écoles', 78.
44. Chartier *et al.*, *L'Éducation*, 278.
45. M. Claeyssen, 'L'Enseignement de la lecture au 18ᵉ siècle', in Baker and Harrigan (eds.), *Making of Frenchmen*, 66–74.
46. L. Trénard, 'L'Enseignement de la langue nationale, 1750–90', in ibid. 107.
47. R. A. Weight, 'Le Meuble brodé de la Salle du Trône de Louis XIV à Versailles', *Rev. Versailles* (1930), 199–206.
48. J. P. Gutton, *La Société et les pauvres: l'exemple de la généralité de Lyon, 1534–1789* (1971), 388.
49. Grèzes, *Saint-Maur*, 592–3.
50. Chartier, *et al.*, *L'Éducation*, 244–5.
51. Grèzes, *Saint-Maur*, 89.
52. Chartier, *et al.*, *L'Éducation*, 245–6.
53. Perrel, 'Les Écoles', 79–82.
54. Schmitt, *L'Assistance*, 82; F. Bridoux, *La Fin du Lys* (1945), 25; B. Pocquet du Haut-Jussé, 'La Vie temporelle des communautés de femmes à Rennes au XVIIᵉ siècle et au XVIIIᵉ siècle', *Ann. Bretagne* (1917), 39, 44–5, 77–8.
55. Mme de Genlis, *Mémoires* (2 vols., 1825), i. 140, 125.
56. Mme Roland, *Mémoires*, ed. Cl. Perroud (2 vols., 1905), ii. 41–4.
57. E. and J. de Goncourt, *La Femme*, 8–10.
58. McManners, *Death*, 33–4.
59. D'Argenson, vi. 185.
60. La marquise du Deffand, *Correspondance complète*, ed. M. de Lescure (2 vols., 1865), ii. p. xlv.
61. Kunstler, *La Vie quotidienne*, 276.
62. L. de Loménie, *Beaumarchais et son temps* (2 vols., 1889), i. 279–83.
63. Diderot, *Correspondance*, ed. G. Roth and J. Varlot (16 vols., 1955–70), vi. 505.
64. Dom E. Lecroq, *Les Annoncionades de Fécamp 1618–1792* (1947), 160–72.
65. M. Fosseyeux, 'Le Cardinal de Noailles et l'administration du diocèse de Paris', *Rev. hist.* (1913), 282–3.
66. E. Lavaquery, *Le Cardinal de Boisgelin, 1732–1804* (2 vols., 1920), i. 57.
67. Gueudré, *Les Monastères d'Ursulines*, ii. 546–9.
68. Guyot, i. 416–18.
69. Deffand, *Correspondance*, i. 401–5 (1767); cf. ii. 468 (1777).
70. A. Lods, 'Les Luthériens d'Alsace devant la Constituante', *Rév. fr.* (1900), 532.
71. F.-X.-J. Droz, *Histoire du règne de Louis XVI* (3 vols., 1839–42), i. 31.
72. Barbier, i. 248–9, 321–3.
73. [Mlle d'Albert], *Confidences d'une jolie femme* (2 vols., 1777; 1st edn., 1775), ii. 214.

74. Choderlos de Laclos, *Les Liaisons dangereuses*.

75. Loménie, *Beaumarchais*, ii. 606, 619; P. Pinsseau, *Gien sous l'ancien régime et la Révolution d'après les mémoires inédits de l'abbé Vallet* (1922), 77–9.

76. P. Tartat, *Histoire de l'Avalonnais* (2 vols., 1958–60), ii. 46.

77. L. Froger, 'Les Établissements de charité à Saint-Cales', *Rev. Maine* (1878), 341.

78. G.-J. Sumeire, *La Communauté de Trets à la veille de la Révolution* (1960), 177–9.

79. J.-F.-M. de Richeprey, *Journal des voyages en Haute-Guienne*, ed. H. Guilhamon (1952), 367.

80. C. Bloch, *L'Assistance et l'État en France à la veille de la Révolution* (1908), 61.

81. C. Jones, *The Charitable Imperative: Hospitals and Nursing in Ancien Régime and Revolutionary France* (1989), 21.

82. Gutton, *La Société*, 394–9.

83. See C. C. Fairchilds, *Poverty and Charity in Aix-en-Provence, 1640–1789* (1976).

84. C. Jones, *Charity and 'Bienfaisance': The Treatment of the Poor in the Montpellier Region, 1740–1815* (1982), 86. The part played by lay charity—especially by pious aristocrats—is evident. See also the full details in K. Norberg, *Rich and Poor in Grenoble, 1600–1814* (1985).

85. P. Delaunay, *Le Monde médical parisien au 18ᵉ siècle*, 2nd edn. (1906), 72–6; A. Gobert, 'Le District des Enfants Trouvés au Faubourg Saint-Antoine', *Rév. fr.* (1936), 141–3; C. Ronan, 'Les Pauvres à Paris au XVIIIᵉ siècle', *Ann.* (1984), 750–2. (There were vast numbers of inmates—in 1788, 6,720 in the Salpêtrière, and 4,094 in the Bicêtre.)

86. Bloch, *L'Assistance*, 138–9.

87. Marais, i. 367.

88. Bloch, *L'Assistance*, 64.

89. J. Imbert, *Le Droit Hospitalier de la Révolution et l'Empire* (1954), 18–20.

90. For an example J. Vinatier, *Treignac-sur-Vévère* (2 vols., 1974), ii. 125.

91. Fairchilds, *Aix-en-Provence*, 134–5.

92. Jones, *Charity and 'Bienfaisance'*, 86.

93. G. Armigon, *Banquiers des pauvres* (n.d.), 82–6, 221.

94. M. Courdurié, *La Dette des collectivités publiques de Marseille au XVIIIᵉ siècle* (1975), 182–96.

95. Schmitt, *L'Assistance*, 310.

96. Gutton, *La Société*, 478; P. D. Bernier, *Essai sur le tiers état rural ou les paysans de Basse-Normandie au XVIIIᵉ siècle* (1891), 68–70.

97. Froger, 'Saint-Cales', 346.

98. See M.-C. Guillerand, *Les Servantes des pauvres de la Providence de Saumur de 1736 à 1814* (1989).

99. Schmitt, *L'Assistance*, 204, 306.

100. P. Coste, 'Une Victime de la Révolution', *Rev. Gascogne* (1904), 161–225.

101. Voltaire, *Essai sur les Mœurs*, in *Œuvres*, xii. 324.

102. *Voyage d'une Française en Suisse et en Franche-Comté* (2 vols., 1790), i. 223.

103. Jones, *Charitable Imperative*, 85.

104. Ibid. 169.

105. Ibid. 45–50, 123.

106. A. Chevallier, *L'Hôtel-Dieu de Paris et les sœurs augustines, 1680–1810* (1901), 416, 444, 463—the basic authority for what follows.

107. D. Roche, *Paris, capitale des pauvres*, European University Institute Working Paper 86/238 (1986), 21–2.

108. Fr. de la Rochefoucauld, *Voyages en France*, ed. J. Marchand (1923), 98.

109. Jones, *Charitable Imperative*, 278.

110. Bloch, *L'Assistance*, 51–2.

111. Y. Forado Cunéo, 'Les Ateliers de charité de Paris, 1788–91', *Rév. fr.* (1933), 322–9.

112. Gutton, *La Société*, 30.

113. J.-P. Poussou, in F.-G. Pariset (ed.), *Bordeaux au XVIIIe siècle* (1968), 365–6.

114. H. Bergues, P. Ariès, *et al., La Prévention des naissances dans la famille: ses origines dans les temps modernes*, I.N.E.D. Cahier 35 (1960), 173, 179–81; M. Cl. Murtin, 'Les Abandons d'enfants à Bourg et dans le département de l'Ain', *Cahiers hist.* (1965), 135–43.

115. L. Lallemand, *Un Chapitre de l'histoire des Enfants Trouvés: la Maison de la Couche à Paris, XVIIe et XVIIIe siècles* (1885), 139–40; J.-J. Rousseau, *Correspondance complète*, ed. R. A. Leigh, ii (1963), 142–4.

116. V. A. Durand, *État religieux des trois diocèses de Nîmes, d'Uzès et d'Alais à la fin de l'ancien régime* (1909), 319–12.

117. R. Mercier, *La Réhabilitation de la nature humaine, 1700–50* (1960), 58.

118. McManners, *Death*, 284.

119. Jones, *Charitable Imperative*, 247 ff.

120. Pocquet du Haut-Jussé, 'La Vie temporelle', 335.

121. Gutton, *La Société*, 389–92.

122. Sumeire, *La Communauté de Trets*, 181–2.

123. F. Cognel, *La Vie parisienne sous Louis XVI* (1882), 49–50.

124. A. Forrest, *The Revolution and the Poor* (1981), 44–6.

125. Delaunay, *Le Monde médical parisien*, 349, 353.

126. Bloch, *L'Assistance*, 89, 116–17.

127. Gutton, *La Société*, 341–2.

128. J. Delumeau, *Le Diocèse de Rennes* (1979), 127.

129. Bloch, *L'Assistance*, 116–17.

130. Ibid. 61, 114.

131. Ibid. 74–5.

132. Jones, *Charitable Imperative*, 111.

133. See T. Gelfand, *Professionalizing Modern Medicine: Paris Surgeons and Medical Science and Institutions in the 18th Century* (1981), and M. Fosseyeux, 'L'Hôtel-Dieu de Paris sous la Révolution', *Rév. fr.* (1914), 41–3.

134. J. Musset, 'Administration hospitalière et l'anticléricalisme municipal à la fin du XVIIIe siècle', *Ann. Normandie* (1980), 318–19.

135. Jones, *Charitable Imperative*, 151–3.

136. E. Laurès, *La Municipalité de Béziers à la fin de l'ancien régime* (1926), 217–19.

137. Y. Bezard, 'L'Assistance à Versailles', *Rev. Versailles* (1919), 145–6.

138. Bloch, *L'Assistance*, 71–3.

CHAPTER 19

1. Guyot, i. 30–40.

2. *P.V. Ass.* viii(2), cols. 1407 ff.

3. J.-A. de Véri, *Journal*, ed. J. de Witte (2 vols., n.d.), i. 199–200.

4. P. Chevallier, *Loménie de Brienne et l'Ordre monastique, 1760–89* (1959), 73–85.

5. Ch. Gérin, 'Les Monastères franciscains et la Commission des réguliers, 1766–89', *Rev. quest. hist.* (1875), 99, 101.

6. Chevallier, *Loménie de Brienne*, i. 44.

7. For the statistics, see L. Lecestre, *Abbayes, prieurés et couvents d'hommes en France. Liste générale d'après les papiers de la Commission des réguliers* (1902).

8. Chevallier, *Loménie de Brienne*, i. 209–10.

9. F. D. Mathieu, *L'Ancien régime en Lorraine et Barrois* (1874), 91–4.

10. Thomas Bentley, *Journal of a Visit to Paris 1776*, ed. P. France (n.d.), 57–8; L. S. Mercier, *Tableau de Paris*, new edn. (12 vols., 1782–8), xii. 40–1.

11. A. Hutchinson, *The Hermit Monks of Grandmont* (1989), 204–74.

12. Chevallier, *Loménie de Brienne*, 214–15.

13. Ibid. i. 174–6.

14. Ibid. i. 137.

15. J. J. Gautier, *Essai sur les mœurs champêtres* (1787), ed. X. Rousseau (1933), 20.

16. P. Dubois, 'Les Capucins dans le Midi: Les Capucins de Varois-Sollies-Pont, 1650–1791', *Bull. Soc. Draguignan* (1965), 72–91.

17. Ch. Collas, *Saint-Louis d'Antin et son territoire* (1932), 64–5.

18. A. Babeau, *La Ville sous l'ancien régime* (2 vols., 1888), ii. 141–4.

19. Bachaumont, xvii. 320 (1767).

20. Restif de la Bretonne, 'Récit d'un incendie', in *Les Nuits de Paris*, ed. M. Bachelin, i. 65. Cf. Barbier, iii. 93–103.

21. L'Abbé Baston, *Mémoires*, ed. J. Loth and C. Verger (3 vols., 1879), i. 104–9, 141.

22. Mme de Genlis, *Mémoires* (2 vols., 1825), i. 38.

23. Chevallier, *Loménie de Brienne*, i. 167–8. For stories of hoarded riches at the top of the Capuchin hierarchy, see R. Reuss, *La Constitution civile du clergé et la crise religieuse en Alsace* (2 vols., 1927), i. 211–13.

24. Chevallier, *Loménie de Brienne*, i. 186–7.

25. A. Playoust-Chaussis, *La Vie religieuse dans le diocèse de Boulogne, 1725–50* (1969), 62.

26. L. Beaumont-Maillet, *Le Grand Couvent des Cordeliers de Paris* (1975), 175–80.

27. Chevallier, *Loménie de Brienne*, i. 123, 137–9, 153–8, 217, 139–41, 178–81, 218.

28. Ibid. i. 183–4, 219–20.

29. P. J. S. Whitmore, *The Order of Minims in 17th-Century France* (1969), 236.

30. Ibid. 32.

31. J. D. Levesque, *L'Ancien Couvent des Frères Prêcheurs d'Angers* (1961), 292–3, 308–9, 325–6.

32. Chevallier, *Loménie de Brienne*, i. 150–1.

33. R. P. Mortier, *Histoire des maîtres-généraux de l'ordre des Frères Prêcheurs* (8 vols, 1904–14), vii. 400–5.

34. Ch. Gérin, 'Les Augustins et Dominicains en France avant 1789', *Rev. quest. hist.* (1877), 79–93.

35. B. Cousin, 'Un Discours . . . l'histoire de Grasse de Père Crespy', *Ann. Midi* (1973), 290–2.

36. F. Duine, 'Les Généraux des paroisses Bretonnes: Saint-Martin de Vitré', *Ann. Bretagne* (1907–8), 481.

37. L. Ampoulange, *Le Clergé et la convocation aux États-Généraux de 1789 dans la sénéchaussée principale de Périgord* (1912), 90.
38. Chevallier, *Loménie de Brienne*, i. 68.
39. P. Feret, *L'Abbaye de Sainte-Geneviève et la Congrégation de France* (2 vols., 1883), ii. 136–9, 153, 163–5, 171–5.
40. L'Abbé Le Gendre, *Mémoires*, ed. M. Roux (1863), 367–8.
41. E. Préclin, *L'Union des Églises gallicane et anglicane: une tentative au temps de Louis XV—P.-F. Le Courayer et Guillaume Wake* (1928).
42. Goevaerts, *Écrivains et savants de l'Ordre de Prémontré* (4 vols., 1895–1917), i. 39, 110, 563–4, 556, 520–4, 362–3; ii. 59–60; iii. 110–29.
43. J. Evans, *Monastic Architecture in France from the Renaissance to the Revolution* (1964), 51–3.
44. Dom G. Charvin, *Statuts, chapitres-généraux et visites de l'Ordre de Cluny* (4 vols., 1965), i. 1–7.
45. G. Charvin, 'À propos d'un projet d'une histoire de l'Ordre de Cluny au XVIIIe siècle', in *Société des Amis de Cluny, Congrès* (1950), 183.
46. L. H. Champly, *Histoire de l'abbaye de Cluny*, rev. R. Champly (1930), 338.
47. G. Charvin, 'Frédéric-Jerôme de la Rochefoucauld, abbé de Cluny, 1747–57', *Rev. Mabillon* (1949), 31; id., 'L'Abbaye et l'Ordre de Cluny à la fin du XVIIIe siècle', ibid. 44–5.
48. L.-J. Lekai, *The Cistercian Ideal and Reality* (1972), 159–65.
49. Guyot, v. 517.
50. Bezard (ed.), *Lettres du président de Brosses à Ch. Loppin de Gémeaux* (1929), 202.
51. Guyot, xi. 114–17.
52. Chevallier, *Loménie de Brienne*, i. 196–200.
53. L.-J. Lekai, 'The Financial Status of the Parisian College of Saint Bernard, 1705–90', *Anal. cist.* (1969), 210–14; and id., 'Introduction à l'étude des collèges cisterciens en France avant la Révolution', ibid. 145–214.
54. L.-J. Lekai, 'Cistercian Monasteries and the French Episcopate on the Eve of the Revolution', *Anal. cist.* (1967), 79–84.
55. N. Tillière, *Histoire de l'abbaye d'Orval* (1967), 240–2, 274.
56. A. Krailsheimer, 'Les Débuts de la réforme de Sept-Fons', *Cîteaux* (1968), 210–11.
57. A. Krailsheimer, 'Sept-Fons de 1700 à 1723', *Cîteaux* (1987), 253.
58. A. Krailsheimer, *Armand-Jean de Rancé, abbot of La Trappe* (1974).
59. Ch. Gérin, 'Les Bénédictins français avant 1789', *Rev. quest. hist.* (1870), 470.
60. A. Morize, *L'Apologie du luxe au XVIIIe siècle: le 'Mondain' et ses sources* (1909), 42; F. Rousseau, *Moines bénédictins martyrs et confesseurs de la foi pendant la Révolution* (1926), 27–8.
61. Le maréchal duc de Croÿ, *Journal, 1718–84*, ed. le vicomte de Grouchy and P. Cottin (4 vols., 1906), ii. 109–15; Fr. de la Rochefoucauld, *Voyages en France*, ed. J. Marchand (1933), 101–2.
62. Up to 1739, more than half died within five years (Krailsheimer, *Rancé*, 92). Average age of death at Saint-Germain-des-Prés was 71, at La Trappe under 40 (M. Ultee, *The Abbey of St Germain des Prés in the 17th Century* (1981), 20).
63. Croÿ, *Journal*, ii. 113. A soldier tries his vocation in Oct. 1718, and is back in his regiment in Jan. 1719 (A. Corvisier, *L'Armée française de la fin du XVIIe siècle au ministère de Choiseul: le Soldat* (2 vols., 1964), ii. 870).

64. M. H. Jette, *La France religieuse au XVIIIe siècle* (1956), 25.

65. J. McManners, 'Voltaire and the Monks', in *Studies in Church History* (1985), 319–42.

66. J. L. Godefroy, 'Figures de moines: Dom Chardon', *Rev. Mabillon* (1944), 82–93.

67. See J. L. Godefroy, *La Congrégation de Saint-Vanne et la Révolution: Dom Charles* (1911).

68. Chevallier, *Loménie de Brienne*, i. 113–18.

69. Dom P. Schmitz, *Histoire de l'Ordre de Saint-Benoît* (7 vols., 1942–56), iv. 31–42.

70. See H. Leclercq, *Dom Mabillon* (2 vols., 1953–7).

71. E. de Broglie, *Mabillon et la société de l'abbaye de Saint-Germain-des-Prés à la fin du 17e siècle* (2 vols., 1888).

72. E. de Broglie, *Bernard de Montfaucon et les Bernardins* (2 vols., 1891), i. 27 ff.

73. Dom L. Deries, 'Dom Pierre Guérin et le chanoine Masclef', *Rev. Mabillon* (1908), 39–67, 151–87.

74. A. Vernière, *Journal de Voyage de Dom Jacques Boyer* (1886).

75. Le Gendre, *Mémoires*, 400.

76. A. de la Borderie, *Correspondance historique des Bénédictins Bretons* (1880), pp. xvii–xxiv, 249–56.

77. L. Lecomte, 'Les Bénédictins et l'histoire des provinces aux XVIIe et XVIIIe siècles', *Rev. Mabillon* (1927), 237 ff.; (1928), 39 ff.

78. L. Deries, 'Un Grand Sauveteur des documents . . . Dom Germain Poirier', *Rev. Mabillon* (1930), 62–6.

79. B. Hauréau, *Histoire littéraire du Maine* (4 vols., 1843), i. pp. xxiii–xxxvii.

80. J. McManners, *French Ecclesiastical Society under the Ancien Régime: A Study of Angers*, 53–4.

81. M. Laurais, 'Les Travaux d'érudition des Mauristes: origine et évolution', *Rev. hist. Église Fr.* (1957), 232.

82. Voltaire to Cideville, 6 May 1733, in Voltaire, *Corresp.* iii. 67 (no. 586).

83. Laurais, 'Les Travaux', 252.

84. Broglie, *Montfaucon*, i. 45–7.

85. J. Ruwet et al. (eds.), *Lettres de Turgot à la duchesse d'Enville, 1764–74 et 1777–80* (1976), 53, 57, 70.

86. Le Glay, *Mission historique de Dom Bévys, Spicilège . . . pour servir à l'histoire des sciences dans le Nord* (Lille, 1858), fasc. i. 45–53.

87. Dom B. Knowles, *Great Historical Enterprises* (1963), 41.

88. Schmitz, *Saint-Benoît*, v. 115–19.

89. *Réponse à la lettre d'un professeur émérite de l'Université de Paris au sujet des exercices de l'école militaire de Sorèz* (1777), cited by A. Sicard, *Les Études classiques avant la Révolution* (1887), 485.

90. A. Rostand, 'L'Œuvre architectural des Bénédictins de Saint-Maur en Normandie, 1616–1789', *Bull. Soc. Normandie* (1939), 88–222; M. Bugner, 'Les Constructions des Bénédictins de Saint-Maur au XVIIe et XVIIIe siècles', *Rev. hist. Église Fr.* (1987), 120–1.

91. J. L. Godefroy, 'Le Chevalier de Folard et les Bénédictins de Saint-Germain-des-Prés', *Rev. Mabillon* (1936), 128.

92. It was the abbé Prévost (E. Harrisse, *L'Abbé Prévost: histoire de sa vie et de ses œuvres* (1896), 250–1).

93. P. Timothée de la Flèche, *Mémoires et lettres . . . 1703–30*, ed. P. Ubald d'Alençon (1907), 73.
94. P. Denis, 'Un Bénédictin janséniste réfugié au Canada', *Rev. Mabillon* (1909), 208–12.
95. Schmitz, *Saint-Benoît*, iv. 50.
96. Chevallier, *Loménie de Brienne*, 120–2.
97. Dom P. Anger, 'Les Mitigations demandées par les moines de Saint-Germain-des-Prés en 1765', *Rev. Mabillon* (1908), 196–229.
98. Chevallier, *Loménie de Brienne*, i. 247–8.
99. Dom A. du Bourg, 'Vie monastique dans l'abbaye de Saint-Germain-des-Prés', *Rev. quest. hist.* (1905), 458.
100. Chevallier, *Loménie de Brienne*, i. 119–22.
101. Dom R.-P. Tassin, *Histoire littéraire de la Congrégation de Saint-Maur* (1770), 197–9, 314–47, 376, 394–5, 421.
102. Dom P. Denis, 'Dom Charles de l'Hostellerie', *Rev. Mabillon* (1909), 8 ff.; (1910), 429 ff.
103. A. de la Borderie, *Correspondance*, pp. xvi, 167–70, 220, 160–3.
104. Dom Th. Réjalot, 'Dom J. P. Deforis et l'abbé Mercier de Saint-Léger', *Rev. Mabillon* (1932), 38 ff.
105. Dom F. Lohier, 'Dom Étienne Maugier, 1753–94', *Rev. Mabillon* (1912–13), 345–9.
106. L. Deries, 'La Vie d'un bibliothécaire, Dom Gourdin, 1739–1825', *Rev. Mabillon* (1928), 211–15.
107. Harrisse, *Prévost*, 15–16, 19–24.
108. Ultee, *St Germain des Prés*, 16, 20–2.
109. 'La Congrégation de Saint-Maur d'après le Journal et les lettres de Dom Dassac, 1752–1826', *Rev. monde catholique* (1893), 59.
110. Dom Pierre Chastelain, 'Journal', ed. H. Jadert, *Trav. Acad. nat. Reims* (1902), 79–90.
111. Harrisse, *Prévost*, 15.
112. L. Deries, 'Poirier', *Rev. Mabillon* (1930), 52–3.
113. L.-J. Lekai, 'The Cistercian Order and the Commission des Réguliers', *Anal. cist.* (1976), 179–209.
114. J. Salmon, *Morimond: les derniers jours de l'abbaye* (1961), 28.
115. Hutchinson, *Grandmont*, 256–71.
116. Ch. Gérin, 'Les Monastères', *Rev. quest. hist.* (1876), 563.
117. S. Lemaire, *La Commission des réguliers* (1926), 92–100.
118. M. Gasnier, *Les Dominicains de la rue Saint-Honoré* (1942), 279–80; M. D. Chapotin, *Le Dernier Prieur du dernier couvent, 1736–1806* (1893), 116–21, 176–7.
119. Lemaire, *La Commission*, 110–23, 231–40.

CHAPTER 20

1. A. Degert, *Histoire des séminaires français jusqu'à la Révolution* (2 vols., 1912), ii. 359.
2. R. Darricau, in *Antoine Godeau, 1605–1672, de la galanterie à la sainteté*, ed. Y. Giraud, Acts et Colloques, Grasse, 17 (1972), 171.

3. Degert, *Histoire*, ii. 374–5. Discussion also of M. Olier, *Traité des saints Ordres* (1675) and L. Habert, *Theologia dogmatica et moralis* (7 vols., 1708), 369–74.

4. *Dictionnaire portatif des cas de conscience*, 2nd edn. (2 vols., Lyon, 1761), i. 422.

5. For Pius XII's rehabilitation of 'attraction' (1912) see E. Farrell, *The Theology of Religious Vocation* (1952), 17–18, 47, 103. I cite occasionally in this section my chapter 'The Bishops of France in the 18th Century', in D. Baker (ed.), *Religious Motivation*, Studies in Church History, 15 (1978), 305–7.

6. [R. Daon], *Conduite des âmes dans la voie du salut* (1750), 86.

7. P. Feret, *La Faculté de Théologie de Paris et ses docteurs les plus célèbres* (7 vols. 1900–9), vi. 142.

8. Mangin, *Science des confesseurs, ou décisions théologiques canoniques, domestiques et morales* (3 vols., 1757), iii. 258. See also the censures of family interests in P. Collet, *Traité des devoirs des gens du monde et surtout des chefs de famille* (1764), 201. A churchman, one should note, could dispose as he willed, within the boundaries of Christian responsibility, of the income coming to him from private sources.

9. L. Tronson, *Correspondance*, ed. L. Bertrand (3 vols., 1904) iii. 301.

10. [J.-L. Brunet, rev. de Maillane], *Le Parfait Notaire apostolique* (2 vols., 1775), i. 252–3.

11. 'Cassanyes et ses mémoires inédits (1758–1843)', *Rév. fr.* (1888), 979.

12. P.-A. Alletz, *La Discipline de l'église de France d'après ses maximes et ses décisions répandues dans la collection des Mémoires du Clergé* (1780), 79.

13. *Le Parfait Notaire*, i. 253. The standard treatise on the theology of minor and major orders in the church and on their ceremonies of initiation was A. Godeau, *Discours sur les Ordres sacrez, ou toutes les cérémonies de l'ordination selon le Pontifical Roman sont expliquées*, 2nd edn. (1658).

14. *Le Parfait Notaire*, i. 259.

15. C. Berthelot du Chesnay, 'Le Clergé diocésain français au XVIIIᵉ siècle et les registres des insinuations ecclésiastiques', *Rev. hist. mod. contemp.* (1963), 245, Autun, 90–200 livres (T. J. Schmitt, *L'Organisation ecclésiastique et la pratique religieuse dans l'archidiaconé d'Autun de 1650 à 1750* (1957), 128); Alsace, 100 livres (A. Schaer, *Le Clergé paroissial catholique en Haute-Alsace sous l'ancien régime, 1648–1789* (1960), 100; Amiens, 100 livres (P. Deyon, *Amiens: capitale provinciale* (1967), 364); Paris, 150 livres (M. Pialès, *Traité des collations et provisions de bénéfices* (8 vols. 1753–6), i. 148).

16. Le marquis de Roux, *Histoire religieuse de la Révolution à Poitiers et dans la Vienne* (1952), 24–5.

17. Leymarie, 'Documents . . . sur la jeunesse de J.-B. Carrier', *Rev. Haute-Auvergne* (1954), 443–4.

18. L. Bassette, *Jean de Caulet, évêque de Grenoble, 1693–1771* (1946), 16; Berthelot du Chesnay, 'Le Clergé diocésain', 255.

19. Berthelot du Chesnay, 'Le Clergé diocésain', 255.

20. *Le Parfait Notaire*, i. 306–11.

21. A. Lestra, *Le Père Coudrin, fondateur de Picpus* (1952), 30.

22. *Le Parfait Notaire*, i. 305.

23. H. Espitalier, 'Les Évêques de Fréjus', *Bull. Soc. Draguignan* (1898–9), 122.

24. 'Une Lettre de Joseph Le Bon', *Rév. fr.* (1913), 229–31.

25. e.g. M. Pialès, *Traité et la dévolution, du dévolut, et des variantes de plein droit* (3 vols., 1757), ii. 189.

26. F. D. Mathieu, *L'Ancien Régime dans la province de Lorraine et Barrois* (1879), 128.

27. A good example: the priory of Andresy, in E. Chartraire, 'Trois recueils de la correspondance des abbés Fenel avec l'abbé Lebeuf et autres', *Bull. Soc. arch. de Sens* (1927), 120.

28. *La Vie de M. Marquis-Ducastel, doyen rural d'Évron et Sonnois, curé de Sainte-Suzanne*, ed. F. Pichon (1873), 7, 11–13, 27. A very able youth might win a free place at a seminary by carrying off academic prizes (see M. Yvart, 'La Vie d'un écolier . . . 1784–92', *Rev. Socs. Haute-Normandie* (1957), 53–72.

29. Marquis-Ducastel, *La Vie*, 101, 107–8.

30. J. McManners, *French Ecclesiastical Society under the Ancien Régime: . . . A Study of Angers* (1960), 140.

31. In the dioceses of Dol, Nantes, Rennes, Saint-Brieuc, and Saint-Malo, a total of a fifth of the livings were at the bishop's disposal, two-fifths shared between bishop and Pope, one-fifth in the patronage of abbeys (C. Berthelot de Chesnay, *Les Prêtres séculiers en Haute-Bretagne au XVIIIe siècle* (1974), 203–4).

32. Pialès, *Traité de la dévolution*, i. 221.

33. Guyot, xlv. 26.

34. Potier de la Germondaye, *Introduction au gouvernement des paroisses* (1777), 22.

35. A. Besnier, *Les Agents généraux du Clergé de France* (1939), 111.

36. Pialès, *Traité de la dévolution*, i. 368–95.

37. A. Sicard, *La Nomination aux bénéfices ecclésiastiques avant 1789* (1896), 12.

38. M. Marion, *Dictionnaire des institutions de la France aux XVIIe et XVIIIe siècles* (2 vols., 1923), i. 43; J.-B. Daranatz, 'Les Ordinations sacerdotales du diocèse de Bayonne au XVIIIe siècle', *Bull. Soc. Bayonne* (1931), 360.

39. M. Pialès, *Traité de l'expectative des gradués, des droits et des privilèges des universités* (4 vols., 1757), iii. 224.

40. Ibid. ii. 451–2.

41. Marion, *Dictionnaire*, ii. 287.

42. For the working of the indult in detail, see Melchior Cochet de Saint-Vallier, *Traité de l'indult du Parlement de Paris* (3 vols., 1747; orig. pub. 1703).

43. Morellet had studied at the Sorbonne with Turgot.

44. Marion, *Dictionnaire*, i. 45.

45. *Le Parfait Notaire*, i. 537 ff. The months varied in different places. For the Trois Évêchés, see E. Martin, *Histoire des diocèses de Toul, de Nancy et de Saint-Dié* (3 vols., 1900–3), ii. 316.

46. Marion, *Dictionnaire*, 431; Pialès, *Traité de la dévolution*, i. 368–9.

47. Guyot, ii. 141–2.

48. Ibid. ii. 138–9.

49. Ibid. ii. 138.

50. Le Gendre, *Mémoires*, ed. M. Roux (1863), 372.

51. Timothée de la Flèche, *Mémoires et lettres, 1703–1730*, ed. P. Ubald d'Alençon (1907), 141.

52. Pialès, *Gradués*, iv. 2.

53. Ibid. iv. 31, 46; *Le Parfait Notaire*, i. 331–2.

54. Marion, *Dictionnaire*, i. 263.

55. Pialès, *Gradués*, iii. 363.

56. Ibid. i. 150–2, 159, 199–205.

57. Ibid. ii. 180–90.
58. Y. Leblanc, 'Pierre Buquet, bibliothécaire de l'Université de Caen . . .', *Bull. Soc. Normandie* (1961–2), 646.
59. Pialès, *Gradués*, iv. 214–18.
60. Ibid. ii. 420–1; *Le Parfait Notaire*, ii. 353–70.
61. A. H. Van der Weil, *Paul-Louis de Mondran, 1734–1795* (1962), 8–11.
62. Marais, ii. 431.
63. Ibid. ii. 62–3.
64. R.-P. Nepveu de la Manoullière, *Mémoires*, ed. G. Esnault (3 vols., 1877–9), i. 19–20.
65. Ibid. ii. 10; Marquis-Ducastel, *La Vie*, 112.
66. Schaer, *Le Clergé paroissial*, 79.
67. Guyot, xiv. 115–26.
68. Mathieu, *L'Ancien Régimen*, 114–15.
69. H. Lancelin, *Histoire du diocèse de Cambrai* (1944), 250.
70. For details on the various provinces, see Pialès, *Traité des commandes et des réserves ou des provisions des bénéfices* (3 vols., 1758), iii. 89–162.
71. B. Coolen, *Helfaut: Essai sur l'administration d'une paroisse sous l'ancien régime* (1939).
72. Guyot, xiv. 122.
73. J. Mahuas, 'Le Concours pour l'obtention des cures dans le diocèse de Vannes au XVIIIe siècle', *Méms. Soc. Bretagne* (1965), 41–52.
74. Ibid. 49–50.
75. Ch. Robert, *Urbain de Hercé, dernier évêque et comte de Dol* (1900), 44.
76. Mathieu, *L'Ancien Régime*, 115.
77. Guyot, lv. 138.
78. M. Perard-Castell, *Traité de l'usage et pratique de la Cour de Rome pour l'expédition des signatures et provisions des bénéfices de France* (2 vols., 1717), i. 70–1.
79. Guyot, iv. 144–6.
80. Pialès, *Traité des collations*, i. 436–7.
81. E. Goiffon, *Monographies paroissiales: paroisses de l'archiprêtré de Nîmes*, 2nd edn. (1898), 307.
82. Ibid. 175 ff.
83. M. Vallery-Radot, *Un Administrateur ecclésiastique à la fin de l'ancien régime: le cardinal de Luynes, archevêque de Sens, 1753–88* (1966), 89–90.
84. Guyot, xlv. 428–9, 441; Daranatz, 'Les Ordinations', 359, 368, 358.
85. Coolen, *Helfaut*, 146.
86. P.-T. Durand de Maillane, *Dictionnaire de droit canonique et de pratique bénéficiale* (2 vols., 1776), cited by L. Châtellier, 'Société et bénéfices ecclésiastiques: le cas alsacien (1670–1730)', *Rev. hist.* (1970), 76–9.
87. Berthelot du Chesnay, 'Le Clergé diocésain', 245.
88. 'Quand it vendit sa primogéniture | Esaü était affamé, | Mais quand il céda sa cure | C'est qu'il avait trop bien diné' (Marion, *Dictionnaire*, i. 45).
89. Letter to Voltaire, 29 May 1764, in la marquise du Deffand, *Correspondance complète*, ed. M. de Lescure (2 vols., 1865), i. 299.
90. A. Krieger and L. Raffin, *La Madeleine* (1937), 47.
91. Châtellier, 'Société', 76–9.
92. Krieger and Raffin, *La Madeleine*, 47–51.

93. Pierre de Vaissière, *Curés de campagne de l'ancienne France* (1933), 72.
94. Cited by Châtellier, 'Société', 81.
95. J.-J. Gautier, *Essai sur les mœurs champêtres* (1787), ed. X. Rousseau (1935), 49.
96. Ch. Bourgeat, 'À propos d'une lettre du comte de Noé', *Rev. Gascogne* (1938), 142.
97. F. Bridoux, *Histoire religieuse du département de Seine-et-Marne pendant la Révolution* (2 vols., 1953), i. 16.
98. Thesis of J. D'Audney, 'The Diocese of Auch, 1650–1730' (Bodl. Lib., 1971).
99. L. Pérouas, *Le Diocèse de la Rochelle de 1648 à 1724: sociologie et pastorale* (1964); T. J. Schmitt, *L'Organisation ecclésiastique et la pratique religieuse dans l'archidia-coné d'Autun de 1650 à 1750* (1957), p. lxvii.
100. J. R. Joly, *Histoire de la prédication* (1767), 519–22.
101. Th. Lhuillier, 'Un Curé de campagne à l'époque de la Révolution: Romain Pichonnier', *Rév. fr.* (1898), 493.
102. V. Lespay (ed.), *Un Curé Béarnais au 18ᵉ siècle: correspondance de l'abbé Tristan*, i (1879), 6–7, 85.
103. C. Baloche, *L'Église Saint-Merry de Paris: histoire de la paroisse et de la collégiale, 700–1910* (2 vols., 1911), i. 448, 563–5; ii. 4–5.
104. Marquis-Ducastel, *La Vie*, 112.
105. Nepveu de la Manoullière, *Mémoires*, ii. 118–19.
106. L. Brochard, *Saint-Gervais, histoire de la paroisse* (1950), 150–1, 154, 162.
107. Y. Castan, *Honnêteté et relations sociales en Languedoc, 1715–80* (1974), 277; A. Poitrineau, *La Vie rurale en Basse-Auvergne au XVIIIᵉ siècle* (1969), 114.
108. Gautier, *Essai*, 49.
109. Perard-Castell, *Traité*, i. 221–2.
110. Guyot, lv. 138; Perard-Castell, *Traité*, i. 210.
111. Pialès, *Traité des collations*, i. 355.
112. Guyot, xlvii. 425–41.
113. *Le Parfait Notaire*, ii. 224.
114. Guyot, xviii. 568 ff.
115. Ibid. xix. 3–4; Pialès, *Traité de la dévolution*, i. 316–18.
116. Guyot, xix. 23–8.
117. Ibid. xix. 3–4.
118. Ibid. xvii. 69.
119. Ibid. xvii. 71.
120. Ibid. xvii. 50–2.
121. Marion, *Dictionnaire*, i. 36–7.
122. Guyot, v. 144.
123. Ibid. xvii. 60–1.
124. Ibid. v. 150, xvii. 67.
125. Ibid. xvii. 63–4.
126. Ibid. xvii. 62.
127. Ibid. xvii. 69.
128. *Le Parfait Notaire*, i. 124.
129. Guyot, vi. 563; *Le Parfait Notaire*, i. 248.
130. Guyot, lxiii. 451–6.
131. Ibid. xxxiii. 424; *Le Parfait Notaire*, ii. 423–4.
132. Marais, i. 124–5.

133. Barbier, ii. 123–4.
134. Pialès, *Traité de la dévolution*, i. 437; Vaissière, *Curés*, 71.
135. Marion, *Dictionnaire*, i. 162.
136. Guyot, xvii. 36–8.
137. Ibid. xvii. 39–41.
138. L. Marcel, *Le Frère de Diderot* (1913), 53–62; Diderot, *Correspondance*, ed. G. Roth and J. Varloot (16 vols., 1955–70), i. 219–20.
139. Pialès, *Traité des collations*, i. 436–8.
140. Guyot, vii. 131–2, lii. 62–4.
141. Ibid. xvii. 41–2.
142. Marion, *Dictionnaire*, ii. 45–6.
143. E. Champion, *La France d'après les cahiers de 1789* (1921), 195–6.
144. C. H. G. B. Jourdain, *Histoire de l'Université de Paris aux XVIIᵉ et XVIIIᵉ siècles* (2 vols., 1888), i. 235. For a list of the patrons of the leading parishes of Paris, see P. de Crousaz-Crétet, *Paris sous Louis XIV* (2 vols., 1922), ii. 9.
145. e.g. Tronson, *Correspondance*, i. 454 (1681); Schaer, *Le Clergé paroissial*, 70.
146. Mathieu, *L'Ancien Régime*, 113.
147. Dom Malaret, prior of Saint-Denis, Paris, to the comte d'Angiviller, 16 Mar. 1788, in 'Les Tombes royales de Saint-Denis', *Le Cabinet historique*, 23 (1876), 144.
148. Marquis-Ducastel, *La Vie*, 110–11.
149. Le Noble, *L'École du monde* (4 vols., 1700), cited by G. Atkinson, *The Sentimental Revolution* (1965), 122.
150. J. F. Marmontel, *Mémoires*, ed. J. Renwick (2 vols., 1972) i. 35, 50–5, 83.
151. A. Monglond, *Le Préromantisme français* (2 vols., 1930), ii. 305.
152. E. Lintilhac, *Vergniaud* (1920), 1–5.
153. J.-B. Thiers, *Traité des superstitions qui regardent tous les Sacremens* (3 vols., 1704; 1st edn. 1696), iii. 403.
154. Collet, *Traité*, 201.
155. J. Brengues, *Charles Duclos* (1971), 396.
156. J. Fabre, *André Chénier* (1955), 14.
157. E. Bernstin, *Jean-Marie Roland et le Ministère de l'Intérieur 1792–93* (1964), 1.
158. A. Cournot, *Souvenirs 1760–1860*, ed. E.-P. Bottinelli (1913), 7–9.
159. R. Reuss, *La Constitution civile du clergé et la crise religieuse en Alsace* (2 vols., 1922), i. 158.
160. Pierre de Vaissière, *Gentilshommes campagnards de l'ancienne France* (1925, 1st edn. 1903), 377–8; Nepveu de la Manoullière, *Mémoires*, i. 22.
161. Marquis-Ducastel, *La Vie*, 26–56.
162. L'Abbé Baston, *Mémoires*, ed. J. Loth and Ch. Verger (3 vols., 1897–9), i. 10–38, 77–8, 152–4.
163. Lestra, *Père Coudrin*, 22, 25–6, 29–30.

CHAPTER 21

1. There were at least 770 abbeys available for the *commende* (P. T. Durand de Maillaine, *Dictionnaire de droit canonique* (4 vols., 1776), i. 2–8).
2. C. A. Sainte-Beuve, *Port-Royal*, ed. Leroy (7 vols., 1912), iii. 112.

3. J.-B. Thiers, *Histoire des perruques* (1777, orig. edn. 1689), 235–9.
4. E. and J. de Goncourt, *Sophie Arnould* (1877), 98–9.
5. M. Souvira, 'La Crise mystique du jeune Diderot', *XVIIIe Siècle* (1987), 315–26.
6. Ph. Auserve, *Delille, poète français* (n.d. [1968]), 7–31; see generally E. Guitton, *Jacques Delille et la poésie de la Nature en France, 1750–1820* (1974).
7. P. Marot, *Recherches sur la vie de François de Neufchâteau* (1960), 49–53.
8. J. F. Marmontel, *Mémoires*, ed. J. Renwick (2 vols., 1972), i. 83.
9. M. Pellisson, *Chamfort* (1895), 17. (Was he the illegitimate son of an ecclesiastic? See C. Arnaud, *Chamfort* (1988), 9, 22–25.)
10. A. Monglond, *Le Préromantisme français* (2 vols., 1930), ii. 305–6.
11. T. Morris, 'L'Abbé Desfontaines et son rôle dans la littérature de son temps', *XVIIIe Siècle* (1961), 20.
12. C. Northeast, *The Parisian Jesuits and the Enlightenment, 1700–1762* (1991), 204–5.
13. For the abbé de Fontenac (Louis-Abel Bonafons), who, after the Jesuits were suppressed, became a journalist and a right-wing propagandist during the Revolution, see W. J. Murray, *The Right-Wing Press in the French Revolution* (1986), 45–7.
14. J. Balcou, *Fréron contre les philosophes* (1975), 12–15; J. Biard-Millérioux, *L'Esthétique d'Eli-Catherine Fréron, 1739–76* (1983), 9.
15. *Encyclopédie ou dictionnaire raisonné des sciences, des arts et des métiers*, i (1751), 12–14 and xvi (1765), 'Tonsure', 413–14; L. Moréri, *Le Grand Dictionnaire historique* (1759), 17–18, copies the *Encyclopédie*; Guyot, i. 32–44; Durand de Maillaine, *Dictionnaire*, i. 42–4; A. Bergier, *Dictionnaire de théologie* (8 vols., 1830 edn.), i. 7–8, viii. 147.
16. For Noailles see B. de Lacombe, *La Résistance janséniste et parlementaire au temps de Louis XV: l'abbé Nigon de Berty, 1702–72* (1948), 24.
17. Bridard de la Garde, *Les Lettres de Thérèse*, in F. C. Green, *La Peinture des mœurs de la bonne société dans le roman français de 1715 à 1761* (1924), 112.
18. Ginguené, *Notice sur la vie de Chamfort*, in S.-R.-N. Chamfort, *Œuvres* (2 vols., 1808), i. 12.
19. L'Abbé Baston, *Mémoires*, ed. J. Loth and C. Verger (3 vols., 1897), i. 22.
20. A. Babeau (ed.), 'Lettres inédites de Grossley, 1758', *Bull. Soc. Aube* (1906), 221–5.
21. Thiers, *Histoire*, 235–9.
22. L. Tronson, *Correspondance*, ed. L. Bertrand (3 vols., 1904), i. 32.
23. B. Plongeron, *La Vie quotidienne du clergé français au 18e siècle* (1964), 81.
24. *Dictionnaire critique, pittoresque et sentencieux* (3 vols., 1768), i, 'abbé'.
25. L. Ampoulange, *Le Clergé et les élections aux États-Généraux de 1789 dans la sénéchaussée principale de Périgord* (1912), 39–46.
26. A. Cournot, *Souvenirs*, ed. E. P. Bottellini (1915), 31–2.
27. J. McManners, *Death and the Enlightenment* (1981), 270–1, 278.
28. *Archives parlementaires*, ed. J. Mavidal (82 vols., 1869–1913), v. 296 (art. 24). The Bicêtre at Paris was a combined gaol, house of correction, and poorhouse.
29. F. Tuloup, *Saint-Malo, histoire religieuse* (1975), 86.
30. Cited by R. Mauzi, *L'Idée du bonheur dans la littérature et la pensée française au XVIIIe siècle* (1960), 167. The *Dictionnaire de Trévoux* treats all abbés as 'abbés

de cour'; so does B. Guy, 'Towards an appreciation of the Abbé de cour', *Yale Fr. St.* (1968), 71–88.

31. Le duc de Broglie, *Le Secret du roi: correspondance secrète de Louis XV et ses agents diplomatiques* (2 vols., 1886), i. 27–30.

32. J. A. Véri, *Journal*, ed. J. de Witte (2 vols., n.d.), i. 7, 87; ii. 115.

33. Saint-Simon, xviii. 271, xx. 346.

34. J. A. Clarke, 'J. P. de Bignon', *Fr. Hist. St.*, viii (1973–4), 215–27; J. Le Brun, 'Censure . . . et littérature religieuse', *Rev. hist. Église Fr.* (1975), 225; D. H. Jarry, 'Le Collège Royal en 1724', *XVIIIe Siècle* (1976), 357–67.

35. P. Girault de Coursac, *L'Éducation d'un roi, Louis XVI* (1972), 193–4.

36. R. Robert, *Contes parodiques et licencieux du 18e siècle* (1987), 22–3.

37. Batteux, *Les Beaux-Arts réduits à un même système*, ed. J. R. Mantou (1990), 267.

38. R. Taton (ed.), *L'Enseignement et la diffusion des sciences en France au XVIIIe siècle* (1964), 273, 586.

39. C. H. G. B. Jourdain, *Histoire de l'Université de Paris aux XVIIe et XVIIIe siècles* (2 vols., 1862–6), ii. 275–6.

40. E. Pease Shaw, *The Case of the Abbé de Moncrif* (1953), 9–47.

41. D'Argenson, vi. 95.

42. Ibid. vii. 396.

43. A. H. Van der Weil, *Paul-Louis de Mondran, 1734–1795* (1962), 27. As a girl, Mme de Genlis saw him, and thought he would end up there (*Mémoires* (2 vols., 1825), i. 69–70).

44. J. Bouchary, *Les Faux-monnayeurs sous la Révolution française* (1946), 10, 23.

45. For their portrayal in eighteenth-century literature, E. Van der Schveren, 'Les Petits Abbés dans la France du 17e et 18e siècle', in *Études sur le 18e siècle* (1991), 166–7.

46. R. Fargher, *Life and Letters in France in the 18th Century* (1970), 7–9.

47. Saint-Simon, x. 334, xi. 106.

48. H. Boivin, 'Les Dossiers de l'abbé Desfontaines aux archives de la Bastille', *Rev. hist. litt. Fr.* (1907), 55–72.

49. D. Charlton, *Grétry and the Growth of Opéra comique* (1986), 339.

50. These two novelettes printed in R. Trousson, *Romans libertins du 18e siècle* (1993), 490 ff. For the life of Voisenon, see Grimm, xi. 150–1 (Nov. 1775); Bachaumont, vi. 132 (Apr. 1772); W. d'Ormesson, *Le Clergé et l'Académie* (1965), 20; J. Comy, *Un Abbé de cour sous Louis XV: M. de Voisenon* (1959).

51. *Rev. rétrospective* (1885), 150 ff.

52. H. Monod-Cassidy, *Un Voyageur philosophe au 18e siècle: l'abbé Jean-Bernard le Blanc* (1941); D'Argenson, vi. 16, 25.

53. G. Gaillard, *Essai sur la fable en France* (1912); Bachaumont, xxvii. 49 (3 Dec. 1782); F. Bluche, *Les Magistrats du Parlement de Paris au 18e siècle* (1956), 369–71.

54. He resigned his benefices before crossing the frontier. Ch. de Brosses, *Lettres familières* (3 vols., 1991 edn.), ii. 717.

55. [Rutlidge], *La Quinzaine Angloise à Paris* (1776), ed. A. Franklin (1902), 51–2.

56. M. de Lescure, *Les Maîtresses du Régent* (1851), 57.

57. G. Rivollet, *Adrienne Lecouvreur* (1925), 102–5.

58. C. Kunstler, *La Vie privée de Marie-Antoinette* (1938), 89.

59. E. Regnault, *Christophe de Beaumont, archevêque de Paris, 1763–81* (2 vols.,

1882), i. 508–9.

60. D'Argenson, v. 392–5.

61. Véri, *Journal*, i. 190–4.

62. J. Dusaulx, *De la passion du jeu depuis les temps anciens jusqu'à nos jours* (2 vols., 1779), i. 216; P. Barbier and F. Vermillot, *Histoire de la France par les chansons: du Jansénisme au Siècle des Lumières* (1957), 192: Voltaire, *Corresp.* viii. 36 (Dec. 1758); Bachaumont, xi. 156–7 (31 Dec. 1776).

63. Saint-Simon, *Mémoires*, ed. A. de Boislisle (41 vols., 1879–1928), xxvii. 163.

64. R. Morel, 'Les Déboires d'un précepteur au XVIIIe siècle. L'abbé Edme Mallet et la princesse de Rohan-Guémené', *Bull. Soc. Seine-et-Marne* (1908–9), 191–203.

65. For the University, J. Nowinski, *Baron Dominique Vivant Denon, 1747–1825* (1970), 20, and Morellet, next note. For battlefield, the case of the prince de Montbarey, see H. Carré, *La Noblesse de France et l'opinion publique au XVIIIe siècle* (1920).

66. L'Abbé Morellet, *Lettres*, ed. D. Medlin *et al.* (2 vols., 1991), i. pp. xxxii–xxxv. The duchesse de la Trémouille gave the abbé Foucher 1,500 livres a year, and he already had an income from the Chastellux family (J.-N. Moreau, *Mes Souvenirs*, ed. C. Hermelin (2 vols., 1892), i. 20–30).

67. H. Duranton, 'Le Métier d'historien au XVIIIe siècle', *Rev. hist. mod. contemp.* (1976), 493–8. The advantage of employing an abbé was that no retirement pension was needed (Carré, *La Noblesse*, 211).

68. J. Sgard, *Corpus Condillac, 1714–80* (1981), 67–9, 81.

69. E. Colombet (ed.), *Revue des provinces de l'Ouest*, ii (1854–5), 259–61.

70. *Souvenirs du baron de Frénilly, 1768–1828*, ed. A. Chuquet (1908), 33–45.

71. Le prince de Ligne, *Mémoires*, ed. A. Lacroix (1861), 30.

72. G. Maugras, *La Cour de Lunéville au XVIIIe siècle* (1906), 195–9. For the abbé Quesnel, see Moreau, *Mes Souvenirs*, i. 18–19.

73. L. Quérard, *La France littéraire* (2 vols., 1827–50), iii. 553, iv. 362, viii. 407.

74. Saint-Simon, xviii. 209–10.

75. Marais, ii. 6, 235.

76. Charles de Mathei, marquis de Valfons, *Souvenirs, 1710–86*, ed. le marquis de Valfons and G. Maurin (1906), 64.

77. A. Rheinwald, 'L'Abbé Huber, la psychologie d'une conversion', *Genava* (1927), 93 ff.; H. Lüthy, *La Banque Protestante en France, de la révocation de l'édit de Nantes à la Révolution* (2 vols., 1961), ii. 68, 219–22.

78. *Journal du duc de Croy, 1718–84*, ed. le vicomte de Grouchy and P. Cottin (4 vols., 1906), ii. 86.

79. Ch. Collé, *Journal historique, 1761–3*, ed. A. J. van Bever (1911), 157–65.

80. E. Dard, *Le Général Choderlos de Laclos, auteur des 'Liaisons dangereuses', 1741–1803* (1936), 147–8.

81. E. S. Mercier, *Tableau de Paris* (12 vols., 1782–8), i. 268. There is an abbé at a lady's *lever* in Badouin's picture *Le Matin*. The puritanical curé Thiers has a diatribe against priests serving as 'domestiques'—business agents, household managers, valets, butlers, horse-dealers, huntsmen, and the mysterious and no doubt disreputable category of 'Quinola' (slang for the knave of hearts) (J. B. Thiers, *Superstitions anciennes et nouvelles* (2 vols., 1732), ii. 250).

82. Cited by J. Fabre, *Lumières et Romantisme* (1963), 142–7.

83. A. Lombard, *L'Abbé Dubos* (1913), 146, 168.

84. Batteux, *Les Beaux-Arts*, 256–7.
85. J. Jacquart, *L'Abbé Trublet, critique et moraliste, 1697–1770* (1926), 101, 121–2, 399.
86. E. Harrisse, *L'Abbé Prévost; histoire de sa vie et de ses œuvres* (1896), 61–2; P. Trahard, *Les Maîtres de la sensibilité française au XVIIIe siècle* (4 vols., 1931–3), i. 91–5. For Maydieu, a tutor, a canon of Troyes and correspondent of Rousseau, see P.-M. Masson, *La Religion de Rousseau* (3 vols., 1916), iii. 176–7.
87. For Saint-Pierre's ordination, J. Drouet, *The Abbé de Saint-Pierre* (1912), 15. For Raynal, H. Jürgen, Lüsebrock, and Tietz, *Lectures de Raynal*, S.V.E.C. (1991), introduction. When called 'ce bougre de prêtre', Desfontaines replied, 'Monsieur, je ne suis pas prêtre'. But this is contradicted by his formal statement to the police when he was arrested for homosexual rape in 1725 (Boivin, 'Les Dossiers').
88. Paul d'Estrée, 'La Mort de l'abbé Desfontaines', *Rev. hist. litt. Fr.* (1908), 126–8.
89. D'Argenson, iv. 65 (May 1743).
90. Grimm, ii. 453 (Dec. 1754). Terrasson died in 1750.
91. R. Granderoute, *Le Roman pédagogique de Fénelon à Rousseau* (2 vols., 1985), i. 305–6, 327; ii. 1070.
92. Sgard, *Corpus Condillac*, 39–68.
93. D'Haussonville, *Le Salon de Mme Necker* (2 vols., 1882), i. 139–40.
94. J. Lough, 'Who were the Philosophes?', in J. M. Fox *et al.* (eds.), *Studies in 18th Century French Literature . . . Robert Niklaus* (1975), 139 ff.
95. A. Jobert, *Magnats polonais et physiocrates français, 1762–1771* (1941), 29.
96. E. Lavaquery (ed.), *Lettres de Piron à Jean-François Le Vayer* (1921), 53 (29 Dec. 1751).
97. C. Daux, *Une Réhabilitation: l'abbé Jean-Martin de Prades* (1902); J. Spink, 'Un Abbé philosophe: l'affaire de l'abbé de Prades', *XVIIIe Siècle* (1971), 145–73; N. Noël, *Une Figure énigmatique parmi les encyclopédistes: l'abbé de Prades* (1973); J. Combes-Malaville, 'Vues nouvelles sur l'abbé de Prades', *XVIIIe Siècle* (1988), 377–97.
98. See V. Pinot, *La Chine et la formation de l'esprit philosophique en France* (1932), as corrected by Northeast, *Parisian Jesuits*, 119–23. Northeast shows the Jesuits facing the contradiction honestly; Prades could well have been following them.
99. J. Renwick, *Marmontel: The Formative Years* (S.V.E.C., 1970), 198–210. The Sorbonne was foolish to allow its list of condemned propositions to be published, for some were unexceptionable (id., 'Marmontel et *Bélisaire*', in J. Ehrard (ed.), *J.-F. Marmontel 1723–99: études* (1972), 63–4).
100. Marmontel, *Mémoires*, ii. 18–21.
101. A sad case of such hero worship in P. Dupont, *Un Poète philosophe: Houdar de la Motte* (1898), 188.
102. J. Ehrard, *L'Idée de Nature en France dans la première moitié du XVIIIe siècle* (2 vols., 1963), ii. 715–17.
103. Fréron's own account in G. Desnoiresterres, *Voltaire et la société française au XVIIIe siècle*, 2nd edn. (8 vols., 1867–76), v. 45–72, 489–90.
104. F. A. and S. L. Kafker, *The Encyclopedists as Individuals: A Biographical Dictionary of the Authors of the* Encyclopédie (1988).

105. L. A. Segal, 'Lenglet du Fresnoy: The Treason of a Cleric', *S.V.E.C.* (1973), 278.

106. R. Hubert, *Les Sciences sociales dans* l'Encyclopédie (1923), 18–19; J. Proust, *Diderot et* l'Encyclopédie (1967), 18–22.

107. J. F. Combes-Malaville, 'L'Incarcération de l'abbé de Prades à Magdebourg', *XVIIIe Siècle* (1993), 338–53.

108. L. Gossman, *Medievalism and the Ideologies of the Enlightenment* (1968), 314; L. Brunel, *Les Philosophes et l'Académie* (1884), 341.

109. R. Darnton, *The Literary Underworld of the Old Régime* (1982), 5.

110. P. Grosclaude, *Malesherbes, témoin et interprète de son temps* (1961), 90–1.

111. J. Wogue, *J.-B.-L. Gresset* (1894), 222–3.

112. G. Wilson, *A Medievalist in the 18th Century: Le Grand d'Aussy and the Fabliaux* (1975), 3–4, 7.

113. M. Badolle, *L'Abbé Jean-Jacques Barthélemy, 1716–1795* (n.d. [1927]), 100, 230–53.

114. G. Bonno (ed.), *Correspondance littéraire de Suard avec le Margrave de Bayreuth*, University of California Publications in Modern Philology (1934), 225 (Oct. 1775).

115. F. de Dainville, *Cartes anciennes de l'Église de France* (1956), 75; Jourdain, *Histoire*, ii. 275–6; C. Chaudon-Adhémar, 'Le Voyage en Sibérie de Chappe d'Auteroche', *XVIIIe Siècle* (1964), 274–94; J. M. Racault, 'L'Observation du passage de Vénus sur le soleil', *XVIIIe Siècle* (1990), 107–20.

116. Bachaumont, iv. 106 (6 Sept. 1768); xxvi. 214–15 (27 Sept. 1784); xxvi. 82–108 (July 1784).

117. E. Esmonin, 'L'Abbé Expilly et ses travaux de statistique', in his *Études sur la France des 17e et 18e siècles* (1964), 274–94.

118. D. Mornet, *Les Sciences de la Nature en France au XVIIIe siècle* (1911), 87; C. Kiernan, *The Enlightenment and Science in 18th Century France* (1973), 154–5.

119. A. Vartarnian, 'Le Frère de Maupertuis', *XVIIIe Siècle* (1982), 305–22.

120. Quérard, *La France littéraire*, i. 32; ii. 158, 193; iii. 54; iv. 572; vii. 472–3.

121. Grimm, viii. 276.

122. D. Lynham, *The Father of Modern Ballet: The Chevalier Noverre* (1950), 55–6; J. Seznec and J. Adhémar, *Diderot, Salons I, 1759–61–63* (1957), 32.

123. Guy, 'Towards an Appreciation', 86. For Allainval see F.C.B.'s edn. of his *École des bourgeois* (1937).

124. Quérard, *La France littéraire*, viii. 191.

125. H. C. Lancaster, *French Tragedy . . . 1715–75* (2 vols., 1977), i. 219–20.

126. *Anecdotes dramatiques* (4 vols., 1775), i. 486–7. Racine first made the joke— to Boileau, 4 Aug. 1695. In the *Apocrypha*, Judith cuts off the head of the Assyrian general Holofernes.

127. *Année littéraire*, 1758, 1760, in C. Barthélemy, *Les Confessions de Fréron* (1876). See also Biard-Milléroux, *L'Esthétique*, 26, 517, 524 and Balcou, *Fréron*, 469. (I have counted the abbé d'Olivet of the Academy as an official apologist. His translation of Cicero's *De natura deorum* was accompanied by notes and an essay refuting its anti-Christian implications. See for him A. C. Kors, *Atheism in France, 1650–1729* (1990), 208–17.

128. Biard-Milléroux, *L'Esthétique*, 524.

129. D. Gembicki, *Histoire et politique à la fin de l'ancien régime: Jacob-Nicolas Moreau, 1717–1803* (1976), 71–3, 82–3. Moreau's *Nouveau mémoire pour servir*

à l'histoire des Cacouacs has been reprinted by Slatkine from the 1828 edn. (1968). The abbé de Saint-Cyr is said to have been a minor chaplain at Versailles.

130. Pluche, *Spectacle de la Nature* (9 vols., 1750 edn.), viii (2), 169 ff.

131. A. Viala, 'Les Idées de l'abbé Pluche sur la société', in A. Viala and M. Labriolle (eds.), *La Régence*, Colloque, Aix-en-Provence 1968 (1970), 308 ff.

132. W. Folkierski, *Entre le Classicisme et le Romantisme: étude sur l'esthétique et les esthéticiens du XVIIIᵉ siècle* (1969), 39 ff.

133. See Lombard, *Dubos*.

134. De la Brétèche, *Saint-Non et Fragonard* (1928); and L. Mascoli, 'Le *Journal du voyage* en Italie de l'abbé de Saint-Non, 1759–61', *XVIIIᵉ Siècle* (1989), 423–38.

135. Lombard, *Dubos*, 51. He was an austere critic, wanting opera shorn of its 'machines', suitable only to impress 'les garçons de boutique nouvellement arrivés à Paris'.

136. J. Chouillet, *La Formation des idées esthétiques de Diderot, 1745–63* (1973), 239, 283.

137. H. J. Martin, *Livre, pouvoir et société à Paris au XVIIᵉ siècle* (2 vols., 1969), ii. 909–19.

138. J. Lough, 'Chaudon's Dictionnaire anti-philosophique', in P. J. Howells *et al.* (eds.), *Studies . . . W. H. Barber* (1985), 307–27. For the *honnête homme* tradition see Ch. 31 below.

139. Mauzi, *L'Idée du bonheur*, 185–6, 387, 401.

140. Aubert, a *tonsuré*, taught much the same lesson in his eight volumes of fables, progressive in politics, prudential in morals. See J. N. Pascal (ed.), *La Fable au siècle des Lumières* (1991), 23 ff.

141. Northeast, *Parisian Jesuits*, 28. The basic discussion is in Cl. Labrosse, 'Les *Mémoires de Trévoux* et le roman, 1730–40', in H. Duranton (ed.), *Études sur la presse au XVIIIᵉ siècle* (1973).

142. Green, *La Peinture*, 20–7.

143. Morris, 'L'Abbé Desfontaines', 174–5, 178.

144. S. Etienne, *Le Genre romanesque en France depuis la parution de la 'Nouvelle Héloïse' jusqu'aux approches de la Révolution* (1922), 171–2, 337.

145. To Delille, the Christian hopes for resurrection, but the consoler is Nature: 'Eh qui n'a pas pleuré quelque perte cruelle? | Loin d'un monde léger, venez donc à vos pleurs, | Venez associer les bois, les eaux, les fleurs. | Tout devient un ami pour les âmes sensibles' (*Les Jardins, ou l'art d'embellir les paysages* (1782), in *Œuvres* (9 vols., 1825), i. 85–6).

146. McManners, *Death*, ch. 10.

GENERAL INDEX

corvées (labour dues) 109–10, 168
Cotte, Robert de 42, 439, 444
coucher, and Louis XV 43–4
Couet, Bernard, abbé 264
Counter-Reformation:
  and charitable institutions 554
  and clergy 3, 348, 360, 615
  and education 516, 533, 546
  and seminaries 198
  and worship 436, 440
Couperin, François II 461, 462, 469
Cournot, A. 369, 395, 652
Court, *see* Versailles
courtesans 239
courts, ecclesiastical 186, 192–8, 223
  and cathedral chapters 400
  and dispensations 108, 195
  and law enforcement 88–9, 91
  officialité diocésaine 179, 192–8, 272, 361
  officialité foraine 193
  officialité métropolitaine/archiépiscopale 192,
    193, 194
  officialité primatiale 193
  powers 196–7
courts, secular
  and bishops 249–50, 254, 266, 354
  and convents 494, 500
  and ecclesiastical courts 25, 156–7, 195,
    361–2
  and General Assembly 156–7
  and marriage 157, 195–6
  and religious Orders 571
  see also *bailliage* court; parlement
courts, seigneurial 108, 111
courts, sovereign:
  and *conseillers clercs* 59–60, 146
  and tithes 139–40
Coustou, Guillaume 42, 437, 444, 557
Coutances diocese:
  and bishops 247, 248, 287, 621
  and clergy 329, 337, 390, 414
  and *conférences ecclésiastiques* 283, 284–5
  and ecclesiastical courts 193
  and maps 262
  and music 451, 453–5
  and parishes 621, 622
  and *prêtres habitués* 394
  and religious Orders 116, 586
  and synods 279–80, 282
  and visitations 268
Couturier, M., Superior of Saint-Sulpice
  50, 231
Coyer, Gabriel-François, abbé 524, 662,
  666

Coypel, Nöel 42
Coysevoix, Antoine 42, 444
crime:
  blasphemy 75–6, 77–8, 195
  and *monitoire* 91–4
  murder 195, 353, 407
  sacrilege 75–9, 195
  theft 76, 77
Croÿ, Emmanuel, duc de 8, 45, 48
curés:
  and bishops 158, 280–2, 286–9
  and career 1–2, 620–1
    appointment 628–34, 640–1
    qualifications 3, 328, 350–1, 625–6
  and diocese:
    and bishop 3, 280–2, 286–9, 362, 363
    and cathedral chapters 430–3
    conférences ecclésiastiques 283–5, 288,
      365, 584
    curé primitif 431
    and religious Orders 494, 506, 529,
      572, 576, 587
    removal from cure 361–2
    synods 280–2
    visitations 190, 270–1, 274–7
  and family 1–2, 386, 617, 632, 634
  and General Assemblies:
    and freehold 361
    representation 144–5, 147, 430
  income 64, 124, 138, 217, 299, 324,
    326–7, 330–46, 359, 620
    and property 100–1, 103–4, 106, 121,
      331–2
    and taxation 156, 170, 171, 345
    and tithe 122–8, 134–5, 137, 139,
      166, 300, 308, 325, 330–5, 338,
      384, 389
    see also *congrue*
  le bon curé 358–83
    dignity and status 358–64
    generosity 370–3, 380–3
    moral reformation 364–70
    and seigneur 373–80
  mentality 346–57
    as authors 351, 355–6
    and journalism 353–4
    reading matter 346–8, 354, 365
    and reform 3, 352
    as teachers 350–1
  and *monitoires* 91–4
  and parish:
    administration 303
    church maintenance 312
    churchwardens 306–7

and official ceremonial 16
and parishes 300
and property rights 114
and republicanism 22
and seigneurs 379–80
and taxation 164
and tithes 140
Frères des écoles Chrétiennes 198, 420,
    473, 475, 515, 529–33
Frères de Saint-Jean-de-Dieu 510, 513–14,
    515–16
Fréron, Élie-Catherine 649–50, 662, 669,
    676–7
Froger, L. 104, 349–50, 352
funerals 195, 308, 338–9, 367
  at sea 63–4
  royal 35, 36, 48
  and surplice-fees 337–40

gabelle (salt tax) 171, 181, 258, 299
Gallican Church:
  bureaucracy 143–4, 150–4, 156, 163,
      188
  central direction 143, 159, 185, 219
  and change 2
  and Four Gallican Articles 20
  and infallibility 205–6
  and interests of the monarchy 58, 121,
      141
  liberties 582, 622, 630, 636
  and primacy 186–8, 193
  and secular society 3–4
  and sovereignty 10, 12, 13, 14
  see also bishops; Church–State relations;
      dioceses; General Assemblies of the
      clergy; parishes; wealth
Gap diocese:
  and chapters 401
  and curés 92–3, 329–30, 337, 343
  and seminaries 201
Gautier, J.-J. 305, 356, 377–8, 393
General Assemblies of clergy 141–73
  agents généraux, see agent-general
  and appointments to benefices 636–7,
      640
  assemblée extraordinaire 146, 159, 162, 171
  and bishops 158, 186, 188, 237
  and *Bureau de l'agence* 151
  bureaucracy 143–4, 150–4, 156, 163,
      188
  and charitable donations 163
  and clerical ambition 148
  and *congrue* 335
  and decline of religion 157–8

and dioceses 216, 271
and doctrine 159–60
and freehold 361
Grande and *Petite Assemblée* 146, 150
and *grands vicaires* 147–8, 153, 192
and grievances 141, 156–7, 162, 188
and heresy 15
and Jansenism 157, 159, 160
and leadership 188
and monarchy 20–1, 24–6, 141, 143–4,
    148–9
procedure 149–50
and religious observance 82
and religious Orders 571, 607, 614
and representation 144–5, 146–8, 152,
    227
and rights of the Church 24–5
and sceptical literature 264
and taxation 141–6, 149, 150–1, 154–6,
    157, 158–9, 160–3, 166–7, 169–72,
    732 n. 66
and tithes 132, 138–9
see also *syndics*
Genlis, Stéphanie-Félicité du Crest, Mme
    de 489, 577, 661, 780 n.43
Génovéfains:
  and almsgiving 506
  and Commission des réguliers 584–5,
      608, 613
Gilles, Jean 447, 469
Girac, François Bareau de, bishop of
    Rennes 153, 248, 257, 271–2
Glandève diocese:
  and bishops 213, 220, 244
  and chapter 178, 399, 401
  and size 178, 180
  and taxation 155, 156
glass 440–1, 443, 444
godparents:
  and church bells 317
  and spiritual affinity 69, 195
Good Friday, Court ceremonies 31
Gossec, François-Joseph 469–70
grace, royal 36
grand aumônier 7, 29–30, 31, 33, 34, 43
  and Court factions 47
  and precedence 36
  and royal *lever* and *coucher* 29, 44
  and royal patronage 49
Grandmontins 166, 574–5, 611
grands jours 302
grands vicaires (vicars-general):
  aristocratic 211, 214, 215, 222, 225–7,
      232–4, 241, 287–8

To Jim

John Man is a historian and travel writer with a special interest in Mongolia and the history of written communication. His *Gobi: Tracking the Desert* was the first book on the subject in English since the 1920s. He is also the author of *The Atlas of the Year 1000*, *Alpha Beta*, on the roots of the Roman alphabet, and *The Gutenberg Revolution*, on the origins and impact of printing. His books *Genghis Khan: Life, Death and Resurrection* and *Attila the Hun* are available in Bantam paperback.

With thanks &
best wishes,

JM.

www.booksattransworld.co.uk

KUBLAI KHAN

From Xanadu to Superpower

JOHN MAN

BANTAM PRESS

LONDON · TORONTO · SYDNEY · AUCKLAND · JOHANNESBURG

TRANSWORLD PUBLISHERS
61–63 Uxbridge Road, London W5 5SA
a division of The Random House Group Ltd

RANDOM HOUSE AUSTRALIA (PTY) LTD
20 Alfred Street, Milsons Point, Sydney,
New South Wales 2061, Australia

RANDOM HOUSE NEW ZEALAND LTD
18 Poland Road, Glenfield, Auckland 10, New Zealand

RANDOM HOUSE SOUTH AFRICA (PTY) LTD
Isle of Houghton, Corner of Boundary Road & Carse O'Gowrie,
Houghton 2198, South Africa

Published 2006 by Bantam Press
a division of Transworld Publishers

A catalogue record for this book is available from the British Library.
ISBN 978 0593 054482 (cased) (from Jan 07)
ISBN 0593 054482 (cased)
ISBN 978 0593 054499 (tpb) (from Jan 07)
ISBN 0593 054490 (tpb)

Typeset in 11½/14½pt Sabon by
Falcon Oast Graphic Art Ltd

Printed in Great Britain by
Mackays of Chatham plc, Chatham, Kent

1 3 5 7 9 10 8 6 4 2

Papers used by Transworld Publishers are natural, recyclable products made from
wood grown in sustainable forests. The manufacturing processes conform to the
environmental regulations of the country of origin.

CONTENTS

KUBLAI IN CONTEXT

This diagram shows, in simplified form, the main characters mentioned in this book,
their relationships, their domains and a rough chronological sequence (GREAT KHANS in CAPITALS).

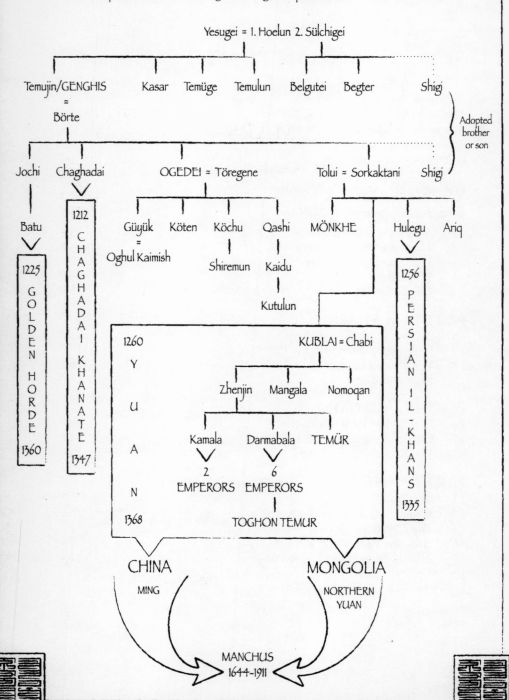

Yesugei ≈ 1. Hoelun 2. Sülchigei

Temujin/GENGHIS   Kasar   Temüge   Temulun   Belgutei   Begter   Shigi
≈
Börte

Adopted brother or son

Jochi   Chaghadai   OGEDEI ≈ Töregene   Tolui ≈ Sorkaktani   Shigi

Batu   1212 CHAGHADAI KHANATE 1347

Güyük   Köten   Köchu   Qashi   MÖNKHE   Hulegu   Ariq
≈
Oghul Kaimish   Shiremun   Kaidu

1225 GOLDEN HORDE 1360

1256 PERSIAN IL-KHANS 1335

Kutulun

1260 Y U A N 1368

KUBLAI ≈ Chabi

Zhenjin   Mangala   Nomoqan

Kamala   Darmabala   TEMÜR

2 EMPERORS   6 EMPERORS

TOGHON TEMUR

CHINA
MING

MONGOLIA
NORTHERN YUAN

MANCHUS
1644-1911

MAPS

ILLUSTRATIONS

Pages with no images credited are all © John Man.

FIRST SECTION
Pages 2 and 3
Tolui and his family, from *Jami al-Tawarikh* by Rashid al-Din, fourteenth-century, Ms sup. pers. 1113 f. 164v, Bibliothèque Nationale, Paris; Karakorum, © Dean Conger/Corbis.

Pages 4 and 5
Alamut: Simon Richmond/Lonely Planet Images; Hassan i Sabbah leading the initiations at Alamut, manuscript illumination by the Boucicaut Master (*fl.*1390–1430): Bibliothèque Nationale, Paris/Bridgeman Art Library; Mongols storming and capturing Baghdad in 1288, from *Jami al-Tawarikh* by Rashid al-Din, fourteenth-century, Ms sup. pers. 1113 f. 180v-181, Bibliothèque Nationale, Paris/Bridgeman Art Library; Mönkhe Khan holds a feast at Karakorum: sixteenth-century illustration of a fourteenth-century Persian history of the Mongols, Werner Forman Archive/Gulistan Library, Teheran.

SECOND SECTION
Pages 2 and 3
Kublai Khan's armies lay siege to the Chinese fortress of O-Chou across a pontoon over the Yangtse River: sixteenth-century illustration of a fourteenth-century Persian history of the Mongols, Werner Forman Archive/Gulistan Library, Teheran;

THIRD SECTION
Page 1
Inset, explosive shell, © John Man; Japanese Invasion Scroll: both courtesy The Art Archive.

Pages 2 and 3
Japanese Invasion Scroll: courtesy The Art Archive; all other photos © John Man.

Pages 4 and 5
Kublai Khan hunting and portrait of Chabi, National Palace Museum, Taipei; portrait of Kublai Khan: courtesy The Art Archive.

Pages 6 and 7
Kublai Khan and the Polo brothers from an illuminated manuscript of 1375, Bibliothèque Nationale, Paris (MS 2810)/akg-images; paiza, © John Man; illumination from the *Chronica Major* of Matthew Paris, Corpus Christi College, Cambridge, MS 16 f. 166v; details from Giotto's *Resurrection*, c.1305, Arena Chapel, Padua, © Photo Scala, Florence; autograph manuscript of Samuel Taylor Coleridge, *Kubla Khan*, 1798, © The British Library Add. Mss. 50847/Heritage Image Partnership; illustration to *Kubla Khan* from A. C. Michael, *A Day With Samuel Taylor Coleridge*, 1912, Mary Evans Picture Library; other photos © John Man.

A NOTE ON SPELLING

The two main systems of transliterating Chinese, Wade–Giles and pinyin, still overlap. Although pinyin is now standard usage, I have used whichever seems more appropriate in each case, keeping the older spelling for names that have become most familiar to western readers in that form as well as for those that appear in a more remote historical context.

Spellings of personal names vary widely. For ease of reading, I have in this book used the more familiar form 'Kublai' rather than, for example, 'Khubilai', 'Qubilai' or 'Kubla'.

'Genghis' is still the most common spelling in English, though the more correct 'Chingis' is coming up fast.

ACKNOWLEDGEMENTS

With thanks to: Charles Bawden, who started it all; Anne Cullen, who introduced me to Zhao Mengfu; Chuluun Dalai, Mongolian Academy of Sciences; Paul Denney and Julie Douglass, for opening the world of trebuchets; Yuefan Deng, Stonybrook University, NY; Luc Kwanten and Lilly Chen, Big Apple-Tuttle Mori, Shanghai; Shizuya Nishimura, Professor Emeritus, Hosei University, Tokyo; Benjamin Ren, for hospitality at Shang-du (Xanadu); Professor Yao Dali, History Department, Fudan University, Shanghai; Yuan-chu Ruby Lam, Department of Chinese, Wellesley College, MA; Igor de Rachewiltz, School of Pacific and Asian Studies, Australian National University, for vital and unstinting guidance through the fog of ignorance; Randall Sasaki, Texas A&M University, for an initial introduction to Kublai's lost fleet, and Kenzo Hayashida, who generously showed me the remains of the Japanese wall in Fukuoka and the finds made by him and his colleagues off Takashima; 'William' Shou (Wei Zhong) and Shijun Cheng, for the Xanadu trip; Helen Tang, the best of Chinese teachers; Jack Weatherford, Macalester College, Minnesota; Doug Young, Simon Thorogood and all at Transworld; Gillian Somerscales, for brilliant editing; and as ever, Felicity Bryan, Michelle Topham *et al*.

KUBLAI KHAN

PROLOGUE:
TO GENGHIS, A GRANDSON

IN 1215, THE WORLD WAS NOT A JOINED-UP PLACE. PEOPLE AND animals alike travelled at an amble. It took days to reach the next town, weeks to cross a country. The great continental land masses were island universes, knowing next to nothing of each other. No-one went from Asia to Australia, except a few inhabitants of Sulawesi, who crossed the Timor Sea to collect sea-cucumbers, then as now a delicacy much in demand in China. No-one from Eurasia visited the Americas, except a few Inuit paddling back and forth across the Bering Strait. In Greenland, communities of Norwegians were thriving in a long warm spell that kept their seas ice-free for a few crucial months, but these hardy voyagers had never been tempted to repeat their forefathers' brief attempt at colonizing the American mainland two centuries before. Ships hugged shorelines; with the remarkable exception of Polynesian canoes island-hopping the Pacific, few yet tackled the open oceans.

But there were signs, if not of globalization, then at least of regionalization. Europe and Asia had a head start, because they were two continents in one. The links between them had once been forged by great empires and cultures: Rome, Persia, China. Now they were forged by religion.

In Europe, Christian scholars from Ireland (and even Iceland) chatted in Latin to their counterparts in Rome, and architects from Assisi to York vied for glory with flying buttresses and tracery; in Reims, they were five years into the creation of one of France's greatest Gothic cathedrals. The church had found new muscle, having ruined much of southern France in a vicious crusade to wipe out the heretical Albigensians. That year the pope condemned them at the 4th Lateran Council (which also, by the way, excommunicated the English barons who had just forced King John to sign away some of his divine right in the Magna Carta).

Europe was reaching outwards as well: a certain Albert, from Buxtehude in north Germany, pushing Christianity into the Baltic regions, had just founded Riga, where he put on a biblical play with the aim of converting the locals. It was the first play the Latvians had ever seen. When Gideon attacked the Philistines on stage, they thought it was for real, and fled for their lives. The same church council that castigated the Albigensians also looked south-east beyond the borders of European Christendom, where there lay a constant affront to Christian sensibilities: Islamic control of what Christians called the Holy Land. There would have to be yet another crusade.

Crusaders had been forging rather unwelcome links between Christian Europe and the Islamic Middle East for over a century, building Christian enclaves in present-day Syria, Lebanon and Israel. Nor was all the hostility directed against the 'heathen'. Nine years earlier, soldiers of the Fourth Crusade, supposedly on their way to Egypt, had shown themselves to be particularly cynical by seizing Constantinople from its Orthodox rulers. In 1215 they held it still, steadily undermining all hopes of a unified Christendom.

Islam, though, was now more than a match for Christianity. Scholars and traders could travel from Spain, across north Africa and the Middle East to Central Asia, and find common roots in Islam's 500-year-old religious community, in 'God's tongue' (Arabic), in the Qur'an and in trade – in slaves, for instance, and gold, both of which flowed from sub-Saharan Africa. A Muslim merchant could travel from Timbuktu to Delhi and be sure of finding some like-minded trader there; and if he went via Baghdad, as he would because it was the heart of Islam, he would mix with Jews, Zoroastrians, Manicheans and Christians of many sects – Nestorians, Monophysites, Gnostics and the Greek Orthodox. Arab captains found it worthwhile to sail the coasts for a year or two all the way to southern China to load up with silks and porcelain.

As for overland links between west and east, they had once been much stronger, thanks to the trade routes known as the Silk Road. Now fewer camel trains made the six-month haul between the world of Islam and China. The Mongols under Genghis Khan had recently assaulted the key Buddhist state of Xi Xia, north of Tibet, in present-day Xinjiang, and few had faith that camel caravans would get through unscathed.

The connections were all very tenuous. But these places and cultures, so distant from each other in time and space, were about to be jolted together, thanks to two events occurring that very year.

The first was a great assault against the major city of north China, today's Beijing. The besiegers were the Mongols, led by Genghis Khan. Genghis had risen from nowhere and nothing – a down-and-out fugitive, in fact – to found a nation, and was now seeking to fulfil his destiny. Having survived many a close call in his youth, he had realized, much to his surprise, that he had been chosen by Heaven to rule. To

3

rule what and whom, exactly? Certainly, his own Mongols. But then, as conquest followed conquest, he saw that the domain accorded him by his divine brief was wider. How wide? North China? Probably. *All* China, although no nomad power had ever managed it? Possibly.

North China, the source of wealth and power, had always lured warrior nomads from beyond the Gobi desert, and had always done its best to defend itself – with walls, armies, bribery, diplomacy and marriages. North China was the traditional enemy, the key to wider empire, and Beijing, the seat of the region's Jin rulers, was the key to north China. It should have fallen the previous year, after a series of long campaigns during which Genghis had neutralized the Tangut empire of Xi Xia and invaded, devastating much of the country north of the Yellow River and besieging Beijing until the Jin emperor capitulated. In 1214 Genghis had left Beijing untaken and unpillaged, thinking that he had a new vassal – only to discover, when the Mongol armies withdrew to the grasslands, that the Jin emperor had decamped, with 3,000 camels and 30,000 cartloads of possessions, to the ancient Chinese capital of Kaifeng, well south of the Yellow River.

Genghis was furious. 'The Jin Emperor mistrusts my word!' he stormed. 'He has used the peace to deceive me!'

Now the Mongols were back, and this time there would be no let-up until Beijing fell, and the whole empire of Jin was Mongol. All through the winter of 1214–15 the Mongol army blockaded the city. There would be no outright assault, for Beijing was too formidable, with 15 kilometres of walls, 900 guard-towers, catapults that could throw boulders and fire-bombs, and vast siege bows that could fire arrows the size of telegraph poles. No: Beijing would be starved into surrender.

So it happened. On 31 May Beijing opened its gates. In the subsequent onslaught, many thousands died; fires burned for a month. A year later, there were still bodies lying about, and disease ran wild. A Muslim envoy reported that the ground remained greasy with human fat.

The fall of Beijing in 1215 unlocked a series of events that changed the course of Eurasian history. It was not yet the end for north China, because Genghis was distracted from his assault by events further west. Four years later a trade delegation to the new Islamic state of Khwarezm was slaughtered in its entirety. With north China neutralized, Genghis was free to turn on his western neighbours in swift vengeance, unleashing devastation on an unprecedented scale and razing the old Silk Road cities of Bukhara, Samarkand, Merv and Urgench. Then he sanctioned an extraordinary campaign of reconnaissance across Georgia and Ukraine, the opening phase of 200 years of Mongol rule in southern Russia. Only when his men returned from this great adventure did Genghis turn once again to the lands across the Gobi. In the summer of 1227, extending his campaign into mountains south of the Yellow River, he died.

His great task remained unfinished. Much of the Islamic world, including Baghdad itself, was still unconquered, as were the Russian steppes, and the remaining pockets of north China, and all of south China – a separate state ruled by the Song dynasty – and beyond that the outlying peoples who must, inevitably, acknowledge the overlordship of Genghis: those on the eastern rim of the Mongol empire (Korea and Japan) and those to the south (present-day Cambodia, Vietnam and Burma) and all those beyond across the rich islands of Indonesia, while way to the west, the Hungarian grasslands would surely be a highway into Christian Europe.

This was the Mongols' Heaven-ordained destiny. Why this should be, Genghis never fathomed, nor did his heirs; they simply accepted that it was so.

Much unfinished business, then: but already on his death Genghis had transformed his world. Never before had East and West been so tightly linked. Mongolian generals now had intimate knowledge of the rivalries of Russian princes, and how to divide them further when the time came. Express riders galloping some 150 kilometres a day, with numerous changes of mount, could deliver a message over the 4,000 kilometres from Beijing to Afghanistan in six weeks, an operation made possible by Mongol control of all the land in between.

What, then, might not be achieved, given an extension of this empire? Traders would bring the wealth of East and West, artists would flock to serve the World-Conqueror, clerics of every religion would bring their insights, scholars would collect and translate books from the greatest libraries, embassies would arrive from rulers of East and West to offer their submissions. The world would be one under Heaven, and at peace. Such was the vision that filled the minds of Genghis's heirs.

It was, of course, a hopeless dream, as time would show. Like all empires, this one would reach limits, divide against itself, and dissolve.

But on 23 September 1215, almost four months after Beijing fell, back in the Mongolian heartland, a royal child was born who, as khan of khans, the Great Khan, would accept the challenge of Genghis's impossible vision and do more than any other leader to make it a reality. With an authority that reached, albeit shakily, from the Pacific to southern Russia, he would become the most powerful man who had ever lived – who *would* ever live until the emergence of the modern super-powers. He would hold nominal sway over one-fifth of the world's populated land masses, perhaps half of all humanity. His name would spread far beyond the areas he conquered, to Europe, to Japan, to Vietnam, to Indonesia: those sea-cucumber gatherers, harvesting their delicacies off northern Australia, would perhaps hear of his attempt to invade Java in 1292. It was the legend of his wealth that, two centuries after his death, would inspire Columbus to head westward on a voyage that ended, not in a new route to an ancient land, but in the chance rediscovery of one long forgotten. Had he not existed, had there been no Mongol empire in China, who, I wonder, would have rediscovered America?

The Great Khan's legacy was an enlarged and unified China, with its present-day borders, give or take a few bits and pieces round the edge. By a strange irony, one of those bits is Mongolia itself, the Great Khan's country of birth. It is a truth only grudgingly acknowledged in China that today's superpower owes its self-image as a geographical entity – the dusty north, the lush south, the huge western deserts, the high fastness of Tibet – to the Mongolian baby born in the year of Beijing's destruction.

The boy was Genghis's grandson, Kublai.

I

SPRING

1

A LIONESS AND HER CUBS

ONE THING YOU NOTICE IN MONGOLIA: THE WOMEN COMMAND attention. In the countryside, crones with walnut faces skewer you with direct, self-confident eyes; tough, red-cheeked girls ride like master-horsemen. In Ulaanbaatar, the capital, you cannot walk from the main square to the department store (there is only one) without passing a beauty radiating elegance, and proud of it. They have a bearing, an assurance, that is more New York than Beijing. Not all, of course, because Mongolia has its share of poverty. But for centuries Mongolia's nomadic, herding traditions ensured that women matched their men in self-reliance. Even today, country women not only cook and mend and raise the children – they hunt and herd if they have to. One of Genghis Khan's decrees reflected an everyday reality: 'Women accompanying the troops carry out the work and duties of the men when these go to war.' They fought as well. In 1220, Genghis's daughter led the final assault on the Persian town of Nishapur, slaying 'all the survivors save only 400 persons who were selected for their craftsmanship'.[1] In family life and in politics alike women have always been a force. Inheritance was through the male line, but widows – upper-class widows, that is – could take over their late husbands' estates, which made some of them rich, powerful and fiercely independent. It is a strange fact that the world's greatest land empire, the very image of masculine dominance, owed its existence and growth to extraordinary women.

As a child, young Genghis was a down-and-out, cared for by his widowed mother Hoelun, who was rejected by her clan and reduced to scrabbling on mountain flanks for juniper berries. It was Hoelun who showed him what it took to survive; how to rebuild family links, call upon traditional friendships, create new ones, forge alliances and reward loyalty, never seeking personal gain, always looking out for ordinary people and their families. If he went wrong, she would rant at him until he saw the error of his ways. When as a teenager he killed his own half-brother, thus ensuring that he would become the unchallenged head of the family, she gave him hell. The Mongols' foundation document, *The Secret History of the Mongols*, records her words in verse. 'You who have destroyed life!' she yells, and compares him to many sorts of animal in acts of viciousness and stupidity. How could he do such a thing when they had nothing going for them except their own unity as a family, at a time when—

> We have no friend but our shadow,
> We have no whip but our horse's tail?

Genghis learned his lesson, and was keen for others to learn it too, because it was surely he who, in his maturity, encouraged his bards to turn this story into song. As emperor,

[1] Ata-Malik Juvaini, *Genghis Khan: The History of the World Conqueror*, trans. and ed. J. A. Boyle.

Genghis honoured – some say feared – his mother all her long life.

The wife Genghis gave to his son Tolui was another one in the same mould. Her name was Sorkaktani, and she is the focus of this chapter, because in 1215, although she could not have had an inkling of the fact, she held the future in her hands – and not just because of the new-born Kublai. Of her five children, two became emperors and a third ruled Persia. Had it not been for her ambition, foresight, good sense and a couple of interventions at crucial moments, Genghis's empire might have dissipated in family squabbles 20-odd years after it was created, and Kublai would never have come into his inheritance.

Sorkaktani was not even a Mongol. She was a Kerait; and her upbringing in this Turkish-speaking group that domi-nated central Mongolia when Genghis was born provided good training in the politics of Inner Asia. The Kerait king, Toghrul – 'falcon' in Turkish – was Sorkaktani's uncle. He was the alpha ruler among the many heads of the clans that grazed the grasslands beyond the Great Wall, with good contacts to the west and south. Toghrul's people had been converted to a form of Christianity by Nestorian missionaries, followers of the heretic Nestorius who had claimed that Christ was both God and man equally, two persons in one, not the single, indivisible Word-Made-Flesh of mainstream Christianity. But Toghrul also had relations with north China, in later life being awarded the title of prince (*wang*), becoming better known to historians as Wang Khan, 'Prince King'. He had been crucial in the fortunes of Genghis's father, who had come to Toghrul's aid on several occasions and become his 'sworn brother'. Under Genghis, the relation-ship had started well, but it went sour, and the two ended up fighting a war from which Genghis emerged as victor.

Toghrul had a younger brother, Jakha, whose story reflects the complexities and dangers of the shifting alliances among the steppe tribes of Inner Asia. Jakha had been raised among the Tangut people of Xi Xia, the Buddhist state of present-day Xinjiang, and rose among them to the rank of commander – *gambu* in Tangut, which became part of his name: Jakha Gambu. As a warlord with his own small army he returned to Mongolia, joining Genghis at a time when Mongols and Keraits were still friends – and, unlike Toghrul, remaining true to him when things went wrong between the Mongols and Keraits. In the decade-long inter-tribal war for national unity, Keraits fought on both sides. When the main body of Keraits was beaten in about 1200, Genghis forged the tribes together with marriages. Jakha had two daughters. The elder, Ibaqa, Genghis took as one of his own wives – quite an honour for her proud and loyal father – though he later handed her on to one of his generals. The younger one, Sorkaktani, he gave to his youngest son, the teenage Tolui, right at the start of his distinguished military career. Over the following years of a marriage punctuated by her husband's long absences on campaigns in China and Muslim lands she produced four sons, so gaining both a motive and a means to win friends and influence people.

Among them, her four boys would dominate much of Asia for 50 years, and redefine the course of its history. But she had a long wait for time's whirligig to spin in her favour.

Sorkaktani's first lucky break, if you can call it that, came when Genghis died in 1227. Genghis had decreed that his third son Ogedei would be his heir as emperor, with all four sons exercising personal authority over their own areas. Jochi, the eldest, had received what is today Russia, from half way across Siberia to the Black Sea; but he had died shortly before Genghis, and the area was inherited by his sons, Orda and Batu. Central Asia from the Aral Sea to Tibet went to Chaghadai. Ogedei's personal estate was Xi Xia (basically, most of western China) and north China. Tolui, the youngest, as tradition demanded, inherited the lands of his father's 'hearth', which in this case meant the whole of Mongolia. This was what would, in due course, give Sorkaktani her power base.

The division involved much wishful thinking, because the borderlands were rather vague and still much disputed by locals. North China was only half conquered; Khwarezm still needed pacifying; Russian princes, though beaten once, would not stay beaten. The strongest position was Tolui's, because he had authority over the heartland with a ready-made corps of civil servants. In addition – since herdsmen were also soldiers – he could in theory have exercised some control over the army. This, though, was a possibility he would not exploit, being not only subject to Ogedei but happily so: the two brothers were very fond of each other. There would be no challenge from Tolui, and thus no reason yet for Sorkaktani to dream of glory for her sons.

Ogedei began his reign with a flurry of martial activity in pursuit of his father's vision, in four huge and independent campaigns. One re-established the Mongols in Iran, seizing it from its Seljuk rulers. An invasion of Korea began a conquest that would not be finalized until 1260. And in 1231 came the return to north China, which had been Genghis's immediate aim when he died. The Mongol forces advanced in three wings, commanded respectively by the greatest of Genghis's generals, the one-eyed Subedei; Ogedei himself; and Tolui, who had conquered several towns on the first invasion 20 years previously.

Sorkaktani's next stroke of luck was that, early in the campaign into north China, her husband Tolui died. *The Secret History* tells of his death in a well-spun account intended to dramatize the loyalty of a younger brother towards his elder, of a general towards his emperor. Soon after the start of the campaign in 1231, Ogedei falls ill. Land

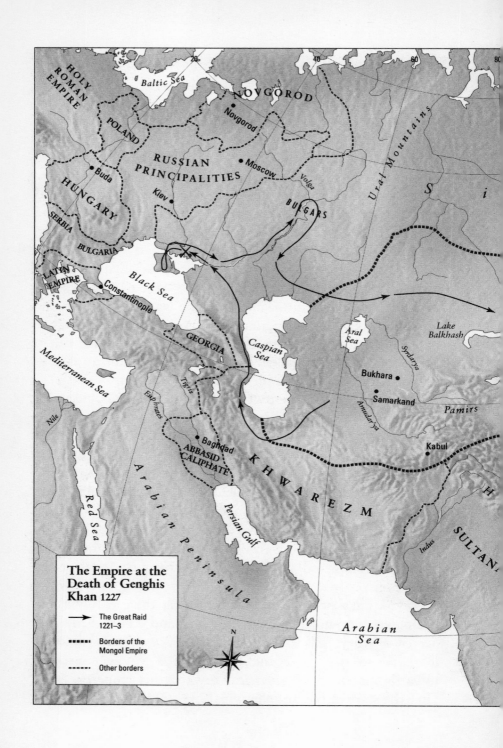

HOLY
ROMAN
EMPIRE

Baltic Sea

NOVGOROD

POLAND

• Novgorod

RUSSIAN
PRINCIPALITIES

• Buda

• Moscow

HUNGARY

Volga

• Kiev

BULGARS

SERBIA

BULGARIA

Ural Mountains

S   i

LATIN
EMPIRE

Black Sea

• Constantinople

GEORGIA

Caspian
Sea

*Aral
Sea*

Lake
Balkhash

Syrdarya

Mediterranean Sea

Tigris

Euphrates

Bukhara •

• Samarkand

Amudarya

Pamirs

Nile

• Baghdad
ABBASID
CALIPHATE

K H W A R E Z M

• Kabul

H

Red Sea

Persian Gulf

A r a b i a n   P e n i n s u l a

SULTAN

Indus

**The Empire at the
Death of Genghis
Khan** 1227

→   The Great Raid
1221–3

▪▪▪▪ Borders of the
Mongol Empire

- - - Other borders

N

*Arabian
Sea*

and water spirits rage within him – delirium tremens prob- ably, the result of a lifetime of alcohol abuse. Shamans go into a huddle to divine the cause. After examining the entrails of slaughtered animals, they state that a sacrifice is needed. But no sooner have the shamans gathered captives, gold, silver, cattle and food for the offering than Ogedei becomes worse. What now? A question arises: Could a member of the khan's family serve as a substitute? Tolui is in attendance, and volunteers to take on Ogedei's illness. But how? Another shamanistic huddle, more advice. Tolui will have to drink an alcoholic potion of some kind, which will attract Ogedei's illness to him. Tolui agrees: 'Shamans, cast your spells and make your incantations!' What he does not know is that Ogedei is suffering not simply an illness but death-pangs. That's the burden he unwittingly assumes. Tolui drinks. The potion works fast. He just has time to consign his family to Ogedei's care before words fail him. 'I have said all I have to say,' he slurs. 'I have become drunk.' On that he passes out, never to regain consciousness. In *The Secret History*'s abrupt words, 'Such was the manner in which he died.' Well, perhaps; or perhaps he just died from drinking too much. Ogedei, distraught at the loss of his brother, never recovered his health. Grief became an excuse for yet more drinking, which he would somehow survive for another ten years.

Tolui's death opened a new chapter for Sorkaktani, as his widow, at the heart of an expanding empire. It was traditional in Mongol society for the widow of a wealthy man to administer her husband's estates until her eldest son was of an age to do so. As it happened, her eldest Mönkhe was already 21, but still Ogedei gave Sorkaktani enduring authority to handle Tolui's estates: her family, an army of her own, a secretariat and the local population, 'all should be under the control of her command and prohibition, her loosening and binding, and should not turn their heads from her commandment'. In essence, Sorkaktani became the queen of Mongolia, though subject to her emperor.

Fate had made her independent, and she, in her forties, was shrewd and ambitious enough to stay that way. When Ogedei proposed that she marry his son (and her nephew) Güyük – an alliance that would have linked the two main family lines – she courteously declined, saying that her prime responsibility was to her own sons. She never did remarry. She ruled well for the next 15 years, earning herself an unrivalled reputation for wisdom and firmness. Reports by outsiders all concurred. 'Among the Tartars this lady is the most renowned, with the exception of the emperor's mother,' wrote one of the pope's envoys, John of Plano Carpini.[2] 'Extremely intelligent and able,' said Rashid ad-Din, going on to praise her 'great ability, perfect wisdom and shrewdness and consideration of the latter end of things'. 'All the princes marvelled at her power of administration,' said a Hebrew physician, Bar Hebraeus, and added a verse quotation: 'If I were to see among the race of women another woman like this, I should say that the race of women was far superior to men.'

Her good sense was apparent in the way she raised her four boys. She made sure they were well educated in traditional Mongol ways and knew all about Genghis's law codes. But the empire was wide, and had many faiths. She knew from her own experience – a Kerait and a Christian married to a Mongol shamanist – how important it was not to alienate allies and subjects. So there were tutors in Buddhism, Nestorianism and Confucianism, and, later, wives who were chosen in Sorkaktani's own image – assertive, dynamic, intelligent, undogmatic and highly independent, thus carrying on the tolerance that had been one of Genghis's more surprising traits. Mönkhe, the eldest son, chose to remain a shamanist, but was married to a Nestorian; Hulegu, later

---

[2] He is referring to Güyük's mother, Töregene, of whom more shortly.

ruler of Islamic Persia, also married a Nestorian. Kublai would marry several times, but his lifelong companion was his second wife Chabi, a famous beauty and an ardent Buddhist.

Meanwhile, the empire grew, and wealth flowed in. Kaifeng, the Jin capital, fell in May 1233, forcing the Jin emperor to flee (he was surrounded near the Song border and committed suicide). Twenty years after Genghis's first invasion, all north China was in Mongol hands. Between 1236 and 1242, a western campaign extended Mongol control across the Russian steppes into Poland and Hungary. At home, Ogedei continued the process started by Genghis of building a sound base for imperial administration, with written laws and censuses and a flow of tax revenue.

Ogedei now saw what Genghis had seen: that an empire of this complexity could not be ruled from a campsite. He needed a capital, a replacement for the old Mongol base of Avraga on the Kherlen river. This place, which still awaits a detailed archaeological survey, stands on the southern edge of the original Mongol heartland, where the Khenti mountains give way to grasslands. To the north lie mountains, forests and safety; to the south, pastures and Gobi and China, the source of trade and booty. For a clan it was a perfect HQ; but not for an empire. Genghis knew the best place from which to rule his newly founded nation. It lay further west, in the valley of the Orkhon river, where previous Turkish empires had ruled. Turks called it Khara Khorum, 'Black Boulder'. Genghis had chosen it as his new capital in 1220, but had done nothing much about it. Ogedei launched his reign in 1228 with a huge gathering in Avraga, where in all probability he supervised the gathering of the tales and information that went into *The Secret History of the Mongols*, but already he had grander plans. It was he, once again, who fulfilled his father's dream, starting to turn Karakorum into a permanent settlement in 1235, just after the conquest of north China, just before the next push westward.

Earthen walls with four gates surrounded a small town, including a palace, with wooden floors, wooden pillars, a tiled roof and nearby cellars for the storage of treasures – recent digs found several statues and some terracotta heads of Buddha. Attached were private apartments, while in front stood a giant stone tortoise bearing an engraved pillar, like those that commonly guard Chinese temples – the very tortoise, perhaps, that still holds a lonely vigil beside Karakorum's replacement, the monastery of Erdene Zuu. Inside, a central aisle led to steps, on which stood Ogedei's throne. Of course, Mongols never did cities – and still don't: as any visitor to Ulaanbaatar will tell you, the zest of the place comes from the people, not the buildings. So it must have been in Karakorum. Soon, one-third of the town was taken up with government departments controlling sacrifices, shamans, merchants, the postal relay system, treasuries and arsenals. But even when Muslim merchants and Chinese craftsmen began to crowd inside the walls, it wasn't much of a town. Friar William of Rubrouck saw it in 1253–4, and was not impressed: 'You should know that discounting the Khan's palace, it is not as fine as the town of St Denis, and the monastery of St Denis is worth ten times that palace.'

Never mind: it was a centre, where previously there had been no centre; and here gathered felt tents (*gers*, as Mongolians call them) by the hundred, wagons by the thousand and animals by the ten thousand. Rich Mongols, of whom by now there were hundreds, each had anything up to 200 ox-drawn wagons, which would be linked into huge trains of 20–30 teams-and-wagons, all strung together lumbering slowly across the open steppe driven by one woman in the lead wagon. Perhaps a visitor would have seen a huge cart, 10 metres across, with axles like masts, drawn by 22 oxen, on which stood the imperial tent. Some doubt that such a vehicle existed, but there are at least three replicas in Ulaanbaatar today, and one of them lumbers round the stadium every July during the National Day celebrations. No-one knows how or where such a monstrosity was used, but in the 1230s it could have creaked its way back and forth between old Avraga and new Karakorum.

Such was Ogedei's headquarters for his newly formed administration.[3] In this his main guide was Genghis's Chinese adviser, an extremely tall (6 feet 8 inches) Khitan from the aristocratic Yeh-lü family, Chu-tsai (Chuzai in pinyin) by name. The Khitans had once ruled north China, until conquered by the Jin in 1125. Chu-tsai's father had chosen to serve the new regime, and in due course Chu-tsai followed, rising to become vice-prefect of Beijing. Although only in his early twenties, he was a famous figure, noted for his brilliance, his height, his sonorous voice and his waist-length beard. He had endured the city's sack in 1215, retired to a monastery for three years to regain his peace of mind, then – such was his reputation – been summoned to meet Genghis in Mongolia. Genghis offered him the job of head of the newly formed chancery, responsible for the scribes who recorded laws and taxes. It was an offer Chu-tsai was not expected to refuse, because, as Genghis said, the Khitans and the Jin had been enemies, and 'I have avenged you.' Chu-tsai had the nerve to point out that he and his father had been loyal servants of the Jin. Did Genghis really expect him to regard his father and his ex-employers as enemies? Genghis took the point, offered him the job anyway, and always thereafter had the greatest respect for 'Long Beard', as he called him. Chu-tsai travelled with Genghis into Muslim lands in 1219 and on

[3] And for this reason it may be resurrected as the seat of Mongolia's government. In 2005, top officials were discussing a startling proposal, backed by the Prime Minister, to build a totally new capital in Karakorum. A decision is supposed to be made in 2006, the 800th anniversary of the founding of the nation by Genghis Khan.

his master's final campaign in China in 1226–7. In 1229 Ogedei made him the provisional head of the new secretariat – in effect, governor – for those parts of north China that had already been conquered, the first civilian official to hold such wide responsibilities. In the same year, Ogedei appointed a foreigner of equal eminence as governor of his Muslim lands. His name was Mahmud, known as Yalavach (Turkish for 'the envoy', because that had been his first job under Genghis).

It was Chu-tsai who did his best to guide Ogedei away from a life of drinking and hunting and towards fiscal prudence. This was a political as well as a personal struggle, because traditionalists at court considered horses and cattle as the only true wealth, despised the land-grubbing Chinese and seriously suggested that the best use for north China was to depopulate all the farms and turn them over to pasture. Who cared what happened to the millions of peasants? They were worthless anyway. Chu-tsai pointed out that such callousness was self-destructive. Better to nurture the peasants and tax them, through officials who would collect silk, grain and silver. In 1230 Chu-tsai proved the system worked: he delivered 10,000 silver ingots. The following year, he was confirmed in his post.

Naturally, his Mongol colleagues were left seething. They saw Chu-tsai's proposals as a plot to deprive them of their just rewards and divert cash from their own pockets into the emperor's coffers. Ogedei didn't help because his response to this sudden influx of cash was simply to become doubly profligate, demanding money both for his military campaigns and to invest in Muslim businessmen, who promised high returns. Chu-tsai's reforms hit a dead end when Ogedei handed over tax collection to a Muslim 'tax farmer' called Abd al-Rahman. His cronies would buy the right to tax, with the freedom to impose whatever interest they wanted – up to 100 per cent per annum (Ogedei considerately banned higher rates). They became the Mongols' loan sharks, setting in motion a vicious circle of scams. The Muslim businessmen would lend Ogedei's money at exorbitant rates of interest to the unfortunate peasants, who needed the loans to make good what had been lost in taxes. The result was predictable: people fled their homes to avoid the tax collectors and their strong-arm gangs. According to one estimate, 50 per cent of the population were either of no fixed abode or enslaved by Mongol officials. Chu-tsai was effectively sidelined, and died three years after Ogedei, a broken man.

Sorkaktani, already a power in the Mongol heartland, benefited from these upheavals, and learned from them. In 1236, two years after Ogedei completed the conquest of north China, she asked for part of Hebei province as her appanage, her personal estate. Ogedei hesitated, but not for long. As Rashid ad-Din said, he 'used to consult her on all affairs of state and would never disregard her advice'. She quickly shamed him into compliance by pointing out that the place was hers by right anyway, because her husband had conquered it.

Travelling to it, she and her family – including the 21-year-old Kublai – would have seen the terrible destruction caused by the Mongol war machine: abandoned farms, overgrown fields, empty villages, refugees. There had been two other barbarian invasions in the past three centuries, but nothing like this. By 1234 the population of the north, perhaps 40 million people in the early thirteenth century, had dropped by three-quarters from 7.6 million households down to 1.7 million. This figure is so astonishing that many scholars simply don't believe it. There must be something wrong with the way the statistics were gathered, but no-one knows what. Perhaps households were broken up. Perhaps millions fled south. In any event, even if the drop was 'only' by a half or two-thirds, the social consequences were catastrophic.

Zhengding (Chen-ting), about 200 kilometres south-west of present-day Beijing, had escaped more lightly than most settled areas because it had been granted to a local warlord who had surrendered to Genghis. He had organized a self-defence force of peasant farmers, who preserved the area as an enclave of peace and stability, providing his son, Shi Tianze, with some good administrative experience. Even so, it was not a place many Mongols would have bothered with. It was famed for its Buddhist temples, pagodas and statues; it still is, and some of them are the same ones that Sorkaktani knew, like the vast 22-metre-high bronze figure of the many-eyed and many-armed Buddhist deity Avalokiteshvara, who waves her 42 arms at tourists in the main temple complex. The area is on the western rim of the great north China plain, where rich farmland gives way to low hills rolling between river valleys. Its 80,000 households, probably over half a million people, would have been totally uninteresting to more traditional Mongols, who saw farmers as dross and farms as potential pastures. Not Sorkaktani. Thanks to Genghis's foresight and Chu-tsai's example, she spotted a chance to build up her personal wealth well away from the city areas ruined by the Mongol invasions. She would nurture her estates and their peasant farmers, flatter the local population by hiring Chinese tutors for her children, and woo them by patronizing Buddhism and Taoism (local rumour even claimed she had abandoned Nestorianism) – and wealth would flow to her and her family in the form of taxes.

The same year, she forged another link in this sensible scheme. Kublai received an estate of his own 100 kilometres south of his mother's, a region of some 10,000 households. Too young to be interested in good government, at first he allowed local officials free rein, with predictable consequences: more oppressive taxation, corruption, protests unheard, the flight of those fit and strong enough to set up house elsewhere, and a dramatic decline in both tax base and tax revenues.

Shocked by this turn of events – or perhaps by his mother's reaction to it – Kublai ordered reforms. New officials were drafted (among them, Shi Tianze from his mother's appanage); tax laws were revised. A decade later, people had returned to their old homes. Kublai had learned an important lesson about business management.

From the mid-1230s, Ogedei drank himself steadily towards death. Wine was his tipple, not the traditional Mongolian mares'-milk *airag*. A special official was appointed by his staff to count the number of goblets he consumed, in a vain attempt to control his consumption. The number went down, apparently, but only because he got himself a bigger goblet.

With a drunkard in charge, princes squabbled. One row involved Ogedei's eldest son Güyük and his cousin Batu, khan of the Golden Horde, the steppe region of what is now Russia from the Caucasus to the Urals. During the 1236–41 invasion of Russia, Poland and Hungary, there was a feast at which both men were present. *The Secret History* quotes Batu's version of what happened, which he sent off across Asia at a gallop. Generally acknowledged as the senior, Batu naturally drank first. Güyük and two other princes took offence and rode away in a huff, throwing insults. They should all be equal! Batu shouldn't be claiming seniority! He was just an old woman with a beard . . . deserved to have his bosom struck with a stick of burning wood . . . have a wooden tail tied to him. Back home, Ogedei backed Batu and blamed his son: 'May he and he alone rot like an egg! He has turned against the bosom of a person who is senior to him!' What was Güyük thinking of, acting so high and mighty as if he had conquered the Muslims all by himself? In his anger, Ogedei disowned Güyük as heir and nominated a grandson, Shiremun, in his place.

In December 1241 the emperor took part in the annual winter hunt, a huge event for which he had had built a fence two days' journey in length to gather wild animals, mainly white-tailed deer and wolves. Then he started a night of heavy drinking, in the company of his favourite Muslim tax farmer, Abd al-Rahman. He died at dawn on 11 December, aged 55. The author of *The Secret History* sums up Ogedei's reign by putting a self-condemnation into his mouth: 'I was at fault to let myself be vanquished by wine. This was indeed one fault of mine.' It was an ignominious end, which was perhaps why he was not buried with his father on the Mongols' sacred mountain, Burkhan Khaldun in northern Mongolia, but on his own private estate in Jungaria, Mongolia's far west.

His widow, Töregene, took over the empire, ignored her husband's will and set about getting the throne for her eldest, Güyük, now aged 35. He couldn't have done it alone, because he was a sickly creature as dedicated to drink as his father. Töregene was one tough lady, the only woman who out-ranked Sorkaktani, according to John of Plano Carpini. She was, says Rashid, 'no great beauty, but of a very masterful nature', and a nasty piece of work by all accounts (though those accounts were written after she had been consigned to the dustbin of history, so perhaps she was not quite so bad as she is painted). She won over most of the family with argu-ments and gifts, but Batu she could not persuade. He refused to come to a *kuriltai*, the great assembly of princes which would elect the next khan, claiming he was suffering from gout. Delays continued for five years, with Töregene constantly shoring up support for her son through intrigue and bribery.

Realizing that Töregene was in a virtually unassailable position, Sorkaktani played a waiting game, remaining quietly supportive of Ogedei's family through the turbulent four-year interregnum. The dispute almost tore the empire apart, with every prince making his own laws for his own entourage, changing what had been written on the orders of Genghis himself. Genghis Khan's youngest brother, Temüge, now well into his seventies, even dared suggest that he, as elder statesman, should be nominated khan without calling an assembly, a claim for which he would pay in due course. Chaos threatened, until Sorkaktani – who had scrupulously refrained from issuing edicts of her own – came out in support of Güyük, giving Töregene a slight but significant majority among the princes. Töregene at last arranged the assembly, which convened in the spring of 1246.

This *kuriltai* was the grandest imperial affair yet, described by Juvaini in his usual flowery style. With the snow gone, the pasture renewed, ring-doves dallying with turtle-doves and melodious nightingales singing, Karakorum became a stage for the display of new-found power and wealth. Nobles by the hundred gathered from every corner of the empire: all of Genghis's scattered descendants, sons and grandsons, cousins and nephews, joined over the course of several weeks by sub-servient leaders from north China, Korea, Russia, Hungary, Turkestan, Azerbaijan, Turkey, Georgia, Syria, even Baghdad, though it was as yet unconquered, arriving to create a satellite city of 2,000 tents. It was a scene 'such as no man had ever seen nor has the like thereof been read of in the annals of history'. Juvaini's words were confirmed by the Italian monk John of Plano Carpini, who had just arrived and was busy gathering inside information from Russians and Hungarians, long-term residents who spoke Latin and French.

The feasting and drinking went on for a week, during which the princes grudgingly offered the throne to Güyük, who, after three routine refusals, accepted. His coronation took place that August at a second tented site in a river valley a few kilometres from Karakorum. Here the tribute was brought, in 500 cartloads of silks, velvet, brocade, gold, silver and furs, displayed in and around Güyük's coronation *ordo*, a huge tent-palace of yellow felt supported by gilded wooden columns. The ceremony – delayed for a few days by a vicious hailstorm – had Güyük crowned on an ivory throne inlaid with gold, made by a Russian goldsmith. It was Sorkaktani who oversaw a gigantic payoff, the tribute being redistributed among everyone, from grizzled companions of Genghis himself down through commanders of a battalion 10,000 strong to platoon chiefs in charge of ten men, from sultans to humble officials, as well as all their dependants.

Together, Güyük and Töregene wrung from the assembled princes a pledge that the throne would remain in Ogedei's direct family. This in effect counteracted Genghis's own will, which specified what should happen if Ogedei's direct descendants were unfit to rule. *The Secret History* underlines the point with a verse: if they prove so worthless that

> Even if one wrapped them in fresh grass,
> They would not be eaten by an ox.
> Even if one wrapped them in fat,
> They would not be eaten by a dog

> – is it possible that among my [other] descendants not even a single one will be born who is good?

So it would have been perfectly acceptable for the princes to look for a khan from another branch of the family – from Tolui's line, for instance. Might not Sorkaktani have pushed Mönkhe forward? He was already 36. But she was not yet ready to enter the fray. It would only further threaten the unity of the empire, and probably endanger her own position. So she held her peace, and went along with those princes who were strong-armed into pledging that the succession would always remain with Ogedei's line, swearing to Güyük that this would hold 'as long as there remains of thy race a piece of flesh such as an ox or dog would not accept wrapped in fat or grass'. It was a pledge that deliberately subverted words attributed to their lord and master, Genghis – a pledge, moreover, with immediate and shocking impact: Genghis's ageing brother Temüge, who had claimed the throne for himself, was put to death. Genghis's *brother*! Executed! There must have been much unhappiness among some of the princes.

Unhappiest of all was Batu. He had, reluctantly, been on his way to the assembly, but too late: Töregene managed to tie up the succession before he arrived, when he and his army were still over 1,000 kilometres away.

But mutterings of discontent persisted. Güyük was never a good choice. He was always in poor health, made worse by drink. He was moody, suspicious, unsmiling. His mother had foisted him upon unwilling relatives and subordinates, and the gifts with which she had bought their acquiescence would not be enough to keep it; indeed, Töregene herself continued to alienate family and officials, notably with her choice of a confidante.

It makes a lurid tale, which started some time before the coronation. Töregene had employed a Muslim woman called Fatima, who had been brought as a captive to Karakorum, where she set up trade managing the local prostitutes. Somehow she wormed her way into Töregene's household and became the queen's close friend and adviser – a sort of female Rasputin. Knowledge of the queen's secret views and court intrigues gave Fatima far too much influence. No minister could do his job without her say-so. She even began issuing her own decrees. Top people had to grovel their way into her good books. Inevitably, they resented her, praying for a come-uppance. It came soon after Güyük succeeded, when his brother fell ill. Someone suggested that Fatima must have bewitched him. To his credit, Güyük tried to reverse the damage. He prised her out of his mother's control, had her accused and tortured until she confessed, and then consigned her to a dreadful death, which graciously conferred upon her the upper-class honour of dying without shedding blood. 'Her upper and lower orifices were sewn up, and she was rolled up in a sheet of felt and thrown into the river.' No doubt most breathed a sigh of relief, but such a conflict between son and mother was no basis for sound rule.

What, meanwhile, of Batu? Still advancing slowly. Güyük suspected rebellion. He mustered his own army and marched westward, ostensibly to check on his estates on the Kazakh–Mongol borders. Once there, he set about preparing a counter-invasion. All this took months, opening a window of opportunity for one of Sorkaktani's most crucial interventions. It was a difficult decision, fraught with danger. If she was discovered, all would be lost – her years of waiting, her careful networking, her hopes for her sons. She would be seen as a traitor and executed, along with her family. This is what she did: recalling the ties of brotherhood between her late husband and Batu's father, she sent a secret message to Batu warning him, in the words of Rashid ad-Din, that Güyük's advance 'was not devoid of some treachery'. Taking advantage of this advance notice, Batu prepared himself for action – unnecessarily, as it turned out, because in April 1248 the two armies were virtually squaring up along the shores of Lake Balkhash when Güyük, always sick and now worn out by travel, died: possibly poisoned, possibly in a fight, but most probably from disease.

Batu, who was content with his own empire in southern Russia, had no interest in promoting himself as the new khan. And he owed Sorkaktani a favour. So he instantly turned his army into a princely assembly and proposed that Sorkaktani's eldest, Mönkhe, should succeed.

Back home, of course, Güyük's sons, under their mother's aegis, demurred, and all set up their own courts, as did Ogedei's favoured grandson Shiremun. Again, the empire was in tatters. Local rulers looked after themselves, wringing whatever they could out of their subjects. Princes used the postal relay system, set up to speed imperial communication, for their own ends, rather like officials of some failing dictatorship using ministerial limos for their own businesses on the side. No-one knew who was going to rule; everyone scrabbled for influence; many sent messages saying they would not even come to a meeting to elect a new khan.

Güyük's widow, Oghul Kaimish, would by tradition have acted as regent until her eldest was fit to rule. But her sons – Ogedei's grandsons – were too young. Besides, she was overwhelmed by events, closeting herself with shamans, trying to achieve her ends by witchcraft. People remembered Genghis's words: that if Ogedei's descendants were unsuitable, then the new khan should be chosen from other lines, that is, from the offspring of Genghis's other three sons. Two of them (Jochi and Chaghadai) had estates so distant that their heirs were out of contention. That left Sorkaktani's children, the offspring of Genghis's youngest son, Tolui, inheritor of the Mongol heartland.

Now at last Sorkaktani went into battle on her own account. She was about 60, and it was her last chance. She had a lot going for her: her own power base, money, respect, influence. The court was torn apart over the Fatima affair. And she had an advantage in that Güyük's offspring were Genghis's great-grandchildren, whereas her own were his grandchildren, a generation closer to the great man. Mönkhe, almost 40, was a good choice, and well qualified. He too had led a Mongol army westwards into Europe in 1238–41, burning Kiev and destroying the Hungarians at the battle of Mohi. Moreover, he had two younger brothers who were also experienced generals, and they would be vital when the empire resumed its Heaven-ordained task of imposing Mongol rule on the world.

The dispute was almost ended in 1250, when the rivals came together at Batu's camp and heard Batu again demand that Mönkhe be elected. But this assembly was not in the Mongol heartland, and carried little weight. The next year, a second assembly, this one in the traditional area near Avraga, confirmed the choice. As if concluding a presidential election,

Mönkhe was all generosity, appeasing and befriending his former opponents and their families. It almost worked, except that Shiremun still had other ideas.

Juvaini picks up the story.

The scene is the princely assembly at Avraga. Imagine a few stone buildings and the surrounding masses of tents and wagons and herds. Everyone is happy that the succession is decided. A falconer named Keshik (*keshig* just means 'guard', but let's follow Juvaini) loses a favourite female camel. He sets out to find it, riding for two or three days here and there. He comes across an army. Who on earth are they? Oh, comes the reply, we are coming to offer Mönkhe our congratulations and obeisance. Reassured, Keshik continues his search. Seeing a broken-down wagon, being mended by a young man, he stops to offer help. Then he notices that the wagon is full of bundles of weapons.

'What are all these arms?' he asks.

'Same as all the other wagons,' the lad replies.

At last Keshik starts to wonder. He strikes up other conversations. Bit by bit, he pieces the story together. These are people 'meditating treason and duplicity and treachery and discord', aiming to launch an attack on Mönkhe while everyone is feasting. Finding his camel, he covers three days' journey in one, barges in on the new emperor and spills the beans. The company is aghast. They don't believe him. He tells his story again, and again. Mönkhe will still not take the threat seriously. His officers remonstrate. At last, it is agreed that Mengeser, chief judge and head of the emperor's guard, will take 3,000 men and investigate. They reach the army, find it to be Shiremun's, and confront him. Shiremun and his officers are flabbergasted: 'The tongue of excuse having turned mute and the leg of advance and withdrawal lame, they saw no hope of departing and no prospect of remaining behind.' Under guard, the leaders troop into Mönkhe's presence, in groups of nine. After three days of interrogations,

Mönkhe comes to his conclusion. It's incredible, inconceivable, cannot be heard by the ear of intelligence nor accepted by the soul of wisdom, but still it is true: they are traitors. Arrests follow, and confessions, and – once Mönkhe has overcome his natural generosity and his urge to forgive – executions. This prisoner is beheaded, that one trampled to death, while others commit suicide with a sword in the stomach.

Purges followed, reaching as far afield as Afghanistan and Iraq. Among the victims was Güyük's widow, Oghul Kaimish, condemned by Mönkhe as viler than a dog, the worst kind of witch; Shiremun's mother; and, in due course, Shiremun himself. It was a terrible blood-letting. Mengeser himself claimed to have tried and executed 77 leaders of the opposition. Many hundreds of others must also have died. The grim episode marked the beginning of a regime more sternly dedicated to Genghis's vision, the new ideology being backed by the official worship of Genghis Khan (the birth of a cult that continues to this day).

And that was how Mönkhe came to absolute power, and how, thanks to Sorkaktani and a good deal of luck, Tolui's line took over from Ogedei's – meaning that, should anything happen to Mönkhe, there was a good chance of the succession passing to Kublai.

Mönkhe brought new vigour to the sacred trust imposed by Genghis, the task of striving for universal domination. He started with a flurry of reforms and plans for expansion. The two went together: renewed conquests would unite his divided people, but only if they stopped working for themselves and worked together; this required the exercise of authority, on the basis of an accurate account of available resources. So there would be a census (actually several censuses) covering the whole empire. This vast project was undertaken through the 1250s, generating a sort of Mongol Domesday Book, enumerating peoples, towns, animals, fields and raw materials from the Pacific coast to the Baltic. There would be no more self-seeking, no more using the postal relay system as a perk of high office. There would be a head tax (based on individuals in Islamic lands and on households in China) paid in cash, an agricultural tax paid in kind and a commercial tax on all businesses. The census also told Mönkhe's secretariat the potential size of his armed forces, and identified in every region households with young men available for military service.

On this basis there would be a push outwards such as the empire had never seen before. Mönkhe put his younger brothers and other relatives in executive charge of the campaigns. Hulegu would move westward, deeper into the Islamic world. Mönkhe himself and Kublai would undertake the final conquest of the Chinese south, the kingdom of Song. The third advance, a minor one by comparison, would be into Korea, under Genghis's nephew, Jochi Khasar. At the heart of this expansion was the triad of brothers – Mönkhe, Hulegu and Kublai – with Mönkhe at the tip, and his two brothers as his right and left wings, west and east, charged with tasks that were mirror images of each other: to extend the power of the empire and of their family, one in the world of Islam, the other in China.

In the meantime, Kublai, having learned from his mother how to take good care of his Chinese estate, had hired a brains trust of half a dozen Chinese advisers, most of whom shared religious and intellectual interests, all of whom were prepared to work with their new overlord, offering guidance in finding his way among China's three great religious traditions – Buddhism, Taoism and Confucianism – and hoping to mould the Mongol leaders into good Chinese rulers. This was quite a remarkable step by Kublai, because it was conducted across a linguistic and cultural gulf. He did not speak Chinese, and very few Chinese spoke Mongol. All communication was through interpreters.

Among the advisers, three were of particular significance.

The first was a brilliant Buddhist monk, Haiyun, who was so clever as a child that he found Confucianism too easy. On the question of happiness and sorrow, he said at the age of seven, he had read Confucius and found him unhelpful. So he turned to Buddhism, and was ordained at the age of nine. When in 1219 the Mongols seized Liangzhou, today's Wuwei in central Gansu province, Haiyun, now aged sixteen, was found wandering with his master amid the devastation and looting, quite unconcerned. A general asked if they were not afraid of being killed by the troops. On the contrary, Haiyun replied calmly, they relied on their protection. Impressed, the commandant of north China, Muqali, brought the pair to the attention of Genghis, who ordered them to be clothed, fed and exempted from taxation. The master died soon afterwards, and the pupil went searching for a religious base, during which he attained enlightenment, expressing his sense of revelation in one of those enigmatic statements that in Buddhism are treated as evidence of wisdom: 'Today for the first time I realize that eyebrows run horizontally while the nose is set vertically.' He rose to become head of several temples, was further promoted by Yeh-lü Chu-tsai, and did a good deal to mitigate Mongol excesses in north China. Once, when asked for advice on hunting by a high official, Haiyun replied sharply that the urgent task of officials was to preserve life, not play games. Later, when the Mongols were debating whether to brand their Chinese subjects on the arm so that they could be identified when they fled, Haiyun again reprimanded his overlords: men were not cattle, he said; and besides, where could they flee, since the Mongols claimed the whole world? The idea was dropped. When Kublai met

Haiyun in Karakorum in 1242, he asked the monk whether Buddhism offered a way to world peace. Haiyun replied that it did, but that understanding was required: Kublai should surround himself with scholars. But the prince was impatient for short cuts. Which of the Three Teachings – Buddhism, Taoism, Confucianism – was the highest? Haiyun replied that in wisdom and sincerity Buddhism was supreme, providing the best guidance for a prince wishing to promote virtue, relieve suffering, resist delusions, accept good advice, shun extravagance, and distinguish right from wrong. Kublai was impressed. When his second son was born in 1243, it was Haiyun who named him: Zhenjin, 'True Gold' – or Jingim, as the Mongols called him.

It was Haiyun, too, who introduced Kublai to another monk: Liu Bingzhong, a painter, calligrapher, poet, mathematician – the multi-talented product of a famous Taoist sect, the Complete Perfection, whose patriarch Ch'ang-ch'un Genghis had summoned all the way to Afghanistan. He later converted to Buddhism, without losing interest in Taoism and Confucianism. While Haiyun eventually returned to run his temple in Beijing, Liu remained on Kublai's staff, devoting his life (in the words of his biographer Hok-Lam Chan) 'to the ideal of modifying Mongol institutions according to Confucian principles'.

The third adviser, Yao Shu, had joined Ogedei's staff in 1235, being sent with raiding forces across the Song frontier, during which he too did his best to restrain Mongol brutality. He later helped found a Confucian academy in Beijing but then, resenting the Mongol administration, retreated to the country for ten years, until Kublai head-hunted him and invited him to Karakorum in 1251. There he became tutor to little Jingim, now eight, Kublai's favourite and his future heir.

Kublai employed other nationalities as well, for he was keen to balance his past and future, local interests and imperial ones, Mongol and Chinese and Turkish. For advice on government, he had his Chinese team; for military matters, he relied on Mongols; for translators and secretaries, Turks. It was a surprisingly large and varied group – some two dozen in all, a shadow cabinet carefully chosen for its political balance, almost as if Kublai were preparing himself for the administration of much more than his own estate.

He was thus well qualified when he asked Mönkhe for an extension of his responsibilities in north China. There was a good strategic reason for such a request – to ensure a reliable flow of supplies for the occupying troops. He had his eye on the rich farmlands along the Yellow River and its tributaries, in today's Shaanxi and Henan provinces, roughly between the ancient capital of Xian and the newer and recently conquered one of Kaifeng. Mönkhe was wary of handing over so much territory all at once, and gave Kublai a choice. His Chinese advisers told him that the land downriver was liable to flooding and saltiness, so he chose an upstream area on the Wei river, an irregular blob almost half the size of England running from the Wei valley southward across mountains to the Song border. Mönkhe was impressed by his reasoning – fewer people, many of them non-Chinese, and tricky to govern, but with greater potential – so he gave him some of Henan as well. In governing these areas, Kublai followed Yeh-lü Chu-tsai's advice, his mother's shrewd practices and Mönkhe's imperial strategy. He allowed the peasants to work, taxed them fairly, and also established 'military farms': colonies dedicated to supplying the troops. It worked. He had his power base – a Chinese one, fanning suspicions among traditionalists back on the grasslands that he was going native.

He was, in a sense. But he could not afford to go the whole way. His mother would have advised him to remain in touch with everything Mongol in its latest imperial manifestation. There was, for instance, its western wing, which in 1251 consisted of present-day eastern Iran and Uzbekistan. For 30 years these regions, with their great Silk Road cities, remained in ruins, while western Islam, and its great capital Baghdad, was still untouched. Sorkaktani herself had kept links with the area, financing the building of mosques and *madrasas* or Islamic colleges – including one in Bukhara with 1,000 students – which, as Muslims noted, was a remarkable thing for a Christian queen to do.

In early 1252 Sorkaktani, now over 70, died. She was buried far to the west in Gansu province, in Zhangye, an ancient garrison town guarding the Silk Road and thus a staging post for Nestorian missionaries. Sorkaktani must have had some early and abiding connection with the town, for her final resting place was said to be the Giant Buddha Temple, famous then and now not only for the size and age of its statue – 34 metres, eleventh century – but for the fact that it is lying down. When I was there in 2005, the statue was undergoing restoration to scrape off 1,000 years of grime. Alone, in gloom, unaware of what to look for, I wandered right around the network of scaffolding, thinking it concealed a decorated wall. I realized only when I glanced up, and saw a huge beatific smile vanishing into darkness above me.

No hint of anything Christian. I began to wonder if I was dealing with a myth. I buttonholed the director, Wu Zhen Ke, who was between meetings to do with the restoration. A dynamic 40-something with a crewcut, he was just the man to ask, because he had written a book about the temple. He was also an enthusiast; information came fizzing out from behind his rimless glasses like shaken champagne. 'In the thirteenth century, this place was maybe five times the size. It contained elements that were both Christian and Buddhist. There is no doubt that Bie Ji [he used a Chinese 'respect name' I had never heard before] was buried here.' Indeed, so close was her connection that some believe she was pregnant with Kublai when she first arrived here, and that he was actually born in the temple. 'Local people, from generation to generation, have always said this.' But Wu, signing a copy of his book, was too careful a scholar to support such a claim. 'We do not have the evidence. Perhaps one day we will unearth some historical relic to prove what they say.' No rituals link the temple with Sorkaktani today, but elsewhere she became a cult figure, and is one of those remembered in the Genghis Khan Mausoleum, Edsen Khoroo – the Lord's Enclosure – the temple in Inner Mongolia where Genghis and his family are worshipped.

Sorkaktani must have approached the end of her days secure in the knowledge that her great work had been accomplished. Her eldest son was khan, the empire reunified, Genghis's dream of world conquest once again becoming more of a reality by the year. Before her death, she would have heard reports of the beginning of Mönkhe's campaign to extend the empire further into Muslim lands, and known that Kublai was due to advance further into China.

She might have guessed, given the character of her boys, that this was a mere beginning. She could not possibly have guessed, however, that Kublai would one day inherit the lot.

2

THE FIRST WAR ON TERROR

HERE ARE CIRCUMSTANCES WHICH MAY SEEM ODDLY FAMILIAR. The leader of a great power needs to unite his people after a divisive election and makes plans for war. Suddenly, by curious chance, a fanatical sect of Muslims with a track record of extreme violence embarks on an underhand assault. Appalled, he turns on the terrorists with overwhelming force. This happened on 9/11/2001; but it *first* happened in the 1250s, when Mönkhe, the newly installed Mongol emperor, heard that a small army of assassins – 40 or 400 of them, the number varying with the source – had been despatched in disguise to kill him. These were killers of a very peculiar and dedicated nature. Like those who flew into the World Trade Center towers, they were quite prepared to die themselves. The threat, the outraged leaders' responses and the consequences were remarkably similar, and the parallels go further: the region at the heart of the conflict, the real danger posed by suicidal Islamic extremists, the vagueness of the current threat, the determination to extend the bounds of empire, the gathering of a massive army, a coalition of allies, overwhelming force, invasion, the fall of Baghdad, much collateral damage, and occupation.

One should not push the comparison too far. The Americans fell upon Iraq after Afghanistan, the Mongols came via Persia and would have come anyway, to fulfil the destiny inherited from Genghis; the Mongol conquest was achieved with a brutality vastly exceeding that of the Bush coalition; and the Mongols intended eternal occupation, whereas America intended regime change and a quick exit. But the echoes are resonant nevertheless, especially to Muslims, many of whom see the Americans as the 'new Mongols'. It is an easy comparison – perhaps too easy, as we see if we take a closer look at the events that added a huge new slab of territory to the empire that would eventually fall to Mönkhe's younger brother, Kublai.

The Mongols knew what they were doing, because they had done it all before, under Genghis Khan, 30 years previously. The army that prepared for the invasion from summer 1252 was formidable, and very well organized. Headed by the emperor's brother Hulegu, it included the best in siege weapons that north China had to offer, including 1,000 mangonel teams, experts in operating these massive catapults which could lob rocks and exploding 'thundercrash' iron bombs 100 metres or more.[1] Governors and secretaries were appointed to administer the newly conquered lands. Vanguards rode off ahead to reserve pastures, places forbidden to non-Mongols and their animals until the army had passed. Herds of mares were gathered along the line of march to provide the troops with their habitual drink of fermented

---

[1] These were almost certainly man-powered 'traction trebuchets', not counterpoise trebuchets, which the Mongols would soon acquire from Muslim engineers, with interesting consequences to be examined in chapter 8.

mare's milk. The invasion force would travel on the same road taken by Genghis, but after 30 years it would have needed a lot of attention. When the army finally left a year later, teams ranged ahead to repair bridges and build ferries – for the leaders and their families, at least: ordinary folk would have made their own way across the rivers, fording, swimming and using animal-skin floats.

This immense operation was greater even than that undertaken by the Mongols in their first move westward under Genghis Khan. Many books for and by non-specialists suggest that any Mongol advance was a storm, a whirlwind, as if it were a new force of nature. In fact, this was as much a migration as a military invasion, a population shift comparable to those that had been regular features of Central Asia for a millennium. The whole mass had to be self-supporting, which was possible because the way westward was across the vast pasture-lands that make an irregular corridor for nomads between Manchuria and the Hungarian plain. As John Masson Smith has pointed out, 'The far-flung campaigns of the Mongols and the extraordinary extent of their empire were to a considerable degree the products of this great logistical boon.'[2]

This particular force (according to Rashid ad-Din) had 15 commanders, each with his battalion; as a battalion was supposedly 10,000-strong, though in practice usually much less, this made something like 100,000–150,000 men in all, probably closer to 100,000. That was just the start. Every man, as usual, had at least five horses, sometimes more, to provide remounts and food – 120 kilos of meat from a butchered horse could feed 100 hungry men. But what set this enterprise apart was that the men had their families along, and each family would also have had some 30 sheep, on average. This was a nation on the move, occupiers and

---

[2] John Masson Smith, 'Ayn Jalut: Mamluk Success or Mongol Failure?'

colonists: perhaps 150,000 people, with 300,000 horses and 1.8 million sheep, all widely dispersed to avoid overgrazing. Horses are usually moved in the morning, grazed in the afternoon and rested at night. The only way to travel really fast was to have fresh mounts ready in advance. This was how the pony express was run in occupied lands. But it could not be done during conquest and occupation. Hulegu's force would have been moving westward a few kilometres a day for a year: not so much a storm, more like a tide, bits of which would flow where required by the demands of conquest and occupation.

The cutting edge, of course, was the cavalry. It was the horses that gave the Mongols their superiority, not because of their strength or endurance, but because of the speed conferred by a regular supply of new mounts. These mounted forces could outflank, outpace, flee, gallop in close to fire their bows point-blank, avoid charges, and harry retreating foes until, like jackals on a buffalo, they would worry their foes to death.

But only if the horses had enough good grazing and enough water; and, though those could be taken for granted on the grasslands that stretched for hundreds of kilometres, it was a big *if* once their edge was reached. The average Mongolian horse needs about 14 kilos of grass a day, an intake that requires some 10.5 hours of grazing, whether or not they are being ridden. Now multiply this by 300,000. A horde of 250,000, with their horses and sheep, would cover 7,000 hectares a day – that's 70 square kilometres; and every day a new 70 square kilometres. This drifting horde of horses, wagons and sheep would be at least 8 kilometres across. Then think of the water needed: over a million gallons a day. Easily supplied by a large river in flood; but once out of the grassland zone, especially in the searing heat of the Middle Eastern summer, pastures dry up and rivers shrink.

The Mongols were about to discover that their reach had rather sharp ecological limits.

*

Whether the plot to murder Mönkhe was real or not is an open question. No-one recorded finding any assassins. But there was good reason to take the threat seriously, because these were not simply assassins, with a lower-case *a*; they were the original Assassins, capitalized: a long-established and notorious menace in the Islamic world, who gave their name to the very idea of murder for political and religious ends.

The story is rooted deep in Islamic sectarianism. Islam, like all the major religions, sowed sub-groups like dragon's teeth, each claiming that it alone was the true heir to the Prophet. All, of course, revered the Qur'an. But doctrinal disputes, political conflict and murder marred Islam from two decades after the Prophet Mohammed died, one of the victims being Mohammed's son-in-law Ali, husband of the Prophet's daughter Fatima. From these seventh-century beginnings grew hideous complexities, with dynasties, races, regions and sects rivalling each other for 500 years, through which we must now weave to trace the origins of the Assassins.

In the early days of Islam, rival leaders evolved a second doctrinal source, the Sunna, or deeds and sayings of both the Prophet and his successors, including some who were not his relatives. Its adherents, the Sunnis, were then opposed by the Shi'ites, the Shi'at Ali ('party of Ali'), who claimed that political authority derived only from Ali, from whose descendants a divinely appointed imam (spiritual leader) would emerge as the Mahdi, 'the guided one'. Since there was no obvious Mahdi, the Shi'ites came to believe that he was being hidden by God. The notion of the 'Hidden Imam' became a central tenet of Shi'ism, one that inspired numerous pretenders and some very strange sub-sects. From the Shi'ites, for instance, arose in the late eighth century the Ismailis, who claimed that Ismail, the disinherited son of the Sixth Imam, represented the true line of authority from Mohammed. Ismail died young, after which his followers claimed that he had been succeeded by 'hidden imams'. This became the creed of a dynasty who claimed descent from Ali's wife, Mohammed's daughter Fatima. The Fatimids, with Ismailism as their faith, built a kingdom in north Africa, then took over Egypt, planning to use this as a base for an anti-caliphate that would seize all Islam. It didn't happen. Fatimid power declined. But Ismaili missionaries, preaching their secretive mystical teachings, remained as active as ever. The sect appealed powerfully to the poor and oppressed, one group becoming notorious for their brutality against mainstream Muslims and established dynasties.

The Ismailis' next transformation was triggered by the Turks, who swept into the Islamic world from the Asian heartland around the year 1000. As the Turks, headed by their rulers the Seljuks, struck westward from their power base in what is now Uzbekistan and Iran, they adopted the orthodox Sunni form of Islam, and turned on the Shi'ites, including the Ismailis, who responded by forming a network of underground cells.

In the second half of the eleventh century, there lived in Rayy (today's Tehran) a man named Hasan i-Sabbah. This Hasan (there are several other unrelated Hasans to come) had friends in high places, including the poet Omar Khayyam. He met one of the secretive Ismaili propagandists, converted, fell foul of the authorities – in the form of Tehran's vizier, Nizam al-Mulk – and fled to Egypt. There he found that Egypt's Fatimid/Ismaili rulers were mere shadows of their former selves, and decided to wage his own war for Ismailism and its Fatimid imam in the heart of Seljuk territory. He and his followers spotted the perfect base: a formidable castle, Alamut, almost 2,000 metres up in the Elburz mountains south of the Caspian Sea. Unfortunately, it was occupied.

Hasan acquired Alamut by converting some of the

garrison, then slipping inside in disguise. Conversions continued. When he was discovered, it was too late. The garrison was his, and so was the castle. The owner received an offer he couldn't refuse – eviction, plus a cheque for 3,000 gold dinars (about £75,000). To his astonishment, the draft was honoured, by a local banker who was one of Hasan's converts.

This, then, is what the Mongols would be up against:

Alamut was a fortress within a natural fortress, the perfect heart for Hasan's intended Ismaili state. Tradition claims that it derives from a local phrase meaning 'eagle's nest' – a good name, if true, because it stood on a peak hundreds of feet above a single approach path, which itself could be entered only from either end of a narrow ravine through which the Alamut river flowed. The rock, in Juvaini's words, 'resembles a kneeling camel with its neck resting on the ground', the castle itself towering up like the load on the camel's hump. Its plastered walls and lead-covered ramparts concealed store cellars cut from the solid rock. A conduit from a stream led water into 'ocean-like tanks', which still gather rainwater today. The castle was some 140 metres long by 10–40 metres wide, overlooking precipitous slopes, steep paths and stairways guarded by lower defence works, with no cover at all for an assault force.

The traveller and writer Freya Stark went there by mule in the 1930s. Starting from Qazvin, she and her guides approached the hills over 30 kilometres of scorching plain, then up shale-covered slopes until, over a ridge, she saw the valley of the Alamut river leading into the Elburz mountains. 'Higher than all, uplifted as an altar with black ridges rising to it through snowfields, Takht-i-Suleiman, Solomon's Throne, looked like a throne indeed in the great circle of its lesser peers. Its white drapery shone with the starched and flattened look of melting snow in the distance.' In a village of mud houses, her host and his sons talked of the snowbound winter, 'when wolves in packs fight the village dogs; of bears and foxes and hunting; and of the mountain streams that swell in spring and wash away the small precipitous fields'. Upstream, a narrow path wound along a canyon wall, through two oases with grey-leafed trees and vines and corn and walnuts. Northwards up a side valley stood the Rock itself, like a ship, broadside on.

> The great Rock looks a grim place. Mount Haudegan (*c.*15,000 feet) behind it rises in shaly slopes with granite precipices above . . . East and west of the rock, far below, run the two streams that form the Qasir Rud (river); they eat their way through scored and naked beds. There is no green of grass until, beyond a neck that joins the castle to this desolate background, one climbs under its eastern lee, reaches the level by old obliterated steps, and from the southern end looks down nearly a thousand feet of stone to the fields and trees of Qasir Khan, the sunny shallow slopes of the northern bank, and beyond the Alamut river, to the glaciers of Elburz.

Further up the Alamut was a cleft in an immense precipice, to which the only approach was through the forests of Mazanderan, up over the 3,500-metre Tundurkhan Pass. It was a perfect hole-in-the-wall sanctuary.

From here, Hasan, the first of the seven lords of Alamut, determined to assert his own peculiar version of Ismailism. He was a formidable leader, self-assured, learned, ascetic, severe, dictatorial and utterly ruthless – he had his two sons executed, one for drinking wine, the other for supposedly plotting to murder an Ismaili missionary. These were desperate times, with Islam corrupted by heresy, and in Hasan's view all means were justified in fighting his cause, which soon acquired a political cutting edge. In 1094, back in Egypt, an army strongman ousted the Fatimid heir, Nizar, had him murdered in prison and installed his own puppet. Hasan believed that Nizar's heirs would produce the Mahdi who would magically reappear to save Islam from impurity and the Turkish invaders. The fact that Nizar *had* no designated heir was only a temporary problem. The line was 'hidden' and would reappear in due course. Meanwhile, Hasan named himself Nizar's deputy and champion. His followers were formally called Nizaris, an offshoot of the Ismaili Shi'ite Muslims, a sect of a sect of a sect of Islam. This 'New Preaching' (as Hasan called it) appealed strongly to country-folk, who, like today's suicide bombers, were desperate to escape war, poverty and uncertainty by devoting themselves to a cause in absolute and unthinking obedience. The world soon knew Hasan's young fanatics as Assassins.

It is a puzzling term. The European word in various spellings derives from the Arabic *hashish*, from which comes the English word for good old Indian hemp, *cannabis sativa*. Some people referred to the Nizaris as *hashishiyya* (or a Persian equivalent) – hashish-users – and that was the term picked up by the Crusaders in the twelfth century when they heard of them in Syria. So everyone assumed that's what they were: killers who took hashish as their secret drug of choice to relax them before going off to stab some high official, and perhaps meet their own deaths. The idea was reinforced in 1818 in the first serious study of the Assassins, written by the Professor of Arabic in Paris's School of Oriental Languages and later Professor of Persian at the Collège de France, Baron Antoine Silvestre de Sacy. After that, it became a conventional wisdom. But it was not so. Hashish was widely known, not a Nizari secret; and no Nizari source mentions it. More likely, the term was an insult applied to this despised and feared group, much as suicide bombers might be referred to as crazies or pot-heads, simply as a put-down for behaviour that struck outsiders as both appalling and irrational.

Other hilltop castles fell to Hasan – Girdkuh, dominating the main road from Khurasan; Shadiz, to the south near

Isfahan; Lamasar; Tabas, near today's Iran–Afghan border. These strongholds, along with several dozen others, gave him an impregnable power base from which to launch his malign campaign. He himself never again left Alamut, where for 35 years he instructed, inspired and organized followers whose obedience extended to the grave. Like those who join Al-Qaeda today, they welcomed death as martyrdom, confident they would be rewarded by an afterlife in paradise.

Later, Hasan's techniques of persuasion became the stuff of legend, as Marco Polo heard when he came by some 20 years after the Assassins had vanished, on his way to China and to fame as the most vivid (if erratic) source on Kublai and his court. In his version, Alamut's stark valley has now become the most beautiful garden ever seen, filled with gilded pavilions and painted palaces, where honey, wine, milk and water flowed in conduits. Damsels played and sang. It was indeed paradise as conjured up in the Qur'an. Here the imam kept a group of lusty teenagers, whom he groomed to become Assassins. He would have them drugged, carried into the garden and, when they awoke, pampered in every way. 'The ladies and damsels dallied with them to their hearts' content, so that they had what young men would have.' Another draught of the sleep-inducing drug, and the young men found themselves back in the real world, bereft, and willing to do anything to regain the joys of paradise. 'Go thou and slay So and So,' the imam told them, 'And when thou returnest my Angels shall bear thee into Paradise. And shouldst thou die, natheless even so will I send my Angels to carry thee back into Paradise.'

Well, there was no garden, and no drug. Hasan did not need either. His first victim was the vizier Nizam al-Mulk, from whom he had fled years before, followed later by his two sons. Dozens more went the same way: the mufti of Isfahan (slain in the mosque), the qadi of Nishapur, the prefect of Bayhaq, the chief of an anti-Ismaili sect: and more,

50 officials being listed as victims in the Assassins' roll of honour. The area was in the throes of civil war, and Ismailism, with its promise of an Islamic renaissance, found many converts. Commanders and officers went out only with armed guards and wearing armour under their clothes. Terror spawned counter-terror, an official persecution of Ismailis with harbingers of modernity – random accusations, round-ups, imprisonments and deaths in custody. Nothing worked. 'Very well, you have killed me,' said one prominent victim to his gaolers. 'But can you kill those in castles?'

A good point. Some castles fell, but Alamut, even after an eight-year siege, remained impregnable. The result: com-promise, and a live-and-let-live arrangement, with occasional assassinations – a prefect here, a governor there, and in 1131 the caliph himself in Baghdad – and occasional unsuccessful reprisals. So it remained after Hasan's death in 1124, with the Assassins slowly gaining more than they lost.

It was another Hasan who injected a further element of revolutionary zeal, which cast the Assassins into outer dark-ness. During the fast of Ramadan in 1164 he gathered his followers and addressed them, placing his pulpit so that no-one faced Mecca. The time had come, he announced: the Hidden Imam had spoken to him and named him, Hasan, as his representative. Thenceforth, the only rules were his. 'The Imam has freed you from the burden of the rules of Holy Law, and has brought you to the Resurrection.' No need for law, for they would be face to face with God through Hasan, who was in spirit the Imam himself, and the true descendant of Nizar. And his first command was that they break the sacred fast by joining him in a banquet, complete with music and wine. Hasan did not enjoy his new status for long. Two years later, his more orthodox brother-in-law stabbed him to death. But the doctrine of the Resurrection, with this Hasan as its messianic leader, became part of Assassin lore.

Not that this should be revealed to the world: it remained

an Ismaili secret, protected by the principle that anything – even a lack of principle – was allowed, if it preserved core Ismaili beliefs. Therefore it was perfectly OK to pretend to other, more mainstream beliefs, if that's what it took to survive. Outward law of any kind, even Ismaili law, was mere 'occultation', under which the truth lay covered. Law, indeed all morality as understood by the outside world, was nothing compared to the inner truth; therein lay the *qiyama*, the Resurrection. It was perhaps this duplicity that explained a sudden, if brief, change of heart expounded in 1210 by the current imam, Jalal al-Din. To the astonishment of his followers and the Islamic world, he announced that it was time for a new conversion, back to old-fashioned Islam. He approached all other Islamic leaders so convincingly that they believed him, until his death allowed a reversion to assassination and brigandry.

There was more, however, to the Assassins than duplicity and violence. They were, after all, asserting what they believed was a truth about God's will. Truth can always do with extra help in the form of reason and science; and so, surprisingly, Ismaili imams were lovers of objective as well as esoteric knowledge. They built a famous library. Scholars were welcomed, one being the famous astronomer and theologian Nasir al-Din Tusi, who lived in Alamut for many years.

They were still there, assassinating now and then, when in 1219 the Mongols attacked their new neighbour to the east, the sultanate of Khwarezm, whose upstart shah had chased out the Seljuks in 1194. In the cataclysm of 1219–22 over a million died, great cities were destroyed, the kingdom shattered. Great turmoil usually favoured the Assassins – more castles to be seized, more converts made with visions of an Islamic renaissance. So it was no wonder that Mönkhe feared for his life, and made the Assassins his first target when he decided to extend the empire westward under Hulegu.

This was a challenge which called for spirited leadership. But the Assassins got nothing of the kind. The incumbent imam, Ala ad-Din, still only in his thirties, was driven crazy by isolation, drink and the uncritical obedience of all around him. It was well known that his mistress was the wife of a good-looking young man named (yes) Hasan, who had been captured by the Mongols during their first incursion, escaped, joined the Assassins, and become a sort of lap-dog for the unstable Ala ad-Din, now favoured, now abused. Made to wear tattered clothing like his eccentric boss, Hasan had most of his teeth broken by blows and a piece cut off 'the instrument of his virility'. To cap it all, 'while Ala ad-Din had commerce with Hasan's wife, he did not avoid Hasan'. Gap-toothed, penis half cut off, buggered and cuckolded: this Hasan had reason enough to resent his master, and so did many others, including Ala ad-Din's own teenage son, Rukn ad-Din. 'In his insanity and melancholy madness,' wrote Juvaini, '[Ala ad-Din] would constantly torment and persecute [the boy] without cause.' He was made to stay with the womenfolk in a room next door to his father's, from which he escaped to wander the castle only in the imam's absences. Terrified of his father's drunken moods, he became convinced that the only hope of survival was to rebel, seize his inheritance and submit to the Mongols. The castle could have held out for years, delayed the Mongol advance, perhaps even retained its independence right through their occupation; but not with this dysfunctional pair at the top.

In November 1255 young Rukn ad-Din was in the midst of planning his move when the Assassin leader went to a nearby valley, apparently to check on a flock of sheep. On the last night of the month, an intruder attacked him and his two sleeping servants. He was found the next morning, 'his head having been severed with a single blow of an axe'. One servant was so badly wounded he died; the other recovered, but could throw no light on the identity of the killer. Some said Rukn himself had done it, but Rukn had been in bed with a fever. No: it had to be Hasan. Indeed, under persuasion, his wife confessed to a knowledge of the plot. Of course, Rukn may have been in on it; indeed, he probably was, because Hasan himself, while out surveying sheep, was decapitated by some unidentified axeman before he could be questioned. His family were all executed and burned, conveniently quickly. And Rukn ad-Din became the new and equally inadequate leader.

Rukn ad-Din was now free to parlay for survival. He decamped to another castle, Maimun-diz, and sent messengers to the local Mongol headquarters in Hamadan to say that he was ready to submit. Fine, came the reply, but Hulegu himself was on his way: submission should be made to him. Rukn began to stall. Five months passed. In May 1256 he sent his brother to Hulegu, now just five days' march away in Damarvand. Fine, said Hulegu, all Rukn had to do now was destroy his castles and come. Rukn wriggled again, begged for more time, made a few token demolitions but kept his main castles intact. As proof of good intent, he said, he would send his six-year-old son as a hostage. When the hostage turned out to be an illegitimate boy fathered on a Kurdish servant-girl, Hulegu sent the child back as of no importance.

Now it was November: Rukn had been prevaricating for almost a year, and the Mongols were upon him. The astronomer Tusi said the stars did not sanction resistance; better capitulate, which Rukn at last did. Hulegu did the proper thing: received him well, as befitted an imam, and handed out Rukn's gifts to the Mongol troops. Rukn was with Hulegu for long enough to fall for a Mongol girl, and was allowed to add her to his harem. He also became obsessed with fighting camels, to which Hulegu responded with a gift of 100 female camels. Apparently, now feeling secure as Hulegu's guest, Rukn did not show due appreciation for this favour. Females don't fight. 'How can I wait for them to breed?' he complained. Yet it suited Hulegu to be magnanimous, for if the imam were treated well he would save the Mongols the trouble of attacking castle after castle.

And it worked: most castles opened their gates. Alamut, Lamasar and Girdkuh did not. The last two held out for years – proof that these castles were indeed virtually impregnable, if determined to resist. At Alamut, the arrival of a Mongol force in November 1256 combined with Rukn's defection persuaded the commander to change his mind after a month. Out trooped the inhabitants; in went the Mongols and burned the place. All its contents would have been lost had not Juvaini, already serving the Mongols, suggested he check out the library, from which he extracted Qur'ans, astronomical instruments and a collection of historical works. The castle was, he noted, in very good shape, and would have been capable of holding out almost indefinitely.

Some 12,000 of the Nizari elite were killed. Rukn ad-Din himself had served his purpose, and eventually would also be despatched, for the Assassins had either resisted or been slow to capitulate. Nevertheless, Hulegu tolerated Rukn for a while longer, aware that the execution of a leader who had voluntarily surrendered would not be a good message to send to other potential vassals. Rukn, however, signed his own death warrant by requesting that he be allowed to present himself to Mönkhe in Karakorum. That suited Hulegu: it would get the young imam out of the way. So Rukn was guided all the way across Central Asia to Mönkhe's court, where, months later, he received the cold shoulder. Go home and destroy your castles, Mönkhe ordered. But on the way home, on the edge of the Khangai mountains, his Mongol escorts took Rukn and his party aside, put his companions to the sword, and – he was, after all, still a leader – kicked him to pulp, thus conferring upon him the honour, due to a leader, of a bloodless death.

*

That was pretty much the end for the Assassins, though a sub-branch in Syria endured until crushed by the Egyptians in 1273; the end of the Assassins themselves, but not of the Nizaris, whose later history is almost as strange as their origins.

Both Persian and Syrian groups split, following different claimants to the leadership.

The line of Syrian imams ended in about 1800. The Persian line endured. In the mid-nineteenth century the current Nizari imam was appointed governor of Qom, with the new title of Agha Khan, which became hereditary from then on. After being dismissed from a second governorship (of Kirman) and becoming embroiled in an uprising, the Agha Khan led his troops and family into Afghanistan, and allied himself with the British in India – who may well have been encouraging him in order to destabilize Persia as part of the Great Game of Anglo-Russian intrigue – just at the moment when the British were chased out of Kabul in the catastrophic defeat of 1842. He finally settled in Bombay in 1848, under British protection. There 'His Highness', as the British styled him, remained for the next 30 years, rebuilding his wealth and raising racehorses.

The present imam, HH Agha Khan IV, Harvard-educated, ministers to his scattered community of several million Nizaris through the Agha Khan Foundation in Switzerland and his headquarters near Paris, supervising the Agha Khan University in Pakistan, some 300 other schools and colleges, and a network of 200 health programmes and institutions, including six hospitals. The British link remains strong. His first wife was Lady James Crichton-Stuart, née Sarah Crocker-Poole, a top fashion model before the marriage; and the largest Nizari community, some 10,000 strong, is in London.

Of all the consequences of the Mongol assault on the world of Islam, this must be the most astonishing. In 1254 Mönkhe, scared by a rumour that a bunch of Assassins are after his blood, launches a campaign to destroy them. It succeeds. Assassins vanish. But in vanishing, they transmute, their imam in the end drawing good from evil, becoming a true father to a people reborn.

For the Mongols, that was half the problem solved. Now they could turn their attention to the rest of this part of the Islamic world: the Abbasid caliphate, and its centre, Baghdad, with which they had unfinished business, having tried and failed to take it in 1238.

In a sense, Hulegu had an easy target. The Abbasid caliphate was already a spent force, divided against itself in innumerable sects – Nusayris, Druzes, Qarmatians, Takhtajis, Zaydis, Sufis. Turks fought Persians, both fought Arabs. Syrians still resented the Abbasid conquest almost 500 years before, and yearned for a messiah to free them. To the east, the great Silk Road cities of Khwarezm – Bukhara, Samarkand, Urgench, Merv – were in ruins from the Mongol assault of 1219–22. At the centre, the royal line of Abbasids was debilitated by luxury. Rather like the Roman empire, as Philip Hitti says in his *History of the Arabs*, 'the sick man was already on his deathbed when the burglars burst open the doors'.

In September 1257 Hulegu, advancing 400 kilometres from the Elburz mountains, sent a message to Baghdad telling the caliph to surrender and demolish the city's outer walls as a sign of good faith. The caliph, al-Mustasim, must know the fate brought upon the world by Genghis Khan, wrote Hulegu.

What humiliation, by the grace of Eternal Heaven, has over-taken the dynasties of the shahs of Khwarezm, the Seljuks, the kings of Daylam [the region where the Assassins had been entrenched] . . . Yet the gates of Baghdad were never closed to any of these races . . . How then should entry be refused to us, who possess such strength and such power?

The caliph, a lacklustre character whose predecessors had been puppets dancing in the hands of their Seljuk masters, could only hope that this menace would pass, as the Seljuk menace had. He was, after all, the spiritual head of all Islam; God was surely on his side. 'O young man,' he foolishly blustered, 'do you not know that from the East to the Maghreb, all the worshippers of Allah, whether kings or beggars, are slaves to this court of mine?' Empty words, as it turned out. Of all the caliph's 'slaves' not a beggar, let alone a king, came to help him.

In November the Mongol army, leaving their families and flocks behind, started their two-month advance on Baghdad from several hundred kilometres away. They came in three columns. One, under Baiju, veteran of the 1238 assault on Baghdad, approached from the north, having crossed the Tigris near Mosul, 325 kilometres upriver. The second was commanded by one of the army's greatest generals, Kitbuqa, who was not a Mongol but a Naiman, one of the tribes blotted up by Genghis 50 years before. His group, the most southerly, advanced due west from today's Lorestan in Iran, while in the centre came Hulegu himself. Descending from the Iranian highlands along the Alwand river, Hulegu ordered his catapult teams to collect wagonloads of boulders as ammunition, since it was known that there were no stones around Baghdad. There was scant opposition. A Muslim force on low-lying ground near Ba'qubah, some 60 kilometres north-east of Baghdad, met with disaster when the Mongols opened irrigation channels, flooded them out, then moved in on the floundering foot soldiers, killing 12,000 of them as they tried to escape the muddy waters. The three columns met at Ctesiphon, 30 kilometres south of Baghdad on the Tigris, aiming to take the newer eastern section of the city, with its Abbasid palace, law college and 150-year-old walls, and then the two bridges that straddled the river on pontoons.

By 22 January 1258, Baghdad was surrounded. With the Tigris blocked upstream by pontoons and downstream by a battalion of horsemen, flight was impossible; one official who tried to escape downriver in a small fleet was turned back by a barrage of rocks, flaming naphtha and arrows that sank three of his boats and killed many of his entourage. The assault began a week later. Rocks from the Mongol catapults knocked chunks off the walls, littering their bases with rubble. To gain better vantage points, the Mongols gathered the rubble and built towers onto which they hauled catapults, the better to aim at the buildings inside. Amid a steady rain of arrows that forced the inhabitants under cover, boulders smashed roofs and pots of flaming naphtha set houses on fire. By 3 February, Mongol forces had seized the eastern walls.

Inside Baghdad, panic reduced the caliph to mush. 'Truth and error remained hidden from him,' in Juvaini's scathing words. He tried sending envoys to sue for peace: first his vizier, along with the city's catholicos, the leader of its Christians, in the hope of appealing through Hulegu's Nestorian wife, the Kerait princess Doquz, cousin of his Nestorian mother Sorkaktani. Doquz was renowned both for her wisdom and for her stout defence of her faith, the outward sign of which was the tent-church she transported wherever she went. Hulegu, with an eye to his powerful, matchmaking mother, had a healthy respect for his wife and her creed. So when she interceded for the Christians of Baghdad, he listened. In messages shot into the city attached to arrows, Hulegu promised that the *qadis* – scholars and religious leaders – including Nestorians, would all be safe, if they ceased resisting. A second embassy sued for peace, and a third; Hulegu ignored them both. The caliph's vizier reported that there was no hope, telling his master that the efforts of his 'hastily gathered rabble are as ineffective as the twitchings of a slaughtered animal'. In the circumstances, he should surrender. 'It is the action of the wise to humble themselves and humiliate themselves.' Give up, he said, hand over the treasures, because that's what they're after; then arrange a marriage so that 'empire and religion shall fuse, so that sovereignty and splendour, caliphate and power become one'.

The caliph wavered, while the city's morale collapsed. Thousands streamed out, hoping for mercy; but since there had been no surrender, all were killed. With survivors cowering in nooks and crannies, the caliph saw he had no chance. On 10 February he led an entourage of 300 officials and relatives to Hulegu's camp to surrender. Hulegu greeted the caliph politely, and told him to order all the inhabitants to disarm and come out of the city.

This they did – only to find themselves penned and slaughtered like sheep for having continued their resistance. Sources speak of 800,000 being killed. All figures should be treated with scepticism, but the Mongols, who were used to mass executions, were quite capable of killing on such a scale. Even if the true figure was one-tenth that amount, it was a massacre of Third Reich proportions. No wonder Muslims refer back to it today as one of the greatest of crimes against their people and religion.

Three days later, the Mongols poured into the empty city and set almost all of it on fire. Mosques, shrines, tombs, houses – all went up in flames. The Nestorians, however, were spared, as Hulegu had promised. While Baghdad burned around them, they found sanctuary with their patriarch in a Christian church. Afterwards, the patriarch was awarded the palace of the vice-chancellor, and no doubt joined other Christians in celebrating Islam's astonishing collapse and their own renaissance.

To crown his victory, Hulegu chose to conduct an exercise in humiliation. Taking over the caliph's Octagon Palace, he threw a banquet for his officers and family members to which he invited his prisoner.

'You are the host, we are your guests,' he taunted. 'Bring whatever you have that is suitable for us.'

The caliph, quivering with fear, volunteered to unlock his treasure rooms, then found that none of his remaining servants could sort out the right keys. Eventually, after locks had been smashed, the attendants brought out 2,000 suits of clothes, 10,000 dinars in cash, jewel-encrusted bowls and gems galore, all of which Hulegu magnanimously divided among his commanders.

Then he turned on the caliph. OK, these were the visible treasures. Now: 'Tell my servants where your *buried* treasures are.'

There was indeed a buried treasure, as perhaps Hulegu already knew: a pool full of gold ingots, which were fished out and distributed.

Next the harem, 700 women, and the 1,000 servants. Oh, please, begged the caliph, not all the women. Hulegu was again magnanimous. The caliph could choose 100 who would be released; the rest were shared out among the Mongol commanders.

Next day, all the possessions from the rest of the palace – royal art treasures collected over 500 years – were stacked in piles outside the gates. Later, some of the booty was sent back to Mönkhe in Mongolia. The rest (according to Rashid ad-Din) joined booty from Alamut, from other Assassins' castles, from Georgia, Armenia and Iran, all of it being taken to a fortress on an island in Lake Orumiyeh (Urmia), a salt lake in Iran's far north-western corner.

And at last, the city foul with the stench of the dead, Hulegu ordered one more set of executions: those of the caliph himself and his remaining entourage. Al-Mustasim and five others, including the caliph's eldest son, met their ignominious deaths in a nearby village. Two days later, the second son was executed. Only the youngest son was spared. He was married off to a Mongol woman, by whom he had two sons. That was the end of the Abbasid line, and the first time in history that all Islam had been left without a religious head.

Now came the peace. Bodies were buried, markets restored, officials appointed. Three thousand Mongols began the task of reconstruction in Baghdad, while others set about securing the rest of Abbasid territory. Most towns, like Al Hillah, opened their gates. Some did not, with the usual consequences: in Wasit, 15 kilometres to the south-east of Baghdad, 40,000 died (according to one source, though again the numbers must be treated with caution; always vague, they were usually exaggerated by anything up to tenfold). Resistance made no difference. The region was Hulegu's from Afghanistan to the Persian Gulf. Georgia and the rump of the Seljuk sultanate – today's eastern Turkey – submitted. Beyond lay Syria and Egypt.

To finish this part of our story we must look forward a few more years before returning to Kublai. Syria, its coast a medley of Crusader states, with an Arab dynasty ruling Aleppo and Damascus inland, was next in line. As Hulegu advanced to the Mediterranean coast the Christians quickly allied themselves to the Mongol conqueror, seeing his anti-Muslim campaign as an extension of their own crusades; their Armenian co-religionists, too, came on board. Magnanimous as before to these Christian allies, Hulegu was as brutal as ever to Muslims. One petty emir ruling in Diyarbakir, in today's south-east Turkey, had made the mistake of crucifying a Christian priest who had been travelling with a Mongol passport. Understandably, he resisted Hulegu's forces, which made things worse for him. As a curtain-raiser to the campaign westward, the Mongols took his stronghold, captured him, and subjected him to a death by a thousand cuts, slicing his flesh away bit by bit, cramming the bits into his mouth, then cutting off his head, which became a sort of talisman as the campaign proper gathered pace. It moved across the Euphrates, reaching Aleppo on 24 January 1260. After a six-day massacre here, the lands were granted to the Crusader king Bohemund VI. Hamah and Hims capitulated. Damascus was abandoned by its sultan, who fled to Egypt, and Kitbuqa personally beheaded its governor. Christians rejoiced, bells rang, wine flowed and a mosque was restored to Christian worship. Six centuries of Muslim domination seemed over. Then the Mongols turned southward, to Nablus, whose garrison was exterminated for resisting, all the while making use of the good pastures on the Syrian borderlands.

Now, at last, for Egypt, which was led by Turkish former slaves, the Mamluks (*mamluk*, owned), who had murdered their way to power only nine years before. At this point, news arrived of an event in Mongolia that changed everything. In August 1259 Mönkhe had died (a development to which we shall return in chapter 5). On hearing this, Hulegu returned to Persia with most of his invasion force, leaving Kitbuqa in command of the remaining 20,000 men.

The current Egyptian sultan, Qutuz, now did something that seemed the height of folly, but turned out to be extremely smart. When Hulegu sent envoys demanding surrender, Qutuz cut off their heads. To the Mongols, the murder of envoys was an act of barbarism that precluded all further communication, including the possibility of capitulation. It was the grossest form of insult. Such an act, famously, had precipitated Genghis's attack on Khwarezm in 1219. Nothing could have been better designed to guarantee invasion. It was, perhaps, an act of defiance: better dead than slaves again!

But it could also have been a deliberate provocation . . .

. . . because Qutuz could well have known that he had a window of opportunity to beat a Mongol force reduced by Hulegu's departure, and teetering on the very edge of sustainability. In Syria, in May, the main rivers – the Quwayq, the Orontes (Asi), the Barada, the A'waj – drop, the pastures wither. The remaining third of the Mongol army could only eat and drink at all because the other two-thirds had gone back eastward. They were shortly to learn a fundamental truth about campaigning in these parts, a truth baldly set out by John Masson Smith: 'Any forces that were small enough to be concentrated amid adequate pasture and water were not large enough to take on the mamluks.' In modern terms, the Mongols were too low on manpower, vehicles and fuel to fight a major battle. A wiser leader might have thought twice. But faced with such an insult, so blatant a challenge, the Mongols had no option but to fight.

In July 1260 a force of some 15,000–20,000 men, perhaps equal to, perhaps rather less than that of the Mongols (no-one knows the numbers for sure), left Egypt for Palestine, re-victualled in Acre and on 3 September, during Ramadan, prepared to meet Kitbuqa's army near Nablus. This was a very different type of army from that of the Mongols. With Egypt's limited pasture, the average Mamluk would have had just one horse, well cared for, bigger and stronger than the pony-size mounts of the Mongols. The Mamluks depended not on speed but on weaponry: bows and arrows, of course, but also lances, javelins, swords, axes, maces and daggers. They were excellent bowmen, with weapons made by expert bowyers (Mongol bows were home-made) and arrows supplied by professional fletchers in amazing quantities. John Masson Smith has calculated that at the battle of Hattin, where Saladin's troops defeated the Crusaders in 1187, they used 1.3 million arrows. The soldiers trained in both speed of fire and accuracy, shooting from a stationary horse. Carrying so much weight, in the open country where the Mongols were at home the Mamluk horses would never have been able to catch their enemies and bring their arms into action; but in a shoot-out the Mongols would lose, as they had once already, at the battle of Parvan in Afghanistan in 1221. In addition, the Mamluk fighters were selected for their physical excellence, whereas the Mongols were ordinary citizen-soldiers, superb only as long as they could choose the terms of battle.

This time, they could not. The place was called Ain Jalut, the Spring of Goliath, because it is here, where the Jezreel valley ends up against the curve of the barren Gilboa hills, that David supposedly slung his fatal stone. No good account of the battle survives, but according to probably the most reliable one,[3] Qutuz arrived after a 50-kilometre march from Acre early on the morning of 3 September, choosing the site for its wooded ridges and good water supply. Behind him were the Gilboa hills, and the rising sun. According to one account, he scattered troops into the nearby slopes and under trees, and arrayed the rest of them at the bottom of the hills. The Mongols must have come around the hills from the Jordan, to meet the Mamluks as they advanced slowly, making a terrifying noise with their kettle-drums. Too late the Mongols, blinded by the sun, discovered that they had been outmanoeuvred. With reinforcements streaming in from Gilboa's side-valleys, the Mamluk cavalry, fresh and well-armoured, closed around the depleted and weakened Mongols. Two Mamluk leaders who had joined the Mongols redefected, reducing the Mongol forces yet further.

The Mongols died almost to a man. According to one account, Kitbuqa was magnificent to the end, spurring on his men until his horse was brought down, he himself caught and

[3] An oral report by Sarim al-Din, assessed in Peter Thorau, 'The Battle of Ayn Jalut: A Re-examination'.

taken before Qutuz. He refused to bow, proclaiming how proud he was to be the khan's servant – 'I am not like you, the murderer of my master!' were his last words before they cut off his head.

It was here, in today's West Bank, that the Mongols' war machine finally ran out of steam. They were not invincible after all. Mongol forces would mount several later attacks on Syria, but could never hold it because, once away from good pastures, they had no natural advantage. Genghis's ambition of a world under Mongol rule had reached its limits in the west. Future expansion would lie in the east, with Kublai.

The Mongols' defeat in 1260 has a peculiar resonance today. Muslims who see the Americans as the 'new Mongols' draw hope from Ain Jalut, for it proves to them that even an apparently overwhelming assault on Islam cannot succeed for ever. To quote one article on the second seizure of Baghdad: 'Fundamentalists believe they have every reason to anticipate victory in this battle, because the story of Baghdad did not end in 1258. The Egyptian mamluks were able to halt the tide of Mongol victories at the Battle of Ayn Jalut in Palestine two years later.'[4] History, of course, has no force apart from individuals willing and able to put its message into practice; and there is no reason to think that lack of fuel will limit the US-led coalition, as lack of pasture limited the Mongols. But Muslims see a message nevertheless, drawing further re-assurance even from the subsequent century-long Mongol occupation of Persia and Iraq. For, long before their rule ended, the Mongols had converted to Islam – proof to some that, whatever the setbacks, Islam will always in the end be victorious.

[4] Husain Haqqani, 'The American Mongols', *Foreign Policy*, May–June 2003.

3

THE TAKING OF YUNNAN

KUBLAI, MEANWHILE, WAS GAZING SOUTH, TOWARDS THE SONG
empire of southern China, a very much greater challenge than
the world of Islam.

Over the 300 years since its foundation, Song China had
become the world's leading power. Its stature had nothing to
do with its geographical size. It had been cut almost in half
when the Jürchen from Manchuria seized the north and its 40
million people in 1125, and was only one-fifth the area of
China today – a good deal smaller than Kublai's homeland.
But southern Song was everything that Mongolia wasn't: 70
million people, probably more, in scores of cities crowded in
and around China's ancient heartland, the fertile plain of the
river the Chinese call the Chang, and Europeans know as
the Yangtze. From the edge of the Tibetan highlands, where it
emerged from precipitous gorges, the river was, as it has
remained, a blessing and a curse, its waters irrigating and
sometimes drowning the rich paddy-fields along its course. It
was also the country's major highway, navigable for 2,700
kilometres, within reach of which lay half a dozen of China's

biggest cities. This was what the Chinese meant when they referred to China as the 'Middle Kingdom', the world between the sea and the mountains, and also between the northern deserts and the wet, hot south, where the forested hills flanking the Yangtze's basin fall away again to lush coastal plains. What a contrast with the Mongols: a people from treeless grasslands and barren gravel plains, with not a fence or a navigable river anywhere, who numbered scarcely 1 per cent of Song's population and had just one little town of their own.

Mere numbers give no clue to Song's real strengths: its cultural depth, economic drive and political unity. The Song had linked six independent kingdoms, creating a nation-state greater than all its neighbours – Tanguts and Tibetans in the west, Nanchao and two Vietnams (as now, but with different names) in the south. True, northern China was lost to its Jürchen conquerors in 1125, along with its capital Kaifeng; but the southern Song preserved their cultural identity, ruling from their new capital, Hangzhou (Linan as it was then). In any case, Jin was not a write-off, because the two Chinese populations shared language and culture, while the two governments, Chinese and Jürchen, rubbed along most of the time, their occasional disputes doing little to disrupt everyday life.

For artistry, wealth, inventiveness, depth of thought – for the quantity and quality of practically any cultural and social trait you care to measure – southern Song was unrivalled. By comparison, Islam was a novelty, an empire united by religion and trade, but divided against itself. Song China exploded with knowledge while Europe hardly stirred in its pre-Renaissance slumber. India? South-east Asia? Japan? Africa? Nothing comparable. The French scholar Jacques Gernet describes what happened under Song rule up until the Mongol invasions as a renaissance, in the European sense of the term – a return to a classical tradition, a diffusion of knowledge, an upsurge of science and technology, a new humanistic view of the world – some of which would flow westward and invigorate Europe. To use the word 'renaissance' invites a comparison between Song and fifteenth-century Italy – which is fair enough in some ways, except that the Song renaissance did not lead on to the outward-looking dynamism of post-medieval Europe: this was a society that favoured continuity and tradition over revolution.

Here is a brief sketch of the world the Mongols were about to challenge, a few flowers plucked at random from a garden that would take lifetimes to explore.

At bottom, the renaissance was fuelled by new methods of growing rice. Life seems to have become marginally easier for the vast mass of peasants, though they are virtually invisible in the records, which, like most official records in most cultures, were written by the literate elite for their masters. More and better food, population growth, trade, new industries (like cotton), people on the move in search of self-improvement, rising incomes from land, the spread of education, more civil servants – all these developments interacted to bring about the boom. Great estates provided income for absentee landlords, who took to living in town. The growth of wealth funded the arts, gardening, fashion, ceramics, architecture. Many peasant farmers, finding themselves landless as the estates of the wealthy expanded, chose to go on the road, taking employment in the army or as servants in the mansions of the rich, or in taverns and teahouses, or as entertainers, or in one of the growing industries – coal-mining, metallurgy, paper-making, printing, salt-making, perhaps in one of the state-funded factories, some of which employed over 3,000 workers. Song porcelain became one of China's glories. Carters crowded the roads, boatmen the rivers and canals.

With the inland frontiers blocked by 'barbarian' kingdoms,

Song China turned seaward. The Yangtze, its tributaries and their canals formed 50,000 kilometres of river highways, along which merchant ships sailed to a coastline dotted with ports that far outclassed their European counterparts and from which sailed ocean-going ships with refined sail-systems designed to take advantage of the regular monsoon winds. Quanzhou was the greatest of these ports, so well known to foreign merchants that it became known to them by its Arabic name, Zayton, possibly a corruption of an old Chinese name, with the advantage of meaning 'olive tree' in Arabic.[1] From here or from the mouth of the Yangtze, a Song captain, setting his course with a compass (an invention taken over from geomancers almost two centuries before it found its way to Europe) would take to the sea in his four- or six-masted junk, made safe with watertight compartments (a feature not seen in Europe until the nineteenth century), with 1,000 people aboard. Foreign trade spread Song coins from Japan to India. Chinese ceramics were exported to the Philippines, Borneo, even Africa.

The examination system for recruiting civil servants, already well established, was enlarged, giving new power to the 20,000 'mandarins' and their 200,000–300,000 employees. Laws curbed the rich and helped the poor. State officials were paid well enough to limit corruption. The state, its income secured by taxes and by monopolies on salt and mining, looked after its people as never before, building orphanages, hospitals, canals, cemeteries and reserve granaries, even funding village schools. Taxes were reformed to win the co-operation of the peasant farmers. The revenues accruing to the state from taxation were immense, and carefully recorded. In the late twelfth century, annual revenues from maritime customs duty alone amounted to 65 million strings of 1,000

[1] Zaytun is supposedly the origin of the English word 'satin'. It's a neat idea, repeated in many books, but it's not true. 'Satin' predates Zaytun.

coins each – that's 65 *billion* coins. Now, coins are cumbersome things, and the monetary system was fraught with inconveniences. Every emperor issued his own currency, and 1,000 coins, strung through square holes, weighed about 6 kilos but were the equivalent of only about 1 ounce of silver (just over $7.00 today), with which one could buy about 60 kilos of rice.[2] Soon after the year 1000, Song had started printing banknotes. Later, commercial organizations began to use cheques, which could be cashed at exchange offices in all major cities.

And how was paper money made? The answer introduces a defining trait of Chinese society in general and Song in particular: the explosion of information. Money was printed as books were – with wood-blocks, images cut into wood in low relief. It was this technique that underpinned the explosion in records and reading matter that had started in the eighth century in China, Japan and Korea. The immense labour of carving each page in reverse inspired the next logical step: printing with movable type, an idea that did not occur – or, at least, was not put into practice – anywhere else until Johannes Gutenberg perfected the revolutionary technique in Germany in the mid-fifteenth century. The story is worth telling, because it would provide the Mongols with one of history's great missed opportunities.

The idea was attributed to a certain Pi Sheng, who in the eleventh century created characters by incising them in wet clay, then baking them. To print them, he chose his characters, fixed them in a frame, inked them, placed cloth or paper on them, and applied a little pressure, rather like taking a brass rubbing. It could not have worked very well, because characters cut into wet clay would hardly be great calligraphy. Still, it was ingenious – but also, in the context of

[2] These coins are still so common that you can pick them up for a few dollars from dealers.

Chinese culture, a dead end: first, because wood-block printing was cheap and efficient, a technology absolutely appropriate for China's script and illustrations; and second, because the use of movable characters was the exact opposite. A typesetter would have needed several thousand characters just to represent the full range of the Chinese script, let alone the extra copies he would need of the many common characters, amounting to tens of thousands of characters in all. The imperial printing works had 200,000 in the eighteenth century; indexed by rhyme, they were stored on several revolving round tables, each 2 metres across. Even then the technique, using ceramic or metal letters, was used only rarely, because it took so long to choose the characters and make up a page. It would not be adapted for mechanical use until the nineteenth century; and today's software has consigned the problem to history.

When Gutenberg devised a similar solution to the problem of reproducing texts, he had several technical advantages – paper with a hard surface and a wine-press being two of them – and a supreme cultural advantage in the alphabet, which meant he only had to make a couple of hundred metal characters – the 26 letters in upper and lower case, in several different versions each, plus punctuation. Perhaps because their script was simpler, it was the Koreans who picked up the idea and ran with it, becoming the first people to use movable metal type in printing the 50-volume *Prescribed Ritual Texts of the Past and Present* in 1234. As it happens, this was shortly before Song fell to the Mongols, who at that moment had within their reach almost all the elements that might have allowed them to develop printing with movable type two centuries before Gutenberg – on which more in chapter 16.

The astonishing growth in books in Song China is proof of just how effective wood-block printing was. Pear wood, with its smooth and even texture, was the wood of choice for most ordinary work, while delicate illustrations were carved into the hard wood of honey locust trees, and for text alone block-cutters worked with soft boxwood. The output was phenomenal. The imperial library in Kaifeng had 80,000 volumes. Soon after the Song came to power, the whole Buddhist canon was published – 260,000 pages in two-page blocks. There were vast official text-collections and encyclopedias with up to 1,000 chapters. A fashion for collections inspired inventories of paintings, calligraphy, stones, coins, inks – anything and everything. Scientific treatises appeared on mushrooms, bamboos, peonies, fruit trees, birds, crabs, citrus fruits and all sorts of technical subjects, one of which (Shen Kua's *Meng-ch'i pi-t'an* or *Dream Pool Essays*) includes the story of Pi Sheng and his movable type. Medicine, geography, maths, astronomy – there were treatises on them all. The print runs were astonishing, ranging into many millions of copies. Of one tenth-century Buddhist collection, 400,000 copies still survive.

Under the influence of the eleventh-century Si-ma Guang, historians developed both literary flair and a concern for good sources, with systematic notes of attribution. Scholars, seeking to escape the stultifying influence of Buddhist theology and stimulated by the fearsomely hard examinations that led to careers, status and income, sought to return to and move beyond Confucian traditions, asserting their faith in reason and evidence and the benefits of education: in short, in the possibility of progress in society and politics. These scholar–officials were deeply concerned with the nature of morality and its implications for life here and now – not, thank goodness, with the nature of God and his supposed ways, as so many Renaissance Europeans would be. Religious disputes bubbled up in plenty, but not religious wars, which are fought by governments, not churches. From these intellectual interests sprang many brilliant men and at least one genius: Shen Gua, a sort of eleventh-century precursor of da Vinci and Darwin who recognized the nature of fossils, theorized that mountains had once been sea-beds, improved astronomical instruments, pioneered advances in mathematics, described how compasses worked, wrote on pharmacology, and took a shrewd interest in politics, history and literature, to list but a few of his accomplishments.

The Song upper classes rejected violent sports – which recalled barbarian and lower-class pleasures – in favour of literature, painting and calligraphy. They loved antiquities: Hung Tsun's *Ku-ch'uan* (*Ancient Coins*), published in the 1190s, was the first book on numismatics. A catalogue of ancient stone and bronze inscriptions records 2,000 of them; it was made by a collector, Zhao Mingcheng, whose wife, Li Qingzhao, was one of the most brilliant poets of her age. In towns, shopkeepers and craftsmen loved storytelling, short musical mimes, puppet-shows and shadow-theatres: traditions that would later stimulate theatre and opera.

A great power culturally, then; but not so great militarily. It was not through lack of numbers – the Song had over a million soldiers in 1045. It was a matter of status and efficiency. The officers were scholar–officials, not professional soldiers, and the soldiers were mercenaries, social dregs raised by recruiters who were the scourge of the countryside. There were no barbarian mercenaries from the northern grasslands, and thus no cavalry to speak of. But inefficiency in the body of the army was countered by some extraordinary technology. As cities grew, so did siege warfare, with a variety of heavy-duty weapons, like the man-powered trebuchets and siege bows which the Mongols would soon adopt. This machinery was combined with the alchemical researches of a previous age. In the early tenth century, gunpowder – based on saltpetre – was used in incendiary devices called 'flying fires': primitive rockets. A century later, Song catapults lobbed bombs and smoke grenades.

It was this great culture that the Mongols were now about to assault, with an odd consequence. It was going to be like squirting water on an oil-fire. The fuel was scattered, along with Mongol forces, flowing westward, infusing Europe with Chinese ideas and discoveries. And the driving force behind this chain of events was Kublai.

Obviously a frontal assault on Song, over the busy, broad and well-defended Yangtze, would risk failure. The Mongols were not in the business of failure. Mönkhe needed something that would give him an edge. It so happened that to the south-west of Song, outside its borders, was a statelet that could, if taken, act as a base from which to open a second front.

Kublai was to be in charge, and about time too. In 1252 he was 37, and had never yet been given responsibility for anything but his own estates. His brother and father had led major campaigns while still in their teens and twenties. A first campaign, an untried leader: Mönkhe was careful to give Kublai the best of help, in the form of one of his most experienced generals, Uriyang-kadai, the 50-year-old son of the legendary Subedei, conqueror of half Asia and much of Russia under Genghis Khan.

Their target was a long way away, and very hard to get to. It was the core of what had between 647 and 937 been a great kingdom, Nanzhao, now reduced to a rump centred on its capital, Dali, after which it is known. Dali, which controlled the road, and thus the trade, between India (through what is now Burma) and Vietnam, was a knot of forested mountains and competing tribes, notoriously difficult to get into, let alone control. In 751, a Tang emperor tried to subdue it and lost 60,000 men.

Not surprisingly, information about Dali/Nanzhao remains scanty and contentious. Thai legends, for instance, refer to Nanzhao as the original homeland of the Thais, where they had ruled in glory until chased away by the Mongols; today, the consensus among scholars is that Thais were insignificant warrior groups living in the far south. Dali's Bai people, a Tibetan–Burmese tribe, had emerged as the dominant group in 937, and since then had retained a sturdy independence for three centuries under its royal family, the Duans. For a region and a culture few westerners have ever heard of, this was no mean place. The Duans ruled an area some 800 kilometres across – half a million square kilometres, about the size of Afghanistan or Texas. Sichuan, to the north, is notoriously wet, so the Chinese dubbed Dali and its surrounding area Yun-nan, 'South of the Clouds'. Dali was a sort of Inner Asian cross between Afghanistan and Switzerland, its tribal rivalries held in check by rulers made rich by trade, and at peace with the Chinese, who had learned enough to leave the place alone to its tangle of tribes, its mountains, its glorious lake and its charming climate. Today, Dali still thrives on its ancient roots and individuality. The Bai inhabitants still wear traditional bright wrap-around shirts and top-heavy head-dresses. Stone houses decorated with wood carvings line cobbled streets. Buddhist pagodas recall old Nanzhao. Artists work the local marble. Tourists wander the old town, or the mountain trails and the lakeside. It reminds ageing hippies of Kathmandu as it used to be. For Mönkhe and Kublai, it was a stepping-stone to further conquest.

The details of this high-risk and challenging enterprise are obscure, but it is worth looking at it as closely as possible because it explains how Yunnan became part of the Mongol empire, and thus a province of modern China.

For strategists back in Karakorum, invasion must have looked a crazy idea. Dali, flanked on one side by the saw-toothed Azure Mountains and on the other by the Erhai lake, offered few approaches, and all were easily defended. But those three centuries of peace had made it complacent. It had no army to speak of. It was a plum, ripe for the picking – if only the Mongols could get there across Song. That would mean gathering their armies in territory newly conquered

from the Tanguts, and then slicing southward for 1,000 kilometres along Song's weakly guarded western borders. It
would have to be done well, which meant careful planning.

Mustering from the late summer of 1252 in the semi-desert
of the Ordos, within the great northern loop of the Yellow
River, Kublai's army took a year to gather itself together: a
cumbersome process that must have involved assembling
huge numbers of wagons and siege machines, all of which
would have to cross rivers and valleys. Eventually, in the
autumn of 1253, this great force headed south-west for 350
kilometres along the Yellow River to the Tao, then south
across the foothills of the Tibetan plateau into what is today
northern Sichuan. This was a pretty remote area, even for the
Mongols, but it had been invaded (conquered would be too
strong a word) by Ogedei's second son, Köten, in 1239.
Kublai camped on the high, bleak grasslands of today's Aba
Autonomous Region, with no trouble apparently from the
locals, the notoriously wild and semi-nomadic Golok tribes-
men, and was ready to attack Dali.

There would not be any need for destruction, if Dali
capitulated. Later, the Chinese *Yuan History* told a story of
how Kublai's Chinese advisers had managed to talk sense into
his naturally violent Mongol soul. One evening, his main
adviser Yao Shu told a story of how a Song general, Cao Bin,
had captured Nanjing without killing 'so much as a single
person; the markets did not alter their openings, and it was as
if the proper overlord had returned'. Next morning, as Kublai
was mounting up, he leaned over to Yao Shu and said: 'What
you told me yesterday about Cao Bin not killing people, that
is something I can do.'

Following normal practice, Kublai sent three envoys ahead
offering Dali the chance to capitulate. Dali's leading minister,
the power behind the Duan ruler, executed them. He must
have been ill-informed, over-confident, or lacking all sense
of history, or all three. Killing envoys was the worst of

diplomatic crimes, a public slap in the face that guaranteed an all-out assault, and who knew what horrors thereafter.

Kublai divided his forces into three. One wing rode eastward, off the high grasslands, down into the Sichuan Basin, by today's Chengdu, replenishing supplies in the newly harvested fields of Dujiangyan, where dams and artificial islands dating back some 1,500 years controlled the Min river. Kublai himself headed south over the grasslands, meeting up with column no. 1 some 350 kilometres and perhaps three days later. All of this would have been well known to those in Dali. Meanwhile, Uriyang-kadai took a difficult – indeed, non-existent – path some 150 kilometres further west, deep into the mountains of western Sichuan, cutting across valleys and ridges to the main road between Dali and Tibet. This would give him a fast two-day run to Dali when the time came. Gao, Dali's leader, massed his forces on the Upper Yangtze, whose headwaters had formed a valley a day's march over a ridge to the east of the city. Dali's army would have looked formidable, but the Mongols had been in this situation many times. A river was no obstacle. They had crossed dozens on their way south. Some of the old hands would have been with Genghis in 1226, when he crossed the Yellow River using sheepskins as floats for rafts. This had been standard procedure there for centuries; even today, you can try it for yourself in Lanzhou, or even further downriver in Shapotou, near the point where Genghis's armies crossed at the start of his last campaign. The crossing was made at night, of course, and in silence. Led by a general named Bayan, of whom more later when he steps into the limelight, the Mongols appeared at dawn on Gao's flank, attacked, inflicted terrible damage and forced a rapid retreat back to Dali.

With Uriyang-kadai galloping in along the lakeside from the north, Dali was now at Kublai's mercy. At this point, given the opposition, you might think that all-out slaughter would follow, in the spirit of Genghis. But Genghis was not all ruthlessness and barbarism. He slaughtered city populations for one main reason: to encourage other cities to surrender. It saves so much trouble when cities surrender. You get booty enough anyway, and it is easier to have subjects made grateful for their survival rather than made bitter and possibly rebellious by brutality. Here, there were no other cities to be conquered. Kublai ordered restraint, proclaiming that the common people should not be punished for the faults of their foolish leaders. Was this all down to his Chinese advisers? I think not. Kublai by now had enough experience of administration to have seen this for himself; but it is only natural that his advisers – and the writers of the *Yuan History* – should give the credit to China's civilizing influence.

It all fell into place quite easily. The leading minister and his underlings who had executed the envoys were themselves executed, but that was all. The king became a puppet in the hands of Kublai's officials. Rather like a prince in British India, he was pampered into subservience, being later awarded the grand-sounding but empty title of Maharajah. Uriyang-kadai, using Dali as his military base, went on to 'pacify' tribes further south and east, penetrating today's north Vietnam, taking Hanoi in 1257, then retreating rather hastily in the face of tropical heat, malaria and some spirited resistance. This is easily said, but it was an immense operation. Yunnan to Hanoi is 1,000 kilometres. In four years the Mongols had marched all the way round Song's western frontiers, meeting hardly any resistance; now they – more specifically, Kublai himself – had all the information needed to plan the next phase of the war against the south.

Yunnan was like a new weight placed on scales: it rebalanced China in interesting ways.

The place was left to its own devices with just a small garrison for almost 20 years, during which the only development of any note – more of a footnote really – was that local officers arranged a brief friendly contact with a tiny neighbouring chiefdom, Kaungai, which was on the upper Irrawaddy, and thus on the main route westward to the Burmese lowlands. This event, entirely insignificant at the time, would acquire significance much later, when Kublai turned an acquisitive eye on Burma.

In 1273 Yunnan's first high-level administrator arrived. Saiyid Ajall was a Turkmen who had survived Genghis's brutal assault on Bukhara in 1220 because his grandfather had surrendered at the head of 1,000 horsemen. Nine years old at the time, the boy was raised in Mongolia and China and went on to make a distinguished career in various government posts, culminating in Yunnan, which, with the help of his son Nasir al-Din, he brought fully into the empire.

The consequences endure in Yunnan's present-day multi-culturalism. Here was an area inhabited by aboriginal populations who were no threat to anyone, and yet found themselves assaulted by Mongols leading a mainly Chinese army. The area was then handed over to a Muslim who made it part of a Mongol–Chinese empire, and was responsible for the introduction of Islam. As a result, it attracted Muslims. Today Yunnan has half a million Muslims as part of its rich amalgam of peoples.

4

IN XANADU

BACK ON HIS CHINESE LANDS, KUBLAI EXPERIMENTED WITH large-scale estate management, almost as if he were honing the skills he would need as a future emperor astride two worlds, Mongol and Chinese. His appanages were beginning to look less like estates and more like miniature kingdoms, especially his main one in the Wei valley. To oversee this substantial slab of territory – 50,000 square kilometres, with a mixture of Chinese and non-Chinese inhabitants – he appointed a 20-year-old Uighur, Lien Xixian, who in turn employed a venerable Confucian, Xu Heng. In the stylized words of the *Yuan History*, both men adopted the high-minded Confucian ideal 'to curb the violent and support the weak'. Together with one of Kublai's other advisers, the Zen Buddhist monk Liu Bingzhong, they re-established schools, banned Mongols from enslaving scholars and printed paper money. In a long memorandum Liu set out the steps Kublai should take to keep society running smoothly and profitably, pointing out that good administration depended on good civil servants, which could only emerge from good schools. In effect, the polymath Liu advised Kublai to act like a Chinese emperor. He should codify the tax and legal systems, reintroduce the civil service examinations and finance the writing of the previous dynasty, the traditional task of a new Chinese ruler. Kublai, however, was not about to go that far. There would be no civil service examinations, because that would mean all his advisers would be Chinese; and there would be no dynastic history of the Jin, because that would be seen by Chinese as proclaiming a new dynasty, which would be seen by Mongols as an attempt to usurp his brother's authority. Perhaps that was what Liu wanted; but not Kublai.

Kublai was already straddling the two worlds, and in 1256 took the first big decision towards making this precarious balance permanent. He needed a better headquarters. He had no town of sufficient stature in his estates. He could not assert traditional Mongol values with a tent-city and mobile palace if he wished to retain the trust of his new Chinese subjects, on whom he now depended for his income. So, perhaps thanks in part to Liu, he decided to create a fixed base, a capital. Why not? Ogedei had one in Karakorum; his brother Hulegu had the choice of many Islamic cities; government in north China demanded no less. But it would have to be done with care. A true Chinese ruler, of course, would have taken over one of the old capitals, maybe Xian or Kaifeng, both within reach of his estates, or even Beijing, now regaining some of its self-respect after Genghis's assault in 1215. But Kublai was not Chinese, and could not afford to seem so in the eyes of his family and fellow Mongols. His Chinese advisers understood the problem, and set out to choose a suitable site.

Kublai knew the general area where his capital needed to be, because there was not a huge range of choices if he was to assert the two cultures equally. It would have to be within

KUBLAI'S HEARTLAND

A stone tortoise (*below*), once a pillar-base, is the sole relic of Karakorum, the capital built on the Mongolian grasslands to administer the empire founded by Genghis Khan. The stupas in the background, built in the seventeenth century from Karakorum's bricks, form the monastery of Erdene Zuu, now one of Mongolia's top tourist attractions. In the mid-thirteenth century, this was the empire's heart for Genghis's children, including his youngest son, Tolui, Kublai's father. In this Persian portrait (*above*), Tolui is shown with his wife, Sorkaktani — Kublai's hugely influential mother.

STRIKING AT THE HEART OF ISLAM

In 1253 Kublai's brother, the khan Mönkhe, sent his other brother Hulegu
to resume the conquest of Islam and extend the Mongol empire westward.
Here (*right*) Mönkhe holds a celebration on the eve of the campaign.
Hulegu first eradicated the notorious sect of Assassins, whose head,
Hassan, supposedly initiated his followers by drugging them (*above*) before
despatching them on murderous missions from his main HQ, the
formidable castle of Alamut in Iran's Elburz mountains (*below*). In 1258,
after destroying the Assassin castles, Hulegu launched a devastating assault
on Baghdad (*below right*) which is still remembered by Muslims today as
one of Islam's greatest disasters.

In Xanadu, Hints of Vanished Splendour

Today, Kublai's summer HQ, Xanadu – Shang-du, 'Upper Capital' – is a long-abandoned site of ridges, grassy plains and distant hills. The palace where Marco Polo met Kublai is an eroded mound (*above*), with little to suggest past glory, except a marble pillar (*left*) displayed in the nearby museum. An original gateway is blocked by a wall of rubble (*below*).

A nearby hill (*above right*) is capped by an *ovoo*, a stone shrine. Xanadu will not remain so wild for long. Nearby is a new, comfortable, Mongolian-style tourist camp (*right*), set up by the energetic and imaginative 'Benjamin' Ren (*below*).

THE COMING OF BUDDHISM

Kublai's commitment both to rule China and to extend his empire led him to build on Mongol contacts with Tibet and with its universalist religion, Buddhism. The link was established in 1244 when the head of Tibet's Saskya sect was summoned from Tibet (*top left*) by Kublai's cousin, Köten (*left*).

The two met near Liangzhou (today's Wuwei), at a place now marked by 108 pagodas, a number sacred in Buddhist theology (*below*).

Here a museum commemorates the occasion and emphasizes the importance of the Mongol–Chinese–Tibetan link, with fine though inauthentic artworks, like murals and bronze busts of the main participants. With the Saskya lama came his two young nephews, one of whom, Phags-pa (*top right*), would become Kublai's Buddhist guru and chief religious adviser.

IN KUBLAI'S NEW CAPITAL, A GREAT BUDDHIST TEMPLE

In 1271, under Phags-pa's guidance, Kublai built the White Pagoda (*below*), which was the largest structure in his new capital, Dadu. The pagoda survives today as one of Beijing's most impressive monuments, and the only Yuan one. Its architect was a Nepalese named Arniko (*inset*), one of many foreign artists and intellectuals employed by Kublai, and now a symbol of Chinese–Nepalese cooperation. The White Pagoda is still a living centre of worship, as the presence of two Tibetan monks showed when I was there in 2005 (*right*).

reach of Beijing, then known as Zhongdu, the Central Capital; it would also have to be on grasslands, in traditional Mongol territory.

The grasslands of Inner Mongolia, now colonized by Chinese spreading from the lowlands, are surprisingly close to Beijing on the map, a mere 250 kilometres, but a world away in practice, even with the fine new roads of today's booming economy. It's a seven-hour drive, which takes you on steep, slow climbs and a great dog's-leg to skirt mountains, stretching the journey by another 100 kilometres. You head north-west, away from the city's dense traffic and noodle-soup pollution, along the expressway that carries over a million tourists a year to the Great Wall. This wonder need not detain us, because it was built long after Kublai's time. Our attention should be on the undulating mountains over which the Wall floats. This was Beijing's last line of natural defences: two tree-covered ranges, the Jungdu and the Xi mountains, all sharp ridges and precipitous ravines, a land-scape like crumpled tinfoil. The ancient route through was once a track along the Juyong Pass, just a few dozen metres across at its narrowest. It cannot accommodate all of an expressway: so while the northbound carriageway, with its tedious lines of bellowing trucks, is cut into the valley wall, the southbound one is out of sight, the other side of the mountains. It was easy to defend, and most armies could be stopped here; but not the Mongols in 1213. They went over the mountains and took it from behind. That's why the Ming, nervous of a Mongol revival, built the Wall across mountains, and why the Wall is actually many walls, its various bits and pieces guarding side-ridges where tough men and sturdy horses could sneak over.

You have now climbed several hundred feet, and are on the half-landing, as it were. It is an easy ride for the next 100 kilometres. Signs in English warn of the dangers of boredom: 'Don't try fatigue driving!', 'Do not drive tiredly!' The next stop, Zhangjiakou, used to be seven hours from Beijing; now it's two if the traffic is light. Zhangjiakou is a historic city, though you wouldn't guess this from the look of the seedy apartment blocks that now swamp the old town's huddle of single-storey houses and alleyways. It once marked the frontier between lowland China and the plateau lands of Mongolia, which is why Mongols (and foreign explorers) called it Kalgan, from the Mongolian for 'gateway'. Through here flowed the trade between Russia, Mongolia and China. A century ago it had 7,000 commercial enterprises, with ox-wagons by the hundred and camels by the hundred thousand passing through its narrow northern gate. In 1917, revolution in Russia killed the place, and its hinterland became famous for banditry. Now it has been resurrected by China's north-ward thrust into its frontier province, Inner Mongolia, while Mongol influence has vanished entirely, as far as I could see. The only sense of its historic role lies in the landscape, the long zigzag haul up on to the farmlands and villages of the Mongolian plateau.

Now you swing eastward, and your mobile beeps a message: Welcome to Inner Mongolia. The plaque on a huge statue of a hand holding a Mongolian horse-head fiddle urges us all to protect the grasslands – protection which they certainly need, because there is not much of them left. At Zhenglan Qi, a new northbound railway line is being built to bring in more farmers and civilize this frontier land with more ploughs and more towns.

Just beyond, though, there are still open spaces that would delight Kublai's soul. This too is a land rich in history, for it was Genghis's campsite on his way south to Beijing, and on his way back from its conquest. That's probably why Kublai directed his advisers' attention here. Led by Liu Bingzhong, the Golden Lotus Advisory Group, as Kublai's brains trust was called, followed the prescribed rituals of geomancy, and identified the site of the place English-speakers know as

Xanadu, and which Kublai would soon call Shang-du, the Upper Capital (as opposed to Da-du, Beijing, the Great Capital, as it became under the Mongols).

There's a legend about the site. It was originally called Lung Gang, Dragon Ridge, so Liu and the Golden Lotus Advisory Group first had to cast a spell to evict the dragon and raise a tall iron pennant endowed with magic powers to prevent its return. There was also a lake in the middle of the open plain. This had to be drained and filled in.

There was nothing much around to build with – hardly a tree, no stone quarries. Xanadu's main palace, the temples, the government buildings, the sub-palaces and officials' houses all had to be started from scratch, with teams of pack animals and wagon trains carting timber and stone (and marble, as you will see) from hundreds of kilometres away.

Kublai was a little wary of calling his new place a capital, perhaps preferring to give the impression this was just a summer camp. For the three years it took to build, and for four years thereafter, it was known as Kai-ping, being renamed Shang-du only in 1263. But it was intended as a capital right from the start, though more for government administration and his own relaxation than a living city; more a Versailles than a Paris.

It had three sections, all squares, nested in the Chinese style of capital cities. The Outer City measured 2.2 kilometres to each side, almost 9 kilometres around in all: nowhere near the '16 miles' mentioned by the unreliable Marco Polo, but large enough to contain a huddle of mud-brick and wooden houses for the mass of ordinary people, crowded into a corner less than a square kilometre in size and carefully separated from its northern section. This was a rectangular parkland, the Emperor's Garden. Here, according to the notice at the site's entrance today, 'auspiciousness reigned'. Marco Polo left a description of it. Deer nibbled meadow-grass, wandering through glades of trees, drinking from streams and fountains. This was Kublai's Arcadia, an artificial version of the Mongolian grasslands, where he could pot a deer with his bow, send a tame snow leopard to seize another, and despatch falcons skimming in pursuit of songbirds. Here, too, he had a pavilion of bamboo, some 15 metres across, from which, sheltered against sun or rain beneath a roof of split canes laid like overlapping roof-tiles, he could watch displays of horse-manship. In these peaceful surroundings, Kublai would also raise his Great Palace Tent, the centre point of Mongol-style assemblies.

In the south-east corner of the Outer City was the Imperial City, 1.4 kilometres square, surrounded by a brick wall some 4 metres high, containing government department buildings, craft houses and several temples, Taoist and Buddhist, all laid out neatly along a grid of streets.

The heart of the place, the Palace City, lay within the Imperial City. Actually, the square that contained the palace was not *quite* a square, being 570 by 620 metres, just over two kilometres around. Six meeting-halls – the halls of Crystal, Auspiciousness, Wisdom, Clarity, Fragrance and Controlling Heaven – were gathered at the feet of the palace itself, the Hall of Great Stability, constructed like all the other buildings in the Chinese style, with curled-up roofs and glazed tiles. Rashid ad-Din says that the palace was built right over the lake that had been in the middle of the site, on a platform of rubble and melted tin, with the result that later the water escaped elsewhere in streams and springs.

After the Mongol dynasty fell in 1368, Xanadu was abandoned. For 600 years it decayed, its great palace, court-yards, buildings and walls eroding away until they were mere mounds, hardly visible in the rolling grasslands. A doctor at the British legation in Beijing, Stephen Bushell, stumbled on the ruins by chance in 1872, and reported seeing blocks of marble, the remains of large temples, 'while broken lions, dragons and the remains of other carved monuments lie about in every direction'. The Japanese did some work there when they occupied Inner Mongolia in the 1930s, after which not much remained. Both before and after the communist takeover of 1949 China showed no interest, for the Mongol dynasty – established by barbarians from beyond the Gobi – was a chapter of the country's history its new rulers would rather forget.

It was here, as every British and American schoolchild used to know, that Kublai decreed a stately pleasure dome, in the dream of Samuel Taylor Coleridge one summer day in 1797, before he was famously interrupted by an unwelcome visitor. Coleridge's vision, and his poem, are fantasy; so it is a surprise to discover that the place and the glory were real, and that by visiting the one you can still sense the other.

When I was first at Xanadu in 1996, there were no signs on the approach roads. My guide was unfazed. 'Under the nose is the mouth,' he remarked with the wisdom of ages, and proved it by asking the way from a couple of farmers. We were able to drive straight into the place, a glorious wilderness, eroded walls rising gently from waving grass and pretty meadow flowers. There was no fence, no entry charge; no custodians blocked the way along the track that cut through the outer wall. The sky was pure Mongolian blue, the breeze gentle, the only sound a cuckoo.

But we were not alone. Half a dozen men were measuring things and setting up bits of string in squares. They were archaeologists from Hohhot, beginning to pick up the threads of research at last. One of them, Wei Jian, an associate professor in the Archaeological Institute, briefed me through my guide. These were the walls, over there the palace. This whole basin used to be called the Golden Flower Plain, and you could see why from the profusion of buttercups mixed in with purples and whites of flowers I didn't recognize.

'You see what a beautiful site it is, protected by the hills.'

I looked at the low wall of hills to the north. They seemed to be very sharply pointed.

'This place was chosen for superstitious reasons. It is an auspicious site. To the north is Dragon Mountain, with Lightning River to the south.'

'The mountains, they look like . . . breasts.'

He laughed. 'They have shrines on the top, piles of stones. There is a story that those with shrines are arranged in the shape of the Seven Gods.' The term he used was the same as the Mongolian name for the constellation we call the Plough, Ursa Major. 'It is something we have to check. We have much to learn.'

I walked through the waving grass towards the palace, and came across a crude little out-of-place statue – Turkish, pre-Mongol – standing as if on guard, brought here perhaps by Kublai's people, or found here and simply left alone. The ground was strewn with rubble which threatened to twist an ankle if I wasn't careful. The base of the palace was still there, an earthen mound about 50 metres long standing some 6 metres above the grass. Despite Rashid's claim, there was no hint of underground dampness, except for what may once have been a well in what was once a courtyard. Or it may have been a flag-holder. The palace mound was flanked by two others – the remains of three great buildings creating a three-sided courtyard. Paths made through the grass by wandering tourists wound to the top of the mound at either end. The front, though, was an almost sheer earth face, punctuated by a line of holes, where long-vanished roof-beams must have held a canopy. I imagined visiting dignitaries dismounting in its shade, before climbing steps to the palace itself, to be received by the emperor himself on his dais.

There is nothing solid up there now, or down below either.

It struck me as odd: a platform of earth has survived 700 years, despite the fierce summer downpours and rock-cracking frosts of winter, yet of the building itself not a trace remains. There is rubble, of course, strewn among the coarse grass. But what of the bricks and tiles? What of the remains of temples and monuments seen by Bushell in 1872? Had the Japanese taken the lot, leaving just the crude remains of stone? I picked up some, all shapeless bits and pieces, nothing about them to suggest what they had once been. A bit of glazing, from a pot, perhaps; the curve of a drab grey roof tile; stones that looked like just stones. But what rubble, what stones: the dust of Xanadu. How on earth would I do them justice?

I was back in 2004. Change was on the way, reflecting change everywhere in China. Now there's a spanking new highway leading east from Zhenglan Qi, and a sign in both Chinese and English to 'Yuan Shang-du', and a newly laid minor road, leading straight north across pasture to a tourist camp of round, white Mongolian tents. The road skirts the tourist camp with two right-angle bends, and leads you to a fence, a gate and a little museum, with two or three attendants and an entrance charge. After that, though, I was on my own, as before. Foreign tourists get no help, for the authorities have not yet appreciated the significance of the place, especially for English-speakers. The few signs were still in Chinese. I was still free to stroll the hummocks and the palace mound and the grass-covered rubble, still free to pick up rubble.

Not for much longer. The archaeologists had been at work. In the courtyard of the museum stands a glass cabinet containing an immense block of white marble, 2 metres high. It was found under the ruins of the palace in 2003, in the wake of two other similar finds which are now in the Hohhot museum. Probably the base of a pillar, it is gorgeously carved with a bas-relief of intertwining dragons and peonies, symbols of both war and peace. Finds like this are finds indeed. They hint at the magnificence of the place, and the skill of Kublai's Chinese artists, and the labour involved – the closest source of marble is 700 kilometres away. They are also new evidence in a rumbling academic dispute about whether the unreliable Marco Polo was ever actually in China at all. Yet he begins his description: 'There is at this place a very fine *marble* palace.' As a plaque near the palace mound states: 'These things testify to Marco Polo's presence.'

The greatest change is not at the site itself, but in the approach to it. The first glimpse of Xanadu is the tourist camp, some 40 small Mongolian tents (*gers*) and three huge concrete ones, with double domes. It is a hint of things to come. The camp is the creation of a local businessman, 'Benjamin' Ren (Chinese who deal with westerners often give themselves western names). Benjamin is remarkable in several ways: handsome, outgoing, generous, ambitious, and driven by a desire to combine business with ecology. Conscious of the ruinous spread of industry and agribusiness into the grasslands, he conceived a plan to plant forests and save pastures. Backed by a rich Indonesian, he bought up a county-sized tract of land, planted no fewer than 15 million trees on half of it, and would have put the rest to pasture had he not discovered it was disastrously overgrazed. Now he's letting it revert to meadowland.

One thing led to another. By chance, his land is right by Xanadu. Speaking good English, he at once saw the potential for tourism, especially with the new road. The tourists would need somewhere to stay. His tourist camp opened in 2003, offering Mongolian *gers*, cunningly adapted with double beds, lighting, running water and toilets, and the double-domed restaurants that employ locals to cook Mongolian banquets and entertain with Mongolian music. In that first year of operation, he hosted 1,500 people, and in 2004 6,000, a number that should multiply sixfold by the time of the Beijing Olympics in 2008.

In the current climate of privatization, I can imagine Benjamin doing deals over the museum and access to the site and the flow of information. Soon, it will be easy, and comfortable, and crowded, and expensive. Unless you go soon, I'm afraid that Xanadu will not be an adventure any more, and you will certainly not be allowed to gather up bits and pieces of broken tile.

But where had they all gone, the remnants seen by Bushell? Benjamin had the answer. In the nearby town of Dolon Nur, many buildings have rather fine brickwork and tiles. This area, remember, was always short of building materials. It seems that Xanadu was mined, brick by brick, tile by tile, by local householders. All that's left is what they couldn't use.

I still have those bits I picked up, and I think I know what to do. I shall grind them to dust and use the dust to fill incisions in a table-top, forming two characters:

上
Shang

都
Du

The emerging capital, half-Mongol and half-Chinese in conception, was still too Chinese for traditional Mongols. Back in Karakorum, there were those who were jealous of Kublai's success and muttered that he was getting above himself, too ambitious by half, dreaming of his own empire by rivalling Mönkhe's capital. And far too rich. Could he perhaps be taking for himself some of the tax receipts that should by rights be coming to Karakorum? Mönkhe heard the talk, wondered if there was any truth in it, and was persuaded to act. In 1257 he sent two tax inspectors to audit Kublai's officials. They found fault, listed 142 breaches of regulations, accused Chinese officials, even had some executed and, with

Mönkhe's authority, took over the collection of all taxes in Kublai's estates. What could Kublai do? He could let loose his guards, and arrest the malign accountants. But that, as his Confucian and Buddhist advisers pointed out, would be outright rebellion. Better to conciliate. He did, first with a two-man embassy that made no impression, and then in person, appealing to Mönkhe as brother to brother. That worked. The two embraced in tears, Kublai all contrition, innocence and loyalty, Mönkhe offering forgiveness and renewed trust. (He was as good as his word: three years later, he had his accountants executed for sedition.)

The fact was that the two brothers needed each other. Kublai's power depended on Mönkhe's support – and Mönkhe had a problem, created by Genghis himself 30 years previously. He had been so impressed by the aged Taoist monk Ch'ang-chun, the one whom Genghis had summoned from China all the way to Afghanistan to teach the ways of Tao, that he had granted Ch'ang-chun's sect freedom from taxation. The Taoists, once the juniors in the hierarchy of religions, had exploited their new-found wealth and status by seizing Buddhist temples. Wealth being a wonderful source of inspiration, Taoist sects had multiplied. There were now 81 of them, according to one account, with ascetics at one end of the scale and at the other fortune-tellers who were hardly more than hooligans, happy to rip paintings and statues from Buddhist shrines.

Buddhists objected, equally violently. They were much strengthened by an influx of priests from Tibet, a region that would soon form part of Kublai's empire (to which chapter 7 returns in more detail). In 1258 Buddhists were all too well aware of the importance of political contacts, and were desperate to have their revenge on the Taoists.

The row had to be stopped, because otherwise there would be no stability in north China, and no secure base from which to undertake the much more important matter of the invasion of Song. Kublai was the key to both problems. In Morris Rossabi's words: 'Though I do not rule out the possibility that the dramatic scene portrayed in the Chinese chronicles occurred, I believe it occurred only after both Mönkhe and Kublai had rationally evaluated the folly of a split between them.'

So the first thing on Kublai's agenda in early 1258 was to convene a conference of Taoist and Buddhist leaders, and knock their heads together. It was quite a conference. To Xanadu came 300 Buddhists and 200 Taoists, held apart by the presence of 200 court officials and Confucian scholars. Kublai was in the chair.

The Taoist case rested on two documents, both of which claimed that Lao-tzu, the sage who had founded Taoism, had undergone 81 incarnations – hence the number of Taoist sects – in one of which he was known as the Buddha. In addition, one document claimed Lao-tzu had died in India, the home-land of Buddhism, not in China. Therefore, they contended, Buddhism was actually Taoism. It was an insulting idea, made worse by the Tao agenda, summarized in their catch-phrase *hua-hu* (convert the barbarians). What they did not appreciate was that Kublai was already almost a Buddhist. His favourite wife, Chabi, was. He had been impressed by his clutch of Buddhist monks and their practical reasons for adopting Buddhist-style good government.

In fact, he did not need to bring his prejudice to bear. The Taoists were not used to debate, and proved a colourless lot. Kublai's Tibetan adviser, Phags-pa, cross-questioned the senior Taoist on the authenticity of their main 'convert the barbarians' text, with its claim that their founder, Lao-tzu, had died in India. How odd that Sima Qien (Ssu-ma Ch'ien in the old orthography), the great first- and second-century historian, did not mention this interesting claim or the document asserting it, the reason being – Phags-pa concluded – that Lao-tzu actually died in China and the document was a forgery. The Taoists, lacking both references and arguments, were left looking foolish. Kublai offered them one last chance: call upon ghosts and demons, prove your magical powers by performing supernatural feats. Naturally, they demonstrated no powers at all.

Kublai delivered his judgement. Buddhism was in, Taoism out. Seventeen Taoist heads were shaved, all copies of the fraudulent texts were to be destroyed, 237 temples were to be restored to the Buddhists. But he was wise enough not to be vindictive, for he knew he could not afford to alienate Tao's many adherents. There would be no executions, merely a return to the status quo earlier in the century, before Ch'ang-ch'un's sudden elevation three decades earlier.

The debate sealed Kublai's return to favour. He had imposed peace with firm executive action, displaying intelligence and moderation. Everyone approved, and he was all set for his next big task, the invasion of southern Song.

5

THE CLAIMANT

AS SUCCESSFUL DICTATORS DO, MÖNKHE DEPENDED ON RAPID AND
all-embracing foreign conquest as a way to pre-empt dissent.
Not that anyone would have put it in those terms, because
that motive was hidden by the overwhelming truth, as the
Mongols saw it, that they had unfinished business with
the world at large. By 1257 Persia and southern Russia were
secure; so now for the rest of China – and then the rest of the
world.

The Mongols were in strong positions, with armies based
in Xanadu (under Kublai) and Yunnan, north China and
what had been Xi Xia. But the task ahead was not simply
formidable. It seemed frankly ludicrous, so vast was the
difference between the two sides.

Song was a land of rivers and forests and mountains, with
none of the open plains that gave the Mongol cavalry its
advantage. The land between the Yellow River and the
southern coast was then, as it is today, China's breadbasket,
including a million square kilometres of fields and canals. Its
capital, present-day Hangzhou (then called Linan) was the

world's most populous city, with 1.5 million people – more than the whole population of Mongolia. A century of imperial spending had turned it into a boom-city. Dominating the southern end of the Grand Canal's exit into Hangzhou Bay, it was among the world's finest ports. Its setting – the Eye of Heaven Mountains, the West Lake – was as beautiful as its palaces. How could the Mongols dare to dream of victory over this one city, let alone the 41 other cities of 100,000 inhabitants or more, let alone the 50 million peasants who crowded the rich lands of the Yangtze basin?

The Mongols did not have resources of their own for such an enterprise. They would have to use north Chinese to fight south Chinese. With the Mongol cavalry virtually useless, everything would depend on Chinese infantry, Chinese siege engines, Chinese engineers. The climate was sub-tropical in summer, the landscape tortuous, the distances immense, diseases rife. Who would bet on success?

At least Mönkhe had a good HQ. Set up 30 years before by Genghis himself, it lay some 200 kilometres south of the Yellow River near the head of a tributary, the Qing Shui river in the billowing foothills of the Liupan mountains, where Genghis had spent the summer of 1227, before he had succumbed to the disease that killed him. It was a good site, because it was out in the open, yet within a day's gallop of the secret valley in the mountains – steep forests, fertile soils, a wealth of medicinal plants – where Genghis had probably been brought in a vain attempt to heal his fatal illness. Now a major archaeological site, Kaicheng was the command centre where the last leader of Xi Xia had surrendered to the ailing – or perhaps already dead – Genghis, only to be murdered. It lay just 70 kilometres from the Song border.

Mönkhe knew well enough the immensity of the task ahead. His plan was to start big, by cutting his opponent in half. Three columns would converge on the Yangtze at Wuchang (now part of the mega-city of Wuhan), the key to the lower Yangtze and thus to the capital, Hangzhou. One of the columns would be Kublai's, advancing from Xanadu, a southward trek of some 1,400 kilometres. Actually, Kublai's involvement was in doubt for a time because he was suffering from gout, the disease that would afflict him all his life. When Mönkhe suggested he be replaced by one of Genghis's nephews, he was indignant. He had just finished sorting out the dispute between Buddhists and Taoists, and was eager for action. 'My gout is better,' he protested. 'How is it fitting that my elder brother should go on a campaign and I should remain idle at home?' Mönkhe let him get on with it. In Wuchang, Kublai would meet up with the two other columns: one under Uriyang-kadai, arriving from Yunnan (almost 1,500 kilometres away), and a third from Kaicheng. Mönkhe himself would be on a separate campaign into the centre of this region, striking south-west for 650 kilometres, taking Chengdu in the heart of Sichuan, and finally turning south-east for 250 kilometres to Chongqing, the river port that was the link between the Yangtze's downriver trade and the over-land route to Tibet.

Mönkhe arranged for the correct rituals to ensure that Heaven would be with him, honouring his grandfather's spirit at his grave on Burkhan Khaldun and scattering milk from his herd of white mares around his palace. Then he headed south, across the Gobi, through what had once been Xi Xia and was now imperial land, to Kaicheng. The summer of 1257 he spent in the Liupan mountains, gathering his forces. The following spring, his army took Chengdu and moved on through Sichuan's mists – so thick, it was said, that dogs bark when they see the sun.

But progress was slow, because conquest had to be accom-panied by administration; so it was early 1259 before he reached Chongqing. Then, further delay: to take Chongqing, he first had to overcome a formidable fortress 60 kilometres to the north. Set on a sheer 400-metre-high ridge called

Fishing Mountain over what is now the town of Hechuan, it dominated three rivers which flowed together before joining the Yangtze. This operation brought Mönkhe to a dead halt. Weeks turned to months, spring to summer. The heat mounted. Disease struck. Several thousand of his men died. Yet, despite urging from his generals, Mönkhe refused to give up.

In August, escaping the heat in the nearby hills and drinking far too much wine with the excuse that it would stave off sickness, he went down with something very serious, probably cholera. If that was it, he had little chance. His bowels turned to water, cramp racked him, and in ten days he was dead.

At this point all military action should have ceased as Mongol leaders refocused their attention on the succession. First came the rituals of burial, which took at least a month, perhaps two: the preparation of the body for travel; the 1,800-kilometre, month-long return to Karakorum, where official mourning took place over four consecutive days in the palaces of high-ranking women, then the final 500-kilometre procession eastward over the grasslands, past the hills that flank present-day Ulaanbaatar, into the Mongols' original heartland, up the Kherlen river, over the ridge that guards its headwater valleys and thus at last to the sacred mountain of Burkhan Khaldun, the burial place of Genghis and his son Tolui. This immense act of reverence should have involved every prince, every noble, every princess, each with his or her entourage of horses and wagons, ending with the pitching of many tents in preparation for the interment. The final burial would have been in the Great Forbidden Place, with its permanent corps of mounted guards patrolling the approaches. A final, smaller group of mourners would have wound along the 20-kilometre valley of the Bogd river, then up the forested slopes to the open plateau that lies beneath Burkhan Khaldun's great arched summit. The site itself was designed to be kept secret: horses trampled the graves, then saplings and coarse grass slowly covered the spots where the earth had been disturbed, while summer rains and winter frosts churned the graves back into the permafrost. So where exactly Genghis, Tolui, Mönkhe and later emperors lie is still a mystery.

Next on the agenda would be the great assembly of the princes and the clan leaders, the *kuriltai*, that would elect the next khan. But by now winter was coming on; so the election would not take place until the following spring, allowing the claimants time to ensure they had the backing they needed.

And what, meanwhile, of Kublai? He had been about to cross the river now known as the Huai, 250 kilometres into Song territory, when news came of Mönkhe's death. He had been on the road for several weeks, covered 1,000 kilometres, opted for speed over security by avoiding the great fortress-town of Xiangyang, and had another 400 kilometres – perhaps ten days' march – to go to reach his rendezvous. There was a Song troop ahead. Scouts were bound to hear of his brother's death, and spread the good news, and inject new heart into the Song opposition. So he had a choice: to sit about doing nothing, and allow the Song time to mount a counter-offensive; to retreat, and abandon conquered territory; or to advance. He knew from experience what was right. When his grandfather had died, he had been twelve: old enough to be part of the plan to keep the death a secret from his main enemy, the Tanguts, in case the news should put new heart into them. He talked the matter over with his number two, Batur. Batur, the same age as Kublai, came from an eminent military family, being the grandson of Genghis's great general Muqali (Mukhali in an alternative spelling). He understood, and between them the decision was made.

They would pretend the news was merely gossip designed to spread fear and despondency. 'Let us pay no attention to this rumour,' Kublai said, according to Rashid ad-Din. 'We have come hither with an army like ants or locusts. How can we turn back, our task undone?'

His advance continued, to the universe of water that was the Yangtze. From the point where it leaves the Three Gorges, 400 kilometres upstream, the Yangtze becomes Amazonian, meandering lazily across rice-rich plains, dropping just 2.5 centimetres every kilometre. It's more inland sea than river, as variable as wet ink on blotting paper. In Kublai's day it hardly had banks at all, so regularly did it spill over them. At this point, it was a maze of meanders and lakes, making a barrier over 10 kilometres wide. It must have taken quite a fleet to cross; but cross he did, because he laid siege to Wuchang, to be joined some three weeks later by Uriyang-kadai's 20,000-strong force from Yunnan. They'd had a hard time, taking fortresses on the mountain passes, losing 5,000 men to disease. Their arrival nearly knocked the heart out of Wuchang. The town must have been on the brink of sur-render when, in early October, Song contingents, released from fighting Mönkhe by his death, arrived to confront Kublai. Somehow, they managed to bypass the Mongols – by river, probably – and enter the city, proof that the besiegers' grip was not as tight as it should have been.

Stalemate.

Kublai faced a tricky decision: to continue the siege of Wuchang, or return to Mongolia to engage with the business of the succession. Increasingly, imperial strategy was being trumped by affairs back home. In December, Kublai decided he could hesitate no longer. But which to choose: finish the job, or pull back?

The Song commander, Jia Sidao, a wily diplomat who undoubtedly knew of the pressures on his adversary, tried to nudge him into withdrawal. Jia, one of the most famous and

controversial men of his age, has an important role to play in
Kublai's story. His grandfather and father had been men of
medium-grade military rank; nothing exceptional, but good
enough to put silver spoons in Jia's young mouth. In his home
town, the Song capital of Hangzhou, he had been one of the
jeunesse dorée, with a penchant for pretty girls, drinking and
gambling. He was also lucky. His sister had been chosen as an
imperial concubine; she became the emperor's favourite, bearing him a daughter, his only surviving child, and rising to the
high rank of Precious Consort in the harem. In 1236 the
emperor had fallen ill and some senior official was going to
suggest pensioning him off. Jia heard of the plot and told his
sister, who told the emperor, who acted to save his throne.
Good jobs followed, and by the time he was 40 Jia was
powerful and rich. He dabbled in art and antiques. He had a
glorious estate in the hills overlooking the West Lake, where
he threw parties for guests by the thousand. With time and
wealth to spare, he was able to indulge a very strange hobby:
he loved to set crickets fighting each other. Indeed, he became
such an expert in crickets and their aggressive ways that he
wrote a handbook on the raising and training of champion
crickets. He had literary pretensions. Another work, a
commonplace book of his thoughts and experiences, was
called *Random Excerpts from the Hall Where One Enjoys
Life*, which he signed pseudonymously 'The Old Man Who Is
Half Idle'. His rivals (of course) called him arrogant and
frivolous, and muttered about the way he siphoned off state
cash to cram his own Xanadu, the Garden of Clustered
Fragrances, with art treasures. In 1259, when he was 46, he
was appointed Chancellor of the Empire, with responsibility
for upgrading Song's shaky finances and armed forces. He
thus found himself in charge of the defence of Wuchang, and
in a position to influence Kublai in his next decision.

Jia chose a high-risk strategy. He made a secret approach to
Kublai to propose terms, an act of duplicity for which he

would pay dearly later. What if the Song paid an annual tribute, in exchange for the Mongols agreeing that the Yangtze should be the new frontier between the states?

Kublai would have none of it. 'Your intentions may be good because you are in favour of peace for the sake of living beings,' he replied through his envoy. 'But now, after we have crossed the Yangtze, what use are these words?'

The Mongols didn't need an agreement to receive what they could simply take; and a treaty designating a new frontier would be a diplomatic inconvenience when the time came to complete the conquest. Better simply to pull back and then return in their own time, especially – and this was the deciding factor – because something rather ominous was afoot back home.

As Kublai learned in a message from his worried wife, his younger brother, Ariq Böke – Ariq the Strong – master of the empire's nomadic heartland, was raising troops, for some unknown reason. It must be to do with the succession, because of the surviving three brothers, Hulegu, ruler of Persia, was not in the running; only Ariq and Kublai were left. Could Kublai possibly return? If Kublai needed a further reason, he had it two days later, when messengers came from Ariq himself, bringing nothing but innocuous greetings and enquiries about Kublai's health. Kublai was suspicious. He asked what their master was doing with the troops he had raised. Disconcerted by the fact that he had heard of Ariq's actions, they wriggled. Troops? What troops? 'We slaves know nothing. Assuredly it is a lie.' Kublai smelt treachery. In a secret meeting with his top generals, he told them he was heading north to find out what was going on.

The fact was that Ariq was a traditionalist. He didn't like to see his brother abandoning the old ways – a Christian wife here, Chinese estates there – and he was seeking support at home to make sure that he would be elected khan at the assembly next spring. But obviously he didn't want Kublai to know his plans. A couple of weeks later, Kublai, having decamped 600 kilometres northward back to the Yellow River, sent Ariq a message asking about the troops – What were they for? Why couldn't they be handed over to him, Kublai, for use against the Chinese? One of Ariq's aides pointed out that Kublai seemed to have guessed what was up. Better to send messengers telling him recruitment had been stopped and reassure him with gifts of falcons and hunting animals.

So it happened. Outwardly, Kublai expressed relief – 'Everyone's mind is set at rest' – but he wasn't fooled. Politics now trumped empire-building. He ordered his generals to abandon the siege of Wuchang instantly, leave a token force as a bridgehead, and head back to Mongolia.

It was, at last, the end of this invasion. Jia soon recaptured what had been taken. Song would remain unconquered for another 20 years. Kublai found all his attention focused on a dispute that would rapidly escalate into civil war.

As 1259 turned to 1260, ploy was followed by counter-ploy, with messages being carried back and forth across the steppes and the Gobi at full gallop, the two would-be emperors dicing for advantage as if they and their supporters were pieces on a vast chessboard. Ariq tried to call an assembly to elect himself khan. It didn't work. It was so obviously intended to bend the rules that several princes did not respond. He tried another stratagem. Come at once, he begged, to mourn our brother. Kublai, now in Beijing, saw that if he did he would be walking into a trap, and stalled. His men were only just back from the campaign, he said. They needed a break. No sooner had Ariq's messengers left than Kublai sent for the force Mönkhe had been leading when he died. Where were they, anyway? Keeping out of the way, apparently, in the land of the Tanguts – what had once been Xi Xia before Genghis took it over.

By now it was spring. Ariq, newly arrived in his summer quarters in the Altai mountains in Mongolia's west, saw he could not afford to wait any longer, could not risk a journey to Karakorum, perhaps because it was within too easy reach of Kublai's armies. He gathered what princes he could, had himself declared khan and sent off messengers proclaiming, as Rashid puts it, that Hulegu, Berke (the new ruler of the Golden Horde in southern Russia), the current ruler of Chaghadai's realm in Central Asia and other princes had all agreed to raise Ariq to the khanate and 'You must pay no attention to the words of Kublai.'

Kublai was incensed. This was outright rebellion, not so much against him personally as against the practice by which the new khan was elected by a conclave of a majority of the princes. It was also a lie. The two khans of Persia and the Golden Horde were not in Mongolia, and anyway were now bitter rivals over both territory and religion. Hulegu had indeed set off for Mongolia after Mönkhe's death, but the disaster of Goliath's Spring had turned him around. Berke had converted to Islam the better to rule his Muslim subjects; Hulegu had been killing Muslims by the thousand. Both princes, one pro- the other anti-Muslim, claimed what is now Azerbaijan. As Hulegu returned to save what he could, Berke took advantage of his cousin's weakness to declare war. What chance such bitter rivals would agree on a new khan?

Ariq had shot himself in the foot. Kublai was not the only one angered by his presumption. Princes and generals who had not responded to Ariq's call rallied to Kublai. To save the empire, there was only one thing to be done: he had to declare himself khan, with as much validity as possible. This could not be done with *total* validity, because that would take a full assembly in Karakorum, which he was not yet ready to hold.

So in early May 1260, those who backed Kublai were called to Xanadu for the ceremony.[1]

The two sides were evenly balanced. Kublai could count on Hulegu; but Hulegu was busy trying to fight off Berke. Then again, Kublai had the resources of north China behind him, which he did his best to secure with a proclamation pointing out his virtues: he would rule with goodness and love, lower taxes, feed the hungry, revere the ancestors, and in brief be everything a thoroughly Chinese emperor ought to be. A flurry of orders set up Chinese-style institutions. Under guidance from his Chinese adviser Wang O, he gave his reign a title: Zhong Tong, 'Moderate Rule'. Some scholars think that this was done to assert Kublai's pro-Chinese credentials by making a link between his rule and the *I Ching* (*Yi Jing* in pinyin), the *Book of Changes*, the 2,000-year-old oracle.

This historical snippet, I think, throws a sharp little spotlight on the choices facing Kublai. His roots were in the grasslands, yet he had Chinese estates; he had been part of the conquest of the north and some of the south, and was set on conquering the rest. Now here he was in a Chinese-style city built on the grasslands, about to declare himself emperor – of what, exactly? A Mongolian empire? A Chinese empire? He needed help to sort out how best to handle this. But he did not, as far as we know, summon Mongolian shamans to examine the scorched and cracked shoulder-bones of sheep. Instead, he called upon a Chinese adept who knew how to cast the *I Ching*.

The *I Ching* holds a unique place in Chinese culture. Both Confucianism and Taoism find themselves reflected in it. At

---

[1] This is Rashid's order of events. Other sources have Kublai's coronation coming first, followed sharply by Ariq's. It doesn't matter very much. Being first would not have affected matters either way.

heart, as Kublai would have known from his advisers, *I* (*Yi*), Change, means the stream of life, symbolized as the Way of Water or Tao, in which, if we can only read the symbols aright, we can see what is arriving from the future and what is of the past and finished. This hugely complex system of divination, which integrates myths, symbols, rituals, land-scapes, character, language and many other human qualities, has roots that reach back 5,000 years into pre-Shang, pre-Bronze Age, pre-writing times, its complexity and (some would say) wisdom growing with each age thereafter. It was one of the Six Classics, the foundation for all study. Everyone, from emperor to street-cleaner, consulted it at times of change and decision, especially at crucial moments when the Mandate of Heaven falls upon a new dynasty, for it offers insight into the unseen world, where events in the physical world are foreshadowed. Depending on your levels of scepticism and creativity, it is either a very impressive piece of mumbo-jumbo or full of astounding truths. Like a vast and complex ink-blot, you can read in it your heaviest problems and find the most startling insights. Nowadays many say, as Jung said, that it is a 'method of exploring the unconscious', of cutting through the clamour of rival thoughts to arrive at a decision. The problem is how to understand what it says, which is where the experts come in.

What Kublai was told was exactly what any Chinese emperor would wish to hear. Imagine the scene. Kublai, in his new palace, is agonizing over what to do. He knows that he must claim the throne, sometime, somewhere. Moreover, he must assert his claim by giving his reign a name, thus im-posing a new calendar, as all new Chinese emperors had done. But should he do it here? Now? And what name should he choose?

The sage prepares his consultation, with the 50 yarrow stalks that will be used to produce one of the 64 six-line diagrams (hexagrams), which will in turn yield a Judgement, an Image and a Commentary. This will be complicated by the fact that the sage speaks Chinese and Kublai doesn't. Everything goes through an interpreter. Each of the six lines that will produce the hexagram must be made by combining random decisions, ritual acts and complex numerical trans- formations. This is, remember, all about understanding change. One stalk is set aside (I can't discover why; perhaps to produce an odd number). The 49 remaining yarrow-stalks are divided into two random heaps. Obeying ancient rules, Kublai slowly transfers stalks from pile to pile and from pile to hand, until he is holding either nine or five stalks between the fingers of his left hand. The stalks are set aside, and given new numerical values. This he does three times. Then the three selections are integrated to produce a final figure, which in turn produces either a broken or an unbroken line, which, depending on the figure, will or will not undergo further transformation. In this case, it is a 'young yang' line, a positive line, unbroken, a line that will not undergo further change. Six times he repeats this procedure, producing six lines. And lo! All six lines are the same. The hexagram is the very first in the time-honoured catalogue, 'The Creative', Qian:

———— ————
———— ————
———— ————
———— ————
———— ————
———— ————

This is highly auspicious. The creative urge emanates from heaven. It consists of two trigrams, both called Qian. The doubling represents action. So the whole sign represents primal power, the power of Heaven, the creative action of both the Deity and his earthly image, the leader. Kublai knows about Heaven, because it was from the Mongol Heaven or sky-god, Tenger, that his grandfather Genghis had received his mandate to rule. If Kublai makes the right decision and becomes ruler, he will inherit that mandate, first as Mongol khan, but then as world conqueror, which will include being Chinese emperor, who, of course, rules only by Heaven's Mandate. Is this his destiny? If so, how best is he to achieve it? He waits, agog.

The sage proclaims the Judgement: 'The Creative works sublime success, furthering through perseverance.'

I can imagine Kublai's inner reaction. '*What??*'

The sage draws breath to explain. When an individual draws this oracle, it means that success will come to him from the primal depths of the universe and that everything depends upon his seeking his happiness and that of others in one way only, that is by perseverance in what is right. One of the attributes of this oracle is a word which is sometimes translated as 'sublime', but which also means 'origin, prime, first, great'. That word is *yuan*.

The sage hasn't finished. The khan's destiny is to display the four attributes of sublimity, potential, power and perseverance. The movement of Heaven is full of power. Thus the superior man makes himself strong and untiring. Because he sees with great clarity causes and effects, he completes the six steps at the right time and mounts towards heaven on them at the right time, as though on six dragons. He towers high above the multitude of beings, and all lands are united in peace.

And more of the same. It is obscure, and mystical, and sounds wonderfully wise in almost any version (this one is from the Cary Baynes translation of Richard Wilhelm's German translation from the Chinese). What Kublai surely got out of it was reassurance that he was on the right track. He also took from the reading a name for the period of his reign: Zhong Tong, an obscure term meaning something like

Central or Moderate Rule. Eventually, once he had been crowned, he would have to assert himself even more firmly with a name for what would surely become a new dynasty. To take such a step now would have seemed too arrogant; but the reading gave him an idea for a dynastic name that would stay with him until the time was right to assume it, a name that expressed everything he wished his dynasty to become: the sublime, the first, the great, the Yuan.

On 5 May 1260, Kublai took the plunge. The princes assembled in Xanadu begged Kublai three times to accept the throne. As tradition dictated, he declined twice; the third time, he graciously accepted. The princes swore their oaths of allegiance, and proclaimed him the new emperor.

Now the empire had two Great Khans, rather as the Christian church had two popes, pope and anti-pope, during the Great Schism of 1378–1417. Here were a khan and an anti-khan. Which would turn out to be which?

Military operations in Song went on hold. Kublai did try for a diplomatic solution by sending envoys to Hangzhou, but Jia's reaction was to arrest them. Through the summer of 1260 the two opposed brothers did more jockeying, each tit-for-tat move raising the stakes. One of Ariq's men, Durchi, who was at Kublai's coronation, fled with the news, only to be chased and captured. Ariq returned to Karakorum to assert his rule from there. Kublai tried to put his own man, Abishqa, the grandson of one of his cousins, in charge of Chaghadai's Central Asian realm, only to hear that the mission – Abishqa, two other princes, 100 men – had all been caught by Ariq, who then had his own candidate crowned khan of Chaghadai's territory. Then came the first armed clash, at an unidentified place, which apparently Ariq lost. In revenge, Ariq had Abishqa, his two royal companions and their 100-man escort all executed.

Kublai closed down the Gobi trade routes, starving Karakorum of the supplies that until then had been imported from China. He could do this because his cousin, Khadan, controlled Xi Xia and the Uighur regions further west. The two of them could blockade the whole 2,300-kilometre arc from Beshbaligh, on the border of Chaghadai's realm, to Xanadu, forcing Ariq as winter came on to turn to the rough farmers and craftsmen of the Siberian valleys to his north. Kublai took no chances. He recruited more troops, bought 10,000 extra horses, ordered 6,000 tonnes of rice – a year's supply – then led his well-supplied army northwards into the heart of Mongolia. Not far from Karakorum he learned of the executions, in revenge for which he executed Durchi.

Ariq, forced to retreat to the valley of the Yenisey, the source of his supplies in Siberia, was becoming desperate. He offered apologies and obedience: 'We, your younger brother, committed a crime and transgressed out of ignorance. You are my elder brother, and . . . I shall go whithersoever you command.'

But he didn't. Skirmishing continued, until the next show-down the following autumn in the grasslands of eastern Mongolia. Two battles were fought, with great loss of life on both sides and no decisive outcome. But Ariq was badly damaged. 'Distraught and bewildered, with a lean and hungry army,' in Rashid's words, he pulled back into the forests and mountains of Siberia. Allies abandoned him. Alghu, his puppet ruler of Chaghadai's realm, refused to help and executed Ariq's officials; the khanate collapsed into raid and counter-raid, and its capital, Almaligh, became a place of 'dearth and famine'. That was where Ariq now fled, hounding his former ally into the depths of Central Asia, while Kublai occupied Karakorum for the winter. In the spring, Ariq found his support draining away, symbolized for his aides when a whirlwind – May in the Central Asian steppes is famous for its winds – tore his audience tent from its 1,000 pegs, smashed its support post and injured many of those inside. To his ministers, it was an omen of coming defeat.

At which moment – early 1262 – he was saved by rebellion against Kublai back home. The trouble came from Shandong, the heart of north China, a rich coastal area near the mouth of the Yellow River. The local warlord, Li Tan, was the son-in-law of one of Kublai's top officials and had helped Mönkhe fight the Song. Kublai thought he was a staunch ally and backed his raids with injections of cash. It seemed a good bet, because Li's son was at court, in effect a hostage. But Li, in control of the local salt and copper industries, was more interested in feathering his own nest than in keeping in with Kublai. He decided that he, as a Chinese, had a better future with the Song than with the Mongols. So he arranged for his son to slip away from Kublai's court, then turned his army loose on local Mongols, seized warehouses, and was clearly intent on establishing his own breakaway kingdom. It took several months to crush him – literally, for his punishment was to be sewn into a sack and trampled to death by horses, the traditional fate reserved by Mongolians for those of princely rank. Kublai followed up by having Li's father-in-law executed as well, and then turned back to the business of dealing with Ariq.

The revolt in Shandong had been a nasty episode, but Kublai came out of it well. Though he would always in future be wary of trusting Chinese, he still consulted his Chinese advisers carefully, and instructed his troops to look after civilians. But he now saw that he needed a better organization to run his war machine. The Bureau of Military Affairs, set up in 1263, drew a clear distinction for the first time between civil and military administration. War would be a sort of Mongol *cosa nostra*, with Chinese excluded, a Mongol-run combination of war ministry and secret service. In establishing this body Kublai was taking an important step away from his grandfather's steppe-based empire, bound together by personal loyalty to Genghis. The Bureau would become a whole parallel bureaucracy, with an elite body of officials owing loyalty not to the person of Kublai, but to his creation, the state.

The winter of 1263–4 was a harsh one for Ariq's army, trapped in Central Asia. Food, weapons and friends were all in short supply. Men and horses starved. Allies – even some members of Ariq's own family – defected. On the wings, Alghu regathered his forces to fight back.

In 1264 Ariq faced the inevitable and came begging for peace, brother submitting to brother. As Rashid describes it, the meeting was full of emotion. Ariq approaches Kublai's huge palace-tent in the traditional manner, raising the flap that covers the door and letting it hang over his shoulder, awaiting the call to enter. Summoned inside, he stands among the secretaries, like a naughty schoolboy. The two brothers stare at each other. If this were a novel, I would tell you that memory carries them back to their childhood, to the years spent under Sorkaktani's stern gaze, to recollections of her virtues: restraint, tolerance, forgiveness. Even Rashid makes it, as they say in film scripts, a moment. Kublai softens. Tears come to the eyes of both men. Kublai beckons.

'Dear brother,' he says, 'in this strife and contention, were we in the right or you?'

Ariq is not quite ready to admit the fault is all his: 'We were then and you are today,' he says. It is almost good enough for Kublai.

Not, however, for the brother of Abishqa, the prince executed by one of Ariq's generals, Asutai. He protests. 'I killed him by the command of the then ruler, Ariq the Strong,' says Asutai, heatedly. 'Today Kublai Khan is ruler of the face of the earth. If he so commands, I will kill you too.'

Another leader utters soothing words. Today is not a time to rake over the past. Today is a time for merrymaking. Kublai approves. Ariq is assigned a place among the princes.

But he is not free. The following day, there is an examination to establish how things had come to this pass. There follows much finger-pointing as commanders dispute who had influenced Ariq the most. These are difficult matters, because Kublai wishes to establish guilt, yet find cause not to execute his own brother.

In the end, ten of Ariq's associates were put to death, while Ariq and Asutai were spared, though remaining under arrest. What to do about Ariq? Kublai summoned his three junior khans – Hulegu, Berke and now Alghu – to discuss the matter, but all three demurred. Hulegu and Berke were still at war, and Alghu only newly restored to power. None of them dared leave home.

Who, then, would rid the khan of his troublesome brother? Not, it seemed, his family; nor Eternal Heaven, either. Ariq was not yet 50 and in fine fettle, a constant reminder that Kublai's claim to the throne was not unchallenged. Then, suddenly, out of the blue, in unexplained circumstances, as Rashid baldly states, Ariq 'was taken ill and died'. Was he murdered? Some suspected so at the time and others have claimed so since. It was certainly a wonderfully convenient solution to an intractable problem.

And then Heaven really did step in. Within a few months of Ariq's death, Hulegu in Persia, Berke of the Golden Horde and Alghu the restored khan of Chaghadai's realm were all dead too. What a waste the past five years had been – all as a result of Ariq's opposition to his brother. The great task of invading China had been put on hold, the stability of Mongol rule across all Eurasia threatened, the Mongol heartland divided against its Chinese territories, the rulers of the three western khanates set at each other's throats. Now, at a stroke, all seemed to be resolved. Never mind that his coronation had not been strictly legal: Kublai was now in direct command of Mongolia, north China, much of Central Asia and some of Song, and overlord of his subsidiary khans in Persia and southern Russia. A portrait of him around this time shows him aged 50, in his prime, in a simple wrap-around gown without adornments. There is something of the sage about him, but his expression is that of a man of uncompromising commitment to the task in hand.

It was time to look south again.

II

SUMMER

6

A NEW CAPITAL

SOME CAPITALS SEEM TO BE BORN GREAT: ROME, PARIS, LONDON. Some have greatness thrust upon them: Brasilia, Canberra, Washington – and Beijing. For 3,000 years Chinese culture was focused by the two great rivers of central China, the Yellow River and the Yangtze. Beijing was no-one's first choice – too far north, no good rivers – until the Mongols' predecessors, the Jin, invaded from Manchuria in the 1120s. With the southern Song ruling from Hangzhou, Beijing became one of three capitals of north China – Zhongdu, 'Central Capital', as it was known.[1] So it was northerners from outside the Chinese heartland who made it a seat of government, and thus drew Genghis's attention to it.

The city that the Mongols seized and devastated in 1215 was small by modern standards, a square of 3.5 kilometres per side. Today a nondescript area just south-west of

[1] Only for a time. Beijing has had many names, and other cities have also been a Beijing (Northern Capital). I have kept these references to a minimum, preferring to call the place Beijing throughout.

Tiananmen Square, with hardly a trace to hint at its former existence, it had by 1260 still not recovered from the destruction meted out by Genghis's army. No doubt the sights and sounds of medieval Beijing would have returned to its alleyways: the twang of tuning forks by which travelling barbers signalled their arrival, the clang of copper bowls from soft-drink sellers, bells sounding the day and night watches, cries of street-vendors everywhere. But the walls and the burned-out palaces were still in ruins. An estate agent showing Kublai's people around would have muttered about its potential. A potential purchaser would have seen nothing but a hopeless mess.

In the 1260s, holding north China as a potter holds unformed clay, Kublai might have made any number of choices. He might have ignored Beijing and ruled from Xanadu. But if he did that he would declare himself for ever an outsider. Seeing the benefits of governing from a Chinese base, he might have chosen to revive an ancient seat of government, like Kaifeng or Xian. But Beijing had two major advantages: of the many possibilities for a Chinese capital in the north, it was the closest both to Xanadu and to Mongolia. In 1263, only seven years after starting to build Xanadu, Kublai decided to make Beijing his main capital. This would complete a sort of stepping-stone progression from the Mongolian grasslands into China, from Karakorum to Xanadu to Beijing. He would abandon Karakorum altogether, henceforth commuting between his two bases, spending summers in Xanadu and winters in Beijing, which was his way of straddling his two worlds. That's why Beijing is China's capital today.

But how best to handle this dilapidated piece of real estate? Incoming dynasties have often made their mark by total demolition and reconstruction (as the Ming would do to Mongol Beijing). Perhaps there was a year of indecision, for in 1261 the walls of the old city were mended, as if he was on the verge of building on the past. But new life in these ancient alleyways, as Kublai's advisers pointed out, would be seething with resentment. To work on the ruins within would have been to accept the agenda of a defeated dynasty and, perhaps, nurture rebellion. Kublai decided on an entirely new capital.

Just north and east of the Jin capital was a perfect site, where runoff from the Western Hills fed Beihai (the North Sea). Here, for 30 years before the Mongols arrived, there had been a playground for the wealthy. The 35-hectare lake at the heart of the parkland had come into existence as the result of a legend. Once upon a time, in the East Sea, there were three fairy mountains where the immortals lived on the miraculous Potion of Immortality. Many searched for the mountains and the potion, but none were successful. In the second century BC Emperor Wu Di of the Han had a lake dug by his palace in his capital, with three islets representing the fairy mountains. Later emperors did the same in their respective capitals. So did the Song in Beijing in the late tenth century, excavating a lake fed by a river from the Western Hills and giving it the by-now-traditional three islands. It was this carefully landscaped beauty spot that the Jin emperor chose for a summer palace in the twelfth century, the Palace of a Myriad Tranquillities; he also built a second retreat on top of today's Jade Island, the city's highest point (now crowned by the seventeenth-century White Dagoba, Beijing's equivalent of the Eiffel Tower). The imperial buildings had been ransacked when Genghis had assaulted Beijing in 1213–15, but the lake was still at the heart of the abandoned and overgrown park. It was natural that Kublai should choose it as the centrepiece of his new city.

With Xanadu representing Kublai's Mongol aspects, the new capital would be thoroughly Chinese. That would have been hard to credit in the autumn of 1263, when the emperor arrived from Xanadu to reclaim an area that would have been half-wilderness after 50 years of neglect. Imagine the lake choked with silt and plants, summerhouses decaying round its edges, and here and there some smallholdings where farmers had dared colonize what had once been royal parkland. With the old capital in ruins, Kublai had nowhere to stay but his tents. Saplings and bushes were cleared and an imperial camp sprang up: a royal area of several grand *gers*, lesser establishments for princes and officials, and hundreds more for contingents of guards, grooms, wagoners, armourers, metalworkers, carpenters and other workers by the thousand, including, of course, architects.

Overall authority for the design was borne by Liu Bingzhong, the mastermind of Xanadu. But among his team of architects was one of particular significance who is not mentioned in the official Chinese sources, for he was an Arab named something like Ikhtiyar al-Din (a rough re-transliteration from the messy Chinese version of his name, Yeh-hei-tieh-erh-ting). We know of him at all only thanks to a Chinese scholar, Chen Yuan, who in the 1930s came across a copy of an inscription dedicated to Ikhtiyar's son, Mohammad-shah. Ikhtiyar had, presumably, proved his worth in Persia after the Mongol conquest a generation before, for he was summoned by Kublai – or, more likely, Liu Bingzhong – to head a department in the Ministry of Works which had something to do with tents (no-one knows what; their manufacture for the imperial household, perhaps). Whatever his duties, he had over the years become an expert in town planning. Now, in his old age, he was selected to oversee Kublai's grand new scheme.

The inscription is worth quoting at length, because it gives a feel for the size of the project and makes explicit Kublai's political aims, as well as honouring its senior architect. In autumn 1266, it says, the court ordered the construction of the new capital's walls and palaces, and it continues:

As the Great Enterprise [whatever that was – perhaps the building of Xanadu] has come to its conclusion, the national influence is in the process of expansion. If the palaces and metropolitan adornments are not beautiful and imposing, they will not be able to command the respect of the empire. Following his appointment, Ikhtiyar laboured at his task ceaselessly, until he had drawn up a grand scheme. The grand astrologer selected a propitious date, and the director of supplies assembled the necessary materials. Detailed plans were prepared for passes and gates, audience halls, roads and residential quarters, informal reception rooms and detached courts, administration offices, shrines, guard houses, store-rooms for clothes, food and utensils, quarters for officers on duty in the imperial household, and so on up to pools, ponds, gardens, parks and places for dalliance, high storeyed structures and beamed pavilions and unadorned verandahs with flying eaves ... In the 12th month [28 December 1266–26 January 1267] a decree was issued ordering [three officials] and Ikhtiyar al-Din to take on together the duties of the Board of Works and carry out the programme of con-structing the palaces and city walls. Measures were taken to provide the necessary equipment, to put in place the pillars and beams, to transport thither stone and brick, timber and earth. Multitudes of artisans participated. Foundations and terraces were laid, solidly and firmly. All met with imperial approval. The services of Ikhtiyar al-Din were highly appreciated, but he was beginning to feel the weight of his advancing years.

Yet in the official Yuan history Ikhtiyar's name is omitted, only his three Chinese junior colleagues being mentioned. 'Either it was left out on purpose,' says Chen, 'or the omission was due to the low regard in which architecture was formerly held.' Well, it sounds to me more like deliberate racism. Kublai, like his grandfather, was happy to employ talent wherever he found it. But Beijing would soon be the vastly imposing imperial capital, with Kublai himself a

Chinese monarch. Look at it from the Chinese point of view: Kublai had imposed a class system with Mongols at the top, followed by Muslims, northern Chinese and southern Chinese. Here was an Arab employed by Mongols showing Chinese how to build a Chinese city. It does not take much to imagine a clique of Chinese official historians wishing to take revenge for their humiliation. Ikhtiyar was simply written out of history – until Chen Yuan deciphered the inscription honouring Mohammad-shah and his father. 'Visitors to Peking in these days are amazed at the grandeur of the palaces and the city walls,' wrote Chen, 'but who would suppose that the man who worked this out was from the country of Arabia?'

Today Beihai Park, once a playground for emperors and princes outside the city walls, is a playground for everyone, right at the heart of the city. For that, Beijingers, picnicking on its banks and paddling its rowing boats, owe Kublai some gratitude. It was he who turned it into an Arcadia that is now a tourist cliché; he who first built a bridge across to Jade Island (replaced late in his reign by the marble Eternal Peace Bridge visitors see today, with its graceful curve); he who landscaped its slopes with rare trees and winding staircases and poetically named temples and pavilions – Golden Dew, Jade Rainbow, Inviting Happiness, Everlasting Harmony; he who made the lake and its island a sight at which foreigners gasped. Marco Polo remarked on the stock of fish, and the metal grating that stopped them escaping into the river at either end. Almost 50 years later, Friar Odoric from Pordenone in north-east Italy admired its multitudes of swans, geese and ducks.

Naturally, Kublai replaced the old palace on the top of Jade Island with a new one, having increased the height of the hill with soil excavated from the lake-bed. This, presumably, was where he held court for a decade (1264–74) while the city proper was under construction.[2] The hilltop palace is now long gone, but recalled by a surprising object standing in its place. In one of the palace's seven halls was a second, miniature palace, and in this was a bed, inlaid with gold and jade, on which Kublai liked to recline as he held court. Beside the bed was an immense jade urn, weighing 3.5 tonnes, intricately carved with dragons cavorting in waves. From this Kublai would dispense wine, 3,000 litres of it. Tossed away by the whirl of events, this extraordinary vessel was rediscovered in the eighteenth century and placed again at the top of the hill, sheltered by its own little pavilion and standing on a new jade base. Rather oddly to western eyes, the stand sports a swastika – not in its malign Nazi version, but with its arms set anti-clockwise in the symbol's original beneficent Zoroastrian form (卐 is the symbol used to represent a temple on Chinese maps). Everyone recognizes the urn's good-luck value. Tourists buy little red charms to hang from the surrounding fence: Good Luck All Life! A Prayer for the Whole Family's Happiness!

Ikhtiyar planned a city that would have the traditional form of previous capitals, including Xanadu. It would be three-in-one: a palace, inner city and outer city in nested rectangles. This design recalled the ground-plans and glory of several previous Chinese capitals, most notably Changan (today's Xian), the Tang capital in the seventh to tenth centuries, possibly the world's greatest city at the time. Kublai would not have known anything of the Terracotta Army that draws tens of thousands of tourists to Xian every year, but he would have known of the power of its dead commander, the First Emperor, unifier of China in the third century BC, builder of roads, canals and the Great

---

[2] See G. N. Kates, 'A New Date for the Origins of the Forbidden City'.

Wall. This was the mantle of power and glory to which Kublai now laid claim.

In August 1267, several thousand workers under Ikhtiyar's direction started to build ramparts over the hills and along the three winding rivers. They used earth, not stone, digging out a moat to give them the raw material. 'It is the custom of that country,' writes Rashid ad-Din, 'to put down two planks, pour damp earth in between, and beat it with a large stick until it is firm. Then they remove the planks and there is a wall.' This was unskilled work, and it went fast. The 382 smallholders who had moved into the area during the years of dereliction were thrown out, with the equivalent of compulsory purchase orders – they all received compensation in 1271. After a year, rammed-earth walls 10 metres thick at the bottom rose for 10 metres, tapering to a 3-metre walkway at the top, so that in cross-section they looked like a decapitated triangle. They made a rectangle of just over 5.5 × 6.5 kilometres, 28 kilometres all the way round, punctuated by eleven gates. Inside, a second wall rose to conceal the Imperial City, and inside that a third wall, within which in due course would lie the palace and its attendant buildings. Actually, Ikhtiyar went one better than Xian, making a fourth set of walls to create a palace-within-a-palace.

From March 1271, 28,000 workers began to build the Imperial City's infrastructure, setting out a network of roads at right-angles, Manhattan-style, each block the property of a top family, complete with its grand house. At the heart, off-centre, just to the right of Beihai lake, was the palace. The nest of walls was designed only in part to provide security. Its unstated purpose, like that of the Kremlin and the Alhambra in Granada (both of which, incidentally, had been built not long before), was political and psychological: to impress all who entered with the awful majesty of the occupant. Imagine your approach, through a gate in the outer bastions, along crowded streets, through another gate – passage through which demands an escort and written permission – into the enclave of the rich and powerful, with their great mansions and gardens and armies of servants, and finally to the empire's innermost sanctuary, the jewel-box that contained the all-powerful embodiment of power, Heaven's own choice to rule the greatest political entity since the Fall of Rome, against which the Arab and Russian empires would have paled. Kublai had his opponents and insecurities; but approaching him would erase thoughts of such things. Long before you were ushered into the divine presence, you would be overwhelmed by a whole thesaurus of royal attributes: might, majesty, power, mystery, and wealth untold.

These were the feelings described by Marco Polo when, in 1275, he came to the place known informally by its Mongol-Turkic name, Khan-balikh, the Khan's City, or Cambaluc as Polo spelled it. To the Chinese, it was Da-du, the Great Capital. He made a particular point of describing the palace and its gardens, all surrounded by 10-metre walls that linked eight fortresses, each a storehouse for its own article of war – bows, saddles, bridles, weapons. Beneath the trees – rarities carried in from distant parts by elephant – grazed deer and gazelle, overlooked by walkways, which were gently slanted so that the rain drained fast before it could soak aristocratic feet. The palace, with a roof of red, yellow, green and blue tiles, was a single-storey building with a vast central hall where 6,000 dinner-guests dined beneath animal frescoes set off by gold and silver decorations. Off limits to all except the elite of the elite lay unknown numbers of private rooms.

Eventually, when all China fell to the Mongols, this would become the capital of the whole united nation, and so it has remained. The heart of today's Beijing, the Forbidden City, was built right over Kublai's creation, its entrance facing south, like the door of any Mongolian tent. The 800 palaces and halls, the 9,000 rooms, the entrance from Tiananmen Square – all these are where they are because Kublai chose to place his palace there.

As the chequerboard of streets and new buildings began to turn a building site into a capital, Kublai had a decision to make. To help his rule become total, to fulfil the ambitions inherited from his grandfather, he needed to make a public statement that Heaven had granted him its mandate, that a new dynasty had been founded. It needed a name. Clearly, a Mongol name would not go down well with his Chinese subjects, especially the southern subjects who would soon be his, if his plans worked out. It was his adviser Liu Bingzhong who came up with the perfect Chinese name, the one that had first suggested itself when Kublai was considering the decision about when to declare himself emperor. It springs straight from the great book of divination, the *I Ching*. The word had been embedded in the Qian oracle cast in Xanadu. Now it found greater justification in a set of words, a magical incantation, associated with the Way of Water or Tao, a formula that evokes life's flow. The words are *yuan heng li zhen*. Each recalls for initiates the sequence of ages through which the *I Ching* evolved; each holds universes of meaning. Right now, it is the first we are interested in: *yuan*.

The dictionary definition of yuan is first, chief, principal, fundamental. But there is much more to it. This, in summary, is what Stephen Karcher has to say about *yuan* in his *Total I Ching: Myths for Change*: Yuan is the ultimate source, the *primum mobile*, the movement behind the absolute origin of the universe. It is the power of spring, and of the east. As well as implying primacy, it also suggests the concepts of 'eldest' and 'the source of thought and growth'. It signifies the good man and a connection with fundamental truths. It is linked to ideas of fundamental rituals, greatness and founding acts.

So Yuan it was, the new name being proclaimed in December 1271. It was chosen with deliberate originality: no previous emperor had chosen a name for his dynasty that was not a place name. Yet its pedigree was impeccable. No name could have better appealed to Chinese sensibilities (which is why, incidentally, it is also the name of today's Chinese unit of currency). Moreover, its vaguely religious overtones hinted at the sublime, linking it to Tenger, the Mongol Heaven. All Kublai's subjects, Chinese and Mongol, would be impressed by their new emperor's choice.

Beijing today is a lagoon swamped by modernity. But below the murky surface of traffic, pollution and new building is a faint image of the old city, a ghostly rectangle defined by one of the innermost road-systems. One hot summer's day, I took the plunge in an attempt to make the ghost real. I decided to follow in the tracks of Emil Bretschneider, botanist, physician at the Russian legation and assiduous historian of the city. In his day, around 1875, Mongol ramparts reared up from countryside criss-crossed by paths and cart-tracks. Forty years later, when the historian Lin Yutang wandered over it, he found it 'completely rural in aspect, with farmsteads and duck-ponds'. It sounded charming.

All charm has long since vanished. Four kilometres north-west of Beihai Park, a tree-covered ridge divides a dual carriageway. It looks like nothing, but it is the remains of Kublai's earthen ramparts. You reach it by dodging cars. Paths of grey brick flanked by ranks of tired grass-clumps led me to the top, for a fine view of high-rises, carriageways and traffic through the soupy air. A notice urged: 'Take care of the grass, because the grass is alive.' There was not much else alive here, and not much of the past either. A modern temple was unused, except for a man with a close-shaven head playing a single-stringed fiddle on his knee. Traffic whizzed where once guards marched and courtiers strolled. A block north there's a canal, once the moat marking the northern limit of Kublai's new estate. I followed it, past what would soon be the main Olympic site, and came upon Yuan Dadu Park, after Kublai's dynasty and the name of Mongol Beijing. Garish little pleasure boats awaited day-trippers. A young man dozed on a bench. Paving stones fringed the ex-ramparts, now nothing but slender trees and pathways. A pillar displayed a bas-relief of Genghis attended by a cloud-borne orchestra and his heirs. This was not real history, but heritage: it was made in 1987, along with the park. But here at least something had survived from the thirteenth century – two stone tortoises bearing rectangular pillars, those symbols of power favoured by the Chinese and adopted by the Mongols. Behind them, Kublai's palatial grounds overflowed with apartment blocks. If you want to get a feel for Kublai's Beijing, best avoid the streets and search for something to set your imagination free.

By 1274 the palace by Beihai was near enough completion for Kublai to hold his first audience in the main hall (though work continued on both walls and palaces for the rest of his reign). He now had a theatre in which to stage the drama of power.

One secret of power is to make a display of it. The modern world has become a bit half-hearted about power-displays. Democracies are embarrassed by it; royalty, if preserved, is pickled in heritage, very pretty but devoid of power-content. But autocrats, the alpha males and sometimes alpha females of history, have always known that power and display work well together. From ancient Persia to Nazi Germany, political dominance has been made palpable by the use of symbols, rituals and ceremonies to act out the ideals with which rulers identify themselves, and through which they assert themselves. Different societies have their own ways of doing this. Roman emperors became gods at their funerals; Nepalese kings proved themselves embodiments of the universal god Vishnu by acts of generosity; in Bali the king showed his power by acting in pageants; Hitler had himself turned into an epic hero by the theatricality of the Nuremberg rallies. As one historian, David Cannadine, points out, kings have ruled as much by divine *rites* as by divine *right*. But underneath the different rites lie fundamental similarities (much debated by anthropologists and historians).

Such rituals and ceremonies assert several things:

- the stability of the state;
- the power of the state over the individual;
- the importance of the power-structure: the hierarchy of ruler, family, court, people;
- the legitimacy of the ruler;
- the ruler's superhuman qualities, connecting him (or occasionally her) with the divine.

One piece of theatre which crops up in several societies is the ceremonial hunt. It was, for instance, one of the most significant events in Charlemagne's Frankish empire after he was crowned emperor in the year 800. It was the natural conclusion to an assembly in which major political crises were resolved, for 'the hunt was an exercise in, and a demonstration of, the virtues of collaboration'.[3] In dramatic form, and in the feast that followed, it symbolized the advantages of collective action, of military and political co-operation.

Kublai, smart enough to see the benefits of ritual but with no experience in their form within Chinese culture, had teams of advisers to guide him. There were precedents galore,

[3] Janet Nelson, 'The Lord's Anointed and the People's Choice: Carolingian Royal Ritual', in David Cannadine and Simon Price, eds, *Rituals of Royalty*.

notably an immense three-volume corpus of imperial rituals recorded half a millennium earlier during the Tang dynasty (618–906), when China was unified, rich and stable.[4] Tang scholars believed these rituals originated in remote antiquity, some 2,000 years BC, and were then modified by the introduction of Confucian practices in the second and first centuries BC. The 150 rituals, the symbolic essence of government, combined cosmology, ethics, and Confucianism, with admixtures of Buddhism and Taoism. Here were rules for sacrifices to gods of heaven and earth, of the five directions, of the harvest, sun, moon, stars, sacred peaks, seas and great rivers; to ancestors; to Confucius. There were rites for recurrent and non-recurrent rituals, for use on sacred Mount Tai, where human and spirit worlds met; rites for the sovereign and for those taking the place of the sovereign, for receiving and entertaining envoys, for the proclamation of victories, for the marriage of dignitaries, for royal congratulations, for investitures, for coming-of-age ceremonies (for all levels down to the sons of sixth-grade officials), for the despatch of memoranda by provincial officials, for procedures to be conducted after bad harvests, illness and mourning . . . and variations of all of these, and more, depending on whether they were conducted by the emperor or a proxy, and for every rank of official from the emperor down to the lowliest, those of the ninth grade. Propitious rituals demanded abstinence at two levels, relaxed or intensive, spread over seven, five or three days, depending on whether the ritual was major, medium or minor. Rules specified the tents, the musical instruments, the positions of participants, the words of prayers. Here were instructions on how villagers should offer cooked meat, jade and silk to the gods of soil and grain. The rituals had their own huge and complex bureau-

[4] David McMullen, 'Bureaucrats and Cosmology: The Ritual Code of T'ang China', in David Cannadine and Simon Price, eds, *Rituals of Royalty*.

cracy, with four divisions – looking after, respectively, sacrifices, imperial banquets, the imperial family and ceremonies for foreigners – and a Board of Rites within the Department of Affairs of State. These demanded hundreds of specialists in ritual; but all the 17,000 scholar-officials of all the other departments were expected to have intimate knowledge of particular rituals in their own areas of expertise.

All of this immense, vastly expensive and horribly cumbersome apparatus was considered absolutely vital to the workings of the state, because it provided a context for human actions and linked these to the cosmos. It maintained the social hierarchy, restrained man's unruly appetites. It picked up where the criminal code left off, for it did not coerce people or punish them. It affirmed the benevolence of the cosmic order, and the emperor's role in mediating between earth and heaven. It was, as it were, a vast social gyroscope that kept society stable (which is one reason why dynasties so often kept going even when moribund, until an end that seemed to come suddenly). Later dynasties followed the Tang lead, producing their own ritual codes. If Kublai wanted to be taken seriously as a Chinese ruler, this was what he had to take on board.

So, in late middle age, Kublai displayed and regimented for all he was worth, which was more than any monarch on earth at the time. If you rule one-third of inhabited Asia and have family ruling the rest; if at the same time your original claim to power is a little shaky; and if you are ageing, overweight, easily out of breath, and wincing on gouty feet – then you would naturally wish to put on as much of a show as you possibly could. In the years after 1274, Kublai commanded more wealth than any monarch in history, and, by heaven, he knew how to use wealth to display and reinforce his power. But he would not pretend to be Chinese, slavishly following Tang precedents in his ceremonies and rituals; his aim was still, as it had long been, to balance

Mongol and Chinese, and his techniques were the well-tried means of inspiring awe – ritual and display that raised him from man to monarch, from monarch to demi-god.

His power base at court, through which his influence spread through China and beyond, was his 12,000-strong court of family, officials and officers; and every individual in this throng had at least three different sets of clothing, each a less lavish match for Kublai's own costumes, one for each of the three main state occasions, the khan's birthday at the end of September, New Year's Day and the annual spring hunt.[5]

Take New Year's Day. This was a festival designed to emphasize both the emperor's Chinese and his Mongol credentials. One of the greatest of Chinese festivals, it was doubly significant under Kublai because his dynastic title, Yuan, means among other things 'first', particularly the first month of the lunar calendar. (Today, the two calendars, lunar and Gregorian, run in parallel.) It was also one of the most important of Mongolian festivals. Still, as always in the countryside, on the first day of the first month – 'White Month' day – one gets up early, puts on one's best clothes, goes out of one's tent, bows to the east and then the other cardinal points, sprinkles milk or vodka to the Blue Sky, flicking some into the air, and returns to honour Buddhist images or – more likely these days – photographs of departed family members. The father of the household tosses some fermented mare's milk to the Blue Sky, children offer silk scarves to parents, hands placed just so in the correct fashion. There are bows and benedictions. Tea is drunk, visits made, old ways recalled, the social network reinforced.

Kublai's court ceremony mixed these simple old private rituals with Chinese court festivities to create a celebration

---

[5] The number of these occasions rose in the sources with the passage of time, often to 4, sometimes to 12 or 13 (*trois* and *treize/tres* being easily interchanged in versions of Polo).

of gargantuan proportions, an overwhelming assertion of personal and state power. Marco Polo describes it. Thousands – 40,000, he says, though we must always remember his habit of tossing out suspiciously large round numbers – dressed in white, all in due order behind the royal family, overflow from the Great Hall into surrounding areas. A high official of some kind – top shaman, Buddhist priest or senior chamberlain, Polo is not sure – calls out 'Bow and adore!' and the whole assembly touches forehead to floor, four times, in a mass kowtow. A song follows, then a prayer from the minister: 'Great Heaven that extends over all! Earth which is under Heaven's guidance! We invoke you and beseech you to heap blessings on the Emperor and the Empress! Grant that they may live ten thousand, a hundred thousand years!' Then each minister goes to the altar and swings a censer over a tablet inscribed with Kublai's name. Officials emerge from every corner with presents of gold, silver and jewellery, many of them in 81 examples, 81 being the doubly auspicious number of nine times nine; treasures are displayed in coffers mounted on contingents of richly adorned elephants and camels.

Then comes the feast. Kublai sits at the high table, which is literally high, placed on a platform, with the princes and their wives immediately below. To one side is a huge buffet table, decorated with animal carvings. The centrepiece is a golden wine-bowl the size of a barrel with four dispensers, from which servants draw wine into golden jugs. Down the hall range ranks of small tables, several hundred of them, flanked by carpets on which sit the guards and their officers. To one side of the dais is an orchestra, its leader keeping a close eye on the emperor.

Polo mentions an odd element in this scene, a significant detail that recalls Kublai's nomad roots. Anyone travelling in Mongolia today would understand. When entering a *ger*, you must take care to step right over the threshold, the bottom bit of the door-frame, without touching it. No-one knows the origins of this superstition, but there's no denying its force. If you kick the threshold by mistake, it is a bad omen; done on purpose, it would be a deliberate insult. Now, it's unlikely that Kublai's Great Hall had actual thresholds to step over. Nevertheless, at each door stand two immense guards, armed with staves, who watch for infringements. Back in Mongolia, a serf might be killed for stepping on a prince's threshold. Nothing so brutal would occur at Kublai's state banquet. But it's still no joke. The guards have orders to humiliate those who infringe the rule, stripping them of their finery or giving them some nominal blows with a stave. To be spared you have to be an ignorant foreigner, in which case a senior official will pounce upon you to explain courtly ways. Once all are seated, the banquet begins, with those at tables being served by butlers. Again, the khan uses ritual to assert his status, for his butlers 'have the mouth and nose muffled with fine napkins of silk and gold, so that no breath or odour from their persons should taint the dish or the goblet presented to the Lord'.

The Lord graciously receives a cup from a butler. The orchestra proclaims the significance of the moment. The cup-bearers and the foodbearers kneel. The Lord drinks. When he deigns to accept food, the same thing happens. These observances punctuate the feast, until the end, when the dishes are removed and it's time for entertainment, a cabaret provided by actors, jugglers, acrobats and conjurors.

Kublai's new Beijing was the centre of hunting on an industrial scale. Under the control of 14,000 huntsmen, the countryside out to 500 kilometres – 40 days' journey, as Polo says – from the city in every direction was dedicated to the business of supplying the court. All large game was the emperor's: boar, deer, bear, elk, wild asses (which can still be found in Mongolia's far west), wild cats of various species.

For his own hunt, Kublai had a zoo of cats, cheetahs and tigers specially trained to hunt and kill larger prey. Cheetahs had long been kept as hunting animals by kings across Asia, but the tigers – Siberian tigers from the northern borders of Kublai's empire – seem to have been a novelty. Polo, who didn't know about tigers, called them lions 'whose skins are coloured in the most beautiful way, being striped all along the sides with black, red and white'. There were eagles, too, trained and deployed by Kazakhs to hunt not just hare and foxes, but deer, wild goats, boar – even wolves, which an eagle attacks with claws and beak, while battering its prey into stupefaction with its wings (hunting with eagles is still alive today in Kazakhstan and western Mongolia). All of these came into their own in spring.

Marco Polo tells us all about it.

It is 1 March. Winter is over, spring approaching. The court prepares for its annual spring hunt, a hunt of such staggering size and opulence that it is easy to forget its underlying purpose. Hidden beneath Chinese wealth lie Mongol roots, the old idea of disparate clans united under one leader. In this ritual, Kublai, grandson of the man who claimed to remain a simple nomad at heart, is playing the nomad himself. The palaces and much of Beijing empty into wagons by the hundred, onto horses by the thousand. For Kublai himself, four elephants are harnessed together, carrying an enormous howdah, a room made of wood, lined on the inside with gold leaf and dressed outside with lion skins. A dozen senior aides ride beside him in attendance. There are 2,000 dog handlers and 10,000 falconers, so Marco says, each with his bird, but we shouldn't take this as exact, because there are also 10,000 tents; it's just an impressively large number. In order not to clog the gateways and the roads, they leave in bunches of a hundred.

Marco says they head south. But if so, the vast array soon swings eastward over the plains and rivers that run between

Beijing and the sea. The emperor makes stately progress on his elephants, say 30 kilometres a day, arriving every evening at a campsite that is a tent-city. Along the way, birds of many species scatter and soar from their new nests.

> And sometimes as they may be going along, and the Emperor from his chamber is holding discourse with his Barons, one of the latter shall exclaim: 'Sire! Look out for Cranes!' Then the Emperor instantly has the top of his chamber thrown open, and having marked the cranes he casts one of his gerfalcons, whichever he please; and often the quarry is struck within his view . . . I do not believe there ever existed in the world or ever will exist, a man with such sport and enjoyment as he has.

Some hunts involve the dogs, huge mastiff-like creatures trained for hunting by their handlers, known as 'wolf-men' (Polo gets the Mongol term right, but thinks it means 'keepers of mastiffs'). 'And as the Lord rides a-fowling over the plains, you will see these big hounds coming tearing up, one pack after a bear, another pack after a stag, or some other beast.'
They are heading towards the spot where the Great Wall now swoops down from highlands to the Pacific. There is no Wall yet, of course, and no danger from the nomads, because the land is all Kublai's. Ahead, through the narrow strip between hills and sea, lie the Manchurian grasslands. After a week, Kublai's elephants bear him into the camp that will be the court's HQ for the next three months. It is a traditional spot, chosen for broad expanses and wealth of game. Falconers and hawkers, with their hooded birds on their wrists and whistles at the ready, scatter over the billowy ground for several kilometres in all directions. The emperor's three tents are ready – a huge one which can hold a whole court of 1,000 people; sleeping quarters; and a smaller audience chamber. Polo does not tell us what shape the tents are, but each has three poles, which probably support the

centre of traditional round tents to remind Kublai of his grassland origins.

What impressed Polo was the decoration of these mobile palace-chambers. They are weatherproofed with tiger skins – Siberian tigers at this stage not being endangered – and lined with ermine and sable, the most valuable of Siberian furs. Consider. A tent that could hold 1,000 people has a circumference of about 125 metres. To cover its walls would take 16,000 pelts, each today costing $50–100 each. That's the equivalent of $1 million, just to line the main tent – without the tiger-skin waterproofing. Spread out all around are the tents of the royal family – Kublai's senior wife Chabi, the three subsidiary wives, and the princes, and the girls from the Ongirad (the Mongol clan that traditionally supplied Genghis's family with mates) brought in for the harem – and the tents of the senior ministers, the attendants, the falconers, grooms, cooks, dog handlers, household staff, secretaries, all with their families, and all of course protected by contingents of soldiers. This was a tent-city, with a population of many thousands, sustained by blood-sport. Every day hawks and falcons bring down cranes, swans, ducks, geese, hare and deer, which the soft-mouthed dogs mark and fetch. Hare, stag, buck, roe – these are designated as royal game, which ordinary people are banned from hunting at this time to ensure a good supply for the imperial forays onto the plains of north-east China.

Meanwhile, the business of the court continues, with conferences and audiences and messengers coming and going and the receipt of ambassadors from abroad. And at the centre of this vast array is the emperor: overweight, gout-ridden, but still eager to reconnect with his roots by riding out over the plain. A portrait of him by the court artist Liu Guan-dao shows him perched heavily in the saddle, wrapped in an ermine coat, with Chabi at his side. He has two attendants. It is a scene of deliberate pseudo-casualness, like a

Cartier-Bresson snapshot, for all four have had their attention caught by something off-camera – someone calling, perhaps: 'Your Majesty! Cranes! Over here!' But there is no bird on the royal wrist, and a whippet awaits an order.

So it continues for two and a half months, until, in mid-May, the immense operation reverses itself, bringing emperor and entourage back to the capital, where, as the summer begins to build, preparations start for the haul northward to Xanadu.

7

EMBRACING BUDDHA,
AND TIBET

UNHAPPILY FOR THOSE WHO WISH IT WERE NOT SO, TIBET IS NOW part of China: threatened, dominated, invaded, colonized, occupied and developed out of any possibility of regaining its independence – or *gaining* it: for China says that Tibet was part of China from way back. But it depends how far back you wish to go. We can see the roots of China's involvement in Tibet by looking back 750 years, which is where Kublai fits in. But there are deeper roots, which take us back another 500 years. It is worth digging them up, because they explain Kublai's role in Tibet's history and thus help us to understand the presence of Chinese troops and colonists in Tibet today.

First, some background to show how thoroughly independent Tibet used to be.

In the seventh century Tibet was an empire, spanning the high heartland and deserts of the north-west, reaching from the borders of Uzbekistan to central China, from halfway across Xinjiang down to the Bay of Bengal. That's 2,250 kilometres from east to west, 1,750 from north to south: an area larger than the Chinese heartland. Indeed, in 763 a Tibetan army briefly captured the Chinese capital Chang-an (today's Xian). Trouble arose around the same time, when Buddhism became the state religion. It made little headway against the Tibetans' original shamanistic faith, Bon. Tensions increased when a ninth-century king became a fanatical advocate of Buddhism. Buddhist monks, deriving wealth and power from their newly founded monasteries, challenged traditional rulers. Bon nobles revolted. In 838 they killed the king by twisting his head off his body and installed his younger brother, who was himself assassinated five years later. Buddhists were persecuted, monasteries destroyed, and the empire collapsed into a patchwork of squabbling minor kings and feudal lords. Politically, Tibet fell into a historical black hole. Without central rule, with the monasteries in ruins, there were few records.

From this wreckage Buddhism re-emerged, in several sects; predominant was the stream called Mahayana, with its complex, mystical belief in the multiple manifestations of Buddha and transcendent beings or *bodhisattvas*. All the sects embraced Tantric Buddhism, with its spells, mystic syllables and diagrams, as the highest and best type of practice, and all took on peculiarly Tibetan forms by adapting Bon chants, rituals and deities.

The seed of revival grew in the east from the action of three Buddhist scholars, later known as the Three Men of Khams, who escaped the persecutions and fled with their books to Amdo, the present-day Chinese province of Qinghai, on the headwaters of the Yellow River. There they lived in a cave, devoting themselves to re-establishing monastic life. From about 950 onwards, a monk from Amdo named Klumes (or kLu-mes in one of several possible transliterations) drove forward the Buddhist renaissance, carrying Buddhism west to the Tibetan heartland. In what is known as the 'second introduction of Buddhism', old monasteries were repaired, new ones founded.

A similar revival occurred in the far west, where a member of the royal family had fled when the empire collapsed. He and his descendants created three tiny kingdoms on the upper Sutlej river, near the borders of present-day India. One in particular, Gu-ge, became a centre for the Buddhist revival in the western Himalayas, then populated by Tibetans. The Gu-ge king became the 'royal monk', Ye-shes-'od (or Yeshe-Ö). He arranged for twenty-one young Tibetans to study in India. Nineteen died there. One of the survivors returned after seventeen years, and went on to become Tibet's most famous medieval scholar, Rinchen Zangpo (958–1055), the 'Great Translator', who founded a monastic complex at Thöling, which remained in use until it was partly ruined in the Cultural Revolution in 1967.

The tenth and eleventh centuries saw intensive programmes of building and restoring monasteries, and translating Sanskrit texts, including one that set out Tibet's 60-year calendar, with its cycle of twelve animals and five elements. The greatest expert on this system was an Indian teacher and master, Atisha. Ye-shes-'od issued an invitation to Atisha, who arrived in Gu-ge at the age of 60 in 1042 – a vital date, because it acts as the base-line for Tibet's lunar calendar. Atisha stayed in Thöling monastery for three years, then travelled in Tibet until his death in 1054. In that time he laid the foundations for Buddhism's fully fledged revival, confirmed in 1076 by a great council in Gu-ge, linking eastern and western Buddhists. The translation of Buddhist literature into Tibetan accelerated. This was to prove vital work for a religion that was to decline in India under the pressure of Islam. Atisha's influence, the translations, the revival of monastic discipline: all this ensured that Tibet was to become the chief inheritor of Indian Buddhism. (Not that this gave Tibet political unity under a single ruler. The struggle between Bon and Buddhism continued until the seventeenth century, when members of the Gelugpa sect killed the last political claimant to the throne, opening the way for the joint spiritual and temporal kings, the Dalai Lamas.)

All of this shows that historically, up until the early thirteenth century, China had no claims on Tibet. Indeed, the opposite applied: Tibet ruled half of present-day China, but looked westward to India for its most significant influence, Buddhism. So on what basis does China claim authority? What is the justification for what happened in the 1950s, the liberation by Mao's army, when 30,000 battle-hardened Communist troops crushed 4,000 Tibetans, the military occupation, the crushing of the 1959 uprising, the flight of the Dalai Lama, the death of hundreds of thousands of Tibetans – over a million, some say – the bombing of the Jokhan, Tibet's most revered religious institution, the subsequent sacking of over 6,000 monasteries, the ruin of a nation?

The justification was, of course, that Tibet became Chinese when it fell to the Mongols.

How did that takeover start? Not in the way that most books claim. Standard accounts say that Genghis's coronation was enough to inspire Tibet to tender voluntary submission. Not so, as Luciano Petech states in the most authoritative recent analysis,[1] calling the suggestion 'a tissue of absurdities'. Nor is there any evidence for a claim that Sorkaktani made an approach in 1215 – the year in which she was supposed to have given birth to Kublai in Zhangye.

The first verifiable link was made in 1239, by Ogedei's second son Köten (Kublai's cousin), who, after campaigning in Sichuan, was given an appanage on the Tibetan borderlands, centred on present-day Wuwei. He invaded briefly the next year, damaging a monastery. The death of Ogedei

[1] 'Tibetan Relations with Sung China and with the Mongols', in Morris Rossabi, ed., *China Among Equals: The Middle Kingdom and its Neighbours.*

delayed any further advance, but in 1244 a rather pressing invitation arrived from Köten for the 62-year-old lama of the Saskya monastery, the other side of Lhasa, not far from the Nepalese border. His words suggest that he had identified Buddhism as the key to political dominance. 'I need to have a master to tell me which path I should take. I have decided to have you. Please come in total disregard of road hardships. If you find excuses in your old age . . . don't you fear that I will answer the matter by sending troops?' With little choice in the matter, the lama started a long journey from the Tibetan highlands, accompanied by two nephews, aged nine and seven, one of whom will be of peculiar significance in Kublai's story. Bear in mind that these events occurred over immense distances: it was 1,700 kilometres from Saskya to Wuwei, across some of the toughest landscapes on earth. The lama arrived at Köten's base in 1246, only to find the Mongol absent attending the great assembly that elected Güyük as the new emperor. On Köten's return, the two agreed that the lama would act as the Mongol agent in Tibet. The lama wrote to various Tibetan leaders suggesting they co-operate: 'There is only one way out, which is to submit to the Mongols.' To seal the pact, the lama's seven-year-old nephew was married to Köten's daughter. As Petech says, by this agreement 'Köten laid the foundations of Mongol influence in Tibet', the influence that one day China would inherit.

Now three deaths occurred in quick succession: of the new emperor Güyük, Köten and the senior lama. The new emperor, eager to assert his rights in the area, sent troops into Tibet, with attendant destruction. He and several princes assumed the patronage of a number of Tibetan sects. One of the princes was Kublai, who thus found himself competing for influence in Tibet with (among others) his brothers Mönkhe, Hulegu and Ariq.

Kublai now made a small gesture of immense significance. He was still only a prince, still under the thumb of his brother

Mönkhe, but with ambitions to extend his influence in north China. Kublai had already realized that he needed to balance his Chinese Confucian and Taoist advisers with a strong Buddhist one, and by happy chance one of the late Saskya lama's two nephews was at a loose end in Köten's HQ. His name was something that looks totally unpronounceable to westerners (Blo-gros rGyal-mtshan), but he would shortly acquire a title, Phags-pa (Noble Guru), which is how he is known to history. Kublai invited the 16-year-old Phags-pa to court. It must have suited them both – the boy grateful to have a sponsor in a chaotic world, already halfway Mongol, and eager for whatever was on offer in Kublai's expanding empire; Kublai well aware that this young priest, the heir to the senior lama of Tibet's most powerful sect yet too young to be viewed with suspicion by Mönkhe, could be the key to the whole country.

In 1251–2 Kublai was back and forth in China's western regions – the Ordos, or Zhangye, or Wuwei – preparing for the invasion of Yunnan. And he had a problem. He needed a rather better justification for conquest than he had inherited from his grandfather and father. Genghis and his immediate heirs had had a powerful but rather limited idea of what the empire was all about. They believed – no: they *knew*, with the utter, impregnable certainty of true believers – that Heaven had given the world into their hands. True, Genghis himself had moved beyond mere brutality to administer his new estates. But still the justification for conquest was, as it were, God's command. Of course, rulers have always claimed divine backing. Certainly every Chinese dynasty had done so, arguing that the very fact of a successful change of dynasty meant that the new emperor had been granted the Mandate of Heaven, and that he and his heirs alone were qualified to apply correctly the rules of good government, the age-old system of Confucian ethics and bureaucracy. But, as Herbert Franke points out in his magisterial analysis of this subject, the Mongols were different. Whatever may or may not have filtered into Genghis's mind from his Chinese neighbours, he was totally uninterested in any Chinese-style Mandate-of-Heaven nonsense, with its goody-goody Confucian veneer. As far as he and his heirs were concerned, the bottom line was that Heaven had given them the world. The Mongols' task was to dominate, and all everyone else had to do was submit. It's there in *The Secret History*: 'Together Heaven and Earth have agreed, Temujin [Genghis's original name] shall be the lord of the land . . . The whole earth is prepared for you . . .' It's there in many statements from the first Europeans to make contact with the Mongols. John of Plano Carpini reported in 1247 that the Mongols intended to conquer the whole world, that only then would there be peace, that Genghis was seen as 'the sweet and venerable Son of Heaven' – *filius Dei dulcis et venerabilis* – and as the only lord on Earth, as God is in Heaven. William of Rubrouck made the same point: *Super terram non sit nisi unus dominus Chingischan* – 'Over the Earth there is to be only one lord, Genghis Khan.' Note the sense of present and future. Genghis remained in some sense alive, in spirit; still does, actually, as anyone can see if they visit his so-called mausoleum in Inner Mongolia, or witness the adoration released by the 800th anniversary of his coronation in 2006.

Even in his life this had proved a rather over-simple prescription. Conquest is not the same as government. Genghis himself had moved beyond conquest, introducing a script, written laws, bureaucracy and some of the rules of administration; and his heirs, overriding the objections of reactionaries, had for the most part drifted in the same direction. As it happened, the fundamental Mongol belief in Tenger proved quite adaptable. Islam and Christianity both acknowledge Heaven. Hence Genghis's religious tolerance, and hence the relative ease with which Mongol rulers in Persia and Central Asia adopted Islam. As Herbert Franke suggests, it is not hard to imagine that, if the Mongols had remained in Hungary after 1242, they would in due course have become Christian.

It was the same with Kublai. The needs of government in his Chinese territories had already demanded that he acquire the trappings of Confucianism. But that was not enough. His gaze was looking beyond traditional Chinese lands, to Yunnan, to Tibet. He had to legitimize his rule in the eyes of Mongols, Chinese and *any other culture that would, as Heaven decreed, form part of the Mongol world-empire*. He found what he was looking for in Buddhism. You may think of Buddhism as a peaceful religion, and therefore unsuitable for an empire dedicated to world conquest, but it is not necessarily so. In Lamaist Buddhism, one of the four god-kings who preside over the four corners of the earth is Vaiśravana, a warrior armed with a lance or cudgel with which to defeat non-believers. He was, if you like, a Buddhist god of war. There is nothing in Lamaist Buddhism incompatible with Mongol imperialism.

It was the teenage Phags-pa who showed Kublai that Buddhism could serve his needs well. For Buddhism offered something that did not exist in the Chinese view of history, or in Islam, or in Christianity: not only did it claim to be a religion of universal truth, it also contained a model of the 'universal emperor', the *cakravartin-raja*, who ruled people of many languages and 'turned the wheel of the Law'. Some previous rulers had experimented with this idea, equating themselves with Buddha, having themselves addressed as a *bodhisattva*, an enlightened being – Emperor Bodhisattva or Saviour of the World Bodhisattva. Buddhism was, in brief, the best way for Kublai to attach himself to a religion that not only was much more than Chinese but also offered an ideology that justified world conquest and world rule. Kublai would become both Caesar and Pope, head of both church and state, the fount of both worldly welfare and spiritual salvation.

The process started in about 1253 – the date is slightly vague, because Kublai was involved with the conquest of Yunnan at the time – when he received a consecration from the 18-year-old Phags-pa, being initiated into the rites of the highest deity of Lamaism, Hevajra, whose cult centred on the Saskya monastery, in which Phags-pa had been raised.

With Yunnan conquered, Kublai returned to Xanadu, bringing with him Phags-pa, a key both to his evolving ideology and to Tibet. Phags-pa concluded his studies, became a full monk, and in 1258, now aged 23, became Kublai's Buddhist guru; for Kublai, shortly to declare himself emperor, needed formally to establish his credentials as a universal ruler.

Phags-pa's status was confirmed when, that same year, he took part in the third and decisive debate set up by Kublai between Buddhists and Taoists. This left him in a strong position when Kublai had himself declared khan in 1260. In the civil war with Ariq that followed, rival sects in Tibet were suspected of siding with Ariq and silenced (temporarily, as it turned out). In 1261, Kublai conferred on Phags-pa the title of National Preceptor and made him the supreme head of the Buddhist clergy in his Chinese domains. Three years later, Kublai gave his protégé the so-called Pearl Document, by which the Buddhist monks were exempted from taxation and granted various other privileges. Soon after, he sent Phags-pa home as abbot of the main Saskya monastery, along with his younger brother. While Kublai sent a scattering of troops to 'pacify' remote corners of Tibet that had hitherto remained beyond Mongol reach, Phags-pa and his brother were supposed to establish Kublai's moral sway over the whole country.

This was not so easy. Locals objected, apparently seeing in Phags-pa not so much a brilliant young mind as a turncoat who had adopted Mongol clothes and manners. The whole project foundered when his brother died in 1267, aged 29; so an army marched in from Qinghai, cowed the opposition and established a Pacification Bureau that would run the country directly. Politically, Phags-pa was sidelined, spending the next few years engaged on a task which we shall get to in a moment. A Mongol named Dashman was given the job of establishing a postal system, with 27 relay stations, and of proclaiming Kublai's sovereignty. By 1269 Tibet was an integral part of Kublai's empire, where it remained for the next 80 years, until the Mongol empire fell apart.

Meanwhile, Kublai had had a startling cultural insight. He had identified a problem that sprang from the nature of Mongol achievements, and from his own ambition; and he wanted Phags-pa to provide the solution.

Kublai had grown up in two worlds, Mongol and Chinese. He spoke Mongol, but struggled with Chinese. Now Xanadu was rising around him, he was surrounded by Chinese advisers, and the vast majority of his subjects were Chinese. Soon, if all went well, there would be millions more.

His problem was this: how to form an administration that actually spanned the two worlds? Sure, Mongol edicts could be written in Mongol, Chinese in Chinese, but the two systems were incompatible.

Mongolian had a fine vertical script, introduced on Genghis's orders by his new vassals the Uighurs, of what is now western China. It was an alphabetical script, which means it could represent most of the sounds of almost any language fairly well (as Latin script does in, for instance, the Latinized version of Chinese, pinyin). However, since the vertical script was devised for Uighur, not Mongolian, it has a number of faults, among them an inability to capture some Chinese sounds. In addition, it has three versions of most letters – initial, medial and final – which gives it about 80 characters (our alphabet having 52, if you count upper and lower case as separate). Still, it works well enough to have survived. It is in everyday use in Inner Mongolia, and quite common in Mongolia itself, if only in academic circles and as a designer-chic escape from the standard and rather less exotic Cyrillic.

Chinese script is infinitely more complex, with thousands of characters, each one representing a syllable, governed by the rule that each must begin with a consonant and end with a vowel or 'n'. In its favour, it works, for Chinese; it is as expressive as any other script; it is beautiful, an art form in its own right; and it has tremendous cultural momentum, in that it has been in existence for 4,000 years – a few characters can be traced right back to their origins in Shang times around 2500 BC – and the Chinese are not about to change it (Mao once played with the idea of trying, but backed off). For Kublai to try to impose Mongolian script on China would have been impossible; it was equally impossible to use Chinese script to write Mongolian. So a system arose whereby documents were first written in Mongol, then translated. But Kublai was wary of allowing Chinese scribes too much authority, so they were not allowed to learn Mongol, and had to rely on non-Chinese interpreters. It was a tedious and cumbersome business.

It gets worse. Genghis had conquered Xi Xia, which was inhabited by Tangut-speakers. Tangut had its own script, which had been invented at the behest of the state's founder, Li Yuan-hao, in the eleventh century. As a model, he chose the script of the region's dominant culture, China. But he also wanted it to be unique to Tangut, a Tibetan language that had no relation to Chinese at all. So he instructed his scholar, Yeli Renrong, to devise something totally new. Tangut's characters, some 6,000 of which are recorded, look like Chinese, but are no more Chinese than the language itself. Since Genghis virtually destroyed the Tangut culture, the language eventually vanished from history. As a result it has only been deciphered quite recently, and Tangut is still in the process of emerging from the darkness into which Genghis cast it. Kublai had many thousands of Tangut subjects. They, too, needed to read his edicts.

Then there was the script of the Khitan, the Manchurian people who had been the Mongols' predecessor dynasty in north China. And Sanskrit, the language towards which his new subjects the Tibetans looked as the fount and origin of their religion. And Tibetan itself, of course, already some 600 years old. Not forgetting Korea, which the Mongols had already attacked once in 1216, and to which Kublai would soon return. And what of those languages of people under the control of Kublai's brother Hulegu, principally Persian?

That's just the languages in which Kublai was directly involved around 1261. If things went as he hoped, if all south China fell to the Mongols, they would be in contact with Burmese, Vietnamese, Japanese and who knew what other cultures. A bureaucratic nightmare loomed. If it went on like this, all administration would be suffocated by translation work.

Once he saw the problem, Kublai also saw an instant solution. Chinese had unified China, welding together diverse dialects with a common script; Kublai wanted a script that would unify the world. Xanadu was ready, Ariq's rebellion had been crushed; Kublai was already thinking about a new capital in what is now Beijing and planning the long-delayed invasion of southern China. He needed to consolidate, to ensure the most efficient management possible as a basis for expansion. On hand was just the man: young Phags-pa, just back from his abortive trip to Tibet. In 1267, Kublai told him to invent the new script, a script in which any language under Heaven could be written.

Phags-pa, fluent in Tibetan, Mongolian and Chinese, and probably with a good knowledge of Uighur and Sanskrit as well, analysed their phonetic demands and modified his own Tibetan script into a sort of International Phonetic Alphabet of some 60 signs, most representing individual vowels and consonants, but including some common syllables. Tibetan reads from left to right, but Phags-pa designed his script to be read vertically, in deference to the Uighur system introduced by the great Genghis. The letters are mostly made of straight lines and right-angles, hence its name in Mongolian: square script. For representing Mongolian and other languages, it is certainly a big advance on Chinese: 'Genghis' in Chinese transliterates as *cheng ji si*; in Phags-pa it is *jing gis*.

After two years of work, it was done. Phags-pa presented his master with his new script in 1269. Kublai was delighted, and conferred on Phags-pa the title of Imperial Preceptor, with income to match. He ordered that all official documentation be recorded in the new script – the 'State Script' as he called it – and set up schools to teach it. It was used on seals and the metal or wood passes – *paiza*, as they are known – which gave authority to high officials to demand goods and service from civilians. 'By the power of Eternal Heaven, by the protection of the Great Blessedness [of Genghis],' ran the text on one of them, 'whoever has no reverence [for this] shall be guilty and die.'

That was the high point of Phags-pa's international influence. He returned to Tibet shortly afterwards as head of the Saskya monastery and sect, which exercised an uneasy sway over the others. Suddenly, in 1280, he died. He was only 45, and there were strong suspicions he had been poisoned. The Tibetan civil administrator was suspected. There was no proof, but justice being rough and Kublai being emperor, he had the man executed anyway.

You can see Kublai's problem, and his solution, set in stone today. If you visit China's prime tourist attraction, the Great Wall at Badaling, just outside Beijing, you will see behind the Wall an ancient arch, Cloud Terrace (Yun Tai), built in

1342 as a gateway to the pass. Its flagstone floor is scarred with parallel tracks by an infinity of wagon-wheels, making it look like an abandoned railway tunnel. If you stand inside and look up, you see that you are surrounded by five flat surfaces carved with intertwining bas-reliefs of warrior kings, buddhas, elephants, dragons, snakes and plants, all framing a Buddhist text in six languages: Sanskrit, Tibetan, Mongol, Tangut, Chinese – and Kublai's answer to this Babel, Phags-pa's 'State Script'.

In fact, the monument confers a significance on the new script that it lacked in practice. It looked good on seals, stone slabs, coins, even porcelain. You still see it today on Mongolian banknotes and the occasional statue, but this is only for display. For routine records it never really took hold. Four more times in the 15 years after his initial proclamation Kublai repeated his order, backed by the creation of a special academy to study and teach the script. His officials handled his demands as bureaucrats always handle orders that make life harder: they said yes, and did nothing. The special schools lacked teachers, because no-one wanted to learn the script, and anyway the officials refused to send their children there.

The trouble with Phags-pa's script had nothing to do with its quality. The problem lay in human nature. Learning a script, however easy, is a demanding business. Writing has grown from nothing only four times in history: in Mesopotamia, Egypt, China and Central America. Each script took many centuries to refine. Once they reach maturity, they spread to other cultures, because they are vital to complex societies. They are incredibly tenacious. Changing a script is the cultural equivalent of growing a new limb. There have been examples of script change by authoritarianism: Kemal Atatürk forced Turkey to shift from Arabic to Latin script in the 1920s; Mongolia's Soviet-style rulers replaced Genghis's vertical script with Cyrillic in 1941. But in both cases the

government wielded overwhelming power over tiny bureau-
cracies and unsophisticated societies. Kublai could employ his
officials to control taxes, armies and records, but he couldn't
control their minds. Trying to overcome the cultural inertia of
his Chinese bureaucracy was like trying to row an iceberg. It
just wasn't going to happen.

In a sense it didn't matter. Kublai's involvement in Tibet had
already done more for his empire than a new script would
ever achieve. By bringing Phags-pa on board, he added a vast
new territory to his domains and established a link between
China and Tibet that was a foundation for their relations
from then on. Under the Manchus it was the Dalai Lama who
ruled, maintaining a nominal independence with Manchu
support, and occasional intervention, until the dynasty's
overthrow in 1911 briefly restored the independence that
Tibet had lost almost seven centuries before. After the 1949
revolution, Mao and his propagandists could thus argue, and
did, that Tibet was an 'inalienable part of China', that Tibet's
independence in the previous 40 years was an illusion based
on China's weakness, and that the Communists were merely
restoring the status quo. It is not an argument that seizes the
moral high ground; go this route, and Britain could reclaim
its empire. In fact, the foundation for the Chinese claim to
Tibet is even shakier than Britain's claim to the USA or India.
At least India and America were seized by the British. The
Chinese claim is based on the fact that Tibet was first occupied by the troops of Genghis's son Ogedei and then his
grandson Kublai, both Mongols. As far as Mongols were
concerned, it was Mongolia that conquered China, Mongolia
that occupied Tibet, Mongolia that established a Mongol
empire. That's what they still assert. Fortunately for China,
Kublai decided to establish a Chinese dynasty, making his
grandfather its posthumous founder, thus turning history

upside down, and allowing official pronouncements like this one in a recent book: 'The Chinese emperor enjoyed paramount authority in the areas under his sovereignty, and these areas included Tibet.'[2]

In Chinese eyes, Genghis and Kublai were actually Chinese. And so, therefore, is Tibet.

End of story.

[2] Wang Jiawei and Nyima Gyaincain, *The Historical Status of China's Tibet*.

8

THE KEY TO CONQUEST

SOME THINGS ARE NON-NEGOTIABLE. FOR KUBLAI, CONQUEST OF Song was one of them. He had tried invasion, and failed. Like his grandfather, Kublai was not to be put off by failure. He would give anything a go if it might work. So when his armies were dealing with Ariq in the north, he turned to soft talk and generosity in the south, hoping to win by charm what he could not yet win by force. But when in 1260 he sent an embassy to Hangzhou to suggest a deal, the envoy never even made it through Song lines. He was detained, and would remain under house arrest for an astonishing 16 years, until released to Kublai's invading armies.

Now why would Song do such a thing? Scholars have tended to put the arrest down to pure dimness, because it gave Kublai a *casus belli*. But more likely the affair grants us an insight into the shadowy world of espionage and counter-espionage.[1] The envoy, Hao Jing, was the protégé of a

---

[1] This paragraph is based on Jennifer W. Jay, *A Change in Dynasties: Loyalism in 13th-Century China*.

northern Chinese general who had gone over to the Mongols after the conquest of Jin in 1234. As a Chinese, and a turn-coat, he would make an effective secret agent. The Song general in charge of the frontier region set his spies to work, and somehow learned the contents of a memo from Hao Jing to Kublai, in which he suggested what Kublai's policy should be. 'There are two ways to conquer countries,' he began: 'by the use of force and by the use of strategy.' Force hadn't worked, therefore strategy was advisable, and this would take a great deal of patience. 'We should thus buy time and gain the confidence of the Song and request that they cede to us some territory and present us annual tributes of cash. When the time is ripe for the conquest we should then first—' and he sketched out an attack plan that was, in essence, the plan eventually adopted by Kublai. So the terms he had come to propose would have been merely a delaying tactic, because Kublai had no intention of keeping the peace long-term. Of course he didn't. His aim was conquest, as Genghis and Heaven had ordained. Hao Jing was on a phoney mission. That's why he was arrested. And once arrested, he could not be released because he would tell Kublai that the Song now knew Kublai's long-term strategy.

Kublai gritted his teeth – he had little choice, given that almost all his troops were dealing with Ariq – and continued to appease. He released unasked 172 merchants who had been arrested for clandestine trading across the Mongol–Song border. He granted land, clothes and oxen to Song defectors, of which there were many. But this was not real peace, as both sides now knew. As soon as he could, Kublai would turn on the south again.

The previous campaign had shown that the Mongols were not yet up to the task. Song was all rivers and cities, exactly what Mongolia and most of north China were not. Cities were the prizes, because that was where the rich lived and the powerful administered – there were no castles such as the

European nobility had, no manorial estates to be plundered. As a result, cities were tough nuts, well supplied with explosives, many of them positioned on rivers, the better to trade and feed themselves. Mongol horsemen might move fast over open land, but as the assaults on Fishing Mountain and Wuchang had shown, horsemen could not guarantee victories against cities set in rivers and mountains. The Mongols needed to beat the Song on their own terms, with (a) better means to take cities and (b) ships. Though they had known of the first – the principles of siege warfare – since Genghis's time, they would now need a vast increase in the scale of their siege machinery. But ships? The only ships they knew were ferries for crossing rivers. To build warships that would carry armies and weapons up and down China's river roads, they would have to start from scratch.

The key, of course, was the mighty Yangtze, beyond whose lower reaches lay the capital, Hangzhou. Now, the Yangtze flows from west to east, while Kublai's armies would be invading from the north. But right in the middle of the Mongol–Song borderland a major tributary, the Han, swung southward, making a river-road straight down to Wuchang, the lower Yangtze – and Hangzhou.

There was just one problem. The Han had its own key, in the form of the town of Xiangyang,[2] which lies on the Han at the junction of two other rivers. Today, Xiangyang and its sister-city across the river, Fancheng, form the super-city of Xiangfan, a knot of roads and railway lines; it thrives on industry and tourists heading for the Wudang mountains to the west, famous for their 72 pinnacles, their Taoist temples and their boxers, who date their *tai ji*-like skills back to Song times. In Kublai's day, Xiangyang was a moated fortress-city

---

[2] Xiangyang has been through all sorts of different versions and spellings – Saianfu in Marco Polo, Sayan-fu in Rashid, Hsiang-yang in more recent, but pre-pinyin times.

and a major trade hub of 200,000 people, linked to Fancheng by a pontoon bridge consisting of boats moored between posts driven into the river-bed. In summer, when bloated by rain, the Han, wide and languid, rolls on southward between the Jing and Dahong hills then meanders out on to lake-spattered lowlands around Wuhan. Xiangyang would have to be eliminated by any army heading south by river.

This was common knowledge on both sides, because the city had been a prime target before – in a Jin assault in 1206–7 and in Ogedei's 1235–41 campaign. It had not fallen either time, but surrendered in 1236 to the Mongols, who held it only briefly before returning north. So Xiangyang was used to taking punishment; and besides, thanks in part to the discovery of Hao's memo, it had been busy rebuilding its defences. It had 6 kilometres of solid stone walls, some 6–7 metres high, set in a rough square just over a kilometre across. Three of the six gates gave directly on to the river, which was a high road for supplies and communication half a kilometre wide when it was in flood, and far too deep to wade; in winter, when the water was low, it became a maze of channels and sandbars; and the moat, fed from the river, was 90 metres across. All of this meant that attackers could not get close enough either to assault the walls with ladders and towers or to undermine them.

This chapter is largely about the answer to this problem – the first of several problems whose solution led on to Kublai's greatest achievement, the recreation of a unified China. In reverse, the argument runs like this: the key to all China was the south, the kingdom of Song; the key to the south was the Yangtze, with its vast population, numerous cities and agricultural wealth; the key to the Yangtze, if approaching from the north, was the Han river; the key to the Han was Xiangyang; and the key that would open Xiangyang to the Mongols was – well, I don't want to give away the story just yet. Let's just say it could not possibly be the old-style Mongol cavalry.

The evidence, I have to admit, is patchy: sources relate the overall progress of the campaign, the difficulties and significance of the siege, a mention of the engineers who solved the problem, the hugely influential consequences. But my reasoning has a step-by-step logic that leads inexorably to a conclusion I would very much like to be true: that, in effect, modern China owes its existence to the device that broke the siege of Xiangyang, a device such as China, and perhaps the world, had never seen before.

Very little of this was in Kublai's mind as he rebuilt his forces after dealing with Ariq. It was four years before his generals told him they were ready, which made it nine years since Kublai had been forced to give up on his first assault on Song. You would think nine years would have been long enough to prepare, but he had no way of knowing that Xiangyang would be such a challenge, and certainly no way of knowing in advance how to deal with it.

It began with Mongols approaching the city in early 1268, under the command of the young (32) and famous Aju – famous because military glory was in the family; he was the son of Uriyang-kadai, who had won Yunnan for Kublai fifteen years before, and the grandson of the now-legendary Subedei, who had masterminded Genghis's and Mönkhe's western campaigns. Almost as soon as he started his advance, Aju found he needed help. 'The forces I am leading consist entirely of Mongol military units [i.e. cavalry],' he wrote to the emperor. 'Encountering barriers of mountains and rivers, stockades and forts, without Chinese army forces I can do nothing.' Kublai complied: infantry arrived, boats were captured and built, and Aju had the amphibious force he thought he needed.

Aju and his army would not have found much in the way of loot to sustain them, because in preparation for a siege city rulers customarily ordered a scorched earth policy, clearing the surrounding countryside of anything that might help the enemy: high buildings, trees, stones, metals, tiles, vegetables, straw, animals, grain. Much of this went into storage inside the walls. A military handbook, *Wu-pei ji-yao* (*The Essentials of Military Preparedness*),[3] lists what had to be stored: lamps, oil, axes, charcoal, sulphur, lime, rafters, nails, needles, mats, hemp, shovels, pestles, stones for pounding textiles, vessels to deal with 'night-soil', brushes, ink, ink-slabs, writing tables – and on and on. Civilians would be trained as militiamen, women organized in cooking gangs, children trained in delivering food and materials. Particular care would have been taken to pre-empt trouble from the disaffected poor – espionage, sabotage – by avoiding harsh treatment: 'The poor are our children who may carry weapons and stand up against the enemy with all their strength,' says the *Essentials*, then quotes the words of a sage, Xu Dong: ' "If a town is besieged, one must first look to the interior peace and only then consider the external enemy." ' The townspeople must draw together. Innkeepers must vouch for their lodgers, abbots for their monks. Itinerant musicians, magicians and fortune-tellers are expelled as potential spies. Families are grouped in tens, with everyone vouching for everyone else. Only long-established employees are kept on, new ones fired. Curfews are kept. Every quarter has its fire-brigade, with its huge water-jars, ladders, and hooks and pulleys to deal with demolition. Specialists prepare their double and triple cross-bows, which could shoot 2-metre arrows some 200 metres, while engineers check their trebuchets.

This is the moment to introduce the trebuchet, a subject that will shortly seize our attention in a big way.

The backbone of Chinese siege technology was the 'traction trebuchet', which has been resurrected in reconstructions. A

---

[3] About 1830, but the practices it quotes are ancient ones.

typical trebuchet consists of a frame about 4 metres high on which pivots an 11–12-metre pole. The pole is on an axle, off-centre, with one section longer than the other. On the long end is a sling, on the short end are ropes, usually attached to a T-bar. The sling is crucial: it lengthens the pole and magnifies its power without increasing the weight. One end is nailed to the head of the pole, the other is attached to a simple hook. In release, it acts like a whip, being dragged up and over like a weighted hook on the end of a fishing line. Centrifugal force carries it in a semi-circle. As it reaches its topmost point, its momentum frees the unattached end, which flies clear, releasing the missile. Each trebuchet has a team of 5–15, depending on its size. A rock weighing no more than a couple of kilos or some sort of incendiary device is loaded in the sling, the team hauls on the other end – hence the term 'traction' – the lever rises, the sling whips round, slips its hook, and releases the rock. The whole operation takes no more than 15 seconds (modern reconstructions show that a good team can fire 5–6 rounds per minute). It is all rather primitive, but effective at close range: over a city wall, and anything up to 100 metres. In the thirteenth century, this was utterly standard siege technology. Traction trebuchets could be made on the spot, or carried in bits on horses, or mounted on wagons. Any army worthy of the name would muster scores, sometimes hundreds of them.

On campaigns, trebuchets formed a whole branch of siege warfare, as the artillery does in modern armies. For one thing, working a trebuchet was demanding, rather like rowing a racing eight. Teams needed to rest. As well as needing its own transport – a few horses, an ox and wagon – each trebuchet had to have several teams, working in relays. These specialized soldiers needed their own food, armour and horses. So each trebuchet, simple as it was, had quite an entourage – large versions demanded 200 men – with tremendous implications for commissariats planning advances, camps, sieges and retreats. They were often made on the spot, and they often needed repair, so imagine also contingents of carpenters. Ropes were of both hemp and leather, alternating, because their qualities varied with the weather (in wet weather, leather shrinks, hemp swells).

Trebuchets were, of course, standard weapons in defence as well as attack. In the siege of 1206–7 Xiangyang had 114 of them. Trebuchet teams would work in relative safety from inside the walls, with an artillery spotter up above to direct them. Before a siege, defenders gathered huge quantities of stone from surrounding areas, for their own use and to deprive the opposition of ammunition.

Whether in attack or defence, trebuchets lobbed more than simple rocks, for all Chinese armies employed experts in explosive devices and chemical warfare. The techniques, based on some 700 years of experimentation by alchemists, had been developed from the first use of gunpowder in war in the early tenth century – a flame-thrower. Rapidly, a whole range of gunpowder-based weapons had appeared: exploding arrows, mines, and bombs thrown by trebuchets. One of these consisted of gunpowder packed into bamboo and surrounded by broken porcelain: the first known use of shrapnel. By the early thirteenth century, about the time of the first Mongol invasions, this had evolved into the much more deadly 'thundercrash bomb', which detonated inside a metal or ceramic casing 5 centimetres thick. The Mongols experienced these when they took the Jin capital Kaifeng in 1232–4:

Among the weapons of the defenders there was the heaven-shaking thundercrash bomb. It consisted of gunpowder put into an iron container; then when the fuse was lit and the projectile shot off there was a great explosion the noise whereof was like thunder, audible for more than a hundred *li* [c.50 kilometres], and the vegetation was scorched and blasted by the heat over more than half a *mou* [400 square metres].

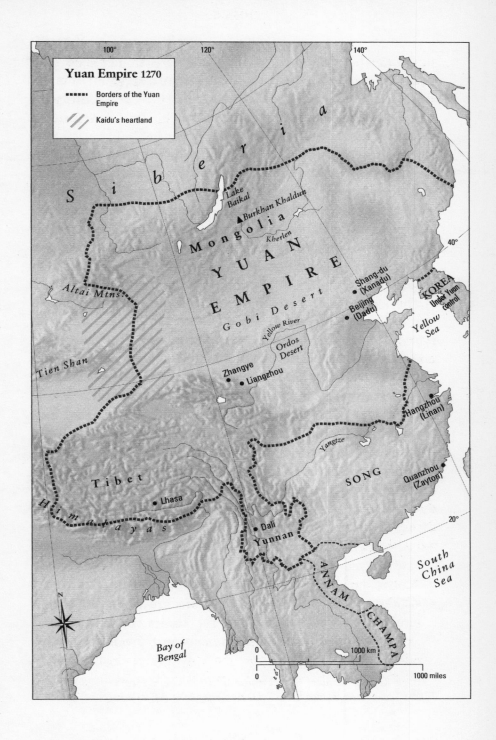

Yuan Empire 1270

▪▪▪▪▪ Borders of the Yuan Empire

⫽⫽⫽ Kaidu's heartland

S i b e r i a

100°   120°   140°

Lake Baikal

▲ Burkhan Khaldun

M o n g o l i a

Kherlen

Y U A N

E M P I R E

Gobi Desert

40°

Altai Mtns.

Shang-du (Xanadu)

Beijing (Dadu)

KOREA
Under Yuan control

Yellow Sea

Yellow River

Tien Shan

Ordos Desert

Zhangye
Liangzhou

Hangzhou (Linan)

Yangtze

T i b e t

SONG

Quanzhou (Zayton)

Lhasa

20°

H i m a l a y a s

Dali

Yunnan

ANNAM

CHAMPA

South China Sea

Bay of Bengal

N

0   1000 km

0   1000 miles

In self-defence, the Mongols dug themselves trenches, covered by cowhides; but the Jin lowered the bombs on chains: 'When these reached the trenches . . . the bombs were set off, with the result that the cowhide and the attacking soldiers were all blown to bits, not even a trace being left behind.'

These bombs were made in large quantities, 'one or two thousand a month', according to a Song official in 1257. He was complaining that current production was down. 'They used to despatch ten or twenty thousand at a time to Xiangyang and Ying-chou,' he said, but now there were not enough. 'The government supposedly want to make preparations for the defence of its fortified cities . . . yet this is all they give us! What chilling indifference!'

The exploding poison devices, the first steps in chemical and germ warfare, are worth a diversion. There were many types. The most repulsive must have been the original dirty weapon, the excrement bomb.[4] I'm inclined to call it the 'shit-and-beetle bomb', after its most bizarre ingredients.

Here is the recipe:

- *7 kilos powdered human excrement*. First gather about 70 kilos of human shit. Dry it, and sift it into a fine powder. This will be the bulk of your poisonous cloud, searing lungs and infecting open wounds. To this add:
- *400g root of aconite*, the herb with hood-shaped flowers whose roots produce some of the deadliest of poisons. Absorbed through the skin, it numbs. Once breathed in or swallowed, it brings on nausea, breathing difficulties, convulsions and heart failure.
- *200g croton oil*. The croton tree grows in India and Indonesia. The oil of its seeds blisters the skin and, if swallowed, inflames the stomach and produces instant diarrhoea.

[4] From Robert Temple, *The Genius of China* (London: Prion, 1999), a distillation of Joseph Needham's massive *Science and Civilisation in China*.

- *400g white arsenic (As$_2$O$_3$) and its compound, arsenic sulphide.* These, in the explosion, would form something like an insecticide spray, which when inhaled in sufficient doses would produce long-term diarrhoea, stomach pain, blood and kidney damage, and death.
- *100g beetles, of the genus Mylabris.* This is the oddest element in this extremely odd mixture. When I first saw it, my imagination went into overdrive. Were the beetles alive? Would they survive an explosion and its poisons? What on earth would be the use of a cloud of poisoned beetles in warfare? A beetles man at the Natural History Museum, Lee Rogers, put me right. *Mylabris* beetles have long been used in traditional Chinese medicine, because in small amounts the chemical they produce, cantharidic acid, stimulates certain organs, including the sexual organs. Indeed, it is the active ingredient in the aphrodisiac known as 'Spanish fly'. A quick bit of Googling reveals that there is a good deal of interest in the chemical at the moment in China because it may be anti-cancerous. But in larger doses, if it gets on the skin, the chemical is a toxin that produces blisters. Hence the common name for these creatures, 'blister beetles'. Once you have gathered your 100g (a few dozen only) of *Mylabris phalerata* or *M. cichorii*, you mash them up, dry them, powder them and add the powder to your poison-bag.

These ingredients were packed into gunpowder, from which ran a fuse. The whole lot was then wrapped in thick paper, tied up with string and covered in a layer of resin, like candle-wax, leaving the fuse sticking out. Weighing some 10–15 kilos, the shit-and-beetle bomb would be placed in its trebuchet sling, lit and fired. This was a specialized weapon, needing a large trebuchet and a team of perhaps a dozen men, who had to cast their lethal package a good 100 metres, or risk being affected by their own poisons.

On both sides all the effort might well end in a balance of forces. For one thing, trebuchets had one huge disadvantage, especially for the defenders. If they used rocks, the cheapest ammunition, they simply supplied ammunition to the other side. The same rocks arced back and forth over the walls, shattering heads, breaking arms, smashing roofs, on occasion in such numbers that the missiles crashed together in mid-air. Whether in defence or attack, think of the rock you would need to attack a city: two shots a minute per device, 100 devices – that's 12,000 rocks per hour, hour after hour, day after day. Where would it all come from? How many men and horses would it take to find it, cut it, transport it? There was thus an incentive to develop more effective projectiles – that is, explosive ones which could scatter poisons, chemicals and shrapnel. But even these were anti-personnel devices, useful only in close-up artillery exchanges, seldom reaching over 100 metres.

It was with these weapons, then, that the siege of Xiangyang began early in 1268, and Aju's advance stopped. The siege was to become a five-year epic, a sort of Chinese Trojan war, with its assaults and attempted break-outs and acts of heroism. The siege even had its equivalent of Troy's dramatic end, though in an act, not of cunning, but of overwhelming force. Unfortunately, since we are in history not prehistory, no bards sang of Xiangyang's heroes, no local Homer spun epic verse; and so, for the first three years of the siege, since we have no tales of heroism to tell, a paragraph of description will have to do.

A proper blockade required boats, 500 of them, built under the supervision of Kublai's admiral Liu Cheng, a senior Song officer who had defected. They took several months to build. Through the summer, the Mongols built fortifications downriver on either side of the Han to bombard Song boats ferrying in supplies. As winter came on again, Aju extended the siege across the river to include Fancheng. An attempt by the Chinese to break out ended in disaster for them: hundreds were captured and beheaded. After that, the Chinese sat tight, with enough supplies reaching them to survive. In spring 1269, Kublai sent in another 20,000 troops to strengthen the besiegers. In August, after 18 months of action and inaction, 3,000 Song boats came up the Han to attack the new Mongol fortifications, and were repulsed with the loss of 2,000 men and 50 boats. Now the Mongols somehow connected up the two sets of downriver fortifications, probably with a chain on pontoons. It could not have worked very well, because the commanders requested another 70,000 troops and 5,000 boats. Even making allowance for the normal inflation of military statistics, this was a massive increase. No doubt, like generals on the Western Front or in Vietnam, they claimed that they could see light at the end of the tunnel, that with one more push it would all be over. The Chinese defenders, re-assured by secret-service officers smuggling in orders, cash and letters sealed inside balls of wax, were equally adamant: there would be no surrender! Several more times the besieged tried to break out. Once, in March 1270, a battalion-strength force – a 'Ten Thousand' – of infantry and horsemen, with 100 boats, mounted an amphibious operation to break through the downriver fortifications; after suffering heavy losses, they retreated back behind the city walls. The catalogue of useless thrusts continued, the Chinese losing 1,000 men in October 1270, 2,000 in August 1271, most of a 3,000-strong force the following month.

What could break the stalemate? As a Mongol general, a Uighur named Ali-haiya, told Kublai, what the Mongols needed was the right sort of artillery. Now, the Mongols already had artillery of many kinds – mangonels, trebuchets, arrow-firing ballistas – having acquired the technology and specialist troops after the siege of Beijing in the year of Kublai's birth.

The problems were Xiangyang's moat and stone walls. The Mongol-Chinese artillery simply didn't have the range or the power to tackle these defences, and no-one in Mongolia or China had the expertise to build bigger, more powerful siege engines.

Kublai, hearing of the problem, also saw the solution. He needed the empire's best siege-engine designers, who happened to be in Persia, 6,000 kilometres away, two-thirds of the way across the empire. This he knew, because he had to hand reports of the siege of Baghdad by his brother Hulegu in 1258. Had not Hulegu had catapults that breached walls? Rashid's words must surely have been echoed by reports in Kublai's archives: 'They set up catapults opposite the Ajami Tower, and breached it.' Ordinary old traction trebuchets could not breach walls. These were machines of a different order.

But even this new secret weapon would not guarantee success. As yet, Xiangyang remained untaken; victory over Song hung in the balance. Yet failure was unthinkable. How could Kublai best fulfil the will of Heaven? Phags-pa advised him what to do. He should seek help from the world of the spirits. Spirit-helpers needed to be approached in the right way, with the correct rites performed in a place impressive enough both to act as a sanctuary for the deity concerned and to assert the emperor's authority as spiritual leader.

Kublai commissioned a temple such as no-one had seen before: Baita Si, the White Pagoda, which still reaches up over central Beijing just to the west of the Forbidden City (it has no connection with the other White Pagoda in Beihai Park). In 2005 I paid the place a visit, vaguely hoping it would bring Kublai to life in some way. It did, mainly because there was one question I had not even thought of yet: to whom or what was Kublai going to pray? I came face to face with the answer, and, without giving away too much, I can tell you it was – well, not scary exactly, but certainly a surprise.

The site on which the White Pagoda would stand was a place of power. People avoided it, because there were reports of fireballs bursting from its low-lying soil (perhaps flares caused by marsh gas). Kublai ordered a dig to see what lay under the ground – and by happy chance someone found ruins, and coins, and a stone tablet engraved with dragons. That was the good omen he needed. Clearly, a dragon-palace had once stood here, making it the ideal location for a royal temple.

Now to define the temple's borders. This he did by means of an ancient Mongol practice for marking a new base. He – or perhaps one of his officers – fired arrows to the four points of the compass, each 200-metre shot specifying the distance to a wall. The original temple was therefore a complex of buildings in a compound about 400 × 400 metres. Later dynasties and the passage of time condemned the outer buildings and walls, reducing the compound to a fraction of its original size, but the pagoda itself, a great inverted ice-cream cone towering over its surrounding huddle of exhibition rooms and offices, remains pretty much as it was in Kublai's day.

Tourists go there to see Buddhas en masse, all official symbols of China's readiness to make everyone part of one great family. The Hall of Ten Thousand Buddhas claims to be one of the greatest collections in the world, with miniature Buddhas from every Buddhist country glittering like jewels. The Hall of Seven Buddhas now has three, four having vanished during the Cultural Revolution. In the Hall of the Great Enlightened One, Emperor Qian Lung's eighteenth-century calligraphy reminds visitors that 'the mind of the Buddha is as bright as a shining pearl'.

The heart of the place is the pagoda itself. To build this, and the complex that would surround it, Kublai naturally chose a

Buddhist: a 27-year-old Nepalese architect and painter named Arniko, who had established his reputation as a teenager in Tibet and then come to China as one of Phags-pa's protégés, making his mark with Kublai in 1265, aged only 21, by rebuilding a bronze statue showing the acupuncture points. He went on to create many other temples and statues around China, continuing almost until his death in 1306 at the age of 62. Everyone is rather proud of Arniko – not surprisingly, given that in the thirteenth century the pagoda, at 374 metres high, was Beijing's tallest building. A statue of him – slim, youthful, fine-featured – stands at its foot, placed there by the Arniko Society of Nepal, unveiled in 2003 in the presence of Nepalese government bigwigs.

I wanted to see inside. With my guide, Silver as she called herself, I climbed steps beside Arniko, and found the way blocked by a wall of corrugated iron. The pagoda was closed for renovation. But there was a door open in the wall. We sneaked inside. To my surprise, I saw two red-robed monks, one solid as a wrestler, the other a lightweight, setting out prayer-flags. Apparently, rituals were still observed here. The monks seemed shy, and I didn't like to intrude with questions. So I wandered round the other side of the pagoda, and was staring up at the huge fat curve of white plaster soaring into the bright autumn sunlight, wondering at the lack of windows and doors, when I heard low chanting. The two monks were performing some sort of a rite; by the time I had hurried back to the front of the building they were closing the door of what looked like a cupboard, and began burning incense and rice. This time there was eye contact, a smile, a nod. Encouraged, I asked Silver to introduce me. The monks were Tibetan. The big one was Tu Dan, the lean one Ganga. How strange, I said, that such a place should still be in use. It always was, came the reply, always protected, always a place to strengthen the relationship between Chinese, Mongols and Tibetans . . .

. . . At which moment we were joined by a man with the

soft, round features of the Beijing professional, who instantly revealed a fine command of English. Benjamin Li was an English graduate and a businessman. He was here because he was an admirer of the temple, and because he was a friend of the two monks. It struck me that he was also some sort of a benefactor, because he pointed out that they lived entirely from donations. A small contribution and an offer to buy lunch produced smiles, and opened the way to more conversation.

Benjamin loved the temple. 'This is a very, very good place, to me, the most important place in Beijing, maybe all China.' He nodded at my look of surprise. 'A *really* good place. Even the Dalai Lama has worshipped here.'

I wanted to know more about its original purpose.

'It was to defeat the Song and unify the country. It was not the only one, you know. There is another, also built by Arniko, in Zhuozhou, Hebei' – 75 kilometres south-west of Beijing – 'called the Protecting-the-Country Temple.'

Still there was something I couldn't quite get. What made this temple and its twin in Hebei so special, then and now? What or whom had Kublai actually worshipped?

'This was created for Kublai, his private family place of worship.' Benjamin paused. I don't think there had been any conscious attempt to keep anything from me, but suddenly the truth about the place came with a rush. 'This temple, you know, was for the worship of a guardian called Mahakala.'

'Mahakala? Who on earth is Mahakala?'

'Mahakala is like . . . a god of war.'

So this was the deity Kublai had hoped to summon to aid him in the struggle with Song. I had never heard of him, but millions across Asia from India to Japan revere him as 'the great black one'. Hindus know him as a form of Shiva, the destroyer. In Tibet, he consumes those who fail to show Buddhism proper respect. I didn't know yet what he looked like, but he was clearly not a god you would wish to meet on a dark night.

As luck would have it, a few days later I was in Ulaanbaatar with the Mongolian scholar and leading Mongolist Shagdaryn Bira, who had researched this very subject. Mahakala was a guardian connected in some way with Hevajra – the deity who was an object of special veneration by Phags-pa's Saskya monastery; the one into whose cult Kublai had been initiated by Phags-pa in 1253. Now, eighteen years later, imperial power had qualified Kublai for the protection of his own personal god. Or, as Bira put it in a paper he was preparing for publication: 'The Khan, having gotten into direct spiritual contact with his tutelary deity Mahakala, the most powerful defender of religion, could pretend to have acquired all his mysterious power in the cause of ruling his empire. Thus the Mongolian khan could enjoy not only the favour of Tenger, but also the favour of the powerful Tantric god.'

And it wasn't just Kublai, as Benjamin explained: 'For Kublai Khan and Phags-pa, and for all the masters since, right down to the tenth Panchen Lama today, the guardian was always Mahakala.'

'And still is?'

'Still is. He is right here. Look behind you.'

And Tu Dan opened the door I had seen him closing earlier, to reveal a little altar surmounted by a peculiarly vivid portrait of Mahakala: a black face, three staring eyes, a ferocious snarl, fangs, a head-dress of skulls set in yellow hair. So that was what the monks had been doing while I was wandering round the pagoda: ministering to Mahakala.

On a shelf along the front of the shrine was a little silver dish of pale liquid. 'Alcohol,' said Benjamin. 'For other bodhisattvas, you may offer flowers, fruits, but nothing alcoholic. But for guardians, especially powerful ones like Mahakala, you give alcohol. With the right prayers it is like, like' – he tapped a word into an electronic Chinese–English dictionary, the type of thing that students and guides tend to carry with them – 'nectar. And food, like the incense and the rice, which gives off the smell that feeds the spirits. We are satisfied by food, but spirits – how can they be satisfied? By smell! Then Mahakala will become your guardian. He brings good luck.'

'He doesn't look like good luck. He looks like a nightmare.'

Benjamin translated, and all three laughed.

'If he is on your side, that's good. He scares away all other spirits.'

I paused, hoping for more insights. 'Can we see inside the pagoda?'

'Not possible. It will not be ready for months. But you can go around again. This time, go the right way, clockwise.'

'What's inside?'

'Mahakala! The real Mahakala!'

One day, I promised myself as we circled the bulbous mass, I would be back, to see him face to face. He may be just a statue, but I shall take no chances. There will be prayers from the likes of Tu Dan and Ganga, and alcohol. I shall make sure he's on my side – as he must have been on Kublai's in 1271, if events are anything to go by.

By way of understanding the problem posed by the walls of Xiangyang, let me introduce you to the strange world of counterweight trebuchets. These machines were the heavy artillery of their day, against which the man-powered traction trebuchets paled into comparative insignificance. In the counterweight trebuchet, manpower was replaced by a box filled with ballast (rocks, earth or lead), the advantage being that the weight could be enormous, the throwing arm lengthened, the missile heavier, the sling extended (without increasing the weight), the range increased, and – if the counterweight and missile remained unchanged between shots – accuracy improved.

Size demanded expertise, which took time to acquire. So the counterweight trebuchet came on the scene quite late, emerging in the Islamic world in the twelfth century and spreading to Europe soon after crusading armies came across it in about 1200. Actually, no-one is quite sure which way it spread. The Chinese called the new engines 'Muslim catapults'; the Muslim writer Rashid ad-Din referred to them as 'Frankish'. Wherever the idea originated, information soon flowed both ways, the machines developing in both Europe and the Islamic world into specialized devices that not only destroyed walls but seized imaginations, influenced strategy and made stars of their engineers (who therefore had a good reason never to record their secrets).

By the end of the fifteenth century, they were gone, blown away by gunpowder. They were only wood, after all, and they took up a lot of space. Once redundant, they became junk, good for beams or planks or firewood. No counterweight trebuchet survived into the twentieth century. One was found during the 1890s in a church in what was then eastern Prussia (now part of Poland), but by the time a museum heard of it, the locals had burned it. No accurate plans have ever been discovered either (probably thanks to the secretiveness of their elitist designers), and all the illustrations are heavily stylized, with vital details of the triggers and pivots omitted by non-technical artists.

Down the years, only very few military-historical specialists have devoted much thought to these machines. To understand them, you have to resurrect them. Today, there is an international sub-culture of 'treb' enthusiasts who do just this. Combining theoretical science, history and practicality, they are all keenly, many obsessively, and some eccentrically dedicated to the business of hurling huge loads as far as possible without the use of explosives. Much of this work is serious reconstructive archaeology, but it also generates extremely odd behaviour, because the forces involved are immense and the results hard to predict, making each machine an individual, often with its own name: Cheesechucker, Son of Cheesechucker, The Flinger Thinger. In 1991 Hew Kennedy, English landowner, inventor and military historian, became intrigued by a machine portrayed by Leonardo da Vinci which appeared to be able to throw dead horses. He designed and built a 30-tonne trebuchet with which he threw half a dozen cars, 60 pianos and many dead pigs, earning himself a good deal of notoriety. Pianos, for some reason, are popular ammunition for hurlers, perhaps because their strings wail wonderfully in mid-throw and they land with a glorious crash of exploding keys. TV channels, which love the combination of power, drama and craziness, have shown keen interest. The US TV programme *Northern Exposure* filmed a catapult built by John Wayne Cyra flinging 200-kilo upright pianos, nine of them, one after the other. The programme went on air in October 1992, the pianos soaring in 100-metre arcs to the tune of 'The Blue Danube'. Ron Toms, a Texan (there are quite a few Texans in this business; they like the power and size), came to trebuchets as a teenager, building a trebuchet and using himself as ammunition, shooting himself 30 feet into the air and landing in a river. He and his friends spent a happy afternoon lobbing themselves into the water, until he increased the counterweight to toss himself further and, as he says, 'The machine self-destructed in mid-throw.' Toms went on to build the big daddy of them all for the TV show *In the Name of Science*. He called his iron monster T. Wrecks: its namesake ate diplodoci; this one spat cars. Websites speak of plans for Thor, with a 100-foot arm and a 25-tonne counterweight, which will supposedly toss Buicks as the war-god tossed thunderbolts. At the time of writing, Thor was still a dream.

Now I, too, am a trebuchet addict because of a visit to Caerphilly Castle, south Wales. The castle contains four reconstructed working catapults, one being a counterweight trebuchet. On the grimly overcast Easter Sunday of 2005 I watched a team of hefty blokes in medieval costume get the machine ready to lob missiles into the moat before a crowd of tourists. They were under the expert eye of Paul Denney, engineer, who with his wife Julie work at the serious, archae-ological end of treb research. This is not a huge machine, weighing in at 10 tonnes, with a counterweight of 2 tonnes. Even so, priming it is quite an operation. It took two men winding the capstan and six others hauling on a rope to cock the machine. With all that weight, all that power being slowly stored, there was a sense of a great beast being harnessed. A hook held the trigger-ring. Someone laid out the sling with its missile. Usually, it's a 2-kilo ball of concrete. In this pre-exhibition test, Paul was using a 5-kilo rock.

'You want to pull the trigger, John?'

'Fire it? Sure.'

'Not "fire". We don't say that. There's no fire involved. That's to do with gunpowder artillery. We say "loose" or "shoot".'

So I did.

There is beauty in what happens when this pent-up energy is released, because it involves only natural elements – wood, iron, rock, rope, gravity – carefully managed. A jerk on the trigger frees the arm. The counterweight drops, the arm rises, the sling follows with its missile. The only sounds are soft, like a giant exhalation: a whisper from the greased axle, the swish of the sling. I had expected a whiplash action, but it's all in slow motion, rather graceful. Away the missile flies. Then the beast resettles with little sounds of satisfaction – sighs from the counterweight swinging back and forth, the clunk of heavy stones rearranging themselves inside, the slap of the empty sling against the waving lever-arm. High up, the rock soars lazily away, spinning in a huge, high arc for seven seconds (I timed it) to splash into the moat 80 metres away.

There was a long moment of awed silence. I was seduced.

I wanted more. Not that I yearned to launch pianos and Buicks. That takes metal, which is cheating. What I wanted was to answer a historical question: how big and how powerful did medieval wooden counterweight trebuchets get? This would take me back to the matter in hand, Kublai's conquest of Song.

King Edward I, Edward Longshanks, almost answered my question, because he was responsible for what was perhaps the biggest European trebuchet. In 1304 he attacked Stirling castle, a key element in Scottish resistance. His army made no impression on its massive walls and well-stocked inhabitants. Edward's response was to order his engineer, named Reginald, to build the biggest counterweight trebuchet he could. Five carpenters and five assistants laboured for three months, and produced the machine called Lup de Guerre, Warwolf. Details are lacking, but it must have had the potential to batter down Stirling's walls. At the very sight of it, so one story goes, the castle surrendered – though Edward refused their surrender until he had tried his giant machine and proved that it worked.

A wooden treb that must approach this size has been built, by a French designer, Renauld Beufette. Its design is authentic, based on the only known plan of a trebuchet, a sketch by a French artist, Villard de Honnecourt, about whom virtually nothing is known except his portfolio of drawings. Beufette's trebuchet is a monster, with a 10-tonne counterweight that can toss 100 kilos 220 metres.

So we know what Kublai was after. We know it was possible. We know the expertise did not exist in China; it had to come from Persia. Nothing could have better shown the advantages of having an empire all run by one family, bound together by a network of transcontinental communications. Off went his letter by pony express. Five weeks later and 6,000 kilometres away, his message was in Tabriz, northern Persia, at the HQ of Kublai's nephew, Abaqa, the Il-khan (subordinate khan) since the death of his father Hulegu in 1265. Abaqa had on hand several designers who had built the counterweight trebuchets used in the sieges of Baghdad, Aleppo, Damascus and Syria's crusader castles. He could spare two of them, Ismail and his assistant Ala ad-Din.[5] In late 1271 the two arrived with their families at Xanadu, and were given an official residence for the winter. The following spring, after building a catapult to demonstrate the principles to the emperor, the two men – plus, apparently, Ismail's son, whom he was training to follow in his footsteps – found themselves in the battle zone, staring at Xiangyang's solid walls, the moat, the broad river and Fancheng, Xiangyang's sibling-city across the river.

Let us put ourselves in the shoes of Ismail. Our task is to sling 100-kilo balls of rock at Xiangyang's walls, given that the moat places us at least 100 metres away. So we are already dealing with a machine too large to be manoeuvrable. That means we must place ourselves and our crew yet further away, out of the range of arrows and poisonous, explosive bombs slung from the walls. So we are at a range of about 200 metres. Beufette's giant would fit the bill nicely. Ismail's machine must have weighed 40 tonnes and towered almost 20 metres high.[6]

There are all sorts of other variables to be assessed, like the exact weight of the counterweight if it happens to get wet; and what happens to the properties of the newly cut lever-arm as it slowly dries out; and at what moment the sling should disengage (earlier for a high trajectory, later for a low one);

[5] Rashid gives completely different names: Taleb and three sons, which sounds like another family altogether. I have not seen a resolution to this, and follow the Chinese sources in the *Yuan History*.
[6] You can get an idea of what was required by checking the website of an Australian group, the Grey Company. Here you will find a link to 'The Algorithmic Beauty of the Trebuchet', which, with the computerized application of some tricky maths, allows you to become a virtual trebuchet engineer.

KUBLAI'S NEW GUARDIAN, MAHAKALA THE TERRIBLE

Kublai found in Buddhism what he needed, spiritually and politically. It was an
established religion that could counteract the influence of Confucianism and Taoism.
It supported his belief that the Mongol sky-god, Tenger, had granted the world to the
Mongols to rule. And its pantheon of deities included the fearsome Mahakala, who, if
accorded proper respect, would scare off other spirits and help in the great task of
conquering the southern Chinese empire of Song. Mahakala, staring from his shrine in
Beijing's White Pagoda, displays his terrifying attributes: a black face, a snarl, a
headdress of skulls, and three eyes.

THE CONQUEST OF SONG

The campaign to conquer Song depended crucially on seizing the town of Xiangyang, which guarded the Han, the main river leading south to the Yangtze. An assault across the Han river using a pontoon bridge (*far left*) was not enough. To crack its great walls, Kublai summoned Muslim catapult-builders, with expertise in building counterweight trebuchets, like the ones used in besieging Baghdad in 1258 (*below left*). Modern trebuchets, like the one in Caerphilly Castle, Wales (*below right*), operate in the same way, with a throwing arm and sling powered by a counterweight (*inset*). Once Xiangyang fell in 1273, the way was open along the Yangtze to the Song capital of Hangzhou (*bottom*), 'without doubt the most noble city and the best in the world' according to Marco Polo.

'la très nobilissime cité de Quins
sans faille la plus noble cité et la
meilleur ce soit au monde

Clay model of medieval Chinese actor (*right*).

IN KUBLAI'S NEW CHINA, OLD TRADITIONS ENDURE

In theatre, painting, calligraphy and other arts, the Chinese continued to follow long-established traditions, generally ignoring the brutality and humiliation brought by the Mongol conquest. Street theatre, perhaps something like that which exists today (*above*) recycled old tales, like *The Romance of the Western Chamber* (*top right*). Potters turned out beautiful ceramics (*middle right*), now known by the dynastic name invented by Kublai – Yuan. Artists created superb paintings that, with rare exceptions, avoided any comment on their Mongol overlords. In his *Sheep and Goat* (*right*), Zhao Mengfu may – just possibly – be contrasting a fat and complacent pro-Mongol 'collaborator' with a scrawny but tough anti-Mongol 'rejectionist'.

How the Khan Made His Mark

To rule his empire, Kublai built his Great
Capital, Dadu, beside the Beihai, 'North Lake'.
Much of his work was replaced by later rulers,
but it can still be seen in the city's geography –
like Beihai's island (*below*), with its curved marble
bridge – and in details, like stele-bearing tortoises
(*left*). Evidence of his administration – his laws,
his economic reforms – exists mainly in
museums and history books.

大明通行寶鈔

壹貫

Kublai and his officials in a Persian view (*top*).

Strings of bronze coins (*left*) from the Song dynasty, superseded by Yuan banknotes (*above*).

A Yuan official – possibly a Muslim, if his beard is anything
to go by – on a tour of duty, guarded by a Mongol.

and the effect of the temperature on the grease that will ease the friction of wooden axles in wooden bearings (unless our Muslim engineers decide to cast bronze-and-metal bearings, which have the remarkable property of wearing so smooth that they are, in effect, self-lubricating). It was Ismail's skill to know all this, and to approach but not overstep the limits of what was possible. And there were still things he could not have known before he arrived, like which timber to use for the lever arm, for all trees differ in their weight and strength, both of which vary again as they dry out.

Now consider the ammunition. Accuracy was crucial. It was no good roughly cutting any old rocks to make approximately 100 kilos, because small variations in weight and shape translate into the difference between hitting and missing a target. A tumbling irregular rock is in chaotic motion, its trajectory unpredictable. If we want to strike a battlement, a tower, or a particular piece of wall several times running, we need missiles of the same weight and of a regular shape, namely spherical. So we need a contingent of stonemasons, a local quarry and good transport.

Speed was vital. That June, 100 Song boats brought 3,000 soldiers downriver, entering the city after a running battle along 50–60 kilometres of river. The only loss, apparently, was the Song general, whose body was found a few days later, still clasping his bow, bobbing against the pontoon bridge across the river. Ismail and Ala ad-Din set their teams to work, felling suitable trees in nearby forests and hewing rocks. If Edward I's Warwolf trebuchet is anything to go by, the work would have taken a good three months: the trees felled and stripped, the timbers shaped for the frame, rocks chipped into spheres, 10 tonnes of ballast gathered for the counterweight, the whole thing being designed so that it could be dismantled by block-and-tackle lifting gear and moved.

Where was the best place to attack? The Mongol general Ariq-khaya decided on an indirect approach by assaulting

Fancheng. In the words of his biography, 'He took the relation of Fancheng to Xiangyang to be like that of the lips to the teeth,' and asked Kublai's permission to switch the focus of the attack to the subsidiary city. Kublai approved. The first thing to do was to isolate Fancheng by destroying the pontoon bridge to prevent supplies being ferried across. Ariq-khaya's biography summarizes the story: 'At the same time, Ismail, a man from the west, had presented a new method of making catapults, and so Ariq-khaya took this man with him to the army. In the first moon [January–February 1273, though the *Yuan History* dates the assault at December 1272] they made catapults and stormed Fancheng.'

Now, if this was the first time Ismail had used his machine, he would have fine-tuned it like an artilleryman, shooting off a couple of ranging shots, then adapting the length of the sling or the setting of the sling-release hook to lob another ball clear over the wall. In artillery terms, he was bracketing. A final bit of fiddling – perhaps slipping a knot to give the lever-arm a few centimetres less of a sweep – and the third shot would have been dead on target. Fancheng's guardians would have watched the ball arc lazily towards them, then smash into the battlements in an explosion of stone that left a nasty hole in the top of the wall. As Ariq-khaya's biography says, Ismail's *hui-hui pao* (Muslim catapult) 'breached the walls . . . [since] the reinforcements from Xiangyang no longer reached the fortress, it was captured'.

Here was an interesting situation. Fancheng had resisted to the end, and everyone knew what happened to cities that did not surrender: the inhabitants were murdered en masse, primarily to terrify other cities into rapid submission. Kublai discouraged such tactics. But the problem of Xiangyang remained unresolved. From the Mongol point of view, Ariq-khaya and Aju agreed there really was no option. The city had to die, very publicly. In the Muslim campaigns, artisans, women and children had often been spared, because they could be enslaved. But there was no point keeping any of these people alive. No distinction was made between young and old, civilian and soldier, man, woman and child. Some 3,000 soldiers and an estimated 7,000 others had their throats cut like cattle, the bodies being piled up in a mound to make sure that the massacre was visible from Xiangyang. In Richard Davis's words, 'Nothing could demoralize Xiangyang's defenders like this grotesque sight and the terrifying message it so forcefully conveyed.'

Then Ismail was told to turn his siege engine on Xiangyang. This must have been quite an operation: dismantling it, dragging and floating and carrying it across the river, reassembling it within range of Xiangyang, 'at the south-east corner of the city', according to the *Yuan History*. Ismail, a master of his art, now knew his machine's abilities very precisely. By triangulation, he would have positioned it, I think, so that its distance from one of Xiangyang's watch-towers was the same as it had been at Fancheng. The missile, we are told, weighed 150 *catties*, which is just short of 100 kilos. The result was astonishing. In the words of Ariq-khaya's biography, 'The first shot hit the watchtower. The noise shook the whole city like a clap of thunder, and every-thing inside the city was in utter confusion.'

On the Mongol side, there then followed a debate among the generals about whether to follow through with an assault, which would, of course, end with another pile of bodies, but with rather less strategic purpose and with understandable revulsion from the Mongols' potential subjects downriver. Ariq-khaya had his own ideas. He went in person to the foot of the wall and called for the city's leader, Lü Wen-huan.

'You have held the city with an isolated army for many years,' he shouted (presumably through an interpreter). 'But now the approaches are cut off even from the birds of the air. My master the emperor greatly admires your loyalty and if you surrender he will give you an honourable post and a generous reward. You may be sure of this, and we certainly shall not kill you.'

Lü, 'suspicious as a fox', hesitated. Ariq-khaya had to snap an arrow and four times repeat a cross-my-heart-and-hope-to-die promise. Finally, Lü believed him, and surrendered the city on 17 March 1273. Ariq-khaya was as good as his word. Lü Wen-huan instantly made himself a traitor in Song eyes and accepted high office on Kublai's side. He would prove a valuable asset in the coming campaign.

It is hard to overstate the significance of this victory. If Song was a castle, Xiangyang was the drawbridge. Not only did it open the way militarily to Song's heartland, but it began to destroy the workings of government. In Hangzhou, the prime minister Jia Sidao – Kublai's old adversary from the Wuchang siege, the rich politician who liked crickets and their pugnacious ways – was in trouble. It was partly his own fault, because he had kept the truth from the Song emperor – or so people believed, which was as damaging to morale.

The story went like this:

In 1270, the emperor had asked Jia if it was true that the siege had been going on for three years.

'The northern troops have already retreated,' replied Jia. 'But who told Your Majesty this?'

'One of my concubines,' came the reply.

According to the Song official history, Jia found out who it was among the several hundred girls at court, accused her on some unrecorded charge – treason, perhaps – and forced her to commit suicide. Apparently, the emperor had not missed the poor girl, but courtiers took note of Jia's high-handedness and townspeople started to exchange jokes and make up derisory songs about him. After that, 'no-one dared speak of the affairs of the frontier', say the annals, which meant that the news of Xiangyang's fall struck the emperor and his court like a ball from a Muslim catapult.

A grateful Kublai awarded Ismail 250 taels of silver – 325 oz or just 9 kg, which would fetch a mere $2,000 today, but was then the equivalent of about ten years' income for an artisan, enough to buy an estate if he had had the time to do so. He didn't, first because he was also appointed the head of the local Muslim artillerymen, and second because the next year he fell ill and died. His work, though, lived on. His position and expertise were inherited by his son, Abu-Bakr, beginning a line of succession from generation to generation that would continue almost until the end of the Yuan dynasty. And from then on, his great creation was known not only as the Muslim (*hui-hui*) catapult, but as 'the Xiangyang catapult'.

This was one of the most famous sieges in Chinese history; so famous that Marco Polo heard its story and loved to tell it. The trouble was that by the time he came to dictate his adventures, he had apparently told the story so many times that he had written major roles for himself, his father and his uncle. His account of the siege of 'Saianfu' is, if you wish to be generous, garbled. To many scholars, it sounds like a flagrant bit of self-promotion. Let's be frank: it's a lie.

This is how Marco's ghost-writer, the romance author Rustichello, recorded in his pseudo-intimate way what Marco told him when the two were in prison in Genoa some 25 years after the event (the quote is from the Yule–Cordier edition of 1903, with its charming archaisms):

> Now you must know that this city held out against the Great Kaan for three years after the rest of Manzi had surrendered [not true: Manzi – i.e. Song – fell in 1279, six years after the siege came to an end]. The Great Kaan's troops made incessant attempts to take it, but they could not succeed because of the great and deep waters that were round about it, so that they could approach from one side only, which was the north. [Northwards was the River Han. Hard to see how

any approach could be made from that direction.] And I tell you they never would have taken it, but for a circumstance that I am going to relate.

You must know that when the Great Kaan's host had lain three years before the city without being able to take it, they were greatly chafed thereat. Then Messer Nicolo Polo and Messer Maffeo and Messer Marco said: 'We could find you a way of forcing the city to surrender speedily;' whereupon those of the army replied, that they should be right glad to know how that should be. All this took place in the presence of the Great Kaan ... Then spoke up the two brothers and Messer Marco, and said: 'Great Prince we have with us among our followers men who are able to construct mangonels which will cast such great stones that the garrison will never be able to stand them, but will surrender incontinently, as soon as the mangonels or trebuchets have shot into the town.'

The Kaan bade them with all his heart have such mangonels made as speedily as possible. Now Messer Nicolo and his brother and his son immediately caused timber to be brought, as much as they desired, and fit for the work in hand. And they had two men among their followers, a German and a Nestorian Christian, who were masters of that business, and these they directed to construct two or three mangonels capable of casting stones of 300 pounds weight. Accordingly they made three fine mangonels, each of which cast stones of 300 pounds weight or more. And when they were complete and ready for use, the Emperor and the others were greatly pleased to see them, and caused several stones to be shot in their presence; whereat they marvelled greatly and greatly praised their work. And the Kaan ordered that his engines should be carried to his army which was the leaguer of Saianfu.

And when the engines were got to the camp they were forthwith set up, to the great admiration of the Tartars. What shall I tell you? When the engines were set up and put in gear, a stone was shot from each of them into the town. These took effect among the buildings, crashing and smashing through everything with huge din and commotion. And when the townspeople witnessed this new and strange visitation they were so astonished and dismayed that they wist not what to do or say. They took counsel together, but no counsel could be suggested how to escape from these engines. They declared they were all dead men if they yielded not, so they determined to surrender . . .

. . . and all this came about through the exertions of Messer Nicolo, and Messer Maffeo, and Messer Marco; and it was no small matter.

It is a good story, but deeply flawed. Young Marco, aged just 21, did not reach Kublai Khan's court until 1275, two years after the great siege was over. There is absolutely no way he or his father and uncle could have had anything to do with devising a catapult, and really no excuse for Marco writing the Polos in and Ismail and Ala ad-Din out. The whole thing reeks of self-serving fantasy – no details of the trebuchets, unnamed 'followers' who never appear again, no mention of Fancheng, vague generalizations about Xiangyang.

Well, he (or his ghost-writer) liked to dramatize – witness the bare-faced claim concerning Yangzhou: 'and Messer Marco Polo himself, of whom this book speaks, did govern this city for three full years, by the order of the Great Kaan'. He didn't; all the governors are listed in the sources; he's not among them. All one can say is that it was not the first time, or the last, that truth (which predominates in Polo) has been pushed aside by a ghost-writer eager for hype: *Oh, come on, Marco! No-one will ever know.*

A couple of points need to be made in Marco's favour. First, many writers who skewer him for bending the truth seem to think that he claims to have been at the siege. He doesn't. The idea and the construction all take place with Kublai in Xanadu, which is where, I guess, he first heard the story and made it his own. Second, the claim to have been governor of Yangzhou appears only in two of the five main editions of his work, all of which are corrupt versions of a lost original. So perhaps along the way Marco's conscience had been at work after all.

In Hangzhou, when the news of the fall of Xiangyang arrived, panic took hold. Suddenly, top people woke up to the threat to their comfortable and civilized ways, their literate discourses, their picnics by the West Lake, their time-honoured rituals, their glorious works of art. It was unthinkable: never before in China's history had barbarians threatened the southern heartland. The court instantly cancelled a state occasion and said the money saved would be spent on strengthening the defences on the Yangtze. To buttress morale, those held responsible for the debacle were not executed, merely demoted. Even the relatives of Lü Wenhuan, the man who had surrendered Xiangyang and joined the Mongols, were told their loyalty was not in doubt. These were, of course, more symptoms of the regime's weakness.

And then: catastrophe upon catastrophe. Without warning, the Emperor Duzong died, aged only 34. Next, the Mountain of Heavenly Visage, the beautiful volcanic range a day's ride west of Hangzhou, shook itself and released devastating landslides and floodwaters. In Chinese, a landslide and an imperial death are different meanings of the same character, *beng* (崩). For leaders, Song had Duzong's four-year-old heir, his ailing grandmother the Empress Dowager, and the discredited prime minister, Jia. Disasters were linking up, like tears in old silk, and there was no-one to patch Song's tattered fabric. Heaven was withdrawing its mandate to rule. An age approached its end.

9

JUGGERNAUT

FOR THIS NEXT VAST AND VITAL CAMPAIGN, KUBLAI WANTED TO
leave no room for error. He retained Aju, the victor of the
Xiangyang siege, but placed him under his dynamic and
widely experienced statesman-general, Bayan.

A word about Bayan. By appointing him, Kublai was playing two royal cards, empire and family, for Bayan's ancestors
had played leading roles in one of *The Secret History*'s more
dramatic tales. It happened five years before Genghis became
khan, when, still bearing the name Temujin, he was fighting
to unify the Mongol clans. As a young man, Temujin/Genghis
had been captured by a rival clan leader, an overweight
character called Tarkutai ('Fatty') Kiriltuk. He had staged an
escape, and then a revenge raid. Defeated and in hiding, Fatty
Kiriltuk is captured by some of his subjects – a man and his
two sons – and dumped in a cart because he is too fat to ride
a horse. His three captors are off to deliver him to Genghis
when his sons gallop up to rescue him. The father, Shiregetu,
leaps on his fat captive, holds a knife to his throat and yells
Back off! And then, to Kiriltuk (to quote *The Secret History*):

If they attack, 'at the very moment I die, I shall die taking you as my death-companion.' OK, shouts Fatty, do as he says; Temujin will spare me; after all, I didn't kill him when I had the chance. The sons retreat. The captors start to ponder. Temujin admires loyalty, doesn't he? Here we are betraying our khan. Surely, Temujin is more likely to kill us for disloyalty than reward us? So they let Kiriltuk waddle away, free. And when they get to Temujin, they are proved right: "Your thought that you could not do away with your rightful lord is correct." So saying, he showed favour.' That was one family's entrée to fame and fortune. Old man Shiregetu was immortalized in legend. On becoming khan in 1206, Genghis made the two sons, Naya and Alak, commanders of 1,000 men; and in addition Naya became one of his top three generals.

Now to the point: the man who held the knife to Kiriltuk's throat, Shiregetu, was Bayan's great-grandfather; Naya his great-uncle; Alak his grandfather, who went on to command in the campaign against Persia in 1219–20, and became a city governor there. Bayan's father was with Hulegu in 1256 and died in action when Bayan was about 20. Bayan himself stayed on working with Hulegu for a decade or so, then came to China to join Kublai as one of his top civilian administrators. In five years, he had won a reputation for calmness and clear thinking under pressure (and also brilliance: he had managed to learn Chinese). Kublai had then picked him in effect to run the Bureau of Military Affairs, under its nominal head, Kublai's eldest son. Now, at the age of only 34, Bayan found himself charged with the task of taking one more giant step towards the fulfilment of the divinely ordained destiny with which his family had been intimately involved for four generations.

This was to be an immense operation. The old days in which victory was all down to the Mongol cavalry were long gone. Cavalry was just one wing among three. The army that

Bayan and Aju gathered around Xiangyang in summer 1274 numbered about 200,000 infantrymen, over half of them northern Chinese, backed by a river fleet of 800 newly built warships and another 5,000 smaller boats for transport, carrying 70,000 sailors, 14 per boat. This was a flexible, amphibious, multinational force. It needed to be, because Song still had 700,000 men at its disposal, and 1,000 warships on the Yangtze.

Victory, yes, of course that would come. But it should be victory with a longer-term purpose, as Kublai had first accepted in the Yunnan campaign. An adviser had urged restraint, and he had listened: 'What you told me about Cao Bin not killing people, that is something I can do.' Now he knew from experience that military victory must be matched by victory of another sort, over the hearts and minds of ordinary people. If the conquest of Song was to last, it would take good government; and that meant minimizing the suffering of civilians. He told Bayan: 'Emulate Cao Bin!'

Bayan's first task in the autumn of 1274 was to get his army down the Han river to the Yangtze, a distance of about 250 kilometres. But the Han was blocked by 100,000 men camped around two fortresses which were linked by a cross-river chain. To avoid another siege, Bayan ordered his troops to bypass this section of river. Shielded by two smaller 10,000-strong columns advancing in parallel a few dozen kilometres on either side, the main force carried the boats overland on bamboo poles, repulsing an attack along the way. No wonder it was a slow haul, averaging 20 kilometres a day. By spring 1275, Bayan and Aju had led their force out of the Han valley into the flood plains of the Yangtze.

Kublai would have been following this campaign with passionate interest, not only because the outcome of the war depended on continued success. He himself had crossed the Yangtze at this very point 15 years before, when Mönkhe's death and Ariq's rebellion had thrown his advance into reverse. He knew all too well the layout of the three cities that form today's Wuhan, the great fortress of Yang-lo downstream, the maze of shallow lakes and inlets, and the broad sweep of the Yangtze which he had crossed in his fruitless attempt to take Wuchang.

Bayan had somehow to overcome that apparently impregnable fortress Yang-lo, which was guarded by a fleet much larger than his own. His only chance of gaining an advantage lay in crossing the well-guarded river and establishing a base on the southern bank. A frontal assault might fail, so he tried a trick. He divided his force, and set one section to attack the fort, forcing the Chinese commander to draw reinforcements from upriver. Then, on a snowy January night, he sent Aju with the other half of his troops 20 kilometres upstream, carrying some of their boats with them. They waded into the icy river and occupied some sandbanks. Come the dawn, they built a pontoon bridge and, overcoming opposition from the depleted enemy forces, made a bridgehead on the south bank. Back downriver again, they took on the Song navy, and somehow – we have no details – won. The commander fled, the shattered Song fleet sailed away downriver, and the fortress surrendered.

The next month was a clear run downriver, much aided by the ex-commander of Xiangyang, Lü Wen-huan, who had also been the boss of many downriver garrisons. A word from him, and commanders surrendered, allowing the Mongol army to advance steadily.

Hangzhou was sliding into desperation. Bayan's reputation grew with every victory. They called him 'Hundred Eyes', because that's what *bai yan* means in Chinese. Jia's status, by contrast, diminished daily as the court officials and ordinary people reviled him for his love of luxury, his accumulated treasures, his wasteful parties. In an attempt to regain his authority, he decided to take command of the army himself. That February, he led a force over 100,000 strong out of the city, a vast throng 40 kilometres long heading westward to intercept Bayan's progress down the Yangtze. Suddenly, the capital was bare of troops, and more were needed.

At this point the emperor's widow, the formidable Dowager Xie, became her people's inspiration. She was no beauty, having an odd-looking dark skin and a cataract in one eye. But she had been a reassuring force for years, generous, restrained, never ambitious to extend her authority beyond the palace. Now she spoke out, urging ordinary people to join the war effort: 'In spite of my old age and decrepitude, I reluctantly took charge of state affairs,' ran her edict. 'How has it come to this present state that deviates from the constants of Heaven and Earth? Three hundred years of virtuous rule – surely this has made an impression on the people . . . Those worthy men with loyal livers and righteous galls [i.e. hearts], come forth and combat the forces that plague the throne and submit your skills.' It worked. By March 1275, all over the country, men were streaming to arms, as many as 200,000 of them.

A month and 250 kilometres later, Jia was in today's Anhui province, deploying his army near Tongling, aiming to block the river. Easier said than done: as Tongling's newish (1995) bridge across the turgid Yangtze shows, the river is 2.6 kilometres wide here, and the hills between which it winds its way are low and far off. Still, at Tongling a slight rise pushes the river in a wide curve, and a midstream island could act as a keystone. Joined by 2,500 warships, many from the bruising defeat at Yang-lo fortress, Jia awaited Bayan's arrival.

Bayan, though, was high on his previous successes, his naval force carrying well-tried contingents of every armed service – the Mongol cavalry (also scouting sideways and ahead), the Chinese infantry, a good supply of turncoat Song commanders full of helpful information about downriver defences, and terrific artillerymen, armed with devices including Ismail's 'Xiangyang catapult', the vast limbs of which did not even need to be carried; they could simply have floated, shepherded by barges.

What shall I tell you (as Marco might have said)? Not much, I'm afraid, because no-one recorded the details. Artillerymen set up the giant trebuchet, which would have a much greater range – several hundred metres – if throwing less weight. Stones rained on to boats, cavalry attacked on shore, infantry were landed on the island, and Jia's demoralized forces scattered, leaving 2,000 boats in Mongol hands.

Jia fled, defeated, humiliated, doomed. Enemies at court petitioned to have him executed, but Dowager Xie, toughened by half a century's experience, would not bend to such pressure. 'Jia Sidao has laboured untiringly through the successive reigns of three emperors,' she replied. 'How, for the failure of one morning, could one bear to abandon the proprieties due to a great official?' Instead, she stripped him of office and banished him to Zhangzhou, on the coast 800 kilometres south. But there was no escape. Along the way, the officer in command, a certain Jeng Hujen, ordered the bearers to taunt the captive with the insulting songs about him they had heard in Hangzhou; and then, when approaching their destination, Jeng killed him. In death, only his faults were remembered, and he was vilified as Song's 'Bad Last Ruler'.

Bayan, meanwhile, continued his victorious progress down-river. Wuwei, He Xian, the local capital of Nanjing all surrendered, inspiring half a dozen other civil leaders to bring their towns into the Mongol camp, and in two cases to commit suicide (the first of many, as we shall see). In Nanjing, Bayan recalled Kublai's long-term scheme of conquest: to hold and to govern, for ever. For four months he paused, setting up a local government for his 30 city conquests and his 2 million new subjects, secured by defences on both sides of the river. From here he opened negotiations with Hangzhou, an exchange hampered by the anti-Mongol antagonism of ordinary people and rank-and-file officials. This would prove to be an increasing problem, because outside the military and higher levels of government people were astonishingly loyal to their land and culture. Already there were the beginnings of guerrilla warfare, which briefly regained several towns for Song. In April, two of Bayan's envoys were murdered by locals before they entered Hangzhou. His next envoy met the same fate.

Now it was summer. The Mongols and northern Chinese wilted in the sticky heat. Bayan was all for pressing on, but was forced to delay because Kublai was faced with another rebellion at home – the subject of the next chapter – and wanted the benefit of Bayan's advice. The delay allowed Aju to fight off a renewed challenge from the Song and mop up other cities, notably Yangzhou and its nearby river-port Zhenjiang. Here, in another great battle, the Song blocked the river with unwieldy seagoing warships all chained together, which, when the little Mongol ships set a few ablaze, acted as a giant fuse that destroyed the lot: another military catastrophe, 10,000 dead, another 10,000 captives (with the usual caution that all the figures are guesstimates). Now the Mongol forces were within 225 kilometres of the Yangtze's mouth; round the nose of the Shanghai peninsula lay Hangzhou. Overland, it was also 225 kilometres. One last push would do it.

Back in the field in September, Bayan planned his final assault, a three-pronged attack by sea and by land. He would lead the central prong of this trident, following the Grand Canal. The main naval and land forces made fast progress. But Bayan's corps hit a problem, in the form of unexpected and dogged resistance from the ancient and prosperous town of Changzhou, noted for its scholars – a key to the southern section of the Grand Canal, and now newly reinforced by 5,000 Song soldiers. Bayan gave them a chance to surrender, firing a message wrapped around arrows: 'If you persist in this senseless and staunch resistance, then not even children will survive the piled corpses and bloodletting. You should reconsider your position promptly, so as not to regret things later.' They did not reconsider, and did not live long enough for regrets. For the second time in this campaign, the Mongols committed urbicide. Bayan stormed the place, took it in two days and had everyone slaughtered: the surviving troops, the civilians, the lot, perhaps 10,000 people in all. Again, as at Fancheng, a vast mound of bodies arose, covering half an acre near the city's eastern gate. Later covered with earth, it survived for over 600 years until well into the last century, with bones sometimes emerging from it.

This massacre, so close to the capital, was intended to encourage immediate capitulation. Its first effect was to spread panic and paranoia. Soldiers mutinied, deserters fled, a senior officer was bludgeoned to death by Jia's replacement. The Empress Dowager did her best to delay the inevitable, with a passionate and self-deprecating plea for mass support. 'The empire's progression toward impending peril is entirely, I regret, due to the insubstantiality of Our moral virtue.' People should recall over 300 years of moral and charitable rule, and come to the capital to 'engage the enemy of their prince'. This second plea for a *levée en masse* also worked, in a sense. They came, by the ten thousand, from the nearby hills and plains; but loyalty was nothing without direction. The newcomers were simply a motley collection of small militias that merely added to the confusion and panic.

For six weeks Dowager Xie sent out envoy after envoy, seeking some sort of settlement. Despite the brash opposition of Jia's replacement, she offered tribute, she offered to divide the country, she offered to honour Kublai as the uncle of the Song's young emperor. Bayan, settling in around Hangzhou, refused to discuss terms. It was total capitulation, or continuing war. But there was no vindictiveness. He gave his assurance that capitulation would buy peace for the people and security for the royal family. He even sent a copy of Kublai's edict to that effect. Some in court advised fighting to the last man, others wanted to abandon the capital altogether, but Dowager Xie decided otherwise. Really, there was no choice. Bayan's naval and land forces met up. The capital was all but surrounded, and weakening daily as soldiers and civilians fled south.

The end, at least of this chapter, came quickly. The new prime minister, Chen Yizhong, scuttled for safety. On 26 January 1276 the Empress Dowager sent a note to Bayan in his HQ 20 kilometres north of the city acknowledging Kublai's overlordship: 'I respectfully bow a hundred times to Your Majesty, the Benevolent, Brilliant, Spiritual and Martial Emperor of the Great Yuan.' A week later, the city's prefect, representing the court, handed over the Song dynastic seal and a memorandum stating the emperor's willingness to give up his title to Kublai and hand over all his territories. Bayan made a triumphal entry into the city, with his commanders and contingents in full array. Hundreds of pretty courtesans trembled at the thought of what might happen to them, and one hundred of them, waiting to be tied up with eunuchs and musicians for the long march north, drowned themselves to avoid finding out. And finally, on 21 February, came the final, formal ceremony of submission, when the five-year-old Emperor Zhao Xian himself led his officials into Bayan's presence and bowed in obeisance towards the north, the direction in which Kublai resided.

Bayan was as good as his word, and Kublai's. When the Mongols had taken Beijing, the Jin capital, in 1215, they had gone on an orgy of destruction and killing. The seizure of this capital was very different: a peaceful handover, a strict ban on unauthorized troops entering the city, the safety of the royal family guaranteed, the royal mausoleum protected, no attempt made to upset the currency or even the style of dress. Mongol-Chinese officers made inventories of troops, civilians, cash and food supplies before removing the treasures for transport northward. Militias were disbanded, regulars incorporated into Bayan's armies. Officials, of course, were all replaced with Mongols, northern Chinese and several Song turncoats; but in other respects, as Bayan reported proudly to Kublai, 'the market places of the nine thoroughfares were not moved and the splendours of a whole era remained as of old'.

An edict from Kublai told everyone to continue their lives as normal. Officials would not be punished; famous sites would be protected; widows, orphans and the poor would be assisted from public funds.

On 26 February the first of two great entourages left Hangzhou for Beijing – 300 officials, 3,000 wagons of booty, the seals of office, the surrender itself. A month later, Bayan, his task completed, left Hangzhou – indeed all of southern China – in the hands of subordinates, and headed north with the second entourage, the royal family: the boy ex-emperor, his mother, the princesses, the concubines, the relatives, leaving the ailing Dowager Xie behind until she was fit enough to travel.

Three months later, in June, this immense throng arrived in the capital, to be welcomed by a Kublai whose joy was such that he had no praise high enough for Bayan. He conferred upon him 20 sets of 'garments of a single colour' – to receive just one being a high honour – and reconfirmed him as co-director of the Bureau of Military Affairs. 'Hundred Eyes' was the empire's hero, genius, saviour: Subedei reborn.

The Empress Dowager and her grandson were then settled in Beijing, where they were given tax-free property. Kublai's wife Chabi took a personal interest in their well-being. The old lady lived out her life with a small official stipend and attendants, and died six years later. And so, officially, the Song dynasty ended not in a bang of destruction, but in a whimper of peace and compassion.

*

But there was another end, an end as different as you can imagine: a messy end, an end of despair and suffering and heartbreak. It made 'a drama of unthinkable intensity', in the words of Richard Davis's powerful study of the conquest of Song.[1] Its prologue came just before the final capitulation, when the Song court sent away the two remaining young princes – Zhao Xia (4) and Zhao Bing (3), brothers of the young Zhao Xian, soon to be on his way to Xanadu – to safety in the far south. With them went a spirit very different from that which marked the ceremonies of capitulation: a spirit of outraged and uncompromising resistance to alien domination. There was heroism here, something redolent of Horatius' words in Macaulay's *Lays of Ancient Rome*:

> And how can man die better
> Than facing fearful odds,
> For the ashes of his fathers
> And the temples of his Gods?

But there was also a tragedy being played out, as a great culture blocked its ears and closed its eyes and chose death when denial was no longer possible.

As the princes fled, the Mongols advanced, and death filled the air: not just imposed death but self-selected death, whether in action or by suicide. Richard Davis, in his evocation of this terrible time, lists 110 named male suicides of prominent, albeit not of the highest rank. There were many hundreds of others at lower levels of government, and many thousands of ordinary people of both sexes and all classes. To take one extreme example: in January 1276,

[1] Richard L. Davis, *Wind Against the Mountain: The Crisis of Politics and Culture in 13th-Century China*.

Ariq-khaya met stiff resistance from Tanzhou (now Changsha), 750 kilometres inland in Hunan province. Resistance was, of course, overcome. The town's leader, Li Fu, made careful arrangements for the mass suicide of his family and household. All made themselves drunk; all were put to the sword by Li Fu's assistant, who then killed his wife and slit his own throat. A military adviser drowned himself with his wife and concubine. A local scholar burned his house, himself, his brother, two sons and some 40 servants. All around the town, so the *Song History* says, people 'annihilated their entire family. No wells in the city were empty of human corpses, while strangled bodies hung in dense clusters from trees.' The Xiang river became thick with the dead. Was this an exaggeration? Were many of those deaths in fact from the assault? Possibly; but when the town fell, Ariq-khaya saw there was no need for further punishment, because the city had in effect committed suicide.

What, meanwhile, of the two small princes and their entourage? They had been taken south, picking up recruits to their cause on the way – not a problem, for their entourage had with them immense amounts of cash. They had then taken to ships, hopping from port to port down the coast, heading for Vietnam. This was no small band of loyalists, but an army of 200,000 carried by a navy of 1,000 ships. There was a terrible storm. The elder of the little princes, Zhao Xia, almost died, and then died anyway on an island not far from Vietnam. By now, the Mongols had overtaken them on land. With the remaining prince, Zhao Bing, the fleet slowly backtracked along the coast to the bay where the Pearl River (Chu Chiang) broadens out west of Hong Kong. Here a dense cluster of islands offered protection.

So all was not yet lost. They found a good island base from which to stage a comeback. To the north were shallows that seemed to exclude enemy warships. At the southern end hills fell sharply into the sea, from which the island took its name:

Yaishan, Cliff Hill. It was here, in the summer of 1278, that the six-year-old prince and his loyal followers – his step-mother the Dowager Consort Yang Juliang, his real mother, a low-level concubine, chief counsellor Lu Xiufu – made their stand, with many of their followers living in warships, many others ashore, racing to throw together simple houses and fortifications.

The Mongol forces were 80 kilometres upriver, in the city that used to be called Canton and is now Guangzhou. In late February 1279 the Song navy's 1,000 ships, well stocked with food and water, prepared for battle. They struck an eye-witness as impressive, the sides of their ships covered with mud-encrusted matting against flaming arrows and incendiary bombs, protected with staves to ward off fire-ships. With the young prince on the flagship the fleet was, according to one account, chained together in preparation for an imminent onslaught.

The Mongol fleet, of only around 300 ships, approached from downriver, round the coast. With their inferior numbers, they were in no hurry to attack. Their commander sent a message giving the Song a chance to surrender. No deal. Now the Mongols discovered they had the advantage of mobility over their chained and anchored enemy. They set a blockade between the Song vessels and the shore, cutting off their water supply, and settled down to await the moment to strike. For two weeks they sat there, trying the occasional raid, but content to observe the tides and weather, while the Song ran out of water.

Then, on the rainy morning of 9 March, one half of the fleet rode the outgoing tide into the flanks of the demoralized and weakened Song; and six hours later the other half struck from the other direction with the rising tide.

The result was a catastrophe for the Song. Accounts speak of the sea turned red by blood, and of 100,000 dead. Scholars agree this is a huge exaggeration, but even the real figure was horrific enough – perhaps 30,000–40,000. The only witness who recorded the details was the loyalist Wen Tianxiang, who was a hostage in one of the Mongol ships. He later captured the horrors he had seen in verse:

> Suddenly this morning the sky darkened;
> wind and rain manifested evil;
> catapults and thunder flashed; arrows descended.
> . . .
> human corpses are scattered like fibres of hemp.
> Foul smelling waves pound my heart to bits.

When they saw what was happening, many – hundreds, perhaps thousands – committed suicide by leaping into the water with weights attached to them. One among them was Lu Xiufu, the adviser to the boy-emperor. And on his back when he jumped he bore the six-year-old prince, the last of his line, the thirteenth generation of Song rulers, still in his gown of royal yellow, with the imperial golden seals strapped around his waist.

So ended the very last of the Song. For Wen Tianxiang, nothing could have better captured the despair of defeat, or better symbolized what was best in Song culture – loyalty that could embrace the ultimate sacrifice. Such high ideals were surely immortal.

> A mountain refuge exchanged for a grave at sea,
> Without empire is to be without family.
> For men with wills of a thousand years,
> Our lives have no limits.

Wen Tianxiang has a significance beyond his presence as an eye-witness of the end of the Song. He was the exemplar of those loyalists who absolutely refused to accept the new regime. From a brief summary of events, you would think that Kublai, once victorious, had an easy time of it. Not so. There was a Song resistance at all levels, finding expression in many ways: by withdrawal, by guerrilla warfare, by assassination and – most strikingly – in suicide.

First see what Wen's high ideals – or rigidity, depending on your point of view – meant in practice. Rich, a brilliant scholar, a noted poet and famously good-looking, he had been a senior figure at court, even involved in negotiations with Bayan. But he was too inflexible to be a great politician – passionate, intolerant, arrogant and a complete pain to work with. Even before the final battle, while the family were fleeing the Mongols as they advanced south, his unwavering loyalty had caused the deaths of his mother and three children. His wife, two concubines and three other children were captured. His wife would be in detention for 30 years. One of the children died; two would remain in permanent exile – 'Young swallows without nests, shivering in the autumn chill,' in their father's mournful words.

After the battle, Wen spent four years in captivity, from which Kublai himself offered to free him if only he would join the Mongol side. He refused, despite the agonizing consequences for his family – his daughters dead, and he unable to collect their bones; his mother dead, and he, unable to perform the funeral rituals, a traitor to Confucian ideals of filial piety. Yet he would not bend – 'The loyal subject cannot serve two masters,' he said – an attitude that proved, in effect, suicidal. He sought death, as martyrs have throughout history, to justify his ideals. In January 1283 a cart carried him to Beijing's firewood market, where he was executed before a huge crowd.

Wen became the epitome of the loyal servant, Song's martyr and an example of how the true loyalist should behave: never mind the bonds of family; loyalty to a master, a cause, was above all. 'When life is exchanged for a cause,' he wrote, 'it is not lived in vain.' For those of a more accommodating temperament, this self-denial is masochistic. To the true believer, it is glorious.

There were many others – many thousands – who chose to die rather than submit; many by killing themselves. This is one of the most astonishing things about the early days of Kublai's rule. Suicide was a well-established response to defeat among honour-bound military men, but among civilians as well as the armed forces there had never been anything like what happened after the Mongol victory over Song. Nothing could more searingly state the strength and depth of Song culture. For 300 years people at all levels of society had lived in relative stability and growing prosperity, governed by officials who, whatever their faults, operated within a framework of dedication to the idea of service and high-minded behaviour. Three hundred years! For such stability, cultural unity, growing wealth and intellectual sophistication, westerners must look back to the Roman empire. The effect on the minds of ordinary people survived the growing weakness of the Song government, symbolized by Hangzhou's corrupting luxuries. All that was merely another sign of impending catastrophe, the main one being the war, which over the previous 45 years had killed millions and displaced millions more in the north, and which was now devastating the south. Intriguingly, where the wars had been worst, in the north, there was no habit of suicide, perhaps because suffering at barbarian hands was routine for Jin's inhabitants, perhaps because they could always flee south. Yet in the south, in Song, many of its bereft inhabitants derived life's very meaning from their culture. With nowhere left to flee to, there was, for these thousands, only one way to assert their free will: by choosing what they considered an honourable death over a life empty of meaning and honour.

There remained one member of the Song royal family: the

Dowager's grandson, Zhao Xian, who as a five-year-old had formally surrendered to Kublai. As he grew to manhood, he became an increasing embarrassment to Kublai. Sources usually say no more than that he was eventually sent away to Tibet to become a monk, and that he died in 1323.

I heard a rather more interesting account of his fate in the Giant Buddha Temple in Zhangye, Gansu province, one of the traditional gateways to Tibet. Director Wu told me the story:

One day, Kublai Khan had a dream. In his dream, a dragon flew up from a certain spot in the palace. Next day, Zhao Xian came to see him. Unfortunately, Kublai found that the lad was standing on the exact spot from which the dragon had ascended. This caused Kublai to realize that Zhao was a danger to the state, and would one day try to overthrow the Yuan dynasty. It was for this reason that he had Zhao sent away to become a monk, right here in the Great Buddha Temple, the burial place of Kublai's mother. Here he remained for many years, until, at the age of 53, he committed suicide.

If true, it is a strange footnote to the end of the Song: the last emperor locked away in a distant monastery, forgotten by the outside world for decades, long outliving the man who had displaced him, until he, like so many of his subjects, escaped despair by choosing death.

III

AUTUMN

10

BURNED BY THE RISING SUN

ON THE VERGE OF ACHIEVING ACTUAL OR NOMINAL DOMINION
over much of Eurasia, having seen his commanders build
and sail warships down the Yangtze, and already making
preparations to pursue the remnants of Song resistance down
1,500 kilometres of coastline, Kublai was in a position to
look outwards across the ocean, to Japan.

Officially, Japan had had remarkably little to do with
China for 400 years, ever since China had persecuted
Buddhists in the middle of the ninth century. The two had no
running disputes, no cause for war; indeed, the opposite,
because there were long-established private trading contacts.
In Japan, Chinese fashions were all the rage among the ruling
classes. Gold, lacquer ware, swords and timber flowed in
from Japan, in exchange for silk, porcelain, perfumes and
copper coins. Monks arriving in Japan in response to an
upsurge in Zen Buddhism brought with them tea, made a
fashionable part of Zen studies by a celebrated monk, Eisai,
around 1200. None of this reflected official policy. But it was
happening under Song rule, and the Song were about to be

targeted by Kublai. It didn't take much imagination for strategists in Xanadu to foresee the Japanese sending aid to the Song. Better take them out fast.

Like other imperialists at other times, Kublai saw an over-riding reason to do this: because it seemed possible. A Korean monk who had become an interpreter at Kublai's court told him Japan would be a pushover: ruled by a figurehead emperor and rival warlords and samurai warriors more interested in their own chivalric codes than in their decrepit coastal defences, it had no large field army nor any experi-enced commanders to match the Mongols. Kublai not only had well-tried armies and commanders with unrivalled experience – he had a new navy; and he had a springboard in the form of Korea, whose southern coast is a mere 200 kilo-metres from Japan.

The Mongols had had experience of Korea since their first invasion in 1231. At that time Korea had proved a tough nut, in the hands of a military clique which had seized power from the king 60 years before in order to fight off barbarians from Manchuria. While the king remained a figurehead for 30 more years, the generals fought the Mongols, much helped by their naval skills, which allowed them to hole up in an off-shore island and supply themselves with food by sea, in effect thumbing their noses at the Mongol cavalry. In response, the Mongols turned to arson, slaughter and theft, all on a vast scale. In their 1254 invasion they had taken some 200,000 captives and devastated much of the country. In 1258 the king and his officials staged a counter-coup, assassinated the military boss and sued for peace, the crown prince himself travelling to China to submit – directly to Kublai, as it happened, because Mönkhe was campaigning far away to the west. It all worked out neatly: both the Korean king and Mönkhe died, and Kublai was left with a new vassal, the former crown prince and now king, Wonjong. In 1271 a joint Korean–Mongol force re-established Wonjong in the old capital, Kaesong, and blotted up what remained of the military opposition. So Kublai had firm enemies in ordinary Koreans and an unwilling vassal in Wonjong. He gave a daughter to Wonjong's son in marriage, so that eventually his grandson would inherit the throne. The two swapped presents, Kublai sending a jade belt and medicines, Wonjong responding with annual missions of tribute – falcons for the imperial hunting grounds and fish skins to be made into soft shoes for Kublai's gouty feet. Korea became a Mongol-Chinese colony, with resident commissioners watched over by Mongol-Chinese troops and served by a corps of Mongolian-speaking interpreters. Kublai was not loved; but he was the power behind the throne. He needed ships; and ships began to roll from Korea's shipyards, first for the conquest of Song, and then to transport a Mongol-Chinese army across to Japan.

By the early 1270s Kublai had engineered a justification for war. In 1266 – with Ariq's rebellion newly crushed, the campaign against Song still being planned – he had sent his first embassy off to Japan, with a demand that the king of this 'little country' submit instantly. The message was rushed through from its point of entry in southern Japan, Hakata (present-day Fukuoka) on Kyushu, 800 kilometres north-east to Kamakura, HQ (or *bakufu*) for Japan's military ruler, the shogun, then halfway back again to the shogun's nominal overlord, the emperor in Kyoto. It caused quite a stir, outrage – 'little country', indeed! – mixed with terror. The emperor drafted a letter offering negotiation, an idea instantly vetoed by the shogun who, after six months, ordered the envoys to leave for home with no answer at all. This was playing for time, with fingers crossed. The court, useless in every practical way, devoted itself to prayer.

Silence seemed to work, because nothing more was heard from Kublai for several years. Kublai's forces were otherwise engaged, embarking on the siege of Xiangyang that would hold the key to the conquest of the south. It was not until September 1271 that another Korean envoy arrived, officially bearing a request to submit, unofficially warning the Japanese to prepare for an attack. Again, there was no official reply, but now vassals were ordered back to their fiefs, and constables and stewards set about strengthening the 30 decrepit coastal castles. At court, prayers became even more fervent. So when in 1272 a Mongol ambassador landed, demanding that his letters be forwarded to the emperor at once, Japanese martial spirit had revived. The shogun, latest in line of the ruling Hojo family, was a feisty 22-year-old called Tokimune; he sent the ambassador packing – a gross insult to Kublai, and nothing less than an invitation to invade.

Kublai was soon ready. In 1273 Xiangyang fell, releasing reserves for action elsewhere; Korea was at last at peace; and there were ships enough around in Korean and Song harbours for the assault. In late October or November 1274 (again, sources vary), some 300 warships and 400–500 smaller craft, with crews of 15,000 and a fighting force of anything up to 40,000 (again, sources vary) left Masan on the south Korean coast to cross the 50 kilometres of sea to the islands of Tsushima, the prehistoric and historic stepping-stone from the mainland to Japan.

On the shore, locals put up a spectacular but hopeless defence which became the stuff of legends, full of Japanese chivalry and Mongol barbarism, of lone warriors issuing dignified challenges, of poisoned Mongol arrows flying like raindrops in spring, of the sea made crimson by blood, of the governor's honourable suicide. Stories tell of 6,000 dead and the Mongols carrying 1,000 heads back to their ships to embark for the next stepping-stone, Iki, 50 kilometres away.

Hearing news of the Mongol advance, Iki's governor sent off to the mainland for help, before the overwhelming assault, the brave but futile defence, the deeds that burned themselves into folk memory – the governor's daughter spirited away by boat only to die at sea in a hail of Mongol arrows; the noble governor and his family accepting death in their burning palace; prisoners nailed by their palms along the prows of Mongol warships.

To invaders, Kyushu's coast is a problem. It has delightful, inviting sandy beaches, but inland is a tangle of steep forested hills which preclude a fast advance. There is only one good harbour, Hakata bay, protected by islands that make natural breakwaters and two headlands that reach westward as if to welcome ships from all mainland Asia to its shallow waters, gentle sandy shores and low-lying hinterland. Japanese warlords advanced from the local administrative centre of Dazaifu, on hills 10 kilometres south-east of present-day Fukuoka, and set up a base nearer the coast. The Mongols first made a tentative landing at Hakata's western end, perhaps thinking to head up a river, then changed their minds and set their army ashore right in the middle of the bay. There, they easily cut through the few disorganized Japanese. As one Japanese account put it, the grandson of the Japanese general fired whistling arrows as the signal for action to start, 'but the Mongols all laughed. Incessantly beating their drums and gongs, they drove the Japanese horses leaping mad with fear. Their mounts uncontrollable, none thought about facing the Mongols.'

Rapidly, the Mongols advanced a kilometre inland to seize a strategic sandstone hillock with steep sides which gave them a good view. The hill, Mount Sohara, is now a park, with rough paths leading up its soft yellow flanks, and the view from its summit is blocked by new buildings. But that summer afternoon, Mongol scouts would have been able to see their own ships riding at anchor in the bay, Dazaifu looming to the south-east, and 5 kilometres to the east the

Japanese camp, from which, within a couple of hours, horsemen approached at the gallop.

Among the Japanese defenders that day was a young warrior named Takezaki Suenaga, from Higo province, a *gokenin* (direct vassal of the shogun) who later acquired enough wealth to commission a series of paintings that were then pasted together to form two scrolls illustrating this and the later invasion of 1281. The scrolls were probably created some time after 1293, by which time Suenaga had become a landowner and guardian of several shrines and temples. He had had something of a struggle to get his deeds of valour officially recognized after the invasions, so it seems likely that he wished to record his own role in the battle and at the same time honour the man who backed him for the official commendation on which his later wealth and influence depended. The Invasion Scrolls passed through various hands, surviving as much by luck as by care – they were once dropped in the sea, which dissolved the glue holding the panels together, leaving the precise sequence in doubt. In the late eighteenth century they were stuck back together, restored and copied, with several much-analysed additions. The scrolls have since become famous as a unique and vivid portrayal of the invasions – and, most scholars agree, an authentic one. They were accompanied by 69 documents – letters, prayers, edicts, battle reports – which have recently been translated and analysed by Thomas Conlan of Bowdoin College, Brunswick, Maine, in an extraordinary book printed back to front, so that the pages of text read backwards and illustrations run from right to left, as the scrolls themselves do. To read it is to be immersed in events by something that is a cross between a comic and a novel.

The section of the scroll depicting the 1274 invasion shows the young Suenaga (aged 29), sporting a trim moustache and goatee beard, advancing through pines with five followers. They carry extraordinarily long bows (by Mongol standards), which they wield with great skill, firing at the gallop, quivers on their backs, protected from head to toe by lamellar armour, made of overlapping metal scales.

Suenaga is a headstrong character. Coming upon one of the Mongol forces, perhaps the one advancing from Mount Sohara, he cannot wait to fight. The text takes over from the pictures:

> Shouting a battle cry, I charged. As I was about to attack, my retainer Togenda Sukemutsu said: 'More of our men are coming. Wait for reinforcements, get a witness, then attack!'
>
> I replied: 'The way of the bow and arrow is to do what is worthy of reward. Charge!' . . .
>
> My bannerman was first. His horse was shot and he was thrown down. I Suenaga and my three retainers were wounded. Just after my horse was shot and I was thrown off, Michiyasu, a *gokenin* from Hizen province, attacked with a formidable squad of horsemen and the Mongols retreated . . . I would have died had it not been for him. Against all odds, Michiyasu survived as well, and so we each agreed to be a witness for the other.

A picture shows Suenaga thrown from his wounded horse, which spouts blood, while a Mongol shell explodes nearby. This shell has been the source of controversy. Though Conlan thinks the image is an eighteenth-century addition to increase the drama, other scholars believe the content is authentic. Either – or, indeed, both – could be the case. As we have seen, the Mongols had long known about explosives, having acquired them after they seized Beijing in 1215. What is shown exploding near Suenaga is a 'thundercrash bomb', a ceramic shell with an explosive core. These were first recorded in 1221, when the Jin of north China, still only partially conquered by Genghis, were besieging the city of Qizhou on the Yangtze. So this could well have been Japan's first experience of explosive weapons.

Delivered how, exactly? Not with counterweight trebuchets, which demanded tonnes of ballast and throwing arms as big as masts – not the sort of thing you would put on a ship. Anyway, the Mongols were not planning to batter down castle walls. Thundercrash bombs were anti-personnel devices, weighing only 3–4 kilos. They could be cast by traction trebuchets, which had been in common use for two centuries. We know the Mongols had thundercrash bombs with them, because several have been found in the remains of one of the Korean/Mongol ships (I'll get to the details later). So whether this particular example was added to the scroll later or not, it captures a truth. With a traction trebuchet, half a dozen men on a ship's prow could easily lob a thundercrash bomb 100 metres as part of an assault to clear the beach.

So far, so brave. It is clear even from this little incident that Suenaga, like any good samurai, is obsessed with individual glory, and not at all concerned at the lack of centralized command. In these circumstances, such tactics had some effect. Good archers were in their element. One warrior, Yamada, made a name for himself by organizing a team of powerful bowmen to fire long range at isolated Mongols, killing three of them, raising laughter and cheers from the Japanese. Another shot a Mongol commander in the face and captured his horse. But individual bravery was not enough. Some of the Mongols galloping back and forth between the beach-head and Mount Sohara managed to burn the local town of Hakata.

As the day died, the Japanese took refuge away from the beach, barricading themselves into Dazaifu. Backed by a hill, it had a rampart of earth and a moat that can still be seen today. It was hardly enough to stop a Mongol army that had become expert in siege warfare. But the Mongols had never mounted an amphibious landing before. They would need food and supplies, in particular more arrows. They had no heavy catapults with them. A siege would take time. And, to cap it all, a storm was brewing. It would be a miserable night for all, worse for the Mongols and Koreans if their boats were caught in the shallows and the troops were trapped on the beach with no means of retreat. Captains urged the troops to retire to the ships to ride out the bad weather at sea, away from the breaking waves. The next day would surely allow another landing, another breakthrough, and victory.

It would not be that easy. In the worsening weather, a flotilla of 300 Japanese open boats crept up the coast towards the Mongol fleet, some bearing a dozen soldiers with bows and swords, some loaded with dry hay to act as fire-ships. These little ships infiltrated the ranks of their massive targets, moving too fast to be caught by the bombs launched by trebuchets or heavy shafts from crossbows, and then in close beneath the outward-curving hulls. Many of Kublai's ships were already on fire as the wind picked up and the Japanese oarsmen headed for the bays and beaches they knew so well, leaving much of the Mongol fleet to the mercy of storm and flames.

The dawn revealed sights both dire (for Mongols) and uplifting (for Japanese): ships scattered by the wind, hulks smouldering, the flotsam of a broken army left behind as the survivors limped for safety in Korea. Korean records claim that 13,000 were drowned.

Kublai did not take this defeat to heart. It had all been down to the weather, nothing to do with Japanese *élan*. Next time, surely – and there would be a next time – the Mongols' natural superiority would tell. Why could not the Japanese see the obvious? He sent another message, another demand for submission.

Neither the Hojo shogun, Tokimune, nor the emperor in

Kyoto had any doubts about what had to be done. A Japanese courtier noted in his diary that the bad weather, though nothing worse than a 'reverse wind', 'must have arisen as a result of the protection of the gods. Most wonderful! We should praise the gods without ceasing. This great protection could only have happened because of the many prayers and offerings to the various shrines ... throughout the realm.' The emperor prayed, and urged all to do likewise, inspiring an upsurge in both Shintoism and Buddhism.

But the gods would only help those who helped themselves. Tokimune ordered Kyushu's coastal provinces to build a wall, and man it, avoidance of military duty being made a criminal offence. Whether this was Tokimune's idea or one of his advisers, it was brilliant and original, for the Japanese had not previously built many military installations, certainly not many that compelled Japan's divided clans and rival provincial governors to collaborate.

The spirit of resistance hardened. When more envoys came from Kublai in May 1275, they were taken to Kamakura and four months later executed (you can see the tomb of their unlucky leader, Du Shizong, in a temple in Fujisawa, close to Kamakura). The shogun might as well have slapped Kublai's face. Court and civil leaders economized, so that the national wealth could be poured into defences. There was even thought of a pre-emptive strike: new ships were built and crews trained. In the end, the military leaders opted for defence, focusing on the building of small, easily manoeuvrable boats that would run rings round the mighty Korean warships. All around Hakata bay clans gathered to build the wall. Since there was no telling when Kublai might strike again, they were in a hurry. But, with no tradition either of co-operation or of large-scale building to guide them, they had to make it up as they went along. Hakata bay's shoreline is almost all sand, backed by dunes and pines, no good at all for building. The wall would have to be of stone.

The result, or some of it, is still visible today, the bits forming several tourist attractions: Genko Borui, the Yuan
Invasion Defensive Wall. Fukuoka has filled in the coastal
inlets here and there, but standing on the beach away from
the port you can easily imagine yourself in Suenaga's saddle.
There are the same sweep of sand, the same mountains at
either end, similar dunes and pines. Of course, sand gathered
over the centuries and stones were snatched for buildings. But
along one 50-metre stretch the sand has been dug away, and
other sections have been rebuilt, so you can still see how the
inexperienced locals responded to the challenge. At least you
can if, like me, you look through the expert eyes of
archaeologist Sumitaka Yanagida, a diminutive, wiry Indiana
Jones figure with flyaway white hair and a jutting jaw.
Having been involved with the wall for 40 years, he supervised its rise to fame as a symbol of Japanese independence
and courage.

Symbolically it's great, yes; but it's no Great Wall. Its main
purpose was to pin horses back on the beach, so it needed to
be no more than 2 metres high. Then there was the problem
of technique. To make stone walls you need good masons,
experts in dry-stone walling and/or cement. The Japanese
lacked all three, and never agreed on a standard blueprint for
construction. There were stones aplenty: granite from one
end, sandstone from the other, some hacked from the mountains, others collected from the beaches at either end where
the sand runs out. Each clan was given a length of wall to
construct, depending on the clan's wealth – 3 metres here, 10
metres there. It seems that each clan collected its own rocks,
dressed them and set them in place, each section coming to an
abrupt end with stones stacked vertically rather than overlapping in proper bricklaying fashion. You can almost hear a
clan leader snorting disdainfully, 'And take care you don't
build any of *their* section!' This is a wall that would have
fallen apart with one ball from a Muslim catapult. At one

point, the wall is a double wall, because at the first attempt the foundations had given way: rather than start again, the clan responsible had simply piled on more rocks. Here the wall is backed by a platform for defenders to stand on; in a second spot it has a walkway protected by a secondary wall; in a third the wall is not solid but hollow, two faces packed with earth. Imagine these variations being repeated along the whole 20-kilometre stretch, imagine the arguments about design, technique and materials – but also imagine the over-riding sense of urgency that forced rivals to swallow their disagreements, and in six months build something that would be impossible for cavalry to take in a frontal assault.

By late 1276, they were ready, with, as it happened, five years to spare.

11

CHALLENGE FROM THE
HEARTLAND

AS A GLANCE AT THE MAP TELLS YOU, CHINA TODAY STRETCHES halfway across Asia. Its western limits are almost on the same longitude as India's western edge. This is surprising, because it is so far beyond the traditional Chinese heartland as defined by its old northern limits, the first Great Wall established by the 'First Emperor' in the third century BC. That wall ended deep in Central Asia; but today's border is as far again beyond. How come China is so big?

The reason for China's size – a major theme of this book – is that Genghis and Kublai made it so. But this leads on to another problem: Kublai's empire stretched way beyond today's borders. This suggests the question should be flipped: how come China is so *small*? Why does it not reach even further into Central Asia?

The answer is that Kublai was limited by the amount of force he could bring to bear on his independent-minded relatives. One reason for this was that they had ready access to horses, which made them as hard to catch as quicksilver. There was nothing much to be done about the more distant parts of the empire – Persia, the Golden Horde of southern Russia – but Central Asia, though far from China's heartland, was on Mongolia's doorstep. In one sense, all of Kazakhstan and a good deal of the other 'stans' to the south were part of Genghis's inheritance and therefore part of Kublai's, and therefore might well have remained in the Chinese sphere. But in this direction Kublai reached his limit. He had moved from beyond the Wall to inside the Wall, and was now constrained by distance and by his own, or rather his troops', inability to pin down his mercurial opponents.

This takes us into a murky backwater of history – the rivalry between Kublai and a distant relative; but it is important because the outcome explains much about the shape of China today. The opposition Kublai met at this time dictated how far he could go. That he went thus far and no further presented an idea of China's western boundary that endured through a time of retreat under the successor dynasty, the Manchus, when these remote regions were ruled again by Mongols. It re-emerged in the eighteenth century with the 'New Kingdom' – Xinjiang (Sinkiang, as it used to be spelled) – when the Manchus regained control, extending the borders once again to the limits defined by Kublai.

This vast and varied region – running from the deserts of Uzbekistan and the grasslands of southern Kazakhstan into the heights of the Tien Shan and the wastes of western China – has no historical unity, but it exerts a strange power to spread trouble. In part this is because it was increasingly Islamic, even in Kublai's day; in part because it is hard for either Islamic realms or China to win permanent control over it. For the same reasons, trouble is brewing again today, with disaffected Islamists wanting to carve out a new state that will suck in China's Islamic far west. It is worth taking a closer look at the great-grand-daddy of this idea, and at how Kublai failed to resolve it.

It was in Central Asia that the real threat to Kublai lay –

real because it came from his own family, from the descendants of Genghis's chosen heir, Ogedei, whose line had been pushed aside by Tolui's powerful widow, Kublai's mother Sorkaktani, in favour of her children; real because it came from Kublai's original homeland, and because opposition here would block the westward flow of goods from China to India, the Islamic world and Europe. If it were allowed to fester, Kublai would be cut off from the wealth that underpinned his power, and would then be as vulnerable as any emperor of old to barbarian hordes sweeping in across the Gobi. Perhaps one day Mongol emperor would fall to Mongol barbarian, some remote cousin with as good a – no, a better – claim to the throne than Kublai himself.

The cousin in question was Kaidu, Ogedei's grandson. This is his story. It is a peculiar one, in that it was played out over Kaidu's rather long life, and over a good deal of Kublai's. For some 40 years, the two ill-matched contestants engaged in a sort of long-distance boxing match, Kaidu the lightweight throwing punches from the northern and western frontiers, occasionally attracting the gaze of his heavyweight opponent, who always had other claims on his attention.

Kaidu never had a hope of actually winning, but his successes highlight another theme, common to many great-power rulers: conquest (if it can be managed at all) is simple, however hard-fought; administration is complicated. Conquest unites subordinates in a great adventure; administration allows free play to character, ambition, the formation of rival groups. Things fall apart, especially at the edges, which in this case was an area 3,000 kilometres from headquarters. It took as long for an official to reach Kaidu as it took an English official to reach America in the 1780s. By the time he got there, who knew what might have happened in the meantime?

*

Born in about 1235, Kaidu had been too young to be caught up in the purges unleashed by Mönkhe against the supporters of Ogedei in 1251, but not too young to be given his own estate when Mönkhe made peace with the survivors the following year. At 16, Kaidu was master of a territory some 2,000 kilometres to the west of Karakorum, a land running down from the Tien Shan into desert, but divided by the lush valley of the Ili river, one of the main routes linking China and the west. This, Asia's geographical dead centre, was his base, where he grew to manhood, far from the ever-more-Chinese world of Kublai. Here he started empire-building on his own account, the new kid on the block elbowing his way into the scrum.

From now on, the story does not come easily, because it means making sense of obscure events, teasing significance from odd references in shadowy sources about petty squabbles. Marco Polo faced the same problem, which he solved, as he often did, by riding roughshod over history and going for a good yarn. In this case, it was not a bad idea, because the gossip he picked up captures something essential about Kaidu and the nature of his rebellion.

Marco remembered Kaidu because of his daughter, Kutulun, another one of those formidable women who stamp their mark on Mongolia's history. Kutulun was famous not for her political skills but for her fighting ability and independent spirit. 'This damsel was very beautiful,' Marco begins, as if opening a fairytale, 'but also so strong and brave that in all her father's realm there was no man who could outdo her in feats of strength . . . so tall and muscular, so stout and shapely withal, that she was almost like a giantess.' Kaidu doted on his Amazonian daughter and wanted to give her in marriage, but she always refused, saying she would only marry a man who could beat her in a wrestling match. Her rule was that a challenger had to put up 100 horses. After 100 bouts and 100 wins, Kutulun had 10,000 horses. Now,

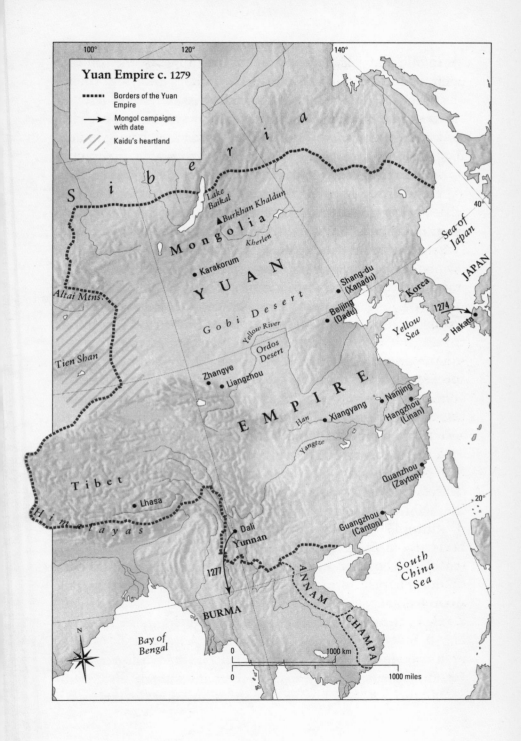

Yuan Empire c. 1279

▪▪▪▪▪ Borders of the Yuan Empire

→ Mongol campaigns with date

▨ Kaidu's heartland

100° 120° 140°

S i b e r i a

Lake Baikal

▲ Burkhan Khaldun

Kherlen

M o n g o l i a

• Karakorum

Y U A N

40°

Altai Mtns.

Gobi Desert

Tien Shan

Shang-du (Xanadu) •

Beijing (Dadu) •

Yellow River

Ordos Desert

Zhangye • Liangzhou •

E M P I R E

Han • Xiangyang •

Yangtze

Nanjing •

Hangzhou (Linan) •

Korea

Sea of Japan

JAPAN

Yellow Sea

1274 → Hakata •

Quanzhou (Zayton) •

T i b e t

Lhasa •

H i m a l a y a s

Dali •
Yunnan

1277

BURMA

Guangzhou (Canton) •

20°

ANNAM

CHAMPA

South China Sea

N

Bay of Bengal

0   1000 km

0   1000 miles

as in all good fairytales, a noble prince appears, the son of a rich and powerful king, both father and son being suspiciously anonymous. So confident is he that he puts up 1,000 horses. Kaidu, eager for a wealthy son-in-law, begs her to lose the fight on purpose. Never, she says: he'll have to beat me fair and square. Everyone gathers to watch the match, which after this great build-up ends in anti-climax. They 'grappled each other by the arms and wrestled this way and that', without either gaining an advantage, until suddenly Kutulun throws her opponent. Shamed, he heads for home, wherever that is, leaving his 1,000 horses behind. Her father swallows his anger at the loss of a good match and proudly takes her on campaigns. She proves a great warrior, sometimes dashing into the enemy ranks to seize some man 'as deftly as a hawk pounces on a bird, and carry him to her father'.

Are we to believe this? Well, some of it. Yes, she existed, because Rashid mentions her; but only in passing, with a rather more jaundiced explanation for her failure to marry. He says the refusal came from her father, 'and people suspected that there was some kind of relationship between him and his daughter'. And Polo's story is rather too reminiscent of others – like the Amazons, or Brünnhilde in the *Nibelungenlied* – to be convincing. What is convincing is the light it throws on Kaidu and the virtues he admired: the traditional pastoral-nomadic virtues of pride, bravery, strength, fighting spirit, independence. He was no lover of scholars, artists or administrators. As Morris Rossabi says, a man with such attitudes would naturally come into conflict with Kublai.

How, then, did things stand with the empire in the early 1260s?

It was no longer a unified empire, but the battleground on which a great family fought over its inheritance. In Central Asia, three Mongol powers battled to increase their own shares: the Golden Horde in today's southern Russia, the Il-Khans in Persia, and Chaghadai's heirs between the Aral Sea and western China. (Actually, there were three-and-a-half powers: there was also a White Horde, ruled by Golden Horde relatives eager to create their own separate estate.) Into this mêlée Kaidu was now elbowing himself, making space in the borderlands where Chaghadai's lands, the Golden Horde and Kublai's China met. All the contestants, of course, acknowledged that they were family, created by Genghis. But who was best suited to wear the mantle of their great forefather? Everything was under strain, pulled by forces over which successive claimants had little control. In the west, Islam drew Mongol rulers; some resisted, some converted, the converts looking to an old enemy, Egypt, for support. In the centre were some who held to traditional nomadic virtues, despising the very cities and cultures they needed for their incomes. In the east, Kublai ruled, for some their nominal overlord, to others a traitor for choosing to be so Chinese.

Kaidu – intelligent, competent and cunning, in Rashid's words – moved steadily into rebellion. In his twenties, he supported Ariq in opposition to Kublai and refused Kublai's summons to his coronation in 1260, with the weak excuse that the pastures were too scanty for his horses. Soon after, all three Central Asian Mongol leaders died – Hulegu in Persia, Alghu in Chaghadai's territory and Berke in the Golden Horde – leaving a power vacuum across all Central Asia. Kaidu grabbed more land, reaching west towards Persia and east into present-day China, relying on the Golden Horde's new ruler as an ally. Kublai tried to bring order to his squabbling family by sending a representative, Baraq, who placed himself in charge of Chaghadai's estate. Baraq and Kaidu fought on the banks of the Syrdar'ya. Kaidu won a great victory, then proposed peace in the name of Genghis.

In 1269 there was a peace conference in Taraz, on the

border of Kazakhstan and Kyrgyzstan, to which the new rulers of all three established Inner Asian Mongol 'nations' came, with Kaidu making a fourth. Three of them – the Golden Horde leaders having no interest in this local matter – divided Transoxania between them, with Baraq and Kaidu, the dominant participants, somehow agreeing to share the trade from Samarkand and Bukhara. The two confirmed their treaty with the great oath that made them *anda* – blood brothers – and by 'drinking gold', as the saying went, which meant exchanging golden cups and toasting each other.

Notice what is happening. Baraq, originally sent by Kublai, and the upstart Kaidu are operating as independent monarchs. No-one checks back with his nominal overlord, Kublai, except (according to an unsourced quotation in the *Yuan History*) to send a rather rude message: 'The old customs of our dynasty are not those of the Han laws. Today, when you remain in the Han territory, build a capital and construct cities, learn a method of reading and writing, and use the Han laws, what will happen to the old customs?' In other words, they were declaring themselves independent of Kublai, because he had turned from the ways of Genghis.

It quickly emerged that the peace conference was a sham. No-one trusted anyone else. Everyone prepared for more fighting. The Golden Horde ruler, Mönkhe Temür, stayed out of it, leaving the other three to scrap, in a vicious round of assaults, alliances and deceptions that we can summarize at speed. Abaqa, Hulegu's successor as Il-Khan, defeated Baraq; Kaidu sent an army to 'help' Baraq, intending to take advantage of his defeat; Baraq died; his commanders defected to Kaidu, along with 30,000 soldiers. As a result of these developments, in late summer 1271 Kaidu was crowned in Taraz, becoming khan of a state 2,500 kilometres from side to side, encompassing today's southern Kazakhstan, most of Uzbekistan and almost all of Kyrgyzstan. This area has no name: Marco Polo refers to it as 'Great Turkey'; others call it

Turkestan (despite its Mongol elements) or Chaghadai's nation, a shifting entity that was never an exact fit with Kaidu's realm. Roughly speaking, it ran from the River Amudar'ya in the west into Xinjiang in the east, from Lake Balkhash in the north down to the Tien Shan – 1.25 million square kilometres in all, which is the size of France, Germany and Italy combined.

This was no mean achievement. Kaidu had proved himself smart enough to exploit his opponents' weaknesses and Kublai's move into the Chinese heartland. He was a commander in the tradition of Genghis himself: tough, austere – he didn't touch alcohol – tolerant of religions other than his own shamanism, and also careful to preserve his tax base, the great Silk Road cities such as Samarkand and Bukhara. Through an efficient chancellor, he introduced his own currency (coins with a high silver content have been found in a dozen cities). He is even credited with building Andizhan, which in the 1280s became a crossroads for trade in the rich Fergana valley. Traditionalist he may have been, but he also took after Genghis in his awareness of the need for administrative skills. He created regiments of cavalry, using the decimal command structure introduced by Genghis to reform units based on established tribal loyalties. In this way, he was able to incorporate many, often rival, Mongol and Turkish tribes. The horsemen, armed with bows and arrows, also used swords and lances. They were reinforced by units of infantry and 'naphtha throwers' – teams expert in the use of trebuchets and other siege engines. How strong were his armies? The sources toss around the figure of 100,000, probably an exaggeration, as almost all such estimates are, though even this is rather smaller than rival forces in Persia, the Golden Horde and Kublai's China. But what they lacked in quantity they made up for in quality. They were terrific at raids: quick advances, hard strikes, rapid retreats.

But economic revival did not last long, and dreams of wider

empire were soon shattered. In the very year of Kaidu's coronation, Kublai took action to bring him to heel. He sent a delegation of six princes led by his fourth son, Nomukhan, to Almaligh, well inside Kaidu's territory, with the aim of persuading him to come to court in Xanadu or Beijing. This must have seemed a good way to force the royal cousins to work together. If so, it backfired disastrously. Kaidu took no notice, keeping his army out of harm's way, securing his western borders. Nomukhan did not have enough cavalry to mount an offensive – his top general told him it would take 110,000 horses to hunt down Kaidu.

This goes to the heart of the problem for Kublai. China did not normally produce horses on this scale. Yuan records show that from Ogedei onwards imperial rulers issued a steady stream of edicts about how horses should be requisitioned.[1] 'As for the people's horses, there is a percentage system,' says one. 'When the number reaches 100, one is taken.' Another, from Kublai in 1293, could apply to Nomukhan's predicament in the mid-1270s: 'Because the rebellious princes [i.e. Kaidu et al.] have not submitted, the time has now come for military operations. Collect 100,000 horses from all the provinces and give the price accordingly.' Herds began to flow from China via the Gansu Corridor, but there was no real chance of sending enough. And anyway, it would surely take Nomukhan time to train his army to use them. Meanwhile, he built up a court and turned himself into yet another warlord.

This stand-off lasted for five useless years, time enough for resentments to grow among the entourage of cousins. The focal point was Tokh-Temür, the son of Tolui's ninth son, famous for his bravery and his skill as an archer. He rode a grey horse because he said blood – 'the adornment and

[1] Sechin Jagchid and C. R. Bawden, 'Some Notes on the Horse-Policy of the Yüan Dynasty'.

decoration of men' – showed up well on it. He was also a hot-head. As Rashid puts it, 'Because of his great bravery his brain was full of rebellion.' Tokh-Temür persuaded another cousin, Mönkhe's son Shiregi, that he had a better claim to the throne than Kublai. One night, they captured both Nomukhan and his senior general, sending the prince off as a prisoner to the Golden Horde as a gift and the general to Kaidu, with a message saying, 'We must not think ill of each other, but unite to drive off the enemy.' But, as often with hot-heads, Tokh-Temür and Shiregi themselves destroyed the unity they sought. Their army turned into a robber band; the two men squabbled about the succession and fought each other; they suffered various defections; eventually they struck eastward into Mongolia, where they occupied Karakorum. Kublai sent troops to drive them out, after which this rebellion petered out. But imposing his will on his unruly family was a task beyond Kublai's reach. He was totally involved in the war against Song, which would last until 1279, and simply gave up trying to control Kaidu's distant realm.

(And what of the unfortunate Nomukhan? He survived the long journey to Crimea as a prisoner to find himself – of course – among cousins. Presumably thinking he might be useful as a pawn, they kept him for ten years. When he was returned to China in 1284, he was given a job as head of the department looking after the northern frontier, but no longer in line for the succession. He died the following year.)

All this was good news for Kaidu. After reoccupying Almaligh, he was free to deal with constant cross-border raids from Persia and several uprisings from disenchanted members of Chaghadai's family. Sitting squarely over the old Silk Road, he presided over a shaky revival. Silver coins underpinned economic stability. Over the next few years, a strategy would become clear. He would build a network of support all around the fringes of the empire, reaching out southward into Tibet and at the same time eastward to

Manchuria. From Almaligh, he would build an arc of yes-men and allies hemming in Kublai's Chinese empire. With Baraq's son Duwa as his right-hand man, he would make good his claim to be the true heir of his grandfather Ogedei, Genghis's appointed successor.

One day, there would have to be a final showdown. It would not come for over twenty years; not in Kublai's life-time. But for the rest of his days, Kublai's hold on Central Asia remained purely nominal.

12

THE KHAN'S NEW CHINA

KUBLAI HAD INHERITED ASTONISHING MANAGERIAL SKILLS. HE
was no intellectual genius, but he had talents that made him
one of the greatest CEOs of all time: he was a superb judge of
character, entirely without personal prejudice, and had the
knack of hiring people who were smarter than he was. Like
his grandfather, he was happy to employ anyone with talent.
His advisers formed an international team. Muslim traders
were headhunted to become financial administrators. He
employed 66 Uighur Turks, 21 of whom were resident commissioners or local officials running Chinese districts, while
several others tutored princes of the royal family. Also like his
grandfather Genghis, he could spot organizational problems
– totally unprecedented ones caused by the novelty of unfold-
ing events – and then, out of the blue, devise solutions that
actually worked. Genghis had taken tribes, broken their
structure and forged a nation, then started to do the same
thing with different cultures to forge an empire. Kublai took
the process further. His mission was conquest, then government, for which his people were doubly unprepared, first

because they had had no government before Genghis and second because, although previous non-Chinese conquerors had taken on north China, none had taken on the whole lot, north and south. Can you think of any precedents in history of such small numbers taking on so much and so many, and succeeding?

Kublai's main fault, as we shall see later, was that he could not be content. How could he be, if he was to be true to his grandfather's mission – to set the bounds of empire wider still and wider, until all the world acknowledged the fact of Mongol supremacy?

At home, by comparison, he was a rock. That, too, was a consequence of his mission. Having seen that China was the key to imperial rule, he needed China to be stable and prosperous, for that would be his foundation for the world rule ordained by Heaven.

To present himself to his subjects as a Chinese ruler, it would not do to go on about the Mongols' divine right. Nor was it enough to be a Buddhist. He also had to be, or at least claim to be, a Confucian. Confucians had always honoured their ancestors. This Kublai did in 1277 by commissioning a Great Ancestral Temple that would prove to his subjects north and south of the Gobi that he was both a good Mongol and a good Chinese. Rising on the south-eastern edge of his new Da-du, the temple's eight chambers were local versions of the Eight White Tents that were already established as travelling shrines to Genghis back in Mongolia, and which centuries later reached their final resting place, Edsen Khoroo, the Lord's Enclosure, south of Dongsheng, Inner Mongolia; in the 1950s, they were replaced by a new shrine, the temple known as the Mausoleum of Genghis Khan. Kublai's original eight-chambered Great Temple commemorated his great-grandparents; Genghis himself; and Genghis's sons, including Kublai's ruling predecessors. Genghis also acquired a Chinese title, T'ai-tsu – the same one given posthumously to the founders of several other dynasties:

Song, Liao, Jin and Ming. It was Kublai, therefore, who gave Genghis his Chinese credentials, and thus founded the belief widespread among Chinese today that Genghis was 'really' Chinese – and thus that all Mongols and Mongolia itself are Chinese.

World rule it was to be then, with China as the foundation stone. From this astonishing ambition came something just as remarkable: not a grim dictatorship, but a revival of much that had vanished from Chinese society during the turmoil of the previous century. For a brief moment, about two decades, all of China underwent something of a renaissance. Kublai, as a foreigner, would never be truly accepted; but he was indisputably the boss; and it is arguable that the changes he brought about improved the lot of his new subjects. Certainly, there were those who were ready to admit that unity with peace under the Mongols was better than disunity with civil war. An epitaph of Kublai might say: He tried to be good.

This is a judgement which conflicts sharply with commonly held opinions about Mongol rule, which is often seen as nothing but a catalogue of abuses, along the following lines.

Almost all the top positions were held by Mongols. They lorded it over the population as the new landowners, the new elite, the new aristocracy. A new class system brought new humiliations: Mongols at the top; then, those from the Muslim lands – Persians, Arabs, Uighurs, Turks – who knew about business and trade; then the 40 million northern Chinese, along with other fringe minorities, like Tatars, Khitans and Koreans; and finally, at the bottom of the heap, the new subjects, the 70 million southern Chinese, who at a stroke were turned from heirs to the richest and most sophisticated culture on earth to subjects and servants. Many were actually enslaved, and a slave trade sprang up. If a Mongol murdered, he was exiled; a Chinese murderer was executed. A Mongol could beat a Chinese with impunity, while the Chinese was forbidden to return the blow. The Chinese were banned from carrying weapons, hunting, military training, raising horses, praying in groups, holding fairs. Curfews were imposed, lights forbidden. The examination system, by which scholar-officials acquired office, was no more. In the ten grades into which Mongols categorized their Chinese subjects, Confucian scholars ranked ninth, below prostitutes, above only the lowest of the low, the beggars.

All this is true. But it is not the whole truth. The scholars, aristocrats and officials represented only a tiny part of Chinese society. Most were peasant farmers and ordinary town-dwellers earning their living by agricultural work, low-level trading and performing the myriad humble jobs that are vital in any large complex, urbanized society. With such a vast population, with such teeming cities, with such a thin upper crust of Mongols, no changes permeated from top to bottom. For ordinary people, the routines of everyday life hardly changed . . .

. . . or actually improved. Stability depended on more than the raw exercise of power. Kublai was the most powerful man of his day, one of the most powerful of all time; yet, as his actions showed, he knew that his power depended only in part on a flow of authority from the top downwards, from him through the court and his army of officials to the masses. It also depended on support flowing from the bottom upwards. Ordinary people had to feel happy and secure, or unrest would fester and spread from below. North China was sick enough as it was, recovering from the half-century of warfare initiated by Genghis back in 1211; the south was seething from his own campaign of conquest; all needed healing.

The foundation of stability was the vast mass of peasant farmers, on whom all depended for food. To look after their interests, Kublai set up a new Office for the Stimulation of Agriculture, with eight officials and a team of experts who organized aid, built 58 granaries that could store almost 9,000 tonnes of grain, arranged tax remissions and banned Mongols from grazing their wandering herds on farmland.

Local councils, each covering 50 households, helped with production, irrigation – and even schools, an idea that proved too revolutionary to work, but did at least show that the emperor was no mere barbarian nomad. Taxes now flowed not directly to the landowner, who in the north was probably a Mongol, but to the government, which then divided the revenue between itself and the landowner. The peasant farmer still paid, but at least Kublai tried to curb abuses. He also insisted that forced labour, which remained vital for large-scale public projects like canals and the postal system, was rather less forced than previously.

Let's see how he ruled. He had had a good start, under the aegis of Genghis's Khitan adviser, the great Yeh-lü Chu-tsai, who successfully set up a decent working bureaucracy, despite opposition from some dyed-in-the-wool traditionalist factions. But Kublai faced a much vaster problem: namely, how to combine steppeland with town and farmland, nomadism with settled cultures, the few with the many. He was not ready simply to abandon the one (from which he derived his core values) and adopt the other. Besides, he also had to take into account his Muslim subjects, a vital component of the empire: his brother Hulegu ruled a good chunk of Islam, and Muslims were important as governors, tax-gatherers, financial advisers and business partners. His response to this many-sided challenge was to make it up as he went along, sometimes finding solutions in the practices of previous dynasties, sometimes devising his own. Over 30 years he created a form of government that was predominantly Chinese, but also uniquely complex and cosmopolitan.

He had one supreme advantage: he was not bound by precedent. Previous emperors had governed through several executive agencies. Kublai saw that this would be a recipe for disaster. He had just one, the Central Secretariat, with him at the top, ranging down through chief councillors (usually two or three, occasionally up to five), privy councillors, assistants, some 200 officials and hundreds of clerical staff, in 18 levels, the status of each minutely defined in terms of precedence, title, salary and perks.[1]

The Secretariat controlled six ministries: Personnel, Revenues, Rites, War, Punishments and Works, each of which had dozens of departments. The Ministry of Works, for instance, had 53 of them, including agencies that handled Buddhist icons, lost-wax casting, a bronze foundry, agate and jade workers, masonry, woodworking, paint, weaving, dyeing, carpets, tents, kilns and leatherworking. Checking up on all ministries and their departments was a Censorate, a sort of National Audit Office, with three national headquarters.

Entirely separate from the civil administration was the Bureau of Military Affairs, the Ministry of War being merely its link to the civil service. This had been established by Kublai after Li Tan's Shandong rebellion in 1262 as the guarantor of his power. The Bureau was hard-core Mongol territory, top secret, staffed by Mongols, with all Chinese excluded to prevent their knowing anything of troop strengths, dispositions or armaments. It controlled all the armed forces, including the appointment of officers, the training of Chinese and Central Asian units, kept the records and conducted all its own auditing procedures. This was perhaps Kublai's greatest stroke of administrative genius. Genghis had created a non-tribal system owing personal loyalty to himself. Kublai had realized that such a huge and enduring establishment as his would be far removed from him as an individual. Its personnel – most of them pen-pushers, not generals – needed to be made loyal to a different entity: not a here-today-gone-tomorrow emperor, but the state.

[1] This section is mostly based on F. W. Mote, *Imperial China 900–1800*.

Then there was the court. Specialized staff took care of the rituals, the protocol, the kitchens, granaries, warehouses, clothing and special food. Teams of artisans supplied gold, silver, porcelain, gems, textiles. There were departments for the hunting facilities and the stud farms. This was a universe unto itself of servants, managers, entertainment specialists, historians, translators, interpreters, astronomers, doctors, librarians, shrine-keepers, musicians and architects.

Other institutions were not under the direct control of any of the above. Three academies were devoted to Mongol studies; a Muslim Bureau of Astronomy gave Muslims their own research facilities; the Commission for Tibetan and Buddhist Affairs – Phags-pa's private empire – acted as a sort of Tibetan government-at-a-distance, supervising the Pacification Bureau in Tibet and the ever-growing Buddhist interests across China: temples, monasteries, other properties.

It was the job of the Bureau of Military Affairs to handle the changeover from conquest to a permanent military administration. The repercussions of this shift would store up trouble for the future. Under Genghis, the Mongol system had drawn every family into its military machine. Families had to be supported with rather more than a salary (which in any case was not a concept that existed in the early days of empire). At first the rewards were booty, then, as territory fell, lands. That was how commanders of 'hundreds' or 'thousands' were supposed to support their troops. Hence the system which gave estates – appanages – to princes and commanders. But with an empire to manage, the appanage system did not work. Few Mongols had the ambition or talent to administer farms. Most were absentee landlords, abandoning their estates to the care of servants who were little more than slaves with no interest in doing a good job. The system tended to collapse of its own accord, leaving the estates ruined, their people destitute. So Kublai stopped awarding appanages.

Mongol landowners sold up and found themselves cast adrift, outside the military system, with no skills, no education, no place back in their homeland, yet still supposedly part of an elite. They were the empire's equivalent of poor whites in the American South. Later, this would be part of the sickness that ate at the soul of Kublai's heirs.

The provinces were another of Kublai's creations. As the tide of Mongol conquest flowed outwards, newly conquered regions were given their own mini versions of the Central Secretariat, and these remained as branches of government in the eleven provinces, which then acquired branches of all the other departments. They were not provincial governments – Kublai wanted his officials governed from the centre, to avoid local empire-building – but they formed the essence of the provincial administrative system set up in succession by the Qing and then by the Communists in 1949. Yunnan, Shaanxi, Sichuan and Gansu all owe their existence to Kublai. The administrations reach right down to the roots. Provinces were sub-divided into prefectures, sub-prefectures and counties, each divided into two classes depending on size, each with its own set of ranked officials, from 3A for the largest prefectures (over 100,000 house-holds) down to 7B for the smallest counties (under 10,000 households).

As CEO, Kublai was committed to Mongolia Inc., which rode high on the wheels of commerce. Craftsmen were favoured with rations of food, clothing and salt, and were exempted from forced labour. Merchants had previously been seen as parasites; now they were encouraged. Trade, mainly with Muslim lands, boomed. Chinese textiles, ceramics and lacquer ware flowed out through the ports; medicines, incense, spices and carpets flowed in.

In some ways, Kublai was the ideal patron of the arts. He

had no pretensions to being an expert himself, but he knew art was tremendously important, and since he wished to appeal to all his subjects, he encouraged artists without distinction of race or creed. He was thus, almost by default, a force for change. Remember the Nepalese architect Arniko, Phags-pa's friend and designer of the White Pagoda? He proved such a hit that he became head of all artisans nation-wide, ending up with a mansion and a rich wife found for him by Kublai's wife Chabi. As a result, some Yuan buildings had Tibetan and Nepalese designs.

Or take ceramics, for which China had been famous, having established ten main kilns in the north and fourteen in the south. The war had largely destroyed ceramic production in the north, and when Kublai came to power he showed no interest in tableware, which you might think would put a damper on the trade as a whole. Exactly the opposite. Southern kilns continued to fill wagons rolling into the great southern port of Quanzhou, the place Marco Polo calls by its Arabic name, Zayton. It was, he says,

> frequented by all the ships of India [i.e. Asia], which bring thither spicery and all other kinds of costly wares. It is the port also that is frequented by all the merchants of Manzi [southern China], for hither is imported the most astonishing quantity of goods and of precious stones and pearls, and from this they are distributed all over Manzi. And I assure you that for one shipload of pepper that goes to Alexandria or else-where, destined for Christendom, there come a hundred such, aye, and more too.

In exchange for these imports, ceramics flowed into the holds of ships bound for South-East Asia, India and the world of Islam – half of which, remember, was ruled by Mongols, who quickly adopted the refined tastes of their subjects. Indeed, Quanzhou/Zayton, from which most goods were exported, was under the thumbs of Persian merchants. With Kublai standing back, the southern kilns could focus on exports, and on experiments to give their customers what they wanted, namely high quality. As a result, as one expert, Margaret Medley, puts it: 'The Yuan marks the beginning of the change-over from stone wares, that is wares fired at high temperatures with bodies varying in colour, to the fine white porcelains, hard, vitrified and translucent, that we now automatically associate with the name of China.' There was more to the revolution. In the Middle East cobalt, an extraordinarily rare metallic element, had long been used to give a blue tinge to statuettes and necklace-beads. It seems someone brought it to Chinese porcelain-makers to see what they could do with it. They made it work: cobalt blue ceramics became famous, exports boomed, and taxes – on kilns, craftsmen and production – rolled into Kublai's coffers. It is a minor irony that Kublai's own indifference led to the creation of techniques and products – the white wares of Fujian, the grey-green celadons of Zhejiang, underglaze blue – which strengthened his economy and for any one example of which a modern collector will pay thousands of dollars.

Working in groups to make use of their wealth, merchants became bankers, lending at 36 per cent annual interest. They and Kublai's government were partners: laws forced merchants to convert their metal coins into paper currency on entry, which gave the government a reserve in metals, which was used to back loans at around 10 per cent annual interest back to the merchant groups, who became, in effect, government-sanctioned loan sharks. From trade, everyone profited. Even the peasants? Why, yes. No doubt Kublai, with a financial adviser at his shoulder, would have argued that merchant wealth translated into government wealth, which financed public works and allowed tax relief to be granted to the needy. Naturally, if peasants chose to get into debt with a loan shark, that was their fault. The government could not be responsible for every merchant banker who sent in the bailiffs to twist the arms of those who had fallen behind on their monthly payments. The majority would benefit. This was trickle-down economics before its time.

Kublai's big success in economics was to extend the use of paper money. Paper money is a great invention, for practical reasons, as the Chinese had discovered almost 300 years before when the Song unified the country and revolutionized it with a booming economy. As we saw in chapter 3, unification, wealth and stability had opened the way to a single currency based on copper coins, which came in cumbersome strings of 1,000. Since rich merchants with nationwide businesses did not like handling such a weight of cash, local governments issued certificates of deposit – so-called 'flying money' – that could be redeemed in other cities. The elements had been in place for centuries, principally paper (AD 105 being the traditional date of its invention), which came to be made from the beaten inner bark of mulberry trees, and printing with carved wood-blocks (eighth century, from Japan). In 1023 the state printed the first banknotes, without taking account of basic economics. One inescapable truth about paper currency is that it is not worth the paper it is printed on. It's all a matter of confidence, based on whatever backs the bills – the economy as a whole, or gold, or in this case coins. By the early twelfth century, 70 million paper 'strings' were in circulation. This was far in excess of anything that could be backed by coins, leading to the first inflation in history. Another problem was forgery, which can be countered by making the designs so elaborate that only authorized institutions can print them – and, of course, by executing the counterfeiters.

Kublai, with the right advice, had both problems under control in an economy of which a modern finance minister would be proud. Four economic pillars – national unity, internal stability, high confidence, good growth – allowed for a far more effective system of paper money than the Song had had. He tried three systems, one backed by reserves of silk, the other two by silver, the last of which became universal, to the astonishment and admiration of Marco Polo. It was the oddest notion – that a whole society should place value on the solidified slurry made from the underbark of mulberry trees – so he goes into it in some detail. He describes the manufacture of the paper, its reduction to notes, the application of an official vermilion stamp, and their introduction into circulation. 'Everybody takes them readily, for wheresoever a person may go through the Great Kaan's dominions he shall find these pieces of paper current, and shall be able to transact all sales and purchases of goods by means of them just as well as if they were coins of pure gold.' Kublai naturally used his own notes to buy wares from foreign traders. 'He buys such a quantity of those precious things every year that his treasure is endless, whilst all the time the money he pays away costs him nothing at all . . . You might say he hath the Secret of Alchemy in perfection.'

Polo could not understand how Kublai created wealth out of paper. In a sense, simply by avoiding what had not worked and doing what did, Kublai almost stumbled on the economic principles of John Maynard Keynes, who asserted that a government can stimulate an economy by borrowing from itself and investing its own money to create the surpluses that allow it to pay itself back. Nothing so sophisticated as borrowing was needed in thirteenth-century China. It was enough that the emperor ensured stability, and preserved confidence in his own currency. This he did by always allowing a free exchange with silver on demand, and by not making the mistake the Song had made: that of printing too much currency, thereby sparking inflation. It is a neat trick, which later dynasties (and many modern governments) could not match. Soon after the Yuan fell in 1368, paper money fell out of use for 400 years.

Another element in Kublai's revolution was a new legal system.[2] Basically, since he had come from outside, all preceding codes, with legal traditions dating back 2,000 years, were suddenly null and void until reinstated. Genghis's legal system, a list of statutes recorded by his adopted kinsman Shigi, did not have the sophistication necessary for a vast and complex society like China's. Advisers quickly began afresh, combining elements of the two systems. How they did it exactly is not known, because only fragments of the texts have survived, but, as one expert wrote in a memorandum in 1266, it would take 30 years to generate all the correct procedures, decrees and precedents. Even then, there would be no unified code applying equally to Mongols, Muslims and Chinese. Draft codes came and went. Meanwhile, day-to-day justice depended, as it had for over 700 years of Chinese history, on the Five Punishments: death by strangulation or decapitation; exile for life to three distances – 1,000, 1,250, or 1,500 kilometres – depending on the seriousness of the crime; penal servitude for up to three years; beating with a heavy stick, from 60 to 100 blows; and beating with a light stick, from 10 to 50 blows. Under Kublai, various adaptations were introduced. The khan's officials had doubts about using strangulation, which did not involve the shedding of blood and was reserved in Mongol tradition for high-born criminals. For the most serious crime – treachery – he revived a seldom-used precedent: death by slow slicing, from which comes the sadistic notion of 'death by a thousand cuts'. Not a thousand, actually, but eight initially – face, hands (2), feet (2), breast, stomach, head – to be increased in stages – 24, 36, 120 – depending on the pain to be inflicted. Mere exile was not considered an adequate sanction, either, mainly because, for a nomad of no fixed abode, being sent somewhere else

[2] This section is based on Paul Heng-chao Chen, *Chinese Legal Tradition Under the Mongols*.

was no great punishment. So exile was replaced by hard labour in salt mines or iron works or some distant military base, backed up by blows with a stick, from one year plus 67 blows to three years plus 107 blows. Beatings were delivered in six degrees of punishment with a light stick (7, 17, 27, 37, 47 and 57 blows), and five degrees with a heavy stick (67–107 blows). 'And many of them', as Marco Polo records, 'die of this beating.'

This sounds grim, but in fact the Yuan code was noted for its leniency. The Song code had listed 293 offences punishable by death. The Yuan had only 135, which contradicts the common view that the Mongols used extreme brutality against all criminals. Indeed, the successor dynasty, the Ming, pushed the number back up again, one official complaining about Kublai's wimpishness. Moreover, the actual number of executions was remarkably low. Between 1260 and 1307, 2,743 criminals were executed (though nine years are missing from the records). An average of 72 executions per year out of a population of 100 million is about half that carried out in the United States when it had an equivalent population in about 1930, since when attitudes have shifted somewhat. Death Row executions in 2002–4 averaged about 60 a year, which, given the size of the population, is half the rate under Kublai Khan. Some things improve with time.

A criminal was also expected to pay compensation to his victims. This practice derived from the Mongolian tradition of paying your way out of trouble. In the Mongolian code, for instance, one statute stipulated that, in a murder case, the perpetrators could escape death 'by paying fines which were: for a Muslim – 40 gold coins; and for a Chinese – one donkey'. Under Kublai, too, certain people could simply pay up: specifically, men over 70 or boys under 15 (unless the crime was a sexual offence against a girl of 10 or under). But in most cases, punishment and compensation went together. If a man beat his sister-in-law to death, for example, he would receive 107 blows with a heavy stick and have to pay for the dead woman's funeral.

Traditionally, officials got off lightly. Not under Kublai. 'Any official who commits an unsuccessful act of rape against the wife of his subordinate shall be punished by 107 blows with a heavy stick and be dismissed from the civil service.'

In other respects, Kublai favoured leniency. Certain criminals received the equivalent of control orders. For first-time robbery-with-violence, the convicted individual was punished, and in addition tattooed on the right arm with the words 'robbery or theft once' and ordered to register with local authorities wherever he went and to serve as an auxiliary policeman for five years: a combination of punishment and community service, of discrimination and surveillance, that reinforced the bonds of society.

How come the world's most powerful man, the head of a regime noted for its iron control, ruled a regime of such relative leniency? Because his people did as they were told, and Kublai knew that justice was justice, and that harshness was counter-productive. In 1287 some 190 people were condemned to death. Kublai ordered reprieves. 'Prisoners are not a mere flock of sheep. How can they be suddenly executed? It is proper that they be instead enslaved and assigned to pan gold with a sieve.' There speaks a man who knew how to get the best from his assets.

So, a conqueror ambitious for ever wider empire, whose troops had been responsible for the death of millions of Chinese, may still come over as a man whose intentions and actions were not all bad. Even from the Chinese point of view, we must grant him some virtues. And this, for those Chinese subjects who had any freedom of choice in the matter, which was not many of them, was a problem, the age-old problem of conquered peoples: whether to oppose the invaders for ever, until death, as the hundreds of known and uncounted unknown suicides would have demanded; or to embrace *disloyalty* – the accusation marked the accused like a plague-spot – accept, kow-tow, collaborate, live and prosper?

There is no easy answer, of course. The passage of time helps. Today's intransigence will seem pig-headed tomorrow; this year's disloyalty will seem like next year's good sense. But still there will be no lasting solution. Even though Kublai proclaimed a Chinese dynasty, even though China accepted and still accepts that fact, the conquest injected a virus of bitterness that would in the end infect and overwhelm Kublai's inadequate heirs.

Let's see how one man struggled to find a way through this moral maze. He is not typical, because he was a master painter, some say a genius, but then who is typical, when everyone with the freedom to do so must make their own choices?

His name was Zhao Mengfu (Chao Meng-fu in the old transliteration). Zhao, a distant relative of the Song royal family, was starting a career as a minor official, aged 25, when his world was shattered by the Mongol invasion. Like many other scholar-officials, he was appalled by the new regime, its boorishness, its crude class structure which put southerners at the bottom of the heap, and by their own helplessness. Without the examinations which offered the educated the chance of a career, they had no hope. He became one of the *yi-min*, the 'leftovers', the rejectionists, who preferred obscurity to collaboration, and retreated to his home town, then Wuxing, now Huzhou, which then and now was famous for its glorious countryside – the huge Taihu lake to the north, the bamboo forests of the Tianmu mountains to the west. In a country retreat, the Gull-Wave Pavilion, he buried himself in classical studies, and discovered prodigious talents. He wasn't the only one. Wuxing's lake and green mountains inspired a loose confederation of masters, the Eight Talents of Wuxing as they became known. In the course of the next seven years, he won fame as a master of three genres, painting, calligraphy and poetry (later to become, many think, the greatest of his age in all three). In 1286 an imperial official arrived in Wuxing, scouting for talent in the name of Kublai. He heard of the Eight, sought them out, and made them all offers of employment in the imperial service.

Zhao accepted. One account says it was his mother who persuaded him, ambitious for him to achieve high office while still young. Some who refused turned against him – a descendant of the first Song emperor serving the Mongols! – and from then the reek of disloyalty hung about him. It was no easy decision, and there was no escape from its consequences. Zhao achieved eminence, in government – as an official in the Ministry of War and provincial administrator – as a scholar, as an artist. But regret for his lost world of lakes and mountains, where he had been his own master, gnawed at him for the rest of his life. As he wrote in one poem:

> Unfortunately I have fallen into the dusty world
> My movements being restricted.
> Before I was as a seagull,
> Now I am a bird inside a cage,
> No one cares about my sad weeping,
> My feathers are falling off every day.

His distress also permeates a painting of a sleek sheep and a miserable-looking goat: simple enough at first glance, less so the deeper you look. In traditional fashion, it includes some of Zhao's beautiful calligraphy, which hints at hidden meanings. 'I have often painted horses, but never before painted sheep or goats,' he notes, as if to say he had painted subjects dear to his horse-loving masters, but not those closer to the people they ruled. 'I did this playfully from life. Although it may not approach the old masters, it does capture something of their spirit.' One commentator, Li Chu-tsing, has argued that there is more here than a reference to ancient artistic traditions. The sheep and the goat are two generals of the Han dynasty (206 BC–AD 220) who were both captured by the Xiongnu, the barbarian empire that lay north of the Great Wall. (The Xiongnu – Hunnu in Mongolian – may have been ancestors of the Huns.) Both generals had a chance to collaborate. One, Su Wu, refused, and was forced to be a shepherd for 20 years. There he is as the haughty sheep, with its fatuous expression and bloated look, ripe for the pot. The other, Li Ling, accepted, and returned home – the scraggy goat, dejected, but at least alive to fight another day.

There's a paradox about Kublai and the arts. He encouraged artists, yet, like many other patrons, could never be a part of China's brilliant artistic tradition. In the eyes of China's artists, the Mongols were and would remain barbarians. But there they were, these great artists, serving the new regime. The inner conflict might have destroyed them. In fact, it stimulated them. Whether collaborators or rejectionists, they might have retreated into traditionalism. In fact, they took the traditions forward.

One reason for this was that, for the first time in 150 years, there was free movement between south and north. Artists from the south, imbued with the pretty, trivial stuff that the southern Song had liked, discovered a tradition of sturdier, freer styles that had dominated the north before the old Song empire had been cut in half by the Mongols' equally 'barbarian' predecessors, the Liao, in 1125.

In his most famous painting, Zhao wraps all this, and more, up together. He combines two artistic traditions, draws on his own experience and emotions, makes a touching gesture to an old friend and reveals something of the pain imposed by the political situation. For six years, his job was Assistant Civil Administrator of Jinan, in Shandong province, just north of the old north–south frontier. Back in his home town in 1295, he rediscovered a friend, Zhou Mi, whose ancestors, three or four generations back, had fled from the Jinan area when it fell to the Jin. He still considered Jinan his home, and dreamed of returning one day. With the country reunified by the Mongols, it was a dream he might have realized – except that he was one of the *yi-min*, the rejectionists who had withdrawn from public life in protest against Mongol rule. Zhao described to his old friend the place of his dreams, as he relates in the inscription. 'I told him about the mountains and rivers of Qi [near Jinan]. Among them, Mount Hua-fu-zhu is the most famous . . . its shape is lofty and precipitous, rising isolated in a most unusual way. So I painted this picture for him, setting Mount Jiao on the east, which is why I call it *Autumn Colours on the Jiao and Hua Mountains*.' It's a deceptively simple scene: marshy land stretching to the horizon, clumps of trees, two contrasting mountains – one a stark double triangle, the other an Ayers Rock lump in the distance – a couple of houses, a tiny fisherman almost lost in the landscape, all washed by a mood of autumnal melancholy. It is not a scene of traditional beauty: there are no towering cliffs and misty forests. Nor is it true to life, for the two mountains are actually far apart. It's more as if, by showing a bleak version of his friend's unseen homeland, he is saying: Don't let's pretend that life is a pretty thing. It's not. It's a tough business. Anyway, what in the end does it all matter, the Mongols, our own petty agonies and divisions? These things pass. Here, in my picture, is what endures: stark mountains, gnarled trees, and hard work.

Autumn Colours is one of the most admired of Chinese paintings, one of many that, in the words of one scholar, James Cahill, 'exhibit an astonishing inventiveness and creativity, offering major stylistic innovations that would change the course of Chinese landscape painting'. Without Kublai, they would not exist. We may question the initial conditions, the brutality of the conquest. But, given those, the outcome could have been worse.

*

Here's an odd thing. The Mongols loved the theatre. They loved it mainly because it was a total novelty. 'There is no evidence of any form of dramatic productions being presented in Mongolian society prior to or during the early empire period,' say two experts on Mongol society, Sechin Jagchid and Paul Hyer, adding wrily, 'It is difficult to develop institutionalised drama in a nomadic society.'

No-one recorded the first performance attended by Mongols – some street show, perhaps, in a town that had the good sense to surrender when Genghis first invaded north China in 1211. I imagine the scene as something like the one I saw in Guyuan, Gansu, one of China's poorest areas in 2002, when a travelling theatre visited: a ragged crowd of two or three hundred sitting on the ground in the main square a good hour before dusk and show time, the curtained stage, the actors behind putting the final touches to their garish make-up. Now we flash back 800 years and see a contingent of Mongols in the background, still on their horses. They have been on campaign for months, and are eager for some light relief. Mongol officers in their lamellar armour and leather helmets dismount and come forward, grim but curious. They are ushered to the front row by trembling townsfolk; there they wait in puzzled silence, until darkness falls. With a rush of fabric, the curtain opens, and footlight candles reveal a fierce-looking man. Mao, for that is his name, speaks directly to the audience:

Mao: I, Mao Yen-shou, am travelling all over the country with the emperor's order to search out beautiful maidens for the palace.
[After a couple of minutes in this vein, a girl named Zhaoqun comes on, incredibly, untouchably, magically beautiful in silk and perfect make-up. Gasps from the armoured front row.]

Zhaoqun: I am Wang Qian, also called Zhaoqun, a native of
          Zikui in Zhengdu. My father, the Elder Wang, has
          worked the land all his life. Before I was born . . .
          [She explains her circumstances: poor family, chosen to
          be a royal concubine at 18, gives offence, is hidden
          away. She's never seen the emperor, and she's sad.]
          . . . Now at night in my solitude, I shall try to play a
          song to while away the time.
          [Plays the lute. The Emperor enters.][3]

The Mongols may not get all the references, but their interpreter is working hard; they are smitten by the beauty of the
girl, they are spellbound by her singing, they hate the villain,
they know all about the emperor, their enemy, and they are
gripped by the story, which, as they will soon learn, is famous
in China. (Still is, actually: the best hotel in Hohhot, the
capital of Inner Mongolia, is named after its heroine.)
Everyone knows of how pretty little Zhaoqun is sent off
across the Great Wall to be the wife of the khan of the
Xiongnu in distant Mongolia. She mourns, she wishes she
were a gold swan flying home, she weeps: it's heartrending.

Something like this must have happened. In 1214–16
Genghis's great general Muqali swept across Manchuria
while Genghis himself was besieging Beijing. Two towns had
the temerity to hold out. As usual in these circumstances,
Muqali said, 'If we let these rebellious bandits live, there
will be nothing with which to admonish later generations.'
He slaughtered them all, except for artisans, craftsmen –
and *actors*.

The traditions were certainly rich enough to seduce the
Mongols. The Chinese had been watching dance shows,

[3] A little authorial licence here. These quotes are actually from a Yuan play, Ma
Zhi-yuan's *Autumn in the Han Palace*, but the story is much older. It is not
impossible that a version was in existence in Song times.

musicals, recitations, storytellings, pageants and variety shows for centuries; divergent traditions emerged in north and south, with a boom in drama under the Song. Archaeological evidence confirms that this was more than street entertainment. Tenth-century tomb-tiles unearthed in Henan in 1958 show actors in traditional dramatic roles, and in Shanxi excavations around 1970 revealed the remains of a brick-and-tile provincial theatre. Even in distant Manchuria, there were a company and a play and music and a leading girl to entertain the invaders. ·

Once in power, Kublai the arts patron made sure his people had theatre, lots of it. But he didn't want just the old stuff. He wanted new writing, designed to appeal to the Mongols and his very international court. That meant it would have to be easy to follow, because Kublai himself did not speak very good Chinese and was unfamiliar with high-flown Song literary traditions. This caused something of a revolution among the Song literati. They had contradictory attitudes towards the theatre, as did Restoration audiences in England. They loved it for its entertainment value, but plays were written in common language, actors were held in low regard and actresses were whores. In brief, from any point of view other than their own, the Song literati were appalling snobs. To create new drama would be prostituting their poetic skills. No-one thought of plays as literature; no-one thought of preserving them. As a result, very little survives from pre-Yuan times.

All this changed under Kublai. At court, there were two bureaux, one responsible for music and acting, the other for staging court rituals and plays. The customer called the tune, and, by comparison with his subjects, the customer had simple tastes. As one of the first translators of Yuan drama, Henry Hart, put it in slightly non-PC terms in 1936: 'Ignorant of literature and of the amenities of civilised life, philosophy and poetry, dainty dancing and soft music had no allure for them. Nurtured on the windswept deserts, exulting in battle and rapine . . . they preferred drama written and acted in the everyday language of common people.'

It was this demand that reinvigorated Chinese drama. Starting in and around Da-du, Kublai's newly built Beijing, a new breed of playwright emerged. Many of them were scholars frustrated by the ending of the examination system, and eager to supplement their meagre clerks' incomes, to win recognition and to find an outlet for their literary skills. They created (as one historian of Chinese drama, Chung-wen Shih, has written) a 'body of works qualitatively and quantitatively unequalled before or after in the Chinese theatre, and making Yuan drama one of the most brilliant genres in Chinese literary history'. This rich field has one disadvantage for the historian. The authors were still embarrassed to have their names associated with their products, so very little is known about them. Fortunately one playwright, Zhong Su-cheng, gathered biographical notes about Yuan writers in *A Register of Ghosts*, its very title a comment on the invisibility of its subjects. Of the 152 listed, 111 are dramatists.

Thousands of plays must have been written, of which some 700 are known by name and 150 have survived, perhaps because they are the best. They are of a type known as 'variety plays', or 'mixed entertainment' – what we would call musicals, except that, with the involvement of fine writers, they are much more than that. They examine contemporary concerns: oppression, injustice, corruption, struggles with authority. They do so in their own terms, of course, not in western ones. Set in a carefully ordered universe, the plays do not display the internal agonies and destructive passions common in western drama from Shakespeare onwards. Some flee the real world for timeless romance, like *The Romance of the Western Chamber*, which derives from a story first written down around 800. A student rescues a beautiful girl from rebels; he woos her; her fierce mother objects; a clever maid helps them; the mother is won round; happy ending. Rewritten several times, the story was turned into a famous drama by Wang Shifu, and has remained popular ever since. I bought a novelized version in Beijing in 2004.

As in Shakespeare, the themes are explored in historical contexts. They could not be set in the present, for fear of giving offence (though mild criticism was OK, if veiled, as one description of a royal command performance reveals: 'If there is any criticism . . . the actors cloak the case in a story to criticise with hidden import; thus no displeasure shadows the emperor's face'). This means that the plays are not time-bound. They try to do what drama should do, which is turn current concerns into timeless themes and present them as entertainments that now and then claim the literary high ground as well.

Let Guan Hanqing (Kuan Han-ch'ing) stand for all, because he was the most prolific of Yuan playwrights. Practically everything about his life is vague. Born by about 1240, he lived to a great age, dying some time before 1330. He wrote 63 or 64 musical plays (the authorship of one is disputed), of which 14 or 18 (another dispute) survive. Most of them are about love, its joys and agonies: love between courtesans and scholars, emperors and concubines, lovers of high and low status. Heroines were his forte. Eleven of the 14 extant plays have at their core strong, brave, determined women, none more so than the star of his best play, *The Injustice to Dou E.* She's a simple village girl, a young widow of 18. A coarse suitor wrongly accuses her of murder. She is dragged into court and beaten by a corrupt magistrate. When she refuses to confess, he threatens to beat her mother-in-law. To save her, Dou E makes a false confession and is condemned to death. On the eve of her execution, she makes three wishes, one of which is that the area should suffer with three years of drought. All her wishes come true, proving that Heaven has heard her prayers. The drought attracts the attention of her father, a high official, who reopens the case. Dou E reappears as a ghost to accuse her accusers. Justice is done, the universe rebalanced.

It was not the plot that made the play a classic, but its poetic language, which gave it an epic grandeur. Dou E is no ordinary girl. Chaste, obedient, self sacrificing, she is a Joan of Arc figure, a symbol of the suffering nation. When she is abused – as the Mongols abused China – the laws of heaven are overturned, corruption and stupidity rule. 'The good suffer poverty and short life,' she sings. 'The wicked enjoy wealth, nobility and long life.' But virtue cannot for ever be despised. Her death spurs Heaven to action, returning justice to an unjust world – great themes that have ensured the play's survival in several later versions, including one performed by the Peking Opera today.

Kublai brought to China a measure of stability and security unknown for centuries. Bearable levels of taxation, the rule of law, a positive, or at worst neutral, policy towards the arts, public works to aid the common good – you might say that he brought a level of happiness to his people. A tiny percentage, the elite – top Mongols, top Chinese officials, Muslim merchants – would have agreed. Would the 100 million less well off? We cannot possibly know, because happiness as we understand it only came to the fore in the eighteenth century. Recently it has emerged as a subject in its own right; now, on the basis of surveys, statistics and analyses, we can look back and argue a case. As Richard Layard points out in *Happiness: Lessons from a New Science*, one definition of happiness is the feeling that today is a little better than yesterday. The vast mass of people in thirteenth-century China started from a pretty low base. They would surely still have feared famine, disease and flood, the tax-man, the loan-shark, the official looking to press-gang men into forced labour; but they also knew that in the previous two generations millions had died and millions more had been driven from their homes, while at least from 1276 onwards they were at peace. They could work with more hope than previously that it would not all go to waste. No-one in medieval China argued that the purpose of government is to increase the sum of human happiness, but somehow Kublai and his officials, working to create stability, continuity and national wealth, managed to achieve, if not the greatest happiness for the greatest number, at least, for 25 or 30 years, a decrease in unhappiness.

IV

WINTER

13

KAMIKAZE

IN 1280, AFTER THE CONQUEST OF THE SOUTH, KUBLAI COULD turn again on Japan. He was now 65, and time was snapping at his heels. But it was more than his age that drove him. He acted like a man obsessed, both with the need to fulfil his grandfather's ambitions for world conquest and with the need to punish this 'little country' for its temerity in resisting him. For an emperor as raw as ever on the subject of his own legitimacy, he was, as always, determined to prove himself, as fast as possible.

Accounts of this campaign have, until recently, been dominated by the Japanese point of view, because they were the victors, and history belongs more to winners than to losers. The story has been often told: how the mighty Chinese fleet was about to crush the hapless, outmoded Japanese samurai when the heavens themselves came to the aid of the Japanese by unleashing a typhoon that swept Kublai's fleet to oblivion. Soon thereafter, the Japanese called the storm the Divine Wind, the *kamikaze* (*kami* also having the sense of 'god', 'spirit' and 'superior'), referring to it as proof that

Japan was under the protection of Heaven. This suited the ruling elite, whose power depended in part on faith in their ability to perform the correct religious rituals. It was to evoke the idea of heavenly protection that the suicide pilots of the Second World War were called *kamikazes*: they were a new Divine Wind that would ensure protection against foreign invasion. Until Japan's defeat in 1945, it was a comforting idea. Yet research since 2001 has revealed it to be a myth. After almost 800 years, it turns out that the Japanese were far more capable than they themselves believed. It was not the Divine Wind that saved them, but Mongol incompetence and Japanese fighting strength.

There was a bad smell about this operation from the beginning. Kublai was out of touch with reality. Like Hitler during the battle for Stalingrad, he seemed to believe that the mere decision to attack would inevitably lead to victory, as if will alone decided military matters. He overrated himself, underrated the opposition, made impossible demands, ignored logistical and command problems, and took no account of the weather, despite what had happened six years before.

To guarantee success, Kublai needed a bigger fleet than before to carry more land forces; and for that he needed the compliance of Korea, his unwilling vassal. But Korea had borne the brunt of the 1274 débâcle. Its grain had been commandeered and its young men drafted as shipbuilders and warriors, leaving only the old and the very young to till the fields. There was no harvest, and no manpower. For five years, Kublai had had to send food aid to keep Korea alive; it was in no condition to provide all the necessary ships. Most would have to come from the south, from the former Song empire and its unwilling inhabitants.

It would be simple, of course, if only Japan would

acknowledge his overlordship. In 1279 yet another embassy
arrived in Japan, with instructions to be extremely polite, in
order to avoid the fate of their predecessors. Unfortunately,
they arrived just at the moment when rumours were spreading fear across the land. A local beauty had vanished in
mysterious circumstances, supposedly abducted by a band of
Mongol spies who had made a base on an uninhabited rocky
islet. It was said their chief had fallen in love with the girl. A
Japanese force had invaded to rescue her. The chief had
dragged her to a cliff-top and threatened to kill her, but she
had cast herself into the sea and had swum to shore, while all
the Japanese were murdered by the Mongol spies. She alone
had survived to tell this dramatic tale. So the story went. It
may or may not have been true; in any event, the government
in Kamakura believed that the three-man delegation from
Kublai was part of the same plot. It didn't help the envoys'
case that Kublai had sent as a gift a golden cockerel engraved
with the insulting words: 'To Hojo Tokimune: I will appoint
thee King of Japan,' implying he would be happy to usurp the
emperor. The three were beheaded, and resolve strengthened.
Foot soldiers and cavalry massed on Kyushu. The barrier
around Hakata bay grew longer and higher, and defences
arose at other possible landing sites – Nagato on the southern
tip of the main island; Harima and Tsuruga, 400 kilometres
up the same coast. Japan braced itself for an assault that was
now seen as inevitable.

Kublai ordered that the fleet should be ready to invade in
little more than a year. If the figures are to be believed, it
would be the biggest fleet ever to set sail, and would remain
the biggest for over 700 years, until exceeded by the Allied
invasion of Normandy on 6 June (D-Day) 1944. It would
combine two forces, one from Korea with a Korean admiral
and the other from south China under a turncoat Chinese,
Fan Wen-hu – one of those who had defected to the Mongols
during their advance down the Yangtze in 1275 – with a

Mongol co-leader, Xin-du. They led a force of about 140,000. According to the *Yuan History*, the Koreans supplied 900 boats, with another 3,500 supposedly coming from the south. The pressure was too much for one area, Fukien (now Fujian), whose trade superintendent had been told to build 200 ships: this, he said, was impossible, and provided 50. The plan was for the troops to be transported in two fleets, 40,000 in the 900 ships from Korea, 100,000 in the 3,500 vessels from Quanzhou in Fukien. The two would link up at the island of Iki, 30 kilometres off the Japanese coast, and then invade the mainland together.

That was the plan. But there's something significant about these figures, which reveals that this plan was highly optimistic. Consider the number: 4,400 is an awful lot of ships, especially if they were warships, as accounts usually suggest. In fact, a little long division shows that this invasion was very unlike the Spanish Armada of 1588, which consisted of 130 massive warships, carrying 27,000 men, about 200 per ship. Kublai's fleet was more comparable to the Allied force that invaded Normandy in 1944: some 156,000 men in around 5,000 vessels (most of which were landing craft), which is 31 per vessel . . .

At which point we should pause and ask: are the figures about Kublai's fleet true? No-one has any idea, because there are no statistics other than the official sources. All estimates should be treated with extreme scepticism. But in this case they are not incredible. Kublai had access to huge numbers of ships that had been massed for the assault on Song down the Yangtze. Only a few years before, the official sources were speaking of a fleet of 3,000, and that was on the Yangtze alone. Since then, all Song, and all its remaining ships, had fallen to the Mongols. Look at it from another angle: Spain in 1588 could muster 27,000 men from a population of about 7 million: a proportion of 1 man-at-arms per 260 civilians. The population of thirteenth-century China was about 50 million.

Proportionally, China could have raised a naval force of 189,000, more than enough to justify the official figures.

If we accept that the southern force was indeed something like 140,000, the implication is clear. Except for a few massive warships, mainly from Korea, what we are dealing with here is a fleet of small landing craft. Now, Portsmouth to Normandy is a mere 170 kilometres, a six-hour crossing by engine-driven ships. When bad weather struck on 2 June, Eisenhower could afford to postpone the invasion by one day, and then order Go! in a 24-hour lull. Kublai would be relying on wind power and oars to propel his 900-strong Korean fleet over 200 kilometres and the 3,500 much smaller vessels from the south over a forbidding 1,400 kilometres. Even with a good wind in the right direction, it would take them six days to reach the rendezvous.

Obviously, Kublai and his commanders aimed to get the conquest over, and have the troops well inland, before the typhoon season started in August. But any experienced sailor would have known in his heart of hearts that it was crazy to plan on a fixed schedule of operations. Kublai, the supreme commander, knew a lot about warfare in large, open spaces, and was perfectly at home wheeling across the Inland Sea, as the Chinese called the gravel and grass of Inner Asia. But he had hardly ever glimpsed the real sea, let alone sailed it, let alone seen what a typhoon could do. Blinded by desperation and isolated by power, he was taking a fearful risk, and there was no-one to tell him the truth.

There were those who sensed trouble ahead. When Yuan officials learned that the Japanese emperor had prayed that the country be saved in exchange for his own life, they reported omens: Mongol soldiers waiting to make the crossing 'saw a great serpent appearing on the surface of the water, and the water smelled of sulphur'. But in Kublai's presence, mouths were buttoned.

*

Things went wrong from the start. The Korean fleet reached Iki as planned around the end of May, and waited . . . and waited. The southern fleet gathered in Quanzhou could not even start on time. A commander fell ill, and had to be replaced. Food rotted in the heat. Epidemics spread. Even when it did finally put to sea, contrary winds drove many ships into ports along the coast.

Eventually, on 10 June, the commander of the Korean fleet occupied Iki anyway; then, after waiting another two weeks, he crossed the small gap and made a landing just north of the Japanese wall at Munakata, only to be forced back to an island in the middle of the bay. He therefore had ample opportunity to recce Hakata bay and confirm the reports he would surely have had from other sources about the defensive wall; after all, it had been there for the past five years. He would have seen the difficulty of fighting his way off the beach, and seen a solution. The wall covered the beach, not the mountains at either end. Genghis had gone over mountains when he took the pass leading to Beijing in 1213. These mountains were nothing by comparison. The Mongols would simply force their way round the edge of the wall, and take it from the rear – the only problem being that they would be highly visible, and strongly opposed. They needed more troops. The Korean fleet could not do the job on its own.

Meanwhile the southern fleet, now a month behind schedule, went straight for the mainland, missing out on Iki and the rendezvous at sea, settling instead for the hilly little island of Takashima in Imari bay, 100 kilometres west of Hakata, the other side of a peninsula. Here they intended to regroup, replenish stores and mount the invasion proper. Now, Takashima will play an important role in this story, so let me introduce it. Takashima – Kite Island – is a pretty place, warm, fertile, famous for its blowfish: *fugu*, a delicacy that has to be carefully prepared because bits of it are deadly poisonous. Though most of its irregular coast offers only steep slopes and rocky bottoms, it has one small harbour where the sea-floor is muddy and shallow – good for holding the wood-and-stone Mongol anchors, with their granite cross-pieces and wooden flukes. Takashima had a few hundred inhabitants, peaceful farmers and fisherfolk utterly unable to resist the Mongol invasion. In a few days, all were slaughtered, right down (so the story goes) to the last family, whose hiding place was revealed by their cockerels. The sole survivor was one old lady who lived to tell the tale. Even today, I was assured, the people of Takashima do not keep cockerels.

It was not a good plan. Takashima is only a kilometre off-shore, but the coast here is steep and backed by forested mountains, ideal for guerrilla warfare. Away from Hakata bay, landing places were few, and at every undefended place Japanese cavalry soon arrived to isolate the soldiers and force the ships back out to sea; all they could do was set up a few useless camps on outlying islands. The Japanese also took the fight out from the shore, rowing nimble little skiffs out at night to cut cables, sneak aboard, cut throats and start fires. True, from the larger ships, siege bows acted like artillery, firing massive arrows that could splinter a Japanese dinghy. But the traction trebuchets which might have been effective inshore against land forces were useless when trying to hit moving targets from moving decks. Kublai's generals bickered in three languages and the greater part of their troops – the Chinese and Koreans – had no heart to fight for their new Mongol masters. The Japanese, with a unified command and years of preparation on home territory behind them, had well-fortified positions from which to stave off assaults and mount counter-attacks.

From the Mongol point of view, the Japanese were every-where, in huge numbers, well able to cover the 20-kilometre length of the wall and beyond, galloping back and forth to congregate wherever a landing threatened. One Yuan source later claimed there were 102,000 of them. But Mongol and Chinese officials were recording a catastrophic defeat and had every reason to exaggerate the strength of the opposition to provide an excuse for failure. Besides, numbers of troops were always, notoriously, exaggerated, sometimes by a factor of ten. A twelfth-century courtier had his servants count an army estimated at 10,000, and found the true number of troops to be 1,080.[1] In this case, historians have made estimates based on duty reports and other documents, which have survived in considerable numbers. The result of two such surveys overlap, with lows of 2,300 and 3,600, highs of 5,700 and 6,000. Now, these figures are based on surviving written sources; many others must have gone missing, and the estimates must be too low. From a population of something like 5 million, the Japanese commanders would surely have been able to muster men in the same proportion as the Spanish in 1588 or indeed their current Mongol and Chinese enemies, which would suggest a force in the order of 20,000 – making about one defender per metre of wall.

There were enough, in any event, to hold back the Mongols, Chinese and Koreans, whose huge superiority in numbers was negated by the difficulty of mounting a joint sea-and-land operation so far from home and by their being hopelessly scattered.

For almost two months, from 23 June to 14 August, the two sides skirmished, reaching no conclusion. The wall was never even tested in battle. The sight of it was enough to put off the Korean fleet, and the joint force never had a chance to approach.

*

[1] William Wayne Farris, *Heavenly Warriors: The Evolution of Japan's Military, 500–1300*, quoted in Thomas D. Conlan (trans. and interpretive essay), *In Little Need of Divine Intervention: Scrolls of the Mongol Invasions of Japan*.

Among those eager to fight was Takezaki Suenaga, whose story continues in the Invasion Scrolls. Suenaga arrives on his horse in full regalia as warriors take up position behind the wall (which appears in one of the illustrations, looking much as its restored sections do today). The enemy are all out at sea. He's desperate to get at them.

'I cannot fight them during this crisis without a ship!'

Gota Goro, his commander, replies: 'If you don't have a ship there's nothing to be done.'

But another *gokenin*, from Hizen – 'I forget his name' – says: 'Let's find a good ship among the damaged craft in the harbour and drive off the pirates!'

'That's right,' Suenaga replies. 'Those troops would be infantry and their boats would be seaworthy craft. I want to cut down at least one of the enemy!'

Suenaga and two companions search for a boat. No luck. As they are on the point of giving up hope, a Japanese war-boat comes by. These war-boats are not impressive: about 8 metres long, riding low in the water, holding no more than ten or eleven people, half of whom are rowers. They are handy for use in the bay, but would be hopeless on the open sea. Gota Goro recognizes this one as belonging to Adachi Yasumori, a senior official, and sends Suenaga and his friends off as messengers. They board a messenger's skiff and row out to the larger vessel. Standing precariously at the bow, Suenaga yells that he has orders to get on board the next boat and fight. Then, without waiting for permission, he jumps aboard.

The captain, Kotabe, is outraged. 'This is the summoned boat [of Adachi]! Only members of his forces can board it! Stay off this boat!'

Suenaga argues. 'In this vital matter I want to aid my lord. Since I just got on the boat, I am not going to get off and wait for another that may never arrive.'

He makes no impression on the captain. 'It is an outrage

for you not to leave a boat when you have been ordered to disembark.'

Suenaga unhappily climbs back into his skiff, and he and his companions row onwards. Another war-boat comes by, this one belonging to an official called Takamasa. Suenaga brings his skiff alongside, though the effort makes him remove his helmet, which gets lost in the chaos. This time Suenaga takes no chances. He comes out with a barefaced lie.

'I am acting on secret orders. Let me on the boat.'

Shouts come from Takamasa's boat: 'You have no orders! Get out of here! There's no room for all of you!'

Suenaga is utterly shameless. Now he tries another tack. 'Since I am a warrior of considerable stature,' he boasts, 'let me alone get on your boat.'

That does the trick. 'We are heading off for battle,' comes the exasperated reply. 'Why must you make such a fuss to Takamasa? Get on!'

He does so, grabbing the shin-guards of one of his companions as a make-shift helmet. Shouts of complaint from the skiff below. But Suenaga ignores them. 'The way of the bow and arrow is to do what is worthy of reward,' he says in the commentary. 'Without even a single follower I set off to engage the enemy.'

He starts to offer advice to Takamasa himself. 'The enemy won't give up until we board them. We have to use grappling-hooks. Once we have them hooked, stab them by impaling them where there is a joint in their armour.' But Takamasa's crew are not properly armed. Nor, come to think of it, is Suenaga. He spots a retainer who has just taken off his helmet, a nice one, braided with yellow and white cords decorated with small cherry blossoms.

'Give me your helmet,' Suenaga says, rather abruptly.

'Sorry. I have a wife and children. What of them if I get killed because of you?'

'Give it to me!'

'Sorry, no. Only I or my lord wears this helmet.'

Suenaga accepts, with pretty bad grace, and prepares for action, making do with his shin-guard helmet and throwing away some of his arrows to lighten his load.

Now the pictures take over. Somehow, Suenaga and five companions have found another punt-like skiff and attacked a Mongol ship, one of the small vessels, only about 10 metres long, with seven Mongol crew and a couple of Chinese officers – hardly the sort of boat to cross a few hundred kilometres of open ocean. Suenaga is first on board, in the bow already. One officer lies dead, his throat cut, and our hero is busy slitting the other's, gripping him by his pigtail, even as his companions are storming the stern. Shortly the boat will be theirs, because a later illustration shows Suenaga with his two heads.

That's the action he wishes to record. Somehow, he returns to shore with his trophy-heads. He reports his deeds to his commander, Gota Goro, whose disapproval at Suenaga's wilfulness is overwhelmed by admiration. 'Without your own boat, you repeatedly lied in order to join the fray. You really are the *baddest* man around!'

On 15 August nature stepped in, with rather more than the 'reverse wind' of 1274. The first typhoon of the season approached, earlier than usual. Nowadays, when tropical cyclones – hurricanes in the Atlantic, typhoons in the Pacific – are named and tracked, their destructive power is a commonplace of news programmes. But to see news footage is not the same as feeling the force. There's no telling whether this particular typhoon ranked as a mere No. 1 on the Saffir–Simpson Scale ('74–95 mph/119–153 kph. Damage limited to foliage, signage, unanchored boats and mobile homes') or a No. 5 super-typhoon ('winds of over 150 mph/249 kph. Complete roof failure . . . catastrophic storm surge damage'). To sailors in small boats, it wouldn't make much difference.

Joseph Conrad, a China hand in his youth, lived through one of these storms, and there is no better evocation of what it is like than his *Typhoon*. Here the storm strikes the *Nan-Shan*, with the stolid Macwhirr as captain, and young Jukes as first mate:

A faint burst of lightning quivered all round, as if flashed into a cavern – into a black and secret chamber of the sea, with a floor of foaming crests.

It unveiled for a sinister, fluttering moment a ragged mass of clouds hanging low, the lurch of the long outlines of the ship, the black figures of men caught on the bridge, heads forward, as if petrified in the act of butting. The darkness palpitated down upon all this, and then the real thing came at last.

It was something formidable and swift, like the sudden smashing of a vial of wrath. It seemed to explode all round the ship with an overpowering concussion and a rush of great waters, as if an immense dam had been blown up to windward. In an instant the men lost touch of each other. This is the disintegrating power of a great wind: it isolates one from one's kind. An earthquake, a landslip, an avalanche, overtake a man incidentally, as it were – without passion. A furious gale attacks him like a personal enemy, tries to grasp his limbs, fastens upon his mind, seeks to rout his very spirit out of him.

Jukes was driven away from his commander . . . The rain poured on him, flowed, drove in sheets. He breathed in gasps; and sometimes the water he swallowed was fresh and sometimes it was salt. For the most part he kept his eyes shut tight, as if suspecting his sight might be destroyed in the immense flurry of the elements . . . After a crushing thump on his back he found himself suddenly afloat and borne upwards. His first irresistible notion was that the whole China Sea had climbed on the bridge. Then, more sanely, he concluded himself gone overboard. All the time he was being tossed, flung, and rolled in great volumes of water, he kept on repeating mentally, with the utmost precipitation, the words: 'My God! My God! My God! My God!' . . .

The motion of the ship was extravagant. Her lurches had an appalling helplessness: she pitched as if taking a header into a void, and seemed to find a wall to hit every time. When she rolled she fell on her side headlong, and she would be righted back by such a demolishing blow that Jukes felt her reeling as a clubbed man reels before he collapses. The gale howled and scuffled about gigantically in the darkness, as though the entire world were one black gully. At certain moments the air streamed against the ship as if sucked through a tunnel with a concentrated solid force of impact that seemed to lift her clean out of the water and keep her up for an instant with only a quiver running through her from end to end. And then she would begin her tumbling again as if dropped back into a boiling cauldron . . .

The sea, flattened down in the heavier gusts, would uprise and overwhelm both ends of the *Nan-Shan* in snowy rushes of foam, expanding wide, beyond both rails, into the night. And on this dazzling sheet, spread under the blackness of the clouds and emitting a bluish glow, Captain MacWhirr could catch a desolate glimpse of a few tiny specks black as ebony, the tops of the hatches, the battened companions, the heads of the covered winches, the foot of a mast. This was all he could see of his ship. Her middle structure, covered by the bridge which bore him, his mate, the closed wheelhouse where a man was steering shut up with the fear of being swept overboard together with the whole thing in one great crash – her middle structure was like a half-tide rock awash upon a coast. It was like an outlying rock with the water boiling up, streaming over, pouring off, beating round – like a rock in the surf to which shipwrecked people cling before they let go – only it rose, it sank, it rolled continuously, without respite and rest, like a rock that should have miraculously struck adrift from a coast and gone wallowing upon the sea.

The *Nan-Shan* was being looted by the storm with a senseless, destructive fury: trysails torn out of the extra gaskets, double-lashed awnings blown away, bridge swept clean, weather-cloths burst, rails twisted, light-screens smashed – and two of the boats had gone already. They had gone unheard and unseen, melting, as it were, in the shock and smother of the wave.

Now imagine that striking wooden sailing ships: not just the warships, which would have been built for storms, but the 3,000 or more little 20- or 30-man craft that came from the south. The Korean sailors knew what was coming. Their admiral ordered his fleet out to sea to avoid being dashed on the rocks. Those who could boarded in order not to be stranded ashore. Many were still clambering aboard or struggling through the shallows when the storm struck. Some 15,000 of the northern force and 50,000 of the southerners died at sea, while hundreds of others perished at Japanese hands, or were tossed to their deaths in the small boats that had remained near the rocky shore.

It was a catastrophe never matched in scale on a single day at sea before or since, and never on land either until the atom bomb destroyed Hiroshima, killing 75,000 at a single blow, in 1945.

No wonder the Japanese soon saw it as an act of the gods, and adopted the idea of divine protection from then on. Both court and military authorities prayed assiduously to keep foreigners at bay. Temples and shrines flourished. Even Suenaga, whose élan had been so evident, ascribed his success as 'a man of the bow and arrow' to the gods. Not that prayer was the only defence, for the wall was maintained and manned constantly for the next 30 years, as a result of which some of it has lasted pretty well to the present day. But the idea of divine intervention became rooted in Japanese culture. Few questioned the conclusion: that Japan had been saved by a divinely ordained typhoon.

Yet there is growing evidence that this was not so; that in reality Japan's salvation was down to the Japanese themselves. It is there in Suenaga's story. Look at his fighting spirit. He's brave, eager to take a risk, but well in control of himself. Although the epitome of the Japanese warrior, he's one among many. There's a terrific sense of common purpose. And it works. He's on the winning side. There's the usual chaos of war, no overall strategy, but all these unco-ordinated actions by individuals are enough to hold back the enemy and take the action to them, out in the bay. Crucially, there is no mention of the typhoon at all. In the Invasion Scrolls, success is down to the Japanese fighters. Suenaga shows respect to the gods with prayers, but there is no hint in either the written account or the pictures that Heaven actually intervenes during or after the action.

Text and pictures together show that, as Conlan puts it, 'the notion of the "divine winds" represented a function of the medieval mindset, which emphasised otherworldly causality, rather than a caustic commentary on the ineptitude of the Japanese defenders, as has commonly been assumed'. He concludes: 'The warriors of Japan were capable of fighting the Mongols to a standstill.' Suenaga and his fellow-fighters were, in the words of Conlan's title, in little need of divine intervention.

Further support comes from marine archaeologists as they try to answer the question: What happened to the armada? Understandably, this is not a subject on which the Chinese records have much to say. The flagship, bearing the admiral, Fan Wen-hu, and a general, Chang Xi, was wrecked on

Takashima. The two mustered other survivors, a couple of thousand of them, who raided the houses and farms of the slaughtered locals for food and repaired one of the wrecks, in which the admiral limped home. The others were mopped up by Japanese, some 1,500 being taken away into slavery. Three were allowed to return, to tell Kublai of the fate of his great armada and its all-conquering army. As for the rest of the fleet, it seemed to have vanished from history and into the belly of the ocean.

Not quite. The story of the victory over the Mongols became part of the Japanese nationalist revival in the 1930s; that was when restoration work first started on the wall around Hakata bay. After the war, a Tokyo University archaeologist, Torao Mozai, began wondering about Kublai's fleet. In the bay, fishermen had found a few anchor-stocks – the great stone cross-pieces that weighed down the anchors and twisted them into the correct position – but these might have come from any one of uncounted ships that had sunk over the centuries. In 1980 he decided to focus on Takashima, where the southern fleet had set up a base, and where it may therefore have sought anchorage to ride out the typhoon. Fishermen showed Mozai a few enigmatic bits of pottery they had found over the years.

Then, suddenly, hard evidence. In 1974 a fisherman, alerted by Mozai's interest, produced something he had dragged up with his clams off the pretty little south-facing harbour of Kazaki: a small square of bronze with a handle on the back and writing engraved on the front in the script devised by Kublai's Tibetan mentor, Phags-pa. It was in Chinese, and it read: 'Seal of Commander of One Thousand'. A Chinese character on the top indicated it was made in 1277. No doubt about it: the remains of one of Kublai's senior officers lay in these murky shallows – and so, probably, did those of his ship. (This little object has since become an iconic symbol of the event and the archaeological research, reproduced in brochures and replicas. The original is in Fukuoka's Kyushu National Museum, which opened in October 2005.)

Inspired, Mozai established a research programme, surveying the sea-bed with sonar and sending down divers. In the mud they found swords, spearheads, stone hand-mills for grinding rice, more anchor-stocks and round stone catapult balls: direct proof that the Mongols had catapults on board.

But Mozai was operating on a shoe-string. His finds were dramatic enough to win backing from the *National Geographic* magazine (see bibliography), but the research needed to be put on a sound, long-term, professional basis. Enter Kenzo Hayashida, newly returned from doing an MA in archaeology – bronze age Greece, of all things – at the University of Pennsylvania. There was no opening in southern Japan for a specialist in Greek archaeology; but there, right on his doorstep, was the possibility of solving one of the great mysteries of Japanese and Chinese history. He joined Mozai in 1981, inherited his role and committed himself to Takashima's silty waters, underpinning his research by working with the local education board and Fukuoka's university. In 1986 he founded the Kyushu and Okinawa Society of Underwater Archaeology, which reports annually on the findings made by him and his team of a dozen volunteer divers.

With a gentle voice and restrained manner, Hayashida has an aura of wisdom. From his half-closed eyelids and rapid blink, I thought at first he was just sleepy. Not so. First impressions gave way before his obvious intelligence and dedication. In English, through which he felt his way with care, as if along a track overgrown after 25 years back in Japan, he guided me through his work, his laboratory on Takashima and the island itself.

Everything about his researches has its problems. First – inexplicably for an island nation – Japan has no tradition, and no single university department, of marine archaeology. Funding is tight. A research project of this significance, now with its own museum, should attract an income from tourists. But – and this is the second problem – Takashima is remote, served by a charming ferry which takes 10 minutes to make the crossing. Though it will soon have a bridge, now half-completed, the island will always be out on a limb, off any tourist route. Third, conditions down in Imari bay are appalling. The bottom is several metres of mud, which swirls up at every touch, quickly reducing vision to zero, forcing a retreat until the waters clear. This is tough, expensive work.

Much of what Hayashida has on Takashima – the museum and his laboratory – he owes to a dramatic find made in 1994, 50 metres or so out from shore: first, two huge granite anchor-stocks, each 1.5 metres long and 300 kilos in weight; then the wooden anchor itself, making a massive 7-metre object weighing a tonne. Even more significant were its ropes: they were made from bamboo, they were intact, and they lay due north across the ocean floor. Further research showed that the granite came from southern China; and carbon-14 dating revealed that the anchor's oak had been cut some time before the 1281 invasion. It was not much of a leap to conclude that this was the anchor of a large Mongol vessel, some 300–400 tonnes, that had been forced northward by the typhoon and sunk, along (presumably) with its commander and his bronze seal of office. But where was the ship itself? And where were all the others?

Tantalizing finds emerged from the gloop, including massive, worm-eaten bits of bulkheads, the cross-pieces that divide large ships into watertight compartments. One of these is 7 metres long, which means the mother-ship was at least that much across – at least, because there is no way of telling which part of the bulkhead it came from, whether at the top or halfway down in the ship's hold. Anyway, this was a big ship: at least 70 metres long, dwarfing anything else in the world. European sailing ships would not approach anything like this size until the nineteenth century. Henry V's *Grace*

Dieu, the largest ship of the early fifteenth century, was paltry by comparison: 38 metres from stem to stern. Nelson's flagship *Victory* was 57 metres long, slightly exceeded by her Spanish and French equivalents. Only as the age of steam approached did the last western sailing ships exceed the dimensions of these Chinese and Korean men-o'-war.

But size was no defence against the typhoon. Perhaps the doomed commander had anchored here, in the lee of a southerly shore, in the hope that the typhoon, swirling anti-clockwise, would head past over land, delivering a glancing blow from the north. In the event, as the mooring-rope revealed, the eye of the typhoon was out at sea, and the blow came from the south, head-on across Imari bay.

Other finds followed, by the hundred, and all of them were brought to Hayashida's laboratory for cleaning. One of the most significant are six of the thundercrash bombs – *tetsahu*, 'iron bombs', as they are known in Japanese, despite the fact that they are ceramic, not iron. Some were even nastier than they looked: one, when X-rayed, was found to be filled with over a dozen metal fragments that would have made extremely effective shrapnel – direct proof that Suenaga and his friends could indeed have been bombarded with thunder-crash bombs in 1274. I was the only person in Hayashida's museum that day, so an assistant opened a cupboard and handed me a couple of *tetsahus*. They made me nervous. I had been wondering about Suenaga and his narrow escape from death for months, and here I was holding the breakable, bar-nacle-encrusted, melon-sized devices that proved the account of the incident was true. What if, for some unfathomable reason, I dropped them? I was happy to hold them, happier to return them.

Next door, in the lab, Hayashida's staff of four minister to almost 4,000 bits, most of them lying in hundreds of tupper-ware containers of fresh water, where they stay for months and sometimes years until clear of all sea-water. Big tanks hold the bulkheads, little ones bits of pottery, scraps of metal, slivers of wood, bowls, even bones. On one side lie anchor-stocks, some so small they would have held mere dinghies. The prize, the one-tonne giant, is in a sealed container the job of which is to impregnate it with a preservative, polyethylene glycol (PEG). It's a painfully slow process that will take a year or two more.

The curator, Akiko Matsu, a round, bustling, enthusiastic woman, showed off some of her favourite finds: a fine celadon bowl, a helmet, a sword, a bundle of arrow-shafts, bits of a bow and a crossbow – and then, carefully packed in cotton-wool, human skulls.

'This one belonged to a young man,' said Hayashida. 'You see how the sea-water erodes the calcium. But we know from its development that he was about twenty. And here, this is from an older man. Look at his teeth. These are the molars. He was in good shape, no cavities at all.'

It is too early to make sense of these finds. They are just a few pieces in a giant jigsaw created by the typhoon, and every typhoon since. What happened then and since has been like tossing 4,000 eggs into a giant blender, then scattering them over mud, then pouring more mud on the top, then trying to make sense of the mess. Four thousand ships! That's millions of bits, most of them scattered – presumably – across the floor of Imari bay. And only 100 or so are ready for display. Hayashida is still right at the beginning, hoping for some other find that will inspire in others a passion to match his own, and allow the research to continue.

Yet it is not too early to point to some tentative con-clusions. Of the pots, almost all are Chinese, not Korean, many of them from the long-established kilns at Yixing in Jiangsu. Indeed, of all the objects, a mere 20 or so are Korean – convincing evidence that the Chinese fleet bore the brunt of the damage.

How come?

What really matters for ocean-going vessels is construction. And here, it seems, there was a good deal of corner-cutting. One of Hayashida's associates, Randall Sasaki, of Texas A&M University, College Station, who has made a study of the 500 or so timber fragments, was surprised to find nail-holes that were suspiciously close together, grouped as if the builders were re-using old timbers.

There's more, from Hayashida. He showed me a square piece of timber with two holes in it. 'It's a mast-step, the bit of wood on which the mast stood, strengthened by two supports which went in these holes. But look: the holes are off-centre. This mast-step was made by someone who didn't know what he was doing.' And, as a final thought, he added: 'You know what is really odd, I think? So far, we have found no evidence of sea-going, V-shaped keels.'

These pieces of evidence, combined with the catastrophic loss of at least one large vessel that should have been able to ride out a typhoon, suggest a startling but logical conclusion: in response to Kublai's insane demands for mass building at high speed, his naval craftsmen improvised. They took any ships available, seaworthy or not. The good ones they put into service; the poor ones they refashioned with the same materials. Except for the new ones built by the Koreans – none of which have yet been found – the vast majority of the invaders' vessels were keel-less river-boats, utterly unsuited to the high seas. Hayashida also wonders about another possibility suggested by the use of bad timbers and poor construction: was opposition to Kublai's plan so strong that workers actually engaged in sabotage? In any event, Kublai's ambitions led inexorably to a massive failure of quality control. I can almost hear the specious words of overseers by the dozen, all proudly stating that orders had been fulfilled, that the boats were all ready. No-one told the emperor that if things got rough, these boats would be death-traps.

Only about 0.5 per cent of the 1.5-square-kilometre site off

Takashima has been searched, let alone the rest of Imari bay. There's surely a lot more still to find, and I would take a bet the finds will reveal more evidence of Mongol-Chinese inadequacy, backing Conlan's point that the Japanese had no need of divine intervention.

True, it was the storm that finally did for the Mongol fleet. True, the ships were poorly built, the strategy flawed. But it was Japanese resistance that denied the Mongols a beachhead. What Kublai needed was a D-Day-style landing: 100,000 troops ashore, then all the equipment – horses, catapults, siege bows and more horses – and a push inland. Instead, the spirited Japanese response delayed landings, while some, like Suenaga, took the battle to the enemy out in the bay, forcing a stalemate which the Mongols showed no sign of breaking.

Was this a campaign Kublai could have won? Frankly, I doubt it. At best, with both fleets acting together, the result was always going to be a close-run thing. Certainly, once the southern fleet got behind schedule, the Mongols were on their way to defeat, victims of the complexity and size of the operation, internal opposition, incompetence and the fog of war. They were a long way from any base, with no back-up. As days stretched into weeks, they would have been running low on food, water and ammunition. Death or dishonourable retreat would have been the only options. The typhoon did not turn the course of the battle; it substituted a quick end for a long-drawn-out collapse. Kublai, with his insane ambitions, had in effect scuppered his own fleet before it set out.

14

MONEY, MADNESS AND A MURDER

THERE'S NOTHING LIKE A MURDER TO REVEAL HIDDEN EMOTIONS. There's nothing like an assassination to reveal a government's faults.

This story shows the beating heart of Kublai's admin-istration. He had created a monster with a prodigious appetite for men, materials and money, and it had to be kept fed. One man seemed to have the secret, and for Kublai that was a good enough reason to ignore the hatred that spread like a plague around his power-obsessed and deeply repellent minister. For 20 years he allowed disaster to ferment, until it cooked up a melodrama more sensational than any fictional thriller, involving a suicidal fanatic, a mad monk, a farcical plot and the murder of the man at the centre of the seething brew. No wonder Marco Polo jumped on the story. But he didn't know the half of it.

The villain of the piece was Ahmad, an Uzbek (as we would now call him) from Banakat, a few kilometres south-west of

Tashkent on the Syrdar'ya. The town was taken by Genghis at the start of his invasion of the Muslim world in 1220, the Mongols slaughtering the garrison and carrying off 'the artisans and a body of youths for siege works'.[1] That must have been about the time he was born. Perhaps his mother was captured along with the young men, because as a boy Ahmad was in the entourage of Chabi; after her marriage in 1239 to Kublai, then a prince of 24, he graduated to Kublai's household, helping with finances and military expenditures, and in this milieu he developed, in the words of his biographer Herbert Franke, a 'relentless craving for total control over government finances'.

When Kublai was enthroned in 1260, Ahmad became responsible for requisitioning provisions for the court. Driven by ambition, he rose fast. The next year he had two jobs, a senior position in the Secretariat and another as transport commissioner. He hated supervision – always a bad sign in an administrator – and asked to be made directly answerable to Kublai himself. His Chinese boss, one of the scholars who had joined Kublai when Jin fell in 1234, was a stickler for doing things through the proper channels. He objected and Kublai agreed, giving his son and heir Zhenjin (Jingim in another spelling) jurisdiction over the Secretariat. It was the first of many such attempts by Ahmad to gain ever more power, the first of many confrontations with his colleagues, and the start of a long-running feud with Zhenjin.

Ahmad's job within the Secretariat was to increase government income, and he was never short of ideas. What if the production of iron tools in government-owned smelting works could be raised, so that the tools could be given to

[1] W. Barthold, *Turkestan Down to the Mongol Invasion*. The rest of this chapter is based on Franke's biography in Igor de Rachewiltz et al., *In the Service of the Khan: Eminent Personalities of the Early Mongol–Yüan Era (1200–1300)*.

farmers in exchange for grain? That would increase grain reserves. What about a sales tax on silver transactions? Then merchants coming into the capital would have to produce a tax receipt. If they couldn't, they would be prosecuted for tax evasion, and have to pay a fine. What about cancelling tax exemptions for monks? And penalizing the salt-producers of Shanxi, whose cheap, low-quality stuff undercut the government's salt?

Kublai loved the result, and Ahmad prospered with a portfolio of jobs. His growing power was matched by his arrogance, and his arrogance by his unpopularity. When his bodyguards started a brawl, one of Kublai's Uighur advisers, Lien Xixian, had him prosecuted and actually beaten. It was not exactly routine, but in a world of rough-and-ready justice it was soon forgotten, and it didn't stop him. What did it matter to him if he was unpopular? Most foreign officials were, as Marco Polo recorded: 'For you should know that all Cathayans [northern Chinese] detested the Great Kaan's rule because he set over them governors who were Tartars, Saracens, or Christians who were attached to his household and devoted to his service, and were foreigners in Cathay.'

In 1266, Ahmad struck gold as head of a new Office for Regulating State Expenditure. To squeeze the last drop out of every available resource, he complained about the quality of linen here, or gold ingots there. He examined schemes for making non-flammable cloth from asbestos, and for exploiting a new silver mine better by smelting some tin from its ore. He wondered how to improve the grain supply to the troops fighting Ariq. He made sure that the empire's tax base was sound: in 1261 north China had 1.4 million tax-paying households; by 1274 it had almost two million.

Disputes around him continued: over his attempt to establish another government department to outflank the Secretariat, and over his objections to the new auditing office, the Censorate. 'Why should we have a Censorate?' he said.

'There's no reason as long as the money and grain come in!' He lost both battles, but shrugged off the outcomes as temporary setbacks. In 1270 he got his department – of State Affairs, the fourth of the great pillars of government, along with the Secretariat, the Bureau of Military Affairs and the Censorate – and also the directorship of political affairs in the Secretariat: both against the advice of senior officials, but in Kublai's eyes he had the magic touch and could do no wrong.

Then, inevitably, came another battle. Ahmad wanted the sole right to appoint his own people, undercutting the role of the Ministry of Personnel, which was controlled by the Secretariat. He appealed to Kublai, who changed the rules for him. But there was no satisfying him. Now he proposed disbanding the Secretariat itself. When two members of his own staff opposed this, he had one demoted, the other fired. In 1272 he succeeded in merging the two councils, with himself as number one, making him Kublai's top official. He had his eldest son Husain made mayor of Beijing. All complaints – there were several attempts to impeach him – were sidelined by Kublai, because nothing was allowed to get in the way of mobilizing resources to fight the Song.

When victory over Song seemed assured, Ahmad was part of the team summoned to advise on how best to exploit the new conquest. One point at issue was whether Song paper currency should be replaced by the Yuan currency. Bayan, the much-lionized commander of the southern forces, had promised there would be no change. Half Kublai's advisers agreed, arguing that such a change would undermine the new regime's credibility among the common people. The others disagreed, probably on the say-so of Ahmad, who saw profit in making the changeover. Kublai had the casting vote and went with Ahmad. The unfortunate southerners were offered a derisory exchange rate: one Yuan note for 50 Song ones.

Now Ahmad was almost supreme, having raised himself above the carefully balanced and frustrating system of

Chinese government and made himself into a Middle Eastern vizier. Luckily for him, around this time several of Kublai's eminent advisers from before his enthronement died of natural causes, among them Liu Bingzhong and Yao Shu. He declared state monopolies on salt, medicinal herbs, copper tools and the sale of iron, which enabled him to manipulate their prices, on which he was able to capitalize. Another of his sons became governor of the southern capital, Hangzhou. He set up transport bureaux in each of the eleven provinces, nominating Muslims to head five of them – a slap in the face for his Chinese colleagues. He had his greatest rival, the Grand Councillor Hantum, sent off with Kublai's son Nomukhan to help put down Kaidu's rebellion in Central Asia, where both vanished for ten years as prisoners of the Golden Horde. Other critics were demoted or thrown into prison, where many died or were executed; some simply vanished, disposed of in sadistic ways, as a grisly find made after his death would suggest.

Ahmad might have got away with ruthlessness, even brutality. Corruption was another matter. He was eternally, fatally acquisitive, proposing through his associates that a property here, a jewel there, or a beautiful horse for his stud would oil the way to this or that appointment. He had a particular eye for women. In Polo's words, 'Whenever he knew of any one who had a pretty daughter, certain ruffians of his would go to the father and say, "What say you? Here is this pretty daughter of yours; give her in marriage [to Ahmad], and we will arrange for his giving such a government or such an office."' All told, according to the Persian historian Rashid ad-Din, he acquired 40 wives and 400 concubines. After his death, when his possessions were listed, he was found to have 3,758 horses, camels, oxen, sheep and donkeys.

Ahmad even took against the great Bayan, old Hundred Eyes, the conqueror of the south. When Bayan arrived to celebrate victory in Beijing, Ahmad made sure he was the first to greet him. Bayan gave him as a personal gift a jade belt-buckle, jade being Heaven's own stone, a symbol of nobility, beauty and purity. He pointed out that it was all he had, because he would not take anything from the Song treasures. This Ahmad took as a veiled criticism of his own sharp practices. He denounced Bayan to Kublai, once for stealing a jade cup, a second time for slaughtering some soldiers who had surrendered. After an examination – grossly humiliating to so eminent a general – both charges were found to be groundless.

Still Kublai remained in thrall to Ahmad's financial acumen, drive, self-confidence and plausibility. Actually, Kublai's behaviour is exactly what you would expect from a political leader. Any prime minister or president today, when confronted by scandal swirling around one of his ministers, will at once declare his full confidence in the minister concerned. On no account must anything be said publicly to give the impression of weakness or poor judgement. Only when meltdown is imminent does the leader accept the inevitable. Kublai clearly thought that he had a grip on events, that he could go on ignoring Ahmad's vices while profiting from his financial wizardry, what with the invasions of Japan and other upcoming foreign adventures to pay for.

In fact, events were about to explode out of anyone's control. A groundswell of opposition was gaining momentum. One former military officer named Zui Pin, a distinguished veteran of the Song campaign and now a senior provincial official, wrote a memo complaining that Ahmad had been empire-building by setting up 200 unnecessary government offices and appointing friends and relatives – some 700 of them, as it later emerged – to posts across the empire. Reluctantly, Kublai authorized action, and relatives were dismissed; but only to be quietly reinstated, Ahmad's Husain among them. Ahmad had his revenge, accusing Zui

Pin and two colleagues of stealing grain and making un-authorized bronze seals. All three were executed in 1280.

But Ahmad had one enemy who was not so easy to handle. Kublai's son and heir Zhenjin absolutely loathed him, his existing antipathy only exacerbated by his admiration for Zui Pin: he had sent officers to save him from execution, but they arrived too late. In Ahmad's presence he tended to lose his temper. Once he punched Ahmad in the face so hard the minister couldn't open his mouth. When Kublai asked what the matter was, Ahmad muttered through clenched teeth that he had fallen off his horse. Another time, he lashed out at Ahmad in the emperor's presence, an outburst that Kublai simply ignored. Ahmad tried to gain some degree of control by proposing he set up a high court of justice that would have authority over all the princes. This was too much even for Kublai. He issued a mild rebuke, saying that he had never heard of anyone trying to censure the imperial clan.

In 1281, more scandals brought matters to a head. Two of Ahmad's protégés almost tripled the taxes in a district in Shaanxi province, from 950,000 to 2,700,000 strings of cash. An old member of the Imperial Guard wrote yet another letter condemning Ahmad for corruption and bribery, for which Ahmad had him sent off to run a provincial iron foundry. Accused of failing to fulfil his quota, he was demoted to the level of clerk; finally his property was confiscated and he was thrown in prison.

And still Kublai trusted him. Indeed, the next spring the emperor promoted him to the rank of Left Chancellor, leaving only the Right Chancellor above him in the official government hierarchy. The dreadful possibility arose that if he were not stopped he and Kublai would end up running the empire together.

Now, at last, a plot was hatched. There were two con-spirators, both highly unstable characters. The driving force was Wang Zhu, a hard military man, a regimental commander so obsessed by his hatred of Ahmad that he had acquired a big brass club with which to kill him. His accomplice was a shady Buddhist monk named Gao, who claimed to be a magician. The two had met on a campaign, when Gao had cast spells that hadn't worked, then killed a man and used the corpse to fake his own suicide. He was now on the run.

In the spring of 1282 Kublai was based in Xanadu, as was usual at this season. Beijing was left to Ahmad, who, in the words of one version in the official history, 'devoted his whole energy to his avarice and his dissipation in a way which the people loathed and resented'. The plotters seized their chance, as the official history relates – in four different and often contradictory versions, which conflict again with Rashid ad-Din and Marco Polo. What follows is my attempt to make sense of the story.

The two plotters hatched a lunatic scheme, involving a crowd of a hundred or so, who would turn up at the city gates purporting to be the entourage accompanying Zhenjin, the heir apparent, who had suddenly decided to return to Beijing for a religious ceremony. It would be night-time, too dark for a quick check of who these people were. The idea was that Ahmad, galvanized by the approach of the one man he feared other than the emperor himself, would lead the way out to greet them, and that would be the moment to strike.

On 26 April Wang Zhu and Gao put the first stage of their complicated scheme into effect. They sent two Tibetan monks to the city council to announce the 'news' and tell the councillors to buy the right equipment for the ceremony. The council members were puzzled. They checked with the guards: no, no orders had been received. So where exactly was the heir apparent? The monks looked embarrassed and could not answer. Suspecting that foul play was afoot, the commander of the guard arrested them.

Next Wang Zhu put his back-up plan into action, sending

a forged letter purporting to be from the heir apparent to the vice-commissioner of the Bureau of Military Affairs telling him, in effect, to go 'to my residence for further orders'. That worked. With the main guards out of the way at Zhenjin's palace, Wang Zhu hurried off to Ahmad, urging him to get all his Secretariat colleagues together to greet the 'prince'. That worked too, but only just. Ahmad sent out a small advance guard to meet the mock-prince and Wang's rent-a-crowd of horsemen, a meeting that took place some 5 kilometres out of town. The guards, of course, saw at once that the whole thing was a scam. The rebels had no alternative: they killed the guards, and proceeded.

At about 10 p.m. they gained entry to one of the city's north gates, and made their way to the west door of the prince's palace.

Here they struck a problem. The guard was ready, and highly suspicious. Where were the prince's usual outriders? they asked. 'We beg first to see these two men, then we will open the gates.'

A pause.

The rebels backed off, worked their way around the palace in the darkness, and tried again, this time at the south door. There had been no time to rush a message across town to warn the guards. The gates opened, and the guards, fooled by another forged note from the 'prince', rushed out to act as his escort.

Now Ahmad and his entourage came out. All the new strangers dismounted, leaving the lone shadowy figure of the mock-prince on his horse. The figure called out to Ahmad. Ahmad stepped forward. Wang and a few followers were right behind him. They led him further forward, then away into the shadows, out of sight. Wang drew from his sleeve his brass club, with which he struck Ahmad a single, fatal blow.

Ahmad's number two was called next, and was killed in the same way.

Now Ahmad's retainers realized something was amiss, and yelled for help. All was sudden chaos, with guards and rebels mixed up in the dark. Gao the counterfeit prince galloped off into the darkness, arrows flew and the crowd scattered, leaving Wang begging to be arrested, certain that the nobility of his act would be recognized.

No such luck. The monk Gao was found two days later. On 1 May, both were condemned to death, along with the commander of the city guard.

Before the axe fell, Wang cried out: 'I, Wang Zhu, now die for having rid the world of a pest! Another day someone will certainly write my story!' The three were beheaded and quartered, a bloody end to an episode that cast doubt on Kublai's ability to judge character or control events.

It was the commander of the Beijing guard who brought the news personally to Kublai, covering some 500 kilometres in a non-stop gallop, changing horses along the post road. It took him two days to reach the emperor in a temporary camp at Tsagaan Nur (White Lake), about 170 kilometres north of Xanadu, where, as Marco Polo says, he was enjoying spring on the grasslands, 'a-hawking with his gerfalcons' for cranes, partridges and pheasants. Kublai at once ordered a return to Xanadu, from where he sent his Vice-Commissioner for Military Affairs, Bolad, to investigate and to ensure that Ahmad had a proper state burial.

Ten days later, Bolad was back with the truth about Ahmad. Kublai flew into a rage, and turned everything upside down: 'Wang Zhu was perfectly right to kill him!' He ordered the arrest of all Ahmad's clan members and associates, right across the empire. Everything he had done was undone; everything he owned was seized.

In a cupboard investigators made a puzzling discovery: two tanned human skins 'with both ears remaining', suggesting

DISASTER IN JAPAN, 1

The Mongol force that invaded Japan in 1274 made landfall in Hakata bay, deploying explosive shells like the one below. It is shown exploding over Takezaki Suenaga and his wounded horse, an incident in the Invasion Scrolls commissioned by Suenaga to commemorate his role in defending his homeland. The scrolls also portray Suenaga in other acts of bravado, before a storm ended Kublai's first attempt at invasion.

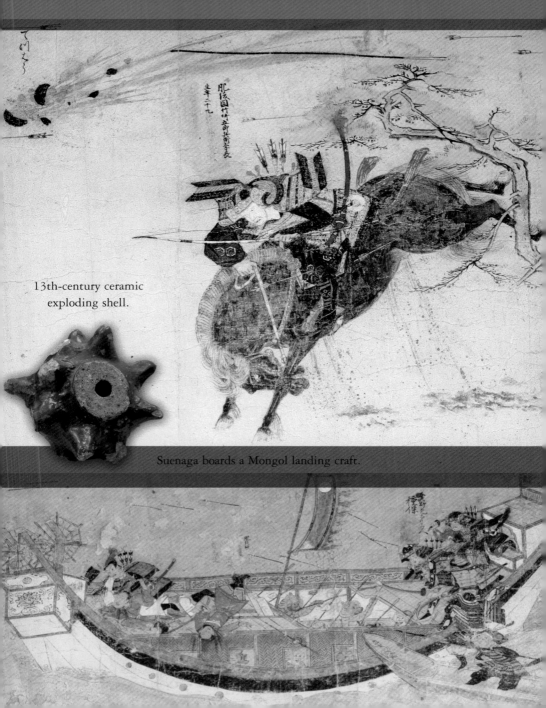

13th-century ceramic exploding shell.

Suenaga boards a Mongol landing craft.

DISASTER IN JAPAN, 2

By 1281, when Kublai launched his second invasion, the Japanese had built a wall round Hakata bay, as the Invasion Scrolls show (*above*), and as visitors to Fukuoka can see for themselves today (*above left*).

Kozaki bay (*below*), Takashima Island, where the anchor-stock and seal were found.

The wall was never tested. The fleets' rendezvous was off Takashima island, where a typhoon struck. The difficult work of raising and cataloguing the detritus of shattered ships is led by Kenzo Hayashida (*left*). He is holding a copy of a famous seal in the script devised by Phags-pa (*inset*), the first hard evidence that the fleets' remains lie scattered on the ocean bed off Takashima. It reads in Chinese: 'Seal of Army Commander.' His thousands of finds include the granite crosspiece, or 'stock' of an anchor which, when restored (*far left*), weighs a tonne.

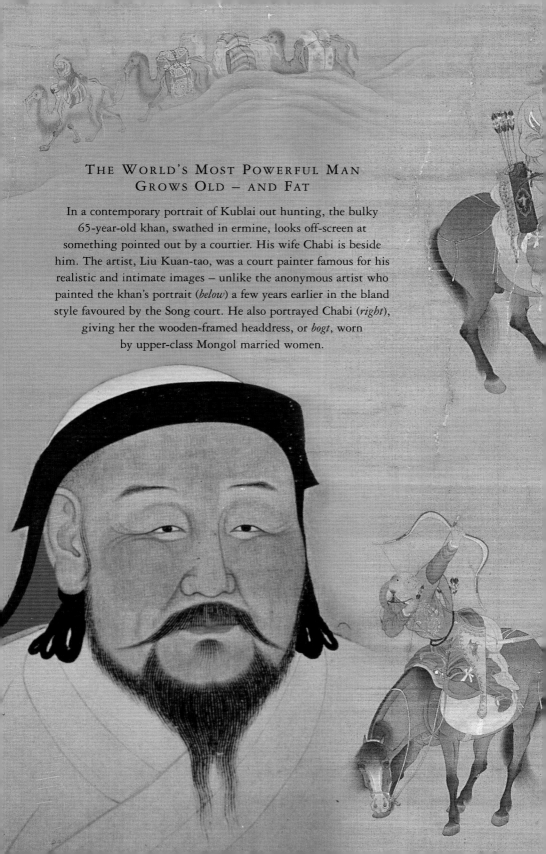

THE WORLD'S MOST POWERFUL MAN GROWS OLD – AND FAT

In a contemporary portrait of Kublai out hunting, the bulky
65-year-old khan, swathed in ermine, looks off-screen at
something pointed out by a courtier. His wife Chabi is beside
him. The artist, Liu Kuan-tao, was a court painter famous for his
realistic and intimate images – unlike the anonymous artist who
painted the khan's portrait (*below*) a few years earlier in the bland
style favoured by the Song court. He also portrayed Chabi (*right*),
giving her the wooden-framed headdress, or *bogt*, worn
by upper-class Mongol married women.

In the West, Legends of Wealth and Cruelty

Kublai became known in Europe mainly thanks to Marco Polo. Kublai helped him return by giving him a passport (*above*), or *paiza* (*inset*). The *paiza* is almost true to life, but Kublai and his minister are shown in western dress, with Kublai wearing a hat in the style of a Byzantine emperor. But his reputation for wealth and pomp was at odds with that of the Mongols themselves, whose invasion of Europe in 1236–41 turned them into murderous barbarians in western eyes (*below*). Possibly, some hint of Phags-pa's script indirectly influenced Giotto's design on the hem of a Roman cloak (*top right*).

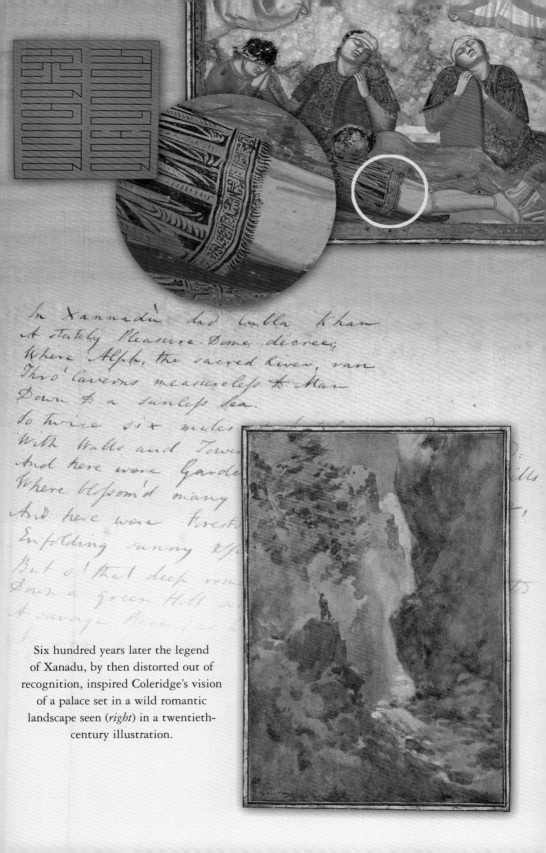

In Xannadu did Cabla Khan
A stately Pleasure-Dome decree;
Where Alph, the sacred River, ran
Thro' Caverns measureless to Man
Down to a sunless Sea.
So twice six miles
With Walls and Towers
And here were Gardens
Where blossom'd many
And here were Forests
Enfolding sunny
But o! that deep romantic
Down a green Hill
A savage place

Six hundred years later the legend of Xanadu, by then distorted out of recognition, inspired Coleridge's vision of a palace set in a wild romantic landscape seen (*right*) in a twentieth-century illustration.

A Secret Burial on a Sacred Mountain

Kublai is buried near his grandfather, Genghis, somewhere on the flanks of Burkhan Khaldun (Khan Khenti), the great ridge in the Khenti Mountains, some 200km east of the Mongolian capital Ulaanbaatar. Though the only way into this remote region is a track along the Kherlen and Bogd rivers, the sacred mountain draws pilgrims who build shrines (*ovoos*) of firs or stones, drape silk scarves (*khatags*), hang prayer flags and leave offerings. One place of worship on the way to the summit is a flat area where Kublai's grandson Kamala built a temple, which has now vanished (*bottom left*). Another, higher up, is a rocky plateau (*bottom right*) with a stunning view over the Bogd river.

that Ahmad had done extremely nasty things to some of his victims, followed by some weird practices. When the investigators questioned the domestic eunuch in charge of the key to the cupboard, he said he didn't know what they were for; but, he added cryptically, 'If they placed the spirit-throne on them when they practised incantations, the answer was very swift.' Whatever Ahmad had been up to, it was nothing to do with Islam. The investigators suspected some sort of cult practice, and their suspicions hardened when they found two silk scrolls painted with images of horsemen surrounding a tent brandishing their swords and aiming their bows as if attacking someone inside. What did it all mean? No-one knew. But the artist was identified and executed, just in case. These disturbing details inspired much talk of magic, which accounts for Marco Polo's remark that Ahmad 'had so wrought upon the Kaan with his sorcery that the latter had the greatest faith and reliance on everything he said'.

Wives and daughters were sent home from his harem, stolen property was returned; his slaves were freed, his herds broken up, his remaining appointees – 581 of them – dismissed. That autumn his four sons were executed, Husain, Beijing's boss, being pickled as an additional disgrace, while the body of one of his brothers was flayed. Ahmad's crimes were publicly proclaimed. Other executions followed, including that of his assistant on the Secretariat, a Muslim protégé who had provided a daughter for Ahmad's harem in exchange for an appointment.

After his murder, Ahmad had been given an official burial. Five weeks later, Kublai ordered his tomb to be opened, his corpse to be beheaded in full public view and then his remains to be thrown outside Beijing's main north gate to be consumed by dogs. As the *Yuan History* laconically reports: 'Officials, gentry and commoners assembled to look on, and expressed approval.'

15

THE LIMITS TO GROWTH

I WONDER WHAT DROVE THE TWO OF THEM, GENGHIS AND HIS grandson Kublai. I think a psychoanalyst would say that both were driven by the same deep sense of insecurity. Genghis had been an outcast as a child, and seemed to have spent the rest of his life building security on a gargantuan scale. Kublai inherited what his grandfather had achieved, but because he was never fully accepted by traditionalist Mongols, his grandfather's people, at a deep level he never felt at ease. Luckily for their subjects, both had extraordinary leadership talents, which they used to push the bounds of empire as far as possible. Genghis did not live long enough to come up against any limits. But Kublai did, and the discovery of them was a shock. Behind all the trappings of greatness, I think there was a spoiled child stamping and refusing to take no for an answer.

Of course, it was all dressed up in ideology. To bring China's millions into the empire was an astonishing achievement, but it was still just one more step towards the realization of that ultimate ambition: to have the world acknowledge his divinely ordained supremacy. It was this drive that lay behind Kublai's determination to expand. There was no threat to be countered, no strategic reason for conquest. It simply had to be done, period. Hence Japan; and hence four other adventures – Burma, Vietnam, Burma again and Java – which revealed how vain this ambition was. He might as well have aimed for the moon. Every adventure should have taught him that he had reached his limits; he refused to learn. Every setback made him more determined to repair the tattered mantle of invincibility, and every effort tore it more. He would go obstinate to the grave.

Hard as it seems to believe, he was even bent on attacking Japan again. In 1283 he ordered southern merchants to build 500 new ships, and two years later commissioned another 200 from the Jürchens in Manchuria. From the Koreans he demanded rice to feed the armies he proposed to send. Only in 1286 did his advisers manage to persuade him to drop the idea, because by then he was deeply embroiled elsewhere.

By the time of the second Japan débâcle, there were long-established links with most of the neighbouring peoples. Trade vessels had gone back and forth. An envoy had come from Annam (today's North Vietnam) in 1265. But trade and envoys were not enough. What Kublai wanted was recognition of his supremacy, the proof of which was tribute. And it was inevitable that he would want such recognition from Burma, because it abutted Yunnan, technically part of China since the Mongol invasion – headed, remember, by Kublai himself – in 1253. Yunnan had been left to its own devices with just a small garrison for 20 years, until in 1273 it acquired its first high-level administrator, Saiyid Ajall, the Turkmen from Bukhara whose grandfather had surrendered to Genghis in 1220. With Yunnan now brought fully into the empire, Kublai decided to send three envoys to demand Burma's submission.

Burma was not about to comply. The king, Narathihipate,

was ruler of a considerable kingdom founded two centuries before by the Burmese, who had migrated into the Irrawaddy's tropical lowlands from the Yunnan highlands, absorbing the rich culture of the indigenous Mons. From their new nation, which they called Mranma (hence today's Myanmar), the Burmese reached out to Sri Lanka, India, Cambodia, Indonesia and China. With Pagan as its capital, it was prosperous, stable, the proud owner of a myriad temples – 5,000 in Pagan alone – that glorified its Buddhist faith. To be told to offer tribute to China was an intolerable insult, especially as the message came from an area the Burmese believed had once been theirs. Added to pride, however, was insecurity. Burma had suffered uprisings and religious schism in the previous century, and the great age of temple-building was over.

Narathihipate was not the man to put things right. He was no true heir to the throne, having seized it by force. His people despised him, calling him 'King Dog's Dung'. Arbitrary and brutal, he kept a close eye on his 3,000 concubines. When he discovered that a favourite had plotted to assassinate him with poison, he had her put in a cage and burned. He wasted resources on an immense pagoda, the Mingalazedi, one of the last of Pagan's great temples – to which, being extremely nervous of assassins, he had a tunnel built from his palace. The pagoda's soft, pinkish bricks, much admired for the way they glowed at sunset, form a huge square-based pyramid on which an inscription records the king's boast that he was 'supreme commander of a vast army, the swallower of 300 dishes of curry daily' – though he wasn't referring to himself alone; he kept his sons and their families in the palace as well in case they turned against him. A Burmese proverb pretty much sums up his achievement: 'The Pagoda is finished, the great country ruined.'

When Kublai's envoys arrived, the king might have placated and negotiated; instead, he threw Kublai's demands back in his face, executing the envoys and then sending a force into the Thai buffer-state of Kaungai, thus virtually guaranteeing invasion.

For the next four years Kublai was otherwise engaged, conquering Song. In 1277 came action. To head the campaign, Kublai chose Saiyid's son Nasir al-Din, who had been helping his father set up Yunnan's administration. What followed was described by Marco Polo (who must have picked up the details later) with his usual admixture of fact and hyperbole.

The Burmese, with 200 war-elephants, had advanced against the invaders over the border along the high valleys, with their steep, forested sides, that lead to what is now the town of Baoshan. Blocking their path were Nasir al-Din's 12,000 men, their backs against a forest slope. Few of the Mongols had seen elephants. Certainly the horses hadn't. When spurred to advance, they refused. So Nasir al-Din ordered his men to dismount, approach on foot and use their bows. A single arrow won't have much effect on an elephant, but hundreds did, as Marco Polo noted:

> Understand that when the elephants felt the smart of those arrows that pelted them like rain, they turned tail and fled, and nothing on earth would have induced them to turn and face the Tartars. So off they sped with such a noise and uproar that you would have trowed the world was coming to an end. And then too they plunged into the wood and rushed this way and that, dashing their castles against the trees, bursting their harness and smashing and destroying everything that was on them.

And destroying everything in their path, including the unfortunate Burmese infantry.

Now the cavalry came into its own, as Polo relates with the zest of a medieval epic poet, describing blows dealt and taken with sword and mace, arms and legs hewn off, and many a wounded man held down among the dead by the sheer weight of numbers. The Burmese fled, the Mongols pursued, using enemy mahouts taken prisoner to capture elephants. 'The elephant is an animal that hath more wit than any other; but in this way at last they were caught, more than 200 of them. And it was from this time forth that the Great Kaan began to keep numbers of elephants.'

Well, probably not 200, because Nasir al-Din, content with his victory, arrived back at Xanadu in July 1279 with just 12 elephants, having walked them over 2,000 kilometres cross-country. It was a victory, of a sort, for the king had fled down the Irrawaddy, earning himself another derogatory nickname: Tarokpliy Man, 'The King Who Ran Away from the Chinese'. But the climate was hellish, disease rampant and Nasir al-Din's troops far from home. All he did after the battle was tally up the households in the area (110,200 of them) and set up some postal stations. There was no conquest of Burma yet; this was unfinished business.

Then there was the matter of Vietnam – or rather, the matters, plural, for in the thirteenth century Vietnam was two kingdoms, Annam (in the north) and Champa. On the assumption that these realms, too, were already an un-acknowledged part of his empire, Kublai gave them both a chance to say so: in person, or by providing population registers that would prove useful for raising taxes and labour, or by delivering young relatives to act as proof of good intentions – that is, in effect, hostages. Annam sent some gifts, nothing more. In 1279 Champa sent an elephant, a rhinoceros and some jewellery. Next time, said Kublai, the king should come in person. In 1280 some more gifts arrived, but no king. It was time to insist.

Kublai placed matters in the hands of a certain Sodu, the

governor in Guangzhou – Canton as it became to Europeans – the closest large port to Champa. His 5,000 troops and 100 vessels landed on the bulge of southern Vietnam, in the lagoon that led to the capital, Vijaya, now the city of Qui Nhon. They took the town, only to discover that the king, Indravarman V, had headed for the hills inland. Sodu foolishly followed, convinced no doubt of quick victory in open combat. Instead, the Vietnamese became guerrillas, inflicting their own version of death by a thousand cuts. Sodu sent for reinforcements, and another 15,000 troops arrived, under Ataqai, a veteran of the Song campaign (he had been Bayan's number two in the final advance on the Song capital, Hangzhou). Yet neither he, nor further reinforcements under another veteran, Ariq-khaya, made any difference. The king remained uncaught, his troops undefeated, his guerrillas extremely effective in keeping the Mongols on edge in the forests of Champa's central highlands.

Some new strategy was called for. It was apparently Sodu's idea, which he proposed on a trip back to Xanadu: What if troops came overland, through Annam? Since Annam was supposedly a Chinese vassal, Kublai could surely send troops across his kingdom with impunity. Kublai liked the idea, and put his son, Toghan, in command, with Sodu as his number two.

But Annam had a new ruler, the third of the ruling Tran dynasty, Tran Nhan Tong; he saw the proposal as a ruse to invade, refused permission, and geared the country to defend itself, which, under Tran leadership, it could do very well. Under an elite of aristocratic officers, all males, except serfs, had to do national service, so a trained army could be called up in days. Accounts are not well sourced, but there is a ring of truth about the fervour they report. At first, the king hesitated. A protracted war would bring terrible destruction, he said to the supreme commander, Tran Hung Dao. Wouldn't it be better to lay down our arms to save the

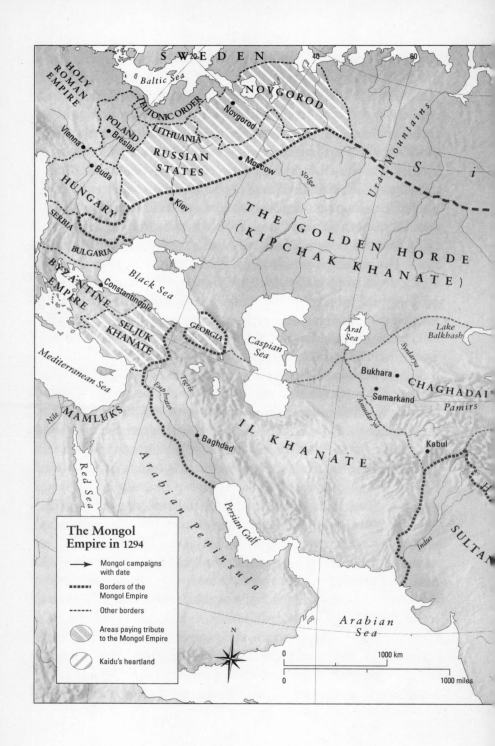

S W E D E N   20   40   60

Baltic Sea

HOLY
ROMAN
EMPIRE

TEUTONIC ORDER

NOVGOROD

Novgorod

LITHUANIA

POLAND
•Breslau

Vienna•

RUSSIAN
STATES

•Moscow

Volga

Ural Mountains

S
i

•Buda

HUNGARY

•Kiev

THE   G O L D E N   H O R D E

SERBIA

BULGARIA

(K I P C H A K   K H A N A T E)

BYZANTINE
EMPIRE

Black Sea

•Constantinople

SELJUK
KHANATE

GEORGIA

*Aral
Sea*

*Lake
Balkhash*

*Caspian
Sea*

Mediterranean Sea

Tigris

Euphrates

Syrdarya

Bukhara•

CHAGHADAI

•Samarkand

Pamirs

Nile

MAMLUKS

Amudarya

I L   K H A N A T E

•Baghdad

•Kabul

Red Sea

A r a b i a n   P e n i n s u l a

SULTAN

Indus

The Mongol
Empire in 1294

→ Mongol campaigns
   with date

▪▪▪▪ Borders of the
      Mongol Empire

- - - Other borders

◯ Areas paying tribute
   to the Mongol Empire

◯ Kaidu's heartland

*Persian
Gulf*

N

*Arabian
Sea*

0   1000 km

0   1000 miles

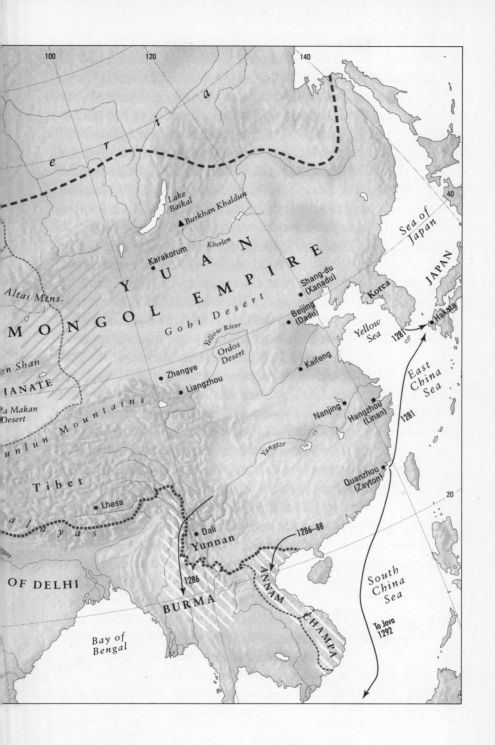

population? 'What would become of our ancestors' land, of our forefathers' temples?' the general is supposed to have replied politely. 'If you want to surrender, please have my head cut off first.' In early 1285, at a national assembly of village elders, Tran Hung Dao, already the embodiment of national resistance, put the matter to the vote: 'The enemy is strong; should we capitulate or fight?' Back came the cry: 'Fight!' But the top people were not setting a good example. The general chastised them in a proclamation much quoted as a classic of Vietnamese literature, a sort of Churchillian call to arms:

> I can neither eat nor sleep, my heart aches, and tears trickle from my eyes, I am enraged at being unable yet to tear the enemy to pieces, pluck out his liver and taste his blood. You who are officers and generals of our royal army . . . you spend your time watching cock-fights, gambling, tending your gardens, looking after your wives and children. You are busy making money and forget about state affairs. But if the country were invaded by the Mongols, your cock's spurs would not be able to pierce their armour, your gambling tricks would not replace military strategy. You may possess immense gardens and fields but even a thousand *taels* of gold could not redeem your lives.

The people responded. Peasants called from their farms had their arms tattooed with 'Death to the Mongols!' and their banners emblazoned: 'Destroy the enemy's strength, repay the king's favour!'

Toghan, gathering an army in China's southern provinces, knew nothing of the opposition, either its spirit or its tactics. He really should have done, for the great Uriyang-kadai had taken the same route in his brief invasion back in 1257, before backing off in the face of Vietnam's intransigence and malarial heat. At first all went well. Toghan, advancing with an army reportedly of 300,000 (some speak of 500,000), a numerical superiority of two to one, forced back the Annamese troops, apparently making a mockery of their tattoos and flags. In June 1285 the Mongols reached Hanoi – Thang Long, as it then was – only to find that Annam's tactics were exactly the same as Champa's. The fall-back had been deliberate. There would be no decisive action. The houses were empty, the gardens stripped of food; the court and people had fled. The Mongols, now reinforced by ships sailing up the Red River, commanded the coast, the Red River delta – but not the interior, the forests and mountains, or the king's base at Thanh Hoa, 170 kilometres to the south. Guerrilla action, disease, lack of food and the fearsome summer heat began to eat away at Toghan's army.

After another month, Tran Hung Dao judged the moment right for a counter-attack. A battle at Chuong Duong, 20 kilometres downriver from Hanoi, carried the Vietnamese back into the capital, forcing the Mongols to retreat across the Red River. Another battle by a little river, the Tay Ket, which joins the Red River's ancient dyke a few kilometres south-east of Hanoi, sealed the Mongol defeat – 50,000 captured, Sodu himself killed and beheaded – leaving the remnants to be harried back to the border.

It took two years for Kublai to reform his shattered force and try again. Toghan clearly needed help, and he was sent it in the form of the veterans Ariq-khaya, Nasir al-Din and one of Kublai's many grandsons, Esen Temür. This time, the strategy would be different: a huge base was to be established just inland from Hai Phong, and a large-scale naval assault mounted as well as a land attack.

Tran Hung Dao's response, in early 1288, was sheer brilliance. On land, his strategy was the same – a scorched-earth withdrawal from inhabited areas, leaving the Mongols with nothing to conquer. Anticipating this, Toghan had prepared for a huge operation with some 500 vessels to bring in reinforcements and food up the Bach Dang river from Hai Phong. It was on the fleet that Tran Hung Dao focused his attention, planning to repeat a tactic first used 300 years before to defeat a Chinese fleet and ensure Vietnamese independence. The first step was to order troops to cut and sharpen hundreds of ironwood stakes. These were then ferried out 5 kilometres into Halong bay, to one of the thousand or more little islands that make the bay a famous beauty-spot (created, according to legend, when a dragon plunged into the sea, carving out crevices and valleys with his tail, and making countless caves in the craggy limestone). In the centre of the island, almost 200 metres up, was a par-ticularly large yet well-hidden cave, into which 1,000 men would fit with ease. Here they settled with their stakes to watch as Toghan's ships slid past to make their way upriver.

Once the ships were out of sight, a small Vietnamese boat crossed from the mainland and picked up the troops and their sharpened stakes. A few kilometres upstream, in an area where the river broadened into mudflats at low tide, they waited for the outgoing waters to reach their lowest level. Then they planted their stakes, one to every square metre – some sticking up vertically, some pointing upstream – running in a zig-zag across the main channel, set just below the level of the water so that small boats would float clear of them. Tran Hung Dao himself came to check the work, so the story goes, thrusting his sword into the ground and twisting his hair into a chignon to get a clear view.

Assaults followed, of which we have no details. The result was that on 22 March (or thereabouts; some accounts mention 3 April or 8 April) the Mongol fleet, harried from the banks and shoreline, retreated downriver. Little Vietnamese boats acting as decoys slipped away above the stakes, a final attack slowed the Mongols, and then they were upon the stakes: many ships were impaled and torn open, fixed in place while others rammed into them, all helpless as Vietnamese fire-boats drifted in from upstream. Sloshing ashore through mud and water, the Mongols were easy prey for the forces ranged along the banks. Toghan was lucky to escape – to face Kublai's fury: the emperor banished his son to Yangzhou, 150 kilometres up the Yangtze from its mouth, and a very long way from court.

Over the years, the river at Bach Dang silted up, and the lines of stakes vanished beneath the river bottom. How do we know any of this is true? Partly because the spot where Tran Hung Dao stuck his sword in the ground to redo his hair was marked with a temple dedicated to him; but mainly because in 1953 the North Vietnamese dredged the river to improve navigation, and found the stakes. On 22 March 1988, the official 700th anniversary of the great victory, the Bach Dang Stake Yard was declared a historic site to commemorate the defeat of the 'northern feudalists'. The island where the stakes were hidden and its huge hidden cave – the Grotto of Wooden Stakes – are now tourist sites; and Tran Hung Dao is still remembered as the national hero who secured Annam's independence.

Kublai's involvement in Vietnam provides striking parallels with more recent events. A powerful ruler conceives the notion that the national interest will be served by sending troops to attack an extremely determined regime in the north. The foreign troops fail to achieve their ends. More troops are sent. Prestige is involved. A world-view must be sustained and it is inconceivable that a minor power can withstand an assault by the mightiest one on earth. For ten years the major power strives to achieve its end, struggling in quagmires and squinting for lights at the end of tunnels, only to be hounded into ignominious retreat.

Yes, there are interesting parallels with America and its war in Vietnam. But just as interesting are the differences. America in the 1960s was in the midst of the Cold War, in grim opposition to the USSR. There was at the time a logic behind the first step into Vietnam. Kublai, on the other hand, specialized in making enemies of people who posed no conceivable threat. It was all down to ideology.

There's a lesson in this on which the spirit of Kublai and the Americans would agree: never, ever, tangle with the North Vietnamese.

After that, there would be no thought of invading Champa. But there was still business to finish in Burma. In 1283 a force of 10,000 from Sichuan had tried to induce the king to submit, but he fled to the hills. Then, trying to avoid further trouble, he sent two monks to beg for peace. They knew they were on weak ground: 'Your majesty, art thou not the Bodhisattva [the future Buddha]? So vast are your domains. Pagan is a small country, but it has the Buddha doctrine which is flourishing. Don't send warriors into it. Come in only after the crops have grown.' Kublai promised, and was as good as his word.

In late 1286, with the defeat in Vietnam behind him, Kublai tried again, with more success that owed much to the internal state of affairs in Burma. King Narathihipate had just been assassinated by his son, Thihathu, who held a knife to his father's throat and forced him to drink poison. This was a kingdom in a state of collapse. The commander, Esen Temür, the grandson who had gained some experience in Vietnam, led his 7,000 troops down the Irrawaddy. When the Mongols reached Pagan, they stripped its monasteries of their gold and silver; then, unable to cope with the climate, they returned home, leaving Burma to more regicide, anarchy and Thai warlords. Dribs and drabs of tribute trickled out of northern Burma. But it was never enough to pay for the wars or satisfy a royal ego.

*

King Kertenagara of Java had done well for himself, having succeeded to one of South-East Asia's most successful kingdoms. Java, especially eastern Java, had a history of mini-empires. Three centuries earlier, one of them, Mataram, had grown rich on rice and spice. Rice grew well on the rich volcanic soil inland, and the island's ships monopolized the cloves, nutmeg and mace of the Spice Islands. Mataram had outperformed its great rival, Srivijaya, on the neighbouring Sumatra, until in 928 the great volcano Merapi, the source of the island's wonderful soil, erupted, spewing ash and rivers of hot mud down river valleys, burying towns and temples several metres deep. Mataram never recovered. But a surviving prince created a brilliant, if brief, successor state. Offered the throne at the age of 20, after four years spent in the refuge of a monastery, Airlangga rebuilt fast, establishing a new base near today's Surabaya, damming rivers, extending irrigation schemes. When he died in 1049, his empire collapsed into two rival kingdoms. One emerged supreme: Singhasari, founded by the orphan, thief and legendary hero Ken Arok in 1222 when he defeated the other, Kediri. It was this new empire of Singhasari that Kertenagara had inherited – a somewhat precarious inheritance, since its survival depended on both keeping control of the spice trade and keeping an eye on Kediri and its would-be rebels. Ambitious for more – indeed, some today see him as a forerunner of Indonesian nationhood – he had allied himself with Champa by marrying a Champa princess, and in 1284 tried and failed to take Bali and, in the other direction, a bit of Sumatra.

Kertenagara was not best pleased, therefore, when an envoy called Meng Chi arrived from Kublai in 1289, bearing a rude demand for submission. Kertenagara punished Kublai for his impertinence by having the envoy's face tattooed, so that when he reported back to court the insult was plain and public. It demanded revenge. Kublai ordered a battle fleet to be made ready in the south commanded by Shi-pi, a veteran of the Song campaign. Under his overall command, ground forces would be led by Kao Xing and naval forces by a Uighur named something like Ikh-Musu. Kublai told them it would be a walkover: 'If you occupy that country, the other smaller states will submit of themselves; you have only to send envoys to receive their allegiance.' For three years they mustered their forces in Quanzhou (Zayton): 1,000 ships, 20,000 troops, a year's supply of grain, 1,000 kilos of silver for new supplies.

So Kertenagara had plenty of time to prepare for the assault; but he misread Shi-pi's strategy. Assuming the commander would work his way southward along the coast, calling in on both Champa and Malaya, he despatched forces there to ambush the Mongol fleet. This was a fatal mistake. Shi-pi covered the 4,000 kilometres to Java non-stop. It was a high-risk strategy – 'The wind was strong and the sea very rough, so that the ships rolled heavily and the soldiers could not eat for many days' – but it paid off. Shi-pi landed his troops in 1293, unopposed because meanwhile Kertenagara had become involved in a war with his neighbouring state, Kediri, and been killed. All the native troops were off fighting in the south.

Shi-pi should have had the walkover Kublai had promised. In fact, he was instantly caught up in local politics. Kertenagara's son-in-law, Vijaya, an equally ambitious and far more devious character, sent him a message offering submission in exchange for help against Kediri, backing his offer with gifts of incense, perfume, rhinoceros horn and ivory. Shi-pi agreed. Vijaya sent details of the territory – on the Brantas river, at the foot of Mount Wilis, 105 kilometres south-west of Surabaya, rich in rice, a harbour on the coast, all explained on a helpful map – and the Mongols went in. A week later, 5,000 of Kediri's troops were dead, their leader had been executed and the place was in Shi-pi's hands.

All that remained was the ceremony to celebrate victory and, of course, accept Vijaya's promised submission. Vijaya requested 200 unarmed men under two officers as an escort back to his capital, Majapahit, supposedly to fetch gifts. On the way, Vijaya's men killed the unarmed escort, and then turned on the Mongol force. Shi-pi fled, leading his troops in a 150-kilometre fighting retreat to the coast, back into the ships, and away for home – where Kublai rewarded him for his failure and the loss of 3,000 men with 17 lashes and the confiscation of one-third of his property.

Two years later Kublai's successor restored Shi-pi to favour. After all, as an adviser pointed out, he had travelled 12,000 kilometres, reached countries never reached before and made a terrific impression on the natives. So ended another disaster, with honour satisfied by self-deception.

For Kublai, this adventure was a fine example of the Law of Unintended Consequences. Setting out to punish one king, Kublai had managed to help his legitimate successor secure the throne and establish a new dynasty and a nation-state. Over the next 50 years Vijaya's new creation, Majapahit, grew into a rich and powerful empire that included a good deal (some say all) of Indonesia – exactly the opposite of what Kublai had intended.

16

HOW THE EAST WENT WEST

FOR MOST OF KUBLAI'S REIGN, THE IMPACT OF CHINA ON THE West was, frankly, fairly negligible. It was only after his death that he became famous, and that was almost entirely thanks to one man who has been much quoted in earlier chapters: Marco Polo.

To understand the difference Marco made, look at what was known of China and Central Asia before Kublai. In the twelfth century, Europeans and Middle Easterners had only the vaguest ideas about China. In Christian Europe, maps were not really maps at all, but diagrams of beliefs in which the Last Judgement and the Garden of Eden were as prominent as land masses and oceans. Monsters had leading roles: men who fed on the smell of apples; the Sciopod, who used his giant foot as a sun-shade. The only continents were Europe, Asia and Africa, which appeared as neat segments of a circle or unshaped blobs. Asia and India were identical; China, simply absent. Arabic geography, of which Europe knew little, was better, but not much. A Spanish Jew, Benjamin of Tudela, travelled from Ceylon to China in the late twelfth century, but recorded few details, and his Hebrew *Itinerary* was unknown to Christian Europe until the sixteenth century. None of the Nestorian Christians who undertook missionary work in Central Asia wrote accounts, or at least none that were copied. Other Christians knew that they were there, and dreamed up another legend, about a non-existent Christian king, Prester John.

So when Genghis's Mongols burst upon Europe, they sprang out of the dark. With Genghis's devastating sweep across Central Asia and into Persia (1219–23), the initial burst of optimism that these were Christians coming to rescue the Crusaders rapidly gave way to fear and trembling. Europeans seized on the name of one group of Mongol subjects, the Tatars, and called all Mongols Tartars – people from Tartarus, the hellish nether regions of antiquity. Minor shocks were like omens of doom. In 1238, the fish-traders of Novgorod forfeited their usual trip to Norfolk for North Sea herring and stayed home to fight the invaders, causing a glut of fish in Yarmouth. The Hungarian king received a threatening letter from Batu, khan of the Golden Horde, Genghis's grandson and Kublai's cousin: 'As for you who dwell in houses and have fortresses and cities – how will you escape my grasp?' Then in 1241, the storm broke. Russia, Poland and Hungary fell. European leaders almost united to fight back. Crusades were proposed, pleas for help and co-operation exchanged between rival leaders. In fact, there was no time to organize anything, because suddenly the Mongols were gone, drawn back home by the death of Ogedei.

After illusion and stark terror came a reality check, in the form of two papal envoys to Karakorum: Giovanni (John), a cleric from what was then Plano (or Piano) Carpini or Carpine, and is now the town of Magione in Umbria, who was at Güyük's election in Karakorum in 1246; and Friar William, from Rubrouck in north-eastern France, who met Mönkhe in 1253–5. Both brought back uncompromising demands from the Mongol khans. 'By the power of God, all lands, from the rising of the sun to its setting, have been made subject to us': that statement in a letter to the pope from Güyük captures their view succinctly. Other envoys were sent to meet the Mongols in the Middle East. As a result, the West acquired detailed, realistic information about Genghis's successors and their people, mainly as a result of Carpini's account, which was leaked before he arrived home. Copies circulated widely (whereas Rubrouck's brilliant report lay uncopied for three centuries). What people read – and heard from Carpini himself, as he toured Europe on his return from the Mongol court – did nothing to calm their nerves. In the event, the direct threat turned out to be over: the Mongols over-reached themselves, then settled back into their new mini-empires in southern Russia and Persia, where they began to engage in the normal activities of states – establishing relations with outside powers, forming alliances and squabbling with each other. Of these states, Europe knew a good deal.

Meanwhile, a new world had emerged in the Far East – Kublai's – of which the West knew nothing. No missionaries were despatched from Rome, nor envoys from any other ruler, until the 1290s – and even then communication was limited, mainly because of linguistic problems. Interpreters were few and bad, no-one stayed long enough to become fluent in either Chinese or Mongol, and anyway the Mongols showed no interest in becoming Christian. True, there were Nestorians among them – notably Kublai's mother, Sorkaktani – but they were so embedded in Mongol and Chinese society as to be no help at all to mainstream Catholics. As the Persian khan Arghun said to the pope in a polite refusal to accept baptism: 'If one prays to Eternal Heaven alone and thinks in the appropriate manner, is it not as if one had accepted baptism?' In brief, they were unconvertible.

The major conduits for information should have been the trade routes. Unfortunately for historians, traders were mainly interested in trade, not travel and social comment. Although several routes were open, thanks to Mongol rule, few made the demanding journey overland themselves. A fourteenth-century anonymous Florentine noted the time taken to travel all the way from Ukraine to Beijing: 250 days, give or take. In addition, scholars now believe that the idea of a peaceful high road across the Pax Mongolica is overstated, because the Mongols were in an almost constant state of bickering or open warfare for most of Kublai's reign. When Hulegu and Berke were fighting each other in the 1260s, both slaughtered each other's traders. Who would risk life and spend 18 months struggling back and forth across Asia to fetch goods you could pick up from middlemen closer to home?

There was always the sea route, of course; but this, for westerners, was even worse. It started in the Persian Gulf, because no-one would be sailing around southern Africa for another two centuries. From there, it took up to two years for Arab ships to reach the East, with the risks along the way of nasty death from pirates, storms and structural collapse of hulls held together by rope (a hazard mentioned by Marco Polo). Again, no-one wrote up the experience.

Some did make the land trek later, after Kublai's death, because there were profits to be made along the way for the lucky and the knowledgeable. But the only ones to have done this in Kublai's time were the Polos, who financed their first journey by selling merchandise in Constantinople, where they bought jewellery which Berke, khan of the Golden Horde in Sarai, took in exchange for unspecified goods that they sold later as they journeyed eastward.

As Venetians and merchants, the Polo family firm of three brothers was uniquely placed for travel eastward. Venice owned bits of Constantinople – recently seized by Latinized

Christians from Greek Orthodoxy – and Acre in Syria, and Soldaia in the Crimea. Venice dominated the trade routes that linked Russia to Egypt, the Middle East to Italy. Fortunes were to be made from Baltic amber, honey, wax, Russian furs and slaves. Around 1260, two brothers, Nicolò and Maffeo, set out to trade in jewels with the Mongols of southern Russia, the Golden Horde. When they arrived, two catastrophes upset their plans. The Greeks retook Constantinople and blinded or killed 50 Venetian merchants; and the two Mongol sub-empires, the Golden Horde and Persia, went to war. There was only one safe direction: due east.

In Bukhara, three years later, a Mongol mission to their overlord's overlord, Kublai, offered to take them to the emperor's court. A year later, they were with Kublai. He questioned them about the papacy and the Roman version of Christianity, and then helped them on their way home, giving them one of the gold or silver tablets (*paiza*) that acted as a combined passport and requisition order, allowing them to make use of official Mongol way-stations on their return journey. He sent them off with a request to bring him 100 men who could act as missionaries, and also some oil from a lamp in Christ's Sepulchre in Jerusalem. This was not just tolerance, but good politics. Kublai was beset by many disputatious clerics of several religions, one of which was Nestorian Christianity. His mother had been a Nestorian. A hundred Christians from a different sect would allow him to create another special interest group, and prevent any one sect becoming dominant.

Back home in 1269, Nicolò was reunited with his son Marco, now 15. Unfortunately for Kublai's request, the pope had died, and a new appointment was much delayed. Two years later, drawn by the wealth and opportunities they had seen in Kublai's China, the brothers set out again, taking Marco with them.

In Acre they consulted an old friend, the archdeacon Teobaldo Visconti, which turned out to be a fortunate decision, because, by an extraordinary coincidence, he was appointed pope and was able to give them official credentials. Three and a half years later – in the summer of 1275 – they were back with Kublai in Xanadu.

Scholars have long debated how much of Marco's account is authentic. Opinions range from very little to almost all. On the minus side, Marco worked with a co-author, Rustichello: a ghost-writer who, since he was a professional author keen to make the book appealing, gave Marco's words a literary spin. There are blatant intimacies and much use of the first person, as if the author is button-holing the reader, and faux-casual asides, like 'Oh, I forgot to mention such-and-such.' Actually, he *was* button-holing, not the reader exactly, but the listener, because this was a time when texts were designed to be read aloud. Later, Marco himself and various editors added, subtracted and rewrote, creating several different versions; there is no original text.

The chattiness, combined with a tabloid habit of being economical with the truth, should often give us pause. Some have even wondered whether he could have plagiarized the lot from other books. To this the short answer is no, he couldn't. The book is crammed with details that no westerner could possibly have known (like the marble of Xanadu). Even his distortions, like the help with making the catapults of Xiangyang, can be put down to exaggeration rather than fantasy. When he and Rustichello were at work in the last years of the century, no-one else in the West had a clue what had been happening in China, so lies could have sold as well as truth. Now, of course, scholars are adept at using other sources to tell truth from falsehood; and on the whole, with a few notable lapses, Marco stands the test.

It is Marco Polo's account of his 17 years in China that told Europe almost all it knew of Kublai. For later historians he was an invaluable eye-witness, because he arrived overland, before the conquest of the south was complete, and plunged right into the heart of China. Others coming later arrived by sea, and saw mainly southern ports. The Polos were there at the heart of things, at Kublai's court, insiders as far as it was possible for foreigners with only a smattering of the language to be: Marco may have picked up some spoken Mongol and Chinese, but he couldn't write either. Kublai used Marco as an envoy, a post which Marco magnifies in importance; in fact he was probably more of a freelance reporter, able to provide an independent view of places, people and events.

So popular were the Polos that Kublai several times refused them permission to leave, finally allowing them to go in order to escort a Mongol princess as a bride to the Mongol ruler of Persia, Arghun. Again he gave them two of his gold passports, so that they should be well taken care of, and told them to deliver messages to all the Christian kings of Europe. In a convoy of 13 four-masted ships, they reached Persia in 1293 or 1294, after two years and many disasters. By then Arghun was dead. The princess was married off to his son, and the Polos arrived back in Venice in 1295.

Somehow, in some scrap between Venice and Genoa, Marco found himself in a Genoese gaol – confined in some comfort, apparently, because it was here that Rustichello ghosted the *Travels*, which was finished before their release, probably in 1300. Marco, now in his mid-forties, married, had three daughters, lived comfortably, and died aged 69 in 1324.

It is hard to know whether people at the time believed his book or not. It was all very far away and extraordinary, and there was nothing else to substantiate it. Some say it was seen as no more than a collection of fables. But Marco makes a whiter-than-white claim right at the beginning, addressing the reader:

> Ye shall find therein all kinds of wonderful things . . . according to the description of Messer Marco Polo, a wise and noble citizen of Venice, as he saw them with his own eyes. Some things indeed there be therein which he beheld not; but these he heard from men of credit and veracity. And we shall set down things seen as seen, and things heard as heard only, so that no jot of falsehood may mar the truth of our book.

But then, if he was lying, he would say that, wouldn't he? Nevertheless, two things carry conviction: the amount of detail and the lack of unsubstantiated legends. It has the ring of truth, and that's what appealed.

The *Travels* must have been immensely popular among the small number of people able to obtain or borrow a copy, for within 25 years it had been translated from its original language, probably a hybrid Franco-Italian, into French, Tuscan, Venetian, German and Latin, each version being re-edited to make it conform to the prejudices of its readers. But what exactly is meant by popularity is anyone's guess. No-one knows how many copies were made, who read them, or how many heard the book being read out loud as if it were an epic being recited by a bard. As one historian of printing, Elizabeth Eisenstein, has written: 'Just what publication meant before the age of printing or just how messages got transmitted in the age of scribes are questions that cannot be answered in general.' All that can be said is that for two centuries the demand for books had been growing steadily, though from a very low base. Most books were religious, and great cathedrals had *scriptoria* of copyists who continued, very slowly, to build libraries that were meagre by later standards, intellectual treasures by their own. Cathedral libraries seldom contained more than 200–300 books. The few great universities boasted not many more. In 1338 the Sorbonne had 338 reference books, carefully chained, and 1,728 books for loan, all of Latin authors, except for one in French, a copy of the epic *Roman de la Rose*. For an individual other than an aristocrat to own a single book was rare, to own one in an everyday language even rarer.

Still the copies multiplied – 85 have survived – many with glorious and utterly spurious illustrations, turning the book into a work of art as much as reportage. Those who took Marco most seriously were his Latin translators, for they were trying to assess China for possible conversion. To one, Francesco Pipino of Bologna, Marco was 'respectable, veracious and devout', as were his father and uncle; a judgement which is then artificially fulfilled by additions describing non-Christian religions as abominations. For Latin clerics at least, Marco was reliable. Some time in the 1330s a Dominican friar, Jacopo d'Acqui, told a story about the dying Marco: 'Because there are many and great things in that book, which are beyond all credence, he was asked by his friends on his death-bed to correct the book by removing everything that went beyond the facts. To which his reply was that he had not told one-half of what he had really seen.'

Slowly, therefore, merchants began to explore the possibilities suggested by Marco. There were enough Genoese making the overland journey by 1330 for Francesco Pegolotti to offer some advice, with rather off-putting casualness: the road to China was 'quite safe by day and by night', he said, unless you happened to die en route, in which case the local warlord would take everything you owned.

Missionaries, too, had taken up the challenge. A Franciscan, John of Montecorvino, set up the first Christian church in Beijing in 1294, the year of Kublai's death. Another Franciscan, Odoric of Pordenone, who arrived in 1322, wrote an account that became almost as famous as Marco's.

Of those early Christians, traces survived that very nearly support one of Marco's more outrageous claims, that for three years he governed the city of Yangzhou. In the autumn of 1951, just after Mao's Communists had taken power, a workforce was knocking down the walls of Yangzhou and using the rubble to build a new road. Workers had spotted a slab of marble with some strange markings on it. They handed it to a local antiquarian, who recognized what looked like scenes from the life of a Christian saint. Puzzled, he crated it up and sent it to a friend near Shanghai, a young Jesuit, Francis Rouleau, who was packing to leave, having been thrown out of the country by the new regime. Rouleau, well aware of the delicacy of researching religious imagery with the Communists looking over his shoulder, took rubbings and photographs. The slab vanished after he left, but from his records he made a report on what he had seen and examined.[1] It was a tombstone, decorated with scenes from the life of St Catherine – suitably so, given the name of the deceased: Katerina Yllionis, who died in July 1342. A few years later another tombstone turned up in Yangzhou, that of Katerina's brother Antonio, who had died in November 1344. Both were the children of Antonio 'Ilioni', as records in his hometown of Genoa spelled him. He had been executor of the estate of a friend who had come to China, done well there and, it seems, founded a little community. Indeed, Odoric mentions staying with Franciscans in Yangzhou in 1322, and also records three Nestorian churches. A Christian community had apparently been there for some time. Long enough, perhaps, for Marco to have been sent by Kublai to take it under his wing? To have been the governor not of the city, but of its Christians, a position that Rustichello either misunderstood or nudged him into upgrading?

[1] Father Francis Rouleau, SJ, 'The Yangchow Latin Tombstone as a Landmark of Medieval Christianity in China'.

In any event, from Marco, merchants and missionaries, news of Kublai filtered into public consciousness.

There's an item of information that Mongolists from time to time toss out that intrigued me. Did you know, they say, that Phags-pa's script is portrayed by the thirteenth- and fourteenth-century master, Giotto? It's one of those insignificant-but-interesting, coffee-time, drinks-party things: *I was talking to this Japanese academic the other day, and he told me . . . Good heavens, that's amazing . . . Giotto? Really? Where? . . . Oh, I think it was something to do with the robe of Christ.* I had heard and read this a few times, and decided to check it out.

Yes, there could be a link between Kublai Khan and Giotto. His name was Rabban (Master) Sauma, a monk who journeyed west from Kublai's realm and was the first known traveller ever to arrive in Europe from China. Sauma was a mirror-image of Marco Polo, with differences: his stay in Europe lasted less than a year, and he was an official envoy who rated top-level meetings. His is a wonderful tale, which vanished in its original Persian form, surviving only in an adulterated Syriac translation undiscovered until the late nineteenth century. The man and his adventures have been superbly resurrected by Morris Rossabi in *Voyager from Xanadu.* 'In these days when multiculturalism is in the air,' he says, 'it seemed fitting to write about a man who flourished in a variety of cultures and who worked to build bridges between them.' But there's more to the story than that: it is one of history's what-ifs, for Sauma very nearly succeeded in forging an alliance between the Mongols and Christian Europe, an alliance that could have changed the course of history. So, for the next few pages, put Giotto out of mind and focus on Sauma.

Sauma was an Önggüd, one of a Turkish tribe that lived on

the Yellow River in today's mid-China and had early on thrown in their lot with Genghis. Living on a major trade route westward, they had converted to Nestorian Christianity, the sect which claimed Christ had two natures, divine and human, and that Mary was the mother of the human, not the god. Declared heretical by Rome, the Nestorians had gone their own way very successfully in Central Asia and China, winning a reputation as good doctors and good businessmen who were remarkably tolerant of local practices. Members included Kublai's mother Sorkaktani and Hulegu's wife. The Önggüd appealed to Genghis because they made good officials. Later, they proved good allies to Kublai in his fight against his cousin Kaidu.

Sauma, born around 1240, joined the priesthood at 25 and became a hermit in mountains 50 kilometres south-west of Beijing. Famous for his asceticism and learning, he would have remained in scholarly seclusion had he not been joined after some years by an eager 15-year-old student named Markos. For a decade master and pupil remained isolated from the world, untouched by the momentous changes going on around them, until Markos became convinced that they should go to Jerusalem to receive the highest level of absolution he could think of. Since the two priests feared neither hardship nor death, Nestorians in Beijing backed them, and so did Kublai. The two priests were good publicity in his efforts to keep the sympathy of the sect to which his mother had belonged. In addition, by chance, this was about the time the Polos returned to Beijing with young Marco, so Kublai could well have been hoping for a boom in East–West contacts overland. Sauma and Markos might be able to bring back western experts who would be useful in his new Beijing. He gave them one of the official golden passes, *paiza*, which allowed them to make use of the postal relay system and to claim care en route. They gathered a caravan of camels, grooms, cooks and guards, and set off, probably in 1275.

It took a long time. The first leg took them back to their homeland on the Yellow River and on through Xinjiang via the Gansu Corridor, skirting the Takla Makan desert to Hotan, the multinational oasis at the base of the Kunlun Mountains. Now they were out of Kublai's protection, into Kaidu's territory. The place had become notorious for brigands. Wisely they headed for Kaidu's camp in Talas, carefully not mentioning either Kublai or Persia, both Kaidu's current enemies. Then on across mountain and desert, enduring heat, bitter winds, avalanches, hunger, thirst and several robberies, and so at last via Tus (today's Mashhad, in north-east Iran) to Kublai's nephew, the Il-khan Abaqa, in his former capital Maragheh; because here, by chance, the Nestorian leader, the Catholicos, Patriarch Mar Denha, was staying. After an emotional meeting and a tour of the local Nestorian sites, they town-hopped westward to Arbil in northern Iraq. Then came a sudden change of plan. The Catholicos summoned them to Baghdad and gave them a new mission: to win the ear of Abaqa for Nestorians. Off then to Tabriz, the Il-khan's new capital, undamaged during the Mongol invasions because, unlike Baghdad, it had surrendered. In this cosmopolitan centre, with its rich markets, many Christian sects and Italian merchants, they showed Abaqa the *paiza* from Uncle Kublai, and received all the recognition the Nestorians wanted, and all the help they needed.

As it happened, there was war further west, so they were stuck; but in great comfort, because the Catholicos promoted them both, Markos to be a metropolitan, equivalent to a bishop, and Sauma to 'visitor general' in China, a sort of roving ambassador (not that he would ever have a chance to perform this role). No, no, they demurred, they wanted a simple life, they wanted to go on with their pilgrimage. But they had no choice. They accepted, and put their travels on hold.

Events now took a most surprising turn. A year later, the Catholicos was dead, and the 36-year-old Markos was appointed to succeed him. For the next five years, he and his middle-aged master were absorbed by local and church politics – the death of Abaqa, a vicious round of in-fighting and final confirmation of their offices.

In 1286 the new Il-khan Arghun found himself needing support against Egyptians and other Muslims, and came up with an extraordinary idea. He wanted to approach Europe to suggest another crusade, Christians and Mongols together against Islam. Considering the horror caused in Europe by the Mongol advance only 40 years before, this sounds totally bizarre; but rather less so, taking into account that there had been some co-operation between Mongols and Christian crusaders 20 years after that. The deal was this: in exchange for Europe's help, Arghun would deliver Jerusalem to them. To set the scheme in motion, he needed a sophisticated, well-travelled, multi-lingual envoy, and Sauma was just the man. He knew Turkish, Chinese and probably Mongol from childhood. Now he knew Persian as well. There were many Italians in the Il-khanate, so interpretation was no problem.

Arghun gave Sauma letters to the pope, the Byzantine Emperor, and the French and English kings. In 1287, the ambassador and three companions left for the Black Sea, where they took a ship to Constantinople. Here he met the Emperor Andronicus, saw the sites, admired relics – and achieved nothing much, for an anti-Muslim coalition meant eastern and western churches working together, which was not about to happen.

And so, in June 1287, he and his small entourage, minus Markos (who as Catholicos had duties closer to home), sailed past Sicily and an erupting Mount Etna, to Naples, and then overland to Rome, only to discover that the pope was dead, and a new one not yet chosen. Sauma was greeted instead, with due respect, by the cardinals. They asked him first about his native land, and his unrecorded reply must have been the first detailed report of Kublai ever heard in Europe. Then they moved rapidly on to his faith, with questions he answered so carefully, emphasizing early church fathers rather than the contentious matters of Christ's nature and the exact status of the Holy Spirit, that the cardinals did not entirely grasp that they were dealing with a supposed heretic. They were hugely impressed with his erudition. 'It is a marvellous thing,' they said, 'that thou who art a Christian, and a deacon of the Throne of the Patriarch of the east, hast come upon an embassy from the King of the Mongols.' But on the matter of a crusade, they could not commit in the absence of a new pope.

He was told all the stories and shown all the sights – the place of Paul's martyrdom (where Paul's severed head had leaped in the air three times, crying 'Christ! Christ! Christ!'), one of Jesus's seamless robes, some wood from Jesus's cradle, the original Crown of Thorns – and appreciatively took all these relics and tales at face value.

But he was anxious to move on. His mission was still only half done. There were the kings of France and England still to see.

Leaving the heat of Italy behind, it took Sauma a month to work his way from inn to inn along France's dusty dirt roads. Now about 60, he must have been near breaking point. But in Paris, France's ambitious teenage king, Philip the Fair, gave him a great reception and a comfortable house. Once recovered, Sauma put his case. Philip seemed to be impressed. If Mongols were ready to help retake Jerusalem, what could Christians do but respond? In fact, he was eager to make a display of strength for reasons of his own – to gain control over English domains in France, to assert French claims to Flanders, to keep the Vatican from siphoning off funds from French church properties.

Assuming that Philip was now a fully paid-up member of

the Mongol–European Alliance, Sauma moved on to Edward I of England, who fortunately was in his French colony, Aquitaine. Sauma reached Bordeaux after a three-week journey in October 1287, identified himself, and was at once invited to see the king. After presenting Arghun's gifts of jewels and silk, Sauma put forward the idea of a crusade. Edward loved it. He himself had vowed to take up the cross that spring. It fitted his plans precisely. Sauma surely believed he had two-thirds of his task done; the final third would fall into place when he returned to Rome.

As if to seal the pact, Edward invited his new ally to give him and his court communion according to his own rite, which differed only in minor respects from the Roman one. This was followed by a feast, which would have been lavish – one of Edward's other banquets fed hundreds of guests with 10 oxen and 59 lambs – though it might have crossed Sauma's mind, as the only person in the world able to make such a comparison, that a few hundred was no match for the 6,000 who dined in Kublai's great hall in Beijing.

Everything now depended on Rome, for without the pope there could be no crusade. Still, however, there was no pope. Winter was closing in. Sauma headed south, to the mildness of Genoa – a garden paradise, as he called it, where he could eat grapes year-round. After three months of growing frustration came the news: *habemus papem*, Jerome of Ascoli, enthroned as Nicholas IV on 1 March 1288.

An invitation followed, and an audience, with a fine speech from Sauma, the delivery of Arghun's gifts and a generous response from Nicholas. Sauma was an honoured guest, he said, and would of course stay for Easter. Sauma was delighted, and asked to celebrate mass. His request was granted and the mass was held, with hundreds watching. No-one understood a thing, but all approved the actions. Sauma countered by asking to receive communion from the pope himself. So it happened, before a huge crowd, on Palm

Sunday, with further celebrations on Passover (Maundy Thursday), Good Friday, Holy Saturday and Easter Day.

Now Sauma requested permission to leave for home. Nicholas demurred, Sauma insisted: he needed to tell his own people of his generous reception. Sauma also took the liberty of asking for some relics. The pope was momentarily fazed: if we gave relics to all who asked, he said, there wouldn't be any left; but, he added, in this case he would provide some – a piece of Jesus's clothing, something of the Virgin's scarf, a few assorted saintly relics; and for Markos, the Catholicos, a bejewelled crown of gold, a purple robe lined with gold thread, socks decorated with pearls and a papal ring . . .

. . . and several letters, confirming the position of Markos and Sauma, and another for Arghun, which at last came to the point. Jesus had given authority to Peter, and thus to all succeeding popes. Arghun should recognize the true faith. As for a crusade, it was up to the pope to proclaim, not others to suggest, because he would bear responsibility for its success or failure. Let Arghun convert, accept papal authority, and God would give him the strength to seize Jerusalem and become a champion of Christianity. In brief: no practical aid, no crusade.

Still, when Sauma reached Persia in September, Arghun was pleased. There was, it seemed, a foundation for peace and diplomacy (and this, remember, was only some 60 years after Genghis's death, and a mere 30 since the destruction of Baghdad and Kublai's succession). There was a three-day banquet for Sauma and the Catholicos.

Of course, the crusade idea was dead in the water. Arghun tried to summon interest in France and England, but got only evasive answers. He himself was sidetracked by challenges from the Golden Horde and rebellious Muslims. He died in 1291, along with his dreams of further conquests. By then, it was too late anyway. The same year the Egyptian Mamluks took Acre, the last Christian outpost in the Middle East, and the crusading era came to an end.

And Sauma ended his days with a fine, new, well-endowed church, spending as much time as possible with his old friend Markos, both no doubt hardly able to believe their transformation from hermit and avid pupil. In late 1293 he fell ill in Baghdad, harboured his strength until Markos arrived to say farewell, and died in January 1294, coincidentally within a month of Kublai himself. With Markos grief-stricken at his graveside, he was buried in Baghdad's main Nestorian church.

What if Nicholas had backed the alliance? The papacy, France, England and the Mongols would have joined the crusaders in defending their castles in Syria, possibly with some strange consequences: Islam pushed out of the Middle East; Jerusalem delivered to the pope, under an English–French–Italian–Mongol administration; Arghun a Christian convert; Christianity taking a leap into Central Asia . . . and all because Kublai had decided that Sauma and Markos had a role to play in his plans.

And now, to echo Marco, I must mention another thing that I had forgotten: Sauma's possible link with Giotto, in the form of strange writing on Christ's robe in one of Giotto's paintings.

Rabban Sauma would surely have had his *paiza* with him in Rome. It would have been seen and admired, its script copied. Twelve years later, Giotto was in Rome, in time for the huge centennial celebrations of 1300 held by Pope Boniface VIII, no doubt gathering ideas to inject into future paintings. In 1305 he was in Padua, about to begin work on his greatest masterpiece, the Arena Chapel frescoes: 67 paintings that cover the whole interior with scenes from the life of Christ. One of the aspects of his originality was his readiness to paint elements of contemporary life into his creations.

Famously, he included in his *Adoration of the Magi* a Star of David that was in fact Halley's Comet, which had made a particularly spectacular appearance in October–November 1301.

I searched every robe of Christ in the Arena Chapel: no strange writing there. But two pictures made me look closer. In the Nativity, the Virgin lies in the stable, rather well dressed given the circumstances. On her dress, just visible beneath her cloak, is a hem displaying some rather oddly familiar designs: squiggles and lines making squares. In the Resurrection fresco, *The Angel at the Tomb*, the same patterns decorate the hems of garments on Roman soldiers who are asleep, unaware of the miracle taking place right beside them; and they are there again on the hem of Mary Magdalene's dress.

I'm sorry to spoil a good story, but these patterns are not Phags-pa's letters. They might, however, just possibly be pastiches of them, the sort of thing that Giotto might have added to provide a touch of exoticism – brought from the mysterious East, moreover, by a Christian. It's a detail; and a bit of a stretch (17 years between Rabban Sauma's visit and Giotto's painting); and perhaps it's mere coincidence. But it's odd, nevertheless. Perhaps there really is a chain of causes and effects linking Xanadu and Padua: a Chinese emperor worried about communicating with his subjects, a brilliant Tibetan monk, a long-distance Turkish Christian traveller, a pope eager for knowledge of the Mongol empire – and an artist injecting a hint of chinoiserie into his masterpiece.

Thinking about the possible transmission of a new script raised a question in my mind. Much of this book has been about Kublai's extraordinary achievements, but the flip side of his life and times is equally intriguing: his failures, his limitations. Given his skills in leadership and his intellectual range, what more might he have done? There is a particular link that might have been made between East and West that would have transformed our world in astonishing ways.

The question is this: why didn't Kublai invent printing with movable type? He had it right there in his hands.

Consider:

Kublai, uniquely placed astride several cultures, knew that no existing script was good enough for his purposes: all were either too hard or too obscure or unacceptable to other members of his imperial family. In theory, Phags-pa's script solved the problem pretty well, even if in practice it did not take root.

Kublai was immersed in books – by the thousand in his own government, by the million in society at large. But the books were not produced by the method invented in the West by Johannes Gutenberg in about 1450: using movable metal type to make up many pages at a time and run them off printing presses. The eastern method of printing, which had been in existence since the fifth century, was to cut text or a picture in reverse into wood, cover this block with ink and print from it onto paper. At first, the technique had been used to make seals, stamps and religious pictures; then, in the late eighth century, the first books appeared. The technology was basic, effective and technically easy, but hampered by fundamental inefficiencies. It took days to make a block, pages could only be printed one at a time, and the information could only be used in that form: the block. Every new page demanded a new block; every new book, many new blocks. Discarded blocks of out-of-print books clogged the yards of printing works. Often, they simply became firewood.

The solution was obvious. If each character had its own block, as in stamps, you could make up any text you liked, and reuse the characters after printing. No need to carve every page; no need for the millions of discarded blocks. Remember Pi Sheng, who supposedly invented printing with movable type in the eleventh century? His idea was to cut his characters in wet clay, in reverse, and bake them. To print, he selected his characters, put them in a frame, inked them, and took a rubbing with cloth or paper. The technique worked; the technology improved and was adopted by the Koreans, whose first book printed with movable metal type appeared in 1234. The Mongols had first invaded Korea in 1216, with much back-and-forth over the next 50 years. It was Kublai who finally made Korea part of the Mongol empire in 1271. So possibly Kublai himself, and certainly his scientific advisers, knew about printing with movable metal type.

They also knew the problems. It was even more trouble than block-printing. The business of choosing the correct character from at least 8,000, maybe 40,000 or more depending on design requirements, offered no advantage in design and not much in speed. Besides, it was an implied threat to two ancient skills, calligraphy and block-carving. True, there were those who remained intrigued by the idea. In 1297 Wang Zhen, a magistrate from Dongping in Shandong province, made 30,000 wooden characters set out in two revolving round tables, which gave easier access to the type. Later, governments produced some astonishing publications with movable type – such as a 1726 encyclopedia of 5,000 volumes that used 250,000 characters – but for day-to-day use this method of printing remained too cumbersome to be more than a technological oddity.

Kublai was thus in a position to see the *real* problem behind both block-printing and movable-type printing: namely, China's writing system. China's script records syllables.[2] It is this that held back Chinese printing until

---

[2] With two exceptions, as I discovered with relief in my first struggles to memorize written characters – the free-floating *r* and *dz* sounds, e.g. in *nar* (where) and *beizi* (cup). These sounds are meaningless on their own, and could thus qualify as 'letters'.

modern techniques and modern demands – mass-market books, newspapers – made it worthwhile to develop the industry in the twentieth century.

But Kublai had the answer, right there, in front of his face. It existed in the form of the alphabetical script adopted from the Uighurs on his grandfather's instigation. It existed again in the alphabetical script devised by Phags-pa. He thus formed another link in the chain that led back 3,400 years to the point when a Middle Eastern immigrant community in ancient Egypt started to adapt hieroglyphs and stumbled upon that revolutionary invention, the alphabet.

Like Chinese, other early writing systems – Egyptian hieroglyphic, Mesopotamian cuneiform – were based on syllables, which seem the natural basic components of language. But language has a much more fundamental level, namely the meaningless bits and pieces of noise that make up syllables. The genius of the alphabet – any alphabet – is that it uses a few symbols, no more than a few dozen, to represent the whole range of linguistic sounds, even non-sounds (like the silent gathering of energy before the little explosion that begins the letter *p*). It is not a one-to-one match between sound and symbol, as is often claimed. Its great strength is its fuzziness, which confers flexibility. It's this quality that allows it to represent any sound in any language, once you have mastered the conventions of that particular system of trans-literation: a Chinese *r* is a sort of buzz (like the *s* in treasure), a French *r* is a Scottish *ch*, a German *r* is a throat-rattle, a child's *r* in English is often a *w* (*w*ound the *w*agged *w*ocks the *w*agged *w*ascal *w*an). This combination of fuzziness and simplicity gives it a massive advantage over scripts based on syllables.

So Kublai had at his disposal several of the major elements that in Gutenberg's hands almost two centuries later helped the Renaissance on its way. Out went scribes and their beautiful, slow ways; in came the printing-press, and a slew of advances, all feeding on each other: mass markets and universal literacy and cheap books and scholars exchanging information and standing on each other's shoulders. Copernicus's ideas were unreadably obscure, but once printed they remained in libraries, waiting for Galileo to confirm them. A scribe took a week to copy a couple of high-quality pages, years to copy a single bible. Gutenberg and his team perfected a whole new technology and printed 180 copies of his famous bible in two years. By 1500, 250 printing operations across Europe were producing 2,000 titles – over 200,000 books – per year. In 1518–25, Germany alone printed a million books each year; and one-third of them were by Martin Luther, whose anti-papal *Ninety-Five Theses* kick-started the Reformation and who has therefore, with some justification, been blamed and praised alike for causing the greatest split in the Christian church. And from the Renaissance and the Reformation sprang a new Europe, a Europe that seized the world, dominated trade, founded nations, discovered new lands – precisely what Genghis and Kublai intended for their empire.

A revolution of this nature might have been initiated under Kublai's aegis. Kublai's China had the technology, the ships, and the intercontinental links by sea and land to back his imperial ambitions. He or his extremely bright advisers might have taken the next steps, which was to turn Phags-pa's script into metal type, set it in frames and start printing. There was even a good financial reason to do this. In Europe, the push came from religion: the need to ensure that all Christian institutions were reading the same approved and error-free Bible. In Kublai's China, the push might well have come from the need to print vast amounts of paper money, with complex designs and several colours to prevent counterfeiting.

Why didn't it happen?

There were several vital technical steps that were missing. One was the right sort of paper. In China, paper was soft and absorbent as toilet-paper, ideal for scribes working with brushes and for block-printing. In Europe, scribes working with quills needed a much firmer, non-absorbent surface, which was the sort of paper Gutenberg needed to produce crisp, tiny lettering. Second, China did not have olives or grapes that needed to be squashed with heavy-duty presses, the devices that Gutenberg adapted to make the printing press. And third, someone would have needed to come up with Gutenberg's astonishing invention of the hand-mould, which could produce several hundred new lead types per day. This device, which now exists only in museums, was fundamental in printing for 500 years.

There is a final, and perhaps fundamentally crucial reason why there was no Yuan printing revolution. The purpose of printing is the transmission of information, and I believe – I am sorry to say this – that the Mongols had no information they wished to transmit. Deep down, what Kublai had created was Mongolia Inc., a vast corporate entity dedicated to creating wealth and power for itself, with nothing at the end save its own eternal survival. This had always been a problem. One of Genghis's main characteristics was his toleration. It was to him clearly true that Heaven had chosen him and his heirs for universal rule. But why this should be so was a mystery. All his life he wondered about it, hoping that perhaps other religions had the answer. His restlessness and tolerance were inherited by his successors, Kublai included – and he had no answers either. There was no great new truth to be promulgated. Nor, of course, did the Mongols have a tradition of great literature or great art. All they could do was to encourage the transmission of the art and literature of their subjects, the Chinese.

There is, therefore, an intellectual and artistic hollowness to the Mongol imperial enterprise. Its aim was purely to conquer and govern and finance itself. And I am not sure that this is enough of a message for any government, let alone one controlling an empire the size of Kublai's. In the end, the Mongols had nothing much to say.

As it was, Gutenberg gets the credit, and Marco Polo's *Travels* moved from script to print, with ever-increasing exposure. Long before the first printed editions – German, in 1477 – came off the press, the route taken by Marco had been closed off by the collapse of the Mongol empire and the Muslim resurgence spearheaded by the Turkish seizure of Constantinople in 1453.

Not wishing to be beholden to Muslim middlemen, Europe's merchants turned again to the sea route to the East. Traditionally, the goods they sought – silks, precious stones and, in particular, spices – were brought by Chinese junks to Malaysia, by Arab ships to India, Persia, Africa and Arabia, and thence via the Red Sea to the Mediterranean. But this was a galling arrangement. Eastern pepper underwent a 50-fold increase in price on its journey to European kitchens. Clearly the thing to do, from the European perspective, was to fetch it yourself. Hence the race to discover and sail around the Cape of Good Hope; and hence Columbus's big idea – to reach the East by sailing round the world the other way, westward.

Let me repeat: his aim was to get to China and the land of the Great Khan. But wait a minute. We are now in the 1490s. Marco's book appeared around 1300. Two centuries have elapsed, *and the Great Khan is still alive?* Of course he can't be. But when the Muslims slammed the door on the overland route in the mid-fourteenth century, it was as if China entered a time-warp for Europeans. No-one had a clue what was happening out there. As far as they were concerned, Kublai Khan was immortal, and no-one seemed to question this extraordinary assumption. As John Larner puts it in *Marco Polo and the Discovery of the World*, 'For Europe, the Great

Khan [i.e. the last Yuan emperor] still lived and reigned 130 years after his expulsion from China.'

Columbus – Cristoforo Colombo – was a rough-and-ready Genoese driven by his obsession, his dream. Having tried for years to get backing from Portugal, he eventually won it from Spain, which turned out rather well for everyone, except America's indigenous peoples. It has become a commonplace of historical writing to say that Columbus was heading for Kublai's China as his first stop because he had read Marco Polo's descriptions of it. Supposedly, he carried the *Travels* with him on his first voyage in 1492 to make sure he could find his way when he got there. Whether this is true or not has been a matter of intense and highly technical controversy among scholars, but there is now a reluctant majority verdict that he didn't. The arguments are well summarized by John Larner. In brief: Columbus *did* own a copy of Marco's book (in Latin, printed in 1490), but, not being a great reader, he seems to have acquired it only *after* his return from the New World, to check what it was he had discovered.

His inspiration for the journey could have come from several sources, for by the fifteenth century Marco had become fully accepted as a reporter rather than a fantasist, and his information was being incorporated into 'maps', if such fanciful creations can be called maps. And Columbus may have had direct access to his ideas as the result of a letter written by a Florentine astrologer and scholar called Pozzo Toscanelli, who was a member of a sort of unofficial pan-European society of scholars. This same group included a Portuguese cleric, Fernão Martins, who became canon of Lisbon and adviser to Alfonso V of Portugal. To him in 1474 Toscanelli sent a map, with a letter: 'I have spoken with you elsewhere about a shorter way, travelling by sea, to the lands of spices than that which you are taking by Guinea . . . It is said that in a most noble port called Zaiton' – which he then describes in Polo-like terms. '[It] is under a prince who is called the Great Khan,' who rules many cities including the 'noble and very great city of Qinsay', which lies in the province of Mangi (southern China) near the province of Cathay (northern China). It happens that Columbus was in Lisbon at the time. As Larner suggests, it is possible that he saw or copied Toscanelli's letter, and thus acquired Marco's information at second hand.

That he had it is certain. When he left in search of Cathay in 1492, he recorded in his journal that his royal backers, Ferdinand and Isabella, had given him letters for 'the Great Khan and for all the kings and lords of India'. When he reaches Cuba, he learns of a river ahead and 'says he will endeavour to go to the Great Khan who he thought was in that region or to the city of Cathay which is in the Great Khan's possession, which he says is very large according to what he was told before he left'. (The reference to Cathay as a city and the words 'what he was told' both suggest an oral source of information rather than a reading of Polo.)

It is an extraordinary chain of causes and effects. Kublai welcomed Marco, who wrote his *Travels*, which indirectly inspired Columbus in his epoch-making voyage. Perhaps this was Kublai's greatest contribution to world history: that he was the magnet that drew Columbus westward, and put the Old World in touch with the New.

By 1492, then, Kublai had become rooted in the western consciousness, no longer as the nightmare his grandfather had been, but as an end-of-rainbow monarch of infinite wealth and glory. It is in this form that he comes through to English-speakers today, thanks to distorted versions of Polo, an opium-induced vision and a famous interruption.

Polo's *Travels* came via an Italian translation (by Ramusio) to the English compiler of voyages of discovery, Richard Hakluyt, whose massive three-volume work appeared in

1598–1600. This, plus Hakluyt's unpublished work, plus additional material, was then edited by his colleague Samuel Purchas into an even larger work published in various editions, concluding with *Hakluytus Post-humus, or Purchas His Pilgrimes* in 1625. In this compendium we read: 'In Xamdu did Cublai Can build a stately Palace, encompassing sixteen miles of plaine ground with a wall, wherein are fertile Meddowes, pleasant Springs, delightful Streames, and all sorts of beasts of chase and game, and in the middest thereof a sumptuous house of pleasures.'

For the famous story of the vision and interruption, we go forward 170 years, to an evening in June 1797. The scene is an isolated hillside farm on Exmoor near the coast between Porlock and Lynton. Enter the poet Samuel Taylor Coleridge, who is staying here. He has been out on a long walk communing with nature and has been suddenly taken short with a terrible stomach upset – dysentery, he calls it. He takes some opium, reads the passage in Purchas, falls asleep and dreams a wilder version of what he has just read. He is dragged from sleep by 'a person on business from Porlock' – one of the most famous incognitos in literary history, kept anonymous because Coleridge was developing a habit, and this (so some have suggested) was probably his dealer. He is aware that he has on the tip of his tongue a poem some 300 lines long. The deal takes an hour, by which time he has forgotten most of the poem. He recalls a few lines, and wrestles together enough a few weeks later to make the 'fragment' that has become one of the most famous poems in the English language:

> In Xanadu did Kubla Khan
> A stately pleasure-dome decree:
> Where Alph, the sacred river, ran
> Through caverns measureless to man
> Down to a sunless sea.

So twice five miles of fertile ground
With walls and towers were girdled round:
And there were gardens bright with sinuous rills,
Where blossomed many an incense-bearing tree;
And here were forests ancient as the hills,
Enfolding sunny spots of greenery.
But oh! that deep romantic chasm which slanted
Down the green hill athwart a cedarn cover!
A savage place! as holy and enchanted
As e'er beneath a waning moon was haunted
By woman wailing for her demon-lover!
And from this chasm, with ceaseless turmoil seething,
As if this earth in fast thick pants were breathing,
A mighty fountain momently was forced:
Amid whose swift half-intermitted burst
Huge fragments vaulted like rebounding hail,
Or chaffy grain beneath the thresher's flail:
And 'mid these dancing rocks at once and ever
It flung up momently the sacred river.
Five miles meandering with a mazy motion
Through wood and dale the sacred river ran,
Then reached the caverns measureless to man,
And sank in tumult to a lifeless ocean:
 And 'mid this tumult Kubla heard from far
Ancestral voices prophesying war!
The shadow of the dome of pleasure
Floated midway on the waves;
Where was heard the mingled measure
From the fountain and the caves.
It was a miracle of rare device,
A sunny pleasure-dome with caves of ice!
A damsel with a dulcimer
In a vision once I saw:
It was an Abyssinian maid,
And on her dulcimer she played,

Singing of Mount Abora.
Could I revive within me
Her symphony and song,
To such a deep delight 'twould win me,
That with music loud and long,
I would build that dome in air,
That sunny dome! those caves of ice!
And all who heard should see them there,
And all should cry, Beware! Beware!
His flashing eyes, his floating hair!
Weave a circle round him thrice,
And close your eyes with holy dread,
For he on honey-dew hath fed,
And drunk the milk of Paradise.

This has, of course, absolutely nothing to do with Kublai, for Xanadu never had any chasms, caves or forests, and certainly boasted no incense-trees, only a slowly flowing river and rolling treeless hills; the sea, which is no less sunny than any other, is two days' hard ride away. It has everything to do with the Quantock hills, the wild Somerset coast, the glorious wooded slopes, a host of literary references, Coleridge's love of nature and a growing addiction to opium. I'm not sure the poetry works all that well today. 'Momently' is an odd word to use twice in six lines. But that's a quibble. It is the surreal mix of images that makes the magic, which is why the name of Kublai Khan echoes in the minds of English-speakers who have never heard of Coleridge.

And why the name of Xanadu does too. Film buffs are surprised to learn that it's a real place, because they know it as Charles Foster Kane's spooky estate in Orson Welles's 1941 film, *Citizen Kane*. Pop enthusiasts of a certain age recall it as a song by Olivia Newton John. IT experts know it as the name given by the visionary Ted Nelson to the idea that all the world's information could be published as hypertext:

Project Xanadu, 'the explicit inspiration for the World Wide Web', as the website puts it, continuing:

> About the name: No, we did not get it from Olivia Newton-John. It is an actual place in Mongolia [China, actually, Ted] which is described in a poem considered by many the most romantic poem in the English language ... This poem's tradition also associates the name 'Xanadu' with memory and lost work, because Coleridge said he lost part of the poem due to a mundane interruption. We chose the name 'Xanadu', with all these connotations, to represent a magic place of literary memory and freedom, where nothing would be forgotten.

Listening to these echoes down the distorting corridors of time, we're a long way from Kublai's Shang-du. But it was he who gave the yell that started it all, and I think he would have been gratified.

17

A HOLY MOUNTAIN,
A SECRET GRAVE

THE TURNING POINT WAS 1281, WHEN KUBLAI WAS 66. HIS EMPIRE
had reached its limits, and there is, by hindsight, a sense of
desperation to his efforts to extend it further. From a modern
perspective, a psychologist might suggest that he, the world's
most powerful man, was fighting off any recognition that
dreams must die, ambitions fade, the body age, and that the
best he could hope for was an empire that endured within
the borders he had set for it.

What was his demon? Depression, for a start. In 1281 his
favourite wife, Chabi, his chief companion and adviser for 41
years, died. In the first 20 years of their marriage, before he
became emperor, she bore and raised four sons, including his
heir Jingim, and five daughters, making sure the children
were educated in all the cultures that surrounded them,
Mongol and Chinese, Buddhist and Confucian. She was
famous for her frugality and good sense. She used to tell the
court ladies to collect old bowstrings, because they could be
used as thread and woven into cloths. She redesigned Mongol
hats, giving them a peak as protection from the sun. She was

not blinded by her husband's successes. After the victory over the Song capital in 1276, she is supposed to have warned him against overweening ambition: 'Your handmaiden has heard that from ancient times there has never been a kingdom that lasted a thousand years.' It was she who made sure the captured Song empress was treated with due respect.

Then there came scandal with the murder of the grasping and unpopular Muslim minister, Ahmad, bringing with it the sudden proof of Kublai's poor judgement. Still, at least the succession was secured, in the form of Jingim, Pure Gold, second son of Kublai and Chabi, now in the prime of life at 38. He had always been the intended heir since the death of an elder brother in childhood. After Ahmad's murder he came into his own, and Kublai rallied enough to take another wife, Nambui, a distant cousin of Chabi's and possibly selected by her before her death in order to give her husband the support he needed. It seemed to work. He was clearly still fit enough to face life because, at the age of almost 70, he managed to make Nambui pregnant. Having borne a son, she began to act as his go-between, protecting him from overwork.

Jingim was increasingly the man in charge, so much so that in 1285 a senior official floated the idea that Kublai abdicate in favour of his son. Somehow, despite Nambui's protection, Kublai heard this, and flew into a rage. In the ensuing crisis, with Kublai no doubt suspecting his son of disloyalty, tragedy struck again. Jingim fell ill from some unspecified disease and died.

There was still a remnant of the old Kublai left; enough for one last effort. He would need it. All this while Kublai's troublesome and ambitious cousin Kaidu had been active in Central Asia, often almost forgotten in China amid the business of administration and foreign adventuring. But he had been busy building support all around the fringes of the empire, reaching out southward into Tibet and at the same time eastward to Manchuria. If Kublai was not careful he would find himself cut off from his own hinterland.

In Tibet, Phags-pa's successor on his death in 1280 had been a 13-year-old boy plucked from the Mongol court, causing much resentment locally. In 1285 one Buddhist sect, the Brigung, turned to violence, attacking the monasteries of Phags-pa's sect, the Saskya. Perhaps this was spontaneous; but Kaidu saw his chance. His protégé Duwa came in to aid the rebels, while at the same time slicing away at Kublai's garrisons and postal relay stations in Uighur lands – today's Xinjiang. Duwa laid siege to the town of Khara-Khocho (now ruins 45 kilometres east of Turpan) for six months, attacking the earthwork walls with a dozen catapults and 100 naphtha-throwers – all to no avail. He gave up only when the town's desperate commander lowered his daughter over the walls as a gift. The following year, Kaidu took Ürümqi (Beshbaligh as it then was), the Uighur capital. In 1288, 1,050 craftsmen abandoned Khotan (Hotan) and Kashgar for safer bases back east. It was all proving too much. The following year Kublai ordered a total retreat from Xinjiang, leaving Kaidu with double his original territory. But only briefly. Kublai despatched a junior grandson at the head of an army. The rebel HQ was destroyed, 10,000 died (so sources claim: it sounds high), the postal relay stations were made good and Mongol authority was restored, turning Tibet into a back-water for the next century.

Meanwhile, Kaidu had been active elsewhere. In 1287 he threatened to link up with a new challenger, a feisty 30-year-old prince named Nayan, a descendant of Genghis's half-brother Belgutei, in Manchuria. Kublai was faced with the grim prospect that all the northern reaches of his empire, a great arc of steppeland from Xinjiang, across his original Mongolian homeland and into Manchuria, would fall away to become the pastoral–nomadic empire to which the rebels aspired. So, to investigate, Kublai picked a hero: Bayan, general, Grand Councillor, conqueror of the Song campaign. (I know Bayan vs Nayan is confusing, but that's the way it was.) According to one source, Bayan was about to accept Nayan's invitation to a banquet when he learned it was a trap, and managed to escape in time. Kublai decided on firm action. Though the details are obscure, he sent Bayan to keep the two rebels apart by occupying Karakorum, while he himself led another army against Nayan.

Marco tells the story in his usual overblown way. In 12 days Kublai gathers his troops, 360,000 cavalry and 100,000 infantry – impossible numbers that we should at once cut by 90 per cent. Even so, 46,000 is a significant force. Astrologers are consulted, and predict victory. Scouts are sent out ahead to arrest anyone they see, thus preventing word of the advance leaking out. Kublai is lifted into his mobile battle-station, a miniature fortress borne by four elephants harnessed together abreast. A 20-day march brings them to a plain, probably somewhere in the vast open spaces of Mongolia's south-eastern steppes. The rebels are surprised, but form up, both sides singing to the accompaniment of 'certain two-stringed instruments'. Then kettle-drums – cauldrons a couple of metres across, covered in buffalo-skin – boom out the order to attack. Arrows fall like rain, men clash with mace, lance and sword, the wounded cry, the battle sounds like thunder, as battles commonly did in the clichés of medieval romances. Kublai wins; Nayan is captured, and executed in the traditional way for princes, without the shedding of blood. 'He was wrapt in a carpet, and tossed to and fro so mercilessly that he died.'

Kaidu, ever the strategist, pulled back westward to avoid a battle, preferring to keep his forces intact for hit-and-run assaults (and also, surely, distracted by conflict that had broken out with Persia, with which he remained in constant enmity for the rest of his life; but that's another story). So there was no showdown; but at least his retreat prevented a possible link-up between the rebels in Central Asia and Manchuria.

With Bayan in control in Karakorum and re-establishing control over surrounding areas, Kaidu, de facto khan of Inner Asia, did not attempt anything large-scale for the next three years. Bayan was blamed for allowing him to escape – some even accused him of collusion with Kaidu, forcing Kublai to relieve him of his command and banish him to Datong in northern Shanxi province to await further orders. Before Bayan went, however, Kaidu was rash enough to return, and this time received a sharp lesson, with the loss of 3,000 men into captivity. That was enough to pen him up in his own territory, behind frontiers garrisoned by Yuan troops. But nor was there any further attempt by Kublai to regain control of Central Asia. The two had reached stalemate.

That stalemate lasted until Kublai's death in 1294, and beyond. His heir, Temür, having abandoned his grandfather's grandiose schemes for overseas expansion, thought he could finally tackle the task of crushing rebellion at home. He was wrong. In September 1301 he sent a massive force, vastly outnumbering Kaidu's, and the two met in a series of four battles in south-west Mongolia, where the Altai mountains begin to fall away into the Gobi's gravel plains. Sources disagree on who won. It seems fair to say it was a draw. So there was no final solution; nor would there be with Kaidu, because, despite the efforts of his Chinese doctors, he died shortly after the battle – of wounds, according to Rashid, or perhaps of sheer exhaustion after 45 years of campaigning. He was, after all, almost 70.

Duwa, now king-maker, crowned Kaidu's first-born, Chapar – not a popular choice: an 'extremely lean and illfavoured' youth, according to Rashid – but remained dominant himself, eliminating all those heirs of Kaidu who had opposed him, until his death. Thereafter Chapar regained control, saw the struggle was in vain and surrendered to the Yuan in 1310, finally making the journey to court that his father had refused to make in 1264, and bringing to an end the challenge to imperial authority from Central Asia.

Personal losses, rebellion, defeat abroad: it was all too much. Kublai turned to food and drink. At court banquets he gorged on boiled mutton, breast of lamb, eggs, saffron-seasoned vegetables in pancakes, sugary tea and, of course, the Mongolian drink of choice: *airag* (fermented mare's milk, otherwise known by its Turkish name, *kumiss*). It was the drink in particular that undermined him. *Airag* and wine – he consumed both in prodigious amounts. As he became less active, as his powers waned, he put on weight, ballooning year by year into extreme obesity. He must have known it would kill him, but he didn't care. Knowing he had not much longer to live, he made peace with the spirit of his lost heir by nominating Jingim's third son, Temür, as his successor.

He also knew where he wanted to be buried: back in the land of his birth, in the heartland of the Mongol people, where the last of the Siberian mountain ranges, the Khenti, begin to give way to grasslands. This was where his grandfather, who had started it all, had been born, and this is where he was buried. Genghis, too, had died far from home, in the Liupan mountains of Ningxia province, just on the verge of the conquest of Xi Xia. For three weeks, his funeral cortège had carried his body northward, back across the Yellow River, along the Helan mountains, into the high grasslands of today's Inner Mongolia, across the Gobi's gravel plains and the grasslands of Mongolia itself, across the Kherlen river to the mountain that had been considered sacred by the Mongols from when they first arrived there some time around AD 800. Its name was Burkhan Khaldun – Holy Khaldun, as it is usually translated (though there are those who say that *burkhan* was nothing but an old word for 'willow'). Genghis knew this area – the two rivers of Kherlen and Onon, the Khenti mountains that give birth to them, the open grasslands they run through – like his own saddle. Burkhan Khaldun was the mountain on which Genghis had often eluded his enemies, on which it had come to him in a revelation (or so his people believed, because he told them so) that he had the backing of the Eternal Sky, Heaven above, to create a nation and an empire. He had promised to give thanks to Burkhan Khaldun every day. The place and the occasion had been captured in oral traditions, and then set down in the Mongols' foundation epic, *The Secret History of the Mongols*, by Shigi, adopted into Genghis's family as a boy. It was inconceivable that Genghis would be buried anywhere else, and equally inconceivable that his people would allow it ever to be desecrated. People often say that no-one knows where Genghis is buried. Don't believe them. Everyone in Mongolia knows within a few square miles where Genghis is buried. It is the exact spot on Burkhan Khaldun's vast, rounded, rocky, forested, scree-covered flanks that is the mystery. Horses were allowed to roam over the site, guards were placed at a suitable distance, trees grew, and to this day the site of the grave is unknown. Today treasure hunters eye Burkhan Khaldun as the place where one day a great find will be made, revealing infinite riches. Mongols say it should never be found, as Holy Genghis intended.

It was surely with a proprietary eye on this spot that in 1292 Kublai put one of his grandsons, Kamala, in charge of Genghis's *ordos*, his tent-palaces and estates. As the Persian historian Rashid ad-Din wrote only a few years after Kublai's death, the estates included

the Great Khorig [Forbidden Precinct] of Genghis Khan, which they call Burkhan Khaldun, and where the great *ordos* of Genghis Khan are still situated. These latter are guarded by

Kamala. There are four great *ordos* and five others, nine in all, and no one is admitted to them. They have made portraits of them [the family] there and constantly burn perfumes and incense.

My guess is that Kublai wanted to make sure that he, Kublai, and not Kaidu or any other rebellious upstart, laid claim to this sacred site. The tent-shrines must already have been in existence when Kamala arrived, guarding a grave site dug 70 years before, and long since overgrown. But tents are temporary things. In due course, nine would later become eight, the Eight White Tents which acted as a travelling shrine, drifting back and forth across Mongol lands until finally settling south of Dongsheng in Inner Mongolia, where they were transformed into today's Genghis Khan Mausoleum. Kamala needed something permanent in which to perform rites honouring Genghis and, in due course, Kublai. As Rashid adds, 'Kamala too has built himself a temple there.'

Burkhan Khaldun appears as Khan Khenti – the King of the Khenti – on maps. There are those who say they are not identical, but I don't believe them, and nor does the government, because every three or four years ministers and MPs by the dozen go there to do honour to the mountain, to Genghis, and also, if they think about it, to Kublai. They travel in many 4×4s, well equipped with winches, because it is quite a trip, as I discovered when I made it in 2002.

From Ulaanbaatar, you take the road east for 100 kilometres to the coal-mining town of Baganuur, an unappealing stack of Communist-era apartment blocks. That's where the paved road runs out. Then you head north over grassy hills, following a loose network of tracks – this is what Mongolians normally mean by a 'road' – which lead you to Möngönmört (meaning At the Silver Horse). You head on, with the Kherlen on your right, into the uninhabited region that is now the

Khan Khenti National Park. The tracks converge on a surprisingly solid wooden bridge (after all, the government comes this way sometimes). Beyond, you're on a single track, often muddy, sometimes impassable after a storm, bouncing through low willow bushes and scattered firs. After 25 kilometres you come to a peat bog and a ridge, the Threshold. If the car can climb the ridge, you are greeted with a stupendous view across the upper Kherlen, and a shocking descent over rutted peat that is either a morass (in wet weather) or as rough as tank-traps. Descending, if you dare, you cross the Kherlen (very shallow, with a stony bottom). At this point Burkhan Khaldun comes into view: 2,452 metres, not very high, but a Schwarzenegger shoulder-muscle of a mountain, a sort of Mongolian Ayers Rock, but seven times the size. Proceed for another 18 kilometres straight ahead, along a valley that closes in on you steadily until you reach a sign and a collection of tree-trunks all leaning together and covered in bits of blue silk and Tibetan prayer-sheets. This is an *ovoo*, a shrine, such as would normally be made of stones, if there were any stones in soil made soft by pine-needles. You are at the base of Burkhan Khaldun, and now you must climb. It will only take you a couple of hours to reach the top.

Very soon you reach a place that was once quite clearly artificially flattened. This area too is considered holy. Here is another silk-draped *ovoo*, with little offerings at its base: vodka bottles, saucers for incense-sticks. This was where Kamala's temple once stood, no doubt about it. In 1961 Johannes Schubert from Leipzig, the first westerner to climb the mountain, found many semi-circular roof tiles and bits of pottery here. Now you have to hunt around for such things. I found two bits of tile, which ignite an imaginary scene whenever I pick them up: the 29-year-old Kamala watching 50 Chinese builders at work on the wooden walls and pillars, while nearby tilers shape local clay into curved roof-tiles which they lay to dry on a tree-trunk covered with sacking.

Later they will be baked in an oven that stands ready nearby.

Kamala would have been keen to get the job done. He knew his grandfather did not have long to live.

And indeed, a year after Kamala returned, Kublai, now well into his 80th year, was hardly able to function except through his wife Nambui.

On 28 January 1294, New Year's Day by the lunar calendar, Kublai was too ill to attend the usual ceremonies in Beijing. No dressing in white, no great reception to receive tributes and praise from visiting vassals, no reviewing the parade of richly caparisoned elephants and white horses, no presiding over the banquet in the Great Hall. Everyone must have known the end was near. A messenger was sent galloping off to the only man who might be able to lift the emperor's spirits: Bayan, still awaiting his next assignment in Datong, 300 kilometres away. Three days later – no more, surely, in these circumstances – Bayan was with the emperor. But there was nothing to be done, except promise eternal loyalty. Kublai knew his end was near, and asked that Bayan be one of the three executors of his will (the others were the chief censor and the director of political affairs on the Secretariat. He weakened steadily, and on 18 February he died.

Two days later, the funeral cortège was ready. Considering Kublai's wealth and the money he had been spending on his campaigns, it would have seemed quite austere. Still, the entourage would have run into the hundreds: members of the family and government who were fit enough for the journey, plus guards, drovers, grooms, cooks, household servants, accompanied by spare horses, carts for the women, carts for the tents, and camels carrying all the paraphernalia suitable for a royal procession that would be on the road for three weeks and 1,000 kilometres. Somewhere quite near the front, behind a guard, would have come Kublai's hearse: a wagon bearing a tent, concealing a large coffin, well-sealed and packed with spices and other preservatives. Covering perhaps 50 kilometres a day – good going for such a crowd – the line would have wound through Beijing's guardian mountains where the Great Wall now runs, over ridges and valleys to the old Mongol–Chinese frontier at Kalgan (today's Zhangjiakou) and up on to the Mongolian plateau; avoiding the right turn to Xanadu – it would mean at least a two-day delay – it would have set out over the Gobi's dusty wastes, until at last the gravel gave way to grassy hills, and the shallow Kherlen, and finally the foothills of the Khenti.

Where he lies I doubt we shall ever know. There is a place, a half-hour's climb above Kamala's temple, where you leave the trees, now stunted and thinned by the height, and step out on to level ground. The summit is still a way ahead, sometimes a breaking wave of rock, sometimes invisible in cloud. The area on which you stand looks like a cemetery. I thought it was when I first saw it, because others think so too. The 'graves' you see are irregular puddles of stone, anything from a metre to three metres across. There are, I would guess, several hundred of them. It is easy to imagine them as graves, the piles of stone as flattened burial mounds. But there was something that didn't fit. The stone-puddles are irregular blobs, and they are all flat. Yet round about were several *ovoos*, stone ones, standing a metre or so high. Enough people come up here today to make and preserve *ovoos*. So why not preserve the 'graves'? And this was on the main path to the summit – not the best place for a secret burial, surely?

I now believe the features to be geological, the result of centuries of frost working magic on loose stones. These cold-weather and permafrost processes are the subject of much study by a rare breed of scientists called cryogeologists. If you glance at a cryogeological textbook, you see patterns – polygons, circles, rings and mounds – that look disturbingly artificial, like fairy rings in stone. Indeed, some early explorers who first saw them in the Arctic landscapes thought they were artificial. But they are all the result of temperature changes that cause minute expansions and contractions in stones, causing them to sort themselves into different sizes and shapes. No-one knows how long it takes, because it happens on geological timescales. They are no more artificial than snowflakes or the polygons of mud in dried-up lakes.

These stony circles suggest a perverse thought. Would not these natural 'graves' offer perfect camouflage for real ones? Who would ever know which among the hundreds was real? Even today, with modern archaeological techniques, it would take millions of dollars and years of work to research them all. Frankly, it's not going to happen.

Of one thing I am certain: Kamala would not have got the wrong place.

A scene replays in my mind whenever I recall my climb. A line of men is winding up through the slender firs, emerging onto this open ground. They are dressed in furs against the bitter cold, and their ornate leather boots with turned-up toes scrape through a thin covering of snow to the hard earth beneath. Six men – no, eight, for their burden is heavy – shoulder two poles that carry a simple coffin draped in blue and yellow silk. There are no lamas in attendance, no Buddhist trappings: this is a return to the austere, nomadic tradition that Genghis loved. Led by a masked shaman with a drum and rattle, the men proceed to the edge of the plateau, where there opens up a stupendous view: a snow-filled valley, a frozen river winding away to distant mountains. It is the land their khan never saw and yet called home.

A small group has been up here for some time, and with gloved hands they have removed stones from one of the hundreds of stony circles. A fire was lit in the shallow depression to melt the iron-hard earth. Slow digging with iron spades has made a grave. Now there is a reverent deposition, followed by prayers and an invocation by the shaman, accompanied by a steady beat on his drum; then the stones are replaced one by one until nothing separates this circle from any other. Kublai is beside his grandfather Genghis, and both are part of the landscape from which they and their empire sprang.

EPILOGUE: THE LEGACY OF THE GREAT KHAN

SHORTLY AFTER KUBLAI'S BURIAL ON BURKHAN KHALDUN, AN assembly was called to decide which of two of his grandsons would succeed him, Kamala or Temür (Temür, Kublai's provisional choice, had never been confirmed as heir). There was a dispute. A matriarch suggested a solution: Kublai had said that whoever knew the sayings of Genghis best was best suited to rule. It was agreed that the two claimants would compete. Temür, the younger, being eloquent and a good reciter, declaimed well, while Kamala, who stammered, could not match him. All cried out: 'Temür knows them better! . . . It is he that is worthy of crown and throne!'

Temür's inheritance was, in theory, astounding. His family ruled China, Korea, Tibet, Pakistan, Iran, most of Turkey, the Caucasus (Georgia, Armenia, Azerbaijan), most of habitable Russia, Ukraine and half of Poland – one-fifth of the world's land area. In fact, as with Kublai's, Temür's hold over the further reaches of this pan-Eurasian empire was nominal. Its nomad roots were a romance in the minds of the soft Mongol aristocracy, who seldom if ever visited Mongolia and who had as much connection with their 'homeland' as New York Irish marching down Fifth Avenue on St Patrick's Day. The empire became a crumbling edifice, its cracks papered over by memories of its founder.

The Golden Horde in southern Russia had begun two centuries of rule still known to Russians as the 'Tartar (or Tatar) Yoke'. Its Mongol rulers – ex-Mongols, as they soon were – turned to Islam, working closely with the rulers of Egypt, with whom they exchanged diplomatic corres-pondence complete with gold lettering and elaborate salutations, all in Turkish. Supposedly every khan had to be one of the Golden Kin, a descendant of Genghis, but as time went on almost any would-be ruler could make that claim. When a resurgent Russia under Catherine the Great annexed the Crimea in 1783, its khan was still proclaiming his Genghisid ancestry.

In Persia, the Il-khans (subordinate khans), as they called themselves, enslaved, plundered and taxed to the limit, entrenching ordinary people in bitter hostility to their rule. Trade favoured cities, which generated enough wealth to enable the Mongols to keep a precarious hold, even as they lost contact with their roots. Hulegu's great-grandson turned Muslim, and fought other Muslims, all with no gain. In 1307, a Mongol embassy to Edward II in England was the final, use-less attempt at self-promotion. Thirty years later, the last of the Mongols died with no heir, and Mongol rule vanished.

In Central Asia, Chaghadai's heirs ruled over a vague expanse constantly riven by religious dissension, wars and internecine strife. Here nomadic traditions remained strong, as did the urge to conquer. Constrained by Mongol rivals east and west, Chaghadai's heirs looked south to Afghanistan and India, invading several times, and inspiring a tradition that endured when Mongol rule fell into the bloody hands of Tamerlane. Though not in a direct line from Genghis, he justified himself as a reincarnation of Genghis – modest roots,

EPILOGUE

heavenly favours, brutal conquest and all. It is this claim that
explains why Tamerlane's descendant Babur called himself
'Mughal' when he seized power in India in the early sixteenth
century, establishing a dynasty that ended when the British
shuffled the last Mughal off the throne in 1857. His name, by
the way, was Bahadur, a distant echo of the Mongol *baatar*,
hero, the second element in the name of Mongolia's capital,
Ulaanbaatar (Red Hero). Modern English contains a fossil
remnant of the same word: a 'mogul', originally a wealthy
Indian, then a wealthy Anglo-Indian, is now a media tycoon.

For another 73 years after Kublai's death, his descendants
in China linked east and west, sharing with distant relatives
the free flow of trade, diplomats and experts. But the
Mongols were on shaky ground. Nomads no longer, they
never became truly Chinese. Though some of Kublai's ten
successors could speak Chinese, not one of them learned to
write it well. Rulers and ruled despised each other. True, there
was a peace dividend: the population rose back towards its
former levels; trade flourished. But Mongol authority
depended on power, and power seeped away.

Successions were disputed, conspiracy and assassination
thrived. In 1328, a two-month civil war ended in executions.
In 1331, plague ravaged parts of China, perhaps the
beginning of the Black Death that would soon spread to
Europe. In Henan province, 90 per cent of the population
died. Then the Yellow River broke its banks, drowned
uncounted thousands and set itself a new course to the sea.
Rebels, sensing that the Mandate of Heaven was being withdrawn, seized the Huai and Yangtze basins. Pirates raided
coastal shipping. In plague-ravaged Henan, rebels known as
Red Turbans even briefly restored the Song dynasty
(1355–60). When the emperor, Toqtoa, tried to restore order
and repair the damage, he did so by printing paper money,
which led to hyperinflation and forced a return to silver and
copper coins.

At last, hatred, corruption, plague, inflation, disaster and disorder, heaped one on another, reached tipping point. In 1368, a former monk drove the last Mongol emperor, Toghon Temür, back to the steppes of Mongolia, leaving some 300,000–400,000 Mongols to fall into the vengeful arms of the Ming. With him went 60,000 of the Mongol elite, trailing back to a land in which they were aliens, and where their deadweight presence ruined the traditional herding economy.

They never accepted their sudden demotion. Their descendants, crowned in Karakorum, went on saying they were the true rulers of China. They said it because they 'knew' a hidden 'truth': that the Ming were actually Mongols. The story, as summarized by Hok-Lam Chan, Associate Professor of Washington University, Seattle, in his *China and the Mongols*, went like this:

The queen of the last Yuan emperor, Toghon Temür, was already pregnant when she was captured and taken as a wife by the incoming Ming emperor in 1368. She said, 'If I give birth soon, they will certainly kill the child.' So she prayed to prolong her pregnancy, and her prayers were answered. She gave birth after twelve months, and the boy was accepted by the first Ming emperor as his heir. There was more: the Ming emperor had made Nanjing his capital, but one day the young Mongol/Ming prince met a man of 'an extraordinary bearing, with a swarthy face, dressed in black robes and riding a black horse', who told him to found a great city with four corners (after the four seasons), nine outer gates (after the planets), and other magical and religious attributes. 'In a golden place in the middle of the city,' the Black Rider said, 'set up a throne of jade, with nine interlaced dragons, and sitting on it become emperor yourself.' Thus did a 'Mongol' prince found modern Beijing, to which the Ming court soon moved.

It is all a legend, of course, with not a scrap of evidence to back it. But, as Hok-Lam Chan concludes, these stories, 'proving' that there was Mongol blood in the Ming emperors and a Mongol inspiration behind the rebuilding of the capital, gained strength in the decades either side of 1500 when Mongolia united again under a khan who claimed the mantle of Kublai, naming himself Dayan, from Da Yuan, Great Yuan, the name Kublai had chosen for his dynasty. The legends were being told and retold until well into the twentieth century.

Nonsense, yes; but there is a smattering of truth in the legends, for the legacy of the two conquerors, Genghis and Kublai, endured down the centuries, and still defines the context of today's geopolitics.

Although Kublai's Chinese territory reached way beyond China's traditional limits, and although successor dynasties claimed to be restoring old China, Kublai's additions dictated their agenda. The Ming adopted them without question. Yunnan, conquered by Kublai as a prince, remained Chinese. So did the Liao river basin in Manchuria, largely populated by Korean captives transplanted from their homeland by Mongol armies. Tibet, unified under Mongol rule, recognized the Ming as overlords, a position which the Ming asserted, if with varying degrees of success. As the Japanese scholar Hidehiro Okada argues, given the non-Chinese origins of these territories, 'the only possible justification of the Ming sovereignty over them was the claim that the Ming emperors were legitimate successors to the Mongol khans'.[1]

In bureaucracy, administration and military structure the Ming also owed a debt to the Mongols. Both civilians and the military, for example, were governed by the decimal system that Genghis had imposed on his new nation and

[1] Hidehiro Okada, 'China as a Successor State to the Mongol Empire', in Reuven Amitai-Preiss and David O. Morgan, eds, *The Mongol Empire and Its Legacy*.

Kublai had adopted for China. It was to lay claim to Mongolia itself that the Ming returned to Beijing. Indeed, as Okada concludes, 'The Ming Dynasty was in all its aspects a shrunken form of the Mongol Empire.'

Same thing with the Manchus when they took over in 1644. Again, no Manchu even thought of giving up territory acquired under Kublai. When the first Manchu emperor was crowned – even before seizing the Chinese throne – he proclaimed himself Vastly Gracious, Harmonious and Holy Khan-Emperor, laying claim to the imperial tradition originating under Genghis in order to legitimize his claim to the eastern half of the old Mongol empire. As Okada writes, the Manchu emperor straddled three worlds: Chinese (as emperor), Mongol (as successor to Genghis) and Tibetan (as patron of Buddhism).

And again with modern China. The far west – Gansu, Ningxia, Xinjiang – had Muslim populations that had more in common with the present-day 'stans' of Central Asia than with the Han regions of the east, but they were considered Chinese because Genghis had conquered Central Asia and Kublai had encouraged Muslim immigration. Western parts of Inner Mongolia had been Tangut territory, the kingdom of Xi Xia until conquered by Genghis and inherited by Kublai. True, his ornery cousin, Kaidu, had controlled a good deal of the west, but that did not make it any less Kublai's. It was on this basis that China regained from Russia areas almost lost in the nineteenth century. Today, it is Kublai's empire that is recalled by China's reach – ironically, minus Mongolia itself, which was allowed to opt for independence and to fall into the Soviet sphere at a time of weakness after the First World War.

It's Mongolia that has a special interest for me. Mongols are very nervous of the Chinese, whom they view as ex-imperial masters itching to pounce. Once I was in the southern Gobi at dusk, looking over immense expanses towards what I thought were clouds, but were not clouds. 'What's that?' I asked my Mongol travelling companion. The answer should have been: the snow-capped peaks of the Tien Shan. Instead he said: 'China. Very dangerous.' Mongols see how the Chinese have moved steadily north since the early twentieth century, beyond the Great Wall, beyond the Yellow River, up on to the Mongolian grasslands. Inner Mongolia is now more Chinese than Mongol. And in commercial terms, pressures on Mongolia itself increase yearly, for Mongolia has valuable resources, especially in the Gobi, that would find a natural outlet in China – with Chinese finance, Chinese transport, Chinese labour. To Chinese, this is as it should be, because, if they pause to think about the matter, which is not often, they would say, as one of my guides put it: Well, of course we know that Mongolia is *really* Chinese, isn't it?

There is, of course, an opposite view north of the Gobi: that China is really Mongolian. But demography rules, and 1,300 million may, in the end, trump two. If Mongolia ever becomes an economic colony of China (no-one speaks of a political takeover), China will shrug her ample shoulders and point out that Mongols have been members of the great family of China for centuries. Any growth in Chinese influence is merely a return to the status quo as established by Genghis, the founder of China's Yuan dynasty, and that dynasty's star, Kublai.

BIBLIOGRAPHY

These are the works that I found particularly useful. The choice is personal, and very selective. Almost all the references are in English. Even in English, they represent only a fraction of the material available to specialists. The best bibliographies for English readers are in Weatherford (English only), and Rossabi and Mote, which also include works in other western and non-western languages.

Abu-Lughod, Janet L., *Before European Hegemony: The World System AD 1250–1350*. Oxford and New York: Oxford University Press, 1989.

Allsen, Thomas, *Culture and Conquest in Mongol Eurasia*. Cambridge: Cambridge University Press, 2001.

Amitai-Preiss, Reuven and Morgan, David O., eds, *The Mongol Empire and Its Legacy*. Leiden and Boston: Brill, 1999.

Atwood, Christopher, *Encyclopedia of Mongolia and the Mongol Empire*. New York: Facts on File, 2004.

Aung-Thwin, Michael, *Pagan: The Origins of Modern Burma*. Honolulu: University of Hawaii Press, 1985.

Barthold, W., *Turkestan Down to the Mongol Invasion*. London, Luzac & Co., 1968.

Bartlett, W. B., *The Assassins: The Story of Medieval Islam's Secret Sect*. Stroud, Glos.: Sutton, 2001.

Bira, Sh., 'Mongolian Tenggerism and Modern Globalism: A Retrospective Outlook on Globalism', *Journal of the Royal Asiatic Society*, vol. 14, London, 2004.

Bira, Sh., 'The Mongolian Ideology of Tenggerism and Khubilai Khan', unpublished paper, 2005.

Bira, Sh., *Studies in Mongolian History, Culture and Historiography*. Ulaanbaatar: International Association for Mongol Studies, 2001, esp. 'Khubilai Khan and Phags-pa bla-ma'.

Biran, Michael, *Qaidu and the Rise of the Independent Mongol State in Central Asia*. Richmond, England: Curzon, 1998.

Boyle: see Juvaini.

Cahill, James, *Hills Beyond a River: Chinese Painting of the Yüan Dynasty 1279–1368*. New York: Weatherill, 1976.

Cannadine, David and Price, Simon, eds, *Rituals of Royalty*. Cambridge: Cambridge University Press, 1992.

Chan, Hok-Lam, *China and the Mongols: History and Legend under the Yüan and Ming*. Aldershot, Hants: Ashgate, 1999.

Chen, Paul Heng-chao. *Chinese Legal Tradition Under the Mongols*. Princeton: Princeton University Press, 1979.

Ch'ên Yüan, 'Western and Central Asians in China Under the Mongols', *Monumenta Serica Monograph XV*, University of California, 1966.

Conlan, Thomas D. (trans. and interpretive essay), *In Little Need of Divine Intervention: Scrolls of the Mongol Invasions of Japan*. Ithaca, NY: Cornell University Press, 2001.

Crump, J. I., *Chinese Theatre in the Days of Kublai Khan*. Tucson: University of Arizona Press, 1980.

Daftary, Farhad, *The Ismāʾīlīs: Their History and Doctrines*. Cambridge: Cambridge University Press, 1990.

Davis, Richard L., *Wind Against the Mountain: The Crisis of Politics and Culture in 13th-Century China.* Cambridge, Mass.: Harvard University Press, 1996.

Delgado, James P., 'Relics of the Kamikaze', *Archaeology,* vol. 56, no. 1 (Jan.–Feb. 2003).

Denney, Paul and Douglas, Julie, trebuchet research at www.artefacts.uk.com.

Eckert, Carter J., et al., *Korea Old and New: A History.* Seoul and Cambridge, Mass.: Ilchokak/Harvard University Press, 1990.

Farris, William Wayne, *Heavenly Warriors: The Evolution of Japan's Military, 500–1300.* Cambridge, Mass.: Harvard Council on East Asian Studies, 1992.

Franke, Herbert, 'Chia Ssu-tao (1213–1275): A "Bad Last Minister"?', in Arthur F. Wright and Denis Twitchett, eds, *Confucian Personalities.* Stanford: Stanford University Press, 1962.

Franke, Herbert, 'Siege and Defence of Towns in Medieval China', in Frank A. Kierman and John K. Fairbank, eds, *Chinese Ways in Warfare.* Cambridge, Mass.: Harvard University Press, 1974.

Franke, Herbert, *From Tribal Chieftain to Universal Emperor and God: The Legitimation of the Yüan Dynasty.* Munich: Bayerische Akademie der Wissenschaft, 1978.

Franke, Herbert, *Studien und Texte zur Kriegsgeschichte der Südlichen Sungzeit* (esp. ch. 4: 'Hsiang-yang: Gelände und Befestigungen'). Wiesbaden: Harrassowitz, 1987.

Franke, Herbert, *China Under Mongol Rule.* Aldershot, Hants: Ashgate, 1994.

Franke, Herbert and Twitchett, Denis, eds, *The Cambridge History of China,* vol. 6: *Alien Regimes and Border States, 907–1368.* Cambridge: Cambridge University Press, 1994.

Gernet, Jacques, *A History of Chinese Civilization,* 2nd edn, trans. J. R. Foster and Charles Hartman. Cambridge: Cambridge University Press, 1996.

Goodman, Jim, *The Exploration of Yunnan*. Kunming: Yunnan People's Publishing House, 2000.

Grey Company, trebuchet website: www.iinet.net.au/~rmine/gctrebs.html.

Groeneveldt, W. P., 'The Expedition of the Mongols Against Java in 1293 AD', *China Review*, vol. 4 (1875–6).

Grousset, Réné, *The Empire of the Steppes*. New Brunswick, NJ: Rutgers University Press, 1970.

Harvey, G. E., *History of Burma*. London: Longmans, Green & Co., 1925.

Heissig, Walther, *The Religions of Mongolia*, trans. Geoffrey Samuel. London: Routledge, 1980.

Herrmann, Albert, *An Historical Atlas of China*. Edinburgh: Edinburgh University Press, 1966.

Hitti, Philip, *History of the Arabs*. Basingstoke: Macmillan, 2002.

Htin Aung, Maung, *A History of Burma*. New York and London: Columbia University Press, 1967.

Jackson, Peter, *The Mission of Friar William of Rubruck*. London: Hakluyt Society, 1990.

Jagchid, Sechin and Bawden, C. R., 'Some Notes on the Horse-Policy of the Yüan Dynasty', *Central Asiatic Journal*, vol. 10 (1965).

Jagchid, Sechin and Hyer, Paul, *Mongolia's Culture and Society*. Boulder, Colo.: Westview, 1979.

Jay, Jennifer W., *A Change in Dynasties: Loyalism in 13th-Century China*. Washington DC: Centre for East Asian Studies, 1991.

Johnson, Dale R., 'Courtesans, Lovers, and "Gold Thread Pond" in Guan Hanqing's Music Dramas', *Journal of Song–Yuan Studies*, vol. 33 (2003).

Juvaini, Ata-Malik, *Genghis Khan: The History of the World Conqueror*, trans. and ed. J. A. Boyle. Manchester:

Manchester University Press/UNESCO, 1958; 2nd edn 1997.

Karcher, Stephen, *Total I Ching: Myths for Change*. London: Time Warner, 2003.

Kates, G. N., 'A New Date for the Origins of the Forbidden City', *Harvard Journal of Asiatic Studies*, vol. 7 (1942–3).

KOSUWA (Kyushu and Osaka Society for Underwater Archaeology), website reports on the Takashima research into Kublai's lost fleet at www.h3.dion.ne.jp/~uwarchae/english.

Langlois, John D., ed., *China Under Mongol Rule*. Princeton: Princeton University Press, 1981.

Larner, John, *Marco Polo and the Discovery of the World*. New York and London: Yale University Press, 1999.

The Legacy Treasure of the Great Dynasty, catalogue of Mongol–Yuan Exhibition, Arthur M. Sackler Museum, Beijing University, 2004.

Lewis, Bernard, *The Assassins: A Radical Sect in Islam*. London: Weidenfeld & Nicolson, 1967.

Li Chu-tsing, *The Autumn Colors on the Ch'iao and Hua Mountains – A Landscape by Chao Meng-fu*. New York: Artibus, New York University, 1964.

Lin Yutang, *Imperial Peking: Seven Centuries of China*. London: Elek, 1961.

Lindner, Rudi Paul, 'Nomadism, Horses and Huns', *Past and Present*, no. 92 (Aug. 1981).

Liu Bin, ed., *Atlas of China*. Beijing: China Cartographic Publishing House, 1989.

Liu Jung-en, trans. and ed., *Six Yüan Plays* (includes *The Injustice Done to Tou Ngo*, a.k.a. *The Injustice to Dou E*). London: Penguin, 1972.

McMullen, David, 'Bureaucrats and Cosmology: The Ritual Code of T'ang China', in Cannadine and Price, eds, *Rituals of Royalty*.

Man, John, *Genghis Khan: Life, Death and Resurrection.* London: Transworld, 2004.

Mansfield, Stephen, *China: Yunnan Province.* Chalfont St Peter, Bucks: Bradt Travel Guides, 2001.

Medley, Margaret, *Yüan Porcelain and Stoneware.* London: Faber, 1974.

Morgan, David, 'The Mongols in Syria, 1260–1300', in Peter Edbury, ed., *Crusade and Settlement.* Cardiff: University College of Wales, 1985.

Morgan, David, *The Mongols.* Oxford, UK and Malden, Mass.: Blackwell, 1986 (many reprints).

Mote, F. W., *Imperial China 900–1800.* Cambridge, Mass. and London: Harvard University Press, 1999.

Moule, A. C., *Quinsai with Other Notes on Marco Polo.* Cambridge: Cambridge University Press, 1957.

Mozai, Takao, 'Kublai Khan's Lost Fleet', *National Geographic*, Nov. 1982.

Needham, Joseph, *Science and Civilisation in China*, vols 5 and 7 on military technology.

Nelson, Janet, 'The Lord's Anointed and the People's Choice: Carolingian Royal Ritual', in Cannadine and Price, eds, *Rituals of Royalty.*

Okada, Hidehiro, 'China as a Successor State to the Mongol Empire', in Amitai-Preiss and Morgan, eds, *The Mongol Empire and Its Legacy.*

Olbricht, Peter, *Das Postwesen in China unter der Mongolenherrschaft im 13. und 14. Jahrhundert.* Wiesbaden: Harrassowitz, 1954.

Peers, C. J., *Medieval Chinese Armies, 1260–1520.* Oxford: Osprey, 1992.

Peers, Chris, *Imperial Chinese Armies (2), 590–1260.* London: Osprey, 1996.

Petech, Luciano, 'Tibetan Relations with Sung China and with the Mongols', in Morris Rossabi, ed., *China Among Equals: The Middle Kingdom and its Neighbours,*

10th–14th Centuries. Berkeley, Los Angeles and London: University of California Press, 1983.

Polo, Marco, *The Travels of Marco Polo: The Complete Yule–Cordier Edition*: Henry Yule's 3rd (1903) annotated translation, with Henri Cordier's notes. New York: Dover, 1993. This is the edition I used. Ronald Latham's edition (translated and introduced by himself), *Marco Polo: The Travels* (Penguin, 1958, still in print) is more accessible. For other editions, see the bibliography in Larner.

Rachewiltz, Igor de, *Papal Envoys to the Great Khans*. London: Faber, 1971.

Rachewiltz, Igor de, trans. and commentary, *The Secret History of the Mongols: A Mongolian Epic Chronicle of the 13th Century*. Leiden and Boston: Brill, 2004.

Rachewiltz, Igor de, et al., *In the Service of the Khan: Eminent Personalities of the Early Mongol–Yüan Era (1200–1300)*. Wiesbaden: Harrassowitz, 1993.

Rashid ad-Din, *The Successors of Genghis Khan*, trans. John Andrew Boyle. New York: Columbia University Press, 1971.

Ratchnevsky, Paul, *Genghis Khan: His Life and Legacy*, trans. and ed. Thomas Haining. Oxford, UK, and Cambridge, Mass.: Blackwell, 1991 (several reprints).

Rossabi, Morris, *Khubilai Khan: His Life and Times*. Berkeley, Los Angeles and London: University of California Press, 1988.

Rossabi, Morris, *Voyager from Xanadu: Rabban Sauma and the First Journey from China to the West*. Tokyo, London and New York: Kodansha, 1992.

Rossabi, Morris, ed., *China Among Equals: The Middle Kingdom and its Neighbours, 10th–14th Centuries*. Berkeley, Los Angeles and London: University of California Press, 1983.

Rouleau, Father Francis, SJ, 'The Yangchow Latin Tombstone as a Landmark of Medieval Christianity',

Harvard Journal of Asiatic Studies, vol. 17, nos 3–4 (Dec. 1954).

Sansom, Sir George, *A History of Japan to 1334*. Folkestone, Kent: Dawson, 1958, 1978.

SarDesai, D. R., *Southeast Asia, Past and Present*. London: Macmillan, 1989.

Saunders, J. J., *A History of Medieval Islam*. London and New York: Routledge, 1965 (many reprints).

Saunders, J. J., *The History of the Mongol Conquests*. Philadelphia: University of Pennsylvania, 1971.

Saunders, J. J., *Muslims and Mongols: Essays on Medieval Asia*. Christchurch, NZ: Whitcoulls, University of Canterbury, 1977.

Shih, Chung-wen, *Injustice to Tou O*. Cambridge: Cambridge University Press, 1972.

Shih, Chung-wen, *The Golden Age of Chinese Drama: Yüan Tsa-chü*. Princeton: Princeton University Press, 1976.

Smith, John Masson, 'Ayn Jalut: Mamluk Success or Mongol Failure?', *Harvard Journal of Asiatic Studies*, vol. 44, no. 2 (Dec. 1984).

Stark, Freya, *The Valleys of the Assassins*. London: John Murray, 1934.

Steinhardt, Nancy, *Chinese Imperial City Planning*. Honolulu: University of Hawaii Press, 1990.

Tarling, Nicholas, ed., *The Cambridge History of Southeast Asia*. Cambridge: Cambridge University Press, 1999.

Temple, Robert, *The Genius of China*, intr. Joseph Needham. London: Prion, 1999 (a good introduction to Needham's massive work).

Thorau, Peter, 'The Battle of Ayn Jalut: A Re-examination', in Peter Edbury, ed., *Crusade and Settlement*. Cardiff: Cardiff Press, 1985.

Toms, Ron, website: www. trebuchet.com.

Turnbull, Stephen, *Siege Weapons of the Far East (1), 612–1300 and (2) 960–1644*. Oxford: Osprey, 2001–2.

Vemming, Peter, trebuchet website at http://www.middelaldercentret.dk. See also his latest reconstruction in http://www.warwicksiege.com.

Wang Jiawei and Nyima Gyaincain, *The Historical Status of China's Tibet*. Beijing: China Intercontinental Press, 1997.

Wang Shifu, *The Romance of the Western Bower*, adapted by Xang Xuejing. Beijing: New World Press, 2000.

Weatherford, Jack, *Genghis Khan and the Making of the Modern World*. New York: Crown, 2004. (Includes the empire and Kublai Khan as well as Genghis.)

Wood, Frances, *Did Marco Polo Go to China?* London: Secker & Warburg, 1995.

Wylie, Turrell V., 'The First Mongol Conquest of Tibet Reinterpreted', *Harvard Journal of Asiatic Studies*, vol. 37, no. 1 (1977).

Yamada, Nabaka, *Ghenko: The Mongol Invasion of Japan*. London: Smith, Elder & Co., 1916.

Yanagida, Sumitaka, *The Mongolian Invasion and Hakata* (in Japanese). Hakata Town, 2001.

Zu An, ed., *Beihai Park*. Beijing: China Pictorial, 1989.

INDEX